South-Western Algebra 1: An Integrated Approach

Content that connects — See pages

	See pages
✓ to other disciplines and other math	112D
✓ to the real world	166D, 221, 275, 330-333, 403
✓ to diverse learning styles	322D
✓ to work and careers	101, 188, 359, 537
✓ and reflects NCTM Standards and state and local curricula	410C

Technology that is integrated — See pages

	See pages
✓ for exploration and discovery	168, 325, 326, 329, 330, 335, 410C
✓ for instruction	15, 65, 322C, 349
✓ for assessment	327, 357

Assessment that is ongoing — See pages

	See pages
✓ to reinforce skills	322-323, 325, 326, 338, 345-347
✓ to integrate into instruction	201, 234, 249, 344
✓ to utilize a variety of assessment techniques	256-261, 364-369
✓ to prepare for standardized tests	274, 291, 358, 366, 368-369

Teacher Support that is comprehensive — See pages

	See pages
✓ full array of support materials	112C-112D
✓ Pacing Guide for traditional, block schedule, and 2-year algebra 1 courses	112D
✓ project starters, management, assessment	114, 128, 145, 150, 163, 324, 340, 352, 367
✓ suggestions for various learning styles	322D, 331, 360
✓ connections to other disciplines	322D, 330, 339, 346
✓ suggestions for diverse student populations	343, 360, 367

Bringing the World into Your Classroom . . .

Connecting the World to Algebra

SOUTH WESTERN

Algebra 1

AN INTEGRATED APPROACH

TEACHER'S ANNOTATED EDITION
PART 2 CHAPTERS 8-14

GERVER, SGROI, CARTER, HANSEN
MOLINA & WESTEGAARD

JOIN US ON THE INTERNET
WWW: http://www.thomson.com
EMAIL: findit@kiosk.thomson.com A service of I(T)P®

South-Western Educational Publishing
an International Thomson Publishing company I(T)P®

Cincinnati • Albany, NY • Belmont, CA • Bonn • Boston • Detroit • Johannesburg • London • Madrid
Melbourne • Mexico City • New York • Paris • Singapore • Tokyo • Toronto • Washington

Editor-in-Chief	Peter McBride
Managing Editor	Eve Lewis
Project Manager	Enid Nagel
Developmental Editor	Janet Heller
Production Coordinator	Patricia M. Boies
Production Consultant	Tamara S. Jones
Marketing Manager	Colleen J. Skola
National Mathematics Consultants	Carol Ann Dana, Everett T. Draper
Art Director	John Robb
Photographic Consultant	Devore M. Nixon
Design Consultant	Elaine St. John-Lagenaur
Editorial Assistant	Mary Schwarz
Marketing Assistant	Dawn Zimmer
Editorial Development and Production	Gramercy Book Services, Inc.
Scans/Prepress/Imaging	Better Graphics, Inc.
Cover Design	Photonics Graphics

About the Cover

The cover design is a collage of real world images from the chapter themes. How many can you find?

The cover design contains ten images which reflect the real world chapter themes in *South-Western Algebra 1: An Integrated Approach.* Those images are a French horn, 1938 Packard Super 8 Convertible Coupe, Super Sonic Transport jet, Earth, stoplight, color palette, leaf, Apple Powerbook 160, astronaut, and a graphing calculator.

ISBN: 0-538-68047-4 Student Edition
ISBN: 0-538-68048-2 Teacher's Annotated Edition Package
ISBN: 0-538-68049-0 Teacher's Annotated Edition Part 1
ISBN: 0-538-68050-4 Teacher's Annotated Edition Part 2
1 2 3 4 5 6 7 8 VH 04 03 02 01 00 99 98 97
Printed in the United States of America

I(T)P®

International Thomson Publishing
South-Western Educational Publishing is an ITP Company. The ITP logo is a registered trademark used herein under License by South-Western Educational Publishing.

CONTENTS
TEACHER'S ANNOTATED EDITION

CONTENTS OF THE STUDENT EDITION

SPECIAL PLANNING PAGES FOR EVERY CHAPTER INCLUDE

THE BIG QUESTION	EXPLORE THE CHAPTER THEME
Chapter Vocabulary	➤ PLANNING GUIDE
Graphic Organizer	➤ PACING GUIDE

ANNOTATED ANSWERS AT POINT OF USE

ADDITIONAL ANSWERS AT END OF EACH CHAPTER

TEACHING PLAN

For Every Lesson	For Algebra Workshops
1 Motivate	1 Motivate
2 Teach	2 Facilitate
3 Summarize	3 Summarize
4 Practice	4 Follow-up
5 Follow-up	

PROFESSIONAL DEVELOPMENT ESSAYS

South-Western Algebra 1: An Integrated Approach is a program that is accessible, innovative, and reflects the spirit of the National Council of Teachers of Mathematics' Standards. It thoroughly addresses the five areas of increased attention called for by NCTM in *Algebra in a Technological World* (1995).

1. **Actively involve students in constructing and applying mathematical ideas** Students have the opportunity to explore, discover, create, invent, hypothesize, and test mathematical ideas in a variety of formats. ***Manipulatives***, both commercially-produced and homemade, are employed throughout the text.

2. **Use problem solving as a means as well as a goal of instruction** Each lesson begins with a discovery activity titled ***Explore***. Problems are posed, dissected, analyzed, and solved. Each chapter offers substantial opportunities to learn and apply a variety of problem solving strategies.

3. **Promote student interaction through the use of effective questioning techniques** Each chapter begins with a series of questions which ask students to both ***look back*** on their mathematical experiences and ***look ahead*** to the material that is yet to come. Many questions are open-ended, allowing students to explore problem situations in a number of ways. ***Sidebar features*** prompt students to analyze the topic at hand though well-planned questions.

4. **Use a variety of instructional formats—small cooperative groups, individual explorations, whole class instruction, and projects** Students are offered a wide range of formats in which learning can take place. ***AlgebraWorks***, a career-oriented exploration, takes on a variety of forms as the text unfolds. Small group, whole class, and individual activities are included. Each chapter contains an ongoing ***Project*** which centers on the chapter theme. Various phases of the project are developed throughout the chapter. Projects usually culminate with a summative activity which is in the form of a written or oral presentation.

5. **Use calculators and computers as tools for learning and doing mathematics** Lessons use material and explorations fully cognizant of the technology which is now readily available to students. Graphing calculator and computer activities are woven into the text. Technology is and integral part of the mathematics classroom of today. In this text, the term **graphing utility** is used to mean a graphing calculator or computer software with graphing capabilities. The use of technology is referenced in each chapter's **Planning Guide** under the column *Technology*. Technology usage is also listed in **Lesson Planning** so teachers have a point-of-use reference. For the student, a calculator icon is sometimes used to indicate *this is a good place to use a calculator.*

1 Data and Graphs

THEME: Entertainment

Applications and Connections

Thematic Chapters

demonstrate that mathematics has a real and relevant connection to students' daily life.
Chapter 1 Theme:

➤ Entertainment

TEACHER'S ANNOTATED EDITION
CHAPTER 1

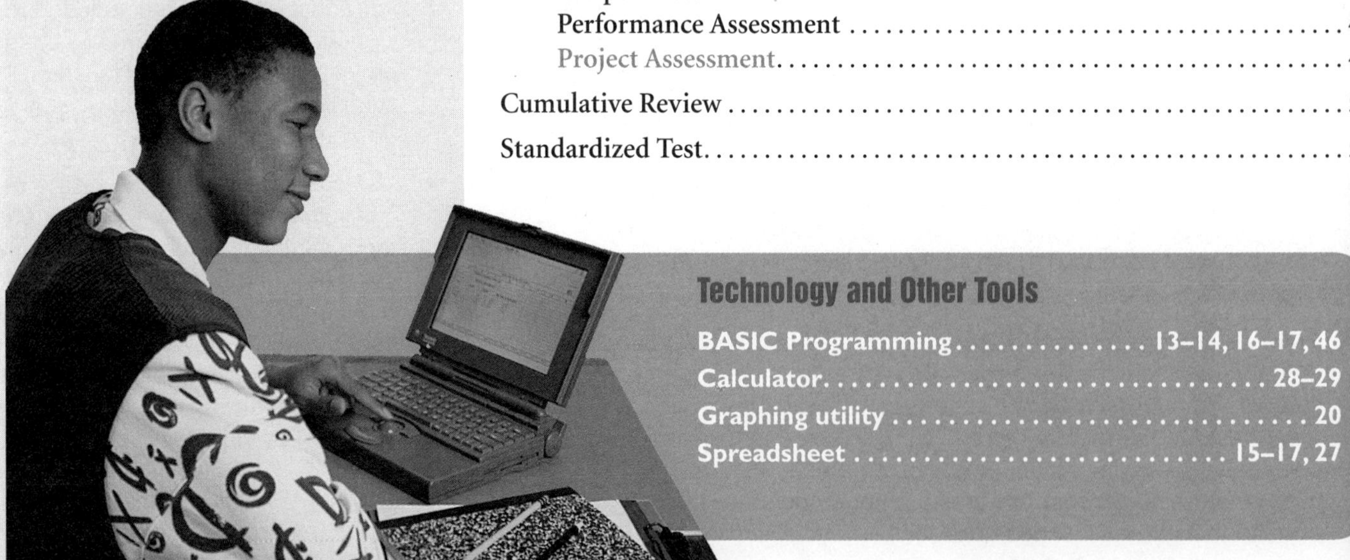

Technology and Other Tools

2 Variables, Expressions, and Real Numbers

THEME: Meteorology: The Science of Weather

Applications and Connections

Technology and Other Tools

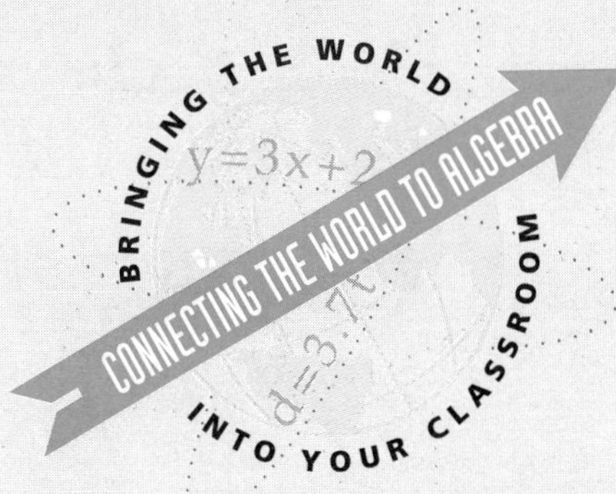

Data Activity focuses on data analysis skills while also providing an opportunity to review arithmetic skills.

➤ Number of Tornadoes PAGES 52–53

TEACHER'S ANNOTATED EDITION
CHAPTER 2

3 Linear Equations

THEME: Health and Fitness

Applications and Connections

Project

Is "Lite" Right? PAGE 114

Projects, based on the theme of each chapter, help develop mathematical understanding and connect algebra to the real world.

TEACHER'S ANNOTATED EDITION CHAPTER 3

Technology and Other Tools

4 Functions and Graphs

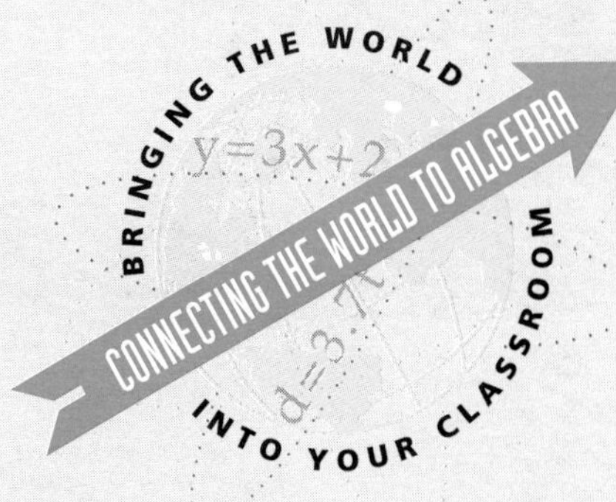

THEME: Sports

Applications and Connections

Technology and Other Tools

AlgebraWorks are career explorations showcasing the algebra in the lesson connected to a career.

TEACHER'S ANNOTATED EDITION
CHAPTER 4

5 Linear Inequalities

THEME: Graphic Arts and Advertising

Explore

PAGES 221, 230, 235, 241, 247

Explore activities actively engage students in discovering mathematical concepts. Working in small groups or in pairs, students will gain insight because they have experienced the math.

Applications and Connections

TEACHER'S ANNOTATED EDITION
CHAPTER 5

Technology and Other Tools

6 Linear Functions and Graphs

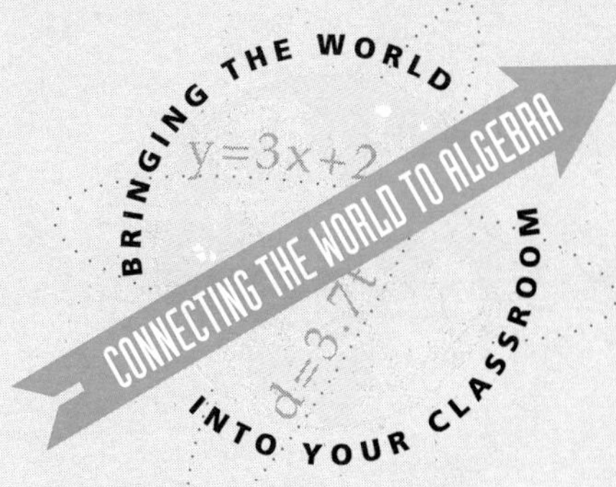

THEME: Save the Planet

Applications and Connections

Technology and Other Tools

Sidebars found in all chapters are Spotlight on Learning, Check Understanding, Communicating About Algebra, Problem Solving Tip, Think Back, Algeblocks Models, and Algebra: Who, Where, When.

TEACHER'S ANNOTATED EDITION
CHAPTER 6

7 Systems of Linear Equations

THEME: Cities and Municipalities

Applications and Connections

Algebra Workshop lessons are guided discovery lessons using manipulatives such as Algeblocks, Graphing Utilities, and other hands-on tools.

TEACHER'S ANNOTATED EDITION
CHAPTER 7

Technology and Other Tools

8 Systems of Linear Inequalities

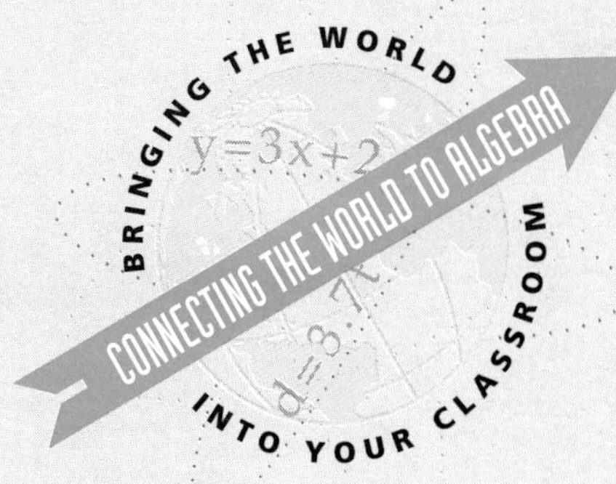

Applications and Connections

Technology and Other Tools

Problem Solving File

lessons provide practice using problem solving strategies, plus one page of nonroutine problems.

TEACHER'S ANNOTATED EDITION CHAPTER 8

9 Absolute Value and the Real Number System

THEME: Traffic

Applications and Connections

Technology and Other Tools

Mixed Review

PAGES 347, 358

Mixed Reviews provide students with ongoing practice of previously learned material. Each Mixed Review contains a standardized test question.

TEACHER'S ANNOTATED EDITION
CHAPTER 9

10 Quadratic Functions and Equations

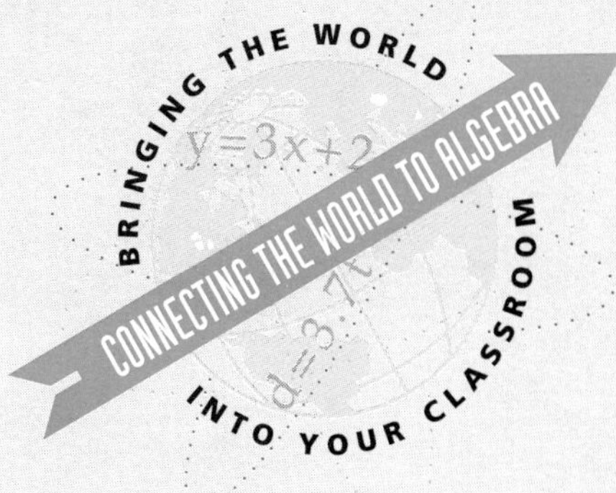

THEME: Business and Industry

Applications and Connections

Technology and Other Tools

Chapter Review

PAGES 508–509

Chapter Reviews in each chapter highlight all of the major topics and definitions in the chapter and provide additional examples and practice items.

TEACHER'S ANNOTATED EDITION
CHAPTER 10

11 Polynomials and Exponen

THEME: Exploring Flight

Applications and Connections

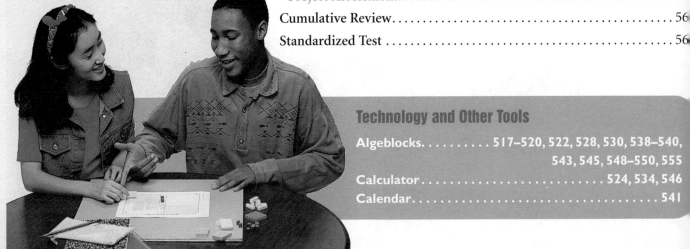

Technology and Other Tools

Chapter Assessment

PAGE 564

Chapter Assessment includes writing questions, standardized test questions, and open-ended questions to assess student understanding.

TEACHER'S ANNOTATED EDITION
CHAPTER 11

12 Polynomials and Factoring

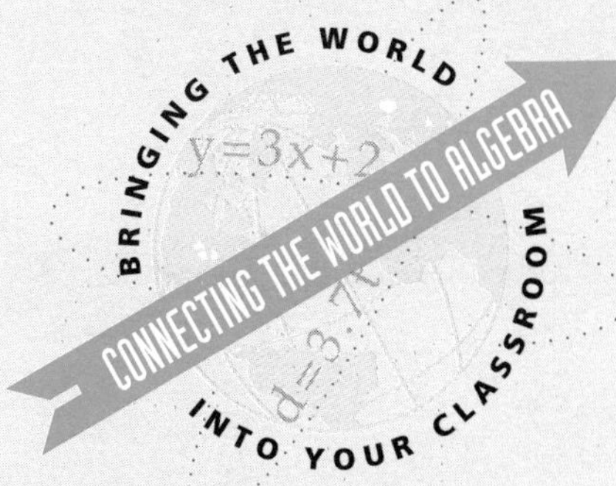

THEME: U.S. Rivers

Applications and Connections

Technology and Other Tools

Performance Assessment

PAGE 609

- Performance assessment options
- Project assessment provides the conclusion to the chapter-long project

TEACHER'S ANNOTATED EDITION
CHAPTER 12

13 Geometry and Radical Expressions

THEME: Travel and Transportation

Applications and Connections

Cumulative Review

PAGE 670

Cumulative Reviews provide ongoing opportunities to maintain math concepts and skills learned previously.

TEACHER'S ANNOTATED EDITION CHAPTER 13

Technology and Other Tools

14 Rational Expressions

BRINGING THE WORLD INTO YOUR CLASSROOM
CONNECTING THE WORLD TO ALGEBRA

THEME: Agribusiness

Applications and Connections

Technology and Other Tools

Also...

Standardized Test

PAGE 727

Standardized Tests get students ready to take standardized tests. Students practice and prepare for answering multiple choice, quantitative comparison, and grid response questions.

TEACHER'S ANNOTATED EDITION CHAPTER 14

CHAPTER 8 SYSTEMS OF LINEAR INEQUALITIES

It is essential that schools and communities accept the goal of mathematical education for every child. However, this does not mean that every child will have the same interests or capabilities in mathematics. It does mean that we will need to examine our fundamental expectations about what children can learn and can do and that we will have to strive to create learning environments in which raised expectations for children can be met.

"Professional Standards for Teaching Mathematics," National Council of Teachers of Mathematics, Reston, Va., 1991, p. 5

The Big Question: Why study systems of linear inequalities?

The solution of a system of linear inequalities leads to one of the most powerful problem solving methods available to introductory algebra students: linear programming. Linear programming problems allow students to consider ways to maximize or minimize results. Although this chapter focuses on consumerism, students will also see applications from business, finance, geometry, health, recreation, sports, and weather.

Vocabulary

boundary
closed half-plane
complement
constraints
event
feasible region
fundamental counting principle
half-plane
linear inequality
linear programming
maximize
minimize
objective function
open half-plane
outcome
probability experiment
probability of an event
sample space
system of linear inequalities
theoretical probability

Using the Graphic Organizer

Project a copy of the Graphic Organizer Transparency for Chapter 8. Explain that the focus of this chapter is on solving systems of linear inequalities. Review the information on the graphic organizer, pointing out that systems of linear inequalities can be solved by graphing either by hand or with a graphing utility.

Ask some preview questions; for example, what methods were you able to use to solve systems of linear equations? Do you think these methods may be helpful when solving systems of linear inequalities?

One way to organize ideas about solving systems of linear inequalities is shown below.

One way to organize ideas about solving a system of linear inequalities is shown.

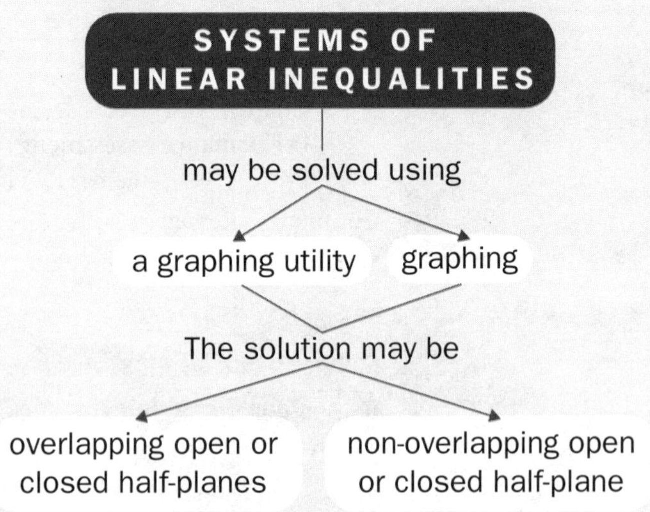

Try It **Use a different plan. Try organizing ideas about the steps used to solve a system of inequalities and the different types of possible solutions.**

xplore the Chapter Theme:

Be a Smart Shopper!

A recent survey showed that there are over 4,000,000 retail sales workers in the nited States. While many work in mall shops, the largest employers re department stores, clothing and ccessory stores, supermarkets, nd car dealerships. Many opportuni-es are available for advancement s companies often select manage-ent trainees from their sales staff. areer paths a sales person may hoose to take are retail manager nd purchasing agent or buyer. etail experience is also valuable hen applying for a position in fields uch as finance, wholesale trade, or anufacturing. Here is a list of char-cteristics and skills expected of etail sales people.

Skills Needed for Success in Retail Sales

1. Organize information in order to plan future purchases.
2. Analyze technical data for decision making.
3. Have self-confidence in your ability to anticipate customers' desires.
4. Be responsible for large amounts of money.
5. Work well both independently and as part of a team.
6. Consult with other professionals when the need arises.
7. Display leadership skills to motivate and direct subordinates.
8. Show patience when dealing with customers.

Investigate Further

Have students identify a retail sales career that interests them. Have students go to the library to find out more information about this career. For example, students might find out about educational requirements including specific courses, degrees, examinations, or licenses. Students should research the average salary range for the career. Have students share their findings in a class discussion about career opportunities.

Here is a list of jobs and educational requirements for careers in retail sales.

Jobs Requiring 1 to 2 Years of Technical Training

Sales Trainee

Retail Manager

Salesperson

Management Trainee

Service Sales Representative

Rental Clerk

Cashier

Counter Clerk

Jobs Requiring 4 + Years of College

Accountant

Marketing Manager

Sales Manager

Financial Officer

Wholesale Buyer

Real Estate Agent

Procurement Service Manager

CHAPTER 8 PLANNING GUIDE

Lessons		Text Pages	NCTM Standards	ASSIGNMENTS Basic	Average	Enriched	Ancillaries	Manipulatives	Technology
	Chapter Introduction	370–372	1, 2, 3, 4, 10, 11				Video Discussion Guide		Video, Transparency 4
8.1	**Graph Linear Inequalities in Two Variables**	373–378	1, 2, 3, 4, 5, 6, 8	1–18, 24–27, MR32–38	1–22, 24–29, MR32–38	1–4, 8–31, MR32–38	W 8.1; R 8.1; P 8.1; E 8.1; Q 8.1; S 21; T 18; M 8	Graph Paper, Straightedge	Graphing Utility, Transparencies 32, 34, 48, 49, 50, 78–80
8.2	**Solve Systems of Linear Inequalities by Graphing**	379–385	1, 2, 3, 4, 5, 6, 8	1–12, 17–26, 30–31, 36, PC1–4, AW1–5	1–14, 17–26, 30–36, PC1–4, AW1–5	13–39, PC1–4, AW1–5	W 8.2; R 8.2; P 8.2; E 8.2; Q 8.2; S 22	Graph Paper, Straightedge	Transparencies 32, 49, 50
8.3	**Algebra Workshop: Use Graphing Utilities to Solve Systems of Inequalities**	386–387	1, 2, 3, 4, 5, 6, 8	1–18	1–18	1–19,	T 19	Graph Paper, Straightedge	Graphing Utility, Transparencies 32, 49–51, 78–80
8.4	**Linear Programming: The Objective Function**	388–393	1, 2, 3, 4, 5, 6, 8	1–14, 17–19, 22–24 MR25–29, PC1–2	1–14, 17–24, MR25–29, PC1–2	3, 7–24, MR25–29, PC1–2	W 8.4; R 8.4; P 8.4; E 8.4; Q 8.4	Graph Paper, Straightedge	Graphing Utility, Transparencies 32, 49–51, 78–80
8.5	**Problem Solving File: Use Linear Programming**	394–397	1, 2, 3, 4, 5, 6, 8	1–15, 18, RPSS1–3	1–18, RPSS1–3	1–18, RPSS1–3	R 8.5; P 8.5	Graph Paper, Straightedge	Graphing Utility, Transparencies 10, 32, 49–51, 78–80
8.6	**Explore Probability: Theoretical Probability**	398–403	1, 2, 3, 4, 5, 11	1–10, 13, 16–17, PC1–2, AW1–4	1–18, PC1–2, AW1–4	1–18, PC1–2, AW1–4	W 8.6; R 8.6; P 8.6; E 8.6; Q 8.6	Dice, Spinner	Transparency 1

NCTM STANDARDS

1. Mathematics as Problem Solving
2. Mathematics as Communication
3. Mathematics as Reasoning
4. Mathematical Connections
5. Algebra
6. Functions
7. Geometry from a Synthetic Perspective
8. Geometry from an Algebraic Perspective
9. Trigonometry
10. Statistics
11. Probability
12. Discrete Mathematics
13. Conceptual Underpinnings of Calculus
14. Mathematical Structure

ANCILLARIES

W = Warm Up
R = Reteaching
P = Extra Practice
E = Enrichment
Q = Lesson Quiz
T = Technology Activity
M = Multicultural Connection
S = Study Skills Activity

ADDITIONAL RESOURCES

pplications	Career Connections	Cooperative Learning	Learning Styles	Strand Integration/ Math Connection
	Chapter Poster			
usiness, 378; Contests, 76; Geometry, 375; ealth, 377; Sports, 377		Paired partners, 373 (Explore/Working Together)	Visual, 373–378; ESL/LEP, 375 (TE); Linguistic/ Interpersonal, 373, 374	Problem Solving, Geometry, Writing, Critical Thinking, Technology, Modeling
usiness, 382; onsumerism, 380, 384; inance, 384; Recreation, 81; Weather, 383	AlgebraWorks: Video Shop Owner, 385	Paired partners, 379 (Explore/Working Together); Small groups/STAD, 384 (Project Connection)	Linguistic/ Interpersonal, 379, 384; Visual, 380–385	Problem Solving, Modeling, Geometry, Writing, Critical Thinking
		Paired partners, 386 (Think Back)	Visual, 386–387; Linguistic/ Interpersonal, 386	Problem Solving, Modeling, Writing, Critical Thinking, Geometry
rafts, 392; Decision laking, 391	Shop Owner, 392	Paired partners, 388 (Explore/Working Together); Small groups/STAD, 393 (Project Connection)	Linguistic/ Interpersonal, 388, 393; ESL/LEP, 390 (TE); Visual, 388–393	Problem Solving, Geometry, Modeling, Writing, Critical Thinking
usiness, 396; ducation, 396; Health, 96	Manufacturer, 396	Paired partners, 397 (Review Problem Solving Strategies)	Visual, Symbolic, 394–397; Linguistic/ Interpersonal, 397	Problem Solving, Technology, Critical Thinking, Writing, Logical Reasoning
usiness, 401; onsumerism, 402	AlgebraWorks: Retail Store Buyer, 403	Paired partners, 398 (Explore); Small groups/STAD, 402 (Project Connection)	Linguistic/ Interpersonal, 398, 400, 402; Visual, 398–403, 399 (TE)	Problem Solving, Probability, Critical Thinking

PACING GUIDE

Lessons	Regular Classes	2-year Algebra 1 Classes	Blocked Classes
8.1	1	2	½
8.2	1	2	½
8.3	1	2	½
8.4	1	2	½
8.5	1	2	½
8.6	1	2	½
Review	1	1	1
Test	1	1	1
Cumulative Test	1	1	1
Total Classes	9	15	6

SESSMENT OPTIONS

dent Edition
apter Assessment
Chapter Test
Performance Assessment
Project Assessment
ndardized Tests

Chapter Resource Book
Chapter Test, Form A
Chapter Test, Form B
Standardized Chapter Test
Portfolio Item: Self-Assessment
Portfolio Assessment Form

MicroExam II

PREVIEW THE CHAPTER

Take a Look Ahead Have students read the previewing suggestions and then scan the chapter looking for new and familiar things. Give students time to make notes in their journals. Discuss student answers to the previewing questions.

Connecting to Career Opportunities Have the students read the descriptions of the AlgebraWorks features for this chapter. Ask students to identify the careers mentioned. **video shop owners and retail store buyers** Ask students: Do you know anyone who works at these jobs? Discuss the types of educational background usually required for each of the careers. For example, while owning a video shop requires no formal training, successful operation demands continual studying of the marketplace; retail store buyers usually have at least a high school diploma and some training beyond that.

Investigate Further Explain to students that as they study this chapter they should look for examples of other careers in business as well as careers in other fields. Ask students to determine one way in which algebra can be used in that career. Encourage students to write questions in their journals about other business careers they would like to learn more about.

USING THE DATA ACTIVITY

Introduce the Data Activity Have students read the introductory paragraph and discuss any interesting experiences they may have had or have heard of regarding use of ATMs.

Skill Focus Read the skills listed and discuss with students what they think each means. Ask students to suggest problems that might involve the skill being discussed.

Study the Data Review the first table. Have the students discuss the relationship between age and ATM

8 Systems of Linear Inequalities

Take a Look AHEAD

Make notes about things that look new.

- Find some graphs that are different from graphs in previous chapters. Explain what is different about them.
- Use the word constraint in a sentence. Try to give a definition or some synonyms.

Make notes about things that look familiar.

- How do you think solving a system of inequalities will be similar to solving a system of equations? How might it be different?
- Review the meaning of the inequality symbols. Make a chart of different word phrases associated with each symbol.

DATA Activity

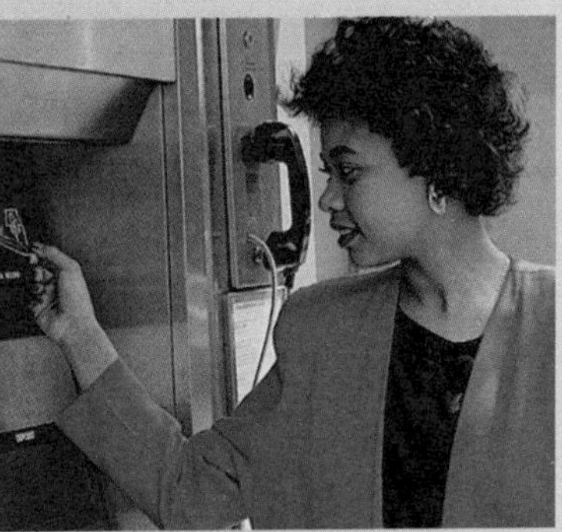

ATM Users

Conveniently located automated teller machines (ATMs) allow customers to bank anytime, day or night. However, there are disadvantages to this banking method. Customers must be careful not to lose their ATM card or to reveal their personal identification number. Computer breakdowns or electrical outages can cause widespread problems. As a result, some people are still reluctant to use ATMs. A bank conducted a survey to gather information about the age and income of ATM users.

SKILL FOCUS

- Calculate experimental probabilities and use values to make predictions.
- Write numbers as decimals, fractions, and percents.
- Draw conclusions from data.
- Make a circle graph.

Be a $mart $hopper

In this chapter, you will see how:

- **Video Shop Owners** use inequalities to determine store income. (Lesson 8.2, page 385)
- **Retail Store Buyers** use probability to make purchasing decisions. (Lesson 8.6, page 403)

ATM USAGE Distribution by Age	
Age (years)	**Percent Using ATMs**
Under 25	7
25 to 34	32
35 to 44	27
45 to 54	15
55 to 64	11
65 to 74	6
75 and over	2

1–4 See Additional Answers.

The tables above and below show the results of the survey conducted by the bank. Use the tables to answer each question.

ATM USAGE Distribution by Income	
Household Income	**Percent Using ATMs**
Under $15,000	14
$15,000 to $24,999	16
$25,000 to $34,999	18
$35,000 to $49,999	23
$50,000 to $74,999	18
$75,000 and over	11

1. Based on this survey, how many in a group of 200 people aged 45 to 54 might be expected to be ATM users?
2. Based on this survey, what is the experimental probability that a person selected at random with a household income of $20,000 per year will be an ATM user? Write your answer as a fraction in lowest terms.
3. How would you describe the person most likely to be an ATM user?
4. **Working Together** For each table, display the information in an accurately drawn circle graph.

usage. Ask them to name factors that they think might cause usage among the youngest and the oldest segments of the population to be low. Students should recognize that although "Under 25" represents almost half of the population, many in that age group have no relationship with a bank. Those over 65 may be least likely to feel comfortable with the technology. As they examine the second table, ask: What percent of ATM users earn less than $50,000? **71%** Discuss how the table can be used to estimate the percent of households falling below a given income.

Complete the Data Activity Have students work individually or with partners to complete the questions.

For Items 1 and 2, students should understand that these tables can be interpreted in several ways. To answer Question 1, for example, students should read the table as "15% of the people between the ages of 45 and 54 use ATMs." To answer Question 2, a similar interpretation is "16% of people with household incomes from $15,000 to $24,999 use ATMs." Using this interpretation, students can answer the first two questions by writing proportions.

For Item 3, have students give the reasons for their choice and then discuss whether their answer seems reasonable from their experience.

For Item 4, you may wish to have students interpret the tables as cumulative frequencies and draw cumulative frequency histograms. For example, the first table can be read as 7% of the people using ATMs are under 25, 39% are under 35, 66% are under 45, and so on.

South-Western Algebra 1 Chapter Theme Video or Videodisc

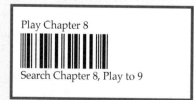

371

INTRODUCING THE PROJECT

Project Goal Discuss the project's big idea: How can algebra be used by consumers to compare the values obtained on different goods and services?

Getting Ready Collect newspaper and magazine advertisements containing fine print disclaimers. Lead a discussion on their complexity. Ask students where else they have seen these types of disclaimers. **in some television and radio commercials**

FACILITATING THE PROJECT

Getting Started Have available several magazines and articles on consumerism. Encourage students to use these to select both a topic for investigating and a format for reporting.

Setting Project Benchmarks Make sure that the students are aware of the project schedule in the Project Planning Calendar and the due dates for each of the benchmarks. You may find the STAD cooperative learning approach appropriate for this activity.

a. Select issues to investigate, consider format for teen consumer report, and begin consumer information list of *Tips for Teens*. (Project/Chapter Opener)
b. Collect data about the services, costs, and requirements for checking accounts at different banks and select the "Top Two Banks for Teens." (Project Connection 8.1)
c. Collect data about the services, costs, and requirements for different book, CD, or video clubs and evaluate the advantages and disadvantages of membership. (Project Connection 8.4)
d. Determine the total cost of an installment purchase including the annual percentage rate of interest. (Project Connection 8.5)
e. Complete the Teen Consumer Report. (Project Assessment)

Suggest that students make subgoals for each goal and include the subgoals in their calendar.

Consumer Report for Teens

Have you ever heard the expression "Read the fine print?" What do you think it means? In a world that offers choices for everything from breakfast cereals to credit cards, you must read labels, advertisements, and contracts carefully before you make a decision. In this project, you will investigate consumer issues and report on where the "real deals" can be found.

PROJECT GOAL

Identify and explore consumer issues of interest to young people.

Getting Started

Work with a group.

1. Begin by brainstorming a list of things you would like to investigate and report on. For example, you may want to compare computer network plans, discount stores, restaurant meals, or air travel costs. Skim the Project Connections so that you do not duplicate the issues in them.
2. Select a final list of three to five issues to investigate.
3. Discuss the format to use for your consumer report. Consider possibilities such as a panel discussion, taped "radio" segments, a video program, or a frequent newsletter for students. Your presentation can be entertaining as well as informative.
4. Begin a *Tips for Teens* list that includes warnings about stores with deceptive practices, notifications of special sales and free concerts, or information about getting the most out of economy sizes of products.

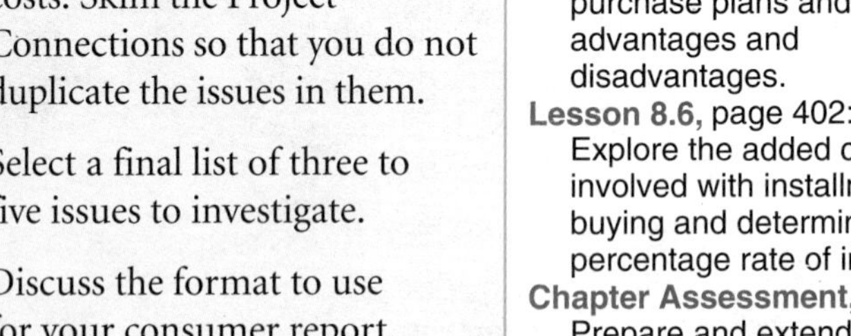

PROJECT Connections

Lesson 8.2, page 384:
Collect data about checking accounts at different banks and compare costs.
Lesson 8.4, page 393:
Evaluate negative option purchase plans and analyze advantages and disadvantages.
Lesson 8.6, page 402:
Explore the added costs involved with installment buying and determine annual percentage rate of interest.
Chapter Assessment, page 407:
Prepare and extend the Teen Consumer Report.

8.1 Graph Linear Inequalities in Two Variables

Explore/Working Together

Work with a partner. Assume that marigolds are $1.00 each and geraniums are $2.00 each.

Ken is planting a flower box garden. He can spend up to $10. Let x represent the number of marigolds he can buy, and let y represent the number of geraniums he can buy.

1. a. If Ken buys only marigolds, what is the greatest number of plants he can buy? the smallest number? Write an ordered pair (x, y) for each of your solutions. 10 marigolds; 0 marigolds; (10, 0); (0, 0)

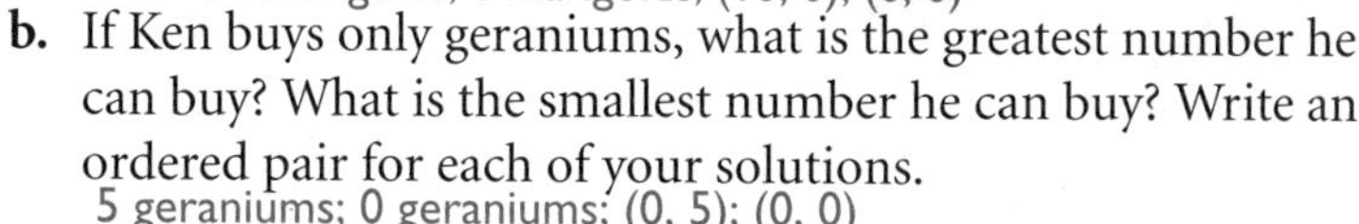

   b. If Ken buys only geraniums, what is the greatest number he can buy? What is the smallest number he can buy? Write an ordered pair for each of your solutions. 5 geraniums; 0 geraniums; (0, 5); (0, 0)

   c. If Ken buys 3 geraniums, what is the greatest number of marigolds he can buy? What is the smallest number he can buy? Write an ordered pair for each of your solutions. 4 marigolds; 0 marigolds; (4, 3); (0, 3)

2. Graph all of the points you found for Questions 1a, 1b, and 1c. Find all combinations of marigolds and geraniums Ken can consider. Graph those points as well. See Additional Answers.

3. What pattern do you notice on your graph? Answers will vary; possible answer: points nearly form the interior of a right triangle.

4. Suppose Ken spends exactly $10 on marigolds and geraniums. Write an equation that represents the number of marigolds and geraniums Ken can buy. $x + 2y = 10$

5. Graph the equation you wrote for Question 4 on the same coordinate plane as the points for the ordered pairs. See Additional Answers.

SPOTLIGHT ON LEARNING

WHAT? In this lesson you will learn
- to determine whether ordered pairs are solutions of linear inequalities.
- to graph linear inequalities.

WHY? Graphing linear equalities in two variables can help you to solve problems in geometry, business, sports, health care, and technology.

Build Understanding

If you replace the equal symbol in any linear equation of two variables with $<$, $>$, $\leq$, $\geq$, or $\neq$, you create a **linear inequality** in two variables.

The points you graphed in Explore are solutions to the linear inequality $x + 2y \leq 10$. In this case, the solutions are found on or below the line $x + 2y = 10$. There are no ordered pairs above the line that are solutions to this linear inequality.

LESSON PLANNING

Objectives
- ▶ Identify solutions of linear inequalities.
- ▶ Graph linear inequalities.

Vocabulary
boundary
closed half-plane
half-plane
linear inequality
open half-plane

Technology/Multimedia
graphing utility

Resources
Warm Up 8.1
Reteaching 8.1
Extra Practice 8.1
Enrichment 8.1
Transparencies 32, 34, 48–49, 78–80
Student Handbook
Lesson Quiz 8.1
Study Skills Activity 21
Technology Activity 18
Multicultural Connection 8, Hispanic: Focus on Numeration

Materials/Manipulatives
graph paper
straightedges

ASSIGNMENTS

Basic: 1–18, 24–27, Mixed Review 32–38

Average: 1–22, 24–29, Mixed Review 32–38

Enriched: 1–4, 8–31, Mixed Review 32–38

1 MOTIVATE

Explore/Working Together After students complete Questions 1–5, ask, why didn't you graph any points below the x-axis or to the left of the y-axis? **Ken could not have bought a negative amount of flowers.** Suppose Ken could spend up to \$16 on pretzels and nuts for a party. Pretzels cost \$1 per pound and nuts cost \$3 per pound. Would the points showing the combinations of pretzels and nuts Ken could buy be the same or different than the points you graphed in Question 2? Explain. **Additional combinations are possible because the area of the enclosed region of $x + 3y \le 16$, $x \le 0$, and $y \le 0$ is greater than the one for Question 2, and because pretzels and nuts can be bought in fractions of a pound as well as in whole pounds.**

2 TEACH

Use the Pages/Build Understanding

Example 1: Ask students how determining whether an ordered pair is a solution of a linear inequality is the same as or different from determining whether it is a solution of a linear equation. **Methods are the same except that for a linear equation the values on both sides of the equation in the last step of the solution must be equal. If the sign in the inequality is < or >, then the values must be compared to see whether one is less than or greater than the other, respectively.**

CHECK UNDERSTANDING

In Example 1c, notice (4, 10) is the solution to the equation $y = 3x - 2$. If the inequality had been $y \le 3x - 2$, how would the solution change?

The point (4, 10) and all other points that are solutions of $y = 3x - 2$ would be solutions of the inequality.

COMMUNICATING ABOUT ALGEBRA

To determine which half-plane contains the solution set of a linear inequality, many people test the origin. Why would they do so? Describe a situation in which testing (0, 0) would not make sense.

See Additional Answers.

PROBLEM SOLVING TIP

Test points from both half-planes to guard against mistakes.

To find whether an ordered pair is a solution to a linear inequality, substitute the values for x and y into the inequality and evaluate.

EXAMPLE 1

Determine whether each ordered pair is a solution of $y < 3x - 2$.

a. (3, 6) **b.** (−4, 2) **c.** (4, 10)

Solution

a.
$y < 3x - 2$
$6 \overset{?}{<} 3(3) - 2$
$6 \overset{?}{<} 9 - 2$
$6 < 7$ **true**

b.
$y < 3x - 2$
$2 \overset{?}{<} 3(-4) - 2$
$2 \overset{?}{<} -12 - 2$
$2 < -14$ **not true**

c.
$y < 3x - 2$
$10 \overset{?}{<} 3(4) - 2$
$10 \overset{?}{<} 12 - 2$
$10 < 10$ **not true**

So, (3, 6) is a solution of $y < 3x - 2$, but (−4, 2) and (4, 10) are not. ◄

The graph of a linear equation divides the coordinate plane into two regions or **half-planes.** The line itself is the **boundary** of each of these two half-planes.

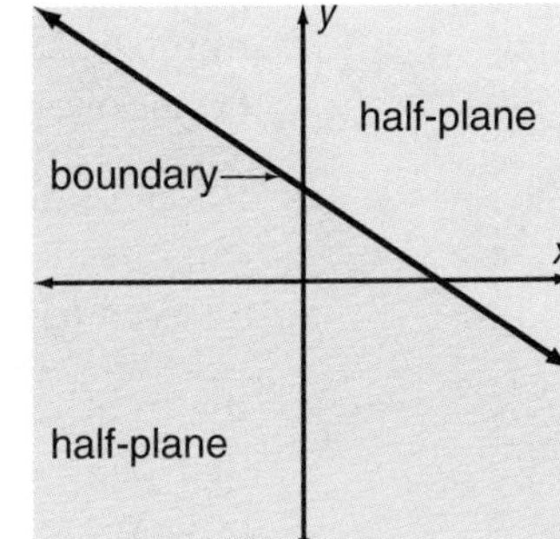

The graph of a linear inequality in two variables includes all points in a half-plane. Shaded half-planes show where solutions can be found. When the inequality symbol is ≤ or ≥, draw the boundary as a solid line. When the inequality symbol is < or >, draw the boundary as a dashed line.

EXAMPLE 2

Graph: $y < 2x + 1$

Solution

Graph the corresponding linear equation $y = 2x + 1$. Because the inequality symbol is <, the boundary line is not a part of the solution. Show the boundary as a dashed line.

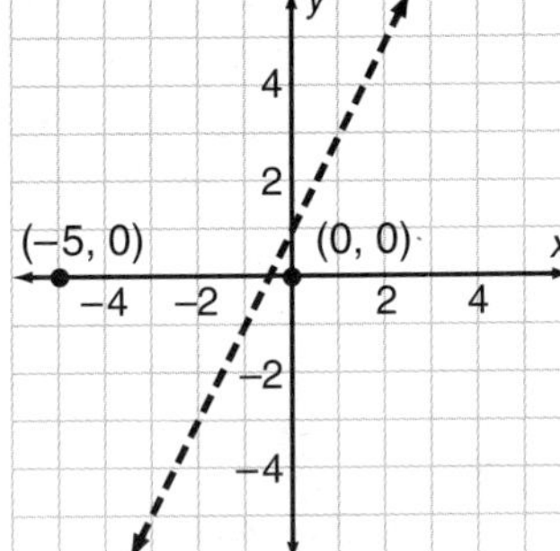

Test points on both sides of the boundary line to determine which half-plane to shade. Choose points that will be easy to substitute, such as (0, 0) and (−5, 0).

(0, 0)
$y < 2x + 1$
$0 \overset{?}{<} 2(0) + 1$
$0 < 1$ **true**

(−5, 0)
$y < 2x + 1$
$0 \overset{?}{<} 2(-5) + 1$
$0 < -9$ **not true**

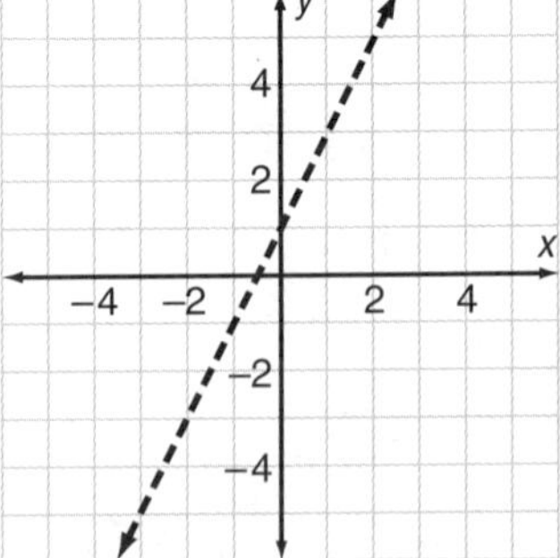

The point (0, 0) is a solution of the inequality, so all other points in the half-plane containing (0, 0) are also solutions of $y < 2x + 1$. Shade that half-plane. ◀

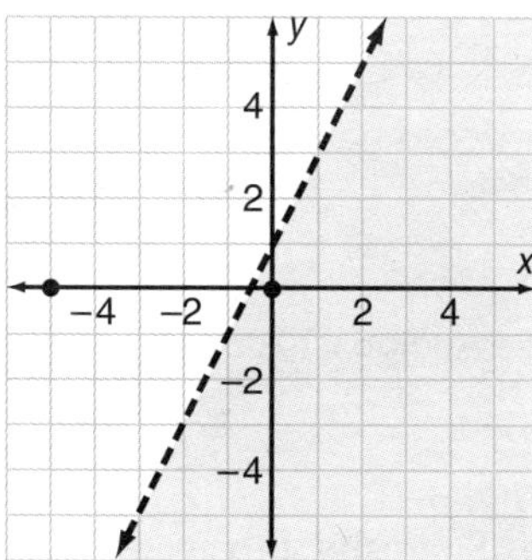

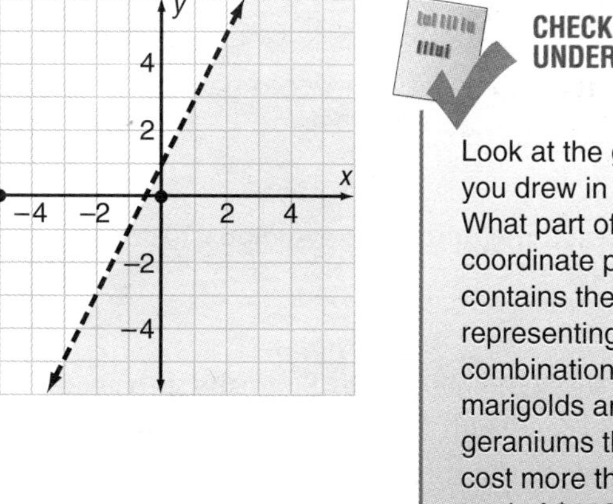

A half-plane that does not include the boundary line, such as the one in Example 2, is an **open half-plane**. A **closed half-plane** is one that includes the boundary line, as in Example 3 below.

EXAMPLE 3

GEOMETRY A certain rectangle has a perimeter of at least 30 cm.

a. Write a linear inequality that represents this situation. Then graph the solution of the inequality.

b. Refer to the graph and name three possible combinations of length and width of this rectangle.

Solution

a. Let x equal the length of the rectangle in centimeters and y equal the width of the rectangle in centimeters.

$$2x + 2y \geq 30$$

Graph the corresponding linear equation. Because the inequality symbol is ≥, the boundary is part of the solution. Show the boundary as a solid line. Test (0, 0) and (10, 10) to see whether either point is a solution of the inequality.

(0, 0)

$$2x + 2y \geq 30$$
$$2(0) + 2(0) \overset{?}{\geq} 30$$
$$0 \ngeq 30$$

(10, 10)

$$2x + 2y \geq 30$$
$$2(10) + 2(10) \overset{?}{\geq} 30$$
$$40 \geq 30$$

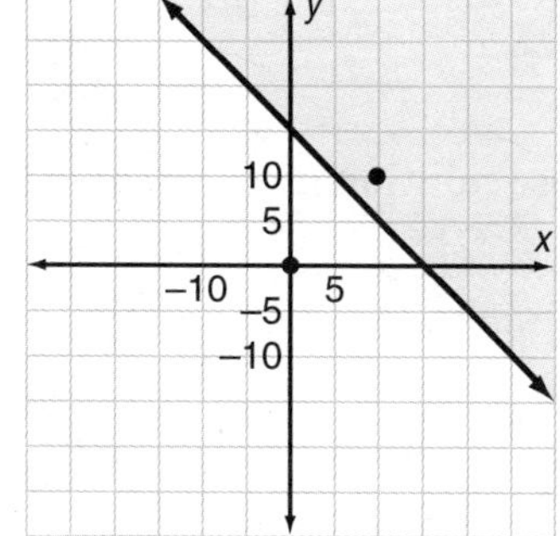

Therefore, shade the half-plane containing the point (10, 10).

b. Both the length and the width of a rectangle must be positive numbers. Therefore, only the ordered pairs in the part of the shaded region that is within Quadrant I represent possible combinations of length and width. Some possible dimensions of the rectangle are 1 cm × 20 cm, 4 cm × 16 cm, or 16.2 cm × 20.5 cm. ◀

CHECK UNDERSTANDING

Look at the graph you drew in Explore. What part of the coordinate plane contains the points representing combinations of marigolds and geraniums that cost more than a total of $10?

the half-plane above the line in Quadrant I

THINK BACK

If a linear equation is not in slope-intercept form, $y = mx + b$, rewrite it in that form before graphing it on a graphing utility. In Example 3, the slope-intercept form of the corresponding linear equation is $y = -x + 15$.

Example 2: Encourage students to test points to determine which half-plane to shade instead of relying solely on the rule of below the line for less than and above the line for greater than. Depending on what the slope of the line is, it can be hard to determine above and below. Also, when $-y$ appears in the original inequality, students sometimes forget to reverse the inequality sign when multiplying by −1. Using test points will also help eliminate graphing errors arising from this mistake.

Example 3: Use this example, as well as the activities in Explore, to point out that when a problem situation is represented by a linear inequality, the real life solution is sometimes represented by only a part of the graph of the inequality.

DIVERSITY IN THE CLASSROOM

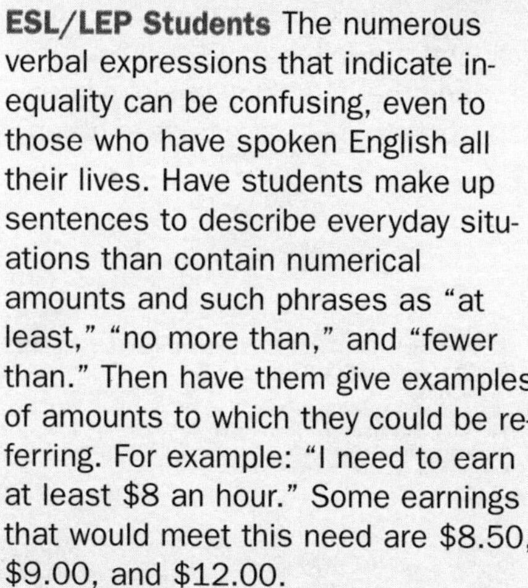

ESL/LEP Students The numerous verbal expressions that indicate inequality can be confusing, even to those who have spoken English all their lives. Have students make up sentences to describe everyday situations than contain numerical amounts and such phrases as "at least," "no more than," and "fewer than." Then have them give examples of amounts to which they could be referring. For example: "I need to earn at least $8 an hour." Some earnings that would meet this need are $8.50, $9.00, and $12.00.

Ongoing Assessment The important concepts are determining whether ordered pairs are solutions of linear inequalities and graphing linear inequalities. To assess these ideas, have students demonstrate how they have applied these concepts and skills in Exercises 1, 4, and 6 of the Try These section.

Guided Practice/Try These If students are having difficulty writing an inequality for Exercise 6, part a, ask leading questions such as these:

- What expression could you write to represent club members who receive tickets and nonmembers who receive tickets? ***x* + *y***
- How would the total number of members and nonmembers who received tickets compare to the number of tickets available? **The total would have to be the same or less than the number available.**

3 SUMMARIZE

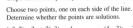

In the Math Journal Have students write a general description of how they would graph a linear inequality. Check to see that they have included the following: if necessary, rewriting the inequality in slope-intercept form to make it easier to graph

NAME ______________ CLASS ________ DATE ________

8.1 GRAPH LINEAR INEQUALITIES IN TWO VARIABLES

RETEACHING

The graph of an inequality in two variables is a half-plane. If the inequality symbol is < or > use a dashed line to show that the boundary line is not part of the solution. Use a solid line to show that the boundary line is part of the solution for an inequality containing ≤ or ≥.

Example
Graph the linear inequality $y < 2x - 1$.

Solution
Graph the boundary line $y = 2x - 1$. Use a dashed line.

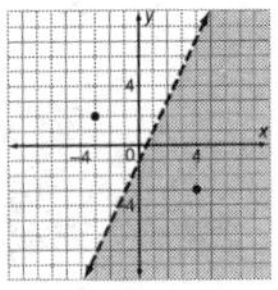

Choose two points, one on each side of the line.
Determine whether the points are solutions.

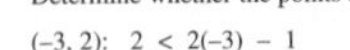

(–3, 2): $2 < 2(-3) - 1$, $2 < -6 - 1$, $2 < -7$ false

(4, –3): $-3 < 2(4) - 1$, $-3 < 8 - 1$, $-3 < 7$ true

(4, –3) is a solution of the inequality. Shade the side of the line that contains (4, –3).

EXERCISES

Graph each inequality.

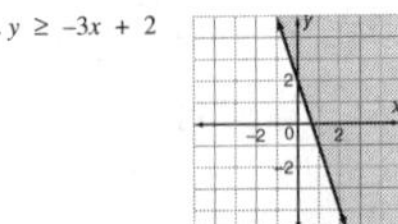

1. $y \geq -3x + 2$

2. $y \leq \frac{1}{4}x - 3$

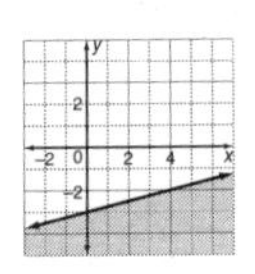

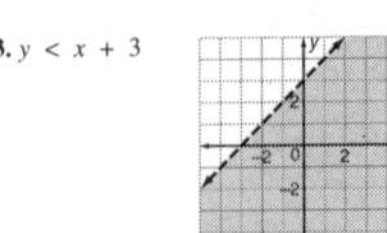

3. $y < x + 3$

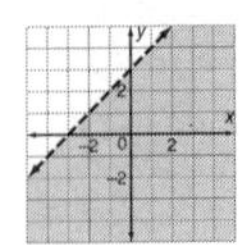

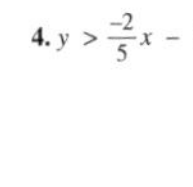

4. $y > \frac{-2}{5}x - 3$

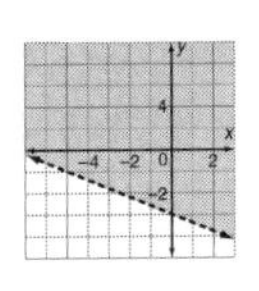

6 South Western Algebra 1: AN INTEGRATED APPROACH

TRY THESE

Determine whether the ordered pair is a solution of the inequality.

1. $y > -4x$; $(-4, 16)$ no
2. $3x - 2y \geq 12$; $(2, -3)$ yes
3. $6x + 3 < 5y$; $(0, 0)$ no

Graph each inequality. See Additional Answers.

4. $y \leq 0.5x - 3$
5. $3x + 4y \geq 8$

6. TICKET GIVEAWAY The Spanish Club at Riverdale High School has received 40 free tickets to the International Festival to be held in Riverdale. These tickets will be given to the first students—club members or nonmembers—who request them.
See Additional Answers.
   a. Write and graph an inequality that represents the number of club members and the number of nonmembers who could receive the tickets.
   b. Based on your graph, name three possible combinations of members and nonmembers who could receive tickets.

7. MODELING Write the inequality whose solution is represented by the graph below.

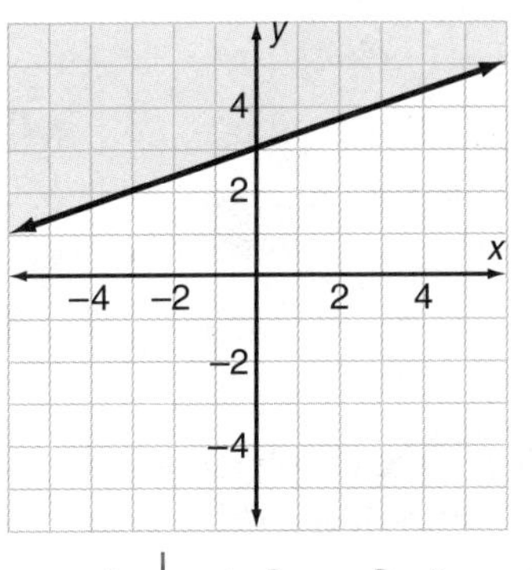

$y \geq \frac{1}{3}x + 3$ or $3y \geq x + 9$

PRACTICE

Determine whether the ordered pair is a solution of the inequality.

1. $y > 5x - 10$; $(3, 5)$ no
2. $2y \leq x$; $(0, 1)$ no
3. $2x + 4y \geq 7$; $(-1, 3)$ yes
4. $3x - y \leq -7$; $(0, 0)$ no

Graph each linear inequality. 5–10 See Additional Answers.

5. $y \leq x - 2$
6. $y > \frac{4}{5}x - 4$
7. $3x + 5y < 20$
8. $2x - y \geq 3$
9. $4x - 3y > 0$
10. $5x + 10y \leq -30$

Write the inequality whose solution is represented by each graph.

11.

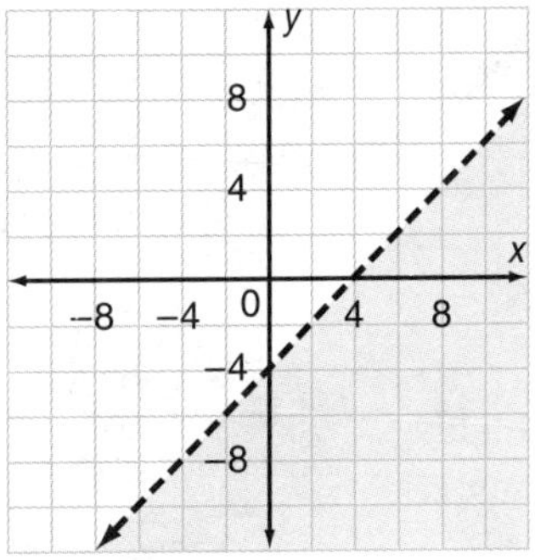

$y < x - 4$

12.

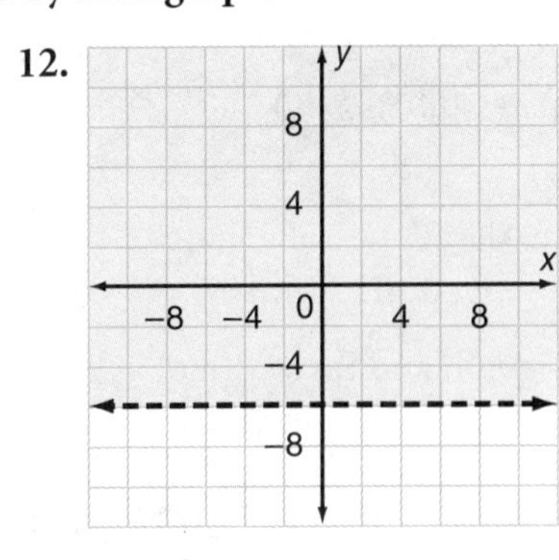

$y > -6$

13.

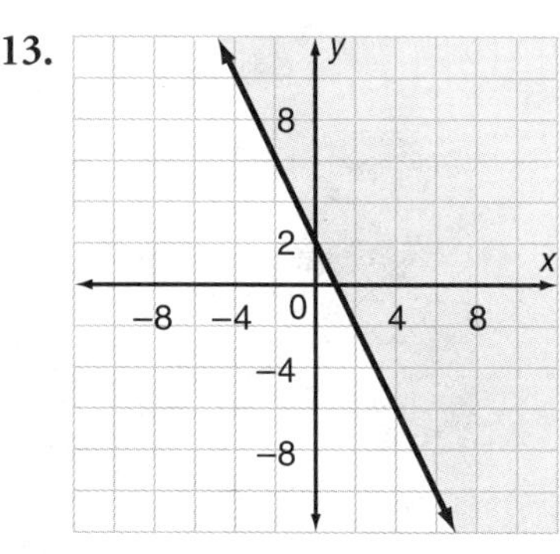

$y \geq -2x + 2$

14.

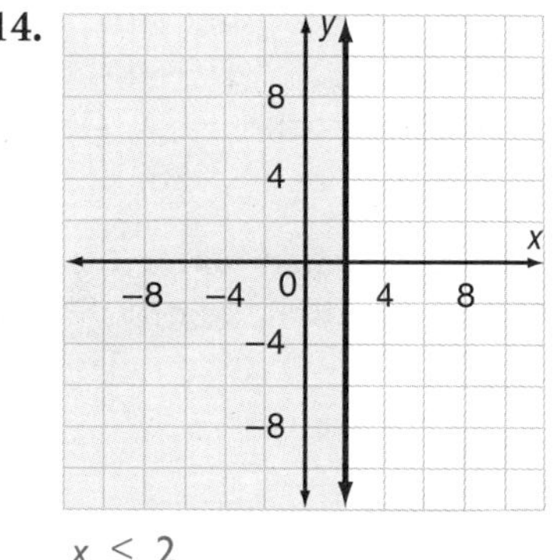

$x \leq 2$

15. **WRITING MATHEMATICS** How is graphing a linear inequality in two variables like graphing an inequality in one variable? How is it different? See Additional Answers.

16. **SPORTS** The Spartans scored 20 points, but they still lost the football game to the Eagles. The Eagles scored field goals (3 points each), as well as touchdowns that were each followed by the extra conversion point (7 points in all).

   a. Write and graph an inequality that represents the combination of field goals and touchdowns the Eagles could have scored.
   See Additional Answers.

   b. Based on your graph, name three possible combinations of field goals and touchdowns the Eagles could have scored. possible combinations: 6 field goals and 1 touchdown; 1 field goal and 4 touchdowns; 3 field goals and 3 touchdowns

EXTEND

Equivalent inequalities are inequalities that have the same solution set. Determine whether each pair of inequalities is equivalent.

17. $y > x$
    $y < -x$ not equivalent

18. $y \geq 3x + 1$
    $3y \geq 9x + 3$
    equivalent

19. $2y > x - 3$
    $x - 3 < 2y$ equivalent

20. $3y > 2x + 6$
    $4y \geq 6x + 8$
    not equivalent

21. **WRITING MATHEMATICS** Describe how to decide whether the inequalities in Exercise 19 are equivalent. See Additional Answers.

22. **HEALTH CARE** A doctor's office schedules 30 min for each new patient and 15 min for each returning patient up to a total of 7 h each day. See Additional Answers.

   a. Write and graph an inequality that represents the combination of new and returning patients that could be scheduled for one day.

   b. Based on your graph, name three possible combinations of new and returning patients that could be scheduled.

the corresponding linear equation; graphing that linear equation and determining whether to use a dashed or solid line; determining and shading the half-plane that contains the solutions.

4 PRACTICE

Practice Extend Exercises 1, 2, and 4 by having students use different inequality signs to rewrite the inequalities so that the ordered pairs given are solutions of the new inequality. **1. ≤ or ≥; 2. >; 4. >**

Extend After students have completed these problems, hold a brief discussion on how office managers and store managers could use the solutions to problems such as those in Exercises 22 and 23.

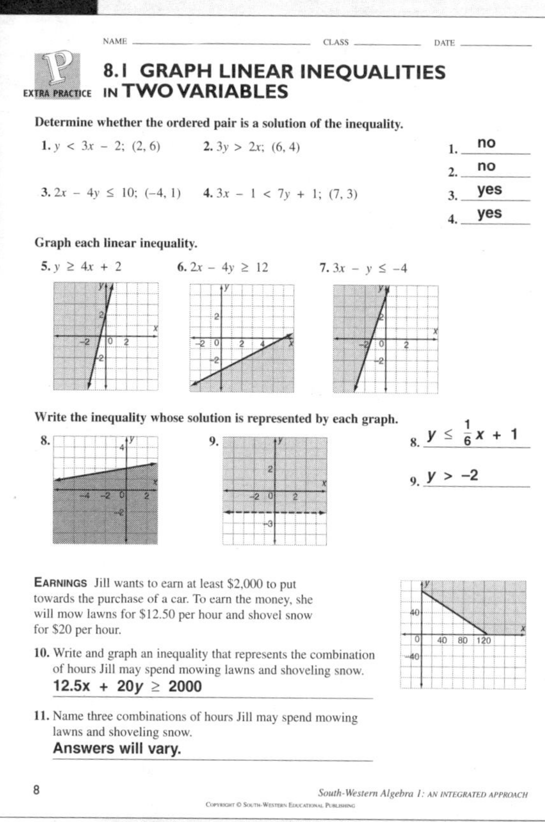

NAME ______ CLASS ______ DATE ______

P EXTRA PRACTICE

8.1 GRAPH LINEAR INEQUALITIES IN TWO VARIABLES

Determine whether the ordered pair is a solution of the inequality.

1. $y < 3x - 2$; (2, 6)
2. $3y > 2x$; (6, 4)
3. $2x - 4y \leq 10$; (−4, 1)
4. $3x - 1 < 7y + 1$; (7, 3)

1. no
2. no
3. yes
4. yes

Graph each linear inequality.

5. $y \geq 4x + 2$
6. $2x - 4y \geq 12$
7. $3x - y \leq -4$

Write the inequality whose solution is represented by each graph.

8.
9.

8. $y \leq \frac{1}{6}x + 1$
9. $y > -2$

EARNINGS Jill wants to earn at least \$2,000 to put towards the purchase of a car. To earn the money, she will mow lawns for \$12.50 per hour and shovel snow for \$20 per hour.

10. Write and graph an inequality that represents the combination of hours Jill may spend mowing lawns and shoveling snow.
$12.5x + 20y \geq 2000$

11. Name three combinations of hours Jill may spend mowing lawns and shoveling snow.
Answers will vary.

8 *South-Western Algebra 1: AN INTEGRATED APPROACH*

Think Critically To write general descriptions in Exercises 24–27, encourage students to look back at graphs they have drawn in this lesson for each type of inequality and identify similarities and differences among them.

5 FOLLOW-UP

Extension Have students look again at Example 3. Ask: If the width of this rectangle is at least 6 cm, how would you modify the graph to represent this? **Draw a line through 6 on the y-axis and parallel to the x-axis. Double-shade the region above this line.**

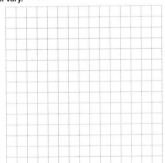

NAME ________ CLASS ________ DATE ________

ENRICHMENT

8.1 GRAPH LINEAR INEQUALITIES IN TWO VARIABLES

Use the graph below to sketch a geometric design made with only straight lines. You may make your lines solid or dashed or a combination of both. Shade one side of each line with colored pencils. Some of your shadings will overlap. Choose colors that will create an interesting effect as they overlap.

After finishing your design, write the inequalites that make up your design. Test a point in each of the shaded regions to be sure your inequality is correct. If possible, graph your design using a graphing utility or graphing software.

Answers will vary.

Equations of lines in your design.

10 *South-Western Algebra 1: An Integrated Approach*

23. **Business/Technology** A shoe store makes an average profit of \$20 on each pair of regularly priced shoes it sells. The store has an average profit of \$5 on each pair of sale priced shoes it sells. The store's goal is to make a daily profit of at least \$1000. See Additional Answers.
   a. Write an inequality that represents the combinations of regularly priced and sale priced shoes that must be sold for the store to achieve its goal. Use a graphing utility to graph this inequality.
   b. Based on your graph, name three possible combinations of the two kinds of shoes the store might sell to achieve its goal.

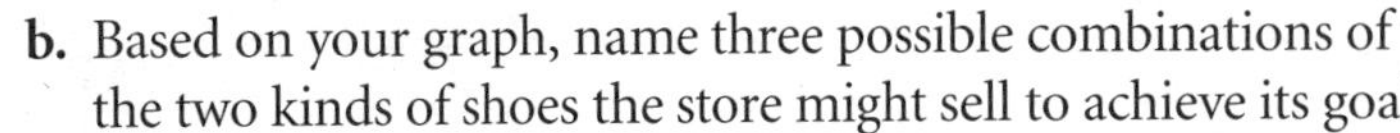

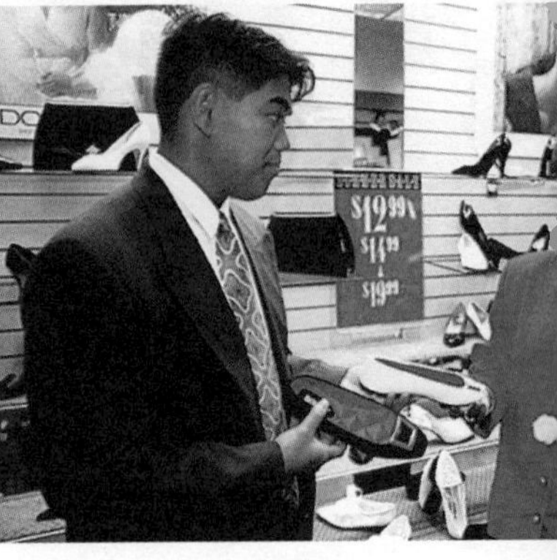

THINK CRITICALLY

Describe each graph. Be sure to include whether the line is dashed or solid and which half-plane is shaded.

24. $y < mx + b$ dashed line; half-plane below the line
25. $y > mx + b$ dashed line; half-plane above the line
26. $y \le mx + b$ solid line; half-plane below the line
27. $y \ge mx + b$ solid line; half-plane above the line
28. Write a linear inequality whose graph is all of Quadrants I and II, as well as the x-axis. $y \ge 0$
29. Write a linear inequality whose graph is all of Quadrants I and IV. $x > 0$
30. **Writing Mathematics** Graph the inequality you wrote for Exercise 29 on both a coordinate plane and a number line. How do the two graphs relate to each other? See Additional Answers.
31. **Writing Mathematics** Write a problem that could be solved by graphing $2x + 0.5y < 10$. Then graph the inequality and name three possible sets of ordered pairs that are in the solution of the inequality. See Additional Answers.

MIXED REVIEW

32. **Standardized Tests** What is the value of the underlined variable in the formula for the given value of A? B; Lesson 3.8

$$A = \pi \underline{r}^2 \text{ when } A = 19.625$$

A. 6.247 B. 2.5 C. 7.85 D. 39

Graph each compound inequality. See Additional Answers. Lesson 5.5

33. $q < -1$ or $q \ge 1$
34. $-2.3 \le a \le 6$

Solve the system using elimination. Lesson 7.4

35. $\begin{cases} 3x + 6y = 3 \\ 2x - 5y = -16 \end{cases}$ (–3, 2)
36. $\begin{cases} 8x - 4y = 2 \\ 4x + 8y = 26 \end{cases}$ (1.5, 2.5)

Graph each linear inequality. See Additional Answers. Lesson 8.1

37. $2x + y \ge -4$
38. $y < 3x - 2$

8.2 Solve Systems of Linear Inequalities by Graphing

Explore/Working Together

Work with a partner. Let x represent the number of lawn seats and y represent the number of reserved seats.

1. Tickets for the Dark Nights concert are $15 for lawn seats and $25 for reserved seats. Each person waiting in line for tickets will buy at least one ticket. Some will buy both types of tickets. Write an inequality that represents the amount of money each person will spend. $15x + 25y \geq 15$
2. Make a list of five ordered pairs that are solutions of the inequality you wrote. possible ordered pairs: (0, 1), (1.5, 2), (2, 0), (2, 2)
3. Cross out any ordered pairs you wrote that could not represent a combination of lawn seat and reserved seat tickets. See Additional Answers.
4. Because the concert is expected to be a sellout, each person is limited to buying 6 tickets. Write an inequality that represents the number of tickets each person will buy. $x + y \leq 6$
5. Cross out any ordered pairs that remain on your list that are not solutions of the inequality you wrote in Question 4. Only ordered pairs with a sum less than or equal to 6 should remain.
6. For an ordered pair to remain on your list, what must be true about it? Possible answer: it must be the solution of both inequalities.

SPOTLIGHT ON LEARNING

WHAT? In this lesson you will learn
- to solve systems of linear equalities by graphing.

WHY? Solving linear inequalities by graphing can help you to solve problems in sales, purchasing, weather, recreation, business, and economics.

Build Understanding

Like linear equations, two or more linear inequalities considered together form a **system of linear inequalities**. If you graph both inequalities in the system on the same coordinate plane, the region in which their graphs overlap contains all the solutions of the system. An ordered pair that is a solution of all the inequalities in a system is a solution of the system. The two inequalities you wrote in Explore form a system of linear inequalities.

LESSON PLANNING

Objective

▶ Solve systems of linear inequalities by graphing.

Vocabulary

system of linear inequalities

Resources

Warm Up 8.2
Reteaching 8.2
Extra Practice 8.2
Enrichment 8.2
Transparencies 32, 49–50
Student Handbook
Lesson Quiz 8.2
Study Skills Activity 22

Materials/Manipulatives

graph paper
straightedges

ASSIGNMENTS

Basic: 1–12, 17–26, 30–31, 36, Project Connection 1–4, AlgebraWorks 1–5

Average: 1–14, 17–26, 30–36, Project Connection 1–4, AlgebraWorks 1–5

Enriched: 13–39, Project Connection 1–4, AlgebraWorks 1–5

1 MOTIVATE

Explore/Working Together After students complete Questions 1–6, ask them to discuss their approach to answering the questions. Watch for students who listed ordered pairs in Question 2 such that they had no pairs remaining on their list after completing the questions. Discuss why this could happen and encourage them to find at least one ordered pair that could have remained on their lists throughout their work.

2 TEACH

Use the Pages/Build Understanding

Example 1: Ask students what the regions of the coordinate plane with single shading only or no shading represent. **ordered pairs that are solutions of one inequality but not the other; ordered pairs that are not solutions of either inequality**

TEACHING TIP

Students may find it easier to see the double-shaded regions of their graphs if they use a different color pencil to graph the solution of each inequality within a system.

Example 2: Ask students whether the following ordered pairs represent possible solutions to the problem and, if not, why they don't: (–3, 15), (4, 3), (10.5, 2) **no; (–3, 15): a negative number of books does not make sense; (4, 3); this is a solution of $5x + 20y < 250$ but not of $x + y \geq 10$; (10.5, 2): a fractional part of a book does not make sense.**

Ongoing Assessment The important concepts and skills are solving systems of linear inequalities by graphing and recognizing the parts of a solution that are solutions of a real world problem. To assess these ideas, have students demonstrate how they have applied these concepts and skills in questions 1, 4, and 11 of the Try These section.

CHECK UNDERSTANDING

What parts of the graph shown in Example 1 contain the points that represent the combinations of lawn and reserved seats that each person in Explore could buy?

Since only positive values of x and y can represent tickets, the part of the double-shaded region in Quadrant I, the x- and y-axes that border Quadrant I, and the segments of the lines $x + y = 6$ and $15x + 25y = 15$ that border the region.

EXAMPLE 1

Graph: $\begin{cases} 15x + 25y \geq 15 \\ x + y \leq 6 \end{cases}$

Solution

First, graph the linear inequality $15x + 25y \geq 15$.

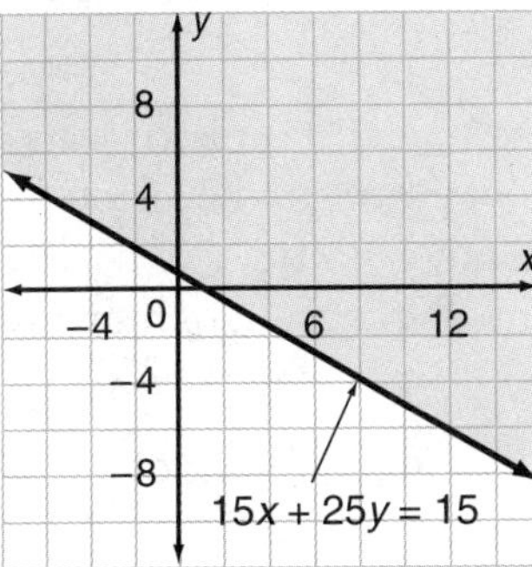

Then graph $x + y \leq 6$ on the same coordinate plane.

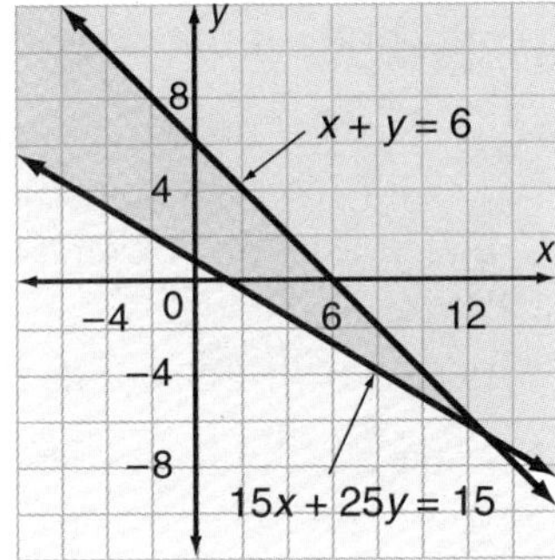

The region with the double shading and the boundary lines of this region contain the points that are solutions of the system. ◄

You can solve real world problems using a system of linear inequalities.

EXAMPLE 2

CONSUMERISM Mrs. Fuentes wants to buy at least 10 books. Each paperback book costs an average of \$10, and each hardcover book costs an average of \$20. Mrs. Fuentes is planning to spend less than \$250 on books.

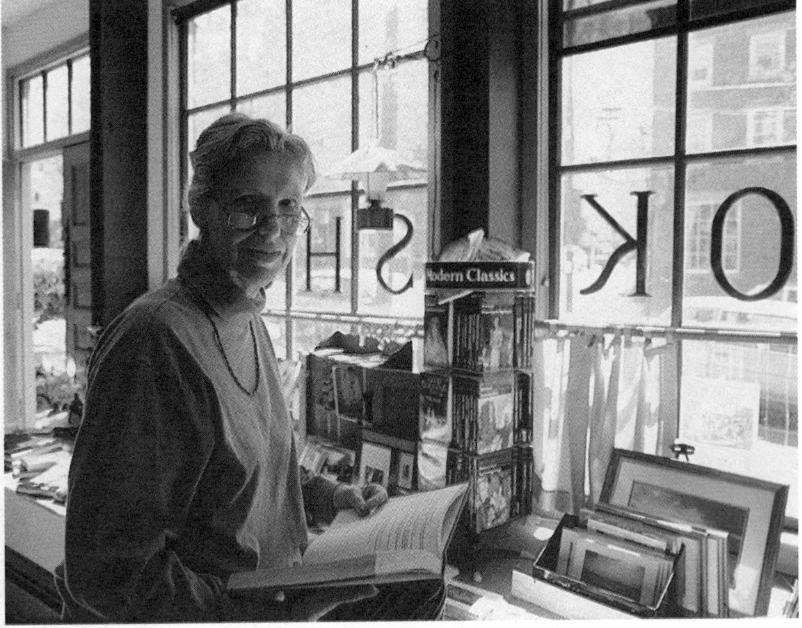

a. Write a system of linear inequalities that represents this situation. Then graph the solution of the system.

b. Based on your graph, name three possible combinations of paperback and hardcover books Mrs. Fuentes could buy.

Solution

a. Let x represent the number of paperback books and y represent the number of hardcover books. The number of books Mrs. Fuentes wants to buy is $x + y \geq 10$. The amount she plans to spend is $10x + 20y < 250$. So, the system of inequalities that represents the situation is

$$\begin{cases} x + y \geq 10 \\ 10x + 20y < 250 \end{cases}$$

Graph $x + y = 10$ with a solid line. Test points on either side of the line, such as (0, 0) and (10, 10), to see which half-plane to shade. Shade above the line, because the point (10, 10) is above the line and makes $x + y \geq 10$ true.

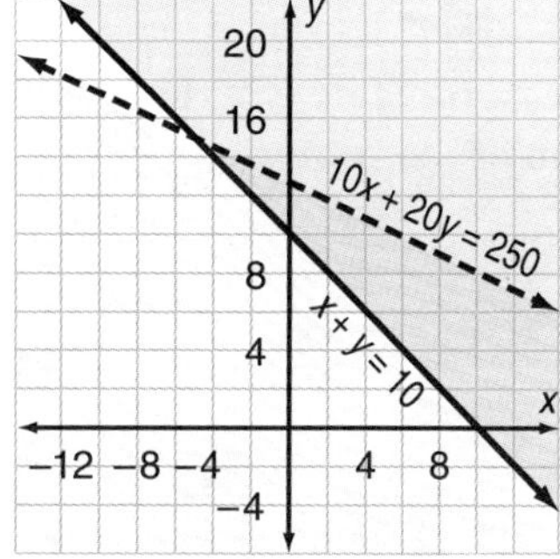

Then graph $10x + 20y = 250$ with a dashed line. Testing points above and below the line shows that the half-plane below the line should be shaded. The solution is the double-shaded region.

b. Select any three points in the double-shaded region. The points representing 12 paperback books and 6 hardcover books, 16 paperback books and 0 hardcover books, and 0 paperback books and 10 hardcover books are all within the double-shaded region. ◄

TRY THESE

Graph each system of linear inequalities. See Additional Answers.

1. $\begin{cases} y > 3x - 1 \\ y \leq -\frac{2}{5}x + 3 \end{cases}$

2. $\begin{cases} 2x + y < 4 \\ 6x - 3y > 18 \end{cases}$

3. $\begin{cases} y < x \\ y \geq -x + 1 \end{cases}$

4. $\begin{cases} 2x - 3y \leq 9 \\ 2y + x < 6 \end{cases}$

5. $\begin{cases} x - y \leq 4 \\ x + y < 3 \end{cases}$

6. $\begin{cases} y \leq -2x + 3 \\ y > 4x - 1 \end{cases}$

7. $\begin{cases} x + y < -1 \\ 3x - y > 4 \end{cases}$

8. $\begin{cases} y > 2x \\ y - x \leq 5 \end{cases}$

9. $\begin{cases} x + 2y \leq 4 \\ x - 2y > 6 \end{cases}$

10. MODELING Write the system of linear inequalities whose solution is represented by the graph at the right. See Additional Answers.

11. Determine whether each ordered pair is a solution of the system represented by the graph at the right.

a. (0, 0) no **b.** (−4, −6) no **c.** (−4, 6) yes **d.** (4, 10) yes

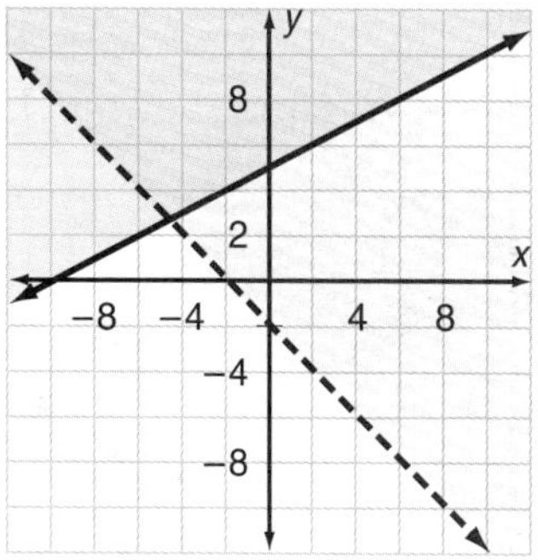

RECREATION While traveling, Mr. Komuro will not drive more than 8 h each day. However, he likes to cover at least 400 km. He averages 60 km/h on the expressways and 40 km/h on the highways.

12. Write and graph a system of linear inequalities that represents the hours and kilometers Mr. Komuro could drive each day. See Additional Answers.

13. Based on your graph, name three possible combinations of roadways Mr. Komuro could drive each day. See Additional Answers.

Guided Practice/Try These If students are having difficulty writing a system of inequalities for Exercise 12, ask questions such as these:

- What expression could you write to represent the hours spent driving on expressways and the hours spent driving on highways? ***x* + *y***
- What is the sum of *x* and *y*? **less than 8**
- What expression could you write to represent the total kilometers driven on expressways? Why? **60*x*; the total kilometers, or distance, equals the rate, 60 mph, times the time, *x***
- How many kilometers does Mr. Komuro like to drive in all? **400 or more**

3 SUMMARIZE

In the Math Journal Have students continue the general description they wrote for Lesson 8.1 to include how they could use the same steps to graph a system of inequalities to find the solution. Check to see that students have included the following steps for graphing each inequality in a system: graphing the corresponding equation, identifying which region of the plane represents the solution of the system, determining whether the half-plane is closed or open, and testing points inside and outside the region.

4 PRACTICE

Practice Extend Exercises 1 and 3 by asking students why those pairs are not solutions. **(5, −2) is only a solution of 2*x* + 3*y* < 9; (10, 3) is not a solution of either inequality.**

Extend Before students begin Exercises 30–35, which involve systems of three inequalities, you may want to ask questions such as these:

- What must be true about solutions of these systems? **They must be solutions of all three inequalities in the system.**
- To graph solutions of these systems, how could you use a method similar to the one you have been using to graph solutions of systems of two inequalities? **Graph the linear equation that corresponds to the first inequality and shade the appropriate half-plane; graph the linear equation that corresponds to the second inequality and shade the appropriate region so that the solution to both the first and second inequalities appears double-shaded; graph the linear equation that corresponds to the third inequality and shade the appropriate region; the solution to all three inequalities will be triple-shaded.**

Sometimes triple-shaded regions are difficult to distinguish from double-shaded regions. Besides shading, another method of indicating half-planes is to use arrows on the appropriate side of the lines. Using this method, for example, the answer for Exercise 30 would look like this.

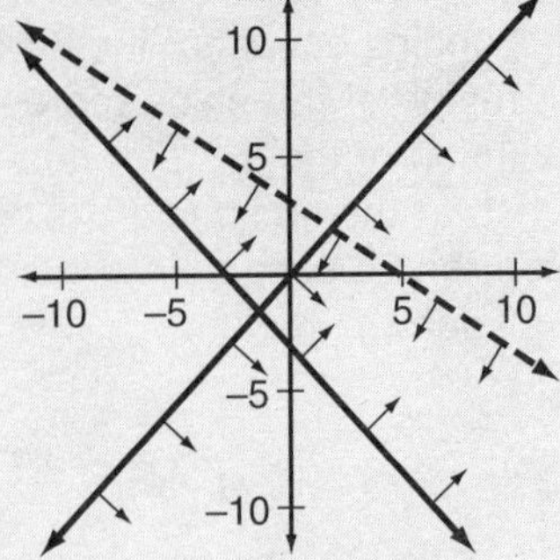

PRACTICE

Refer to the graph at the right. State whether each ordered pair is a solution of the system.

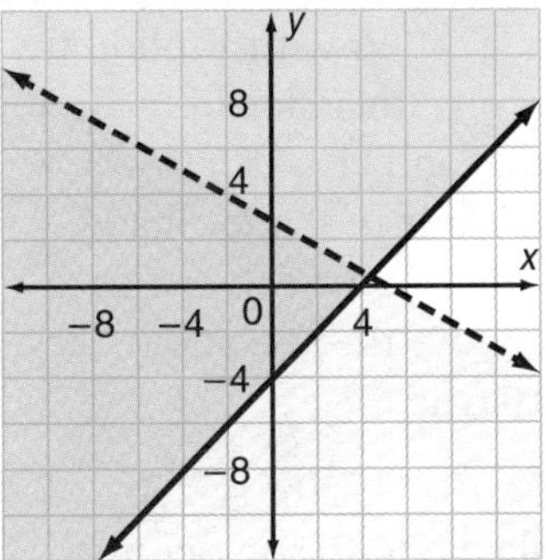

$$\begin{cases} y \geq x - 4 \\ 2x + 3y < 9 \end{cases}$$

1. $(5, -2)$ no **2.** $(-1, 2)$ yes

3. $(10, 3)$ no **4.** $(-10, -6)$ yes

Graph each system of inequalities. See Additional Answers.

5. $\begin{cases} y > -3 \\ y < 2x + 4 \end{cases}$ **6.** $\begin{cases} y < 2x + 4 \\ y > 2x - 3 \end{cases}$ **7.** $\begin{cases} x + 4y \geq -8 \\ x - 2y \geq -6 \end{cases}$ **8.** $\begin{cases} 2x + 5y > -10 \\ 3x - 4y \geq 12 \end{cases}$

9. $\begin{cases} y \geq 1 - x \\ y \leq x - 1 \end{cases}$ **10.** $\begin{cases} 5x + 2y \geq 12 \\ 2x + 3y \leq 10 \end{cases}$ **11.** $\begin{cases} x + y \leq 9 \\ x - y \geq 3 \end{cases}$ **12.** $\begin{cases} x - y \leq -6 \\ 3x - y > -2 \end{cases}$

13. $\begin{cases} y > 4x - 1 \\ y < -2x + 3 \end{cases}$ **14.** $\begin{cases} y < -3x + 2 \\ y \geq \frac{x}{3} + 5 \end{cases}$ **15.** $\begin{cases} y < 3x + 3 \\ y > -3x + 3 \end{cases}$ **16.** $\begin{cases} x - 6y \leq -5 \\ 2x - 3y > 0 \end{cases}$

Write the system of inequalities whose solution is represented by each graph.
See Additional Answers.

17.

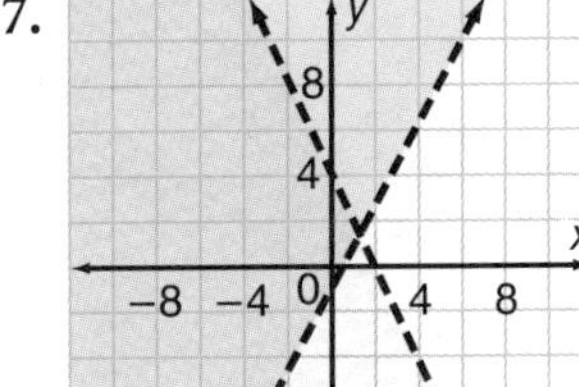

18.

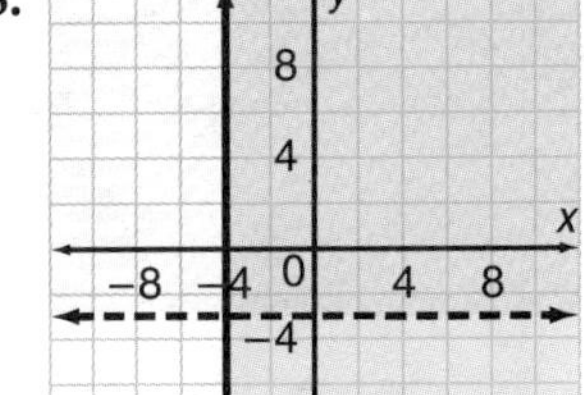

19.

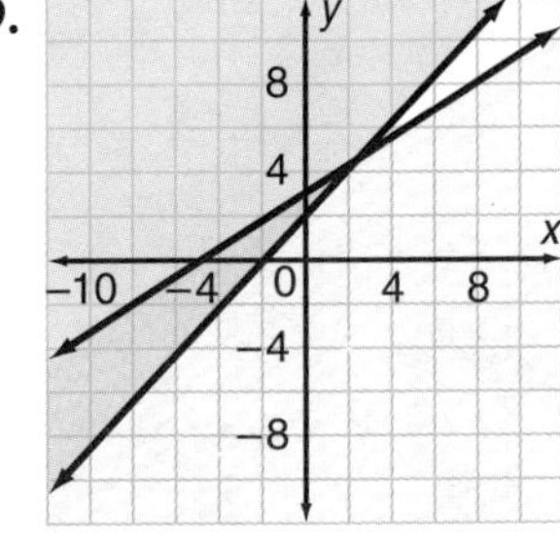

20. WRITING MATHEMATICS Explain how you determined the systems of inequalities for the graphs shown in Exercises 17–19. See Additional Answers.

21. BUSINESS During the spring Mr. Wilson assembles lawn furniture. It takes him $\frac{3}{4}$ h to assemble a chair and 1 h to assemble a table. He earns \$50 for each chair and \$80 for each table. He works no more than 50 h each week, but he likes to assemble enough lawn furniture to generate more than \$3000 income. See Additional Answers.

a. Write and graph a system of linear inequalities that represents the combination of chairs and tables Mr. Wilson assembles in a week.

b. Based on your graph, name three possible combinations of chairs and tables Mr. Wilson could assemble in a week.

Think Critically For Exercises 36–39, students may find it helpful to try to graph the solutions described and then write the systems represented by the graphs. For Exercise 39, students might think that the system $x \geq 0$ and $x < 0$ represented the entire coordinate plane. It would do so if the solution were the union of the two half-planes. Remind students that the solution to a system is the intersection, not the union of the two inequalities. In this instance, the intersection is the null set.

EXTEND

State whether the indicated part of the coordinate plane at the right includes a solution of $y < x + 5$, of $2x + y \leq 3$, of the system of both inequalities, or of neither inequality.

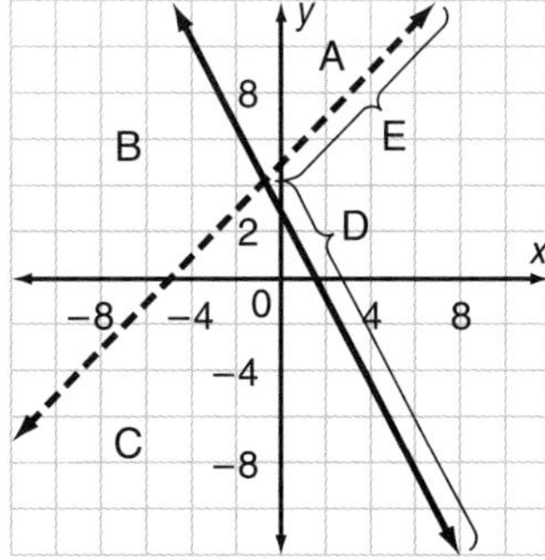

22. A neither

23. B $2x + y \leq 3$

24. C both

25. D both

26. E neither

Write a system of linear inequalities whose solution represents each of these parts of the coordinate plane.

27. Quadrant I $\begin{cases} x > 0 \\ y > 0 \end{cases}$

28. Quadrant III and the axes that border it $\begin{cases} x \leq 0 \\ y \leq 0 \end{cases}$

29. Quadrant IV and the x-axis that borders it $\begin{cases} x > 0 \\ y \leq 0 \end{cases}$

Graph each system of linear inequalities.
30–33 See Additional Answers.

30. $\begin{cases} y < x \\ y \geq -x - 3 \\ 3x + 5y < 15 \end{cases}$

31. $\begin{cases} 2y - x \geq 0 \\ x + 5y < 15 \\ y > x + 1 \end{cases}$

32. $\begin{cases} x > -1 \\ y \leq x + 2 \\ y > 2x \end{cases}$

33. $\begin{cases} x > 0 \\ x + y \leq 5 \\ x - y > 3 \end{cases}$

34. WEATHER The average monthly temperature is the average of the average monthly high temperature and the average monthly low temperature. During July, the average temperature in Buenos Aires, Argentina was less than 60°F. The average low was greater than 40°F. See Additional Answers.

a. Write and graph a system of three linear inequalities that represents this situation. (*Hint:* Let x represent the average low temperature and y represent the average high temperature. Then write one inequality to compare the average low and the average high.)

b. Based on your graph, name three possible combinations of average monthly high and low temperatures for that July in Buenos Aires.

NAME ______ CLASS ______ DATE ______

RETEACHING

8.2 SOLVE SYSTEMS OF LINEAR INEQUALITIES BY GRAPHING

Example
Graph the system of linear inequalities.

$\begin{cases} y \leq 4x + 3 \\ y < -x + 2 \end{cases}$

Solution
Graph the system of linear equations.

$\begin{cases} y = 4x + 3 \\ y = -x + 2 \end{cases}$

Use a dashed line when < or > is in the inequality.

For each line, shade the side containing solutions of that inequality. The region of the graph shaded twice contains all the points that are solutions of the system of inequalities.

EXERCISES
Graph the system of linear inequalities.

1. $\begin{cases} y \leq -3x \\ x - y \geq -4 \end{cases}$

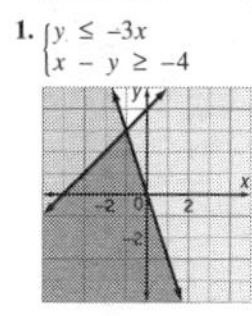

2. $\begin{cases} y > -6 \\ 3x - 2y \leq 6 \end{cases}$

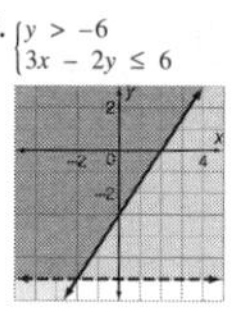

3. $\begin{cases} -x + 3y > -3 \\ 3x + 4y \leq 12 \end{cases}$

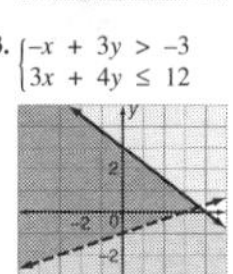

4. $\begin{cases} y \geq -x + 6 \\ y < 2x - 8 \end{cases}$

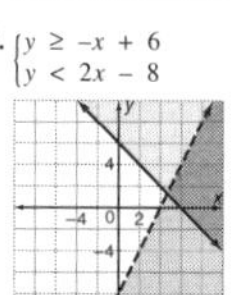

14

South-Western Algebra 1: AN INTEGRATED APPROACH

5 FOLLOW-UP

Extension
Show students a sketch of the following graph that a new business owner made to display his projected income and expenses during the first year of business.

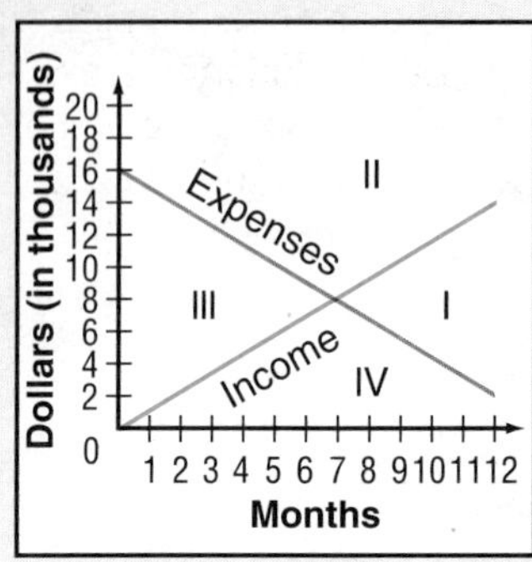

NAME ______ CLASS ______ DATE ______

8.2 SOLVE SYSTEMS OF LINEAR INEQUALITIES BY GRAPHING

EXTRA PRACTICE

Refer to the graph at the right. State whether each ordered pair is a solution of the system.

$$\begin{cases} y > -2x + 5 \\ -2x + 3y \le -6 \end{cases}$$

1. (6, 0) — 1. **yes**
2. (3, −1) — 2. **no**
3. (10, 4) — 3. **yes**

Graph each system of linear inequalities.

4. $\begin{cases} y \ge -3 \\ y \le -2x + 4 \end{cases}$

5. $\begin{cases} x - y > 3 \\ 6x + 3y \le 9 \end{cases}$

6. $\begin{cases} -2x - 5y > -10 \\ -x + y \ge -7 \end{cases}$

Write the system of linear inequalities whose solution is represented by each graph.

7. — 7. $\begin{cases} y \ge -3x + 3 \\ y > 2x - 6 \end{cases}$

8. — 8. $\begin{cases} y \le 3 \\ y \ge -5x \end{cases}$

16 South-Western Algebra 1: AN INTEGRATED APPROACH

35. FINANCE Mr. and Mrs. Patel plan to invest a maximum of $10,000. They will invest part of this amount in a mutual fund that pays an average of 8% annual interest and part in certificates of deposit that pay 5% annual interest. They would like to earn at least $500 interest the first year. Because the mutual fund has been paying a higher interest, they will invest more in the mutual fund than in the certificates of deposit.
See Additional Answers.
    a. Write and graph a system of three linear inequalities that represents this situation.
    b. Based on your graph, name three possible combinations of amounts the Patels could invest in the mutual fund and in certificates of deposit.

THINK CRITICALLY

Write and graph a system of two inequalities whose solution is described by each of the following. If it is not possible to do so, explain why.
See Additional Answers.

36. all points in a region bounded by two lines that do not intersect
37. no solution
38. all points in one line
39. all points in the coordinate plane

PROJECT Connection

Many students have part-time jobs to earn their own money. A good way to keep track of that money is by opening a checking account. Different banks may offer the same basic accounts, but service charges, interest rates, and minimum balance requirements can vary widely.

1. The different types of checking accounts usually offered by banks are cost-per-check accounts, minimum balance accounts, free checking accounts, and negotiable order of withdrawal (NOW) accounts. Make a table of information about each type of account at several local banks, including costs per check, monthly service charges, minimum balances, and possible interest rates.
2. Express the total monthly cost of each account as a function of number of checks used. Graph the functions. Are the graphs linear? Explain.
3. For interest-bearing accounts, write a verbal model and then a formula for determining the total amount earned or charged monthly.
Answers will vary. Amount earned or charged = interest − charge for checks − service charges.
4. Use your findings to name the "Top Two Banks for Teens."

Career
Video Shop Owner

Shop owners are faced with decisions about inventory and pricing. For a video shop owner, considerations include determining the number of copies of new films needed, deciding how to price the newest films relative to older ones, determining how to dispose of videos that are no longer rented, and whether or not to begin a club.

Decision Making

1. Some video shops charge a set rate per day for rentals. Videos 'n More charges $3.00 per day or less, depending on whether the film is a new release, an older film, or a public service video. If a customer rents x videos for one day, write an inequality that represents the store's income, y. $y \leq 3x$
2. Videos 'n More is considering offering the option of a club with a membership fee of $20.00 per year. Club members would be charged $2.00 or less per video, depending on the type of video. Suppose a club member rents x videos for one day. Write an inequality that represents the store's income, y. Write another inequality that describes at least how much annual income the store will receive from a club member. $y \leq 20 + 2x$; $y \geq 20$
3. Graph the three inequalities on the same coordinate plane. Create an ad the store owner could use if the store offered the club option. (*Hint*: Determine the fewest number of rentals for which the two plans produce the same income.) See Additional Answers.
4. If a customer rented at most two videos per month, which plan would be best? See Additional Answers.
5. If you were the owner of Videos 'n More, would you offer the club option to your customers? Explain your reasoning. See Additional Answers.

Then ask these questions.

1. What does the intersection of the lines indicate? **the point at which income equals expenses, or when there is no longer a loss**
2. Which region represents profit? Which represents loss? **region I; region III**
3. What is the approximate projected net profit or loss? (Hint: Determine the areas for the region of profit and the region of loss.) **approximate net loss of $40,000 for the first 12 months**

Project Connection This activity presents further aspects of the activity introduced on page 372. Encourage the students to justify their choice of the Two Top Banks for teens.

AlgebraWorks Have students research rates at various video shops in your area and graph their possible annual cost at each shop. Based on their current viewing habits and the graph, have them decide which shop and/or club plan would be best for them.

NAME ______________ CLASS ________ DATE ________

E ENRICHMENT

8.2 SOLVE SYSTEMS OF LINEAR INEQUALITIES BY GRAPHING

PRICING Mr. Tooley is in charge of setting the price for CDs to insure that Toontown Music makes a profit. Let x represent the retail price per CD and y represent the number of sales. After looking at past sales records, Mr. Tooley wrote the following inequalities, which describe facts about the company's sales history.

$x \leq \$25$
$y \geq 6{,}000$
$y \leq -600x + 18{,}000$

Mr. Tooley also knows that $y \geq 0$ and $x \geq 0$. This will keep the graph in the first quadrant because the solution must be positive.

1. Use the grid above to graph the system of inequalities. Where do the solutions to the inequalities lie? — 1. **in the triangle enclosed by the lines**
2. Based on your graph, what is the highest whole dollar price Mr. Tooley should set for one CD? — 2. **$20.00**
3. The third inequality in the system describes the company's earning potential. According to that inequality, how many sales could the company make if they priced their CDs at that price? — 3. **less than 6000**
4. How much money could the company receive in sales if they priced their CDs at $19.00? — 4. **less than $114,000**
5. How many sales would the company make if they priced their CDs at $5.00? — 5. **less than 15,000**
6. How much money could the company receive in sales if they priced their CDs at $5.00? — 6. **less than $75,000**
7. Based on the graph, write three possible prices for CDs and the number of sales that could be made. What price do you think will bring in the most income?
Answers will vary.

18 *South-Western Algebra 1:* AN INTEGRATED APPROACH

LESSON PLANNING

Objectives

- Use a graphing utility to solve systems of linear inequalities.
- Compare systems of linear inequalities to systems of linear equations.

Technology/Multimedia
graphing utility

Resources
Transparencies 32, 34, 49–51, 78–80
Student Handbook
Technology Activity 19

Materials/Manipulatives
graph paper
straightedges

ASSIGNMENTS

Basic: 1–18

Average: 1–18

Enriched: 1–19

1 MOTIVATE

Think Back Be sure students recall how to graph a system of equations with a graphing utility.

2 FACILITATE

Explore For Question 8, be sure students understand that the points of intersection represent solutions. For Question 10, students should see that the solid boundary lines and their intersections are part of the triple-shaded region.

8.3 Algebra Workshop

Use Graphing Utilities to Solve Systems of Inequalities

SPOTLIGHT ON LEARNING

WHAT? In this lesson you will learn

- to solve systems of linear inequalities using a graphing utility.

WHY? Knowing how to use a graphing utility to solve systems of inequalities can help you solve real world problems.

Think Back

Work with a partner. Use a graphing utility.

1. Graph: $\begin{cases} 3x - 2y = 7 \\ 4x + 6y = 5 \end{cases}$ See Additional Answers.
2. Refer to your graph to find the solution of the system of equations. How did you determine the solution? (2, –0.5); This is the point of intersection of the graphs of the equations.

You can also use a graphing utility to solve systems of inequalities.

Explore

3. Use a graphing utility to graph these systems of linear inequalities, which correspond to the system of linear equations you graphed in Explore. (If your graphing utility does not shade for inequalities, copy the graph of the boundary lines onto paper and shade the half-planes.) See Additional Answers.

   a. $\begin{cases} 3x - 2y \le 7 \\ 4x + 6y \le 5 \end{cases}$ **b.** $\begin{cases} 3x - 2y < 7 \\ 4x + 6y < 5 \end{cases}$ **c.** $\begin{cases} 3x - 2y > 7 \\ 4x + 6y \ge 5 \end{cases}$

4. At what point do the boundary lines intersect? Does this point represent a solution of each system of inequalities? (2, –0.5); yes for a; no for b and c
5. Do any other parts of these graphs represent solutions of the systems? If so, describe them. See Additional Answers.
6. Use your graphing utility to graph this system of linear equations and the corresponding system of inequalities. See Additional Answers.

   a. $\begin{cases} y = 4 \\ -x + 3y = 6 \\ 2x + y = -12 \end{cases}$ **b.** $\begin{cases} y \le 4 \\ -x + 3y \ge 6 \\ 2x + y \ge -12 \end{cases}$

Refer to the graph of the system in Question 6a.

7. Name three points at which the lines intersect. (–8, 4), (6, 4), (–6, 0)
8. Do these points represent solutions of the system? Explain. See Additional Answers.

   Refer to the graph of the system in Question 6b.

9. Name three points at which the lines intersect. (–8, 4), (6, 4), (–6, 0)
10. Does any part of this graph represent solutions of the system? If so, which part? the triple-shaded region, including the boundary

Making Connections

Refer to the graphs you have drawn in this workshop to answer these questions.

11. How are the graphs of corresponding systems of linear equations and inequalities the same? How are they different? See Additional Answers.

12. How are the representations of the solutions of systems of linear equations and systems of linear inequalities the same? How are they different? See Additional Answers.

13. How does the number of solutions for a system of linear equations compare with the number of solutions for a system of linear inequalities? See Additional Answers.

ALGEBRA: WHO, WHERE, WHEN

In calculus, inequalities are important in defining and determining the limit (maximum or minimum value) of any function.

Summarize

14. Modeling Write the system of inequalities represented by the graph at the right.

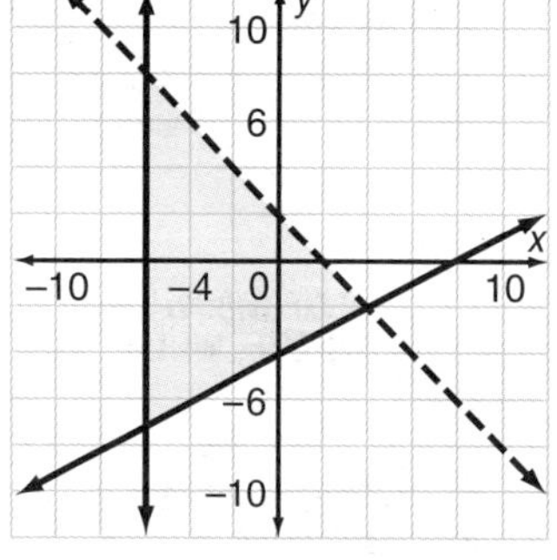

$$\begin{cases} y < -x + 2 \\ x \geq -6 \\ y \geq \frac{1}{2}x - 4 \end{cases}$$

15. Writing Mathematics Consider the graph of the system of linear equations that corresponds to this system of linear inequalities.

$$\begin{cases} y \leq 4x + 1 \\ y < -\frac{1}{2}x \end{cases}$$

Does the intersection point of the graph represent a solution to the system of inequalities? Explain your reasoning. See Additional Answers.

Thinking Critically Match each graph below to the system of inequalities it represents.

16. c

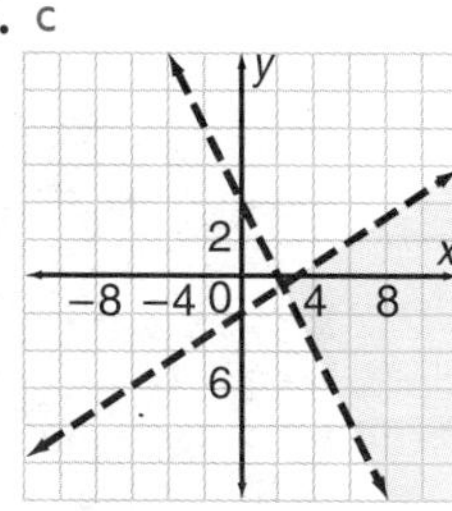

17. b

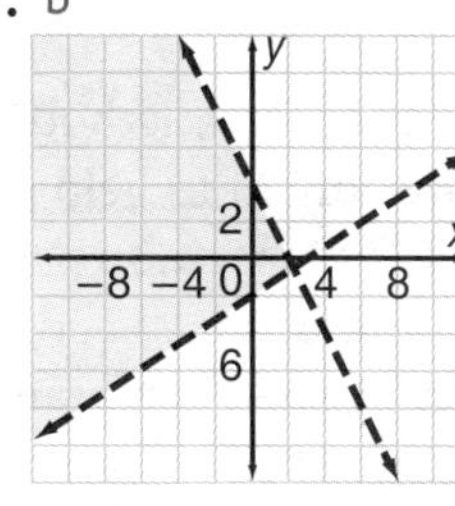

18. a

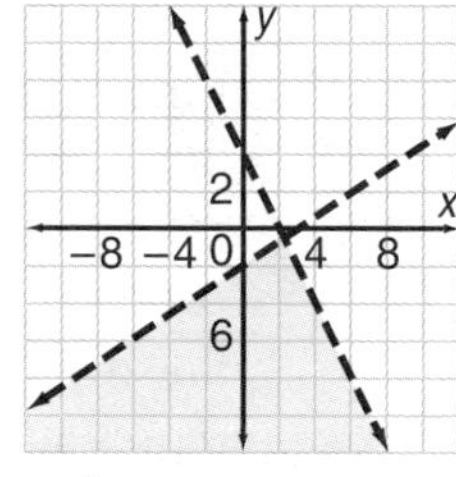

a. $\begin{cases} 2x + y < 4 \\ 2x - 3y > 6 \end{cases}$ **b.** $\begin{cases} 2x + y < 4 \\ 2x - 3y < 6 \end{cases}$ **c.** $\begin{cases} 2x + y > 4 \\ 2x - 3y > 6 \end{cases}$

19. Going Further Write a system of three inequalities that forms a triangle with its base parallel to the x- or y-axis. Find the area of your triangle. See Additional Answers.

Make Connections After students answer Questions 11–13, have them share their findings with the class.

Technology Graphing utilities differ in whether they shade for inequalities, if there is any order in which the inequalities need to be entered, and whether it can show dashed boundary lines.

3 SUMMARIZE

Modeling Students should use the same strategies for Question 14 as in Lesson 8.2 for writing the system represented by a graph.

Writing Mathematics For students having difficulty with Question 15, ask questions such as these:

- What type of boundary line would you draw for the graph of each inequality? **solid; dashed**
- Which types of lines contain points that are solutions of an inequality? **solid lines only**

Thinking Critically For Questions 16–18, encourage students to first write the inequalities in slope-intercept form before they identify which boundary line corresponds to which inequality.

Going Further For Question 19, suggest that students first draw the figure described.

4 FOLLOW-UP

Other Explorations Have students write a system of four inequalities whose graph forms a parallelogram, a rectangle, or a trapezoid. Have students trade systems with a partner and have the partner graph the systems.

LESSON PLANNING

Objective

▶ Use linear programming techniques to find minimum and maximum values.

Vocabulary

constraints
feasible region
linear programming
maximize
minimize
objective function

Technology/Multimedia

graphing utility

Resources

Warm Up 8.4
Reteaching 8.4
Extra Practice 8.4
Enrichment 8.4
Transparencies 32, 49–51, 78–80
Student Handbook
Lesson Quiz 8.4

Materials/Manipulatives

graph paper
straightedges

ASSIGNMENTS

Basic: 1–14, 17–19, 22–24, Mixed Review 25–29, Project Connection 1–2

Average: 1–14, 17–24, Mixed Review 25–29, Project Connection 1–2

Enriched: 3, 7–24, Mixed Review 25–29, Project Connection 1–2

8.4 Linear Programming: The Objective Function

SPOTLIGHT ON LEARNING

WHAT? In this lesson you will learn

- to use linear programming to find minimum and maximum values.

WHY? Understanding linear programming can help you to determine maximum profits and minimum cost in manufacturing and other business applications.

ALGEBRA: WHO, WHERE, WHEN

When you make a telephone call, the circuiting system searches available paths for the fastest route using the *simplex method*, an application of linear programming developed in 1947 by mathematician George Danzig. The computer visualizes the network of possible connections as edges of a geometric solid, checking each corner as a possible connection for the call.

Explore/Working Together

Work with a partner.

1. Graph: $\begin{cases} 4x - 2y > -10 \\ x + y < 5 \\ 2x - 4y < 16 \end{cases}$ See Additional Answers.

2. Select ten different points that represent solutions of this system of inequalities. Which point has the greatest sum of the coordinates? Which has the least sum? Answers will vary. The greatest sum approaches 5. The least sum approaches −13.

3. In which region(s) of the graph did you find the points having greater coordinate sums? having lesser sums? See Additional Answers.

4. Write the ordered pairs for the vertices of the triangle formed by the boundary lines of the system. How do the sums of the coordinates of these points compare with the greatest and least sums you found in Question 2? See Additional Answers.

5. Examine the graph of a system of inequalities at the right. What do you think the greatest sum of the coordinates of a point in the shaded region is? What do you think the least sum is? Explain your thinking. See Additional Answers.

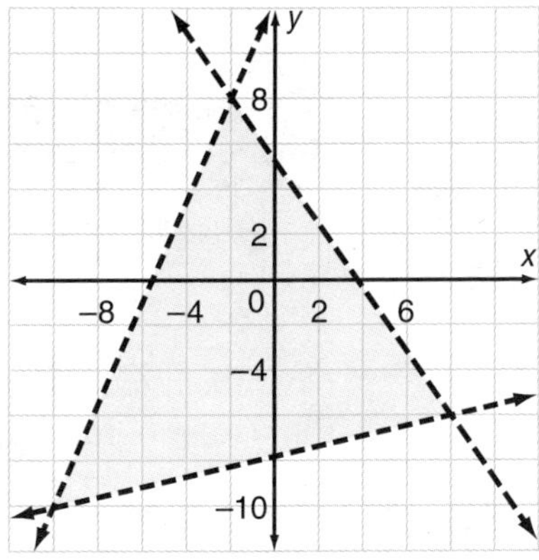

6. Test points within the shaded region. Was your thinking in Question 5 correct? Answers will vary. Answer given for Question 5 will be confirmed.

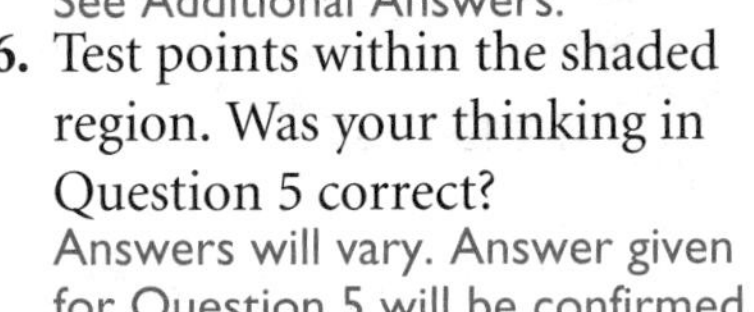

Build Understanding

Linear programming is a method used in business and government to help manage resources and time. **Constraints** are conditions that limit business activity. In linear programming such constraints are represented by inequalities. The intersection of the graphs of a system of constraints includes all possible solutions and is known as the **feasible region**. The vertices of the feasible region represent minimum and maximum values, as you found in Explore.

EXAMPLE 1

FUND RAISING The Student Council sells hot dogs and beverages at a concession stand during sports events. The following constraints must be considered.

- At each game council members always sell at least half as many hot dogs as beverages.
- At each game they always sell at least 150 beverages.
- There is space to refrigerate only 300 hot dogs for each game.

a. Should council members expect to sell 250 hot dogs and 400 beverages?

b. Should they expect to sell 200 hot dogs and 500 beverages?

c. What is the least number of hot dogs council members should expect to sell at a game?

d. What is the greatest number of beverages they should expect to sell at a game?

Solution

Let x represent the number of hot dogs and y represent the number of beverages. Write an inequality to represent each constraint.

- at least half as many hot dogs as beverages $\quad x \geq \frac{1}{2}y$ or $y \leq 2x$
- at least 150 beverages $\quad y \geq 150$
- space for only 300 hot dogs $\quad x \leq 300$

Graph the system of inequalities. Write ordered pairs for the vertices of the shaded region. The triangular shaded region is the feasible region and represents all solutions that satisfy the constraints.

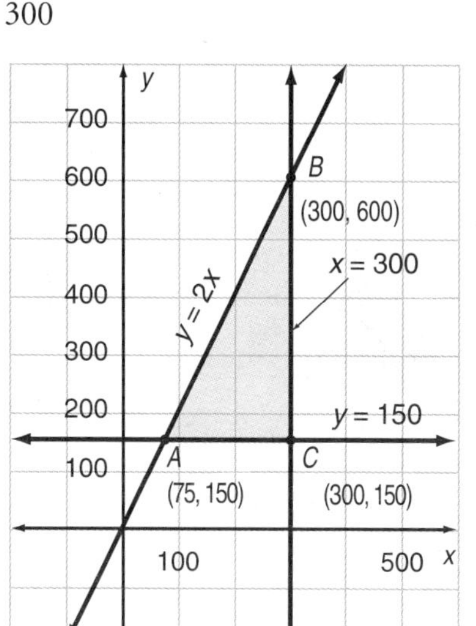

a. The ordered pair (250, 400) represents 250 hot dogs and 400 beverages. The point representing this ordered pair is within the feasible region, so this is a possible expectation.

b. The ordered pair (200, 500) represents 200 hot dogs and 500 beverages. The point representing this ordered pair is *not* within the feasible region, so this is not a possible expectation.

c. The ordered pair for vertex A (75, 150) represents the least number of hot dogs and beverages. So the least number of hot dogs the Student Council should expect to sell is 75.

d. The ordered pair for vertex B (300, 600) represents the greatest number of hot dogs and beverages. So the greatest number of beverages the Student Council should expect to sell is 600. ◄

CHECK UNDERSTANDING

Name some constraints that a business may have to consider.

possible answers: amount of money available, cost of materials, production capability, demand for product or service

THINK BACK

Recall the inequality symbols:
$\leq$: "is at most"
$<$: "is less than"
$\geq$: "is at least"
$>$: "is greater than"
$\neq$: "is not equal to"

1 MOTIVATE

Explore/Working Together Because of the important role that vertices play in using linear programming techniques, it is important for students to discover how the sums of the coordinates of the vertices compare to the sums of the coordinates of other points within the graph of the solution of the system of inequalities. As students work on Question 2, encourage them to select points throughout the *entire* region.

2 TEACH

Use the Pages/Build Understanding

Example 1: Make sure students understand what each part of the graph represents by discussing the answers to questions a–d, as well as asking questions such as these.

- What do the points in the triple-shaded region represent? **all the solutions to the system of inequalities that satisfy the constraints; all the points that have whole number coordinates represent possible combinations of hot dogs and beverages that could be sold**
- What does the ordered pair for vertex C represent? **the least number of beverages the Student Council should expect to sell even if it sells the greatest number of hot dogs**

Example 2: Ask students to explain each expression in the objective function. **P = total profit, or the profit from the sale of both hot dogs and beverages; $0.65x$ is the profit per hot dog times the total number of hot dogs sold; $0.35y$ is the profit per beverage times the total number of beverages sold** Have students refer to the table to find the minimum profit the Student Council could expect to make. **$101.25** Then have them compare (1) finding the maximum and minimum profits by substituting the coordinates of the vertices of the feasible region in the objective function (2) their discovery in Explore that the greatest and least sums of the coordinates occur near the intersection of the boundary lines.

DIVERSITY IN THE CLASSROOM

ESL/LEP Students Discuss the common meanings of *feasible, maximum,* and *minimum.* Then ask these questions.

- Would it be feasible for the manager at your part-time job to plan to have you work Monday through Friday mornings? Saturday and Sunday afternoons? Explain. **probable answers: no, because I am at school then; yes, I have nothing else I am required to do then**
- Is a speed limit a minimum or a maximum quantity? **maximum**
- Is a recommended daily amount of a vitamin a minimum or a maximum quantity? **minimum**

Ongoing Assessment The important concepts and skills are using linear programming techniques to find minimum and maximum values. To assess these ideas, have students demonstrate how they have applied these concepts and skills in Exercises 1, 3, and 8 of the Try These section.

Guided Practice/Try These After students have completed the exercises in this section, have them describe some of the solutions. Encourage students who used different methods to explain their work and compare results. At this point, students should not be required to understand the exact meaning of the constraints and objective functions, such as those given in Exercises 8 and 9. Discuss factors that contribute to determining profit and cost. In the next lesson, students will write both constraints and objective functions.

CHECK UNDERSTANDING

Describe the set of numbers that lie within a region if the inequalities $x \geq 0$ and $y \geq 0$ are included as boundaries for that region.

zero and all positive real numbers

Solutions to linear programming problems are often restricted to the first quadrant of the coordinate plane. The feasible region for Example 1 is completely within the first quadrant. When this is not the case, include $x \geq 0$ and $y \geq 0$ as constraints, if necessary.

Business people use linear programming to determine how to make the most (maximum) profit with the least (minimum) cost. You can write an equation representing a quantity such as profit or cost. This equation is called the **objective function**. By substituting values within the constraints, you can find the values that **maximize** or **minimize** the objective function. The maximum or minimum values of the objective function will occur at or near a vertex of the feasible region.

EXAMPLE 2

PROFIT At its concession stand, the Student Council makes a profit of \$0.65 on each hot dog sold and \$0.35 on each beverage sold. The objective function for profit is $P = 0.65x + 0.35y$. What is the maximum profit the Student Council should expect to make?

Solution

Substitute the coordinates for the vertices of the feasible region in the objective function.

Vertex	$P = 0.65x + 0.35y$	Profit, P
(75, 150)	$0.65(75) + 0.35(150)$	\$101.25
(300, 150)	$0.65(300) + 0.35(150)$	\$247.50
(300, 600)	$0.65(300) + 0.35(600)$	\$405.00

The maximum profit is \$405.00. To do this, the Council must sell 300 hot dogs and 600 beverages, the coordinates at point B. ◄

TRY THESE

Graph the given constraints to determine the feasible region. Determine whether each point is within the feasible region.

1. Constraints: $y \leq x - 3,\ x \leq 8,\ y \geq 0$; point (1, 4) The point is not within the region.
2. Constraints: $y \leq 2x + 6,\ y \geq -3 - 2x,\ x \leq 0,\ y \geq 0$; point (–1, 2) The point lies within the region.

For the given vertices of each feasible region in Exercises 3–7, find the minimum and maximum value of the objective function and name the coordinates at which each occurs.
See Additional Answers.

	Objective Function	Vertices
3.	$P = x + 3y$	(0, 0), (3, 0), (0, 7), (4, 2)
4.	$P = 2x + 5y$	(2, 3), (3, 6), (1, 6), (0, 5)
5.	$P = 4x + 2y$	(0, 1), (9, 1), (2, 7), (6, 3)
6.	$C = 5x + y$	(10, 10), (10, 20), (20, 20), (30, 10)
7.	$C = 3x + y$	(0, 0), (0, 8), (4, 3), (5, 0)

8. Graph the given constraints to determine the feasible region. Then find the minimum cost C for a business whose cost is given by the objective function $C = x + 2y$. Name the point at which it occurs. minimum is 8 at (2, 3)

$x + y \leq 6 \quad 2x - y \leq 4 \quad x \geq 2 \quad y \geq 3$

9. Graph the given constraints to determine the feasible region. Then find the maximum profit P given by the objective function $P = 2x + y$. Name the point at which it occurs.

$y \leq x + 6 \quad y \geq 3x - 1 \quad x \geq 0 \quad y \geq 0$ maximum is 16.5 at (3.5, 9.5)

10. WRITING MATHEMATICS Why should the feasible region for many linear programming problems be restricted to Quadrant I? See Additional Answers.

PRACTICE

For Exercises 1–3, graph the given constraints to determine the feasible region. Then determine whether each point is within the feasible region.

1. Constraints: $y \leq -2x + 7,\ y \geq -x + 2,\ x \geq 0,\ y \geq 0$; point (1, 4)
The point lies within the region.
2. Constraints: $3y - x \geq 0,\ y \leq -2x + 9,\ x \geq 0,\ y \geq 0$; point (5, 4)
The point is not within the region.
3. Constraints: $2x - y \leq 2,\ 2y - x \leq 8,\ y \geq 2$; point (1, 3)
The point lies within the region.

For the given vertices of each feasible region in Exercises 4–8, find the minimum and maximum value of the objective function and name the coordinates at which each occurs.
See Additional Answers.

	Objective Function	Vertices
4.	$P = x + 4y$	(0, –1), (4, 0), (3, 2), (0, 1)
5.	$P = 2x - 3y$	(3, 1), (2, 4), (0, 5), (0, 0)
6.	$P = -x + 6y$	(–2, 0), (3, 0), (4, 3), (0, 1)
7.	$R = 3x - 2y$	(0, 0), (–2, –3), (–3, 3), (0, 1)
8.	$C = 4x + 5y$	(0, 2), (2, 3), (4, 0), (0, 6)

9. Graph the given constraints to determine the feasible region. Then find the maximum value of the objective function $P = x + 4y$. Name the point at which it occurs.

$y + x \geq 0 \quad x + 2y \leq 6 \quad x \leq 0 \quad y \leq 3$ maximum is 12 at (0, 3)

10. Graph the given constraints to determine the feasible region. Then find the minimum value of the objective function $C = 4x + 3y$. Name the point at which it occurs.

$2y \leq 22 - x \quad 3x \leq 30 - 2y \quad x \leq 6 \quad y \geq 3$ minimum is 9 at (0, 3)

11. Graph the given constraints to determine the feasible region. Then find the maximum value of the objective function $P = 4x + y$. Name the point at which it occurs.

$x \geq 4 \quad 4y - x \geq 4 \quad y \leq -3x + 53 \quad y - x \leq 5$ maximum is 69 at (16, 5)

12. Graph the given constraints to determine the feasible region. Then find the minimum value of the objective function $C = x + 5y$. Name the point at which it occurs.

$3y + 2x \geq 3 \quad x \geq 0 \quad x \leq 6 \quad y + x \leq 16 \quad 3y - 4x \leq 9$ minimum is –9 at (6, –3)

3 SUMMARIZE

In the Math Journal Have students write a paragraph that describes, for any given set of constraints, where the feasible region is and what it represents. **The feasible region is in the most heavily-shaded region. It represents all the points that are solutions of all the inequalities that satisfy the constraints.**

4 PRACTICE

Practice For Exercises 13–14, students will first need to find the minimum value of each objective function and then compare them.

Extend After students have completed Exercises 17–19, have them discuss whether a real business situation could occur that would not have an upper or lower bound. For example, a company might state that the market was so strong for sales of its

NAME ______ CLASS ______ DATE ______

8.4 LINEAR PROGRAMMING: THE OBJECTIVE FUNCTION

You can find maximum and minimum values for an equation that represents profit or cost. This equation is called the objective function.

Example
Find the minimum and maximum value for the profit function $P = x + 3y$, given the following constraints.

$x + 2y \geq 80$
$y \leq \left(\frac{1}{3}\right)x + 40$
$x \leq 60$

The constraints are graphed at the right.

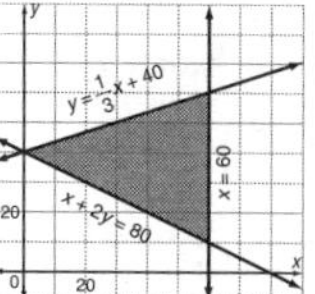

Solution
Identify the lines that bound the region containing solutions of the system of constraints. Identify the coordinates of the intersection points.

The solution for the system is the triple-shaded triangular area that is bounded by lines that intersect at (0, 30), (60, 60), and (60, 10).

Substitute the values of the coordinates in the profit equation and solve.

(0, 30) $P = 0 + 3(30) = 0$
(60, 60) $P = 60 + 3(60) = 240$
(60, 10) $P = 60 + 3(10) = 90$

The minimum is 90 at (0, 30) and (60, 10).
The maximum is 240 at (60, 60).

EXERCISES
Use the constraints given in the graph below to determine the minimum and maximum values of each objective function.

$y \leq -x + 5,\ x \leq 3,\ y \geq 1,\ x \geq 0$

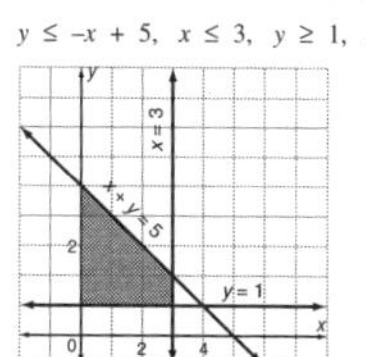

1. $P = 5x + 4y$
min: 4 at (0, 1); max: 23 at (3, 2)
2. $C = 2x + 5y$
min: 5 at (0, 1); max: 25 at (0, 5)
3. $P = 3x - 2y$
min: –10 at (0, 5); max: 7 at (3, 1)
4. $C = 6x - 6y$
min: –30 at (0, 5); max: 12 at (3, 1)

22 *South-Western Algebra 1: AN INTEGRATED APPROACH*

T-shirts that there was no limit on how many could be sold. However, is there really no limit? Ask students to suggest conditions that might impose limits on the manufacture of the shirts. **availability of fabric, factory limits on production** For Exercise 21, ask students to explain why the graphs miss the feasible region. ***M* is already the minimum value, so any value less than *M* would be less than the minimum value.**

Think Critically For students having difficulty with Exercise 22, ask questions such as these.

- What expression could represent the cost of materials to make x bracelets? **0.50*x***
- to make y necklaces? **1.25*y***
- How does the cost of making *x* bracelets and *y* necklaces compare to $10.00? **The cost is less than $10.00.**

Point out that the information given about profit is incorporated in the objective function given in Exercise 23.

NAME ______ CLASS ______ DATE ______

P EXTRA PRACTICE

8.4 LINEAR PROGRAMMING: THE OBJECTIVE FUNCTION

Determine whether each point is within the feasible region given by the constraints. Write yes or no.

1. Constraints: $y \leq 3x + 1$, $y > -x + 5$, $x \leq 10$, $x \geq 0$; Points (2, 6), (4, 8) — 1. **yes; no**
2. Constraints: $3x + 2y > 6$, $y \geq 2x + 3$, $x \leq 6$, $x \geq 0$; Points (–1, 2), (2, 6) — 2. **no; no**
3. Constraints: $y \leq 4x + 4$, $2x + y \leq 16$, $x \geq 0$, $y \geq 0$; Points (1, 10), (2, 6) — 3. **no; yes**

For the given vertices of each feasible region, find the minimum and maximum value of the objective function and name the coordinates at which each occurs.

Objective Function	Vertices
4. $P = 2x + y$	(4, 0), (6, 0), (2, 7), (0, 7)
5. $P = 3x + 3y$	(0, 10), (10, 6), (10, 2), (0, 2)
6. $P = x + 4y$	(2, 1), (5, 1), (8, 7), (11, 7)

4. **minimum 7 at (0, 7); maximum 12 at (6, 0)**
5. **minimum 6 at (0, 2); maximum 48 at (10, 6)**
6. **minimum 6 at (2, 1); maximum 39 at (11, 7)**

7. Find the maximum and minimum values for $P = 2x + 5y$, given the following constraints. Name the point at which each occurs.
$y \geq -x - 3$, $-y \leq 2x$, $x \leq 6$, $x \geq 0$, $y \leq 0$
maximum is 42 at (6, 6); minimum is –33 at (6, –9)

8. Find the maximum and minimum values for $P = x + 4y$, given the following constraints. Name the point at which it occurs.
$y + 2x \geq 4, 2x - y \leq 6, y \leq 4$
maximum is 21 at (5, 4); minimum is $-\frac{3}{2}$ at $\left(\frac{5}{2}, -1\right)$

24 South-Western Algebra 1: AN INTEGRATED APPROACH

Decision Making A shop owner can use either of two objective functions for determining her costs.

$$C = 4x + 4y \quad \text{or} \quad C = 3x + 2y$$

She has determined the constraints as follows.

$$y + 2x \leq 12 \quad x + y \leq 8 \quad x \geq 0 \quad y \geq 2$$

13. Graph the given constraints to determine the region. Name the vertices of the feasible region. (0, 8), (4, 4), (5, 2), (0, 2)
14. Use the vertices to determine which objective function she should use to minimize her costs. $C = 3x + 2y$

Farming Manuel needs to plant 210 acres on his farm. From crop *x* he will earn $400 an acre and from crop *y* he will earn $350 an acre. He must plant at least 40 acres of crop *x* and 50 acres of crop *y*. Soil conditions do not permit him to plant more than 80 acres of crop *x*. State regulations will allow the acres for crop *y* to be no more than twice the number of acres for crop *x*.

$$x \geq 40 \quad y \geq 50 \quad x \leq 80 \quad y \leq 2x \quad x + y \leq 210$$

15. Graph the given constraints to determine the feasible region. Name the vertices of the feasible region. (40, 50), (40, 80), (70, 140), (80, 130), (80, 50)
16. Use the objective function $P = 400x + 350y$ to find how many acres he should plant to maximize his earnings. 80 acres of crop *x* and 130 acres of crop *y*

EXTEND

For the given objective function and constraints in Exercises 17–19, state whether there is a minimum value, a maximum value, or both. If a minimum or maximum value does not occur, explain why. See Additional Answers for graphs.

17. $T = 6x + 3y$
Constraints: $3x + y \geq 8,\ 2y - 4 \leq 8x,\ x \geq 0,\ y \geq 0$
There is a minimum value but no maximum value, because the graph of the constraints is unbounded.
18. $W = 3x - 4y$
Constraints: $2x \leq y + 5,\ 0 \leq y \leq 3,\ x \geq 0$ There are both minimum and maximum values.
19. $R = x + 3.5y$
Constraints: $y \leq 2x + 1,\ y \geq -x + 1,\ x \geq 0,\ y \geq 0$
There is a minimum value but no maximum value, because the graph of the constraints is unbounded.
20. For the given objective function and constraints, find the minimum and name the point at which it occurs. minimum is 5 at (2, 3)

$$C = x + y$$
Constraints: $3x + 2y \geq 12,\ x + 3y \geq 11,\ x \geq 0,\ y \geq 0$

21. Substitute the minimum value *M* you determined in Exercise 20 and graph the equations $x + y = M - 1$ and $x + y = M - 2$. What do you notice?
For any value less than *M*, the graph misses the feasible region.

THINK CRITICALLY

JEWELRY MAKING Sherry is starting a business making friendship bracelets and necklaces. She must consider the following constraints.

- Materials cost \$0.50 for a bracelet and \$1.25 for a necklace. She has no more than \$10.00 with which to begin.
- She believes she can make at least 2 necklaces per week.
- She believes she can make at least 5 bracelets per week.
- Also, Sherry expects to be able to make a profit of \$1.00 on each bracelet and \$2.00 on each necklace.

22. Write inequalities to represent the constraints. Then graph the system of inequalities.
See Additional Answers.

23. How is the objective function $P = x + 2y$ related to the data in the Exercise?
It represents that profit P is \$1.00 on each bracelet and \$2.00 on each necklace.

24. Use the objective function given in Exercise 23 to find the maximum profit Sherry should expect to make. How many necklaces and how many bracelets would she have to make to maximize her profit? 15 bracelets and 2 necklaces

MIXED REVIEW

25. STANDARDIZED TESTS Which of the following expressions has a value of –6? C; Lessons 2.6 and 2.7

A. $(-3)(-5) - (1)(-9)$ **B.** $(-3)(-5) + (1)(-9)$

C. $(-3)(5) - (-1)(9)$ **D.** $(3)(5) + (-1)(9)$

Evaluate the function for $x = -2$. Lesson 4.6

26. $y = x^2 - 4x + 7$ 19

27. $y = x^4 - 3x^3 + x - 4$ 34

28. $y = 3x^2 - 7x + 12$ 38

29. $y = 2x^5 - 4x^3 + 12x - 6$ −62

PROJECT Connection

An ad for a book, CD, or video club may read "Receive six selections for \$2.99." By accepting the merchandise, you may also be agreeing to purchase additional selections under the club's *negative option plan*. These plans work as follows: If you want the selection, do nothing. If you do not want it, you must direct the seller not to send it by returning a "negative option" form that comes with the announcement of the selection.

1. Find ads for several different clubs. Make a table summarizing features such as what you receive as a joining bonus, how many selections you must buy over what period of time, whether future selections are offered at a discount from list price, how and when you can cancel your membership, if there are shipping charges, and how you must notify the seller that you do not want a selection.
2. Compare the total cost for the amount of merchandise you receive from the plan with the cost if the same items were purchased at local stores. Draw graphs showing the total costs of different numbers of items. Do the clubs really offer good deals? What are the advantages and risks of belonging?

5 FOLLOW-UP

Extension

Have students work in small groups and list the careers they are interested in pursuing. Then have them identify situations in their present experience or that they could anticipate in the future careers where linear programming might be useful in solving problems.

Project Connection

This activity presents further aspects of the project introduced on page 372. Encourage students to use the information from their tables and graphs to support their discussion of the advantages and risks of belonging to a book, CD, or video club.

NAME ________ CLASS ________ DATE ________

ENRICHMENT

8.4 LINEAR PROGRAMMING: THE OBJECTIVE FUNCTION

For each given objective function and constraints, list all vertices. Not all vertices will be integral. Use the techniques learned in Chapter 7 and your graphing utility to determine points of intersection. Find the minimum and maximum value of the function if possible.

1. $C = 4x - 3y$

Constraints: $4x + 3y \le -7,\ x > y,\ 2x + 6y > -23$

Vertices $(-1, -1), \left(1\frac{1}{2}, -4\frac{1}{3}\right), \left(-2\frac{7}{8}, -2\frac{7}{8}\right)$

Maximum 19 at $\left(1\frac{1}{2}, -4\frac{1}{3}\right)$ Minimum $-2\frac{7}{8}$ at $\left(-2\frac{7}{8}, -2\frac{7}{8}\right)$

2. $R = 8x - 5.4y$

Constraints: $10x - 3y < 16,\ y > -2x,\ x - 15.5y \ge -89.6$

Vertices $(1, -2), (3.4, 6), (-2.8, 5.6)$

Maximum -2.8 at $(1, -2)$ Minimum -52.69 at $(-2.8, 5.6)$

3. $P = -14x + 27y$

Constraints: $4x - 10y < 16,\ 2x + 5y < 26,\ y \le 5,\ -2x + 5y \le 17\frac{1}{2}$

Vertices $\left(8\frac{1}{2}, 1\frac{4}{5}\right), \left(2\frac{1}{8}, 4\frac{7}{20}\right)$

Maximum none Minimum none

4. $G = 23x + 7y$

Constraints: $-2x + 8y \ge 12,\ 16x + 4y < 91,\ -2x + 8y \le 63,\ 8x - 8y > -87,\ 7x + 6y > 72\frac{1}{4}$

Vertices $\left(5, 2\frac{3}{4}\right), \left(3\frac{1}{2}, 8\frac{3}{4}\right), \left(-4, 6\frac{7}{8}\right), \left(\frac{1}{2}, 1\frac{5}{8}\right)$

Maximum $\left(3\frac{1}{2}, 8\frac{3}{4}\right)$ Minimum $\left(-4, 6\frac{7}{8}\right)$

26 *South-Western Algebra 1: AN INTEGRATED APPROACH*

LESSON PLANNING

Objective
▶ Use linear programming to solve problems.

Technology/Multimedia
graphing utility

Resources
Reteaching 8.5
Extra Practice 8.5
Transparencies 10, 32, 49–51, 78–80
Student Handbook

Materials/Manipulatives
graph paper
straightedges

ASSIGNMENTS

Basic: 1–15, 18, Review Problem Solving Strategies 1–3

Average: 1–18, Review Problem Solving Strategies 1–3

Enriched: 1–18, Review Problem Solving Strategies 1–3

1 MOTIVATE

Introduction In this lesson students will apply linear programming techniques to typical business situations.

2 TEACH

Use the Pages/Problem Ask students what information represents constraints on the Spirit Club. **the bulleted items** What does the objective function represent? **cost**

Use the Pages/Explore the Problem If students need help writing the constraints, ask questions such as these.

8.5 Problem Solving File

Use Variables

Use Linear Programming

SPOTLIGHT ON LEARNING

WHAT? In this lesson you will learn
- to use linear programming as a model for determining maximum profits and minimum costs under constraints.

WHY? Linear programming can help you solve problems in sales, manufacturing, and transportation.

All businesses want to maximize profits and minimize costs. Linear programming is a model for determining maximum profit or minimum costs under a set of constraints. Recall that the value to be maximized or minimized is the objective function.

Problem

The Spirit Club is selling both long- and short-sleeved T-shirts. The club pays $4 per short-sleeved shirt and $5 per long-sleeved shirt. Each shirt is then silk-screened. From experience, members know the following.

- They always sell at least as many long- as short-sleeved shirts.
- They can silk-screen at least 30 shirts per week but no more than 50.
- Their supplier can provide them with no more than 25 long-sleeved shirts per week.

How many of each type of shirt should the Spirit Club produce weekly to minimize their costs?

CHECK UNDERSTANDING

For this problem, are the constraints $x \geq 0$ and $y \geq 0$ needed? If so, how do they appear in the graph?

Yes. They appear as the y- and x-axes, respectively.

PROBLEM SOLVING TIP

Set your graphing utility so that integers are displayed when using the TRACE feature.

Explore the Problem

First, define the variables. Let x represent the number of short-sleeved shirts produced, and let y represent the number of long-sleeved shirts produced.

1. Express the constraints in terms of x and y. $y \geq x, x + y \geq 30, x + y \leq 50, y \leq 25, x \geq 0, y \geq 0$

Next, write an objective function for cost.

2. If the cost of producing one short-sleeved shirt is $4, write an expression for the cost of producing x short-sleeved shirts. $4x$
3. At a cost of $5 per long-sleeved shirt, write an expression for the cost of producing y long-sleeved shirts. $5y$
4. Since the only costs being considered are for the purchase of shirts, what equation represents the club's total costs C? $C = 4x + 5y$
5. Graph the constraints on a graphing utility. Use the TRACE feature to find the vertices of the feasible region. (15, 15), (5, 25), (25, 25)

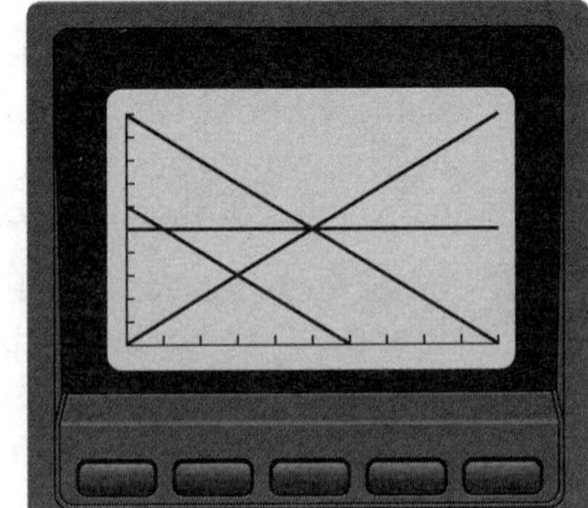

Write an Equation

Draw a Diagram

6. Copy and complete the following table to evaluate the objective function $C = 4x + 5y$ for the (x, y) value at each vertex.

Vertex	$C = 4x + 5y$	Cost
(15, 15)	4(15) + 5(15)	______ $135
(5, 25)	4(5) + 5(25)	______ $145
(25, 25)	4(25) + 5(25)	______ $225

7. At which vertex is the cost function a minimum? (15, 15)

8. What combination of shirts should the club produce to minimize its costs? What will be the minimum cost?
15 short-sleeved, 15 long-sleeved; $135

Investigate Further

Given the constraints in the problem, assume that the club can sell short-sleeved shirts for $6 and long-sleeved shirts for $8.

9. What is the club's profit on one short-sleeved shirt? on one long-sleeved shirt? $2; $3

10. Write an expression for the profit on x short-sleeved shirts. Write an expression for the profit on y long-sleeved shirts. $2x$; $3y$

11. Write the objective function for the club's profit from both short- and long-sleeved shirts. $P = 2x + 3y$

12. Copy and complete the following table.

Vertex	$P = 2x + 3y$	Profit
(15, 15)	2(15) + 3(15)	______ $75
(5, 25)	2(5) + 3(25)	______ $85
(25, 25)	2(25) + 3(25)	______ $125

13. At which vertex will the maximum profit be earned? What will the profit be for that number of shirts? (25, 25); $125

14. Consider this statement, in reference to the original problem and Questions 1–13: "If club members want to maximize their profits, they will have to spend more than the minimum. If they want to minimize their costs, they will earn less than the maximum profit." How does this statement apply to the problem?
See Additional Answers.

PROBLEM SOLVING PLAN

- Understand
- Plan
- Solve
- Examine

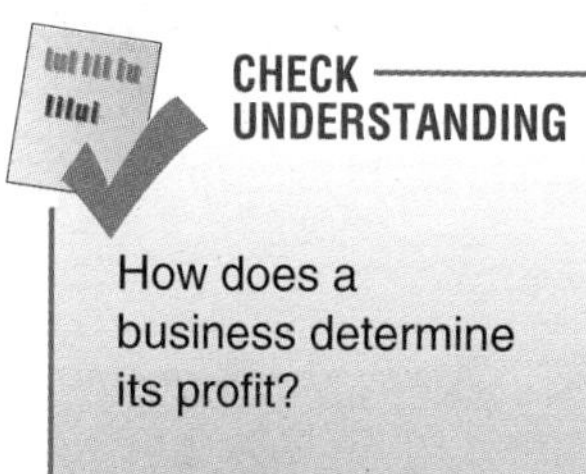

CHECK UNDERSTANDING

How does a business determine its profit?

It finds the difference between total income and total costs.

- Since the club always sells at least as many long- as short-sleeve shirts, what is the relationship between x and y? $\mathbf{y \geq x}$
- The total number of shirts the club can produce per week is $x + y$. What inequality shows that the total is at least 30? $\mathbf{x + y \geq 30}$ What inequality shows that the total is no more than 50? $\mathbf{x + y \leq 50}$

Ask students who use the TRACE feature on their graphing utility why they should set it so integers are displayed. **Only whole numbers of shirts can be produced.**

Use the Pages/Investigate Further Have students compare Problems 1–8 and 9–14. They should recognize that the constraints are the same, so the x- and y-values for the vertices of the feasible region are the same. The objective functions, however, differ. One is cost and the other is profit.

3 SUMMARIZE

In the Math Journal Have students describe how linear programming techniques can be applied to determine maximum or minimum values. They should include writing inequalities to represent the constraints, graphing the constraints to find the vertices of the feasible region, writing an objective function to represent the value to be maximized or minimized, and substituting the x- and y-values at each vertex of the feasible region.

4 PRACTICE

Apply the Strategy For Problems 15–16, ask questions to help students write constraints and an equation for the objective function. For

Problem 18, have students work in pairs or small groups.

TEACHING TIP

Problems 15–16 may first appear complex to some students. Encourage students to work each problem one step at a time.

5 FOLLOW-UP

Extra Practice

ComPuter Corporation manufactures two styles of computers. A desktop costs \$500 to produce and requires 50 hours of labor, while a portable costs \$400 and requires 60 labor hours. ComPuter has up to \$18,000 to invest and at most 2100 hours of labor available. Desktops sell for \$800 and portables for \$700.

1. Express the constraints in terms of x and y. **$50x + 60y \leq 2100$; $500x + 400y \leq 18{,}000$; $x \geq 0$; $y \geq 0$**

NAME ______ CLASS ______ DATE ______

RETEACHING

8.5 PROBLEM SOLVING FILE: USE LINEAR PROGRAMMING

FUNDRAISING The Holyoke Marching Band will hold two raffles. Each ticket for the first will sell for \$2. Each band member can sell at least one ticket for the first raffle. Each ticket for the second raffle will sell for \$0.50. At least one-fourth of the students will buy one ticket each. There are 50 band members and 1600 students. The band can afford to print only 1000 tickets. How many of each type should they print and sell to maximize their income?

Step 1: Let x represent the number of tickets for raffle 1. Let y represent the number of tickets for raffle 2.

Step 2: Write the constraints in terms of x and y.

$x + y \leq 1000$

$x \geq 50$

$y \geq 400$

Step 3: Graph and find the vertices of the feasible region.

Step 4: Write an objective function. Evaluate it for the (x, y) value at each vertex.

Tickets for second raffle: 200, 400, 600, 800, 1000
Tickets to first raffle: 0, 200, 400, 600, 800, 1000
$x + y = 1000$
$y = 400$
$x = 50$

Vertex	$2x + 0.5y$	Income
(50, 950)	2(50) + 0.5(950)	\$575
(50, 400)	2(50) + 0.5(400)	\$300
(600, 400)	2(600) + 0.5(400)	\$1400

The band should print 600 tickets for the first raffle and 400 tickets for the second raffle. If all the tickets are sold, they will earn \$1400.

EXERCISES

FOOD PRODUCTION A company makes gourmet peanut butter from type A peanuts and a store brand from type B peanuts. Each day the company can receive a maximum of 650 lb of type A peanuts and 800 lb of type B peanuts. They can produce no more than 1200 lbs of peanut butter daily. They make \$1.35 profit per pound of gourmet peanut butter and \$0.75 per pound of store brand peanut butter.

1. What will the variables x and y represent?
2. Write the constraints in terms of x and y.
3. Graph and name the vertices of the feasible region.
4. Write an objective function for profit P. Evaluate it for each vertex. To maximize profits, how many pounds of each type of peanut should the company

1. **x = lbs of type A; y = lbs of type B**
2. **$x \leq 650$; $y \leq 800$; $x + y \leq 1{,}200$**
3. **(0,0; (0, 800) (400, 800); (650, 550); (650, 0)**
4. **$P = 1.35x + 0.75y$; 650 lb type A, 550 lb type B; \$1290**

28 South-Western Algebra 1: AN INTEGRATED APPROACH

Use a Graph | Write an Expression

Apply the Strategy

15. **SKI MANUFACTURE** A manufacturer makes two types of snow skis, slalom and cross-country. It takes 6 h to make a pair of cross-country skis and 4 h to make a pair of slalom skis. One hour is required to finish each type. The maximum number of hours of labor available is 96 for manufacture and 20 for finishing. The profit is \$45 for each pair of cross-country skis and \$30 for each pair of slalom skis. See Additional Answers.
    a. Express the constraints in terms of x and y.
    b. Graph the constraints. Find the vertices of the feasible region.
    c. Write an objective function for profit P and evaluate it for the (x, y) value at each vertex.
    d. To maximize profit, how many pairs of each type of ski should the company produce? What will the maximum profit be?

16. **SCHOOL FIELD TRIP** A school is planning a field trip and will rent buses and vans for the trip. Each bus carries up to 60 students, requires 4 chaperons, and costs \$1000 to charter. A van carries up to 10 students, requires 2 chaperons, and costs \$100 for gas. At least 300 students plan to attend, and 36 parents will chaperon. See Additional Answers.
    a. Express the constraints in terms of x and y.
    b. Graph the constraints. Find the vertices of the feasible region.
    c. Write an objective function for cost C and evaluate it for the (x, y) value at each vertex.
    d. To minimize cost, how many of each type of vehicle should the school rent? What is the minimum cost?
17. **EXERCISE EQUIPMENT** A sports equipment company makes stationary bicycles and rowing machines. On a given day, the company can make no more than 110 pieces. The cost to produce a bicycle is \$75; a rower, \$125. The company can spend no more than \$10,000 per day on production. A bicycle sells for \$125, and a rower sells for \$200. To maximize profit, how many of each type should the company produce per day? What is the maximum profit? See Additional Answers.
18. **WRITING MATHEMATICS** Describe two services or products you could provide. Determine constraints that might apply to your business. Base the constraints on performance or production time, operating costs, and profits. Determine a relationship between the constraints that makes sense. See Additional Answers.

Make a Model | Write an Equation | Make a Table

1–3 See Additional Answers.

REVIEW PROBLEM SOLVING STRATEGIES

A Strange and Moving Story

1. The diagram shows the room arrangement at the Hotel Strange. Room 102 is currently empty. Luggage for five different families is in the other five rooms.

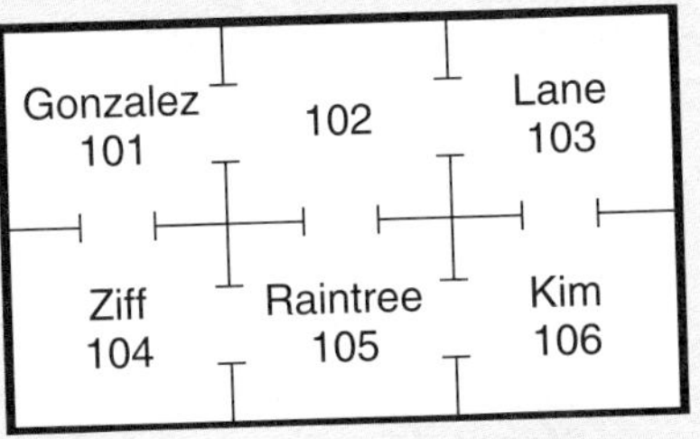

Mr. Bumbler, the desk clerk, realizes that the Lanes and the Kims were given each other's rooms, so their luggage must be switched. To prevent further mixups, Mr. Bumbler insists that luggage for two families cannot be in the same room at the same time. Because of the odd arrangement of rooms, Mr. Bumbler knows that some of the other families will also have to be moved. He is not concerned about the other families returning to their original rooms, as long as the Lanes and the Kims are switched. Finally, Mr. Bumbler wants to complete the switch in as few moves as possible.

a. Work with a partner. Decide on a strategy for solving the problem. Also decide on a method for recording the moves.

b. Compare your solution with those of others. Did anyone make the switch in fewer moves?

2. There are 100 dogs at Pampered Paws Kennel. Each day, the dogs eat 100 lb of food. Large dogs eat 3 lb a day, medium dogs eat 2 lb, and small dogs eat $\frac{1}{2}$ lb. How many dogs of each size are at the kennel if there are five times as many medium dogs as large ones?

a. How many unknowns are there in the problem? How will you represent them algebraically?

b. How many facts are given in the problem? Is this enough to solve the problem? Why?

c. How many of each size dog are there?

d. Could you have solved this problem using another strategy? If so, do you think one method is more efficient?

A Burning Question

3. After his electricity went out, Mr. Choi took out two candles. Both were the same length, but the label on candle A said that it would burn for 4 h while the label on candle B said it would burn for 5 h. Mr. Choi lit both candles at the same time and let them burn until the electricity was restored. He discovered that what remained of one candle was exactly four times the length of what was left of the other. How long were the candles burning? You may use the questions below to guide your thinking, or solve the problem on your own and explain your method.

a. Let t represent the number of hours that the candles were burning, and let x represent the original length of each candle. How much of its original length does candle A burn in t hours? How long is candle A after t hours?

b. How much of its original length does candle B burn in t hours? How long is candle B after t hours?

c. After t hours, how is the remaining length of candle B related to the remaining length of candle A?

d. How long were the candles burning? How much of the original length of each candle remained?

2. Graph the constraints and find the vertices of the feasible region.

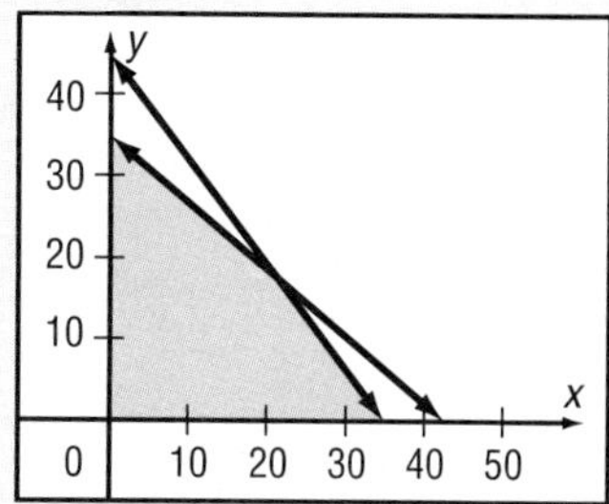

(0, 0), (0, 35), (24, 15), (36, 0)

3. Write an objective function for profit P and evaluate it for the (x, y) value at each vertex. **$P = 800x + 700y$**

(x, y)	$800x + 700y$	Profit, P
(0, 0)	800(0) + 700(0)	$0
(0, 35)	800(0) + 700(35)	$24,500
(24, 15)	800(24) + 700(15)	$29,700
(36, 0)	800(36) + 700(0)	$28,800

4. To maximize its profit, how many of each type of computer should the company manufacture? What is the maximum profit? **24 desktop computers and 15 laptop computers; $29,700**

NAME ______ CLASS ______ DATE ______

P EXTRA PRACTICE **8.5 PROBLEM SOLVING FILE: USE LINEAR PROGRAMMING**

Computer Networks Online time for GlobalNet is $3.00 per hour. Time on InterWorld is $2.50 per hour. Data Management Company needs to access both computer networks. Data Management spends at least twice as much time on GlobalNet as on InterWorld. They spend at least 10 hours each month on InterWorld. The total online time necessary is at least 30 hours per month, but would never exceed 90 hours.

1. Let x represent the hours the company uses GlobalNet. Let y represent the hours they use InterWorld. Write inequalities to express the constraints given.
$y \geq 10$; $x \geq 2y$; $x + y \leq 90$; $x + y \geq 30$

2. Graph the constraints.

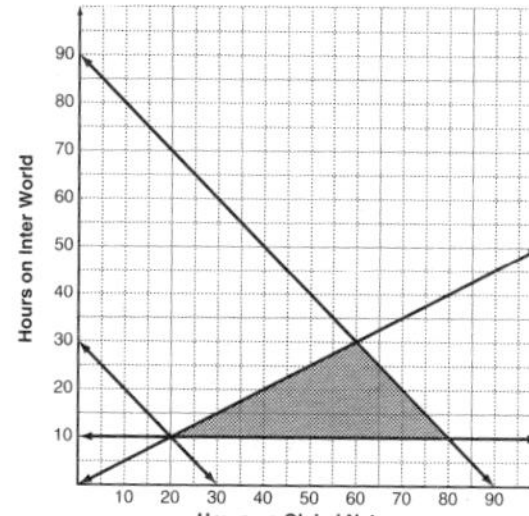

3. Identify the vertices of the feasible region.
(20, 0); (60, 30), (80, 0)

4. Write the objective function for the cost C to access time on both networks.
$C = 3x + 2y$

5. What is the maximum that Data Management company should budget each month for the use of time on these networks?
$255

30 South-Western Algebra 1: An Integrated Approach

LESSON PLANNING

Objectives

- Determine the sample space for a probability experiment.
- Determine the theoretical probability of an event.

Vocabulary

complement
event
fundamental counting principle
sample space
theoretical probability

Resources

Warm Up 8.6
Reteaching 8.6
Extra Practice 8.6
Enrichment 8.6
Transparency 19
Student Handbook
Lesson Quiz 8.6

Materials/Manipulatives

dice
spinners divided into three equal sections labeled 0, 5, and 6

ASSIGNMENTS

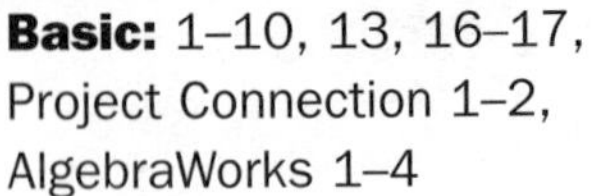

Basic: 1–10, 13, 16–17, Project Connection 1–2, AlgebraWorks 1–4

Average: 1–18, Project Connection 1–2, AlgebraWorks 1–4

Enriched: 1–21, Project Connection 1–2, AlgebraWorks 1–4

1 MOTIVATE

Explore Use this section to review students' understanding of experimental probability which was covered in Lesson 1.8. After students have completed the activities, ask them, on the basis of the games they

8.6 Explore Probability: Theoretical Probability

SPOTLIGHT ON LEARNING

WHAT? In this lesson you will learn

- to determine the sample space for a probability experiment.
- to determine the theoretical probability of an event.

WHY? You can use theoretical probability to solve problems involving sales inventory, game theory, and genetics.

Explore

Imagine playing a game with one standard die and a spinner like the one shown. You or your partner chooses the die or the spinner. The other person then takes the other objects. A game consists of one throw of the die and one spin of the spinner. Whichever player shows the greater number wins the game.

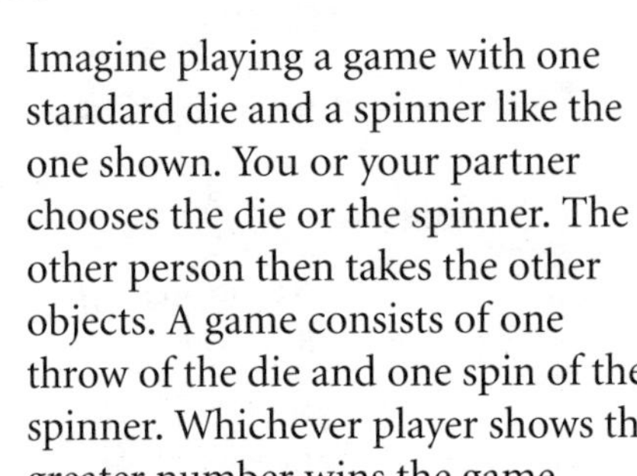

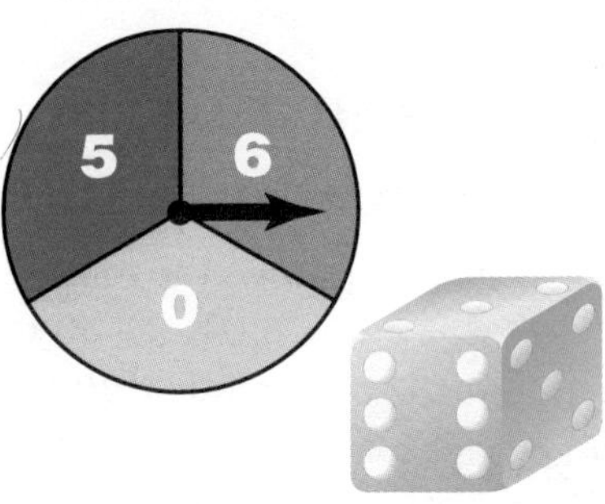

1. If you had first choice, which would you choose to have the greater chance of winning? Answers will vary.
2. What would you need to know in order to have enough information to choose? See Additional Answers.
3. How many games would you want to play before deciding which, if either, player has an advantage? Answers will vary. Some students wi want to play 50 or 100 games before making a guess.
4. Use a die and a spinner like the one shown. Play the game until you are convinced that one is better. Which one is it? answers will vary; probable answer: the spinner

Build Understanding

The game described in Explore is a **probability experiment**. To find out without experimenting which device is more favorable involves **theoretical probability**.

Recall that the **probability of an event**, $P(E)$, is the ratio

$$P(E) = \frac{\text{number of favorable outcomes}}{\text{total number of outcomes in the sample space}}$$

In the Explore game, each combination of numbers that results from a throw of the die and a spin of the spinner is a possible **outcome** of the experiment. Each of the outcomes is equally likely. Any one of the possible outcomes of the experiment constitutes an **event**. Together, all possible outcomes of a probability experiment make up the **sample space** for the experiment.

EXAMPLE 1

What is the sample space for the game in Explore in which the die is rolled once and the spinner is spun once?

Solution

Two methods for determining the sample space are shown below.

a. Use a tree diagram.

Spinner	Die	Outcomes	Spinner	Die	Outcomes	Spinner	Die	Outcomes
0	1	0, 1	5	1	5, 1	6	1	6, 1
	2	0, 2		2	5, 2		2	6, 2
	3	0, 3		3	5, 3		3	6, 3
	4	0, 4		4	5, 4		4	6, 4
	5	0, 5		5	5, 5		5	6, 5
	6	0, 6		6	5, 6		6	6, 6

b. Use a table of ordered pairs.

Spinner \ Die	1	2	3	4	5	6
0	(0, 1)	(0, 2)	(0, 3)	(0, 4)	(0, 5)	(0, 6)
5	(5, 1)	(5, 2)	(5, 3)	(5, 4)	(5, 5)	(5, 6)
6	(6, 1)	(6, 2)	(6, 3)	(6, 4)	(6, 5)	(6, 6)

Both methods of display show that the sample space for the experiment or game in Explore consists of 18 possible outcomes. ◄

You can also use the **fundamental counting principle** to count outcomes in a sample space.

FUNDAMENTAL COUNTING PRINCIPLE

If one activity can be done in m ways and, for each of the m ways, a second activity can be done in n ways, then both can be done in mn ways.

total number of possible outcomes $= m \cdot n$

The fundamental counting principle can be applied to more than two activities.

EXAMPLE 2

Use the fundamental counting principle to determine the number of possible outcomes for the game in Explore.

Solution

The game consists of two activities, rolling the die and spinning the spinner. For one roll of the die there are 6 possible outcomes. For one spin of the spinner there are 3 possible outcomes. Using the fundamental counting principle, there are $3 \cdot 6$ or 18 possible outcomes. ◄

ALGEBRA: WHO, WHERE, WHEN

The modern theory of probability began in a series of letters written in 1654 between the mathematician Blaise Pascal and another mathematician, Pierre Fermat. The discussion centered on a problem: A player is given eight throws of a die to throw a one. The game is interrupted after only three throws. How should the player be compensated?

ALGEBRA: WHO, WHERE, WHEN

The earliest book dealing with the theory of probability was the *Art of Conjecturing* (1713) by Jacques Bernoulli.

played, what the probability is that the spinner player will win. **Answers will vary.** Then discuss why each pair of students who played the games did not find the same probability.

2 TEACH

Use the Pages/Build Understanding Be sure students understand the meanings of the key terms event, outcome, sample space, and probability.

DIVERSITY IN THE CLASSROOM

Visual Learners To help students see that the order in which activities take place does matter, have them make a graph of the sample space of an event such as throwing two dice.

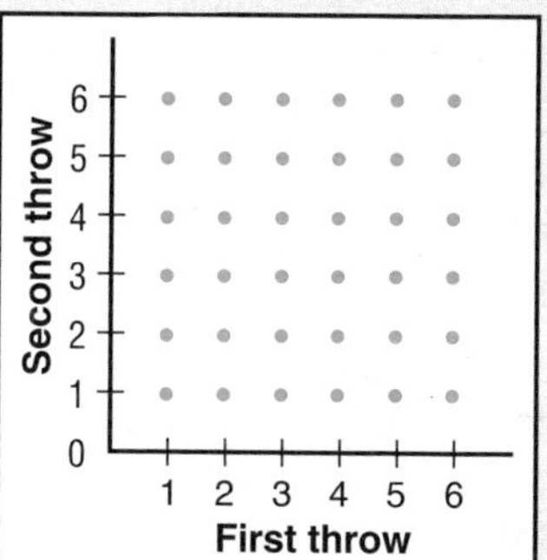

Then ask questions such as the following with regard to the ordered pairs represented in the graph.

- Which point indicates throwing a 2 and then a 3? **(2, 3)**
- Which point indicates throwing a 3 and then a 2? **(3, 2)**
- Are these points the same points or different points? **different**
- In how many ways can you throw a 4 and a 5? What shows this? **two ways; the two distinct points, (4, 5) and (5, 4)**

Example 1: In determining the number of outcomes in the sample space, a common error is to disregard order. Be sure that students understand that (5, 6) is a different outcome than (6, 5).

Example 2: Ask students how the numbers used in the application of the fundamental counting principle relate to the format of the tree diagram and table of ordered pairs in Example 1. **The numbers are the same as the number of trees and branches or as the number of rows and columns.**

Example 3: Have students compare the probabilities found in this example to the decisions they made in the Explore.

Example 4: Ask students why there are three possible outcomes in the event "choose a large brown jacket." **Three jackets fit the description: a large brown leather jacket, a large brown suede jacket, and a large brown cotton jacket.**

Ongoing Assessment The important concepts and skills are determining the sample space for a probability experiment and determining the theoretical probability of an event. To assess these ideas, have students demonstrate how they have applied these concepts and skills in Exercises 2, 5, and 7 of the Try These section.

Guided Practice/Try These Students should be aware that the answer to Exercise 5 is needed to solve Exercises 6 and 7. For students who are having difficulty with Exercise 5, suggest that they write a multiplication expression for the fundamental counting principle, using words for the types of shirt characteristics. **sleeve lengths times colors times directions of stripes times sizes** Then have them substitute the number of possible outcomes for each characteristic in the verbal expression. Then they can find the product. **2 • 6 • 3 • 10 = 360**

3 SUMMARIZE

In the Math Journal Have students describe a probability experiment that involves two activities. Then have them describe and demonstrate how to use tree diagrams,

THINK BACK

What is the greatest value that can be found for the probability of any event? the least value? What do each of these values indicate?

greatest: 1 means certainty; least: 0 means impossibility

COMMUNICATING ABOUT ALGEBRA

Use the information in Example 4. How could you determine the probability that a jacket chosen at random isn't a small cotton one?

Find P(small, cotton) and subtract it from 1.

You can use theoretical probability to find out which you would choose in order to have the greater chance of winning, the spinner or the die.

EXAMPLE 3

What is each player's probability of winning the game in Explore? Which player is more likely to win?

Solution

Refer to the sample space in Example 1. There are 18 possible outcomes in the sample space. For the event "spinner player wins," there are 9 outcomes.

$$P(\text{spinner player wins}) = \frac{9}{18}, \text{ or } \frac{1}{2}$$

For the event "die player wins," there are 7 outcomes.

$$P(\text{die player wins}) = \frac{7}{18}$$

The spinner player is more likely to win. ◄

Since there are two possible ties, the P(a player wins) is $\frac{16}{18}$, or $\frac{8}{9}$. The event "game ends in a tie" is the same as "no player wins." Because the sum of the probabilities of all outcomes in the sample space is 1, to find P(no player wins), you can subtract P(a player wins) from 1.

$$P(\text{no player wins}) = 1 - \frac{8}{9} = \frac{1}{9}$$

In general, the events A and *not* A are **complements** and

$P(A) + P(\text{not } A) = 1$, or
$P(A) = 1 - P(\text{not } A)$, or
$P(\text{not } A) = 1 - P(A)$

EXAMPLE 4

A shop sells jackets in smooth leather, suede, or cotton. Each is available in four sizes (small, medium, large, and extra large) and three colors (brown, tan, and green). The store has one of each possible jacket. What is the probability that a jacket chosen at random is large and brown?

Solution

Use the fundamental counting principle to determine the number of outcomes in the event "choose a large brown jacket" and the total number of outcomes.

Number of Outcomes in the Event	Total Number of Outcomes
material • size • color	material • size • color
3 • 1 • 1 = 3	3 • 4 • 3 = 36

$$P(\text{large, brown}) = \frac{3}{36} = \frac{1}{12}$$ ◄

TRY THESE

Use the following information to solve Exercises 1–4. You will toss a coin and draw a card from a standard deck of 52 cards.

1. How many different outcomes are there in the sample space? 104
2. Show a table of ordered pairs for the event "tossing a head and drawing a red card." How many outcomes are in the event? See Additional Answers.
3. What is the probability of tossing a head and picking a red card? $\frac{26}{104}$ or $\frac{1}{4}$
4. What is the probability of tossing a tail and picking the ace of clubs? $\frac{1}{104}$

BUSINESS INVENTORY The Shirt Gallery has long- and short-sleeved shirts. They are available in blue, white, tan, yellow, green, and pink, as well as with diagonal, vertical, and horizontal stripes. Every shirt is available in ten different sizes.

5. What is the least number of shirts the store must carry in inventory to have one of each possible selection? 360 shirts
6. If the Shirt Gallery keeps the minimum number of shirts in stock, how many will be
   a. short-sleeved? 180
   b. blue? 60
   c. long-sleeved and yellow? 30
   d. short-sleeved, pink, with vertical stripes? 10
7. What is the probability that a shirt chosen at random will be green with vertical stripes? $\frac{1}{18}$

PRACTICE

Use the following information to solve Exercises 1–5. A license plate in one state consists of two digits from 0 to 9, the first of which cannot be zero, followed by three letters.

1. If the two digits are known, how many different license plates are possible? 26^3, which is 17,576
2. If the three letters are known, how many different license plates are possible? 90
3. How many different license plates are possible for the given conditions? $90 \cdot 26^3$, which is 1,581,840
4. If you try to remember the license plate but can only recall the two numbers and first letter, what is the probability that you can guess the rest of the plate in one guess? $\frac{1}{676}$
5. How many different plates can have the same letter used three times? $26 \cdot 90$, which is 2340
6. An ice-cream store advertises that it has 28 different flavors and 12 different toppings. How many different cups can be made with one flavor and one topping? $28 \cdot 12$, which is 336
7. If the middle digit of a three-digit area code must be either 0 or 1, and the first digit cannot be 0, how many area codes are possible? $9 \cdot 2 \cdot 10$, which is 180
8. In Exercise 7, if you dial three digits at random, what is the probability that you will dial a three-digit sequence that is an actual area code? $\frac{180}{1000} = \frac{9}{50}$
9. A restaurant offers a complete meal that consists of three courses. If the choice is one each of six appetizers, eight main courses, and five desserts, how many different complete meals are possible? $6 \cdot 8 \cdot 5 = 240$

ordered pairs, and the fundamental counting principle to find the total number of possible outcomes in the sample space.

4 PRACTICE

Practice For Exercise 6, ask how many different cups can be made with two different flavors and one topping. **$28 \cdot 27 \cdot 12$, or 9072** Students must realize that once they have chosen a flavor for the first scoop, the number of choices for the second scoop is decreased by 1.

NAME ______ CLASS ______ DATE ______

R RETEACHING

8.6 EXPLORE PROBABILITY: THEORETICAL PROBABILITY

Pete's Pizza Parlor makes three different types of crusts for their pizzas. They offer 20 different toppings. What is the probability that a customer will order randomly a two-topping pizza in which one of the toppings is onions.

Step 1: Calculate the total number of choices.

$3 \cdot 20 \cdot 19 = 1140$ (crusts · topping choices · topping choices)

Step 2: Calculate the number of pizzas for which one topping is onions.

$3 \cdot 1 \cdot 19 = 57$ (crusts · topping choices (onions) · topping choices)

Step 3: Write a fraction and simplify.

$\frac{\text{Number of pizzas with onions}}{\text{Total number of choices}} = \frac{57}{1140} = \frac{1}{20}$

The probability that a customer will order a two-topping pizza with onion is $\frac{1}{20}$.

EXERCISES

RETAIL A clothing store sells 8 different shirts and jeans in 4 different colors (blue, white, black and gray).

1. How many different combinations of jeans and shirts are possible? 1. **32**
2. How many different combinations can be made with the pair of black jeans? 2. **8**
3. If you choose randomly, what is the probability that you will buy a pair of black jeans? 3. $\frac{1}{4}$
4. What is the probability that you will buy either black or gray jeans? 4. $\frac{1}{2}$

COLLECTING Jo has a key chain collection. Some are souvenirs and some are not. Some key chains have words on them and some do not. All of the key chains are either solid red, green, blue, black, yellow, or striped.

5. If Jo has one key chain with each of the characteristics described, how many key chains does she have? For example, one key chain might be red with words and be a souvenir. 5. **24**
6. What is the probability that Jo will randomly choose a blue souvenir key chain with words? 6. $\frac{1}{24}$

34 *South-Western Algebra 1: AN INTEGRATED APPROACH*

Extend For Exercises 12–14, students should begin by showing the sample space for each game. This will make it easier for them to find the correct number of outcomes in the sample space. For example, the sample space for the game in Exercise 12 consists of 36 outcomes, not 11 (each sum from 2 through 12).

Think Critically For Exercises 15–18, students should recognize that there is more than one sequence in which each event may occur. This fact will be evident if they list all 16 possible outcomes.

5 FOLLOW-UP

Extra Practice
Use the following information for Exercises 1–3. You will spin a spinner divided into ten equal sections numbered 1 through 10 and throw a die.

1. How many different outcomes are there in the sample space? **60**

NAME ______ CLASS ______ DATE ______

EXTRA PRACTICE
8.6 EXPLORE PROBABILITY: THEORETICAL PROBABILITY

Use the following information to solve Exercises 1–6.

SECURITY A code to enter a high security building is a three-digit number followed by two letters from A to F.

1. How many different codes are possible? 1. 36,000
2. If the two letters are known, how many different codes are possible? 2. 1000
3. What is the probability that the first number of a code is 0? 3. $\frac{1}{10}$
4. What is the probability that any of the numbers in the code is 0? 4. $\frac{3}{10}$
5. If you try to remember the code but can only recall the three numbers, what is the probability that you can guess the rest of the code in one guess? 5. $\frac{1}{36}$
6. If you could only remember the two letters, what is the probability that you can guess the rest of the code in one guess? 6. $\frac{1}{1000}$
7. A pizza parlor has 12 choices of toppings. If you want to purchase a three-topping pizza, how many choices do you have if the three toppings must all be different? 7. 1,320
8. Mr. Reilly gives ten-question multiple choice quizzes. If each question has four choices, how many different outcomes are possible if you are guessing? 8. 1,048,576
9. In Exercise 8, if you knew the answers for seven questions, what is the probability you'd guess the remaining three answers correctly? 9. $\frac{1}{64}$
10. A tile company has 5 different styles of tile in 8 different colors and 4 different designs. How many different selections do they have? 10. 160
11. The tile company in Exercise 10 wants to offer 400 different selections. If they only plan on adding more designs, how many more designs should they add? 11. 6
12. Two coins are tossed and one die is rolled. What's the probability of getting 2 heads and an even number? 12. $\frac{1}{8}$

36 *South-Western Algebra 1:* AN INTEGRATED APPROACH

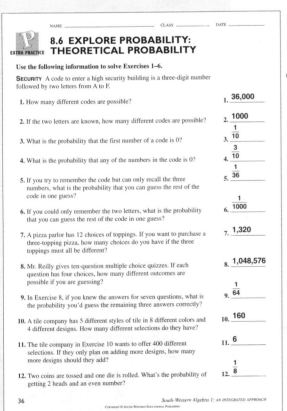

10. In Exercise 9, what is the greatest number of main courses that the restaurant can remove from its menu and still allow at least 150 different meals to be chosen?
three choices can be removed: solve $6 \cdot (8 - x) \cdot 5 = 150$
11. On a five-question true/false quiz, what is the probability of answering all five questions correctly by guessing? $\left(\frac{1}{2}\right)^5 = \frac{1}{32}$

EXTEND

For Exercises 12–14, decide whether the games described give each player an equal chance of winning. If not, name the player who has the advantage and explain why. Assume dice are labeled 1 to 6. See Additional Answers.

12. Two dice are rolled and the numbers are added. Player A wins if the sum is even; player B wins if the sum is odd.
13. Two dice are rolled and the numbers are multiplied. Player A wins if the product is even; player B wins if the product is odd.
14. Three coins are tossed. Player A wins if all three show either heads or tails. Player B wins if any one coin is different from the other two. For each win, Player A scores 3 points. For each win, Player B scores 1 point.

THINK CRITICALLY

Use the following information to solve Exercises 15–19. A husband and wife are planning to have four children. Assume that having a boy or a girl is equally likely. (*Hint:* List all possible outcomes.)

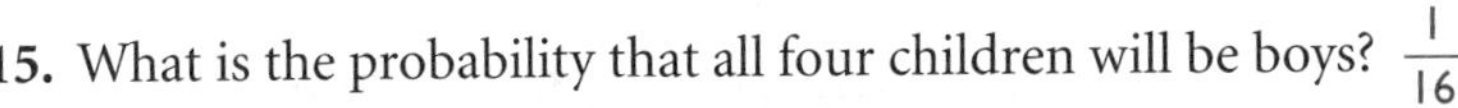

15. What is the probability that all four children will be boys? $\frac{1}{16}$
16. What is the probability that all four children will be of the same sex? $\frac{1}{8}$
17. What is the probability of having three girls and one boy? of having three boys and one girl? $\frac{1}{4}$; $\frac{1}{4}$
18. What is the probability of having two boys and two girls? $\frac{3}{8}$
19. What is the sum of all the probabilities in Exercises 16–18? Explain this result.
See Additional Answers.

PROJECT *Connection*

Suppose you want to purchase an expensive item, such as a computer. If you do not have enough cash to pay for the item, you might consider *installment buying*. You pay part of the price as a *down payment* at the time of purchase and the remainder in equal monthly installments. Buying on an installment plan is a form of credit, and you should expect to pay extra for credit. Suppose, for example, you can buy a $1200 computer for a down payment of $240 and 12 monthly payments of $90 each.

1. Determine the total price you will pay for the computer. How much extra are you paying for an installment plan? $1320; $120
2. What percent of the list price of the computer does the extra cost in Question 1 represent? If you paid the total installment price in a single payment at the end of the year, that percent would be the interest rate. Since you make monthly payments, the *annual percentage rate* (APR) of interest is actually higher. Determine the APR using this formula.

$$\text{APR} = (24 \cdot \text{extra cost}) \div [(\text{list price})(\text{number of payments} + 1)]$$ 10%; 18.46%

Career
Retail Store Buyer

The buyer for a retail store selects and purchases the merchandise to be sold by the store. Some of the decisions the buyer makes are based on probabilities.

Decision Making

Colors	Sizes	Styles
white	small	crewneck
grey	medium	hooded
black	large	
red	X large	
blue	XX large	
green	XXX large	
yellow		
pink		
purple		

1. The buyer for Ace Sports wants to purchase the line of sweatshirts described in the table at the left. The shirt manufacturer is offering a special introductory purchase price if the buyer purchases three of each possible shirt. How many shirts is this? $3(9 \cdot 6 \cdot 2) = 324$ shirts
2. Suppose the buyer takes advantage of the special introductory offer. What is the probability that the first customer will select a large, blue, hooded sweatshirt? $\frac{3}{324} = \frac{1}{108}$
3. What is the probability that the first sweatshirt sold will be a red crewneck sweatshirt? $\frac{18}{324} = \frac{1}{18}$
4. A buyer relies on statistics from market trend reports and sales reports to predict which items are most likely to sell. Below are portions of the Ace Sports sales report for last year. The shirt manufacturer offers the same special rate for larger orders as long as the wholesale buyer purchases at least three of each shirt. Based on the statistics in the table below at the right, how many of each shirt would you recommend for the wholesale buyer? See Additional Answers.

Total Plain Sweatshirts Sold: 1500		
Styles	**Sizes**	**Colors**
Crewneck: 1150	Small: 80	White: 191
Hooded: 350	Medium: 152	Grey: 296
	Large: 220	Black: 143
	X Large: 465	Red: 360
	XX Large: 435	Blue: 375
	XXX Large: 148	Green: 135

2. What is the probability of showing two even numbers? **15/60 or 1/4**
3. What is the probability of showing a 10 and a 6? **1/60**
4. A paint store offers True Color ready-mixed paint in two ceiling colors, eight wall colors, and three trim colors. Provided that all colors coordinate with each other, from how many different combinations of ceiling, wall, and trim paints does a customer have to choose? **48**

Project Connection This activity presents further aspects of the project introduced on page 372. Review how to find what percent one number is of another.

AlgebraWorks After students complete the exercises, ask them to identify which problems involve theoretical probability and which involve experimental probability. **2–3; 4**

NAME ______________ CLASS ________ DATE ________

E ENRICHMENT

8.6 EXPLORE PROBABILITY: THEORETICAL PROBABILITY

Everyone inherits traits from his or her parents. For example, a child can inherit hair traits from one parent and eye traits from the other. Genetics is the branch of science that considers the inheritance of traits, based on possible patterns from parental genes. In this activity you will look at the possible outcomes for hair and eye color in your family.

Answers for all questions will vary.

1. Think about the characteristics of your parents' hair and eyes. Describe these characteristics in the chart at the bottom of the page. 1. ________
2. Considering just your parents' characteristics, how many possible outcomes are there? 2. ________
3. Considering only your parents' characteristics, what was the probability of you having blue eyes and straight blond hair? (Hint: If neither of your parents have black hair, the probability of you having black hair is zero.) 3. ________

If neither of your parents has black hair, but one of your grandparents does, you have a slight chance of having a brother or sister with black hair. One of your parents may carry the trait of black hair as a recessive gene.

4. Consider the hair and eye characteristics of both sets of grandparents. Describe those characteristics in the chart. Fill in what you know. 4. ________
5. Considering both your parents' and grandparents' characteristics, how many possible outcomes are there? 5. ________
6. Considering both your parents' and grandparents' characteristics, what was the probability of you having blue eyes and straight blond hair? 6. ________

HAIR			EYES		
Color	Density (thin/thick)	Waviness (curly, straight, etc.)	Color	Color Blindness (yes/no)	Sight (perfect/far-sighted, etc.)

38 South-Western Algebra 1: AN INTEGRATED APPROACH

Introduction The Chapter Review emphasizes the major concepts, skills, and vocabulary presented in this chapter and can be used for diagnosing students' strengths and weaknesses. Page references direct students to appropriate sections for additional review and reteaching.

Using Pages 404–405 Ask students to scan the Chapter Review and ask questions about any section they find confusing. Exercises 1–4 review key vocabulary.

Informal Evaluation Have students write or state a list of questions that they asked themselves as part of solving a particular problem in the review. These questions may give you insight into students' methods of analyzing problems and give you suggestions for improving their problem solving skills.

Follow-Up Have students solve this problem: The objective function $P = 3x + y$ exists under the following constraints:

$$x + y \le 7$$
$$x + 2y \le 8$$
$$x \ge 0$$
$$y \ge 0$$

a. In which quadrant of the coordinate plane will the feasible region be found? Explain how you know. **The feasible region will be found in Quadrant 1, given the fact that $x \ge 0$ and $y \ge 0$.**

b. Find the vertices of the feasible region. **(0, 0), (0, 4), (6, 1), (7, 0)**

c. At which vertex will the objective function be maximized? **(7, 0)**

d. Find the maximum value of the objective function under the given constraints. **Maximum value is 21.**

Have students write word problems that can be solved using a system of linear inequalities. Students should exchange and solve each others' word problems.

CHAPTER REVIEW

VOCABULARY

Choose the word from the list at the right that completes each statement.

1. If an inequality is written with ≤ or ≥, the boundary line is shown as a(n) __?__. d
2. A(n) __?__ half-plane does not include the boundary line. c
3. In a probability experiment, the set of all possible outcomes is called the __?__. b
4. In linear programming, the maximum or minimum value of the objective function will occur at a(n) __?__ of the feasible region. a

a. vertex
b. sample space
c. open half-plane
d. solid line

Lesson 8.1 GRAPH LINEAR INEQUALITIES IN TWO VARIABLES pages 373–378

- A **linear inequality** in two variables is an inequality of the form

$$y < mx + b, y > mx + b, y \le mx + b, \text{ or } y \ge mx + b,$$

in which x and y are variables and m and b are constants. To determine whether an ordered pair is a solution of a linear inequality, substitute the values for the variables and evaluate the inequality.

- The graph of a linear equation separates the coordinate plane into three parts: points on the line, points above the line, and points below the line. Points above the line and below it form two **half-planes**. The line forms the **boundary** of each of the half-planes.
- The graph of a linear inequality in two variables includes all points in a half-plane. For inequalities with ≤ or ≥, the half-plane includes the boundary line and is a **closed half-plane**.
- For inequalities with < or >, the half-plane does not include the boundary line and is an **open half-plane**.

Tell whether the ordered pair is a solution of the linear inequality.

5. $y \le 3x - 6$; (1, 1) no
6. $3y > x$; (0, 0) no
7. $2x + y > 4$; (4, 6) yes

Graph each linear inequality. See Additional Answers.

8. $y \le x + 3$
9. $3x + 6y \le 12$
10. $3x - 2y > 6$

Lesson 8.2 SOLVE SYSTEMS OF LINEAR INEQUALITIES BY GRAPHING pages 379–385

- If you graph a **system of linear inequalities** on a coordinate plane, the region in which their graphs overlap contains the solution set of the system.

Graph each system of linear inequalities. See Additional Answers.

11. $\begin{cases} y \le x + 1 \\ y \ge 2x - 2 \end{cases}$
12. $\begin{cases} 3y < x + 6 \\ y > -2x + 3 \end{cases}$
13. $\begin{cases} x - 4y \le 4 \\ 3x - 2y \ge 0 \end{cases}$

Lesson 8.3 USE GRAPHING UTILITIES TO SOLVE SYSTEMS OF INEQUALITIES	pages 386–387

- You can use a graphing utility to solve a system of inequalities.

Use a graphing utility to solve each set of inequalities. See Additional Answers.

14. $\begin{cases} y > 3 \\ y < x + 3 \end{cases}$ **15.** $\begin{cases} y < 3 \\ y > x + 3 \end{cases}$ **16.** $\begin{cases} y > 3 \\ y > x + 3 \end{cases}$

Lesson 8.4 LINEAR PROGRAMMING: THE OBJECTIVE FUNCTION	pages 388–393

- **Linear programming** is a technique in which graphs of linear inequalities are used to find a maximum value for profit or a minimum value for costs. The inequalities represent **constraints**, or restrictions, that limit business activity.
- The region containing possible solutions is the **feasible region**. The expression to be maximized or minimized is called the **objective function**. A maximum or minimum value always occurs at a vertex of a feasible region.
- To avoid negative solutions, the inequalities $x \geq 0$ and $y \geq 0$ are included as constraints.

17. Find the maximum profit P for the objective function $P = 2x + 3y$ if P is subject to the following constraints. Name the point at which it occurs. maximum is 24 at (0, 8)

$y \geq x + 5 \quad 2x + y \leq 8 \quad x \geq 0 \quad y \geq 0$

Lesson 8.5 USE LINEAR PROGRAMMING	pages 394–397

- You can use linear programming to set up a model to determine the conditions under which costs will be minimized or profits maximized for a given set of constraints.

18. The Home Ec Club plans to sell two kinds of pies at the Health Fair, apple and blueberry. They sell apple pies for $3 each and blueberry pies for $2 each. Members sell at least as many blueberry pies as apple pies. They can make at least 20 pies but no more than 40. They can get only enough blueberries for 20 pies.

a. What expression represents the profits P to be maximized? $P = 3x + 2y$

b. Write expressions for the constraints. $x + y \geq 20, x + y \leq 40, y \geq x, y \leq 20$

c. Use a graph to find how many of each type of pie the club should sell to maximize profits. See Additional Answers.

Lesson 8.6 EXPLORE PROBABILITY: THEORETICAL PROBABILITY	pages 398–403

- In a probability experiment, the set of all possible outcomes is called the **sample space**. The number of possible outcomes can be found by the **fundamental counting principle**. To apply the principle, find the product of the number of possible outcomes of each activity.
- The **theoretical probability** P for each event E in an experiment is the ratio

$$P(E) = \frac{\text{number of outcomes in } E}{\text{total number of outcomes in the sample space}}$$

19. You toss three number cubes. What is the total number of outcomes in the sample space? 216

Study Skills Tip Students should be aware that not all topics in mathematics are equally challenging. Therefore, they should not assume that they have to devote the same amount of time to every section of a chapter. Their success with the chapter review can serve as a guide to the relative amounts of time they should spend studying the material. In this sense, studying for a test can mirror taking the test: students should first work with the material with which they feel most comfortable and then undertake the more challenging parts.

For Your Portfolio Have students gather samples from their project, homework, quizzes, and class work that portray efforts to meet each of their goals for this chapter. On a cover page for each representative work have students write the related goal, why the work is included in the portfolio, and what the teacher should look for when reviewing the work. On a general cover page have students write a self-evaluation of how well they have met each of their goals for this chapter. The general cover page should conclude with goals for the next chapter and the students' reasons for choosing these goals.

The Chapter Test is comprised of a variety of test-item types as follows:

writing	12
traditional	1–8, 10–11, 14–19
verbal	9, 13, 20–22

TEACHING TIP

The writing item provides an opportunity for students to demonstrate a knowledge of process as well as end result. Suggest that before they begin answering the questions, students should look over the entire test and determine the order in which they will work. Some students may be more successful if they save the open-ended writing question until after they have completed the other test questions.

The table below correlates the Chapter Test items with the appropriate lesson(s).

Item	Lesson	Item	Lesson
1–2	8.1	13	8.6
3–8	8.2	14–19	8.4
9	8.2	20–21	8.4
10–12	8.4	22	8.5

CHAPTER ASSESSMENT

CHAPTER TEST

Tell whether the ordered pair is a solution of the linear inequality.

1. $y > 4x - 3$; (4, 1) no
2. $3x - y < 4$; (2, 2) no

Graph each system of inequalities. See Additional Answers.

3. $\begin{cases} x \le 2 \\ y \ge -4 \end{cases}$
4. $\begin{cases} y - x < 2 \\ y + 2x < 6 \end{cases}$
5. $\begin{cases} x + 3y \le -9 \\ x - y \ge 0 \end{cases}$
6. $\begin{cases} y < 2x + 4 \\ y > -2x + 4 \end{cases}$
7. $\begin{cases} x - 3y \ge -1 \\ 3x - 4y \le 2 \end{cases}$
8. $\begin{cases} x + 2y \le 3 \\ -2x - 4y \le 3 \end{cases}$

9. Carla plans to buy at least 16 CDs and books as graduation gifts. CDs will cost her an average of \$12, and books will cost an average of \$16. Carla wants to spend no more than \$288. See Additional Answers.
   a. Write and graph a system of linear inequalities to represent the situation described above.
   b. Name three combinations of single CDs and albums that Carla could buy.

Graph each system of inequalities.

10. $\begin{cases} y - x \ge 0 \\ x + y \le 8 \\ x \ge 2 \end{cases}$
11. $\begin{cases} x \ge 1 \\ y \le 1 \\ x - y \le 7 \end{cases}$

12. WRITING MATHEMATICS Write a paragraph to explain how you used the data in Question 9 to write the system of inequalities. Answers will vary.
13. A restaurant offers a three-course meal. If there is a choice of seven appetizers, nine main courses, and seven desserts, how many different complete meals are there? 7 • 9 • 7, or 441

Use the graphs of $y = -2$, $y = x$, and $y = 10 - 2x$, shown at the right, to name the numbered region that contains the solution set of each system given.

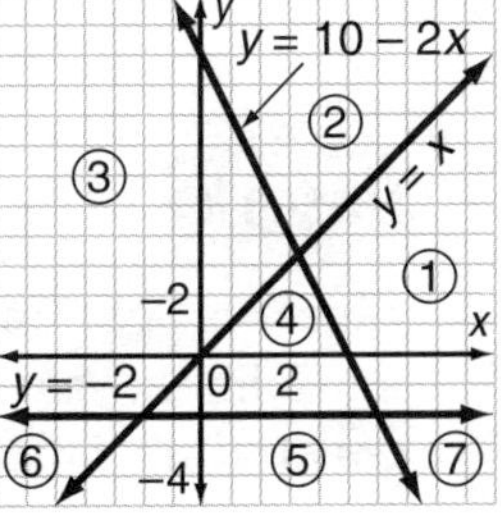

14. $\begin{cases} y > -2 \\ y < x \end{cases}$ 1, 4
15. $\begin{cases} y < -2 \\ y < x \end{cases}$ 5, 7
16. $\begin{cases} y > x \\ y > -2 \end{cases}$ 2, 3
17. $\begin{cases} y > x \\ y < -2 \end{cases}$ 6
18. $\begin{cases} y < x \\ y < 10 - 2x \\ y > -2 \end{cases}$ 4
19. $\begin{cases} y > -2 \\ y > x \\ y < 10 - 2x \end{cases}$ 3

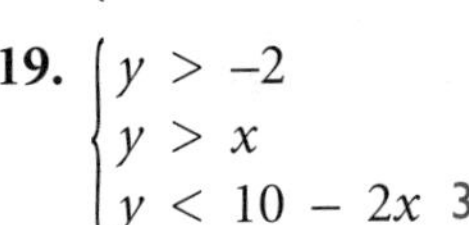

For the given objective function and constraints, find the maximum profit or minimum cost and name the point at which it occurs.

20. $P = 5x + 3y$; $x + y \le 6; x - y \le 4; x \ge 0; y \ge 0$ maximum of 28 at (5, 1)
21. $C = 2x + y$; $x + y \ge 6; x - y \ge 4; x \ge 0; y \ge 0$ minimum of 11 at (5, 1)
22. Joe's Heavy Hauling has 8 five-ton trucks, 7 ten-ton trucks, and 12 drivers. Joe hauls 420 tons of cement per day. The five-ton trucks can make 8 trips a day. The ten-ton trucks can make six trips per day. The cost is \$40 per day for a five-ton truck and \$60 for a ten-ton truck, not including drivers' salaries. See Additional Answers.
    a. Write an equation for the objective function representing cost. Then write inequalities for the constraints. Graph the system.
    b. If all 12 drivers are to work, how many trucks of each type must be used to minimize the cost?

For Performance Assessment see Additional Answers.

PERFORMANCE ASSESSMENT

QUILT MODELS Many quilt patterns are based on simple shapes such as squares and triangles.

1. Write the systems of inequalities that generate the green square and each of the blue triangles on this quilt pattern.
2. Find a quilt pattern or other folk art design that you like. Copy the design onto graph paper and draw coordinate axes. Use equations and systems of inequalities to describe as many lines and regions in the design as you can.

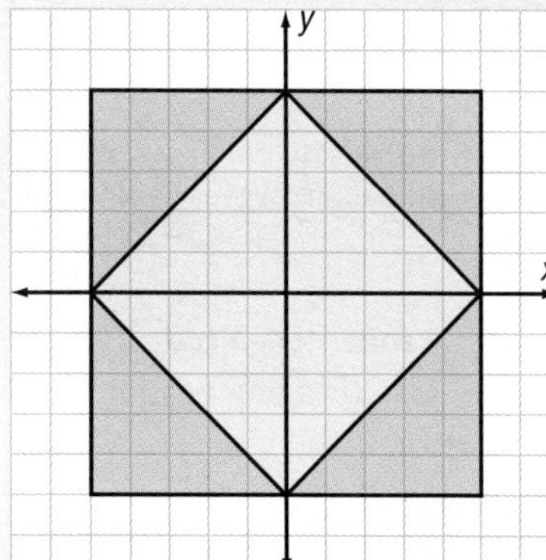

BAKE SALE Find recipes for two items you could prepare for a charity bake sale. The recipes should each require different amounts of two main ingredients, such as shortening and flour or eggs and flour. Make up numbers for how much of these ingredients you might have on hand. Then estimate how much they could sell for at the sale. Show how to write and solve a linear programming problem to determine how to maximize the profit from your baking.

PARALLELOGRAM PROBLEM Draw coordinate axes on a piece of graph paper. Shade a parallelogram that is not a rectangle and has an area of 48 square units. (Recall that area is the product of the base and the height.) Write the system of inequalities that describes the shaded area.

PROJECT ASSESSMENT

PROJECT *Connection* If your group has not already decided the format for your Teen Consumer Report, do so now. Plan a schedule for completing the report and determine responsibilities for each group member. Make any necessary arrangements for using school equipment such as video cameras or computers.

1. Think about how you can build student interest in attending your presentation. Let your target audience know why your project is important to them and when they should expect to read, watch, or listen to it.
2. Create a "What you have learned" quiz to distribute after your presentation.
3. Find out about consumer protection agencies or better business bureaus in your area. If possible, include a brief interview with a representative from one of these groups in your report. Ask about issues important to young people.
4. Invite all students to contribute to your *Tips for Teens* or alert you about misleading consumer practices. Update your audience regularly.

Performance Assessment

The activities on page 407 give students with different learning styles opportunities to demonstrate their understanding of concepts in this chapter. The activities may be used in addition to or instead of the Chapter Test on the previous page.

Quilt Models (Visual) In writing the system of inequalities for the square and the triangles, students should realize that although there appear to be 16 inequalities necessary (3 for each triangle, 4 for the square), there are actually fewer: one side of the square is included in each of the triangles. Their ability to recognize this before determining the necessary inequalities is one indicator of under- standing.

Bake Sale (Visual) Check to see that students are using reasonable numbers for the amounts of each ingredient on hand, the amounts needed for each recipe, and the selling price of each of the baked goods. Check to see whether students can select numbers that lead to manageable inequalities for the given constraints and whether their constraints match values chosen for amounts needed and amounts on hand.

Parallelogram Problem (Visual) A good indicator of understanding is students' ability to determine the slopes of the sides of the parallelogram. Check to see whether students have chosen to position the parallelogram so that the slopes of the sides are most easily found.

Project Assessment

Project Connection Work together to determine the best format for your project. Consider suggestions from class members and use professionally produced literature as a guide. Discuss ways to involve students outside your group or class.

NAME ______ CLASS ______ DATE ______

FORM B **CHAPTER 8 TEST**

Write the letter of the best answer for Questions 1–4.

1. Which ordered pair is a solution of $5x + 4y > 40$? 1. c

NAME ______ CLASS ______ DATE ______

FORM A **CHAPTER 8 TEST**

Write the letter of the best answer for Questions 1–4.

1. Which ordered pair is a solution of $5x + 3y < 30$? 1. d
   a. (8, –2) b. (7, –1) c. (3, 6) d. (–2, 10)
2. Which describes the graph of $4x - 3y \le 24$? 2. a
   a. a half plane above the solid line through (0, –8) and (6, 0)
   b. a half plane below the solid line through (0, –8) and (6, 0)
   c. a half plane above the dashed line through (0, –8) and (6, 0)
   d. a half plane below the dashed line through (0, –8) and (6, 0)
3. Which ordered pair is a solution of the system? 3. a
   $\begin{cases} x - 3y \le 9 \\ y + x > 6 \end{cases}$
   a. (7, 1) b. (0, 0) c. (1, 4) d. (–1, –1)
4. Which numbered region in the graph represents the solution of the system below? 4. d
   $\begin{cases} y - x \le 4 \\ 2x + y \ge 1 \end{cases}$
   a. 1 b. 2
   c. 3 d. 4

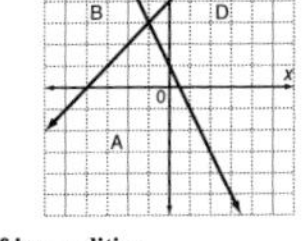

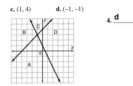

Graph each inequality or system of inequalities.

5. $12x - 8y \le 24$

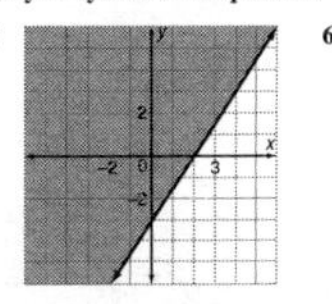

6. $\begin{cases} y + x \le 5 \\ 2x - 3y \ge 6 \end{cases}$

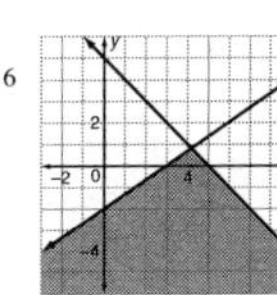

Questions 7 and 8 refer to the following situation.

An objective function is $P = 6x + 2y$. The feasible region has vertices at (10, 0), (10, 2), (8, 10), (0, 10). For which vertex is P

7. a maximum? 8. a minimum? 7. (8, 10) 8. (0, 10)

42 South-Western Algebra 1: AN INTEGRATED APPROACH

CHAPTER 8 TEST Form A, page 2 NAME ______

Questions 9-12 refer to the following situation.

CRAFTS Juan sells two sizes of dried wreaths. He makes a profit of \$14 for each large wreath and \$10 for each small wreath he sells. It takes him 3 hours to make each large one and 2 hours to make each small one. He has enough material for no more than 6 large wreaths or 9 small wreaths. He can work a maximum of only 24 hours. Let x represent the number of large wreaths and y the number of small ones.

9. What objective function could he write to express the maximum profit P? 9. $P = 14x + 10y$
10. Write inequalities for the constraints.
    $3x + 2y \le 24,\ x \le 6,\ y \le 9,\ x \ge 0,\ y \ge 0$
11. Graph the system.

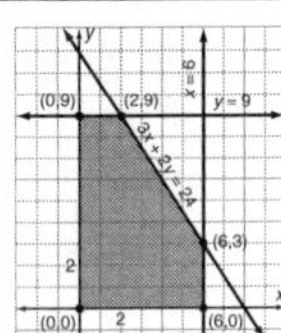

12. Use your graph to determine how many of each type he should make to have the maximum profit.
    2 large and 9 small give a maximum profit of \$118
13. A car dealer sells one make of car that comes in three body styles and 12 colors. If the dealer wanted to have one car of each type that a customer might want, how many cars would the dealer need to have on the lot? 13. 36
14. You dial a 3-digit number at random using any of the digits from 0 through 9. How many 3-digit numbers could you possibly dial? 14. 1000

For Question 15, use a separate sheet of paper if necessary.

15. WRITING MATHEMATICS Write a problem that could be solved by applying the fundamental counting principle.
    Answers will vary. Accept any problem that requires multiplication of m possible activities by n activities.

44 South-Western Algebra 1: AN INTEGRATED APPROACH

• • • CUMULATIVE REVIEW • • •

Graph each linear inequality. See Additional Answers; Lesson 8.1

1. $y \ge \frac{1}{2}x + 1$ **2.** $y < -2x + 3$

A bag contains 4 blue marbles, 3 red, 2 yellow, and 1 green marble. Use this bag of marbles for Questions 3–6. Lesson 8.6

3. Find $P(\text{yellow})$ as a fraction. $\frac{1}{5}$
4. Find $P(\text{red})$ as a decimal. 0.3
5. Find $P(\text{orange})$. 0
6. WRITING MATHEMATICS Maria picked a red marble out of a bag, put it back, and then picked a blue marble. After 20 picks, she had chosen a red marble 8 times. She concluded that $P(\text{red}) = 0.4$. Is she correct? Explain. See Additional Answers. Lessons 1.8 and 8.6
7. Four hamburgers and 3 orders of fries cost \$4.65. Five hamburgers and 2 orders of fries cost \$4.85. How much does one hamburger and one order of fries cost? \$1.30; Lesson 7.7
8. The money a shopkeeper takes in varies directly with the number of customers that enter the shop. After 8 customers, the shopkeeper had \$30. How many customers would he need in order to take in \$135? 36; Lesson 6.7

Use the line graph for Questions 9 and 10.

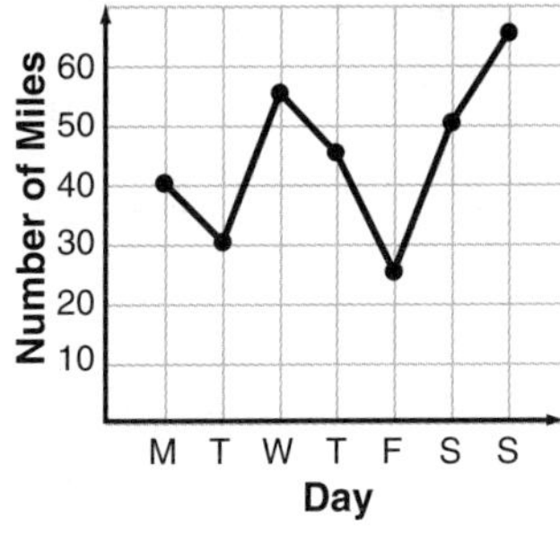

9. On which day did the riders ride 50 mi? Saturday; Lesson 1.4
10. To the nearest mile, find the mean number of miles covered each day. 44 mi; Lessons 1.4 and 1.7

Solve each system of inequalities by graphing.

11. $\begin{cases} y > \frac{2}{3}x - 2 \\ y < -x + 1 \end{cases}$ **12.** $\begin{cases} 3x - 2y \le 6 \\ x + y \ge 4 \end{cases}$

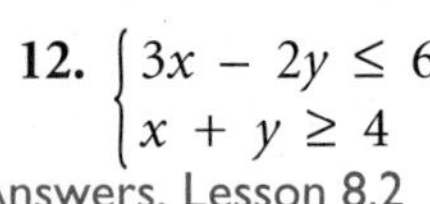

See Additional Answers. Lesson 8.2

13. TECHNOLOGY Explain the importance of knowing which half-plane should be shaded when solving a system of inequalities on a graphing utility. See Additional Answers. Lesson 8.3

Solve each equation.

14. $n + 18 = 15$ –3; Lesson 3.3
15. $\frac{h}{-12} = -6$ 72; Lesson 3.4
16. $4(2d + 5) = 12$ –1; Lesson 3.6
17. $\frac{1}{4}x + 3 = 16 - \frac{2}{5}x$ 20; Lesson 3.7
18. A company makes a profit of \$0.26 per unit sold. How many units does the company need to sell in order to earn a profit of at least \$2000.00? at least 7693 units; Lesson 5.3
19. WRITING MATHEMATICS Describe the difference in appearance of the graph of $x > 3$ and $x + y > y + 3$. See Additional Answers. Lessons 5.1 and 8.1
20. Use Cramer's Rule to find the solution for x in the following system of equations. 2; Lesson 7.6
    $$\begin{cases} 3x - 7y = 13 \\ 5x + 2y = 8 \end{cases}$$
21. STANDARDIZED TESTS The point at which the two lines $2x - 5y = 22$ and $15y = 6x - 22$ intersect is E; Lesson 7.5
    A. (11, 0)
    B. (6, –2)
    C. (16, 2)
    D. They are the same line.
    E. They do not intersect—they are parallel.

• • • STANDARDIZED TEST • • •

QUANTITATIVE COMPARISON In each question compare the quantity in Column 1 with the quantity in Column 2. Select the letter of the correct answer from these choices:

A. The quantity in Column 1 is greater.
B. The quantity in Column 2 is greater.
C. The two quantities are equal.
D. The relationship cannot be determined by the information given.

Notes: In some questions, information which refers to one or both columns is centered over both columns. A symbol used in both columns has the same meaning in each column. All variables represent real numbers. Most figures are not drawn to scale.

	Column 1		Column 2
1.	the slope of the line through points, (4, –2) and (–2, 4)	B; Lessons 6.2 and 6.5	the slope of a horizontal line
2.	the product of the coordinates of a point on the x-axis	C; Lesson 4.3	the product of the coordinates of a point on the y-axis

3. $\begin{cases} 3b - a = 5 \\ 4b + 2a = 0 \end{cases}$

	Column 1		Column 2
3.	$a + b$	A; Lesson 7.4	ab
4.	-3^2	B; Lesson 2.2	$(-3)^2$
5.	(rolling a 7) with two number cubes	A; Lesson 8.6	P(rolling a 10) with two number cubes

6.

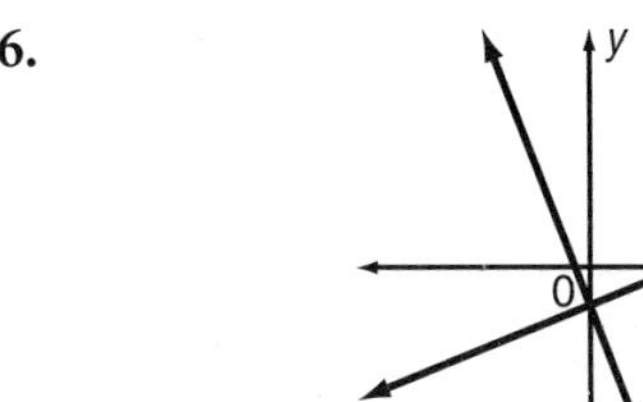

B; Lesson 6.2

Column 1	Column 2
the absolute value of the slope of line a	the absolute value of the slope of line b

	Column 1		Column 2
7.	x = amount of sales per week $\$1000 \le x \le \$2000$		
	weekly salary of \$150 plus 8% of sales	D; Lesson 4.4	weekly salary of \$100 plus 12% of sales
8.	the product of the the slopes of two diagonal parallel lines	A; Lesson 6.3	the product of the the slopes of two diagonal perpendicular lines
9.	$y = x - 3$		
	y	B; Lesson 4.3	x

10.

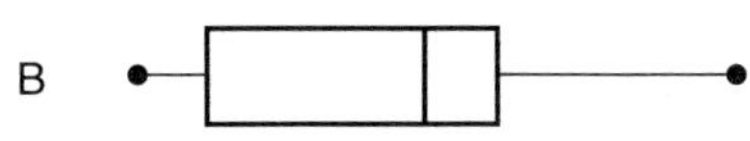

Column 1		Column 2
the median of boxplot A	B; Lesson 5.6	the median of boxplot B

	Column 1		Column 2
11.	$a < b$		
	$2a$	D; Lesson 5.1	b
12.	the weakest possible correlation of two variables	C; Lessons 6.6 and 8.6	the probability of an impossible event
13.	$\begin{vmatrix} 3 & n \\ -2 & m \end{vmatrix}$	D; Lesson 7.6	$\begin{vmatrix} -2 & m \\ 3 & n \end{vmatrix}$
14.	$f(x) = x^2 - 3$		
	the least value in the domain	B; Lessons 4.2 and 4.6	the least value in the range
15.	$(5 - 3)^2$	B; Lesson 2.8	$5^2 - 3^2$

Answers

1. A	**9.** A
2. B	**10.** A
3. C	**11.** D
4. E	**12.** C
5. B	**13.** 7
6. E	**14.** 240
7. C	**15.** 72
8. B	**16.** 4.4

CHAPTER 8 Standardized Test, page 2 NAME ____________

8. A shop sells T-shirts in 3 sizes, 5 colors, and 2 collar styles. If the shop has one of each kind of shirt in stock, how many different kinds of shirts are available?

A. 3 + 5 + 2 **B.** 3 • 5 • 2

12. a code number has 3 digits; each may be from 1 to 9

Column 1	Column 2
number of codes if the first digit must be 1, 2, or 3	the number of codes codes if the last digit must be 7, 8, or 9

NAME ____________ CLASS ________ DATE ________

CHAPTER 8 STANDARDIZED TEST

Standard Five-Choice For Questions 1–8, fill in the best choice on the answer grid provided.

1. Which is a solution of $y < 5x - 3$?

A. (1, –3) **B.** (–3, 1)
C. (0, –2) **D.** (0, –3)
E. (–3, 0)

2. Which of the following describes the graph?

A. $2x + 4y > -12$
B. $2x - 4y > -12$
C. $2x + 4y < -12$
D. $2x - 4y < -12$
E. none of these

3. Which is a solution of the system?

$\begin{cases} y - 4x < -2 \\ 3x + 2y \ge 6 \end{cases}$

A. (1, 0) **B.** (0, 5)
C. (3, 0) **D.** (0, –3)
E. (–3, 0)

4. Which system of inequalities is shown by the graph?

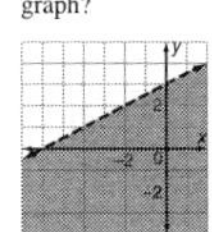

A. $\begin{cases} y + 2x < 4 \\ 2y > x - 2 \end{cases}$ **B.** $\begin{cases} y + 2x > 4 \\ 2y < x - 2 \end{cases}$

C. $\begin{cases} y + 2x \le 4 \\ 2y \ge x - 2 \end{cases}$ **D.** $\begin{cases} y + 2x \ge 4 \\ 2y < x - 2 \end{cases}$

E. none of these

5. The constraints for a feasible region are $y \le x + 4$, $x + y \le 6$, $x \ge 0$, and $y \ge 0$. Which graph shows the feasible region?

A. **B.** **C.** **D.**

E. none of these

6. An objective function is $P = 3x + 5y$. The feasible region has vertices at (0, 0), (12, 0), (5, 3), (6, 6), and (10, 4). Which vertex represents a maximum value?

A. (0, 0) **B.** (12, 0)
C. (5, 3) **D.** (6, 6)
E. (10, 4)

7. Sue works at a restaurant that pays \$4 an hour and at a store that pays \$5 an hour. She cannot work more than 20 hours a week. She must work at least 6 hours a week at the restaurant but no more than 8 hours at the store. What is the maximum amount she can earn in a week?

A. \$100 **B.** \$80 **C.** \$88
D. \$64 **E.** None of these

Chapter Opener

DATA ACTIVITY, PAGES 370–371

1. 30 people
2. $\frac{4}{25}$ or 0.16
3. Answers will vary. A person aged 25 to 34 with a household income of $35,000 to $49,000.
4. **ATM Use by Age Group**

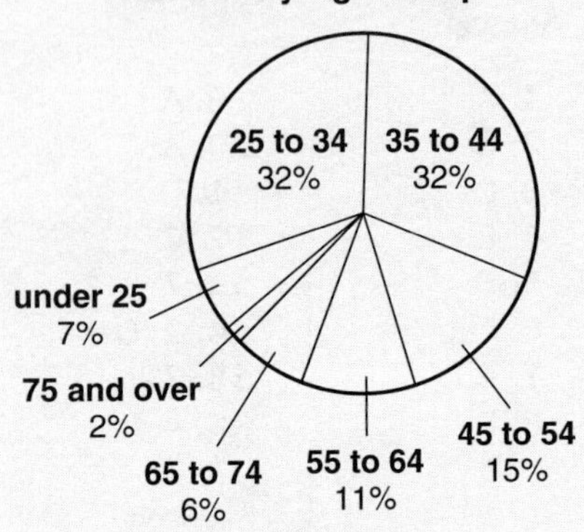

ATM Use by Income

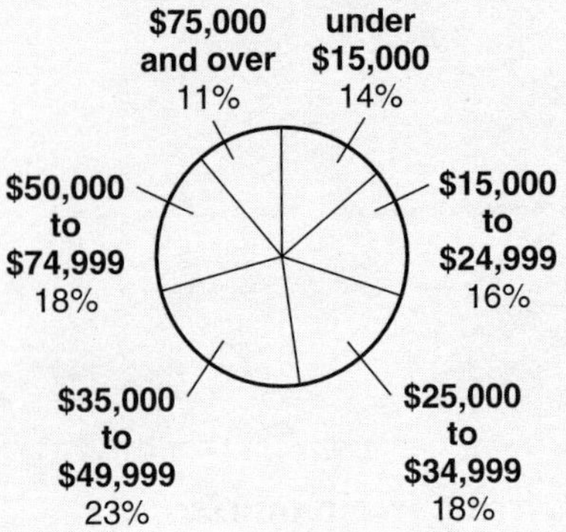

$75,000 and over 11%
under $15,000 14%
$50,000 to $74,999 18%
$15,000 to $24,999 16%
$35,000 to $49,999 23%
$25,000 to $34,999 18%

Lesson 8.1

EXPLORE, PAGE 373

2.

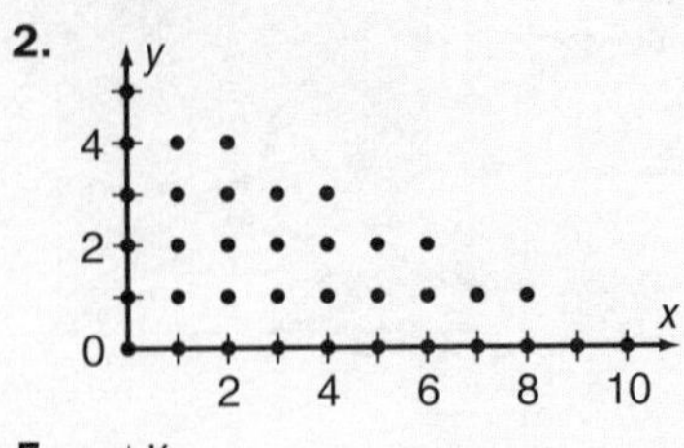

5.

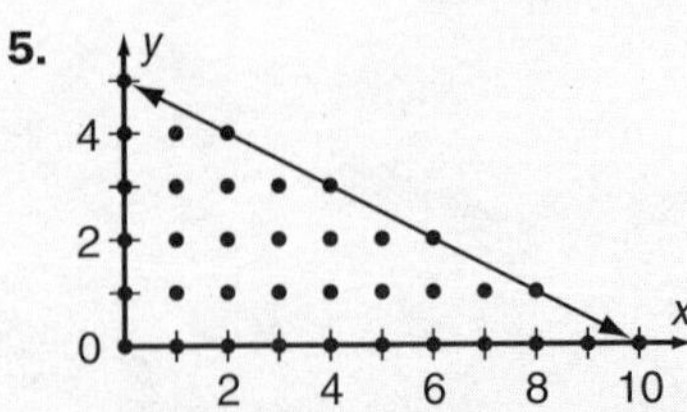

COMMUNICATING ABOUT ALGEBRA, PAGE 374

evaluating the expressions is easy because x and y terms become equal to zero when (0, 0) is substituted; when the boundary line passes through the origin

TRY THESE, PAGE 376

4.

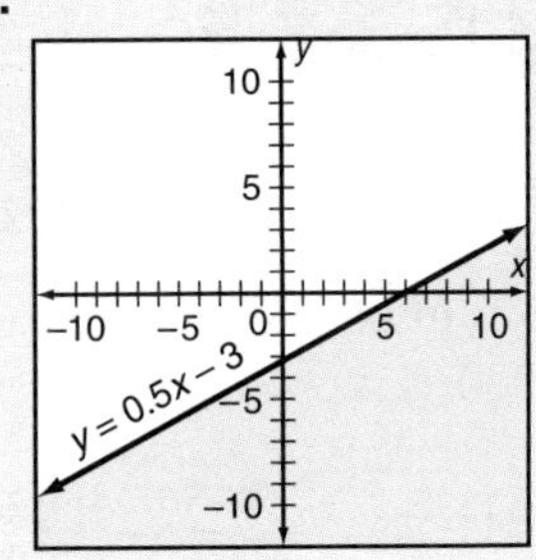

5.

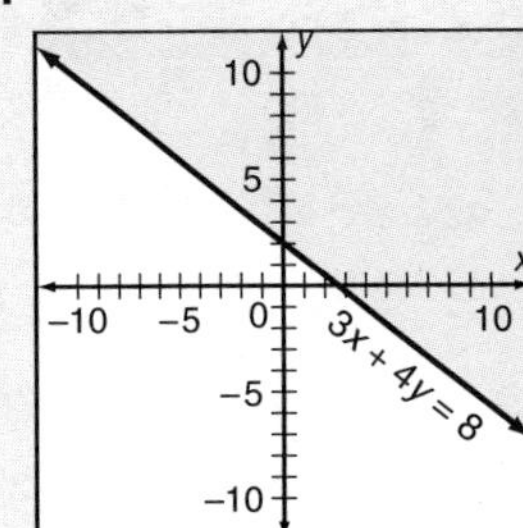

6. a. $x + y \leq 40$

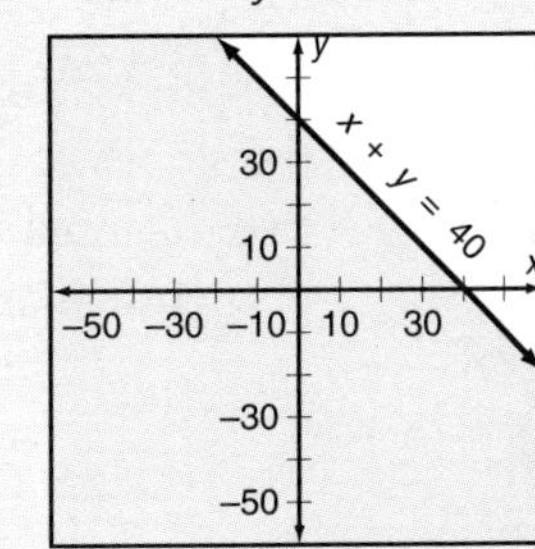

b. possible combinations: 20 members and 20 nonmembers; 10 members and 15 nonmembers; 15 members and 10 nonmembers

PRACTICE, PAGES 376–377

5.

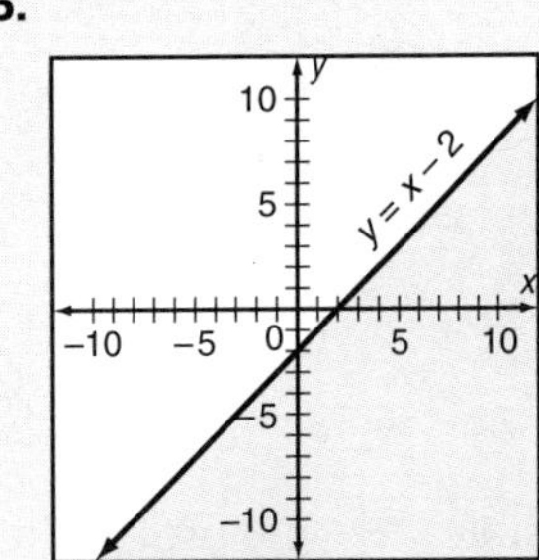

6.

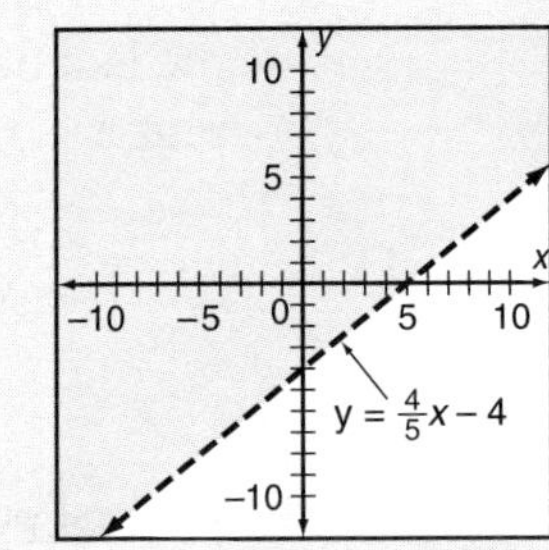

7.

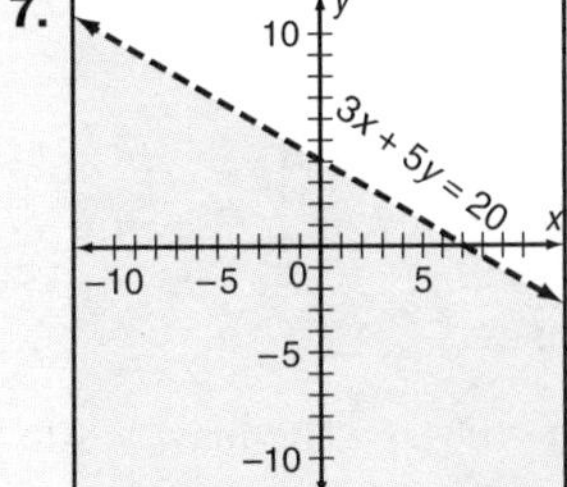

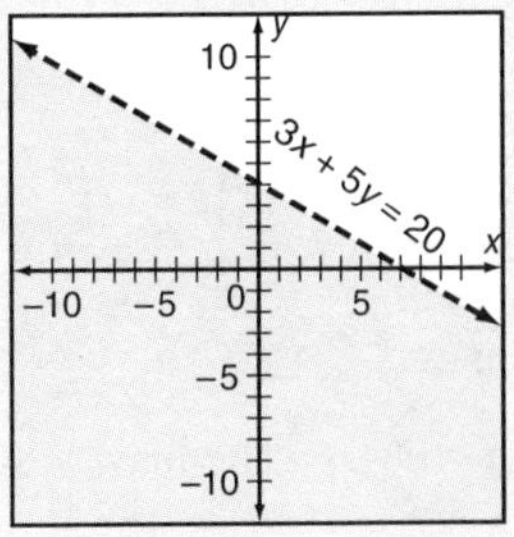

8.

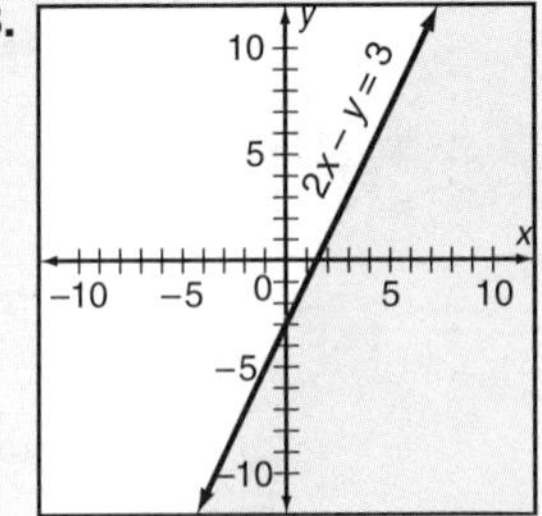

9.

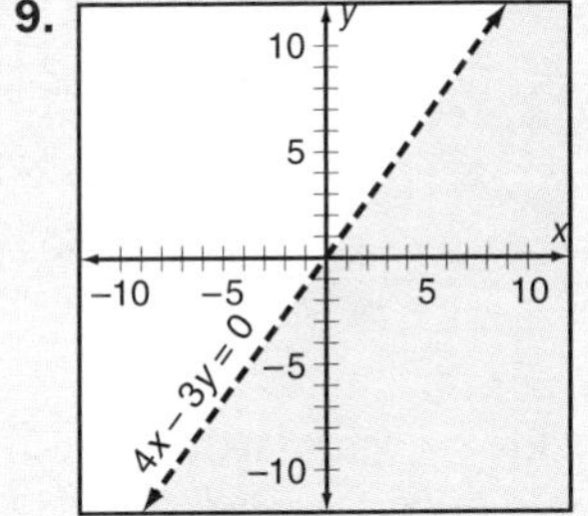

10.

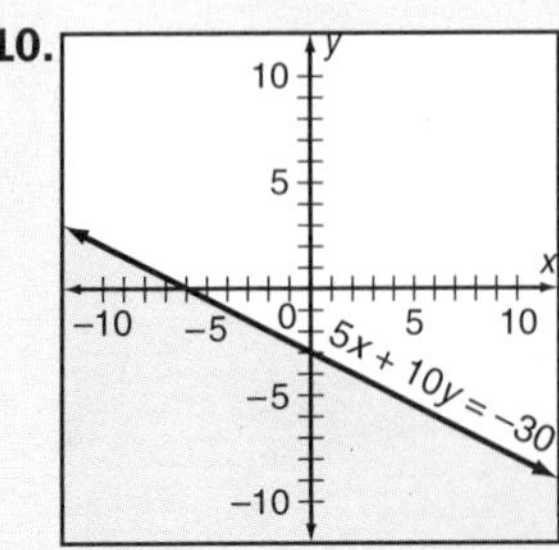

15. Possible answer: Same—you must determine whether a line or point is included in the graph and which half-plane or part of the number line contains the solution set; different—a linear inequality in two variables is graphed on a coordinate plane and the solutions are ordered pairs of real numbers; an inequality in one variable is graphed on a number line and the solutions are real numbers.

16. a. $3x + 7y > 20$

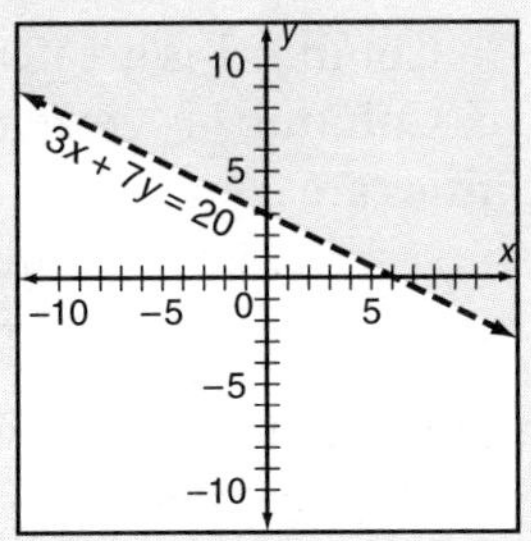

EXTEND, PAGES 377–378

21. Possible answer: Write both inequalities in the slope-intercept form to see if the coefficients, constants, and inequality symbols all match each other.

22. a. $30x + 15y \leq 420$, $0.5x + 0.25y \leq 7$, or $2x + y \leq 28$

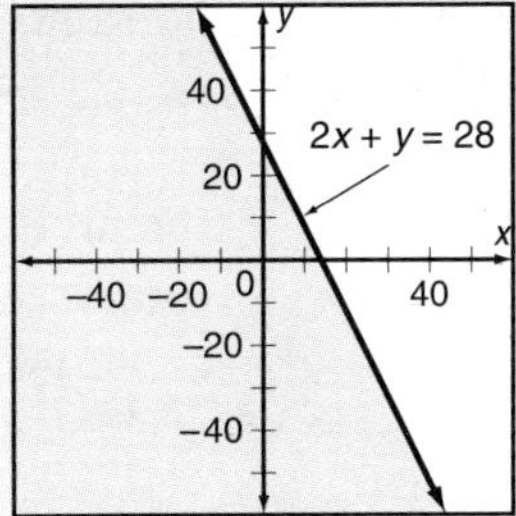

b. possible combinations: 4 new and 19 returning patients; 14 new and 0 returning patients; 5 new and 10 returning patients

23. a. $20x + 5y \geq 1000$

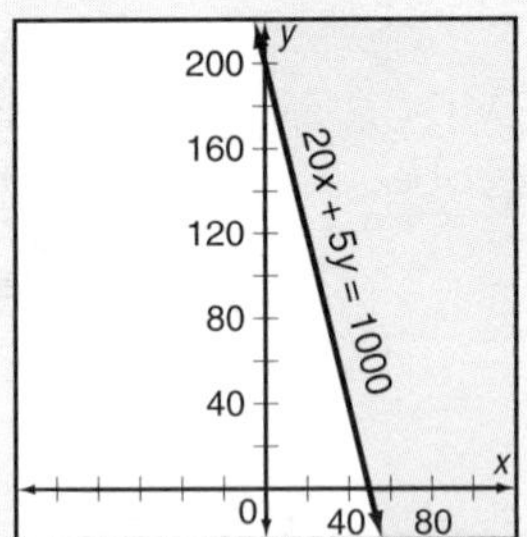

b. possible combinations: 50 regular and 0 sale pairs; 145 regular and 120 sale pairs; 8 regular and 168 sale pairs

THINK CRITICALLY, PAGE 378

30. The number line is the x-axis of the coordinate plane, and the graph on the number line is the shaded part of the graph on the coordinate plane.

31. Possible problem: Ted and his friends bought hamburgers for \$2 each and beverages for \$0.50 each. They spent less than \$10. What possible combinations of hamburgers and beverages could they have bought? Possible combinations: 2 hamburgers and 5 beverages; 1 hamburger and 10 beverages; 3 hamburgers and 6 beverages.

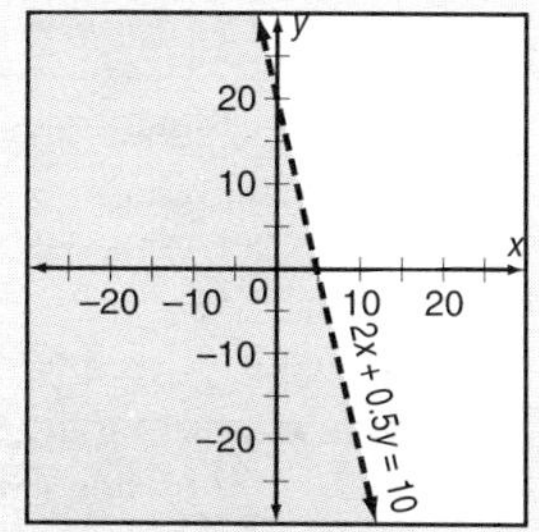

MIXED REVIEW, PAGE 378

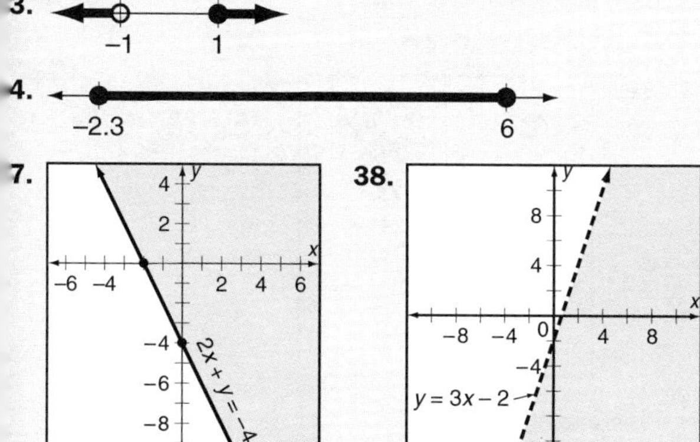

Lesson 8.2

EXPLORE/WORKING TOGETHER, PAGE 379

3. Only ordered pairs consisting of two whole numbers, at least one of which is not zero, should remain.

TRY THESE, PAGE 381

1.

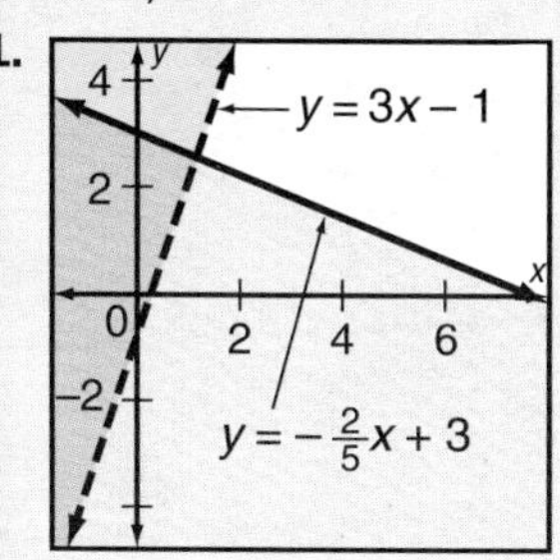

2.

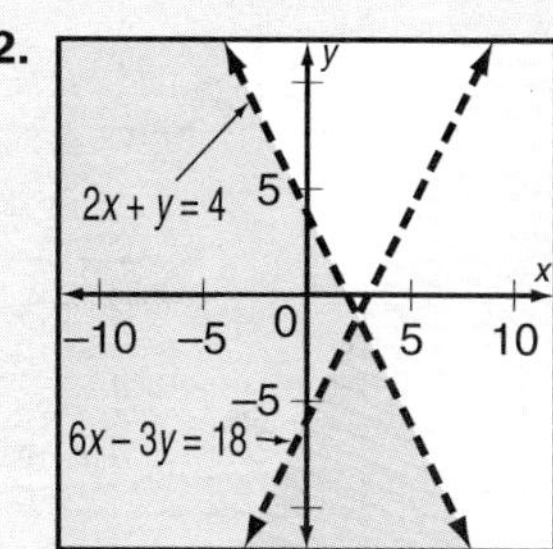

3.

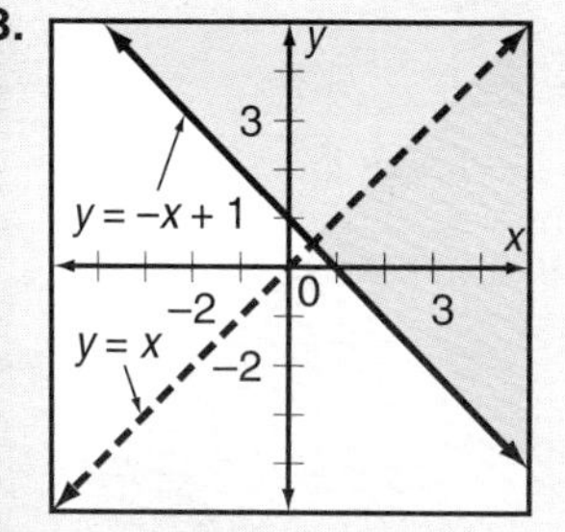

4.

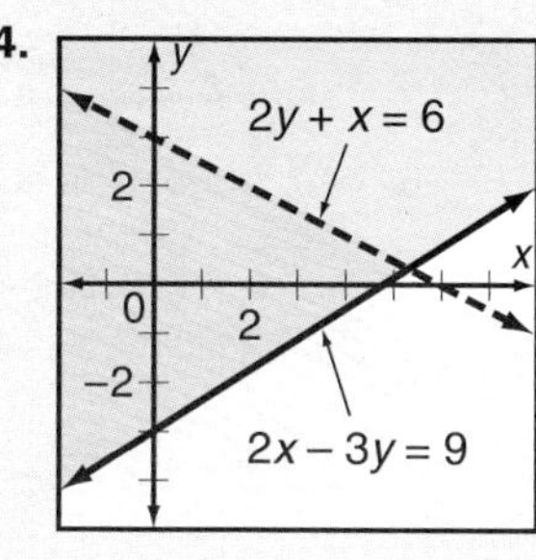

5.

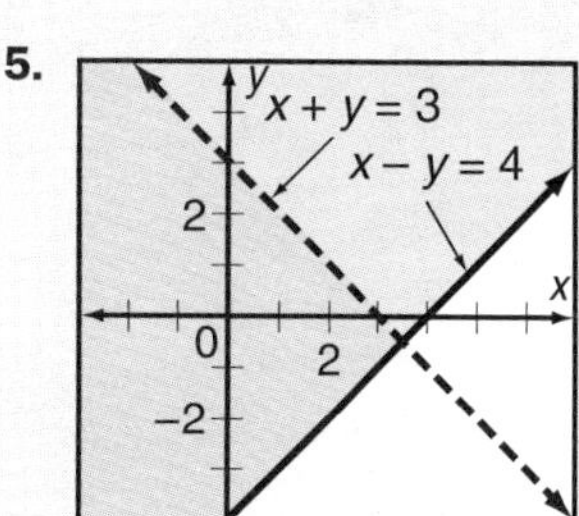

6.

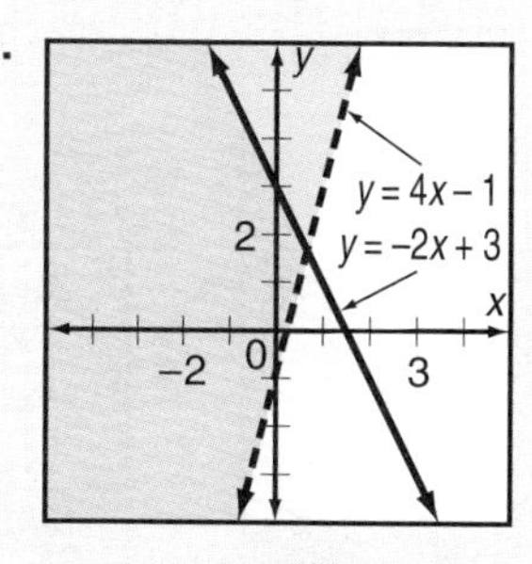

7.

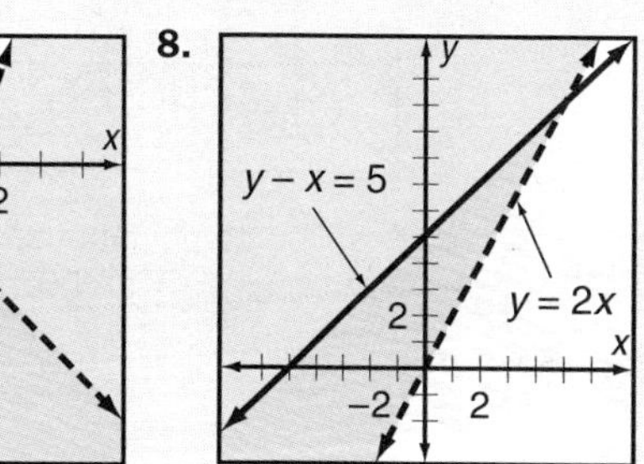

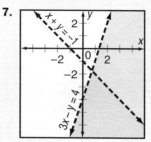

8.

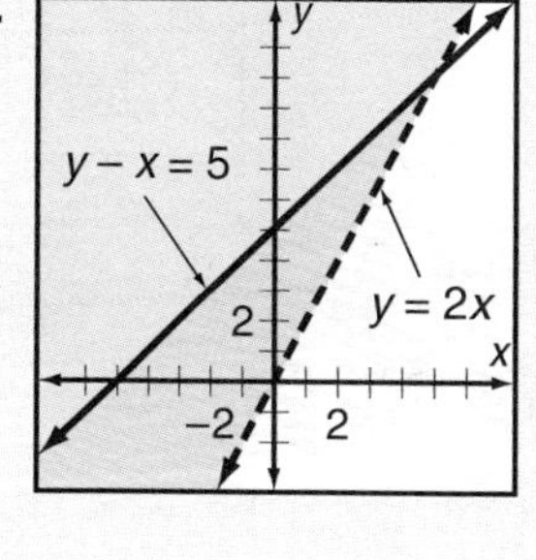

9.

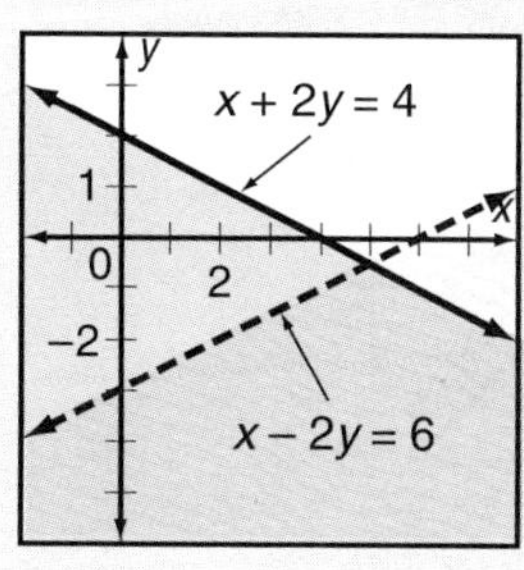

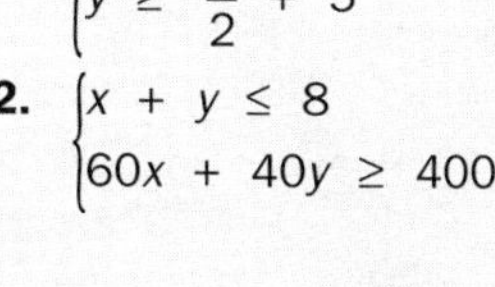

10. $\begin{cases} y > -x - 2 \\ y \geq \dfrac{x}{2} + 5 \end{cases}$

12. $\begin{cases} x + y \leq 8 \\ 60x + 40y \geq 400 \end{cases}$

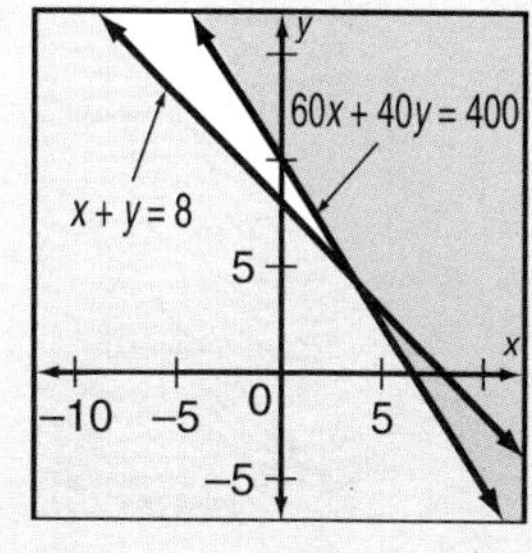

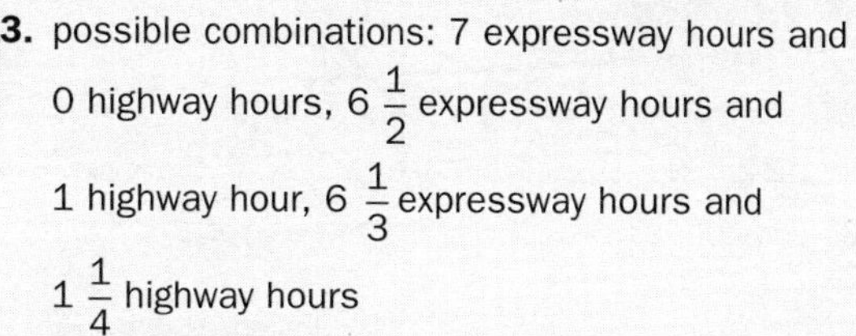

13. possible combinations: 7 expressway hours and 0 highway hours, $6\frac{1}{2}$ expressway hours and 1 highway hour, $6\frac{1}{3}$ expressway hours and $1\frac{1}{4}$ highway hours

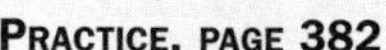

PRACTICE, PAGE 382

5.

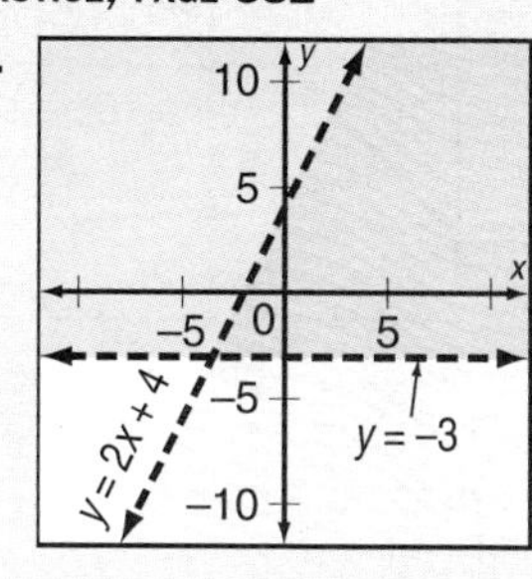

6.

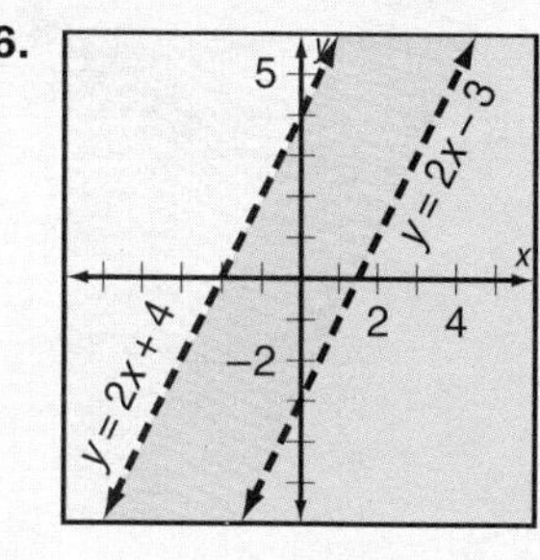

7.

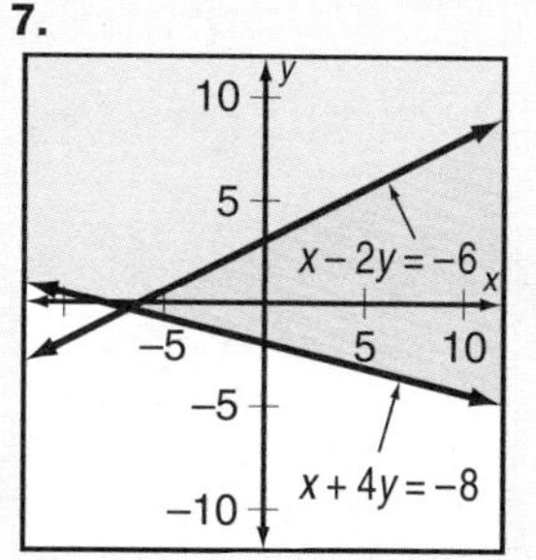

8.

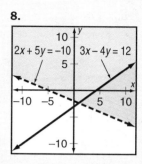

$2x + 5y = -10$
$3x - 4y = 12$

9.

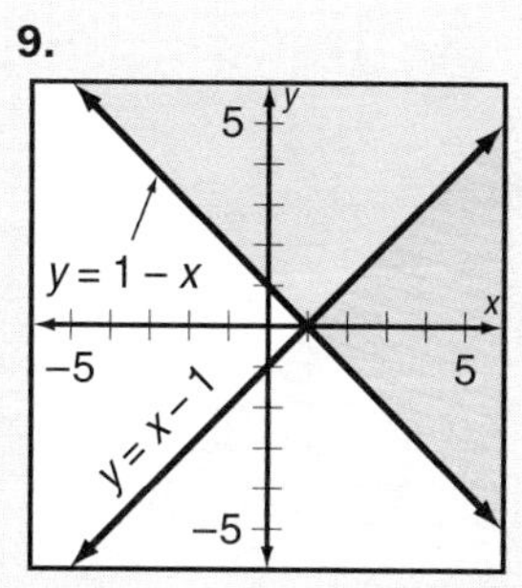

10.

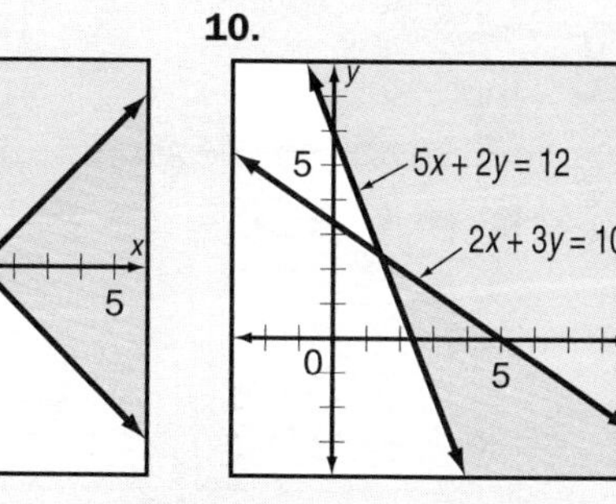

11.

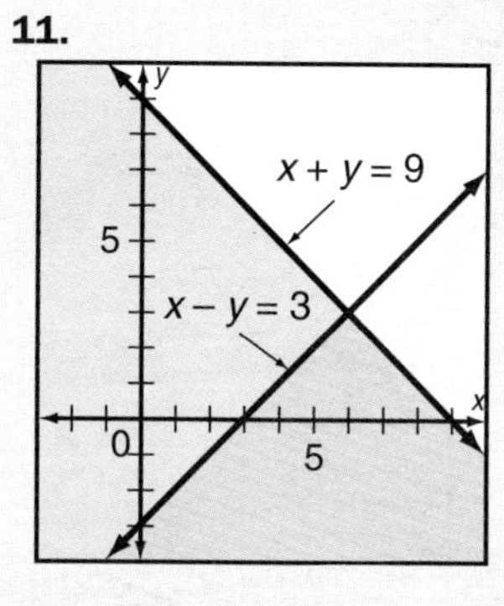

12.

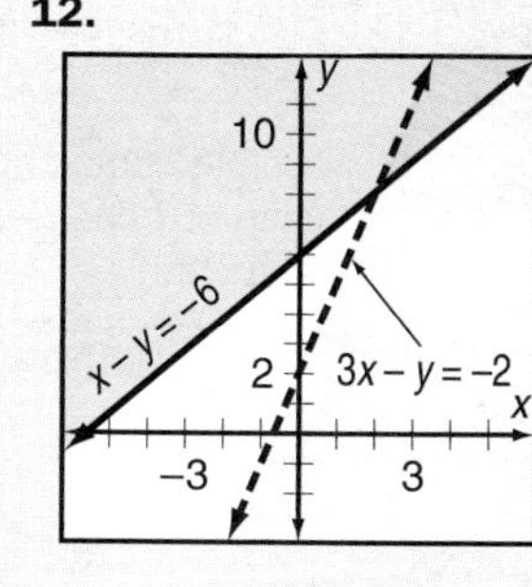

13.

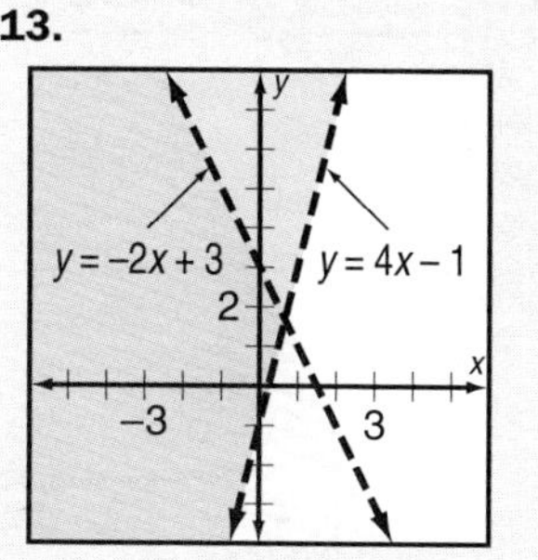

14.

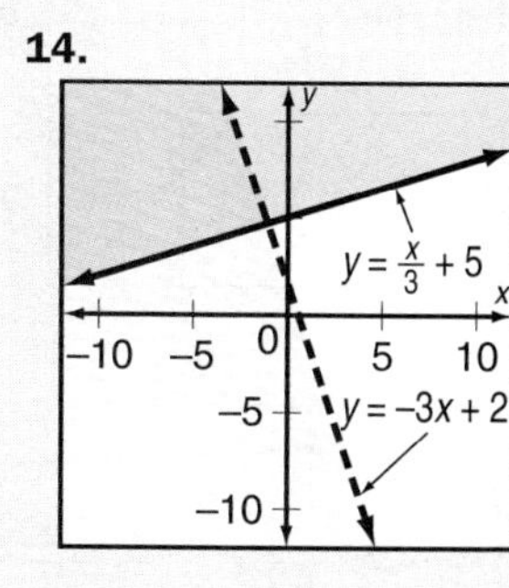

15.

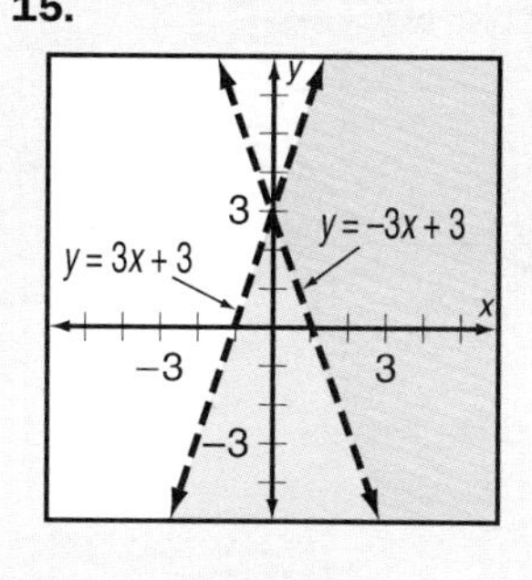

16.

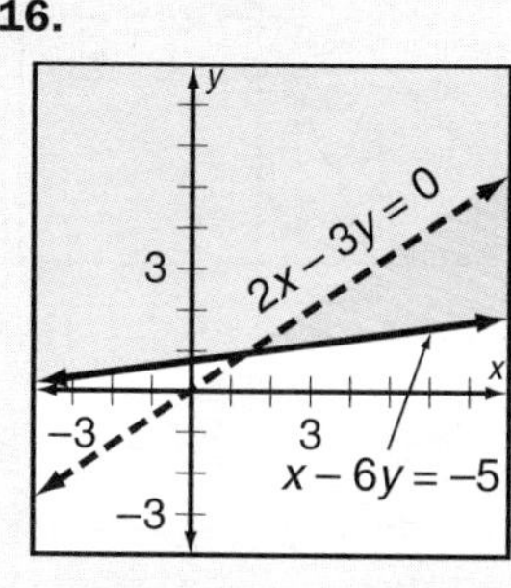

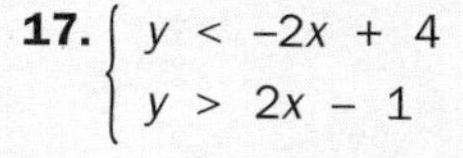

17. $\begin{cases} y < -2x + 4 \\ y > 2x - 1 \end{cases}$

18. $\begin{cases} x \geq -4 \\ y > -3 \end{cases}$

19. $\begin{cases} y \geq x + 2 \\ y \leq \frac{3}{5}x + 3 \end{cases}$

20. Possible answer should include identifying the y-intercept, determining the slope, determining whether shading is above or below each line to indicate > or <, and determining whether each line is dotted or solid to indicate whether or not "or equal to" applies.

21. a. $\begin{cases} \frac{3}{4}x + y \leq 50 \\ 50x + 80y > 3000 \end{cases}$

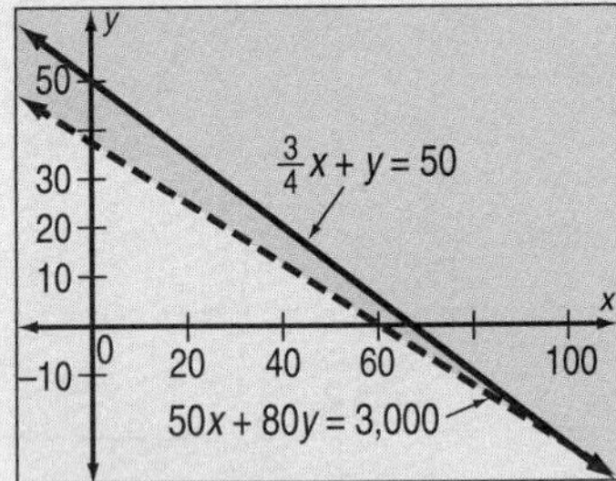

b. possible combinations: 0 chairs and 50 tables, 10 chairs and 35 tables, 50 chairs and 10 tables

EXTEND, PAGES 383–384

30.

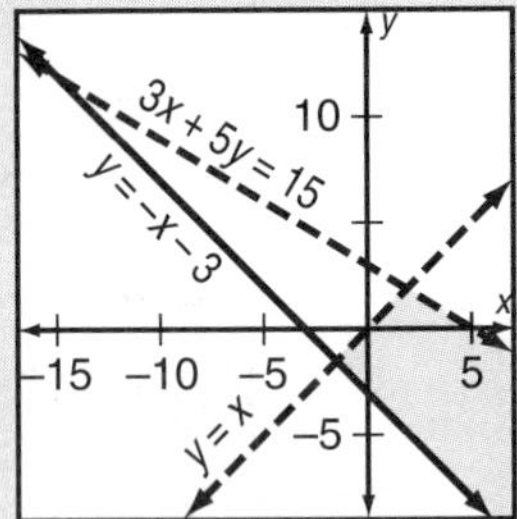

31.

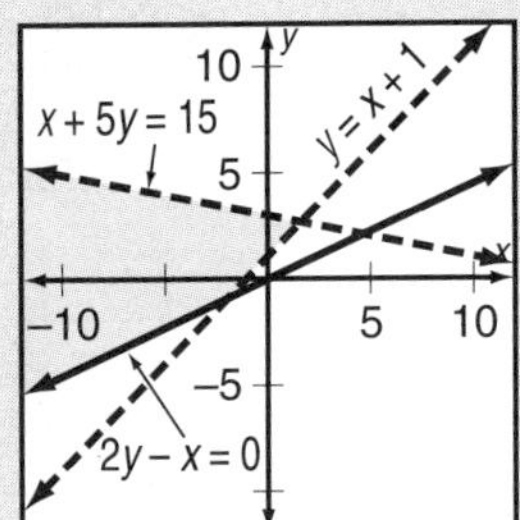

32.

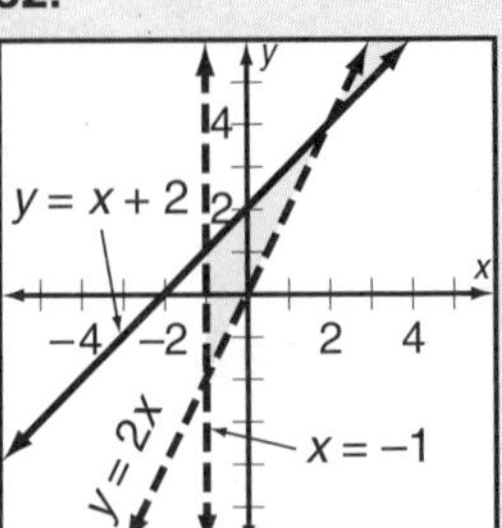

33.

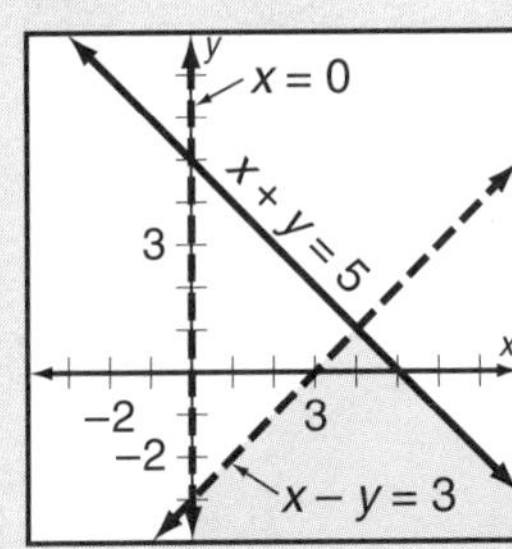

34. a. $\begin{cases} \frac{(x + y)}{2} < 60 \\ x > 40 \\ x > y \end{cases}$

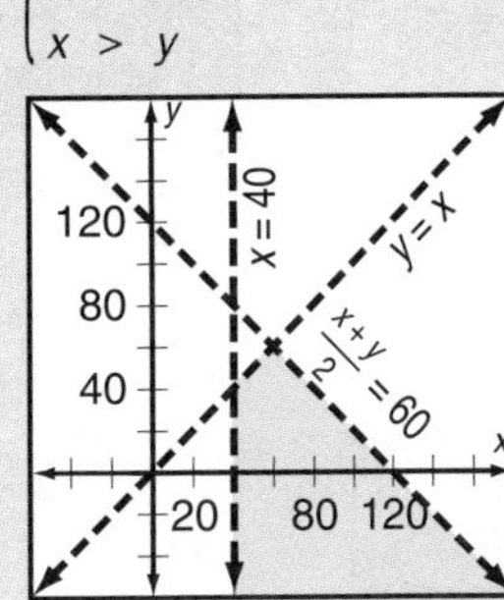

b. Possible combinations: 50°F and 60°F, 45°F and 55°F, 55°F and 62°F

35. a. $\begin{cases} x + y \leq 10{,}000 \\ 0.08x + 0.05y \geq 500 \\ x > y \end{cases}$

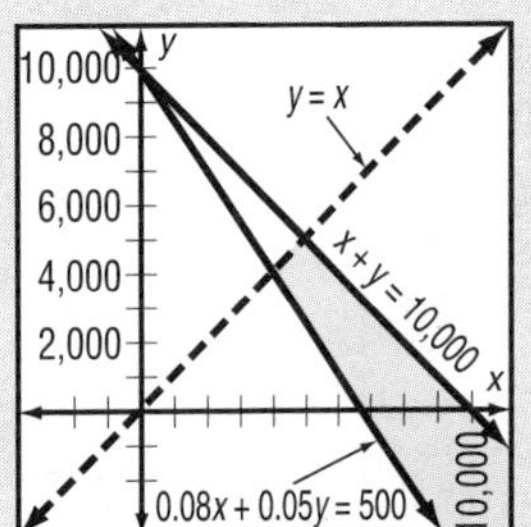

b. possible combinations:
$5000 in mutual funds and $4000 in CDs,
$6000 in mutual funds and $3000 in CDs,
$9000 in mutual funds and $1000 in CDs

36. Possible answer:
$\begin{cases} y \leq x + 4 \\ y \geq x - 6 \end{cases}$

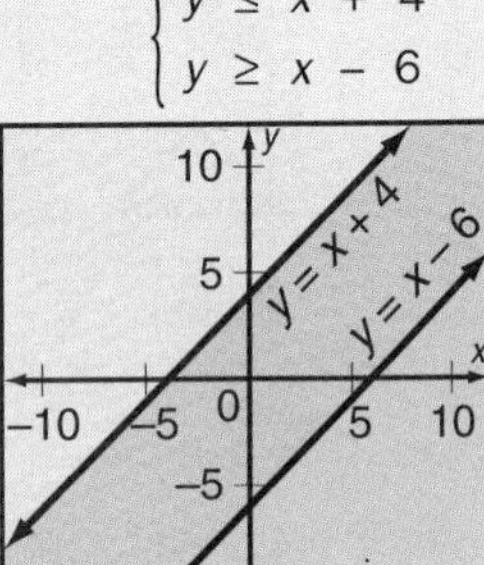

37. Possible answer:
$\begin{cases} y \geq x + 4 \\ y \leq x - 6 \end{cases}$

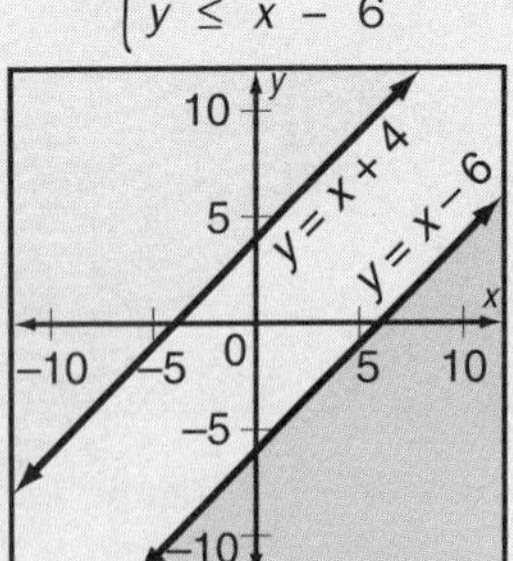

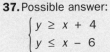

38. Possible answer:
$\begin{cases} y \geq x + 4 \\ y \leq x + 4 \end{cases}$

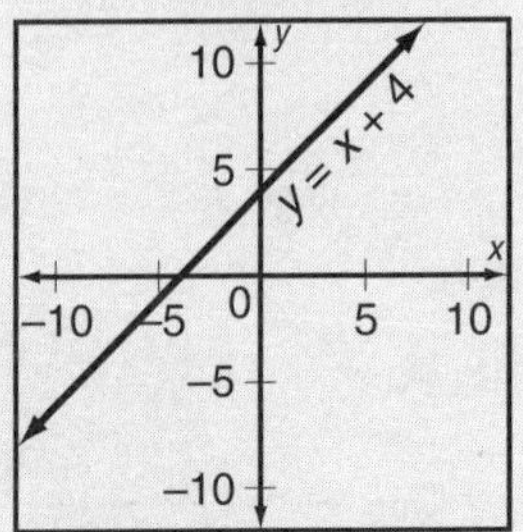

39. Not possible; because coordinate plane extends to infinity in all directions, it is impossible to write equations for boundary lines of a region that includes the entire plane.

ALGEBRAWORKS, PAGE 385

3. Answers will vary. Possible ad: Do you watch more than two new release videos a month? If so, this club's for you!

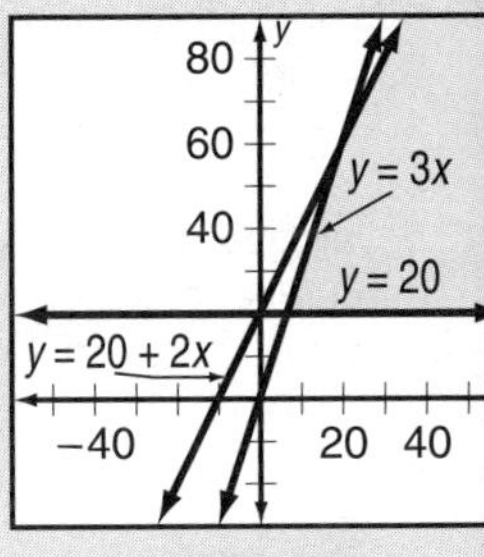

4. If the customer were to rent new releases only, the club would be the better plan. If the customer expected to rent both new and older releases, the set rate plan would probably be better.

5. Answers will vary. Possible answer: Yes; most people rent more than two videos per month, and they usually rent new releases, so the club plan would appeal to new customers.

Lesson 8.3

THINK BACK, PAGE 386

1.

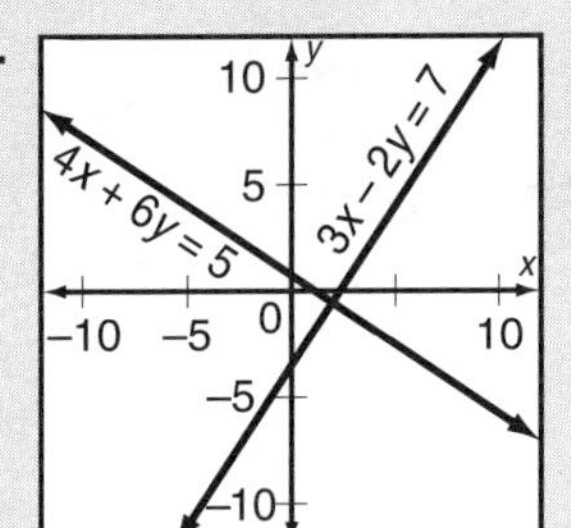

EXPLORE, PAGE 386

3. a.

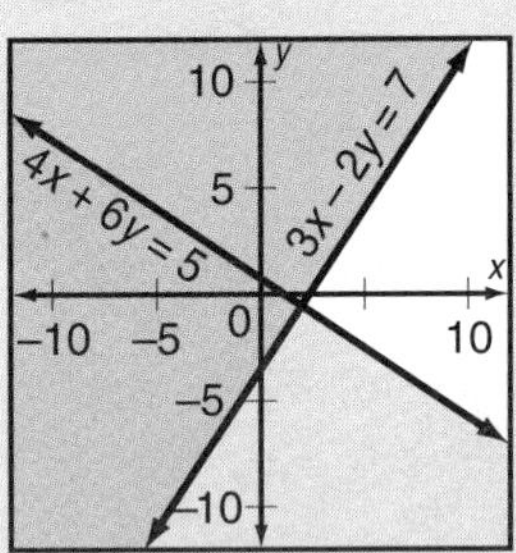

b.

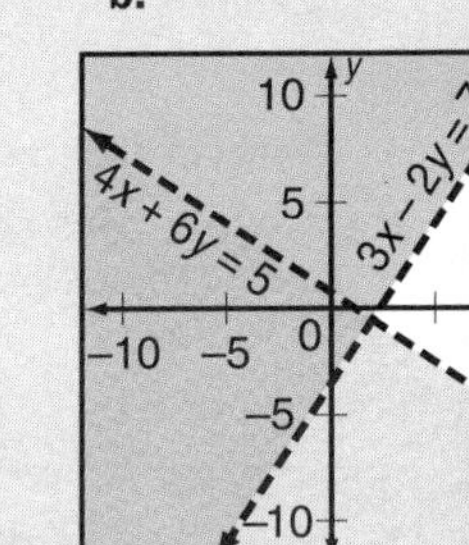

c.

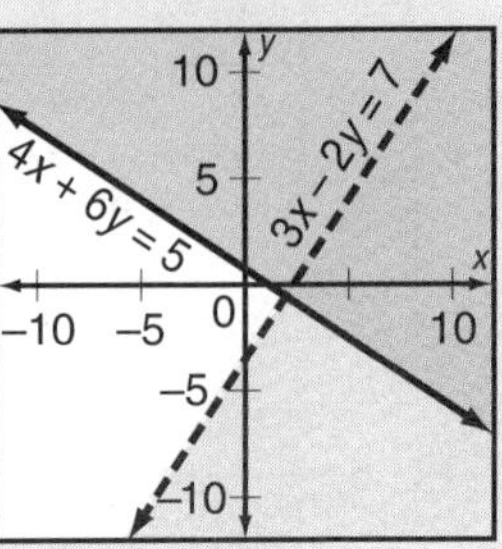

5. Yes; the double-shaded areas indicating the intersection of half-planes and any parts of the boundary lines that fall within the double-shaded areas.

6. a.

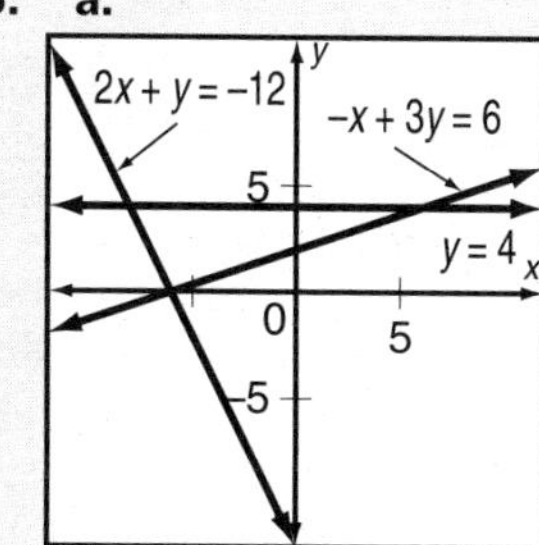

b.

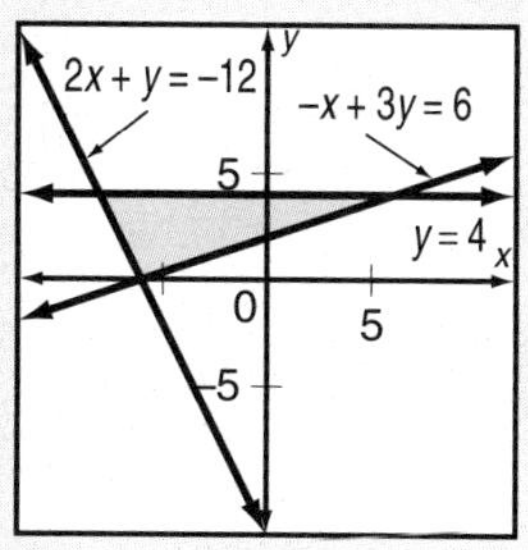

8. No; any solution would be represented by a point at which all three lines intersect, but there is no such point in the graph of this system. Each intersection point is a solution to a different pairing of the three equations.

Making Conections, page 387

11. Graphs of corresponding systems consist of the same lines and points of intersection; graphs of systems of inequalities also consist of half-planes and intersections of half-planes. Boundary lines of systems of inequalities may be dashed; lines representing equations are never dashed.

12. Both types of representations are intersections; solutions of systems of equations are represented by the intersection of lines, and solutions of systems of inequalities are represented by the intersection of half-planes and, in some cases, boundary lines.

13. Provided that no equations or inequalities in the system are equivalent, both types of systems could have zero or one solution. Systems of inequalities could have an infinite number of solutions.

Summarize, page 387

15. No; the intersection point of the graph of the system of equations is the intersection point of the boundary lines for the systems of inequalities. However, none of the points along the boundary line of $y < -\frac{1}{2}x$ are solutions of that inequality.

19. Answers will vary. Possible answer:

$$\begin{cases} y \geq 2 \\ y \leq x \\ x \leq 7 \end{cases}$$

area = 12.5 square units

Lesson 8.4

Explore/Working Together, page 388

1.

3. near the boundary line for $x + y < 5$; near the intersection of the boundary lines for $4x - 2y > -10$ and $2x - 4y < 16$

4. (0,5), (6,–1), (–6,–7); Earlier sums may have been very close to vertex sums. No earlier sum was greater than the greatest vertex sum or less than the least vertex sum.

5. greatest sum is close to 6; least sum is close to –20; the sums of the coordinates of the vertices are 6, 2, and –20

Try These, pages 390–391

3. minimum 0 at (0, 0); maximum 21 at (0, 7)
4. minimum 19 at (2, 3); maximum 36 at (3, 6)
5. minimum 2 at (0, 1); maximum 38 at (9, 1)
6. minimum 60 at (10, 10); maximum 160 at (30, 10)
7. minimum 0 at (0, 0); maximum 15 at (4, 3) and (5, 0)
10. Possible answer: The values represented by x and y are usually positive. For example, a negative number of hot dogs does not make sense.

Practice, pages 391–392

4. minimum –4 at (0, –1); maximum 11 at (3, 2)
5. minimum –15 at (0, 5); maximum 3 at (3, 1)
6. minimum –3 at (3, 0); maximum 14 at (4, 3)
7. minimum –15 at (–3, 3); maximum 0 at (0, 0) and (–2, –3)
8. minimum 10 at (0, 2); maximum 30 at (0, 6)

Extend, page 392

17.

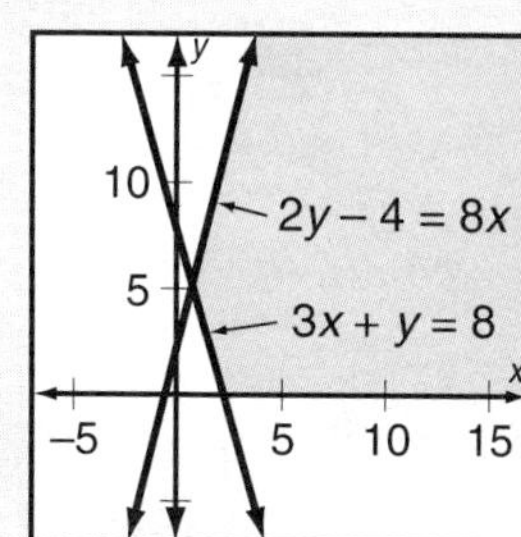

18.

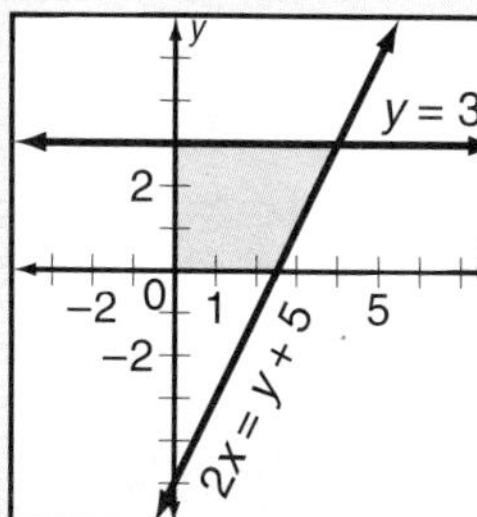

19.

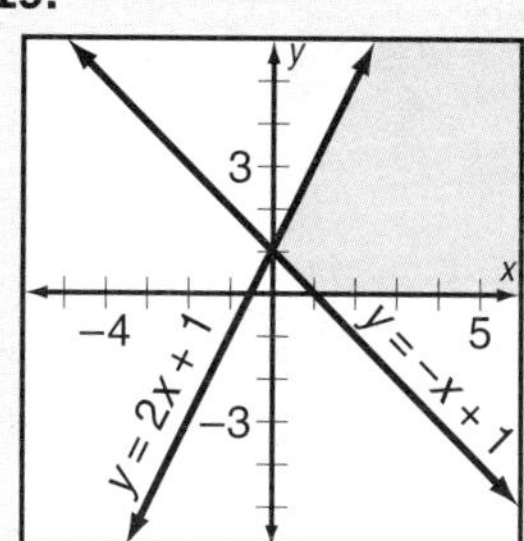

20., 21.

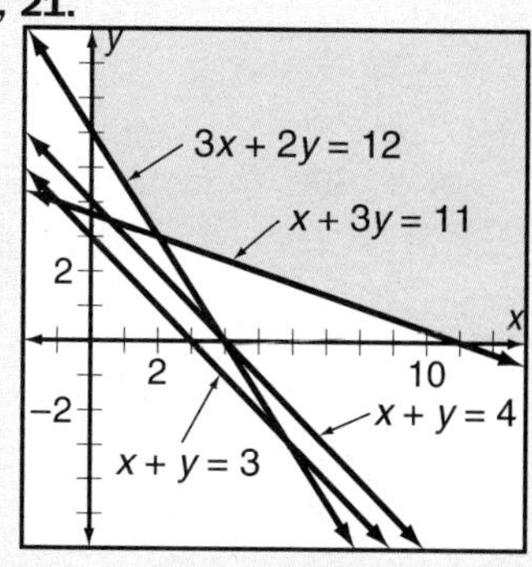

Think Critically, page 393

22. $0.50x + 1.25y \leq 10$
$x \geq 5$
$y \geq 2$

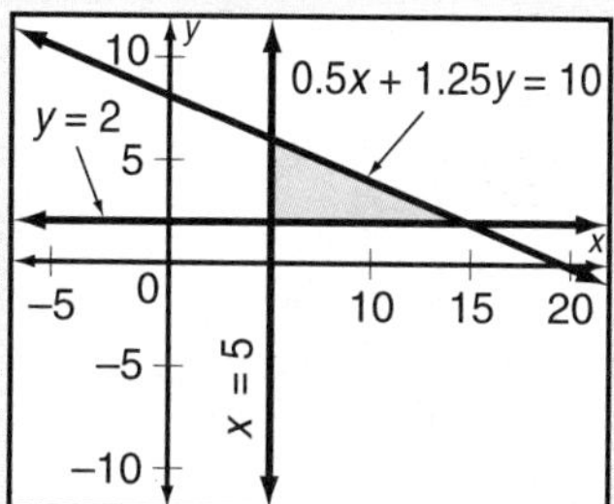

Project Connection, page 393

2. Answers will vary. Advantages include convenience, time savings, no transportation costs. Disadvantages include ending up with items you don't want if you forget to notify the seller.

Lesson 8.5

Apply the Strategy, page 396

14. The minimum cost, \$135, will produce a profit of \$75. To earn the maximum profit, \$125, the club must purchase \$225 worth of shirts.

15. a. Let x represent number of cross-country skis. Let y represent number of slalom skis.
$6x + 4y \leq 96$
$x + y \leq 20$
$x \geq 0$
$y \geq 0$

b. (0, 0), (0, 20), (16, 0), (8, 12)

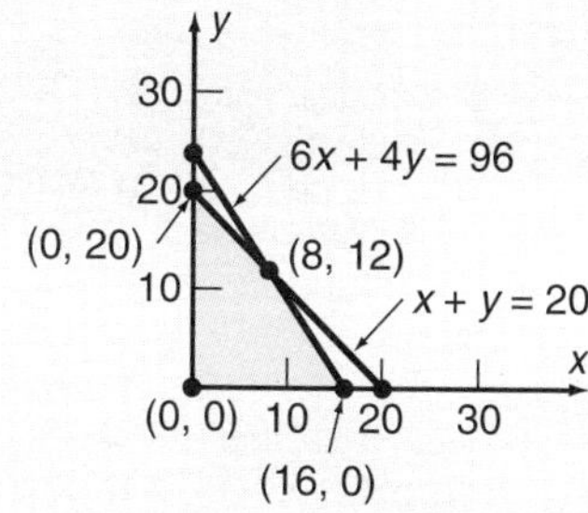

c. $P = 45x + 30y$

Vertex	$P = 45x + 30y$	Profit, P
(0, 0)	45(0) + 30(0)	\$0
(0, 20)	45(0) + 30(20)	\$600
(16, 0)	45(16) + 30(0)	\$720
(8, 12)	45(8) + 30(12)	\$720

d. 16 pairs of cross-country skis and 0 pairs of slalom skis or 8 pairs of cross-country skis and 12 pairs of slalom skis; \$720

16. a. Let x represent number of buses. Let y represent number of vans.

$60x + 10y \geq 300$

$4x + 2y \leq 36$

$x \geq 0$

$y \geq 0$

b. (5, 0), (9, 0), (3, 12)

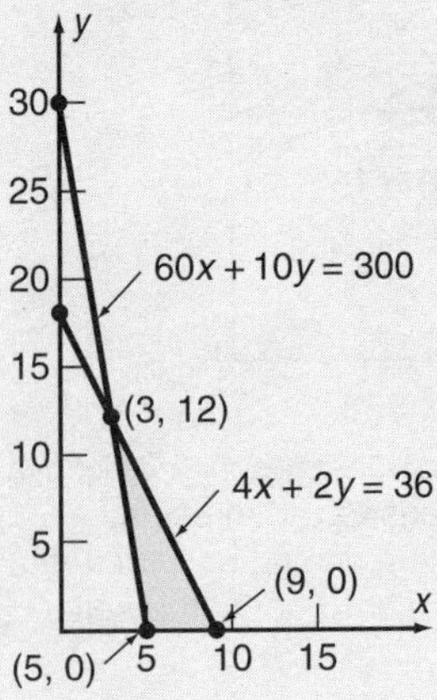

c. $C = 1000x + 100y$

Vertex	$C = 1000x + 100y$	Cost, C
(5, 0)	1000(5) + 100(0)	\$5000
(9, 0)	1000(9) + 100(0)	\$9000
(3, 12)	1000(3) + 100(12)	\$4200

d. 3 buses and 12 vans; \$4200

17. 75 bicycles and 35 rowers; $P = 50(75) + 75(35) = \$6375$

18. Answers will vary. Students should realize that, in general, for a business to produce two products or offer two services, higher production costs for one of the products or services must be offset by higher profits from that product or service.

Review Problem Solving Strategies, page 397

A Strange and Moving Story

students may draw diagrams or make a physical model with paper slips; shortest solution: Lane to 102, Kim to 103, Raintree to 106, Lane to 105, Gonzalez to 102, Ziff to 101, Lane to 104, Raintree to 105, Kim to 106, Gonzalez to 103, Raintree to 102, Lane to 105, Ziff to 104, Raintree to 101, Gonzalez to 102, Kim to 103, Lane to 106 (17 moves)

Yip, Woof, Grr!

a. 3; possible answer: let l represent large dogs, m represent medium dogs, and s represent small dogs

b. There are three facts that relate the quantities; this is enough to solve because three equations in three unknowns can be written.

c. 5 large, 25 medium, 70 small;

$s + m + l = 100,\ 3l + 2m + \frac{1}{2}s = 100,$

$m = 5l$

d. Answers will vary; guess-and-check could be used, but many students may feel that writing equations is more efficient.

A Burning Question

a. $\frac{tx}{4}$; $x - \frac{tx}{4}$

b. $\frac{tx}{5}$; $x - \frac{tx}{5}$

c. four times the length of candle A;

$x - \frac{tx}{5} = 4\left(x - \frac{tx}{4}\right)$

d. $3\frac{3}{4}$ h; candle A was $\frac{1}{16}$ its original length, candle B was $\frac{1}{4}$ its original length.

Lesson 8.6

Explore, page 398

2. possible answers: what the probability is of rolling a particular number on the die and on the spinner; what the probability is of the number rolled on the die being greater than the number spun on the spinner

Try These, page 401

2. 26: head and any of 13 hearts; head and any of 13 diamonds

(H, ♥A) (H, ♥2) (H, ♥3) (H, ♥4) (H, ♥5) (H, ♥6) (H, ♥7) (H, ♥8) (H, ♥9) (H, ♥10) (H, ♥J) (H, ♥Q) (H, ♥K) (H, ♦A) (H, ♦2) (H, ♦3) (H, ♦4) (H, ♦5) (H, ♦6) (H, ♦7) (H, ♦8) (H, ♦9) (H, ♦10) (H, ♦J) (H, ♦Q) (H, ♦K)

Extend, page 402

12. The game is fair; each player has a probability of $\frac{18}{36}$ of winning each round.

13. The game is unfair; $P(A\ wins) = \frac{27}{36}$, or $\frac{3}{4}$, or $\frac{1}{2}$; $P(B\ wins) = \frac{9}{36}$, or $\frac{1}{4}$, of the time

14. The game is fair; $P(Player\ A\ wins) = \frac{2}{8}$, or $\frac{1}{4}$; $P(Player\ B\ wins) = \frac{6}{8}$, or $\frac{3}{4}$; since $P(B)$ is 3 times as great as $P(A)$, A should get 3 times as many points to make the game fair.

Think Critically, page 402

19. Exercises 16–18 include the sample space of all possible outcomes for a family with four children. The sum of all possible outcomes in a probability experiment is exactly 1.

Algebra Works, page 403

4. Answers will vary but should reflect proportions o styles, sizes, and colors similar to those in the sales report. Yellow, pink, and purple were not included in the sales report, possibly because these colors were not in inventory or because no sold. Possible recommendations for these colors may be cautious or may take into consideration t popularity of purple.

Chapter Review, pages 404–405

8.

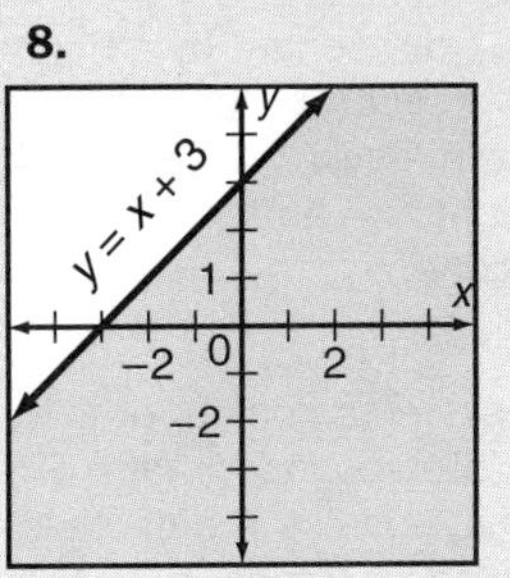

9.

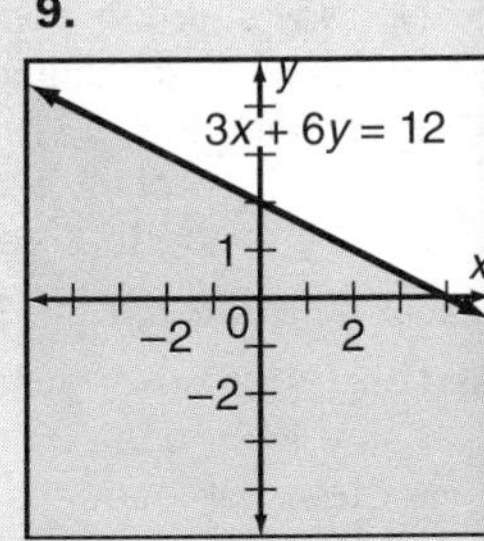

10.

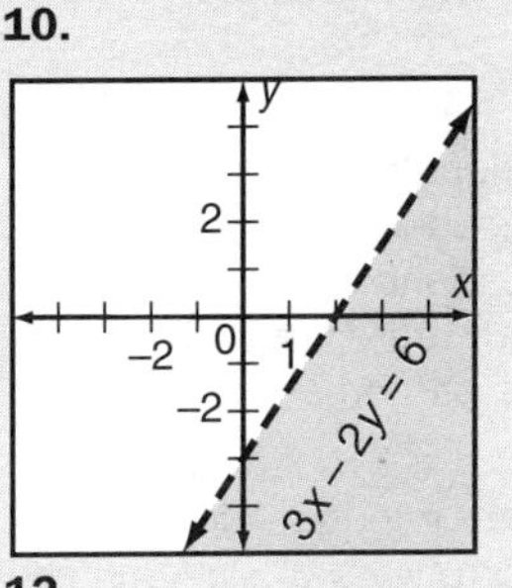

11.

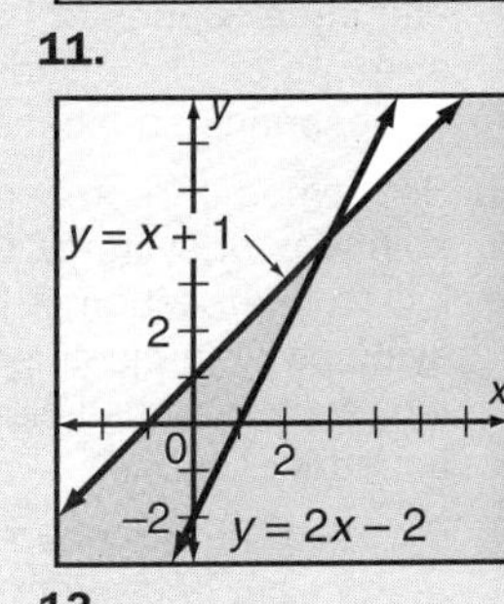

12. **13.**

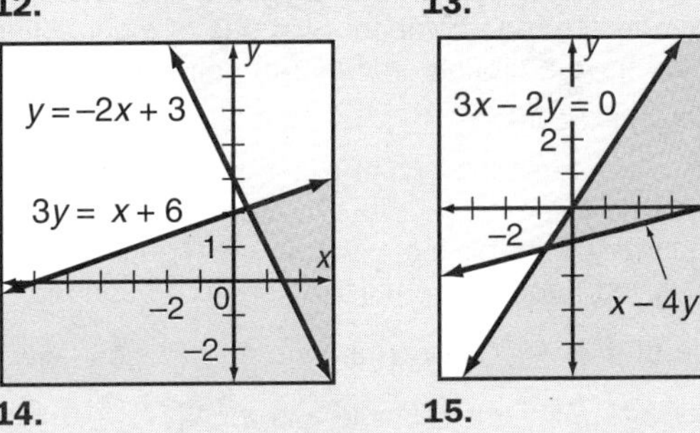

14.

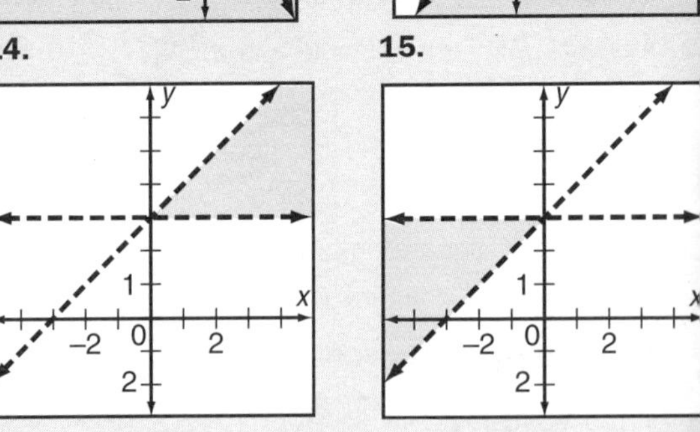

15.

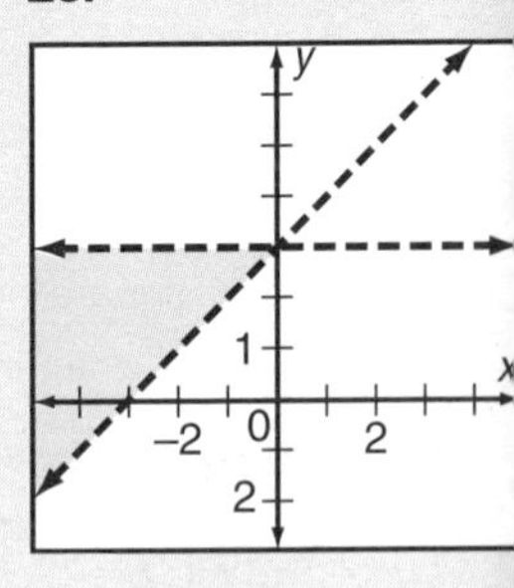

16.

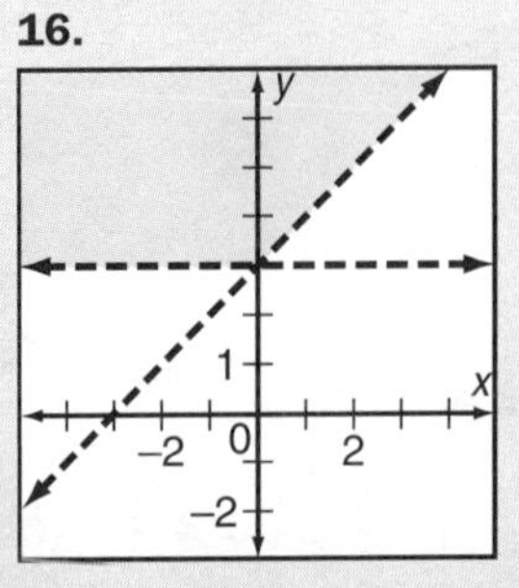

8. c. The maximum profit given the constraints is \$100 earned by selling 20 apple pies and 20 blueberry pies.

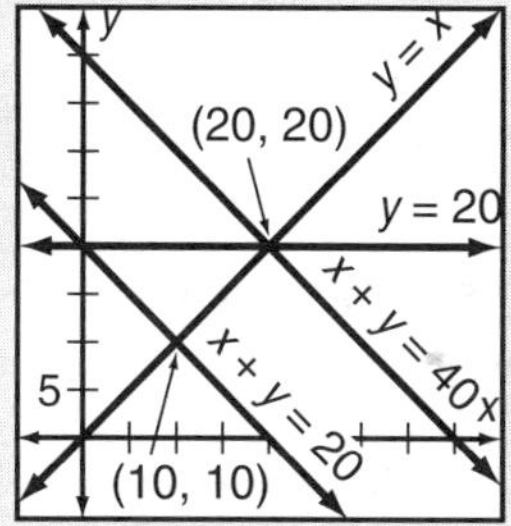

Chapter Assessment

CHAPTER TEST, PAGE 406

3.

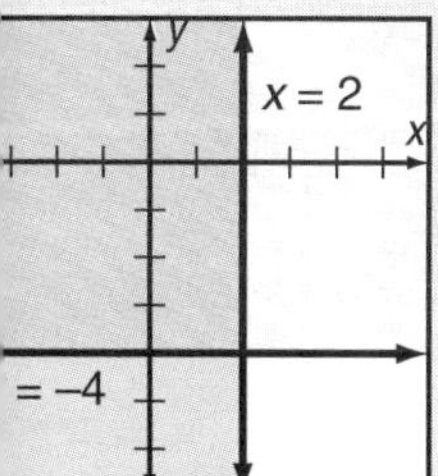

4.

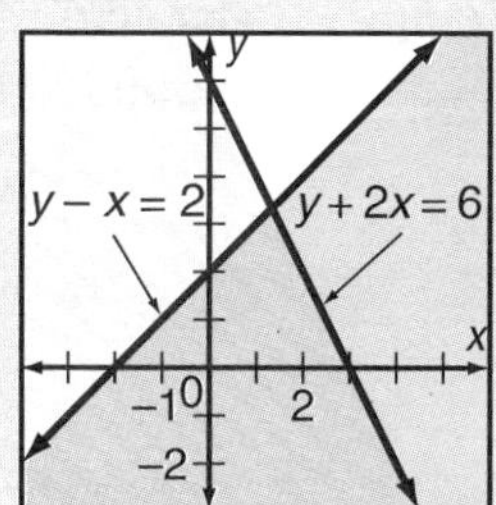

5.

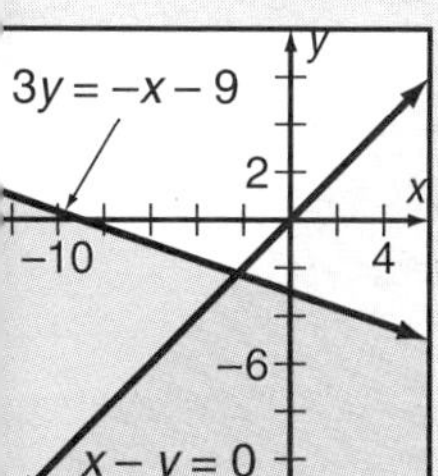

6.

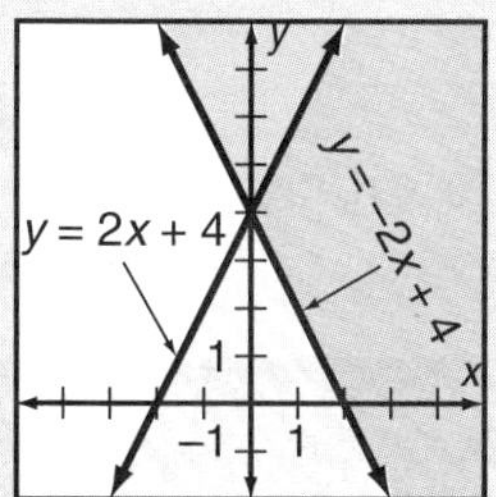

7.

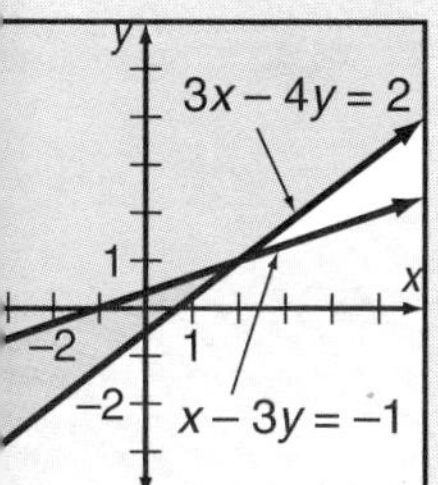

8.

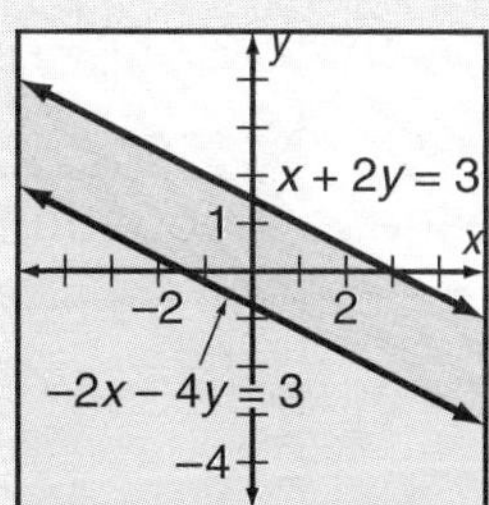

9. a. $x + y \geq 16$

$12x + 16y \geq 288$

$x \geq 0$

$y \geq 0$

b. 10 CDs and 8 books

16 CDs and 2 books

8 CDs and 8 books

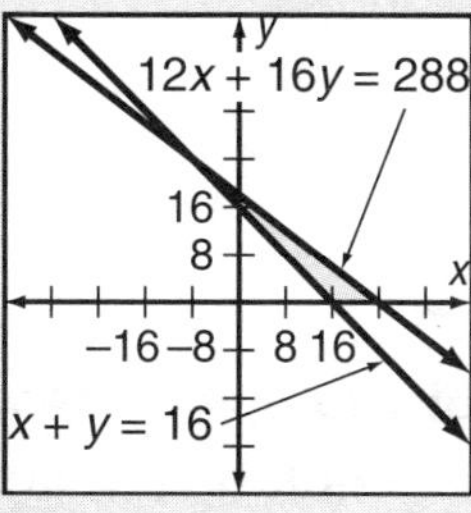

10.

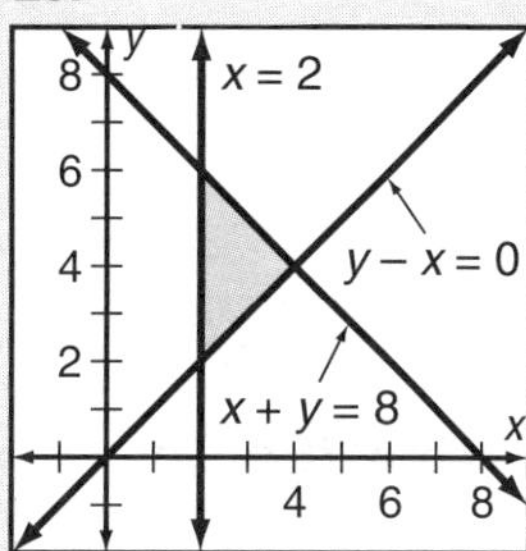

11.

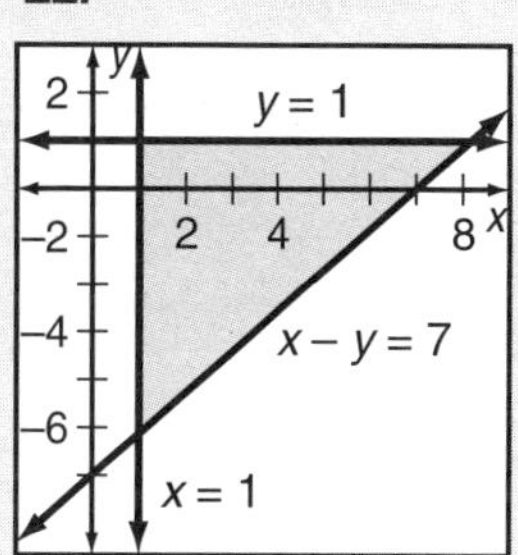

22. a. $C = 40x + 60y$

$x \leq 8$

$y \leq 7$

$x + y \leq 12$

$x \geq 0$

$y \geq 0$

$40x + 60y \geq 420$

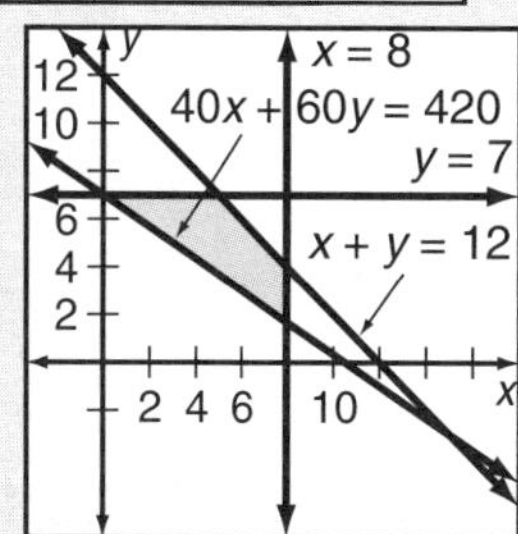

b. Since all 12 drivers are to work, only whole number values of x and y adding up to 12 can be considered. There are vertices at (5, 7) and (8, 4). So, 8 five-ton trucks and 4 ten-ton trucks must be used.

PERFORMANCE ASSESSMENT, PAGE 407

QUILT MODELS

Square:
$x + y \leq 5$
$x - y \geq 5$
$x + y \geq -5$
$x - y \leq -5$

Triangle upper right:
$x + y \geq 5$
$y \leq 5$
$x \leq 5$

Triangle lower right:
$y \geq x - 5$
$x \leq 5$
$y \geq 5$

Triangle upper left:
$y \leq 5$
$x \geq -5$
$y \geq x + 5$

Triangle lower left:
$y \geq -5$
$x \geq -5$
$x + y \leq -5$

CUMULATIVE REVIEW, PAGE 408

1. $y \geq \frac{1}{2}x + 1$

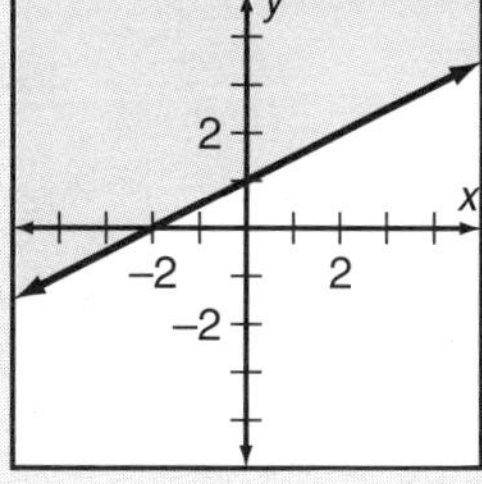

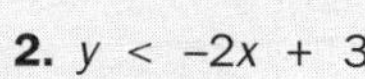

2. $y < -2x + 3$

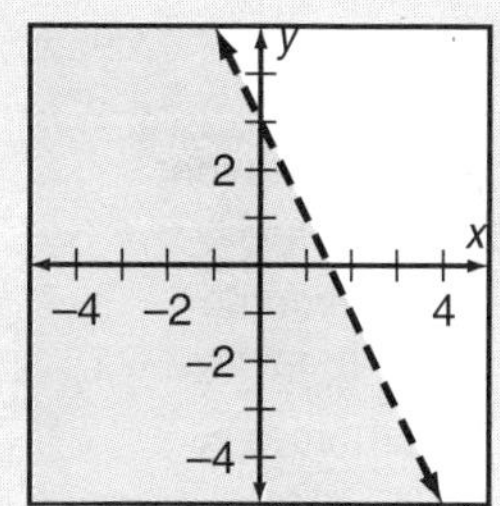

6. No; 0.4 is Maria's experimental probability of choosing a red marble on her next selection. This probability will change after each successive selection.

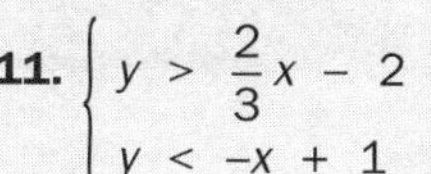

11. $\begin{cases} y > \frac{2}{3}x - 2 \\ y < -x + 1 \end{cases}$

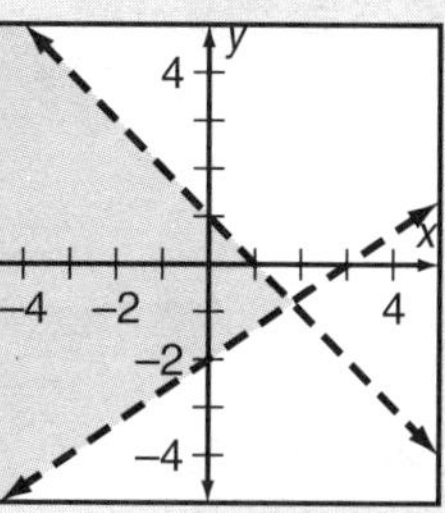

12. $\begin{cases} 3x - 2y \leq 6 \\ x + y \geq 4 \end{cases}$

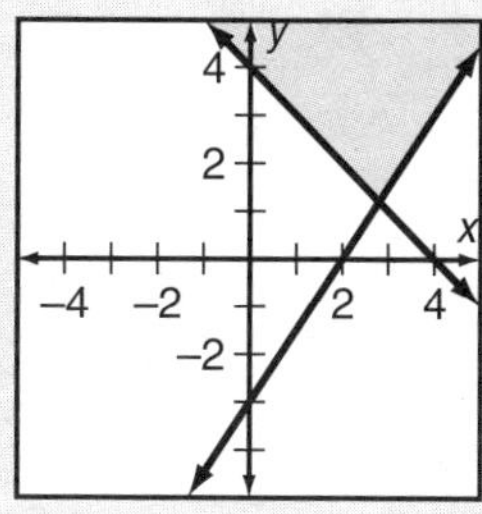

13. Answers will vary. Many graphing utilities will not automatically shade the half-plane.

19. Since $x > 3$ is a single-variable inequality, the graph would be on a number line. The other is a two-variable inequality and would be graphed on a coordinate plane.

CHAPTER 9 ABSOLUTE VALUE AND THE REAL NUMBER SYSTEM

All young Americans should be equipped to work in, contribute to, benefit from, and enjoy our technological society. Integrating mathematics, science, and technology and/or connecting one to the other in a planned way with an emphasis on conceptual thinking and problem solving is essential to successful achievement . . .

Curriculum Instruction and Assessment, University of the State of New York, Albany, NY, 1994, page 13

The Big Question: Why study absolute value and the real number system?

Solving absolute value equations and inequalities gives students the ability to solve a variety of problems. An absolute value equation is solved by expressing it as a disjunction. An absolute value inequality is solved by expressing it as either a disjunction or a conjunction. Although the theme of this chapter is traffic, students will also find applications from astronomy, design, economics, education, engineering, physics, social studies, and travel.

Vocabulary

absolute value function	quotient property of square roots
complete	radical
compound inequalities	radical symbol
conjunction	radicand
dense	rational number
disjunction	real numbers
elements	reflection
finite	reflexive property
horizontal shift	set
infinite	subset
irrational number	substitution property
line of reflection	symmetric property
line of symmetry	symmetry
line symmetry	transformations
principal square root	transitive property
product property of square roots	translation
proof	trichotomy property
properties of equality	vertical shift

Using the Graphic Organizer

Project a copy of the Graphic Organizer Transparency for Chapter 9. Explain that the focus of this chapter is on absolute value and the real number system. Review the information on the graphic organizer, pointing out that students may find absolute values in both equations and inequalities.

Ask some preview questions; for example, what does it mean to say that absolute value refers to distance, not direction? Why is the absolute value of any nonzero number positive?

One way to organize ideas about absolute value and real numbers is shown below.

One way to organize ideas about absolute value and real numbers is shown.

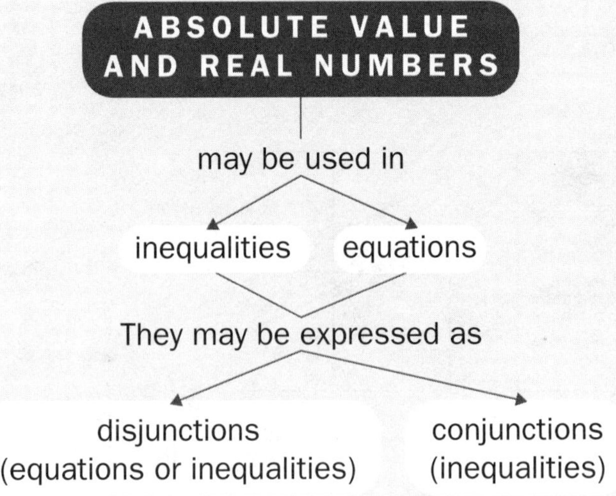

Try It Use a different plan. Try organizing ideas about the specific types of graphs that correspond to absolute value equations and inequalities.

xplore the Chapter Theme:

Traffic

To some degree, the problem of traffic is faced by all Americans. Even air travelers ace problems as acute as travelers sing roads and highways. There is a ide range of industries and occupa-ons involved in the movement of eople from place to place. This ncludes positions from maintenance orkers to facility managers. As our opulation increases, the prospect is or continued growth in travel and affic-related careers.

Skills Needed for Success in Traffic-Related Careers

1. Understand the laws relating to transport and traffic.
2. Make decisions based on an understanding of law.
3. Concentrate on work for extended periods without being distracted.
4. Read and understand technical manuals.
5. Keep skills up to date as technology changes.
6. Diagnose problems and determine solutions.
7. Relate well to customers and appreciate their problems.
8. Work well under pressure imposed by safety and time considerations.

Investigate Further

Have students identify a traffic-related career that interests them. Have students to go to the library to find more information about this career. For example, students might find out about educational requirements including specific courses, degrees, examinations, or licenses required. Students should research the average salary range for the career. Have students share their findings in a class discussion about career opportunities.

Here is a list of jobs and educational requirements for traffic-related careers.

Jobs Requiring 1 to 2 Years of Technical Training	Jobs Requiring 4 + Years of College
Law Enforcement Officer	Air Traffic Controller
Road Maintenance Worker	Tire Company Engineer
Toll Collector	Commercial Pilot
Truck Driver	Airport Manager
Truck Mechanic	Turnpike Supervisor
Auto Mechanic	Civil Engineer
Diesel Mechanic	Automotive Engineer

CHAPTER 9 PLANNING GUIDE

Lessons		Text Pages	NCTM Standards	ASSIGNMENTS Basic	Average	Enriched	Ancillaries	Manipulatives	Technology
	Chapter Introduction	410–412	1, 2, 3, 4, 10				Video Discussion Guide		Video, Transparency 5
9.1	**Algebra Workshop: Absolute Value**	413–415	1, 2, 3, 4, 5, 6, 8	1–31	1–31	1–32	S 23 M 9	Graph Paper	Graphing Utility, Transparencies 32, 33, 53, 78–80
9.2	**Graph Absolute Value Functions**	416–423	1, 2, 3, 4, 5, 6, 8	1–24, 29–32, 34, 36–38, 42, 44, 47–49, PC1–3	1–32, 34–52, PC1–3	5–52, PC1–3	W 9.1; R 9.1; P 9.1; E 9.1; Q 9.1; T 20; S 24	Uncooked Spaghetti, Graph Paper	Graphing Utility, Transparencies 32, 33, 53, 54 78–80
9.3	**Absolute Value Equations**	424–429	1, 2, 3, 4, 5, 8, 10	1–20, 22–26, 28–33, 35–36, 38–39, 41–42, 44, PC1–4	4–33, 35–45, PC1–4	4–47, PC1–4	W 9.3; R 9.3; P 9.3; E 9.3; Q 9.3	Uncooked Spaghetti	Graphing Utility Transparencies 32, 54–56, 78–80
9.4	**Absolute Value Inequalities**	430–436	1, 2, 3, 4, 5, 8	1–44, 47, 50, 52, 54, 56, 58, 61, 64a–c, MR65–71, AW1–7	5–59, 61, 64a–c, MR65–71, AW1–7	9–64, MR65–71, AW1–7	W 9.4; R 9.4; P 9.4; E 9.4; Q 9.4; T 21	Uncooked Spaghetti	Transparencies 18, 55, 56
9.5	**The Real Number System**	437–444	1, 2, 3, 4, 5, 8, 14	1–7, 12–18, 22–25, 27–30, 32–36, 42, 44–46, 50–51, 54–55, 58–61, PC1–3, AW1–8	1, 7–51, 53–56, 58–62, PC1–3, AW1–8	7–63, PC1–3, AW1–8	W 9.5; R 9.5; P 9.5; E 9.5; Q 9.5	Number Lines	Calculator, Transparencies 15, 17, 18, 78–80
9.6	**Properties of Equality and Order**	445–451	1, 2, 3, 4, 5, 10, 14	1–31, 34, 40, MR41–47, AW1–5	2–31, 34, 36–40, MR41–47, AW1–5	3–40, MR41–47, AW1–5	W 9.6; R 9.6; P 9.6; E 9.6; Q 9.6		Calculator, Transparency 18, 78–80
9.7	**Problem Solving File: Use Multiple Representations**	452–455	1, 2, 3, 4, 5, 8	1–15, RPSS1–3	1–15, RPSS1–3	1–15, RPSS1–3	R 9.7; P 9.7		Transparencies 10, 34

NCTM STANDARDS

1. Mathematics as Problem Solving
2. Mathematics as Communication
3. Mathematics as Reasoning
4. Mathematical Connections
5. Algebra
6. Functions
7. Geometry from a Synthetic Perspective
8. Geometry from an Algebraic Perspective
9. Trigonometry
10. Statistics
11. Probability
12. Discrete Mathematics
13. Conceptual Underpinnings of Calculus
14. Mathematical Structure

ANCILLARIES

W = Warm Up
R = Reteaching
P = Extra Practice
E = Enrichment
Q = Lesson Quiz
T = Technology Activity
M = Multicultural Connection
S = Study Skills Activity

ABSOLUTE VALUE AND THE REAL NUMBER SYSTEM

ADDITIONAL RESOURCES

ɅApplications	Career Connections	Cooperative Learning	Learning Styles	Strand Integration/ Math Connection
	Chapter Poster			
		Paired partners, 413–414 (Think Back/Working Together/Explore)	Linguistic/Interpersonal, 413–414; Visual, Symbolic, 413–415	Problem Solving, Geometry, Technology, Writing, Critical Thinking
)esign, 422; Engineering, ɁL20; Geometry, 423; ;ocial Studies, 422; 'raffic, 423		Small groups/TAI, 423 (Project Connection)	Linguistic/Interpersonal, 417, 419, 423; Visual, 416–423; ESL/LEP, 418 (TE); Tactile, 423	Problem Solving, Geometry, Technology, Writing, Critical Thinking
:ducation, 428; Health, 427; Income, 428, 429; ;cience, 426–427, 428; raffic, 429		Small groups/TAI, 429 (Project Connection)	Kinesthetic/Tactile, Visual, 424, 425–429; Linguistic/Interpersonal, 425, 426, 429	Problem Solving, Technology, Geometry, Writing, Critical Thinking, Estimation
:ducation, 433; :ecreation, 434; Sales, ‑34; Science, 435; Travel :32–433	AlgebraWorks: Tire Company Engineer, 436		Linguistic/Interpersonal, 431, 432; Kinesthetic/Tactile, 431; Visual, 430–436; Linguistic Learners, 431 (TE)	Problem Solving, Geometry, Writing, Critical Thinking, Statistics, Estimation
;eometry, 443; Number heory, 443; Physics, ‑40, 442; Sports, 441; raffic, 443	AlgebraWorks: Law Enforcement Officer, 444	Small groups/TAI, 443 (Project Connection)	Linguistic/Interpersonal, 440, 443; Visual, 437, 439, 440, 443, 444	Problem Solving, Sets, Technology, Geometry, Number Theory, Writing, Critical Thinking, Statistics
stronomy, 449; conomics, 447; Travel, 48	AlgebraWorks: Market Research Analyst, 451	Paired partners, 445 (Explore) (TE)	Visual, 445, 446–449, 445–451; Visual Learners, 446 (TE)	Problem Solving, Geometry, Sets, Logic, Writing, Critical Thinking, Technology, Statistics
esign, 454; Economics, 54			Visual, 452–455	Problem Solving, Geometry, Writing, Patterns

PACING GUIDE

Lessons	Regular Classes	2-year Algebra 1 Classes	Blocked Classes
9.1	1	2	½
9.2	1	2	½
9.3	1	2	½
9.4	1	2	½
9.5	1	2	½
9.6	1	2	½
9.7	1	2	1
Review	1	1	1
Test	1	1	1
Cumulative Test	1	1	1
Total Classes	10	17	7

SESSMENT OPTIONS

ıdent Edition
apter Assessment
Chapter Test
Performance Assessment
Project Assessment
ındardized Tests

Chapter Resource Book
Chapter Test, Form A
Chapter Test, Form B
Standardized Chapter Test
Portfolio Item: Self-Assessment
Portfolio Assessment Form

MicroExam II

PREVIEW THE CHAPTER

Take a Look Ahead Have students read the previewing suggestions and then scan the chapter looking for new and familiar things. Give students time to make notes in their journals. Discuss student answers to the previewing questions.

Connecting to Career Opportunities Have the students read the descriptions of the AlgebraWorks features for this chapter. Ask students to identify the careers mentioned. **tire company engineers, law enforcement officers, and market research analysts** Ask students if they know anyone who works at these jobs. Discuss the types of educational background required for each of the careers. For example, engineers and market research analysts at least have undergraduate degrees; law enforcement officers have at least a high school diploma and considerable further training.

Investigate Further Explain to students that as they study this chapter they should look for examples of other careers involved with traffic as well as careers in other fields. Ask students to determine one way in which algebra can be used in that career. Encourage students to write questions in their journals about other traffic-related jobs they would like to learn more about.

USING THE DATA ACTIVITY

Introduce the Data Activity Have students read the introductory paragraph and identify some ways in which they think traffic delays are responsible for such large losses of money.

Skill Focus Read the skills listed and discuss with students what they think each means. Ask volunteers to suggest problems that might involve the skill being discussed.

9 Absolute Value and the Real Number System

Take a Look AHEAD

Make notes about things that look new.

- What different sets of numbers make up the real numbers? How are these sets of numbers related?
- In this chapter, several new properties of numbers and equality will be added to those you already know. Skim the lesson to identify the names of these properties. How might the name relate to the meaning of the property?

Make notes about things that look familiar.

- Recall your work with absolute value in Chapter 5. When is a compound statement containing *and* true? When is a compound statement containing *or* true?
- How is the mathematical usage of the term *dense* similar to its everyday usage? How is it different?

DATA Activity

Right Lane Closed Ahead!

Nobody enjoys being stuck in traffic, but road congestion is more than just an annoyance— it's a feature of daily life that costs individuals and businesses billions of dollars and contributes significantly to the serious problem of air pollution. The Federal Highway Administration compiles extensive data on road travel and delays. The results for selected cities are shown in the table on the opposite page.

SKILL FOCUS

- Add, subtract, multiply, and divide real numbers.
- Determine the mean of a set of data.
- Use ratios to compare.
- Use estimation.
- Construct graphs.

TRAFFIC

In this chapter, you will see how:

- **Tire Company Engineers** use algebra to represent characteristics of ride, handling, and wear. (Lesson 9.4, page 436)
- **Law Enforcement Officers** apply formulas to determine the speed at which a vehicle was traveling by its breaking distance. (Lesson 9.5, page 444)
- **Market Research Analysts** for a long-distance telephone company collect and organize data to attract customers. (Lesson 9.6, page 451)

1–5 See Additional Answers.

Road Congestion

City	Daily Vehicle Miles, thousands	Vehicle Hours of Delay	Delay and Fuel Cost, $ millions
New York, NY	80,920	1,512,740	6,040
Boston, MA	22,080	349,860	1,390
Cincinnati, OH	10,890	39,520	160
St. Louis, MO	18,720	138,450	540
Atlanta, GA	24,600	229,090	910
Miami, FL	8,350	222,270	870
Dallas, TX	22,650	241,530	980
Phoenix, AZ	7,050	179,560	700
Los Angeles, CA	106,680	1,752,200	7,000
Seattle, WA	18,200	255,630	1,020

Use the table above to answer the questions.

1. Determine the mean number of daily vehicle miles for the cities shown. Is the mean a useful statistic for this set of data?
2. Would it be correct to claim that the traffic delays in Phoenix are worse than those in New York? Explain.
3. Estimate the total delay and fuel cost for the cities shown. Describe the method you use.
4. Select one column from the table. Make a graph to display the data in that column.
5. **Working Together** Select a trip you can all take together, such as going to school or to the mall. Take the trip during a period of light traffic and again during heavy traffic. Make a graph to show how travel times compare.

Study the Data Before students examine the data, have them use an almanac or atlas to find the populations of each of the cities in the table. Then have them look for ratios that seem surprising. For example, Los Angeles, with a population half of New York City, records more than 20 million additional vehicle miles daily. Students can compare the number of square miles within each city. Other comparisons students can consider are the extensiveness of the city's mass transit system and the average age of the population. This latter point may be especially interesting for Miami and Phoenix, two popular retirement destinations.

Complete the Data Activity

For Item 1, have students determine the median number of vehicle miles for the cities and compare the mean (32,014,000) to the median (20,400,000).

For Item 2, students can calculate the ratio of delay hours to miles for each city. Students will find that, using this ratio, Miami appears to have the worst delays.

For Items 3 and 4, be sure students understand how to express each of the numbers in the final column in terms of billions of dollars. For example, they should know that the total for New York City is approximately $6 billion and for St. Louis approximately one-half billion dollars.

For Item 5, have students discuss the appropriateness of different types of graphs for displaying the data.

South-Western Algebra 1 Chapter Theme Video or Videodisc

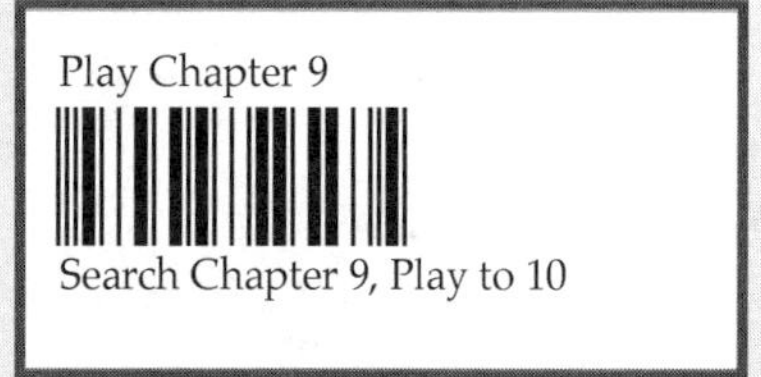

Play Chapter 9
Search Chapter 9, Play to 10

INTRODUCING THE PROJECT

Project Goal Discuss the project's big idea: How can algebra be used to analyze data about individual and group travel habits?

Getting Ready Ask students to think of a travel destination for which they have two or more choices of transportation methods. Lead a discussion on what factors influence their decision in choosing a method and the benefits of each method. Where quantifiable factors such as distance and cost are mentioned, have students make a comparison using the language of inequalities.

FACILITATING THE PROJECT

Getting Started Have available several maps, each with a different scale. Briefly review the use of proportions in interpreting map scales.

Setting Project Benchmarks Make sure that the students are aware of the project schedule in the Project Planning Calendar and the due dates for each of the benchmarks. You may find the TAI cooperative learning approach appropriate for this activity.

a. On a detailed street map, show the straight–line distance between home and school for each group member. (Project/Chapter Opener)

b. Determine an absolute value graph showing the distance traveled to and from school as a function of time spent traveling. (Project Connection 9.2)

c. Compare absolute value equations based on map distance and actual distance between home and school. (Project Connection 9.3)

d. Plan and conduct a survey of people's transportation habits. (Project Connection 9.5)

e. Use graphs, equations, and survey results to prepare travel profiles for group members and for the community. Plan your presentation. (Project Assessment)

Suggest that students make subgoals for each goal and include the subgoals in their calendar.

Which Way To Go?

Even when you have a destination in mind, there may be several different routes and methods of transportation that you can use to reach it. Traveling by car may be convenient and fast, but bicycling is good exercise and probably less expensive. Many people keep track of mileage, gasoline costs, and transportation time and use the data for travel decisions, household budgeting, or business purposes. In this project you will find out about people's travel habits, including your own.

PROJECT GOAL

To collect, analyze, and compare data about individual and group travel habits.

Getting Started

Work in groups.

1. Discuss methods of transportation used regularly by each person. Find out which places (other than school) are common destinations. Make a frequency table showing how often group members visit these destinations each week.
2. Obtain a detailed street map of your city, town, or county and a different colored pencil for each group member. Mark the location of your school. Have each member locate his or her home on the map and draw a straight line connecting home to school.
3. Have each member use the map scale to estimate the straight-line distance from home to school. Organize the information in a table or graph.
4. Discuss why the straight-line distance may not match the actual distance traveled to school. Plan how to find the actual distance. You will use this actual distance in a Project Connection.

PROJECT *Connections*

Lesson 9.2, page 423:
Determine an absolute value graph that shows the distance to and from home to school as a function of time.

Lesson 9.3, page 429:
Write absolute value equations using map distances and actual distances.

Lesson 9.5, page 443:
Plan and conduct a survey to learn more about people's travel habits.

Chapter Assessment, page 459:
Prepare travel profiles for the group and the community.

9.1 Algebra Workshop
Absolute Value

Think Back/Working Together

Work with a partner. Recall that the absolute value of a number x is the distance between x and 0 on a number line. The absolute value of a number x is written $|x|$.

1. Evaluate each expression.
   a. $|4|$ 4 b. $|-3.5|$ 3.5 c. $|0|$ 0 d. $\left|-\frac{1}{2}\right|$ $\frac{1}{2}$ e. $|-\pi|$ π

2. Use the information from Exercise 1 to complete the following definition of absolute value.

   $|x| = \square$ if $x \geq 0$ x $|x| = \square$ if $x < 0$ $-x$

3. Solve each equation. If there is no solution, explain.
   a. $|x| = 5$ $x = 5$, $x = -5$ b. $|x| = 0$ $x = 0$ c. $|-x| = -2$ no solution; absolute value cannot be negative d. $|-x| = \frac{1}{2}$ $x = \frac{1}{2}$, $x = -\frac{1}{2}$

Explore

You can use a graphing utility to graph absolute value equations. The equation $y = |x|$ is graphed at the right. A standard viewing window (x and y range from –10 to 10) with an x-scale and y-scale of 2 is used. The ABS (absolute value) function is used for $|x|$.

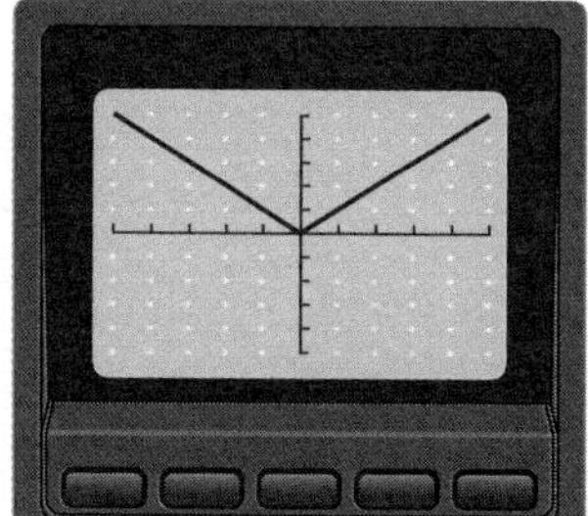

4. What letter of the alphabet best describes the shape of the graph? V

5. If you can fold a drawing of a figure so that the part on one side coincides with the part on the other side, the figure is said to have **symmetry**. The fold is called a **line of symmetry**. Does the graph have a line of symmetry? Explain. Yes, the y-axis is a line of symmetry.

6. Why is the graph located only in Quadrants I and II? See Additional Answers.

7. Graph $y = |x|$ on your graphing utility. Use the TRACE feature to find the vertex of the graph. (0, 0)

You can add or subtract a positive number from the equation $y = |x|$ to obtain an equation of the form $y = |x| \pm c$, which means $y = |x| + c$ or $y = |x| - c$. 8–9 See Additional Answers.

8. Graph $y = |x| + 3$ on the same set of axes (that is, without clearing your screen from Question 7). How is the graph of $y = |x| + 3$ similar to the graph of $y = |x|$? How is it different? Where is its vertex? What is its line of symmetry?

9. Graph $y = |x| - 4$ on the same set of axes. How is the graph of $y = |x| - 4$ similar to the graph of $y = |x|$? How is it different? Where is its vertex? What is its line of symmetry?

SPOTLIGHT ON LEARNING

WHAT? In this lesson you will learn
- to graph absolute value equations using a graphing utility.
- to shift absolute value graphs vertically and horizontally.

WHY? A graphing utility can help you to understand vertical and horizontal shifts in graphs of absolute value equations.

LESSON PLANNING

Objectives
- ▶ Graph absolute value equations using a graphing utility.
- ▶ Shift absolute value graphs vertically and horizontally.

Vocabulary
symmetry
line of symmetry

Technology/Multimedia
graphing utility

Resources
Transparencies 78–80
Student Handbook
Study Skills Activity 23
Multicultural Connection 9, Hispanic American: Focus on Higher Education

ASSIGNMENTS

Basic: 1–31

Average: 1–31

Enriched: 1–32

1 MOTIVATE

Think Back After students complete Exercises 1–2, ask them to give examples for Exercise 2. **possible example: $|3| = 3$ since $3 \geq 0$; $|-3| = -(-3) = 3$ since $-3 < 0$** For Exercise 3 part c, ask why an absolute value cannot be a negative number. **The absolute value of a number represents distance which is always positive.**

2 FACILITATE

Explore For Exercise 7, have students use the TRACE feature to locate other points on the graph. **examples: (1, 1), (−2, 2), (2, 2), (−3, 3)** After students have completed Exercises 1–7, have them work with partners for Exercises 8–18. Tell students that ± is read "plus or minus." So, $y = x \pm b$ is read "y equals x plus or minus b"; and means "$y = x + b$ or $y = x - b$."

For Exercise 18, ask students what the coordinates are for the vertex of the graph $y = |x - b| - c$. **(b, $-c$)**

Make Connections For Exercises 19–21, ask students how many units graphs will move in each case. **2 units right and 4 units down; 5 units left; 6 units left and 6 units up**

3 SUMMARIZE

Writing Mathematics Have students give examples of equations in $y = |x \pm b| \pm c$ form, graph them, and then describe how much and in what direction the graph of each example is shifted from the graph of $y = |x|$.

Thinking Critically For Exercise 30, have students give examples of $y = a|x|$ for values of $a > 1$ and for values of a when $0 < a < 1$. **possible examples: $y = 5|x|$; $y = 0.2|x|$** For Exercise 31, ask students how the graph of $y = -|x|$ is different from the graph of $y = |-x|$. **The graph of $y = -|x|$ is below the x-axis with all values for y negative; the graph of $y = |-x|$ is the same as the graph of $y = |x|$ which is above the x-axis with all values for y positive.**

Algebra Workshop

PROBLEM SOLVING TIP

Recall that your calculator has a built-in order of operations. If you enter the equation $y = |x + 2|$ as ABS x + 2 instead of ABS(x + 2), you will obtain the graph of $y = |x| + 2$.

10. Draw a conclusion about the type of shift that occurs when a positive number c is added to or subtracted from the right side of the equation $y = |x|$. The graph is shifted vertically.
11. Clear your screen. Graph a new equation of the form $y = |x| \pm c$. Have your partner use your graph to identify the equation you entered. Then switch roles with your partner. Answers will vary.

You can add or subtract a positive number from x within the absolute value bars to obtain an equation of the form $y = |x \pm b|$.

12–13, 17 See Additional Answers.

12. Clear your screen. Graph $y = |x + 2|$ and $y = |x|$ on the same set of axes. How is the graph of $y = |x + 2|$ similar to the graph of $y = |x|$? How is it different? Where is its vertex? What is its line of symmetry?
13. Clear your screen. Graph $y = |x - 3|$ and $y = |x|$ on the same set of axes. How is the graph of $y = |x - 3|$ similar to the graph of $y = |x|$? How is it different? Where is its vertex? What is its line of symmetry?
14. Draw a conclusion about the type of shift that occurs when a positive number b is added to or subtracted from x within the absolute value bars. The graph is shifted horizontally.
15. Clear your screen. Graph a new equation of the form $y = |x \pm b|$. Have your partner use your graph to identify the equation you entered. Then switch roles with your partner. Answers will vary.
16. Predict how the graph of the equation $y = |x \pm b| \pm c$ will be shifted from the graph of $y = |x|$. Answers will vary; the graph will be shifted horizontally and vertically.
17. Clear your screen. Graph $y = |x + 3| - 1$ and $y = |x|$ on the same set of axes. How is the graph of $y = |x + 3| - 1$ similar to the graph of $y = |x|$? How is it different? Where is its vertex? What is its line of symmetry?
18. Clear your screen. Graph a new equation of the form $y = |x \pm b| \pm c$. Have your partner identify the equation you entered by studying the graph. Then switch roles with your partner. Where is the vertex of the graph of $y = |x + b| + c$? $(-b, c)$

COMMUNICATING ABOUT ALGEBRA

Reading from left to right in the equation $y = |x + 3| - 1$, the horizontal shift takes place first. Would the same graph result from entering $y = -1 + |x + 3|$? Discuss whether order matters when you perform these shifts.

Order does not matter in performing these operations.

Make Connections

- You have just learned that adding or subtracting a positive number c from the equation $y = |x|$ produces a vertical shift. Adding or subtracting a positive number b within the absolute value bars of the equation $y = |x|$ produces a horizontal shift.

Use the words *up*, *down*, *left*, and *right* (you can combine them) to indicate the direction in which the graph of each equation is shifted from the graph of $y = |x|$.

19. $y = |x - 2| - 4$ right and down **20.** $y = |x + 5|$ left **21.** $y = |x + 6| + 6$ left and up

Determine the equation of each graph. Then verify your answer using a graphing utility. Each tick mark is one unit.

22. 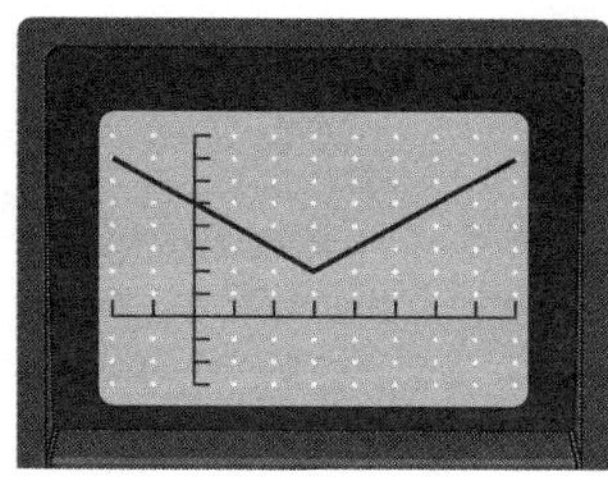
$y = |x - 3| + 2$

23. 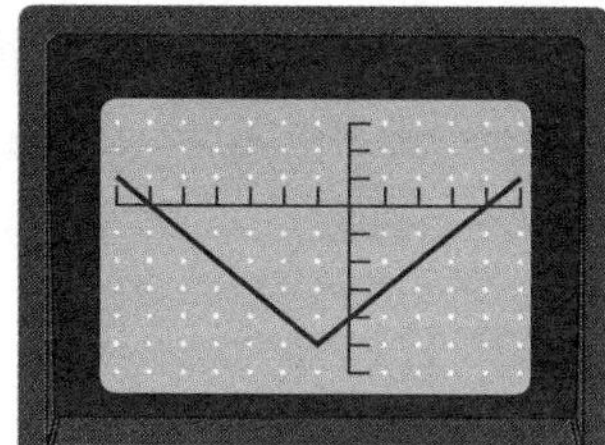
$y = |x + 1| - 5$

24. 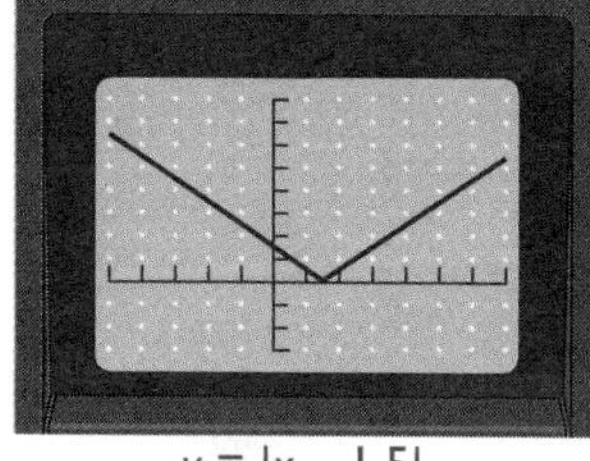
$y = |x - 1.5|$

Write an equation of the form $y = |x \pm b| \pm c$ whose graph represents each of the following shifts from the graph of $y = |x|$.

25. 3 units down and 4 units left $y = |x + 4| - 3$

26. 1.5 units up and 7.5 units right $y = |x - 7.5| + 1.5$

27. 2.5 units down and 4.5 units right $y = |x - 4.5| - 2.5$

28. 1.8 units up and 4.8 units left $y = |x + 4.8| + 1.8$

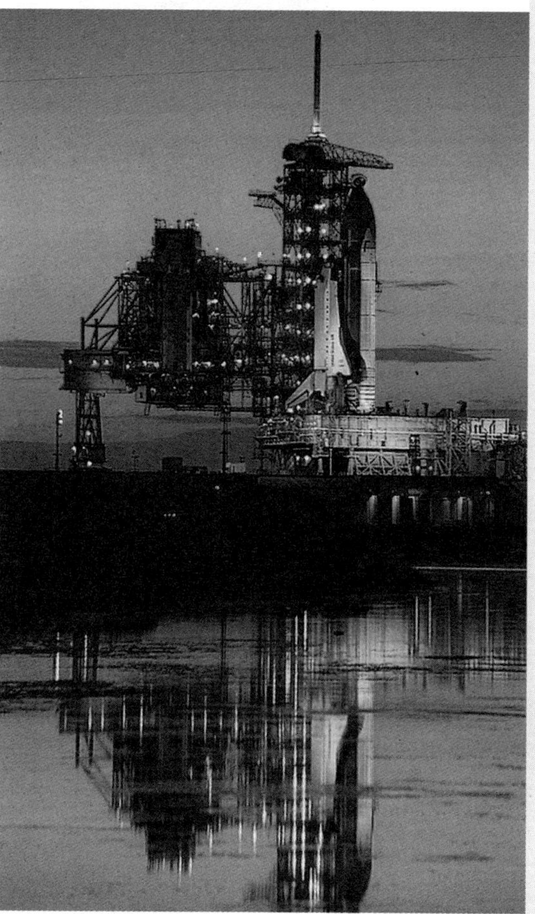

Summarize

29. **Writing Mathematics** Write a paragraph that explains how to determine how much and in what direction the graph of $y = |x \pm b| \pm c$ is shifted from the graph of $y = |x|$. Answers will vary.

30. **Thinking Critically** How is the graph of $y = a|x|$ different from the graph of $y = |x|$ if $a > 1$? if $0 < a < 1$? See Additional Answers.

31. **Thinking Critically** How is the graph of $y = -|x|$ different from the graph of $y = |x|$? Over what line is the graph of $y = -|x|$ a reflection of the graph of $y = |x|$? it is upside down; x-axis

32. **Going Further** Would you obtain the same graph by reflecting the graph of $y = |x|$ over the x-axis and then shifting it up 3 units as you would if you shifted it up 3 units and then reflected it over the x-axis? Does order matter when shifting and reflecting this absolute value graph? no; yes

Going Further For Exercise 32, ask students to graph the results of each case of shifting and reflecting the graph $y = |x|$ and to share their graphs.

4 FOLLOW-UP

Other Explorations Have students use their graphing utilities to graph examples of the equation $y = a|x|$ when $a < -1$ and when $-1 < a < 0$. Have them describe how graphs are different from the graph of $y = |x|$. **When $a < -1$, the graphs will be steeper; when $-1 < a < 0$, graphs will be less steep, or closer to the x-axis; in both cases the graphs will be reflected over the x-axis.**

Making Connections Design Explain to students that computer-generated designs rely on mathematical equations to define them. The design below uses four equations: $y = |x|$, $y = |x + 2| - 4$, $y = |x + 4| - 8$, and $y = -|x - 2| + 8$. Ask students to identify which equation describes which graph in the design.

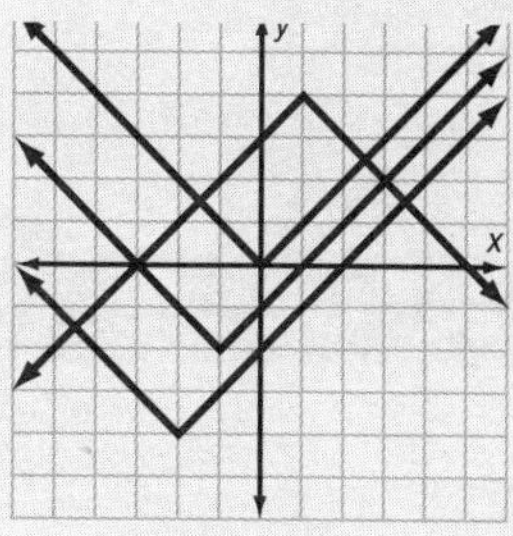

$y = |x|$
$y = |x + 2| - 4$
$y = |x + 4| - 8$
$y = -|x - 2| + 8$

LESSON PLANNING

Objective

► Graph absolute value functions using a table of values or a graphing utility.

Vocabulary

absolute value function
horizontal shift
line of reflection
line of symmetry
reflection
transformations
translation
vertical shift

Technology/Multimedia

graphing utility

Resources

Warm Up 9.2
Reteaching 9.2
Extra Practice 9.2
Enrichment 9.2
Transparencies 34, 53, 54, 78–80
Student Handbook
Lesson Quiz 9.2
Study Skills Activity 24
Technology Activity 20

Materials/Manipulatives

graph paper

ASSIGNMENTS

Basic: 1–24, 29–32, 34, 36–38, 42, 44, 47–49, Project Connection 1–3

Average: 1–32, 34–52, Project Connection 1–3

Enriched: 5–52, Project Connection 1–3

9.2 Graph Absolute Value Functions

SPOTLIGHT ON LEARNING

WHAT? In this lesson you will learn

- to graph absolute value functions using a table of values or a graphing utility.

WHY? Graphing absolute value functions can help you solve problems involving engineering, geometry, and fashion.

Explore

1. On a coordinate plane draw a triangle in Quadrant I so that it does not touch either axis. Label the vertices of the triangle A, B, and C.
   Answers will vary.
2. Fold the paper back along the y-axis. Trace your triangle in Quadrant II, labeling the vertices A', B', and C'.
   See Additional Answers.
3. Unfold the paper. What is the relationship of points A and A' to the y-axis? of B and B'? of C and C'?
   See Additional Answers.

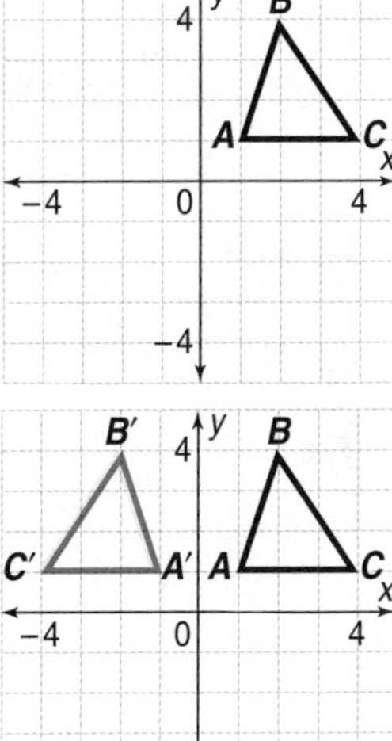

Build Understanding

The **absolute value function** is denoted by $f(x) = |x|$. The corresponding absolute value equation is $y = |x|$, where x is any real number and y is any number that is greater than or equal to 0.

The graphs of $y = x$ and $y = |x|$ are shown below.

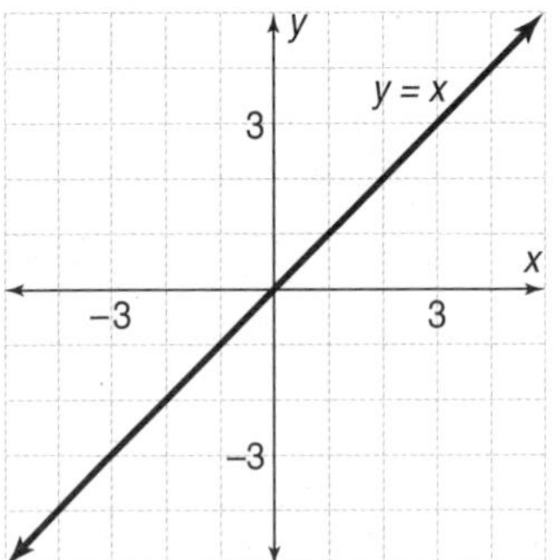

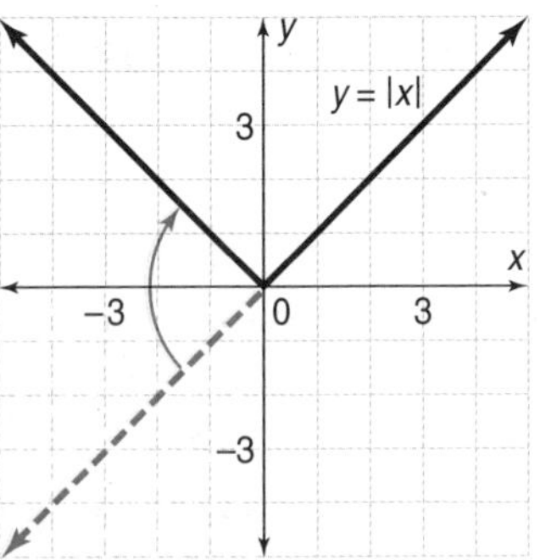

The graph of $y = x$ is a straight line that extends through Quadrants I and III. The graph of $y = |x|$ is V-shaped, has a vertex at (0, 0), and opens upward in Quadrants I and II. The Quadrant III portion of the graph of $y = x$ has been "flipped" over the x-axis into Quadrant II. This flip is called a **reflection**, and the x-axis is called the **line of reflection**.

If you fold the graph of $y = |x|$ along the y-axis, the Quadrant I portion will fit exactly over the Quadrant II portion. The graph is said to have **line symmetry**, and the y-axis is the **line of symmetry**.

A **translation** of a graph is a slide or shift that produces the same graph in a new position. For example, when a number is added to or subtracted from the right side of the equation $y = |x|$, a *vertical shift* occurs.

The simplest form of a function is called a **parent function**. For linear functions, $y = x$ is the parent function, and for absolute value functions, $y = |x|$ is the parent function.

EXAMPLE 1

Graph each equation. Identify its vertex and line of symmetry from the graph.

a. $y = |x| + 2$ **b.** $y = |x| - 3$

Solution

a.

x	y
−4	6
−2	4
0	2
2	4
4	6

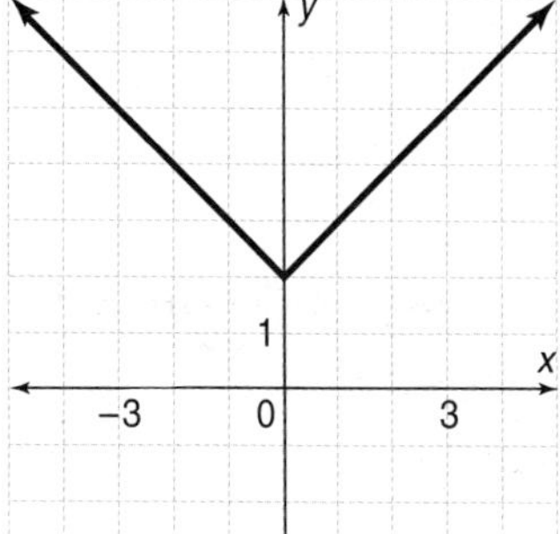

Vertex: (0, 2)
Line of symmetry: y-axis

b.

x	y
−4	1
−2	−1
0	−3
2	−1
4	1

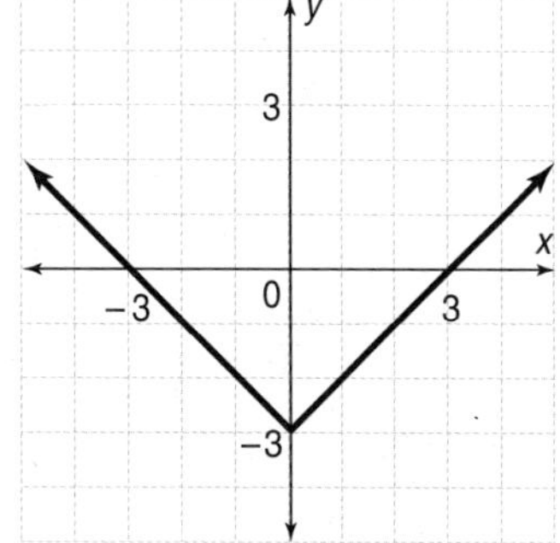

Vertex: (0, −3)
Line of symmetry: y-axis

VERTICAL SHIFT

The graph of $y = |x| + c$ is shifted c units *up* from the graph of $y = |x|$ when c is positive and c units *down* when c is negative.

When a number is added to or subtracted from x within the absolute value bars of the equation $y = |x|$, a *horizontal shift* occurs.

COMMUNICATING ABOUT ALGEBRA

Discuss whether or not the graph of an absolute value equation could be nonsymmetric.

Possible answer: The graph would be nonsymmetric if the domain were restricted to all nonnegative values or all nonpositive values.

PROBLEM SOLVING TIP

You can use a table of values to help you plot the graph.

CHECK UNDERSTANDING

Locate any lines of symmetry in the photo of the suspension bridge. Can you also locate any part of the bridge tower structure that resembles the absolute value graph?

Answers will vary. A possible line of symmetry is a vertical line through the center of the tower of the bridge. Absolute value graph shapes can be seen in the structure of the bridge.

1 MOTIVATE

Explore After students do the activities, ask them to fold their papers along the x-axis and trace triangle $A'B'C'$ in Quadrant III. Have them label the vertices of the new triangle A'', B'', and C''. Their graphs should show the reflection of triangle $A'B'C'$ over the x-axis. Ask them to describe the relationship of the points A' and A'', of B' and B'', and of C' and C'' to the x-axis. **Each point of each pair of points is the same distance from the x-axis.** Ask students to show what will happen if they reflect triangle ABC over the x-axis and reflect triangle $A''B''C''$ over the y-axis. **Both reflections should yield the same triangle.**

2 TEACH

Use the Pages/Build Understanding Ask students what they remember about a function. **For every value of x there is exactly one value of y.** Have them show that $f(x) = |x|$ is a function. **Students may show the vertical line test on the graph.** Ask students what the line of reflection is in Explore. **y-axis** Ask them what the line of symmetry is in Explore. **y-axis** Ask students to describe what a translation of the original triangle in Explore might look like. **The triangle will be in a new position.**

Example 1: Ask students to name other points on the graph of $y = |x| + 2$. **Possible points are (1, 3), (−1, 3), (3, 5), and (−3, 5).** Ask how the graph of $y = |x| + 2$ compares with the graph of $y = |x|$. **It is shifted 2 units up.** Ask how the graph of $y = |x| - 3$ compares with the graph of $y = |x|$. **It is shifted 3 units down.** Be sure students understand that in the equation $y = |x| + c$ the plus sign preserves the intuitive connection of positive with up and negative with down when $c > 0$.

Example 2: Ask students to name points on the graph of $y = |x + 3|$. **Possible points are (–1, 2), (–2, 1), (–4, 1), (2, 5), (1, 4), and (3, 6).** Ask students how the graph of $y = |x + 3|$ compares with the graph of $y = |x|$. **It is shifted 3 units to the left.** Ask how the graph of $y = |x - 1|$ compares with the graph of $y = |x|$. **It is shifted 1 unit to the right.**

DIVERSITY IN THE CLASSROOM

ESL/LEP Students Some students may have difficulty in distinguishing the terms *vertical* and *horizontal.* They may find it helpful to remember that horizontal "models" the horizon. It stretches away to the right and to the left of the position of the viewer. Thus, a horizontal shift moves from right to left or left to right.

Example 3: Ask students to name points on the graphs of $y = 2|x|$, $y = 1/2|x|$, and $y = -|x|$. **Possible points are (–2, 4), (–1, 2), (0, 0), (1, 2), and (2, 4); (–4, 2), (–2, 1), (0, 0), (2, 1), and (4, 2); (–4, –4), (–2, –2), (0, 0), (2, –2), and (4, –4)** Ask students to describe what they think the graph of $y = -2|x|$ looks like. **The graph of $y = -2|x|$ is the reflection of $y = 2|x|$ over the *x*-axis; it is V-shaped and opens downward.** Ask students to give an example of an absolute value function whose graph is steeper than the graph of $y = |x|$. **Accept any equations $y = a|x - b| + c$ for any real numbers *b* and *c* and for $a > 1$.** Ask them to give an example of an absolute value function whose graph opens downward. **Accept any equations $y = a|x + b| + c$ for any real numbers *b* and *c* and for $a < 0$.**

CHECK UNDERSTANDING

Write an equation for an absolute value function whose graph is shifted right 4 units and up 3 units from the graph of $y = |x|$.

$y = |x - 4| + 3$

ALGEBRA: WHO, WHERE, WHEN

One of the earliest known uses of transformations occurs in an Egyptian mathematical scroll called the Rhind papyrus (1650 B.C.). Some of the material is thought to have been handed down from the architect Imhotep (ca. 3000 B.C.).

EXAMPLE 2

Graph each equation. Identify its vertex and line of symmetry from the graph.

a. $y = |x + 3|$ **b.** $y = |x - 1|$

Solution

a.

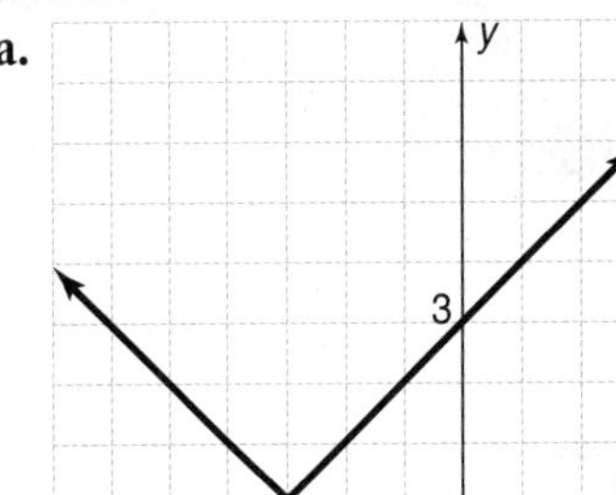

Vertex: (–3, 0)
Line of symmetry: $x = -3$

b.

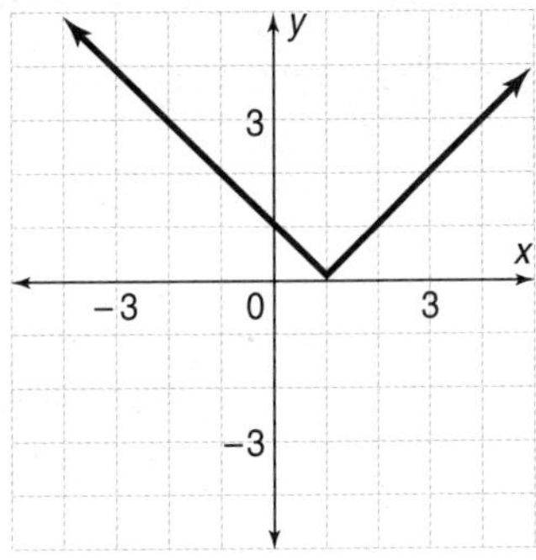

Vertex: (1, 0)
Line of symmetry: $x = 1$

HORIZONTAL SHIFT

The graph of $y = |x - b|$ is shifted *b* units to the *right* from the graph of $y = |x|$ when *b* is positive and *b* units to the *left* when *b* is negative.

The translations you have seen in this lesson are two types of **transformations**. A third type of transformation occurs in equations of the form $y = a|x|$.

EXAMPLE 3

Graph each equation. Tell how each graph differs from the graph of $y = |x|$.

a. $y = 2|x|$ **b.** $y = \frac{1}{2}|x|$ **c.** $y = -|x|$

Solution

a.

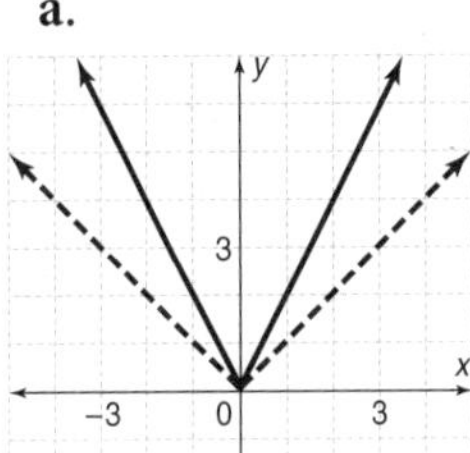

b.

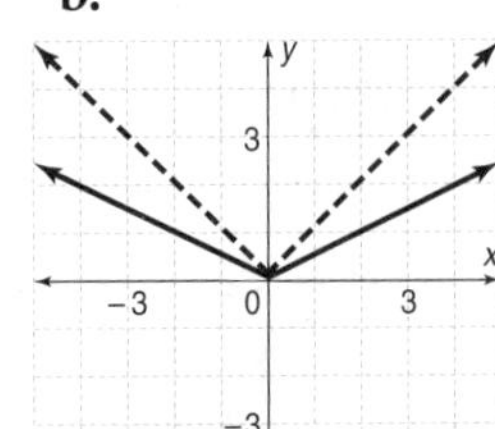

c.

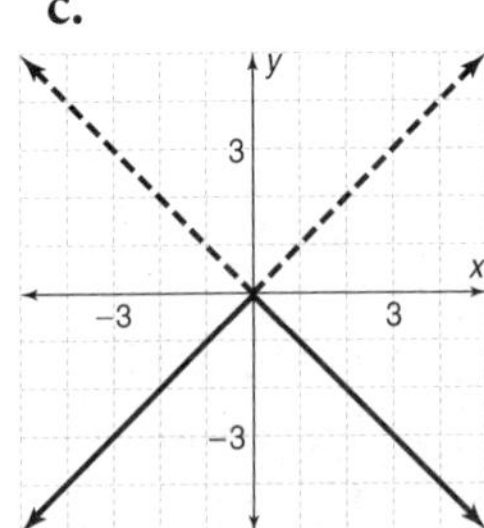

a. The graph of $y = 2|x|$ is V-shaped, but the rays that form the V are farther away from the *x*-axis than those of $y = |x|$.

b. The graph of $y = \frac{1}{2}|x|$ is V-shaped, but the rays that form the V are closer to the x–axis than those of $y = |x|$.

c. The graph of $y = -|x|$ is the reflection of the graph of $y = |x|$ over the x-axis. It is V-shaped and opens downward. ◀

All three types of transformations may occur in one equation of the form $y = a|x - b| + c$. You can determine the x-coordinate of the vertex of the graph by setting the expression within the absolute value bars equal to zero and solving for x.

$$x - b = 0$$
$$x = b \quad \text{Solve for } x.$$

To determine the y-coordinate of the vertex, substitute this value of x into the original absolute value equation and solve for y.

If the vertex of an absolute value graph is at (b, c), then the equation of the line of symmetry is $x = b$.

COMMUNICATING ABOUT ALGEBRA

The graphs of the equations in Example 3 show different V-shapes. Explain what effect the value of a has on the shape of the graph $y = a|x|$.

The greater the value of the coefficient a, the narrower the V. The closer the value of the coefficient is to 0, the wider the V. When $a < 0$, the graph points downward.

EXAMPLE 4

Graph $y = 3|x + 2| + 1$ and indicate how it differs from the graph of $y = |x|$. Identify its vertex, line of symmetry, and shape.

Solution

The graph of $y = 3|x + 2| + 1$ has been shifted up one unit and to the left by two units. It is V-shaped, but the rays that form the V are farther away from the x-axis.

To find the x-coordinate of the vertex, set the expression inside the absolute value symbol equal to zero and solve for x.

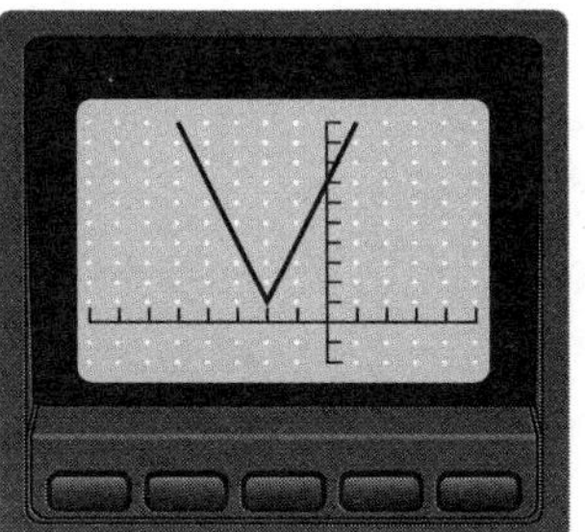

$$x + 2 = 0$$
$$x = -2$$

To find the y-coordinate, substitute the x-coordinate into the original equation and solve for y.

$$y = 3|-2 + 2| + 1$$
$$y = 1$$

So, the vertex is $(-2, 1)$, the line of symmetry is $x = -2$, and the graph is V-shaped with its sides farther from the x-axis than the graph of $y = |x|$. ◀

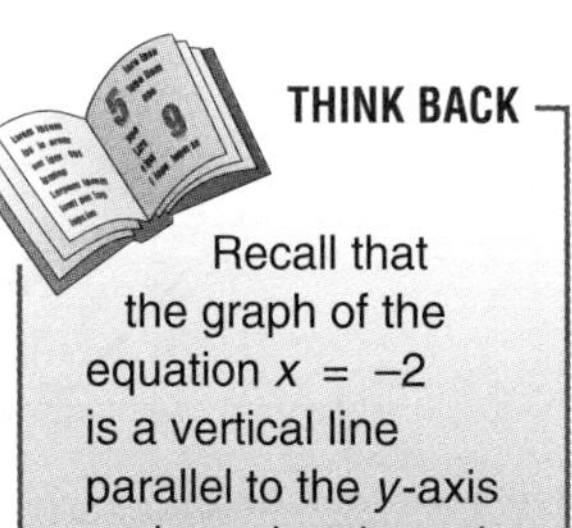

THINK BACK

Recall that the graph of the equation $x = -2$ is a vertical line parallel to the y-axis and passing through $(-2, 0)$.

You can use the skills you developed in this lesson to determine the equation of an absolute value graph.

Example 4: Ask students to name some points on the graph of $y = 3|x + 2| + 1$. **Possible points are (0, 7), (–1, 4), (–2, 1), (–3, 4), and (–4, 7).** Ask students to describe what they think the graph of $y = 3|x + 2|$ looks like. **the same as the graph of $y = 3|x + 2| + 1$ but shifted 1 unit down with a vertex of (–2, 0)**

Example 5: Have students describe what each graph looks like as compared to the graph of $y = |x|$. **$y = |x| + 4$: the graph is shifted up 4 units; $y = -|x - 4|$: the graph is shifted to the right 4 units and opens downward; $y = -|x| + 4$: the graph is shifted 4 units up and opens downward; $y = -|x + 4|$: the graph is shifted to the left 4 units and opens downward**

Ongoing Assessment The important concepts and skills are determining vertices and lines of symmetry of absolute value functions, matching equations with graphs, and graphing absolute value functions using a table of values or a graphing utility. To assess these ideas, have students demonstrate how they have applied these concepts and skills in Exercises 2, 14, 15, and 17 of the Try These section.

Guided Practice/Try These For Exercises 9–12, ask students what the vertex is of each graph. **The vertex for each is (0, 0).** For Exercises 13–16, ask students which equations indicate a vertical shift and which indicate a horizontal shift. In which direction? How many units? **vertical shift up 2 units: $y = |x| + 2$; vertical shift down 2 units: $y = |x| - 2$; horizontal shift left 2 units: $y = |x + 2|$; horizontal shift right 2 units: $y = |x - 2|$**

3 SUMMARIZE

In the Math Journal Have students describe how to graph an absolute value function using a table of values and how to graph an absolute value function using transformations of the graph of $y = |x|$. **Answers will vary.** Have them choose the method they prefer and graph $y = 4|x - 1|$.

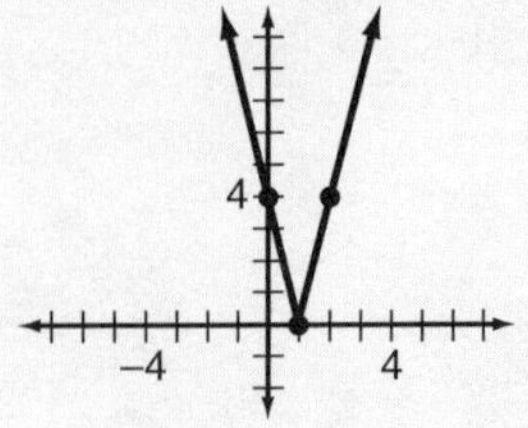

EXAMPLE 5

ENGINEERING A truss is a framework of beams that supports a bridge or roof. The triangular truss in the graph at the right can be represented by an absolute value equation. Which of the following equations represents the graph?

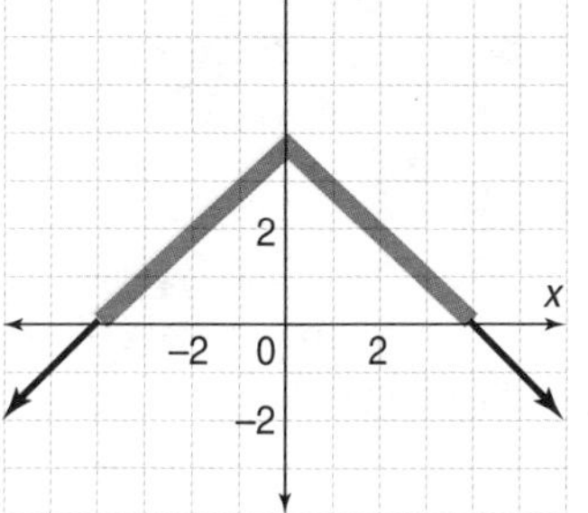

a. $y = |x| + 4$ **b.** $y = -|x - 4|$

c. $y = -|x| + 4$ **d.** $y = -|x + 4|$

Solution

The vertex of the graph is at (0, 4). There is no horizontal shift. Only options a and c do not have a horizontal shift. The graph opens downward, so there must be a negative sign in front of the absolute value bars. The correct answer is c. Check by graphing the equation. ◄

TRY THESE

Determine the vertex and line of symmetry for the graph of each equation.

1. $y = |x - 2.5|$ (2.5, 0); $x = 2.5$
2. $y = |x + 4|$ (−4, 0); $x = -4$
3. $y = |x| - 1.5$ (0, −1.5); $x = 0$
4. $y = |x| + 2.5$ (0, 2.5); $x = 0$
5. $y = |x + 4| - 9$ (−4, −9); $x = -4$
6. $y = |x - 3| - 3$ (3, −3); $x = 3$
7. $y = -|x + 3| - 1$ (−3, −1); $x = -3$
8. $y = -|x - 1| + 2$ (1, 2); $x = 1$

Tell how each graph differs from the graph of $y = |x|$. See Additional Answers.

9. $y = 4|x|$
10. $y = \frac{1}{4}|x|$
11. $y = -2|x|$
12. $y = -\frac{1}{2}|x|$

Match each equation with its graph.

13. $y = |x + 2|$ d
14. $y = |x| + 2$ c
15. $y = |x - 2|$ a
16. $y = |x| - 2$ b

a.

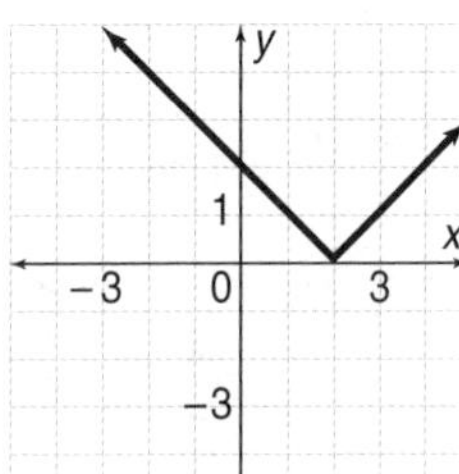

b.

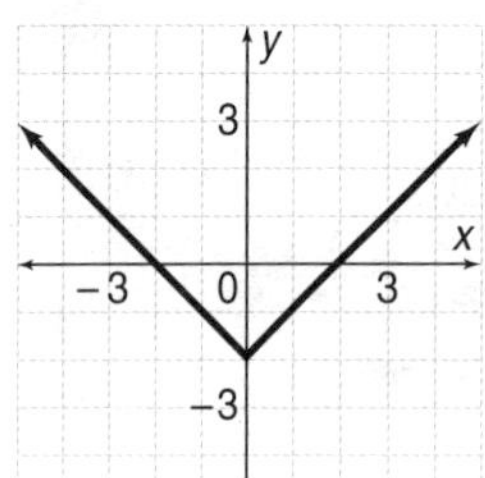

c. **d.**

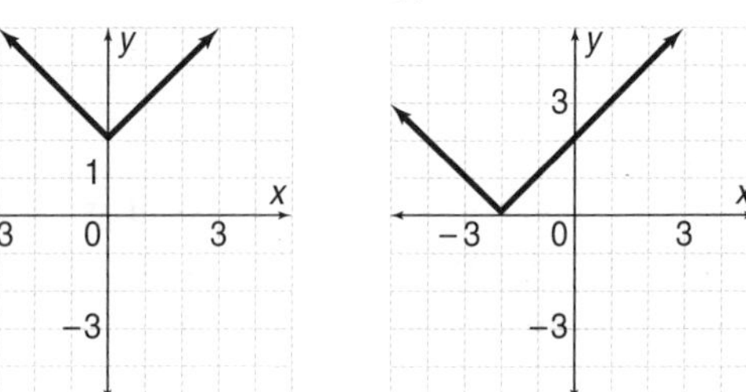

Graph each equation. See Additional Answers.

17. $y = |x - 2| + 3$
18. $y = |x + 1| - \frac{1}{2}$
19. $y = 2|x + 1.5|$
20. $y = -2|x - 1.5|$

21. WRITING MATHEMATICS Write an equation that represents the graph of the equation $y = |x|$ shifted 2 units to the right and 8 units downward. $y = |x - 2| - 8$

22. WRITING MATHEMATICS Explain how the graph of $y = a|x - b| + c$ differs from the graph of $y = |x|$. Answers will vary.

PRACTICE

Determine the vertex and the line of symmetry for the graph of each equation.

1. $y = |x| - 4$ (0, −4); $x = 0$

2. $y = |x| + 5$ (0, 5); $x = 0$

3. $y = |x - 1.5|$ (1.5, 0); $x = 1.5$

4. $y = |x + 0.5|$ (−0.5, 0); $x = -0.5$

5. $y = |x - 4| - 3$ (4, −3); $x = 4$

6. $y = |x + 3| - 3$ (−3, −3); $x = -3$

7. $y = -|x + 1| - 2$ (−1, −2); $x = -1$

8. $y = -|x - 3| + 2$ (3, 2); $x = 3$

Explain how the graph of each equation differs from the graph of $y = |x|$. See Additional Answers.

9. $y = 3|x|$

10. $y = \frac{1}{3}|x|$

11. $y = -\frac{1}{5}|x|$

12. $y = -5|x|$

Match each equation with its graph.

13. $y = |x + 1|$ b

14. $y = |x| + 1$ d

15. $y = |x - 1|$ c

16. $y = |x| - 1$ a

a.

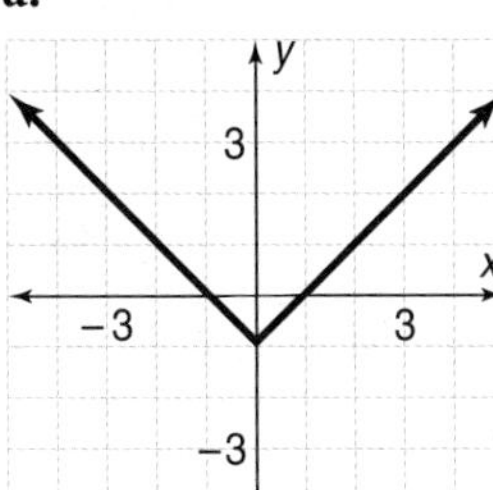

b.

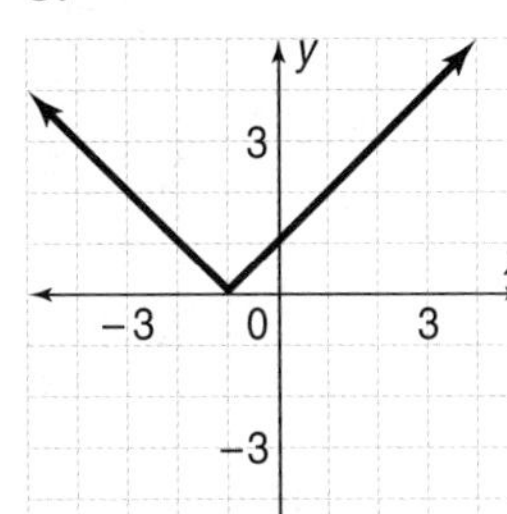

c.

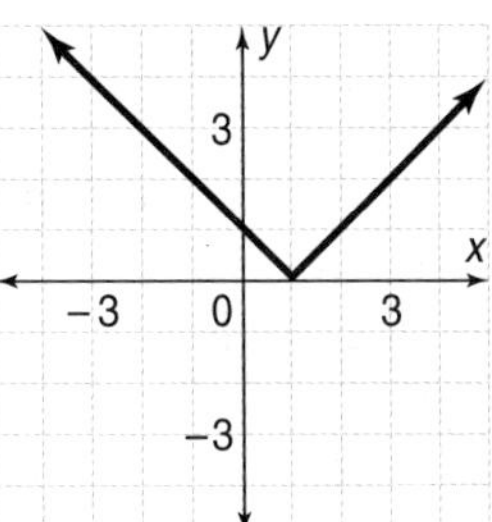

d.

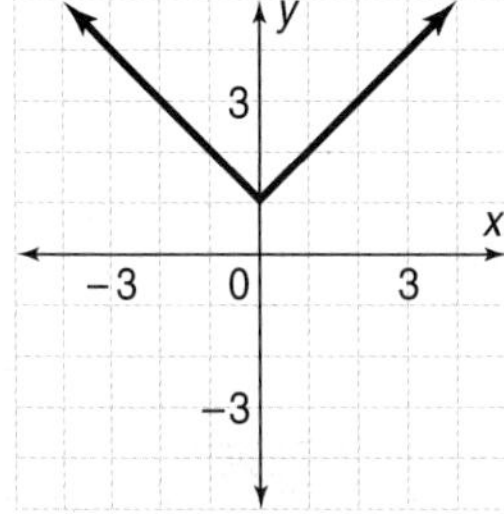

Match each equation with its graph.

17. $y = |x + 2| - 3$ d

18. $y = -|x - 3| + 2$ b

19. $y = -|x + 2| + 3$ a

20. $y = |x + 3| - 2$ c

a.

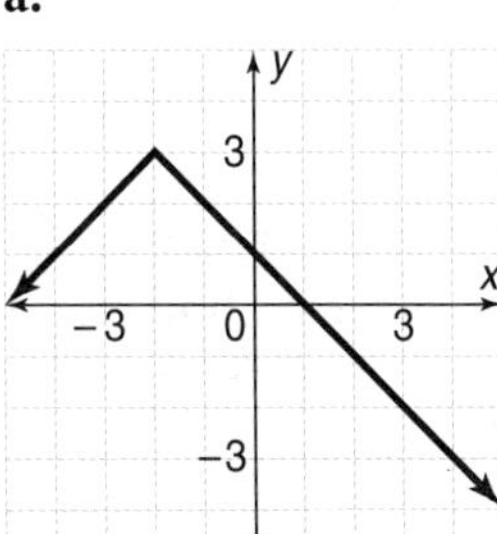

b.

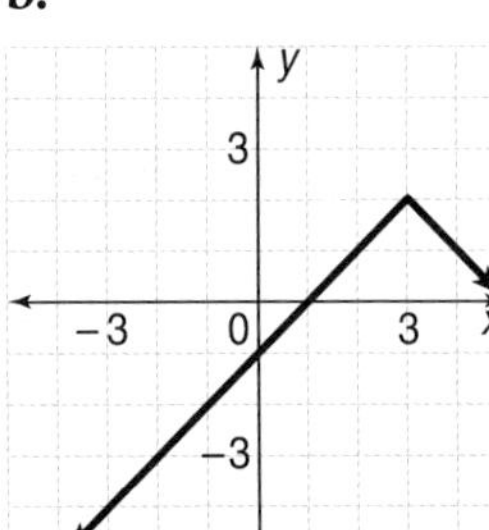

c.

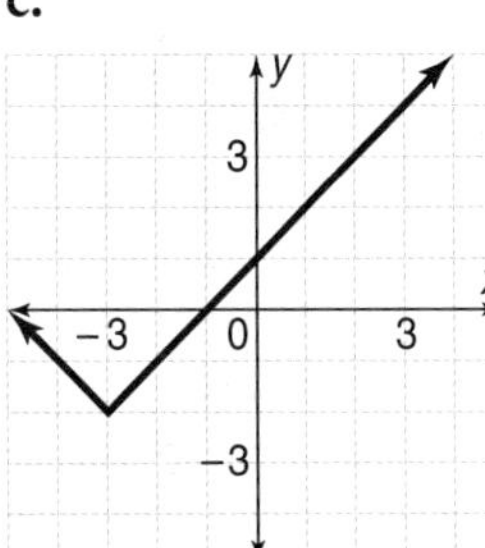

d.

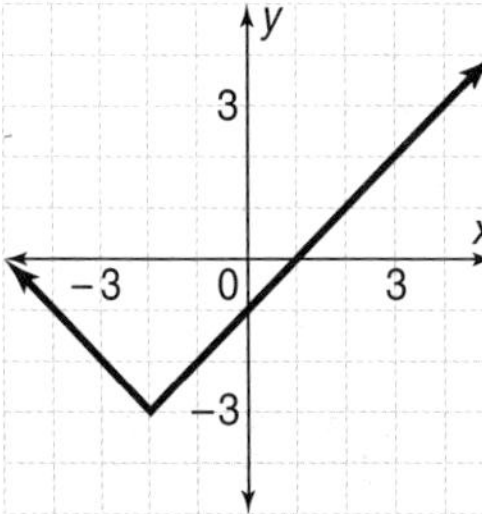

Graph each equation. See Additional Answers.

21. $y = |x - 3| + 2$

22. $y = |x + 2| - 2$

23. $y = 2|x - 2.5|$

24. $y = 0.5|x - 2| - 1.5$

25. $y = -2|x + 0.5|$

26. $y = 3|x + 3| + 3$

27. $y = 2|x - 2| - 2$

28. $y = -\frac{1}{2}|x + 2.5| - 1$

29. WRITING MATHEMATICS Write an equation of the form $y = a|x - b| + c$ that reflects the graph of $y = |x|$ over the x-axis and then moves it 5 units right and 2 units down. $y = -|x - 5| - 2$

30. WRITING MATHEMATICS The graph of the equation $y = a|x|$ has a right angle at its vertex when $a = 1$. For what values of a will the vertex angle be acute and when will it be obtuse? Explain your reasoning. See Additional Answers.

4 PRACTICE

Practice For Exercises 13–16, remind students that each graph is a vertical or horizontal shift of the graph $y = |x|$ in a particular direction. Ask students how Exercises 17–20 differ from Exercises 13–16. **In Exercises 17–20 each graph is the result of both a horizontal and a vertical shift of the graph $y = |x|$; those in Exercises 13–16 are the result of either a vertical or a horizontal shift.** Suggest that students graph at least some of the Exercises 21–28 using a table of values and then have them check their answers using a graphing utility. For Exercise 29, point out that the new graph involves three transformations—two translations (a vertical shift and a horizontal shift) and a reflection.

Extend For Exercise 43, ask students if there are any other lines of symmetry and what they might be. **Yes, there are infinitely many; any line which passes through the center of the circle.**

NAME ______________ CLASS ________ DATE ________

9.2 GRAPH ABSOLUTE VALUE FUNCTIONS

The absolute value function is graphed using the equation $y = |x|$. This graph forms a 90° angle, a **V**. The y-axis is a line of symmetry and the point of the **V** is the vertex of the graph. It is transformed by moving the vertex up or down (vertical shift) or right or left (horizontal shift) and by changing the width or the direction of the **V**.

Example 1

Graph $y = |x| - 4$.

Identify its vertex and line of symmetry.

Solution

x	y
−4	0
0	−4
4	0

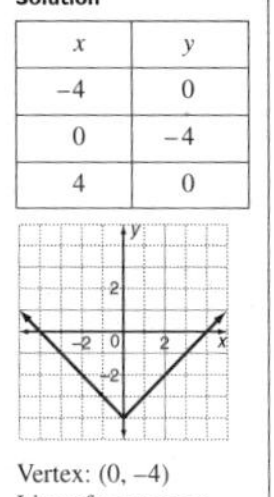

Vertex: (0, −4)
Line of symmetry: y-axis

Example 2

Graph $y = |x - 4|$.

Identify its vertex and line of symmetry.

Solution

x	y
−4	8
0	4
4	0

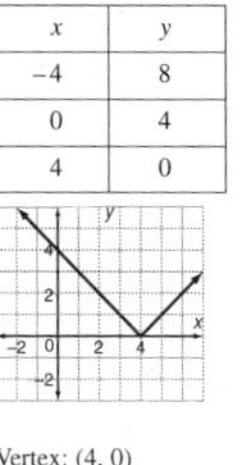

Vertex: (4, 0)
Line of symmetry: $x = 4$

Example 3

Graph $y = -\frac{1}{4}|x|$.

Tell how it differs from that of $y = |x|$.

Solution

x	y
−4	−1
0	0
4	−1

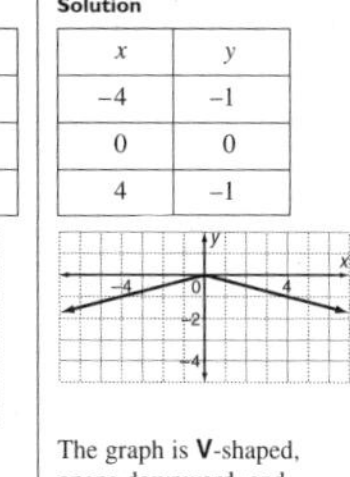

The graph is **V**-shaped, opens downward, and the rays of the **V** are closer to the x-axis.

EXERCISES

Identify the vertex and line of symmetry for the graph of each equation.

1. $y = |x| + 3$

2. $y = |x| - 2.5$

3. $y = |x - 2|$

4. $y = -|x + 2| - 4$

1. (0, 3); $x = 0$
2. (0, −2.5); $x = 0$
3. (2, 0); $x = 2$
4. (0, −4); $x = -2$

6 *South-Western Algebra 1: AN INTEGRATED APPROACH*

Think Critically For Exercise 47, ask students how the graph of $y = |x|$ differs from the graph of $y = |-x|$. **It is exactly the same since absolute value function makes all *y*-values positive.** For Exercise 49, have students discuss why the graphs are not the same. **The negative sign is negated when inside the absolute value symbol but is not when outside it.**

5 FOLLOW-UP

Extension Have students graph the equation $y = ||x| - 4|$. Tell students to first graph the equation $y = |x| - 4$. Then have them use reasoning about absolute values to complete the graph. **Students should reason that the negative values of *y* of the graph of $y = |x| - 4$ become positive when the absolute value function is applied. Thus, positive *y*-values remain positive and negative *y*-values become positive, as well.**

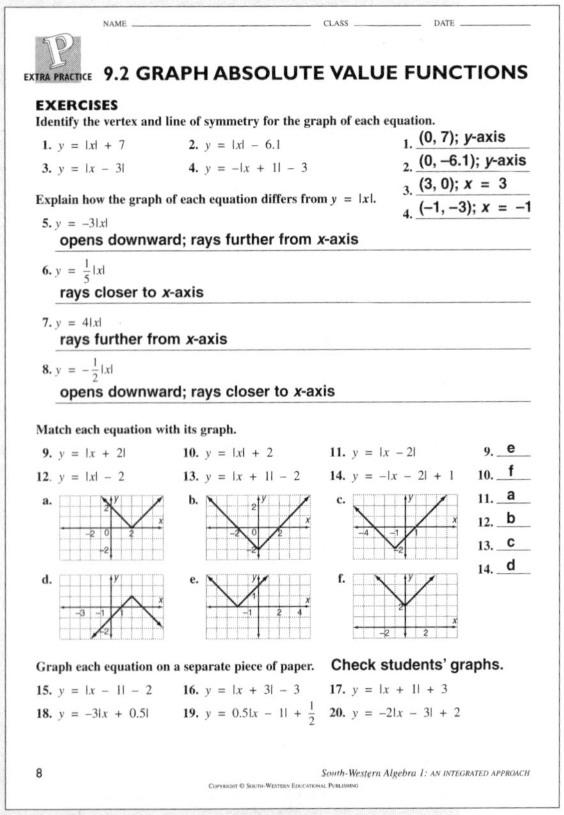

NAME ______________ CLASS ________ DATE ________

EXTRA PRACTICE **9.2 GRAPH ABSOLUTE VALUE FUNCTIONS**

EXERCISES

Identify the vertex and line of symmetry for the graph of each equation.

1. $y = |x| + 7$ **2.** $y = |x| - 6.1$

3. $y = |x - 3|$ **4.** $y = -|x + 1| - 3$

1. (0, 7); *y*-axis
2. (0, –6.1); *y*-axis
3. (3, 0); $x = 3$
4. (–1, –3); $x = -1$

Explain how the graph of each equation differs from $y = |x|$.

5. $y = -3|x|$
opens downward; rays further from *x*-axis

6. $y = \frac{1}{5}|x|$
rays closer to *x*-axis

7. $y = 4|x|$
rays further from *x*-axis

8. $y = -\frac{1}{2}|x|$
opens downward; rays closer to *x*-axis

Match each equation with its graph.

9. $y = |x + 2|$ **10.** $y = |x| + 2$ **11.** $y = |x - 2|$

12. $y = |x| - 2$ **13.** $y = |x + 1| - 2$ **14.** $y = -|x - 2| + 1$

a. b. c. d. e. f.

9. e
10. f
11. a
12. b
13. c
14. d

Graph each equation on a separate piece of paper. Check students' graphs.

15. $y = |x - 1| - 2$ **16.** $y = |x + 3| - 3$ **17.** $y = |x + 1| + 3$

18. $y = -3|x + 0.5|$ **19.** $y = 0.5|x - 1| + \frac{1}{2}$ **20.** $y = -2|x - 3| + 2$

8 *South-Western Algebra 1: AN INTEGRATED APPROACH*

Write an equation that represents each graph. (*Hint:* Find the value of x when $y = 0$. Use that value to find a.)

31.

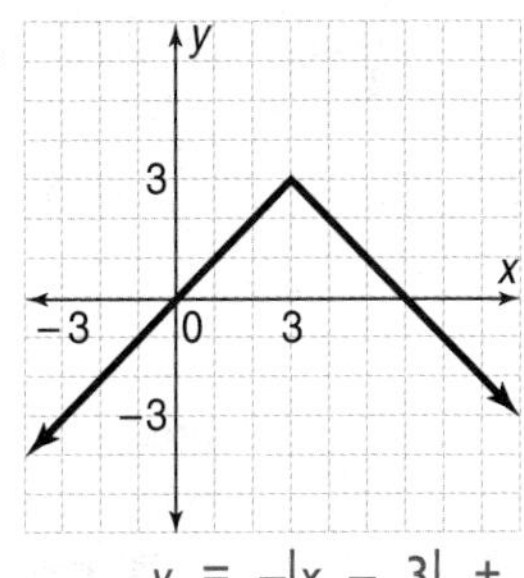

$y = -|x - 3| + 3$

32.

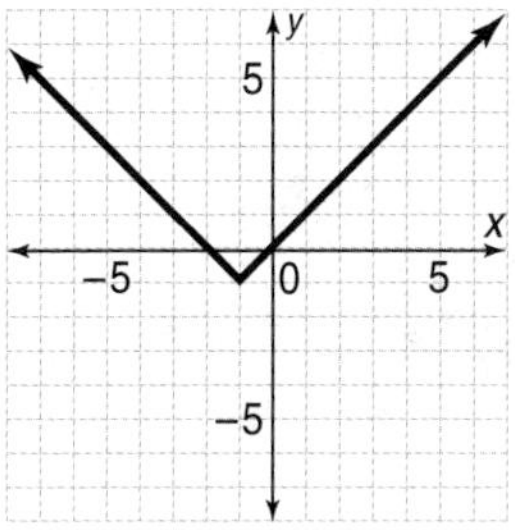

$y = |x + 1| - 1$

33. FASHION DESIGN The width of neckties that are considered fashionable changes frequently. As the width of a tie changes, the V at the bottom of the tie changes. Ties may be designed using a grid such as the one shown with three ties. Write an absolute value equation for the triangular shape at the bottom of each tie.

A: $y = |x| - 3$, B: $y = 2|x| - 3$, C: $y = 3|x| - 3$

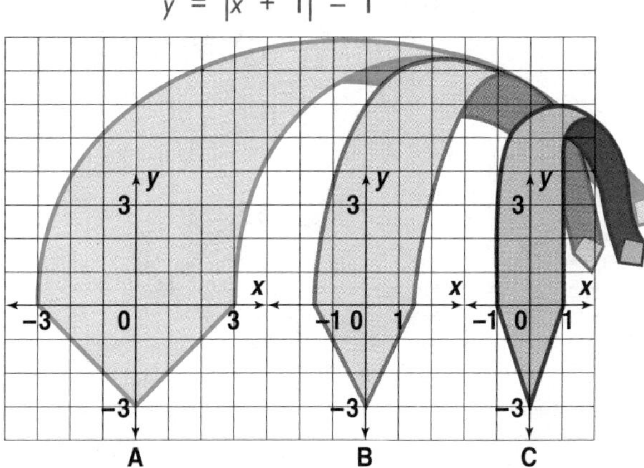

EXTEND

34. TECHNOLOGY Use a graphing utility to estimate the coordinates of the points at which the graphs of $y = |2x|$ and $y = -|2x| + 2$ intersect. (–0.5, 1); (0.5, 1)

35. TECHNOLOGY Use a graphing utility to estimate the coordinates of the points at which the graphs of $y = |2x| - 1$ and $y = -|2x| + 3$ intersect. (–1, 1); (1, 1)

INTERNATIONAL FLAGS The graphs of the absolute value equations in this lesson have vertical lines of symmetry of the form $x = r$, where r is a real number. If you graph $y = |x|$ and $y = -|x|$ on the same coordinate plane, the x- and y-axes are both lines of symmetry. Some figures have the line $y = x$ as a line of symmetry. Flags from six different countries are shown below. Imagine a flag is placed on a coordinate plane where the center of the flag is at (0, 0). Determine the line or lines of symmetry for each flag.

36. Vietnam *y*-axis

37. Israel *x*-axis, *y*-axis

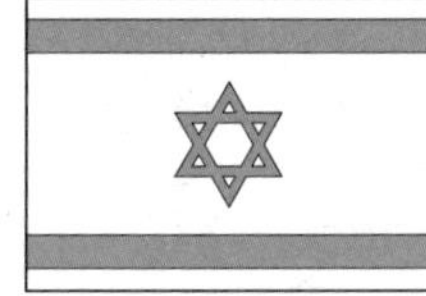

38. Finland *x*-axis

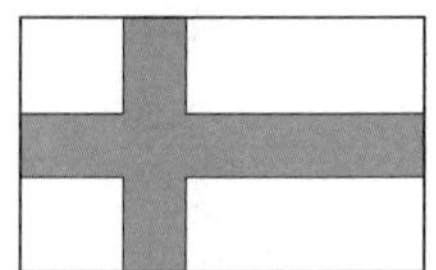

39. Switzerland

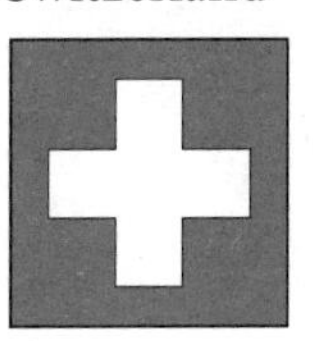

x-axis, *y*-axis, $y = x$, $y = -x$

40. Rwanda none

41. Nigeria *x*-axis, *y*-axis

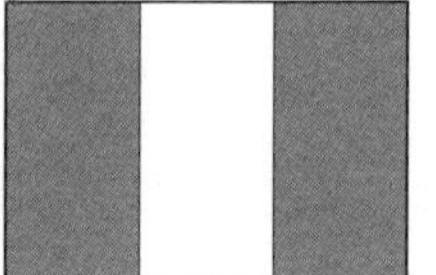

GEOMETRY Copy each figure. Then draw and/or describe all the lines of symmetry. See Additional Answers.

42. 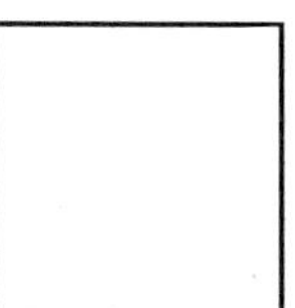 **43.** **44.** **45.** 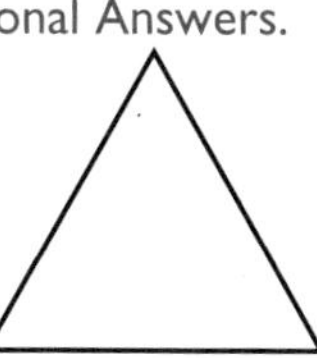 **46.**

THINK CRITICALLY

47. Graph $y = -x$ and $y = |-x|$. What portion of the graph of $y = -x$ must be reflected to obtain the graph of $y = |-x|$? What is the line of reflection? the portion in Quadrant IV is reflected into Quadrant I; x-axis

48. Graph $y = -x$ and $y = -|x|$. What portion of the graph of $y = -x$ must be reflected to obtain the graph of $y = -|x|$? What is the line of reflection? the portion in Quadrant II is reflected into Quadrant III; x-axis

49. The graph of $y = |2x|$ is the same as the graph of $y = 2|x|$. Is it also true that the graph of $y = |-2x|$ is the same as the graph of $y = -2|x|$? Verify your solution. no

50. Do the graphs of $y = -3x$ and $y = |-3x|$ ever overlap? Write the equation of another graph, half of which overlaps the graph of $y = -3x$. yes; possible answers: $y = -|3x|$ and $y = |3x|$

51. Write the equation of an absolute value function that intersects the graph of $y = |x|$ in exactly two points. answers will vary; possible answer: $y = -|x| + 1$

52. Write the equation of an absolute value function that does not intersect the graph of $y = -|x|$. answers will vary; possible answer: $y = -|x| + 1$

PROJECT *Connection*

In this activity, you will graph the distance between your home and school compared to the time you spend traveling.

1. Use the actual route, method of travel, and distance you determined earlier. Decide on the equal time intervals (such as every 5 min) you will use to record distances. Estimate the distance you have traveled at each time interval. Record each distance on your way to school and on your way home as a distance from home. Travel the same route each way. Record each time as total time you spend traveling so when you start home add to the amount of time you had previously.
2. Graph the data. Show time on the horizontal axis and distance from school on the vertical axis. Do the points for each part of the round trip lie on or near a straight line? If not, explain why.
Points will not be linear if rate of travel varied.
3. Draw a line connecting your starting point to the school point. Draw another line connecting the school point to the home point again. Describe the graph. Compare your graph with those of other group members.

Answers will vary.

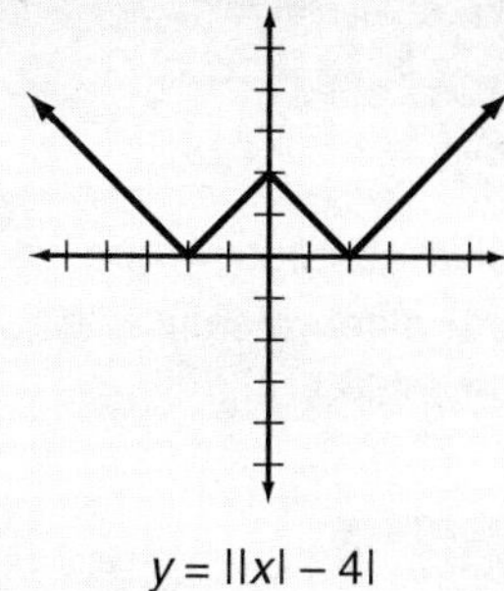

$y = ||x| - 4|$

Project Connection This activity presents further aspects of the project introduced on page 412. Have students discuss ways they can measure distance when they are not traveling by car.

NAME ______ CLASS ______ DATE ______

ENRICHMENT **9.2 GRAPH ABSOLUTE VALUE FUNCTIONS**

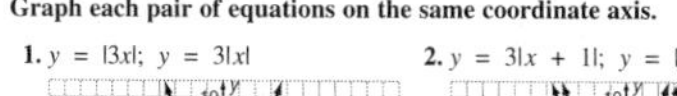

Graph each pair of equations on the same coordinate axis.

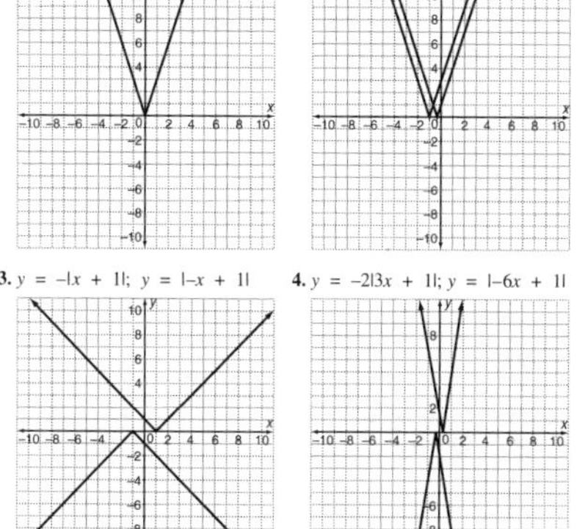

1. $y = |3x|$; $y = 3|x|$ **2.** $y = 3|x + 1|$; $y = |3x + 1|$

3. $y = -|x + 1|$; $y = |-x + 1|$ **4.** $y = -2|3x + 1|$; $y = |-6x + 1|$

5. In Exercise 1, how did the two equations compare?
The graphs of the two equations are exactly the same.

6. In Exercises 2–4, how does the coefficient outside the absolute value sign affect the graph of an equation?
The distance of the rays from the *x*-axis does not change. Only the vertex changes, and if the coefficient is negative, the direction of the graph as well.

7. What is the vertex of the graph of an absolute value function of the form $y = |cx + b|$?
$(-b/c, 0)$

10 *South-Western Algebra 1: AN INTEGRATED APPROACH*

LESSON PLANNING

Objective

- ▶ Solve absolute value equations both algebraically and by using a graphing utility.

Vocabulary
disjunction

Technology/Multimedia
graphing utility

Resources
Warm Up 9.3
Reteaching 9.3
Extra Practice 9.3
Enrichment 9.3
Transparencies 34, 53–56, 78–80
Student Handbook
Lesson Quiz 9.3

Materials/Manipulatives
uncooked spaghetti

ASSIGNMENTS

Basic: 1–20, 22–26, 28–33, 35–36, 38–39, 41–42, 44, Project Connection 1–4

Average: 4–33, 35–45, Project Connection 1–4

Enriched: 4–47, Project Connection 1–4

1 MOTIVATE

Explore This section will help students understand that absolute value represents a distance. After students have answered Questions 1 and 2, ask them to describe what is meant by a line of symmetry of an absolute value equation in two variables. **It is a line equidistant from each**

9.3 Absolute Value Equations

SPOTLIGHT ON LEARNING

WHAT? In this lesson you will learn

- to solve absolute value equations both algebraically and by using a graphing utility.

WHY? Solving absolute value equations can help you solve problems involving radiology, science, health and fitness, economics, and veterinary medicine.

Explore

1. Use a straightedge and graph paper to make two identical number lines that extend from –5 to 5 in increments of 1 unit. Cut out the number lines as shown below. Label one number line as the "zero finder" and the other as the "solution finder." Obtain two pieces of uncooked spaghetti.

2. Use the number lines and spaghetti to solve the equation $|x - 2| = 3$ in the following manner.

   a. Set $x - 2$, the expression within the absolute value bars, equal to zero to obtain $x = 2$.

   b. Align the 2 on the second number line with the 0 on the zero finder.

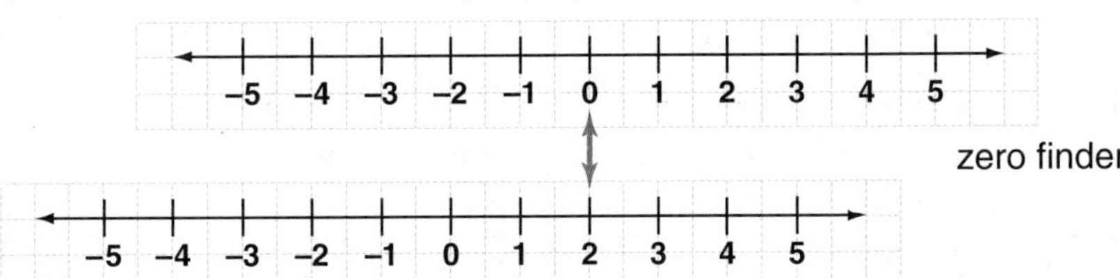

   c. Since you are looking for numbers that are 3 units from $|x - 2|$, place a piece of spaghetti vertically on 3 in the zero finder. Place another piece of spaghetti vertically on –3 on the zero finder.

   d. The pieces of spaghetti intersect the solution finder at $x = -1$ and $x = 5$. These values are the solutions to the equation $|x - 2| = 3$.

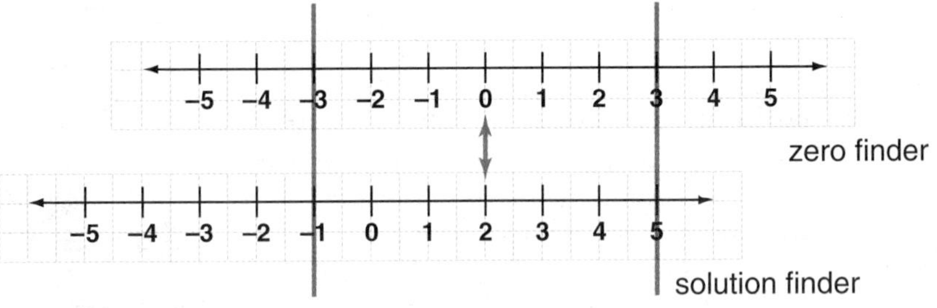

   e. Check the solutions by substituting in the original equation.

3. Work in the same way to solve $|x + 1| = 2$. What numbers do the pieces of spaghetti cross on the solution finder? 1, –3

Build Understanding

In the previous lesson you found the line of symmetry for two-variable absolute value equations. In Explore you found the *point of symmetry* for one-variable absolute value equations by setting the absolute value expression equal to zero and finding equal distances from both sides of the point of symmetry to solve the original equation.

Recall that the absolute value of a number x is the distance between x and 0 on a number line. Since distance is positive, the absolute value of an expression must be positive. For example, the distance between 0 and 2 is 2, so $|2| = 2$. Since distance is positive, the distance between 0 and –2 is also 2, and $|-2| = 2$.

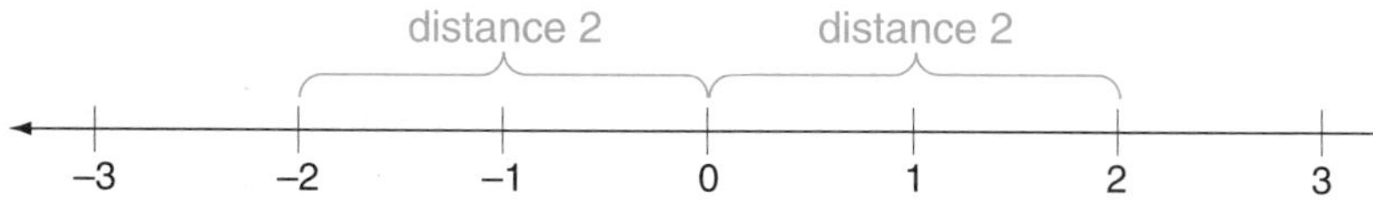

An algebraic way to state this is

$$|x| = x \quad \text{if } x \geq 0 \qquad \text{and} \qquad |x| = -x \quad \text{if } x < 0$$

A **disjunction** is two statements joined by the word *or*. A disjunction is true if at least one of the statements is true. The equation $|x| = 5$ is equivalent to the disjunction

$$x = 5 \text{ or } x = -5$$

EXAMPLE 1

Express as a disjunction: $|3x - 5| = 15$

Solution

$$3x - 5 = 15 \quad \text{or} \quad 3x - 5 = -15$$

To solve an absolute value equation, begin by writing it as a disjunction. Then solve the two resulting equations.

EXAMPLE 2

Solve and check: $|2x - 1| = 4$

Solution

$2x - 1 = 4$	or	$2x - 1 = -4$	Write a disjunction.
$2x = 5$	or	$2x = -3$	Add 1 to both sides.
$x = 2.5$	or	$x = -1.5$	Divide both sides by 2.

To check, substitute both solutions into the original equation.

$$|2x - 1| = 4 \qquad\qquad |2x - 1| = 4$$
$$|2(2.5) - 1| \stackrel{?}{=} 4 \qquad\qquad |2(-1.5) - 1| \stackrel{?}{=} 4$$
$$4 = 4 \checkmark \qquad\qquad 4 = 4 \checkmark$$

The solutions are 2.5 and –1.5.

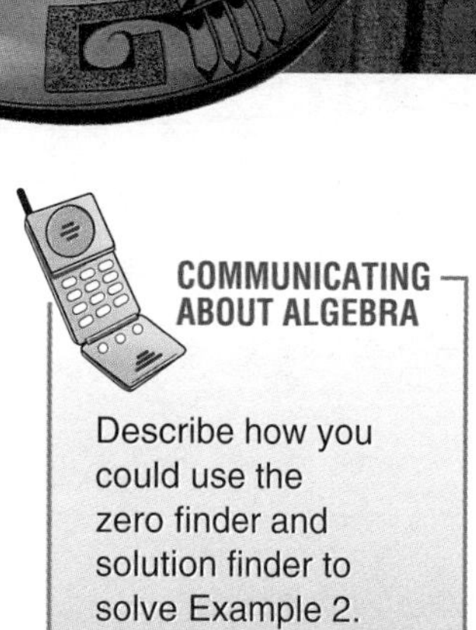

COMMUNICATING ABOUT ALGEBRA

Describe how you could use the zero finder and solution finder to solve Example 2.

See Additional Answers.

solution. Ask them what a point of symmetry might mean. **a point that is equidistant from each solution of an abso-lute value equation with one variable** Ask what the point of symmetry is for the absolute value equation $|x - 2| = 3$. **2** Tell students that the absolute value equation means that the distance between x and 2 is 3.

2 TEACH

Use the Pages/Build Understanding Point out that in Question 2 of Explore, the number 2 on the "zero finder" is the point of symmetry. Ask students what the point of symmetry is for the equation in Question 3. **–1**

Example 1: Have students give examples of an absolute value equation and its disjunction. **possible examples: $|x| = 8$: $x = 8$ or $x = -8$; $|4x - 2| = 1$: $4x - 2 = 1$ or $4x - 2 = -1$**

Example 2: Stress the importance of writing the disjunction and recording the steps as shown in the example. Explain that such a practice will facilitate checking for possible errors and correcting them. Also stress the importance of checking both solutions in the original equation.

Example 3: Stress the importance of first isolating the absolute value part of the equation before writing the disjunction.

Example 4: After students have worked through Example 4 using their graphing utilities, have them read Communicating About Algebra and use their graphing utilities to solve $|2x + 1| = 5$ using the method involv-ing three equations. Then ask them to use their graphing utilities to solve $|-x + 6| = 10$ using whichever method they prefer. **−4, 16**

Example 5: Ask students how they can write the minimum weight and the maximum weight. **110 − 11 = 99 and 110 + 11 = 121** Ask students to name the point of symmetry. **110**

Ongoing Assessment The important concepts and skills are solving absolute value equations algebraically and by using a graphing utility. To assess these ideas have students demonstrate how they have applied these concepts and skills in Exercises 1, 4, and 16 of the Try These section.

To solve some absolute value equations, you must first isolate the expression containing the absolute value symbol.

EXAMPLE 3

Solve and check: $2|2z + 4| - 5 = 11$

Solution

$$2|2z + 4| - 5 = 11$$
$$2|2z + 4| = 16 \quad \text{Add 5 to both sides.}$$
$$|2z + 4| = 8 \quad \text{Divide both sides by 2.}$$

$$2z + 4 = 8 \text{ or } 2z + 4 = -8 \quad \text{Write a disjunction.}$$
$$2z = 4 \text{ or } 2z = -12 \quad \text{Subtract 4 from both sides.}$$
$$z = 2 \text{ or } z = -6 \quad \text{Divide both sides by 2.}$$

To check, substitute both solutions into the original equation.

$$2|2z + 4| - 5 = 11 \qquad 2|2z + 4| - 5 = 11$$
$$2|2(2) + 4| - 5 \stackrel{?}{=} 11 \qquad 2|2(-6) + 4| - 5 \stackrel{?}{=} 11$$
$$11 = 11 ✓ \qquad 11 = 11 ✓$$

The solutions are 2 and −6.

Some absolute value equations have no solution. For example, the absolute value equation $|x + 5| = -3$ has no solution because the absolute value of an expression cannot be negative.

You can also use a graphing utility to solve an absolute value equation.

COMMUNICATING ABOUT ALGEBRA

Solve Example 4 in a different way by graphing three equations. Name the three equations. Which method do you prefer?

$y_1 = 2x + 1$, $y_2 = 5$, $y_3 = -5$; answers will vary

EXAMPLE 4

TECHNOLOGY Use a graphing utility to solve $|2x + 1| = 5$.

Solution

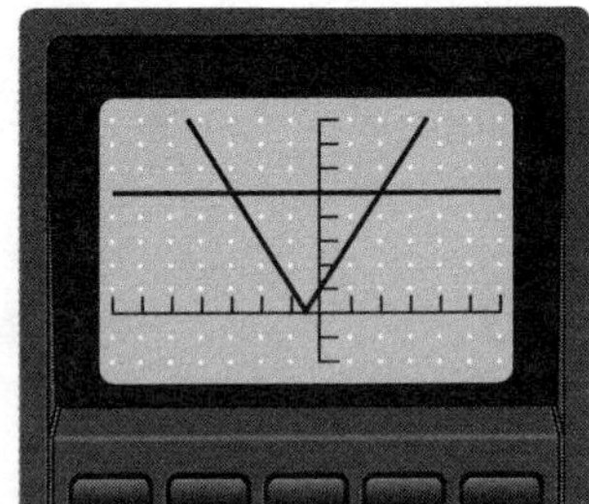

Graph $y_1 = |2x + 1|$ and $y_2 = 5$ on the same set of axes. Use the TRACE and ZOOM features to find the x-values of the two points of intersection, which are −3 and 2. These are the solutions to the equation $|2x + 1| = 5$.

You can use absolute value equations to model real world events.

EXAMPLE 5

RADIOLOGY A hospital ultrasound machine can measure with a 10% tolerance the weight of an unborn baby. This means that the weight x of the unborn baby will be measured as $x \pm 0.1x$. Suppose an unborn baby weighs 110 oz. Determine the maximum and minimum weights of the unborn baby.

Solution

Since the weight x of the baby is within 10% of 110 oz, the maximum and minimum weights must be $0.1(110) = 11$ oz above or below 110 oz. Write an absolute value equation for this situation.

$$|x - 110| = 11$$
$$x - 110 = 11 \quad \text{or} \quad x - 110 = -11 \qquad \text{Write a disjunction.}$$
$$x = 121 \quad \text{or} \quad x = 99 \qquad \text{Add 110 to both sides.}$$

The maximum and minimum weights of the baby are 121 oz and 99 oz, respectively. ◀

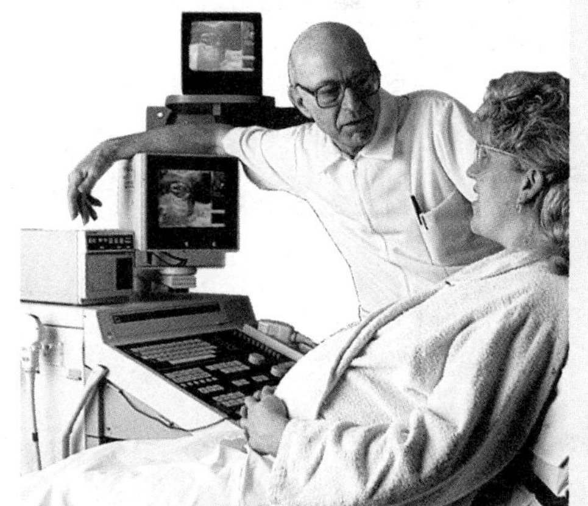

TRY THESE

Express each absolute value equation as a disjunction.

1. $|2x - 3| = 12$ $\quad 2x - 3 = 12$ or $2x - 3 = -12$
2. $|3x - 2| = 10$ $\quad 3x - 2 = 10$ or $3x - 2 = -10$
3. $|2x + 5| = 17$ $\quad 2x + 5 = 17$ or $2x + 5 = -17$

Solve and check each equation. If an equation has no solution, write "no solution."

4. $|x - 2| = 6$ $\quad -4, 8$
5. $|x - 3| = 9$ $\quad -6, 12$
6. $|6 - x| = 4$ $\quad 2, 10$
7. $|8 - x| = 2$ $\quad 6, 10$
8. $|2x - 7| = 5$ $\quad 1, 6$
9. $|2x - 9| = 11$ $\quad -1, 10$
10. $3|x - 5| = 6$ $\quad 3, 7$
11. $4|x - 3| = 16$ $\quad -1, 7$
12. $2|3z + 1| - 3 = 9$ $\quad -\frac{7}{3}, \frac{5}{3}$
13. $2|4w - 1| + 2 = 12$ $\quad -1, \frac{3}{2}$
14. $-|x + 4| - 3 = 12$ $\quad$ no solution
15. $-|x + 5| - 5 = 5$ $\quad$ no solution

Use a graphing utility to solve each equation.

16. $|x + 1| = 5$ $\quad -6, 4$
17. $|x + 3| = 2$ $\quad -5, -1$
18. $|6 - x| = 2$ $\quad 4, 8$

19. **SCIENCE** The volume of a liquid in a graduated cylinder is 30 mL. Write an equation that represents the volume if the cylinder is accurate to 5%. $|x - 30| = 1.5$

20. **HEALTH AND FITNESS** A fitness study concluded that the optimal amount of body fat for a male is 15% ± 3% of total body weight. Determine the maximum and minimum optimal percentages of body fat for a male. $|x - 15| = 3$; max 18%, min 12%

21. **WRITING MATHEMATICS** Write about a real world situation in your classroom involving a maximum and minimum. Write an absolute value equation to model the situation. Answers will vary.

PRACTICE

Express each absolute value equation as a disjunction.

1. $|4x| = 12$ $\quad 4x = 12$ or $4x = -12$
2. $|2x| = 10$ $\quad 2x = 10$ or $2x = -10$
3. $|3x + 4| = 11$ $\quad 3x + 4 = 11$ or $3x + 4 = -11$
4. $|2x + 1| = 8$ $\quad 2x + 1 = 8$ or $2x + 1 = -8$
5. $|5x - 1.5| = 8.5$ $\quad 5x - 1.5 = 8.5$ or $5x - 1.5 = -8.5$
6. $|6x - 4.1| = 9.1$ $\quad 6x - 4.1 = 9.1$ or $6x - 4.1 = -9.1$

Solve and check each equation. If an equation has no solution, write "no solution."

7. $|2w| = 16$ $\quad -8, 8$
8. $|-5t| = 15$ $\quad -3, 3$
9. $\left|-\frac{1}{2}q\right| = -16$ $\quad$ no solution
10. $|x - 2| = 4$ $\quad -2, 6$
11. $|8 - x| = 5$ $\quad 3, 13$
12. $|7 - x| = 3$ $\quad 4, 10$

Guided Practice/Try These For Exercises 4–15, remind students to first write the disjunction. For Exercise 12, ask students whether it is easier to add 3 to both sides first or to divide both sides by 2 first. Why? **It is easier to add 3 to both sides first, because then 12 is evenly divisible by 2.** Suggest that for Exercises 16–18 students try both methods described in the lesson for using a graphing utility to solve absolute value equations.

3 SUMMARIZE

In the Math Journal Ask students to write a paragraph that answers the following question and justifies their answer.

Is it true that $|a - b| = |b - a|$? **Yes, because the distance between *a* and *b* is the same as the distance between *b* and *a*; $|a - b| = |-(a - b)| = |b - a|$.**

NAME ________ CLASS ________ DATE ________

RETEACHING 9.3 ABSOLUTE VALUE EQUATIONS

An absolute value equation of the form $y = |x|$ has two solutions. One is $y = x$, and the second one is $y = -x$. These can be written as a disjunction, an *or*-statement. $y = x$ or $y = -x$. To solve an absolute value equation, first get the absolute value part of the equation all by itself. Next, write the disjunction and then solve the two equations that form the disjunction.

Example Solve and check: $3|2x - 8| + 5 = 23$

Solution

$3\|2x - 8\| + 5 = 23$		
$3\|2x - 8 = 18$		Subtract 5 from both sides.
$\|2x - 8\| = 6$		Divide both sides by 3.
$2x - 8 = 6$ or	$2x - 8 = -6$	Create a disjunction.
$2x = 14$	$2x = 2$	Add 8 to both sides.
$x = 7$	$x = 1$	Divide both sides by 2.

Check Substitute each solution into the original equation.

$3\|2x - 8\| + 5 = 23$	$3\|2x - 8\| + 5 = 23$
$3\|2(7) - 8\| + 5 = 23$	$3\|2(1) - 8\| + 5 = 23$
$3\|6\| + 5 = 23$	$3\|-6\| + 5 = 23$
$23 = 23$	$23 = 23$

EXERCISES

Express each absolute value equation as a disjunction.

1. $|x - 4| = 6$ $\quad x - 4 = 6$ or $x - 4 = -6$
2. $|x + 3| = 7$ $\quad x + 3 = 7$ or $x + 3 = -7$
3. $|-x + 2| = 27$ $\quad -x + 2 = 27$ or $-x + 2 = -27$
4. $|-x - 9| = 18$ $\quad -x - 9 = 18$ or $-x - 9 = -18$

Solve and check each equation.

5. $|2x + 3| = 7$
6. $|4x - 5| = 1$
7. $|3x - 2| = 14$
8. $5|4x + 3| = 15$
9. $3|2x - 7| = 21$
10. $2|2x + 3| = 8$

5. $2, -5$
6. $\frac{3}{2}, 1$
7. $\frac{16}{3}, -4$
8. $0, -\frac{3}{2}$
9. $7, 0$
10. $\frac{1}{2}, -\frac{7}{2}$

14 *South-Western Algebra 1: AN INTEGRATED APPROACH*

4 PRACTICE

Practice For Exercises 14–21, remind students to first isolate the absolute value expression. Before students begin Exercises 22–27, review the two methods given in the lesson for using a graphing utility to solve absolute equations.

Extend For Exercise 31, ask students why they must reject one of the solutions. **because it produces a false statement when substituted in the original equation: $|-6.25| \neq -6.25$; absolute value must be positive**

Think Critically For Exercise 44, ask students to describe how they solved for *x*. **Write a disjunction: $ax = b$ or $ax = -b$; divide both sides by a: $x = b/a$ or $x = -b/a$.**

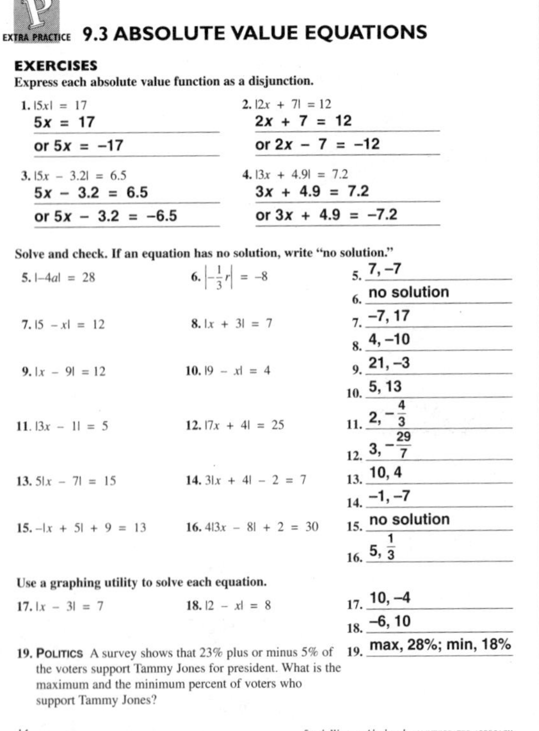

NAME ______ CLASS ______ DATE ______

EXTRA PRACTICE **9.3 ABSOLUTE VALUE EQUATIONS**

EXERCISES

Express each absolute value function as a disjunction.

1. $|5x| = 17$ — $5x = 17$ or $5x = -17$
2. $|2x + 7| = 12$ — $2x + 7 = 12$ or $2x - 7 = -12$
3. $|5x - 3.2| = 6.5$ — $5x - 3.2 = 6.5$ or $5x - 3.2 = -6.5$
4. $|3x + 4.9| = 7.2$ — $3x + 4.9 = 7.2$ or $3x + 4.9 = -7.2$

Solve and check. If an equation has no solution, write "no solution."

5. $|-4a| = 28$
6. $\left|-\frac{1}{3}r\right| = -8$
7. $|5 - x| = 12$
8. $|x + 3| = 7$
9. $|x - 9| = 12$
10. $|9 - x| = 4$
11. $|3x - 1| = 5$
12. $|7x + 4| = 25$
13. $5|x - 7| = 15$
14. $3|x + 4| - 2 = 7$
15. $-|x + 5| + 9 = 13$
16. $4|3x - 8| + 2 = 30$

Use a graphing utility to solve each equation.

17. $|x - 3| = 7$
18. $|2 - x| = 8$

19. **POLITICS** A survey shows that 23% plus or minus 5% of the voters support Tammy Jones for president. What is the maximum and the minimum percent of voters who support Tammy Jones?

Answers:
5. 7, −7
6. no solution
7. −7, 17
8. 4, −10
9. 21, −3
10. 5, 13
11. $2, -\frac{4}{3}$
12. $3, -\frac{29}{7}$
13. 10, 4
14. −1, −7
15. no solution
16. $5, \frac{1}{3}$
17. 10, −4
18. −6, 10
19. max, 28%; min, 18%

16 *South-Western Algebra 1: AN INTEGRATED APPROACH*

Solve and check each equation. If an equation has no solution, write "no solution."

13. $|2x - 5| = 7$ −1, 6
14. $3|x - 4| = 10$ $\frac{2}{3}, \frac{22}{3}$
15. $8|3z + 1| - 6 = 18$ $-\frac{4}{3}, \frac{2}{3}$
16. $3|2w + 1| + 3 = 12$ −2, 1
17. $-|x + 4| + 12 = 3$ −13, 5
18. $2|2x + 3| + 3 = 3$ $-\frac{3}{2}$
19. $2|x + 3| + 3 = 9$ −6, 0
20. $4|x + 2| - 5 = 3$ −4, 0
21. $\frac{1}{2}|4x - 2| + 6 = 12$ $-\frac{5}{2}, \frac{7}{2}$

Use a graphing utility to solve each equation.

22. $|x + 1| = 5$ −6, 4
23. $|x + 3| = 2$ −5, −1
24. $|6 - x| = 2$ 4, 8
25. $|5 - x| = 7$ −2, 12
26. $\frac{1}{2}|5y - 4| + 4 = 6$ $0, \frac{8}{5}$
27. $\frac{1}{2}|3y - 4| + 4 = 10$ $-\frac{8}{3}, \frac{16}{3}$

28. **SALARY AND BENEFITS** A law firm pays a bonus of \$10,000 to any associate who charges fees for 2,000 ± 50 hours per year. Determine maximum and minimum hours for which an associate can earn a \$10,000 bonus. $|x - 2{,}000| = 50$; max 2,050; min 1,950

29. **VETERINARY MEDICINE** Joline adopted a kitten from the local animal shelter. Her veterinarian estimated the kitten's age at 9 ± 3 mo. Determine the maximum and minimum ages of the kitten. $|x - 9| = 3$; max 12 mo; min 6 mo

30. **WRITING MATHEMATICS** Describe the graph of an absolute value equation that has no solution. Provide such an equation and sketch its graph. The graphs of y_1 and y_2 would have no point of intersection; answers will vary; $|x + 3| = -4$ is an example.

EXTEND

31. Some absolute value equations may have only one solution. What are the possible solutions of $|x - 5| = 5x$? Check your possible solutions in the original equation. Which possible solution must you reject? What is the solution? $-\frac{5}{4}, \frac{5}{6}; -\frac{5}{4}; \frac{5}{6}$

Solve and check each equation.

32. $|x - 4| = 2x$ $\frac{4}{3}$
33. $|x - 3| = 4x$ $\frac{3}{5}$
34. $\frac{1}{4}|5 - 2x| = 2 - x$ $\frac{3}{2}$

ESTIMATION Estimate the solutions of each equation to the nearest integer. Check your solutions to see how accurate they are.

35. $|x - 2.1| = 4.1$ −2, 6
36. $|x - 2.9| = 9.9$ −7, 13
37. $|8 - 0.9x| = 4.9$ 3, 13

COLLEGE ADMISSION Havenhearst College accepts students with mathematics SAT scores of 700 ± 100 and high school grade-point averages of 3.5 ± 0.5.

38. Determine the maximum and minimum mathematics scores accepted at Havenhearst. $|x - 700| = 100$; max 800, min 600
39. Determine the maximum and minimum high school grade-point averages accepted at Havenhearst. $|x - 3.5| = 0.5$; max average 4.0, min average 3.0

SALARY AND BENEFITS The SKS Corporation established the following salary grade levels for middle management.

LEVEL	LOW	MIDDLE	HIGH
1	\$ 18,000	\$ 25,000	\$ 32,000
2	\$ 23,000	\$ 31,000	\$ 39,000
3	\$ 36,000	\$ 45,000	\$ 54,000
4	\$ 50,000	\$ 61,000	\$ 72,000

40. Determine the maximum and minimum salaries at each level. level 1: $|x - 25{,}000| = 7{,}000$; level 2: $|x - 31{,}000| = 8{,}000$; level 3: $|x - 45{,}000| = 9{,}000$; level 4: $|x - 61{,}000| = 11{,}000$

THINK CRITICALLY

41. Write an absolute value equation that has two solutions, one of which is 0. answers will vary; possible answer: $|3x - 1| = 2x + 1$
42. Write an absolute value equation that has only one solution, which cannot be 0. answers will vary; possible answer: $|x + 1| = 2x$
43. Describe the graph of an absolute value equation with only one solution, which is not 0. y_1 would be V-shaped and y_2 would be a line that intersects y_1 in exactly one point

Solve each equation for *x*. Assume *a*, *b*, *c*, *d*, and *e* are positive numbers.

44. $|ax| = b$ $\;-\frac{b}{a}, \frac{b}{a}$
45. $|cx - d| = e$ $\;\frac{d-e}{c}, \frac{d+e}{c}$
46. $-|x + c| = d$ no solution
47. $|x - 4| = 2x + c$ $\;\frac{4-c}{3}, -c - 4$

PROJECT Connection

Use the map on which you drew a straight line connecting your home and school.

1. First, make a copy of the map you drew. Let zero represent the location of your home. Mark off units on the line you drew so that the coordinate of the school is the actual distance from your home. Determine the midpoint of your distance line. Then write an absolute value equation with solutions that place you at school and at home. How did knowing the midpoint help you? See Additional Answers.
2. Write another absolute value equation using the distances on the map instead of actual distances. See Additional Answers.
3. How are your two equations related? The ratio M'/M is the map scale.
4. Compare your equations with those of other group members. How are the equations alike? Why? How do they differ? Why? Answers will vary.

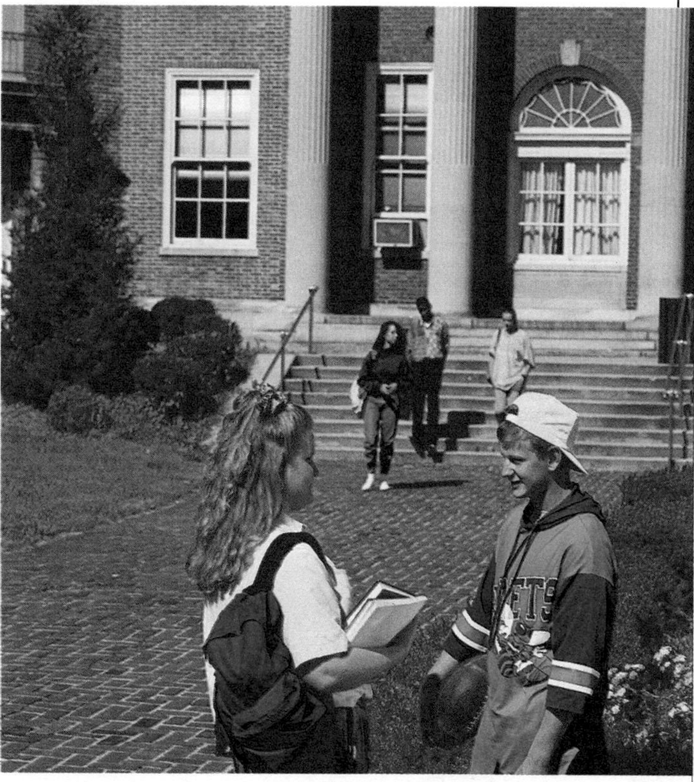

5 FOLLOW-UP

Extension Have students describe how to algebraically find the slope of each ray of the graph of the absolute value equation $y = -4|x + 4| + 8$. **Find the vertex: $x + 4 = 0$, $x = -4$; $y = -4|-4 + 4| + 8$, $y = 8$; vertex is $(-4, 8)$; find the x-intercepts: $0 = -4|x + 4| + 8$, $x = -2$ or $x = -6$; use the vertex and x-intercepts to find the rise/run for each ray: $m_1 = (8 - 0)/(-4 + 6) = 4$ and $m_2 = (8 - 0)/(-4 + 2) = -4$; 4 and -4 are the slopes.**

Project Connection This activity presents further aspects of the project introduced on page 412. To write the absolute value equations, students need to understand that the absolute value of zero minus half the map or actual distance is equivalent to the absolute value of the whole distance minus half the map or actual distance.

NAME ________ CLASS ________ DATE ________

ENRICHMENT **9.3 ABSOLUTE VALUE EQUATIONS**

Use what you know about absolute value to answer the following questions. Test a few examples to be sure.

1. For what values of a does $a|x| = |ax|$?
   For all a that are non-negative.
2. For what values of a does $|a| \cdot |x| = |ax|$?
   All values of a.
3. For what values of a does $\frac{|x|}{a} = \left|\frac{x}{a}\right|$?
   For all a that are non-negative.
4. For what values of a does $\frac{|x|}{|a|} = \left|\frac{x}{a}\right|$?
   All values of a.

Solve and check. If an equation has no solution, write "no solution."

5. $\frac{|x + 7|}{-2} = 6$
6. $\frac{|x + 7|}{|-2|} = 6$
7. $\frac{|4x - 2|}{|-2|} = 7$
8. $\left|\frac{3x + 4}{3}\right| = 10$
9. $-4\left|\frac{8x - 16}{4}\right| = 21$
10. $\left|\frac{2x - 1}{6}\right| + 7 = 11$
11. $\frac{-2|2x + 7|}{|4|} = -11$
12. $\frac{5|3x + 17|}{|-2|} + 2 = 37$
13. $-7\left|\frac{4x + 1}{3}\right| + 5 = -9$
14. $6\left|\frac{10x - 15}{-5}\right| = 36$
15. $\frac{2}{3}\left(\frac{|18x - 6|}{|-6|}\right) - 18 = 12$
16. $\frac{-4}{7}\left(\left|\frac{8x + 6}{2}\right|\right) - 13 = 15$

Answers:
5. **no solution**
6. **5, −19**
7. **−3, 4**
8. **$8\frac{2}{3}, -11\frac{1}{3}$**
9. **no solution**
10. **12.5, −11.5**
11. **7.5, −14.5**
12. **$-1, -10\frac{1}{3}$**
13. **1.25, −1.75**
14. **−1.5, 4.5**
15. **$-14\frac{2}{3}, 15\frac{1}{3}$**
16. **no solution**

18

South-Western Algebra 1: AN INTEGRATED APPROACH

LESSON PLANNING

Objective

- ▶ Solve absolute value inequalities algebraically and by using a number line.

Vocabulary

compound inequalities
conjunction
disjunction

Materials/Manipulatives

uncooked spaghetti

Resources

Warm Up 9.4
Reteaching 9.4
Extra Practice 9.4
Enrichment 9.4
Transparencies 18, 53–56
Student Handbook
Lesson Quiz 9.4
Technology Activity 21

ASSIGNMENTS

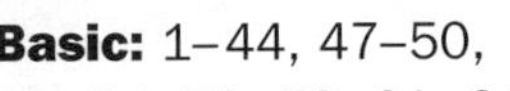

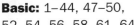

Basic: 1–44, 47–50, 52, 54, 56, 58, 61, 64a–c, Mixed Review 65–71, AlgebraWorks 1–7

Average: 5–59, 61, 64a–c, Mixed Review 65–71, AlgebraWorks 1–7

Enriched: 9–64, Mixed Review 65–71, AlgebraWorks 1–7

1 MOTIVATE

Explore To help students understand Question 5, have partners use a number line extending from –10 to 10 with increments of 1 unit and two pieces of uncooked spaghetti. Ask students how they can represent set *A* using one piece of spaghetti and the number line. **Place one end of the spaghetti at –2 just above the number line with the rest of the**

9.4 Absolute Value Inequalities

SPOTLIGHT ON LEARNING

WHAT? In this lesson you will learn
- to solve absolute value inequalities algebraically and by using a number line.

WHY? Solving absolute value inequalities can help you solve problems involving travel, test-taking, games, blood chemistry, and tire design.

ALGEBRA: WHO, WHERE, WHEN

Many of the symbols used in algebra today were first introduced by the English mathematician Thomas Harriot (1560–1621). He was the first to use the inequality symbols < and >. In 1585, Harriot joined Sir Walter Raleigh on a trip to North America. He was the first noted European mathematician to go to North America.

Explore

- In the circle diagram at the right, the universal set U is $\{-4, -3, -2, -1, 0, 1, 2, 3, 4, 5, 6, 7\}$. Set A includes the integers greater than or equal to –2, and set B includes the integers less than or equal to 5. The shaded region represents the intersection of sets A and B.

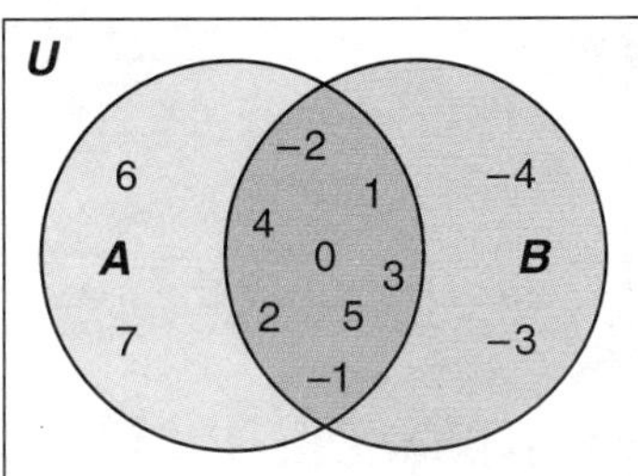

1. What numbers are included in set A? in set B? in set A but not in set B? in set B but not in set A? in the intersection of sets A and B? See Additional Answers.

Let x represent any integer. The graph below shows the solution set of the conjunction

$x \geq -2$ *and* $x \leq 5$

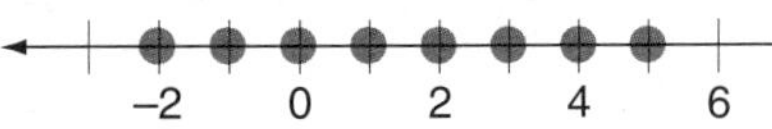

2. How many solutions are there? 8
3. Why are there solid dots at $x = -2$ and $x = 5$? because –2 and 5 are included in the solution
4. What would open dots indicate? See Additional Answers.
5. If x were not limited to integers, would the number of solutions be different? Explain. See Additional Answers.

Build Understanding

- The double-shaded area in the circle diagram in Explore is where circles A and B overlap. The overlapping represents a *conjunction*. A **conjunction** is two statements connected by the word *and*.

The graph of $|x| < 4$ below contains points less than 4 units from 0. The solution is the conjunction

$-4 < x$ *and* $x < 4$

which can be written $-4 < x < 4$.

The graph of $|x| > 4$ below contains points more than 4 units from 0. The solution is the disjunction

$x < -4$ *or* $x > 4$

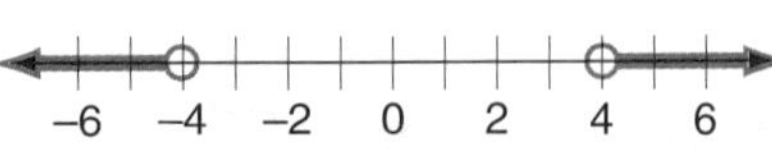

These conjunctions and disjunctions are called **compound inequalities**.

You can solve absolute value inequalities of the form $|ax \pm b| < c$ or $|ax \pm b| > c$ by expressing each inequality as a compound inequality.

EXAMPLE 1

Solve $|x + 2| < 3$. Graph the solution.

Solution

Number Line Method

First, find the point of symmetry.

$$x + 2 = 0$$
$$x = -2$$

Align 0 with -2. Place spaghetti on 3 and -3 on the zero finder.

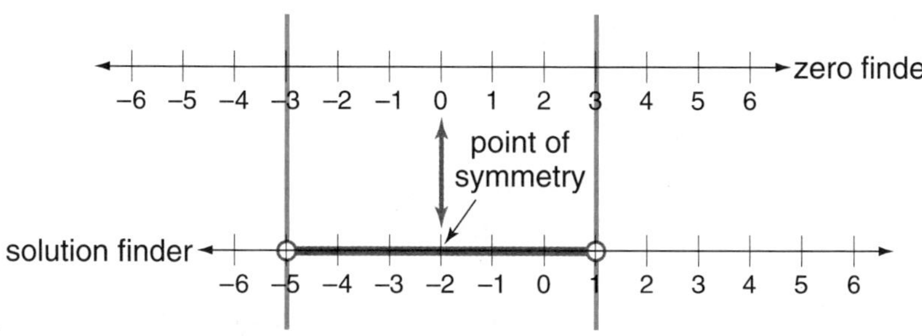

The spaghetti intersects the solution finder at -5 and 1. Since the absolute value is "less than," the distance from the point of symmetry is less than 3. The solution is $-5 < x < 1$. Place open dots on -5 and 1. Connect them.

Algebraic Method

$|x + 2| < 3$ means $-3 < x + 2$ *and* $x + 2 < 3$.

$-3 < x + 2$ and $x + 2 < 3$
$-5 < x$ $\quad x < 1$ Solve for x.

The solution is $-5 < x < 1$.

When the inequality is "greater than" or "greater than or equal to," the solution is a disjunction.

EXAMPLE 2

Solve $|2x - 3| > 5$. Graph the solution.

Solution

Use the algebraic method.

$|2x - 3| > 5$ means $2x - 3 < -5$ *or* $2x - 3 > 5$.

$2x - 3 < -5$ or $2x - 3 > 5$
$x < -1$ $\quad x > 4$ Solve for x.

The solution is $x < -1$ *or* $x > 4$.

CHECK UNDERSTANDING

Example 1 shows a conjunction and Example 2 shows a disjunction. How can you tell which is which by looking at the inequality symbols?

If the absolute value of an expression is less than some positive number, it can be written as a conjunction. If the absolute value of an expression is greater than some positive number, it can be written as a disjunction.

COMMUNICATING ABOUT ALGEBRA

Describe how you could use the number line method to solve Example 2.

See Additional Answers.

spaghetti extending toward 10. How can they represent set B? **Place one end of the other piece of spaghetti at 5 just above the first piece of spaghetti with the rest of the spaghetti extending toward −10.** Ask students how they can tell which numbers are in the solution set of the conjunction $x \geq -2$ and $x \leq 5$. **The part of the number line where the pieces of spaghetti overlap represents the real numbers in the solution set.** What are they? **all real numbers greater than or equal to −2 and all real numbers less than or equal to 5; $-2 \leq x \leq 5$**

2 TEACH

Use the Pages/Build Understanding

Ask what the solution of $|x| < 6$ is. **the conjunction $-6 < x$ and $x < 6$ or $-6 < x < 6$** Ask what the solution of $|x| > 6$ is. **the disjunction $x < -6$ or $x > 6$** Have students graph each solution on a separate number line.

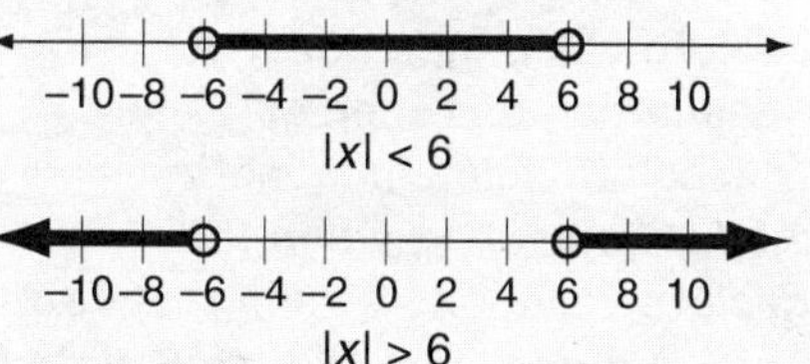

DIVERSITY IN THE CLASSROOM

Linguistic Learners Some students may find it easier to remember how to write absolute value inequalities as conjunctions and disjunctions if they think of the greater than symbol > as "more than." "More" has the word "or" in it, so it must be a disjunction.

Example 1: For the number line method, ask students why they count 3 units on either side of the point of symmetry. **because the distance**

from x to −2 is less than 3 units Ask students how to solve $-3 < x + 2$ and $x + 2 < 3$ for x. **Subtract 2 from both sides.** Ask students how they can check the solutions $-5 < x < 1$. **Substitute values for x that are greater than −5 and less than 1 into the original inequality; for example, $|0 + 2| < 3$.** Point out that substituting either −5 or 1 in the original inequality will not help them check because the result will be an equality: $|-5 + 2| = 3$ and $|1 + 2| = 3$.

Example 2: Ask why the number line method is not used to solve Example 2. **because the point of symmetry is a fraction** Have students read Check Understanding. Make sure they understand the distinction between conjunction and disjunction. Ask them to give an example of each. **Possible examples: conjunction: $|x + 1| < 4$; disjunction: $|x - 2| > 1$**

Example 3: Ask students how the method for solving absolute value inequalities is similar to that for solving absolute value equations. **You must first isolate the absolute value expression.** How is it different? **For absolute value equations, you write a disjunction and then solve for x; for absolute value inequalities, you write a disjunction when the absolute value expression is greater than (>) a number and a conjunction when the absolute value expression is less than (<) a number and then solve for x.** Ask students to explain why $6.5 \geq z$ and $z \geq -2.5$ can be written as $-2.5 \leq z \leq 6.5$. **Because $-2.5 \leq z \leq 6.5$ is the same as $-2.5 \leq z$ and $z \leq 6.5$; these two expressions are the same as $z \geq -2.5$ and $6.5 \geq z$.**

Example 4: Point out that by looking at the graph it is clear that 115 is the point of symmetry or midpoint. Ask students how they can find the midpoint between 100 and 130. **Add 100 and 130 and divide the result by 2.** Have students read and discuss Communicating About Algebra.

CHECK UNDERSTANDING

In Example 3, why is the order of the inequality signs reversed in the last line of the solution?

It is reversed because both sides of each inequality are divided by a negative number.

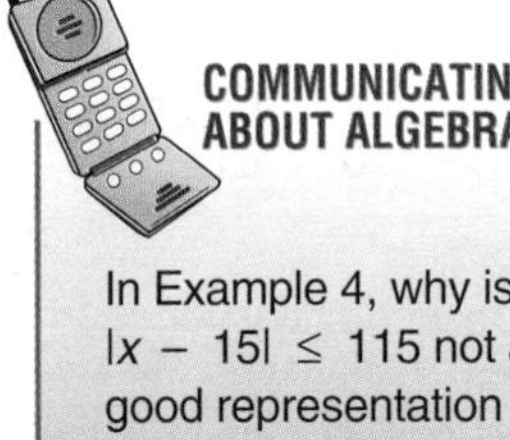

COMMUNICATING ABOUT ALGEBRA

In Example 4, why is $|x - 15| \leq 115$ not a good representation of the data?

See Additional Answers.

Be sure to isolate the absolute value on one side of the inequality before you express it as a compound inequality.

EXAMPLE 3

Solve $2|4 - 2z| - 3 \leq 15$. Graph the solution.

Solution

$2|4 - 2z| - 3 \leq 15$

$2|4 - 2z| \leq 18$ Add 3 to both sides.

$|4 - 2z| \leq 9$ Divide both sides by 2.

$|4 - 2z| \leq 9$ means $-9 \leq 4 - 2z$ *and* $4 - 2z \leq 9$.

$-9 \leq 4 - 2z$ and $4 - 2z \leq 9$

$-13 \leq -2z$ $\qquad -2z \leq 5$

$6.5 \geq z$ $\qquad z \geq -2.5$ Divide both sides by −2. Reverse the inequality.

The solution is $-2.5 \leq z \leq 6.5$.

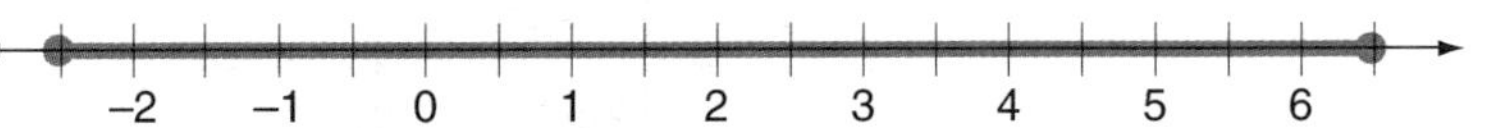

Some inequalities have no solution. For example, $|3x - 7| < -2$ has no solution because absolute value cannot be negative.

Absolute value inequalities are useful in representing real world data.

EXAMPLE 4

TRAVEL A private commuter airline charges customers a flat rate for all flights from its home airports to destinations that are between and including 100 mi and 130 mi away. Choose the graph that best represents this situation. Then write the absolute value equation that represents the situation.

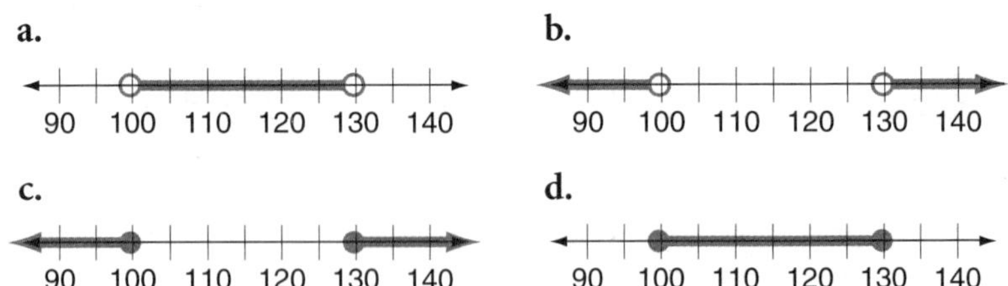

Solution

Eliminate graphs **b** and **c** because they do not indicate values between 100 and 130. Eliminate graph **a** because it does not include 100 and 130. The correct answer is **d**.

The number 115 represents the point of symmetry or the midpoint between the solutions to the inequality, 100 and 130. So, this situation can be modeled by the absolute value inequality $|x - 115| \leq 15$.

The following rules summarize the algebraic method for solving absolute value inequalities. You can replace $<$ with $\le$ and $>$ with $\ge$ in these rules.

> **For all real numbers a, b, and c where $b \ge 0$ and $c \ge 0$,**
>
> **If $|ax + b| < c$, then $-c < ax + b$ and $ax + b < c$.**
> **If $|ax - b| < c$, then $-c < ax - b$ and $ax - b < c$.**
>
> **If $|ax + b| > c$, then $ax + b < -c$ or $ax + b > c$.**
> **If $|ax - b| > c$, then $ax - b < -c$ or $ax - b > c$.**

You may prefer to solve an absolute value inequality using a number line. If the inequality is $|x - b| < c$, then its solutions are those values of x that are less than c units from the point of symmetry b. If the inequality is $|x - b| > c$, then its solutions are those values of x that are more than c units from b.

TRY THESE

Write a compound inequality that is equivalent to each absolute value inequality.

1. $|x + 3| < 6$ $-6 < x + 3$ and $x + 3 < 6$
2. $|x - 4| > 7$ $x - 4 < -7$ or $x - 4 > 7$
3. $|2x - 4| \ge 6$ $2x - 4 \le -6$ or $2x - 4 \ge 6$
4. $|3x + 5| \le 9$ $-9 \le 3x + 5$ and $3x + 5 \le 9$

Use the number line method to solve each absolute value inequality. Graph the solution. See Additional Answers for graphs.

5. $|z + 3| < 5$ $-8 < z < 2$
6. $|x - 4| \le 3$ $1 \le x \le 7$
7. $|t - 5| \ge 2$ $t \le 3$ or $t \ge 7$
8. $|w + 2| > 4$ $w < -6$ or $w > 2$

Match each equation with its graph.

9. $|x| \le 5$ c
10. $|2 - x| > 1$ a
11. $|x + 2| \ge 1$ d
12. $|x - 3| < 2$ b

a. 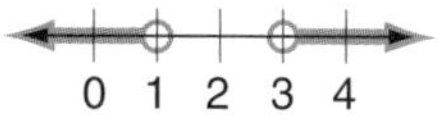

b. 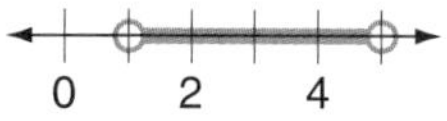

c. 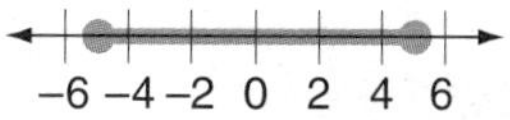

d. 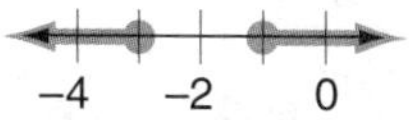

Solve each inequality. For Exercises 13–16, also graph each solution. See Additional Answers for graphs.

13. $|2q - 7| \ge 1$ $q \le 3$ or $q \ge 4$
14. $|9x - 6| > 12$ $x < -\frac{2}{3}$ or $x > 2$
15. $|3t + 5| < 7$ $-4 < t < \frac{2}{3}$
16. $|4x - 2| \le 6$ $-1 \le x \le 2$
17. $|2x| \ge 0$ all reals
18. $|2x - 8| < 0$ no solution

19. GRADING Ms. Hewlett indicated that those students with semester averages from 82 to 88 would receive a B. Write an absolute value inequality that represents this range. $|x - 85| \le 3$

20. WRITING MATHEMATICS Explain the similarities and differences between the graphs of $|x - b| < c$ and $|x - b| > c$. See Additional Answers.

21. WRITING MATHEMATICS What is the solution of $|x - 9| < -4$? Explain. See Additional Answers.

Ongoing Assessment The important concepts and skills are solving absolute value inequalities algebraically and by using a number line. To assess these ideas, have students demonstrate how they have applied these concepts and skills in Questions 5, 13, and 15 of the Try These section.

Guided Practice/Try These For Exercises 5–8 and 13–16, remind students to check both solutions of each inequality.

3 SUMMARIZE

In the Math Journal Write a paragraph explaining how the graph of $|x| < 4$ represents real number values between -4 and 4 and how the graph of $|x| > 4$ represents real number values that are *not* between -4 and 4. **In the inequality $|x| < 4$, x represents numbers less than 4 units from the origin. The graph of $|x| < 4$ contains those points $-4 < x < 4$. In the inequality $|x| > 4$, x represents numbers greater than 4 units from the origin. The graph of $|x| > 4$ must contain those points that are more than 4 units from the origin in either direction, that is, $x < -4$ or $x > 4$.**

4 PRACTICE

Practice For Exercises 9–16, ask if it is possible to use the number line method for each problem. **Yes, the number line method is possible because all of the absolute value expressions are in the form $|x - b|$, where the coefficient of $x = 1$.** For Exercise 47, remind students that sometimes problems include extra information which is not necessary in order to solve the problem.

Extend For Exercises 50–53, ask why some inequalities have only one solution. **because the other solution produces a false statement when substituted in the original inequality**

Think Critically For Exercise 64, ask students what types of numbers they could consider. **all real numbers** Have students discuss their answers to Exercise 64 and give examples.

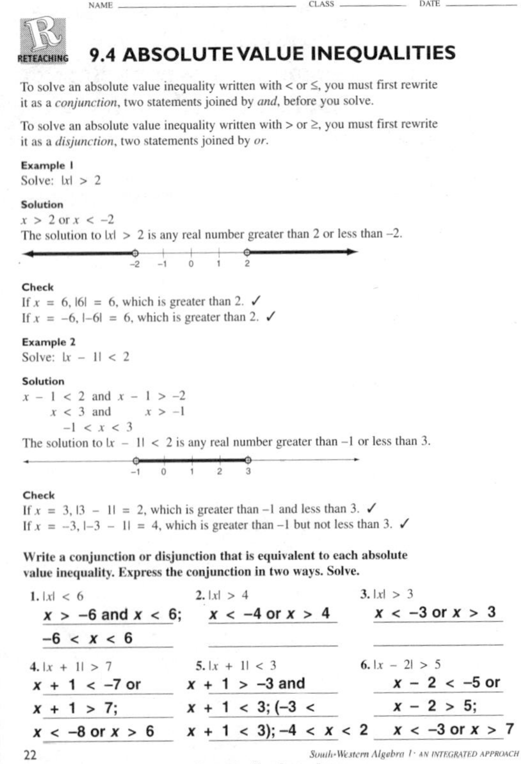

NAME ______________ CLASS ________ DATE ________

RETEACHING

9.4 ABSOLUTE VALUE INEQUALITIES

To solve an absolute value inequality written with $<$ or $\leq$, you must first rewrite it as a *conjunction*, two statements joined by *and*, before you solve.

To solve an absolute value inequality written with $>$ or $\geq$, you must first rewrite it as a *disjunction*, two statements joined by *or*.

Example 1
Solve: $|x| > 2$

Solution
$x > 2$ or $x < -2$
The solution to $|x| > 2$ is any real number greater than 2 or less than -2.

Check
If $x = 6$, $|6| = 6$, which is greater than 2. ✓
If $x = -6$, $|-6| = 6$, which is greater than 2. ✓

Example 2
Solve: $|x - 1| < 2$

Solution
$x - 1 < 2$ and $x - 1 > -2$
$x < 3$ and $x > -1$
$-1 < x < 3$
The solution to $|x - 1| < 2$ is any real number greater than -1 or less than 3.

Check
If $x = 3$, $|3 - 1| = 2$, which is greater than -1 and less than 3. ✓
If $x = -3$, $|-3 - 1| = 4$, which is greater than -1 but not less than 3. ✓

Write a conjunction or disjunction that is equivalent to each absolute value inequality. Express the conjunction in two ways. Solve.

1. $|x| < 6$ $x > -6$ and $x < 6$; $-6 < x < 6$
2. $|x| > 4$ $x < -4$ or $x > 4$
3. $|x| > 3$ $x < -3$ or $x > 3$
4. $|x + 1| > 7$ $x + 1 < -7$ or $x + 1 > 7$; $x < -8$ or $x > 6$
5. $|x + 1| < 3$ $x + 1 > -3$ and $x + 1 < 3$; $(-3 < x + 1 < 3)$; $-4 < x < 2$
6. $|x - 2| > 5$ $x - 2 < -5$ or $x - 2 > 5$; $x < -3$ or $x > 7$

22 *South-Western Algebra 1 · AN INTEGRATED APPROACH*

PRACTICE

Write a compound inequality that is equivalent to each absolute value inequality.

1. $|x + 1| < 5$ $-5 < x + 1$ and $x + 1 < 5$
2. $|x + 2| < 3$ $-3 < x + 2$ and $x + 2 < 3$
3. $|x - 4| > 6$ $x - 4 < -6$ or $x - 4 > 6$
4. $|x - 3| > 5$ $x - 3 < -5$ or $x - 3 > 5$
5. $|2x - 2| \leq 6$ $-6 \leq 2x - 2$ and $2x - 2 \leq 6$
6. $|3x - 3| \leq 15$ $-15 \leq 3x - 3$ and $3x - 3 \leq 15$
7. $|2x + 5| \geq 3$ $2x + 5 \leq -3$ or $2x + 5 > 3$
8. $|3x + 5| \geq 13$ $3x + 5 \leq -13$ or $3x + 5 \geq 13$

Solve each absolute value inequality. Graph the solution. See Additional Answers for graphs.

9. $|z + 1| < 3$ $-4 < z < 2$
10. $|z + 3| < -7$ no solution
11. $|x - 5| > 2$ $x < 3$ or $x > 7$
12. $|x - 4| > 2$ $x < 2$ or $x > 6$
13. $|x - 0.5| \leq 3.5$ $-3 \leq x \leq 4$
14. $|t - 1.5| \leq 4.5$ $-3 \leq t \leq 6$
15. $|w + 2.5| \geq 3.5$ $w \leq -6$ or $w \geq 1$
16. $|q + 3.5| \geq -2.5$ all reals

Match each equation with its graph.

17. $|x - 2| \leq 3$ b
18. $|3 - x| > 2$ d
19. $|x + 3| \geq 2$ c
20. $|x| < 3$ a

a. –2 0 2
b. 0 2 4
c. –6 –4 –2 0
d. 0 2 4 6

Solve each inequality. For Exercises 21–28, also graph each solution. See Additional Answers for graphs.

21. $|2q - 4| \geq 6$ $q \leq -1$ or $q \geq 5$
22. $|3x - 9| > 6$ $x < 1$ or $x > 5$
23. $|3t + 5| < 10$ $-5 < t < \frac{5}{3}$
24. $|4x - 2| \leq 10$ $-2 \leq x \leq 3$
25. $|3z - 6| > 12$ $z < -2$ or $z > 6$
26. $|3z - 1| \geq -7$ all reals
27. $|2q + 5| \leq 9$ $-7 \leq q \leq 2$
28. $|5z - 10| < 5$ $1 < z < 3$
29. $|5x| > 0$ $x \neq 0$ (all reals except $x = 0$)
30. $|6x| \geq 0$ all reals
31. $|5x + 4| < 0$ no solution
32. $|2x - 9| < -5$ no solution
33. $\left|\frac{1}{2}x - 1\right| > 0$ $x \neq 2$ (all x except $x = 2$)
34. $\left|\frac{1}{4}x - 2\right| > 0$ $x \neq 8$ (all x except $x = 8$)
35. $\left|2 - \frac{1}{2}x\right| > -4$ all reals
36. $\left|4 - \frac{1}{2}x\right| \geq 2$ $x \leq 4$ or $x \geq 12$
37. $|6 - 2x| < 12$ $-3 < x < 9$
38. $|5 - 2x| \leq 7$ $-1 \leq x \leq 6$
39. $|2x + 4| \leq 0$ $x = -2$
40. $|3x + 9| \leq 0$ $x = -3$
41. $2|1 + 2z| + 5 \leq 9$ $-\frac{3}{2} \leq z \leq \frac{1}{2}$
42. $3|1 + 3x| - 6 < 12$ $-\frac{7}{3} < x < \frac{5}{3}$
43. $4 - |5 - t| \geq 1$ $2 \leq t \leq 8$
44. $3 - |4 - t| > 1$ $2 < t < 6$
45. $\left|\frac{8 - 4x}{3}\right| < 2$ $\frac{1}{2} < x < \frac{7}{2}$
46. $\left|\frac{5 - 3x}{2}\right| > 4$ $x < -1$ or $x > \frac{13}{3}$

47. **ARCADE GAMES** One arcade game consists of a ramp with slots at one end that are labeled 1–6. To win at this game, you must roll 6 balls down the ramp to get a total score less than 11 or more than 31. Write an absolute value inequality that models the situation in which you would lose the game. $|x - 21| \leq 10$

48. **AUTOMOTIVE SALES** An automobile salesman estimates that he will sell 30 ± 5 red cars next year. Write an absolute value inequality that models this estimate. $|x - 30| \leq 5$

49. **WRITING MATHEMATICS** Write about a real world situation concerning food in which it is important to know the numbers within a specific range. Write an absolute value inequality to model this situation. Possible answer: One health program recommends that people consume from 15 g to 45 g of fat per day; $|x - 30| \leq 15$.

EXTEND

Some absolute value inequalities with the variable on each side of the equation have solutions that are single inequalities instead of compound inequalities. Solve each inequality.

50. $|x + 2| \leq x + 2$ $x \geq -2$
51. $|x - 2| < 5x$ $x > \frac{1}{3}$
52. $|3 - x| > 3 - x$ $x > 3$
53. $|5 - x| \geq 3x$ $x \leq \frac{5}{4}$

ESTIMATION Estimate the solutions to each inequality to the nearest integer. Check to see how accurate your estimates were.

54. $|x - 3.1| \le 7.1$ $-4 \le x \le 10$

55. $|x - 1.9| < 8.9$ $-7 < x < 11$

56. $|7 - 0.9x| > 3.9$ $x < 3$ or $x > 11$

57. $|5 - 1.1x| \ge 3.1$ $x \le 2$ or $x \ge 8$

HEMATOLOGY Lab technicians use the reference ranges below when measuring the blood chemistries of patients. A portion of the lab report for a patient is shown below.

58. Write an absolute value inequality that represents the normal range for glucose. $|x - 93| \le 23$

Chemzyme	Result	Normal Range
Glucose	110	70–116
Creatinine	1.3	0.7–1.4
GGTP	33	0–45

59. Write an absolute value inequality that represents the normal range for creatinine, a kidney function indicator. $|x - 1.05| \le 0.35$

60. Write an absolute value inequality that represents the normal range for GGTP, a liver function indicator. $|x - 22.5| \le 22.5$

THINK CRITICALLY

61. Write an absolute value inequality that has $x \ne 0$ as its solution. $|x| > 0$

62. Write an absolute value inequality that has no solution. (Do not use inequalities of the form $|x - b| < 0$ or $|x + b| < 0$.) answers will vary; example: $|5x - 4| \le 4x - 5$

63. Use the following strategy for solving the inequality $|x| \ge c$. Explain your answer.
Since < includes all numbers that ≥ does not, any real number that does not satisfy $|x| < c$ must satisfy $|x| \ge c$.

- Solve the inequality $|x| < c$.
- Conclude that the solutions of $|x| \ge c$ are the real numbers that do not satisfy $|x| < c$.

64. Under what circumstances, if any, are the following equations true? See Additional Answers.

a. $|a + b| = |a| + |b|$ **b.** $|a \cdot b| = |a| \cdot |b|$ **c.** $|a - b| = |a| - |b|$ **d.** $\left|\frac{a}{b}\right| = \frac{|a|}{|b|}$

MIXED REVIEW

65. **STANDARDIZED TESTS** Choose the value that correctly represents the expression in simplified form. C; Lesson 2.8

$$2(100 - 5^2)^2 - 3(8 + 2)^3$$

A. 14,250 **B.** 15,750 **C.** 8,250 **D.** −2,845

Express the equation of each line in slope-intercept form. Lesson 6.4

66. $3x - 7 = 4y + 3$ $y = \frac{3}{4}x + -\frac{5}{2}$

67. $5y - 5 = 2x + 11$ $y = \frac{2}{5}x + \frac{16}{5}$

Solve each system of linear equations using substitution. Lesson 7.3

68. $\begin{cases} x + 3y = 15 \\ 4x = 24 \end{cases}$ (6, 3)

69. $\begin{cases} x + 7y = 30 \\ -2y = -8 \end{cases}$ (2, 4)

Solve each absolute value inequality algebraically. Lesson 9.4

70. $|2x + 6| > 15$ $x < -10.5$ or $x > 4.5$

71. $|3x - 7| < 21$ $-\frac{14}{3} < x < \frac{28}{3}$

5 FOLLOW-UP

Extension Have students describe how to solve the absolute value inequality $2 < |x + 1| < 4$. Have them graph the solution. **Rewrite the conjunction in two separate inequalities: $2 < |x + 1|$ and $|x + 1| < 4$.**

$|x + 1| > 2$ and $|x + 1| < 4$

Solve $|x + 1| > 2$.

$x + 1 < -2$ or $x + 1 > 2$
$x < -3$ or $x > 1$

Solve $|x + 1| > 4$.

$-4 < x + 1$ and $x + 1 < 4$
$-5 < x$ and $x < 3$
$x < -3$ or $x > 1$ and $-5 < x < 3$

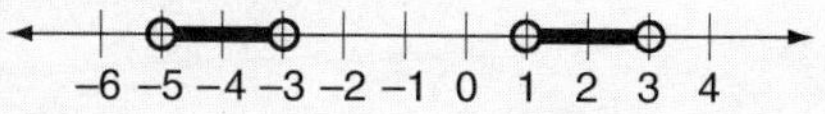

NAME ______ CLASS ______ DATE ______

EXTRA PRACTICE **9.4 ABSOLUTE VALUE INEQUALITIES**

EXERCISES

Write a compound inequality that is equivalent to each absolute value inequality.

1. $|x - 7| < 8$ **2.** $|x + 5| > 4$ **3.** $|3x - 1| \ge 8$ **4.** $|2x + 5| \le 9$

1. $x - 7 > -8$ and $x - 7 < 8$
2. $x + 5 < -4$ or $x + 5 > 4$
3. $3x - 1 \le -8$ or $3x + 1 \ge 8$
4. $-9 \le 2x + 5 \le 9$

Solve each absolute value inequality. Graph the solution. Check students' graphs.

5. $|a - 4| < 7$ **6.** $|t + 6| > 2$ **7.** $|z - 8| < 4$ **8.** $|m + 3.6| \ge 9.4$ **9.** $|3r + 6| \le 9$ **10.** $|4t - 7| \ge 25$ **11.** $|5b - 3| > -2$ **12.** $|4x - 3| \ge 5$ **13.** $\left|4 - \frac{1}{2}d\right| > -2$ **14.** $\left|2 + \frac{1}{3}b\right| < 5$ **15.** $|7y + 1| < 0$ **16.** $\left|\frac{1}{3}x - 2\right| > 0$ **17.** $|3x - 2| \le 11$ **18.** $|5x + 10| \le 0$

5. $a > -3$ and $a < 11$
6. $t < -8$ or $t > -4$
7. $z > 4$ and $z < 12$
8. $m \le -13$ or $m \ge 5.8$
9. $-5 \le r \le 1$
10. $t \le -4.5$ or $t \ge 8$
11. all reals
12. $x \le -\frac{1}{2}$ or $x \ge 2$
13. all reals
14. $-21 < b < 9$
15. no solution
16. all x except $x = 6$
17. $-3 \le x \le 4\frac{1}{3}$
18. $x = -2$

Match each inequality with its graph.

19. $|x - 4| \le 2$ **20.** $|2 - x| > 4$ **21.** $|x + 2| \ge 2$

19. b
20. c
21. a

22. **PROFIT AND LOSS** If between 125 and 145 students attend the dance, the class makes a profit. Write an absolute value inequality that represents the necessary attendance to make a profit.

22. $|x - 135| \le 10$

24 *South-Western Algebra 1: AN INTEGRATED APPROACH*

AlgebraWorks Ask students how they can determine the absolute value inequality for Exercise 5. **Find the point of symmetry and the distance between the point of symmetry and the minimum and maximum: 1,400 – 1,100 = 300, 300 ÷ 2 = 150, 150 is the distance; 150 + 1,100 = 1,250, 1,250 is the point of symmetry; $|x - 1{,}250| \le 150$.**

Ask students how to determine the absolute value inequality for Exercise 6. **The maximum load for 4 tires is 4 times that for 1 tire or from 4,400 to 5,600: 5,600 – 4,400 = 1,200, 1,200 ÷ 2 = 600; 600 + 4,400 = 5,000; $|x - 5{,}000| \le 600$.**

NAME ______________ CLASS ________ DATE ________

ENRICHMENT **9.4 ABSOLUTE VALUE INEQUALITIES**

The property of sums of absolute values states when a and b are real numbers, $|a + b| \le |a| + |b|$

Example
Estimate $|-4n|$ when $|2n| \le 4$ and $|-6n| \le -1$

Solution
From the property of sums of absolute values you know $|2n + (-6n)| \le |2n| + |-6n|$. Since $|2n| \le 4$ and $|-6n| \le -1$,

$|2n| + |-6n| \le 4 + (-1)$ addition property of inequality
$|2n + (-6n)| \le 4 + (-1)$ substitution
$|-4n| \le 3$ simplify

Use the property of sums of absolute values to solve.

1. $|3g| \le -4$ and $|h| < 6$
   Estimate: $|3g + h|$
2. $|-3x| < 10$ and $|5x| < -12$
   Estimate: $|2x|$
3. $|a - 6| \le 4$ and $|b - 10| < 5$
   Estimate: $|(a + b) - 16|$
4. $|2x - 1| \le 7$ and $|-3x + 5| \le 2$
   Estimate: $|-x + 4|$
5. $|3x + 7| \le 21$ and $|-2x - 5| \le -6$
   Write an inequality that estimates the value of the sum of the two absolute values.
6. $|4r^2 - 6r + 1| \le 14$ and $|8r^2 + 4r - 6| \le 16$
   Write an inequality that estimates the value of the sum of the two absolute values.
7. $|2c - 1| \le 10$ and $|3c + 5| \le -6$
   Write an inequality that estimates the value of the sum of the two absolute values.
8. $|4s - 7| \le 10$, $|2s + 10| \le 11$, and $|-5s - 2| \le -6$
   Write an inequality that estimates the value of the sum of the three absolute values.
9. Show that $|x - y| \ge |x| - |y|$.
   $|(x - y) + y| \le |x - y| + |y|$
   $|x| \le |x - y| + |y|$
   $|x| - |y| \le |x - y| + |y| - |y|$
   $|x| - |y| \le |x - y|$
   Likewise, $|x - y| \ge |x| - |y|$

1. < 2
2. < -2
3. < 9
4. < 9
5. $|x + 2| < 15$
6. $|12r - 2r - 5| < 30$
7. $|5c + 4| < 4$
8. $|s + 1| < 15$

26 *South-Western Algebra 1: AN INTEGRATED APPROACH*

Career
Tire Company Engineer

Tire company engineers design tires that have specific characteristics of ride, handling, and wear. All the information about the tire is molded onto the tire sidewall.

The most common size tire in the United States is the P205/70R14. The "P" stands for passenger car. The 205 is the section width of the tire in millimeters. The 70 is the aspect ratio, which is a measure of the handling of the car. The lower the aspect ratio, the higher the performance. The "R" stands for radial construction, and the 14 is the diameter of the wheel in inches.

Decision Making

A car maker's 1996 sedan has P195/60R15 tires, and the same maker's turbo sedan has P205/50R16 tires.

1. Which tires have the larger section width? turbo sedan
2. Which tires have the higher aspect ratio? regular sedan
3. Which tires have the higher performance? turbo sedan
4. How much greater is the radius of the turbo sedan tire than that of the regular model? $\frac{1}{2}$ in.

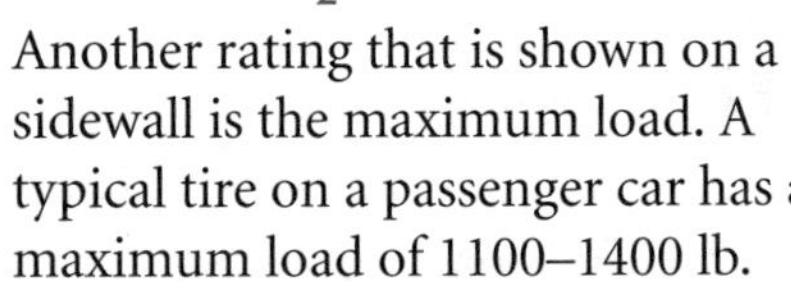

Another rating that is shown on a sidewall is the maximum load. A typical tire on a passenger car has a maximum load of 1100–1400 lb.

5. Express the maximum load on one tire as an absolute value inequality. $|x - 1250| \le 150$
6. Express the maximum load on the four tires as an absolute value inequality. $|x - 5000| \le 600$
7. A P205/70R14 tire has a sidewall that is 5.7 in. high. It is expected to last for approximately 60,000 mi. How many rotations will the tire make in its lifetime? See Additional Answers.

9.5 The Real Number System

Explore

For Questions 1–3, begin with a new number line. Consider the interval between 0 and 2.

0 1 2

1. Divide each unit interval between 0 and 2 into 2 equal parts. Locate and graph the numbers $\frac{1}{2}$, 1, $\frac{3}{2}$, and 2.
2. Divide each unit interval between 0 and 2 into 3 equal parts. What numbers can you locate and graph as a result? $\frac{1}{3}, \frac{2}{3}, 1, \frac{4}{3}, \frac{5}{3}, 2$
3. Divide each unit interval between 0 and 2 into 4 equal parts. What numbers can you locate and graph as a result?
See Additional Answers.
4. Suppose your number line is p units long and you divide each unit interval into q equal parts (p and q are both integers > 1). What numbers can you locate and graph as a result?
See Additional Answers.
5. If you continue indefinitely, do you think you will eventually be able to locate and graph every point on the number line? Explain.
Answers will vary. You cannot locate every point on the number line this way because not every number can be expressed as the quotient of two integers.

Build Understanding

You have worked with whole numbers, integers, and rational numbers throughout this book. Each of these groups of numbers forms a set of numbers. A **set** of numbers is any group of numbers with one or more common attributes.

Enclosing numbers in braces, { }, indicates that they form a set. You have studied sets of numbers, such as {0, 2, 4, 6}. The **elements** of this set are 0, 2, 4, and 6. The set is said to be **finite** because each element of the set can be listed. The set of all even numbers is **infinite** because its elements go on indefinitely, without limit (indicated by ellipsis points, . . .). The following are also infinite sets.

Natural or counting numbers: {1, 2, 3, 4, . . .}
Whole numbers: {0, 1, 2, 3, 4, . . .}
Integers: { . . . , –4, –3, –2, –1, 0, 1, 2, 3, 4, . . .}

Set A is a **subset** of a set B if every element of A is also an element of B. For example, the set of whole numbers is a subset of the set of integers because every whole number is also an integer.

Recall that a **rational number** is a number that can be expressed as $\frac{a}{b}$, where a and b are integers and b does not equal zero. A rational number can be expressed as either a terminating decimal such as 5.2 or a nonterminating repeating decimal such as $5.\overline{12}$.

SPOTLIGHT ON LEARNING

WHAT? In this lesson you will learn
- to express a rational number as the quotient of two integers.
- to identify the subsets of the real number system.
- to find the principal square root of a number.

WHY? Understanding the real numbers can help you solve problems involving physics, sports, geometry, and law enforcement.

CHECK UNDERSTANDING

Name the sets of numbers listed at the left that are subsets of the integers.

natural numbers, whole numbers

THINK BACK

Recall that the bar used in $5.\overline{12}$ is a symbol for the repeating decimal 5.12121212. . . .

LESSON PLANNING

Objectives
- ▶ Express a rational number as the quotient of two integers.
- ▶ Identify the subsets of the real number system.
- ▶ Find the principal square root of a number.

Vocabulary
elements
finite
infinite
irrational number
principal square root
rational number
real numbers
subset

Technology/Multimedia
calculator

Resources
Warm Up 9.5
Reteaching 9.5
Extra Practice 9.5
Enrichment 9.5
Transparencies 15, 18
Student Handbook
Lesson Quiz 9.5

Materials/Manipulatives
number lines

ASSIGNMENTS

Basic: 1–7, 12–18, 22–25, 27–30, 32–36, 42, 44–46, 50–51, 54–55, 58–61, Project Connection 1–3, AlgebraWorks 1–8

Average: 1, 7–51, 53–56, 58–62, Project Connection 1–3, AlgebraWorks 1–8

Enriched: 7–63, Project Connection 1–3, AlgebraWorks 1–8

1 MOTIVATE

Explore For Questions 1–3, have students draw or use a new number line 2 units long for each question. For Question 4, have students give examples for different values of p and q. **possible example: $p = 3$, $q = 2$; 1/2, 2/2 = 1, 3/2, 4/2 = 2, 5/2, 6/2 = 3**

2 TEACH

Use the Pages/Build Understanding Have students read Check Understanding and then ask them what set is a subset of the set of whole numbers. **natural numbers**

Example 1: Ask students how they can express 0 as a rational number. **0/a, where a is any integer except zero**

Example 2: Ask why the number is multiplied by 100 to move the decimal two places and not by 10 or 1,000 to move the decimal one or three places. **to move the decimal point exactly two places so that the decimal part of the new number begins with .57; then the decimal part of both numbers is the same and they drop out when you subtract**

Example 3: Ask students to give examples of other repeating decimals. **possible examples: $0.\overline{3}$, $1.\overline{18}$** Ask them to express 7/6 in decimal form. **$1.1\overline{6}$** Ask students why the bar goes only over 6 and not over 16. **Only 6 repeats, 1.16666 . . . , not 16: 1.161616 . . . .**

PROBLEM SOLVING TIP

You can often use mental math to compute numbers involving multiples of 10. For example:

$$\frac{3600}{12}$$

Use only 36 when you divide by 12. 36 ÷ 12 = __?__. Then multiply by 100, which adds two zeros.

EXAMPLE 1

Write each of the following numbers as the quotient of two integers.

a. -6 **b.** 3.05 **c.** $4\frac{1}{2}$

Solution

a. $-6 = \frac{-6}{1}$ **b.** $3.05 = 3\frac{5}{100} = \frac{305}{100}$ **c.** $4\frac{1}{2} = \frac{9}{2}$

Example 1 demonstrates that the set of rational numbers includes integers, decimals, and fractions. You can also express a nonterminating repeating decimal as the quotient of two integers.

EXAMPLE 2

Write $0.\overline{57}$ as the quotient of two integers.

Solution

Let $n = 0.575757\ldots$. Note that two decimal places are repeated.

$100n = 57.575757\ldots$ Multiply both sides of the equation by 100 to move the decimal two places.

$n = 0.575757\ldots$

$99n = 57$ Subtract the first equation from the second.

$n = \frac{57}{99} = \frac{19}{33}$ Solve for n.

EXAMPLE 3

Express each quotient as a rational number in decimal form.

a. $\frac{7}{2000}$ **b.** $\frac{-56}{4}$ **c.** $\frac{323}{37}$

Solution

a. *Calculator method* Divide 7 by 2000. The result is 0.0035.

Mental math method Think of the denominator 2000 as 2 • 1000. First divide 7 by 2, then divide the result by 1000.

$7 \div 2 = 3.5$

$3.5 \div 1000 = 0.0035$

b. $-56 \div 4 = -14$

The integer –14 is already in decimal form because the decimal point is assumed to be to the right of the integer.

c. $323 \div 37 = 8.729729729\ldots$

To the right of the decimal point, the digits 729 repeat forever. Write the number using a bar over the first 729 to indicate which group of digits repeats. The result is $8.\overline{729}$.

An **irrational number** cannot be expressed as the quotient of two integers. It is represented as a decimal that neither repeats nor terminates. Examples are 1.45445444544445 . . . , $\sqrt{5}$ and π.

The diagram at the right shows the relationships between the subsets of real numbers. Notice that the rational numbers and irrational numbers have no common elements. The **real numbers** are composed of the rational and irrational numbers.

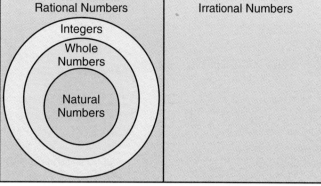

Real Numbers

Rational Numbers | Irrational Numbers

Integers

Whole Numbers

Natural Numbers

EXAMPLE 4

List all subsets of the real numbers to which each number belongs.

a. -3.2 **b.** 6 **c.** 0 **d.** $\sqrt{17}$

Solution

a. -3.2: rational numbers, real numbers

b. 6: natural numbers, whole numbers, integers, rational numbers, real numbers

c. 0: whole numbers, integers, rational numbers, real numbers

d. $\sqrt{17}$: irrational numbers, real numbers ◄

The inverse process of squaring a number is finding its square root. Since 6^2 equals 36, 6 is a square root of 36. However, since $(-6)^2 = 36$, -6 is also a square root of 36. Every positive real number has one positive square root and one negative square root. The non negative square root of a number k is called the **principal square root**. It is denoted $\sqrt{k}$. The symbol $\sqrt{\ }$ is called a **radical symbol**, the number under the radical symbol is called the **radicand**, and an expression such as $\sqrt{36}$ is called a **radical**. The negative square root of a number k is indicated by $-\sqrt{k}$.

The product and quotient properties of square roots can be used to find the square root of a number.

PRODUCT PROPERTY OF SQUARE ROOTS

For all real numbers a and b, where $a \geq 0$ and $b \geq 0$,

$$\sqrt{ab} = \sqrt{a} \cdot \sqrt{b}$$

QUOTIENT PROPERTY OF SQUARE ROOTS

For all real numbers a and b, where $a \geq 0$ and $b > 0$,

$$\sqrt{\frac{a}{b}} = \frac{\sqrt{a}}{\sqrt{b}}$$

ALGEBRA: WHO, WHERE, WHEN

Irrational numbers were first called *incommensurable* ("unmeasurable") *numbers.* The mathematician Pythagoras (580–500 B.C.) taught that all measurements could be expressed as ratios of whole numbers. The discovery that lengths such as the diagonal of a unit-square could not be expressed as a ratio led to the concept of irrational numbers.

CHECK UNDERSTANDING

Why are perfect squares always positive?

Whether you multiply two positive numbers or two negative numbers, the result is positive.

Example 4: Ask students to determine to which subset each number belongs. **-3.2, 6, and 0 are rational because they can be expressed as the quotient of two integers ($-32/10$, $6/1$, and $0/8$). Since 17 is not the square of an integer, $\sqrt{17}$ is not a rational number; $\sqrt{17}$ is a nonterminating, nonrepeating decimal and thus is irrational.**

Next have students consider the irrational numbers π and $\sqrt{2}$. Explain that although we often express π as 3.14 or 22/7, it is not possible to get an exact value for π since it is an irrational number.

Make Connections

History In 240 B.C. Archimedes calculated π to be between 223/71 and 22/7. Tsu Ch'ung-chih represented π as 355/113. A recent fractional representation of π is 754/240. Stress that π is an irrational number and that these are only approximate representations of π.

Similarly, we often use 1.414 to approximate $\sqrt{2}$. Have students use their calculators to find the $\sqrt{2}$.

Before students discuss the product and quotient properties of square roots following Example 4, have them work with partners to explore properties of square roots. Ask them to set up charts like the one below and fill in values for a and b. Have them complete three or four rows, and then ask them to describe any patterns they see. Students should see that $\sqrt{a} \cdot \sqrt{b} = \sqrt{a \cdot b}$ and that $\sqrt{a}/\sqrt{b} = \sqrt{a/b}$.

a	b	$\sqrt{a}$	$\sqrt{b}$	$\sqrt{a} \cdot \sqrt{b}$	$\sqrt{a \cdot b}$	$\sqrt{a}/\sqrt{b}$	$\sqrt{a/b}$
4	25	2	5	$2 \cdot 5 = 10$	$\sqrt{100} = 10$	2/5	2/5

Example 5: Ask students why 1089 was factored to 9 • 121 and not 3 • 363. **because 9 and 121 are perfect squares**

Example 6: Ask students to find $\sqrt{-16}$ using a calculator. Ask them what happens. **The calculator registers an error.** Why? **because the square root of a negative number is not defined for real numbers**

Example 7: Ask students what the word *oscillation* means. **a single swing of the pendulum in one direction**

Ongoing Assessment The important concepts and skills are identifying subsets of the real number system, expressing a rational number as the quotient of two integers, and finding the principal square root of a number. To assess these ideas, have students demonstrate how they have applied these concepts and skills in Exercises 5, 8, and 25 of the Try These section.

Guided Practice/Try These In connection with Exercises 2–6, ask students which sets are subsets of other sets and which sets have no numbers in common. **naturals: subset of wholes, integers, rationals, reals; wholes: subset of integers, rationals, reals; integers: subset of rationals, reals; rationals: subset of reals; irrationals: subset of reals; rationals and irrationals have no numbers in common** Stress that the real number system is made up of rational numbers and irrational numbers. Every real number is either rational or irrational and no real number is both rational and irrational. Have a student explain how to write the decimal in Exercise 8 as the quotient of two integers. **4.11 = 4 11/100** For Exercise 33, point out that, for convenience, batting averages are not written with a leading zero in sports reports.

COMMUNICATING ABOUT ALGEBRA

Using the definition of square root, explain why a negative radicand can not have a real number square root.

The square root of a number is any number times itself whose product is equal to the radicand. It is not possible to have a negative product when two real numbers with the same sign are multiplied.

CHECK UNDERSTANDING

In Example 7, why is the length of the pendulum converted to 125 cm? If you wanted to leave the length of the pendulum in meters, how could you convert the formula to accommodate meters?

See Additional Answers.

EXAMPLE 5

Determine each square root.

a. $\sqrt{1089}$ **b.** $-\sqrt{0.49}$ **c.** $\sqrt{-25}$ **d.** $\sqrt{\frac{324}{361}}$

Solution

a. $\sqrt{1089} = \sqrt{9 \cdot 121} = \sqrt{9} \cdot \sqrt{121} = 3 \cdot 11 = 33$

b. $-\sqrt{0.49} = -0.7$

c. $\sqrt{-25}$ has no real square root since there is no real number whose square is –25.

d. $\sqrt{\frac{324}{361}} = \frac{\sqrt{324}}{\sqrt{361}} = \frac{18}{19}$

The real numbers can be graphed on a real number line. You can use a calculator to find decimal approximations of irrational square roots.

EXAMPLE 6

Approximate the square root to the nearest hundredth using a calculator. Then graph each on the same number line.

a. $\sqrt{75}$ **b.** $\sqrt{224}$ **c.** $-\sqrt{21}$ **d.** $-\sqrt{0.004}$

Solution

a. $\sqrt{75} \approx 8.66$ **b.** $\sqrt{224} \approx 14.97$

c. $-\sqrt{21} \approx -4.58$ **d.** $-\sqrt{0.004} \approx -0.06$

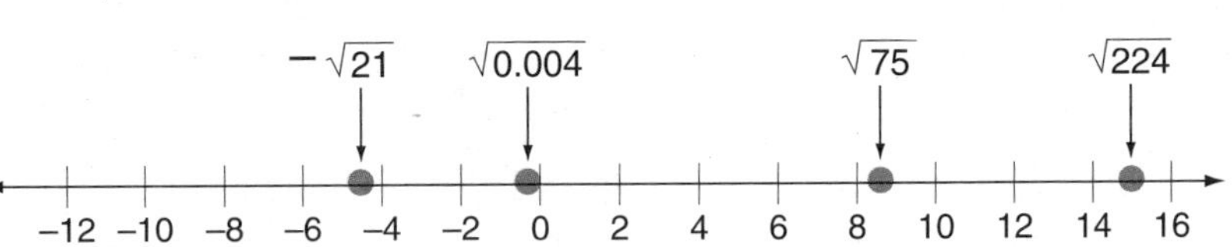

A number in front of a radical means that the radical is multiplied by that number. So $8\sqrt{5}$ means 8 times $\sqrt{5}$.

EXAMPLE 7

PHYSICS The formula $T = 2\pi\sqrt{\frac{L}{g}}$ represents the period of oscillation of a pendulum, where T is the period of oscillation, L is the length of the pendulum in centimeters and $g = 980$ cm/s^2, the force of gravity. Approximate the period of oscillation for a pendulum of length 1.25 m to the nearest hundredth of a second.

Solution

There are 100 cm in 1 m, so 1.25 m = 125 cm.

$$T = 2\pi\sqrt{\frac{L}{g}}$$

$$T = 2\pi\sqrt{\frac{125}{980}} \approx 2.24$$

The period of oscillation is approximately 2.24. ◄

TRY THESE

1. Graph and label each of the following real numbers on the same number line. See Additional Answers.

   a. $-\frac{\pi}{2}$ b. $0.\overline{8}$ c. -2.8 d. $\sqrt{11}$ e. $-3\frac{1}{4}$

List the subsets of the real number system to which each number belongs.

2. -4.4 rationals, reals
3. $\sqrt{13}$ irrationals, reals
4. -15 integers, rationals, reals
5. $\frac{0}{13}$ wholes, integers, rationals, reals
6. $7\frac{1}{5}$ rationals, reals

Write each as the quotient of two integers.

7. -3 $\frac{-3}{1}$
8. 4.11 $\frac{411}{100}$
9. $5\frac{3}{7}$ $\frac{38}{7}$
10. 6.06 $\frac{606}{100}$
11. 0.01 $\frac{1}{100}$
12. $0.\overline{7}$ $\frac{7}{9}$
13. $0.\overline{35}$ $\frac{35}{99}$
14. $0.\overline{2}$ $\frac{2}{9}$
15. $0.\overline{123}$ $\frac{41}{333}$
16. $0.\overline{753}$ $\frac{251}{333}$

Write each as a rational number in decimal form.

17. $\frac{9}{20}$ 0.45
18. $\frac{451}{8}$ 56.375
19. $\frac{-7}{5}$ −1.4
20. $\frac{-336}{21}$ −16
21. $\frac{27}{33}$ $0.\overline{81}$

Determine each square root. Do not use a calculator.

22. $\sqrt{\frac{225}{256}}$ $\frac{15}{16}$
23. $\sqrt{-36}$ not a real number
24. $-\sqrt{0.81}$ −0.9
25. $\sqrt{2704}$ 52
26. $\sqrt{3.61}$ 1.9

Approximate the square root to the nearest hundredth using a calculator.

27. $\sqrt{82}$ 9.06
28. $\sqrt{179}$ 13.38
29. $-\sqrt{47}$ −6.86
30. $-\sqrt{111}$ −10.54
31. $\sqrt{0.88}$ 0.94
32. $\sqrt{0.69}$ 0.83

33. **SPORTS** In 1985, Dwight Evans had a batting average of 0.263. Show that this number can be expressed as the quotient of two integers. If he was at bat 617 times, how many hits did he get? $\frac{263}{1000}$, 162

34. **WRITING MATHEMATICS** For which real numbers is $\sqrt{x} > x$?
If $0 < x < 1$, then $\sqrt{x} > x$.

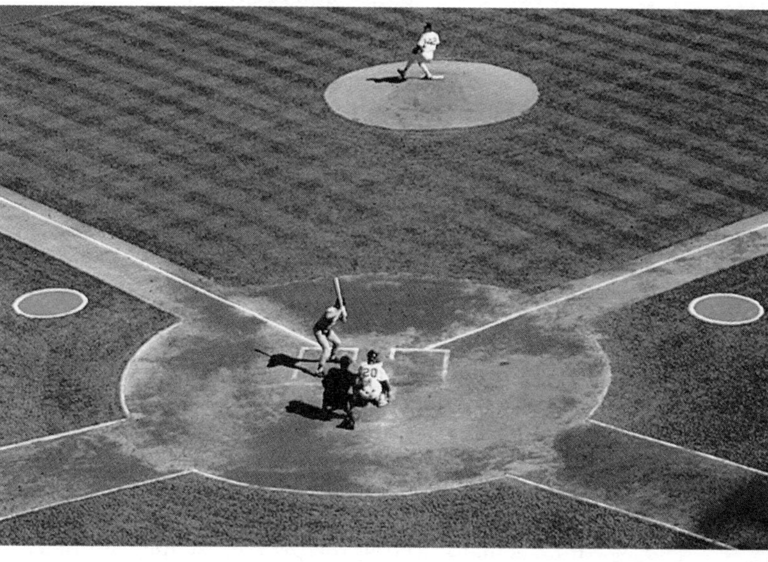

3 SUMMARIZE

In the Math Journal Ask students if $\sqrt{8}$ is a rational number and to write a brief paragraph explaining their answer. **no, because 8 is not the square of an integer and therefore $\sqrt{8}$ cannot be expressed as the quotient of two integers**

4 PRACTICE

Error Alert For Exercise 32, watch for students who incorrectly round from the thousandths place. The calculator shows 8.774964387. These students round the 4 in the thousandths place to 5 and then round the 7 in the hundredths place to 8. Students should focus on the hundredths place. The number to the right of the hundredths place is 4, and 4 < 5. So, the correct answer is 8.77.

For Exercise 42, make sure that students understand that they need to solve for t. Ask students how they determined how many seconds the object is falling. **Substitute the given values for d and g in the formula and then solve for t: $100 = (1/2)(9.8)t^2$, $200 = 9.8t^2$, $200/9.8 = t^2$, $\sqrt{200/9.8} = t$, ≈ 4.5.**

Extend Have students give examples of perfect cubes and their cube roots. **possible examples: $\sqrt[3]{1} = 1$, $\sqrt[3]{8} = 2$, $\sqrt[3]{64} = 4$, $\sqrt[3]{-1} = -1$** Ask volunteers to describe how they solved Exercise 50. **let $l = 2w$; Area = $l \cdot w$, Area = $2w \cdot w = 16$; so, $2w^2 = 16$, $w^2 = 8$, $w = \sqrt{8}$; $w \approx 2.83$; $l = 2w$; $2 \cdot 2.83 = 5.66$; $l \approx 5.66$**

Think Critically Have students discuss their answers to Exercises 58–59. Have them give examples for each. **possible examples: (58) $\sqrt{4+9} \neq \sqrt{4} + \sqrt{9}$ since $\sqrt{4+9} = \sqrt{13}$ and $\sqrt{13} \approx 3.61$ and $\sqrt{4} + \sqrt{9} = 2 + 3 = 5$; $3.61 \neq 5$; (59) $\sqrt{16-9} \neq \sqrt{16} - \sqrt{9}$ since $\sqrt{16-9} = \sqrt{7}$ and $\sqrt{7} \approx 2.65$ and $\sqrt{16} - \sqrt{9} = 4 - 3 = 1$; $2.65 \neq 1$**

PRACTICE

1. Graph and label each of the following real numbers on the same number line. See Additional Answers.
   a. $\frac{\pi}{3}$ b. $0.\overline{2}$ c. -1.6 d. $-\sqrt{15}$ e. $-1\frac{1}{4}$

List the subsets of the real number system to which each number belongs.

2. -3.33 rationals, reals
3. $\frac{0}{-9}$ wholes, integers, rationals, reals
4. 99 naturals, wholes, integers, rationals, reals
5. $\sqrt{1.69}$ rationals, reals
6. $6\frac{1}{8}$ rationals, reals
7. $-0.\overline{3}$ rationals, reals
8. $\sqrt{25}$ naturals, wholes, integers, rationals, reals
9. $\sqrt{26}$ irrationals, reals
10. $6.\overline{0}$ naturals, wholes, integers, rationals, reals
11. $7\frac{1}{2}$ rationals, reals

Write each as the quotient of two integers.

12. -4 $\frac{-4}{1}$
13. 5.22 $\frac{522}{100}$
14. $10\frac{1}{6}$ $\frac{61}{6}$
15. 0.078 $\frac{78}{1000}$
16. $0.\overline{5}$ $\frac{5}{9}$
17. $0.\overline{12}$ $\frac{4}{33}$
18. $-0.\overline{96}$ $-\frac{32}{33}$
19. $0.\overline{167}$ $\frac{167}{999}$
20. $0.\overline{779}$ $\frac{779}{999}$
21. $0.\overline{157}$ $\frac{157}{999}$

Write each as a rational number in decimal form.

22. $\frac{21}{50}$ 0.42
23. $\frac{756}{400}$ 1.89
24. $\frac{-17}{8}$ −2.125
25. $\frac{1664}{32}$ 52
26. $\frac{568}{1111}$ $0.\overline{5112}$

Determine each square root. Do not use a calculator.

27. $\sqrt{\frac{900}{529}}$ $\frac{30}{23}$
28. $\sqrt{-144}$ not a real number
29. $-\sqrt{0.64}$ −0.8
30. $\sqrt{1764}$ 42
31. $\sqrt{2.89}$ 1.7

Approximate the square root to the nearest hundredth using a calculator.

32. $\sqrt{77}$ 8.77
33. $\sqrt{151}$ 12.29
34. $-\sqrt{59}$ −7.68
35. $-\sqrt{166}$ −12.88
36. $\sqrt{0.67}$ 0.82
37. $\sqrt{0.56}$ 0.75
38. $\sqrt{0.05}$ 0.22
39. $\sqrt{0.09}$ 0.3
40. $-\sqrt{1122}$ −33.50
41. $-\sqrt{2233}$ −47.25

42. **PHYSICS** Galileo's formula states that the distance d, in meters, covered by a falling object can be calculated using $d = \frac{1}{2}gt^2$, where $g = 9.8 \text{ m/s}^2$ and t represents time in seconds. If an object falls a distance of 100 m, for how many seconds is it falling? about 4.5 s

43. **PHYSICS** Use Galileo's formula in Exercise 42 to determine how many seconds it takes for a ball to fall to the ground from the top of a table that is 100 cm high. about 0.45 s

44. **WRITING MATHEMATICS** For what numbers is the square root of a real number a rational number? The square root of a real number is a rational number if the real number is a perfect square.

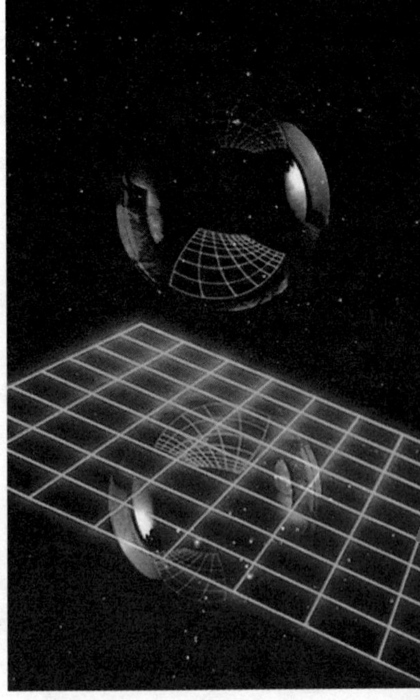

EXTEND

You know that the positive square root of a number k, denoted by $\sqrt{k}$, is called the principal square root. The principal cube root of a number k is denoted by $\sqrt[3]{k}$. Any real number k has exactly one real number cube root, the solution to the equation $x^3 = k$. It may be either positive or negative. You use the cube root function in your calculator to find the principal cube root of a real number k.

NAME ______ CLASS ______ DATE ______

RETEACHING **9.5 THE REAL NUMBER SYSTEM**

The real numbers are the rational and irrational numbers. A *rational number* can be written as the quotient of two integers, when the divisor is not zero. The set of rational numbers includes natural or counting numbers, whole numbers, and integers. Rational numbers can be expressed as either terminating decimals or nonterminating repeating decimals.

The following are rational numbers: $\frac{4}{5}, \frac{19}{3}, \frac{-7}{1}, \frac{3}{1}, \frac{0}{3}$, 0.1666 . . ., 0.125

An *irrational number* is a number that cannot be written as the quotient of two integers. It is a decimal that does not repeat or terminate. The number 3.727727772 . . . is irrational.

Example 1
List all subsets of the real numbers to which each number belongs.
a. 18 b. −6.4 c. $\sqrt{5}$

Solution
a. 18 natural numbers, whole numbers, integers, rational numbers, real numbers
b. −6.4 integers, rational numbers, real numbers
c. $\sqrt{5}$ irrational numbers, real numbers

Example 2
Write $0.\overline{324}$ as the quotient of two integers.

Solution
Let $n = 0.324324\ldots$ 3 digits repeat
$1000n = 324.324324\ldots$ multiply by 10^3
$-\ 1n = 0.324324\ldots$ subtract n
$999n = 324$
$\frac{999n}{999} = \frac{324}{999}$
$n = \frac{324}{999} = \frac{36}{111}$

EXERCISES

List all subsets of the real numbers to which each number belongs.

1. 0 2. $\frac{17}{5}$

1. whole, integers, rationals, reals
2. rationals, reals

Write each as a quotient of two integers.

3. $0.\overline{86}$ 4. −3.61
5. $7\frac{5}{9}$ 6. 13

3. $\frac{86}{99}$ 4. $-\frac{361}{100}$
5. $\frac{68}{9}$ 6. $\frac{13}{1}$

Write each as a rational number in decimal form.

7. $\frac{19}{50}$ 8. $-\frac{37}{8}$
9. $\frac{123}{999}$ 10. $\frac{5}{9}$

7. 0.38 8. −4.625
9. $0.\overline{123}$ 10. $0.\overline{5}$

30 *South-Western Algebra 1:* AN INTEGRATED APPROACH

Determine each cube root to the nearest hundredth.

45. $\sqrt[3]{27}$ 3.00 **46.** $\sqrt[3]{-27}$ −3.00 **47.** $-\sqrt[3]{0.027}$ −0.30 **48.** $\sqrt[3]{-990}$ −9.97 **49.** $\sqrt[3]{75}$ 4.22

50. GEOMETRY The area of a rectangle whose length is double its width is 16 cm^2. Find its length and its width to the nearest hundredth of a centimeter. 5.66 cm, 2.83 cm

51. GEOMETRY The area A of a circle is given by the formula $A = \pi r^2$, where r is the radius. If $A = 122$ cm^2, find the radius of the circle to the nearest hundredth of a centimeter. 6.23 cm

52. GEOMETRY The volume V of a sphere with radius r is given by the formula $V = \frac{4}{3}\pi r^3$. If $V = 905$ $in.^3$, find the radius of the sphere to the nearest hundredth of an inch. 6.00 in.

53. NUMBER THEORY Name three perfect squares between 80 and 130. 81, 100, 121

THINK CRITICALLY

Determine which number is the greatest in each group.

54. $\sqrt{13}$, $\sqrt{7}$, $\sqrt{18}$, or $\sqrt{21}$ $\sqrt{21}$

55. $\sqrt{\frac{1}{13}}$, $\sqrt{\frac{1}{7}}$, $\sqrt{\frac{1}{18}}$, or $\sqrt{\frac{1}{21}}$ $\sqrt{\frac{1}{7}}$

56. $\sqrt[3]{27}$, $\sqrt[3]{64}$, $\sqrt{64}$, or $\sqrt{27}$ $\sqrt{64}$

57. $\sqrt[3]{0.027}$, $\sqrt{0.027}$, $\sqrt[3]{0.064}$, or $\sqrt{0.064}$ $\sqrt[3]{0.064}$

Tell whether each statement is *true* or *false*. If it is false, explain why.

58. $\sqrt{a+b} = \sqrt{a} + \sqrt{b}$ false; answers will vary

59. $\sqrt{a-b} = \sqrt{a} + \sqrt{b}$ false; answers will vary

60. Why are there no real square roots of negative real numbers? See Additional Answers.

61. When is a rational number a perfect square? See Additional Answers.

62. For what values of x is $\sqrt{3x-6}$ real? $x \geq 2$

63. For what values of x is $\sqrt{4x+12}$ real? $x \geq -3$

PROJECT *Connection*

In this activity, you will work with your group to plan and conduct a survey of people's transportation habits. Some examples of the type of information you may want to collect follow.

- What means of transportation do people use to go to work or school?
- What percent of people surveyed use public transportation?
- Do people drive alone or do they carpool?
- What percent of people work at home?
- What is the average travel time (in minutes) to work or school?

1. Each group member should try to survey at least ten people.
2. Tally the group results and discuss the conclusions that can be drawn from the data. Prepare tables and graphs to communicate the results.
3. Compare your results with other groups. Explore whether pooling all the data leads to different conclusions.

5 FOLLOW-UP

Extension Have students explore a method for finding square roots without using the square root key on their calculators. Tell them that one method is the divide-and-average method. The first step is to try any reasonable number as a possible square root for the given number; then divide the radicand by that number, and then take the average of the number and the quotient. **example:**

find : $\sqrt{2304}$; try 40; 2,304/40 = 57.6; 40 + 57.6 = 97.6; 97.6/2 = 48.8; try 48; 2,304 ÷ 48 = 48; $\sqrt{2304}$ = 48.

Project Connection This activity presents further aspects of the project introduced on page 412. Review the characteristics of a good survey question. Good survey questions are short, clear, and unbiased. An example of a biased question is, "Do you like corn better than green beans?" An unbiased question would be, "What is your favorite vegetable?"

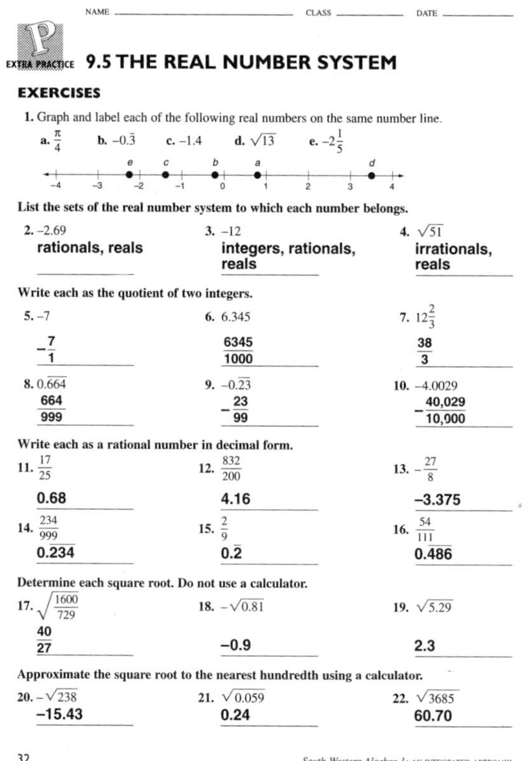

NAME ______ CLASS ______ DATE ______

EXTRA PRACTICE **9.5 THE REAL NUMBER SYSTEM**

EXERCISES

1. Graph and label each of the following real numbers on the same number line.

a. $\frac{\pi}{4}$ **b.** $-0.\overline{3}$ **c.** -1.4 **d.** $\sqrt{13}$ **e.** $-2\frac{1}{5}$

List the sets of the real number system to which each number belongs.

2. −2.69 rationals, reals **3.** −12 integers, rationals, reals **4.** $\sqrt{51}$ irrationals, reals

Write each as the quotient of two integers.

5. −7 $-\frac{7}{1}$ **6.** 6.345 $\frac{6345}{1000}$ **7.** $12\frac{2}{3}$ $\frac{38}{3}$

8. $0.\overline{664}$ $\frac{664}{999}$ **9.** $-0.\overline{23}$ $-\frac{23}{99}$ **10.** −4.0029 $-\frac{40,029}{10,000}$

Write each as a rational number in decimal form.

11. $\frac{17}{25}$ 0.68 **12.** $\frac{832}{200}$ 4.16 **13.** $-\frac{27}{8}$ −3.375

14. $\frac{234}{999}$ $0.\overline{234}$ **15.** $\frac{2}{9}$ $0.\overline{2}$ **16.** $\frac{54}{111}$ $0.\overline{486}$

Determine each square root. Do not use a calculator.

17. $\sqrt{\frac{1600}{729}}$ $\frac{40}{27}$ **18.** $-\sqrt{0.81}$ −0.9 **19.** $\sqrt{5.29}$ 2.3

Approximate the square root to the nearest hundredth using a calculator.

20. $-\sqrt{238}$ −15.43 **21.** $\sqrt{0.059}$ 0.24 **22.** $\sqrt{3685}$ 60.70

32 *South-Western Algebra 1: AN INTEGRATED APPROACH*

AlgebraWorks For Exercise 4, ask students how they determined by what factor the braking distance increases. **$2s = 2\sqrt{20b}$; since $2 = \sqrt{4}$, $2\sqrt{20b} = \sqrt{4} \cdot \sqrt{20b}$, $\sqrt{4} \cdot \sqrt{20b} = \sqrt{4 \cdot 20b}$** Ask students how to determine by what factor the braking distance increases when the speed is tripled. **$3s = 3\sqrt{20b}$; Since $3 = \sqrt{9}$, $3\sqrt{20b} = \sqrt{9} \cdot \sqrt{20b} = \sqrt{9 \cdot 20b}$; braking distance increases by a factor of 9.** For Exercise 5 ask students how they determined the number of feet the car would be traveling. **Find braking distance: $s = \sqrt{20b}$, $45 = \sqrt{20b}$; square both sides and solve for b: $2025 = 20b$, $101.15 = b$.**

Some students may want to do research to find the arithmetical method for taking the square root of a number. Students can report to the class on their findings.

Career
Law Enforcement Officer

When law enforcement officers investigate accident scenes, they measure the length of a skid mark to determine how fast a car was traveling. The table below shows the information in a highway code.

Speed, mi/h	Reaction Distance, ft	Braking Distance, ft	Stopping Distance, ft
10	10	5	15
20	20	20	40
30	30	45	75
40	40	80	120
50	50	125	175
60	60	180	240

Decision Making 2–3, 8 See Additional Answers.

Use the table above to answer the following questions.

1. If the car's speed is x mi/h, what is the reaction distance in feet? x ft
2. Verify that speed s is related to braking distance b by the formula $s = \sqrt{20b}$ using three ordered pairs (speed, braking distance).
3. Write an expression for stopping distance.
4. If speed doubles, by what factor does braking distance increase? 4
5. Over how many feet would a car traveling at 45 mi/h brake? What is its stopping distance? 101.25 ft; 146.25 ft

Investigating officers use the formula $s = \sqrt{30fd}$ to estimate the speed s in miles per hour of a car that skids a distance of d ft. The variable f represents the coefficient of friction, which is determined by the type and condition of the road. The table below shows values of f for two road conditions, wet and dry.

	Concrete	Tar
Wet	0.4	0.5
Dry	0.8	1.0

6. At 65 mi/h, approximately how many feet would you skid on a wet tar road? 281.67 ft
7. Suppose the car in Question 6 had been traveling at half the speed. By what factor could you multiply your answer to determine the skid distance? $\frac{1}{4}$
8. The driver of the car involved in an accident claimed to be going 35 mi/h. The officer measured the skid to be 200 ft. Write up the report as if you were the officer.

NAME ______ CLASS ______ DATE ______

ENRICHMENT

9.5 THE REAL NUMBER SYSTEM

Closure A set of numbers is said to be "closed" under an operation if, when that operation is performed on any numbers within the set, the result is also a member of the set.

Sometimes sets of numbers are not closed under all operations. Some examples follow.

The set of whole numbers is closed under addition.
If two or more whole numbers are added, the sum will always be a whole number.

The set of whole numbers is NOT closed under subtraction.
The difference of some pairs of whole numbers does not always result in another whole number. For example, $5 - 7 = -2$. Negative numbers are not in the set of whole numbers. Thus, the set of whole numbers is not closed under subtraction.

Determine whether the following sets are closed under the operation indicated in parentheses. Write *closed* or *not closed*.

1. Whole numbers (×)
2. Whole numbers (÷)
3. Integers (–)
4. Integers (×)
5. Integers (÷)
6. Rational Numbers (+)
7. Rational Numbers (÷)
8. Real Numbers (–)
9. Natural Numbers (÷)
10. Even Numbers (+)
11. Odd Numbers (×)
12. Negative Numbers (×)
13. Real numbers between 0 and 1 (×)
14. Real numbers between 0 and 1 (+)

1. closed
2. not closed
3. closed
4. closed
5. not closed
6. closed
7. closed
8. closed
9. not closed
10. closed
11. closed
12. not closed
13. closed
14. not closed

34 South-Western Algebra 1: AN INTEGRATED APPROACH

9.6 Properties of Equality and Order

Explore

1. Use the two clues to graph the three numbers a, b, and c on a number line.
   See Additional Answers.
   - The graph of b is to the right of a.
   - The graph of a is to the right of c.
2. Where is the graph of b in relation to the graph of c?
   b is to the right of c
3. What is the order of the numbers on the number line? c, a, b
4. Express each clue using an inequality symbol. Then express your answer to Question 3 using inequality symbols.
   $b > a$, $a > c$; $c < a < b$ or $b > a > c$
5. Use the two clues to graph the three numbers d, e, and f.
   See Additional Answers.
   - The graph of d is to the left of f.
   - The graph of f is to the left of e.
6. Where is the graph of d in relation to the graph of e?
   d is to the left of e
7. What is the order of the numbers on the number line? d, f, e
8. Express each clue about d, e, and f using an inequality symbol. Then express your answer to Question 7 using inequality symbols.
   $d < f$, $f < e$; $d < f < e$ or $e > f > d$

SPOTLIGHT ON LEARNING

WHAT? In this lesson you will learn
- to order real numbers.
- to use the properties of equality.

WHY? Understanding the properties of order and equality helps you to solve problems involving finance, transportation, astronomy, and market research.

Build Understanding

In the previous lesson, you graphed real numbers on a number line. Each real number is associated with exactly one point on the number line. Each point on the number line is associated with a unique real number. The real numbers are said to be **complete** because of this one-to-one correspondence between the real numbers and the points on the number line.

Number lines help when comparing real numbers. As Explore illustrates, one number can be less than a number, greater than a number, or equal to a number, just as your test score can be less than, greater than, or exactly the same as the test score of another person. These relationships can be summarized in the *trichotomy property*.

TRICHOTOMY PROPERTY

For all real numbers a and b, one and only one of the following is true:

$a = b \quad a < b \quad a > b$

ALGEBRA: WHO, WHERE, WHEN

The idea that the points on a line can be put into one-to-one correspondence with the real numbers was first stated by two German mathematicians, Georg Cantor (1845–1918) and J.W.R. Dedekind (1831–1916).

LESSON PLANNING

Objectives
- ▶ Order real numbers.
- ▶ Use the properties of equality.

Vocabulary
complete
dense
proof
reflexive property
substitution property
symmetric property
transitive property
trichotomy property

Technology/Multimedia
calculator

Resources
Warm Up 9.6
Reteaching 9.6
Extra Practice 9.6
Enrichment 9.6
Transparency 18
Student Handbook
Lesson Quiz 9.6

ASSIGNMENTS

Basic: 1–31, 34, 40, Mixed Review 41–47, AlgebraWorks 1–5

Average: 2–31, 34, 36–40, Mixed Review 41–47, AlgebraWorks 1–5

Enriched: 3–40, Mixed Review 41–47, AlgebraWorks 1–5

1 MOTIVATE

Explore After students have completed Questions 1–8, have them work with a partner and substitute numbers for a, b, and c in Questions 1–4 and for d, e, and f in

Questions 5–8. Ask students if the same answers hold true for positive numbers, negative numbers, fractions or decimals, and zero. **Students should see that the same answers hold true for all real numbers.** Ask students to state a rule for each of the two cases. **For all real numbers, if $b > a$ and $a > c$, then $b > c$ and if $d < f$ and $f < e$, then $d < e$.**

2 TEACH

Use the Pages/Build Understanding
Ask students to give an example of values of a and b for each case of the trichotomy property. **Possible example: If $a = 4$ and $b = 4$, $a = b$ and $a \not< b$ and $a \not> b$; if $a = 3$ and $b = 4$, then $a < b$ and $a \neq b$ and $a \not> b$; if $a = 4$ and $b = 3$, then $a > b$ and $a \neq b$ and $a \not< b$.**

Example 1: Ask students how they can determine where to graph each number on the number line. **Answers will vary; one method is to convert each number to a decimal: $-\sqrt{2} \approx -1.41$, $-4/3 \approx -1.33$, $-3/4 = -0.75$, $-1 = -1$, $-\sqrt{3} \approx -1.73$, $-\sqrt{1/4} = -0.5$, $-1/3 \approx -0.33$.** Have students classify each number as rational or irrational. **irrational: $-\sqrt{2}$, $-\sqrt{3}$; rational: $-4/3$, $-3/4$, -1, $-\sqrt{1/4}$, $-1/3$**

DIVERSITY IN THE CLASSROOM

Visual Learners Show that the negative half of the number line is a reflection of the positive half of the number line.

Example 2: After students have read through the example, have them work and discuss the activity in Check Understanding. Ask them how many points on the number line are between 2.89 and 2.9. **an infinite number**

CHECK UNDERSTANDING

Find three numbers located between 2.89 and 2.9 other than the numbers in Example 2. Take the smallest of these and find three numbers between 2.89 and it. Would you ever find a number n, such that $n > 2.89$, for which there is no number between n and 2.89?

answers will vary; answers will vary; no

EXAMPLE 1

Graph the numbers $-\sqrt{2}, -\frac{4}{3}, -\frac{3}{4}, -1, -\sqrt{3}, -\sqrt{\frac{1}{4}}$, and $-\frac{1}{3}$ on a real number line. Then order them from least to greatest.

Solution

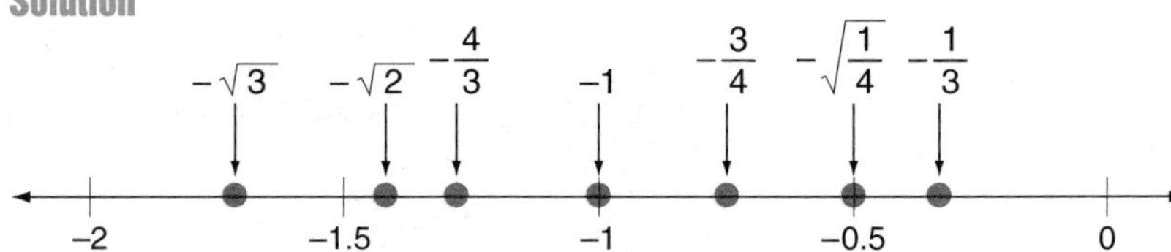

From the number line, list the numbers from least to greatest.

$$-\sqrt{3}, -\sqrt{2}, -\frac{4}{3}, -1, -\frac{3}{4}, -\sqrt{\frac{1}{4}}, -\frac{1}{3}$$ ◄

The real numbers are said to be **dense**. That is, no matter how close two real numbers appear to be, another real number can be found between them. For example, the numbers 0.4491, 0.4495, and 0.4499 are just three of the numbers between 0.449 and 0.45.

EXAMPLE 2

Name three numbers between 2.89 and 2.9.

Solution

The choices are endless; examples include 2.891, 2.8913, and 2.89999. ◄

You have studied and applied properties of real numbers throughout this book. In fact, you used some of them earlier in this chapter to solve absolute value equations and inequalities. These four *properties of equality* are true for all real numbers.

PROPERTIES OF EQUALITY

For all real numbers a, b, and c,

$a = a$	Reflexive Property
If $a = b$, then $b = a$.	Symmetric Property
If $a = b$ and $b = c$, then $a = c$.	Transitive Property
If $a = b$, then a may replace b or b may replace a in any statement.	Substitution Property

Mathematicians use the properties of equality to *prove* other statements. A **proof** is a logical sequence of statements that show another statement to be true. Properties, definitions, and already proven facts can be used as reasons for each statement in a proof.

EXAMPLE 3

Prove: For all real numbers x and y, if $x = y$, then $x - y = 0$.

Solution

Statements	Reasons
1. $x = y$	1. given
2. $x - y = x - y$	2. reflexive property
3. $x - y = y - y$	3. substitution property
4. $x - y = 0$	4. additive inverse property

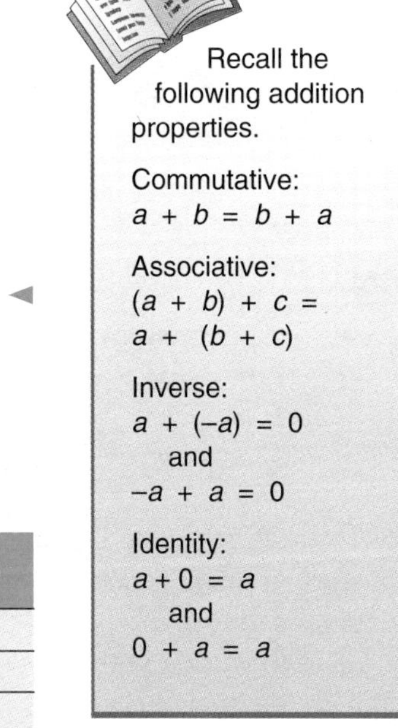

THINK BACK

Recall the following addition properties.

Commutative:
$a + b = b + a$

Associative:
$(a + b) + c = a + (b + c)$

Inverse:
$a + (-a) = 0$ and $-a + a = 0$

Identity:
$a + 0 = a$ and $0 + a = a$

Properties of real numbers are used to interpret real world data.

EXAMPLE 4

THE STOCK MARKET The 1994 performance of the Dow Jones industrial average was mixed. The performance of 6 of the 30 companies that make up the 1994 index are displayed in the table.

Company	% Change
Woolworth	−40.9
AT&T	−4.3
Exxon	−3.8
McDonald's	2.6
Merck	10.9
Union Carbide	31.3

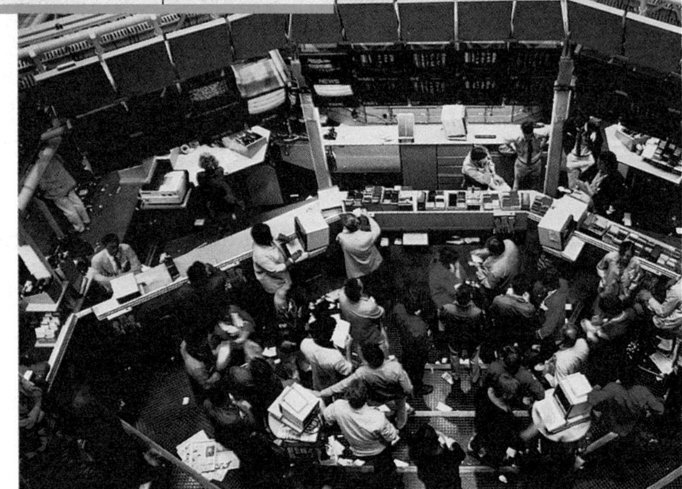

a. Which two companies experienced the greatest percentage increases?

b. Which two companies experienced the greatest percentage decreases?

c. Which company experienced the greatest percentage change?

Solution

Order the percent change from least to greatest.

a. Merck and Union Carbide

b. Woolworth and AT&T

c. Woolworth

TRY THESE

Graph each set of numbers on the real number line. Then order them from least to greatest. See Additional Answers for graphs.

1. $\sqrt{5}, 4, -3, 2, -1, 0$ $\quad -3, -1, 0, 2, \sqrt{5}, 4$

2. $3, -3.5, 2.5, -\sqrt{2}, -2, 1$ $\quad -3.5, -2, -\sqrt{2}, 1, 2.5, 3$

3. $1.2, 1.8, \frac{5}{4}, \frac{3}{2}, \frac{3}{4}$ $\quad \frac{3}{4}, 1.2, \frac{5}{4}, \frac{3}{2}, 1.8$

4. $-\sqrt{3}, -1.25, -1.5, -\frac{7}{4}, -2, -\frac{1}{2}$ $\quad -2, -\frac{7}{4}, -\sqrt{3}, -1.5, -1.25, -\frac{1}{2}$

Find three numbers between each pair of numbers. Answers will vary.

5. 1.1 and $1.\overline{1}$
examples include 1.101, 1.102, 1.103

6. 0.17 and $0.1\overline{7}$
examples include 0.171, 0.172, 0.173

Have students give examples of each property of equality by substituting real number values for a, b, and c. **possible example: reflexive property: $-\sqrt{5} = -\sqrt{5}$; symmetric property: if 4 = 2 + 2, then 2 + 2 = 4; transitive property: if 6 = 3 + 3 and 3 + 3 = 2 • 3, then 6 = 2 • 3; substitution property: if 0 = 5 + (−5) and x = 5 + (−5), then x = 0**

Example 3: Explain that a proof is an argument to convince another person that something is true. One way to do that is to provide a reason for every statement in the argument. Arguments begin with a fact or given information and systematically develop towards the conclusion. Ask students how substitution was used in step 3 of the proof. Have them state the substitution property using x and y as used in that step of the proof. **The variable y was substituted for x; since $x = y$, y may replace x in the statement $x - y = x - y$.** Have students review the addition properties in Think Back. Ask them why the additive inverse property was used as a reason for $y - y = 0$. **It is equivalent to $y + (-y)$ which equals zero.** Ask students to prove that for all real numbers y, $y - y = 0$.

Statements	Reasons
1. $y + (-y) = 0$	**additive inverse property**
2. $y + (-y) = y - y$	**definition of subtraction**
3. $0 = y - y$	**substitution property**
4. $y - y = 0$	**symmetric property**

Example 4: Ask which company experienced the least percentage change. **McDonald's** Ask students to name all possible percent changes, in tenths, between −3.8 and −4.3. **−3.9, −4.0, −4.1, −4.2**

Ongoing Assessment The important concepts and skills involve ordering real numbers and using the properties of equality. To assess these ideas, have students demonstrate how they have applied these concepts and skills in Exercises 1, 5, and 7 of the Try These section.

Guided Practice/Try These For Exercises 1–4, ask students to explain how to graph irrational numbers on the number line. **Find an approximate decimal value and then compare with other decimal values.** For Exercises 12 and 13, have students concentrate on one group at a time, for example Westchester or the U.S. Ask students how they found the increase or decrease in each category. **Subtract the percentage in 1980 from that in 1990; a negative percentage represents a decrease and a positive percentage represents an increase.**

3 SUMMARIZE

In the Math Journal Have students list the four properties of equality in their journals and give examples of each. Have them explain how mathematicians prove statements. **Answers will vary.**

4 PRACTICE

Practice Remind students to be careful when rounding numbers. Have them find $\sqrt{6}$ and $\sqrt{7}$ to the nearest thousandth, to the nearest hundredth, and to the nearest tenth. **2.449, 2.45, 2.4; 2.646, 2.65, 2.6** Make sure students focus on the number to the immediate right of the place to which they are to round.

Determine which property of equality is demonstrated in each statement.

7. If $6 = 3 \cdot 2$, then $3 \cdot 2 = 6$. symmetric
8. If $24 \div 2 = 12$ and $12 = 4 \cdot 3$, then $24 \div 2 = 4 \cdot 3$. transitive
9. $7 = 7$ reflexive
10. $8 = 5 + 3$. Since $16 \div 8 = 2$, then $16 \div (5 + 3) = 2$. substitution
11. Prove: For all real numbers a, b, and c, if $a = b$, then $ac = bc$.

Statements	Reasons
1. $a = b$	1. given
2. $ac = ac$	2. ______ reflexive property
3. $ac = bc$	3. ______ substitution property

TRANSPORTATION Despite advertisements encouraging people to form carpools to drive to work and the increase in high occupancy lanes on the highways, the percentage of commuters traveling in carpools in representative New York counties and in the entire United States decreased from 1980 to 1990. This information is displayed in the chart to the right.

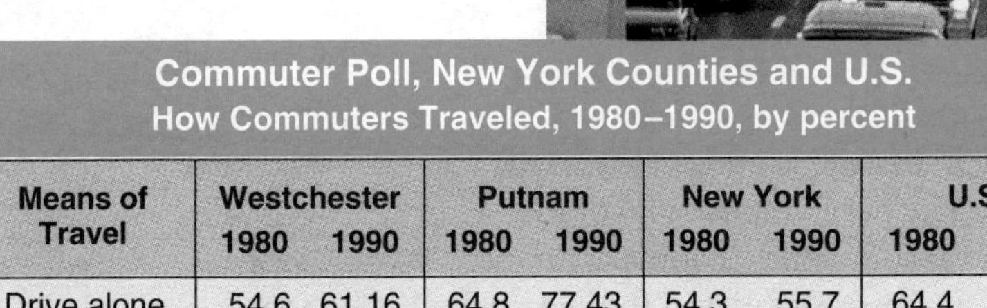

Commuter Poll, New York Counties and U.S.
How Commuters Traveled, 1980–1990, by percent

Means of Travel	Westchester 1980	Westchester 1990	Putnam 1980	Putnam 1990	New York 1980	New York 1990	U.S. 1980	U.S. 1990
Drive alone	54.6	61.16	64.8	77.43	54.3	55.7	64.4	73.2
Carpool	15.7	10.20	24	11.71	18.4	19.75	19.7	13.4
Bus	5	4.94	1.1	0.59	8.2	6.69	4.1	3
Rail	12.6	12.47	4.5	5.14	3.4	2.9	0.6	0.6
Bicycle	0.2	0.14	0.1	0.06	0.4	0.25	0.5	0.5
Walk	7.2	5.43	2.6	1.59	9.2	7.18	5.6	5.6
Other	4.7	5.71	2.9	3.48	6.1	7.52	5.2	3.7

12. Which mode of transportation experienced the greatest percentage point increase? drive alone
13. Which mode of transportation experienced the greatest percentage point decrease? carpool
14. **WRITING MATHEMATICS** Write a paragraph in your own words explaining how to order $\sqrt{3}$, 1.7, $1\frac{71}{100}$, 1.732, and $1.\overline{732}$. Answers will vary.

PRACTICE

Graph each set of numbers on the real number line. Then order them from least to greatest. See Additional Answers for graphs.

1. $-\sqrt{6}, 5, -4, 3, -2, 0$ $\quad -4, -\sqrt{6}, -2, 0, 3, 5$
2. $5, -5.5, 4.5, -4, 3.5, \sqrt{20}$ $\quad -5.5, -4, 3.5, \sqrt{20}, 4.5, 5$
3. $1.3, 1.8, \frac{6}{5}, \frac{8}{5}, \frac{19}{10}$ $\quad \frac{6}{5}, 1.3, \frac{8}{5}, 1.8, \frac{19}{10}$
4. $-1.75, -1.5, -\frac{5}{4}, -1, -\frac{3}{4}$ $\quad -1.75, -1.5, -\frac{5}{4}, -1, -\frac{3}{4}$

Write each set of numbers in order from least to greatest.

5. $\frac{5}{8}, \frac{4}{7}, \frac{6}{9}$ $\quad \frac{4}{7}, \frac{5}{8}, \frac{6}{9}$
6. $\frac{14}{17}, \frac{16}{19}, \frac{13}{16}$ $\quad \frac{13}{16}, \frac{14}{17}, \frac{16}{19}$
7. $1\frac{6}{7}, \frac{15}{7}, 2.1$ $\quad 1\frac{6}{7}, 2.1, \frac{15}{7}$
8. $2\frac{5}{9}, 2\frac{2}{3}, 2.5$ $\quad 2.5, 2\frac{5}{9}, 2\frac{2}{3}$
9. $-0.151, -0.1501, -0.1511$ $\quad -0.1511, -0.151, -0.1501$
10. $-3.343, -3.434, -3.43$ $\quad -3.434, -3.43, -3.343$

Find three numbers between each pair of numbers. Answers will vary.

11. 3.1 and 3.11 examples include 3.101, 3.102, 3.103

12. 5.7 and 5.75 examples include 5.71, 5.72, 5.73

13. 4.118 and $4.\overline{118}$ examples include 4.11801, 4.11802, 4.11803

14. 3.345 and $3.\overline{345}$ examples include 3.3451, 3.3452, 3.3453

Determine which property of equality is demonstrated in each statement.

15. $-3 = -3$ reflexive

16. $7 = 9 - 2$; since $21 \div 7 = 3$, then $21 \div (9 - 2) = 3$. substitution

17. If $4 = 8 \div 2$, then $8 \div 2 = 4$. symmetric

18. If $30 \cdot 2 = 60$ and $60 = 54 + 6$, then $30 \cdot 2 = 54 + 6$. transitive

19. Prove: For all real numbers x, y, and z, if $x = y$, then $x + z = y + z$.

Statements	Reasons
1. $x = y$	1. given
2. $x + z = x + z$	2. ______ reflexive property
3. $x + z = y + z$	3. ______ substitution property

20. Prove: For all real numbers x, y, and z, if $x + y = z$, then $x = z - y$.

Statements	Reasons
1. $x + y = z$	1. given
2. $x + y - y = z - y$	2. ______ subtraction property
3. $x + 0 = z - y$	3. ______ additive inverse property
4. $x = z - y$	4. ______ zero property of addition

ASTRONOMY The asteroids are approximately 30,000 pieces of rocky debris located between the orbits of Mars and Jupiter. The first asteroid was discovered in 1801 by Father Piazzi. Karl Friedrich Gauss calculated its orbit. Data for the first ten asteroids to be discovered are given in the chart.

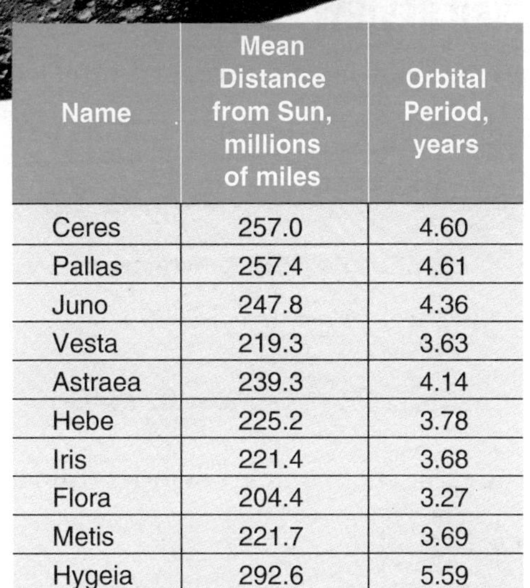

Name	Mean Distance from Sun, millions of miles	Orbital Period, years
Ceres	257.0	4.60
Pallas	257.4	4.61
Juno	247.8	4.36
Vesta	219.3	3.63
Astraea	239.3	4.14
Hebe	225.2	3.78
Iris	221.4	3.68
Flora	204.4	3.27
Metis	221.7	3.69
Hygeia	292.6	5.59

21. Which asteroid has the least mean distance from the sun? Flora

22. Which asteroid has the greatest mean distance from the sun? Pallas

23. Order the ten asteroids from shortest to longest orbital period. Flora, Vesta, Iris, Metis, Hebe, Astraea, Juno, Ceres, Pallas, Hygeia

24. **WRITING MATHEMATICS** Use a dictionary to find the definition of the word *symmetric.* Compare and contrast the meaning of this word as it is used in the properties of equality in this lesson and as it is used in Lessons 9.1 and 9.2 in relation to the graphs of absolute value equations. Answers will vary.

For Exercises 11–14, suggest that students first graph the two given numbers on a number line, allowing generous space for the interval and then locate numbers within that interval. For Exercises 19 and 20, remind students to use only mathematical properties as reasons.

Extend Have students discuss Exercises 25–29. Have them test negative numbers and zero as well as positive numbers. Ask why they should do so. **because negative numbers and zero sometimes yield different results than positive numbers do, and it is important to test all possibilities** Ask if their answers hold true for ≤ and ≥ as well. **yes**

Think Critically Have students give examples to justify their answer to Exercise 34. **Possible example: All three statements are true; −3 = −3, −3 ≤ −3, and −3 ≥ −3.** For Exercises 36–38, make sure that students understand that in the properties of equality, *a*, *b*, and *c* represent distinct real numbers.

NAME ______ CLASS ______ DATE ______

RETEACHING **9.6 PROPERTIES OF EQUALITY AND ORDER**

Every real number can be paired with exactly one point on the number line. Likewise, every point on the number line is paired with only one real number. Because of this "one-to-one" pairing, or correspondence, between every point on the number line and every real number, the real numbers are *complete.*

Where a number point, or graph of a number, is on the number line in relation to another number point determines how that number compares in value to the other number. Points to the left of any number point represent numbers less than that number. Points to the right represent numbers greater than that number. Any number is either equal to (=), less than (<), or greater than (>) another number.

Example

Graph the numbers. Then order them from least to greatest.

$-\sqrt{5}, -\frac{5}{4}, -2, -\sqrt{\left(\frac{1}{64}\right)}, -\frac{3}{8}, -\frac{3}{4}$

Solution

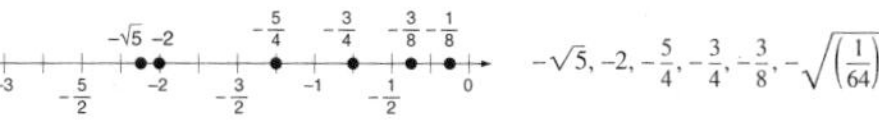

$-\sqrt{5}, -2, -\frac{5}{4}, -\frac{3}{4}, -\frac{3}{8}, -\sqrt{\left(\frac{1}{64}\right)}$

EXERCISES

1. Graph the numbers on the real number line. Then order them from least to greatest.

$-\sqrt{3}, -\sqrt{\frac{4}{25}}, -\sqrt{\frac{36}{25}}, -\sqrt{\frac{25}{4}}, -\frac{15}{4}$

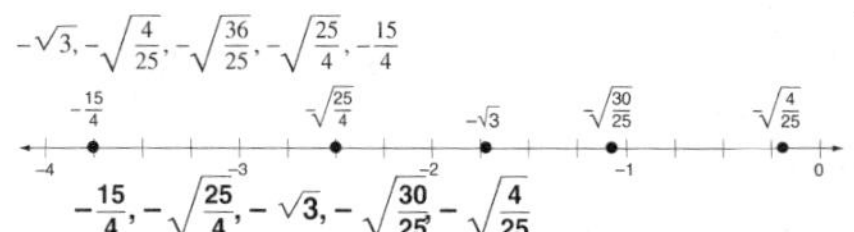

$-\frac{15}{4}, -\sqrt{\frac{25}{4}}, -\sqrt{3}, -\sqrt{\frac{30}{25}}, -\sqrt{\frac{4}{25}}$

Write each set in order from least to greatest.

2. $3.8, 3\frac{2}{3}, \frac{15}{3}$

3. $\frac{7}{8}, \frac{7}{10}, \frac{7}{12}$

4. $5\frac{3}{8}, 5\frac{2}{5}, 5\frac{1}{3}$

5. −0.479, −0.794, −0.497

2. $3\frac{2}{3}, 3.8, \frac{15}{3}$

3. $\frac{7}{12}, \frac{7}{10}, \frac{7}{8}$

4. $5\frac{1}{3}, 5\frac{2}{5}, 5\frac{3}{8}$

5. −0.794, −0.497, −0.479

38 *South-Western Algebra 1: AN INTEGRATED APPROACH*

5 FOLLOW-UP

Extension Students can use the properties of equality to prove many statements about equality. Tell students that sometimes they can be proved with only a few steps; others take a number of steps. Give students the following proof and ask them to give reasons for each step.

Prove: For all real numbers, a, b, and c, if $a = b$, then $ac = bc$.

Statement	Reason
1. $a = b$	**Given**
2. $ac = ac$	**Reflexive property**
3. $ac = bc$	**Substitution property**

NAME ______ CLASS ______ DATE ______

EXTRA PRACTICE **9.6 PROPERTIES OF EQUALITY AND ORDER**

EXERCISES

Graph each set of numbers on the real number line. Then order them from least to greatest. Check students' graphs.

1. $\sqrt{7}, 3, -3, 2, 0, -1$ **2.** $6.7, 6.2, \frac{13}{2}, \frac{63}{10}, \frac{34}{5}$

1. $-3, -1, 0, 2, \sqrt{7}, 3$
2. $6.2, \frac{63}{10}, \frac{13}{2}, 6.7, \frac{34}{5}$

Write each set in order from least to greatest.

3. $\frac{6}{11}, \frac{5}{9}, \frac{4}{7}$ **4.** $\frac{15}{19}, \frac{13}{17}, \frac{11}{15}$

5. $2.2, 2\frac{3}{8}, \frac{9}{4}$ **6.** $-0.213, -0.2123, -0.2143$

3. $\frac{6}{11}, \frac{5}{9}, \frac{4}{7}$
4. $\frac{11}{15}, \frac{13}{17}, \frac{15}{19}$
5. $2.2, \frac{9}{4}, 2\frac{3}{8}$
6. $-0.2143, -0.213, -0.2123$

Find three numbers between each pair of numbers.

7. 6.07 and 6.078 **8.** 5.875 and $5.\overline{875}$

7. 6.071, 6.072, 6.073
8. 5.87551, 5.87552, 5.87553

Determine which property of equality is demonstrated in each statement.

9. If $9 + 3 = 12$, then $12 = 9 + 3$. — 9. symmetric property

10. If $\frac{36}{18} = \frac{16}{8}$ and $\frac{16}{8} = \frac{30}{15}$, then $\frac{36}{18} = \frac{30}{15}$. — 10. transitive property

11. If $6 = 9 - 3$ and $2.7 \div 0.3 = 9$, then $6 = (2.7 \div 0.3) - 3$ — 11. substitution property

12. Prove: For all real numbers x, y, and z. If $x = z - y$, then $x + y = z$.

Statements	Reasons
1. $x = z - y$	1. given
2. $x + y = z - y + y$	2. addition property
3. $x + y = z + 0$	3. additive inverse property
4. $x + y = z$	4. zero property of addition

40 *South-Western Algebra 1: AN INTEGRATED APPROACH*

EXTEND

The transitive property holds true for inequalities as well as equalities.

a. If $a < b$ and $b < c$, then $a < c$.
b. If $a > b$ and $b > c$, then $a > c$.

25. Provide a numerical example for part a of this property. Answers will vary; Example: if $2 < 3$ and $3 < 4$, then $2 < 4$.

26. Provide a numerical example for part b. Answers will vary; Example: if $8 > 7$ and $7 > 5$, then $8 > 5$.

27. Does the reflexive property hold for inequalities? Provide an example. No; a number is not less than itself; $3 \nless 3$.

28. Does the symmetric property hold for inequalities? Provide an example. No; if $3 < 4$, then $4 \nless 3$.

29. Does the substitution property hold for inequalities? Provide an example. No; if $2 < 3$ and $2 + 4 < 7$, then $3 + 4 < 7$ is a false statement.

TECHNOLOGY On some calculators, you can use the TEST menu to determine whether an inequality is true. If the statement is true, the calculator displays a 1. If the statement is false, the calculator displays a 0. Determine whether each of the following is true or false.

30. $0.889 > \frac{8}{9}$ true **31.** $\frac{8}{9} < -0.889$ false **32.** $0.11 < \frac{1}{9}$ true **33.** $\frac{1}{4} < 0.252525$ true

THINK CRITICALLY

34. Can you replace the $<$ symbol with the $\leq$ symbol and the $>$ symbol with the $\geq$ symbol in the trichotomy property? Explain. No; the trichotomy property states that only one statement can be true at a time.

35. Write a property similar to the trichotomy property for $=$ and $\neq$. For all real numbers a and b, one and only one of the following properties is true: $a = b$; $a \neq b$.

36. Is the reflexive property true for $\neq$? Provide an example. No; $a \neq a$ is false.

37. Is the symmetric property true for $\neq$? Provide an example. Yes; if $a \neq b$, then $b \neq a$.

38. Is the transitive property true for $\neq$? Provide an example. No; if $5 \neq 7$ and $7 \neq 5$, then $5 \neq 5$ is false.

39. Is the substitution property true for $\neq$? Provide an example. No; if $3 \neq 4$ and $3 + 5 \neq 9$, then $4 + 5 \neq 9$ is a false statement.

40. Is $-x < x$ for all x? Explain. (Assume $x \neq 0$.) No; if $x = -5$, then $-(-5)$ is not less than -5.

MIXED REVIEW

Find the following measures of central tendency for these scores. Lesson 1.7

89, 92, 88, 77, 92, 83, 69, 98, 72, 95.

41. mean 85.5 **42.** mode 92 **43.** median 88.5 **44.** range 29

45. STANDARDIZED TESTS Which is the value of the function for $x = 8$? B; Lesson 2.2

$$f(x) = \frac{x^2 - x}{4}$$

A. 16.5 **B.** 14 **C.** 11.5 **D.** 18

Write each set of numbers in order from least to greatest. Lesson 9.6

46. $\frac{17}{19}, \frac{13}{16}, \frac{17}{21}$ $\frac{17}{21}, \frac{13}{16}, \frac{17}{19}$ **47.** $-0.161, 0.1601, -0.1611$ $-0.1611, -0.161, 0.1601$

Career
Market Research Analyst

Telephone companies constantly seek ways to increase communication traffic on their lines. A market research analyst for Phone, Inc., a long-distance telephone company, analyzes the company's services and compares them to those of its competitors. To help the advertising department decide on an appropriate advertising campaign, the analyst may point out the areas in which the company has a price advantage over the competition.

Over 85% of the long-distance telephone market is controlled by three major companies, Phone, TelCo, and ABC, Inc. Each carrier has more than one plan. Although the three major carriers offer basic rates that are similar, the market researcher points out that Phone offers advantages for those people who have heavy night and weekend usage. The analyst compiles the following data based on 5% of calls made during the daytime, 25% in the evening, and 70% during night/weekend hours.

	10 calls/ 108 min	30 calls/ 318 min
PHONE Plan A	\$17.53	\$39.07
PHONE Plan B	\$19.41	\$45.35
TELCO Plan A	\$19.98	\$46.00
TELCO Plan B	\$19.51	\$46.66
ABC, INC Plan A	\$21.08	\$49.69
ABC, INC Plan B	\$19.61	\$45.35

Decision Making

1, 2, 4 See Additional Answers.

1. Order the plans from least expensive to most expensive based on 10 calls/108 min.
2. Order the plans from least expensive to most expensive based on 30 calls/318 min.
3. Do you think the time percentages used represent average customer usage? If not, suggest percentages for daytime, evening, and night/weekend usage that you think are more typical and should be compared.
   Answers will vary.
4. Name two types of discounts that a long-distance carrier can offer other than those based on the time of day of the call.
5. What other factors could affect a customer's choice of company and plan? Why might a customer be interested in rate history as well as current prices?
   Answers will vary.

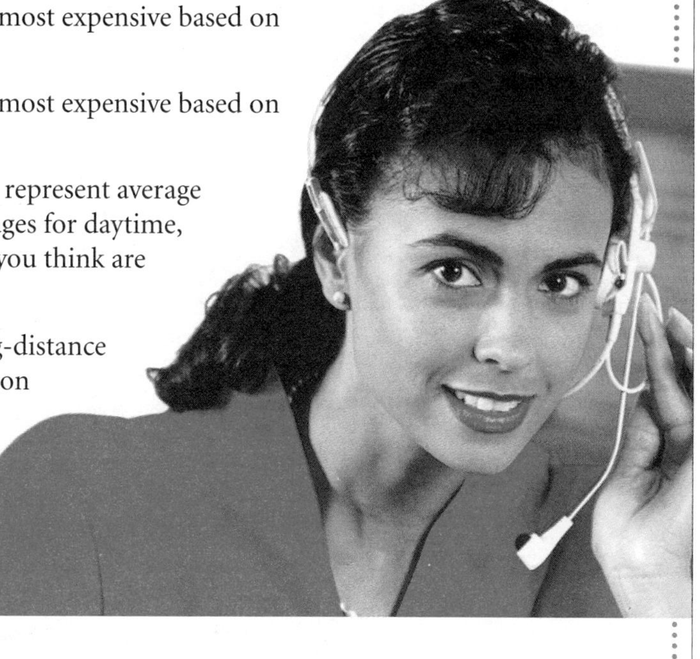

AlgebraWorks For Exercises 1 and 2, ask students how they determined the order of the plans from least expensive to most expensive. **Answers will vary; possible answers: graph each number on the real number line or use place value to order the costs for the plans.** Ask students which method they prefer and why. **Answers will vary.** Ask students which telephone plan they prefer and why. **Answers will vary.**

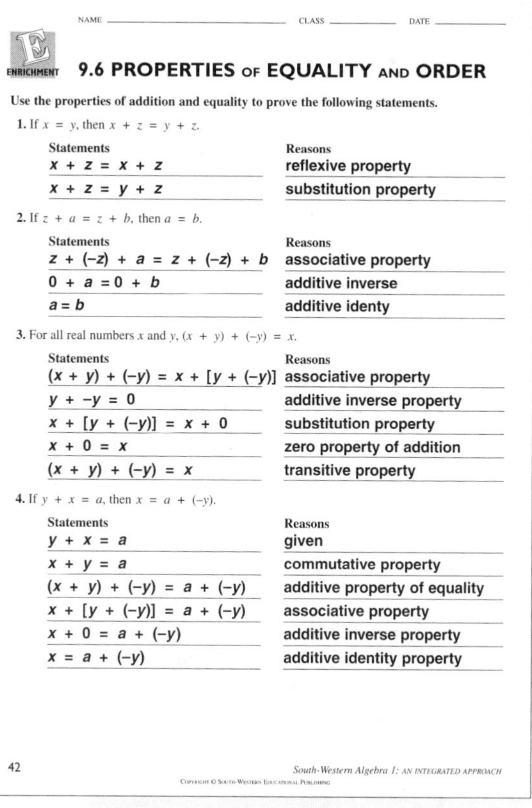

NAME ______ CLASS ______ DATE ______

ENRICHMENT **9.6 PROPERTIES OF EQUALITY AND ORDER**

Use the properties of addition and equality to prove the following statements.

1. If $x = y$, then $x + z = y + z$.

Statements	Reasons
$x + z = x + z$	reflexive property
$x + z = y + z$	substitution property

2. If $z + a = z + b$, then $a = b$.

Statements	Reasons
$z + (-z) + a = z + (-z) + b$	associative property
$0 + a = 0 + b$	additive inverse
$a = b$	additive identy

3. For all real numbers x and y, $(x + y) + (-y) = x$.

Statements	Reasons
$(x + y) + (-y) = x + [y + (-y)]$	associative property
$y + -y = 0$	additive inverse property
$x + [y + (-y)] = x + 0$	substitution property
$x + 0 = x$	zero property of addition
$(x + y) + (-y) = x$	transitive property

4. If $y + x = a$, then $x = a + (-y)$.

Statements	Reasons
$y + x = a$	given
$x + y = a$	commutative property
$(x + y) + (-y) = a + (-y)$	additive property of equality
$x + [y + (-y)] = a + (-y)$	associative property
$x + 0 = a + (-y)$	additive inverse property
$x = a + (-y)$	additive identity property

42 *South-Western Algebra 1: AN INTEGRATED APPROACH*

LESSON PLANNING

Objective

- Use different strategies, including generating a table of numbers, making a graph, and writing an equation or formula, to solve problems.

Resources
Reteaching 9.7
Extra Practice 9.7
Transparencies 10, 34
Student Handbook

ASSIGNMENTS

Basic: 1–15, Review Problem Solving Strategies 1–3

Average: 1–15, Review Problem Solving Strategies 1–3

Enriched: 1–15, Review Problem Solving Strategies 1–3

1 MOTIVATE

Introduction Tell students that they will be generating a table, making a graph, and writing an equation or formula to solve problems and make predictions.

2 TEACH

Use the Pages/Problem Ask what information is given in the problem. **average weekly income for miners in 1970 and 1990** Ask what they need to find. **a representation of income as a function of the year and predicted income for miners for year 2000** Ask what information they need to represent the income as a function of the year? **the rate of change in the weekly income**

9.7 Problem Solving File

Use Multiple Representations

SPOTLIGHT ON LEARNING

WHAT? In this lesson you will learn
- to use more than one of these approaches to solve problems.
- to create tallies, graphs, or write equations to solve problems.

WHY? Generating tables, making graphs, and writing equations are different approaches that help you to solve problems involving economics and design.

Many mathematical problems require different approaches, such as generating a table of numbers, making a graph, or writing an equation or a formula. Trying different approaches may help you understand a problem. Sometimes, one approach is more efficient than the others.

Problem

Government agencies take interest in earnings trends. For example, in 1970 the average weekly income of mining workers was \$164; in 1990 the average weekly income for this group was \$604. If the rate of change in the weekly income was about the same each year, how can the weekly income be represented as a function of the year? What is the predicted income for mining workers in the year 2000?

THINK BACK

Recall that the slope of the graph of a linear function may be used to represent either a constant or an average rate of change in one quantity with respect to another.

Explore the Problem

1–3, 5–6 See Additional Answers.

1. Use a graph. Let x represent time and use the last two digits of the year (so that 70 represents 1970 and 100 represents 2000). Using the given information, what two points can you plot? Use these points to graph the function. Describe your graph.
2. How can you find the yearly rate of change? What is this rate?
3. Use a table. Generate a table of weekly incomes for the period 1970–1980. Which was the first year that weekly income exceeded \$300? Does the result agree with your graph above?
4. Use an equation. Use the information for 1970 and the slope-intercept method to write an equation that gives income as a function of the year. (*Hint:* Begin with $y = m(70) + b$.) $y = 22x - 1376$
5. How could you use each of the methods to predict earnings for the year 2000? Carry out the work and compare your results.
6. WRITING MATHEMATICS Which method was most useful for making your prediction? Explain. What are some advantages of each method? Describe situations where each would be useful.

Investigate Further

Analysts for government agencies often compare earnings in several industries. Consider these data for workers in construction trades: in 1970 the average weekly income was \$195; in 1990 it was \$526. Assume a constant yearly rate of change.

Write an Equation | Make a Table

7. a. Which group had the higher income in 1970, mining or construction workers? a–c See Additional Answers.

   b. Which group had the higher income in 1990?

   c. What can you conclude about the yearly rate of change in income for construction workers as compared to mining workers? Explain.

8. Use the same set of axes as for the mining graph. Plot two points and draw the construction income graph. Describe the graph and explain what information you gain from it. See Additional Answers.

9. a. Find the yearly rate of change in construction income. Use this result to add a column for construction workers to the table you made for Question 3. a–b See Additional Answers.

   b. Explain how you can determine from the table when the income for the two groups was approximately the same. Compare with your results using the graph.

10. a. Write an equation that determines the weekly construction income as a function of the year. Which method did you use? a–b See Additional Answers.

    b. To show the graph of this equation on a graphing utility, what range values would you use?

11. How could you use elimination or substitution to determine when weekly income for both groups was equal? Why might you not want to use this approach? Solve the equation $22x - 1376 = 16.55x - 963.5$; calculations may be tedious.

12. Predict the income for construction workers in the year 2000. Which representation did you use? Explain how to use a different representation to check your result. $691.50; answers will vary

PROBLEM SOLVING PLAN

- Understand
- Plan
- Solve
- Examine

CHECK UNDERSTANDING

In Question 4, try writing the equation using the point-slope method. Show that both methods result in the same equation.

using the point-slope formula, $\frac{604 - 164}{90 - 70} = \frac{y - 604}{x - 90}$ results in $y = 22x - 1376$

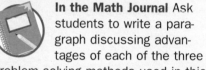

Use the Pages/Explore the Problem For Question 1, ask students to explain why 100 is used as the value for x to represent the year 2000. **Possible answer: the year 2000 is 1970 + 30 and 70 + 30 is 100.** For Question 3, ask students how they generated a table of weekly incomes. **Since the yearly rate of change is $22, add $22 for each successive year.**

Use the Pages/Investigate Further The problem given is similar to the one in the previous section. **Both problems give an average weekly income and use a constant rate of change to predict income for other years.**

3 SUMMARIZE

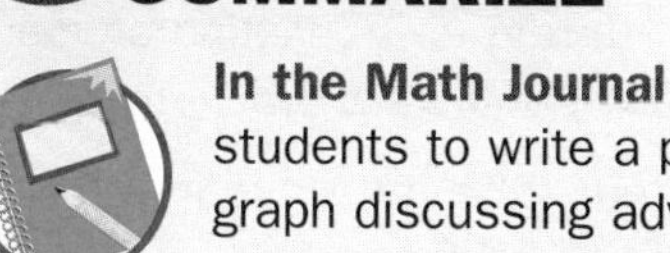

In the Math Journal Ask students to write a paragraph discussing advantages of each of the three problem solving methods used in this lesson: use a table, use a graph, and use an equation or formula.

4 PRACTICE

Apply the Strategy For Problem 13, ask what the slope of the graph represents. **the average rate of change in income per year** For Problem 14b, suggest that students draw a diagram to represent each instance and count the different colored tiles until they see a pattern.

5 FOLLOW-UP

Extra Practice The birth rate per 1,000 people in the United States was 14.0 in 1975 and 15.7 in 1992. Let 75 represent 1975 and 92 represent 1992.

1. Graph the rate of change in the birth rate from 1975 to 1992.

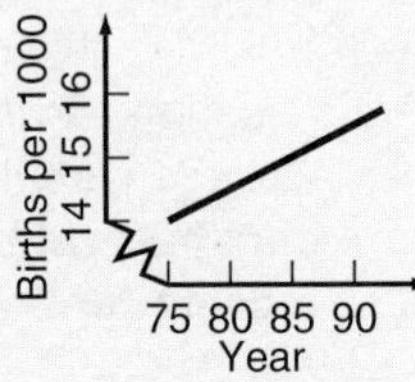

2. What is the average rate of change per year in the birth rate from 1975 to 1992? Use this information to write an equation that determines the birth rate as a function of year. **0.1; $y = 0.1x + 6.5$**

3. Predict the birth rate in the year 2000. **16.5**

NAME ______ CLASS ______ DATE ______

RETEACHING

9.7 PROBLEM SOLVING FILE: USE MULTIPLE REPRESENTATIONS

Equations, tables, and graphs can all be used to help solve word problems. Each of these representations can provide different information.

Equations – When data increases or decreases at the same rate, you can use a linear equation. An equation is helpful when you need to solve for one of the variables.

Tables – A table can help you sort data. If you need to refer to a finite set of data to answer a question, referring to a table may be the easiest option.

Graphs – A pictorial representation can often help you draw more conclusions about a set of data. A graph can help you see the larger picture and help you predict unknown information.

EXERCISES

PHYSICAL GROWTH Todd's grandfather gave him a sunflower seedling 2 inches tall for his garden. At the end of 4 weeks the plant was 38 inches tall. After 8 weeks the plant stood 74 inches tall. Assume that the sunflower grew at a constant rate each week.

1. Graph the data. Let x represent the number of weeks of growth. Using the given information, what two points can you plot? 1. **(4, 38) (8, 74)**
Check students' graphs.
2. What was the weekly growth rate of the plant? 2. **9 in./wk**
3. Use your graph from Exercise 1 to write a set of ordered pairs showing the height of the sunflower plant from 4 weeks to 8 weeks.
(4, 38), (5, 47), (6, 56), (7, 65), (8, 74)
4. How many weeks did it take for the plant to reach a height of 56 inches? 4. **3.6 wk**
5. How tall was the plant after 7 weeks? 5. **65 in.**
6. Write an equation that gives the height in inches of the plant as a function of weeks of growth. 6. **$y = 9x + 2$**
7. The plant grew to its full height after 12 weeks. How tall was it at that time? 7. **110 in.**
8. What representation did you use to answer Question 7?
Answers will vary.
9. Describe how you could use a different representation to answer Question 7?
Answers will vary.

44 *South-Western Algebra 1: AN INTEGRATED APPROACH*

Apply the Strategy

13. **ECONOMICS** In 1970 the average weekly income of transportation workers was \$133. In 1990 the weekly average was \$442.

   a. Make a prediction about the slope of the transportation workers' graph and how this graph would look in comparison with the mining and construction workers' graphs. Then construct the graph for the transportation workers' incomes to check your prediction. See Additional Answers.

   b. What is the average rate of change in income per year for transportation workers over the 20-year period? Use this information to write an equation that determines their average weekly income as a function of the year.
   \$15.45; $y = 15.45x - 948.5$

   c. Predict the income for transportation workers in the year 2000.
   \$596.50

PROBLEM SOLVING TIP

Use the values of x and y for one of the years given to find the value of b in the equation for weekly income.

14. **DESIGN** Leroy has red, blue, and green square tiles. He creates square designs according to these rules.

   - Outside corner tiles must be red.
   - Other outside tiles must be blue.
   - Inside tiles must be green.

   corner / outside / inside

   b–d, f–g See Additional Answers.

   a. A 3×3 design is shown. Color or label a 4×4 design. How many tiles of each color did you use? R = 4; B = 8; G = 4

   b. Make a table to show how many tiles of each color you need for a 2×2, a 3×3, . . . , a 10×10 design.

   c. On one set of axes, graph the number of each color tile as a function of side length. Does it make sense to connect the points? Explain.

   d. Which color increases most quickly? Describe the change for each of the other colors. Explain how either the table or the graph can be used to answer these questions.

   e. Write a formula for the number of tiles of each color in an $n \times n$ design. $R = 4(n^0)$; $B = 4(n - 2)$; $G = (n - 2)^2$

   f. Find the number of each color tile for a 100×100 design. Which method is most useful this time?

   g. How many tiles are in a 100×100 design? Why? How can you check your answers to Question 14 f?

15. **WRITING MATHEMATICS** Write a paragraph about why it is useful to be able to use more than one method to solve a problem.
   Answers will vary.

Guess and Check | Look for a Pattern | Write an Expression

REVIEW PROBLEM SOLVING STRATEGIES

1–3 See Additional Answers.

WHAT'S IT WORTH TO YOU?

1. Jan's Jewels is having a contest. Displayed in the window is a necklace of 33 pearls. A sign near the necklace gives the information at the right.

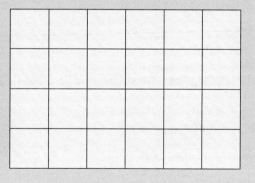

The middle pearl in this necklace is the most valuable. From one end of the necklace, the pearls have been arranged so that each successive pearl is worth $100 more than the preceding one, up to and including the center pearl. From the other end, the pearls increase in value by $150, up to and including the center pearl. The whole necklace is worth $65,000. What is the value of the center pearl?

Anyone who solves the problem gets a 33% discount on any purchase, including the necklace. (You didn't think Jan's would give the necklace away, did you?)

a. Can the pearls at each end have equal values? Explain.
b. Will you solve this problem using one or two variables?
c. How can you write two different expressions for the value of the center pearl?
d. What equation can you write for the value of the whole necklace?
e. What is the value of the center pearl? What is the value of the pearl at each end?
f. How much would a contest winner pay for the necklace?

FIND A PATTERN

2. Without listing them all, can you tell how many numbers are in this list?

2, 5, 8, 11, 14, . . . , 683

Explain your reasoning.

CAN DO!

3. A case of soup cans holds 24 cans in four rows and six columns. Draw X's to show how to arrange 18 cans in the case so that there are an even number of cans in each row and each column. (You may want to use small circles to represent cans.)

Review Problem Solving Strategies

What's It Worth to You? The strategy is use algebra.

Find a Pattern Strategies are find a pattern and solve a simpler problem. Students should note that the difference between each term and the following one is 3. Suggest that students create a similar list beginning with 3 and let n equal the number of terms in the series.

Can Do Strategies are guess and check and draw a diagram. Students should see tht 24 ÷ 18 does not have a remainder of zero. So, one of the rows will have a greater number of cans than the other three.

NAME ______ CLASS ______ DATE ______

EXTRA PRACTICE

9.7 PROBLEM SOLVING FILE: USE MULTIPLE REPRESENTATIONS

POPULATION In 1975 the population of the town of Ashton Lake was 12,500. By 1995 the population had grown to 34,000. Assume a constant yearly growth in population.

1. What has been the yearly rate of population growth for Ashton Lake? 1. 1,075/year
2. What was the first year the population of Ashton Lake was over 25,000? 2. 1987
3. Write an equation that gives the population as a function of the year. 3. $y = 1075x + 12{,}500$
4. Predict the population in the year 2010. Assume the rate of growth remains the same. 4. 50,125

POPULATION In 1975 the population of the town of Greenfield was 15,200. By 1995 the population had grown to 33,400. Assume a constant yearly growth in population.

5. Which city, Ashton Lake or Greenfield, had the largest population in 1989? 5. Greenfield
6. Make a graph showing the population increases for both Ashton Lake and Greenfield. Explain what information you gain from the graph. Check students' graphs. Answers will vary.
7. What was the first year that Ashton Lake's population was greater than Greenfield's population? 7. 1992
8. Predict Greenfield's population in the year 2010 if the rate of growth remains the same. 8. 47,050
9. Which representation did you use to answer Question 8? Describe how to answer the same question using a different representation. Answers will vary
10. What if Greenfield has a population boom in the year 2000 increasing their population to 40,000, then their growth rate returns to the same as it had been since 1975? Which city would have the larger population in 2020? 10. Ashton Lake

46 South-Western Algebra 1: AN INTEGRATED APPROACH

Introduction The Chapter Review emphasizes the major concepts, skills, and vocabulary presented in this chapter and can be used for diagnosing students' strengths and weaknesses. Page references direct students to appropriate sections for additional review and reteaching.

Using Pages 456–457 Ask students to scan the Chapter Review and ask questions about any section they find confusing. Exercises 1–5 review key vocabulary.

Informal Evaluation Give students a chance to review the material with partners or groups. Ask them to explain how they helped one another without actually giving answers to the particular problems. This technique provides another means of understanding students' thinking processes.

Follow-Up Have students solve this problem: A circus side show performer tells a 42-year-old that she will guess his age to within five years.

- **a.** Does the situation represent a conjunction or disjunction? **conjunction**
- **b.** Let x represent the customer's actual age. Write an absolute value inequality to represent the situation. $|x - 42| \le 5$
- **c.** Solve the inequality. Explain the results in terms of the problem. **$37 \le x \le 47$; the performer is correct if she guesses anywhere within the range of 37 to 47 years**

Have students write word problems that can be solved by using absolute value equations or inequalities. Students should exchange problems and write equations or inequalities to solve each others' word problems.

CHAPTER REVIEW

VOCABULARY

Choose the word from the list that completes each statement.

1. A(n) __?__ is a sentence formed by joining two open sentences by the word *or*. e
2. The __?__ of a number is the distance between zero and the point representing the number on a number line. c
3. A(n) __?__ is a number that neither repeats nor terminates. a
4. A(n) __?__ is a number that can be expressed as the quotient of two integers. d
5. A(n) __?__ is a sentence formed by joining two open sentences by the word *and*. b

a. irrational number
b. conjunction
c. absolute value of a number
d. rational number
e. disjunction

Lesson 9.1 ABSOLUTE VALUE pages 413–415

- Graphing utilities may be used to graph absolute value equations.

Use a graphing utility to graph each absolute value equation. See Additional Answers.

6. $y = |x| - 5$ **7.** $y = |x| + 5$ **8.** $y = |x - 5|$ **9.** $y = |x + 5|$

Lesson 9.2 GRAPH ABSOLUTE VALUE FUNCTIONS pages 416–423

- The graph of $y = |x - b| + c$ will be shifted upward or downward from the graph of $y = |x|$ depending on the value of c. It will be shifted left or right depending on the value of b.
- Determine the vertex and line of symmetry before you graph an absolute value function.

Determine the vertex and line of symmetry for the graph of each equation. Graph the absolute value function. See Additional Answers for graphs.

10. $y = |x + 4| - 1$ $(-4, -1); x = -4$
11. $y = |x - 4| + 1$ $(4, 1); x = 4$
12. $y = 2|x - 2| + 3$ $(2, 3); x = 2$
13. $y = -\frac{1}{2}|x - 2| + 3$ $(2, 3); x = 2$

Lesson 9.3 ABSOLUTE VALUE EQUATIONS pages 424–429

- To solve an absolute value equation, express it as a disjunction. Then solve the two resulting equations.

Solve and check each equation. If an equation has no solution, write "no solution."

14. $|6x| = 36$ $-6, 6$
15. $|x - 5| = 8$ $-3, 13$
16. $|3 + x| = 9$ $-12, 6$
17. $-3|4g + 2| - 3 = 7$ no solution

Lesson 9.4 ABSOLUTE VALUE INEQUALITIES pages 430–436

- To solve an absolute value inequality, express it as either a disjunction or a conjunction. Then solve the two resulting inequalities.

Solve each inequality. Graph each solution. See Additional Answers for graphs.

18. $|x - 2| < 7$ $-5 < x < 9$

19. $|z + 1| > 4$ $z < -5$ or $z > 3$

20. $|3w + 6| \le 12$ $-6 \le w \le 2$

21. $|5 + 3x| \ge 0$ all reals; graph is the number line

22. REPORT CARDS Miko's teacher told the class that any students with grade averages from 94 to 100 would receive an A. Write an absolute value inequality representing this range. $|x - 97| \le 3$

Lesson 9.5 THE REAL NUMBER SYSTEM pages 437–444

- A **rational number** can be expressed as $\frac{a}{b}$, where a and b are integers and $b \neq 0$. It can be represented as either a terminating decimal or a nonterminating, repeating decimal. An **irrational number** cannot be expressed as the quotient of two integers and is represented as a decimal that neither terminates nor repeats.
- To determine the square root of a number, use the product property of square roots and the quotient property of square roots.

Write each as a rational number in decimal form.

23. $\frac{2}{11}$ $0.\overline{18}$

24. $\frac{5}{9}$ $0.\overline{5}$

25. $\frac{11}{20}$ 0.55

26. $\frac{323}{19}$ 17

27. $\frac{5}{18}$ $0.2\overline{7}$

Determine each square root if it is a real number.

28. $-\sqrt{0.49}$ -0.7

29. $\sqrt{-36}$ not a real number

30. $\sqrt{\frac{625}{961}}$ $\frac{25}{31}$

31. $\sqrt{4096}$ 64

Lesson 9.6 PROPERTIES OF EQUALITY AND ORDER pages 445–451

- The real number line can be used to order real numbers. The real numbers are **dense**; that is, between any two real numbers there is another real number.
- The properties of equality can be used to prove other statements.

Complete each of the following exercises.

32. Graph $-\frac{2}{3}, -\sqrt{2}, -\sqrt{\frac{1}{9}}, -2, \frac{3}{8}$, and $-\sqrt{5}$ on a number line. Order them from least to greatest. See Additional Answers.

33. Prove: For all real numbers a, b, and c, if $a = b$, then $a - c = b - c$. See Additional Answers.

Lesson 9.7 USE MULTIPLE REPRESENTATIONS pages 452–455

- Using different methods to solve a problem can help you understand it better.

34. ENERGY CONSUMPTION In 1980 the total amount of energy consumed by the United States was 2364.4 million metric tons (in coal equivalents). In 1990 the amount was 2572.3 million metric tons. Construct a graph showing the rate of change in energy consumption from 1980 to 1990. Extend the graph to the year 2000 and give an approximate estimate of the energy consumption in that year. 2800 million metric tons; see Additional Answers for graph

Study Skills Tip You may wish to work with students to create a general procedure for them to evaluate their own solutions to open-ended problems. This will give students some insight into the kinds of things test evaluators look for. The procedure might include some or all of the following:

The solution contains:

- a clear, coherent explanation
- a clear and simple diagram
- a clear understanding of the problem's mathematics
- responses to all parts of the problem
- examples and/or counterexamples
- strong arguments supporting your position.

For Your Portfolio Have students gather samples from their project, homework, quizzes, and class work that portray efforts to meet each of their goals for this chapter. On a cover page for each representative work have students write the related goal, why the work is included in the portfolio and what the teacher should look for when reviewing the work. On a general cover page have students write a self-evaluation of how well they have met each of their goals for this chapter. The general cover page should conclude with goals for the next chapter and the student's reason for choosing these goals.

The Chapter Test is comprised of a variety of test-item types as follows:

writing	1
traditional	2–5, 7–14, 19–26
verbal	16, 28
standardized test	6, 15, 17–18, 27

TEACHING TIP

The writing item provides an opportunity for students to demonstrate a knowledge of process as well as end result. Suggest that before they begin answering questions, students should look over the entire test and determine the order in which they will work. Some students may be more successful if they save the open-ended writing question until after they have completed the other test questions.

The table below correlates the Chapter Test items with the appropriate lesson(s).

Item	*Lesson*	Item	*Lesson*
1–6	*9.2*	**16**	*9.7*
7–10	*9.3*	**17–27**	*9.5*
11–14	*9.4*	**28**	*9.7*
15	*9.5*		

CHAPTER ASSESSMENT

CHAPTER TEST

1. WRITING MATHEMATICS Write a paragraph explaining how the graph of $y = 3|x - 1| + 4$ differs from the graph of $y = |x|$.
See Additional Answers.

Determine the vertex and the line of symmetry for the graph of each equation.

2. $y = -2|x|$ $(0, 0); x = 0$

3. $y = |2x + 6| - 7$ $(-3, -7); x = -3$

4. $y = |x + 1| + 5$ $(-1, 5); x = -1$

5. $y = -6|x - 2| + 3$ $(2, 3); x = 2$

6. STANDARDIZED TESTS Choose the equation that represents the graph of $y = |x|$ shifted 3 units left and 5 units downward. C

A. $y = |x - 3| - 5$ **B.** $y = |x + 5| + 3$

C. $y = |x + 3| - 5$ **D.** $y = |x - 3| + 5$

Solve each equation. If an equation has no solution, write "no solution."

7. $|x + 3| = 2$ $-5, -1$

8. $|x - 8| = 3$ $5, 11$

9. $3|4x - 1| - 7 = 5$ $-\frac{3}{4}, \frac{5}{4}$

10. $4|3x + 2| + 6 = 2$ no solution

Solve each inequality. Graph each solution.
See Additional Answers for graphs.

11. $|t + 7| > 2$ $t < -9$ or $t > -5$

12. $|w - 5| < 1$ $4 < w < 6$

13. $|2x + 5| \geq 1$ $x \leq -3$ or $x \geq -2$

14. $\frac{1}{2}|3 - 5x| > 0$ all reals

15. STANDARDIZED TESTS Which set lists the elements in order from least to greatest? D

A. $-\frac{6}{3}, \frac{7}{8}, -\sqrt{7}, \frac{5}{3}$ **B.** $-\sqrt{7}, -\frac{6}{3}, \frac{5}{3}, \frac{7}{8}$

C. $-\sqrt{7}, \frac{5}{3}, -\frac{6}{3}, \frac{7}{8}$ **D.** $-\sqrt{7}, -\frac{6}{3}, \frac{7}{8}, \frac{5}{3}$

Solve the problem.

16. The birth rate per 1000 people in Japan was 17.2 in 1975 and 9.7 in 1992. Predict the approximate birth rate in the year 2000 if this trend continues. about 6.2

STANDARDIZED TESTS Which item lists all the subsets of the real numbers to which each of the following numbers belong?

I. natural **II.** whole **III.** integers
IV. rational **V.** irrational **VI.** real

17. $-\frac{12}{4}$ A

A. III, IV, and VI **B.** I, II, III, IV, and VI

C. IV, V, and VI **D.** I, II, III, and VI

18. $\sqrt{21}$ C

A. III, V, and VI **B.** IV and VI

C. V and VI **D.** IV, V, and VI

Determine each square root if it is a real number.

19. $\sqrt{1.44}$ 1.2

20. $-\sqrt{121}$ -11

21. $\sqrt{484}$ 22

22. $\sqrt{-1681}$ not a real number

Write each as the quotient of two integers.

23. -4.17 $\frac{-417}{100}$

24. 0.091 $\frac{91}{1000}$

25. $0.\overline{8}$ $\frac{8}{9}$

26. $0.\overline{16}$ $\frac{16}{99}$

27. STANDARDIZED TESTS Which of the following numbers represents the rational number $\frac{17}{6}$ in decimal form? C

A. 2.83 **B.** $2.\overline{83}$

C. $2.8\overline{3}$ **D.** 2.8333

Solve the problem.

28. A clothing store pays each salesperson a yearly bonus of $1,000 if they achieve total sales of $75,000 ± $5,000 for the year. Write an inequality for the maximum and minimum sales for which a person can earn the bonus.
$|x - 75{,}000| \leq 5{,}000$

PERFORMANCE ASSESSMENT

USE THE REAL NUMBER LINE Write absolute value equations in the form of $|ax + b| < c$ and $|ax + b| > c$ for positive, negative, and zero values for a and b and positive values for c. Show how to model solutions of the different absolute value equations using the real number line and strands of colored yarn and tape.

BUILD PERFECT SQUARES Cut out 100 squares of construction paper each 1 in. × 1 in. Use the method shown to find the first 10 perfect squares.

$1 = 1 \cdot 1 = 1^2 \rightarrow \sqrt{1} = 1$

2, not a square

3, not a square

$4 = 2 \cdot 2 = 2^2 \rightarrow \sqrt{4} = 2$

ABSOLUTE VALUE PATTERNS Graph $y = |x|$ using a black marker. Then on the same coordinate grid, graph each of the following absolute value equations using the color listed.

$y = \lvert x - 1\rvert$	Red
$y = \lvert x - 2\rvert$	Blue
$y = \lvert x - 3\rvert$	Yellow
$y = \lvert x - 4\rvert$	Green
$y = \lvert x - 5\rvert$	Orange

Then on a separate coordinate grid, graph $y = |x|, y = \frac{1}{4}|x|, y = \frac{1}{3}|x|, y = \frac{1}{2}|x|, y = 2|x|,$ $y = 3|x|$, and $y = 4|x|$ using a different color for each. Graph other types of absolute value equations to make different patterns.

MAKE PREDICTIONS Find out what the population of your town or city was in 1970 and what it is today. Make a prediction based on this information as to what the population might be in the year 2000 if the current trend continues.

PROJECT ASSESSMENT

PROJECT Connection Use the graphs, equations, and results of your survey to prepare travel profiles of your group and the community.

1. As a group, discuss and agree upon the key ideas about travel habits that you wish to communicate. Plan how to arrange your material to support these ideas. Consider a large poster, bulletin board display, computer slide show, or video.
2. Research and include national statistics for some of the items in your survey. One source of information is the *Statistical Abstract of the United States*, a government publication available in most public libraries.
3. In a section of your presentation called "Into the Future," verbally or visually describe solutions to some of the transportation problems you have identified. Be creative!

Performance Assessment

The activities on page 459 give students with different learning styles opportunities to demonstrate their understanding of concepts in this chapter. The activities may be used in addition to or instead of the Chapter Test on the previous page.

Use the Real Number Line (Kinesthetic/Visual) Check to see that students are discriminating between conjunctions and disjunctions as well as recognizing the difference between an inequality symbol alone as opposed to an inequality or equals symbol. You may wish to ask students to demonstrate or explain how they would check their solutions.

Build Perfect Squares (Visual) A good indicator of understanding is a student's ability to recognize a pattern that is developing. After finding several perfect squares, you may wish to suggest that students generalize the pattern, write the remaining perfect squares, and explain how they knew which numbers would be perfect squares.

Absolute Value Patterns (Visual) After students have drawn the patterns, ask them to name any other equation that fits the pattern and to describe how the graph will look.

Make Predictions (Linguistic/Visual) Check to see the number of significant digits students use to describe their prediction. Ask them to explain why they wrote the number as they did.

Project Assessment

Project Connection As a class, have students compare the types of presentations chosen by groups. Have them discuss the effectiveness of each type and what results they can hope to obtain from the work.

CUMULATIVE REVIEW

Graph each equation. See Additional Answers; Lesson 9.2

1. $y = |x + 3|$
2. $y = |x| - 4$
3. $y = 2|x|$

Solve each inequality. Then graph the solution. See Additional Answers; Lessons 5.4 and 9.4

4. $|4x + 2| \geq 10$
5. $|2x - 5| < 7$
6. $12 - 3(6n + 5) + 4n < \frac{1}{2}(10n - 6)$

Solve each system of equations.

7. $\begin{cases} 9x - 5y = 22 \\ y = 3x - 8 \end{cases}$ (3, 1); Lesson 7.3
8. $\begin{cases} 7x - 4y = 11 \\ 8y - 14x = -11 \end{cases}$ no solution; Lesson 7.5

Use the two scatter plots for Questions 9–11.

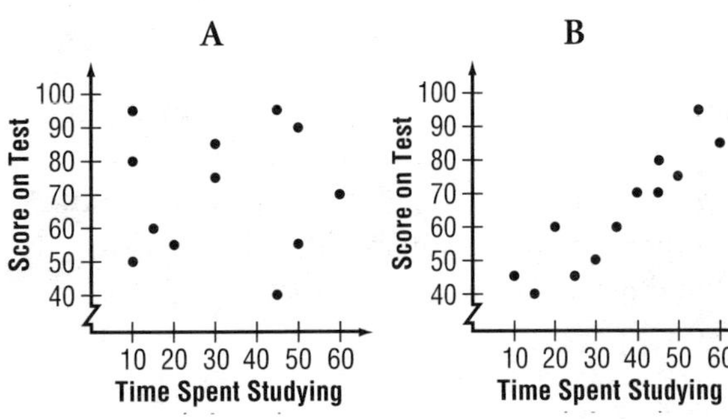

9. Which scatter plot shows the stronger correlation? B; Lesson 6.6

10. STANDARDIZED TESTS Consider statements I–IV as they pertain to scatter plots A and B.

   I. Scatter plot B shows a correlation close to 1.
   II. Scatter plot A shows a correlation close to –1.
   III. Scatter plot A shows a weak correlation.
   IV. Scatter plot B shows that the longer you study, the higher your test score can be.

   Which statements are true? D; Lesson 6.6

   A. I and II B. I and IV
   C. II and III D. I, III, and IV

11. WRITING MATHEMATICS If you were the teacher, would you be pleased with the results in scatter plot A? Why or why not? See Additional Answers; Lesson 6.6

12. A concession stand sells hot dogs for \$1.50 each and hamburgers for \$2.00 each. It costs the owner of the stand \$0.30 per hot dog and \$0.60 per hamburger. For the big game, the owner decides that a total of 500 hot dogs and hamburgers should be enough, but does not want to spend more than \$240 to purchase the food. How many hot dogs and hamburgers should the owner purchase in order to maximize profits? 200 hot dogs and 300 hamburgers; Lesson 8.5

Solve for the variable indicated in each formula.

13. $A = P + Prt$ for r $\frac{A - P}{Pt}$; Lesson 3.8
14. $SA = 2\pi r^2 + 2\pi rh$ for h $\frac{SA - 2\pi r^2}{2\pi r}$; Lesson 3.8

Identify the property illustrated.

15. If $c = a \cdot b$ and $a \cdot b = d$, then $c = d$. transitive; Lesson 9.6
16. $(10 + 13) + 24 = 10 + (13 + 24)$ associative property of addition; Lesson 2.5
17. $7 \cdot \frac{1}{7} = 1$ multiplicative inverse property; Lesson 2.7
18. $x + 5 = x + 5$ reflexive; Lesson 9.6
19. WRITING MATHEMATICS Explain how the commutative properties and the symmetric property are similar and different. See Additional Answers; Lessons 2.5, 2.7, and 9.6

Graph each inequality. Then determine whether (2, –3) is a solution. See Additional Answers; Lesson 8.1

20. $4x + 2y \leq 7$
21. $3x - y < 5$

Compare the expressions. Use <, =, or >.

22. $(5 - 3)^2$ ■ $5^2 - 3^2$ <; Lesson 2.8
23. $-(-3)^3$ ■ $-(-2)^6$ >; Lesson 2.2
24. $|-5 - 7|$ ■ $|-5| + |-7|$ =; Lesson 2.2

NAME ______ CLASS ______ DATE ______

FORM B

CHAPTER 9 TEST

Write the letter of the best answer for Questions 1–6.

1. Which ordered pair names the vertex of the graph of $y = |x - 4| + 3$? 1. d

---

NAME ______ CLASS ______ DATE ______

FORM A

CHAPTER 9 TEST

Write the letter of the best answer for Questions 1–6.

1. Which ordered pair names the vertex of the graph of $y = |x + 7| - 5$? 1. b

   a. (7, –5) b. (–7, –5) c. (–7, 5) d. (7, 5)

2. Which equation represents the line of symmetry for the graph of $y = |x - 8| + 6$? 2. a

   a. $x = 8$ b. $x = -8$ c. $x = 5$ d. $x = -5$

3. Which graph represents the graph of $y = |x| - 5$? 3. b

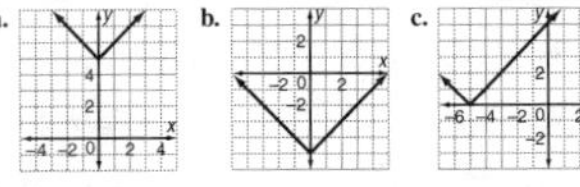

4. Which conjunction or disjunction represents the solution of $|4x + 8| < 24$? 4. c

   a. $x > 4$ or $x < -8$ b. $-4 < x < 8$
   c. $-8 < x < 4$ d. $x > 8$ or $x < -4$

5. Which number represents $\sqrt{0.64}$? 5. d

   a. 0.32 b. 3.2 c. 0.08 d. 0.8

6. Which property of equality is demonstrated by the following statement? 6. b
   If $20 \div 5 = 4$, then $4 = 20 \div 5$.

   a. reflexive b. symmetric
   c. transitive d. substitution

Solve each equation. If an equation has no solution, write *no solution*.

7. $|x - 27| = 3$ 7. 30, 24
8. $|4x + 1| = 43$ 8. 10.5, –11
9. $|3x + 1| = -10$ 9. no solution
10. $6|2x + 1| = 18$ 10. 1, –2

Solve each inequality.

11. $|x + 5| > 1$ 11. $x > -4$ or $x < -6$
12. $|4x - 1| \leq 17$ 12. $-4 \leq x \leq 4.5$

50 *South-Western Algebra 1:* AN INTEGRATED APPROACH

CHAPTER 9 TEST Form A, page 2 NAME ______

Write each as a quotient of two integers.

13. –3.19 13. $-\frac{319}{100}$
14. 0.087 14. $\frac{87}{1000}$
15. $0.\overline{4}$ 15. $\frac{4}{9}$
16. $0.\overline{13}$ 16. $\frac{13}{99}$

Determine each square root if it is a real number.

17. $\sqrt{400}$ 17. 20
18. $-\sqrt{225}$ 18. –15
19. $\sqrt{-81}$ 19. not real
20. $\sqrt{1.69}$ 20. 1.3

Write each set of numbers in order from least to greatest.

21. $\frac{3}{8}, \frac{2}{7}, \frac{1}{3}$ 21. $\frac{2}{7}, \frac{1}{3}, \frac{3}{8}$
22. –0.139, –0.1309, –0.1319 22. –0.139, –0.1319, –0.1309

List the sets of the real number system to which each number belongs. Use the following Roman numerals to designate each set.

I. natural II. whole III. integers
IV. rational V. irrational VI. real

23. –2.333 23. IV, VI
24. $-\sqrt{25}$ 24. III, IV, VI
25. $\sqrt{7}$ 25. V, VI
26. $-\frac{0}{2}$ 26. II, III, IV, VI

Solve.

27. RETAIL SALES A store owner tells his employees anyone with sales between \$900 and \$1100 would get a day off with pay. Write an absolute value inequality for this range of sales. 27. $|x - 1000| = 100$

28. SALARY TRENDS In 1980 Molly was making \$340 per week. In 1995 she was making \$520 per week. Predict how much she will make in the year 2000 if this trend continues. 28. \$580

For Question 29, use a separate sheet of paper if necessary.

29. WRITING MATHEMATICS Write a paragraph explaining how the graph of $y = 2|x| - 3$ differs from the graph of $y = |x|$.
   The rays that form the V of $y = 2|x| - 3$ are closer together than those of $y = |x|$, and the graph is shifted 3 units downward.

52 *South-Western Algebra 1:* AN INTEGRATED APPROACH

STANDARDIZED TEST

STANDARD FIVE-CHOICE Select the best choice for each question.

1. The solution to $|3x - 2| \geq 5$ is C; Lesson 9.4
   A. $-5 \leq x \leq 5$
   B. $x \leq 3$ or $x \geq 7$
   C. $x \leq -1$ or $x \geq \frac{7}{3}$
   D. $-1 \leq x \leq \frac{7}{3}$
   E. $x \geq \frac{7}{3}$

2. If $A = 8$, $B = 4$, and $C = 6$, then which expression in BASIC will output 16? D; Lesson 1.3
   A. PRINT C / B * A
   B. PRINT A * B – C
   C. PRINT C * A / B
   D. PRINT C * B – A
   E. none of these

3. All of the following numbers are irrational except B; Lesson 9.5
   A. $\sqrt{5}$
   B. 1.833333...
   C. π
   D. $-\sqrt{8}$
   E. all are irrational

4. After three tests, Juan has an 86% average. What does he need to get on the next test to raise his average to 90%? E; Lessons 1.7 and 3.6
   A. 90%
   B. 94%
   C. 98%
   D. 100%
   E. he can't do it—he needs more than 100%

5. Which of the following cannot be the result of solving a linear system of equations? C; Lessons 7.1 and 7.5
   A. no solutions
   B. one solution
   C. two solutions
   D. infinite number of solutions
   E. all are possible

6. Which of the following equations can be solved by first subtracting 5 from both sides and then multiplying both sides by 3? D; Lesson 3.6
   A. $3x - 5 = 10$
   B. $3x + 5 = 14$
   C. $\frac{1}{3}x - 5 = 7$
   D. $\frac{1}{3}x + 5 = 11$
   E. none of these

7. Consider statements I–III as each applies to the correlation coefficient, r. D; Lesson 6.6
   I. $|r| \leq 1$
   II. $r = 0.6$ indicates a weak correlation
   III. $r = 0.9$ and $r = -0.9$ indicate the same strength of correlation

   Which statement is true?
   A. II only
   B. III only
   C. I and II
   D. I, II, and III
   E. none are true

8. All of the following functions have a domain of all real numbers except A; Lesson 4.2
   A. $y = \sqrt{x} + 2$
   B. $y = 5$
   C. $y = x^2 - 3$
   D. $y = |x - 4|$
   E. two of the above

9. Which graph shows the solution of $3(3 - 2x) > 4x - 1$? B; Lesson 5.4
   A. –4 –3 –2 –1 0 1 2 3 4
   B. –4 –3 –2 –1 0 1 2 3 4
   C. –4 –3 –2 –1 0 1 2 3 4
   D. –4 –3 –2 –1 0 1 2 3 4
   E. –2 –1 0 1 2 3 4 5 6

Answers

1. C	**15.** B
2. E	**16.** A
3. A	**17.** C
4. B	**18.** A
5. B	**19.** B
6. D	**20.** 0.7
7. E	**21.** –13
8. E	**22.** 1.1
9. D	**23.** 19
10. C	**24.** –95
11. C	**25.** –76
12. A	**26.** –19
13. C	**27.** –23
14. A	**28.** 278

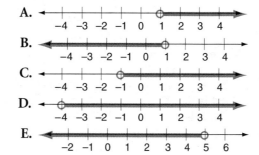

CHAPTER 9 Standardized Test, page 2 NAME ______

QUANTITATIVE COMPARISON For Questions 11–19, fill in A if the quantity in Column 1 is greater, B if the quantity in Column 2 is greater, C if the two quantities are equal, and D if the relationship cannot be determined.

GRID RESPONSE For Questions 20–28, mark your answer on the answer grid provided.

Write each as a rational number in decimal form.

NAME ______ CLASS ______ DATE ______

CHAPTER 9 STANDARDIZED TEST

STANDARD FIVE-CHOICE For Questions 1–10, fill in the best choice on the answer grid provided.

1. Which ordered pair names the vertex of the graph of $y = |x - 3| + 5$?
   A. (3, –5) B. (–3, 5)
   C. (3, 5) D. (–3, –5)
   E. (–3, 0)

2. Which equation represents the graph?
   A. $y = |x + 2| + 1$
   B. $y = |x - 2| - 1$
   C. $y = |x + 1| - 2$
   D. $y = |x - 1| + 2$
   E. None of these

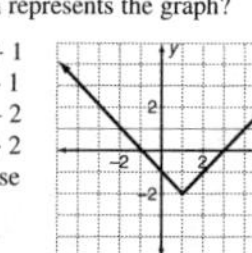

3. Which description shows how you could shift the graph of $y = |x|$ to obtain the graph of $y = |x - 3| - 5$?
   A. 3 units right and 5 units down
   B. 3 units left and 5 units down
   C. 5 units left and 3 units up
   D. 5 units right and 3 units up
   E. None of these

4. Which is the solution for $|x - 3| = 12$?
   A. 9, –15 B. –9, 15 C. –9, –15
   D. 9, 15 E. None of these

5. Which conjunction or disjunction represents the solution for $|2x + 4| > 10$?
   A. $-7 < x < 3$ B. $x > 3$ or $x < -7$
   C. $-3 < x < 7$ D. $x > 7$ or $x < -3$
   E. None of these

6. Which graph represents the solution for $|2x - 6| \leq 4$?
   A. –6 –5 –4 –3 –2 –1 0 1 2 3 4 5 6
   B. –6 –5 –4 –3 –2 –1 0 1 2 3 4 5 6
   C. –6 –5 –4 –3 –2 –1 0 1 2 3 4 5 6
   D. –6 –5 –4 –3 –2 –1 0 1 2 3 4 5 6
   E. –14 –13 –12 –11 –10 –9 –8 –7 –6 –5 –4 –3 –2

7. Which set lists the elements in order from least to greatest?
   A. $-\frac{7}{8}$, –1.7, –1.07, –1.007
   B. –1.007, –1.07, –1.7, $-\frac{7}{8}$
   C. –1.07, –1.7, –1.007, $-\frac{7}{8}$
   D. $-\frac{7}{8}$, –1.7, –1.07, –1.007
   E. –1.7, –1.07, –1.007, $-\frac{7}{8}$

8. Which item lists all the subsets of the real numbers to which $\sqrt{35}$ belongs?
   I. natural II. whole III. integers
   IV. rational V. irrational VI. real
   A. III. V, and VI B. IV and VI
   C. III and VI D. IV, V, and VI
   E. V and VI

9. Which represents $\sqrt{0.36}$?
   A. 0.18 B. 1.8 C. 0.06
   D. 0.6 E. 6

10. Which represents $\frac{4}{15}$ in decimal form?
    A. 0.26 B. $0.\overline{26}$ C. $0.2\overline{6}$
    D. 0.026 E. 2.6

South-Western Algebra 1: AN INTEGRATED APPROACH 57

Chapter Opener

Data Activity, pages 410–411

1. 32,014,000 mi; Answers will vary. The mean is much higher than the data values for eight of the ten cities due to the extreme values of NY and LA. However, it is also useful to see how these large cities affect the national average.
2. Answers will vary. The ratio of hours of delay to miles driven is higher for Phoenix than New York.
3. Answers will vary. Students may round to nearest billion or half billion or use clustering. Accept a range of $18–20 billion.
4. Answers will vary.

Lesson 9.1

Explore, pages 413–414

6. The absolute value function yields y-values ≥ 0. The y-values are positive only in Quadrants I and II.
8. It has the same V-shape; it is shifted up 3 units; its vertex is (0, 3); its line of symmetry is the y-axis.

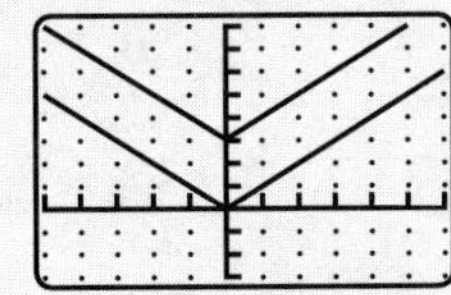

9. It has the same V-shape; it is shifted down 4 units; its vertex is (0, –4); its line of symmetry is the y-axis.

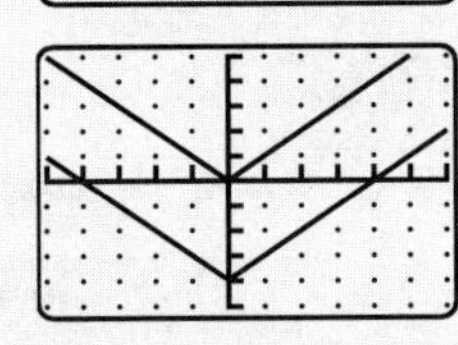

12. It has the same V-shape; it is shifted left 2 units; its vertex is (–2, 0); its line of symmetry is $x = -2$.

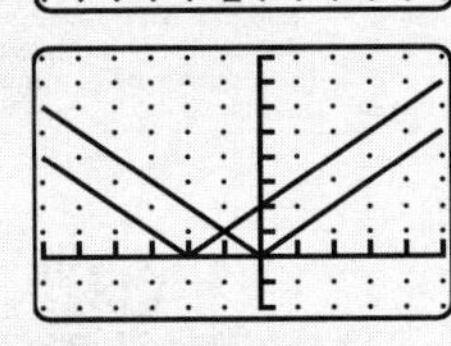

13. It has the same V-shape; it is shifted right 3 units; its vertex is (3, 0); its line of symmetry is $x = 3$.

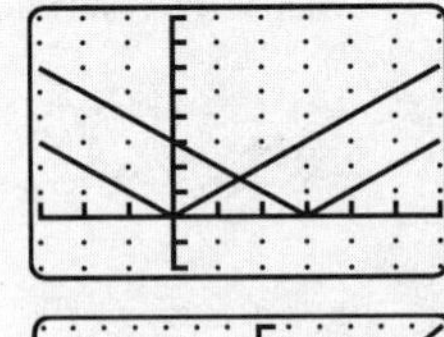

17. It has the same V-shape; it is shifted 3 units left and 1 unit down; its vertex is (–3, –1); its line of symmetry is $x = -3$.

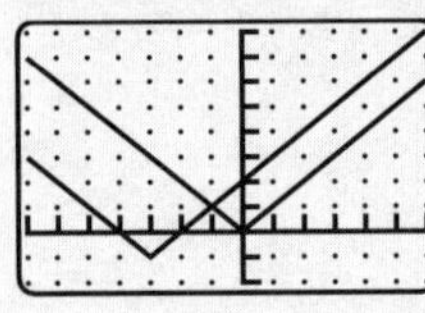

Summarize, page 415

30. Answers will vary. The rays that form the V are steeper or farther from the x-axis than those of $y = |x|$ if $a > 1$. The rays that form the V are closer to the x-axis or less steep than those of $y = |x|$ if $0 < a < 1$.

Lesson 9.2

Explore, page 416

2. The graph should show a reflection of the original triangle over the y-axis.
3. A and A' are equal distances from the y-axis. B and B' are equidistant from the y-axis. C and C' are equidistant from the y-axis.

Try These, page 420

9. The rays that form the V in the graph of $y = 4|x|$ are farther from the x-axis than those of $y = |x|$.
10. The rays that form the V in the graph of $y = \frac{1}{4}|x|$ are closer to the x-axis than those of $y = |x|$.
11. The rays that form the V in the graph of $y = -2|x|$ are farther from the x-axis than those of $y = |x|$. The graph opens downward, unlike the graph of $y = |x|$.
12. The rays that form the V in the graph of $y = -\frac{1}{2}|x|$ are closer to the x-axis than those of $y = |x|$. The graph opens downward, unlike the graph of $y = |x|$.

17.

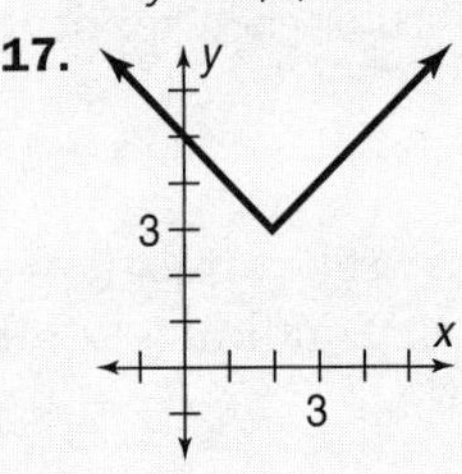

18.

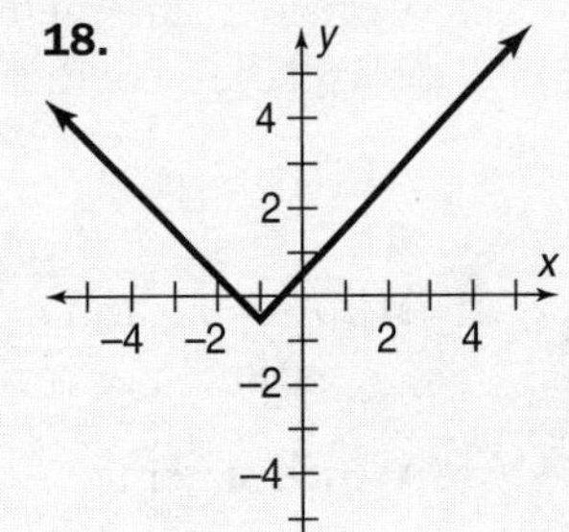

19.

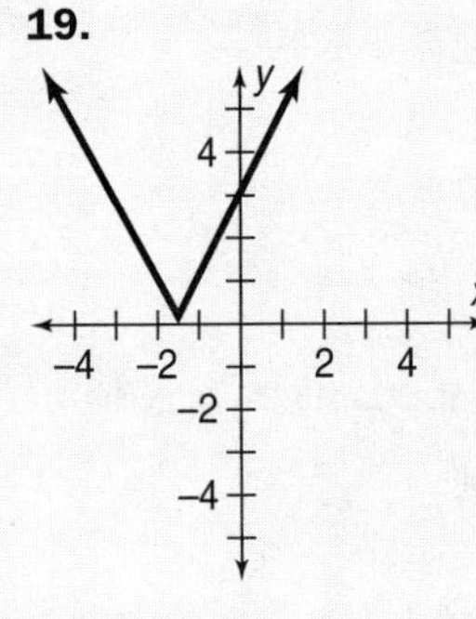

20.

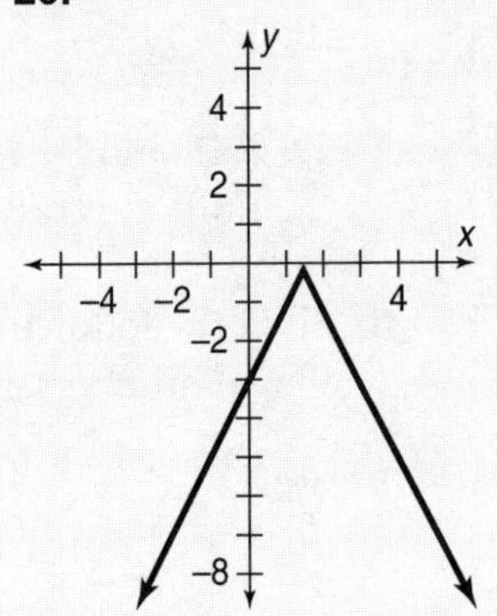

Practice, pages 421–422

9. The rays that form the V in the graph of $y = 3|x|$ are farther from the x-axis than those of $y = |x|$.
10. The rays that form the V in the graph of $y = \frac{1}{3}|x|$ are closer to the x-axis than those of $y = |x|$.
11. The rays that form the V in the graph of $y = -\frac{1}{5}|x|$ are closer to the x-axis than those of $y = |x|$. The graph opens downward, unlike the graph of $y = |x|$.
12. The rays that form the V in the graph of $y = -5|x|$ are farther from the x-axis than those of $y = |x|$. The graph opens downward, unlike the graph of $y = |x|$.

21.

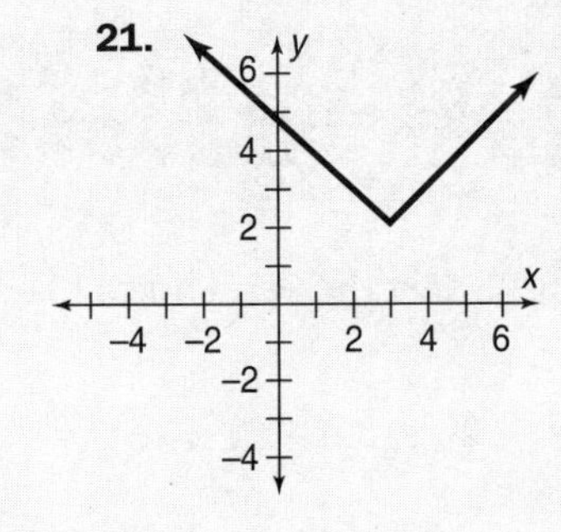

22.

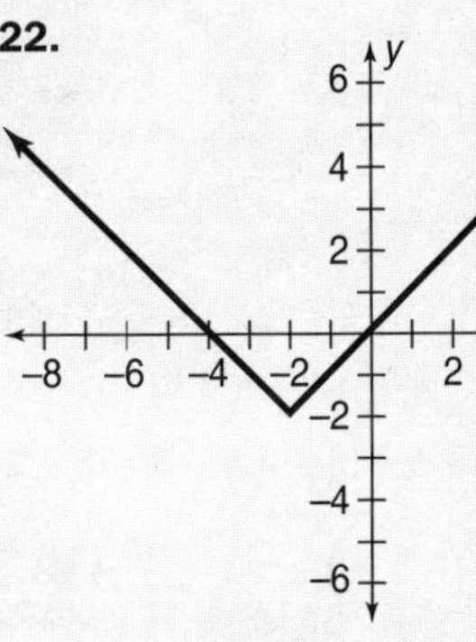

23.

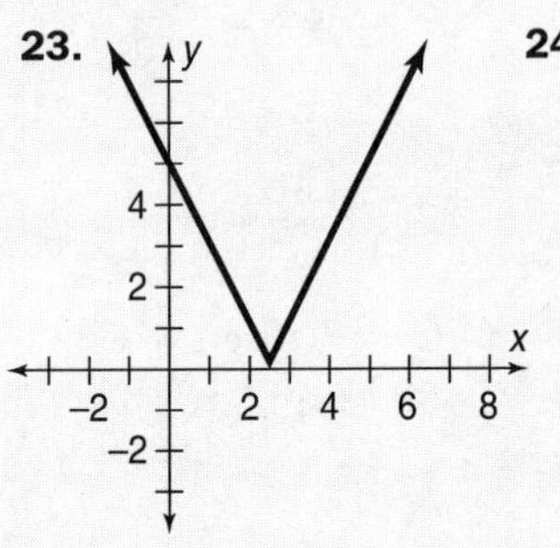

24.

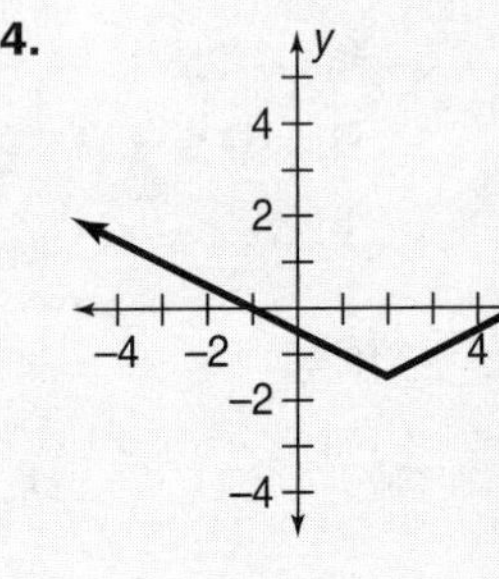

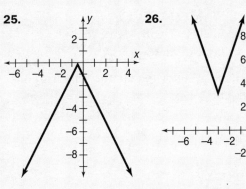

25. 26.

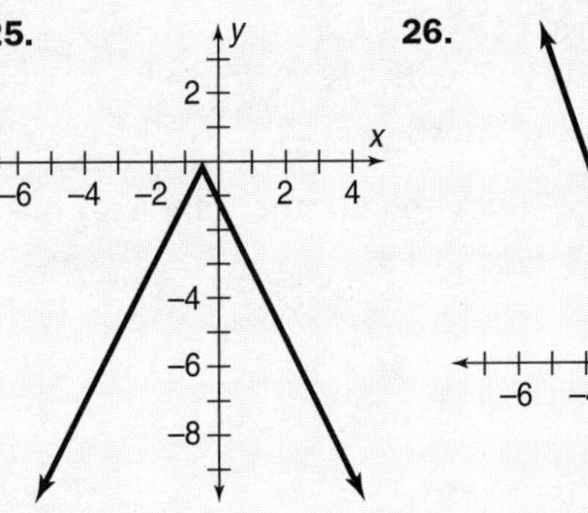

27. 28.

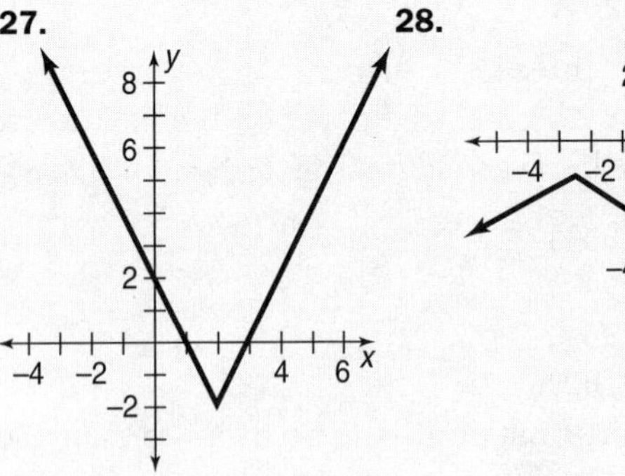

30. Angle will be obtuse when $a < 1$ because the rays of an obtuse angle will be closer to the x-axis. Angle will be acute when $a > 1$ because the rays that form an acute angle will be farther from the x-axis.

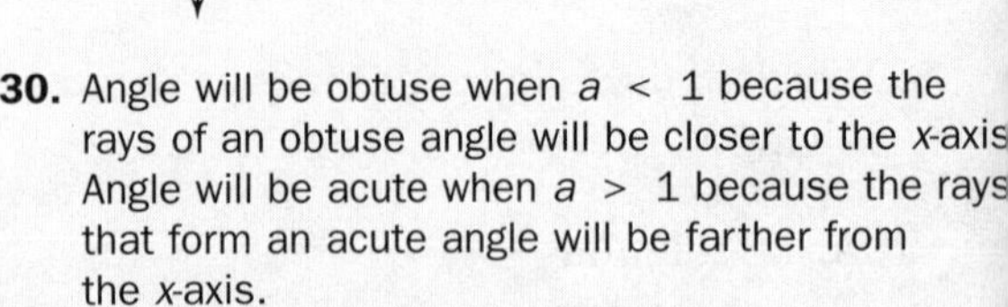

Extend, pages 422–423

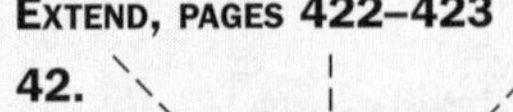

42.

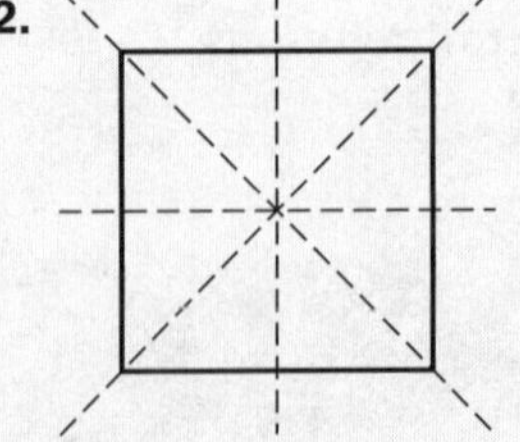

43. any line passing through the center of the circle

44.

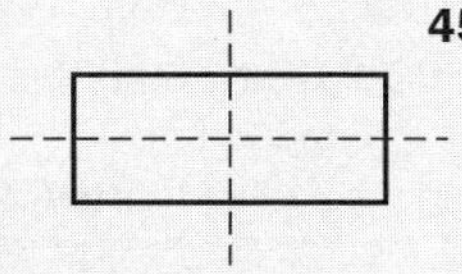

45.

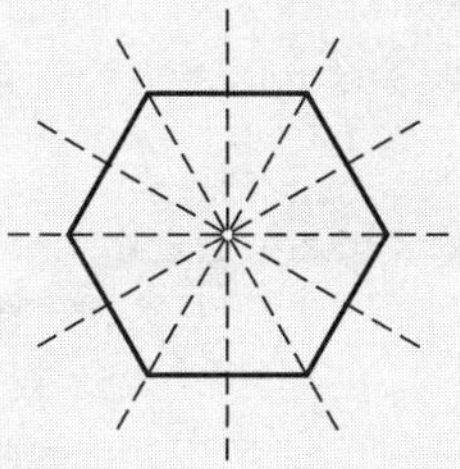

46.

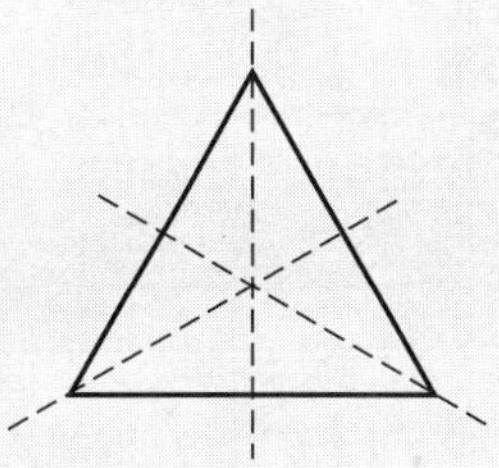

.esson 9.3

OMMUNICATING ABOUT ALGEBRA, PAGE 425

ince $|2x - 1| = 4$ means $2x - 1 = 4$ or $2x - 1 = -4$, then $x - 0.5 = 2$ or $x - 0.5 = -2$. herefore, $|x - 0.5| = 2$. So, set the 0 of the zero inder over 0.5 on the solution finder. Place spaghetti n 2 and –2 of the zero finder. Read the solutions on he solution finder: 2.5 and –1.5.

ROJECT CONNECTION, PAGE 429

1. Equations should be of the form $|x - M| = M$ where M is the midpoint of the actual distance.
2. Equations should be of the form $|x - M^1| = M^1$ where M^1 is the midpoint of the map distance.

.esson 9.4

XPLORE, PAGE 430

1. –2, –1, 0, 1, 2, 3, 4, 5, 6, 7; –4, –3, –2, –1, 0, 1, 2, 3, 4, 5; 6 and 7; –4 and –3; –2, –1, 0, 1, 2, 3, 4, 5
4. The numbers between, but not including, –2 and 5 were solutions.
5. yes; there would be an infinite number of solutions, since all rational numbers ≥ –2 and ≤ 5 would be solutions

OMMUNICATING ABOUT ALGEBRA, PAGE 431

ince $|2x - 3| > 5$ means $2x - 3 < -5$

r $2x - 3 > 5$, then $x - \frac{3}{2} < -\frac{5}{2}$

r $x - \frac{3}{2} > \frac{5}{2}$. Let $x - \frac{3}{2} = 0$; $x = \frac{3}{2}$ is the

oint of symmetry. Place the 0 of zero finder over $\frac{3}{2}$,

nd place the spaghetti on $\frac{5}{2}$ and $-\frac{5}{2}$ of the zero

nder. Read the solutions on solution finder: –1 and 4.

COMMUNICATING ABOUT ALGEBRA, PAGE 432

The solution is $-100 \le x \le 130$, and nobody can travel –100 mi.

TRY THESE, PAGE 433

5.

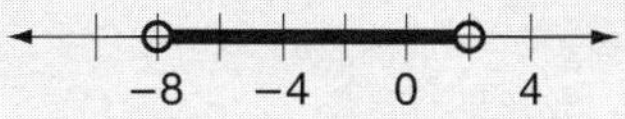

6.

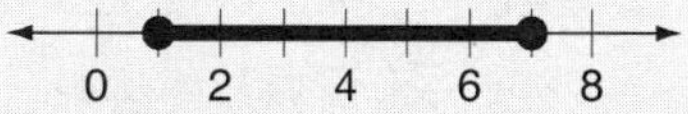

7.

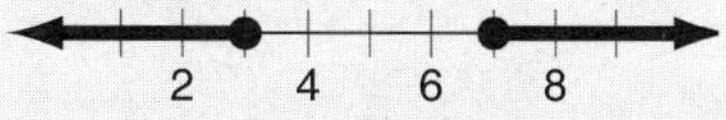

8.

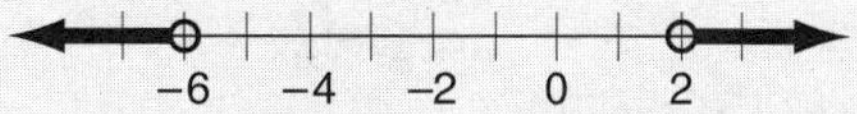

13.

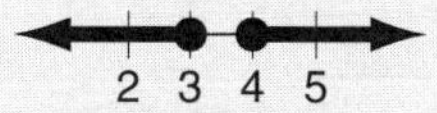

14.

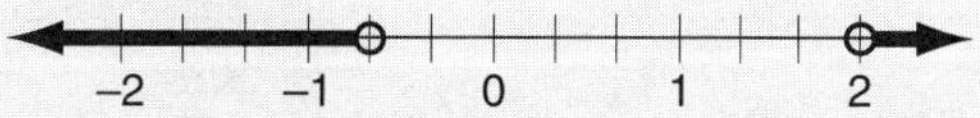

15.

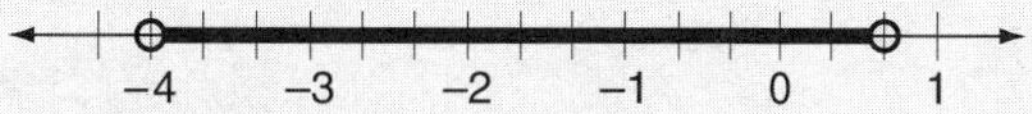

16.

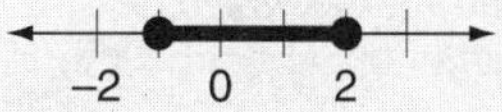

20. Answers will vary. They are similar because they both have open circles at $-c + b$ and $c + b$. They are different because the graph of $|x - b| < c$ has a line connecting $-c + b$ and $c + b$, whereas the graph of $|x - b| > c$ has a ray extending left from $-c + b$ and another ray extending right from $c + b$.

21. The equation has no solution. Absolute value cannot be negative.

PRACTICE, PAGE 434

9.

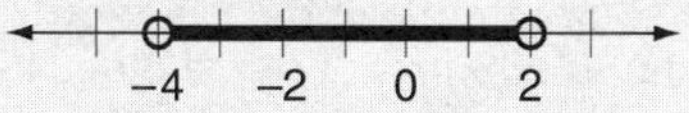

11.

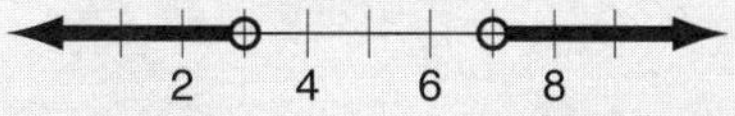

12.

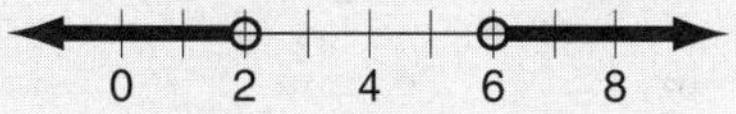

13.

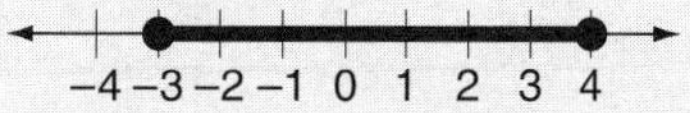

14.

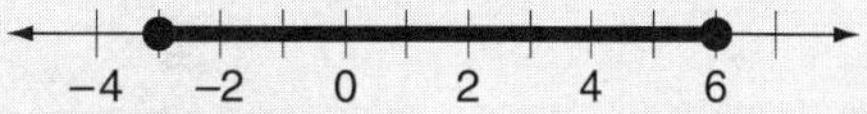

15.

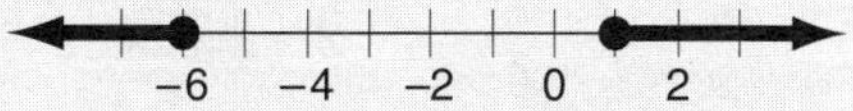

16.

21.

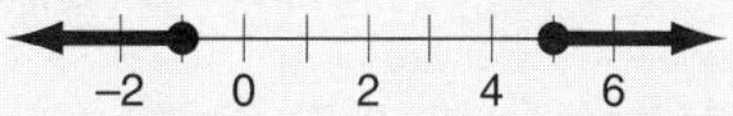

22.

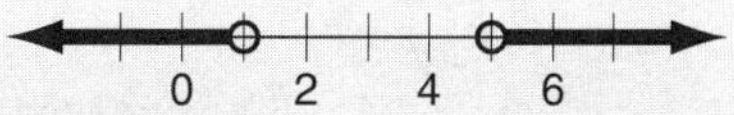

23.

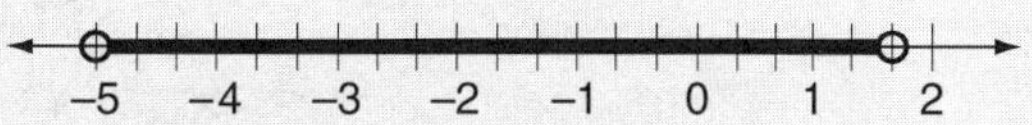

24.

25.

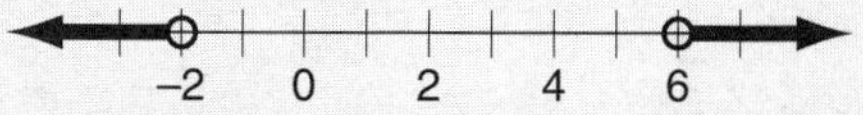

26.

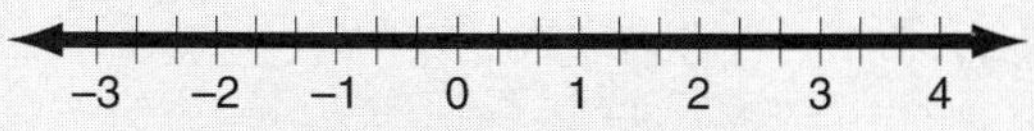

27.

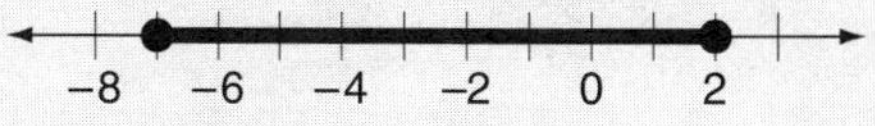

28.

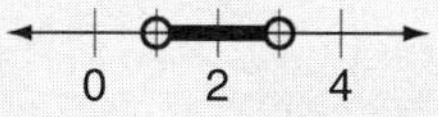

THINK CRITICALLY, PAGE 435

64. **a.** if a and b are both positive, if a and b are both negative, or if $a = 0$ or $b = 0$

b. for all values of a and b

c. if a and b are both positive and $a > b$, if a and b are both negative and $b > a$, if $b = 0$, or if a and b are both 0

d. for all values of a and b except $b = 0$

ALGEBRAWORKS, PAGE 436

7. $60{,}000 \text{ mi} = (60{,}000 \text{ mi})\left(\frac{5{,}280 \text{ ft}}{\text{mi}}\right)\left(\frac{12 \text{ in.}}{\text{ft}}\right)$ $= 3{,}801{,}600{,}000$ in. The radius of the wheel is $14 \div 2 = 7$ in. The radius of the wheel plus the height of the tire sidewall is $7 + 5.7 = 12.7$ in. In one rotation, a point on the tire travels $(2)(\pi)(12.7 \text{ in.}) = 25.4\pi$ in. So, $3{,}801{,}600{,}000 \div 25.4\pi \approx 47{,}641{,}215$ rotations.

Lesson 9.5

EXPLORE, PAGE 437

3. **0, $\frac{1}{4}$, $\frac{1}{2}$, $\frac{3}{4}$, 1, $\frac{5}{4}$, $\frac{3}{2}$, $\frac{7}{4}$, 2**

4. numbers of the form $\frac{1}{q}, \frac{2}{q}, \ldots \frac{pq}{q}$

CHECK UNDERSTANDING, PAGE 440

It is converted to 125 cm because the formula is expressed in terms of centimeters. You can convert the formula to $T = 2\pi\sqrt{\frac{L}{9.8}}$, where L is in meters and 9.8 represents g in terms of m/s^2.

TRY THESE, PAGE 441

1.

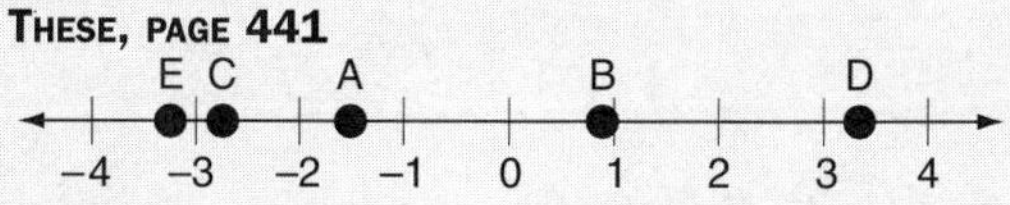

PRACTICE, PAGE 442

1.

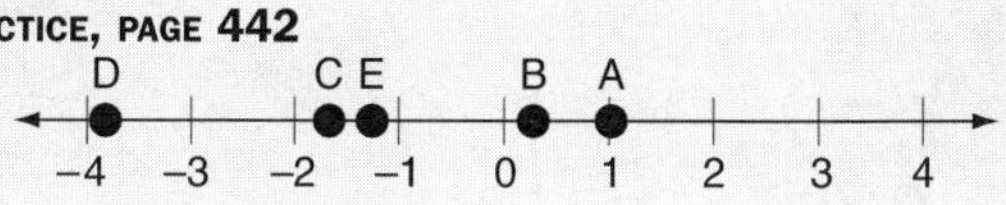

THINK CRITICALLY, PAGE 443

60. The square of every real number is either positive or zero. Therefore, negative numbers do not have square roots in the real number system.

61. A rational number k is a perfect square if there is a number x such that $x^2 = k$.

ALGEBRAWORKS, PAGE 444

2. $10 = \sqrt{20(s)}$; $20 = \sqrt{20(20)}$;
$30 = \sqrt{20(45)}$; $40 = \sqrt{20(80)}$;
$50 = \sqrt{20(125)}$; $60 = \sqrt{20(180)}$

3. stopping distance = braking distance + thinking distance, or $\frac{s^2}{20} + s$

8. Answers will vary; for each type of road surface condition, the length of the skid mark shows that the speed was greater than 35 mi/h.

Lesson 9.6

EXPLORE, PAGE 445

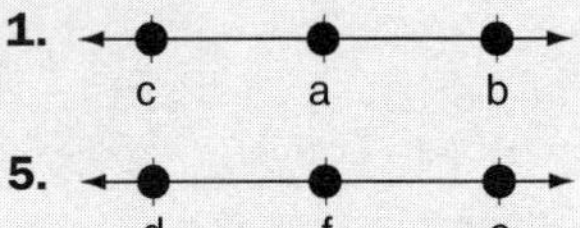

TRY THESE, PAGES 447–448

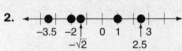

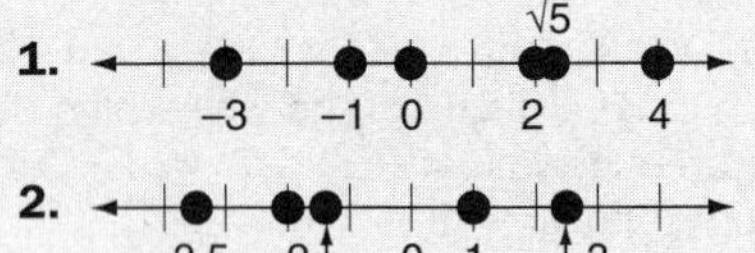

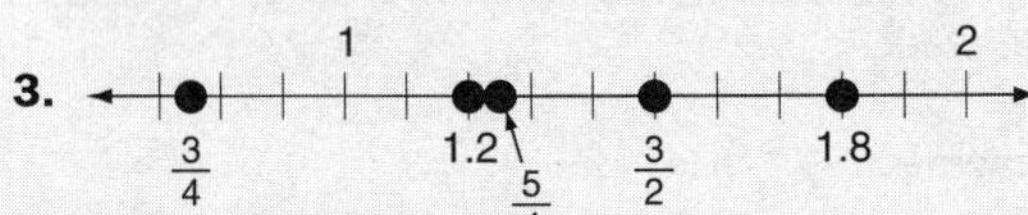

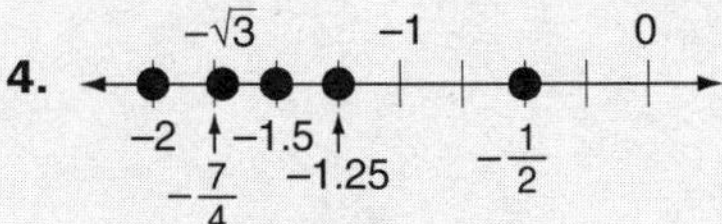

PRACTICE, PAGES 448–449

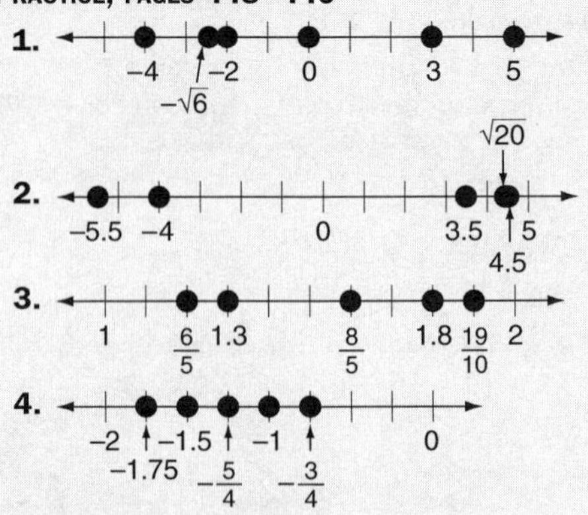

ALGEBRAWORKS, PAGE 451

1. Phone plan A, Phone plan B, TelCo Plan B, ABC, Inc Plan B, TelCo Plan A, ABC, Inc Plan A

2. Phone plan A, Phone plan B and ABC, Inc Plan B (tied), TelCo Plan A, TelCo Plan B, ABC, Inc Plan A

4. answers will vary; possible answer: discounts on total amount of bill; discounts on calls made to certain locations frequently called by the customer

Lesson 9.7

EXPLORE THE PROBLEM, PAGE 452

1. (70, 164), (90, 604) The graph is linear.

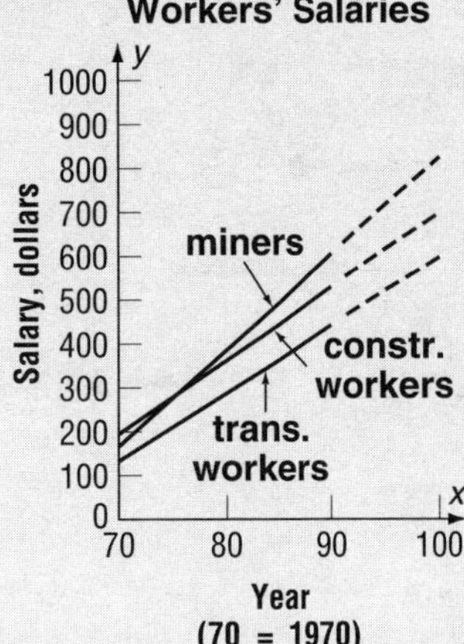

2. $\frac{\text{total change}}{\text{years}} = \frac{604-164}{20} = \frac{440}{20} = \$22/\text{year}$

3. The year 1977 was the first in which income rose above $300; the graph should confirm the fact.

Year	Average Weekly Income	Year	Average Weekly Income
1970	164	1976	296
1971	186	1977	318
1972	208	1978	340
1973	230	1979	362
1974	252	1980	384
1975	274		

5. Continue the table to the year 2000, and extend the graph to show income for the year 2000. Graph: Substitute 100 for 2000 in the equation and solve. The weekly income of miners in the year 2000 will be $824.

Year	Wkly Avg Income	Year	Wkly Avg Income	Year	Wkly Avg Income
1981	406	1988	560	1995	714
1982	428	1989	582	1996	736
1983	450	1990	604	1997	758
1984	472	1991	626	1998	780
1985	494	1992	648	1999	802
1986	516	1993	670	2000	824
1987	538	1994	692		

6. Answers will vary. Students may feel that the equation gives a single answer most directly; a graph presents information and trends visually; a table might be helpful when information needs to be available for ready reference.

INVESTIGATE FURTHER, PAGES 452–453

7. a. construction workers ($195 as opposed to $164 for miners)
   b. miners ($604 as opposed to $526 for construction workers)
   c. The yearly rate for miners increased more rapidly than the rate for construction workers

8. See the graph for Exercise 1. The y-value for the construction workers' graph is greater than the y-value for the miner's graph; the construction workers' graph rises more gradually because the rate of change per year is smaller.

9. a. $16.55

Year	Average Weekly Income	Year	Average Weekly Income
1970	195	1976	294.30
1971	211.55	1977	310.85
1972	228.10	1978	327.40
1973	244.65	1979	343.95
1974	261.20	1980	360.50
1975	277.75		

   b. Find the year in each column that has values closest to being equal (1975). The point of intersection of the graphs should confirm the fact.

10. a. $y = 16.55x - 963.5$; methods will vary
    b. Answers will vary.
    Xmin = 70
    Xmax = 100
    Xscl = 10
    Ymin = 0
    Ymax = 900
    Yscl = 100

APPLY THE STRATEGY, PAGE 454

13. a. The slope of the transportation workers' gra[ph] would rise more slowly because the average yearly increase is less. The graph for Exercise 1 supports the prediction.

14. b.

Square	Red	Blue	Green
2 x 2	4	0	0
3 x 3	4	4	1
4 x 4	4	8	4
5 x 5	4	12	9
6 x 6	4	16	16
7 x 7	4	20	25
8 x 8	4	24	36
9 x 9	4	28	49
10 x 10	4	32	64

c. Each point represents a discrete whole number. A connecting line would have no meaning.

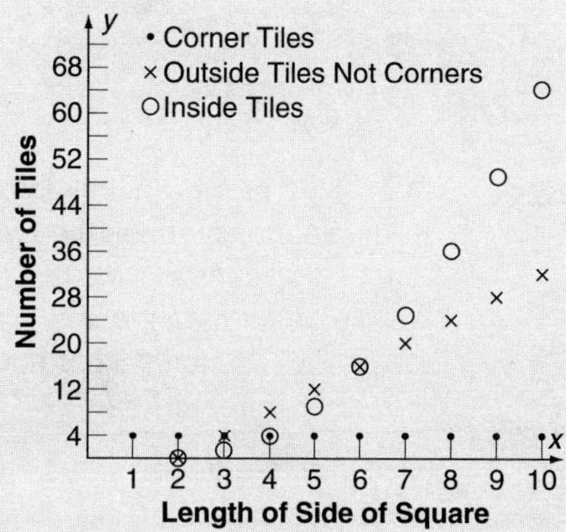

d. green; the number of red tiles is constant; the blue tiles increase by 4 for each larger-size square; in the graph; the slope of the lines shows the rate of increase; the table shows the increases in number of tiles of each color for each size square

f. $R = 4$; $B = 392$; $G = 9604$; formulas

g. 10,000; $100 \bullet 100 = 10{,}000$; find the sum of all colors of tiles—if answers are correct the sum will be 10,000

EVIEW PROBLEM SOLVING STRATEGIES, PAGE 455

HAT'S IT WORTH TO YOU?

a. No; the pearl at the \$100 end must be worth more than the one at the \$150 end in order for the values to be equal by the center.

b. Answers will vary. Use two variables, x and y, to represent the value of each end pearl.

c. answers will vary; $x + 16(150) = y + 16(100)$

d. $17x + 136(150) + 16y + 120(100) = 65{,}000$ (Students must be careful to include the center pearl only once in the equation. The value of each pearl from one end, including the center pearl, is x, $x + 150$, $x + 2(150) \ldots x + 16(150)$, and so on. The sum of these terms is $17x + (136)150$. From the other end, the value of the pearls is the sum of y, $y + 100$, $y + 2(100)$, . . . , $y + 15(100)$).

e. \$3,000; the pearl at the \$100 end is worth \$1400; the pearl at the \$150 end is worth \$600

f. \$43,550

IND A PATTERN

28 numbers; if the list had started with (3, 6, 9, . . . , 684), the value of any term would be n; solve the equation $3n = 684$, since the list starts ith 2 and lists every third number, the value would be ound by $3n - 1 = 683$

CAN DO!

Answers will vary; possible arrangement is shown.

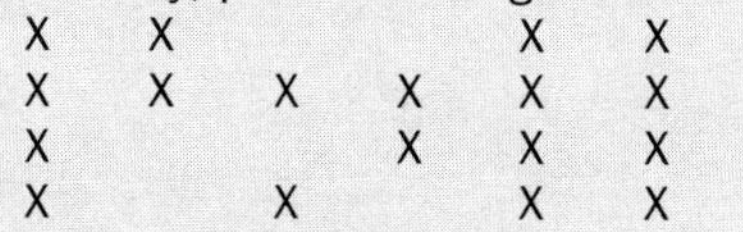

Chapter Review, pages 456–457

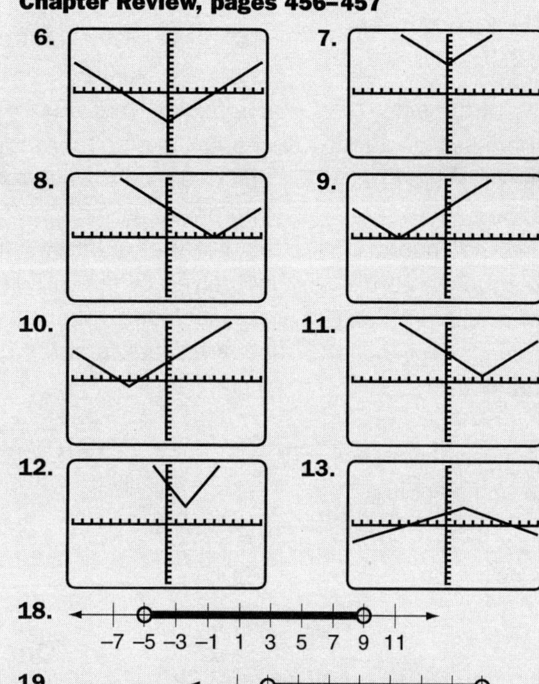

18.

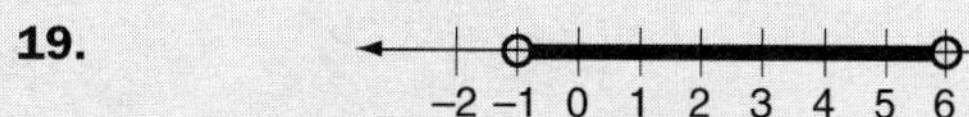

19.

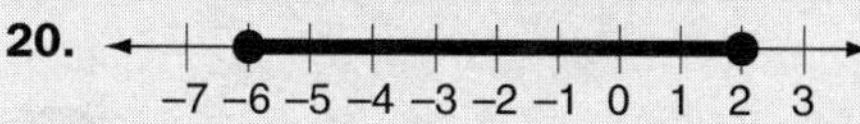

20.

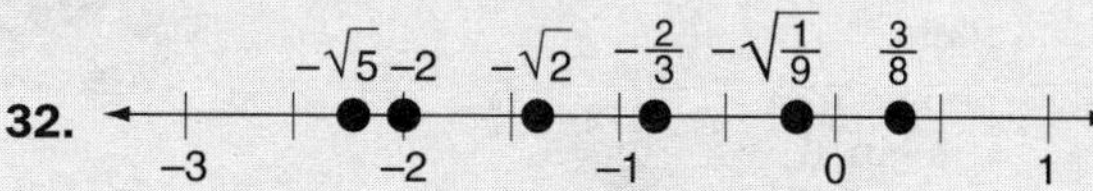

32.

$-\sqrt{5}$ −2 $-\sqrt{2}$ $-\frac{2}{3}$ $-\sqrt{\frac{1}{9}}$ $\frac{3}{8}$

−3 −2 −1 0 1

33.

Statement	Reason
1. $a = b$	given
2. $a - c = a - c$	reflexive property
3. $a - c = b - c$	substitution property

34.

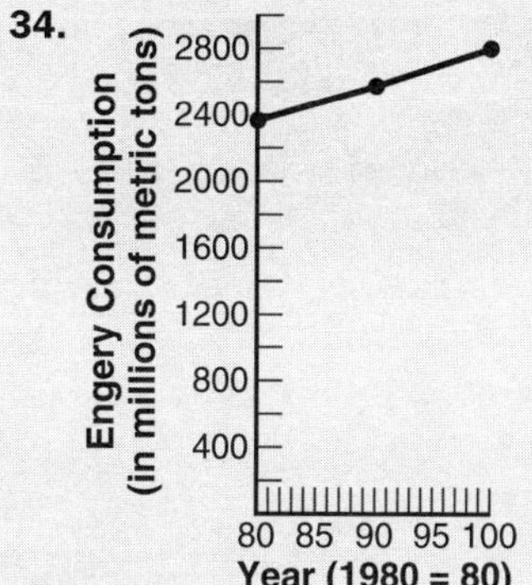

Chapter Assessment, pages 458–459

CHAPTER TEST, PAGE 458

1. The rays that form the graph of $y = 3|x - 1| + 4$ are farther from the x-axis than those of $y = |x|$. The graph is shifted 1 unit to the right and 4 units upward.

11.

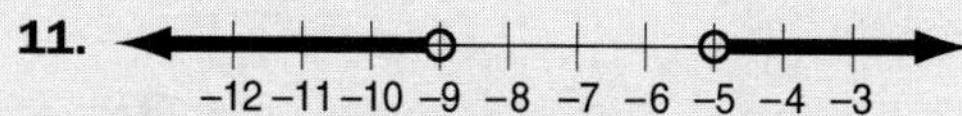

12.

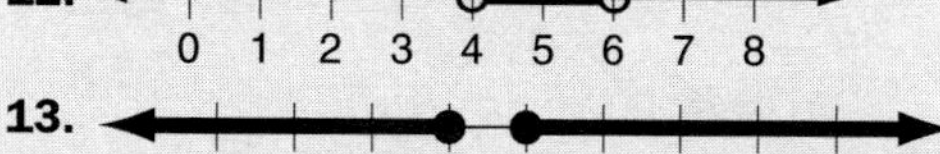

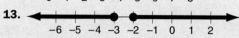

13. −6 −5 −4 −3 −2 −1 0 1 2

14. graph is the real number line

CUMULATIVE REVIEW, PAGE 460

1. **2.**

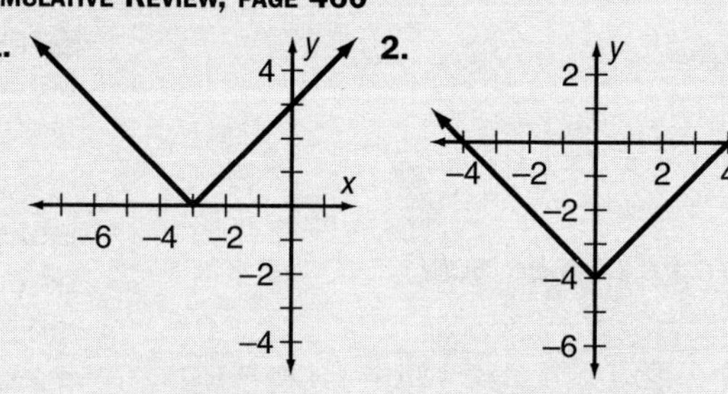

3.

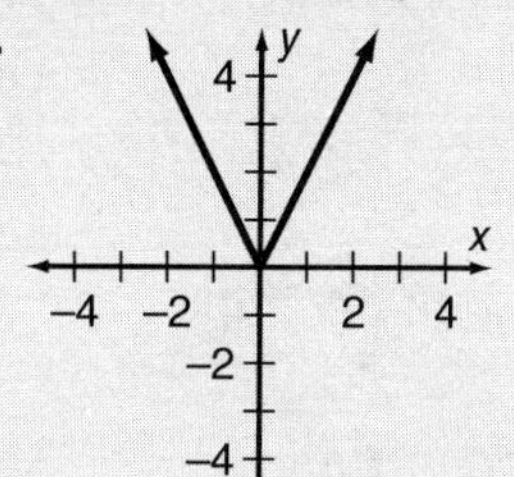

4. $x \leq -3$ or $x \geq 2$;

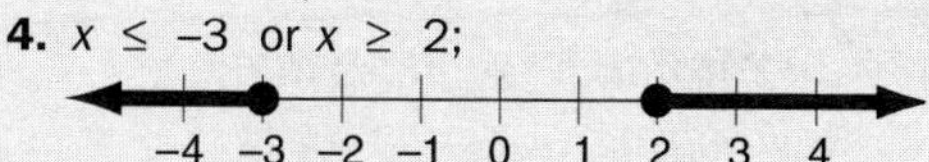

5. $-1 < x < 6$;

6. $n > 0$;

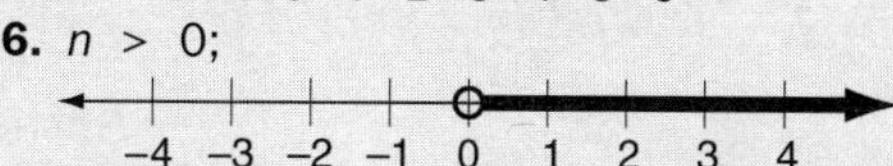

11. No. Students did not really have to study in order to do well, and those who studied longer did not do too well.

19. They are similar in that they both involve a change of order. They are different in that the commutative properties apply to an expression with an operation, and the symmetric property applies to both sides of the equation.

20. yes;

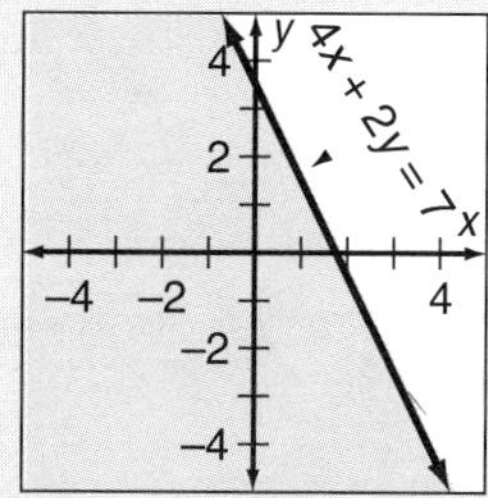

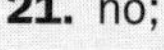

21. no;

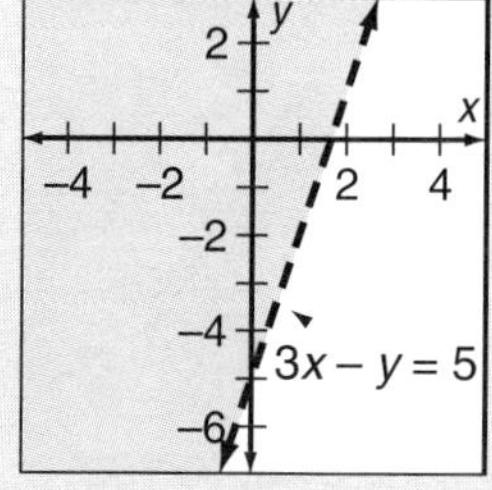

CHAPTER 10 QUADRATIC FUNCTIONS AND EQUATIONS

The evidence from exemplary programs is clear: In mathematics, the American dream of equal educational opportunity for all need not be a myth. The dream can be achieved. We know how to do it. We know where it is being done. And we know why it must be done. The nation cannot afford to ignore this opportunity.

"Moving Beyond Myths: Revitalizing Undergraduate Mathematics," National Research Council, Washington, D.C., 1991, page 44

The Big Question: Why study quadratic functions and equations?

Quadratic equations of the type $ax^2 + bx + c = 0$ represent quadratic functions. They may be solved by graphing, by using the square root property, or by using the quadratic formula. Quadratic equations are used in a variety of problem solving situations. While this chapter focuses on business and industry, students will also encounter applications from engineering, finance, science, travel, and urban planning.

Vocabulary

axis of symmetry
discriminant
line symmetry
maximum
minimum
parabola
point of reflection
quadratic equation
quadratic formula
quadratic function
roots
square root method
square root property
standard form
vertex
x–intercepts

Using the Graphic Organizer

Project a copy of the Graphic Organizer Transparency for Chapter 10. Explain that the focus of this chapter is on quadratic functions and equations. Review the information on the graphic organizer, pointing out that quadratic equations can be solved by several different methods, including graphing, using square roots, and the quadratic formula.

Ask some preview questions; for example, do you think the graphs of quadratic equations will be linear? What does it mean to say that a quadratic function cannot have a power of x greater than 2?

One way to organize ideas about solving quadratic equations is shown below.

One way to organize ideas about quadratic equations is shown.

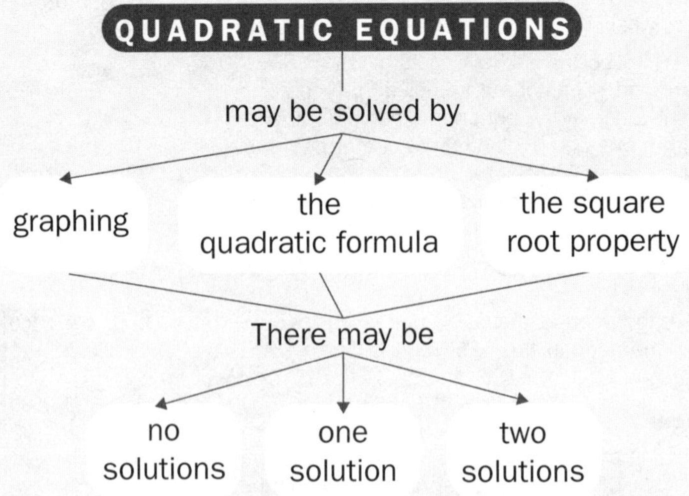

Try It Use a different plan. Try organizing various forms of quadratic equations and their graphs.

Explore the Chapter Theme:

Business and Industry

Many business owners start their own company after working for someone else in the same field. They feel they can provide an equal or better product or service at less cost than the company they have been working for. The opportunity to begin a business is always available. However, since every field will almost certainly be highly competitive, success is never guaranteed. Here is a list of skills and characteristics needed to begin a business.

Skills Needed for Success in Business and Industry

1. Have a good understanding of the product or service you intend to market and sell.
2. Use good judgement when responding to competition.
3. Develop customer relations skills.
4. Be self–disciplined enough to manage your income and allocate it where necessary.
5. Organize and direct the work of others.
6 Motivate employees.
7. Understand how changes in the economy can affect your business and develop techniques for responding to change.

Investigate Further

Have students identify a business career that interests them. Have students go to the library to find more information about this career. For example, students might find out about educational requirements including specific courses, degrees, examinations, or licenses required. Students should research the average salary range for the business. Have students share their findings in a class discussion about career opportunities.

Here is a list of jobs and educational requirements needed for business and industry.

Jobs Requiring 1 to 2 Years of Technical Training	Jobs Requiring 4 + Years of College
Retail Store Owner	Business Analyst
Restaurant Owner	Engineer
Travel Agency Owner	Budget Analyst
Fast Food Franchisee	Cost Estimator
Service Station Operator	Management Consultant
Health Club Operator	Economist
Video Rental Shop Owner	Banker
Consultant	Attorney
	Accountant

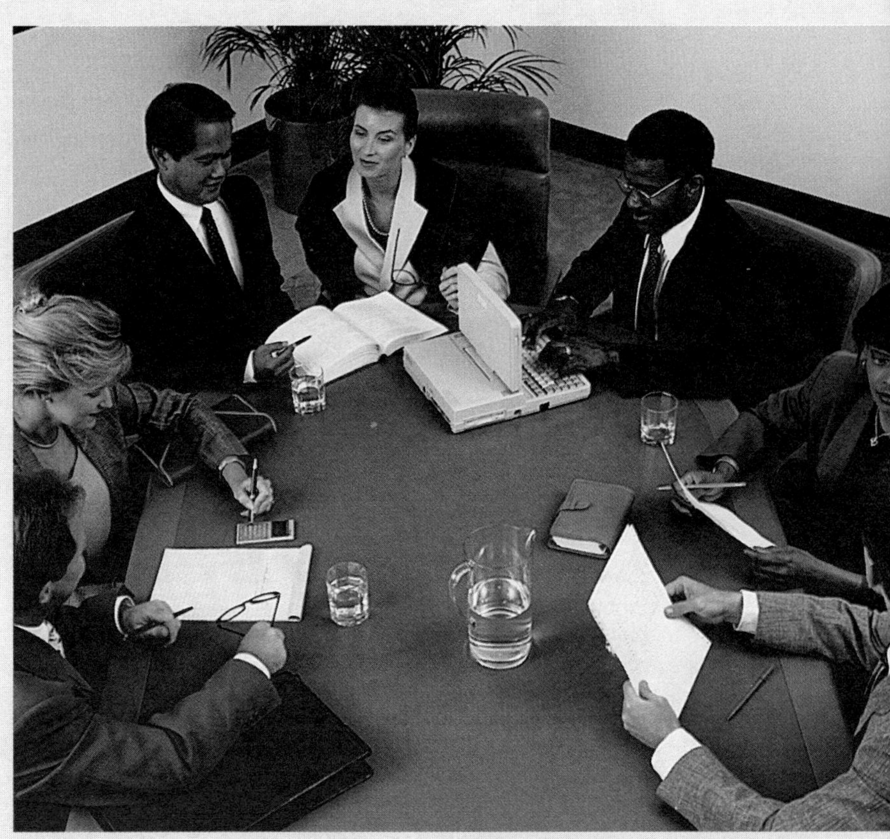

CHAPTER 10 PLANNING GUIDE

Lessons		Text Pages	NCTM Standards	ASSIGNMENTS Basic	Average	Enriched	Ancillaries	Manipulatives	Technology
	Chapter Introduction	462–464	1, 2, 3, 4, 5, 10				Video Discussion Guide		Video, Transparency 57
10.1	**Algebra Workshop: Explore Quadratic Functions**	465–467	1, 2, 3, 4, 5, 6, 8	1–16, 18–21	1–21	1–21	M10		Graphing Utility, Transparencies 32, 35, 58
10.2	**Graphs of Quadratic Functions**	468–476	1, 2, 3, 4, 5, 6, 8	1–31, 40–41, MR46–52, AW1–6	4–38, 40–41, 44–45, MR46–52, AW1–6	4–45, MR46–52, AW1–6	W 10.2; R 10.2; P 10.2; E 10.2; Q 10.2; T 22, T 23; S 26	Graph Paper	Graphing Utility, Transparencies 32, 35, 58, 59
10.3	**Solve Quadratic Equations by Graphing**	477–482	1, 2, 3, 4, 5, 6, 8	1–12, 16–19, 22–28, 31–36, 38–39, MR43–51, PC1–3	1–40, MR43–51, PC1–3	7–42, MR43–51, PC1–3	W 10.3; R 10.3; P 10.3; E 10.3; Q 10.3; T 24		Graphing Utility, Transparencies 32, 58, 59
10.4	**Solve Quadratic Equations Using Square Roots**	483–489	1, 2, 3, 4, 5, 6, 8, 10	1–28, 32–36, 38, 41–45, 50, MR51–57, PC1–4, AW1–8	3–37, 41–49, MR51–57, PC1–4, AW1–8	9–50, MR51–57, PC1–4, AW1–8	W 10.4; R 10.4; P 10.4; E 10.4; Q 10.4	Deck of Cards	Calculator
10.5	**The Quadratic Formula**	490–497	1, 2, 3, 4, 5	1–35, 40, 45–46, MR49–55, PC1–3, AW1–5	4–37, 40–44, 47–48, MR49–55, PC1–3, AW1–5	10–48, MR49–55, PC1–3, AW1–5	W 10.5; R 10.5; P 10.5; E 10.5; Q 10.5; T 25		Graphing Utility, Transparency 60
10.6	**Problem Solving File: Maximizing Area**	498–501	1, 2, 3, 4, 5, 6, 8	1–13, 15–16	1–16	1–16	R 10.6; P 10.6	Graph Paper	Graphing Utility, Transparencies 10, 32
10.7	**Explore Statistics: Using Quadratic Models**	502–507	1, 2, 3, 4, 5, 6, 8, 10	1–13, MR15–22	1–14, MR15–22	1–14, MR15–22	W 10.7; R 10.7; P 10.7; E 10.7; Q 10.7	Graph Paper	Graphing Utility, Transparency 32

NCTM STANDARDS

1. Mathematics as Problem Solving
2. Mathematics as Communication
3. Mathematics as Reasoning
4. Mathematical Connections
5. Algebra
6. Functions
7. Geometry from a Synthetic Perspective
8. Geometry from an Algebraic Perspective
9. Trigonometry
10. Statistics
11. Probability
12. Discrete Mathematics
13. Conceptual Underpinnings of Calculus
14. Mathematical Structure

ANCILLARIES

W = Warm Up
R = Reteaching
P = Extra Practice
E = Enrichment
Q = Lesson Quiz
T = Technology Activity
M = Multicultural Connection
S = Study Skills Activity

ADDITIONAL RESOURCES

Applications	Career Connections	Cooperative Learning	Learning Styles	Strand Integration/ Math Connection
	Chapter Poster			
		Paired partners, 465 (Think Back/Working Together); Small groups, 466 (Make Connections); Paired partners, 467 (Make Connections)	Visual, 465–467; Linguistic/ Interpersonal, 465–467	Problem Solving, Technology, Modeling, Writing, Critical Thinking, Geometry
Business, 472; Engineering, 471, 473; Finance, 475; Physics, 474; Urban Planning, 473	AlgebraWorks: Pizza Parlor Owner, 476; Civil Engineer, 471, 473		Visual. Symbolic, 468–476; Tactile/ Visual 471 (TE); Linguistic/ Interpersonal, 469, 470	Problem Solving, Geometry, Technology, Writing, Critical Thinking
Business, 481, 482; Physics, 479–481; Travel, 481		Small groups, 477 (Explore/Working Together); Small groups, 482 (Project Connection)	Visual, 477–482; ESL/LEP, 478 (TE) Linguistic/ Interpersonal, 482	Problem Solving, Geometry, Technology, Writing, Critical Thinking
Business, 488; Finance, 486; Geometry, 487; Physics, 485–486	Window Washer, 485; AlgebraWorks: Amusement Park Ride Designer, 489	Small groups, 483 (Explore/Working Together) Small groups, 488 (Project Connection)	Linguistic/ Interpersonal, 484, 488; Visual, 483, 487–488, 485 (TE)	Problem Solving, Writing, Critical Thinking, Geometry, Technology, Statistics, Probability
Business, 493, 495–496; Number theory, 495; Physics, 494	Rig Outfitters, 493; AlgebraWorks: Satellite Antenna Engineer, 497	Small groups, 496 (Project Connection)	Linguistic/ Interpersonal, 491, 496; Interpersonal, 493 (TE); Visual, 490, 497	Problem Solving, Technology, Writing, Critical Thinking, Number Theory, Statistics
			Visual, 498–501; ESL/LEP, 499 (TE)	Problem Solving, Geometry, Writing, Logical Reasoning, Measurement
Computers, 504; Science, 505, 506	Dentist, 502; Physical Anthropologist, 502; Chemist, 506	Small groups, 502 (Explore/Working Together)	Visual, 502–507; Linguistic/ Interpersonal, 502, 504; Kinesthetic, 502, 504 (TE)	Problem Solving, Geometry, Statistics, Writing, Critical Thinking

PACING GUIDE

Lessons	Regular Classes	2-year Algebra 1 Classes	Blocked Classes
10.1	1	2	½
10.2	1	2	½
10.3	1	2	½
10.4	1	2	½
10.5	1	2	½
10.6	1	2	½
10.7	1	2	1
Review	1	1	1
Test	1	1	1
Cumulative Test	1	1	1
Total Classes	10	17	7

ASSESSMENT OPTIONS

Student Edition
Chapter Assessment
- Chapter Test
- Performance Assessment
- Project Assessment

Standardized Tests

Chapter Resource Book
Chapter Test, Form A
Chapter Test, Form B
Standardized Chapter Test
Portfolio Item: Self-Assessment
Portfolio Assessment Form

MicroExam II

PREVIEW THE CHAPTER

Take a Look Ahead Have students read the previewing suggestions and then scan the chapter looking for new and familiar things. Give students time to make notes in their journals. Discuss student answers to the previewing questions.

Connecting to Career Opportunities Have the students read the descriptions of the AlgebraWorks features for this chapter. Ask students to identify the careers mentioned. **pizza parlor owners, amusement park ride designers, and satellite antenna engineers** Ask students if they know anyone who works at these jobs. Discuss the educational background usually required for each career. For example, amusement park ride designers and satellite antenna engineers usually have undergraduate degrees. Pizza parlor owners may have a high school diploma and some additional training.

Investigate Further Explain that as they study this chapter students should look for examples of other careers in business or industry as well as careers in other fields. Ask students to determine one way in which algebra can be used in that career. Encourage students to write questions in their journals about careers in business and industry they would like to learn more about.

USING THE DATA ACTIVITY

Introduce the Data Activity Have students read the introductory paragraph and identify some unknowns that potential business owners should consider before starting a business. **competition, the state of the economy, the size of a potential market, and the possibility of their product becoming obsolete**

Skill Focus Discuss the skills listed. Ask students to suggest problems that might involve each skill.

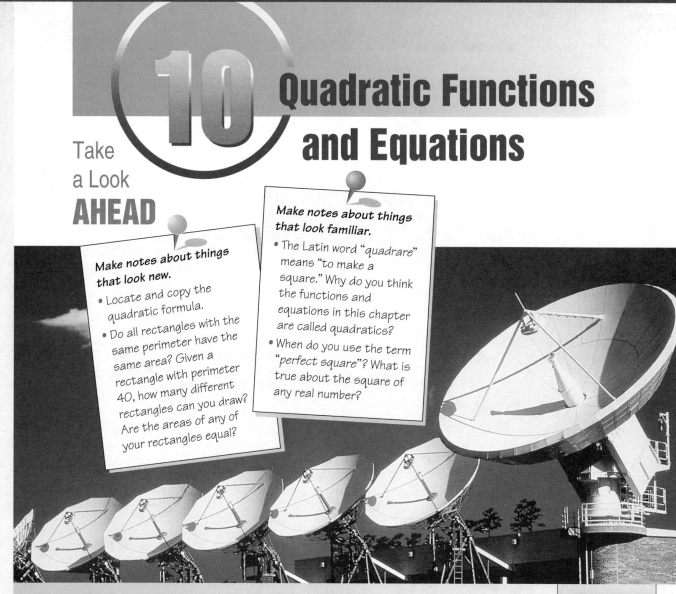

10 Quadratic Functions and Equations

Take a Look AHEAD

Make notes about things that look new.

- Locate and copy the quadratic formula.
- Do all rectangles with the same perimeter have the same area? Given a rectangle with perimeter 40, how many different rectangles can you draw? Are the areas of any of your rectangles equal?

Make notes about things that look familiar.

- The Latin word "quadrare" means "to make a square." Why do you think the functions and equations in this chapter are called quadratics?
- When do you use the term "perfect square"? What is true about the square of any real number?

DATA Activity

Business Risk

Running a business can be exciting, but it also involves risk. For a business to grow and prosper, its owners and managers must understand their potential market, plan carefully, and always watch expenses. Business successes and failures also provide private and government analysts with important statistics for evaluating the condition of the national economy. The table on the next page gives data about businesses and failures during the 1980s and early 1990s.

SKILL FOCUS

- Construct and interpret a line graph.
- Compare real numbers.
- Add, subtract, multiply, and divide real numbers.
- Determine equivalent rates.

A BUSINESS INDUSTRY

In this chapter, you will see how:

- **Pizza Parlor Owners** use algebra to provide their customers with a better value for the money than their competitors do. (Lesson 10.2, page 476)
- **Amusement Park Ride Designers** use algebra to create thrilling but safe rides. (Lesson 10.4, page 489)
- **Satellite Antenna Engineers** use parabolas to design effective satellite dish antennas. (Lesson 10.5, page 497)

1–5 See Additional Answers.

Business Failures

Year	Total Number of Businesses, in 1000s	Number of Failures	Year	Total Number of Businesses, in 1000s	Number of Failures
1981	2,745	16,794	1987	6,004	61,111
1982	2,806	24,908	1988	5,804	57,098
1983	2,851	31,334	1989	7,694	50,361
1984	4,885	52,078	1990	8,038	60,747
1985	4,990	57,078	1991	8,218	88,140
1986	5,119	61,616	1992	8,805	96,857

Use the table to answer the following questions.

1. Make a line graph showing the total number of businesses for each year.
2. Use your graph to determine the two periods during which the greatest business growth occurred.
3. Is it accurate to say that more businesses failed in 1992 than in 1986? In what way is this statement misleading?
4. One method that business analysts use to make meaningful comparisons is to determine a rate of failure. In this situation, they might calculate the number of businesses that failed per 10,000 of the total number of businesses. Determine this rate to the nearest whole number for each year shown in the table.
5. **Working Together** Consult local business organizations and/or the Chamber of Commerce to find out how many businesses opened and how many closed during the last 2 years. Would you want to open a new business?

Study the Data As students examine the table, ask them to compare the change in total number of businesses in the U.S. from 1981 to 1992. Discuss the different ways of reporting this information. **they can find the difference in the number of businesses between the two years: approximately 6,060,000; they can find how many times greater the number in 1992 was than in 1981: approximately 3.2 times as great**; **or they can report the percent increase between the two years: approximately 220%** Ask them to imagine they work for the U.S. Department of Commerce and choose a method to report the change to the American people. Have them justify their choice.

Complete the Data Activity

For Item 1, students should be aware that the total number of businesses given for each year is an estimate. In drawing a graph and labeling the vertical axis in millions, the degree of accuracy of the data is further decreased. However, since the purpose of this graph is mainly to determine a trend, this data is sufficiently accurate.

For Item 2, have students verify their decisions from the graph by calculating the slope of the segments they have chosen.

For Items 3, 4 and 5, be sure students recognize the difference between comparing the absolute values of the numbers of failures and the number of failures as a percent of the total number of businesses. They should understand that economic data in general has no value unless it can be related to previously existing conditions.

South-Western Algebra 1 Chapter Theme Video or Videodisc

Play Chapter 10

Search Chapter 10, Play to 11

INTRODUCING THE PROJECT

Project Goal Discuss the project's big idea: How can algebra help in research about industry and the stock of corporations in a particular industry?

Getting Ready Provide magazines and newspaper articles dealing with business and industry. These can range from business periodicals to articles from local newspapers. From the articles, students should be able to discern what makes industries and companies successful.

FACILITATING THE PROJECT

Getting Started Provide a list of the 500 largest U.S. corporations. This will give students ideas about how industries are categorized. They can also use this list to contact corporations for information.

Setting Project Benchmarks Make sure that the students are aware of the project schedule in the Project Planning Calendar and the due dates for each of the benchmarks.

a. Read newspaper stock market reports and identify the listing for the selected corporations. (Project/Chapter Opener)

b. Prepare a set of facts about a corporation's stock market activity. (Project Connection 10.3)

c. Construct a graph that shows the daily high, low, closing price, and number of shares traded for a corporation. (Project Connection 10.4)

d. Construct an historical timeline for a corporation. Make predictions about the corporation's future. (Project Connection 10.5)

e. Analyze, organize, and display results of corporate research. (Project Assessment)

Suggest that students make subgoals for each goal and include the subgoals in their calendar.

PROJECT

The Company Picture

The stock market offers people the opportunity to earn money on their money. Investors who know about industries, corporations, and the workings of the market itself can optimize their chances of making profitable choices. While there is never a guarantee of success in financial investing, it is no accident that most good decisions are based on solid research. In this project you will gain some experience in building knowledge about a potential investment.

PROJECT GOAL

To combine algebra and research skills to learn about an industry and the recent stock activity of corporations in that industry.

Getting Started

Work in small groups. Look over the Project Connections to familiarize yourself with the materials required for activities. You need to request information immediately so that it will be available for your corporate summary.

1. Select an industry that interests your group.
2. Use the stock market section of your newspaper to name several corporations in that industry. Each group member should be responsible for one corporation.
3. Learn how to read the stock market reports in the newspaper. Identify the listing for your corporation.

PROJECT Connections

Lesson 10.3, page 482: Contact corporations to secure information and learn about stocks and stock markets.
Lesson 10.4, page 488: Construct a special graph to display daily stock activity for a selected corporation.
Lesson 10.5, page 496: Analyze corporate information, prepare a timeline, and explore models to fit data.
Chapter Assessment, page 511: Groups present reports on industries, corporations, and stock markets, determine the success of imaginary investments, and speculate on the future.

Internet Connection
www.swalgebra1.com

10.1 Algebra Workshop
Explore Quadratic Functions

Think Back/Working Together

Work with a partner. Recall the slope-intercept form of a linear equation $y = mx + b$. The graph of this equation is a line with slope m and y-intercept b.

1. Copy and complete the table at the right for the equation $y = 2x - 5$.

x	y	Change in y
–2	–9	
		2
–1	–7	
		2
0	–5	
1		
2		
3		
4		
10		
25		

y: –3, –1 1, 3, 15, 45
change in y: 2, 2, 2, 2, 12, 30

2. a. How much does y change for every *unit* increase in x? 2
   b. What do you observe about this change? It is constant.
   c. How did you determine y when $x = 25$? See Additional Answers.
3. How can you answer Question 2a without making a table? Read the value of m from the equation. For $y = 2x - 5$, $m = 2$.
4. Determine the slope of the line that contains the points (10, 15) and (25, 45).
   compute the slope: $\frac{45 - 15}{25 - 10} = \frac{30}{15} = 2$

Explore

A **quadratic equation** is an equation of the form

$$y = ax^2 + bx + c$$

where a, b, and c are real numbers and $a \neq 0$.

5. Use a graphing utility to graph the equations $y_1 = 2x - 5$ and $y_2 = 2x^2 - 5$ on the same set of axes. Discuss the differences between the two equations and the two graphs. See Additional Answers.
6. What letter of the alphabet best describes the shape of the graph of $y_2 = 2x^2 - 5$? U

SPOTLIGHT ON LEARNING

WHAT? In this lesson you will learn
- to identify the characteristics of quadratic functions.
- to compare and contrast linear and quadratic equations.
- to note the effects of parameter changes on the graphs of quadratic equations.

WHY? Using a graphing utility helps you solve problems about the track of a roller coaster, in physics, and in business.

LESSON PLANNING

Objective
- Use a graphing utility to explore characteristics of quadratic functions and their graphs.

Vocabulary
quadratic equation

Technology/Multimedia
graphing utility

Resources
Transparencies 32, 35, 58, 78–80
Student Handbook
Study Skills Activity 25
Multicultural Connection 10, Asian: Focus on Kites

ASSIGNMENTS

Basic: 1–16, 18–21

Average: 1–21

Enriched: 1–21

1 MOTIVATE

Think Back Be sure that students understand how to complete the last column in the table. Point out that for the first seven values of x, the value of x increases by 1 for each new entry in the table. Ask a student how he or she would describe a change from –9 to –7. **The value increases by 2.** Point out that 2 is the change in y when x is increased by 1.

Use the following table to show students that in linear equations, the change in y is the coefficient of x multiplied by –1.

x	$ax + b$	
0	b	
		$-a$
1	$a + b$	
		$-a$
2	$2a + b$	
		$-a$
3	$3a + b$	

2 FACILITATE

Explore Direct students' attention to the definition of a quadratic equation at the beginning of Explore. For Questions 5 and 6, some students may need help with their graphing utilities. For Question 7, check to see if students understand how to complete the table. Point out how Difference Column 1 asks for the change in y while Difference Column 2 asks for the *change* in the change in y. Have students work in groups for Questions 7–10.

Make Connections As students answer Question 11, make sure that students' tables should have three columns, as in the table for Question 7.

Technology When entering functions on some graphing utilities, it is important that students use the negative sign key when the coefficient of the first term is negative. Students who try to use the subtraction key may get an error message.

Check to see that tables are correctly filled out before students answer Question 12.

3 SUMMARIZE

Writing Mathematics For Question 18, explanations should include that solutions for both linear and quadratic functions are ordered pairs. Differences should include that: the graph of a linear function is a straight line, but the graph of a quadratic function is a curve; the rate of change in y per unit increase in x is constant for a linear function but not for a quadratic function; quadratic functions of the form $y = ax^2 + bx + c$ have a minimum or maximum point, while linear functions do not.

Algebra Workshop

7. Copy and complete the following table for the equation $y = 2x^2 - 5$.

x	y	Difference Column 1 (Change in y)	Difference Column 2 (Change in the change in y)
−4	27		
		14	
−3	13		4
		10	
−2	3		
−1			
0			
1			
2			
3			
4			

y: −3, −5, −3, 3, 13, 27

column 1: −6, −2, 2, 6, 10, 14

column 2: 4, 4, 4, 4, 4

8. What do you notice about the rate of change in y per unit increase in x? (See Difference Column 1.)
It is not constant. It can be positive or negative.

9. Compare the table in Question 7 to the table in Explore. Why do you think the numbers in Difference Column 1 change in the table in Question 7? See Additional Answers.

10. What do you notice about the change in the change in y? (See Difference Column 2.) It is constant.

Make Connections

COMMUNICATING ABOUT ALGEBRA

Discuss a possible relationship between the sign of a in $y = ax^2 + bx + c$ and the sign of the values in Difference Column 2. Use additional equations to test your hypothesis.

The sign of the constant difference is the same as the sign of a.

11. Work in a group of four students. Assign one of the following four quadratic equations to each member of your group, and complete a table for each equation similar to the table in Question 7. Use consecutive integer values of x from −4 to 5 in the x-column. See Additional Answers.

a. $y_1 = x^2 - x - 6$ **b.** $y_2 = x^2 - 2x - 3$

c. $y_3 = 3x^2 + x + 2$ **d.** $y_4 = -2x^2 + 4$

12. Compare your tables in Question 11. Do the values of y increase or decrease as x increases? See Additional Answers.

13. Based upon the results you obtained for Questions 7 and 11, draw conclusions about the behavior of the numbers in Difference Column 1 and in Difference Column 2. See Additional Answers.

14. Work with a partner. Use your graphing utility to graph each of the following equations on the same set of axes. Then draw a conclusion about the effect on the graph of $y = x^2$ of adding or subtracting a constant to the right side of the equation. The function $y = x^2$ is called the **parent function** of the quadratic functions. See Additional Answers.

$y_1 = x^2 \quad y_2 = x^2 + 3 \quad y_3 = x^2 + 6 \quad y_4 = x^2 - 4$

15. Use a graphing utility to graph a quadratic equation of the form $y = x^2 + c$. Have your partner identify the equation you entered by studying the graph. Then switch roles with your partner. Answers will vary.

16. Use your graphing utility to graph each of the following sets of equations on the same coordinate plane. Then draw a conclusion about the effect on the graph $y = x^2$ of multiplying x^2 by a constant. See Additional Answers.

Set I:	Set II:
$y_1 = x^2$	$y_1 = x^2$
$y_2 = 3x^2$	$y_2 = -x^2$
$y_3 = 5x^2$	$y_3 = -3x^2$
$y_4 = \frac{1}{2}x^2$	$y_4 = -\frac{1}{2}x^2$

17. Use a graphing utility to graph a quadratic equation of the form $y = ax^2$ where $a > 0$. Have your partner identify the equation you entered by studying the graph. Then switch roles with your partner.

COMMUNICATING ABOUT ALGEBRA

The constants and coefficients in equations are called *parameters* of the equations. Look in a dictionary to compare the various meanings of *parameter.* Discuss the similarities and differences in meaning you find. Explain how the presence of parameters in a quadratic equation can change the graph of the function.

Answers will vary. A constant added to a quadratic equation translates the graph vertically. A constant added to the variable before it is squared changes the graph horizontally. A change in the coefficient of the squared term changes the width of the parabola.

Summarize

18. **Writing Mathematics** Explain the similarities and differences between linear functions and quadratic functions. Create examples to illustrate your points. Answers will vary.

19. **Modeling** Graph $y = (x - 3)^2 - 5$. Imagine the curve as the track of a roller coaster. At what point does the track reach its lowest point? at the vertex (3, –5)

20. **Thinking Critically** Will the graphs of $y_1 = x^2 + 3x + 4$ and $y_2 = x^2 + 3x + 6$ ever intersect? Explain. no; y_2 is a vertical translation of y_1 by 2 units

21. **Going Further** Use your graphing utility to graph each of the following equations on the same set of axes. Then draw a conclusion about the effect on the graph of $y = x^2$ of adding a constant to x before squaring the quantity.

$y_1 = x^2 \quad y_3 = (x + 3)^2$

$y_2 = (x - 2)^2 \quad y_4 = \left(x - \frac{1}{2}\right)^2$

The graph is shifted horizontally to the left or right. See Additional Answers for graph.

Modeling Mathematics Since the graph of the equation for Question 19 is a model of a roller coaster, ask students what the x-coordinate and y-coordinate represent. **the time of the ride (x) and the height of the roller coaster's path (y)** Since the lowest point has the y-coordinate –5, the x-axis must represent a horizontal line above ground level.

Thinking Critically For Question 20, some students may approach the problem algebraically. If the graphs intersect, then there is a value of x for which $x^2 + 3x + 4 = x^2 + 3x + 6$. After subtracting $x^2 + 3x$ from each side of the equation, the result is 4 = 6, which is never true. Therefore, the assumption that the two graphs intersect is false.

Going Further For Question 21, help students see the pattern by having them graph $y_1 = x^2$ and $y_2 = (x - 2)^2$ and then $y_3 = (x + 3)^2$. Students should notice that $y = (x - h)^2$ moves the graph of $y = x^2$ horizontally by h units to the right if h is positive and h units to the left if h is negative. They can then test their conjecture by graphing $y_4 = (x - 1/2)^2$.

4 FOLLOW-UP

Other Explorations Following is another example of modeling with a quadratic function.

The average monthly temperature in degrees Fahrenheit in Honolulu, Hawaii, can be approximated using the quadratic equation $y = -0.232x^2 + 3.386x + 67.218$, where x is the month of the year (Jan = 1, Feb = 2, . . . , Dec = 12). Use a graphing utility to graph this equation. Then determine the maximum average monthly temperature and the month in which it occurs. Round to the nearest whole number. **80°, July (7)**

LESSON PLANNING

Objective
- ▶ Graph quadratic equations of the form $y = ax^2 + bx + c$.

Vocabulary
axis of symmetry
line of symmetry
maximum
minimum
parabola
point of reflection
quadratic function
vertex

Technology/Multimedia
graphing utility

Resources
Warm Up 10.2
Reteaching 10.2
Extra Practice 10.2
Enrichment 10.2
Transparencies 32, 35, 58, 59, 78–80
Student Handbook
Lesson Quiz 10.2
Study Skills Activity 26
Technology Activities 22, 23

Materials/Manipulatives
graph paper
graphing utility

ASSIGNMENTS

Basic: 1–31, 40–41, Mixed Review 46–52, AlgebraWorks 1–6

Average: 4–38, 40–41, 44–45, Mixed Review 46–52, AlgebraWorks 1–6

Enriched: 4–45, Mixed Review 46–52, AlgebraWorks 1–6

10.2 Graphs of Quadratic Functions

SPOTLIGHT ON LEARNING

WHAT? In this lesson you will learn
- to graph quadratic equations of the form $y = ax^2 + bx + c$

WHY? Graphing quadratic equations can help you solve problems in civil engineering, urban planning, and credit card trends.

Explore

1. Graph $y = x^2 - 6x + 8$ on a graphing utility. Find the vertex (highest or lowest point) of the equation. (3, –1)
2. Would you expect the graphs of
   $y = 2(x^2 - 6x + 8) = 2x^2 - 12x + 16$ and
   $y = 3(x^2 - 6x + 8) = 3x^2 - 18x + 24$
   to have the same vertex as the graph of $y = x^2 - 6x + 8$? Why? No. Answers will vary.
3. Would you expect the vertices of the graphs of
   $y = 2x^2 - 12x + 16$ and
   $y = 3x^2 - 18x + 24$
   to have the same x-coordinate as the vertex of the graph of $y = x^2 - 6x + 8$? Why? Yes. Answers will vary.
4. Verify your answers to Questions 2 and 3 using your graphing utility. Find the vertices of the graphs of
   $y = 2x^2 - 12x + 16$ and
   $y = 3x^2 - 18x + 24$ (3, –2); (3, –3)
5. Without graphing, predict the vertices of the graphs of
   $y = 4(x^2 - 6x + 8) = 4x^2 - 24x + 32$ and
   $y = -(x^2 - 6x + 8) = -x^2 + 6x - 8$ (3, –4); (3, 1)

Build Understanding

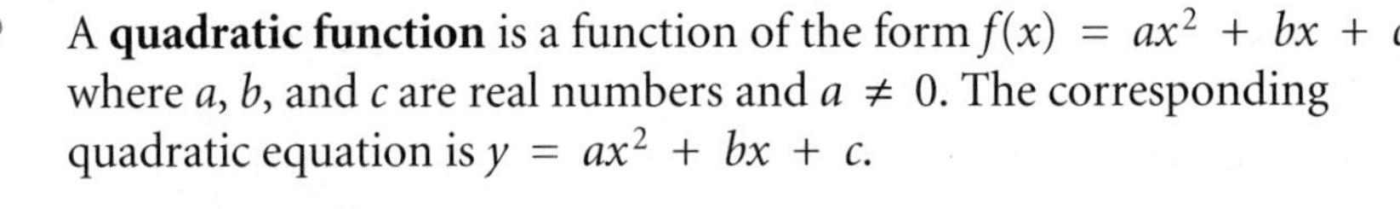

A **quadratic function** is a function of the form $f(x) = ax^2 + bx + c$ where a, b, and c are real numbers and $a \neq 0$. The corresponding quadratic equation is $y = ax^2 + bx + c$.

CHECK UNDERSTANDING

If $a = 0$ in the equation $y = ax^2 + bx + c$, is the equation still quadratic?

No, it becomes a linear equation.

The graph of a quadratic equation is U-shaped and is called a **parabola**. If the leading coefficient a is positive, the parabola opens upward. If the leading coefficient a is negative, the parabola opens downward. The point where a parabola has its **maximum** (highest) point or **minimum** (lowest) point is called the **vertex** of the parabola.

EXAMPLE 1

Use a table of values for each equation to graph $y = x^2$ and $y = -x^2$.

Solution

Make a table of ordered pairs for each equation as shown at the top of page 469. Graph each point. Then connect the points with a smooth curve. Both graphs have vertices at (0, 0). The graph of $y = x^2$ opens upward, so the vertex is the minimum point. The graph of $y = -x^2$ opens downward, so the vertex is the maximum point.

x	y
−3	9
−2	4
−1	1
0	0
1	1
2	4
3	9

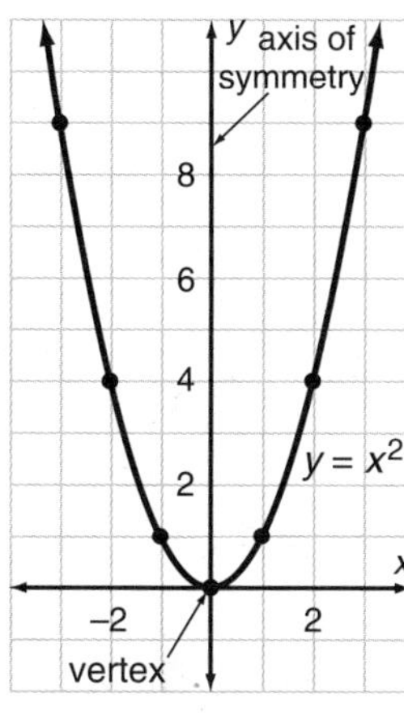

x	y
−3	−9
−2	−4
−1	−1
0	0
1	−1
2	−4
3	−9

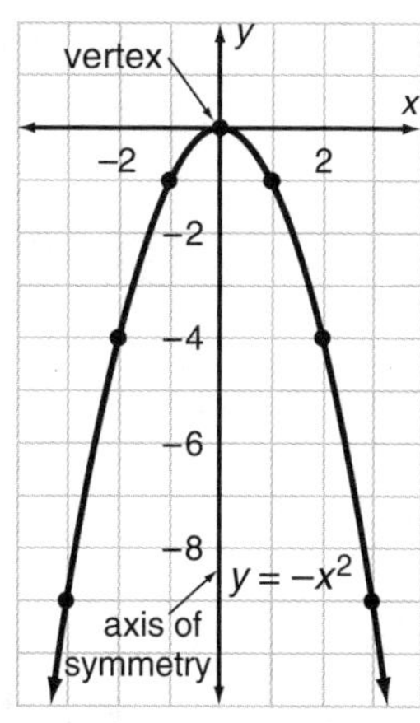

If you fold either graph along the y-axis, $x = 0$, one side fits exactly over the other. The graph is said to have **line symmetry**. For these two graphs the y-axis is the **axis of symmetry**. The vertex of a parabola is the point where the axis of symmetry intersects the graph. Each point on the graph has a corresponding **point of reflection** across the axis of symmetry. On the graph of the parent function $y = x^2$, the reflection of $(-3, 9)$ is $(3, 9)$.

When a quadratic equation is in the form $y = ax^2 + bx + c$, the x-value of the vertex is $x = \frac{-b}{2a}$. To find the y-value of the vertex, substitute the x-value into the original equation and solve for y. Use the x-value of the vertex to write the equation of the line of symmetry, $x = \frac{-b}{2a}$.

EXAMPLE 2

For the equation $y = 3x^2 - 24x + 40$,

a. Determine the coordinates of the vertex of the graph.
b. Write the equation for the axis of symmetry.
c. Determine whether the vertex is a maximum or a minimum.

Solution

a. For $y = 3x^2 - 24x + 40$, $a = 3$ and $b = -24$.

$$x = \frac{-b}{2a} \qquad \text{Equation of the line of symmetry.}$$

$$x = \frac{-(-24)}{2(3)} = 4 \qquad \text{Substitute and solve.}$$

Substitute 4 for x in the original equation and solve for y.

$$y = 3x^2 - 24x + 40$$
$$= 3(4)^2 - 24(4) + 40 = -8$$

The vertex is the point $(4, -8)$.

b. Write the equation of the line of symmetry, $x = 4$.

c. Since $a = 3$, the graph opens upward. The vertex is a minimum. ◄

CHECK UNDERSTANDING

How do the graphs of $y = x^2$ and $y = -x^2$ appear to be related?

The graphs are the same but reflected over the x-axis.

CHECK UNDERSTANDING

Name three other points and their reflections that are on the graph of $y = x^2$.

See Additional Answers.

COMMUNICATING ABOUT ALGEBRA

Study some of the graphs you drew earlier in the lesson. How is the x-coordinate of the vertex of a parabola related to the x-coordinates where the graph crosses the x-axis?

See Additional Answers.

1 MOTIVATE

Explore Some students may expect that both the x- and y-coordinates would change. Refer to this question after discussing the equation of the axis of symmetry so that students can make the connection.

2 TEACH

Use the Pages/Build Understanding

Example 1: Emphasize that the function $y = x^2$ has a minimum but no maximum value for y and $y = -x^2$ has a maximum but no minimum. Show that the graph continues for values less than −3 and greater than 3 by extending the table.

Example 2: Ask the students to consider a general equation $y = ax^2 + bx + c$. Ask which of the coefficients determine the equation of the axis of symmetry. ***a* and *b*** Ask which of the coefficients determine whether the vertex is a minimum or maximum. ***a*** Stress the importance of substituting carefully in the equation $x = -b/2a$. Encourage students to use parentheses around b, especially with negative values, to avoid making a mistake with signs.

Example 3: Point out that the ratio of the x-coefficient to the x^2-coefficient determines the axis of symmetry. This explains why the equation of the axis of symmetry does not change when only the value of c, the constant term, changes.

Example 4: Ask students how finding the axis of symmetry can help determine which values of x to evaluate in a table of the function. **Using x-values to the left and right of the x-coordinate of the axis of symmetry will help to locate the vertex of the parabola.**

Example 5: Ask students to explain why 987 was subtracted from 1000 to find the position of the drainpipe. **The engineers would actually excavate the roadbed from A to a point along the roadbed 13 feet below point A.** Students should understand that the vertex of the parabola is not measured from sea level but from point A. You may want to ask students to find the elevation (y-value) at point B. **Let $x = 1500$ in the equation. The corresponding y-value is 1018 or 18 feet above the elevation at point A.**

THINK BACK

Write an equation for an absolute value function whose graph is shifted right 4 units and up 3 units from the graph of $y = |x|$.

$y = |x - 4| + 3$

COMMUNICATING ABOUT ALGEBRA

What happens to the graph of $y = ax^2 + bx + c$ when $|a|$ increases? What happens when $|a|$ decreases?

When $|a|$ increases, the graph narrows. When $|a|$ decreases, the graph widens.

Recall that graphs of quadratic equations shift up or down, right or left, and are wide or narrow, depending on the equation.

EXAMPLE 3

Graph on the same pair of axes and compare the graphs.

a. $y = x^2$, $y = x^2 + 2$, and $y = x^2 - 3$

b. $y = x^2$, $y = (x + 2)^2$, and $y = (x - 3)^2$

c. $y = x^2$, $y = \frac{1}{2}x^2$, and $y = 2x^2$

Solution

a. The three graphs have the same shape, the same axis of symmetry, and open upward.

Graph of $y = x^2 + 2$
Vertex: (0, 2)
Axis of symmetry: y-axis, $x = 0$
Shifted up 2 units.

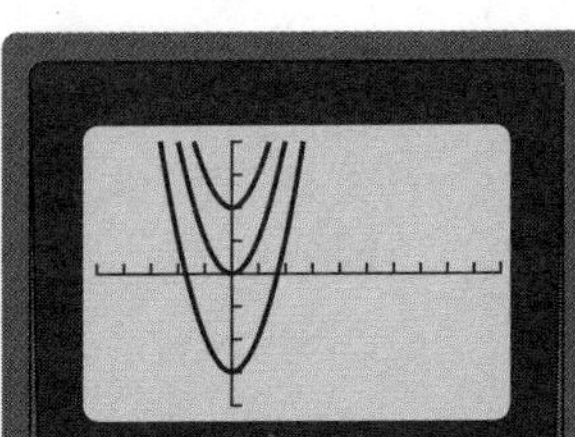

Graph of $y = x^2 - 3$
Vertex: (0, –3)
Axis of symmetry: y-axis, $x = 0$
Shifted down 3 units.

b. The three graphs have the same shape and open upward.

Graph of $y = (x + 2)^2$
Vertex: (–2, 0)
Axis of symmetry: $x = -2$
Shifted left 2 units.

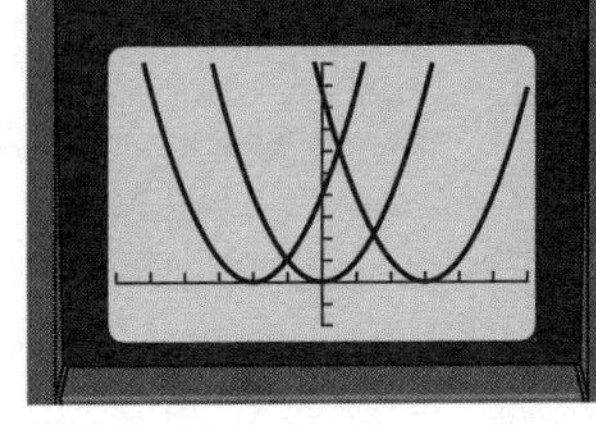

Graph of $y = (x - 3)^2$
Vertex: (3, 0)
Axis of symmetry: $x = 3$
Shifted right 3 units.

c. The three graphs open upward, have the same vertex (0, 0), and have the y-axis, $x = 0$, as the axis of symmetry.

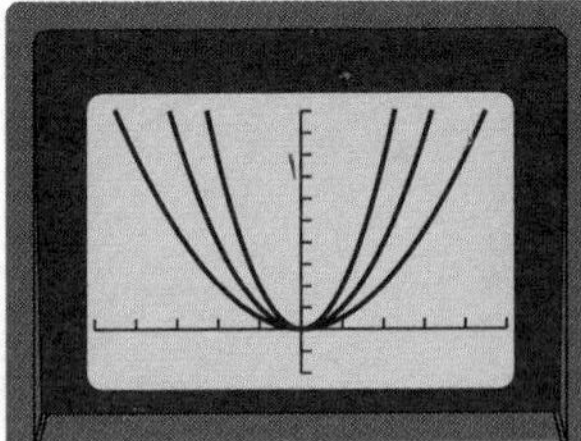

Compared to the graph $y = x^2$, the graph of $y = \frac{1}{2}x^2$ is wider and the graph of $y = 2x^2$ is narrower. ◄

The graph of a quadratic equation of the form $y = ax^2 + bx + c$, in which $a \neq 1$, $b \neq 0$, and $c \neq 0$, exhibits all types of transformations from the graph of $y = x^2$.

EXAMPLE 4

Graph: $y = -2x^2 + 4x + 3$

Solution

Since a is negative, the graph opens downward. The x-coordinate of the vertex is $\frac{-4}{2(-2)} = 1$. The y-coordinate is $-2(1)^2 + 4(1) + 3 = 5$.

The vertex is at (1, 5). The axis of symmetry is the line $x = 1$.

x	−2	−1	0	1	2	3	4
y	−13	−3	3	5	3	−3	−13

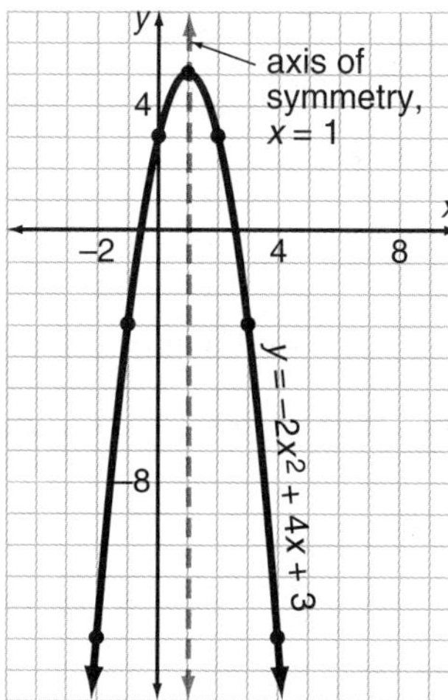

Knowing the coordinates of the vertex of a parabola is often useful in real world applications.

EXAMPLE 5

CIVIL ENGINEERING Engineers building a highway must find a curve that will make a smooth roadbed connecting point A at an elevation of 1000 ft to point B directly above a point that is 1500 ft away horizontally. The curve giving the smoothest roadbed is called a *transition curve*. It is a parabola modeled by the equation $y = 0.000038x^2 - 0.045x + 1000$. A storm drain is to be installed at the lowest point on the transition curve. Find the coordinates of the position of the storm drain to the nearest foot.

Solution

Find the vertex of $y = 0.000038x^2 - 0.045x + 1000$.
The x-coordinate of the vertex is

$$x = \frac{-b}{2a} = \frac{-(-0.045)}{2(0.000038)} = 592 \quad \text{To the nearest foot}$$

Substitute the value for x in the equation to find the y-coordinate.

$$y = 0.000038(592)^2 - 0.045(592) + 1000$$
$$= 987 \quad \text{To the nearest foot}$$

So, the coordinates of the storm drain are (592, 987).

In the graph at the right, the y-coordinate of the vertex indicates that the elevation of the low point of the curve will be 1000 − 987 or 13 ft less than the elevation of point A. The x-coordinate shows that the low point for the storm drain is 592 ft from a point directly below point A and 908 ft from a point directly below point B.

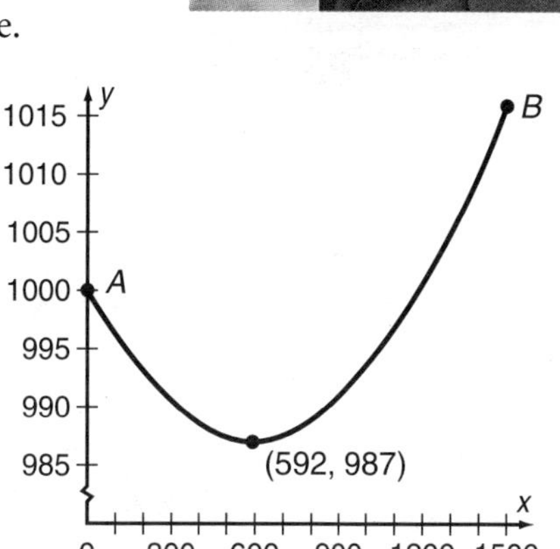

Tactile/Visual Learners When teaching the changes in $y = x^2$ when certain parameters are changed, have students draw and label a set of coordinate axes that shows the graph of $y = x^2$. Then have them graph $y = x^2 - 4$ on a separate sheet of graph paper. By placing one graph over the other and holding them up to the light, students can see that the graph moves but does not change shape. Try several examples from Practice Exercises 13–18 using the graph of $y = x^2$ as a reference.

Ongoing Assessment The important concepts and skills involve graphing a quadratic equation. To assess these ideas, have students demonstrate how they have applied these concepts and skills in Exercises 1, 8, 10, and 15 of the Try These section.

Guided Practice/Try These For Exercises 10–15, ask students to explain which parameter produces which effect on the graph of $y = x^2$. Exercises 16–18 apply the concept in Example 3. Students should use the graph of $y = x^2$ as a reference and determine how each given equation differs from that graph.

3 SUMMARIZE

In the Math Journal Write a paragraph describing the graph of a quadratic equation of the form $y = ax^2 + bx + c$ as well as the properties that are used to sketch its graph. **a U-shaped parabola; it is symmetrical and has an axis of symmetry and a vertex that is either a maximum or a minimum**

4 PRACTICE

Practice For Exercises 4–12, remind students to be careful of signs when substituting in $x = -b/2a$ and in the function. For Exercises 19–21, remind students that each graph should be compared to the graph of $y = x^2$. For students who will make a table of values for Exercises 25–27, suggest that they find the x-coordinate of the vertex first and then choose x-values to the right and left of that value.

TRY THESE

Determine whether the graph of each equation opens upward or downward.

1. $y = -2x^2 + 10$ downward
2. $y = 0.1x^2 - 6x + 9$ upward
3. $y = 4(x - 3)^2 - 15$ upward

Determine the vertex and axis of symmetry for the graph of each equation.

4. $y = 5x^2$ $(0, 0), x = 0$
5. $y = -7x^2$ $(0, 0), x = 0$
6. $y = 3x^2 + 4$ $(0, 4), x = 0$
7. $y = -3x^2 + 15$ $(0, 15), x = 0$
8. $y = 4x^2 - 2x + 15$ $\left(\frac{1}{4}, \frac{59}{4}\right), x = \frac{1}{4}$
9. $y = -3x^2 - 5x - 9$ $\left(-\frac{5}{6}, -\frac{83}{12}\right), x = -\frac{5}{6}$

Tell how each graph differs from the graph of $y = x^2$.

10. $y = x^2 - 7$ 7 units down
11. $y = x^2 + 6$ 6 units up
12. $y = 4x^2$ narrower
13. $y = \frac{1}{4}x^2$ wider
14. $y = (x - 5)^2$ 5 units to the right
15. $y = (x + 8)^2$ 8 units to the left

For Exercises 16–18, match the equation with its graph.

16. $y = 3x^2$ c
17. $y = x^2 + 3$ a
18. $y = (x - 3)^2$ b

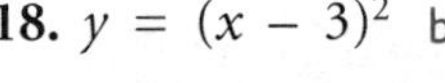

a.

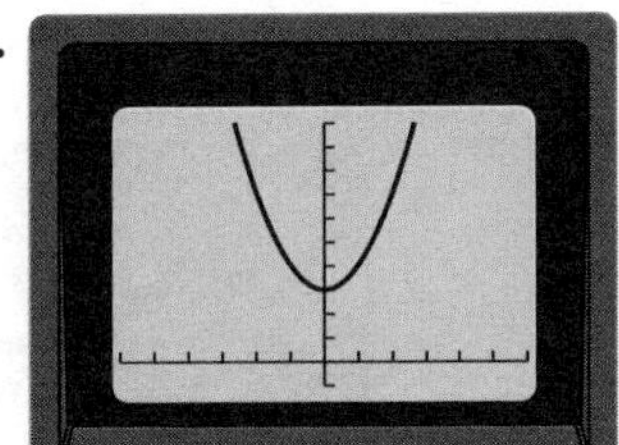

b.

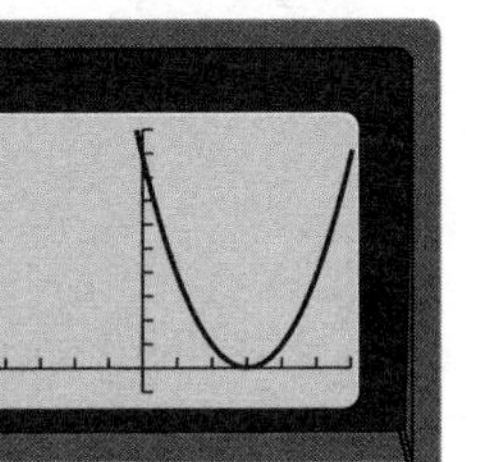

c.

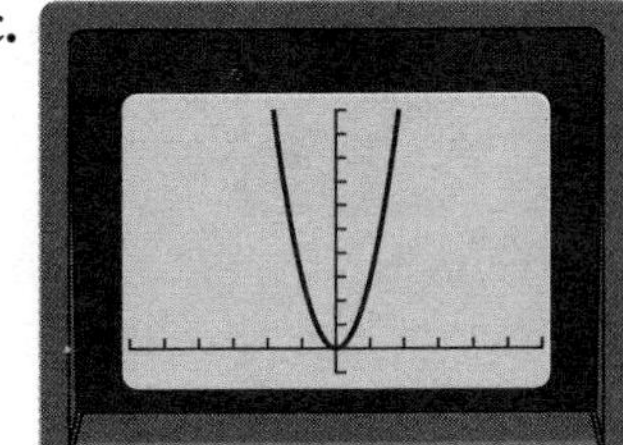

Graph each equation. Show and label the vertex and axis of symmetry for each. See Additional Answers.

19. $y = x^2 - 2x + 3$
20. $y = \frac{1}{4}x^2 - 3$
21. $y = -2x^2 - 4x - 2$

22. **BUSINESS** A business supply store found that pens that sell for x dollars have a profit in thousands of dollars modeled by the equation $y = -x^2 + 8x - 4$. What price will give the maximum profit, and what is the profit at that price? $4.00, $12,000.00

23. **WRITING MATHEMATICS** Explain why the axis of symmetry of the graph of $y = ax^2 + bx + c$ is either the y-axis or parallel to the y-axis. See Additional Answers.

PRACTICE

Determine whether the graph of each equation opens upward or downward.

1. $y = 2x^2 + 10$ upward
2. $y = -x^2 + 9x + 15$ downward
3. $y = \frac{1}{2}x^2 + 3x + 12$ upward

Determine the vertex and axis of symmetry for the graph of each equation. 8–12 See Additional Answers.

4. $y = -66x^2$ $(0, 0), x = 0$
5. $y = 82x^2$ $(0, 0), x = 0$
6. $y = 7x^2 + 3$ $(0, 3), x = 0$
7. $y = -2x^2 + 14$ $(0, 14), x = 0$
8. $y = 3x^2 - 4x - 11$
9. $y = -5x^2 - 10x - 15$
10. $y = \frac{1}{2}x^2 - 6x - 2$
11. $y = -\frac{1}{2}x^2 - 4x + 14$
12. $y = \frac{1}{4}x^2 + 6x - 5$

Tell how each graph differs from the graph of $y = x^2$.

13. $y = x^2 - 10$ 10 units down
14. $y = x^2 + 16$ 16 units up
15. $y = 3x^2$ narrower
16. $y = \frac{1}{3}x^2$ wider
17. $y = (x + 25)^2$ 25 units to the left
18. $y = (x - 18)^2$ 18 units to the right

For Exercises 19–21, match the equation with its graph.

19. $y = 4x^2$ c
20. $y = x^2 - 4$ b
21. $y = (x + 4)^2$ a

a. 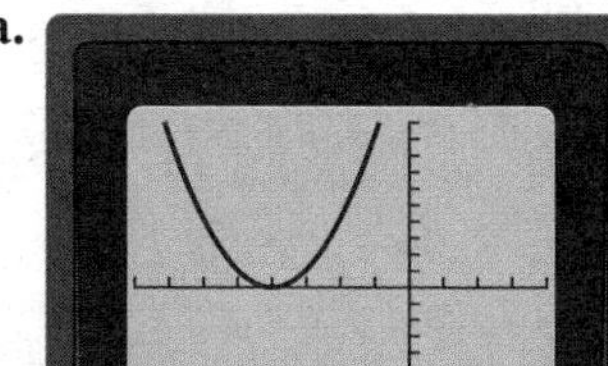

b. 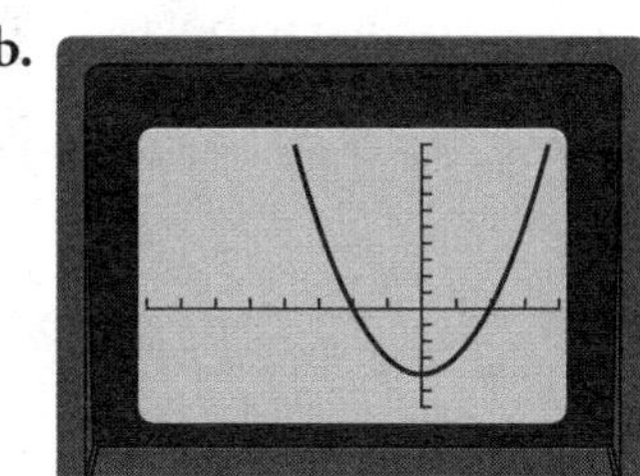

c. 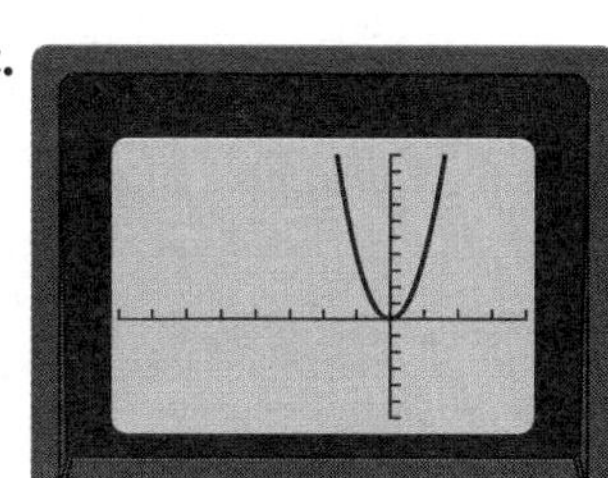

For Exercises 22–24, match the equation with its graph.

22. $y = 2x^2 + 4x - 1$ b
23. $y = -\frac{1}{2}x^2 - 2x + 1$ a
24. $y = -\frac{1}{4}x^2 + 2x + 1$ c

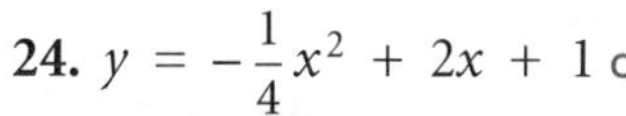

a.

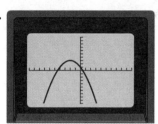

b. 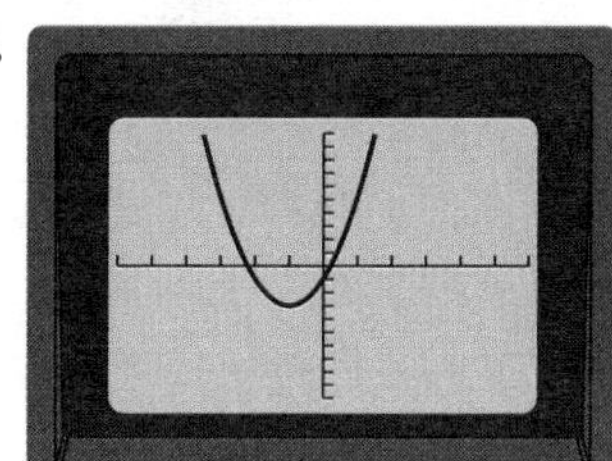

c. 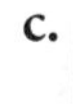 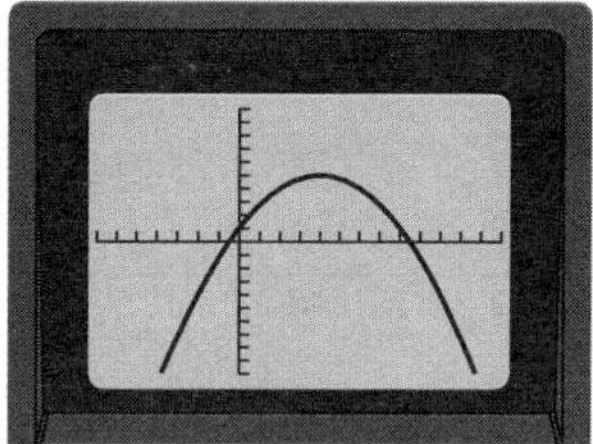

Graph each equation. Show and label the vertex and the axis of symmetry.
See Additional Answers.

25. $y = x^2 + 2x - 1$
26. $y = 0.5x^2 - 1.5$
27. $y = -2x^2 + 8x - 8$

28. Urban Planning The city council is considering lowering the city bus fare. They determined that the daily revenue from people riding the bus can be represented by $R(x) = -50x^2 + 200x + 19{,}800$ where x represents the number of \$0.05 decreases off the current fare of \$1.10. What fare will yield the highest revenue? \$1.00

29. Civil Engineering Engineers are designing a transition curve for a stretch of highway on a mountain from point A with an elevation of 100 ft to point B directly below a point that is horizontally 1000 ft away. They want a lookout station at the highest point (summit) on the curve. The curve is modeled by

$$y = -0.00004x^2 + 0.025x + 100$$

Determine the coordinates of the summit to the nearest hundredth.
See Additional Answers.

Extend For Exercises 31–34, students use a previously learned skill, solving a system of three linear equations. Ask students how the three equations were obtained. **Substituting values of x and y into the general form of the quadratic and writing a linear equation for each ordered pair given.** Before students graph the sets of equations in Exercises 38 and 39, ask them how they know the graphs will intersect. **because, in each set, one opens upward and one opens downward; also, neither graph is shifted to the left or right but only vertically, the first downward and the second upward**

Think Critically For Exercises 42 and 43, remind students to consider the effect of both positive and negative replacements for *h*, *b*, and *c*. For Exercise 44, suggest that students try a few numerical examples until they see a pattern.

5 FOLLOW-UP

Extra Practice Determine whether the graph of each equation opens upward or downward.

1. $y = 0.5x^2 - 3x - 4$ **upward**
2. $y = -3x^2 + 5x + 100$ **downward**

Determine the vertex and axis of symmetry for the graph of each equation.

3. $y = x^2 - 4x + 3$ **(2, –1), $x = 2$**
4. $y = -x^2 - 2x + 5$ **(–1, 6) $x = -1$**
5. $y = 3x^2 - 2x + 1$ **(1/3, 2/3), $x = 1/3$**

Tell how each graph differs from $y = x^2$.

6. $y = 2.5x^2$ **narrower**
7. $y = x^2 - 5$ **5 units down**
8. $y = (x + 5)^2$ **5 units to the left**

NAME ______ CLASS ______ DATE ______

10.2 GRAPHS OF QUADRATIC FUNCTIONS

RETEACHING

The graph of a quadratic equation of the form $y = ax^2 + bx + c$ is a *parabola*. A parabola has a vertex and an axis of symmetry as shown to the right. The axis of symmetry goes through the vertex.

To determine the axis of symmetry, use the equation $x = -\frac{b}{2a}$.

To find the coordinates of the vertex, substitute the x-value of the axis of symmetry and use it to find the corresponding y-value.

To determine whether the parabola opens upward or downward, look at the original equation. If a is positive, the parabola opens upward. If a is negative, the parabola opens downward.

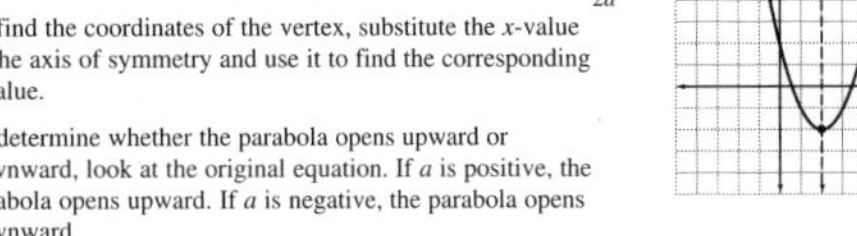

Example

For the equation $y = x^2 + 6x - 3$, find
a. the equation of the axis of symmetry
b. the coordinates of the vertex
c. whether the parabola opens upward or downward

Solution

a. From the equation, $a = 1$, $b = 6$, and $c = -3$.
axis of symmetry: $x = -\frac{b}{2a} = -\frac{6}{2(1)}$
$x = -3$

b. $y = (-3)^2 + 6(-3) - 3$
$y = -12$
The coordinates of the vertex are (–3, –12).

c. Since $a = 1$, the parabola opens upward.

EXERCISES

1. $y = 2x^2 - 8x + 5$
axis of symmetry: $x = 2$
vertex: (2, –3)
parabola opens: upward

2. $y = -x^2 + 4x + 1$
axis of symmetry: $x = 2$
vertex: (2, 5)
parabola opens: downward

3. $y = 3x^2 - 2$
axis of symmetry: $x = 0$
vertex: (0, –2)
parabola opens: upward

4. $y = -3x^2 - 9x + 1$
axis of symmetry: $x = \frac{3}{2}$
vertex: $\left(-\frac{3}{2}, 7\frac{3}{4}\right)$
parabola opens: downward

6 *South-Western Algebra 1: AN INTEGRATED APPROACH*

30. **WRITING MATHEMATICS** Ramiro says that if a parabola that opens upward and a parabola that opens downward are drawn on the same axes, they must intersect twice. Sultan says that the two parabolas do not have to intersect. Ariel says that they intersect 3 or 4 times, and Joelle says that they intersect only one time. Determine the different number of ways in which these parabolas can intersect. Provide examples and draw graphs.
They can intersect in 0, 1, or 2 points; see Additional Answers for graph.

EXTEND

If you know the coordinates of three points on a parabola with an equation of the form $y = ax^2 + bx + c$, you can solve for the values of a, b, and c. For example, if the points (0, 5), (1, 12), and (–1, 4) are solutions, then

$$\text{I.}\quad a(0)^2 + b(0) + c = 5 \qquad c = 5$$

$$\text{II.}\quad a(1)^2 + b(1) + c = 12 \qquad a + b + c = 12$$

$$\text{III.}\quad a(-1)^2 + b(-1) + c = 4 \qquad a - b + c = 4$$

Substitute 5 for c in Equations II and III and then add them.

$$a + b + 5 = 12 \quad \text{Equation II}$$
$$a - b + 5 = 4 \quad \text{Equation III}$$

$$2a \quad + 10 = 16$$
$$2a = 6$$
$$a = 3 \quad \text{Solve for } a.$$

Substitute $a = 3$ and $c = 5$ into Equation II: $3 + b + 5 = 12$. So, $b = 4$. Check these values in Equation III. The quadratic equation that has points (0, 5), (1, 12), and (–1, 4) as solutions is $y = 3x^2 + 4x + 5$.

Determine an equation of the form $y = ax^2 + bx + c$, given the points that satisfy the equation.

31. (0, 4), (1, 5), (–1, 9) $y = 3x^2 - 2x + 4$
32. (0, 2), (1, –4), (–1, 12) $y = 2x^2 - 8x + 2$
33. (–1, 1), (4, 26), (0, –2) $y = 2x^2 - x - 2$
34. (4, 12), (–2, 9), (0, 6) $y = 0.5x^2 - 0.5x + 6$

PHYSICS Galileo found that the height h of an object t seconds after being released can be modeled by the equation $h = \frac{1}{2}at^2 + vt + s$ where a is the acceleration due to gravity, v is the upward speed of the object upon release, and s is the starting height of the object. On earth, a is approximately –32 ft/s² in customary units or –9.8 m/s² in metric units.

35. Ricky threw a ball straight up with a speed of 25 ft/s. His hand was 6 ft above the ground when he released the ball. Write the equation that represents the height of the ball in the air as a function of time. $h = -16t^2 + 25t + 6$

36. Graph the equation you found in Exercise 35. What is the maximum height to the nearest hundredth of a foot that the ball attains? 15.77 ft; see Additional Answers for graph

37. **Credit Card Trends** During each of the years 1990–1994, bank credit card offers can be approximated by the quadratic equation $C = 104.143x^2 - 19{,}026.286x + 869{,}356.657$ where C represents millions of bank credit card offers for the year and x represents the last two digits of the year. Use the equation to estimate the number of bank card offers made in 1994.
about 1,093 million, or about 1.093 billion

38. **Technology** Use a graphing utility to determine to the nearest hundredth the coordinates of the points at which the graphs of $y = 2x^2 - 7$ and $y = -2x^2 + 4$ intersect. (–1.66, –1.5), (1.66, –1.5)

39. **Technology** Use a graphing utility to determine to the nearest hundredth the coordinates of the points at which the graphs of $y = x^2 - 5$ and $y = -3x^2 + 16$ intersect. (–2.29, 0.25); (2.29, 0.25)

THINK CRITICALLY

40. Write an equation of the form $y = ax^2$ whose graph will intersect the graph of $y = -2x^2$ in exactly one point. $y = 2x^2$

41. Find the vertex of the graph of $y = ax^2 + c, a \neq 0$. $(0, c)$

42. Compare the effect that h has on the graph of the quadratic equation $y = (x + h)^2$ with the effect that b has on the graph of the absolute value equation $y = |x + b|$.
See Additional Answers.

43. Compare the effect that c has on the graph of the quadratic equation $y = ax^2 + c$ with the effect that c has on the graph of the absolute value equation $y = a|x| + c$.
See Additional Answers.

44. If the graph of $y_1 = ux^2 - 5$ is narrower than the graph of $y_2 = vx^2 - 5$, is $u > v$ or $u < v$? $u > v$

45. Explain why the graphs of all equations of the form $y = ax^2$ have the same vertex and axis of symmetry. See Additional Answers.

MIXED REVIEW

Solve each equation. Lesson 3.6

46. $3x - 7 = 5x + 20$ $x = -13.5$

47. $\frac{1}{2}(6x - 4) = 4(2x + 5)$ $x = -\frac{22}{5}$

48. **Standardized Tests** Choose the correct slope and y-intercept of the line $3y - 4 = 6x$ C; Lesson 6.2

A. $6; -4$ B. $-2; \frac{4}{3}$ C. $2; \frac{4}{3}$ D. $6; 4$

Compare the graph of each equation to the graph of $y = |x|$. See Additional Answers. Lesson 9.2

49. $y = 2|x - 1| + 3$

50. $y = \frac{1}{2}|x + 3| - 1$

Determine the vertex and the equation for the line of symmetry for the graph of each equation. Lesson 10.2

51. $y = 2x^2 - 8x - 17$ $(2, -25); x = 2$

52. $y = -4x^2 + 12x - 22$ $\left(\frac{3}{2}, -13\right); x = \frac{3}{2}$

Extension Ask students to tell whether this statement is *true* or *false* and to explain their answer.

If the graphs of $y = mx^2$ and $y = nx^2$ have exactly one point in common, then m and n must have opposite signs.

False. The statement is true for any m and n where $m \neq n$.

Make Connections
Sports For the following, students should use a set of coordinate axes with no numerical labels. Ask students to sketch the path of a softball as it leaves the pitcher's hand, travels through the air and lands in the catcher's glove. What kind of equation could model this path? **a quadratic equation** What would x represent? **the time after the ball is thrown** What would y represent? **the height of the ball** How do you think a coach could use the model to help the pitcher? **Answers will vary. The coach might suggest different ways of pitching and analyze the result of changes in speed.** What other paths in sports could be analyzed using a

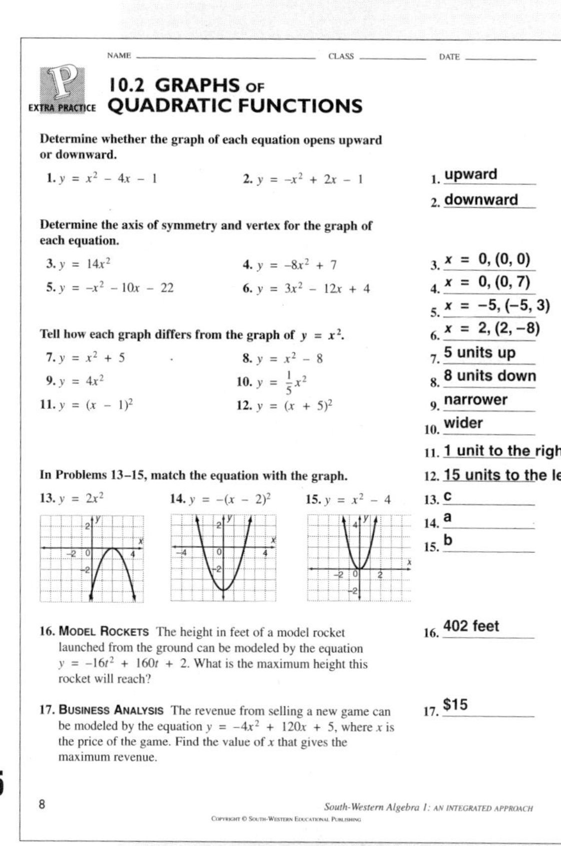

NAME ______ CLASS ______ DATE ______

EXTRA PRACTICE

10.2 GRAPHS OF QUADRATIC FUNCTIONS

Determine whether the graph of each equation opens upward or downward.

1. $y = x^2 - 4x - 1$
2. $y = -x^2 + 2x - 1$

1. upward
2. downward

Determine the axis of symmetry and vertex for the graph of each equation.

3. $y = 14x^2$
4. $y = -8x^2 + 7$
5. $y = -x^2 - 10x - 22$
6. $y = 3x^2 - 12x + 4$

3. $x = 0, (0, 0)$
4. $x = 0, (0, 7)$
5. $x = -5, (-5, 3)$
6. $x = 2, (2, -8)$

Tell how each graph differs from the graph of $y = x^2$.

7. $y = x^2 + 5$
8. $y = x^2 - 8$
9. $y = 4x^2$
10. $y = \frac{1}{5}x^2$
11. $y = (x - 1)^2$
12. $y = (x + 5)^2$

7. 5 units up
8. 8 units down
9. narrower
10. wider
11. 1 unit to the right
12. 15 units to the left

In Problems 13–15, match the equation with the graph.

13. $y = 2x^2$
14. $y = -(x - 2)^2$
15. $y = x^2 - 4$

13. c
14. a
15. b

16. **Model Rockets** The height in feet of a model rocket launched from the ground can be modeled by the equation $y = -16t^2 + 160t + 2$. What is the maximum height this rocket will reach?

16. 402 feet

17. **Business Analysis** The revenue from selling a new game can be modeled by the equation $y = -4x^2 + 120x + 5$, where x is the price of the game. Find the value of x that gives the maximum revenue.

17. \$15

8 *South-Western Algebra 1: An Integrated Approach*

quadratic model? **possible answers: path of the ball after it hits the bat; path of a football**

AlgebraWorks After students have answered the questions, ask how a pizzeria owner may use the differences in area to determine the price of a larger pizza. **Use a ratio of area to price.** If a store owner charges $8 for a 14-inch pizza, how much, to the nearest 50 cents, should be charged for a 16-inch pizza? **$10.50**

NAME ______ CLASS ______ DATE ______

E ENRICHMENT **10.2 GRAPHS OF QUADRATIC FUNCTIONS**

Materials: graphing calculator

Investigate the effect of multiplying or dividing x or y by a constant.

1. Graph the function $y = x^2 + 2x + 1$ on your graphing utility.

If you divide y by 2, you get the equation $\frac{y}{2} = x^2 + 2x + 1$ which is the same as $y = 2x^2 + 4x + 2$.

2. Graph the function $y = 2x^2 + 4x + 2$ on the graphing utility along with the graph from Exercise 1.

3. Describe how the two graphs are alike and how they are different. **Possible answer: graphs have same axis of symmetry and same x-intercepts; second graph is narrower than the first graph**

Clear the previous two graphs from the screen.

4. Graph the function $y = x^2 - 3x - 10$ on the graphing utility.

5. Graph the function $y = \left(\frac{x}{2}\right)^2 - 3\left(\frac{x}{2}\right) - 10$ on the same screen as Exercise 4.

6. Describe how the two graphs are alike and how they are different. **Possible answer: graphs have same y-intercept but different axes of symmetry; second graph is wider than the first**

The graphs in Exercises 1 and 2 illustrate the effect of a vertical scale change of 2. The graphs in Exercises 3 and 4 illustrate the effect of a horizontal scale change of 2.

7. Design a function that will have a vertical scale change of 2 and a horizontal scale change of 4 from the function $y = x^2 - 5x + 4$. **$y = 2(\frac{x}{4})^2 - 10(\frac{x}{4}) + 8$**

10 South-Western Algebra 1: AN INTEGRATED APPROACH

Career
Pizza Parlor Owner

Small businesses such as local butchers, hardware stores, shoe stores, and bakeries face tremendous competition from malls, department stores, discount stores, and warehouse stores. National chains are forcing many small downtown stores out of business.

The traditional "pizza parlor" faces competition from national chains and pizza delivery businesses. In the true spirit of competition, some pizza parlor owners offer better value than their competition.

The area of a pizza can be represented by $A = \pi r^2$, a quadratic equation in which r represents the radius of the pizza.

Decision Making

1. Pizzas are often priced according to diameter. Determine the area of a pizza with an 18-in. diameter to the nearest square inch. Use $\pi = 3.14$. 254 in.^{2}
2. Express the area of the pizza as a function of its radius. Use a graphing utility to draw the graph of the resulting equation and describe it. $A = \pi r^2$; the graph is an upward curve; see Additional Answers for graph
3. To promote the business, Rossi's pizza parlor owner, who regularly sells pies with 16-in. diameters, is now offering 20-in. pies for the same price. Determine the difference in the areas of the pizzas to the nearest square inch. $100\pi - 64\pi = 36\pi$ in.$^2 \approx 113$ in.^{2}
4. Best Pizza also sells 16-in. pies for the same price as Rossi's. It is now offering a free 10-in. pie with the purchase of a regular 16-in. pie. Their advertisements claim, "We give more—10 inches of free pizza to Rossi's 4 inches of free pizza!" Find the area of the free 10-in. pizza to the nearest square inch. 25π in.$^2 = 79$ in.^{2}
5. Is Best Pizza making an accurate claim? Explain why or why not. See Additional Answers.
6. Use the graph of $A = \pi r^2$ to show that adding 2 in. to the radius of a 14-in.-diameter pie does not add the same amount of pizza as adding 2 in. to the radius of an 18-in.-diameter pie. See Additional Answers.

10.3 Solve Quadratic Equations by Graphing

Explore/Working Together

1. Guess and check until you find as many solutions as you can for each equation. (*Hint:* One equation has only one solution, one equation has no solutions, and two have two solutions.)

   a. $x^2 - 4x = 0$ 0, 4

   b. $x^2 - 25 = 0$ 5, –5

   c. $x^2 - 2x + 1 = 0$ 1

   d. $x^2 + 1 = 0$ no solutions

2. Use a graphing utility to graph $y = x^2 - 4x$. How many times does the graph cross the x-axis? Use the ZOOM and TRACE features to determine where the graph crosses the x-axis. How do these points compare to the answer for Question 1a? twice; at (0, 0) and at (4, 0); the x-coordinates match the solutions to the equation $x^2 - 4x = 0$

3. Use a graphing utility to graph $y = x^2 - 25$. How many times does the graph cross the x-axis? Use the ZOOM and TRACE features to determine where the graph crosses the x-axis. How does this relate to the answer for Question 1b? See Additional Answers.

4. Use a graphing utility to graph $y = x^2 - 2x + 1$. How does this graph relate to the answer for Question 1c? See Additional Answers.

5. Use a graphing utility to graph $y = x^2 + 1$. How does this graph relate to the answer for Question 1d? See Additional Answers.

SPOTLIGHT ON LEARNING

WHAT? In this lesson you will learn
- to solve quadratic equations by graphing.
- to determine the number of real solutions of a quadratic equation.

WHY? Solving quadratic equations by graphing will help you to solve problems in physics, business technology, and travel.

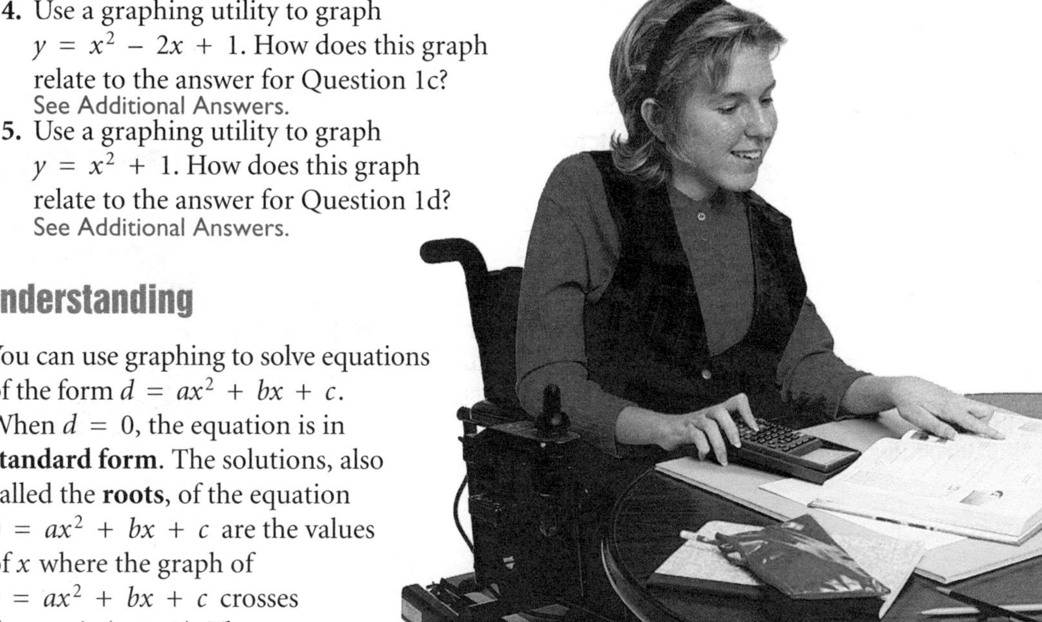

Build Understanding

You can use graphing to solve equations of the form $d = ax^2 + bx + c$. When $d = 0$, the equation is in **standard form**. The solutions, also called the **roots**, of the equation $0 = ax^2 + bx + c$ are the values of x where the graph of $y = ax^2 + bx + c$ crosses the x-axis ($y = 0$). These values are the ***x*-intercepts** of the graph.

LESSON PLANNING

Objectives
- ▶ Use graphing to solve quadratic equations.
- ▶ Determine the number of real solutions of a quadratic equation.

Vocabulary
roots
standard form
x-intercepts

Technology/Multimedia
graphing utility

Resources
Warm Up 10.3
Reteaching 10.3
Extra Practice 10.3
Enrichment 10.3
Transparencies 32, 58, 78–80
Student Handbook
Lesson Quiz 10.3
Technology Activity 24

ASSIGNMENTS

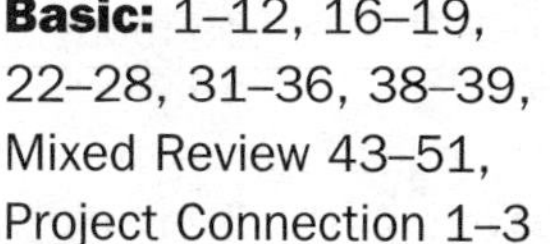

Basic: 1–12, 16–19, 22–28, 31–36, 38–39, Mixed Review 43–51, Project Connection 1–3

Average: 1–40, Mixed Review 43–51, Project Connection 1–3

Enriched: 7–42, Mixed Review 43–51, Project Connection 1–3

1 MOTIVATE

Explore/Working Together For students who have trouble guessing, suggest that they approach

Question 1 by systematically substituting values for x in each equation. They can start with 0 and go on to ±1, ±2, and so on.

When they have finished answering Questions 1–5, ask students to name the coordinates of the points where the graph of $y = x^2 - 9$ crosses the x-axis and what those points mean for the equation $x^2 - 9 = 0$. **The graph crosses at (–3, 0) and (3, 0) and shows that the solutions of the equation are –3 and 3.**

2 TEACH

Use the Pages/Build Understanding

DIVERSITY IN THE CLASSROOM

ESL/LEP Students The word *roots* has several meanings and students may have trouble associating it with a solution to a quadratic equation. Ask them what the word for "the solution to an equation" is in their language and to write that in their notebooks as a definition for "roots" of an equation.

Example 1: Point out that the function $y = x^2 - 2x - 8$ has many different values for y. Ask why the solutions to the equation are the x-intercepts of this graph. **The solutions to the equation $0 = x^2 - 2x - 8$ are the values of x when the value of y is 0. These are the x-intercepts on the graph.**

Example 2: Ask students to compare the two methods. **Method A requires an algebraic step before graphing. Method B requires graphing two equations on the same set of axes. In both methods the solutions of the equation are found in the x-coordinates of the points of intersection, either of the graph with the x-axis or of the graphs of the two equations.**

CHECK UNDERSTANDING

In Example 2, what equations would you graph to solve the equation $0 = x^2 - 4x + 3$ using Method B?

$y = 0; y = x^2 - 4x + 3$

EXAMPLE 1

Solve $0 = x^2 - 2x - 8$ by finding the x-intercepts of its related graph.

Solution

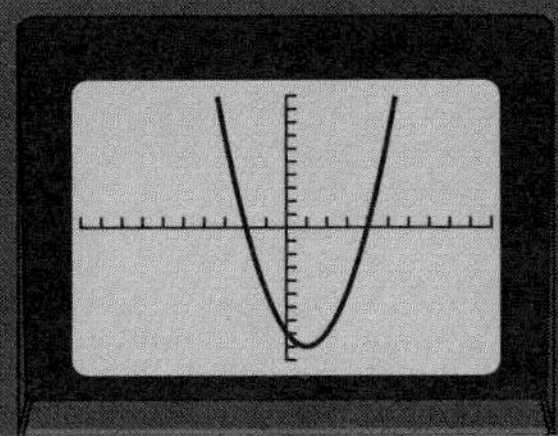

Graph the equation $y = x^2 - 2x - 8$ on a graphing utility. Use the ZOOM and TRACE features to determine the x-intercepts of the graph. The x-intercepts are –2 and 4. So, the solutions are –2 and 4.

Check

Substitute the solutions into the original equation.

$$0 = x^2 - 2x - 8 \qquad\qquad 0 = x^2 - 2x - 8$$
$$0 \stackrel{?}{=} (-2)^2 - 2(-2) - 8 \qquad\qquad 0 \stackrel{?}{=} 4^2 - 2(4) - 8$$
$$0 = 0 \ \checkmark \qquad\qquad 0 = 0 \ \checkmark$$

When $d \neq 0$, you can use your graphing utility to solve equations of the form $d = ax^2 + bx + c$ using either of two methods.

EXAMPLE 2

Solve the equation $12 = x^2 - 4x + 15$ using methods A and B below.

Solution

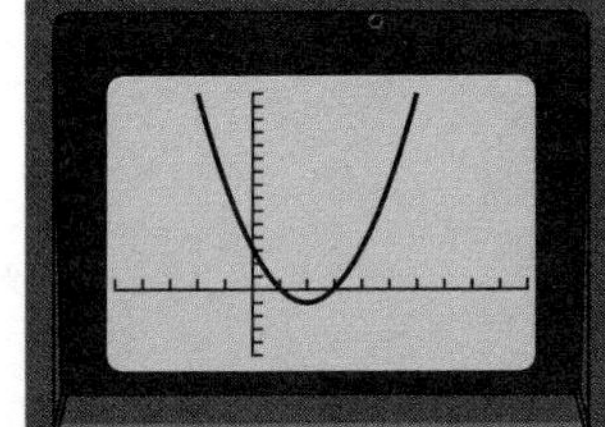

Method A Rewrite $12 = x^2 - 4x + 15$ as $0 = x^2 - 4x + 3$. Graph the equation $y = x^2 - 4x + 3$ on your graphing utility. Use the ZOOM and TRACE features to determine the x-intercepts of the graph. The x-intercepts are 1 and 3. So, the solutions are 1 and 3.

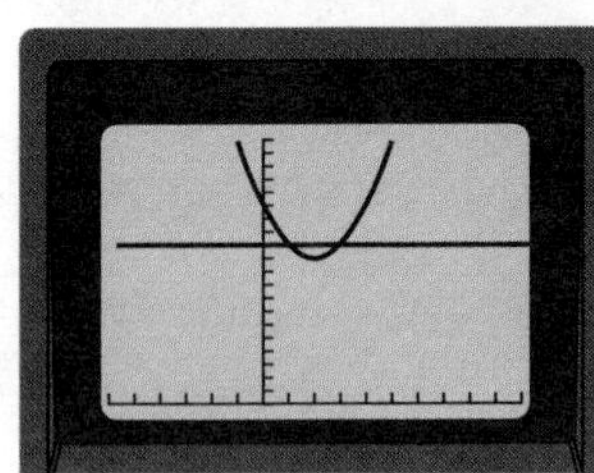

Method B Graph each side of the equation. Graph $y = 12$ and $y = x^2 - 4x + 15$ on the same set of axes. Use the ZOOM and TRACE features to determine the points of intersection of the two equations. The points of intersection are (1, 12) and (3, 12), so the solutions are 1 and 3.

As you saw in Explore, a quadratic equation may have one, two, or no real solutions. If its graph crosses the x-axis at two points, then the equation has two solutions. If its graph touches the x-axis at only one point, then the equation has one solution. If its graph neither touches nor crosses the x-axis at any point, then the equation has no real solutions.

EXAMPLE 3

Graph the related equation to decide how many solutions it has.

a. $0 = x^2 + 2x + 1$ **b.** $0 = x^2 + 2x - 3$ **c.** $0 = x^2 + 2x + 3$

Solution

a. one solution **b.** two solutions **c.** no solutions

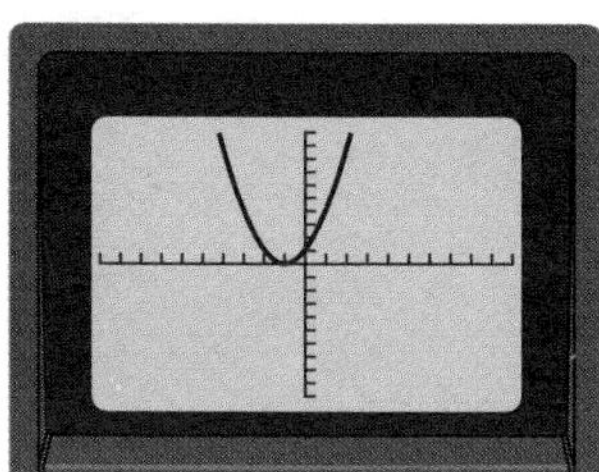
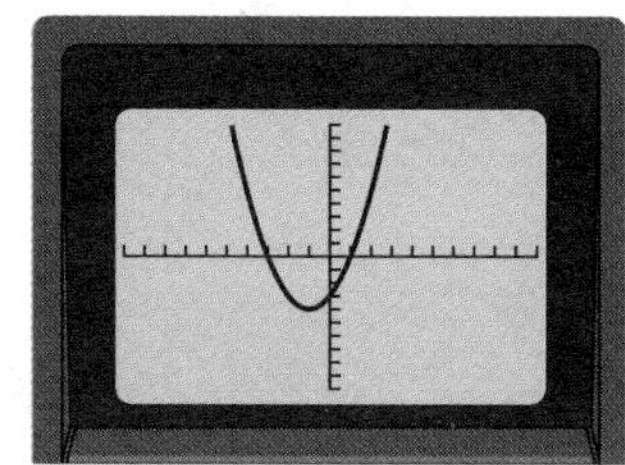
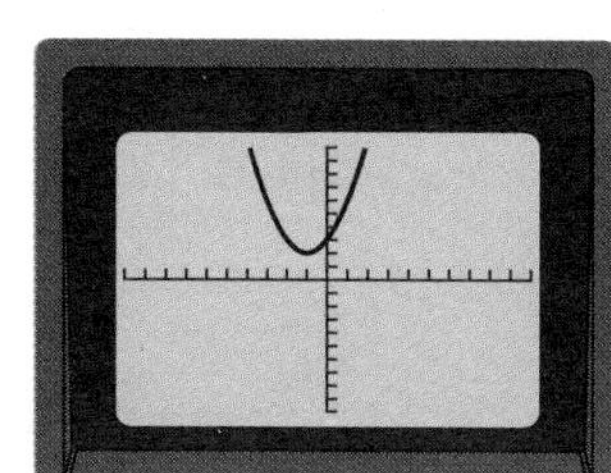

Recall that the height h of an object t seconds after being released is modeled by the equation $h = \frac{1}{2}at^2 + vt + s$ where a is the acceleration due to gravity, v is the upward speed of the object upon release, and s is the initial height. On Earth, a is approximately -32 ft/s^2.

EXAMPLE 4

PHYSICS A toy rocket is launched from ground level with an upward speed of 120 ft/s.

a. Write an equation that represents the height of the rocket as a function of time.
b. After how many seconds will the rocket be 150 ft above ground?

Solution

a. In this example, $a = -32$ ft/s, $v = 120$ ft/s, and $s = 0$.

$$h = \frac{1}{2}(-32)t^2 + 120t$$
$$h = -16t^2 + 120t$$

b. The equation $150 = -16t^2 + 120t$ represents the time at which the rocket is 150 ft above the ground. Rewrite the equation as $0 = -16t^2 + 120t - 150$, then graph the function $y = -16x^2 + 120x - 150$ on your graphing utility. Use the TRACE and ZOOM features to determine the x-intercepts of the graph. The x-intercepts are 1.58 and 5.92 to the nearest hundredth.

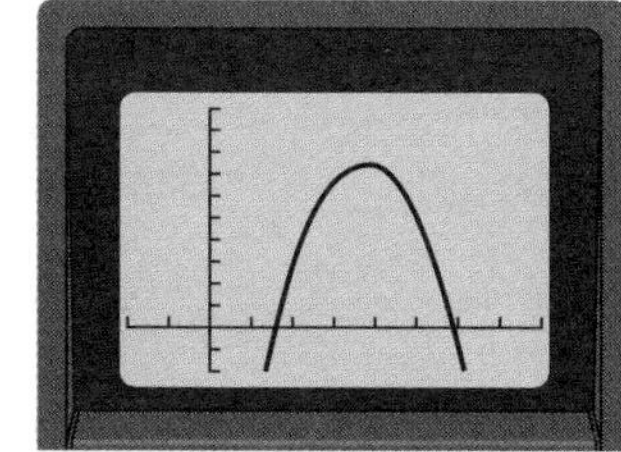
x-scale: 1 y-scale: 10

The rocket is at a height of 150 ft on its way up at $t = 1.58$ s and again on its way down at $t = 5.92$ s.

CHECK UNDERSTANDING

Can the vertex ever be the solution to the equation? Explain.

yes; when the vertex lies on the x-axis

PROBLEM SOLVING TIP

To help you decide what viewing window (range) to use, first determine the coordinates of the vertex. Decide if the graph opens upward or downward. Then choose your window to include the vertex and surrounding points of the graph.

Example 3: After students have finished discussing this example, ask them to experiment with the graphing utility and see if they can find three other equations, one with one real solution, one with two real solutions, and one with no real solutions. Tell students that "no solutions" means there are no real-number solutions and that the graph of such an equation does not intersect the x-axis. These types of equations have complex number solutions which are taught in the second course in algebra.

Example 4: Ask students to explain how the facts in the problem relate to the equation given in the paragraph above Example 4. Point out that if the facts in the problem are given in metric units (meters per second) they would need the metric value for acceleration due to gravity, which is –9.8 m/s.

Ongoing Assessment The important concepts and skills are to use graphs to find solutions to quadratic equations and to determine the number of real solutions of a quadratic equation. To assess these ideas, have students demonstrate how they have applied these concepts and skills in Exercises 7, 10, 16, and 17 of the Try These section.

Guided Practice/Try These In Exercises 4–6, point out that there are many equivalent equations for any particular equation. Have students check their answers to Exercises 7–15 by substituting the solutions in the equation. Point out that rounded decimal answers can be checked by taking the rounding into consideration when evaluating the substitution.

3 SUMMARIZE

In the Math Journal Ask students to write a paragraph that explains the two different ways to use a graphing utility to solve an equation such as $3 = x^2 + 2x - 5$.

Error Alert Watch for students who look for the x-intercepts of, for example, $y = x^2 + 2x - 3$ to solve $5 = x^2 + 2x - 3$. These students have not recognized that the equation is not in standard form. Students must either graph $y = x^2 + 2x - 8$ or, in addition to the graph displayed already, must graph $y = 5$ and find the x-coordinates of the points of intersection of the two graphs.

4 PRACTICE

Practice For Exercises 4–6, remind students that an equivalent equation is formed if the same number has been added to each side of the equation. In Exercise 31, when students

NAME ______ CLASS ______ DATE ______

RETEACHING

10.3 SOLVE QUADRATIC EQUATIONS BY GRAPHING

Finding the coordinates of the vertex will help you determine a good range to use when you are using a graphing utility to solve a quadratic equation.

Example
Solve by graphing: $0 = x^2 - 2x - 7$

Solution
Find the coordinates of the vertex: $x = \frac{-b}{2a} = \frac{-(-2)}{2(1)} = 1$

$y = 1^2 - 2(1) - 7 = -8$

The coordinates of the vertex are $(1, -8)$.

For the range of x-values, try subtracting 5 and adding 5 to the x-coordinate of the vertex.
Xmin = –4, Xmax = 6

For the y-values, try a range that includes the y-coordinate of the vertex and a y-value on the opposite side of the horizontal axis.
Ymin = –10, Ymax = 10

After you have an appropriate viewing window, use the ZOOM and TRACE features to determine the x-intercepts to the nearest hundreth. The x-intercepts are –1.83 and 3.83. So, the solutions are –1.83 and 3.83.

EXERCISES

For each equation, find the coordinates of the vertex. Then, suggest a range of values to be used on a graphing utility. Solve each equation by finding the x-intercepts of its graph.

1. $0 = x^2 + 3x - 11$
Vertex: (–1.5, **13.35**)
Range: Xmin **–6.5** Xmax **–3.5**
Ymin **–14** Ymax **14**
x-intercept: **–5.14, 2.14**
solution: **–5.14, 2.14**

2. $0 = x^2 - 4x - 9$
Vertex: (2, **–13**)
Range: Xmin **–3** Xmax **7**
Ymin **–14** Ymax **14**
x-intercept: **–1.61, 5.61**
solution: **–1.61, 5.61**

3. $0 = -2x^2 + 8x + 17$
Vertex: **(2, 25)**
Range: Xmin **–3** Xmax **7**
Ymin **–26** Ymax **26**
x-intercept: **5.5, –1.54**
solution: **5.5, –1.54**

4. $0 = x^2 + 20x - 150$
Vertex: **(–10, –250)**
Range: Xmin **–30** Xmax **10**
Ymin **–300** Ymax **300**
x-intercept: **–25.81, 5.81**
solution: **–25.81, 5.81**

14 *South-Western Algebra 1: AN INTEGRATED APPROACH*

TRY THESE

Rewrite each equation in the form $0 = ax^2 + bx + c$.

1. $7 = 3x^2 - 4x + 15$
$0 = 3x^2 - 4x + 8$
2. $4 = 8 - 2x^2 + 5x$
$0 = -2x^2 + 5x + 4$
3. $2 = 2 - 3x + \frac{1}{2}x^2$
$0 = \frac{1}{2}x^2 - 3x$

Determine whether each equation is equivalent to $8 = 4x^2 - 6x - 2$.

4. $-8 = -4x^2 + 6x - 2$ not equivalent
5. $0 = 4x^2 - 6x - 10$ equivalent
6. $10 = 4x^2 - 6x$ equivalent

Solve each equation by finding the x-intercepts of its related graph.

7. $0 = x^2 + 2x - 15$ –5, 3
8. $0 = -x^2 + 3x + 4$ –1, 4
9. $0 = x^2 - 10x + 25$ 5

Rewrite each equation in standard form. Then solve each equation by finding the x-intercepts of its graph. Round decimals to the nearest hundredth.

10. $6 = x^2 + 4x - 6$
$0 = x^2 + 4x - 12$; –6, 2
11. $8 = -x^2 + 6x + 1$
$0 = -x^2 + 6x - 7$; 1.59, 4.41
12. $-25 = -x^2 + x - 5$
$0 = -x^2 + x + 20$; –4, 5

Solve each equation by graphing $y = d$ and $y = ax^2 + bx + c$ on the same set of axes and then finding the x-coordinates of their points of intersection. Round decimals to the nearest hundredth.

13. $12 = x^2 - 2x - 3$
–3, 5
14. $-5 = -x^2 + 2x + 1$
–1.65, 3.65
15. $1 = 2x^2 - 2x - 8$
–1.68, 2.68

Use a graphing utility to determine the number of solutions to each equation.

16. $0 = 3x^2 - 6x + 2$ 2
17. $0 = 4x^2 + 5x + 2$ 0
18. $0 = x^2 - 8x + 16$ 1

19. PHYSICS If the rocket discussed in Example 4 is launched from the moon, where the acceleration due to gravity is –5.32 ft/s^2, after how many seconds will it be at a height of 150 ft? Round to the nearest hundredth.
1.29 and 43.83

20. WRITING MATHEMATICS Explain how to use a graphing utility to find the solution(s) to a quadratic equation in standard form. Answers will vary.

PRACTICE

Rewrite each equation in the form $0 = ax^2 + bx + c$.

1. $9 = 2x^2 - 5x + 12$
$0 = 2x^2 - 5x + 3$
2. $3 = 6 - x^2 + 3x$
$0 = -x^2 + 3x + 3$
3. $5 = 5 - 5x + \frac{1}{4}x^2$
$0 = \frac{1}{4}x^2 - 5x$

Determine whether each equation is equivalent to $5 = 3x^2 - 4x - 4$.

4. $9 = 3x^2 - 4x$ equivalent
5. $0 = 3x^2 - 4x - 9$ equivalent
6. $-5 = 3x^2 - 4x - 14$ equivalent

Solve each equation by finding the x-intercepts of its related graph. Round decimals to the nearest hundredth.

7. $0 = x^2 - 2x - 24$ –4, 6
8. $0 = x^2 - x - 30$ –5, 6
9. $0 = -x^2 - 3x + 10$ –5, 2
10. $0 = -x^2 + 4x + 12$ –2, 6
11. $0 = x^2 - 12x + 36$ 6
12. $0 = x^2 + 6x + 9$ –3
13. $0 = 2x^2 - 7x + 2$ 0.31, 3.19
14. $0 = 3x^2 - 8x - 2$ –0.23, 2.90
15. $0 = -4x^2 + 2x + 4$ –0.78, 1.28

Rewrite each equation in standard form. Then solve each equation by finding the x-intercepts of its graph. Round decimals to the nearest hundredth.

16. $4 = x^2 + 2x - 4$
$0 = x^2 + 2x - 8$; $-4, 2$

17. $48 = x^2 + 8x - 17$
$0 = x^2 + 8x - 65$; $5, -13$

18. $9 = x^2 - 18x - 31$
$0 = x^2 - 18x - 40$; $-2, 20$

19. $-10 = -x^2 + 2x - 6$
$0 = -x^2 + 2x + 4$; $-1.24, 3.24$

20. $2 = 3x^2 + 4x - 1$
$0 = 3x^2 + 4x - 3$; $-1.87, 0.54$

21. $5 = 4x^2 - 2x + 1$
$0 = 4x^2 - 2x - 4$; $-0.78, 1.28$

Solve each equation by graphing $y = d$ and $y = ax^2 + bx + c$ on the same set of axes and then finding the x-coordinates of their points of intersection. Round decimals to the nearest hundredth.

22. $5 = x^2 - 4x$ $-1, 5$

23. $-6 = -x^2 + 3x + 6$
$-2.27, 5.27$

24. $1 = 3x^2 - x - 4$
$-1.14, 1.47$

Use a graphing utility to determine the number of solutions to each equation.

25. $0 = 4x^2 - 12x + 9$ 1

26. $0 = 3x^2 + x + 4$ 0

27. $0 = x^2 - 8x + 14$ 2

28. $0 = 4x^2 - x + 5$ 0

29. $0 = x^2 + 5x - 3$ 2

30. $0 = 9x^2 + 6x + 1$ 1

31. BUSINESS TECHNOLOGY On January 17, 1995, the Prodigy on-line information service became the first consumer computer network to open its electronic portals to the Internet service known as the World Wide Web. The number (in trillions) of packets (bundles of data) traversing a major Internet conduit between May 1993 and December 1994 can be modeled with the equation $y = 0.052x^2 - 0.551x + 1.7$ where x is the month ($x = 1$ corresponds to May 1993, $x = 2$ corresponds to June 1993, . . . , and $x = 20$ corresponds to December 1994). In which month was the number of packets approximately 2 trillion? April 1994

32. PHYSICS On Mars the acceleration due to gravity is -12.2 ft/s^2. A ball is thrown from a point 5 ft above the ground straight upward at a speed of 20 ft/s. Use the formula for Example 4 to write the equation that represents the height of the ball as a function of time. Determine after how many seconds the ball will be 10 ft off the ground.
$h = -6.1t^2 + 20t - 5$; 0.27, 3.01

33. WRITING MATHEMATICS Describe the graph of $y = ax^2 + bx + c$ if the quadratic equation $0 = ax^2 + bx + c$ has no solutions.
Answers should indicate that the parabolic graph has no x-intercepts.

EXTEND

TRAVEL PLEASE GO AWAY! travel agency offers a vacation package to Europe at a discounted rate. They have calculated that their per-person profit on the purchase can be modeled by the equation $y = -x^2 + 60x$ where x is the number of people who buy the package.

34. If their profit was \$371 per person, how many people went to Europe?
7 or 53

35. If their profit was \$704 per person, how many people went to Europe?
16 or 44

36. Determine the number of travelers that will provide the agency with the maximum profit per person. What is the maximum profit per person? 30; \$900

37. If more than a certain number of people accept this package, the agency will lose money. What is the maximum number of people that can use this package before the agency begins to lose money? 60

graph the equation, they must disregard the negative solution because it is unreasonable. The other solution is a little more than 11. Then they must find the twelfth month. **April 1994**

Extend For Exercises 34–37, help students to understand why the profit-per-person equation is not linear. Help students understand that the cost of a chartered airplane is the same whether a few people get on it or if it is full. Therefore, the profit per person is less if there are fewer people. Ask students to use this example to explain why, past the number required to reach maximum profit, a large number of people can also decrease the profit per person. **If another airplane is needed, the cost of providing the tour increases.**

Think Critically For Exercise 39, discuss students' solutions and ask students to generalize about the values of c that result in no solution. **any value of c greater than 4** Ask students to explain their methods for solving Exercises 40 and 41.

NAME ________ CLASS ________ DATE ________

EXTRA PRACTICE **10.3 SOLVE QUADRATIC EQUATIONS BY GRAPHING**

Rewrite each equation in the form $0 = ax^2 + bx + c$.

1. $7 = 3x^2 - 5x + 1$ **2.** $8 = x^2 + 2x - 41$

3. $10 = 4x - x^2 - 3$ **4.** $-3 = 8 + 7x - x^2$

Determine whether each equation is equivalent to $3 = 2x^2 + x - 8$.

5. $0 = 2x^2 + x - 11$ **6.** $5 = 2x^2 + x - 10$

Rewrite each equation in standard form. Then solve each equation by finding the x-intercepts of its graph. Round decimals to the nearest hundredth.

7. $-2 = x^2 + 7x + 10$ **8.** $5 = x^2 + 6x - 2$

9. $4 = x^2 + 5x - 62$ **10.** $-3 = x^2 + 2x - 2$

11. $7 = x^2 + 3x - 8$ **12.** $3 = x^2 - 4x - 10$

Solve each equation by graphing $y = d$ and $y = ax^2 + bx + c$ on the same set of axes and then finding the x-coordinates of their points of intersection. Round decimals to the nearest hundredth.

13. $-1 = x^2 + 3x - 19$ **14.** $3 = x^2 + 2x - 12$

15. $6 = x^2 - 4x + 8$ **16.** $10 = x^2 - x - 8$

17. $5 = x^2 + 3x - 17$ **18.** $-4 = x^2 - 2x - 9$

19. PHYSICS The height of an object thrown in the air can be modeled by the equation $y = -16x^2 + 80x + 20$ where x is the number of seconds after it is thrown. Find to the nearest second when it will reach the ground.

1. $0 = 3x^2 - 5x - 6$
2. $0 = x^2 + 2x - 12$
3. $0 = -x^2 + 4x - 13$
4. $0 = -x^2 + 7x + 11$
5. equivalent
6. not equivalent
7. $-4, -3$
8. $-7, 1$
9. $-11, 6$
10. -1
11. $-5.65, 2.65$
12. $-2.12, 6.12$
13. $-6, 3$
14. $-5, 3$
15. 0.59, 3.41
16. 4.77, -3.77
17. $-6.42, 3.42$
18. $-1.45, 3.45$
19. 5 seconds

16 *South-Western Algebra 1: AN INTEGRATED APPROACH*

5 FOLLOW-UP

Extension The function $h = -16t^2 + 500$ represents the height h in feet of an object falling from 500 feet above the ground at t seconds after it is dropped. Ask students how they can use this equation to find the length of time (to the nearest second) for the object to reach the ground. **When h is 0, the object is on the ground. Graph $y = -16x^2 + 500$ on a graphing utility and find the value of x for which $y = 0$; $x = 6$ to the nearest second.**

Project Connection This activity presents further aspects of the project introduced on page 464. Review the procedure for changing very large and very small numbers from standard to scientific notation.

NAME ________ CLASS ________ DATE ________

10.3 SOLVE QUADRATIC EQUATIONS BY GRAPHING

A graphing utility can be used to find solutions to equations with an exponent greater than 2. These equations may have one or more solutions that are real numbers.

Example
Find any real number solutions of $x^3 - 8 = 0$.

Solution
Graph $y = x^3 - 8$ on a graphing utility. Find any value of x for which $y = 0$.

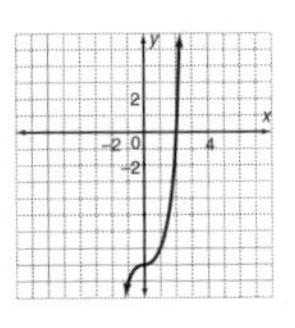

You can see from the graph that $x = 2$ when $y = 0$, so 2 is a real number solution of the equation.

EXERCISES
Use a graphing utility to find all the real number solutions of these polynomial equations.

1. $x^3 + 8 = 0$ — 1. **−2**
2. $2x^3 - 8x = 0$ — 2. **−2, 0, 2**
3. $x^4 - 16 = 0$ — 3. **−2, 2**
4. $x^4 - 10x^2 + 9 = 0$ — 4. **−3, −1, 1, 3**
5. $x^5 - 13x^3 + 36x = 0$ — 5. **−3, −2, 0, 2, 3**
6. $x^5 - 5x^3 + 4x = 0$ — 6. **−2, −1, 0, 1, 2**
7. What do you notice about the relationship between the number of real number solutions of the polynomial equation and the degree of that equation?
The number of real number solutions of a polynomial equation is sometimes less than, but never greater than, the degree of the equation.
8. Predict the greatest number of real number solutions of this equation:
$x^7 - 11x^5 + 19x^3 - 9x = 0$
Number of real number solutions cannot be greater than **7**.

18 *South-Western Algebra 1: AN INTEGRATED APPROACH*

THINK CRITICALLY

38. Find a value of c such that the equation $y = x^2 - 4x + c$ will have only one solution. 4
39. Find two values of c such that the equation $y = x^2 - 4x + c$ will have no real solutions.
Answers will vary; examples include 6 and 10; any value of c, such that $c > 4$, is correct.
40. Write a quadratic equation that has two real solutions.
Answers will vary; an example is $0 = x^2 + x - 42$ with solutions −7, 6.
41. Write a quadratic equation that has two real solutions, one of which is a solution to the equation you wrote in Question 40.
Answers will vary; an example is $0 = x^2 - x - 30$ with solutions −5 and 6.
42. Graph to determine the solutions to the equation $x^2 - 6x + 5 = 0$. How do the solutions relate to the axis of symmetry?
The solutions are reflections of each other over the axis of symmetry.

MIXED REVIEW

43. **Standardized Tests** Which is the slope-intercept form of the equation $9x + 3y = 12$?
C; Lesson 6.3

A. $y = 3x + 4$ **B.** $y = 3x - 4$
C. $y = -3x + 4$ **D.** $y = 27x - 36$

Determine the number of solutions each system of equations has. Lesson 7.5

44. $\begin{cases} 2x + 3y = 6 \\ -12 + 4x = -6y \end{cases}$ infinitely many

45. $\begin{cases} 5x + 4y = 13 \\ 4x + 6y = 16 \end{cases}$ one

Demonstrate that each of the following numbers can be written as the quotient of two integers. Answers will vary; sample answers are provided. Lesson 9.5

46. -8 $\frac{-8}{1}$
47. 5.33 $\frac{533}{100}$
48. $-9\frac{1}{2}$ $\frac{-19}{2}$
49. 0.095 $\frac{19}{200}$

Rewrite each equation in standard form. Solve each equation by finding the x-intercepts of its graph. Lesson 10.3

50. $-6 = x^2 + 5x$ $0 = x^2 + 5x + 6$; −2, −3
51. $-2 = -x^2 + 3x + 1$
$0 = -x^2 + 3x + 3$; −0.79, 3.79

PROJECT Connection

In this activity, you will begin researching the industry and corporation you selected.

1. Obtain the address and/or telephone number of your corporation.
2. Contact each corporation immediately, by business letter or telephone. Explain the purpose of your project and request a copy of the Annual Report and any other available information (some companies have videos). Have the material sent to your home address. Send a thank you letter when you receive the information.
3. Research and summarize information on stocks and stock markets. You will need this information for the graph you will construct in the next Project Connection. Prepare a set of six to ten "attention-getting" facts using very large or very small numbers as they relate to market activity (for example, trading volume, total worth of corporations, amount of time for an electronic transaction). Consider using scientific notation for your data.

10.4 Solve Quadratic Equations Using Square Roots

Explore/Working Together

1. If you are the first person chosen by your teacher, select three cards from the deck in your teacher's hand. Assign the number on the first card to be a, the number on the second card to be b, and the number on the third card to be c in the equation $ax^2 + b = c$.
2. Write the resulting equation on the chalkboard.
3. Select a student to use mental math in solving the equation.
4. After that student provides you with an answer, solve the equation algebraically on the board.
5. Discuss whether the equation has a real number solution and, if so, discuss whether the solution is rational or irrational.
6. If the student you selected has the correct answer, repeat Steps 1–5. If that student does not have the correct answer, your teacher will select a new student to pick three cards.
7. After the class finishes the game, write the conditions under which the equation $ax^2 + b = c$ has no real solutions.
When $c - b$ is a negative number, the equation has no real solutions.

SPOTLIGHT ON LEARNING

WHAT? In this lesson you will learn
- to use the square root method of solving quadratic equations of the form $ax^2 + b = c$.

WHY? The square root method for solving quadratic equations can help to solve problems in banking, physics, and geometry.

Build Understanding

Recall that every positive real number k has one positive and one negative square root. This fact is stated in the *square root property*.

SQUARE ROOT PROPERTY

If $x^2 = k$, then $x = \sqrt{k}$ or $x = -\sqrt{k}$ for any real number k, $k > 0$.

If $k = 0$, then the equation $x^2 = 0$ has one solution, which is 0.

CHECK UNDERSTANDING

The square root property states that k in $\sqrt{k}$ must be greater than or equal to zero. Why is $\sqrt{k}$ not defined for $k < 0$?

The property applies to real numbers. There is no real number whose square can be a negative number. So $\sqrt{-k}$ cannot be a real number and $\sqrt{-k}$ has no real square root.

To solve a quadratic equation of the form $ax^2 + b = c$, you can use the square root property. First solve for x^2 and then take the square root of both sides. This technique is called the **square root method** of solving quadratic equations.

Since $x^2 = 4$, $x = 2$ or $x = -2$. To indicate this you can write $x = \pm 2$. Therefore, when taking the square root of both sides of an equation, write $\pm\sqrt{}$ to indicate both the positive square root and the negative square root.

LESSON PLANNING

Objective

▶ Use the square root method of solving quadratic equations of the form $ax^2 + b = c$.

Vocabulary

square root method
square root property

Technology/Multimedia

calculator

Resources

Warm Up 10.4
Reteaching 10.4
Extra Practice 10.4
Enrichment 10.4
Student Handbook
Lesson Quiz 10.4

Materials/Manipulatives

deck of cards

ASSIGNMENTS

Basic: 1–28, 32–36, 38, 41–45, 50, Mixed Review 51–57, Project Connection 1–4, AlgebraWorks 1–8

Average: 3–37, 41–49, Mixed Review 51–57, Project Connection 1–4, AlgebraWorks 1–8

Enriched: 9–50, Mixed Review 51–57, Project Connection 1–4, AlgebraWorks 1–8

1 MOTIVATE

Explore/Working Together Prepare a standard deck of playing cards by removing all face cards and jokers from the deck. Explain to students that the black cards are positive integers, red cards are negative integers, and aces are worth 1. Before beginning this activity, remind students that $\sqrt{k}$ is the principal, or positive, square root of k. Suggest that when students solve equations, they may express answers with square root signs. Have students read the Check Understanding on page 483. Then ask them to explain why $x^2 = k$ can have no real solution if $k < 0$. **There is no real number whose square will result in a negative number.** Tell students that the square root of a negative number is called an imaginary number.

2 TEACH

Use the Pages/Build Understanding

Example 1: Tell students that the square root method cannot be used unless the equation is in the form $x^2 = k$. In the check, ask students why parentheses should be used when substituting –9 in the original equation. **to prevent mistakes in signs when simplifying the expression**

Example 2: Display the step in the equation in which both sides are divided by 4. Ask students what happens to the 4 on the left side of the equation. **Both sides of the equation are divided by 4.** Remind students to be careful about order of operations when finding decimal approximations like $\frac{1 + 2\sqrt{3}}{2}$.
They must either use parentheses around the numerator or find $\sqrt{3}$ on the calculator first, then multiply it by 2, add 1, and take half of the result.

Example 3: When they have read this example, ask students to find the time for an object to fall from a height of 200 meters. **approximately 6.39 s**

THINK BACK

Recall the product and quotient properties of square roots.

For real numbers $a \geq 0$ and $b \geq 0$,

$$\sqrt{ab} = \sqrt{a} \cdot \sqrt{b}$$

For real numbers $a \geq 0$ and $b > 0$,

$$\sqrt{\frac{a}{b}} = \frac{\sqrt{a}}{\sqrt{b}}$$

PROBLEM SOLVING TIP

In Example 2, think of the expression $2x - 1$ as a "chunk." Then let $p = 2x - 1$. The equation becomes $4p^2 = 48$. After you find $p = \pm\sqrt{12}$, replace p with $2x - 1$ and solve the two equations $2x - 1 = \sqrt{12}$ or $2x - 1 = -\sqrt{12}$.

COMMUNICATING ABOUT ALGEBRA

Do all equations of the form $ax^2 + b = c$ where $c < 0$ have no real solutions?

See Additional Answers.

EXAMPLE 1

Solve: $2x^2 + 5 = 167$

Solution

$$2x^2 + 5 = 167$$
$$2x^2 = 162 \quad \text{Subtract 5 from both sides.}$$
$$x^2 = 81 \quad \text{Divide both sides by 2.}$$
$$x = \pm\sqrt{81} \quad \text{Take the square root of both sides.}$$
$$x = \pm 9 \quad \text{Simplify.}$$

Check

Substitute both solutions in the original equation.

$2x^2 + 5 = 167$	$2x^2 + 5 = 167$
$2(9)^2 + 5 \stackrel{?}{=} 167$	$2(-9)^2 + 5 \stackrel{?}{=} 167$
$2(81) + 5 \stackrel{?}{=} 167$	$2(81) + 5 \stackrel{?}{=} 167$
$162 + 5 \stackrel{?}{=} 167$	$162 + 5 \stackrel{?}{=} 167$
$167 = 167$ ✓	$167 = 167$ ✓

Therefore, the solutions are 9 and –9. ◄

You can also use the square root method to solve quadratic equations when an expression such as $(2x - 1)$ is squared.

EXAMPLE 2

Solve: $4(2x - 1)^2 = 48$

Solution

$$4(2x - 1)^2 = 48$$
$$(2x - 1)^2 = 12 \quad \text{Divide both sides by 4.}$$
$$2x - 1 = \pm\sqrt{12} \quad \text{Take the square root of both sides.}$$

$$2x - 1 = 2\sqrt{3} \quad \text{or} \quad 2x - 1 = -2\sqrt{3}$$
$$x = \frac{1 + 2\sqrt{3}}{2} \qquad x = \frac{1 - 2\sqrt{3}}{2}$$

Check

Use your calculator or computer to determine a decimal approximation for each solution. Store each result in a memory.

$$(1 + 2\sqrt{3}) \div 2 \approx 2.232050808 \quad \text{Store in memory A.}$$
$$(1 - 2\sqrt{3}) \div 2 \approx -1.232050808 \quad \text{Store in memory B.}$$

Substitute each stored value in the original equation.

$4(2x - 1)^2 = 48$	$4(2x - 1)^2 = 48$
$4(2A - 1)^2 \stackrel{?}{=} 48$	$4(2B - 1)^2 \stackrel{?}{=} 48$
$48 = 48$ ✓	$48 = 48$ ✓

The solutions to the nearest hundredth are 2.23 and –1.23. Note that if you round the solution before you store it in memory, you may only get a number close to 48. ◄

You can use the square root method to determine the time it takes for an object in free fall to descend a specific distance. Galileo found that the formula that models an object in free fall is $d = \frac{1}{2}at^2$ where d is the distance that the object has fallen, a is the acceleration due to gravity, and t is the elapsed time. The value of a varies depending on the location on Earth's surface. At sea level, the value of a is approximately -9.8 m/s^2.

EXAMPLE 3

PHYSICS A window washer accidentally dropped his watch from a top floor window 60 m above the ground. The acceleration due to gravity is approximately -9.8m/s^2. In how many seconds will the watch hit the ground?

Solution

The watch falls 60 m downward, which can be represented by -60 m.

$$d = \frac{1}{2}at^2$$

$$-60 = \frac{1}{2}(-9.8)t^2 \quad \text{Substitute.}$$

$$-60 = -4.9t^2 \quad \text{Multiply.}$$

$$\frac{-60}{-4.9} = t^2 \quad \text{Solve for } t^2.$$

$$\pm\sqrt{\frac{-60}{-4.9}} = t \quad \text{Take the square root.}$$

$$\pm 3.50 \approx t$$

The watch will hit the ground in about 3.50 s.

ALGEBRA: WHO, WHERE, WHEN

One of the earliest persons to investigate freely falling objects was the Greek philosopher Aristotle (384–322 B.C.). Aristotle's investigations led him to conclude that heavy objects fall faster than light ones. Not until Galileo investigated this problem (1564–1642) did scientists accept the idea that all objects fall at the same acceleration.

TRY THESE

Solve each equation. Use the product and quotient properties to simplify the radicals.

1. $x^2 = 81$ $-9, 9$
2. $x^2 = 100$ $-10, 10$
3. $x^2 + 2 = 50$ $\pm 4\sqrt{3}$
4. $x^2 - 3 = 72$ $\pm 5\sqrt{3}$
5. $\frac{1}{2}x^2 + 3 = 23$ $\pm 2\sqrt{10}$
6. $\frac{1}{2}x^2 - 8 = 44$ $\pm 2\sqrt{26}$
7. $(x - 1)^2 = 25$ $-4, 6$
8. $(x - 1)^2 = 64$ $-7, 9$
9. $2(x + 1)^2 = 162$ $8, -10$
10. $3(x - 4)^2 = 108$ $-2, 10$
11. $3\left(x + \frac{2}{3}\right)^2 = \frac{1}{3}$ $-1, -\frac{1}{3}$
12. $2\left(x + \frac{3}{4}\right)^2 = \frac{1}{8}$ $-1, -\frac{1}{2}$

Solve each equation. Round your answers to two decimal places.

13. $x^2 - 5 = -6$ no real number solution
14. $x^2 - 10 = -10$ 0
15. $4x^2 - 3 = 18$ ± 2.29
16. $2x^2 - 7 = 13$ ± 3.16
17. $3x^2 - 4 = 16$ ± 2.58
18. $3(x - 3)^2 = 17$ $0.62, 5.38$
19. $5(x - 2)^2 = 12$ $0.45, 3.55$
20. $6\left(x - \frac{1}{2}\right)^2 = 3$ $-0.21, 1.21$
21. $5(x + 0.5)^2 = 7.5$ $-1.72, 0.72$

Ongoing Assessment The important concepts and skills involve solving quadratic equations of the form $ax^2 + b = c$ by using the square root method. To assess this idea, have students demonstrate how they have applied it in Exercises 2, 6, 14, and 18 of the Try These section.

Guided Practice/Try These For Exercises 1–12, students may leave answers in simplest radical form. In Exercises 13–21, they must express each answer as the decimal approximation of a square root.

Error Alert Watch for students whose first step in solving Exercise 17 is $3x - 4 = 4$. When students see a number that is an expression containing a perfect square on one side of the equation, they may want to take the square root immediately. Remind them that they cannot take the square root of only part of one side of an equation.

DIVERSITY IN THE CLASSROOM

Visual Learners For students who are having trouble identifying when to take the square root of both sides of the equation, have them use highlighter or colored pencil to outline the expression being squared. Then when that expression has been isolated they can use the square root property.

3 SUMMARIZE

In the Math Journal Have students write a paragraph that describes equations for which the square root method for solving can be used. **When the side that contains the variable is a squared expression such as x^2 or $(x - 2)^2$ or a multiple of a squared expression, there is no first-degree term in x, and the other side is a positive integer.**

4 PRACTICE

Practice Exercise 10 can be solved in two ways. For both methods, begin by adding 5 to each side. Since $4x^2$ is a squared expression, you can take the square root of each side: $2x = \pm\sqrt{288}$, $2x = \pm 12\sqrt{2}$. Then divide both sides by 2: $x = \pm 6\sqrt{2}$. The other method would involve dividing both sides by 4 before taking the square root.

Extend Be sure that students read the text and example above Exercises 35–40 before attempting these exercises.

Think Critically For Exercises 44–45, students may want to try some numerical examples to help them see the pattern. Geometry formulas can be found in the Geometry Quick Notes starting on page 728 of the student book.

22. **BANKING** The formula for determining the amount of money A that you will have at the end of 2 years if you deposit a principal of P in an account in which the interest rate is $r\%$ compounded annually is $A = P\left(1 + \frac{r}{100}\right)^2$. Determine the interest rate paid by this account if you deposit \$400 and it grows to \$441 in 2 years. 5%

23. **WRITING MATHEMATICS** Explain in your own words the conditions under which a quadratic equation of the form $ax^2 + b = c$ will have two real number solutions, one real number solution, and no real number solutions. See Additional Answers.

PRACTICE

Solve each equation. Express radicals in simplest form.

1. $x^2 = 49$ $-7, 7$
2. $x^2 = 121$ $-11, 11$
3. $x^2 = \frac{25}{81}$ $\pm\frac{5}{9}$
4. $x^2 - \frac{16}{64} = 0$ $\pm\frac{1}{2}$
5. $x^2 = \frac{361}{484}$ $\pm\frac{19}{22}$
6. $x^2 + 6 = 0$ no real number solution
7. $x^2 + 3 = 0$ no real number solution
8. $x^2 + 4 = 112$ $\pm 6\sqrt{3}$
9. $x^2 + 6 = 86$ $\pm 4\sqrt{5}$
10. $4x^2 - 5 = 283$ $\pm 6\sqrt{2}$
11. $3x^2 - 4 = 290$ $\pm 7\sqrt{2}$
12. $(x - 1)^2 = 64$ $-7, 9$
13. $(x - 4)^2 = 225$ $-11, 19$
14. $\frac{1}{2}x^2 + 4 = 158$ $\pm 2\sqrt{77}$
15. $\frac{1}{2}x^2 + 5 = 250$ $\pm 7\sqrt{10}$
16. $3(x + 5)^2 = 75$ $0, -10$
17. $5(x + 6)^2 = 80$ $-2, -10$
18. $3(2x + 5)^2 = 300$ $-7.5, 2.5$
19. $2(3x + 4)^2 = 180.5$ $-4.5, \frac{11}{6}$
20. $2\left(x - \frac{5}{6}\right)^2 = \frac{1}{18}$ $\frac{2}{3}, 1$
21. $5(x + 0.3)^2 = 4.05$ $-1.2, 0.6$
22. **BANKING** If you invest \$1440 in a savings account in which the interest is compounded annually, and the principal grows to \$1690 in 2 years, what is the interest rate on the account? (*Hint:* Use the formula in Exercise 22 of Try These.) $8\frac{1}{3}\%$

Solve each equation. Round your answers to two decimal places.

23. $3x^2 - 5 = 16$ ± 2.65
24. $4x^2 - 10 = 25$ ± 2.96
25. $5x^2 + 9 = 38$ ± 2.41
26. $3x^2 + 7 = 70$ ± 4.58
27. $x^2 + 8 = 81$ ± 8.54
28. $2(x - 3)^2 = 55$ $-2.24, 8.24$
29. $5(x - 6)^2 = 82$ $1.95, 10.05$
30. $7(x - 0.6)^2 = 3$ $-0.05, 1.25$
31. $5(x - 0.8)^2 = 12$ $-0.75, 2.35$
32. **PHYSICS** Students conducting a physics experiment dropped an egg from a window 222 m above the ground. In how many seconds will the egg reach the ground? (*Hint*: Use the formula given for Example 3.) 6.73 sec
33. **WRITING MATHEMATICS** Explain why one square root that is a solution to a quadratic equation in certain real world applications may be meaningless. Provide an example of such a situation. Answers will vary. Possible answer: a deposit in a savings account grows. Therefore, the interest rate cannot be negative.
34. **GEOMETRY** Alejandro is using posterboard to construct a cone for his geometry class. He has determined that the volume V should be 18π cm^3. He is ready to cut the circle for the base of the cone. Determine the radius of the circular base if the height h of the cone is 6 cm. $\left(\textit{Hint}: \text{Use the formula } V = \frac{1}{3}\pi r^2 h.\right)$ 3 cm

EXTEND

The square root method of solving a quadratic equation can be used to solve quadratic inequalities of the form $ax^2 + b < c$ or $ax^2 + b > c$. The following shows how you can solve a quadratic inequality such as $3x^2 + 7 < 82$.

a. Solve the corresponding quadratic equation.

$$\begin{aligned} 3x^2 + 7 &= 82 \\ 3x^2 &= 75 \\ x^2 &= 25 \\ x &= \pm 5 \end{aligned}$$

b. Use the solutions to divide the real number line into three sections. Test a value from each section.

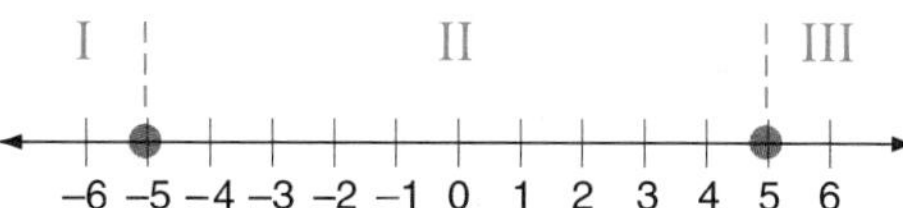

c. Check each of these sections by trying a test value in the section.

- Try $x = -7$ from Section I: $3(-7)^2 + 7 < 82$, which is false.
- Try $x = 0$ from Section II: $3(0)^2 + 7 < 82$, which is true.
- Try $x = 6$ from Section III: $3(6)^2 + 7 < 82$, which is false.

d. The solution is $-5 < x < 5$.

Use the above method to solve each inequality.

35. $x^2 > 144$ $x < -12$ or $x > 12$ **36.** $x^2 < 225$ $-15 < x < 15$ **37.** $2x^2 - 6 > 66$ $x < -6$ or $x > 6$

38. $4x^2 - 8 < 392$ $-10 < x < 10$ **39.** $4(x - 2)^2 < 16$ $0 < x < 4$ **40.** $3(x + 1)^2 > 147$ $x < -8$ or $x > 6$

GEOMETRY The surface area S of a sphere can be calculated by using the formula $S = 4\pi r^2$ where r represents the radius of the sphere.

41. If the surface area of a sphere is 100 m^2, determine its radius to the nearest hundredth. Use 3.14 for π. 2.82 m

42. Write an equation for the surface area of an enclosed hemisphere. Then determine its radius to the nearest hundredth if the surface area of an enclosed hemisphere is 100 m^2. Solve using 3.14 for π.
$S = 3\pi r^2$; 3.26 m

43. GEOMETRY The surface area of a cube can be calculated using the formula $S = 6x^2$ where x is the length of a side. If the surface area of a cube is 350 m^2, determine the length of a side to the nearest hundredth. 7.64 m

THINK CRITICALLY

44. If the radius of a sphere is doubled, by what factor is the surface area multiplied? 4

45. If the side x of a cube is doubled, by what factor is the surface area multiplied? 4

46. If the height from which an object goes into free fall is doubled, by what factor is the time for the object to reach the ground multiplied? $\sqrt{2} \approx 1.41$

47. Derive a formula that allows you to determine the amount of money A that you will have at the end of 4 years if you deposit P in an account in which the interest rate is r% compounded annually. $A = P\left(1 + \frac{r}{100}\right)^4$

5 FOLLOW-UP

Extension Ask students to describe the conditions under which $ax^2 + b = c$ will have solutions that are rational. **when the value of $\frac{(c - b)}{a}$ is a perfect square**

Making Connections

Finance A formula that relates the amount deposited P to the total amount plus interest A in an account that pays r% compounded quarterly for t years is $A = P\left(1 + \frac{r}{400}\right)^t$.

Ask students to determine when an investor would use this formula solved for A and when the investor would solve it for P. **to determine how much money will be in the account after a given principal P has been invested at a given rate of interest for a given number of quarters; to determine how much money would have to be invested at a given rate of interest for a given amount of time in order to yield a given amount**

NAME ______ CLASS ______ DATE ______

10.4 SOLVE QUADRATIC EQUATIONS USING SQUARE ROOTS

The square root property states that if $x^2 = k$, then $x = \sqrt{k}$ or $x = -\sqrt{k}$ for a real number k, where $k > 0$.
To solve an equation, you must use properties of equality to find an equivalent equation that has the squared expression isolated on one side.

Example
Solve: $2(x - 1)^2 = 98$

Solution

$$\begin{aligned} 2(x - 1)^2 &= 98 \\ (x - 1)^2 &= 49 && \text{Divide each side by 2.} \\ x - 1 &= \pm 7 && \text{Take the square root of each side.} \\ x - 1 = 7 &\text{ or } x - 1 = -7 \\ x = 8 &\text{ or } x = -6 \end{aligned}$$

Check

$$\begin{aligned} 2(8 - 1)^2 &= 98 \\ 2(7)^2 &= 98 \\ 2(49) &= 98 \\ 98 &= 98 \checkmark \end{aligned} \qquad \begin{aligned} 2(-6 - 1)^2 &= 98 \\ 2(-7)^2 &= 98 \\ 2(49) &= 98 \\ 98 &= 98 \checkmark \end{aligned}$$

Therefore, the solutions are 8 and –6.

EXERCISES
Solve each equation.

1. $3(x - 2)^2 = 48$
$(x - 2)^2 = 16$
$x - 2 =$ **±4**
$x =$ **4 + 2,**
or $x =$ **−4 + 2**

2. $5(x + 2)^2 = 20$
$(x + 2)^2 = 4$
$x + 2 =$ **±2**
$x =$ **2 − 2,**
or $x =$ **−2 − 2**

3. $(x + 1)^2 = 36$ **4.** $(x - 3)^2 = 4$

5. $4(x + 5)^2 = 100$ **6.** $3(x - 1)^2 = 300$

7. $5(2x + 5)^2 = 45$ **8.** $2(x - 7)^2 = 50$

9. $3(x - 4)^2 = 1.08$ **10.** $4(x + 3)^2 = 9$

1. **6, −2**
2. **0, −4**
3. **5, −7**
4. **5, 1**
5. **−10, 0**
6. **11, −9**
7. **−1, −4**
8. **12, 2**
9. **4.6, 3.4**
10. **−1.5, −4.5**

22 *South-Western Algebra 1: AN INTEGRATED APPROACH*

Project Connection This activity presents further aspects of the project introduced on page 464. To be sure students know how to interpret the sample graph, ask some questions such as the following. What was the closing price of one share on Monday? **$37\frac{3}{4}$** What was the number of shares traded on Friday? **5000** On what day was the daily low the same as the closing price? **Tuesday** What does the graph for Friday's price represent? **The price remained unchanged throughout the day.**

48. Derive a formula that allows you to determine the amount of money A that you will have at the end of 2 years if you deposit P in an account in which the interest rate is r% compounded semi-annually. $A = P\left(1 + \frac{r}{200}\right)^4$

49. If you deposited \$800 in an account that pays 8.1% simple interest per year for 2 years, will you have more or less money than you would have if you deposited \$800 in an account that pays 8% compounded annually for 2 years? Explain. less; in the simple interest account, you would have \$929.60; in the compounded account, you would have \$933.12

50. In an equation of the form $ax^2 + b = c$, does c have to be a perfect square to solve the equation by the square root method? Explain. no; it can be any real number such that $c - b \geq 0$

MIXED REVIEW

51. **STANDARDIZED TESTS** One number cube having faces labeled 1, 2, 3, 4, 5, and 6 is rolled. What is the probability of rolling a number divisible by 3? D; Lesson 1.8

    A. $\frac{1}{2}$ **B.** $\frac{1}{6}$ **C.** $\frac{1}{4}$ **D.** $\frac{1}{3}$

Which property of real numbers is demonstrated below? Lesson 2.7

52. $2 \cdot \frac{1}{2} = 1$ multiplicative inverse

53. $5(0) = 0$ multiplication property of zero

Determine the vertex and the line of symmetry for the graph of each equation. Lesson 9.2

54. $y = |x - 5| + 1$ (5, 1); $x = 5$

55. $y = |x + 4| - 2$ (−4, −2); $x = -4$

Solve each equation. Round your answer to the nearest hundredth. Lesson 10.4

56. $3(x + 3)^2 = 18$ −5.45, −0.55

57. $4(x - 5)^2 = 29$ 2.31, 7.69

PROJECT Connection

In this activity, you will construct a special type of graph that gives information about the daily high, daily low, closing price, and the number of shares traded of a corporation's stock. Examine the sample graph shown.

1. On a sheet of paper, draw and label the axes for the *Price of One Share* graph.
2. Label the middle of the vertical axis with today's closing price. This will allow space to graph the price if it rises or falls. Use intervals of $\frac{1}{4}$ dollar.
3. On another sheet of graph paper, draw and label the axes for the *Sales* graph. Do not set the range of numbers for the vertical axis. Use a table to record daily sales data. At the end of the project, examine your high and low sales figures and then decide how to label the vertical axis.
4. At the end of the project, combine or redraw the two graphs so that all the information is clearly displayed as shown at the right.

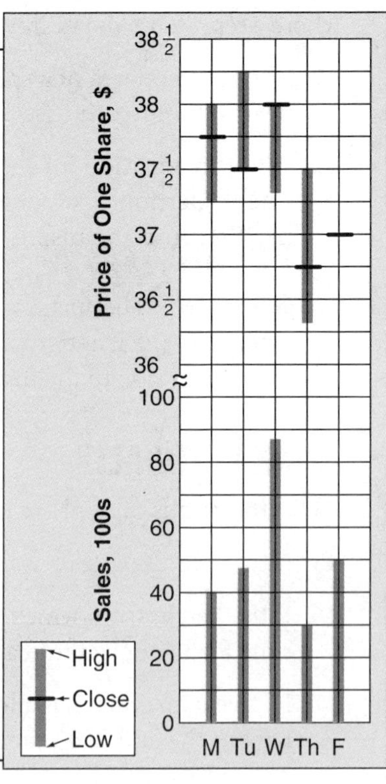

NAME ______ CLASS ______ DATE ______

EXTRA PRACTICE

10.4 SOLVE QUADRATIC EQUATIONS USING SQUARE ROOTS

Solve each equation. Express radicals in simplest form.

1. $x^2 = 36$
2. $x^2 = 169$
3. $x^2 = \frac{49}{64}$
4. $x^2 - \frac{144}{225} = 0$
5. $x^2 + 15 = 0$
6. $x^2 + 8 = 0$
7. $x^2 + 3 = 21$
8. $x^2 + 31 = 156$
9. $2x^2 - 9 = 15$
10. $6x^2 - 110 = 82$
11. $(x - 1)^2 = 49$
12. $(x - 5)^2 = 196$
13. $\frac{1}{4}x^2 + 13 = 103$
14. $\frac{1}{3}x^2 + 27 = 150$
15. $4(x + 6)^2 = 144$
16. $7(x + 3)^2 = 28$
17. $4(5x + 1)^2 = 289$
18. $2(3x + 3)^2 = 760.5$
19. $4\left(x - \frac{5}{8}\right)^2 = \frac{9}{16}$

Solve each equation. Round your answers to two decimal places.

20. $4x^2 - 9 = 30$
21. $6x^2 + 3 = 58$
22. $3(x - 7)^2 = 8$
23. $9(x - 0.5)^2 = 42$
24. **PHYSICS** The kinetic energy of an object is the energy it possesses due to its motion. The formula for kinetic energy is $k = \frac{1}{2}mv^2$ where k is the kinetic energy of the object, m is the mass in grams of the object and v is the velocity in meters per second of the object. Find v when $k = \frac{24\text{gm}^2}{\text{s}^2}$ and $m = 3\text{g}$.

Answers:
1. −6, 6
2. −13, 13
3. $\pm\frac{7}{8}$
4. $\pm\frac{4}{5}$
5. no real solution
6. no real solution
7. $\pm 3\sqrt{2}$
8. $\pm 5\sqrt{5}$
9. $\pm 2\sqrt{3}$
10. $\pm 4\sqrt{2}$
11. −6, 8
12. −9, 19
13. $\pm 6\sqrt{10}$
14. $\pm 3\sqrt{41}$
15. 0, −12
16. −1, −5
17. 1.5, −1.9
18. −7.5, −5.5
19. $\frac{1}{4}$, 1
20. ±3.12
21. ±3.03
22. 8.63, 5.37
23. 2.66, −1.66
24. 4 m/s

24 *South-Western Algebra 1: AN INTEGRATED APPROACH*

Career
Amusement Park Ride Designer

The most exciting amusement park rides feel like a free fall for the rider. The acceleration due to gravity on earth is -32 ft/s^2. A ride designer can use $d = -16t^2$, derived from Galileo's formula, to model the distance traveled by the ride as a function of time. The speed of the ride after t seconds is $32t$. The ride designer must also consider the following issues.

- How high should the ride be?
- How many seconds should the free fall last?
- What speed is too slow to be exciting?
- What speed is too fast to be safe?
- How much money will rides of different heights cost to build?
- How much distance should be allowed for the safe braking of the ride?

Decision Making

1. If a ride drops 36 ft, how many seconds is the rider in free fall? 1.5 s
2. Use your answer to Question 1 to determine the speed at which the ride is dropping when it has dropped 36 ft. 48 ft/s
3. If a ride drops 72 ft, how many seconds is the rider in free fall? 2.12 s
4. Use your answer to Question 3 to determine the speed at which the ride is dropping when it has dropped 72 ft. 67.84 ft/s

A speed of 60 mi/h is equivalent to 1 mi/min. There are 5280 ft in a mile.

5. Convert a speed of 60 mi/h to feet per second. 88 ft/s
6. Determine the speed on the ride after 1 second and convert your answer to miles per hour. 32 ft/s = 21.82 mi/h
7. Determine the speed on the ride after 2.5 seconds and convert your answer to miles per hour. 80 ft/s = 54.55 mi/h
8. What do you think is a reasonable time for this ride?

Answers will vary. Responses should be between 1 and 2 min.

AlgebraWorks Have students research the tallest, fastest, or longest roller coaster ride. Some students may want to design their own roller coaster rides.

NAME ______ CLASS ______ DATE ______

ENRICHMENT

10.4 SOLVE QUADRATIC EQUATIONS USING SQUARE ROOTS

Imaginary Numbers

By the square root property, the solution of the equation $x^2 = k$ is the $\sqrt{k}$ and $-\sqrt{k}$ for any real number $k > 0$. If $k = 0$, there is one solution, 0, since $(0)^2 = 0$.

Suppose that $k < 0$. The equation $x^2 = -1$ has no real solution since there is no real number x such that $x \cdot x = -1$. However, $x^2 = -1$ has a solution in the set of *imaginary numbers*. Imaginary numbers are represented by i such that

$$i = \sqrt{-1} \qquad (i)^2 = -1 \qquad (-i)^2 = -1$$

For any real number a, where $a > 0$, $\sqrt{-a} = i\sqrt{a}$

So, $\sqrt{-3} = i\sqrt{3}$ and $\sqrt{-25} = i\sqrt{25} = 5i$.

These numbers allow us to solve the equation $x^2 = k$ for any real number k.

Example 1 Solve: $x^2 = -6$

Solution $x = \pm\sqrt{-6}$
$x = \pm i\sqrt{6}$

Example 2 Solve: $(x - 3)^2 = -4$

Solution $x - 3 = \pm\sqrt{-4}$
$x - 3 = \pm i\sqrt{4}$
$x - 3 = \pm 2i$
$x = 3 + 2i$ and $x = 3 - 2i$

Solve each equation.

1. $x^2 = -9$ **2.** $x^2 = -16$
3. $x^2 = -3$ **4.** $x^2 = -7$
5. $x^2 + 2 = -12$ **6.** $x^2 - 5 = -41$
7. $(x - 2)^2 = -2$ **8.** $(x + 4)^2 = -4$
9. $2x^2 = -32$ **10.** $6x^2 = -48$
11. $2(x + 3)^2 = -50$ **12.** $3(x - 1)^2 = -15$
13. $5(x - 2)^2 = -10$ **14.** $-2(x + 5) = 8$

An *imaginary number* (I) is a product of a real number and an imaginary number. A *complex number* (C) is the sum of a real number and an imaginary number. Label each I or C.

15. $-7i$ **16.** $8 + 2i$
17. $3i$ **18.** $i - 5$
19. $6i$ **20.** $-8 - i$

1. $3i, -3i$
2. $4i, -4i$
3. $i\sqrt{3}, -i\sqrt{3}$
4. $i\sqrt{7}, -i\sqrt{7}$
5. $i\sqrt{14}, -i\sqrt{14}$
6. $6i, -6i$
7. $2 \pm i\sqrt{2}$
8. $-4 \pm$
9. $4i, -4i$
10. $2i\sqrt{2}, -2i\sqrt{2}$
11. $-3 \pm$
12. $1 \pm i\sqrt{5}$
13. $2 \pm i\sqrt{2}$
14. $5 \pm 2i$
15. I
16. C
17. I
18. C
19. I
20. C

26 *South-Western Algebra 1:* AN INTEGRATED APPROACH

LESSON PLANNING

Objectives

- Solve quadratic equations of the form $ax^2 + bx + c = 0$ using the quadratic formula.
- Use the discriminant to determine the number of real solutions of a quadratic equation.

Vocabulary
discriminant
quadratic formula

Technology/Multimedia
graphing utility

Resources
Warm Up 10.5
Reteaching 10.5
Extra Practice 10.5
Enrichment 10.5
Transparencies 60, 78–80
Student Handbook
Lesson Quiz 10.5
Technology Activity 25

ASSIGNMENTS

Basic: 1–35, 40, 45–46, Mixed Review 49–55, Project Connection 1–3, AlgebraWorks 1–5

Average: 4–37, 40–44, 47–48, Mixed Review 49–55, Project Connection 1–3, AlgebraWorks 1–5

Enriched: 10–48, Mixed Review 49–55, Project Connection 1–3, AlgebraWorks 1–5

1 MOTIVATE

Explore In the chart for Question 1, ask students how the expressions above the fourth and fifth columns differ. **In the fourth, the sign between –b and the radical**

10.5 The Quadratic Formula

SPOTLIGHT ON LEARNING

In this lesson you will learn

- to solve quadratic equations of the form $ax^2 + bx + c = 0$ by using the quadratic formula.
- to use the discriminant to determine the number of real solutions of a quadratic equation.

WHY? Using the quadratic formula can help you solve problems about business, physics, and satellite antenna engineering.

Explore

1. Copy and complete the chart.

a	b	c	$\frac{-b + \sqrt{b^2 - 4ac}}{2a}$	$\frac{-b - \sqrt{b^2 - 4ac}}{2a}$
1	–7	12		
1	5	6		
1	6	5		
1	1	–2		

4, –2, –1, 1   3, –3, –5, –2

Use a graphing utility to find the solutions to each quadratic equation below.

2. $x^2 - 7x + 12 = 0$ 3, 4
3. $x^2 + 5x + 6 = 0$ –3, –2
4. $x^2 + 6x + 5 = 0$ –5, –1
5. $x^2 + x - 2 = 0$ 1, –2
6. What similarities do you notice between your answers to Question 1 and Questions 2–5? See Additional Answers.
7. What does your answer to Question 6 suggest about the expressions $\frac{-b + \sqrt{b^2 - 4ac}}{2a}$ and $\frac{-b - \sqrt{b^2 - 4ac}}{2a}$? See Additional Answers.

Build Understanding

The two algebraic expressions in Explore are formulas for finding the solutions to any quadratic equation of the form $ax^2 + bx + c = 0$, known as the *quadratic formula.*

QUADRATIC FORMULA

For a quadratic equation of the form $ax^2 + bx + c = 0$ where a, b, and c are real numbers and $a \neq 0$,

$$x = \frac{-b \pm \sqrt{b^2 - 4ac}}{2a}$$

EXAMPLE 1

Use the quadratic formula to solve $x^2 + 6x - 16 = 0$.

Solution

In $x^2 + 6x - 16 = 0$, $a = 1$, $b = 6$, and $c = -16$.

$$x = \frac{-b \pm \sqrt{b^2 - 4ac}}{2a}$$ Write the quadratic formula.

$$x = \frac{-6 \pm \sqrt{6^2 - 4(1)(-16)}}{2(1)}$$ Substitute known values.

$$x = \frac{-6 \pm \sqrt{36 + 64}}{2} \quad \text{Simplify.}$$

$$x = \frac{-6 \pm \sqrt{100}}{2} \quad \text{Simplify under the radical symbol.}$$

$$x = \frac{-6 \pm 10}{2} \quad \text{Determine the value of the radicand.}$$

Check

Check your solutions in the original equation.

$$\begin{array}{rcl} x^2 + 6x - 16 &=& 0 \\ 2^2 + 6(2) - 16 &\stackrel{?}{=}& 0 \\ 0 &=& 0 \checkmark \end{array} \qquad \begin{array}{rcl} x^2 + 6x - 16 &=& 0 \\ (-8)^2 + 6(-8) - 16 &\stackrel{?}{=}& 0 \\ 0 &=& 0 \checkmark \end{array}$$

The solutions are $x = \frac{-6 + 10}{2} = 2$ and $x = \frac{-6 - 10}{2} = -8$.

You must write a quadratic equation in the standard form $ax^2 + bx + c = 0$ before you apply the quadratic formula.

EXAMPLE 2

Use the quadratic formula to solve $3x^2 = -5 - 10x$.

Solution

Write $3x^2 = -5 - 10x$ in standard form as $3x^2 + 10x + 5 = 0$. In $3x^2 + 10x + 5 = 0$, $a = 3$, $b = 10$ and $c = 5$.

$$x = \frac{-b \pm \sqrt{b^2 - 4ac}}{2a} \quad \text{Write the quadratic formula.}$$

$$x = \frac{-10 \pm \sqrt{10^2 - 4(3)(5)}}{2(3)} \quad \text{Substitute known values.}$$

$$x = \frac{-10 \pm \sqrt{100 - 60}}{6} \quad \text{Simplify.}$$

$$x = \frac{-10 \pm \sqrt{40}}{6} \quad \text{Simplify under the radical symbol.}$$

$$x = \frac{-10 \pm 2\sqrt{10}}{6} \quad \text{Write } \sqrt{40} \text{ as } \sqrt{4} \cdot \sqrt{10} = 2\sqrt{10}.$$

$$x = \frac{-5 \pm \sqrt{10}}{3} \quad \text{Divide each term by 2.}$$

The solutions are $x = \frac{-5 + \sqrt{10}}{3}$ and $x = \frac{-5 - \sqrt{10}}{3}$. Check your solutions in the original equation.

In Lesson 10.3, you graphed equations to determine whether a quadratic equation has zero, one, or two real number solutions. Another method is to use $b^2 - 4ac$, the expression under the radical symbol in the quadratic formula, to determine the number of real number solutions. The expression $b^2 - 4ac$ is called the **discriminant**.

COMMUNICATING ABOUT ALGEBRA

What other methods besides the quadratic formula can be used to solve any quadratic equation of the form $ax^2 + bx + c = 0$?

graphing or taking the square root of $-\frac{c}{a}$ if $b = 0$

ALGEBRA: WHO, WHERE, WHEN

The quadratic formula is one of the oldest and most useful formulas in mathematics. No one knows just where it was first derived or by whom. However, versions of the formula were used as early as 2000 B.C. in ancient Babylonia, now the area of the Middle East known as Iraq.

expression is positive; in the fifth, the sign is negative. Have a student explain how the equations in Questions 2, 3, and 4 related to the chart in Question 1. **The values of *a*, *b*, and *c* in each line of the table correspond to the coefficients of one of these equations, respectively.**

2 TEACH

Use the Pages/Build Understanding

Example 1: Stress the importance of correctly substituting *a*, *b*, and *c* in the formula. Suggest that students use a chart like the one in Explore when using the quadratic formula.

Example 2: Be sure students understand that the quadratic equation must be in standard form before the quadratic formula can be applied.

Example 3: Ask a student to use the quadratic formula to justify the rules about the discriminant. **(1) If the expression under a radical is negative, there is no real solution; (2) the expression $(-b \pm 0)/2a$ has only one value, $-b/2a$; (3) if the expression under the radical is positive, it has some value *v*, so the expressions $(-b + v)/2a$ and $(-b - v)/2a$ represent two different values for *x*.**

Make Connections

Language The word *discriminant* is related to the word *discriminate*. Ask students to look up the two words and discuss how the meanings relate to determining something about the roots of an equation. **Although *discriminate* can mean making judgments based on social or ethnic differences, the meaning students should focus on is the basic general meaning: to mark distinguishing characteristics of things. A *discriminant* is something that helps distinguish differences between things, in this case the kinds of roots an equation has.**

Example 4: After reading the example, ask students why there are two solutions although they were asked to find a value that gives exactly one solution. **There are two different values of *k* that will give a quadratic equation that has exactly one solution.**

Example 5: To help students understand business vocabulary, ask them to consider the business of selling lemonade. The total revenue is the money collected from selling the lemonade. The total cost includes the cost of supplies to make the lemonade, cups for serving, and all other expenses involved in the selling. The profit is revenue less cost. Ask what it would mean if the profit were a negative number. **They lost money because expenses exceeded revenues.**

CHECK UNDERSTANDING

Describe the graphs of a quadratic function whose related equation has each of the following discriminants: greater than zero, less than zero, and equal to zero. Give examples.

The graph intersects the x-axis twice, does not intersect the x-axis, intersects the x-axis once. Examples will vary.

For a quadratic equation of the form $ax^2 + bx + c = 0$, the discriminant is $b^2 - 4ac$.

- **If $b^2 - 4ac > 0$, the equation has two real solutions.**
- **If $b^2 - 4ac = 0$, the equation has one real solution.**
- **If $b^2 - 4ac < 0$, the equation has no real solutions.**

EXAMPLE 3

Use the discriminant to determine the number of real solutions for each quadratic equation.

a. $x^2 - 4x + 4 = 0$

b. $x^2 - 4x + 5 = 0$

c. $x^2 - 4x - 2 = 0$

Solution

a. $b^2 - 4ac = (-4)^2 - 4(1)(4) = 16 - 16 = 0$
one real solution

b. $b^2 - 4ac = (-4)^2 - 4(1)(5) = 16 - 20 = -4$
no real solutions

c. $b^2 - 4ac = (-4)^2 - 4(1)(-2) = 16 - (-8) = 24$
two real solutions ◄

You can also use the discriminant to find values for one of the coefficients of a quadratic equation if you know the number of solutions the equation has.

EXAMPLE 4

Determine the values of k for which the equation $4x^2 + kx + 25 = 0$ has exactly one solution.

Solution

Since the equation has exactly one solution, $b^2 - 4ac = 0$ for $a = 4$, $b = k$, and $c = 25$.

$$b^2 - 4ac = 0$$

$$k^2 - 4(4)(25) = 0 \quad a = 4, b = k, c = 25$$

$$k^2 - 400 = 0 \quad \text{Solve for } k.$$

$$k^2 = 400$$

$$k = \pm 20$$

The equation has exactly one solution when $k = 20$ or $k = -20$. ◄

The quadratic formula can be used to solve real world problems.

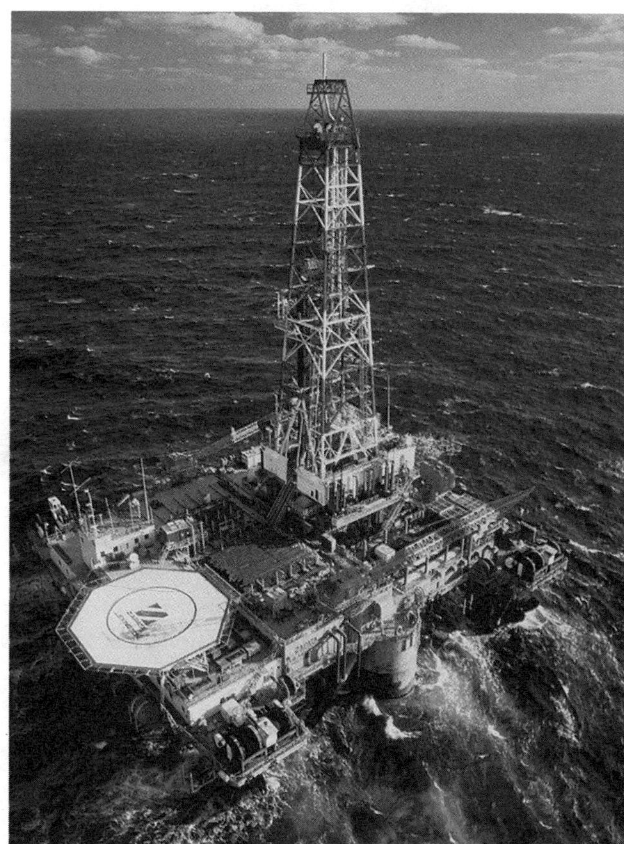

EXAMPLE 5

BUSINESS Rig Outfitters makes equipment for oil companies. The projected revenue on pipe connectors is modeled by the function $R(x) = 20x^2 + 82x + 600$ where x is the number of connectors produced in hundreds. The cost to produce these items can be modeled by the function $C(x) = 4x^2 + 12x + 1296$. Assume that the company sells every connector it produces. The company determined that it made a profit of \$300 on these connectors.

a. If profit is defined as revenue minus cost, write an equation that models profit.

b. Solve the equation in **a** to determine the number of connectors that the company sold.

Solution

a. $P(x) = R(x) - C(x)$

$$\begin{aligned} P(x) &= 20x^2 + 82x + 600 - (4x^2 + 12x + 1296) \\ &= 20x^2 - 4x^2 + 82x - 12x + 600 - 1296 \\ &= (20 - 4)x^2 + (82 - 12)x - 696 \\ &= 16x^2 + 70x - 696 \end{aligned}$$

Since $P(x) = 300$, $16x^2 + 70x - 696 = 300$ or $16x^2 + 70x - 996 = 0$.

b. Use the quadratic formula, with $a = 16$, $b = 70$, and $c = -996$.

$$x = \frac{-b \pm \sqrt{b^2 - 4ac}}{2a}$$ Quadratic formula.

$$x = \frac{-70 \pm \sqrt{(70)^2 - 4(16)(-996)}}{2(16)}$$

$$x = \frac{-70 \pm 262}{32}$$

$x = -10.375$ or $x = 6$

Since x is in hundreds, the company sold 600 connectors. ◄

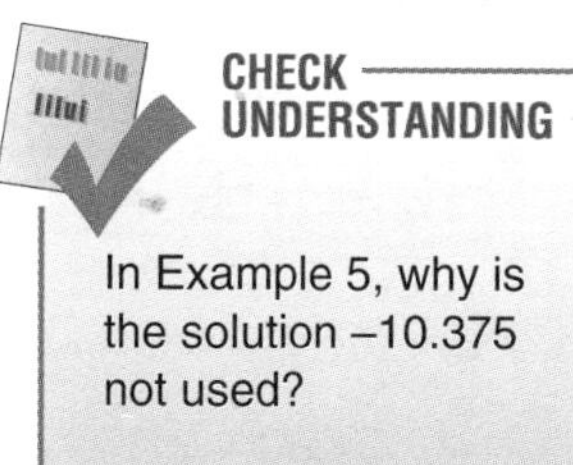

CHECK UNDERSTANDING

In Example 5, why is the solution –10.375 not used?

It is meaningless because the company cannot sell a negative number of items.

Ongoing Assessment The important concepts and skills are solving quadratic equations by using the quadratic formula and using the discriminant to find the number of real solutions to a quadratic equation. To assess these ideas, have students demonstrate how they have applied these concepts and skills in Exercises 4, 7, 11, and 14 of the Try These section.

Error Alert Watch for students who, when using the quadratic formula, divide only one of the terms in the numerator by 2. Remind students that each term over the fraction bar must be divided by 2.

Guided Practice/Try These For Exercises 10–18, students should make sure that the equation is in standard form before they use the quadratic formula.

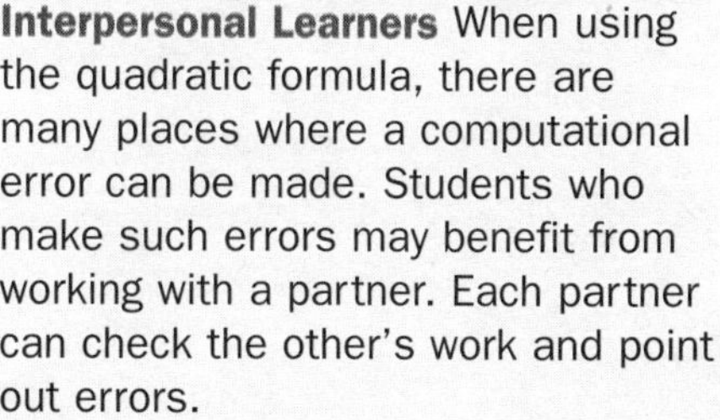

DIVERSITY IN THE CLASSROOM

Interpersonal Learners When using the quadratic formula, there are many places where a computational error can be made. Students who make such errors may benefit from working with a partner. Each partner can check the other's work and point out errors.

3 SUMMARIZE

In the Math Journal Ask students to write a description outlining each step needed to use the quadratic formula.

4 PRACTICE

Practice In Exercises 14–17 and 20, 22, 24, and 25 remind students to first write all equations in standard form. Encourage students who are making errors to write more steps of their work and to place parentheses around negative numbers when substituting them in the formula.

TRY THESE

Determine the value of the discriminant for each equation.

1. $2x^2 + 4x + 9 = 0$ −56 **2.** $-x^2 - 6x + 12 = 0$ 84 **3.** $16x^2 + 16x + 4 = 0$ 0

Use the discriminant to determine the number of real solutions to each quadratic equation.

4. $x^2 - 4x - 5 = 0$ 2 **5.** $x^2 + 3x + 52 = 0$ 0 **6.** $x^2 + 4x + 4 = 0$ 1

7. $9x^2 + 6x + 1 = 0$ 1 **8.** $6x^2 - 2x - 8 = 0$ 2 **9.** $2x^2 + 2x + 4 = 0$ 0

Use the quadratic formula to solve each equation. Round answer to the nearest hundredth where necessary.

10. $x^2 - 9x + 8 = 0$ 1, 8 **11.** $x^2 - 7x - 8 = 0$ −1, 8 **12.** $x^2 - 6x = -8$ 2, 4

13. $x^2 = 10 - 3x$ −5, 2 **14.** $4x^2 + 3x = 5$ −1.55, 0.80 **15.** $2x^2 + 4x = 7$ −3.12, 1.12

16. $3x^2 = 2x + 2$ 1.22, −0.55 **17.** $5x^2 - x - 3 = 0$ 0.88, −0.68 **18.** $2x^2 - 6x + 3 = 0$ 0.63, 2.37

Determine the values of k for which each equation has exactly one solution.

19. $x^2 + 12x + k = 0$ 36 **20.** $kx^2 + 12x + 9 = 0$ 4, 0 **21.** $16x^2 + kx + 1 = 0$ ±8

22. PHYSICS A small rocket is fired from a height of 60 ft above ground level. Its height at any given time can be modeled by the function $h(t) = -16t^2 + 300t + 60$. Use the quadratic formula to determine the time, to the nearest second, at which the rocket will be 20 ft from the ground. 19 s

23. WRITING MATHEMATICS Explain in your own words how the value of the discriminant relates to the number of solutions that an equation has. Answers will vary.

PRACTICE

Determine the value of the discriminant for each equation.

1. $3x^2 + 3x + 8 = 0$ −87 **2.** $-x^2 - 8x + 6 = 0$ 88 **3.** $25x^2 + 20x + 4 = 0$ 0

Use the discriminant to determine the number of real solutions to each quadratic equation.

4. $x^2 + x + 1 = 0$ 0 **5.** $x^2 + 4x - 6 = 0$ 2 **6.** $x^2 + 10x + 25 = 0$ 1

7. $36x^2 + 12x + 1 = 0$ 1 **8.** $6x^2 - 3x - 5 = 0$ 2 **9.** $2x^2 + 3x + 6 = 0$ 0

Use the quadratic formula to solve each equation.

10. $x^2 - 10x + 9 = 0$ 1, 9 **11.** $x^2 - 6x - 7 = 0$ −1, 7 **12.** $x^2 - 9x + 18 = 0$ 3, 6

13. $x^2 - 11x + 30 = 0$ 5, 6 **14.** $x^2 + 2x = 35$ −7, 5 **15.** $x^2 - 7x = 30$ −3, 10

16. $x^2 = 4x + 45$ −5, 9 **17.** $x^2 = -4x + 21$ −7, 3 **18.** $6x^2 + x - 35 = 0$ $-\frac{5}{2}, \frac{7}{3}$

19. BUSINESS The revenue function for SRB Company can be approximated by the function $R(p) = -16p^2 + 320p + 20{,}000$ where p represents the price of their product. If the revenue is $10,000, use the quadratic formula to determine the price of their product to the nearest dollar. $37.00

Use the quadratic formula to solve each equation. Round decimal answers to the nearest hundredth.

20. $10x^2 - 3x = 1$ $-\frac{1}{5}, \frac{1}{2}$ **21.** $14x^2 - 3x - 5 = 0$ $-\frac{1}{2}, \frac{5}{7}$ **22.** $20x^2 = 4x + 24$ $-1, \frac{6}{5}$

23. $x^2 + 5x - 2 = 0$ −5.37, 0.37 **24.** $x^2 + 4x = 1$ −4.24, 0.24 **25.** $2x^2 - 4x = 12$ −1.65, 3.65

26. $6x^2 - 6x - 7 = 0$ −0.69, 1.69 **27.** $3x^2 + 10x + 4 = 0$ −2.87, −0.46 **28.** $5x^2 + 12x - 2 = 0$ −2.56, 0.16

Determine the values of k for which each equation has exactly one solution.

29. $x^2 + 14x + k = 0$ 49 **30.** $kx^2 - 30x + 25 = 0$ 9 **31.** $25x^2 + kx + 16 = 0$ ±40

32. NUMBER THEORY Find a number whose square is 80 greater than twice the number. −8, 10

33. WRITING MATHEMATICS Describe the graph of a quadratic equation whose discriminant is negative. See Additional Answers.

EXTEND

If s_1 and s_2 are the solutions of a quadratic equation of the form $ax^2 + bx + c = 0$ and $a = 1$, then $x^2 - (s_1 + s_2)x + s_1s_2 = 0$. For example, if a quadratic equation has −4 and 3 as its solutions, then

$$x^2 - (s_1 + s_2)x + s_1s_2 = 0$$
$$x^2 - (-4 + 3)x + (-4)(3) = 0$$
$$x^2 + x - 12 = 0$$

This equation has −4 and 3 as its solutions.

Write a quadratic equation having the given solutions.

34. 5 and −6 $x^2 + x - 30 = 0$ **35.** 7 and −3 $x^2 - 4x - 21 = 0$ **36.** $\frac{1}{2}$ and $-\frac{1}{4}$ $8x^2 - 2x - 1 = 0$

37. 7 and $-\frac{1}{2}$ $2x^2 - 13x - 7 = 0$ **38.** 10.5 and −10.5 $x^2 - 110.25 = 0$ **39.** c and $-c$ $x^2 - c^2 = 0$

NUMBER THEORY For each exercise, use the sum and the product of the numbers to write a quadratic equation. Then use the quadratic equation to solve for the numbers.

40. The sum of two numbers is 30 and their product is 216. $x^2 - 30x + 216 = 0$; 12, 18

41. The sum of two numbers is −37 and their product is −650. $x^2 + 37x - 650 = 0$; 13, −50

42. The sum of two numbers is −26 and their product is 153. $x^2 + 26x + 153 = 0$; −9, −17

Extend In Exercises 36 and 37, students will get an equation with fractional coefficients. Ask them how they can rewrite the equations so that they have no fractions. **multiply each term by a common denominator**

Think Critically Some students may answer Exercises 43 and 44 by giving one or two values of k that work. Encourage them to make a general statement about the values of k that will produce each result. Students should see that the answer in each case is an inequality, not an equation.

NAME ______ CLASS ______ DATE ______

RETEACHING **10.5 THE QUADRATIC FORMULA**

Follow these steps when using the quadratic formula.

1. Put the equation in standard form, $ax^2 + bx + c = 0$.
2. Substitute in the formula for a, b, and c. Use parentheses around negative numbers.
3. Simplify under the radical sign first. Then simplify the numerator.

Example
Solve: $x^2 - 3x = 10$

Solution
Write $x^2 - 3x = 10$ in standard form as $x^2 - 3x - 10 = 0$.
Use $a = 1$, $b = -3$, and $c = -10$.

$x = \frac{-b \pm \sqrt{b^2 - 4ac}}{2a}$ Write the quadratic formula.

$= \frac{-(-3) \pm \sqrt{(-3)^2 - 4(1)(-10)}}{2(1)}$ Substitute known values.

$= \frac{3 \pm \sqrt{9 - (-40)}}{2}$ Simplify.

$= \frac{3 \pm \sqrt{49}}{2}$ Simplify under the radical.

$x = \frac{3 + 7}{2}$ $x = \frac{3 - 7}{2}$ Write as two equations.

$x = \frac{10}{2} = 5$ $x = \frac{-4}{2} = -2$ Simplify each equation.

The solutions are 5 and −2.

EXERCISES
Solve using the quadratic formula. Round decimals to the nearest hundredth.

1. $x^2 - 4x = -4$ 2. $2x^2 - 2 = 3x$
3. $x^2 - 4x = 12$ 4. $x^2 - 11 = 10x$
5. $3x^2 - 2x = 1$ 6. $x^2 - 20 = x$
7. $3x + 5 = x^2$ 8. $x^2 - 8x = 11$

1. 2
2. $-\frac{1}{2}$, 2
3. −2, 6
4. 11, −1
5. $-\frac{1}{3}$, 1
6. 5, −4
7. 1.19, −4.19
8. 9.20, −1.20

30 *South-Western Algebra 1: AN INTEGRATED APPROACH*

5 FOLLOW-UP

Extra Practice Use the discriminant to determine the number of real solutions to each quadratic equation.

1. $x^2 + 2x + 8 = 0$ **0**

2. $9x^2 - 12x + 4 = 0$ **1**

3. $x^2 - 3x - 7 = 0$ **2**

Use the quadratic formula to solve each equation. Round decimal answers to the nearest hundredth.

4. $x^2 - 5x - 36 = 0$ **−4, 9**

5. $x^2 = x + 56$ **−7, 8**

6. $2x^2 + 3x = 8$ **1.39, −2.89**

7. $3x^2 - 2x - 1 = 0$ **−1/3, 1**

8. Determine the values of k for which $x^2 - 32x + k = 0$ has exactly one solution. **256**

NAME ____________ CLASS ________ DATE ________

EXTRA PRACTICE **10.5 THE QUADRATIC FORMULA**

Determine the value of the discriminant for each equation.

1. $2x^2 + 4x + 5 = 0$ **2.** $-10x^2 - 3x + 7 = 0$

3. $x^2 - 7x = 1$ **4.** $3x^2 + x = 18$

Use the discriminant to determine the number of real solutions to each quadratic equation.

5. $4x^2 + 3x + 1 = 0$ **6.** $x^2 + 7x - 2 = 0$

7. $12x^2 - 12x + 3 = 0$ **8.** $5x^2 - 2x - 1 = 0$

Use the quadratic formula to solve each equation. Round decimal answers to the nearest hundredth.

9. $x^2 - 11x + 18 = 0$ **10.** $x^2 - 2x - 3 = 0$

11. $x^2 - 6x = 7$ **12.** $x^2 + 8 = 6x$

13. $x^2 + 2x + 1 = 0$ **14.** $x^2 + 25 = 10x$

15. $2x^2 + x = 3$ **16.** $5x^2 + 9x - 2 = 0$

17. $3x^2 + 16x + 13 = 0$ **18.** $10x^2 = 12x - 2$

19. $3x^2 + 6x = 42$ **20.** $13x^2 - 2x = 20$

Determine the values of k for which each equation has exactly one solution.

21. $16x^2 + kx + 16 = 0$ **22.** $4x^2 + 20x = k$

23. GEOMETRY The area of a rectangle is 25 inches. The length is 5 inches more than twice the width. What are the length and width of this rectangle?

1. −24
2. 289
3. 53
4. 217
5. 0
6. 2
7. 1
8. 2
9. 9, 2
10. 3, −1
11. 7, −1
12. 2, 4
13. −1
14. 5
15. $-\frac{3}{2}, 1$
16. $\frac{1}{5}, -2$
17. $-1, -\frac{13}{3}$
18. $1, \frac{1}{5}$
19. −4.87, 2.87
20. 1.32, −1.17
21. ±32
22. −25
23. 10", 2.5"

32 *South Western Algebra 1:* AN INTEGRATED APPROACH

THINK CRITICALLY

43. For what values of k are there two real solutions to the quadratic equation $x^2 + 6x + k = 0$? $k < 9$

44. For what values of k are there no real solutions to the quadratic equation $-x^2 - 5x + k = 0$? $k < -6.25$

Use the quadratic formula to solve each equation for x.

45. $(x - a)^2 - (x - a) - 5 = 0$ $\frac{2a + 1 \pm \sqrt{21}}{2}$

46. $(x - a)^2 - (x - a) = 6$ $a - 2, a + 3$

47. Describe the solutions to the equation $ax^2 + bx + c = 0$ if $\sqrt{b^2 - 4ac}$ is a perfect square. The solutions are rational numbers.

48. Use the quadratic formula to determine where the graph of $y = 2x^2 - 7x - 4$ crosses the x-axis. See Additional Answers.

MIXED REVIEW

49. STANDARDIZED TESTS Which is the mean of the set of numbers? C; Lesson 1.7

18, 44, 76, 6, 16

A. 30 **B.** 160
C. 32 **D.** 18

Determine whether each relation is a function. Lesson 4.2

50. $\{(3, 4), (4, 5), (5, 6)\}$ function

51. $\{(1, 3), (2, 5), (2, 7)\}$ not a function

Express each absolute value equation as a disjunction. Lesson 9.3

52. $|4 - 3x| = 21$ $4 - 3x = 21$ or $4 - 3x = -21$

53. $\left|2x - \frac{1}{2}\right| = \frac{1}{4}$ $2x - \frac{1}{2} = \frac{1}{4}$ or $2x - \frac{1}{2} = -\frac{1}{4}$

Use the quadratic formula to solve each equation. Lesson 10.5

54. $0 = 2x^2 - 37x + 105$ $\frac{7}{2}, 15$

55. $12x^2 + 2x - 2 = 0$ $-\frac{1}{2}, \frac{1}{3}$

PROJECT Connection

Read the material your corporation sent. Collect any other information you can find about your corporation in books, magazines, and other media.

1. Highlight important dates, people, and inventions that directly affected your corporation. Then find out about events that occurred in American history as your industry and corporation developed. Use the information to make a timeline that can include photographs and technical drawings.
2. Interpret at least one graph from your company's Annual Report. Consider using a different method to display the data.
3. Identify data in the Annual Report that might fit a linear or quadratic model. Use a graphing utility to determine the equation of the model. What predictions can you make for the corporation's future based on the equation?

Career
Satellite Antenna Engineer

"Satellite dish" antennas allow some homeowners to receive hundreds of television channels. Engineers use parabolas and quadratic equations to ensure that these antennas work correctly.

Geometrically, a *parabola* is the set of all points that are the same distance from a given line and a fixed point not on the line. This fixed point is called the *focus* of the parabola and the given line is called the *directrix*. Parabolic antennas reflect microwaves (represented by the parallel lines in the diagram) so that they converge at the focus of the parabola.

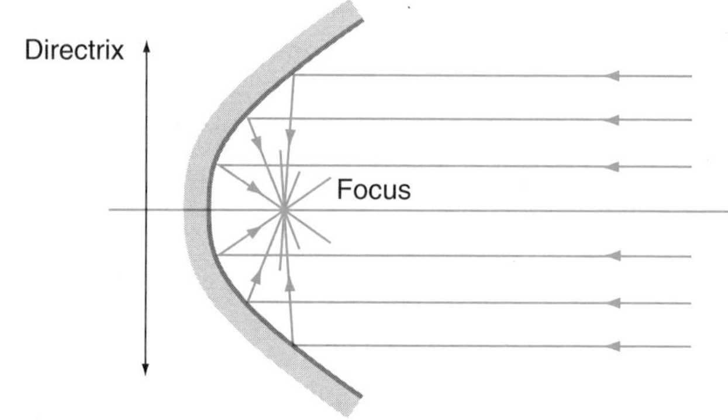

The structure of the satellite dish must support its weight and stand up to wind. If it bends, the incoming parallel waves will not be reflected correctly. Two factors in its construction are the area and circumference of the large circle created by the dish. To construct a particular antenna, an engineer begins with the parabola described by the function $f(x) = 0.04x^2$ on the domain $-9 \text{ ft} \le x \le 9 \text{ ft}$. The parabola is spun about its axis of symmetry to create a parabolic antenna.

Decision Making

1. Graph the parabola described by the function $f(x) = 0.04x^2$ with X-min: -9, X-max: 9, X-scl: 1, Y-min: -1, Y-max: 5, and Y-scl: 1. See Additional Answers.
2. Determine the circumference of the edge of the parabolic antenna. 18π ft
3. Determine the area of the circle formed by the edge of the antenna. $81\pi \text{ ft}^2$
4. Determine the depth of the antenna from its vertex to the plane of the circle formed by the edge. 3.24 ft
5. If the parabola $g(x) = 0.05x^2$ were used to create a dish with the same diameter as $f(x)$ above, which would have greater depth?

$g(x) = 0.05x^2$

Extension Ask students to look at Example 4 and tell whether they can find a value for k that gives exactly one solution for any values of a and c. Have them explain their answer. **The product $4ac$ must be a perfect square for there to exist a value for k that gives the equation exactly one solution.**

Project Connection This activity presents further aspects of the project introduced on page 464. Show some sample timelines and review various methods of displaying data.

AlgebraWorks If any students have seen satellite antennas, ask them to estimate how large they are. For Question 2, students must see that the first task is determining the radius of the circle. **9 ft since the equation of the axis of symmetry is $x = 0$ and the limits on x are -9 and 9 (Note that the smaller satellite dishes are 18 inches in diameter.)** For Exercise 4, the students need to find the value of y when $x = 9$. In Exercise 5, the value of $y = 0.05x^2$ when $x = 9$ is 4.05, so the dish formed by $y = 0.95x^2$ is $4.05 - 3.24$, or 0.81 ft deeper.

NAME ______ CLASS ______ DATE ______

ENRICHMENT **10.5 THE QUADRATIC FORMULA**

If the discriminant of a quadratic equation is negative, the equation has no real solutions. If it is positive, you can determine whether the real solutions are rational or irrational.

Examine the following.

Equation:	**a.** $x^2 - 2x - 15 = 0$	**b.** $x^2 + 3x - 5 = 0$
Discriminant:	64	29
Real Solutions:	5, −3	$\frac{-3 \pm \sqrt{29}}{2}$
Equation:	**c.** $x^2 - 18x + 65 = 0$	**d.** $x^2 - 4x + 2 = 0$
Discriminant:	64	8
Real Solutions:	13, 5	$2 \pm \sqrt{2}$

1. It would appear that when the discriminant is a perfect square, the real solutions of the equation are rational numbers. Based on what you know about the quadratic formula, explain why the above statement is true.
When the discriminant is a perfect square, the simplified radical is a rational number, so the whole expression is rational. When the discriminant is not a perfect square, an irrational number is part of the expression.

Use the discriminant to determine the number of real solutions. Tell whether those solutions are rational or irrational.

2. $x^2 - 5x = 14$
3. $x^2 - 2 = x$
4. $x^2 + 2x = 9$
5. $x^2 = 7$
6. $x^2 + 16 = 8x$
7. $x^2 - 2x = 120$
8. $x^2 - 6x + 12 = 0$
9. $x^2 - 3x = 7$
10. $2x^2 - 5x = 9$
11. $3x^2 + 14x = 5$

2. **2; rational**
3. **2; rational**
4. **2; irrational**
5. **2; irrational**
6. **1; rational**
7. **2; rational**
8. **0**
9. **2; irrational**
10. **2; irrational**
11. **2; rational**

34 *South-Western Algebra 1: AN INTEGRATED APPROACH*

LESSON PLANNING

Objective

▶ Use quadratic equations to solve problems involving maximizing area.

Technology/Multimedia
graphing utility

Resources
Reteaching 10.6
Extra Practice 10.6
Transparencies 10, 34, 78–80
Student Handbook

Materials/Manipulatives
graph paper

ASSIGNMENTS

Basic: 1–13, 15–16

Average: 1–16

Enriched: 1–16

1 MOTIVATE

Introduction Ask students to draw a rectangle having a perimeter of 20 cm and to label its length and width. Have students share the dimensions they wrote. They should discover that more than one rectangle has such a perimeter. Then have them compute the area of their rectangle to demonstrate that rectangles with the same perimeter can have different area measures.

DIVERSITY IN THE CLASSROOM

ESL/LEP Students Make sure students correctly interpret each problem. Ask them to restate the problems in their own words so that you can evaluate their understanding.

10.6 Problem Solving File

Use Variables

Maximizing Area

SPOTLIGHT ON LEARNING

WHAT? In this lesson you will learn
- to use quadratic equations to solve problems involving maximizing area.

WHY? Many construction and landscaping problems involve maximizing area or minimizing cost.

Many problems involve determining shape for a given set of conditions. You can analyze such problems by using diagrams, tables, graphs, and equations.

Problem

Your community is building a children's playground. A local construction company has donated 200 ft of fencing for the project. The playground will be in the shape of a rectangle, having the greatest possible area for the given perimeter. If you use all of the available fencing, what should the length and width of the rectangle be?

Explore the Problem

Start by examining rectangles with whole-number dimensions and a constant perimeter of 200 ft.

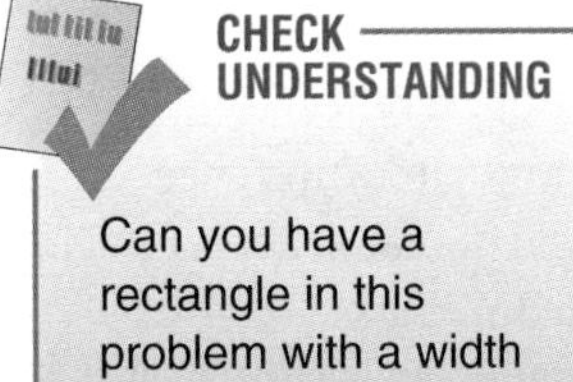

CHECK UNDERSTANDING

Can you have a rectangle in this problem with a width of 100 ft? Explain.

No, there would be no fencing left for the length.

1. Suppose the rectangle has a width of 10 ft. Explain how you determine the length of this rectangle. What is the area?
   $l = 90$ ft since $2w = 20$, $200 - 20 = 180$, $180 \div 2 = 90$; $A = 900$ ft^2
2. If you make the width 20 ft, then what must the length be? What is the area? Does it appear that the dimensions of the rectangle have an effect on area even when the perimeter is constant?
   80 ft; 1600 ft^2; yes, the area changes
3. Write an equation that expresses the relationship between length and width for rectangles with a perimeter of 200 ft.
   $2l + 2w = 200$ or $l + w = 100$
4. Copy and complete the table. Compare the table of widths, lengths, and areas below. Look for patterns. See Additional Answers.

w	l	A	w	l	A	w	l	A	w	l	A
5 ft			30 ft			55 ft			80 ft		
10 ft			35 ft			60 ft			85 ft		
15 ft			40 ft			65 ft			90 ft		
20 ft			45 ft			70 ft			95 ft		
25 ft			50 ft			75 ft			99 ft		

5. As widths increase, for what values do areas increase as well?
   As widths increase from 5 to 50 ft, areas increase.

6. How would you predict the results for widths greater than 50 ft?
See Additional Answers.
7. What is the most efficient shape for the playground?
a 50-ft square
8. Use the data from your table. Are there any rectangles whose dimensions are not shown in the table but which might have greater area? Make a graph of area as a function of width.
See Additional Answers.
9. If you had 350 ft of fencing and wanted to enclose the maximum rectangular area, what would the dimensions and the area be? (Dimensions do not have to be whole numbers.)
a square with sides of 87.5 ft; 7,656.25 ft^2

PROBLEM SOLVING PLAN

- Understand
- Plan
- Solve
- Examine

Investigate Further

For rectangles with a constant perimeter of 200 ft, you know that $2l + 2w = 200$ or $l + w = 100$. So, $l = 100 - w$. The area can be expressed as a function of width.

$$A = w(100 - w) = 100w - w^2 = -w^2 + 100w$$

10. What type of function is $A(w) = -w^2 + 100w$?
a quadratic function
11. Graph this area function for $0 \le w \le 100$. How can knowing the shape and position of the graph of $B(w) = w^2$ help you to graph $A(w) = -w^2 + 100w$? See Additional Answers.
12. What are the coordinates of the vertex of the graph you drew above? Does this result agree with the solution you found by making a table? See Additional Answers.

CHECK UNDERSTANDING

Use what you learned in Lesson 10.1 and your description in Question 11 to write an equivalent equation for $A(w)$.

$A(w) = (w - 50)^2 + 2500$

Apply the Strategy

Draw a diagram to help you analyze each of the questions below.

13. Suppose you have 120 ft of fencing to enclose a rectangular area for a garden. You plan to use a house wall as one side of the garden.
    a. If the width is w, write an expression for the length.
    $l = 120 - 2w$
    b. Write an expression for the area as a function of width.
    $A(w) = w(120 - 2w)$ or $120w - 2w^2$
    c. Use any strategy you choose. Find the dimensions of the rectangle having the maximum area and determine the area.
    $l = 60$ ft, $w = 30$ ft, $A = 1800$ ft^2
    d. How could you have used your fencing to make a square with one side being the wall? Determine the dimensions and the area for this square.
    See Additional Answers.

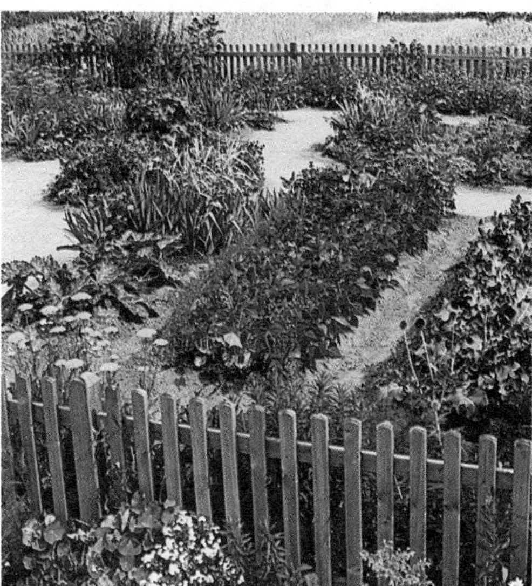

2 TEACH

Use the Pages/Problem Have students read and discuss the problem. Then, ask what information is given in the problem. **There is 200 ft of fencing available to enclose a rectangle.** Ask them to restate the question in the problem. **What are the dimensions of a rectangle with a perimeter of 200 ft that will give the greatest possible area?**

Use the Pages/Explore the Problem Check students' answers to Question 4 before continuing so that students will have a correctly filled-in table from which to answer the rest of the questions. For Question 7, ask students to state how their investigation of the problem helped them to answer this question. **The most efficient shape was a square, so it makes sense to look for a square in this situation.**

Use the Pages/Investigate Further After students give the equation for Problem 10, ask them to name the values of the coefficients *a*, *b*, and *c*. **$a = -1$, $b = 100$, and $c = 0$** Ask why, in Exercise 11, the values of *w* are restricted to between 0 and 100. **Neither dimension of the rectangle can be equal to or greater than 100 and still give a perimeter of 200. So, *w* must be either greater than 0 or less than 100.**

3 SUMMARIZE

In the Math Journal Ask students to explain the different strategies they can use to find the maximum area for a given perimeter. **Answers will vary. Possible answers include make a table, sketch a function, or use a graphing utility.**

4 PRACTICE

Apply the Strategy Ask how Problem 15 is different from the previous problems in the lesson. **The area is fixed, and you want to find the minimum perimeter.** Ask how the result in 15c is similar to the result in the problem given in the beginning of the lesson. **A square is still the most efficient shape for the given area.**

NAME ____ CLASS ____ DATE ____

RETEACHING

10.6 PROBLEM SOLVING FILE: MAXIMIZING AREA

In order to solve problems that involve maximum area, you can draw and carefully label a diagram.

Example

A rectangular lot will be enclosed by 200 meters of fencing. What is the maximum area that can be enclosed?

Solution

For a rectangle with a perimeter of 200 m, you know that $2l + 2w = 200$ or $l + w = 100$.
Draw a diagram. Let x represent the length of the lot. Then, $100 - x$ represents the width.

$$A = x(100 - x)$$
$$= 100x - x^2$$

x

100 − x

Make a table or graph the function to find which value of x will give the maximum value for A.

The maximum area, 2500 m^2, is found when $x = 50$.

EXERCISES

Solve. Use a diagram to help analyze the problem.

1. The side of the house can be used to enclose a rectangular garden. If 80 feet of fence are available, what dimensions should the garden have to enclose the maximum area? 1. **40 ft × 20 ft**

x

80 − 2x

2. What is the maximum rectangular area that can be enclosed by 40 meters of fencing? 2. **100 m^2**

3. A rectangular area of 6400 square feet must be enclosed with a wooden fence. What are the dimensions of a rectangle that will require the least amount of fencing? 3. **80 ft × 80 ft**

36 South-Western Algebra 1: AN INTEGRATED APPROACH

Use a Formula | Write an Expression

14. Suppose you had 120 ft of fencing and a house wall to use as one side. You plan to use some of the fencing to partition your garden into two sections, one for vegetables and one for flowers. The partition will make a right angle with the house wall.

   a. If the width of the rectangle is w, write expressions for the length and the area as a function of width.
   $l = 120 - 3w$; $A(w) = w(120 - 3w)$ or $120w - 3w^2$
   b. Find the dimensions of the rectangle with maximum area and find the area. If you wanted each section to have equal area, how would you partition the garden?
   $w = 20$; $l = 60$; area $= 1200$ ft^2; make two 20 by 30 rectangles
   c. If you wanted each section of the garden to be a square, what would be the dimension of the whole garden? What would be the area of each square section? See Additional Answers.
   d. Suppose you wanted the garden to be a square with the partition dividing it equally. What would be the area of each section? See Additional Answers.

15. Suppose you want to enclose a rectangular garden area of 400 ft^2. You want to know what dimensions will minimize the cost of fencing you will use. (Assume all dimensions are whole numbers.)
   a. How is this problem different than the others you have solved in this lesson? In the other problems, perimeter was constant; in this problem, the area is constant.
   b. Will the dimensions of the rectangle make any difference as long as the rectangle has an area of 400 ft^2? Justify your answer with examples. See Additional Answers.
   c. Find the shape with the minimum perimeter by making a table for different lengths and widths.
   The most efficient shape is a 20-ft square.
   d. If the width of the rectangle is w, write an expression for the length in terms of w. $l = \frac{400}{w}$
   e. Write an expression for the perimeter as a function of the width. Use a graphing utility to graph this function. Describe the graph and how you can use it to solve the problem.
   See Additional Answers.

16. WRITING MATHEMATICS Write a paragraph explaining the importance of drawing a diagram to help you solve problems.
   Answers will vary but may include that diagrams help in understanding and analyzing the problem.

Use a Model | Make a List | Draw a Diagram

I–3 See Additional Answers.

REVIEW PROBLEM SOLVING STRATEGIES

WELL, WELL!

1. One day, Sharla was watching her friend Randy digging a well.

"How deep is the well so far?" Sharla asked.

"Guess," said Randy. "I'm exactly 5 ft 10 in. tall."

"How much deeper will you dig?" asked Sharla.

"I'm going to dig twice as deep as I've gone already," answered Randy, "and then my head will be twice as far below the ground as it is now above the ground."

Drawing a diagram may help you understand the relationships in the problem.

a. How many inches tall is Randy?

b. Let x represent the number of inches above ground Randy's head is at present. Represent the current depth of the well.

c. Using the expression you wrote in Question b, represent the final depth of the well in terms of x.

d. Have you used all the information in the problem? What other expression can you write?

e. How far above ground is Randy's head? What is the present depth of the well? How deep will the well be when completed?

REVA'S GLASSES

2. Reva took a small glass and filled it half full with pure orange juice. Then she took another glass, which was twice the size of the first glass, and filled it one-third full of pure orange juice. Then she filled each glass to capacity with water and poured the contents of both into a large pitcher. Then Reva figured out what part of the mixture was orange juice and what part was water. Can you figure it out? Use these hints if you need them.

a. What part of the total contents of the pitcher came from the smaller glass? What part of the total contents was the juice from the smaller glass?

b. What part of the total contents came from the larger glass? What part of the total contents was the juice from the larger glass?

Measurement Marks

3. Suppose you have an unmarked piece of wood that you know is 12 in. long.

12 in.

You want to be able to measure all lengths from 1 to 12 in. using the piece of wood only once for each length you measure. What is the least number of marks you must make on the wood, and where would you place them? Explain.

5 FOLLOW-UP

Extra Practice A rectangular lot will be enclosed by 800 meters of fencing. Determine the dimensions of the rectangle that will give the maximum area. **200 m by 200 m; A = 40,000 square meters**

Review Problem Solving Strategies Have students work individually or in groups to solve these problems.

Well, Well The strategies used to solve this problem are draw a diagram and write an expression.

Reva's Glasses The strategies used to solve this problem are draw a diagram and use logical reasoning.

Measurement Marks The strategies used to solve this problem are draw a diagram and guess and test.

NAME ______ CLASS ______ DATE ______

EXTRA PRACTICE

10.6 PROBLEM SOLVING FILE: MAXIMIZING AREA

Solve. Draw a diagram to help you analyze each problem.

1. A rectangular play area is to be enclosed with 100 feet of fencing.
   a. What is the maximum area possible of the play area?
   b. What dimensions of length and width will give the maximum area?

1. a. 625 ft^2 b. 25 ft by 25 ft

2. A garden is to be enclosed by 90 feet of fencing and the side of a building.
   a. What is the maximum rectangular area possible that can be enclosed?
   b. What dimensions of length and width will give the maximum area?

2. a. 1012.5 ft^2 b. 45 ft by 22.5 ft

3. A farmer wants to plant 1600 square yards of land in soybeans. What dimensions of length and width would enclose an area that size with the least amount of fencing?

3. 40 yd; 40 yd

4. What is the maximum rectangular area that can be enclosed with 360 meters of fencing?

4. 8100 m^2

5. What are the dimensions of a rectangular plot with the maximum possible area if one side of a barn and 60 yards of fencing can be used to enclose it?

5. 15 yd; 30 yd

6. A rectangular lot will be enclosed by a cement wall. The area must measure 2500 square meters.
   a. What are the dimensions of the lot that will use the least amount of wall length?
   b. What is the least possible length of wall that can be used?

6. a. 50 m by 50 m b. 200 m

7. A bus shelter will enclose a rectangular area and be completely open on one side.
   a. If there is 25 feet of enclosing material available, what is the maximum area that can be sheltered?
   b. What are the dimensions of the shelter with maximum area?

7. a. 78.125 ft^2 b. 12.5 ft by 6.25 ft

38 *South-Western Algebra 1:* AN INTEGRATED APPROACH

LESSON PLANNING

Objectives

- Recognize when a quadratic model fits a set of data.
- Find the best-fitting parabola for a set of data and compare predicted and actual values.

Technology/Multimedia
graphing utility

Resources
Warm Up 10.7
Reteaching 10.7
Extra Practice 10.7
Enrichment 10.7
Transparencies 34, 78–80
Student Handbook
Lesson Quiz 10.7

Materials/Manipulatives
graph paper

ASSIGNMENTS

Basic: 1–13, Mixed Review 15–22

Average: 1–14, Mixed Review 15–22

Enriched: 1–14, Mixed Review 15–22

1 MOTIVATE

Explore/Working Together Ask the students why they think Question 3 suggests using the *y*-axis as the axis of symmetry and the origin as the vertex. **These are convenient choices that make it easier to read ordered pairs on the curve.** For Question 7, if students do not use graphing utilities or if some graphing utilities do not give the coefficient of correlation, ask how else they may

10.7 Explore Statistics: Using Quadratic Models

SPOTLIGHT ON LEARNING

WHAT? In this lesson you will learn

- to recognize when a quadratic model fits a set of data.
- to find the best-fitting parabola for a set of data and compare predicted and actual values.

WHY? Using quadratic models can help you to solve problems about computer viruses, expansion of water, and solubility.

Explore/Working Together

An animal's teeth reveal much about its diet and way of life. Humans, like all mammals, have four kinds of specialized teeth: *incisors*, chisel-like teeth used for cutting; *canines* and *premolars*, for gripping and tearing; and *molars*, for crushing and breaking. Dentists and physical anthropologists describe the shape of the arrangement of human teeth as a *parabolic dental arcade.*

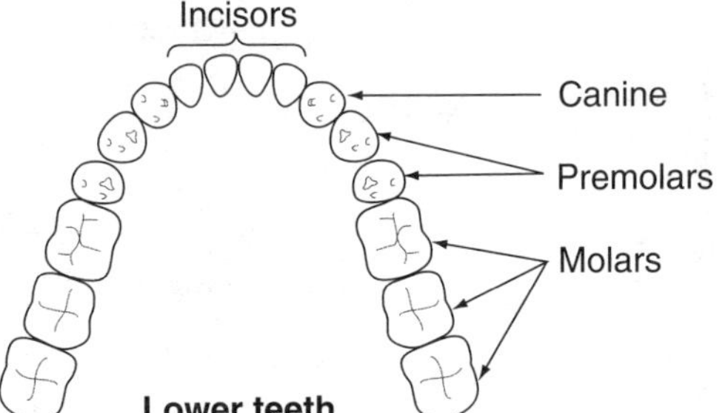

You can find a quadratic equation that describes your dental arcade. Each member of your group will need a sheet of graph paper, plain paper, and a graphing utility that does quadratic regression.

1. Take an impression of your bite by biting the plain sheet of paper.
2. Draw a parabolic curve through the center of the impression as shown at the right.

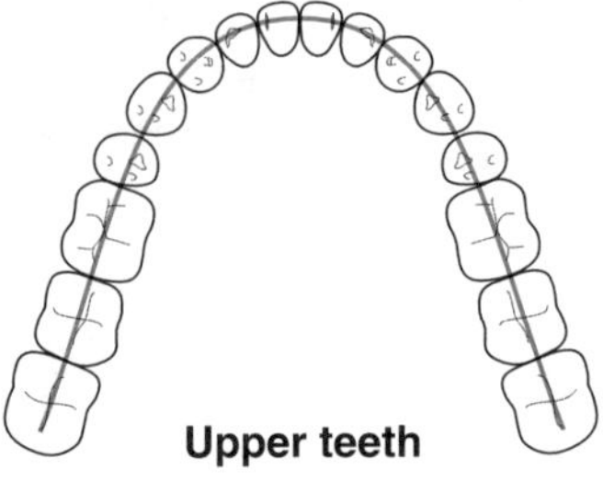

3. Draw a set of axes on the graph paper. Using the y-axis as the axis of symmetry and $(0, 0)$ as the vertex, trace the parabola. Answers will vary.

4. Pick ten points on the parabola and estimate their coordinates, to the nearest tenth. Answers will vary.
5. Use a graphing utility to draw a scatter plot of these ten points. Answers will vary.
6. Use your graphing utility to find a quadratic equation that approximates the scatter plot. Answers will vary.
7. Describe how well the parabola approximates the scatter plot. Answers will vary.
8. Compare and discuss your work with other groups. In general, were the equations a good fit for the data? Answers will vary.

Build Understanding

A linear model is of the form $y = ax + b$. One type of nonlinear model, the quadratic, is of the form $y = ax^2 + bx + c$. You can make a scatter plot to decide if a data set shows a linear or quadratic relationship.

EXAMPLE 1

Decide whether each data set shows a *linear relationship*, a *quadratic relationship*, or *neither*.

a. (1.3, 1.4) (2.5, 4.8) (3, 7) (0, 1) (–1.5, 4.7) (–2.2, 8)
b. (1.3, 5.5) (2.3, 1.7) (4, 7.7) (0, 0) (–1, –2.3) (–2.5, 8.1)
c. (0, 2.7) (1.3, 3.6) (2.1, 3.9) (3.0, 4.5) (3.5, 5.1) (4.5, 5.7)

Solution

Make scatter plots of each data set. Examine the plots to see if the points appear to lie near a line or a parabola.

a.
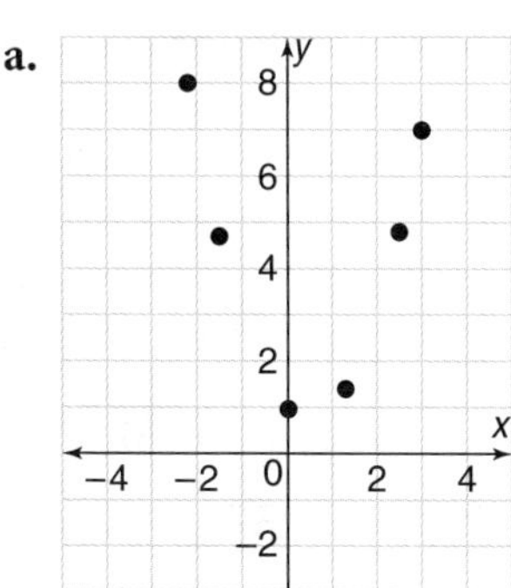

b.
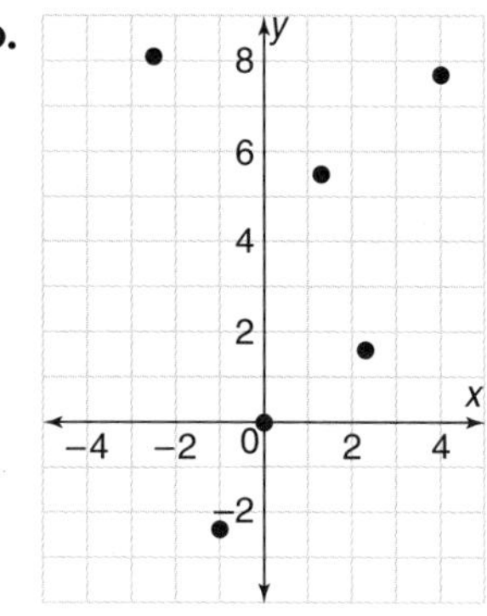

c.
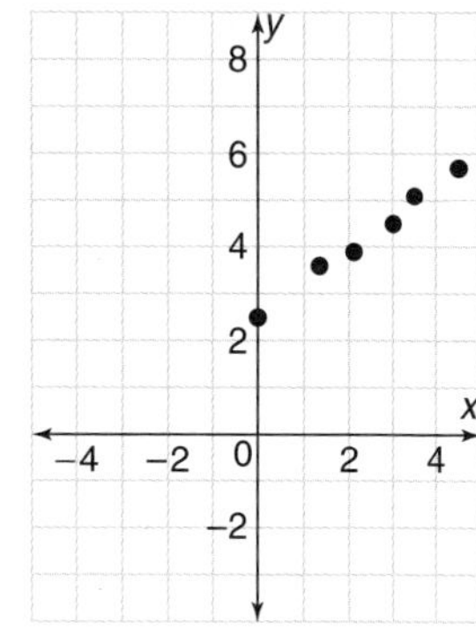

a. The points appear to lie near a parabola. The data show a quadratic relationship.

b. The points do not appear to lie near a line or a parabola. The data show neither a linear nor quadratic relationship.

c. The points lie near a line. The data show a linear relationship. ◄

be able to determine how well the equation fits the data. **They can substitute their data points in the equation to see if most of them come close to satisfying the equation.**

2 TEACH

Use the Pages/Build Understanding

Example 1: Since all that is required is a recognition of the type of relationship, students can graph the data points and look for a possible pattern. Remind them that a linear relationship either increases or decreases, but a quadratic relationship does both. Ask students whether the parabola appears to have a minimum or a maximum point. **The parabola would appear to open upwards, so it will have a minimum point.**

Example 2: Ask students to describe a computer virus. **Computer viruses can enter a computer and run without the user's knowledge. Most are destructive, changing or deleting data or interfering with normal operation.** Ask students to explain how viruses can be spread from one computer to another. **Viruses can be spread over networks (computers linked by data transfer cables), over modems (which link computers over phone lines), or through disks.** For parts b and c, point out that to find the percent error, the amount of error is divided by the actual value, not by the predicted value.

Ongoing Assessment The important concepts and skills are to recognize when a quadratic model fits a set of data, to find the best-fitting parabola for a set of data, and to compare predicted and actual values. To assess these ideas, have students demonstrate how they have applied these concepts and skills in Exercises 1, 2, 5, and 7 of the Try These section.

DIVERSITY IN THE CLASSROOM

Kinesthetic Learners Have kinesthetically-oriented students place a piece of string on a scatter plot and move it around until it forms a curve or line that seems to be a good fit for the data points. Explain that the graphing utility computes the coefficients for a curve or line that seems to fit most of the data.

Guided Practice/Try These Remind students that when plotting the scatter plots for Exercises 1–4, they should use the same scale on both axes to get an accurate idea of the shape of the plot. For Exercise 7, students may want to use a graphing utility to check the given equation.

3 SUMMARIZE

In the Math Journal Ask students to write a paragraph that describes the difference between the actual value and the predicted value for the y-values in a scatter plot of a data set. **The actual value is the value of y given x in an ordered pair of data. The predicted value is the y-value determined from a function of x based on the data.**

COMMUNICATING ABOUT ALGEBRA

For Example 2, discuss why an industry analyst might hypothesize that the financial loss due to viruses might increase more rapidly in the years following 1994.

Possible answer: if the number of computers in use is increasing more and more rapidly, so will the problems caused by viruses.

Many nonlinear relationships in the real world can be approximated by a quadratic model. However, as the next example shows, you must be careful when rounding.

EXAMPLE 2

COMPUTER VIRUSES Businesses and individuals lose time and productivity when a virus infects their computers, making progress impossible. The table below shows financial losses caused by viruses during the years 1990–1994.

Year, last two digits	90	91	92	93	94
Loss, billions of dollars	0.1	0.3	0.7	1.4	2.7

a. Find the equation that best fits the data.

b. Check to see how well the curve fits the data for 1992.

c. Round the coefficients to the nearest hundredth and check to see how well the curve fits the data for 1992.

Solution

a. A scatter plot of the data shows that a linear model may not be the best one. The points seem to rise more rapidly in the later years and suggest the appearance of a parabola. Use a quadratic model and a graphing utility to find

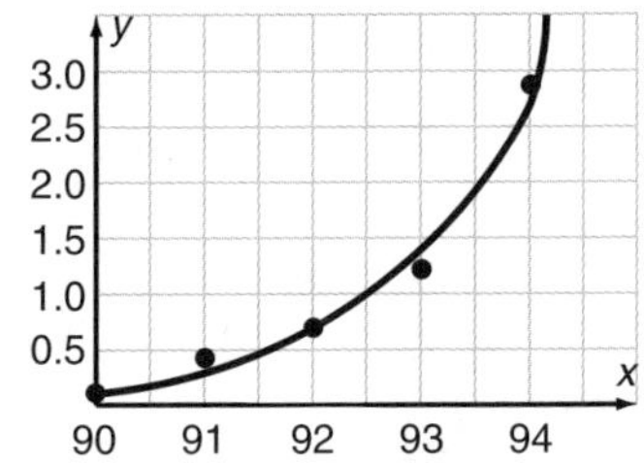

$$y = 0.1785714286x^2 - 32.22714286x + 1454.151429$$

b. Substitute 92 for x in the quadratic equation in **a** and find the value of y.

$$\begin{aligned} y &= 0.1785714286(92)^2 - 32.22714286(92) + 1454.151429 \\ &= 0.6828575504 \end{aligned}$$

Subtract the predicted value from the actual value to find the error.

Error	=	Actual Value	–	Predicted Value

$$\begin{aligned} &= 0.7 - 0.6828575504 \\ &= 0.0171424496 \end{aligned}$$

The percent error is $\dfrac{(0.0171424496)100}{0.7}$ or about 2.45%. Because the percent error is small, the quadratic model is a good fit.

c. With rounded coefficients, the equation is

$$y = 0.18x^2 - 32.23x + 1454.15$$

Substitute 92 for x in the new equation and find the value of y.

$$y = 0.18(92)^2 - 32.23(92) + 1454.15$$
$$= 12.51$$

Find the error.

$$\text{error} = 0.7 - 12.51$$
$$= -11.81$$

The percent error is $\frac{(-11.81)100}{0.7}$ or about −1687%. The percent error is large. ◀

Why was the percent error in Example 2c so large? You can verify that rounding the coefficient of the x^2 term contributed most of the error. Rounding the coefficient of the x^2 term magnifies the errors from rounding, especially if the x^2 term is relatively large. Rounding coefficients can destroy the accuracy of the regression equation.

TRY THESE

Make a scatter plot for each set of data. Tell whether each data set shows a *linear relationship*, a *quadratic relationship*, or *neither*.

See Additional Answers for graphs.

1. (0, 0) (5, 99.6) (10, 148.9) (12.5, 156) (20, 100.5) (25, 0.8) quadratic
2. (−2, −3.1) (−1, −1.75) (1, 0.85) (3, 3.4) (5, 6) (8, 9.8) linear
3. (1, 2) (2, 0) (3, 5) (4, 3) (6, 4) (9, 9) (12, 2) neither
4. (−5, 6.2) (−2, 1) (0, 0) (1, 0.3) (3, 2.3) (6, 9) quadratic

EXPANSION OF WATER Density, or mass/unit volume, decreases as temperature increases for most liquids. For a certain range of temperature, the density of water increases as it is warmed from its frozen state at 0°C and then decreases as it is warmed further. The table shows values for the density of water at different temperatures.

Temperature, °C	Density, g/cm³
0	0.99986
1	0.99993
2	0.99997
3	0.99999
4	1.00000
5	0.99999
6	0.99997
7	0.99993
8	0.99987
9	0.99981

5. Make a scatter plot of the data. (*Hint:* Use intervals of 0.00005 from 0.99970 to 1.00000 on the vertical axis.) What type of relationship does the data show?
   quadratic; see Additional Answers for graph
6. For which temperature interval does the density of water increase? What is the maximum density?
   0° to 4°; max = 1.00000 g/cm³
7. Using a graphing utility, a researcher determined that the equation $y = -0.000008x^2 + 0.000065x + 0.999867$ modeled the data in the table. What is the predicted value for 4°C. What is the percent error? 0.999999; 0.0001%
8. Use the model to predict the density at 10°C.
   0.999717 g/cm³

4 PRACTICE

Practice For Exercise 1, tell students to use a separate set of axes for each substance, titling each graph substance *A*, *B*, and so on. Remind students that they will need the results from Exercise 3 for Exercise 4, so they should be sure to label their answers clearly.

Extend Check students' answers to Exercise 9 before having them go on to Exercises 10–12, which rely on a correct answer to Exercise 9. Ask students why they think they are asked not to round their answers to Exercise 9. **Rounding can result in a large error, as they discovered in Exercise 2.**

Think Critically To help students answer Exercise 14, display a parabola and cover half of it so that students can see that the relationship can also appear linear. Point out that one of the models will have a higher coefficient of correlation than the other for the given data.

NAME ______ CLASS ______ DATE ______

RETEACHING

10.7 EXPLORE STATISTICS: USING QUADRATIC MODELS

A graphing utility gives the coefficients for a, b, and c in a quadratic model $y = ax^2 + bx + c$. To find the predicted y-value for a certain x-value, substitute the value of x in the equation. Usually, you round the coefficients to a given place value.

Example

The graphing utility reads
$a = 1.324987342$
$b = -2.145632998$
$c = 5.1187642187$

Round coefficients to three decimal places. Find the value of y when $x = 100$.
$y = 1.325x^2 - 2.146x + 5.119$ ← Coefficients rounded.
$y = 1.325(100)^2 - 2.146(100) + 5.119$
$y = 1.325(10{,}000) - 2.146(100) + 5.119$
$y = 13{,}250 - 214.6 + 5.119$
$y = 13{,}040.519$

EXERCISES

For each set of coefficients, write the quadratic equation. Round decimals to three decimal places. Then find the value of y for the given value of x.

1. $a = 0.004523112$, $b = 3.285534263$, $c = 1.033251628$. Find y when $x = 5$.
   1. $y = 0.005x^2 + 3.286x + 1.033$; $y = 17.588$
2. $a = 32.12313134$, $b = 3.123449832$, $c = -45.3242755$. Find y when $x = 10$.
   2. $y = 32.123x^2 + 3.123x - 45.324$; $y = 3198.206$
3. $a = 4.384738219$, $b = -3.26372612$, $c = 8.237661237$. Find y when $x = -2$.
   3. $y = 4.385x^2 - 3.264x + 8.238$; $y = 32.306$
4. $a = 0.002345635$, $b = 0.053123438$, $c = 35.48372112$. Find y when $x = 3$.
   4. $y = 0.002x^2 + 0.053x + 35.484$; $y = 35.661$

42 *South-Western Algebra 1: AN INTEGRATED APPROACH*

5 FOLLOW-UP

Extension A graphing utility will give a quadratic equation for any set of data that is entered. Ask students to discuss how they can decide whether or not an equation model is appropriate. Ask them to discuss problems involving an equation that does not fit the data well. **By looking at a scatter plot or finding the percent error, you can judge how good a fit an equation is. One problem with using an equation that is not a good fit is that you may base a decision on a prediction that is not accurate.**

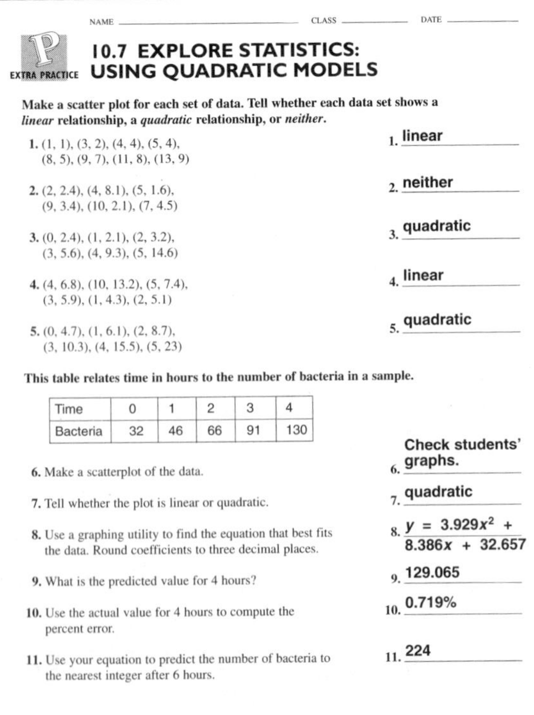

NAME ____________ CLASS ________ DATE ________

EXTRA PRACTICE

10.7 EXPLORE STATISTICS: USING QUADRATIC MODELS

Make a scatter plot for each set of data. Tell whether each data set shows a *linear* relationship, a *quadratic* relationship, or *neither*.

1. (1, 1), (3, 2), (4, 4), (5, 4), (8, 5), (9, 7), (11, 8), (13, 9) — 1. **linear**
2. (2, 2.4), (4, 8.1), (5, 1.6), (9, 3.4), (10, 2.1), (7, 4.5) — 2. **neither**
3. (0, 2.4), (1, 2.1), (2, 3.2), (3, 5.6), (4, 9.3), (5, 14.6) — 3. **quadratic**
4. (4, 6.8), (10, 13.2), (5, 7.4), (3, 5.9), (1, 4.3), (2, 5.1) — 4. **linear**
5. (0, 4.7), (1, 6.1), (2, 8.7), (3, 10.3), (4, 15.5), (5, 23) — 5. **quadratic**

This table relates time in hours to the number of bacteria in a sample.

Time	0	1	2	3	4
Bacteria	32	46	66	91	130

6. Make a scatterplot of the data. — 6. **Check students' graphs.**
7. Tell whether the plot is linear or quadratic. — 7. **quadratic**
8. Use a graphing utility to find the equation that best fits the data. Round coefficients to three decimal places. — 8. $y = 3.929x^2 + 8.386x + 32.657$
9. What is the predicted value for 4 hours? — 9. **129.065**
10. Use the actual value for 4 hours to compute the percent error. — 10. **0.719%**
11. Use your equation to predict the number of bacteria to the nearest integer after 6 hours. — 11. **224**

44 *South-Western Algebra 1: AN INTEGRATED APPROACH*

PRACTICE

SOLUBILITY You can make a chemical solution by dissolving a substance such as sugar in water. The amount of a substance that can be dissolved in a given liquid is a function of the temperature of the liquid. A chemist collected data on the solubility of several substances in water.

GRAMS OF SUBSTANCE PER 100 GRAMS OF WATER						
Temperature, °C	0	20	40	60	80	100
Substance A	179	204	238	287	362	487
Substance B	28.0	34.2	40.1	45.8	51.3	56.3
Substance C	128	144	162	176	192	206
Substance D	13.9	31.6	61.3	116	167	245
Substance E	73	87.6	102	122	148	180

1. Make a separate scatter plot for each substance. For which substances does the temperature–solubility relationship appear to be linear? For which does the relationship appear quadratic? Indicate if there are any for which you are undecided.
   See Additional Answers.
2. Use a graphing utility to find the quadratic equation that best fits the data for substance E. Round coefficients to three decimal places.
   $y = 0.006x^2 + 0.456x + 74.121$

3. Use your equation from Exercise 2 to predict values for 0°C and 100°C. 74.121; 179.721
4. Use the actual values for 0° and 100° to compute the percent error. Do you think rounding the coefficients produced an acceptable model?
   1.54%; 0.155%; answers will vary, but the model seems acceptable
5. Use a graphing utility to find the linear equation that best fits the data for substance C. Round coefficients to three decimal places. $y = 0.783x + 128.857$
6. Compare the predicted and actual values for substance C at 60°C. Does the linear model appear to be a good fit? predicted: 175.837; actual: 176; percent error 0.093%; yes, linear model is a good fit

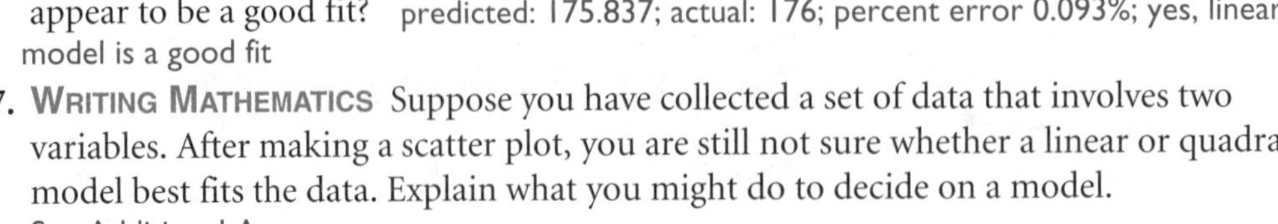

7. **WRITING MATHEMATICS** Suppose you have collected a set of data that involves two variables. After making a scatter plot, you are still not sure whether a linear or quadratic model best fits the data. Explain what you might do to decide on a model.
   See Additional Answers.

EXTEND

You can construct and solve a system of equations to find an equation of a quadratic model. To determine the coefficients a, b, c, you will need three equations. Exercises 8–11 show the procedure.

8. Use the solubility data for substance A at 0°C, 40°C, and 80°C. Substitute the coordinates of each point into the equation $y = ax^2 + bx + c$. Write a system of three equations for a, b, c. $c = 179$; $1600a + 40b + c = 238$; $6400a + 80b + c = 362$

9. Solve the system for a, b, c. Do not round. $a = 0.0203125$; $b = 0.6625$; $c = 179$

10. Use your results to write a quadratic equation of the form $y = ax^2 + bx + c$. $y = 0.0203125x^2 + 0.6625x + 179$

11. What values does your model predict for 60°C and 100°C? Do you think the equation is a good fitting model? 291.875; 448.375; the equation does not seem to be a good fit at higher temperatures

12. Use a graphing utility to find the quadratic equation that best fits the data. Round coefficients to three decimal places. What are the predicted values for 60°C and 100°C? $0.03x^2 - 0.017x + 185$; 291.98; 483.3

THINK CRITICALLY

Write *true* or *false*.

13. If two variables do not have a quadratic relationship, then they have a linear relationship. false

14. A set of data involving two variables can have both a linear model and a quadratic model. true

MIXED REVIEW

15. STANDARDIZED TESTS Identify the property illustrated. D; Lesson 2.5

$$9 + (13 + 26) = (9 + 13) + 26$$

A. commutative property of addition

B. identity property of addition

C. inverse property of addition

D. associative property of addition

16. Solve and graph: $-2m + 3 > -5$ $m < 4$; also see Additional Answers for graph; Lesson 5.4

Determine the slope of the line passing through each pair of points. Lesson 6.2

17. (3, –9), (4, –12) –3

18. (4, –4), (9, 6) 2

Solve each system of equations. Lessons 7.3 and 7.4

19. $\begin{cases} 25x - 10y = 41 \\ 5x + 15y = 100 \end{cases}$ (3.2, 2.9)

20. $\begin{cases} m = 16 + n \\ -m - n = 0 \end{cases}$ (8, –8)

Use the function $f(x) = x^2 + 6x + 8$. Lesson 10.2

21. Find the vertex. (–3, –1)

22. Find the axis of symmetry. $x = -3$

Make Connections

Art Show students some examples of string art. (The art teacher at your school may be able to provide examples.) Ask students how this kind of art relates to the scatter plots they looked at in this lesson. **Pins are placed in a canvas or board and connected by string so that a design or pattern is revealed. The design may resemble a mathematical curve.**

NAME ______ CLASS ______ DATE ______

10.7 EXPLORE STATISTICS: USING QUADRATIC MODELS

During the year, the amount of daylight changes.

1. Describe the pattern of the change. Explain why a quadratic model would provide a better fit than a linear model.
The amount of daylight increases and then decreases. It is quadratic rather than linear since a linear model would either increase or decrease.

2. Use an almanac to complete the following table.

Day of the Year	Date	Amount of Daylight	
		Hours: Minutes	Total Minutes
x			y
25	1/25	______	______
50	2/19	______	______
75	3/14	______	______
100	4/8	______	______
125	5/3	______	______
150	5/28	______	______
175	6/22	______	______
200	7/17	______	______
225	8/11	______	______
250	9/5	______	______
275	9/30	______	______
300	10/25	______	______
325	11/19	______	______
350	12/14	______	______

3. Use a graphing utility to plot the day of the year x and the number of minutes of daylight y. Write the quadratic equation with coefficients rounded to the nearest thousandth.
Answers will vary. For 1996 data: $-0.013x^2 + 4.633x + 463.484$

4. Use your equation to find the predicted value for Day 40, February 9th.
Answers will vary. For above equation, $y = 628.004$

5. Use the almanac to find the number of minutes of daylight for Day 40. Compare with your answer to Question 4 and compute the percent error.
Answers will vary. For Question 4, 9 min; 1.5%

46 *South-Western Algebra 1:* AN INTEGRATED APPROACH

Introduction The Chapter Review emphasizes the major concepts, skills, and vocabulary presented in this chapter and can be used for diagnosing students' strengths and weaknesses. Page references direct students to appropriate sections for additional review and reteaching.

Using Pages 508–509 Ask students to scan the Chapter Review and ask questions about any section they find confusing. Exercises 1–4 review key vocabulary.

Informal Evaluation After completing the Chapter Review, have students write a short paragraph describing the steps they used to reach any incorrect solutions. This may help them in discovering their own error patterns and give you insight into their thinking. Make sure students understand this material before moving on to the assessment stage.

Follow-Up Have students solve this problem: The area of a square room with a 2-foot by 4-foot closet cut out of the room is given by the formula $x^2 - 8 = 161$ where x is the length of one side of the room.

a. What method is the most appropriate for solving the quadratic equation? **using square roots**
b. Find the values of x that are solutions to the equation. **$x = \pm 13$**
c. Which solution makes sense in terms of the problem? Explain your reasoning. **Only 13 makes sense since −13 as a room length has no meaning.**

Have students write word problems that can be solved by using quadratic equations. Students should exchange and solve each other's word problems.

• • • CHAPTER REVIEW • • •

VOCABULARY

Choose the word from the list that completes each statement.

1. Every point on the graph of a function $y = ax^2 + bx + c$ has a point of reflection over the __?__ of the graph. b

2. The intersection of a parabola and its axis of symmetry is called the __?__. d

3. "The solutions of the equation $ax^2 + bx + c = 0$ can be expressed in terms of a, b, and c." This statement refers to the __?__. c

4. The number of real solutions to a quadratic equation can be found by evaluating the __?__. a

a. discriminant
b. line of symmetry
c. quadratic formula
d. vertex

Lesson 10.1 EXPLORE QUADRATIC FUNCTIONS — pages 465–467

- The graph of $y = x^2$ is translated vertically when a constant is added or subtracted, and horizontally when a constant is added to x before squaring the quantity. The graph of $y = ax^2$ is wider than $y = x^2$ for $-1 < a < 1$ and $a \neq 0$ and narrower for $a < -1$ or $a > 1$.

Match each in equation with its graph.

5. $y = x^2 + 4$ c

6. $y = 3x^2$ a

7. $y = (x - 4)^2$ b

a.

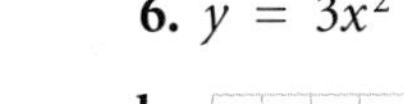

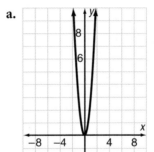

b.

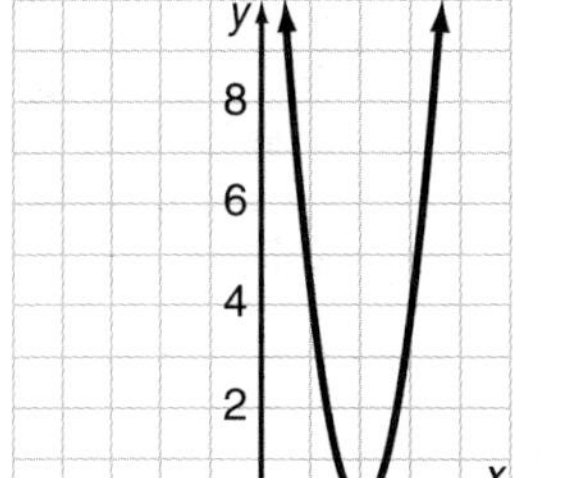

c.

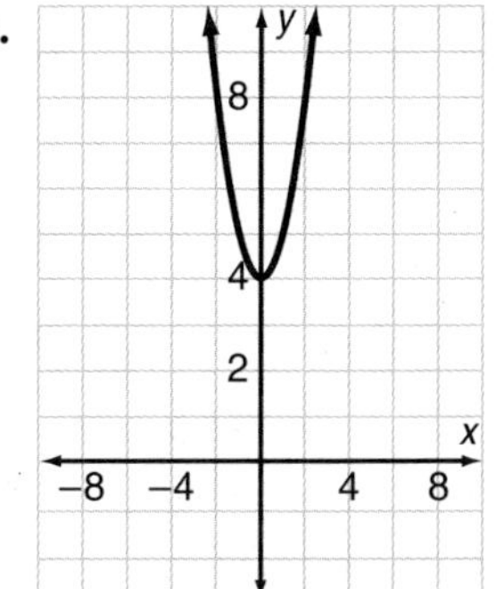

Lesson 10.2 GRAPHS OF QUADRATIC FUNCTIONS — pages 468–476

- The graph of $y = ax^2 + bx + c$ opens upward for $a > 0$ and downward for $a < 0$.
- The x-value of the vertex of the graph $y = ax^2 + bx + c$ is $-\frac{b}{2a}$. To find the y-value, substitute the x-value in the equation and solve for y.

Determine the coordinates of the vertex and the equation of the axis of symmetry for the graph of each equation.

8. $y = x^2 + 5$
(0, 5); $x = 0$

9. $y = 2x^2 - 4x + 11$
(1, 9); $x = 1$

10. $y = x^2 + 6x - 1$
(−3, −10); $x = -3$

Lesson 10.3 SOLVE QUADRATIC EQUATIONS BY GRAPHING pages 477–482

- To solve a quadratic equation of the form $ax^2 + bx + c = 0$, find the x-intercepts of the graph of $y = ax^2 + bx + c$.
- To solve a quadratic equation of the form $ax^2 + bx + c = d$, rewrite the equation as $ax^2 + bx + c - d = 0$. Alternatively, graph both $y_1 = ax^2 + bx + c$ and $y_2 = d$ and find the x-values of their intersection.

Solve each equation. Round decimals answers to the nearest hundredth.

11. $x^2 - 3x + 2 = 0$ 1, 2 **12.** $x^2 - x = 20$ −4, 5 **13.** $x^2 + 4x - 7 = 0$ 1.32, −5.32

Lesson 10.4 SOLVE QUADRATIC EQUATIONS USING SQUARE ROOTS pages 483–489

- To solve a quadratic equation of the form $ax^2 + b = c$, use the square root property.

Solve. Express answers in simplest radical form.

14. $x^2 - 49 = 0$ ± 7 **15.** $2x^2 = 64$ $\pm 4\sqrt{2}$ **16.** $3x^2 - 1 = 47$ ± 4

Lesson 10.5 THE QUADRATIC FORMULA pages 490–497

- To solve a quadratic equation of the form $ax^2 + bx + c = 0$, use the quadratic formula.
- Use the discriminant to determine the number of real solutions of a quadratic equation.

Solve. Round decimal answers to two decimal places.

17. $x^2 + 7x + 10 = 0$ −2, −5 **18.** $4x^2 - 12x + 9 = 0$ 1.5 **19.** $x^2 - x = 5$ 2.79, −1.79

Determine the number of solutions.

20. $x^2 - 4x - 1 = 0$ two **21.** $x^2 + 3x + 6 = 0$ zero **22.** $2x^2 + 7x = 9$ two

Lesson 10.6 MAXIMIZING AREA pages 498–501

- You can determine a maximum area for a given shape by solving a quadratic equation.

Solve.

23. A rectangular herb garden will be enclosed by 12 yards of low fencing. Determine the dimensions of the rectangle that will give the maximum area. 3 yards by 3 yards

Lesson 10.7 EXPLORE STATISTICS: USING QUADRATIC MODELS pages 502–507

- A **scatter plot** may reveal that a set of data has a quadratic relationship. Use a graphing utility to find a quadratic equation that models the data.

Solve.

24. A set of data has a y-value of −5 when $x = 2$. A graphing utility gives the function $y = 0.286x^2 - 2.857x + 0.071$ as a model for this data. Determine the percent error for $x = 2$ between the actual and predicted values. 10%

Study Skills Tip Emphasize to students that studying takes preparation. Before they sit down to study for an exam, students should have all materials from a chapter well organized and within easy reach. This includes class notes, quizzes, homework, calculator, and anything else they might need. Suggest that as they study, they summarize each lesson in one or two sentences to reassure themselves that they understand the material.

For Your Portfolio Have students gather samples from their project, homework, quizzes, and class work that portray efforts to meet each of their goals for this chapter. On a cover page for each representative piece of work have students write the related goal, why the work is included in the portfolio, and what the teacher should look for when reviewing the work. On a general cover page have students write a self-evaluation of how well they have met each of their goals for this chapter. The general cover page should conclude with goals for the next chapter and the student's reason for choosing these goals.

The Chapter Test is comprised of a variety of test-item types as follows:

writing	23
traditional	1–14, 16–21, 24–27
verbal	28–31
standardized test	15, 22

TEACHING TIP

The writing item provides an opportunity for students to demonstrate a knowledge of process as well as end result. Suggest that before they begin answering questions, students should look over the entire test and determine the order in which they will work. Some students may be more successful if they save the open-ended writing question until after they have completed the other test questions.

The table below correlates the Chapter Test items with the appropriate lesson(s).

Item	Lesson	Item	Lesson
1–4	10.2	23	10.3, 10.4, 10.5
5–14	10.4	24–28	10.5
15	10.2	29	10.6
16–22	10.3	30	10.5
22	10.3	31	10.7

CHAPTER ASSESSMENT

CHAPTER TEST

Determine the coordinates of the vertex and the equation of the axis of symmetry of each equation.

1. $y = x^2 - 4x + 1$ (2, −3), $x = 2$
2. $y = 2x^2 + 8x - 5$ (−2, −13), $x = -2$
3. $y = x^2 - 8x + 15$ (4, −1), $x = 4$
4. $y = x^2 + 6x + 2$ (−3, −7), $x = -3$

Solve each equation. Express answers in simplest radical form.

5. $x^2 - 3x + 2 = 0$ 2, 1
6. $x^2 - 8x = -16$ 4
7. $x^2 - 70 = 11$ ±9
8. $3x^2 - 12x = -4$ $2 \pm \frac{2\sqrt{6}}{3}$
9. $x^2 - 2x - 48 = 0$ −6, 8
10. $x^2 + 6x - 9 = 0$ $-3 \pm 3\sqrt{2}$
11. $x^2 + 6x + 9 = 15$ $-3 \pm \sqrt{15}$
12. $x^2 + 49 = 14x$ 7
13. $x^2 + 6 = 48$ $\pm\sqrt{42}$
14. $x^2 - 2x - 2 = 0$ $1 \pm \sqrt{3}$

15. STANDARDIZED TESTS Which is the equation of the graph shown? B

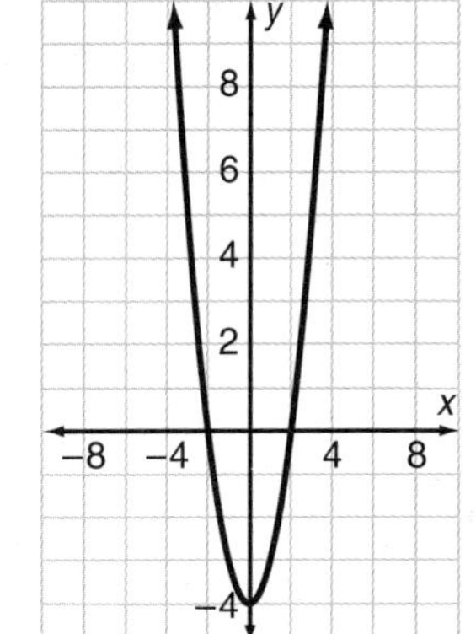

A. $y = (x + 2)^2$

B. $y = x^2 - 4$

C. $y = (x - 2)^2$

D. $y = x^2 + 4$

Solve each equation. Round decimal answers to the nearest hundredth.

16. $x^2 - 7x + 12 = 0$ 3, 4
17. $x^2 + 4x - 14 = 0$ 2.24, −6.24
18. $2x^2 + x = 10$ 2, −2.5
19. $3x^2 - 16 = 2x$ 2.67, −2
20. $x^2 = 11$ ±3.32
21. $2x^2 - 108 = 20$ ±8

22. STANDARDIZED TESTS Which of the following equations is equivalent to $x^2 - 3x + 4 = 0$? B

A. $x^2 - 3x = 4$ B. $x^2 - 3x + 1 = -3$
C. $x^2 - 4 = 3x$ D. $x^2 - 3x - 2 = 2$

23. WRITING MATHEMATICS Write a paragraph explaining how to solve a quadratic equation of the form $ax^2 + bx + c = d$. See Additional Answers.

Use the discriminant to determine the number of real solutions of each equation.

24. $x^2 - 10x + 25 = 0$ one
25. $x^2 + 5x = 12$ two
26. $2x^2 - x + 23 = 9$ zero
27. $x^2 + 3x - 5 = 7$ two

Solve each problem. Round decimal answers to the nearest hundredth.

28. The revenue y from ticket sales for a concert can be modeled by the equation $y = -5x^2 + 250x + 70$, where x is the price of the ticket. Find the ticket price that will give the maximum revenue. $25

29. Andrea is enclosing a rectangular area for a vegetable garden near the back of her house. One wall of the house will form one side of the garden. Andrea plans to use 50 ft of fencing. Determine the dimensions of the enclosed garden that will produce a maximum area. 25 ft by 12.5 ft

30. The height of a rocket launched from the ground can be modeled by the equation $y = -16x^2 + 90x$, where x is the number of seconds after launching and y is the height in feet. Find the number of seconds it will take for the rocket to reach the ground after launching. 5.62 s

31. The equation $y = 0.198x^2 - 0.396x + 1.102$ models the following data: (0, 1), (3, 2), (5, 4), (6.7, 7), (7.5, 9), (8, 11).

   a. Find the predicted value of y for $x = 5$. 4.072

   b. Find the percent error for the predicted and actual values of y for $x = 5$. 1.8%

For Performance Assessment see Additional Answers.

PERFORMANCE ASSESSMENT

"WEIGHTLESS" EQUATIONS The equation $d = -9.8t^2$ can be used to determine the time t in seconds it takes for an object to reach the ground in free fall from a height d meters above the ground.

a. Use the equation to help you answer this question: If a brick and a nickel are dropped from a 10-meter height at the same moment, which object will hit the ground first?

b. Test your answer by performing an experiment. Hold a heavy book in one hand and a coin in the other. Drop them simultaneously from the same height. What do you notice?

c. Make a conjecture about your results.

USING A GRAPHING UTILITY Write three quadratic equations. Graph them with a graphing utility. Discuss with a partner how each graph relates to its equation. For each graph, determine the vertex and locate the axis of symmetry. Find the x-values for which the value of the function is 0.

DESIGN A POSTER Draw a parabola on posterboard. Label the vertex, the axis of symmetry, and the x-intercept or intercepts. On the poster, display the standard form of a quadratic equation, the quadratic formula, the algebraic expression for the discriminant, and a table that shows how to interpret the discriminant.

OUTLINING STEPS Make a list of steps you need to take to solve a quadratic equation. Give your list to a partner who will use it to solve an equation. Revise the steps if necessary. Then exchange roles with your partner.

PROJECT ASSESSMENT

PROJECT Connection Work with your teacher to determine when a class Business Week can be held. Groups will organize the results of their research and take turns presenting an in-depth look at different industries and corporations and the working stock market. Here are some ideas for related activities.

1. Create a collage of logos of the corporations your group followed. See if your classmates can identify the corporations associated with each logo.
2. Pretend that each member of your group purchased 100 shares of stock in his or her chosen corporation. How much did each of you "invest" initially? What was the total value of your imaginary stock portfolio at the beginning and at the end of the project? Who came out ahead and who came out behind? Could you identify trends for the stock market or the industry in general? Were there reasons for individual corporate performance?
3. As a class, brainstorm new products or services for each industry studied. Speculate on the future of each industry and how it might be affected by technological advances.

Performance Assessment

The activities on page 511 give students with different learning styles opportunities to demonstrate their understanding of concepts in this chapter. The activities may be used in addition to or instead of the Chapter Test on the previous page.

"Weightless" Equations (Kinesthetic/Visual/Symbolic) Some students may immediately notice that the weight of an object is not a variable in the equation. These students can also benefit from this activity: Have pairs of students drop objects from a predetermined height and measure their fall time using a stop watch. They can then compare their experimental results to those expected from the formula.

Use a Graphing Utility (Visual/Symbolic) As an indicator of understanding, look for students' ability to explain how changing an equation would change the vertex and/or axis of symmetry.

Design a Poster (Linguistic/Visual) As an extension, have students write a short paragraph describing one or more applications of the quadratic function with which they have become familiar during this chapter.

Outlining Steps (Linguistic/Symbolic) To check for complete understanding, make sure students include in their directions the need to consider the form of the equation before beginning to solve.

Project Assessment

Project Connection As a class, have students make a list of the industries/corporations the groups chose to study. Discuss why these industries caught their interest and how this relates to the choices people make in both investments and careers.

CUMULATIVE REVIEW

Graph each equation. Give the coordinates of the vertex. See Additional Answers for graphs.

1. $y = x^2 - 6x + 9$ (3, 0); Lesson 10.2
2. $y = 2x^2 + 8x - 10$ (−2, −18); Lesson 10.2
3. $y = -|x| + 3$ (0, 3); Lesson 9.2
4. $y = 3x - 2$ no vertex; Lesson 6.3

Solve each equation by graphing. Round decimals to the nearest hundredth.

5. $x^2 - 3x + 1 = 7$ (−1.37, 4.37); Lesson 10.3
6. $5x^2 + 2x - 3 = 4x - 1$ (−0.46, 0.86); Lesson 10.3

Write three numbers that are between the two given numbers. Lesson 9.6

7. 5.06 and 5.07 Examples include 5.061, 5.065, 5.069
8. $\frac{1}{2}$ and $\frac{3}{4}$ Examples include $\frac{9}{16}, \frac{5}{8}, \frac{11}{16}$
9. The Nut Hut sells cashews for \$6.50 per pound and almonds for \$2.25 per pound. Customers have suggested a mixture of cashews and almonds, so that the cost per pound would be \$4.50. The owner agrees to make 20 pounds of the mixture on a trial basis. To the nearest tenth, how many pounds of each kind of nut will be needed to make the mixture? 10.6 lb of cashews, 9.4 lb of almonds; Lesson 7.7
10. Arrange the numbers in order from least to greatest. See Additional Answers; Lesson 9.5

$$-3.94, -\sqrt{17}, \frac{-11}{3}, -3.943$$

11. What percent of 5 is 6? 120%; Lesson 3.5
12. About 800 runners entered the 10 K race. It was determined that 28% of the runners finished the race in less than 32 minutes. How many runners was this? 224; Lesson 3.5

Write the equation of each line described.

13. passes through (3, 1) and (−2, −4) $y = x - 2$; Lesson 6.4
14. passes through (−4, 2) and (4, 2) $y = 2$; Lesson 6.5
15. passes through (5, −4) and parallel to the y-axis $x = 5$; Lesson 6.5

Use the bar graph for Questions 16–18.

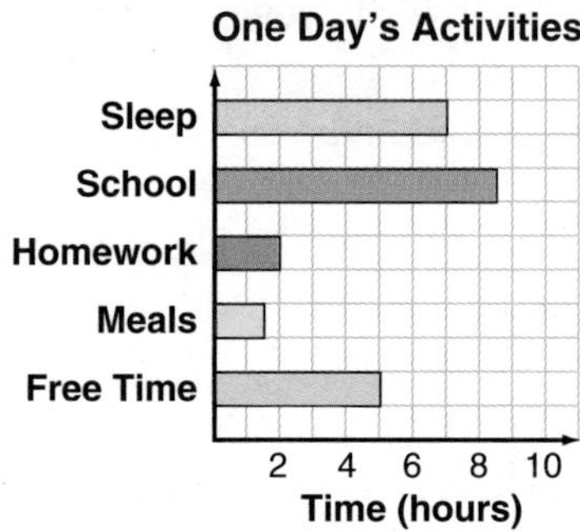

16. At which activity was 7 hours spent? sleep; Lesson 1.4
17. How much time was spent on homework? 2 hours; Lesson 1.4
18. WRITING MATHEMATICS What other type of graph might have been used to represent these data? Why? See Additional Answers. Lesson 1.4

Solve each quadratic equation. Use the product and quotient properties to simplify the radicals. See Additional Answers. Lesson 10.4

19. $3(x + 1)^2 = 24$
20. $9x^2 + 5 = 45$
21. Benny asked Jenny to try to guess the number he was thinking of. Jenny guessed 26. Benny said that Jenny was close, that she was only off by at most 7. In what range was Benny's number? Write an absolute value inequality and solve. $|n - 26| \le 7$; $19 \le n \le 33$; Lesson 9.4
22. A deli offers five different kinds of lunch meat, three kinds of bread, and six different kinds of cheese. If customers can order one kind of lunch meat on a sandwich with one kind of cheese on one type of bread, how many different sandwiches can a customer order? 90; Lesson 8.6

Solve each inequality. Then graph the solution. See Additional Answers for graphs.

23. $3x - 5 > -2$ $x > 1$; Lesson 5.4
24. $-3x \le 9$ and $x + 2 < 5$ $-3 \le x < 3$; Lesson 5.5

NAME ______ CLASS ______ DATE ______

FORM B **CHAPTER 10 TEST**

Write the letter of the best answer for Questions 1–7.

1. Which is the equation of the graph shown? 1. a

NAME ______ CLASS ______ DATE ______

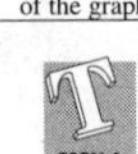

FORM A **CHAPTER 10 TEST**

Write the letter of the best answer for Questions 1–7.

1. Which is the equation of the graph shown? 1. b
   a. $y = (x - 1)^2$ b. $y = (x + 1)^2$ c. $y = x^2 + 1$ d. $y = x^2 - 1$
2. Which is the vertex of the graph of $y = 2x^2 - 8x + 10$? 2. d
   a. (−4, 74) b. (−2, 34) c. (4, 10) d. (2, 2)
3. Which is the equation of the axis of symmetry for the graph of $y = x^2 - 6x + 11$? 3. a
   a. $x = 3$ b. $x = -3$ c. $x = -6$ d. $x = 38$
4. To find the solutions for $x^2 - 8x = -7$, you could find the x-intercepts of the graph for which equation? 4. a
   a. $y = x^2 - 8x + 7$ b. $y = x^2 - 8x$ c. $y = x^2 - 8x - 7$ d. $y = -7$
5. Which of the following shows the solutions for $x^2 + 3 = 15$? 5. c
   a. $\pm 3\sqrt{2}$ b. ± 12 c. $\pm 2\sqrt{3}$ d. ± 6
6. Which equation is the standard form for $6x^2 = 3x + 1$? 6. d
   a. $6x^2 - 3x = 1$ b. $6x^2 - 3x + 1 = 0$ c. $6x^2 + 3x - 1 = 0$ d. $6x^2 - 3x - 1 = 0$
7. What is the value of the discriminant of $x^2 - 10x + 9 = 0$? 7. a
   a. 64 b. 36 c. 5 d. −16

Determine the coordinates of the vertex and the equation of the axis of symmetry for the graph of each equation.

8. $y = x^2 + 7$ 8. (0, 7), $x = 0$
9. $y = 2x^2 - 4x + 1$ 9. (1, −1), $x = 1$

Solve each equation. Express answers in simplest radical form.

10. $x^2 - 144 = 0$ 10. ±12
11. $4x^2 = 128$ 11. $\pm 4\sqrt{2}$
12. $x^2 + 1 = 50$ 12. ±7
13. $4(x + 4)^2 = 100$ 13. 1, −9

50 South-Western Algebra 1: AN INTEGRATED APPROACH

CHAPTER 10 TEST Form A, page 2 NAME ______

Solve each equation. Round decimal answers to the nearest hundredth.

14. $x^2 - 3x - 10 = 0$ 14. 5, −2
15. $x^2 + 7x = 30$ 15. 3, −10
16. $5x^2 + 2x - 1 = 0$ 16. 0.29, −0.69
17. $6x^2 - x = 1$ 17. 0.5, −0.33

Use the discriminant to determine the number of solutions to each equation.

18. $x^2 - 12x + 36 = 0$ 18. 1
19. $x^2 + 4x + 6 = 0$ 19. 0
20. $2x^2 + x - 6 = 0$ 20. 2
21. $3x^2 - 8x = 5$ 21. 2

Solve each problem. Round decimal answers to the nearest hundredth.

22. BUSINESS The revenue y from sales of a certain type of lawn chair can be modeled by the equation $y = -4x^2 + 240x + 80$, where x is the price of each chair. Find the chair price that will give the maximum revenue. 22. \$30
23. Suppose you have 80 feet of fencing to enclose a rectangular pen. You can use one side of a garage as a side of the pen. Determine the dimensions of the pen that will produce a maximum area. 23. 20 m by 40 m
24. PHYSICS If a ball is thrown upward at a speed of 40 feet per second from a point 5 feet above the ground, then the height of the ball above the ground can be modeled by the equation $y = -16x^2 + 40x + 5$. Find the time it will take the ball to hit the ground. 24. 2.6 sec
25. The equation $y = 0.092x^2 + 0.403x + 0.973$ models the following data: (0, 1), (3, 3), (5, 5), (6.5, 8), (7.5, 9), (8, 10). Find the predicted value of y for $x = 5$. Then find the percent error for the predicted and actual values of y for $x = 5$. 25. 5.288, −5.76%

For Question 26, use a separate sheet of paper if necessary.

26. WRITING MATHEMATICS Describe the graph of the quadratic equation $0 = ax^2 + bx + c$ if the equation has two real solutions. Answers should indicate that the parabolic graph has two x-intercepts.

52 South-Western Algebra 1: AN INTEGRATED APPROACH

• • • STANDARDIZED TEST • • •

STUDENT PRODUCED ANSWERS Solve each question and on the answer grid write your answer at the top and fill in the ovals.

Notes: Mixed numbers such as $1\frac{1}{2}$ must be gridded as 1.5 or 3/2. Grid only one answer per question. If your answer is a decimal, enter the most accurate value the grid will accommodate.

1. $\begin{bmatrix} -12 & x + y \\ -3y & w \end{bmatrix} = \begin{bmatrix} -4x & z \\ 15 & 2z \end{bmatrix}$ −4; Lesson 1.6

Find the value of w.

2. Solve the system of inequalities. Find the product of m and n. −36; Lesson 7.4

$$\begin{cases} 5m + 8n = 13 \\ 4m - 5n = 56 \end{cases}$$

3. Find the product of the integer solutions of $|x - 2| < 2$. 6; Lesson 9.4

4. Find the value of the discriminant for the equation $x^2 + 8x = 5$. 84; Lesson 10.5

5. If $f(x) = 4x + 5$ and $g(x) = 2x^2 - 7x + 3$, find $f(-2) + g(4)$. 4; Lessons 4.4 and 4.6

6. A reporter asked the people attending the movie to rate the movie on a scale of 0 to 4. The results are shown in the table at the right.

Score	Frequency
0	6
1	15
2	25
3	42
4	12

Find the mean rating score given by the people at the movie. 2.39; Lessons 1.2 and 1.7

7. Solve the equation $-3x^2 + 10x - 5 = 0$. Grid the greater solution. 2.72; Lesson 10.3

8. A store buys a certain item for $3.50. The store gives the item a selling price by marking it up 32%. Omitting the dollar sign, find the amount of the store's selling price for the item. 4.62; Lesson 3.5

9. Find the slope of a line perpendicular to the line $2x - 9y = 14$. $-\frac{9}{2}$; Lesson 6.3

10. Evaluate the expression $a + b \cdot a - b$ if $a = 3$ and $b = -4$. −5; Lesson 2.2

11. A bag contains 4 red rubber balls, 3 blue rubber balls, and 1 black rubber ball. Azure gets to choose 3 balls and keep them. Azure's favorite color is blue. What is the probability that Azure will get the 3 blue balls with the three picks? Enter the answer as a fraction. $\frac{1}{56}$; Lesson 8.6

12. Solve the equation

$$4n + \frac{1}{2}(5 - 2n) = 5(n + 2).$$

Find $|n|$. $\frac{15}{4}$; Lessons 3.7 and 2.3

13. A football team has scored 31, 27, 35, 24, and 14 points in its five games. They still have two games to play. What is the least number of points the team needs to total in the two games so that they have an average of at least 28 points per game? 65; Lesson 5.7

14. A homeowner wants to plant a vegetable garden and enclose it with 60 ft of fencing. The garden is to be adjacent to the house so it only has to be fenced on three sides. If the garden is to be rectangular, what is the greatest number of square feet the homeowner can enclose? 450; Lesson 10.6

15. Two weeks ago, a worker was earning $100 per week. Last week, the worker's salary was reduced by 10%. This week, the worker's salary was increased by 10%. Omitting the dollar sign, find the worker's current weekly salary. 99; Lesson 3.5

Answers

1. B	**14.** C
2. A	**15.** A
3. A	**16.** A
4. E	**17.** B
5. C	**18.** 4
6. E	**19.** 5
7. B	**20.** 0.5
8. C	**21.** 1
9. C	**22.** 124
10. A	**23.** 24
11. A	**24.** 3
12. B	**25.** 12
13. A	

CHAPTER 10 Standardized Test, page 2 NAME ______

Quantitative Comparison For Questions 12–17, fill in A if the quantity in Column 1 is greater, B if the quantity in Column 2 is greater, C if the two quantities are equal, and D if the relationship cannot be determined.

Grid Response For Questions 18–25, mark your answer on the answer grid provided.

Determine the solutions of each equation. Write the larger solution in the grid. Round decimal answers to the

NAME ______ CLASS ______ DATE ______

CHAPTER 10 STANDARDIZED TEST

Standard Five-Choice For Questions 1–11, fill in the best choice on the answer grid provided.

1. Which is the vertex of the graph of $y = 4x^2 - 16x + 1$?
   A. (2, 1) B. (2, −15) C. (−2, 15) D. (−2, 49) E. (−2, −15)

2. Which is the axis of symmetry of the graph of $y = x^2 - 6x + 3$?
   A. $x = 3$ B. $x = -3$ C. $x = 13$ D. $x = -6$ E. $x = 4$

3. Which is the equation of the graph shown?
   A. $y = x^2 + 2$ B. $y = x^2 - 2$ C. $y = (x - 2)^2$ D. $y = (x + 2)^2$ E. none of these

4. To find the solutions for $x^2 + 4x = 4$, you could find the x-intercepts of the graph for which equation?
   A. $y = x^2 + 4$ B. $y = x^2 - 4$ C. $y = x^2 + 4x + 4$ D. $y = 4$ E. $y = x^2 + 4x - 4$

5. Which equation is the standard form of $6x^2 - 2x = -1$?
   A. $6x^2 - 2x - 1 = 0$ B. $6x^2 + 2x + 1 = 0$ C. $6x^2 - 2x + 1 = 0$ D. $6x^2 + 2x - 1 = 0$ E. All of these

6. Which item shows the solutions for $3x^2 + 6 = 24$?
   A. ± 3 B. $\pm 3\sqrt{2}$ C. $\pm\sqrt{10}$ D. $\pm 2\sqrt{6}$ E. $\pm\sqrt{6}$

7. What is the value of the discriminant for $2x^2 - 3x + 1 = 0$?
   A. 9 B. 1 C. 2 D. $\frac{3}{4}$ E. $\frac{1}{8}$

8. For what values of k will $x^2 + kx + 4 = 0$ have exactly one solution?
   A. ±2 B. ±3 C. ±4 D. 0 E. 1

9. Which shows the solutions of $3x^2 - 8x - 3 = 0$?
   A. $3, \frac{1}{3}$ B. $-3, -\frac{1}{3}$ C. $3, -\frac{1}{3}$ D. $-3, \frac{1}{3}$ E. None of these

10. Suppose you have 100 feet of fencing to enclose a rectangular area for a pen. One side of a barn will be used as a side of the pen. Which dimensions for the pen will give the largest area?
    A. 25 ft by 50 ft B. 20 ft by 60 ft C. 24 ft by 52 ft D. 50 ft by 50 ft E. 40 ft by 10 ft

11. A set of data has a y-value of 3 when $x = 1$. A graphing utility gives the function $y = 0.986x^2 + 2.125x + 0.093$ as a model for the data. What is the percent error for $x = 1$ between the actual and predicted values of y?
    A. 6.8% B. 0.68% C. 0.068% D. 68% E. None of these

South-Western Algebra 1: AN INTEGRATED APPROACH 57

Chapter Opener

DATA ACTIVITY, PAGES 462–463

1.

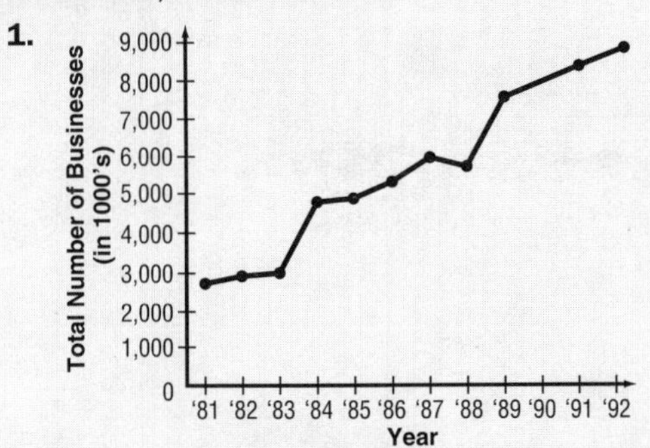

2. 1983–1984, 1988–1989
3. Yes. Answers will vary. There were more failures, but there were also more businesses in '92 than in '86. A type of rate is needed to make a comparison.
4. 1981: 61; 1982: 88; 1983: 110; 1984: 107; 1985: 115; 1986: 120; 1987: 102; 1988: 98; 1989: 65; 1990: 76; 1991: 107; 1992: 110
5. Answers will vary.

Lesson 10.1

THINK BACK/WORKING TOGETHER, PAGE 465

2. c. x changes 15 units and y changes 30 units

EXPLORE, PAGES 465–466

5. Answers will vary.

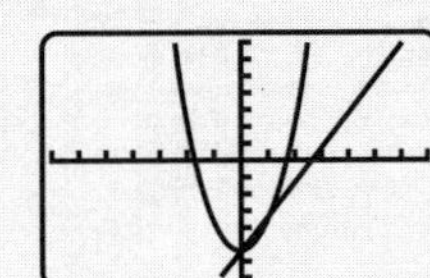

9. Answers will vary.

MAKE CONNECTIONS, PAGE 466–467

11. a. $y_1 = x^2 - x - 6$

x	y	Difference Column 1 (Change in y)	Difference Column 2 (Change in the change in y)
−4	14		
−3	6	−8	
−2	0	−6	2
−1	−4	−4	2
0	−6	−2	2
1	−6	0	2
2	−4	2	2
3	0	4	2
4	6	6	2
5	14	8	2

b. $y_2 = x^2 - 2x - 3$
Table will resemble the one in 11a, except the change in the change in y will be 2.

c. $y_3 = 3x^2 + x + 2$
Table will resemble the one in 11a, except the change in the change in y will be 60.

d. $y_4 = -2x^2 + 4$
Table will resemble the one in 11a, except the change in the change in y will be −4.

12. y_1, y_2, y_3 decrease then increase; y_4 increases, then decreases
13. As x increases, the values in Difference Column 1 may increase or decrease. The values in Difference Column 2 remain constant.
14. The graph is translated vertically.

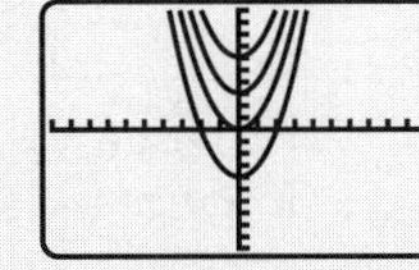

16. When $a > 0$, the graph opens upward; when $a < 0$, it opens downward. The graph also changes shape. When $|a| > 1$, the graph narrows; when $|a| < 1$, the graph widens.

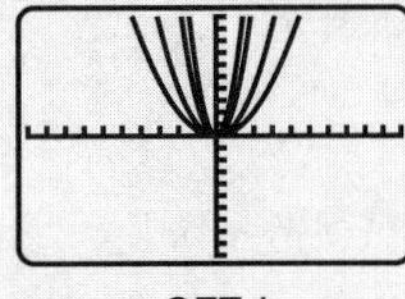

SET I

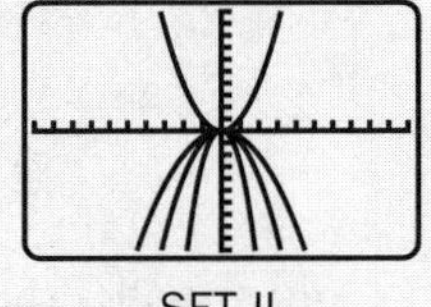

SET II

SUMMARIZE, PAGE 467

21.

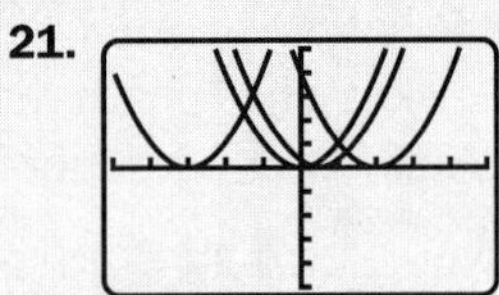

Lesson 10.2

CHECK UNDERSTANDING, PAGE 469

Answers will vary. Examples include (−1, 1) and (1, 1), (−2, 4) and (2, 4) and (0.5, 0.25) and (−0.5, 0.25).

COMMUNICATING ABOUT ALGEBRA, PAGE 469

The x-coordinate of the vertex is the value midway between the two x-intercepts.

TRY THESE, PAGE 472

19.

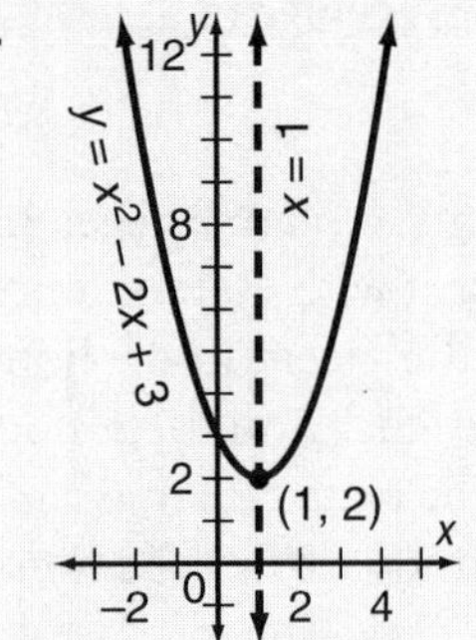

20.

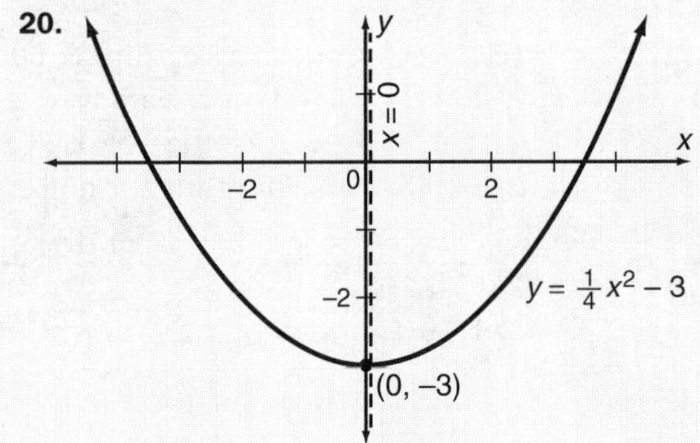

21.

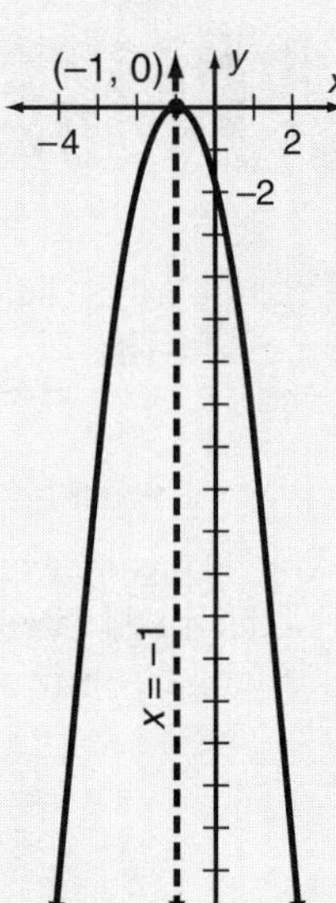

23. Since the equation of the axis of symmetry is $x = \frac{-b}{2a}$, which is a vertical line, it must be parallel to the y-axis. If $b = 0$, it is the y-axis.

PRACTICE, PAGES 472–474

8. $\left(\frac{2}{3}, -\frac{37}{3}\right)$, $x = \frac{2}{3}$
9. (−1, −10), $x = -1$
10. (6, −20), $x = 6$
11. (−4, 22), $x = -4$
12. (−12, −41), $x = -12$

25.

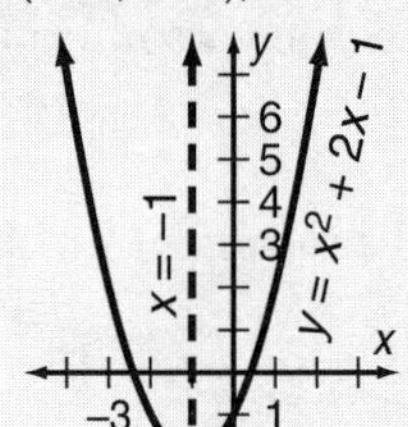

26.

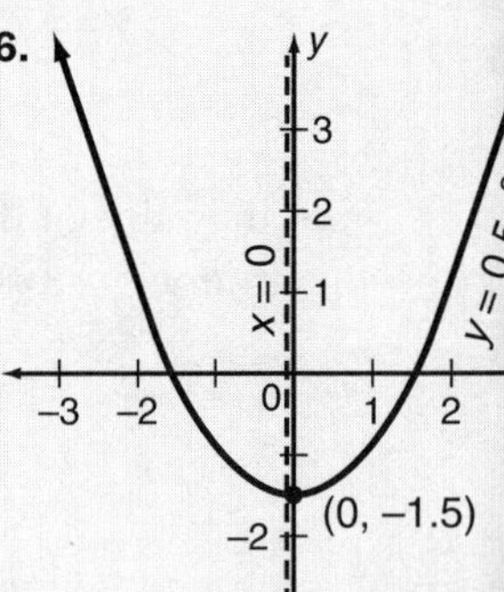

27.

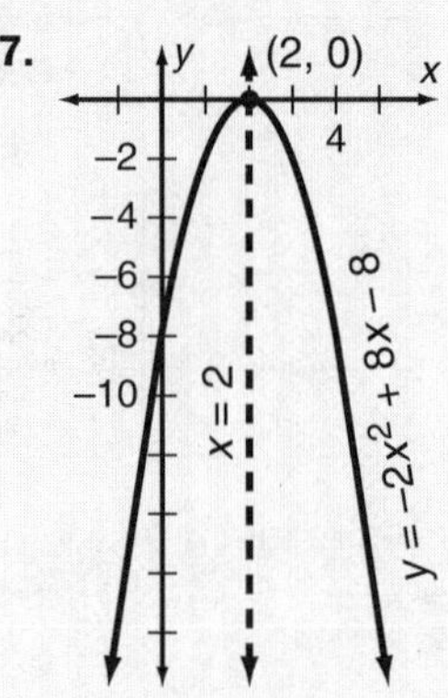

29. (312.50, 103.91); the high point will be 3.9 ft above point A and 312.5 ft from point A

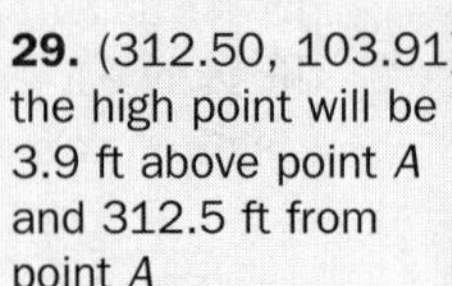

30.

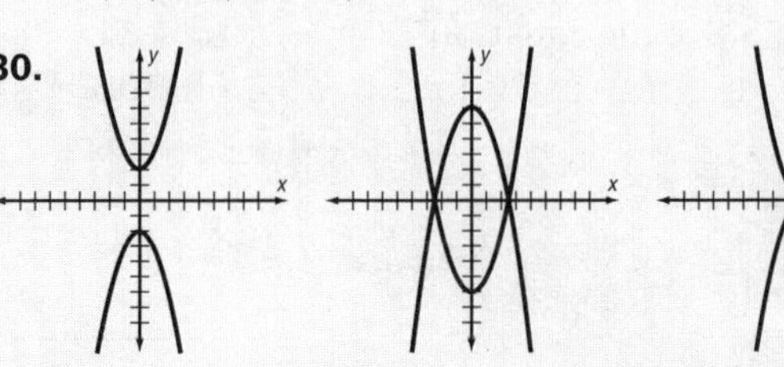

EXTEND, PAGES 474–475

36.

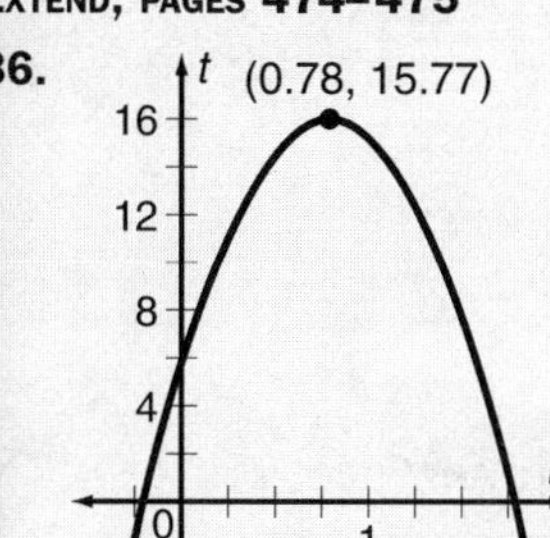

THINK CRITICALLY, PAGE 475

42. Both move the graph to the left if they are positive and to the right if they are negative.

43. c moves each graph up c units if c is positive and down c units if c is negative.

45. They all have a vertex of (0, 0).

Since $\frac{-b}{2a} = \frac{0}{2a} = 0$, $x = 0$. Since $y = a(0)^2$, $y \neq 0$. The equation of their axes of symmetry is $x = 0$.

MIXED REVIEW, PAGE 475

49. up 3 units; right 1 unit; rays closer to y-axis

51. down 1 unit; left 3 units; rays farther from y-axis

ALGEBRAWORKS, PAGE 476

2.

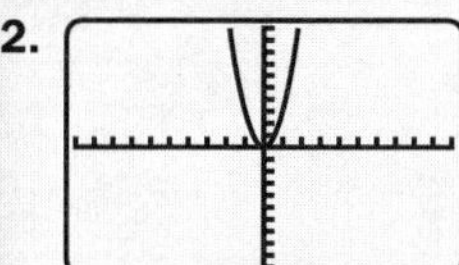

5. No. Best Pizza is giving 79 in.^{2} of free pizza, whereas Rossi's is giving 113 in.^{2} of free pizza.

6. Adding 2 in. to the radius of a 14-in.-diameter pie adds about 101 in.^{2} to the area. Adding 2 in. to the radius of an 18-in.-diameter pie adds about 126 in.^{2} to the area.

Lesson 10.3

EXPLORE/WORKING TOGETHER, PAGE 477

3. twice; at (5, 0) and at (–5, 0); the x-coordinates match the solutions to the equation $x^2 - 25 = 0$

4. The graph touches the x-axis once at (1, 0) and the x-coordinate matches the solution to the equation $x^2 - 2x + 1 = 0$.

5. The graph does not cross the x-axis and there are no solutions to the equation $x^2 + 1 = 0$.

Lesson 10.4

COMMUNICATING ABOUT ALGEBRA, PAGE 484

o. If $c - b \geq 0$, there is at least one real solution.

TRY THESE, PAGE 486

3. two real solutions when $\frac{c - b}{a} > 0$

one real solution when $\frac{c - b}{a} = 0$

no real solutions when $\frac{c - b}{a} < 0$ or when $a = 0$

Lesson 10.5

EXPLORE, PAGE 490

6. For each row, the values in the last two columns are the solutions of the quadratic with values of a, b, c.

7. They are formulas for finding the solutions to the quadratic equation $ax^2 + bx + c = 0$.

PRACTICE, PAGES 494–495

33. The parabola has no x-intercepts.

THINK CRITICALLY, PAGE 496

48. $\frac{7 \pm \sqrt{49 - 4 \bullet 2 \bullet (-4)}}{2 \bullet 2} = \frac{7 \pm 9}{4}$,

$x = 4$ or $x = -\frac{1}{2}$

The graph crosses the x-axis at 4 and $-\frac{1}{2}$.

ALGEBRAWORKS, PAGE 497

1.

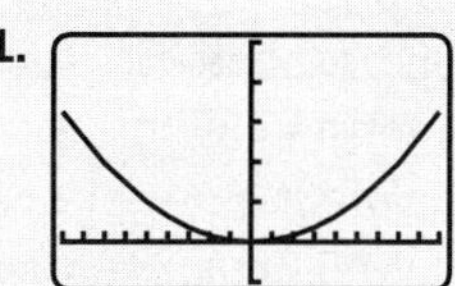

Lesson 10.6

EXPLORE THE PROBLEM, PAGES 498–499

4. l: 95 ft, 90 ft, 85 ft, 80 ft, 75 ft, 70 ft, 65 ft, 60 ft, 55 ft, 50 ft, 45 ft, 40 ft, 35 ft, 30 ft, 25 ft, 20 ft, 15 ft, 10 ft, 5 ft, 1 ft

A: 475 ft^2, 900 ft^2, 1275 ft^2, 1600 ft^2, 1875 ft^2, 2100 ft^2, 2275 ft^2, 2400 ft^2, 2475 ft^2, 2500 ft^2, 2475 ft^2, 2400 ft^2, 2275 ft^2, 2100 ft^2, 1875 ft^2, 1600 ft^2, 1275 ft^2, 900 ft^2, 475 ft^2, 99 ft^2

6. For every rectangle with a width greater than 50 ft, there is an "equal" rectangle with width less than 50 ft.

8. There are no rectangles with an area greater than that of a 50-ft square.

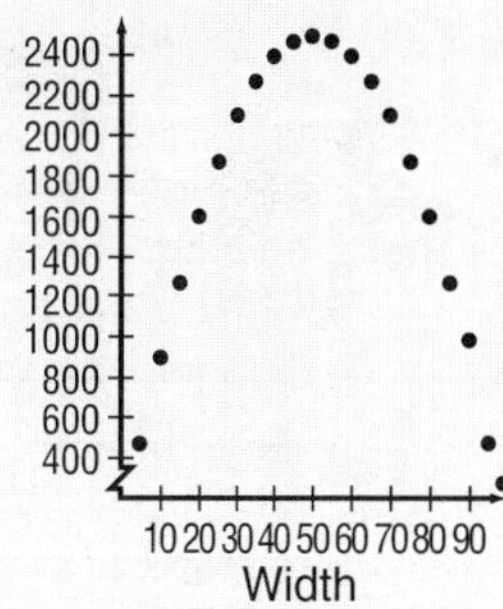

INVESTIGATE FURTHER, PAGE 499

11. The graph of $-w^2 + 100w$ is the graph of w^2 reflected over the x-axis, and translated right 50 units and up 2500 units.

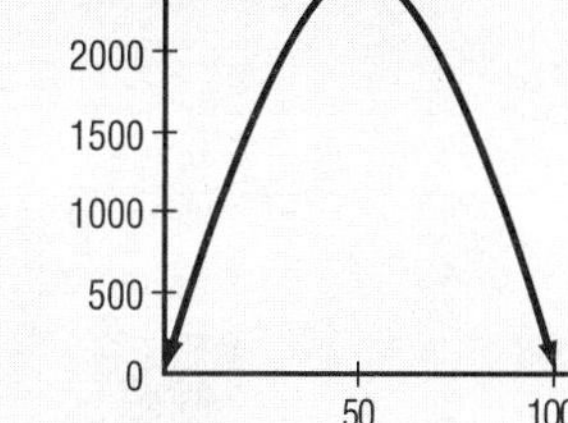

12. (50, 2500); yes

APPLY THE STRATEGY, PAGES 499–500

13. **d.** Divide the total fencing by 3. Each side must be 40 ft; $A = 1600$ ft^2.

14. **c.** The garden would be 24 by 48 ft; each section would be 576 ft^2.

d. 450 ft^2

15. **b.** Yes; the amount of fencing will change.
For a 4×100 rectangle, $P = 208$;
for a 5×80 rectangle, $P = 170$;
for an 8×50 rectangle, $P = 116$;
for a 10×40 rectangle, $P = 100$;
for a 20×20 rectangle, $P = 80$.

e. $P(w) = 2w + 2\left(\frac{400}{w}\right) = 2w + \left(\frac{800}{w}\right)$

Descriptions will vary.

REVIEW PROBLEM SOLVING STRATEGIES, PAGE 501

WELL, WELL

a. 70 in. **b.** $70 - x$ **c.** $2(70 - x)$

d. no; $70 + 2x$ to represent the final depth of the well

e. 17.5 in.; 52.5 in.; 105 in. or 8 ft 8 in.

REVA'S GLASSES

The juice from the small glass was $\frac{1}{6}$ of the total contents of the pitcher, and the juice from the larger glass was $\frac{2}{9}$ of the total. Add: $\frac{7}{18}$ of the total was juice, so $\frac{11}{18}$ was water.

MEASUREMENT MARKS

4 marks are needed; one possible set includes marks at 2, 5, 8, and 11

Additional Answers continued on page 671D

CHAPTER 11 POLYNOMIALS AND EXPONENTS

Today's mathematics opens doors to tomorrow's jobs. As successive waves of immigrants have used this country's educational system to secure better lives for themselves and their children, so today's children the world over are using mathematical training as a platform on which to build up their lives. America's children deserve the same chance.

"Everybody Counts. A Report to the Nation on the Future of Mathematics Education." Board on Mathematical Sciences [and] Mathematical Sciences Education Board, National Research Council. 1989 National Academy of Sciences, Washington, D.C., page 1

The Big Question: Why study polynomials and exponents?

Polynomials are algebraic expressions that include variables, powers of variables, numbers, and sums, differences, and products of these elements. Exponents appear in polynomials and in scientific notation. Polynomials can be used to model many real life phenomena in science, social science, and business. Although the theme of this chapter is flight, the students will also see applications from astronomy, biology, chemistry, demography, finance, history, physics, recreation, sports, and travel.

Vocabulary

- binomial
- constant rate of speed
- degree of a monomial
- degree of a polynomial
- degree of a variable
- FOIL
- monomial
- polynomial
- properties of exponents:
  - negative exponents
  - power of a power
  - power of a product
  - power of a quotient rule
  - product of powers
  - quotient rule
- reciprocal
- scientific notation
- simplest form
- standard notation
- term
- trinomial
- uniform rate of speed
- zero property of exponents

Using the Graphic Organizer

Project a copy of the Graphic Organizer Transparency for Chapter 11. Explain that the focus of this chapter is performing operations with polynomials. Tell students that the graphic organizer shows one way to organize ideas about polynomials and exponents. Review the information on the graphic organizer, pointing out that operations on polynomials use the distributive property and properties of exponents.

Ask some preview questions; for example, what property allows you to simplify an expression like $3x + 2x$? How is the expression y^2 different from y^5? How are these two expressions the same?

One way to organize ideas about polynomials and exponents is shown below.

One way to organize ideas about polynomials and exponents is shown.

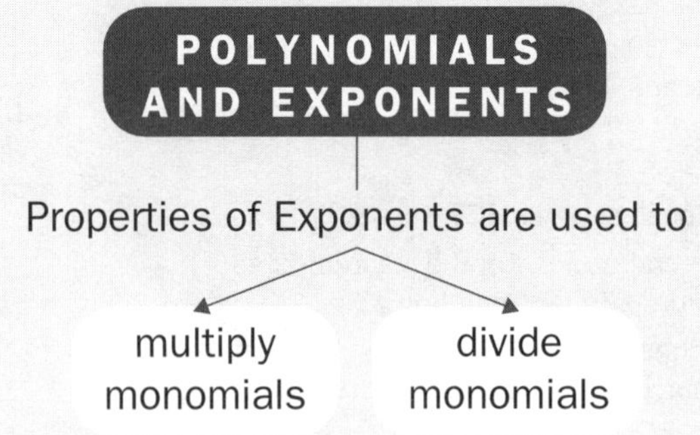

Distributive Property of Multiplication-Addition is used to

add polynomials | subtract polynomials | multiply polynomials

Try It Use a different plan. Try organizing the ideas pertaining to each operation.

Explore the Chapter Theme:

Exploring Flight

One frontier of the twentieth century has been flight and space exploration. Aerospace ngineers design, develop, test and elp manufacture commercial and nilitary aircraft, missiles, and pacecraft. In addition to engineering obs, there are many different jobs equiring technical skills in nanufacturing, computers, and obotics. The benefits of flight xploration exceed what has actually een accomplished in terms of ransport. Photographs from irplanes and spacecraft have added remendously to our knowledge of arth and the solar system.

Skills Needed for Success in Aerospace Careers

1. Work with a team that includes engineers, technicians, and computer operators.
2. Use mathematical and scientific knowledge to develop designs for specific projects.
3. Use computer modeling and computer assisted design (CAD) to test design ideas.
4. Use analytical thinking skills to process data from computer simulations and other design tests.
5. Write and speak clearly to be able to communicate ideas and to make reports.
6. Accept the challenge to go beyond current achievements in science and technology.
7. Work cooperatively; be able to contribute ideas and respond to ideas from others.
8. Use critical thinking skills to troubleshoot design and/or manufacturing problems.
9. Be curious and able to look at problems creatively.

Investigate Further

Have students identify a career related to exploring flight that interests them. Tell students to go to the library and find more information about the career. For example, students might find out about educational requirements including specific courses, degrees, examinations, or licenses required. Students should research the average salary range for the career. Have students share their findings in a class discussion about career opportunities.

Here is a list of jobs and educational requirements for jobs related to exploring flight.

Jobs Requiring 1 to 2 Years of Technical Training

- Aerial Photographer
- Aircraft Mechanic
- Machinist
- Model-Development Technician
- Tool Programmer
- Mechanical Engineering Technician
- Computer Operator

Jobs Requiring 4 + Years of College

- Aerospace Engineer
- Electro-Optical Engineer
- Electromagnetic Engineer
- Electrical Engineer
- Computer Programmer
- Systems Engineer
- Engineering Project Manager

CHAPTER 11 PLANNING GUIDE

Lessons	Text Pages	NCTM Standards	ASSIGNMENTS Basic	Average	Enriched	Ancillaries	Manipulatives	Technology
Chapter Introduction	514–516	1, 2, 3, 4, 8, 10				Video Discussion Guide		Video, Transparency 6
11.1 Algebra Workshop: Multiply and Divide Variables	517–520	1, 2, 3, 4, 5, 8	1–41	1–41	1–42	S 27; M 11	Algeblocks, Quadrant Mats, 517–520	Transparencies 12, 21
11.2 Multiply Monomials	521–526	1, 2, 3, 4, 5, 8, 11, 14	1–28, 33, 35, 41–46, PC1–4, AW1–4	3–39, 41–46, PC1–4, AW1–4	3–8, 11–46, PC1–4, AW1–4	W 11.2; R 11.2; P 11.2; E 11.2; Q 11.2; S 28	Algeblocks, Quadrant Mats, 522	Transparencies 12, 21, 62
11.3 Divide Monomials	527–531	1, 2, 3, 4, 5, 8, 14	1–19, 21–24, 27, 29, 33–36, MR38–51	3–27, 29–30, 33–36, MR38–51	9–37, MR38–51	W 11.3; R 11.3; P 11.3; E 11.3; Q 11.3; T 26	Algeblocks, Quadrant Mats, 528, 530	Transparencies 12, 21, 62
11.4 Scientific Notation	532–537	1, 2, 3, 4, 5	1–24, 26–28, 30, 32, 34, 35, 37, PC1–5, AW1–7	1–32, 34–38, PC1–5, AW1–7	1–39, PC1–5, AW1–7	W 11.4; R 11.4; P 11.4; E 11.4; Q 11.4; T 27		Calculators, Transparency 6
11.5 Algebra Workshop: Add and Subtract Expressions	538–540	1, 2, 3, 4, 5, 8	1–40	1–40	1–41		Algeblocks, Quadrant Mats, 538–540	Transparencies 12, 13
11.6 Add and Subtract Polynomials	541–547	1, 2, 3, 4, 5, 8	1–28, 33–36, MR38–47, PC1–8	1–30, 33–36, MR38–47, PC1–8	3–37, MR38–47, PC1–8	W 11.6; R 11.6; P 11.6; E 11.6; Q 11.6	Algeblocks, Quadrant Mats, 543, 545	Calculator, Transparencies 12, 13, 78–80 Graphing Utility
11.7 Algebra Workshop: Patterns in Multiplying Polynomials	548–550	1, 2, 3, 4, 5, 8	1–35	1–35	1–36		Algeblocks, Quadrant Mats, 548–550	Transparencies 12, 21
11.8 Multiply Polynomials	551–557	1, 2, 3, 4, 5, 8	1–30, 33–35, 37, 39–41, 44, 46–47, PC1–3	3–42, 44–47, PC1–3	4–47, PC1–3	W 11.8; R 11.8; P 11.8; E 11.8; Q 11.8	Graph Paper	Transparencies 34, 64, 65
11.9 Problem Solving File: Rate, Time, and Distance Problems	558–561	1, 2, 3, 4, 5	1–16	1–16	1–17	R 11.9; P 11.9		Transparency 1

NCTM STANDARDS

1. Mathematics as Problem Solving
2. Mathematics as Communication
3. Mathematics as Reasoning
4. Mathematical Connections
5. Algebra
6. Functions
7. Geometry from a Synthetic Perspective
8. Geometry from an Algebraic Perspective
9. Trigonometry
10. Statistics
11. Probability
12. Discrete Mathematics
13. Conceptual Underpinnings of Calculus
14. Mathematical Structure

ANCILLARIES

W = Warm Up
R = Reteaching
P = Extra Practice
E = Enrichment
Q = Lesson Quiz
T = Technology Activity
M = Multicultural Connection
S = Study Skills Activity

ADDITIONAL RESOURCES

pplications	Career Connections	Cooperative Learning	Learning Styles	Strand Integration/ Math Connection
	Chapter Poster			
		Paired partners, 517 (Think Back/Working Together)	Linguistic/Interpersonal, 517–519; Tactile, Kinesthetic, 517–520; Visual, 517–520	Problem Solving, Modeling, Critical Thinking, Geometry
eronautics, 525; eometry, 525; Physics, 25; Probability, 525; cience, 525	AlgebraWorks: Machinist, 526	Paired partners, 521 (Explore/Working Together); Small groups, 525 (Project Connection)	Linguistic/Interpersonal, 521–523, 525; Tactile/ Kinesthetic, 521, 522; Visual, 521–522, 524–526	Problem Solving, Modeling, Patterns, Number Theory, Writing, Critical Thinking, Geometry, Probability
stronomy, 531; emography, 531; eometry, 530		Paired partners, 527 (Explore/Working Together)	Visual, 527–528, 530–531; Tactile/ Kinesthetic, 528, 530; Linguistic/ Interpersonal, 527, 529	Problem Solving, Patterns, Modeling, Writing, Geometry, Number Theory, Critical Thinking
eronautics, 536; stronomy, 533–535; iology, 535; Chemistry, 35; History, 535; Physics, 35; Science, 536	AlgebraWorks: Aerial Photographer, 537	Small groups, 536 (Project Connection)	Visual, 532–536, 534 (TE); Linguistic/ Interpersonal, 534, 536	Problem Solving, Patterns, Number Theory, Writing, Critical Thinking
		Paired partners, 538 (Explore)	Linguistic/Interpersonal, 538; Tactile/Kinesthetic, 538–540; Visual, 538–540	Problem Solving, Modeling, Writing, Critical Thinking
eronautics, 546–547; eometry, 544–545; avel, 546		Small groups, 547 (Project Connection)	Linguistic/Interpersonal, 542, 547; Tactile/Kinesthetic, 543; Visual, 541, 543–545, 547	Problem Solving, Patterns, Writing, Critical Thinking, Geometry, Modeling
		Paired Partners, 548 (Explore)	Linguistic/Interpersonal, 548, 550; Tactile/Kinesthetic, Visual, 548–550	Problem Solving, Modeling, Writing, Critical Thinking
eronautics, 557; emography, 557; nance, 556; Geometry, 55–556; History, 556		Paired partners, 551 (Explore/Working Together); Small groups, 557 (Project Connection)	Visual, 551–553, 555–557; Tactile, 557; Linguistic/Interpersonal, 551, 552, 557	Problem Solving, Modeling, Critical Thinking, Writing, Geometry
ecreation, 560; Sports, 60; Travel, 560			Visual, 558–561; Symbolic, 558–561	Problem Solving, Writing, Logical Reasoning

PACING GUIDE

Lessons	Regular Classes	2-year Algebra 1 Classes	Blocked Classes
11.1	1	2	½
11.2	1	2	½
11.3	1	2	½
11.4	1	2	½
11.5	1	2	½
11.6	1	2	½
11.7	1	2	½
11.8	1	2	½
11.9	1	2	1
Review	1	1	1
Test	1	1	1
Cumulative Test	1	1	1
Total Classes	12	21	8

SESSMENT OPTIONS

udent Edition
apter Assessment
Chapter Test
Performance Assessment
Project Assessment
ndardized Tests

Chapter Resource Book
Chapter Test, Form A
Chapter Test, Form B
Standardized Chapter Test
Portfolio Item: Self-Assessment
Portfolio Assessment Form

MicroExam II

PREVIEW THE CHAPTER

Take a Look Ahead Have students read the previewing suggestions and then scan the chapter looking for new and familiar things. Give students time to make notes in their journals. Discuss student answers to the previewing questions.

Connecting to Career Opportunities Have the students read the descriptions of the AlgebraWorks features for this chapter. Ask students to identify the careers mentioned. **machinists and aerial photographers** Ask students if they know anyone who works at these jobs. Discuss the types of educational background usually required for each of the careers. For example, machinists usually have received additional technical training after high school while some aerial photographers may get on-the-job training.

Investigate Further Explain to students that as they study this chapter they should look for examples of other careers related to flight. Ask students to determine one way in which algebra can be used in that career. Encourage students to write questions in their journals about other jobs related to flight that they may want to learn more about.

USING THE DATA ACTIVITY

Introduce the Data Activity Have students read the introductory copy and identify some milestones in the history of flight of which they are aware.

Skill Focus Read the skills listed and discuss with students what they think each means. Ask students to suggest problems that might involve the skill being discussed.

11 Polynomials and Exponents

Take a Look AHEAD

Make notes about things that look new.

- Look for places where you will be expected to multiply and divide terms with exponents in them.
- Locate two different pages where negative exponents appear. What will you be doing with negative exponents?

Make notes about things that look familiar.

- Find five different examples of subtraction in this chapter.
- What other operations are used in this chapter?

DATA Activity

Up, Up, and Away

Each of the seven aircraft in the Hall of Air Transportation at the National Air and Space Museum in Washington, D.C., played a role in the development of air transportation. In the early years of commercial aviation, most revenue came from mail routes flown by planes such as the Pitcairn PA-5 Mailwing. Although the 10-seat Boeing 247D expanded passenger travel, it was the Douglas DC-3 that changed the industry. With 21 seats, it was the first plane to make a profit transporting people.

SKILL FOCUS

- Add, subtract, multiply, and divide real numbers.
- Round decimal numbers.
- Determine ratios.
- Use scaled dimensions.
- Estimate metric and customary units.

Exploring FLIGHT

In this chapter, you will see how:

- **Machinists** use equations to help them determine how much force is required by a metal punch machine to make rivet holes in sheets of metal. (Lesson 11.2, page 526)
- **Aerial Photographers** use equations to help them compare the distance between objects in a photograph to the actual distance between real objects on the ground. (Lesson 11.4, page 537)

1–6 See Additional Answers.

	Pitcairn PA-5 Mailwing	Boeing 247D	Douglas DC-3
Wingspan	10.05 m	22.55 m	28.95 m
Length	6.67 m	15.72 m	19.66 m
Height	2.83 m	3.70 m	5 m
Maximum Weight	1,139 kg	7,623 kg	11,430 kg

Use the table to answer the following questions.

1. How much greater is the wingspan of the Douglas DC-3 than that of the Boeing 247D?
2. What is the ratio of the Pitcairn's length to its height? Round to one decimal place.
3. If you were making a scale model of the Douglas DC-3 where 2 cm represents 0.5 m, how long would your model be? Round to one decimal place.
4. What is the wingspan of the Boeing 247D expressed in feet?
5. When expressed in customary units, would the Boeing's maximum weight be closer to 18,600 lb or 16,800 lb?
6. **Working Together** Research some of the highlights in the development of air transportation and prepare a timeline of major events in the history of flight.

Study the Data The chart compares three different early airplanes according to four measures. Ask students to explain what each measure means. **wingspan: length from tip of one wing to tip of other wing; length: distance from nose to end of tail; height: distance from ground to uppermost point; maximum weight: the greatest possible weight the plane is designed to carry** Point out that all measures are in S.I. (metric) units.

Complete the Data Activity

For Item 1, make sure students compare the correct measures and subtract them.

For Item 2, point out that length should be in the numerator and height in the denominator of the ratio fraction. Have students use calculators to find the decimal equivalent of the ratio.

For Item 3, have students write a proportion. If x represents the length of the model in centimeters, then they must solve the proportion $2/0.5 = x/19.66$.

For Item 4, students must use a conversion factor. One meter equals 3.28 feet so students can multiply 22.55 by 3.28. They should round their answers to two decimal places.

For Item 5, students can estimate. One kilogram equals 2.2 pounds. The students may estimate that the weight of the Boeing is 8000 kg and therefore the weight in pounds would be about 16,000 lb.

For Item 6, books on the history of flight, encyclopedias, and almanacs will all contain information students can use in the timeline.

South-Western Algebra 1
Chapter Theme Video or Videodisc

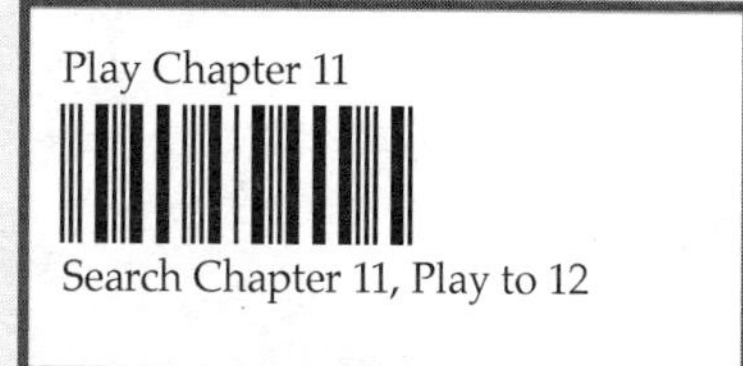

Play Chapter 11
Search Chapter 11, Play to 12

INTRODUCING THE PROJECT

Project Goal Discuss the project's big idea: How do makers of airplanes know their planes will fly? How do they test their ideas?

Getting Ready Collect pictures or articles that show new aircraft designs. Use them as a springboard for discussion about the process of design.

FACILITATING THE PROJECT

Getting Started Encourage the whole class to get involved in the rule making. The class should decide whether to create a paper airplane that goes farthest or one that stays airborne longer. Form small teams of students to work on the project.

Setting Project Benchmarks Make sure that the students are aware of the project schedule in the Project Planning Calendar and the due dates for each of the benchmarks. You may find the TGT cooperative learning approach appropriate for the Project Assessment stage of this activity.

a. Research ways of constructing paper airplanes. (Project/Chapter Opener)

b. Explore aspect ratio and the effects of drag on aircraft flight. (Project Connection 11.2)

c. Find the center of gravity on a paper airplane. (Project Connection 11.4)

d. Explore how a parachute's size and shape affect its drop time. (Project Connection 11.6)

e. Demonstrate how the design of an airplane's wing affects the plane's lift (Bernoulli's principle). (Project Connection 11.8)

f. Determine design features that give the best performance. (Project Assessment)

Suggest that students make sub-goals for each goal and include subgoals in their calendar.

Aspects of Flight

Flying, gliding, and soaring above mountaintops is easy for birds, but thousands of years passed from when humans started wondering about flight until they figured out how flight works. Building a machine that could lift itself and several hundred people off the ground and stay airborne for long distances was no easy task. During this project, you will explore different aspects of flight and make a paper airplane for a team competition.

PROJECT GOAL

To make a paper airplane that will fly the greatest distance or stay airborne the longest.

Getting Started

1. As a class, discuss rules for a paper airplane competition. For example, does the plane have to be folded from a single sheet of paper? Are there any size limitations? How many "extra" materials, such as rubber bands, tape, clips, string, and so on, is each team allowed to use?

2. Research ways of constructing paper airplanes. Many books are available on the subject. One is *Paper Airplane Book* published by the American Association for the Advancement of Science. Another is *Experimenting with Air and Flight* by O.H. Walker.

PROJECT Connections

Lesson 11.2, page 525: Learn how two different types of drag affect aircraft performance.
Lesson 11.4, page 536: Experiment to locate a paper airplane's center of gravity.
Lesson 11.6, page 547: Construct several model parachutes to determine design features that work best.
Lesson 11.8, page 557: Find out what Bernoulli's principle is and how an aircraft is able to lift off.
Chapter Assessment, page 565: Have the group airplane competition. Record and analyze data to determine design features that give best performance.

11.1 Algebra Workshop
Multiply and Divide Variables

Think Back/Working Together

- To multiply integers using Algeblocks, use a Quadrant Mat and unit blocks. Work with a partner. Set up unit blocks on the Quadrant Mat as shown at the right.

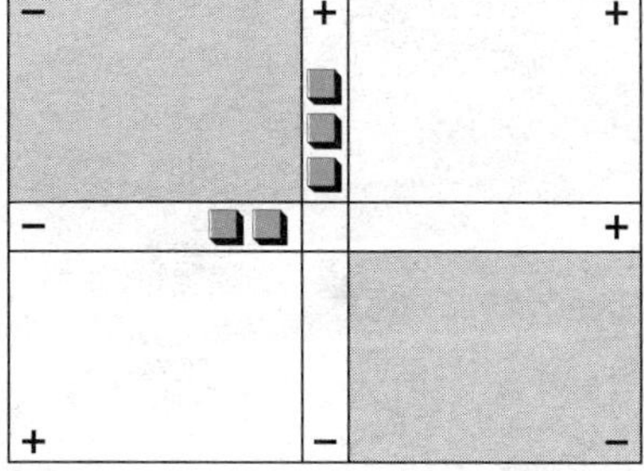

1. What multiplication is shown? $-2(3)$
2. Use unit blocks to complete the model. What is the product? -6
3. With blocks, make a model that shows that the product of two negative integers is positive. models will vary, possible answer: $-2(-3) = 6$

Explore

- The Quadrant Mat can be used to model multiplication with variables.

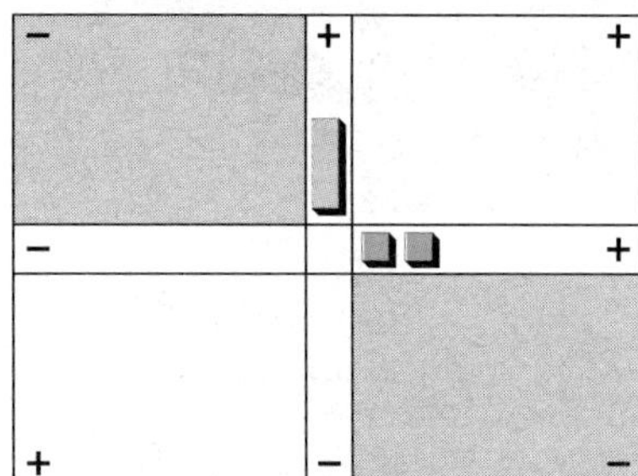

4. What multiplication is shown at the right? $2(x)$
5. Use Algeblocks to complete the model for this product. Write an expression for the product. $2x$

Write a multiplication sentence for each model.

6. 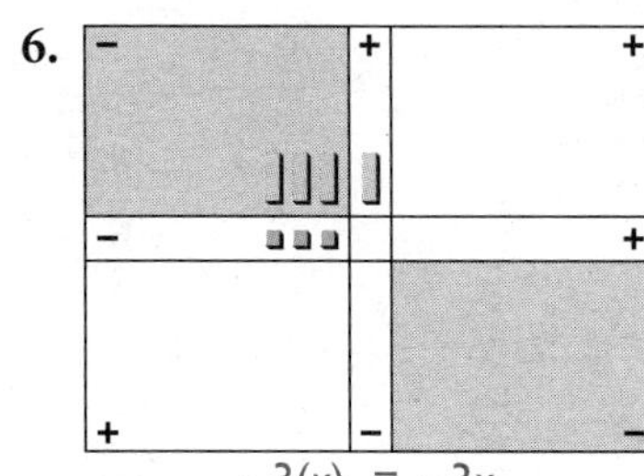

$-3(x) = -3x$

7. 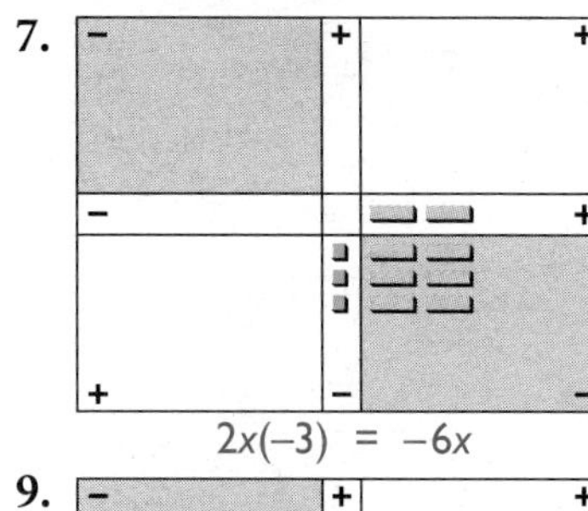

$2x(-3) = -6x$

8. 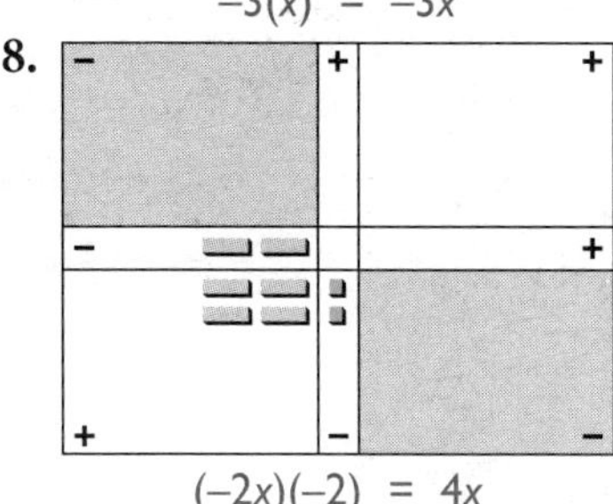

$(-2x)(-2) = 4x$

9. 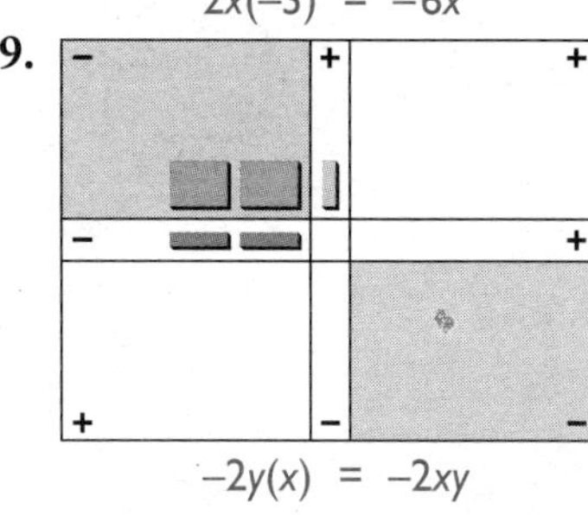

$-2y(x) = -2xy$

SPOTLIGHT ON LEARNING

WHAT? In this lesson you will learn
- to use Algeblocks to model multiplication and division of variables.

WHY? Algeblocks can help you to understand multiplication and division of variables useful in solving a variety of practical problems.

ALGEBLOCKS MODEL

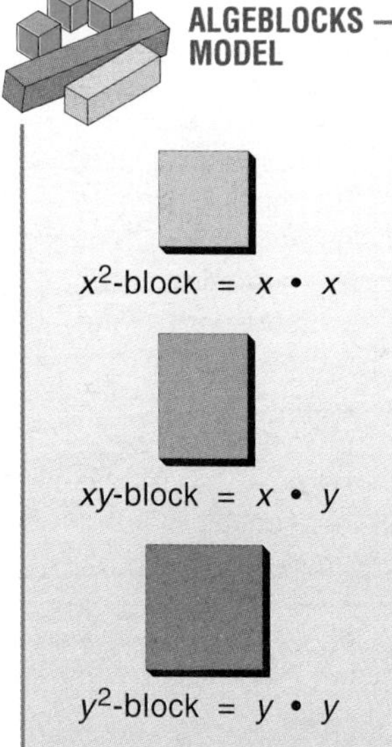

LESSON PLANNING

Objective

▶ Model multiplication and division of variables using Algeblocks.

Resources

Transparencies 12, 21
Student Handbook
Study Skills Activity 27
Multicultural Connection 11, African American: Focus on Space

Materials/Manipulatives

Algeblocks
Quadrant Mats

ASSIGNMENTS

Basic: 1–41

Average: 1–41

Enriched: 1–42

1 MOTIVATE

Think Back/Working Together Have students share their models for Question 3. Then have them model 3(–2) and explain how this model differs from that of –2(3). **Different parts of each axis were used to model each expression.**

Explain that since multiplication and division are inverse operations, Algeblocks can also be used to show division. Show students the following model and ask them what division the model shows. **$-8 \div 2$**

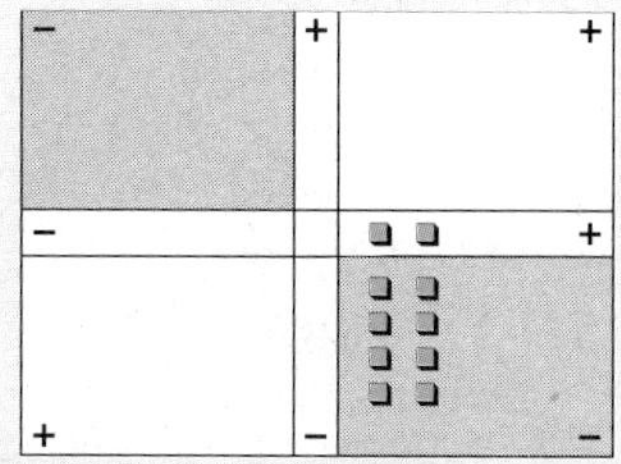

Ask how they can determine the quotient. **the vertical axis shows the answer; –4** Have students take turns modeling other examples of multiplication and division with their partners determining what multiplication or division is shown and giving the quotient.

2 FACILITATE

Explore After students have completed Exercises 4 and 5, ask them to describe how to model –2*x*. **the same as 2*x* except place the two unit blocks on the negative part of the horizontal axis** After students have completed Exercise 12, ask them to write the following numbers in factored form and then to simplify each: 4^3, 2^5, $(-1/2)^3$, $(-3)^4$, $-(-2)^7$. $\mathbf{4^3 = 4 \cdot 4 \cdot 4 = 64}$; $\mathbf{2^5 = 2 \cdot 2 \cdot 2 \cdot 2 \cdot 2 = 32}$; $\mathbf{(-1/2)^3 = -1/2 \cdot -1/2 \cdot -1/2 = -1/8}$; $\mathbf{(-3)^4 = -3 \cdot -3 \cdot -3 \cdot -3 = 81}$; $\mathbf{-(-2)^7 = -(-2 \cdot -2 \cdot -2 \cdot -2 \cdot -2 \cdot -2 \cdot -2) = -(-128) = 128}$ Have students work individually to complete Exercises 18–23. Ask a student to describe how to use Algeblocks to show the product for Exercise 21. **Place three *x*-blocks on the positive part of the horizontal axis and two *y*-blocks on the negative part of the vertical axis. Form a rectangle using *xy*-blocks in the quadrant bounded by these blocks and matching the *x*- and *y*-sides. Read the answer, –6*xy*, from the mat.** Have students discuss Exercises 24 and 25. Then have them work individually to complete Exercises 26–32 and compare their answers.

Algebra Workshop

Remember, an exponent tells you how many times a number or variable is used as a factor. For example, 2^3 means $2 \cdot 2 \cdot 2$ and x^2 means $x \cdot x$.

10. Using unit blocks, make a square that is 3 units on each side. Write an expression with an exponent for the number of blocks in the square. 3^2

11. Using unit blocks, make a cube that is 2 units wide, 2 units long, and 2 units high. Write an expression with an exponent for the number of blocks in the cube. 2^3

12. Which is greater in value, 3^2 or 2^3? How do you know? See Additional Answers.

COMMUNICATING ABOUT ALGEBRA

After you complete the multiplication models, think about the numerical and variable parts of the factors and their product in each problem. With a partner, discuss the relationships you notice.

See Additional Answers.

Use Algeblocks to complete the following products. Write an algebraic expression for the product. Check students' models.

13. 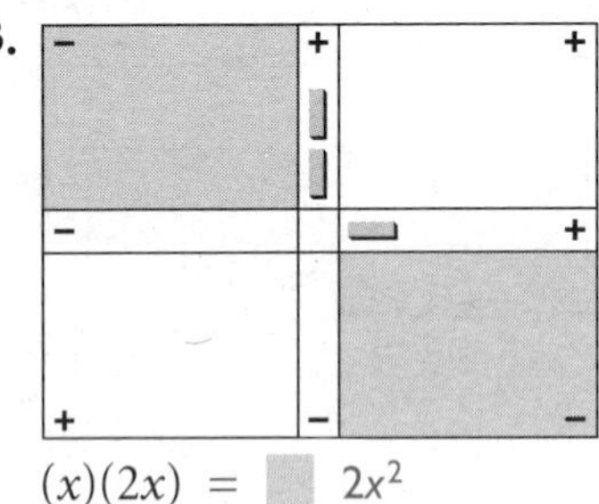

$(x)(2x) = \square$ $2x^2$

14. 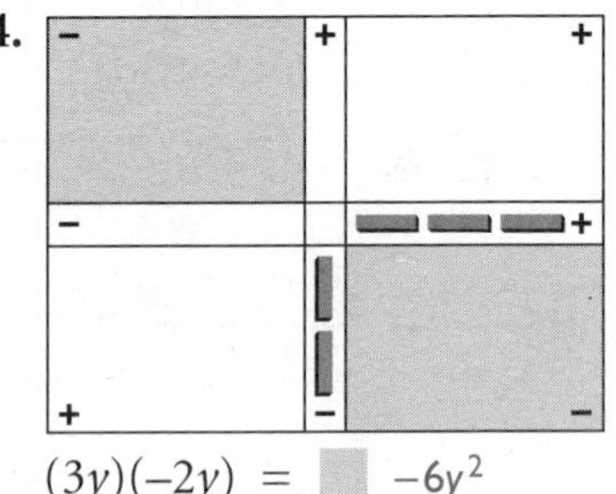

$(3y)(-2y) = \square$ $-6y^2$

15. 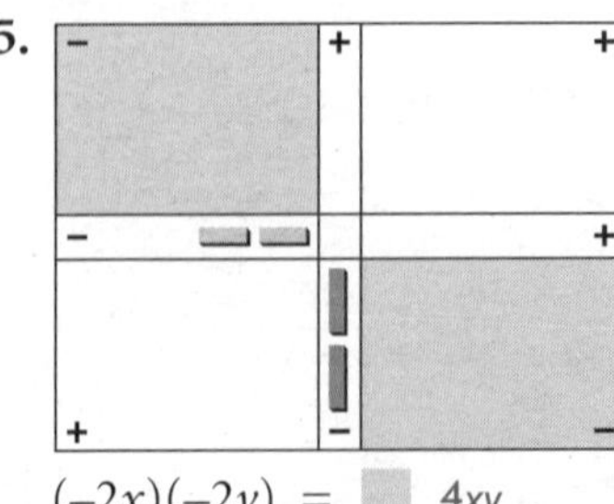

$(-2x)(-2y) = \square$ $4xy$

16. 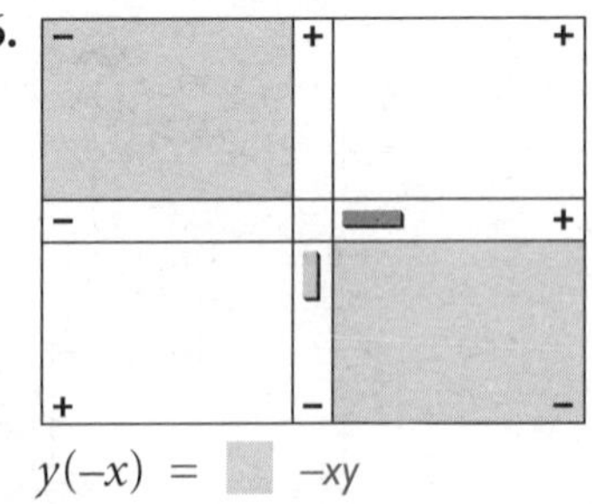

$y(-x) = \square$ $-xy$

17. Describe how you would use Algeblocks to show the product of $(-3x)(-2x)$. See Additional Answers.

Find each product.

18. $(2x)(5x)$ $10x^2$ 19. $(-3x)(3x)$ $-9x^2$ 20. $(-4y)(2y)$ $-8y^2$

21. $(3x)(-2y)$ $-6xy$ 22. $(-x)(2y)$ $-2xy$ 23. $(-y)(-2y)$ $2y^2$

Since multiplication and division are inverse operations, you can use Algeblocks to show division.

24. The diagram shows a way of using Algeblocks to find the quotient for $-4xy \div 2x$. How will you complete the problem? What is the quotient? See Additional Answers.

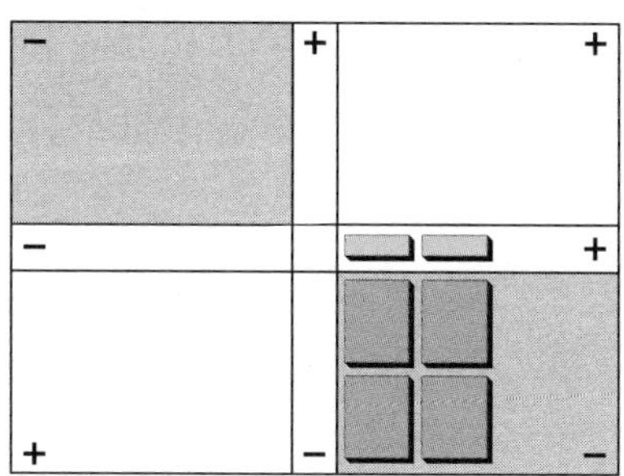

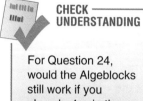

25. Describe how to use Algeblocks to find a quotient such as $2x^2 \div 2x$. See Additional Answers.

Complete each division using Algeblocks. Write an algebraic expression for the quotient.

26. 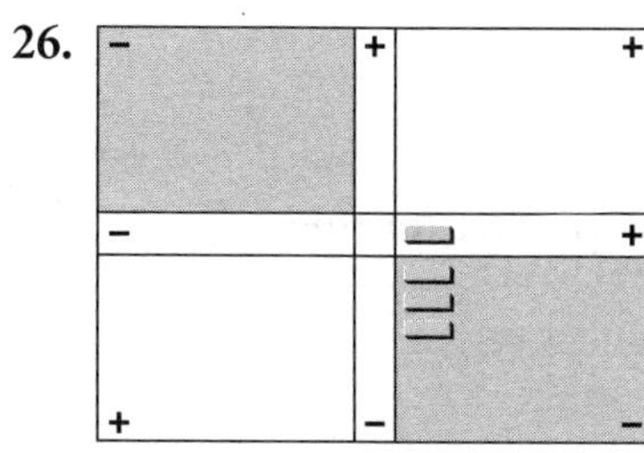

$-3x \div x = \square$ -3

27. 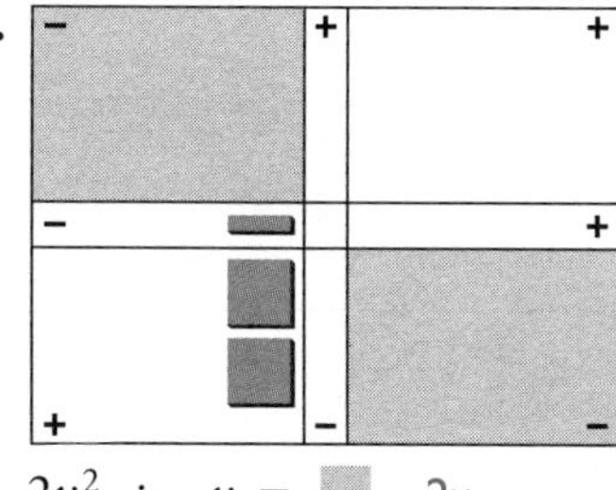

$2y^2 \div -y = \square$ $-2y$

28. 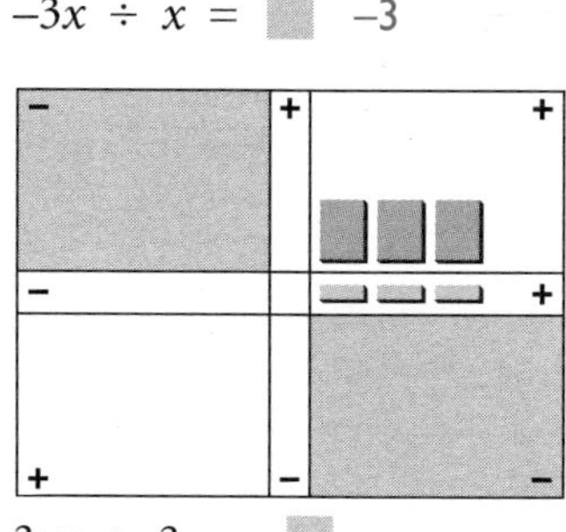

$3xy \div 3x = \square$ y

29. 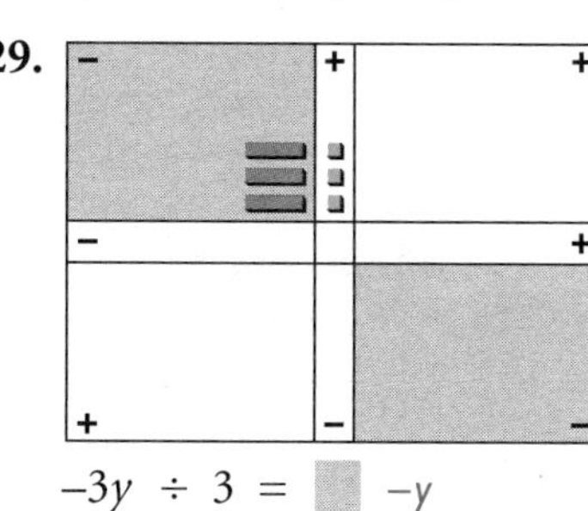

$-3y \div 3 = \square$ $-y$

Find each quotient.

30. $\frac{-6y}{3y}$ -2 31. $\frac{2xy}{x}$ $2y$ 32. $\frac{-4x^2}{-2x}$ $2x$

CHECK UNDERSTANDING

For Question 24, would the Algeblocks still work if you placed $-4xy$ in the *other* negative region? Draw a sketch showing your model.

See Additional Answers.

COMMUNICATING ABOUT ALGEBRA

Discuss the patterns you noticed in your division models. How do the numerical and variable parts of the dividend and divisor relate to the numerical and variable parts of the quotient?

See Additional Answers.

Make Connections Have students work with partners to complete Exercises 33 and 34. For Exercises 36 and 37, have students find the product and quotient without Algeblocks and then verify their answers using Algeblocks. Have students find the product of $3y$ and $4x$ and the quotient of $16xy \div 2y$ without using Algeblocks. **$12xy$; $8x$**

Make Connections Geometry Multiplying a variable by itself or by another variable can be used to represent the area of a rectangle. Write an expression representing the area of each of the following rectangular figures.

- The length of a rectangular garden is twice its width. **$2w^2$**
- One side of a rectangular room is three times the width of the window. An adjacent side is five times the width of the door. **$15xy$**

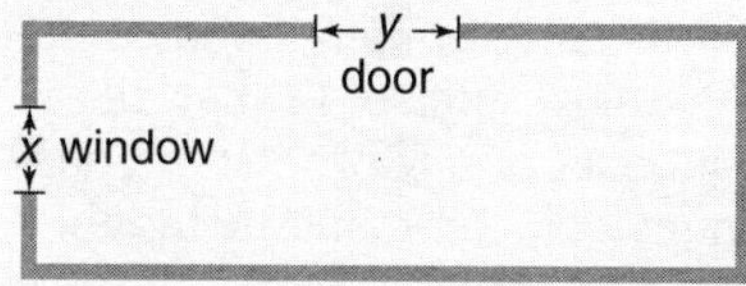

3 SUMMARIZE

Modeling For Exercises 38 and 39, ask students what each rectangle and what each square shown in the models represents. ***x*; x^2** Ask how they can determine from an Algeblocks model whether a variable has a positive or negative coefficient. **If the blocks are on the right part of the horizontal axis or the top part of the vertical axis, the coefficient is positive; if the blocks are on the left part of the horizontal axis or the bottom part of the vertical axis, the coefficient is negative.**

Thinking Critically Ask students to give examples for Exercises 40 and 41. **possible examples: $(3x^2)(4x) = 12x^3$;**

$$\frac{18x^5}{3x^2} = 6x^3$$

Going Further Students should realize that for Exercise 42 they can find the product of any two factors and then multiply the result by the third factor. For example, $2x \bullet 2 = 4x$ and $4x \bullet 3y = 12xy$, so $V = 12xy$.

4 FOLLOW-UP

Other Explorations Ask students to describe how they could use Algeblocks to solve Exercise 42. **Represent 3*y* in the positive horizontal axis and 2*x* in the positive vertical axis. Add another layer of blocks to the blocks in each axis to represent a height of 2. Then make a rectangle 2 layers high. Each layer will have a width of 2 *x*-blocks and a length of 3 *y*-blocks.**

Algebra Workshop

CHECK UNDERSTANDING

Explain the relationship between the *x*-block, x^2-block and x^3-block.

The x^2-block represents the 2-dimensional model of the *x*-block.
The x^3-block represents the 3-dimensional model of the *x*-block.

Make Connections

33. What shape do you use to model $x(x)$? How many dimensions does the shape have? Write the algebraic expression for the product. square; 2 (length and width); x^2
34. What shape would you use to model $x^2(x)$? How many dimensions does the shape have? Write the algebraic expression for the product. cube; 3 (length, width, and height); x^3
35. Can you make a physical model for x^4? Explain. See Additional Answers.
36. How could you find the product of $2x$ and $3x^3$ without using Algeblocks? Justify your answer. See Additional Answers.
37. How could you find the quotient of $5x^6 \div 10x$ without using Algeblocks? Justify your answer. See Additional Answers.

Summarize

38. MODELING Write a multiplication sentence for this Algeblocks model. $(x)(-3x) = -3x^2$

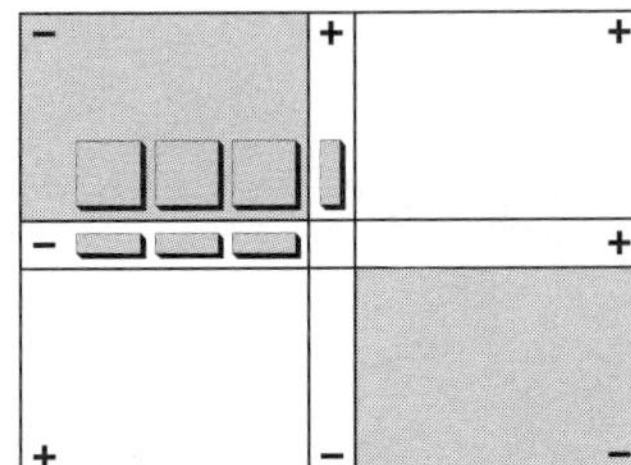

39. MODELING Write a division sentence for this Algeblocks model. $2x^2 \div (-x) = -2x$ or $2x^2 \div (-2x) = -x$

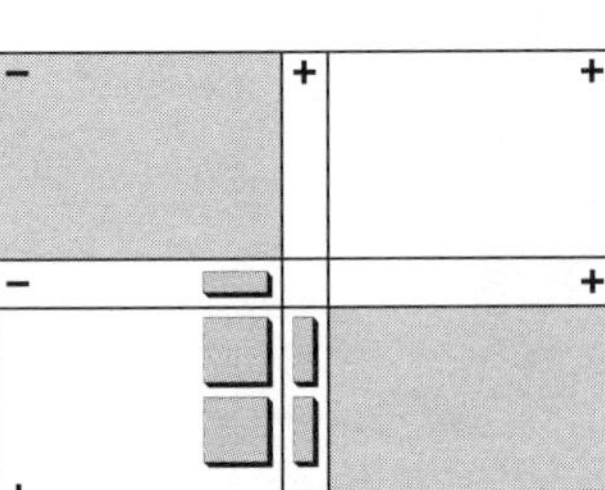

40. THINKING CRITICALLY When both factors contain the same variable, what is true about the variable and its exponent in the product? See Additional Answers.
41. THINKING CRITICALLY When the dividend and divisor have the same variable, what is true about the variable in the quotient? See Additional Answers.
42. GOING FURTHER Write an expression for the volume of the figure shown at the right. $12xy$

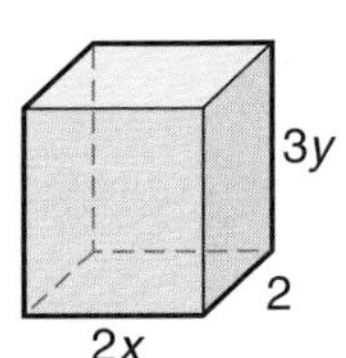

11.2 Multiply Monomials

Explore/Working Together

Work with a partner.

1. Fold a blank sheet of paper in half. How many regions are formed by one fold? 2

2. Continue to fold the sheet in half. Copy and complete this table to record the number of regions formed from each additional fold.

Fold Number	1	2	3	4	5
Number of Regions	2	?	?	?	?

4 8 16 32

3. What do you observe from the table about the number of regions? How is the number of regions related to the number of folds? See Additional Answers.

4. Predict the number of regions that will be formed by 10 folds. $2^{10} = 1024$

5. Suppose the paper is folded into thirds each time. Describe the pattern of the number of regions as the number of folds increases. number of regions triples with each fold

Build Understanding

A **monomial** is a single term that is a number, a variable, or the product of a number and one or more variables. A monomial can be made of any combination of numerical and variable factors. The variable must not appear in the denominator of a fraction or under a radical sign.

These expressions are monomials.

$$\frac{4}{5}x \qquad 3y^2 \qquad 17 \qquad -5x^2y^3 \qquad m \qquad \sqrt{2}xy$$

The following expressions are *not* monomials because they have more than one term, have a variable in the denominator, or have a variable under a radical sign.

$$x + 2 \qquad 3x + y + 5x \qquad \frac{5y}{2z} \qquad 3\sqrt{a}$$

The **degree of a variable** in a monomial is the number of times the variable occurs as a factor in the monomial. In the monomial $7x^2y^4$, the degree of x is 2 and the degree of y is 4.

The **degree of a monomial** is the sum of the degrees of all the variable factors. To find the degree of any monomial, add the degrees of the variables in the monomial. The degree of $7x^2y^4$ is $2 + 4 = 6$. The degree of a nonzero real number is zero. The monomial 0 has no degree.

SPOTLIGHT ON LEARNING

WHAT? In this lesson you will learn
- to recognize monomials.
- to multiply monomials using properties of exponents.

WHY? Multiplying monomials helps you solve problems involving gravity, electricity, and machines.

THINK BACK

In the algebraic expression $2x^5$, 2 is the coefficient, x is the base, and 5 is the exponent. The exponent indicates how many times the base is used as a factor.

ALGEBRA: WHO, WHERE, WHEN

Chu Shih-chieh, a Chinese mathematician who flourished about 1280–1303, wrote a book entitled *Ssu-yüan yü-chien* that deals with equations of degrees as high as fourteen.

LESSON PLANNING

Objective

▶ Multiply monomials using properties of exponents.

Vocabulary

degree of monomial
degree of a variable
monomial
properties of exponents

Resources

Warm Up 11.2
Reteaching 11.2
Extra Practice 11.2
Enrichment 11.2
Transparencies 12, 21, 62
Student Handbook
Lesson Quiz 11.2
Study Skills Activity 28

Materials/Manipulatives

Algeblocks
Quadrant Mats

ASSIGNMENTS

Basic: 1–28, 33–35, 41–46, Project Connection 1–4, AlgebraWorks 1–4

Average: 3–39, 41–46, Project Connection 1–4, AlgebraWorks 1–4

Enriched: 3–8, 11–46, Project Connection 1–4, AlgebraWorks 1–4

1 MOTIVATE

Explore/Working Together To help students having difficulty defining the number of regions as a function of the number of folds, have them that they write the number of regions as products of 2. **2, 2 • 2, 2 • 2 • 2, 2 • 2 • 2 • 2, 2 • 2 • 2 • 2 • 2**

2 TEACH

Use the Pages/Build Understanding
Ask students to give examples of expressions that are monomials and expressions that are not monomials. **possible examples: 4, 3*xy*, –2*z*, (2/3)h^5; 1/*x*, 5*b* + 1, *x* + *y***

Example 1: Ask students how they know that the degree of $9x^6$ is 6. ***x* is raised to the 6th power which means that the variable *x* occurs six times: 9 • *x* • *x* • *x* • *x* • *x* • *x*.** Have students read and discuss Communicating About Algebra.

Example 2: After students have discussed Example 2, ask them to describe how to find the product of $-3x^2(4xy)$ using the factor method shown in Example 2. **$-3x^2(4y) = -3 \cdot x \cdot x \cdot 4 \cdot y = (-3 \cdot 4) \cdot (x \cdot x) \cdot y = -12x^2y$**

Example 3: For part b, ask students why $y^3 \cdot y^{10}$ was written as y^{13}. **because $y^3 \cdot y^{10} = y^{3+10} = y^{13}$** For part c, ask them where the –1 came from in the expression $-4(-1)(x^3)(y^6 \cdot y^8)$. **it is the coefficient of x^3y^8**

Example 4: For part a, ask students another way to determine $(2^3)^2$. **$(2^3)(2^3) = (2 \cdot 2 \cdot 2)(2 \cdot 2 \cdot 2) = 2^6$** Ask students to compare the values of $(2^2)^3$ and $(2^3)^2$. Why is this true? **They are equal because multiplication is commutative**

Example 5: For part c, ask students why –8 was not squared. **because –8 is not within the parentheses with the terms to be squared**

TEACHING TIP

Although students may understand each property of exponents as they work with each separately, they may become confused when applying all the properties at once. Stress the definition of exponents. Suggest that they write a simple example for each property and express the monomial in factored form.

COMMUNICATING ABOUT ALGEBRA

In Example 1a, suppose that the coefficient was written as 3^2 instead of 9, so that the monomial was 3^2x^6. How would that affect the degree of the monomial?

It would not affect the degree of the monomial because only the exponents of the variables—not the coefficients—are considered.

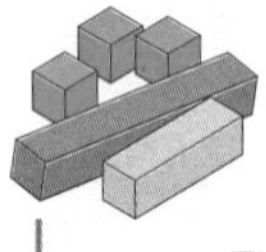

ALGEBLOCKS MODEL

Find the product of 2*y* and –2*x*. Model the factors.

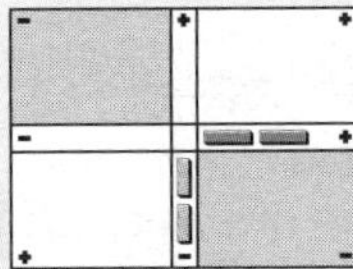

Complete the rectangles for the product.

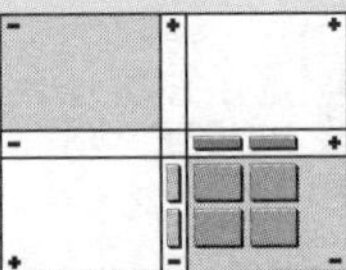

Read the product from the mat: –4*xy*.

EXAMPLE 1

Find the degree of each monomial.

a. $9x^6$ **b.** $-2y$ **c.** $5x^3y^4$ **d.** -7

Solution

a. The degree of $9x^6$ is 6, the exponent of the variable *x*.

b. The degree of $-2y$ is 1, since $-2y = -2y^1$. If a variable has no written exponent, its exponent is 1.

c. The degree of $5x^3y^4$ is 7. The degree of *x* is 3, the degree of *y* is 4, and the sum of 3 and 4 is 7.

d. The degree of –7 is 0. ◄

When monomials are multiplied, you can use the commutative and associative properties of multiplication to rearrange the factors.

EXAMPLE 2

Find the product of $-3x$ and $4xy$.

Solution

The product of $-3x$ and $4xy$ is the product of all five factors.

$$-3x(4xy) = -3 \cdot x \cdot 4 \cdot x \cdot y$$

You can use the commutative property to order the factors so that coefficients are together and like variables are together.

$$-3 \cdot x \cdot 4 \cdot x \cdot y = -3 \cdot 4 \cdot x \cdot x \cdot y$$

By the associative property, you can group numbers and variables.

$$(-3 \cdot 4) \cdot (x \cdot x) \cdot y = -12x^2y$$

Therefore, the product $-3x(4xy) = -12x^2y$. ◄

When monomials having the same base are multiplied, you can see a pattern.

$$x^2 \cdot x^3 = (x \cdot x)(x \cdot x \cdot x) = x^5$$

$$y^3 \cdot y^4 = (y \cdot y \cdot y)(y \cdot y \cdot y \cdot y) = y^7$$

$$a \cdot a^3 = a(a \cdot a \cdot a) = a^4$$

This pattern suggests the following property.

PROPERTY OF EXPONENTS: PRODUCT OF POWERS

For any real number *a* and all positive integers *m* and *n*,

$$a^m \cdot a^n = a^{m+n}$$

EXAMPLE 3

Find each product.

a. $x^5 \cdot x^7$ b. $3y^3(-2y^{10})$ c. $-4y^6(-x^3y^8)$

Solution

a. $x^5 \cdot x^7 = x^{5+7} = x^{12}$

b. $3y^3(-2y^{10}) = 3(-2)(y^3 \cdot y^{10}) = -6y^{13}$

c. $-4y^6(-x^3y^8) = -4(-1)(x^3)(y^6 \cdot y^8) = 4x^3y^{14}$ ◄

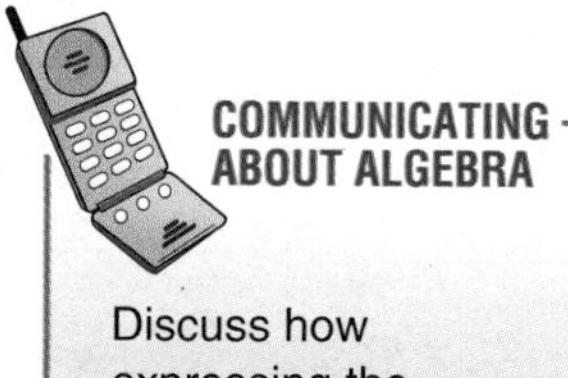

Discuss how expressing the product of x^2 and x^3 differs from expressing the product of x^2 and y^3.

See Additional Answers.

A number or a monomial in exponential form can be raised to a power. You could write the factors, then use exponents to write the product.

$$(2^2)^3 = (2^2)(2^2)(2^2) = (2 \cdot 2)(2 \cdot 2)(2 \cdot 2) = 2^6$$

$$(a^2)^3 = (a^2)(a^2)(a^2) = (a \cdot a)(a \cdot a)(a \cdot a) = a^6$$

Comparing the exponents in the original expression to the exponents in the final expression suggests the following property.

PROPERTY OF EXPONENTS: POWER OF A POWER

For any real number a and all positive integers m and n,
$$(a^m)^n = a^{mn}$$

EXAMPLE 4

Simplify.

a. $(2^3)^2$ b. $(x^7)^3$ c. $(y^4)^{10}$

Solution

a. $(2^3)^2 = 2^{3 \cdot 2} = 2^6 = 64$

b. $(x^7)^3 = x^{7 \cdot 3} = x^{21}$

c. $(y^4)^{10} = y^{4 \cdot 10} = y^{40}$ ◄

When a product is raised to a power, each factor is raised to that power.

$$(3x^2)^4 = (3x^2)(3x^2)(3x^2)(3x^2)$$
$$= (3 \cdot 3 \cdot 3 \cdot 3)(x^2 \cdot x^2 \cdot x^2 \cdot x^2) = 3^4 \cdot (x^2)^4 = 81x^8$$

This pattern suggests the following property.

PROPERTY OF EXPONENTS: POWER OF A PRODUCT

For any real numbers a and b and positive integer m,
$$(ab)^m = a^mb^m$$

Ongoing Assessment The important concepts and skills involve recognizing and multiplying monomials, and using the properties of exponents. To assess these ideas, have students demonstrate how they have applied these concepts and skills in Exercises 4, 7, and 12 of the Try These section.

Guided Practice/Try These For Exercise 3, ask students why the degree of the monomial is not zero since there is no visible exponent. **The unwritten exponent is 1, since $m = m^1$.** For Exercises 5–8, remind students to group coefficients and like variables together. For Exercise 15, ask how the product for $(-2m)^6$ differs from that of $-(2m)^6$. **The negative sign is inside the parentheses for $(-2m)^6$, and thus is acted on by the exponent 6, resulting in a positive product. In $-(2m)^6$ it is outside the parentheses, and thus is not acted on by the exponent, resulting in a negative product.**

3 SUMMARIZE

Communicating About Algebra Tell students that the power of a product property of exponents states that $(ab)^m = a^m b^m$. Ask them if it is also true that $(abcd)^m = a^m b^m c^m d^m$. Have them justify their answer. **It is true; justification will vary.**

4 PRACTICE

Practice For Exercises 9–20, remind students to group coefficients and like variables together and then apply the properties of exponents. Ask which property they should use for these exercises. **product of powers** Ask them which properties they should use to simplify Exercises 21–32. **power of a power and power of a product**

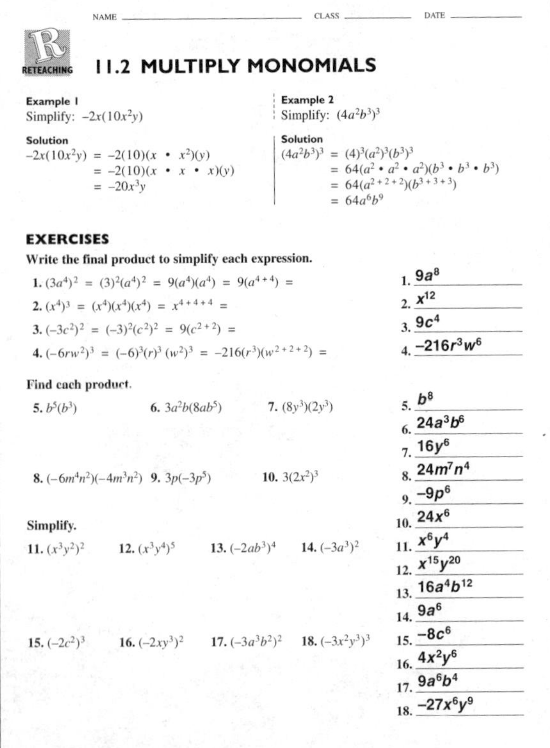

NAME ______________ CLASS ________ DATE ________

RETEACHING

11.2 MULTIPLY MONOMIALS

Example 1
Simplify: $-2x(10x^2y)$

Solution
$$-2x(10x^2y) = -2(10)(x \cdot x^2)(y) = -2(10)(x \cdot x \cdot x)(y) = -20x^3y$$

Example 2
Simplify: $(4a^2b^3)^3$

Solution
$$(4a^2b^3)^3 = (4)^3(a^2)^3(b^3)^3 = 64(a^2 \cdot a^2 \cdot a^2)(b^3 \cdot b^3 \cdot b^3) = 64(a^{2+2+2})(b^{3+3+3}) = 64a^6b^9$$

EXERCISES

Write the final product to simplify each expression.

1. $(3a^4)^2 = (3)^2(a^4)^2 = 9(a^4)(a^4) = 9(a^{4+4}) =$ **$9a^8$**
2. $(x^4)^3 = (x^4)(x^4)(x^4) = x^{4+4+4} =$ **x^{12}**
3. $(-3c^2)^2 = (-3)^2(c^2)^2 = 9(c^{2+2}) =$ **$9c^4$**
4. $(-6rw^2)^3 = (-6)^3(r)^3(w^2)^3 = -216(r^3)(w^{2+2+2}) =$ **$-216r^3w^6$**

Find each product.

5. $b^5(b^3)$ **b^8**
6. $3a^2b(8ab^5)$ **$24a^3b^6$**
7. $(8y^3)(2y^3)$ **$16y^6$**
8. $(-6m^4n^2)(-4m^3n^2)$ **$24m^7n^4$**
9. $3p(-3p^5)$ **$-9p^6$**
10. $3(2x^2)^3$ **$24x^6$**

Simplify.

11. $(x^3y^2)^2$ **x^6y^4**
12. $(x^3y^4)^5$ **$x^{15}y^{20}$**
13. $(-2ab^3)^4$ **$16a^4b^{12}$**
14. $(-3a^3)^2$ **$9a^6$**
15. $(-2c^2)^3$ **$-8c^6$**
16. $(-2xy^3)^2$ **$4x^2y^6$**
17. $(-3a^3b^2)^2$ **$9a^6b^4$**
18. $(-3x^2y^3)^3$ **$-27x^6y^9$**

6 *South-Western Algebra 1:* AN INTEGRATED APPROACH

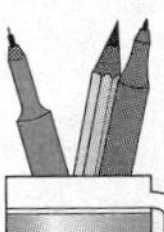

PROBLEM SOLVING TIP

Use the exponent key on a calculator to find powers of numbers quickly.

EXAMPLE 5

Simplify.

a. $(-2x^2)^5$ **b.** $(5xy^7)^3$ **c.** $-8(2x^3)^2$

Solution

a. $(-2x^2)^5 = (-2)^5(x^2)^5 = -32x^{10}$

b. $(5xy^7)^3 = (5)^3(x)^3(y^7)^3 = 125x^3y^{21}$

c. $-8(2x^3)^2 = -8(2^2x^6) = -8(4x^6) = -32x^6$

TRY THESE

Find the degree of each monomial.

1. y^{10} 10
2. $4b^2$ 2
3. $-5m$ 1
4. $2ab^3c^2$ 6

Find each product.

5. $3a(-2a^3)$ $-6a^4$
6. $-2b^4(b^8)$ $-2b^{12}$
7. $-6c^3d(-3c^8d^2)$ $18c^{11}d^3$
8. $10ef^2(-ef^5)$ $-10e^2f^7$

Simplify.

9. $(3^2)^3$ 729
10. $(x^8)^4$ x^{32}
11. $(z^{14})^2$ z^{28}
12. $(4a^3)^2$ $16a^6$
13. $(-3b)^3$ $-27b^3$
14. $(-2c^2d)^4$ $16c^8d^4$
15. $-(2m)^6$ $-64m^6$
16. $-3(x^3y)^4$ $-3x^{12}y^4$
17. **WRITING MATHEMATICS** Make a chart summarizing the three properties of exponents presented in this lesson. Make up one example for each property. See Additional Answers.

PRACTICE

Find the degree of each monomial.

1. $3x^2$ 2
2. $4a^3$ 3
3. $-9c^8$ 8
4. $-m^5$ 5
5. $2x$ 1
6. $-6de$ 2
7. $3x^2y^4$ 6
8. $-a^4b^5$ 9

Find each product.

9. $a^3(a^4)$ a^7
10. $b^6(b^2)$ b^8
11. $2x^3(-5x^2)$ $-10x^5$
12. $8y^4(3y^4)$ $24y^8$
13. $5g(-4g^9)$ $-20g^{10}$
14. $-6h^3(-7h)$ $42h^4$
15. $2a^2b(9ab^5)$ $18a^3b^6$
16. $(-3p^5q^2)(-pq^7)$ $3p^6q^9$
17. $(-2m^3n^3)(7m^4n)$ $-14m^7n^4$
18. $(-5x^6y^9)(3x^9y^6)$ $-15x^{15}y^{15}$
19. $3xyz(-4x^2z^3)$ $-12x^3yz^4$
20. $(-8a^4b^2)(-9a^3b^2)$ $72a^7b^4$

Simplify.

21. $(a^3)^4$ a^{12}
22. $(b^2)^4$ b^8
23. $(3c^2)^3$ $27c^6$
24. $(5d^7)^2$ $25d^{14}$
25. $(6a^2b^3)^3$ $216a^6b^9$
26. $(-4x^9y^3)^2$ $16x^{18}y^6$
27. $(-3gh^7)^3$ $-27g^3h^{21}$
28. $(-2j^4k)^5$ $-32j^{20}k^5$
29. $(-2x^4yz^2)^3$ $-8x^{12}y^3z^6$
30. $-2(-3x^6y^{12}z^5)^4$ $-162x^{24}y^{48}z^{20}$
31. $-1(-4a^5b^3)^3$ $64a^{15}b^9$
32. $3(-2m^6n^5)^4$ $48m^{24}n^{20}$

33. **FALLING OBJECTS** The formula $d = |-16t^2|$ is used to find the distance d in feet that an object falls in t seconds. How far will a brick fall in 5 s? 400 ft

34. **GEOMETRY** Express the volume of the box at the right in terms of x. $6x^3$

3x

x

2x

EXTEND

Simplify.

35. $(3x^4y)^2(-4xy^3)$ $-36x^9y^5$

36. $(-ab^5)^5(7a^4b^2)$ $-7a^9b^{27}$

37. $(p^3q^7)(-2p^2q^4)^3$ $-8p^9q^{19}$

38. Write an expression for the result of n doublings of a quantity x. 2^nx

39. **ELECTRICITY** Ohm's law is the formula $E = IR$ where E is the voltage in volts in an electrical circuit, I is the current in amperes of the circuit, and R is the resistance in ohms. The formula $W = EI$ can be used to find the power of the circuit in watts. Use these two formulas to write a formula for W in terms of I and R only. $W = I^2R$

40. **PROBABILITY** Write an expression for finding the probability of getting all heads on n tosses of a coin. (*Hint:* Look at the case for $n = 1$, 2, and 3 and find a pattern.) $\frac{1}{2^n}$

THINK CRITICALLY

Find the value of n that makes each statement true.

41. $9x^n(7x^5) = 63x^8$ 3

42. $(5a^nb^3)^2 = 25a^8b^6$ 4

43. $(-q^3r^5)^n = -q^{15}r^{25}$ 5

44. Does $(a^m)^n = (a^n)^m$? Justify your answer. yes; $(a^m)^n = a^{mn}$; $(a^n)^m = a^{nm}$; since m and n are integers, $mn = nm$

45. If $x^p(x^q) = x^{2p+1}$, write a formula for q in terms of p. $q = p + 1$

46. **GEOMETRY** The volume of a cube is $V = s^3$ where s is the length of a side. How much more volume does a cube with side of length $2x$ have than a cube with side of length x? Justify your answer. eight times; if the side equals $2x$, then the volume is $(2x)^3 = 8x^3$, and since the volume of a cube with side x is x^3, the volume of the other cube is 8 times greater

PROJECT *Connection*

Aircraft must overcome the effects of drag in order to fly.

1. *Parasitic drag* is energy lost moving air around the aircraft's body. To model parasitic drag, hold a large piece of cardboard in front of you and run. Is it easier or harder to run with it? Why? See Additional Answers.
2. *Induced drag* is energy lost as the aircraft rises and air must be moved around the rising wing. One way to lower induced drag is to increase the *aspect ratio* defined as $A = \frac{b^2}{S}$ where b represents wing span and S represents wing area. If the wing area is held constant, what effect would increasing the wing span by 1 ft have on the aspect ratio? It would increase by $\frac{2b+1}{s}$.
3. The wing area S is defined as wing span times average chord length, or bc. Find another way to express the aspect ratio. $\frac{b}{c}$
4. Using this new expression, explain how a designer could increase the aspect ratio. increase b or decrease c

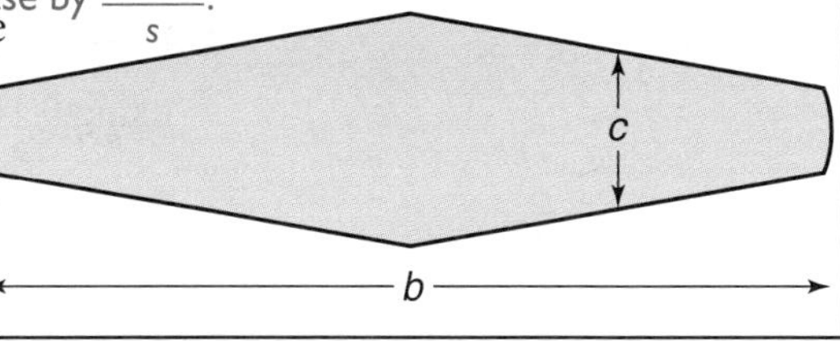

Extend For Exercise 35, ask students what they should do first. **Simplify $(3x^4y)^2$.** For Exercise 36, ask students what the coefficient is for the monomial $-ab^5$. **(−1)** Have students explain how they found their answers to Exercise 38.
Possible answer:

Number of Times Doubled	1	2	3	...	n
Result	$2x$	$4x$	$8x$	...	2^nx
Power of 2	2^1	2^2	2^3	...	2^n

Think Critically For Exercise 41, suggest that students first simplify the monomial and then solve for n.

Project Connection This activity presents further aspects of the project introduced on page 516. Students can answer Question 2 by substituting numbers in the formula and looking for a pattern. If $b = 2$, then $b^2 = 4$. If $b = 3$, then $b^2 = 9$. If $b = 4$, then $b^2 = 16$. Since 9 is 5 greater than 4 and 16 is 7 greater than 9, the pattern shows that increasing b by 1 results in an increase of $2b + 1$.

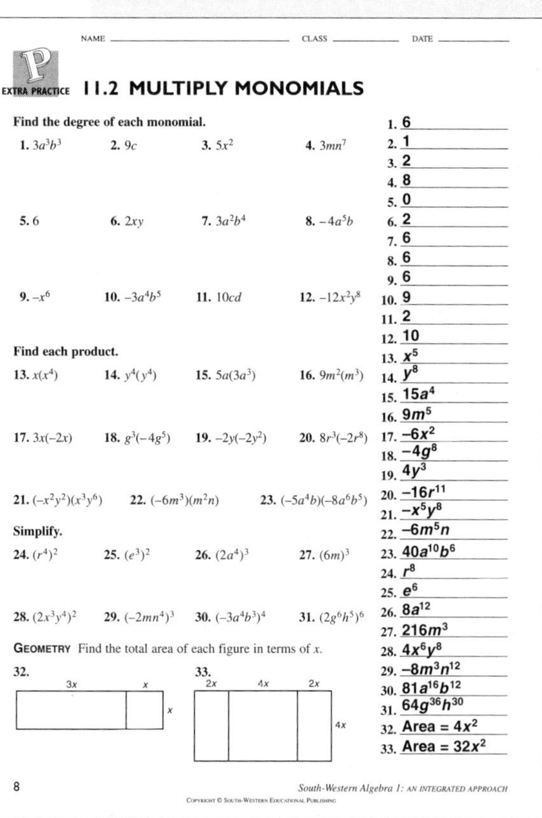

NAME ____ CLASS ____ DATE ____

EXTRA PRACTICE **11.2 MULTIPLY MONOMIALS**

Find the degree of each monomial.

1. $3a^3b^3$ 2. $9c$ 3. $5x^2$ 4. $3mn^7$

5. 6 6. $2xy$ 7. $3a^2b^4$ 8. $-4a^5b$

9. $-x^6$ 10. $-3a^4b^5$ 11. $10cd$ 12. $-12x^2y^8$

Find each product.

13. $x(x^4)$ 14. $y^4(y^4)$ 15. $5a(3a^3)$ 16. $9m^2(m^3)$

17. $3x(-2x)$ 18. $g^3(-4g^5)$ 19. $-2y(-2y^2)$ 20. $8r^3(-2r^8)$

21. $(-x^2y^2)(x^3y^6)$ 22. $(-6m^3)(m^2n)$ 23. $(-5a^4b)(-8a^6b^5)$

Simplify.

24. $(r^4)^2$ 25. $(e^3)^2$ 26. $(2a^4)^3$ 27. $(6m)^3$

28. $(2x^3y^4)^2$ 29. $(-2mn^4)^3$ 30. $(-3a^4b^3)^4$ 31. $(2g^6h^5)^6$

GEOMETRY Find the total area of each figure in terms of x.

32. 3x, x, x

33. 2x, 4x, 2x, 4x

1. 6
2. 1
3. 2
4. 8
5. 0
6. 2
7. 6
8. 6
9. 6
10. 9
11. 2
12. 10
13. x^5
14. y^8
15. $15a^4$
16. $9m^5$
17. $-6x^2$
18. $-4g^8$
19. $4y^3$
20. $-16r^{11}$
21. $-x^5y^8$
22. $-6m^5n$
23. $40a^{10}b^6$
24. r^8
25. e^6
26. $8a^{12}$
27. $216m^3$
28. $4x^6y^8$
29. $-8m^3n^{12}$
30. $81a^{16}b^{12}$
31. $64g^{36}h^{30}$
32. Area = $4x^2$
33. Area = $32x^2$

8 *South-Western Algebra 1: AN INTEGRATED APPROACH*

5 FOLLOW-UP

Extension Have students answer each of the following questions.

- What do you do with the exponents when you add like variables? **You do nothing with them.**
- What do you do with the exponents when you multiply like variables? **You add them.**
- What do you do with the exponents when you raise a power to a power? **You multiply them.**

Then have them brainstorm ways of remembering these properties of exponents.

AlgebraWorks Be sure that students use correct procedures in transforming formulas. For Question 1, watch for students who, find the value of the numerator and forget to divide by 3.78. For Question 4, encourage students to see that this is equivalent to keeping the numerator of a fraction constant and decreasing the denominator, which results in a greater number.

NAME ______________ CLASS ________ DATE ________

ENRICHMENT **11.2 MULTIPLY MONOMIALS**

Integers can be expressed exponentially as powers and as powers of powers. For example, 64 can be expressed as 8^2, as 4^3, as $(2^2)^3$, as $(2^3)^2$, or as 2^6.

Express the following positive integers in as many exponential forms as you can. **Answers will vary.**

1. 4 = 1. 2^2
2. 16 = 2. $2^4 = 4^2$
3. 256 = 3. $16^2 = 4^4 = (2^4)^2 = (2^2)^4 = 2^8$
4. 512 = 4. $2^9 = (2^3)^3$
5. 1024 = 5. $4^5 = 2^{10} = (2^5)^2 = (2^2)^5$
6. 4096 = 6. $2^{12} = 4^6 = (2^6)^2 = (2^2)^6 = (2^3)^4 = (2^4)^3$
7. 16,284 = 7. $2^{14} = (2^7)^2 = (2^2)^7$
8. 65,536 = 8. $2^{16} = (2^8)^2 = (2^2)^8 = (2^4)^4$
9. 262,144 = 9. $2^{18} = (2^9)^2 = (2^2)^9 = (2^6)^3 = (2^3)^6$

Express these powers of three in as many exponential forms as you can. Then write the number in standard form. **Answers will vary.**

10. 3^4 = 10. $9^2 = (3^2)^2 = 81$
11. 3^6 = 11. $(3^2)^3 = (3^3)^2 = 729$
12. 3^8 = 12. $(3^2)^4 = (3^4)^2 = 6561$
13. 3^9 = 13. $(3^3)^3 = 19,683$
14. 3^{12} = 14. $(3^6)^2 = (3^2)^6 = (3^4)^3 = (3^3)^4 = 531,441$

15. Suppose that you wanted to determine the power of 3 that is a square, a cube, a sixth power, and a ninth power. How could you find that number quickly?
Find the LCM of 2, 3, 6, and 9, which is 18. Then determine the eighteenth power of 3.

16. What power of 3 is a square, cube, sixth power, and an eighth power? 16. 3^{24}

10 *South-Western Algebra 1: AN INTEGRATED APPROACH*

Career
Machinist

Machinists build and maintain machines used in mass production. They are involved in the manufacturing of most factory-made items, including airplanes. They must understand how many different kinds of machines work.

Airplanes are constructed from many sheets of metal. A metal punch machine is used to punch holes in a metal sheet. Two pieces of metal are joined together with rivets hammered through the holes. Usually rivet holes are punched in either a single row or a double row.

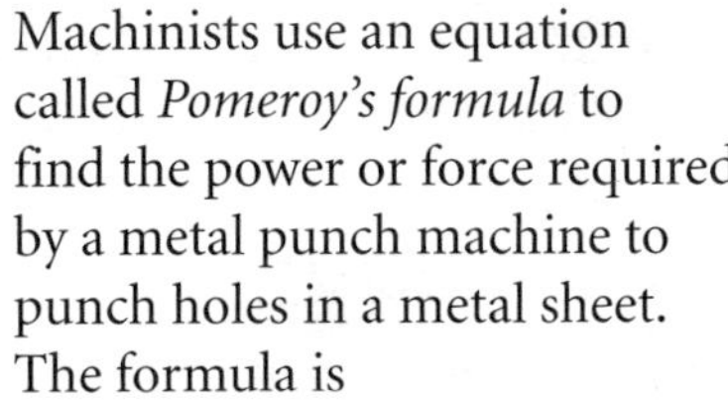

Machinists use an equation called *Pomeroy's formula* to find the power or force required by a metal punch machine to punch holes in a metal sheet. The formula is

$$P = \frac{t^2 dN}{3.78}$$

where P represents the power needed in horsepower (hp), t is the thickness of the metal in inches, d is the diameter of the hole in inches, and N is the number of holes to be punched at once.

Decision Making

1. Find the power needed to punch eight 2-in. diameter holes at the same time in a sheet of metal that is $\frac{1}{16}$-in. thick. Round to the nearest thousandth. 0.017 hp
2. A machinist wants to punch as many holes as possible at one time. Solve Pomeroy's formula for N, the number of holes punched at once. $N = \frac{3.78P}{t^2 d}$
3. How many holes $1\frac{1}{2}$ in. in diameter can be punched at once using 0.1 hp on metal $\frac{3}{16}$-in. thick? 7 holes
4. At a constant power, how can you increase the number of holes that can be punched at once? decrease the thickness of the metal and/or the diameter of the holes

11.3 Divide Monomials

Explore/Working Together

Work with a partner.

1. Complete the table.
2. How does the exponent of the expression in the left column of the table change as you move down the table? decreases by 1 each time
3. How does the expression in the right column of the table change as you move down the table? halves each time

Expression	Value	
2^6		64
2^5		32
2^4		16
2^3		8
2^2		4
2^1		2

4. Based on the pattern in the table, what should be the next entry below 2^1? What should its value be? 2^0; 1
5. Continue the pattern by writing the next three entries and their values. See Additional Answers.
6. Rewrite each expression you wrote for Question 5 in the form $\frac{1}{2^n}$. What do you notice? See Additional Answers.

SPOTLIGHT ON LEARNING

WHAT? In this lesson you will learn
- to use properties of exponents to divide monomials.
- to use negative and zero exponents.

WHY? Dividing monomials helps you solve problems in geometry, demography, and astronomy.

Build Understanding

Dividing two monomials is similar to simplifying fractions to lowest terms. To write the fraction $\frac{15}{25}$ in lowest terms, a common factor of 5 is used to divide both numerator and denominator. So, $\frac{15}{25} = \frac{3}{5}$.

EXAMPLE 1

Simplify: $\frac{16x^5}{2x^2}$

Solution

$$\frac{16x^5}{2x^2} = \frac{2 \cdot 8 \cdot x \cdot x \cdot x \cdot x \cdot x}{2 \cdot x \cdot x}$$ Rewrite the variable terms without exponents.

$$= \frac{8 \cdot x \cdot x \cdot x}{1}$$ Divide both numerator and denominator by their common factor, $2 \cdot x \cdot x$.

$$= 8x^3$$

◄

LESSON PLANNING

Objectives
- ▶ Divide monomials using properties of exponents.
- ▶ Use negative and zero exponents.

Vocabulary
properties of exponents

Resources
Warm Up 11.3
Reteaching 11.3
Extra Practice 11.3
Enrichment 11.3
Transparencies 12, 21, 62
Student Handbook
Lesson Quiz 11.3
Technology Activity 26

Materials/Manipulatives
Algeblocks
Quadrant Mats

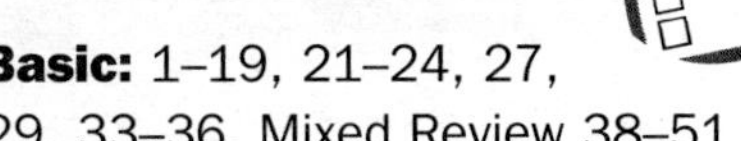

ASSIGNMENTS

Basic: 1–19, 21–24, 27, 29, 33–36, Mixed Review 38–51

Average: 3–27, 29–30, 33–36, Mixed Review 38–51

Enriched: 9–37, Mixed Review 38–51

1 MOTIVATE

Explore/Working Together For Question 4, ask students how they determined the answer. **2 ÷ 2 = 1**

2 TEACH

Use the Pages/Build Understanding

Example 1: Ask students why the first step in the solution does not express 16 in the complete factored form of 2 • 2 • 2 • 2. **because 2 is the greatest common factor of 16 and 2, the coefficients of the numerator and the denominator**

Example 2: Stress that if students become confused when finding quotients, they should write the expression in factored form and divide both the numerator and denominator by their common factors.

Example 3: For part a, show students that any number divided by itself is 1, so $y^6/y^6 = 1$. For part b, ask students how the coefficient –3 was determined. **$-9 \div 3 = -3$**

Example 4: For part a, remind students that the coefficient –5 is not effected by the exponent –3. Some students may tend to rewrite the expression as $1/-5a^3$ instead of $-5/a^3$. Ask students to simplify $3x^{-2}$. **$3/x^2$**

ALGEBLOCKS MODEL

Find the quotient of $4xy$ and $-2x$. Model the divisor and the dividend.

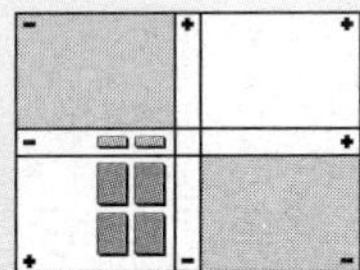

Make the other dimension of the rectangle.

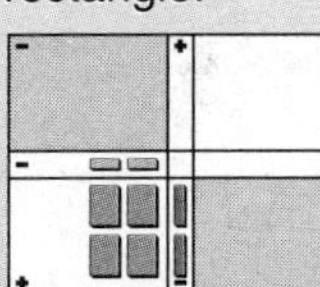

Read the quotient from the mat: $-2y$.

ALGEBRA: WHO, WHERE, WHEN

In 1484, Nicholas Chuquet, a French physician, wrote *Triparty en la science des nombres*, which contained an early form of exponential notation, including a notation for zero and negative exponents.

The following examples suggest that when monomials with the same base are divided, the exponents of the bases can be subtracted.

$$\frac{y^4}{y} = \frac{y \cdot y \cdot y \cdot y}{y} = y^3 \qquad y^{4-1} = y^3$$

$$\frac{a^7}{a^3} = \frac{a \cdot a \cdot a \cdot a \cdot a \cdot a \cdot a}{a \cdot a \cdot a} = a^4 \qquad a^{7-3} = a^4$$

The pattern is summarized in the following property.

PROPERTY OF EXPONENTS: QUOTIENT RULE

For any real number a, $a \neq 0$, and positive integers m and n,

$$\frac{a^m}{a^n} = a^{m-n}$$

EXAMPLE 2

Find each quotient.

a. $\dfrac{-10a^7b^4}{2ab}$ b. $\dfrac{4w^5z^7}{-10z^4}$

Solution

a. $\dfrac{-10a^7b^4}{2ab} = -5a^{7-1}b^{4-1} = -5a^6b^3$

b. $\dfrac{4w^5z^7}{-10z^4} = \dfrac{-2w^5z^3}{5}$

In Explore you saw that $2^0 = 1$. Any base raised to the zero power is 1. This is summarized in the following property.

ZERO PROPERTY OF EXPONENTS

For any real number a, $a \neq 0$,

$$a^0 = 1$$

EXAMPLE 3

Simplify each expression.

a. $\dfrac{y^6}{y^6}$ b. $\dfrac{-9x^5y^0}{3x}$ c. $4^3 \cdot 6^0 - 3^4$

Solution

a. $\dfrac{y^6}{y^6} = y^{6-6} = y^0 = 1$

b. $\dfrac{-9x^5y^0}{3x} = \dfrac{-9x^{5-1}(1)}{3} = -3x^4$

c. $4^3 \cdot 6^0 - 3^4 = 64 \cdot 1 - 81 = 64 - 81 = -17$

Also in Explore you saw that $2^{-1} = \frac{1}{2}$ and that $2^{-3} = \frac{1}{2^3}$. Any base raised to a negative power is the reciprocal of the base raised to the positive power. This is summarized in the following property.

> **PROPERTY OF NEGATIVE EXPONENTS**
>
> **For any real number a, $a \neq 0$, and any positive integer n,**
>
> $$a^{-n} = \frac{1}{a^n}$$

EXAMPLE 4

Simplify each expression. Write with positive exponents.

a. $-5a^{-3}$ **b.** $3^0 \cdot 5^{-2} \cdot 4^2$ **c.** $\frac{x^4y^3}{x^7y^2}$

Solution

a. $-5a^{-3} = \frac{-5}{a^3}$

b. $3^0 \cdot 5^{-2} \cdot 4^2 = 3^0 \cdot \frac{1}{5^2} \cdot 4^2$
$= 1 \cdot \frac{1}{25} \cdot 16$
$= \frac{16}{25}$

c. $\frac{x^4y^3}{x^7y^2} = x^{4-7} \cdot y^{3-2}$
$= x^{-3}y$
$= \frac{y}{x^3}$ ◄

When a fraction is raised to a power, both the numerator and the denominator are raised to that power.

> **PROPERTY OF EXPONENTS: POWER OF A QUOTIENT RULE**
>
> **For all real numbers a and b, $b \neq 0$, and any positive integer m,**
>
> $$\left(\frac{a}{b}\right)^m = \frac{a^m}{b^m}$$

EXAMPLE 5

Simplify each expression. Write with positive exponents.

a. $\left(\frac{3}{10}\right)^3$ **b.** $\left(\frac{5x^3}{2y}\right)^2$ **c.** $\left(\frac{2}{3}\right)^{-2}$

Solution

a. $\left(\frac{3}{10}\right)^3 = \frac{3^3}{10^3} = \frac{27}{1000}$

b. $\left(\frac{5x^3}{2y}\right)^2 = \frac{(5x^3)^2}{(2y)^2} = \frac{25x^6}{4y^2}$

c. $\left(\frac{2}{3}\right)^{-2} = \left(\frac{3}{2}\right)^2 = \frac{3^2}{2^2} = \frac{9}{4}$ ◄

COMMUNICATING ABOUT ALGEBRA

Write the reciprocal of a^n in two different ways. Show why each expression is the reciprocal of a^n. Compare and discuss the expressions you wrote with those of your classmates.

$\frac{1}{a^n}$, a^{-n};
$a^n \cdot a^{-n} = a^{n-n} = a^0 = 1$,
and
$a^n \cdot \frac{1}{a^n} = \frac{a^n}{a^n} = a^{n-n} = 1$.
Since the product in each is equal to 1, a^{-n} and $\frac{1}{a^n}$ must be reciprocals, or multiplicative inverses, of a^n.

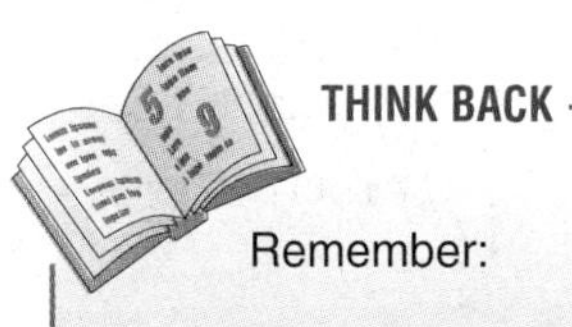

THINK BACK

Remember:

$$\frac{1}{\frac{2}{3}} = \frac{3}{2}$$

Example 5: For part b, ask students how $\frac{(5x^3)^2}{(2y)^2}$ was expressed as $\frac{25x^6}{4y^2}$ and what properties of exponents were used.

$\frac{(5x^3)^2}{(2y)^2} = \frac{5^2(x^3)^2}{2^2y^2}$**; power of a power**

Ongoing Assessment The important concepts and skills are using properties of exponents to divide monomials and using negative and zero exponents. To assess these ideas, have students demonstrate how they have applied these concepts and skills in Exercises 3, 6, and 14 of the Try These section.

Guided Practice/Try These For Exercise 6, ask students if w^0 will be 1 for all values of w. **It will be 1 for all values except 0; 0 raised to any power has no meaning.**

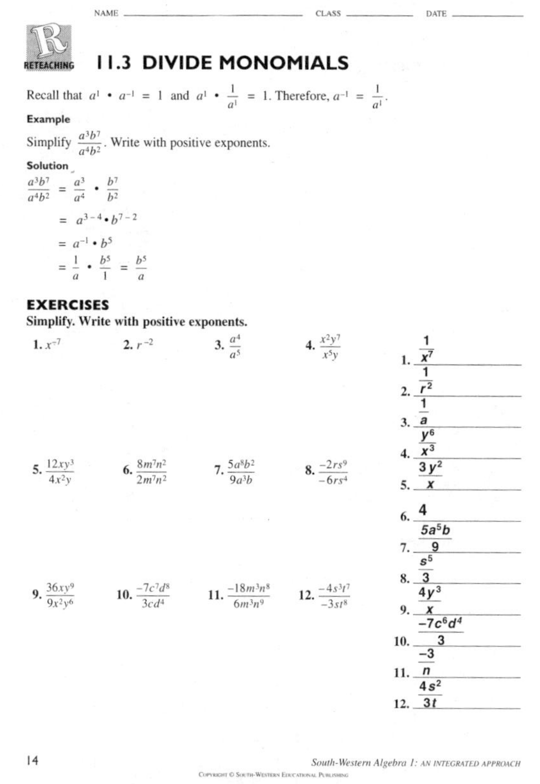

NAME ______ CLASS ______ DATE ______

RETEACHING

11.3 DIVIDE MONOMIALS

Recall that $a^1 \cdot a^{-1} = 1$ and $a^1 \cdot \frac{1}{a^1} = 1$. Therefore, $a^{-1} = \frac{1}{a^1}$.

Example

Simplify $\frac{a^3b^7}{a^4b^2}$. Write with positive exponents.

Solution

$\frac{a^3b^7}{a^4b^2} = \frac{a^3}{a^4} \cdot \frac{b^7}{b^2}$
$= a^{3-4} \cdot b^{7-2}$
$= a^{-1} \cdot b^5$
$= \frac{1}{a} \cdot \frac{b^5}{1} = \frac{b^5}{a}$

EXERCISES

Simplify. Write with positive exponents.

1. x^{-7} **2.** r^{-2} **3.** $\frac{a^4}{a^5}$ **4.** $\frac{x^2y^7}{x^5y}$

5. $\frac{12xy^3}{4x^2y}$ **6.** $\frac{8m^7n^2}{2m^7n^2}$ **7.** $\frac{5a^8b^2}{9a^3b}$ **8.** $\frac{-2rs^9}{-6rs^4}$

9. $\frac{36xy^9}{9x^2y^6}$ **10.** $\frac{-7c^7d^8}{3cd^4}$ **11.** $\frac{-18m^3n^8}{6m^3n^9}$ **12.** $\frac{-4s^3t^7}{-3st^8}$

1. $\frac{1}{x^7}$
2. $\frac{1}{r^2}$
3. $\frac{1}{a}$
4. $\frac{y^6}{x^3}$
5. $\frac{3y^2}{x}$
6. 4
7. $\frac{5a^5b}{9}$
8. $\frac{s^5}{3}$
9. $\frac{4y^3}{x}$
10. $\frac{-7c^6d^4}{3}$
11. $\frac{-3}{n}$
12. $\frac{4s^2}{3t}$

14

South-Western Algebra 1: AN INTEGRATED APPROACH

3 SUMMARIZE

In the Math Journal Have students discuss different ways to simplify $(x^{-3}/y^4)^{-2}$. **possible answer: $(x^{-3}/y^4)^{-2} = (1/x^3y^4)^{-2} = (x^3y^4)^2 = (x^3)^2 \cdot (y^4)^2 = x^6y^8$**

4 PRACTICE

Practice Suggest that before students simplify each expression they determine if the denominator will have a variable. Ask students when the denominator will have a variable. **when the positive exponents for like variables are greater in the denominator than in the numerator** Remind students that they can check their answers using the factored form. For Exercise 22, ask students how the diameter of a sphere is related to its radius. ***d* = 2*r***

NAME ________ CLASS ________ DATE ________

EXTRA PRACTICE 11.3 DIVIDE MONOMIALS

Simplify. Write with positive exponents.

1. 6^{-2} 2. 1^{-2} 3. $8^0 - 2^{-2}$ 4. $5^2 - 12^0$

5. 4^{-3} 6. $\left(\frac{2}{3}\right)^2$ 7. $\left(\frac{2}{5}\right)^{-2}$ 8. $\left(-\frac{1}{3}\right)^{-2}$

9. $\frac{4a3b}{2b}$ 10. $\frac{12bc^6}{6c^5}$ 11. $\frac{15p^2q^5}{5p^2q}$ 12. $\frac{6r^8s^4}{3r^6s}$

13. $\frac{-12u^9v^7}{-2u^9v^7}$ 14. $\frac{-24vw^2}{4vw}$ 15. $\frac{-16a^5b^2}{-4ab}$ 16. $\frac{3m^4n^9}{5m^3n^8}$

17. $\frac{14ab^4}{-2ab}$ 18. $\frac{20m^3n^2}{4m^6n^5}$ 19. $\frac{42x^{10}y^3}{7x^3y^9}$ 20. $-\frac{10m^7n^4}{5m^8n^4}$

Answers: 1. $\frac{1}{36}$ 2. 1 3. $\frac{3}{4}$ 4. 24 5. $\frac{1}{64}$ 6. $\frac{4}{9}$ 7. $\frac{25}{4}$ 8. 9 9. $2a^3$ 10. $2bc$ 11. $3q^4$ 12. $2r^2s^3$ 13. 6 14. $-6w$ 15. $-4a^4b$ 16. $\frac{3mn}{5}$ 17. $-7b^3$ 18. $\frac{5}{m^3n^3}$ 19. $\frac{6x^7}{y^6}$ 20. $-\frac{2}{m}$

21. **ELECTRICITY** The formula $t = \frac{1000C}{Wc}$ gives the length of time t in hours that an electrical appliance has been in use, where C is the total cost of operation in cents, c is the cost per kilowatt hour and W is the number of watts used. Find t if $C = x^2y^2$, $W = x^3y$, and $c = xy$.
$t = \frac{1000x^2y^2}{x^3y(xy)} = \frac{1000x^2y^2}{x^4y^2} = \frac{1000}{x^2}$

22. **DISTANCE FORMULA** The formula $d = rt$ gives the distance traveled in time t at an average rate r. Find r if $d = a^4b^7$ and $t = a^5b^2$.
$r = \frac{d}{t} = \frac{a^4b^7}{a^5b^2} = \frac{b^5}{a}$

16 *South-Western Algebra 1: AN INTEGRATED APPROACH*

TRY THESE

Simplify. Write with positive exponents.

1. $-\frac{-15x^7}{5x^5}$ $3x^2$
2. $\frac{-24a^4}{-3a^3}$ $8a$
3. $\frac{6a^{12}b^4}{2a^4b^2}$ $3a^8b^2$
4. $\frac{20p^9q}{-4p^3q}$ $-5p^6$
5. 100^0 1
6. w^0 1
7. 4^{-2} $\frac{1}{16}$
8. 3^{-3} $\frac{1}{27}$
9. $\frac{-3g^3h^2}{-9g^5h^4}$ $\frac{1}{3g^2h^2}$
10. $\frac{15km^4}{5k^2m^3}$ $\frac{3m}{k}$
11. $\frac{6p^3q^4}{3p^3q^3}$ $2q$
12. $\frac{-r^2s^5}{rs^6}$ $\frac{-r}{s}$
13. $\left(\frac{4}{5}\right)^3$ $\frac{64}{125}$
14. $\left(\frac{-3}{4}\right)^{-2}$ $\frac{16}{9}$
15. $\left(\frac{2x^4}{y^3}\right)^5$ $\frac{32x^{20}}{y^{15}}$
16. $\left(\frac{-3a}{2b^4}\right)^3$ $\frac{-27a^3}{8b^{12}}$
17. **MODELING** Write a division sentence for the Algeblocks at the right. $4x^2 \div -2x = -2x$

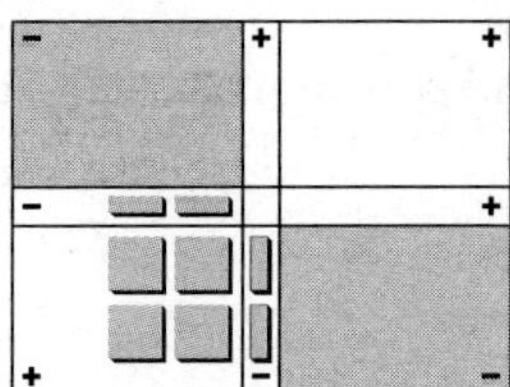

18. **WRITING MATHEMATICS** Write the rules of exponents presented in the lesson. Use words instead of symbols. Make up one example for each rule. See Additional Answers.

PRACTICE

Simplify. Write with positive exponents.

1. $\frac{-16a^7}{-2a^6}$ $8a$
2. $\frac{9b^4}{-3b^2}$ $-3b^2$
3. $\frac{12a^6b^4}{-4a^5b}$ $-3ab^3$
4. $\frac{-5c^4d^6}{7c^2d^5}$ $\frac{-5c^2d}{7}$
5. $\frac{6x^0y^3}{y^2}$ $6y$
6. $\frac{-7cd^0}{14c}$ $-\frac{1}{2}$
7. $\frac{62yz^4}{14y^5z^4}$ $\frac{31}{7y^4}$
8. $\frac{-2p^2q^7}{8p^4q}$ $\frac{-q^6}{4p^2}$
9. $2^4 \cdot 5 - 7^0$ 79
10. $8^2 + 2 \cdot 5^0$ 66
11. $9^0 \cdot 2^{-3} \cdot 6$ $\frac{3}{4}$
12. $5^{-2} \cdot 3^{-2} \cdot 4^0$ $\frac{1}{225}$
13. $\frac{-52x^7y}{-4x^3y^3}$ $\frac{13x^4}{y^2}$
14. $\frac{35rs^4}{-7rs^{10}}$ $-\frac{5}{s^6}$
15. $\frac{12s^2t^3}{-4st^4}$ $\frac{-3s}{t}$
16. $\frac{-8t^2v}{-10tv^4}$ $\frac{4t}{5v^3}$
17. $\left(\frac{2}{3}\right)^4$ $\frac{16}{81}$
18. $\left(\frac{1}{2}\right)^{-3}$ 8
19. $\left(\frac{2c^4}{5d}\right)^2$ $\frac{4c^8}{25d^2}$
20. $\left(\frac{-3g^5}{2h^3}\right)^3$ $\frac{-27g^{15}}{8h^9}$
21. **GEOMETRY** The volume of the rectangular solid shown is $4x^2y$. Find the height. x

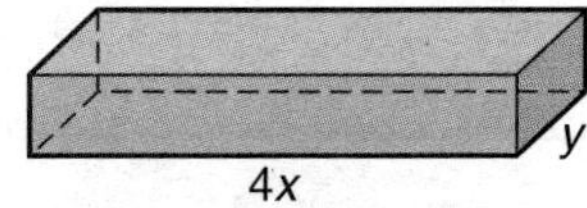

22. **GEOMETRY** The formula for the volume of a sphere is $V = \frac{4\pi r^3}{3}$ where r is the radius of the sphere. Write a formula for the volume that uses d, the diameter. $V = \frac{\pi d^3}{6}$

EXTEND

Simplify. Write with positive exponents.

23. $\frac{(2a^3b)^4(4ab^3)}{(3b)^2}$ $\frac{64a^{13}b^5}{9}$
24. $\frac{(4c^2)(-cd^4)^5}{8c^4}$ $\frac{-c^3d^{20}}{2}$
25. $\frac{(g^2h^4)^2(-2gh)^3}{(4g^3h^5)^2}$ $\frac{-gh}{2}$
26. $\frac{(3s^4t^5)^2(-st)^4}{(5s^4t^5)^2}$ $\frac{9s^4t^4}{25}$
27. $\left(\frac{2wx}{5w^4x^3}\right)^{-2}$ $\frac{25w^6x^4}{4}$
28. $\left(\frac{-y^2z^5}{3yz^3}\right)^{-3}$ $\frac{-27}{y^3z^6}$
29. **WRITING MATHEMATICS** Explain how you could use positive and negative exponents to evaluate $\frac{6}{K^2}$ when $K = \frac{2}{3}$. See Additional Answers.

Demography The annual growth rate of the population of the Dominican Republic is 2.2%. The expression $p(1.022)^t$ will give an estimate of the population t years from now, if p is the present population.

30. Write an expression for the population t years ago. $p(1.022)^{-t}$

31. Estimate the population two years ago if the population is now 7,800,000. 7,467,802

32. **Astronomy** The force of gravitation between two objects is given by the formula $F = \frac{GmM}{r^2}$ where F is the force, G is a gravitational constant, m is the mass of one object, M is the mass of the other object, and r is the distance between the objects. Suppose that m is doubled, M is tripled, and r is doubled. Describe the effect on F. Explain your answer. See Additional Answers.

THINK CRITICALLY

Find a value of n that makes each statement true. Assume that none of the bases is 0.

33. $h^{-3} \cdot h^n = 1$ 3

34. $(ab^3)^n = 1$ 0

35. $\left(\frac{cd^6}{c^5d^n}\right)^2 = \frac{d^8}{c^8}$ 2

36. If $\frac{p^a}{p^b} = p^2$, write a formula for a in terms of b. $a = b + 2$

37. Suppose $\frac{x^p}{x^q} = x^n$, $p > 0$, $q > 0$, and $n < 0$. Compare p and q. Justify your answer. See Additional Answers.

MIXED REVIEW

Solve. Lesson 3.7

38. $6x + 5 = 3x - 13$ −6

39. $7y + 2(y - 1) = 4y + 18$ 4

40. $2z = 9z + 28$ −4

41. Graph these points on the coordinate plane. See Additional Answers. Lesson 4.3

a. $(7, 0)$ b. $(0, -2)$ c. $(-1, -4)$ d. $(1, -3)$

42. Using the graph you made for Exercise 41, connect the points consecutively to form a closed figure. Is the figure a triangle? Justify your answer. See Additional Answers. Lesson 4.3

Solve. Lesson 5.4

43. $2x - 1 > -7$ $x > -3$

44. $5 - 3x \geq 26$ $x \leq -7$

45. $4x + 1 < -1$ $x < -\frac{1}{2}$

46. $4 > 5x - 1$ $x < 1$

47. **Standardized Tests** Which system has the solution (9, 2)? C; Lesson 7.3

A. $\begin{cases} x = 3y \\ x + 2y = -35 \end{cases}$ B. $\begin{cases} y = -2x \\ x - y = -27 \end{cases}$ C. $\begin{cases} x = 4y + 1 \\ 2x + y = 20 \end{cases}$ D. $\begin{cases} y = x + 3 \\ 2x - y = 2 \end{cases}$

Simplify. Write with positive exponents. Lesson 11.3

48. $\frac{-14b^9}{-7b^7}$ $2b^2$

49. $\frac{-5x^6y^4}{x^8y^5}$ $\frac{-5}{x^2y}$

50. $\left(\frac{4a^2}{3b^3}\right)^3$ $\frac{64a^6}{27b^9}$

51. $\left(\frac{1}{3}\right)^{-4}$ 81

Error Alert Watch for students who give the answer $-5s^6$ for Exercise 14. These students are subtracting and writing the positive result in the numerator even though the greater exponent occurs in the denominator. The correct solution is

$$\frac{35rs^4}{-7rs^{10}} = -5s^{-6} = \frac{-5}{s^6}$$

Extend For Exercises 23–28, ask students what they must do before finding the quotient of each expression. **Simplify the various parts of each expression.**

Think Critically For Exercises 33 and 34, ask when $x^k = 1$. **when $k = 0$**

5 FOLLOW-UP

Extension Have students use a graphing utility to graph $y = 2^x$. Ask if the graph will cross the x-axis. If so, where? If not, why not? **No, because $2^x \neq 0$ for any values of x.**

NAME ______________ CLASS ________ DATE ________

11.3 DIVIDE MONOMIALS

You can work with units of measure similar to the way you work with monomials.

Example

In the formula for force when $F = m \cdot a$ the metric unit of force is newtons. One newton is equal to $\frac{1\text{ kg} \cdot \text{m}}{\text{s}^2}$. How many newtons are there when $m = 200$ g and $a = \frac{5\text{ m}}{\text{s}^2}$?

Solution

$$F = m \cdot a = 200\text{ g} \cdot \frac{5\text{ m}}{\text{s}^2}$$

$$= 200\text{ g} \cdot \frac{1\text{ kg}}{1000\text{ g}} \cdot \frac{5\text{ m}}{\text{s}^2} \quad \text{Convert g to kg.}$$

$$= \frac{200 \cdot 5}{1000} \cdot \frac{\text{g} \cdot \text{kg} \cdot \text{m}}{\text{g} \cdot \text{s}^2} \quad \text{Use associative property to regroup.}$$

$$= \frac{1\text{ kg} \cdot \text{m}}{\text{s}^2} = 1\text{ newton}$$

So, when $F = \frac{1\text{ kg} \cdot \text{m}}{\text{s}^2}$, force is 1 newton.

EXERCISES

1. Another formula for force is $F = \frac{k \cdot q_1 \cdot q_2}{r^2}$. Find the force when $k = \frac{9\text{kg} \cdot \text{km}^3}{\text{s}^2 \cdot c^2}$, $q_1 = 0.00004\ c$, $q_2 = 0.00001\ c$ (c is coulombs, a unit of electrical charge) and $r = 3$ m. Remember to convert units if necessary.
0.4 newtons or 0.4 $\frac{\text{kg m}}{\text{s}^2}$

2. How did the units for Question 1 compare to those in the Example?
They are the same.

3. The metric unit of power is the watt. One watt is equal to $\frac{1\text{ kg} \cdot \text{m}^2}{\text{s}^3}$. The formula for power is $P = \frac{F \cdot d}{t}$. Find the power when $F = 1$ newton, $d = 3.6$ km, and $t = 1$ h. Remember to convert units if necessary.
1 watt or $\frac{1\text{ kg} \cdot \text{m}^2}{\text{s}^3}$

4. Another formula for power is $P = \frac{WI}{q}$. Find the power if $W = \frac{1\text{ kg} \cdot \text{m}^3}{\text{s}^2}$, $I = \frac{5\text{ c}}{\text{s}}$, and $q = 0.5$ c.
10 watts or $\frac{10\text{ kg} \cdot \text{m}^2}{\text{s}^3}$

5. How did the units for in Question 4 compare to those in the Question 3?
They are the same.

18 South-Western Algebra 1: AN INTEGRATED APPROACH

LESSON PLANNING

Objectives

- ▶ Write numbers in scientific notation.
- ▶ Compute with numbers written in scientific notation.

Vocabulary

scientific notation
standard notation

Technology/Multimedia

calculator

Resources

Warm Up 11.4
Reteaching 11.4
Extra Practice 11.4
Enrichment 11.4
Transparencies 62, 63
Student Handbook
Lesson Quiz 11.4
Technology Activity 27

ASSIGNMENTS

Basic: 1–24, 26–28, 30, 32, 34, 35, 37, Project Connection 1–5, AlgebraWorks 1–7

Average: 1–32, 34–38, Project Connection 1–5, AlgebraWorks 1–7

Enriched: 1–39, Project Connection 1–5, AlgebraWorks 1–7

1 MOTIVATE

Explore Have students make a chart for 2.4×10^n where n is an integer from –5 to 5. Ask students what patterns they notice. **Each exponent names the number of places the decimal point moves to the right of 2 for positive exponents or to the left of 2 for negative exponents.**

11.4 Scientific Notation

SPOTLIGHT ON LEARNING

WHAT? In this lesson you will learn

- to write large and small numbers using scientific notation.
- to compute with numbers written in scientific notation.

WHY? Using scientific notation helps you to work with very large and very small numbers in solving problems in astronomy, history, physics, chemistry, and aerial photography.

Explore

1. Copy and complete the chart.

Exponential Expression										
10^5	10^4	10^3	10^2	10^1	10^0	10^{-1}	10^{-2}	10^{-3}	10^{-4}	10^{-5}
				10		0.1				
Value										

100,000; 10,000; 1,000; 100; 1; 0.01; 0.001; 0.0001; 0.00001

2. What patterns do you notice? Possible patterns are that the bases are all 10 and that each exponent names the number of places the decimal point moves to the right of 1 (positive exponent) or to the left of 1 (negative exponent).

Build Understanding

Any number in decimal form, such as 12.456, 1,000,000,000, or 0.0083, is in **standard notation**. Large numbers, such as for the distance between planets, and small numbers, such as for the size of an atom, take up a great deal of space when written in standard notation. To conserve space, **scientific notation** is used to write such numbers. In scientific notation a number is written as a product of a number between 1 and 10 and a power of 10.

SCIENTIFIC NOTATION

A number written in the form $m \times 10^n$ where $1 \le m < 10$ and n is any integer.

CHECK UNDERSTANDING

Is 12.64×10^3 written in scientific notation? Explain.

no; the first number is greater than 10

Example 1 shows the use of scientific notation for large numbers.

EXAMPLE 1

Write each number in scientific notation.

a. 8,000

b. 3,456,000

Solution

a. $8{,}000 = 8{,}000.$

$8{,}000$ (decimal places counted 1 2 3)

$= 8.000 \times 10^?$

$= 8 \times 10^3$

Move the decimal point left so that it shows a number between 1 and 10. To find the exponent of 10, count the number of decimal places you moved the decimal point to the left.

b. $3{,}456{,}000 = 3.456000 \times 10^? = 3.456 \times 10^6$ ◄

Scientific notation is often used by astronomers to express distances in the universe.

EXAMPLE 2

ASTRONOMY The sun is approximately 93,000,000 mi from Earth. Write this distance in scientific notation.

Solution

$$93{,}000{,}000 = 9.3 \times 10^7$$

In scientific notation, the distance between Earth and the sun is 9.3×10^7 mi. ◄

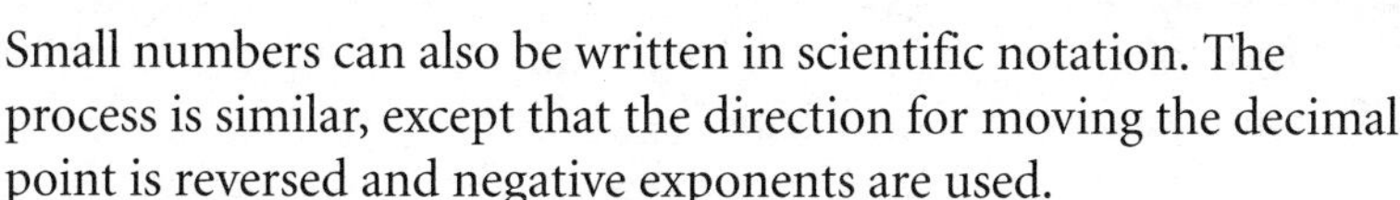

Small numbers can also be written in scientific notation. The process is similar, except that the direction for moving the decimal point is reversed and negative exponents are used.

EXAMPLE 3

Write each number in scientific notation.

a. 0.0006

b. 0.000000792

Solution

a. $0.0006 = 0006. \times 10^?$
$= 6 \times 10^{-4}$

Move the decimal point to the right of the first nonzero digit.

b. $0.000000792 = 0000007.92 \times 10^?$
$= 7.92 \times 10^{-7}$ ◄

CHECK UNDERSTANDING

To write 7,350,000 in scientific notation, would you use a positive number or a negative number for the exponent? to write 0.00894?

positive number; negative number

To write numbers in standard notation, reverse the process.

EXAMPLE 4

Write each number in standard notation.

a. 4.03×10^6 **b.** 5.2×10^{-5} **c.** 2.86×10^{-8}

Solution

a. $4.03 \times 10^6 = 4\,030000.$
$= 4{,}030{,}000$

Move the decimal point to the right 6 places.

b. $5.2 \times 10^{-5} = .00005\,2$
$= 0.000052$

Move the decimal point to the left 5 places.

c. $2.86 \times 10^{-8} = .00000002\,86$
$= 0.0000000286$ ◄

Move the decimal point to the left 8 places.

CHECK UNDERSTANDING

When changing from scientific notation to standard notation, how do you know in which direction to move the decimal point?

positive exponent, move to the right; negative exponent, move to the left

2 TEACH

Use the Pages/Build Understanding

Example 1: After students have read through part *a*, ask what they should first do in order to write 12,300 in scientific notation. **Decide that the decimal will be placed after the 1.** Ask them how they should choose the exponent for 10. **It will be the number of places the decimal is moved.**

Example 2: Have students read 93,000,000 miles. **93 million miles** Have them explain why 9.3×10^7 is a number written in scientific notation. **because $1 \leq 9.3 < 10$ and it is multiplied by a power of 10**

Example 3: After students have read Example 3, point out that in Example 1 the exponents are positive and in Example 3 they are negative. Ask students how they can remember when the exponent should be positive and when it should be negative. **Possible answer: It will be positive for numbers whose absolute value is greater than or equal to 1 and negative for numbers whose absolute value is between 0 and 1**

Example 4: For part a, ask students how they know to move the decimal point 6 places to the right. **+6 is the exponent of 10** For part b ask how they know to move the decimal point 5 places to the left. **–5 is the exponent of 10.**

Example 5: Ask students to describe the associative and commutative properties of multiplication and to give examples. **The associative property states that groupings may be changed without changing the product: $3 \cdot (1/3 \cdot 4) = (3 \cdot 1/3) \cdot 4$; the commutative property states that numbers may trade places without changing the product: $3 \cdot 4 \cdot 1/3 = 3 \cdot 1/3 \cdot 4$.** Ask students to explain why $10^5 \cdot 10^4 = 10^9$. **The exponents are added because of the product of powers property of exponents.**

Example 6: Ask why 135.24×10^{12} is not in scientific notation. **135 is not greater than or equal to 1 and less than 10**

Ongoing Assessment The important concepts and skills are writing numbers in scientific notation and computing with numbers in scientific notation. To assess these ideas, have students demonstrate how they have applied these concepts and skills in Exercises 6, 9, and 11 of the Try These section.

Guided Practice/Try These For Exercises 1–8, ask students how they determined where to place the decimal point. **The decimal is placed to the right of the first nonzero digit.** Ask a student to describe how to evaluate the expression in Exercise 13. **$(7.6 \times 10^4)^2 = 7.6^2 \times (10^4)^2 = 57.76 \times 10^8 = 5.776 \times 10^1 \times 10^8 = 5.776 \times 10^9$**

COMMUNICATING ABOUT ALGEBRA

Discuss the conditions under which you could add numbers that are expressed in scientific notation.

when all the numbers are expressed using the same power of 10

PROBLEM SOLVING TIP

Most calculators can show scientific notation for very large and very small numbers. The number to the right of the E is the exponent for the 10. For example, 4.68E4 is 4.68×10^4.

Numbers written in scientific notation can be multiplied and divided using properties of exponents.

EXAMPLE 5

Find the product of 4.2×10^5 and 2.31×10^4.

Solution

Use the associative and commutative properties to rearrange the factors. Use the product of powers property for exponents to multiply the powers of 10.

$$(4.2 \times 2.31)(10^5 \times 10^4) = 9.702 \times 10^9$$

Sometimes, you must rewrite the number you get after computing so that your answer is in scientific notation.

EXAMPLE 6

ASTRONOMY The star Vega in the constellation Lyra is 23 light-years away from Earth. A *light-year* is the distance light travels in 1 year, 5.88×10^{12} mi. Find the distance from Earth to Vega in miles. Write the distance in scientific notation.

Solution

Find the product of 23 and 5.88×10^{12}.

$$23 \times 5.88 \times 10^{12} = (23 \times 5.88) \times 10^{12} = 135.24 \times 10^{12}$$

Rewrite 135.24 in scientific notation.

$$135.24 \times 10^{12} = (1.3524 \times 10^2) \times 10^{12} = 1.3524 \times 10^{14}$$

The star Vega is 1.3524×10^{14} mi from Earth.

TRY THESE

Write each number in scientific notation.

1. 3,250,000,000 3.25×10^9
2. 109,000,000 1.09×10^8
3. 72,000,000 7.2×10^7
4. 923,000,000 9.23×10^8
5. 0.00315 3.15×10^{-3}
6. 0.000072 7.2×10^{-5}
7. 0.0000054 5.4×10^{-6}
8. 0.000432 4.32×10^{-4}

Evaluate. Write each result in scientific notation.

9. $(3.5 \times 10^4)(2.1 \times 10^5)$ 7.35×10^9
10. $(1.4 \times 10^7)(4.5 \times 10^8)$ 6.3×10^{15}
11. $\dfrac{9.6 \times 10^9}{1.2 \times 10^2}$ 8×10^7
12. $\dfrac{8.4 \times 10^6}{2.1 \times 10^3}$ 4×10^3
13. $(7.6 \times 10^4)^2$ 5.776×10^9
14. $(6.8 \times 10^6)(9 \times 10^9)$ 6.12×10^{16}

15. **ASTRONOMY** The mean distance of Venus to the sun is 67.2 million miles. Write this number in scientific notation. 6.72×10^7

16. **WRITING MATHEMATICS** Describe the steps used in writing 0.00062 in scientific notation. See Additional Answers.

PRACTICE

Write each number in standard notation.

1. 5.12×10^8 512,000,000
2. 9.7×10^{10} 97,000,000,000
3. 1.2×10^{-5} 0.000012
4. 6.5×10^{-4} 0.00065

Write each number in scientific notation.

5. 314,000 3.14×10^5
6. 4,300,000 4.3×10^6
7. 23,000,000 2.3×10^7
8. 610,000,000 6.1×10^8
9. 0.000415 4.15×10^{-4}
10. 0.00103 1.03×10^{-3}
11. 0.000008 8×10^{-6}
12. 0.000032 3.2×10^{-5}

Evaluate. Write each answer in scientific notation.

13. $(2.4 \times 10^5)(1.3 \times 10^9)$ 3.12×10^{14}
14. $(4 \times 10^6)(2.1 \times 10^8)$ 8.4×10^{14}
15. $\dfrac{9 \times 10^7}{3 \times 10^4}$ 3×10^3
16. $\dfrac{7.4 \times 10^{10}}{2 \times 10^6}$ 3.7×10^4
17. $(2 \times 10^5)^2$ 4×10^{10}
18. $(3 \times 10^6)^2$ 9×10^{12}
19. $(4.6 \times 10^4)(9 \times 10^{15})$ 4.14×10^{20}
20. $(8.1 \times 10^5)(7.5 \times 10^{11})$ 6.075×10^{17}

Write the number in each problem in scientific notation.

21. **ASTRONOMY** The distance from Mercury to the sun is 57,900,000 mi. 5.79×10^7

22. **HISTORY** Archimedes wrote that the Greeks had traditional number names only for numbers through myriad myriads. (A myriad was equal to 10,000.) What was the largest number the Greeks could name? 1×10^8

23. **PHYSICS** The wave length of red light is 0.0000065 m. 6.5×10^{-6}

24. **BIOLOGY** The number of hairs on the average human head is 1.5×10^5. There are approximately 5×10^9 people in the world. About how many human hairs are there in the world? 7.5×10^{14}

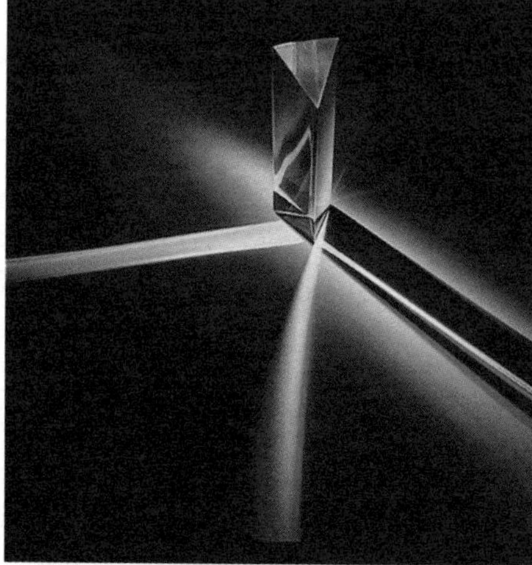

25. **CHEMISTRY** The cross-sectional area of a molecule is about 1.5×10^{-25} mm^2. What are the fewest number of molecules necessary to cover the head of a pin of diameter 2.25 mm? 2.65×10^{25} molecules

EXTEND

Estimate. Write each estimate using scientific notation. Answers will vary.

26. $(9.23 \times 10^7)^2$ 8×10^{15}
27. $(1.09 \times 10^9)^4$ 1×10^{36}
28. $\dfrac{2.03 \times 10^6}{3.98 \times 10^3}$ 5×10^2
29. $\dfrac{3.13 \times 10^{10}}{8.6 \times 10^4}$ 3×10^5
30. $(7.35 \times 10^4)(8.19 \times 10^9)$ 6×10^{14}
31. $(4.7 \times 10^7)(8.3 \times 10^9)$ 4×10^{17}

3 SUMMARIZE

In the Math Journal Explain that often very large numbers and very small numbers are expressed in words such as *2.5 million* or *one billionth.* Have students find examples of very large numbers and very small numbers which are expressed in words in newspapers and magazines. Have them record the examples in their journals and describe how to write the numbers in scientific notation. Ask them also to collect any examples of numbers written in scientific notation and describe how to record those numbers in standard notation.

4 PRACTICE

Practice For Exercises 13–20, remind students to be sure that the number multiplied by a power of 10 is greater than or equal to 1 and less than 10.

NAME ____________ CLASS ________ DATE ________

RETEACHING

11.4 SCIENTIFIC NOTATION

The associative property can help you understand multiplication of numbers written in scientific notation.

Example
Multiply: $(2.34 \cdot 10^3)(7.5 \cdot 10^4)$.

Solution
$(2.34 \cdot 10^3)(7.5 \cdot 10^4)$

$= 2.34 \times 10^3 \times 7.5 \times 10^4$

$= (2.34 \times 7.5)(10^3 \times 10^4)$ Rearrange the factors to separate the powers of 10.

$= 17.55(10^3 \times 10^4)$ Multiply the decimal numbers.

$= 17.55 \times 10^7$ Multiply the powers of 10.

$= 1.755 \times 10^8$ Write the solution in scientific notation.

EXERCISES

Evaluate. Write each answer in scientific notation.

1. $(2.3 \times 10^5)(4.1 \times 10^4)$ **(9.43×10^9)**
2. $(1.6 \times 10^8)(2.2 \times 10^6)$ **(3.52×10^{14})**
3. $(1.8 \times 10^4)(1.2 \times 10)$ **(2.16×10^5)**
4. $(3.9 \times 10^3)(1.2 \times 10^7)$ **(4.68×10^{10})**
5. $(7.5 \times 10^5)(4.2 \times 10^6)$ **(3.15×10^{12})**
6. $(8.1 \times 10^2 \times 9.2 \times 10^4)$ **(7.452×10^7)**
7. $\dfrac{7.5 \times 10^4}{3.0 \times 10^2}$ **(2.5×10^2)**
8. $\dfrac{5.2 \times 10^8}{4.0 \times 10^5}$ **(1.3×10^3)**
9. $\dfrac{8 \times 10^7}{2 \times 10^5}$ **(4×10^2)**
10. $\dfrac{7.13 \times 10^9}{3.1 \times 10^5}$ **(2.3×10^4)**
11. $(2.5 \times 10^2)^2$ **(6.25×10^4)**
12. $(3.8 \times 10^4)^2$ **(1.444×10^9)**
13. $(4.2 \times 10^6)^2$ **(1.764×10^{13})**
14. $(2.9 \times 10^8)^2$ **(8.41×10^{16})**

22 *South-Western Algebra 1: AN INTEGRATED APPROACH*

Extend For Exercise 32, answers will vary slightly depending on the value for π students use. Students will need to use the formula for the circumference of a circle to solve the problem.

Think Critically Have students describe how they found p for Exercise 35. **possible answer:** $4.23 \times 10^6 = 423 \times 10^p$, $4.23 \times 10^6 = 4.23 \times 10^2 \times 10^p$, $10^6 = 10^2 \times 10^p$, $10^6 = 10^{2+p}$, $6 = 2 + p$, $4 = p$ Have students describe how they found p for Exercise 38. **possible answer:** $6.7 \times 10^{-4} = p \times 10^{-8}$, $6.7 \times 10^{-4}/10^{-8} = p$, $6.7 \times 10^{-4}/10^{-8} = p$, $6.7 \times 10^8/10^4 = p$, $6.7 \times 10^{8-4} = p$, $6.7 \times 10^4 = p$, $67{,}000 = p$

NAME ______ CLASS ______ DATE ______

EXTRA PRACTICE 11.4 SCIENTIFIC NOTATION

Write each number in standard notation.

1. 1.23×10^7 **12,300,000**
2. 6.09×10^4 **60,900**
3. 4.81×10^5 **481,000**
4. 2.2×10^8 **220,000,000**
5. 9.1×10^5 **910,000**
6. 8.04×10^2 **804**
7. 5.5×10^4 **55,000**
8. 8.3×10^7 **83,000,000**
9. 2.3×10^{-2} **0.023**
10. 3.4×10^{-4} **0.00034**
11. 5.7×10^{-5} **0.000057**
12. 7.7×10^{-3} **0.0077**

Write each number in scientific notation.

13. 1,200,000 $\mathbf{1.2 \times 10^6}$
14. 13,500,000 $\mathbf{1.35 \times 10^7}$
15. 43,000,000 $\mathbf{4.3 \times 10^7}$
16. 91,500 $\mathbf{9.15 \times 10^4}$
17. 0.0042 $\mathbf{4.2 \times 10^{-3}}$
18. 0.00056 $\mathbf{5.6 \times 10^{-4}}$
19. 0.000261 $\mathbf{2.61 \times 10^{-4}}$
20. 0.00308 $\mathbf{3.08 \times 10^{-3}}$

Evaluate. Write each answer in scientific notation.

21. $(3.2 \times 10^3)(1.7 \times 10^5)$ $\mathbf{5.44 \times 10^8}$
22. $(2.6 \times 10^9)(2.1 \times 10^8)$ $\mathbf{5.46 \times 10^{17}}$
23. $(7.4 \times 10^5)(6.3 \times 10^6)$ $\mathbf{4.662 \times 10^{12}}$
24. $(9.1 \times 10^6)(4.7 \times 10^3)$ $\mathbf{4.277 \times 10^{10}}$
25. $\frac{9.6 \times 10^8}{8.0 \times 10^3}$ $\mathbf{1.2 \times 10^5}$
26. $\frac{7.4 \times 10^7}{3.7 \times 10^2}$ $\mathbf{2.0 \times 10^5}$

Write each number in scientific notation.

27. **GEOLOGY** The movement of a glacier is approximately 0.0005 km per hour. $\mathbf{5.0 \times 10^{-4}}$
28. **COMPUTERS** A *micron* is a unit of measure 0.001 mm in length. A computer microchip may be 0.25 microns in width. What is the width of a microchip in mm? $\mathbf{(1.0 \times 10^{-3})(2.5 \times 10^{-1}) = 2.5 \times 10^{-4}}$ **mm**

24 South-Western *Algebra 1:* AN INTEGRATED APPROACH

Use scientific notation to solve each problem.

32. **AERONAUTICS** The equatorial radius of Earth is about 4000 mi. How long will it take a caped superhero traveling at 600 mi/h to fly around Earth at a constant altitude of 100 mi directly over the equator? 4.2913×10^1 h

33. **SPEED OF SOUND** The speed of sound through air varies with the air temperature. At 0°C, the speed of sound is 330 m/s. At 1000°C, it is 700 m/s. Find the number of meters per second increase for each degree Celsius. See Additional Answers.

34. **WRITING MATHEMATICS** Compare finding products and quotients using standard and scientific notation. What do you think are the advantages and disadvantages of each system? See Additional Answers.

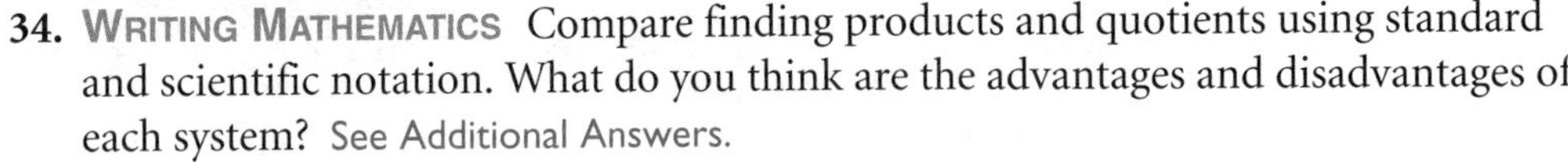

THINK CRITICALLY

Find the value of p that will make each sentence true.

35. $4.23 \times 10^6 = 423 \times 10^p$ 4
36. $9.1 \times 10^{-7} = 0.091 \times 10^p$ −5
37. $5.3 \times 10^7 = p \times 10^6$ 53
38. $6.7 \times 10^{-4} = p \times 10^{-8}$ 6.7×10^4 or 67,000
39. If $(a \times 10^m)(b \times 10^n) = c \times 10^{m+n+1}$, in scientific notation, what must be true about the product, ab? $ab > 10$

PROJECT Connection

1. Make a plane by folding an $8\frac{1}{2}$ by 11 in. sheet of paper as shown.
2. Use a ruler. Along the bottom of the plane, mark off and label every $\frac{1}{2}$ cm starting at the front.
3. Place a paper clip on the first mark, fly the plane, and record the distance. Repeat this test for each mark. For consistency, the same student should "pilot" the plane each time. Decide if you want one or more tests for each mark to collect reliable data.
4. Identify the two marks for which the plane seems to fly best, then test-fly with the clip between these marks to determine final placement. Graph and label your results.

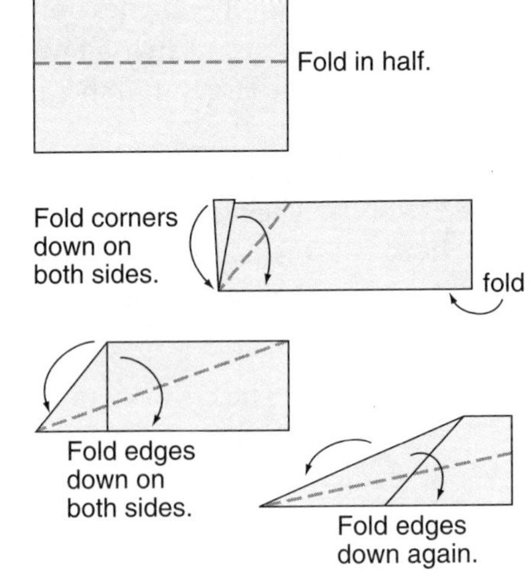
Fold in half.
Fold corners down on both sides.
fold
Fold edges down on both sides.
Fold edges down again.

5. When you have found the best spot for the paper clip, turn the plane upside down and hang it with a thread placed through the clip. How does the plane hang? You have just located the *center of gravity* of your plane. Discuss why this point is important when landing an aircraft. See Additional Answers.

Career
Aerial Photographer

Industries and the government employ aerial photographers, who use scientific notation to determine the actual size or distance between objects appearing on a photo.

A photographer has taken an aerial photo and wants to determine the actual length of a road between two points for the photo caption. First he needs to determine the 1–1 scale factor.

The diagram shows the relationship between the actual length of the road *AB* and the length of the image of the road *PQ* on the photo. The camera lens is at *C*, the focal length *f* of the camera is 150 mm, and the height above ground *H* of the camera is 0.96 km.

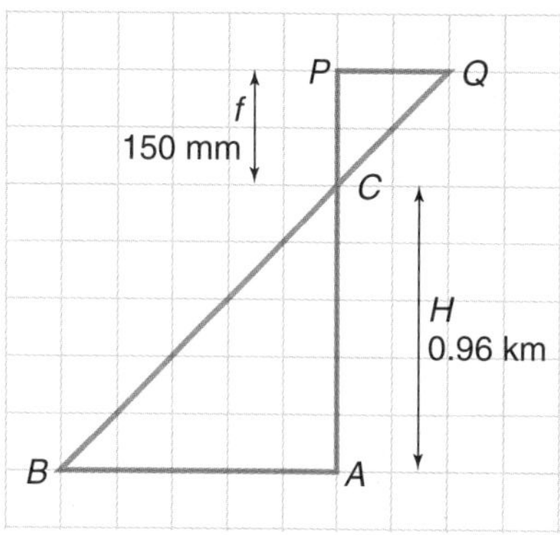

Decision Making

The ratio of the image length *PQ* to the actual length *AB* is the same as $\frac{f}{H}$. The ratio $\frac{f}{H}$ is called a 1–1 scale factor when the numerator and denominator are in the same units.

1. Change *f*, 150 mm, to meters. 0.150 m
2. Change *H*, 0.96 km, to meters. 960 m
3. Write the values you found for *f* and *H* in Questions 1 and 2 in scientific notation. 1.5×10^{-1}, 9.6×10^{2}
4. Find the 1–1 scale factor $\frac{f}{H}$ in scientific notation. 1.5625×10^{-4}
5. Use the proportion $\frac{PQ}{AB} = \frac{f}{H}$ to find the actual length of the road *AB* if the image length *PQ* is 225 mm. 1440 m or 1.44 km

Photo resolution is the smallest actual length whose image can be measured on the photograph. With current technology, it is possible to make measurements on a photograph to the nearest micron (10^{-6} m).

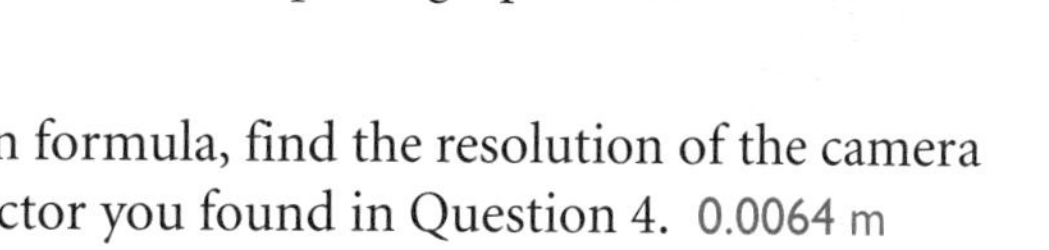

6. Using the proportion formula, find the resolution of the camera with the 1–1 scale factor you found in Question 4. 0.0064 m
7. Name three posible applications for aerial photography. Answers will vary.

5 FOLLOW-UP

Extra Practice Have students rewrite each number in standard notation to find each sum. Then have them write their answers in standard notation.

1. $10^4 + 10^2$ **1.01×10^4**
2. $10^{-3} + 1^{-1}$ **1.01×10^{-1}**
3. $10^3 + 10^{-3}$ **1.000001×10^3**
4. $10^5 + 10^4 + 10^{-2}$ **1.1000001×10^5**

Project Connection This activity presents further aspects of the project introduced on page 516. Be sure students label the half-centimeter marks so they can indicate their results.

AlgebraWorks Some students may have studied ratios of similar triangles in a previous course Tell them that ∠ CBA ≈ ∠ CQP and ask why the ratio of the image length and the actual length is the same as the ratio *f*/H. **The sides of similar triangles are proportionate, meaning that the ratios of their corresponding sides are equal.**

NAME ______________ CLASS ________ DATE ________

ENRICHMENT

11.4 SCIENTIFIC NOTATION

To measure large distances in space, astronomers created the astronomical unit (AU). This unit is equivalent to the average distance from the Sun to the Earth, approximately 148,000,000 km or 1.48×10^8 km. The table gives the approximate distances from the Sun to each planet in millions of kilometers.

Planet	Distance from the Sun		AU
	Millions of km	Scientific Notation	
Mercury	57.9	5.79×10^7	0.4
Venus	108.2	1.082×10^8	0.7
Earth	148	1.48×10^8	1.0
Mars	228.0	2.280×10^8	1.5
Jupiter	788.4	7.884×10^8	5.3
Saturn	1424.6	1.4246×10^9	9.6
Uranus	2866.9	2.8669×10^9	19.4
Neptune	4486.0	4.486×10^9	30.3
Pluto	5889.7	5.8897×10^9	39.8

1. Complete the Scientific Notation column with each planet's distance from the Sun. Use the data you entered to answer Questions 2–5. Write your answers in scientific notation and round to the nearest tenth.
2. How many astronomical units from the Sun is Mercury?
   $(5.79 \times 10^7) \div (1.48 \times 10^8) = 0.39 = 0.4$ AU
3. Which planet is approximately 5 AU from the Sun?
   Jupiter: $(7.784 \times 10^8) \div (1.48 \times 10^8) = 5.3$
4. Approximately how many times greater is Neptune's distance from the Sun than Mercury's?
   approximately 77.5 times: $(4.486 \times 10^9) \div (5.79 \times 10^7) = 77.5$
5. Complete the table by writing the remaining planetary distances from the Sun in astronomical units.

LESSON PLANNING

Objective

► Model addition and subtraction of algebraic expressions using Algeblocks.

Resources

Transparencies 12, 13
Student Handbook

Materials/Manipulatives

Algeblocks
Basic Mats

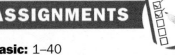

ASSIGNMENTS

Basic: 1–40

Average: 1–40

Enriched: 1–41

1 MOTIVATE

Think Back For Exercise 1, ask students how they can determine like terms. **Like terms have like variables with identical exponents.** Ask students to name the like terms. **$4x$ and $-2x$; $3y$ and $-y$** Have a student describe how to model the expression with Algeblocks. **Place four x-blocks on the positive part, two x-blocks on the negative part, three y-blocks on the positive part, and one y-block on the negative part; remove two zero pairs of x-blocks and one zero pair of y-blocks.** After students have completed Questions 1–7, ask how they can revise the rule they stated in Question 5. **After combining terms, the number of unlike terms will always be less than or equal to the number of different terms in the original expression.**

11.5 Algebra Workshop
Add and Subtract Expressions

SPOTLIGHT ON LEARNING

WHAT? In this lesson you will learn
- to model addition and subtraction of algebraic expressions with Algeblocks.

WHY? Algeblocks can help you to understand addition and subtraction of algebraic expressions useful in solving problems involving geometry and astronomy.

Think Back

1. Use Algeblocks and the Basic Mat to model $4x + 3y - 2x - y$. Combine like terms and remove any zero pairs, sketching each step. Write the resulting algebraic expression. See Additional Answers.
2. How many kinds of unlike terms were in the original expression in Question 1? How many terms did your algebraic expression for Question 1 have? 2 kinds of unlike terms; 2 terms
3. Model $x + 4 - 2x - 6$. Combine like terms and remove any zero pairs, sketching each step. Write the resulting algebraic expression. See Additional Answers.
4. How many kinds of unlike terms were in the original expression in Question 3? How many terms did your algebraic expression for Question 3 have? 2 kinds of unlike terms; 2 terms
5. What pattern do you notice in Questions 2 and 4? See Additional Answers.
6. Model $3x + 2 - y + 1 - 2x - y - x$. Combine like terms and remove any zero pairs, sketching each step. Write the resulting algebraic expression. See Additional Answers.
7. How many kinds of unlike terms were in the original expression in Question 5? How many terms did your algebraic expression for Question 5 have? Why are they different? 3 kinds of unlike terms; 2 terms; the sum of the x-terms was 0, which eliminated the x-terms

Explore

COMMUNICATING ABOUT ALGEBRA

Compare your results for Exercises 11–13 with the results of other students. Did everyone write the terms in the same order? Does it matter?

Work with a partner and Algeblocks.

8. Model the following addition. See Additional Answers.

$$(x^2 + 2x) + (2x^2 - 5x)$$

9. How many different kinds of blocks are on the mat? What do the different kinds of blocks represent? 2; x^2 and x
10. Group blocks that are alike together. Remove any zero pairs from the mat. Write an algebraic expression for the blocks that are left. $3x^2 - 3x$ or $3x^2 + (-3x)$

Use Algeblocks to find each sum.

11. $(3x^2 - 2x + 4) + (5x - 3)$ $3x^2 + 3x + 1$
12. $(x^3 + 4x + 3) + (-2x + 3)$ $x^3 + 2x + 6$
13. $(3xy + 5x - 3y) + (-2xy - 3x - 1)$ $xy + 2x - 3y - 1$

14. **WRITING MATHEMATICS** Make up an addition exercise that has the answer $3x + y - 5$.
answers will vary; possible answer: $(2x + y) + (x - 5)$
15. Combine the expression $2x - 3$ with its opposite, $-2x + 3$, on the same mat. Find the sum. Explain your answer.
See Additional Answers.

Use Algeblocks to model each of the following. First model the expression inside the parentheses. Then move each piece to the opposite side of the mat. Record the result.

16. $-(x + 2)$ $-x - 2$ 17. $-(2xy - y)$ $-2xy + y$ 18. $-(x^2 + y^2)$ $-x^2 - y^2$ 19. $-(-x + 3)$ $x - 3$
20. Model $(4x - 2) - (2x - 3)$ by adding the opposite of $2x - 3$ to $4x - 2$. What is the result? $2x + 1$
21. What is the opposite of $2x^2 + x - 3$? If you combined the original expression, $2x^2 + x - 3$, with its opposite, what would you find?
$-2x^2 - x + 3$; the result is 0
22. Model $(3x^2 + 4x + 2) - (2x^2 + x - 3)$. Remember to add the opposite of the expression being subtracted. $x^2 + 3x + 5$

Find each difference.

23. $(3x - 2) - (x + 4)$ $2x - 6$ 24. $(2xy + y) - (3xy - x)$ $-xy + y + x$
25. $(3x^2 + 4x - 1) - (2x^2 - 7)$ $x^2 + 4x + 6$ 26. $(2y^2 - 3y) - (y^2 + 3y)$ $y^2 - 6y$

Make Connections

27. Use the distributive property to show that $3x + 2x = 5x$.
$3x + 2x = (3 + 2)x = 5x$

Which of these expressions can be simplified by combining like terms? Write *yes* or *no*.

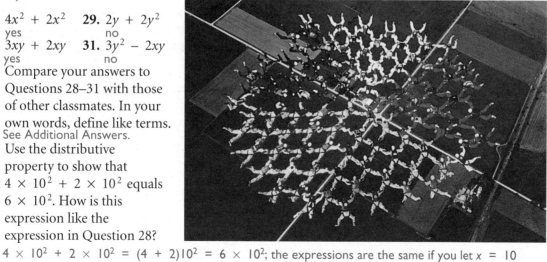

28. $4x^2 + 2x^2$ yes 29. $2y + 2y^2$ no
30. $3xy + 2xy$ yes 31. $3y^2 - 2xy$ no
32. Compare your answers to Questions 28–31 with those of other classmates. In your own words, define like terms.
See Additional Answers.
33. Use the distributive property to show that $4 \times 10^2 + 2 \times 10^2$ equals 6×10^2. How is this expression like the expression in Question 28?

$4 \times 10^2 + 2 \times 10^2 = (4 + 2)10^2 = 6 \times 10^2$; the expressions are the same if you let $x = 10$

2 FACILITATE

Explore Have students share how they found each sum for Questions 11–13. For Questions 16–19, have students read the expressions as; for example, *the opposite of* x + 2. For Question 22, remind students that adding the opposite yields the same result as subtracting.

Make Connections For Question 27, ask students what the distributive property states. **For any real numbers *a*, *b*, and *c*, $a(b + c) = ab + bc$.** For Questions 28–31, have students identify the like and unlike terms. For Question 35, ask students to describe another way to change the form of the numbers so that they can add. **change all of the numbers to multiples of 10^7 or 10^9: 29×10^7, 47×10^7, 72.8×10^7, 339.2×10^7, 70×10^7, 2.8×10^7; 0.29×10^9, 0.47×10^9, 0.728×10^9, 3.392×10^9, 0.7×10^9, 0.028×10^9**

Make Connections Geometry Have students use the Pythagorean theorem to solve for the length of each side of the right isosceles triangle to the nearest tenth of a centimeter. **($a^2 + b^2 = c^2$, $x^2 + x^2 = 8^2$, $2x^2 = 64$, $x^2 = 32$, $x = \sqrt{32}$, $x \approx 5.7$ cm)**

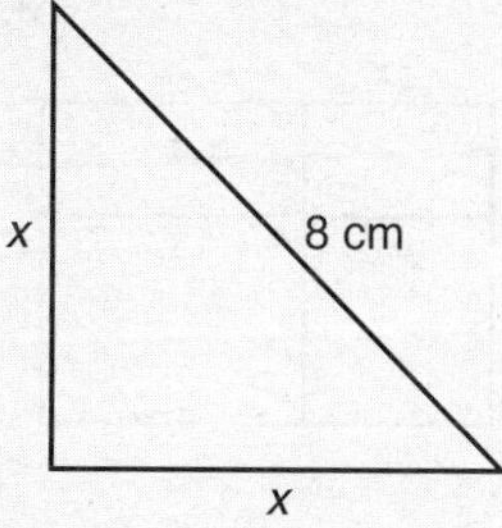

3 SUMMARIZE

Modeling For Question 37, ask students to model another pair of expressions, comprised of one that can and one that cannot be simplified.

Writing Mathematics For Questions 38 and 40, have students share their answers and give examples. **possible examples: (38) $3x + 2x^2 + 4x + x^2 = 3x + 4x + 2x^2 + x^2 = 7x + 3x^2$; (40) $(3x + 2x^2) - (4x + x^2) = 3x + 2x^2 + (-4x - x^2) = 3x + 2x^2 + (-4x) + (-x^2) = 3x + (-4x) + 2x^2 + (-x^2) = -x + x^2$**

Thinking Critically For Question 39, ask students to give examples of an algebraic expression and its opposite. **possible examples: $4x^2 + 2$ and $-4x^2 + (-2)$ or $-4x^2 - 2$; $x^2 - x$ and $-x^2 + x$.**

Going Further For Question 41, ask students how they determined which terms could be combined. **Like terms can be combined, and like terms consist of those terms with the same variable or variables raised to the same power.**

4 FOLLOW-UP

Other Explorations Have students use Algeblocks to find the area of the large rectangle formed by the sum of the areas of the smaller rectangles. Have them write the total area as a polynomial in simplest form. **$2x^2 + 7x + 6$**

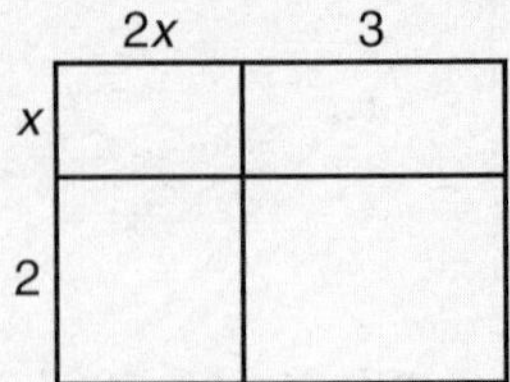

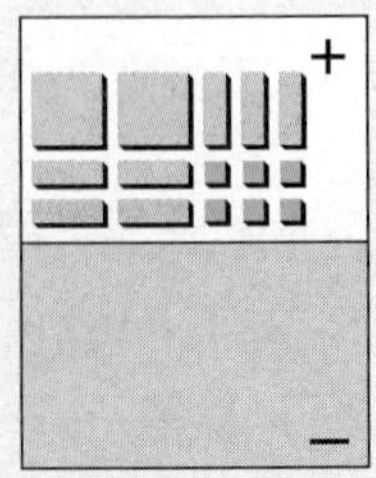

Algebra Workshop

The numbers below represent the total population of the world by region.

North America: 290,000,000	Asia: 3,392,000,000
Latin America: 470,000,000	Africa: 700,000,000
Europe: 728,000,000	Oceania: 28,000,000

34. Rewrite each number in scientific notation. See Additional Answers.

35. Note that the numbers you wrote for Question 34 do not have the same exponent for 10. How could you change the form of some of the numbers so that you can add them? (The new forms will not be in scientific notation.) See Additional Answers.

36. Add to find the total population of the world. Write the answer in scientific notation. 5.608×10^9

Summarize

37. **Modeling** The mat at the left shows Algeblocks for $3x + 2x$. The mat at the right shows $3x^2 + 2x$.

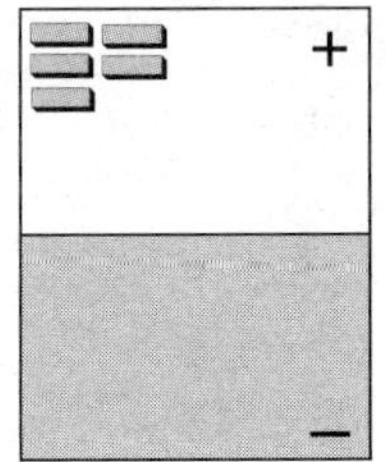

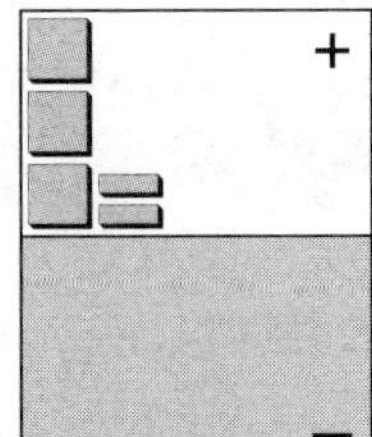

   a. Are the two mats different from one another? See Additional Answers.
   b. Use the mats to simplify $3x + 2x$. Can $3x^2 + 2x$ be simplified? Explain. $5x$; no; the blocks are not the same and cannot be combined

38. **Writing Mathematics** Write a paragraph describing how to add two algebraic expressions. See Additional Answers.

39. **Thinking Critically** How can you find the opposite of an algebraic expression? How is the opposite of an expression like the opposite of a number? See Additional Answers.

40. **Writing Mathematics** Write a paragraph describing how to do the subtraction $(6x^2 - y) - (x - y)$. See Additional Answers.

41. **Going Further** Which terms in the expression $3x^4 + 2x^3 + 2x + 5x^4 + 4x^3 + 3x + 12$ can be combined? Simplify the expression.
$3x^4$ and $5x^4$, $2x^3$ and $4x^3$, and $2x$ and $3x$; $8x^4 + 6x^3 + 5x + 12$

11.6 Add and Subtract Polynomials

Explore

Here is a mathematical trick you can play using the numbers in a calendar.

January 1997						
S	M	T	W	T	F	S
			1	2	3	4
5	6	7	8	9	10	11
12	13	14	15	16	17	18
19	20	21	22	23	24	25
26	27	28	29	30	31	

1. A 3×3 arrangement of numbers has been chosen on the calendar at the right. Find the sum of the nine circled numbers. 153
2. Multiply 9 by the center number of the 3×3 arrangement. What do you notice?
This product is equal to the sum of the nine numbers.
3. Choose a different 3×3 arrangement on a different month in a calendar. Does the same relationship appear? Describe a shortcut for finding the sum of the nine numbers in a 3×3 arrangement for any month in a calendar. Multiply the center number by 9.
4. The matrix at the right shows an algebraic expression for each number in any 3×3 arrangement on a calendar if the center number of the arrangement is x. Show that these expressions work for the dates circled in the calendar in Question 1.
See Additional Answers.

$$\begin{bmatrix} x-8 & x-7 & x-6 \\ x-1 & x & x+1 \\ x+6 & x+7 & x+8 \end{bmatrix}$$

5. Use the algebraic expressions in the matrix to show that the sum of the nine expressions will always be $9x$. Explain how you found your answer. See Additional Answers.

SPOTLIGHT ON LEARNING

WHAT? In this lesson you will learn
- to recognize polynomials.
- to determine the degree of a polynomial.
- to add and subtract polynomials.

WHY? Adding and subtracting polynomials helps you to solve problems in geometry, aeronautical design, and automotive safety.

Build Understanding

The expressions in the matrix in Question 4 of Explore are all *polynomials*. A **polynomial** is either a monomial or a sum or difference of monomials. Each monomial is a **term** of the polynomial. For example, the polynomial $x^2 + y^2 + 2xy + 5$ has four terms. Some polynomials have special names. A polynomial of two terms is a **binomial**. A polynomial of three terms is a **trinomial**.

THINK BACK

A monomial is a number, a variable, or the product of numbers and variables. The degree of a monomial is the sum of the exponents of its variable factors.

LESSON PLANNING

Objectives
- ▶ Determine the degree of a polynomial.
- ▶ Add and subtract polynomials.

Vocabulary
binomial
degree of a polynomial
like terms
polynomial
simplest form
term
trinomial

Technology/Multimedia
calculator
graphing utility

Resources
Warm Up 11.6
Reteaching 11.6
Extra Practice 11.6
Enrichment 11.6
Transparencies 12, 13, 78–80
Student Handbook
Lesson Quiz 11.6

Materials/Manipulatives
Algeblocks
Basic Mats

ASSIGNMENTS

Basic: 1–28, 33–36, Mixed Review 38–47, Project Connection 1–8

Average: 1–30, 33–36, Mixed Review 38–47, Project Connection 1–8

Enriched: 3–37, Mixed Review 38–47, Project Connection 1–8

1 MOTIVATE

Explore After students have completed Questions 1–3, have them share their findings and ask if the rule works for any 3 x 3 arrangement. **yes** For Question 5, students could also find the sum by adding each term or by adding rows. Have students repeat Questions 1–5 for a current calendar and year. Ask if this mathematical trick works for all months and for all years. Have them discuss why or why not. **Yes, the algebraic matrix from Question 4 works for all months and years; since there are always 7 days in a week the pattern is always the same.**

2 TEACH

Use the Pages/Build Understanding Have students read the section. Explain that the prefixes *mono, bi, tri,* and *poly* mean one, two, three, and many respectively. Ask students to name other common words with these prefixes and to discuss their meanings.

Example 1: Ask why the polynomial in part a is a trinomial. **because it consists of three terms** Ask students to explain how they determined the degree of each monomial in part a. **The degree is the exponent of each variable.** Show students $3 = 3x^0$ and ask them why it is or is not true. **It is true because $x^0 = 1$ when $x \neq 0$ and $3 \cdot 1 = 3$.** For part b, ask students what type of polynomial $x^2y^3 + 4y^4$ is, and have them explain how they know. **binomial because it consists of two terms**

Example 2: Ask what the degree of each polynomial is. **3; 9**

Example 3: For adding in vertical form, stress the importance of aligning like terms one under the other.

COMMUNICATING ABOUT ALGEBRA

Compare the degree of a constant term and the degree of a variable term.

You could think of 3 as $3x^0$, or you could think of that a constant has no variable factor and therefore no exponent.

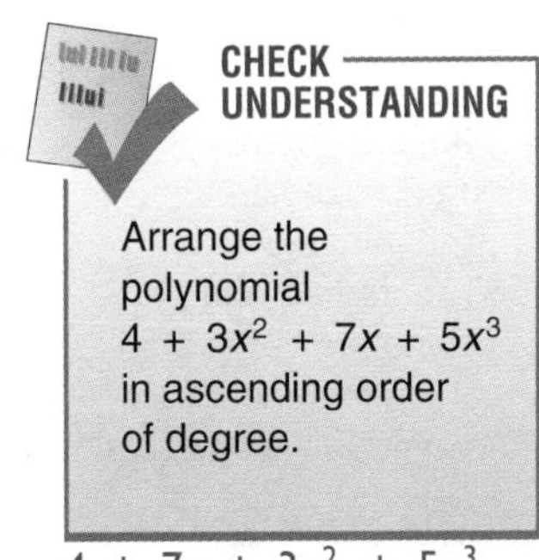

CHECK UNDERSTANDING

Arrange the polynomial $4 + 3x^2 + 7x + 5x^3$ in ascending order of degree.

$4 + 7x + 3x^2 + 5x^3$

The **degree of a polynomial** is the greatest degree of any of its terms.

EXAMPLE 1

Determine the degree of each polynomial.

a. $2x^2 + 5x + 3$

b. $x^2y^3 + 4y^4$

Solution

a. The degree of each term of the trinomial $2x^2 + 5x + 3$ is

$$\begin{array}{lccc} & 2x^2 & + 5x & + 3 \\ & \uparrow & \uparrow & \uparrow \\ \text{degree:} & 2 & 1 & 0 \end{array}$$

Since the greatest degree of any of the terms is 2, the degree of the trinomial is 2.

b. Since the degree of x^2y^3 is 5 (the sum of the exponents of its variable factors) and the degree of $4y^4$ is 4, the degree of the binomial $x^2y^3 + 4y^4$ is 5.

Polynomials are usually arranged so that the degrees of one variable in the terms are either in ascending or descending order.

EXAMPLE 2

Arrange the terms of each polynomial in descending order of degree of the variable x.

a. $4 + 3x^2 + 7x + 5x^3$

b. $3x^2y^5 + 7xy^8 + 2x^3y^2$

Solution

For descending order, the term with the greatest degree should appear first.

a. $5x^3 + 3x^2 + 7x + 4$

b. $2x^3y^2 + 3x^2y^5 + 7xy^8$

Recall that the terms $4x^2$ and $-7x^2$ are **like terms** because they have the same variable with the same exponent. Like terms can be combined by using the distributive property.

$$\begin{aligned} 4x^2 + (-7x^2) &= [4 + (-7)]x^2 \\ &= -3x^2 \end{aligned}$$

Polynomials are added by combining their like terms.

EXAMPLE 3

Add the following polynomials.

$$(2x^2 + 3x - 2) + (x^2 - 3)$$

Solution

One way to find the sum is to use the commutative and associative properties to rearrange the terms of the two polynomials so that like terms are together.

$$(2x^2 + 3x - 2) + (x^2 - 3)$$
$$= (2x^2 + x^2) + 3x + [-2 + (-3)]$$

Then use the distributive property to combine like terms by adding their coefficients.

$$= (2 + 1)x^2 + 3x + [-2 + (-3)]$$
$$= (3)x^2 + 3x + (-5)$$
$$= 3x^2 + 3x - 5$$

Another way to find the sum is to write the polynomials in vertical form, with like terms aligned in columns.

$$\begin{array}{r} 2x^2 + 6x - 4 \\ +\ 2x^2 \qquad - 5 \\ \hline 4x^2 + 6x - 9 \end{array}$$

There is no x-term; leave a space.
Like terms are combined in each column.

The sum of the two polynomials is $4x^2 + 6x - 9$. ◄

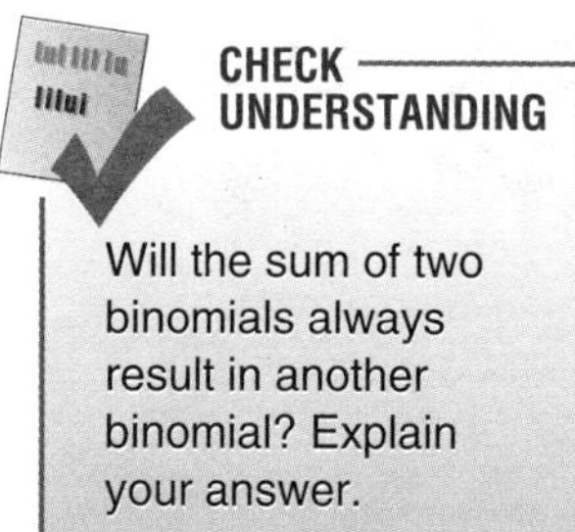

CHECK UNDERSTANDING

Will the sum of two binomials always result in another binomial? Explain your answer.

See Additional Answers.

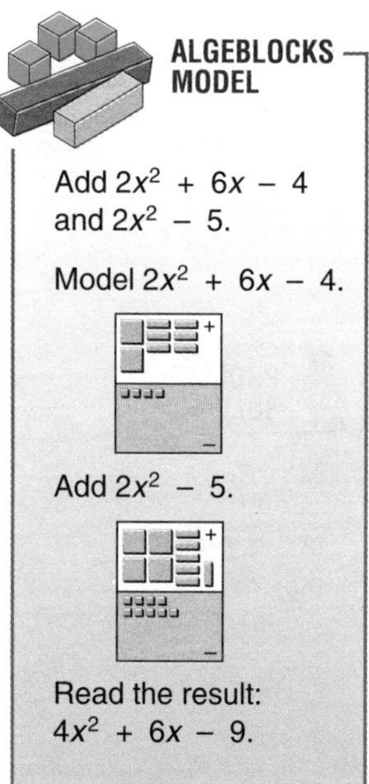

ALGEBLOCKS MODEL

Add $2x^2 + 6x - 4$ and $2x^2 - 5$.

Model $2x^2 + 6x - 4$.

Add $2x^2 - 5$.

Read the result: $4x^2 + 6x - 9$.

Recall that you can subtract a number by adding its opposite.

$$a - b = a + (-b)$$

The opposite of a polynomial is the opposite of each of its terms.

EXAMPLE 4

Find the opposite of each polynomial.

a. $2x + 7$

b. $x^2 + 4x - 2$

Solution

a. The opposite of $2x + 7$ is $-(2x + 7) = -2x - 7$.

b. The opposite of $x^2 + 4x - 2$ is $-x^2 - 4x + 2$. ◄

To subtract two polynomials, add the opposite of the polynomial being subtracted.

Example 4: First have students give examples of subtracting real numbers by adding their opposites. **possible examples: 7 – 4 = 7 + (–4) = 3, 8 – (–2) = 8 + 2 = 10** Then have students describe in words how to find the opposite of a polynomial. **Find the opposite of each term in the polynomial.**

Example 5: Ask students to identify the properties used in the first three steps of the solution **definition of subtraction, commutative and associative properties, distributive property**

Technology
Explain that graphing utilities and matrices can be used to add and subtract polynomials. Stress that the coefficients for like terms must be in the same position in each matrix.

- $(12x^2 + 36xy - 16y^2) + (24x^2 - 13xy - 48y^2)$

  $A = [12\ 36\ {-16}]$
  $B = [24\ {-13}\ {-48}]$
  $A + B =$

  [36 23 –64] so $(12x^2 + 36xy - 16y^2) + (24x^2 - 13xy - 48y^2) = 36x^2 + 23xy - 64y^2$

- $(12x^3 + 16x^2 - 25x + 52) - (43x^3 - 12x + 16)$

  $A = [12\ 16\ {-25}\ 52]$
  $B = [43\ 0\ {-12}\ 16]$
  $A - B =$

  [–31 16 –13 36] $(12x^3 + 16x^2 - 25x + 52) - (43x^3 - 12x + 16) = -31x^3 + 16x^2 - 13x + 36$

Example 6: Ask students to identify the like terms in the lengths of the triangle. **x, $2x$, and $3x$; 5, 9, and 2**

Ongoing Assessment The important concepts and skills involve determining the degree of a polynomial and adding and subtracting polynomials. To assess these ideas, have students demonstrate how they have applied these concepts and skills in Exercises 3, 11, and 15 of the Try These section.

Guided Practice/Try These For Exercises 4–5, ask students what steps they follow in arranging the polynomials in descending order. **Find the degree of the variable *x* in each monomial and list the monomial with the highest degree of the variable *x* first, the next highest degree next, and so on.** For Exercise 9, ask students to list the like terms. Ask how many different terms the sum will have. **$7x^2y$ and $2x^2y$, $-3xy$ and $4xy$, $8y$; 3**

3 SUMMARIZE

In the Math Journal Have students write a paragraph explaining how to recognize like terms. **They are numbers with no variables, or they have the same variable or product of variables with the same exponents for all like variables.**

4 PRACTICE

Practice For Exercises 7–22, remind students that to subtract a polynomial, they add its opposite. For Exercise 23, ask students what they will need to do to find the area of the shaded area. **Subtract the area of the small rectangle from the area of the large rectangle.** For Exercise 24, ask students how they can find the surface area of the rectangular prism. **Add the areas of each side of the rectangular prism or use the formula, $SA = 2(A_1 + A_2 + A_3)$, where A_1, A_2, and A_3 are the areas of the top and two adjoining sides.**

CHECK UNDERSTANDING

Show with an example that when a polynomial and its opposite are added, the result is 0.

possible example: $x + 2 + (-x - 2) = 0$

PROBLEM SOLVING TIP

After adding or subtracting polynomials, write the answer in descending order of one variable.

EXAMPLE 5

Subtract: $(5y^2 + 2y - 2) - (3y^2 + 7y - 8)$

Solution

Write the opposite of $3y^2 + 7y - 8$, then combine like terms.

$$\begin{aligned} &(5y^2 + 2y - 2) - (3y^2 + 7y - 8) \\ &= 5y^2 + 2y - 2 + (-3y^2 - 7y + 8) \\ &= 5y^2 - 3y^2 + 2y - 7y - 2 + 8 \\ &= (5 - 3)y^2 + (2 - 7)y + (-2 + 8) \\ &= 2y^2 - 5y + 6 \end{aligned}$$

The difference is $2y^2 - 5y + 6$.

A polynomial is in **simplest form** when it contains no like terms.

EXAMPLE 6

GEOMETRY Find the perimeter of the triangle. Write the answer in simplest form.

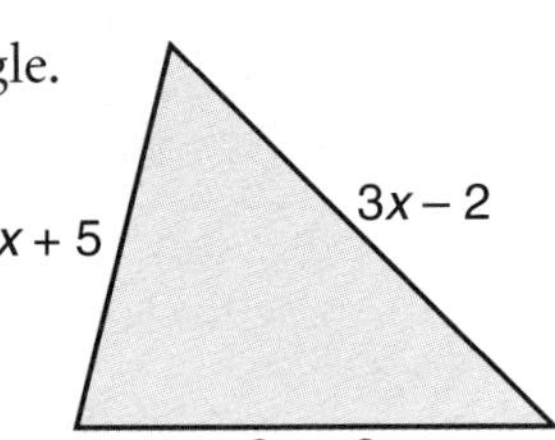

Solution

Find the perimeter by adding the lengths of each side.

$$\begin{array}{r} x + 5 \\ 2x - 9 \\ + \ 3x - 2 \\ \hline 6x - 6 \end{array}$$

In simplest form, the perimeter of the triangle is $6x - 6$.

TRY THESE

Give the degree of each polynomial.

1. $2x^6 - 11x^4$ 6
2. $-6y^2 + 2y + 9$ 2
3. $9xy + 5x^2y$ 3

Arrange each polynomial in descending order of degree of the variable *x*.

4. $4x + 8 + 2x^3 + 3x^2$ — $2x^3 + 3x^2 + 4x + 8$
5. $6xy^3 - 2x^4y + 3x^2y^2 + 9$ — $-2x^4y + 3x^2y^2 + 6xy^3 + 9$

Add.

6. $\begin{array}{r} 5x - 11 \\ + \ 6x - 1 \\ \hline \end{array}$ $11x - 12$
7. $\begin{array}{r} -2x^2 + 6x - 9 \\ + \ 4x^2 - 3x + 4 \\ \hline \end{array}$ $2x^2 + 3x - 5$
8. $8x + 2y + (7y - 8)$ $8x + 9y - 8$
9. $7x^2y - 3xy + (8y + 2x^2y + 4xy)$ $9x^2y + xy + 8y$

Find the opposite of each polynomial.

10. $-3x + 9$ $3x - 9$
11. $8a^2 + 2a - 7$ $-8a^2 - 2a + 7$
12. $9b^4 - 1$ $-9b^4 + 1$
13. $a + 2b + c$ $-a - 2b - c$

Subtract.

14. $\begin{array}{r} 7a - 2 \\ -(4a + 1) \\ \hline \end{array}$ $3a - 3$

15. $\begin{array}{r} 3b^2 + 2b - 1 \\ -(-2b^2 - 7b + 4) \\ \hline \end{array}$ $5b^2 + 9b - 5$

16. $(6h + 2m) - (4h + 5m - 1)$ $2h - 3m + 1$

17. $(9p^2 + 5p + 3q) - (6q^2 + 7q)$ $9p^2 + 5p - 4q - 6q^2$

18. **MODELING** Show the sum of $(x^2 + 2x + 1) + (x^2 - 3x - 4)$ using Algeblocks. See Additional Answers.

19. **WRITING MATHEMATICS** In your own words, explain what like terms are. Tell how like terms are involved in the addition and subtraction of polynomials. See Additional Answers.

20. **GEOMETRY** Find the perimeter of the figure at the right and express it in simplest form. $13x$

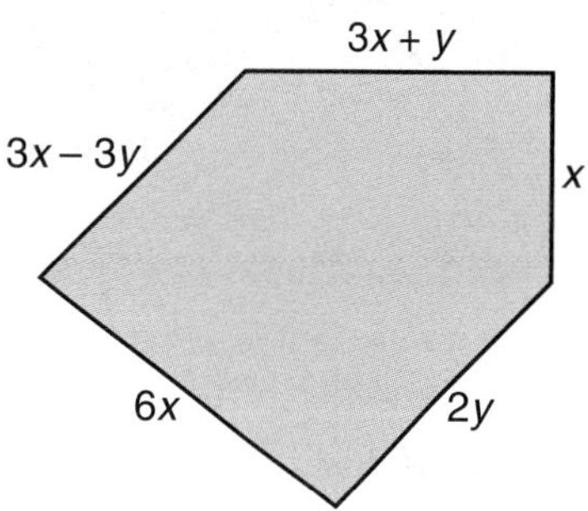

PRACTICE

Find the degree of each polynomial.

1. $10x^2 - 25$ 2
2. $6x + 4x^3 + x^5$ 5
3. $8a^2b - 2a^2b^2$ 4
4. $11c^3 + 4cd^2 - 6d^7$ 7
5. $9yz + 2y^2z^5 + 3z^3$ 7
6. $100 - g^4$ 4

Perform the indicated operation. 7–14 See Additional Answers.

7. $\begin{array}{r} 4a - 3b + 5c \\ + 8a + 3b - 7c \\ \hline \end{array}$

8. $\begin{array}{r} 5r + 3s + t \\ + r + 9s + 7t \\ \hline \end{array}$

9. $\begin{array}{r} -4p + q - 8 \\ + p + 5q + 17 \\ \hline \end{array}$

10. $\begin{array}{r} 4x^2 - 8x \\ + 9x^2 - 2x \\ \hline \end{array}$

11. $\begin{array}{r} 2a + 4b - c \\ -(6a + 3b + 5c) \\ \hline \end{array}$

12. $\begin{array}{r} x - y + z \\ -(x + y - z) \\ \hline \end{array}$

13. $\begin{array}{r} 8y^4 + 7y^2 - 3 \\ -(2y^4 - y^2 + 7) \\ \hline \end{array}$

14. $\begin{array}{r} z^3 + 4z^2 - z \\ -(3z^3 - 2z^2 + 5z) \\ \hline \end{array}$

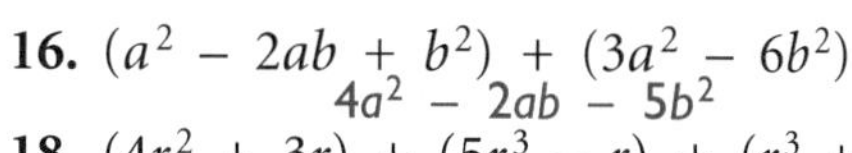

15. $(5x + 7y - 10) + (3y - 14)$ $5x + 10y - 24$

16. $(a^2 - 2ab + b^2) + (3a^2 - 6b^2)$ $4a^2 - 2ab - 5b^2$

17. $(a + 2b) + (b - c) + (3a + 5c)$ $4a + 3b + 4c$

18. $(4r^2 + 3r) + (5r^3 - r) + (r^3 + 4r)$ $6r^3 + 4r^2 + 6r$

19. $(7d - 8d^2 + d^3) - (3d + d^2 - 4d^3)$ $5d^3 - 9d^2 + 4d$

20. $(8k - 3k^2) - (9k + 2)$ $-3k^2 - k - 2$

21. $(8x^2 + 5xy - y^2) - (6x^2 - 3xy + y^2)$ $2x^2 + 8xy - 2y^2$

22. $(4b^2 - 3b) - (7b + 6)$ $4b^2 - 10b - 6$

23. **GEOMETRY** Write a polynomial for the area of the shaded region shown below. $32x^2$

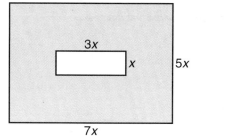

3x x 5x 7x

24. **GEOMETRY** Find the surface area of the rectangular prism shown below. Write the answer in simplest form. $12x^2 + 40xy$

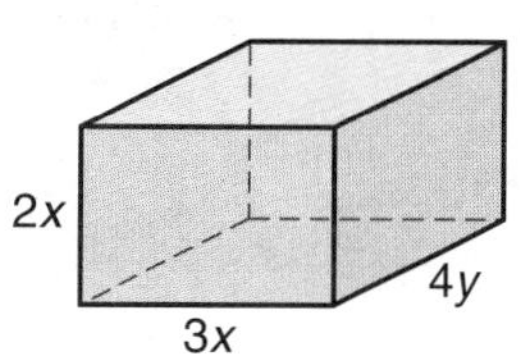

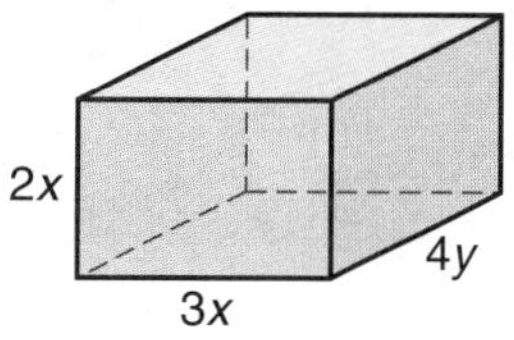

Extend For Exercise 25, ask students what they must do before subtracting $4x + y$. **Find the sum of $x + 3y$ and $8x - 2y$.** Ask students how Exercises 29 and 30 are like Exercises 27 and 28. **They both require substitution.** Ask a student to describe how to solve Exercise 29. $\mathbf{y^2 + 2y - 3 = (-2g)^2 + 2(-2g) - 3 = (-2)^2(g)^2 + -4g - 3 = 4g^2 - 4g - 3}$

Think Critically For Exercises 35 and 36, ask students how they can find the missing term. **Simplify the polynomial and solve for ■.** Some students may find this concept easier to understand if they replace the ■ with the variable T to represent the missing term.

NAME ______ CLASS ______ DATE ______

11.6 ADD AND SUBTRACT POLYNOMIALS

To add two polynomials, combine their like terms. To subtract one polynomial from another, you can add its opposite.

Example
Subtract: $(x + 4) - (2x - 3)$

Solution
Write the opposite of $2x - 3$, then combine like terms.

$$\begin{aligned} &(x + 4) - (2x - 3) \\ &= x + 4 + (-2x + 3) \\ &= x - 2x + 4 + 3 \\ &= -x + 7 \end{aligned}$$

EXERCISES

Complete each addition.

1. $\begin{array}{r} 3x^2 - 2x + 1 \\ + x^2 + 6x - 3 \\ \hline \end{array}$
2. $\begin{array}{r} 4x^2 - 5y \\ + 3x^2 + 6y \\ \hline \end{array}$
3. $\begin{array}{r} 3x^2 - 4y^2 \\ + 5x^2 - 2xy + 7y^2 \\ \hline \end{array}$

Complete each subtraction.

4. $\begin{array}{r} 4x^2 - 2x \\ - x^2 + 8x \\ \hline \end{array}$
5. $\begin{array}{r} 6y^2 + 7y + 5 \\ - 3y^2 + y + 3 \\ \hline \end{array}$
6. $\begin{array}{r} x^2 - 6x + 4 \\ - 3x^2 - 5x - 2 \\ \hline \end{array}$

Perform the indicated operation.

7. $(5x + 3) + (8x - 6)$
8. $(-2m - 4) + (9m + 7)$
9. $(4a^2 - 6a + 12) - (5a^2 + 8a - 17)$
10. $(3r^2 - 7r + 15) - (7r^2 - r - 9)$

1. $4x^2 + 4x - 2$
2. $7x^2 + y$
3. $8x^2 - 2xy + 7y^2$
4. $3x^2 - 10x$
5. $3y^2 + 6y + 2$
6. $2x^2 - x + 6$
7. $13x - 3$
8. $7m + 3$
9. $-a^2 - 14a + 29$
10. $-4r^2 - 6r + 24$

30 South-Western Algebra 1: AN INTEGRATED APPROACH

5 FOLLOW-UP

Extension Have students find the area of a quilt border which is x inches wide. Have students write a polynomial expression for the amount of material needed for the border. Then have them use the expression to find the amount of material needed for a 4-inch border.

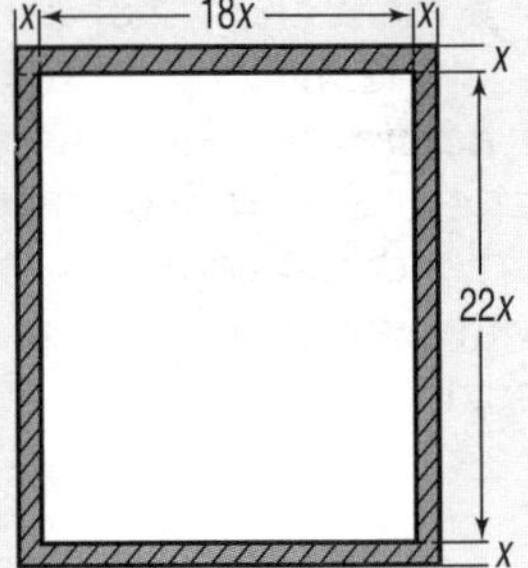

Total Width = $x + 18x + x = 20x$, Total Length = $x + 22x + x = 24x$, Total Area = $(20x)(24x) = 480x^2$; Interior Width = $18x$, Interior Length = $22x$, Interior Area = $(18x)(22x) = 396x^2$; Border Area = Total Area – Interior Area = $480x^2 - 396x^2 = 84x^2$

NAME ______________ CLASS ________ DATE ________

EXTRA PRACTICE **11.6 ADD AND SUBTRACT POLYNOMIALS**

Give the degree of each polynomial.

1. $a^3 - 3a + 4$ **3**
2. $x^2y^6 + 2xy^4$ **8**
3. $-9e^2 - 4e^7$ **7**

Perform the indicated operation.

4. $4m - 2n - 8$ $+ 9m + 6n + 1$ **$13m + 4n - 7$**
5. $7e + 9f - 4$ $- (3e - 8f + 2)$ **$4e + 17f - 6$**
6. $5x^2 - 6x$ $- (6x^2 + 6x)$ **$-x^2 - 12x$**
7. $(r - 3r^2 + 5r^3) + (2r + 7r^2 - 9r^3)$ **$3r + 4r^2 - 4r^3$**
8. $(13e - 8e^3) - (4e + 1)$ **$-8e^3 + 9e - 1$**
9. $(-10x - 7x^3 + x^2) - (-4x^2 + 9x - x^3)$ **$-6x^3 + 5x^2 - 19x$**
10. $(2y + 3y^4 - 4y^3) + (-3y^3 - 4y^4 - y)$ **$-y^4 - 7y^3 + y$**

Solve.

11. **BANKING** The value of $1000 invested at $r\%$ simple interest at the end of one year is $1000(1 + \frac{r}{100})$. Write a polynomial to express the value of x dollars invested at $r\%$ simple interest for one year. **$x(1 + \frac{r}{100}) = x + \frac{xr}{100}$**
12. **TAXI RATES** The cost for a taxi ride is $1.50 for the first mile and $1.25 for each additional mile. The formula for the cost is $C = \$1.50 + \$1.25(n - 1)$, where n is the number of miles ridden. Write a polynomial to express the cost of a ride if the cost for the first mile increases to $1.75 and the cost for each additional mile increases to $1.50. **$C = 1.75 + 1.50(n - 1)$**

32 *South-Western Algebra 1: AN INTEGRATED APPROACH*

EXTEND

25. Subtract $4x + y$ from the sum of $x + 3y$ and $8x - 2y$. $5x$
26. Subtract $x^2 + x + 2$ from the sum of $2x + 3$ and $4x^2 + x - 7$. $3x^2 + 2x - 6$

Use a calculator to evaluate each polynomial for $x = 0.6$.

27. $2x^2 + 7x - 3.2$ 1.72
28. $x^3 - 5x^2 + 4x - 7$ −6.184

Evaluate each polynomial for $y = -2g$.

29. $y^2 + 2y - 3$ $4g^2 - 4g - 3$
30. $2y^3 - 5y^2 + y - 3$ $-16g^3 - 20g^2 - 2g - 3$

AERONAUTICAL DESIGN The total gross weight W_g of an airplane can be expressed by the polynomial $W_{st} + W_e + W_f + W_p$, where W_{st} is the structural weight of the empty plane less the weight of the engines, W_e is the weight of the engine or propulsion system, W_f is the weight of the fuel, and W_p is the weight of the payload (passengers and cargo). Use this information to answer Questions 31–32.

31. For a particular airplane with a particular engine, which of the terms in this polynomial are constants? W_{st} and W_e
32. Suppose the total gross weight cannot exceed a certain limit. The amount of fuel determines the distance that the plane can travel. Assuming that W_g is at the limit, what is the effect on another of the variables if the amount of fuel and its weight W_f are increased? Payload (W_p) must be decreased.

DRIVING SAFETY The polynomial $x + \frac{x^2}{20}$ is the stopping distance of the car under ideal conditions in feet, after the brakes are applied. The variable x is the speed of the car in miles per hour before braking. Use this information to answer Questions 33–34.

33. Find the stopping distance if the car has been traveling at 40 mi/h. 120 ft
34. A common formula is to leave one car length (approximately 20 ft) between your car and the car in front of you for each 10 mi/h of the speed at which you are traveling. Does this work based on the polynomial given here? Explain. See Additional Answers.

THINK CRITICALLY

Find the missing term.

35. $(3x^2 + 2x - 4) + (\square + 5x^2 - 9) = 8x^2 - 5x - 13$ $-7x$
36. $(x^2y + 5xy - 9y^2) - (3x^2y - 2y^2 + \square) = -2x^2y + 9xy - 7y^2$ $-4xy$
37. Is the following *true* or *false*? Explain. The opposite of $a - b$ is $b - a$. See Additional Answers.

Project Connection This activity presents further aspects of the project introduced on page 516. Check that students use the correct formula for finding the area of a circle. Review the procedure for making a scatter plot from a data set.

MIXED REVIEW

Evaluate. Round decimals to the nearest hundredth. Lesson 2.2

38. $z = \sqrt{121}$ 11 **39.** $z = \sqrt{289}$ 17 **40.** $z = \sqrt{47}$ 6.86 **41.** $z = \sqrt{103}$ 10.15

Solve. Lesson 3.5

42. A sales representative receives 4% commission on total sales. To earn $450, what amount of sales does she need? $11,250

43. The population of Briarwood decreased by 2.5% from last year. If the population last year was 20,000, what was is this year? 19,500

Write in standard notation. Lesson 11.4

44. 3.4×10^6 3,400,000 **45.** 1.02×10^8 102,000,000 **46.** 4.8×10^{-7} 0.00000048 **47.** 3.03×10^{-5} 0.0000303

You will be exploring different sizes and shapes of parachutes. You will need several sheets of paper, tape, thread, scissors, a ruler, a clothespin, a stopwatch, and a compass.

1. Cut out squares of paper with side lengths of 8 in., 10 in., 12 in., and 14 in. For each square, tape a piece of thread to each corner. The pieces of thread should be the same length and about double the length of one side of the square. Tape the pieces of thread together underneath the chute and clip the clothespin over them.

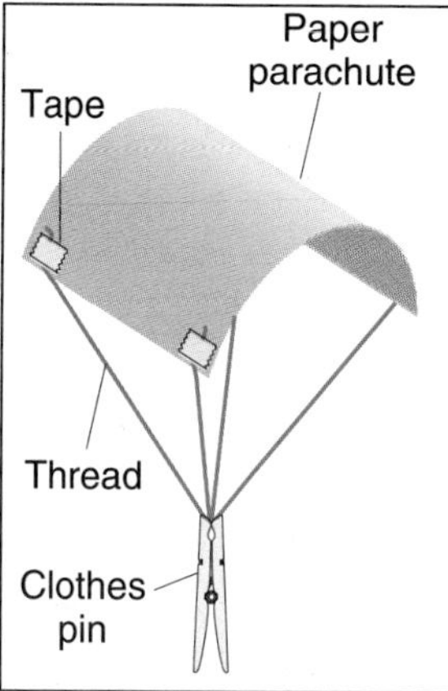

2. Drop each square parachute from a high place. (Stand on a chair or partway up a staircase and drop the chute. Be careful!) Time and record how long each parachute takes to hit the ground. For each chute, do at least three trials and average the times. Answers will vary.

3. Repeat the experiment with circular chutes of the same area as the square chutes. Explain how you determine the radii of your circles. See Additional Answers.

4. Make a scatter plot for each data set, using different colors to represent the square chutes and the circular chutes. Answers will vary.

5. From your graph, estimate the drop time of a 16-by-16-in. square parachute. Answers will vary.

6. Estimate the drop time of a circular parachute with equal area. Answers will vary.

7. Which parachute style works better, the square or the circular? Why do you think this is so? Answers will vary.

8. What do you think would happen if you cut a small hole in the center of the chute? Test your prediction. Summarize your findings.
The hole will make the chute more stable and it will fall more slowly.

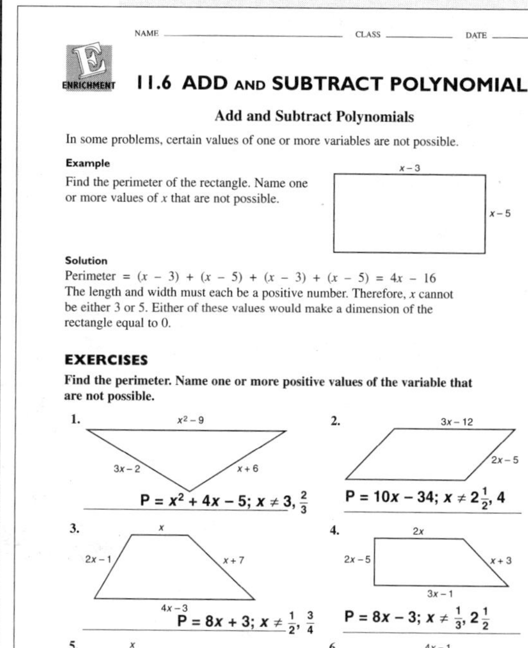

NAME ______ CLASS ______ DATE ______

ENRICHMENT **11.6 ADD AND SUBTRACT POLYNOMIALS**

Add and Subtract Polynomials

In some problems, certain values of one or more variables are not possible.

Example

Find the perimeter of the rectangle. Name one or more values of x that are not possible.

Solution

Perimeter $= (x - 3) + (x - 5) + (x - 3) + (x - 5) = 4x - 16$
The length and width must each be a positive number. Therefore, x cannot be either 3 or 5. Either of these values would make a dimension of the rectangle equal to 0.

EXERCISES

Find the perimeter. Name one or more positive values of the variable that are not possible.

1. $P = x^2 + 4x - 5$; $x \neq 3, \frac{2}{3}$

2. $P = 10x - 34$; $x \neq 2\frac{1}{2}, 4$

3. $P = 8x + 3$; $x \neq \frac{1}{2}, \frac{3}{4}$

4. $P = 8x - 3$; $x \neq \frac{1}{3}, 2\frac{1}{2}$

5. $P = 20x - 12$; $x \neq \frac{2}{3}, \frac{1}{2}, \frac{4}{5}$

6. $P = 16x - 8$; $x \neq 1, \frac{1}{2}, \frac{3}{5}$

34 South-Western Algebra 1: AN INTEGRATED APPROACH

LESSON PLANNING

Objective

▶ Use Algeblocks to multiply polynomials.

Resources

Transparencies 12, 21
Student Handbook

Materials/Manipulatives

Algeblocks
Quadrant Mats

ASSIGNMENTS

Basic: 1–35

Average: 1–35

Enriched: 1–36

1 MOTIVATE

Think Back Ask how the product $(-3x)(2y)$ compares to that of $(3x)(-2y)$. **The products are the same.** Have students give examples of two other factors that will give the same product. **possible example: $(-x)(6y)$, $(x)(-6y)$**

2 FACILITATE

Explore Have a student describe how to model the product in Exercise 9. **Place two x-blocks on the positive part of the horizontal axis and one x-block and one y-block on the positive part of the vertical axis; form a rectangle in the enclosed quadrant; write a monomial for each different part of rectangle, $2x^2$ and $2xy$; the product is the sum of the monomials, $2x^2 + 2xy$.** Ask students how they found the answer for Exercise 23, part c. **Add all the monomials.**

11.7 Algebra Workshop
Patterns in Multiplying Polynomials

SPOTLIGHT ON LEARNING

In this lesson you will learn
- to use Algeblocks to multiply polynomials.

WHY? Algeblocks can help you to understand that multiplication of polynomials is useful in solving a variety of practical problems.

Think Back

To use Algeblocks in multiplying two monomials, place the blocks for one factor along the horizontal axis and place the blocks for the other factor along the vertical axis of a Quadrant Mat.

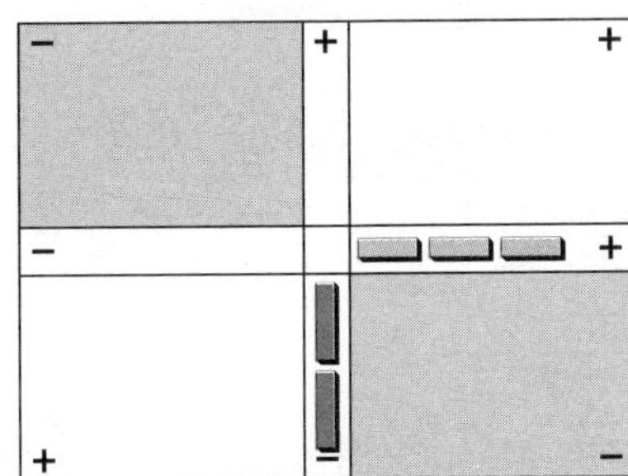

1. What multiplication is shown by the Algeblocks at the right? $(3x)(-2y)$
2. Use Algeblocks to model the multiplication. Read the product from the mat. $-6xy$
3. Write two factors whose product is $-2x^2$. answers will vary; possible answer: $x(-2x)$

Explore

Work with a partner. Use Algeblocks to multiply $2x(x - 2)$.

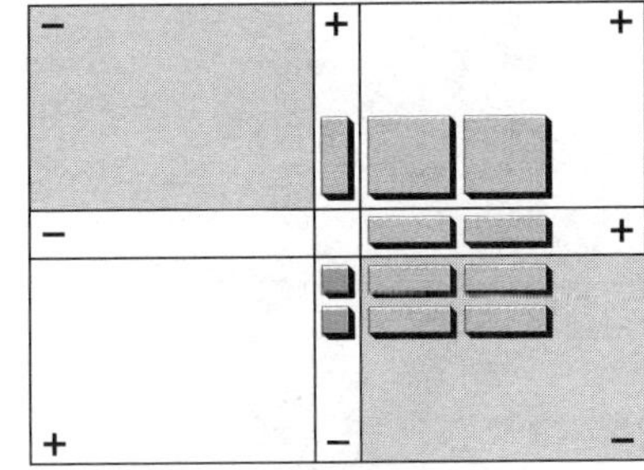

4. Place blocks for the first factor, $2x$, along the horizontal axis. Place blocks for the second factor, $x - 2$, along the vertical axis. Which regions will you use to model the multiplication? the two regions to the right of the vertical axis
5. Model the multiplication. Write the product that matches each area. $2x^2, -4x$
6. The total product is the sum of the rectangular areas. Write a polynomial for the sum. $2x^2 - 4x$

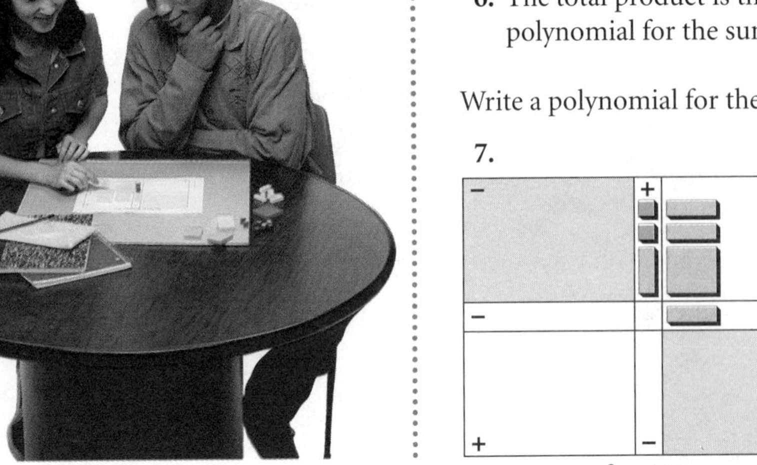

Write a polynomial for the product shown on each Quadrant Mat.

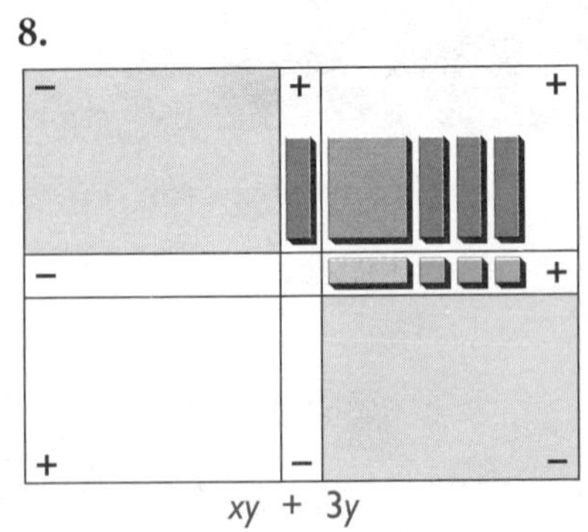

7. $x^2 + 2x$

8. $xy + 3y$

Use Algeblocks to model these products.

9. $2x(x + y)$ $2x^2 + 2xy$

10. $y(y + 2)$ $y^2 + 2y$

11. $-3x(2x + 1)$ $-6x^2 - 3x$

12. $-2y(x - y)$ $-2xy + 2y^2$

13. Use the distributive property to simplify $2x(x - 2)$. Explain how the product relates to the Algeblocks model completed in Question 5. See Additional Answers.

You can use Algeblocks to multiply two binomials.

Multiply: $(2x + 1)(x - 3)$

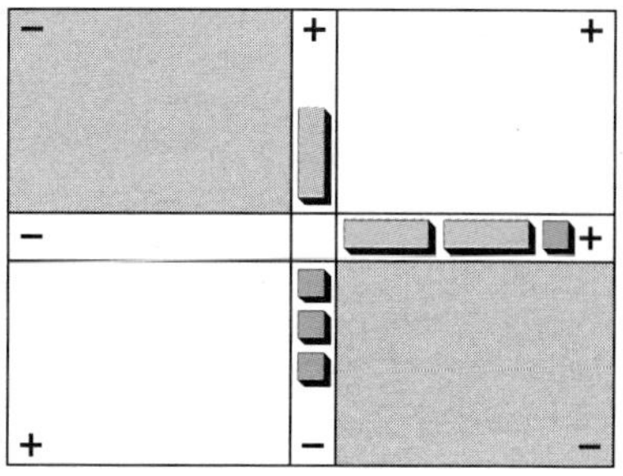

14. Place the first factor along the horizontal axis and the second along the vertical axis. Arrange the pieces as shown at the right.

15. Model the multiplication. Notice that within the large rectangle are smaller rectangles made up of blocks that are the same size and shape. Write a monomial for each of these smaller rectangles. $2x^2, -6x, x, -3$

16. Write a polynomial for the entire rectangular area. Can the polynomial be simplified? If so, how?
$2x^2 + (-6x) + x + (-3)$; yes; $2x^2 - 5x - 3$

Use Algeblocks to model each product.

17. $(x + 2)(x + 3)$
$x^2 + 5x + 6$

18. $(x - 1)(x + 4)$
$x^2 + 3x - 4$

19. $(x + 1)(x - 4)$
$x^2 - 3x - 4$

20. $(x + 3)(x - 2)$
$x^2 + x - 6$

21. $(2y + 2)(y - 2)$
$2y^2 - 2y - 4$

22. $(x + 1)(x + 2)$
$x^2 + 3x + 2$

23. The mat to the right shows Algeblocks that model the multiplication problem $(x + 1)(x - 2)$ and its product. Note the four circled rectangles.

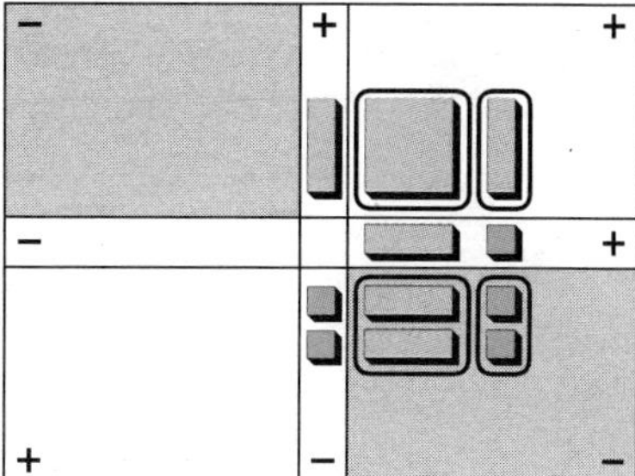

a. Write the two factors that form each circled rectangle. $(x)(x), (x)(-2), (1)(x), (1)(-2)$

b. Write a monomial for each circled rectangle. $x^2, -2x, x, -2$

c. Write a simplified polynomial for the entire product. $x^2 - x - 2$

Make Connections For Exercise 24, have a student show how to use the distributive property to simplify $(x + 1)(x - 2)$. **$(x + 1)(x - 2) = x(x - 2) + (1)(x - 2) = x^2 - 2x + x - 2 = x^2 + (-x) - 2 = x^2 - x - 2$** For Exercises 29 and 30, ask students if they could use a different value for x to check the product. If so, have them give an example, and if not, have them explain why not. **yes, as long as you substitute the same value for x in both the factors and the product; for Exercise 29, let $x = 3$: $(3 - 3)(3 - 4) = 0$ and $3^2 - 7(3) + 12 = 9 - 21 + 12 = 0$**

Make Connections
Geometry Have students find the area of the trapezoid if Area = $1/2h(b_1 + b_2)$ where h represents the height and b_1 and b_2 represent the lengths of the bases. **$4x^2 - 1$**

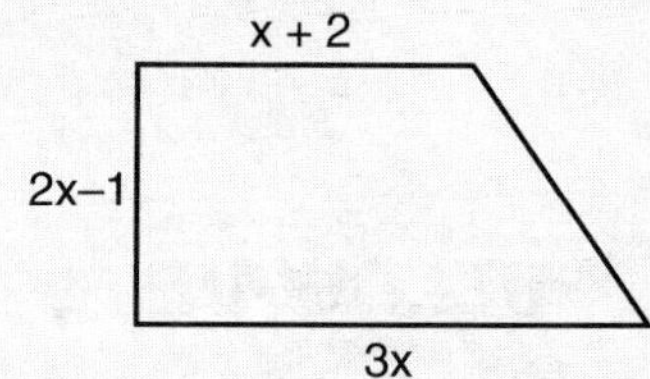

3 SUMMARIZE

Modeling After students have completed Exercises 31 and 34, have them model $(y + 2)y$ and its product and $(x + 2)(x + 1)$ and its product. Have students compare these models and products with the ones shown in the text. **The factors on the horizontal and vertical axes are reversed, and the products are the same.**

Thinking Critically For Question 33, ask students how many terms will result when two binomials in simplest form are multiplied. **If the second binomial has both terms in common with the first binomial, then terms in the product can be combined and there will be two or three terms; otherwise, there will be four terms.**

Writing Mathematics For Exercise 35, ask students to give an example. **possible example: $(x - 1)(2x + 3) = x(2x + 3) + (-1)(2x + 3) = 2x^2 + 3x + (-2)x + (-3) = 2x^2 + 3x - 2x - 3 = 2x^2 + x - 3$**

Going Further For Question 36, ask students how many times they used the distributive property. **three times: once to form the sum of two products and then twice to form the sum of three products in each case**

4 FOLLOW-UP

Other Explorations Have students use Algeblocks to model $(2x + 1)(x + 1)$. Ask them what the length and the width of the largest rectangle is. **$2x + 1$; $x + 1$** Ask students to express the area as one polynomial. **$2x^2 + 3x + 1$**

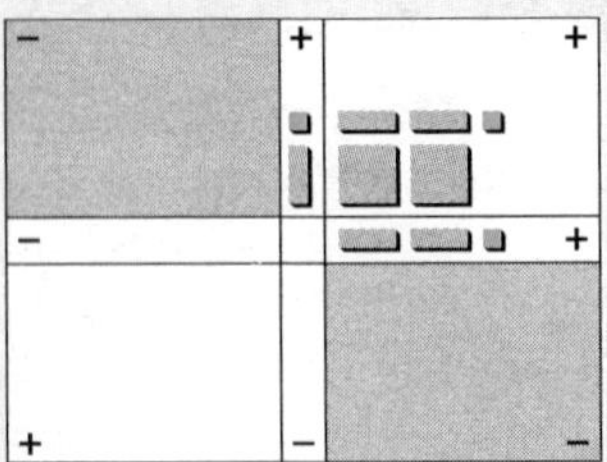

Algebra Workshop

COMMUNICATING ABOUT ALGEBRA

For Question 25, how will your work look different if you multiply $(x - 3)(2x + 1)$? Will the product be the same?

The products will appear in a different order; yes, the product will be the same.

Make Connections

24. Look at your answers in Question 23a. How does the distributive property of multiplication relate to these products? See Additional Answers.

25. In Questions 14–16, you used Algeblocks to find $(2x + 1)(x - 3)$. In using algebra to multiply two binomials, you use the distributive property twice to form the sum of four products.

$$(2x + 1)(x - 3) = (2x)(x - 3) + 1(x - 3)$$
$$= (2x)(x) + (2x)(-3) + (1)(x) + (1)(-3)$$

   a. Complete each product. $2x^2 + (-6x) + x + (-3)$
   b. Simplify the polynomial. $2x^2 - 5x - 3$

Use the distributive property to multiply.

26. $(x - 3)(x - 4)$ $x^2 - 7x + 12$
27. $(x + 7)(x - 5)$ $x^2 + 2x - 35$
28. $(2y - x)(y + 2x)$ $2y^2 + 3xy - 2x^2$

You can check to see that the product of two binomials is correct by substituting values for the variable.

29. Substitute $x = 5$ in the expression $(x - 3)(x - 4)$. What value for the expression did you get? 2

30. Substitute $x = 5$ in the expression you got as an answer to Question 26. Is this the same value you got in Question 29? What does this tell you about your answer to Question 29? See Additional Answers.

Summarize

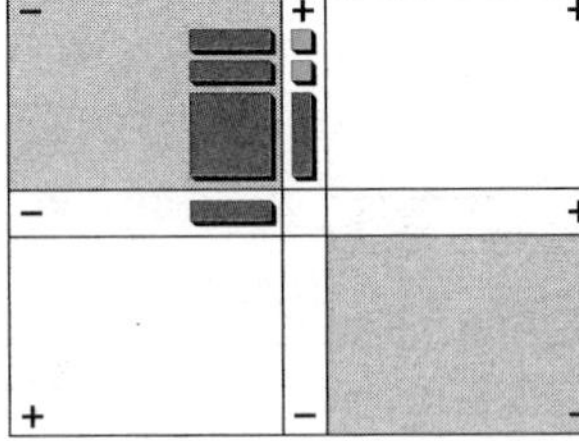

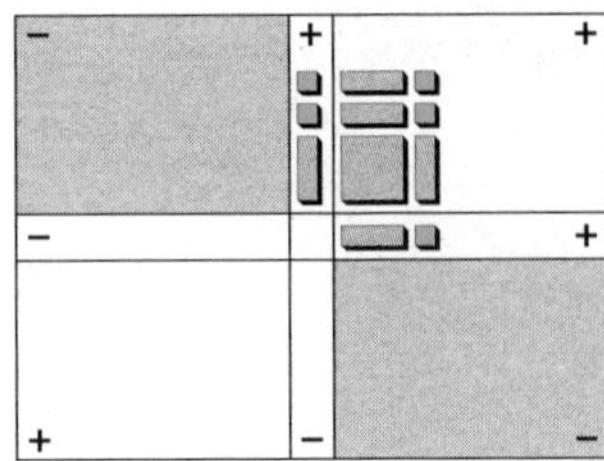

31. **MODELING** Write the two factors and the product for the model on the mat at the top left. $-y(y + 2)$; $-y^2 - 2y$

32. **WRITING MATHEMATICS** Describe how to multiply a polynomial by a monomial. See Additional Answers.

33. **THINKING CRITICALLY** If a polynomial in simplest form is multiplied by a monomial, how many terms will the product have? the same number of terms as the polynomial

34. **MODELING** Write the two factors and the product for the model on the mat at the bottom left. $(x + 1)(x + 2)$; $x^2 + 3x + 2$

35. **WRITING MATHEMATICS** Write a paragraph describing how to use the distributive property to multiply two binomials. See Additional Answers.

36. **GOING FURTHER** Write out each step necessary to multiply $(x + 3)(x^2 - 2x + 5)$. Then find the total product.
$x(x^2 - 2x + 5) + 3(x^2 - 2x + 5) =$
$x(x^2) + x(-2x) + x(5) + 3(x^2) + 3(-2x) + (3)(5)$;
$x^3 + x^2 - x + 15$

11.8 Multiply Polynomials

Explore/Working Together

Work with a partner.

Below are five arrangements of unit squares. While the first arrangement consists of only one square, the rest include more squares than you may notice at first.

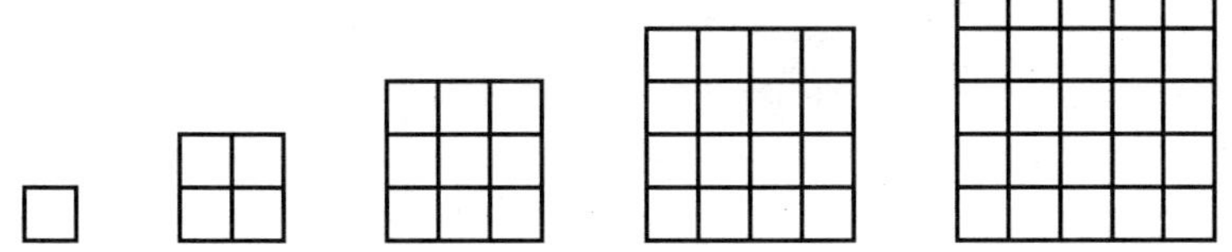

1. Study each arrangement of unit squares carefully. Then copy and complete this table in which n is the number of units of the side of the largest square.

	n					
	1	2	3	4	5	
Number of 1 X 1 Squares						1, 4, 9, 16, 25
Number of 2 X 2 Squares						0, 1, 4, 9, 16
Number of 3 X 3 Squares						0, 0, 1, 4, 9
Number of 4 X 4 Squares						0, 0, 0, 1, 4
Number of 5 X 5 Squares						0, 0, 0, 0, 1
Total Number of Squares						1, 5, 14, 30, 55

A polynomial can model this problem.

2. In each polynomial below, substitute each value of n from the table to determine which polynomial will always give you the correct total number of squares. (More than one correct answer is possible.) a, b, and d

   a. $\frac{n(n + 1)(2n + 1)}{6}$ b. $\frac{(n^2 + n)(2n + 1)}{6}$

   c. $\frac{n^3 + 3n^2 + 2}{6}$ d. $\frac{2n^3 + 3n^2 + n}{6}$

3. More than one polynomial works for any given value of n. What does that tell you about those polynomials?
They are the same or equivalent.

4. Use a polynomial model to determine the number of squares on a checkerboard, which is an 8×8 square. 204

SPOTLIGHT ON LEARNING

WHAT? In this lesson you will learn
- to multiply polynomials.

WHY? Multiplying polynomials helps you to solve problems in geometry, finance, demography, and history.

LESSON PLANNING

Objective
▶ Multiply polynomials.

Vocabulary
FOIL

Resources
Warm Up 11.8
Reteaching 11.8
Extra Practice 11.8
Enrichment 11.8
Transparencies 34, 64, 65
Student Handbook
Lesson Quiz 11.8

Materials/Manipulatives
graph paper

ASSIGNMENTS

Basic: 1–30, 33–35, 37, 39–41, 44, 46–47, Project Connection 1–3

Average: 3–42, 44–47, Project Connection 1–3

Enriched: 4–47, Project Connection 1–3

1 MOTIVATE

Explore/Working Together For Question 1, show the following method for counting all 2 x 2 squares within a 5 x 5 square to students having difficulty. Have students find all the 2 x 2 squares in the second and third rows, then the third and fourth rows, and in the fourth and fifth rows.

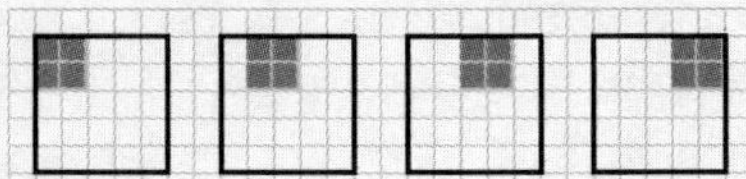

2 TEACH

Use the Pages/Build Understanding

Example 1: Before reading the solution, ask students how many sums will be formed by using the distributive property in part a and in part b. Have them explain how they know. **two because there are two terms to be multiplied by the monomial 2*x*; three because there are three terms to be multiplied by the monomial *y***

Have students read the paragraph following Example 1. Ask what the area of the entire rectangle shown in the first diagram is. **$x(x + 2)$, since the area of a rectangle is the product of the width and the length** Ask what x^2 and $2x$ written inside the rectangles represent. **x^2 is the area of the small square; $2x$ is the area of the small rectangle** Ask students how they can use this information to determine the product of $x(x + 2)$. **Since the area of the entire rectangle equals the sum of the areas of its parts, $x(x + 2) = x^2 + 2x$.**

COMMUNICATING ABOUT ALGEBRA

Show how you can multiply 43 by 25 by multiplying two binomials. (Use the expanded form of each number, 40 + 3 and 20 + 5.)

See Additional Answers.

Build Understanding

The distributive property of multiplication over addition can be used to multiply a polynomial by a monomial.

EXAMPLE 1

Find the product.

a. $2x(x + 6)$ **b.** $y(y^2 - 3y + 4)$

Solution

a. $2x(x + 6) = 2x(x) + 2x(6)$
$= 2x^2 + 12x$

b. $y(y^2 - 3y + 4) = y(y^2) + y(-3y) + y(4)$
$= y^3 + (-3y^2) + 4y$
$= y^3 - 3y^2 + 4y$

The diagram at the right shows an area model for multiplying $x(x + 2)$.

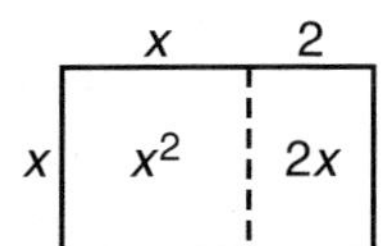

A similar diagram can model the product of two binomials. This rectangle has a width of $x + 2$ and a length of $x + 3$. Notice that the total area $(x + 2)(x + 3)$ consists of four smaller areas, x^2, $3x$, $2x$, and 6. The total area is the simplified polynomial $x^2 + 5x + 6$.

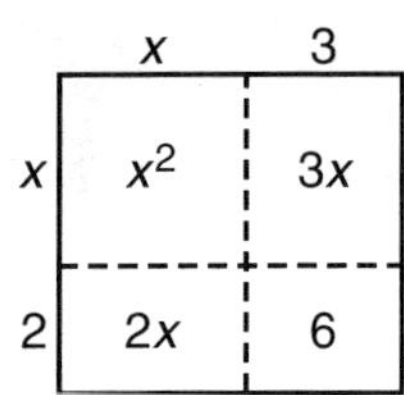

To multiply two binomials, use the distributive property twice.

EXAMPLE 2

Find the products.

a. $(x + 4)(x - 3)$ **b.** $(2y - 1)(y - 5)$

Solution

a. $(x + 4)(x - 3) = x(x - 3) + 4(x - 3)$
$= x(x) + x(-3) + 4(x) + 4(-3)$
$= x^2 + (-3x) + 4x + (-12)$
$= x^2 + x - 12$

b. $(2y - 1)(y - 5) = 2y(y - 5) + (-1)(y - 5)$
$= 2y(y) + (2y)(-5) + (-1)(y) + (-1)(-5)$
$= 2y^2 + (-10y) + (-y) + 5$
$= 2y^2 - 11y + 5$

Any two polynomials can be multiplied using the distributive property. FOIL is a mnemonic device, or memory aid, for remembering which terms to multiply when multiplying two binomials.

The following is an example of how **FOIL** works in finding the product of $w + 3$ and $w - 5$. Multiply the First terms, the Outer terms, the Inner terms, and the Last terms.

$$\begin{aligned}
&\quad\quad\quad\quad\quad\quad\quad\;\; \text{F} \quad\; \text{O} \quad\;\; \text{I} \quad\;\; \text{L}\\
(w + 3)(w - 5) &= w^2 - 5w + 3w - 15\\
&= w^2 - 2w - 15 \quad \text{Combine like terms.}
\end{aligned}$$

Sometimes you may prefer to multiply vertically.

EXAMPLE 3

Find the product of $x + 2$ and $x^2 + 4x - 3$.

Solution

Arrange the work vertically so that like terms are in the same column.

$$\begin{array}{rrrrl}
 & x^2 & + 4x & - 3 & \\
 & & x & + 2 & \\
\hline
 & 2x^2 & + 8x & - 6 & \quad 2(x^2 + 4x - 3)\\
x^3 & + 4x^2 & - 3x & & \quad x(x^2 + 4x - 3)\\
\hline
x^3 & + 6x^2 & + 5x & - 6 & \quad \text{Combine like terms.}
\end{array}$$

The product is $x^3 + 6x^2 + 5x - 6$. ◄

CHECK UNDERSTANDING

How would you use an area model to multiply a binomial by a trinomial?

Possible response: make a 3×2 multiplication table with the trinomial on one side and the binomial on the adjacent side.

As you practice multiplying binomials, you will notice patterns. Sometimes the product of two binomials is not a trinomial but another binomial.

EXAMPLE 4

Find the products. Describe the pattern.

a. $(x - 4)(x + 4)$ **b.** $(2x + 7)(2x - 7)$

Solution

a.
$$\begin{aligned}
&(x - 4)(x + 4)\\
&= x(x + 4) + (-4)(x + 4)\\
&= x(x) + x(4) + (-4)(x) + (-4)(4)\\
&= x^2 + 4x + (-4x) + (-16) \quad \text{Opposite middle terms.}\\
&= x^2 - 16
\end{aligned}$$

b.
$$\begin{aligned}
&(2x + 7)(2x - 7)\\
&= 2x(2x - 7) + 7(2x - 7)\\
&= 2x(2x) + 2x(-7) + 7(2x) + 7(-7)\\
&= 4x^2 + (-14x) + 14x + (-49) \quad \text{Opposite middle terms.}\\
&= 4x^2 - 49
\end{aligned}$$
◄

CHECK UNDERSTANDING

Do you think $(3x + 2)(2 - 3x)$ fits the pattern described in Example 4? Explain.

Yes; by the commutative property $3x + 2 = 2 + 3x$. So, one binomial is a sum and the other is a difference of the same terms.

Example 2: Show students this diagram for $(x + 4)(x - 3)$.

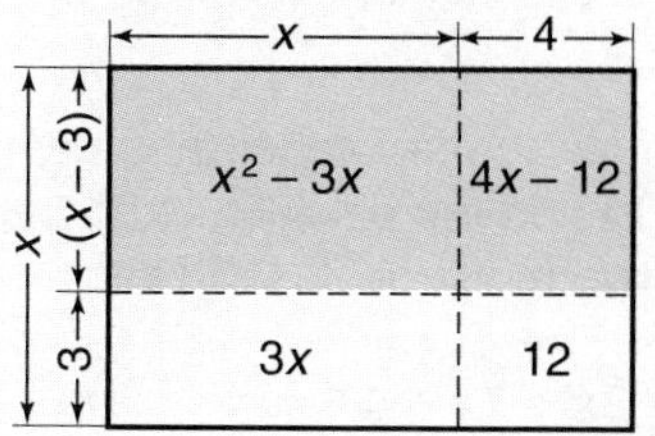

The dimensions of the shaded region are $x + 4$ and $x - 3$. The area of the shaded region is $(x^2 - 3x) + (4x - 12)$, which simplifies to $x^2 + x - 12$.

Example 3: Stress the importance of arranging terms in order so that like terms are in the same column. Ask students why this is important. **because only like terms can be combined** Ask what it means to write a polynomial in standard form. **Arrange the terms according to degree in descending order.** Encourage students to rewrite each polynomial in standard form before multiplying. Also suggest that they use zero as a marker for missing terms. For example, rewrite $(x + 1)(x^3 + x^2 + 2)$ as $(x + 1)(x^3 + x^2 + 0x + 2)$. Ask how multiplying vertically is like finding the product using the distributive property. **In both methods each term of the second polynomial is multiplied by each term in the first polynomial.**

Example 4: Ask students to describe how to use the FOIL method to find the product. $\mathbf{(x - 4)(x + 4) = x^2 + 4x + (-4x) + (-16) = x^2 - 16}$ Point out that in both part *a* and part *b* the middle terms are opposites and are zero pairs. Have students give another example of this type and give the product. **possible example:** $\mathbf{(7 - x)(7 + x) = 49 - x^2}$

Example 5: Ask students what they notice about the middle terms of the product in each case. **It is twice the product of the two terms of the binomial.**

Example 6: Ask students to describe how to find the product using the distributive method. $\mathbf{(x + 5)(x + 3) = x(x + 3) + 5(x + 3) = x^2 + 3x + 5x + 15 = x^2 + 8x + 15}$

Ongoing Assessment The important concepts and skills are multiplying polynomials and recognizing special cases of binomial products. To assess these ideas, have students demonstrate how they have applied these concepts and skills in Exercises 8, 11, and 13 of the Try These section.

Guided Practice/Try These Ask students which exercises show special cases of polynomial products and describe them. **Exercises 11 and 12 each show the square of a binomial; Exercises 13 and 14 each show two binomials with identical terms where one binomial is a sum and the other a difference.** For Exercise 15, ask students to draw an area model to represent the product.

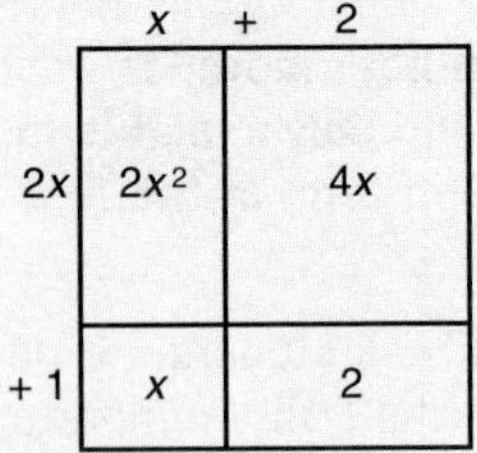

Have students discuss their answers to Exercise 16.

3 SUMMARIZE

In the Math Journal Have students describe how to find products using the distributive, the FOIL, and the vertical methods of multiplication. Have them give an example to show how to use each method. **Examples will vary.**

CHECK UNDERSTANDING

Do you think $(8x + 5)(8x^2 + 5)$ fits the pattern shown in Example 5? Explain.

No; the terms $8x$ and $8x^2$ are not the same, so the product is not the square of a binomial.

The product in Example 4 reveals a pattern. When you multiply two binomials with identical terms, where one binomial is a sum and the other is a difference, the product is the difference of the squares of the first and second terms.

PRODUCT OF A SUM AND A DIFFERENCE

$$(a + b)(a - b) = a^2 - b^2$$

Another pattern for multiplying binomials involves the square of a binomial.

EXAMPLE 5

Find the products. Describe the pattern.

a. $(y - 5)^2$ **b.** $(2x + 3)^2$

Solution

a.
$$\begin{aligned} &(y - 5)^2 \\ &= (y - 5)(y - 5) \\ &= y(y - 5) + (-5)(y - 5) \\ &= y(y) + (y)(-5) + (-5)y + (-5)(-5) \quad \text{Identical middle terms.} \\ &= y^2 + (-5y) + (-5y) + 25 \\ &= y^2 + (-10y) + 25 \\ &= y^2 - 10y + 25 \end{aligned}$$

b.
$$\begin{aligned} &(2x + 3)^2 \\ &= (2x + 3)(2x + 3) \\ &= 2x(2x + 3) + 3(2x + 3) \quad \text{Identical middle terms.} \\ &= 2x(2x) + 2x(3) + (3)2x + 3(3) \\ &= 4x^2 + 6x + 6x + 9 \\ &= 4x^2 + 12x + 9 \end{aligned}$$

The products in Example 5 reveal a pattern. When you square a binomial, the product is a trinomial whose first and last terms are the squares of the terms and whose middle term is twice the product of the two terms.

SQUARE OF A BINOMIAL

$$(a + b)^2 = a^2 + 2ab + b^2 \text{ and}$$
$$(a - b)^2 = a^2 - 2ab + b^2$$

Multiplying binomials and polynomials can help solve many real world problems.

EXAMPLE 6

GEOMETRY The shaded area of the figure at the right is 63 ft². Solve for x.

Solution

The area of the shaded region of the figure can be determined by subtracting the area of the square from the area of the larger rectangle.

$$\text{area of rectangle} - \text{area of square} = 63$$
$$(x + 5)(x + 3) - x^2 = 63$$
$$(x^2 + 8x + 15) - x^2 = 63 \quad \text{Multiply.}$$
$$8x + 15 = 63 \quad \text{Combine like terms.}$$
$$x = 6 \quad \text{Solve for } x.$$

So, the unknown length in the figure is 6 ft. ◄

TRY THESE

Multiply. Simplify each product.

1. $x(3x + 5)$ $3x^2 + 5x$
2. $c(c^2 + 9c)$ $c^3 + 9c^2$
3. $-4(y + 2)$ $-4y - 8$
4. $-3(2z - 7)$ $-6z + 21$
5. $(x + 7)(x + 8)$ $x^2 + 15x + 56$
6. $(g + 4)(g - 6)$ $g^2 - 2g - 24$
7. $(2x + 1)(x - 4)$ $2x^2 - 7x - 4$
8. $(z - 3)(2z - 3)$ $2z^2 - 9z + 9$
9. $(a - 2)(a^2 - 3a + 2)$ $a^3 - 5a^2 + 8a - 4$
10. $(k + 4)(k^2 - 4k + 1)$ $k^3 - 15k + 4$
11. $(a + 2)^2$ $a^2 + 4a + 4$
12. $(b - 6)^2$ $b^2 - 12b + 36$
13. $(x - 5)(x + 5)$ $x^2 - 25$
14. $(2y - 1)(2y + 1)$ $4y^2 - 1$
15. **MODELING** What multiplication problem and product are modeled on the mat shown at the right? $(x + 2)(2x + 1) = 2x^2 + 5x + 2$

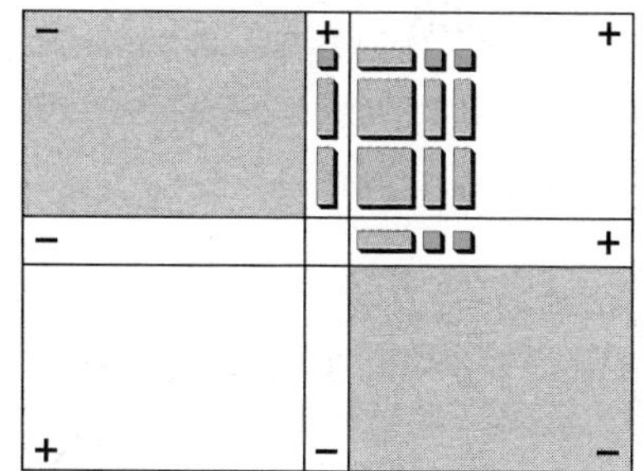

16. **WRITING MATHEMATICS** Explain why $(x + 5)^2 \neq x^2 + 25$ for all values of x. See Additional Answers.

PRACTICE

Multiply. Simplify each product.

1. $x(x - 5)$ $x^2 - 5x$
2. $2y(y - 3)$ $2y^2 - 6y$
3. $-5z(2z + 3)$ $-10z^2 - 15z$
4. $-2k(k + 9)$ $-2k^2 - 18k$
5. $-3m(2m - 4)$ $-6m^2 + 12m$
6. $-7g(3g - 1)$ $-21g^2 + 7g$
7. $2xy(x^2 - y^2)$ $2x^3y - 2xy^3$
8. $3ab(a^2 - 2b^2)$ $3a^3b - 6ab^3$
9. $(x + 2)(x + 5)$ $x^2 + 7x + 10$
10. $(y + 7)(y + 3)$ $y^2 + 10y + 21$
11. $(a - 6)(a - 4)$ $a^2 - 10a + 24$
12. $(b - 2)(b - 4)$ $b^2 - 6b + 8$
13. $(c - 5)(c + 3)$ $c^2 - 2c - 15$
14. $(d + 9h)(d + 4h)$ $d^2 + 13dh + 36h^2$

4 PRACTICE

Practice For Exercises 1–32, ask students what methods they can use to find products of polynomials. **distributive, FOIL, area model, and vertical methods** Suggest that students check their answers using a different method from the one they used to find the product. Ask students how they can find the area of the polygon in Exercise 33. **Draw a dotted line vertically to define two smaller rectangles with the measures $3x$ by x and $2x$ by 5 and respective areas $(3x)(x)$ and $5(2x)$; or draw a dotted line horizontally to define two smaller rectangles with the measures $x + 5$ by $2x$ and $3x - 2x$ by x and respective areas $(x + 5)(2x)$ and $(3x - 2x)(x)$ or $(x)(x)$.**

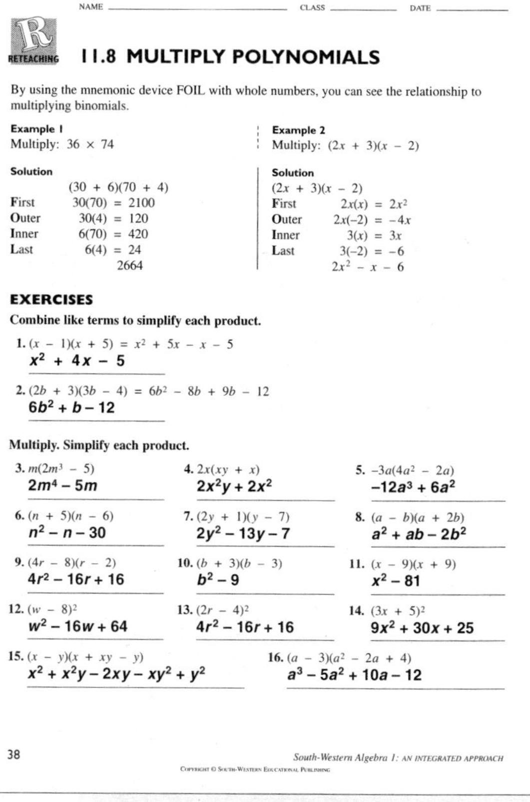

NAME ________ CLASS ________ DATE ________

RETEACHING **11.8 MULTIPLY POLYNOMIALS**

By using the mnemonic device FOIL with whole numbers, you can see the relationship to multiplying binomials.

Example 1
Multiply: 36×74

Solution
$(30 + 6)(70 + 4)$
First $30(70) = 2100$
Outer $30(4) = 120$
Inner $6(70) = 420$
Last $6(4) = 24$
2664

Example 2
Multiply: $(2x + 3)(x - 2)$

Solution
$(2x + 3)(x - 2)$
First $2x(x) = 2x^2$
Outer $2x(-2) = -4x$
Inner $3(x) = 3x$
Last $3(-2) = -6$
$2x^2 - x - 6$

EXERCISES

Combine like terms to simplify each product.

1. $(x - 1)(x + 5) = x^2 + 5x - x - 5$ **$x^2 + 4x - 5$**
2. $(2b + 3)(3b - 4) = 6b^2 - 8b + 9b - 12$ **$6b^2 + b - 12$**

Multiply. Simplify each product.

3. $m(2m^3 - 5)$ **$2m^4 - 5m$**
4. $2x(xy + x)$ **$2x^2y + 2x^2$**
5. $-3a(4a^2 - 2a)$ **$-12a^3 + 6a^2$**
6. $(n + 5)(n - 6)$ **$n^2 - n - 30$**
7. $(2y + 1)(y - 7)$ **$2y^2 - 13y - 7$**
8. $(a - b)(a + 2b)$ **$a^2 + ab - 2b^2$**
9. $(4r - 8)(r - 2)$ **$4r^2 - 16r + 16$**
10. $(b + 3)(b - 3)$ **$b^2 - 9$**
11. $(x - 9)(x + 9)$ **$x^2 - 81$**
12. $(w - 8)^2$ **$w^2 - 16w + 64$**
13. $(2r - 4)^2$ **$4r^2 - 16r + 16$**
14. $(3x + 5)^2$ **$9x^2 + 30x + 25$**
15. $(x - y)(x + xy - y)$ **$x^2 + x^2y - 2xy - xy^2 + y^2$**
16. $(a - 3)(a^2 - 2a + 4)$ **$a^3 - 5a^2 + 10a - 12$**

38 *South-Western Algebra 1: AN INTEGRATED APPROACH*

Error Alert Watch for students who forget to multiply the second polynomial by the second term in the first binomial. In Exercise 19, for example, some students might not multiply $3p - 2q$ by q. Their answer will be $6p^2 - 4pq$ instead of the correct answer, $6p^2 - pq - 2q^2$.

Extend For Exercises 39 and 40, ask students how they can find the area of the shaded region. **Subtract the area of the square from the area of the triangle.** For Exercise 42, explain that the model is similar to the area model they used earlier in the lesson.

15. $(g^2 + 7)(g^2 - 2)$ $g^4 + 5g^2 - 14$
16. $(h^3 + 8)(h^3 - 1)$ $h^6 + 7h^3 - 8$
17. $(2m - 1)(m + 3)$ $2m^2 + 5m - 3$
18. $(3n + 4)(n + 5)$ $3n^2 + 19n + 20$
19. $(2p + q)(3p - 2q)$ $6p^2 - pq - 2q^2$
20. $(4q + r)(5q + r)$ $20q^2 + 9qr + r^2$
21. $(x - 2)(x + 2)$ $x^2 - 4$
22. $(s + 9)(s - 9)$ $s^2 - 81$
23. $(3r - 2)(3r + 2)$ $9r^2 - 4$
24. $(4t + 5)(4t - 5)$ $16t^2 - 25$
25. $(v - 6)^2$ $v^2 - 12v + 36$
26. $(g + 8)^2$ $g^2 + 16g + 64$
27. $(2w + 8)^2$ $4w^2 + 32w + 64$
28. $(3x - 2)^2$ $9x^2 - 12x + 4$
29. $(x + 3)(x^2 + 4x - 3)$ $x^3 + 7x^2 + 9x - 9$
30. $(y + 5)(y^2 - 3y - 8)$ $y^3 + 2y^2 - 23y - 40$
31. $(a - b)(a^2 - 2ab - 3b^2)$ $a^3 - 3a^2b - ab^2 + 3b^3$
32. $(p + 2)(p^2 - 5p - 1)$ $p^3 - 3p^2 - 11p - 2$
33. **Geometry** Find the area of the figure at the right. $3x^2 + 10x$

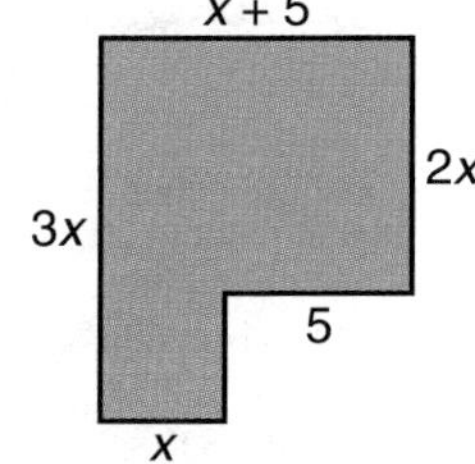

34. **Compound Interest** The formula for the amount of money A in an account that earns compound interest is $A = p(1 + r)^t$, where p is the principal (money invested), r is the rate of interest per time period, and t is the number of time periods.
    a. Find A when $p = \$1000$, $r = 0.04$, and $t = 3$. $1124.86
    b. Write the formula for A when $p = \$2000$ and $t = 2$. Write the formula as a polynomial in r without parentheses. $A = 2000 + 4000r + 2000r^2$

EXTEND

Simplify.

35. $(q - 2)^3$ $q^3 - 6q^2 + 12q - 8$
36. $(a + 5)^3$ $a^3 + 15a^2 + 75a + 125$
37. $(g + 3)(g - 1)^2$ $g^3 + g^2 - 5g + 3$
38. $(k - 1)(k + 2)^2$ $k^3 + 3k^2 - 4$
39. **Geometry** Find x if the shaded area of the triangle measures 54 m². 4.5 m

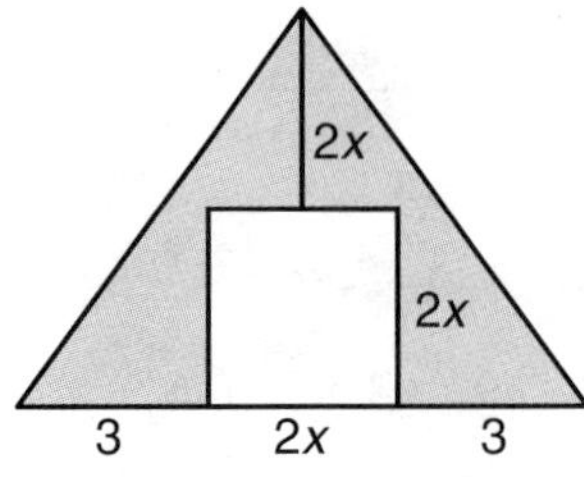

40. **Geometry** Find the value of x in the triangle at the right if the shaded area is 255 cm². $x = 15$ cm

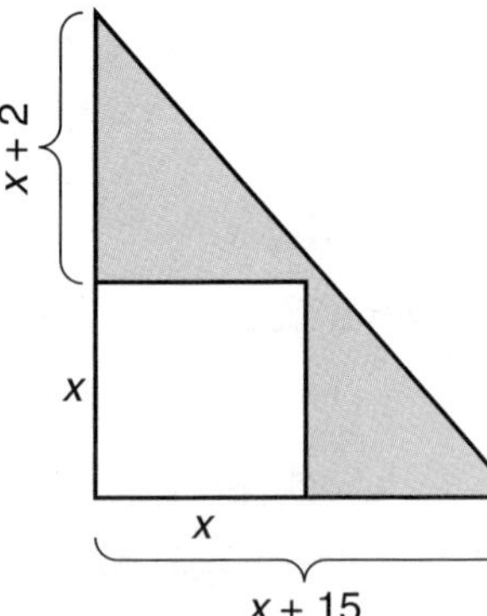

41. **Geometry** A rectangle is 5 ft longer than it is wide. Its area is 66 ft². Find the width of the rectangle. (*Hint:* Guess and check your answer.) 6 ft
42. **History** The relationship $(a + b)(a - b) = a^2 - b^2$ was known to astronomers of Mesopotamia (Iraq) by 2000 B.C. They could demonstrate this fact by a geometric model. Draw a geometrical model for this product. See Additional Answers.

NAME ______ CLASS ______ DATE ______

EXTRA PRACTICE **11.8 MULTIPLY POLYNOMIALS**

Multiply.

1. $a(a^2 + 4)$ **$a^3 + 4a$**
2. $m(m - 9)$ **$m^2 - 9m$**
3. $x(x^2 - 6x)$ **$x^3 - 6x^2$**
4. $-2x(x - 5)$ **$-2x^2 + 10$**
5. $-y(y + 3)$ **$-y^2 - 3y$**
6. $-7a(a^2 - 2a)$ **$-7a^3 + 14a^2$**
7. $4ab(2a^2 - b)$ **$8a^3b - 4ab^2$**
8. $-2mn(-m + n)$ **$2m^2n - 2mn^2$**
9. $-8x(xy - x^2)$ **$-8x^2y + 8x^3$**
10. $(p - 3)(p + 4)$ **$p^2 + p - 12$**
11. $(t + 1)(t - 2)$ **$t^2 - t - 2$**
12. $(e - 4)(e - 4)$ **$e^2 - 8e + 16$**
13. $(x + 2)(2x - 3)$ **$2x^2 + x - 6$**
14. $(m - 5)(3m - 1)$ **$3m^2 - 16m + 5$**
15. $(r - 9)(r + 9)$ **$r^2 - 81$**
16. $(2x - 3)^2$ **$4x^2 - 12x + 9$**
17. $(3g - 5)^2$ **$9g^2 - 30g + 25$**
18. $(n + 4)^2$ **$n^2 + 8n + 16$**
19. $(a - 3)(a^2 - 5a - 7)$ **$a^3 - 8a^2 + 8a - 21$**
20. $(x + 4)(x^2 - 2x + 1)$ **$x^3 + 2x^2 - 7x + 4$**
21. $(a + b)(a^2 + 5)$ **$a^3 + a^2b + 5a + 5b$**
22. $(y + 3)(2y^2 + y + 6)$ **$2y^3 + 7y^2 + 9y + 9$**
23. **Distance** A car travels at a rate of $8x + 3$ miles per hour. How far can it travel at that rate in $x - 2$ hours? **$8x^2 - 13x - 6$ miles**
24. **Distance** In Question 23, if $x = 7$, what is the car's rate of speed? How many hours does it travel, and what distance is covered? **59 miles per hour, 5 hours, 295 miles**
24. **Geometry** The perimeter of a square is $8x + 24$. Write the area of the square as a polynomial. **$4x^2 + 24x + 36$**

40 South-Western Algebra 1: AN INTEGRATED APPROACH

43. **DEMOGRAPHY** If p is the present population of a region and r is the percent increase of the population per year, an expression for the size of the population after y years is $p\left(1 + \frac{r}{100}\right)^y$. Find the population of Uganda two years from now if the present population is 19,800,000 and the rate of increase is 3%. 21,005,820

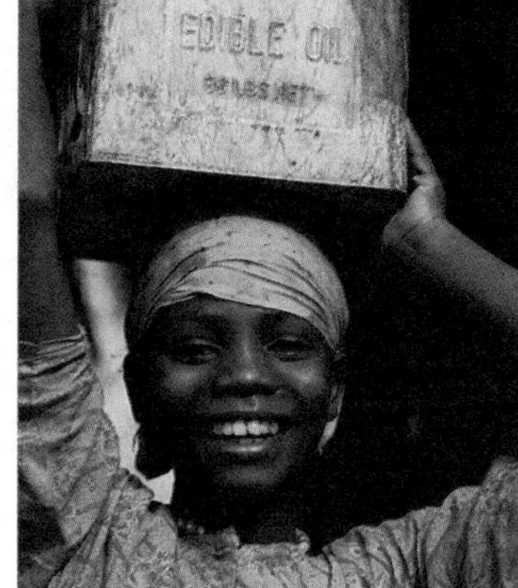

THINK CRITICALLY

Find the value of n that will make each statement true.

44. $(x + n)(x - 8) = x^2 - 12x + 32$ $n = -4$

45. $(2y - 6)(y + n) = 2y^2 + 8y - 42$ $n = 7$

46. Are there any values of a and b that make this statement true: $(a + b)^2 = a^2 + b^2$? Justify your answer. If either $a = 0$ or $b = 0$, the statement is true.

47. If a and b are positive integers, which is greater, $(a + b)^2$ or $a^2 + b^2$? Justify your answer. Since $(a + b)^2 = a^2 + 2ab + b^2$, it is $2ab$ greater than $a^2 + b^2$.

PROJECT Connection

Perform this experiment to find out about *lift* and the design of an airplane wing.

1. Cut a piece of paper 3 in. by 11 in. Fold it to make a 3 by $5\frac{1}{2}$-in. piece, but do not crease the fold. With ends together, slide one side of the folded paper so that it is $\frac{1}{2}$ in. shorter than the other end and tape it down. The top of the paper should have a slight curve, like a wing. Put your pencil through the folded end, curved side up. Blow across the paper. What happens? The wing should rise.

You have just demonstrated *Bernoulli's principle* (discovered in 1738 by Swiss mathematician Daniel Bernoulli), which states that as the speed of a gas or liquid increases, the pressure decreases. The velocity of the air passing over the curved wing increases to "catch up" with the air flowing below. Pressure decreases above the wing, lift is created, and the plane rises.

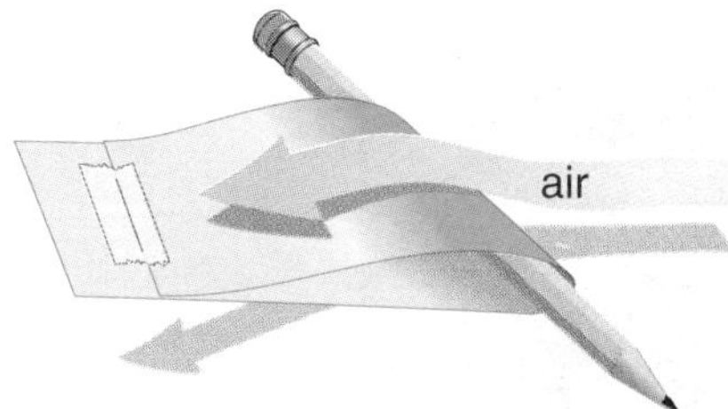

2. Bernoulli derived an equation for the pressure difference P, measured in newtons per square meter (N/m²):

$$P = \frac{1}{2}d(v_1^2 - v_2^2)$$

where d represents air density in km/m, v_1 represents velocity in m/s above wing, and v_2 represents velocity in m/s below wing. When an airplane is traveling at 192 km/h, $v_1 = 59.2$ m/s, $v_2 = 55.7$ m/s, and $d = 1.29$ km/m³. Determine P to one decimal place. 259.4 N/m²

3. Show that Bernoulli's equation can be expressed as $P = \frac{1}{2}d(v_1 - v_2)(v_1 + v_2)$.

Think Critically For Exercises 44 and 45, suggest that students use the FOIL method to help them find a value of n.

5 FOLLOW-UP

Extra Practice Tell students to use the product of a sum and difference to find each product.

1. Since 48 = 50 – 2 and 52 = 50 + 2, find the product of 48 • 52. **2500 – 4 = 2496**
2. Since 21 = 30 – 9 and 39 = 30 + 9, find the product of 21 • 39. **900 – 81 = 819**
3. Find the product of 91 • 89. **8100 – 1 = 8099**

Project Connection This activity presents further aspects of the project introduced on page 516. For Question 3, if students substitute a for v_1 and b for v_2 they will see that the original expression involves the difference of the squares of the first and second terms.

NAME ______ CLASS ______ DATE ______

ENRICHMENT **11.8 MULTIPLY POLYMIALS**

The Pythagorean Theorem states that the square of the hypotenuse of a right triangle is equal to the sum of the squares of the two legs. This is often written $c^2 = a^2 + b^2$. Many mathematical proofs have been given for this theorem. This one is reported to have been developed by U.S. President James Garfield.

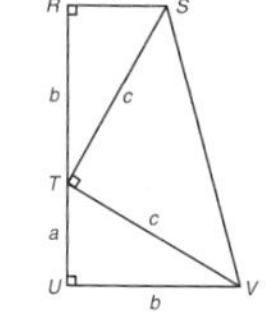

In the figure, triangles TUV, RST, and STV are all right triangles and $RSVU$ is a trapezoid.

Answer the following questions in terms of side lengths a, b, and c.

1. What is the area of triangle TUV?
   $\left(\frac{1}{2}\right)ab$
2. What is the area of triangle TRS?
   $\left(\frac{1}{2}\right)ab$
3. What is the area of triangle STV?
   $\left(\frac{1}{2}\right)c^2$
4. Write the area of trapezoid $RSVU$ as the sum of the 3 triangles.
   $A = \left(\frac{1}{2}\right)ab + \left(\frac{1}{2}\right)ab + \left(\frac{1}{2}\right)c^2 = ab + \left(\frac{1}{2}\right)c^2$
5. Recall that the formula for the area of a trapezoid in terms of its base lengths and height is $A = \frac{1}{2}(h)(b_1 + b_2)$. Write the area of trapezoid $RSVU$ in terms of a and b.
   $A = \frac{1}{2}(a + b)(a + b) = \left(\frac{1}{2}\right)(a + b)^2 = \frac{1}{2}(a^2 + 2ab + b^2) = \left(\frac{1}{2}\right)a^2 + ab + \left(\frac{1}{2}\right)b^2$
6. Write an equation in which the area found in questions 4 and 5 are set equal to each other and simplify to show that $c^2 = a^2 + b^2$.
   $ab + \left(\frac{1}{2}\right)c^2 = \left(\frac{1}{2}\right)a^2 + ab + \left(\frac{1}{2}\right)b^2$
   $\left(\frac{1}{2}\right)c^2 = \left(\frac{1}{2}\right)a^2 + \left(\frac{1}{2}\right)b^2$
   $c^2 = a^2 + b^2$

42 *South-Western Algebra 1: AN INTEGRATED APPROACH*

LESSON PLANNING

Objective
▶ Use the formula $d = rt$ to solve problems that involve uniform motion.

Vocabulary
constant rate of speed
uniform rate of speed

Resources
Reteaching 11.9
Extra Practice 11.9
Transparency 10
Student Handbook

ASSIGNMENTS

Basic: 1–16, Review Problem Solving Strategies 1–3

Average: 1–18, Review Problem Solving Strategies 1–3

Enriched: 1–20, Review Problem Solving Strategies 1–3

1 MOTIVATE

Introduction After students have read the introductory paragraph, tell them that the formula $d = rt$, known as the distance formula, is used widely in business as well as in mathematics and physics.

11.9 Problem Solving File

Use Variables

Rate, Time, and Distance Problems

SPOTLIGHT ON LEARNING

WHAT? In this lesson you will learn
- to apply the formula $d = rt$ to solve problems that involve uniform motion.

WHY? Equations involving rate, time, and distance help you to solve problems about travel, hiking, recreation, and sports.

If an object such as an automobile or an airplane travels at a constant, or *uniform*, rate of speed r, then the distance d traveled by the object during time t is given by the formula $d = rt$.

When you read a problem, note whether the situation involves motion in the same direction, motion in opposite directions, or a round trip.

Problem

Dan and Fran are truck drivers. Dan, averaging 55 mi/h, begins a 200-mi trip from their company's Chicago depot to Indianapolis at 7:00 A.M. Fran sets out from the Indianapolis depot at 8:00 A.M. the same day and travels to Chicago at 45 mi/h in the opposite direction on the same road. At what time will Dan and Fran pass each other?

Explore the Problem

1. Let t represent the amount of time Fran travels from 8:00 A.M. until the trucks pass each other. How long will Dan have been traveling when the trucks pass? $t + 1$ h
2. A table like the one below can help you to organize information about the problem. Complete the table.

	Rate, mi/h	x Time, h	= Distance, mi
Dan	55	$(t + 1)$	$55(t + 1)$
Fran	45	t	$45t$

3. A diagram can help you write an equation. Remember, the trucks are traveling toward each other.

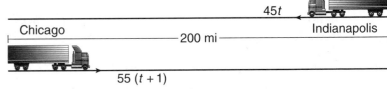

When the trucks pass, what will be true about the distance Dan has traveled from Chicago and the distance Fran has traveled from Indianapolis? Show this relationship algebraically. See Additional Answers.

4. Solve the equation and interpret your solution. See Additional Answers.
5. Check your result. (*Hint:* When the trucks pass, how far will each have traveled?) See Additional Answers.

Investigate Further

When problems involve a round trip along the same route, you know that the distances each way are equal.

A jet traveled from New York to Mexico City at an average speed of 500 mi/h. Because of a very strong west-to-east tailwind, the average speed for the return trip was 600 mi/h. The return trip from Mexico City took 42 min less than the trip going. What is the air distance between New York and Mexico City?

PROBLEM SOLVING PLAN

- Understand
- Plan
- Solve
- Examine

6. Notice that the units do not match for all of the data. Identify what needs to be changed and then change it. 42 min; 0.7 h
7. To find the distance, first find the time for each part of the trip. Let t represent the number of hours for the trip to Mexico City. How should you represent the time for the return trip? $t - 0.7$ or $t - \frac{7}{10}$
8. Draw a diagram and complete the table.

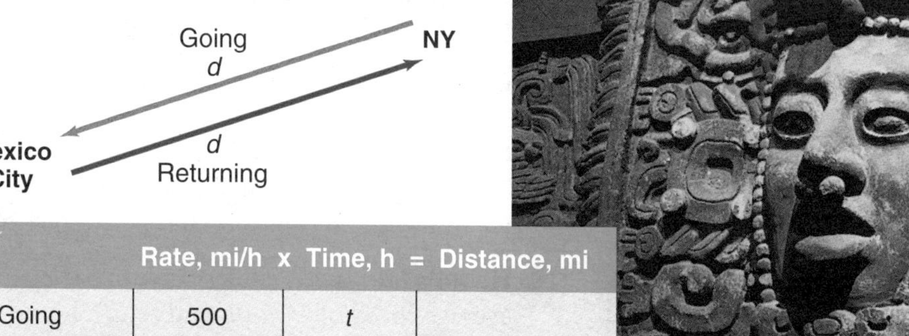

	Rate, mi/h	x Time, h	= Distance, mi
Going	500	t	$500t$
Returning	600	$t - 0.7$	$600(t - 0.7)$

9. You know that the distances are equal. Write an equation in which you can solve for t. $500t = 600(t - 0.7)$
10. Solve the equation. Explain how to use your result to find the distance between the two cities. $t = 4.2$ h, so $500 \cdot 4.2 = 2100$ mi
11. How long was the return trip? Using the return time, find the distance. $4.2 - 0.7 = 3.5$ h; $3.5 \cdot 600 = 2100$ mi
12. **Writing Mathematics** Write a problem about your commute to and from school that requires the distance formula to solve. Then solve the problem. See Additional Answers.

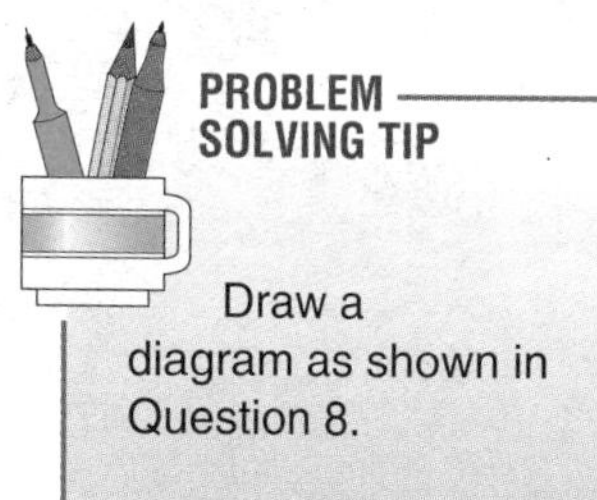

PROBLEM SOLVING TIP

Draw a diagram as shown in Question 8.

2 TEACH

Use the Pages/Problem Have students read the problem and consider whether the situation involves motion in the same direction, motion in opposite directions, or a round trip. **They travel the same route in opposite directions going towards each other.**

Use the Pages/Explore the Problem For Question 1, ask students to how long Dan will have been traveling when the trucks pass. **He will have been traveling one hour longer or $t + 1$.** To help students answer Question 3, have them draw a point on their diagrams where the trucks might meet. This will help them see that the sum of the distances must be 200 mi.

Use the Pages/Investigate Further Ask students how the problem is similar to the one in the previous section. How is it different? **Both problems involve rate, time, and distance; this problem involves round trip motion instead of motion in opposite directions.** For Question 9, ask students how they know that the distances are equal. **The problem involves a round trip.**

3 SUMMARIZE

In the Math Journal Ask students to write a paragraph describing how to determine what to let the variable represent when they are considering more than one unknown in the problem. Ask how they could solve the first problem differently by letting t represent a different rate. **Let t represent the amount of time Dan travels from 7:00 A.M. until the trucks pass each other: $55t + 45(t - 1) = 200$; $t = 2.45$ or 2 h 27 min; add 2 h 27 min to 7:00 A.M. to get 9:27.**

4 PRACTICE

Apply the Strategy Remind students to draw a diagram and make a chart to represent each problem. For Problem 16, ask them how they can represent Mr. Gonzalez's and Mrs. Gonzalez's rates of speed. **Let r represent Mr. Gonzalez's rate of speed and let $r + 8$ represent Mrs. Gonzalez's rate of speed.** For Problem 17, ask students what type of motion their diagram will represent. **motion in opposite directions** Ask them if this problem is like one they have already solved. **yes, the first problem in the lesson** Ask students if Problem 18 is like one they have already solved. **yes, the second problem in the lesson**

NAME ______________ CLASS ________ DATE ________

RETEACHING

11.9 RATE, TIME, AND DISTANCE PROBLEMS

Reading a problem carefully and making a table can help you solve problems of rate, time, and distance.

Example

A train leaves a station traveling at an average speed of 40 miles per hour. Two hours later another train leaves the same station traveling the same direction on an adjacent track. If the second train averages 60 miles per hour, in how many hours are the trains beside each other?

Solution

Complete a table.

	Rate	Time	Distance (rate × time)
First train	40	t	$40t$
Second train	60	$t - 2$	$60(t - 2)$

The distances are equal, so

$40t = 60t - 120$

$20t = 120$

$t = 6$

The trains will be beside each other after 6 hours.

EXERCISES

1. Two planes take off at the same time flying in opposite directions. One plane travels at twice the speed of the other. After 3 hours, they are 1,620 miles apart. What is the average speed of each plane?
180 mph, 360 mph

2. A train leaves a station averaging 30 miles per hour. Three hours later another train leaves a station 330 miles away, traveling toward the first on an adjacent track. If the second train averages 50 miles per hour, after how long will they pass?
6 hours; (first train: 180 mi, second train: 150 mi)

3. Samantha and Darren live 4.5 mi. apart. Samantha leaves her house walking at 3 mi/h and Darren leaves his house and runs at 6 mi/h. If they are moving toward each other, how long will it be until they meet?
0.5 h

4. One boat leaves the pier travelling at 40 mi/h. Three hours later a second boat leaves the same pier going 60 mi/h in the same direction. How long will it be until the second boat passes the first?
9 h

44 *South-Western Algebra 1: AN INTEGRATED APPROACH*

Draw a Diagram | Write an Expression

Apply the Strategy

HIKING Darrell and Ivan are spending a month at a summer camp in the mountains. One morning Darrell leaves camp and hikes along a mountain trail at 4 km/h. Thirty minutes later, his friend Ivan sets out along the same route, following after him at a rate of 6 km/h. How long will it take Ivan to catch up with Darrell?

13. Draw a diagram. What kind of motion will you show—in the same direction, in opposite directions, or a round trip? same direction

14. Let t represent Ivan's hiking time. Is Darrell's time more or less than Ivan's? Represent Ivan's time. Darrell's time is more; $t + 0.5$

15. When Ivan catches up to Darrell, what will be true about the distance each of them has walked? What equation fits the information? Solve your equation. Interpret and check your result. See Additional Answers.

16. COMMUTING Mr. and Mrs. Gonzalez leave home at the same time in separate cars. Mrs. Gonzalez travels north at a rate of speed that is 8 mi/h faster than that of her husband, who travels south. At the end of 3 h, Mr. and Mrs. Gonzalez's two cars are 300 mi apart. How fast was Mrs. Gonzalez traveling? How far south is Mr. Gonzalez after 3 h? 54 mi/h; 138 mi

17. RAIL TRAVEL A passenger train averaging 62 mi/h begins the 355-mi trip from Glenville to Lintown at 12:00 noon. A freight train traveling 48 mi/h leaves Lintown at 2:00 P.M. the same day and travels to Glenville on an adjacent track. At what time will the two trains pass each other? 4:06 P.M.

18. RECREATION The Padillas drive to Safari and Surf at an average speed of 54 mi/h and return home on the same highway at an average speed of 46 mi/h. If the trip to the theme park takes 20 min less than the trip home, how far is the park from the Padillas' home? 103.5 mi

SPORTS Jason and Jackson are entered in the 26-mi Aeolian Marathon. Jason's average rate is 5 mi/h and Jackson's average rate is 8 mi/h. Both runners start at the same moment.

19. How far behind will the slower runner be when the faster one finishes the race? 9.75 or $9\frac{3}{4}$ mi

20. If they start at 9:30 A.M., at what time will Jason and Jackson be 5.1 mi apart? 11:12 A.M.

Guess and Check | Make a Table | Solve a Simpler Problem

REVIEW PROBLEM SOLVING STRATEGIES

1–3 See Additional Answers.

THE EMPTY ENVELOPE, PLEASE!

1. An assistant is sending copies of the sales meeting agenda to 27 of the company's representatives. After all the envelopes are addressed and sealed, the assistant discovers that one copy has fallen on the floor. Not wanting to open all the envelopes, the assistant decides to use a simple pan balance to determine which envelope is empty. What is the least number of weighings the assistant will need for 27 envelopes? Explain the method.

Swimmer's Puzzle

2. Each of nine swimmers has been assigned a lane for a 200-meter freestyle race. The leftmost lane is Lane 1. When a friend asks Joel in which lane he will be swimming, Joel replies, "The number of swimmers to the right of me multiplied by the number of swimmers to the left of me is 3 less than it would have been if my lane was 3 places to the right of where I will be." In which lane will Joel be swimming? Explain how you solved the problem. (*Hint:* You do not need algebra.)

3. Bill's Bargain Basement is selling everything in the store at a 15% discount. Across the street, Good Buys is offering a discount of $1 on each $5 spent in the store. Where would you shop? Explain your shopping strategy. Use a graph to support your reasoning.

$1 DISCOUNT ON EACH $5 SPENT

SHOP HERE! 15% OFF ON EVERYTHING

5 FOLLOW-UP

Extra Practice
Solve the problem.

1. For Problem 17, determine the distance each train will have traveled at the time they pass each other. **passenger: 254.2 mi; freight: 100.8 mi**

Review Problem Solving Strategies Have students work individually or in groups to solve these problems.

The Empty Envelope, Please! Possible strategies for solving this problem are use logical thinking and draw a diagram.

Swimmer's Puzzle Possible strategies for solving the problem include making a table or a combination of guess and check and draw a diagram.

Shopper's Special Possible strategies for solving this problem include: graph a system of equations and make a table.

NAME ________ CLASS ________ DATE ________

EXTRA PRACTICE **11.9 RATE, TIME, AND DISTANCE PROBLEMS**

Solve.

1. The Johnsons are taking two cars to their family for the holidays. Mr. Johnson leaves at 8:00 AM. At 9:00 AM, Mrs. Johnson leaves, traveling on the same road, but 10 miles per hour faster than her husband. If they are alongside one another at 1:00 PM, how fast is each traveling?
   Mr. Johnson: 40 mi/h; Mrs. Johnson: 50 mi/h
2. How far will the Johnsons have traveled when they are alongside one another?
   200 miles
3. Two trains leave a depot at the same time traveling in opposite directions. The passenger train averages 15 mi/h faster than the freight train. After 6 hours, the trains are 630 miles apart. How fast is the passenger train traveling?
   60 mi/h
4. After how many hours will the trains be 840 miles apart?
   8 hours
5. On her way to a business meeting, Mrs. Butler drove an average of 55 mi/h. On the return trip over the same roads, she was only able to average 45 mi/h. If the return trip took 2 hours more than the trip out, how many hours did she drive in all?
   20 hours
6. How far from her home was the meeting Mrs. Butler attended?
   495 miles
7. A car and truck start towards each other at the same time from cities 315 miles apart. The car averages 48 miles per hour, the truck 42 mph. After how many hours will they pass?
   3.5 hours
8. If the car's driver plans to stay on the same road for 50 miles past where the truck began its trip, how much farther must the car travel?
   197 miles: 315 – 48(3.5) = 147; 147 + 50 = 197

46 *South-Western Algebra 1: AN INTEGRATED APPROACH*

Introduction The Chapter Review emphasizes the major concepts, skills, and vocabulary presented in this chapter and can be used for diagnosing students' strengths and weaknesses. Page references direct students to appropriate sections for additional review and reteaching.

Using Pages 562–563 Ask students to scan the Chapter Review and ask questions about any section they find confusing. Exercises 1–3 review key vocabulary. Exercises 4–7, 21–24, and 29–31 ask students to model problems using Algeblocks.

Informal Evaluation Have students explain how they arrived at any incorrect answers. They may find their own mistakes and give you some clues as to the nature of their errors. Make sure students understand this material before moving on to the assessment stage.

Follow-Up Have students solve this problem: the length of a rectangle is twice the width. The area of the rectangle is 72 ft^2. Find the dimensions.

a. Let x represent the width in feet. The length can be represented by $2x$. The area of the rectangle is the product of the length and width, so the equation for x is $x(2x) = 72$ or $2x^2 = 72$. **The solution of the equation is $x = 6$. The width is 6 feet; the length is 12 feet.**

Have students write problems that involve operations with polynomials. Students should exchange and solve each others' word problems.

CHAPTER REVIEW

VOCABULARY

Choose the word from the list that completes each statement.

1. The __?__ is the greatest degree of any of its terms. b
2. A base raised to a negative power is the __?__ of the base raised to a positive power. c
3. The __?__ is the sum of the degrees of all the variable factors. a

a. degree of a monomial
b. degree of a polynomial
c. reciprocal

Lesson 11.1 MULTIPLY AND DIVIDE VARIABLES — pages 517–520

- Algeblocks may be used to model multiplication and division of variables.

Use Algeblocks to model the multiplication or division.

4. $(-3y)(y)$ $-3y^2$
5. $3x^2 \div x$ $3x$
6. $(-2x)(-3y)$ $6xy$
7. $-2xy \div (-2y)$ x

Lesson 11.2 MULTIPLY MONOMIALS — pages 521–526

- To multiply monomials, use the properties of exponents.

Simplify.

8. $z^4(z^2)$ z^6
9. $3a^4(-2a^3)$ $-6a^7$
10. $-4x^2y^5(3xy^2)$ $-12x^3y^7$
11. $-2a^3bc(-3ab^3c^2)$ $6a^4b^4c^3$

Lesson 11.3 DIVIDE MONOMIALS — pages 527–531

- To divide monomials use the zero property of exponents, the quotient rule, and the property of negative exponents.

Simplify. Write with positive exponents.

12. $\dfrac{-3x^5}{-x^3}$ $3x^2$
13. $\dfrac{12a^8}{-2a^5}$ $-6a^3$
14. $\dfrac{4p^6q^5}{16pq^7}$ $\dfrac{p^5}{4q^2}$
15. $\dfrac{5x^3y^0}{-x^2}$ $-5x$
16. $\left(\dfrac{3g^2}{2h^4}\right)^3$ $\dfrac{27g^6}{8h^{12}}$

Lesson 11.4 SCIENTIFIC NOTATION — pages 532–537

- A number is written in scientific notation when it is written as a product of a number greater than or equal to 1 and less than 10 and a power of 10.

Evaluate. Write the answers in scientific notation.

17. $(1.8 \cdot 10^6)(2.5 \cdot 10^4)$ $4.5 \cdot 10^{10}$
18. $\dfrac{6.3 \cdot 10^8}{2 \cdot 10^5}$ $3.15 \cdot 10^3$
19. $1{,}200{,}000{,}000 \cdot 2$ $2.4 \cdot 10^9$
20. $0.000000023 \cdot 3$ $6.9 \cdot 10^{-8}$

Lesson 11.5 ADD AND SUBTRACT EXPRESSIONS pages 538–540

- Algeblocks may be used to model addition and subtraction of algebraic expressions.

Use Algeblocks to model the addition or subtraction.

21. $(3x - y) + (2y - x)$ $2x + y$

22. $(x^2 + y) + (-3x^2 + 2y)$ $-2x^2 + 3y$

23. $(4x - 3) - (x + 2)$ $3x - 5$

24. $(3x + y) - (2y - x)$ $4x - y$

Lesson 11.6 ADD AND SUBTRACT POLYNOMIALS pages 541–547

- To add polynomials, combine like terms.
- To subtract a polynomial, add its opposite.

Perform the indicated operation.

25. $\begin{array}{r} 4r + 2s - t \\ + \ 7r - 3s + 2t \\ \hline 11r - s + t \end{array}$

26. $\begin{array}{r} 7x^2 + 2x - 8 \\ -(4x^2 - 5x + 2) \\ \hline 3x^2 + 7x - 10 \end{array}$

27. $(3a + 2b) + (-a - 4b + 6c)$ $2a - 2b + 6c$

28. $(4x^2 + xy - 6) - (x^2 - 2xy - 9)$ $3x^2 + 3xy + 3$

Lesson 11.7 PATTERNS IN MULTIPLYING POLYNOMIALS pages 548–550

- Algeblocks may be used to model multiplication and division of variables.

Use Algeblocks to model the multiplication.

29. $(x + 2)(2x + 1)$ $2x^2 + 5x + 2$

30. $(-x + 1)(x - 2)$ $-x^2 + 3x - 2$

31. $(x - 1)(x + 3)$ $x^2 + 2x - 3$

Lesson 11.8 MULTIPLY POLYNOMIALS pages 551–557

- To multiply polynomials use the distributive property, the FOIL method, an area model, or the vertical method.

Multiply. Simplify each product.

32. $k(k + 4)$ $k^2 + 4k$

33. $-5x(3x - y)$ $-15x^2 + 5xy$

34. $2ab(3a^2 - 4b^2)$ $6a^3b - 8ab^3$

35. $(a + 3)(a + 1)$ $a^2 + 4a + 3$

36. $(x - 2)(x + 4)$ $x^2 + 2x - 8$

37. $(2r + s)(r - s)$ $2r^2 - rs - s^2$

38. $(y + 6)(y - 6)$ $y^2 - 36$

39. $(b + 2)^2$ $b^2 + 4b + 4$

40. $(y - 2)(y^2 + 3y - 4)$ $y^3 + y^2 - 10y + 8$

Lesson 11.9 RATE, TIME, AND DISTANCE PROBLEMS pages 558–561

- Use diagrams and charts to solve rate, time, and distance problems.

Draw a diagram and make a chart to solve.

41. At 10:30 A.M. Lizzie left Boston, driving at 54 mi/h. At 10:50 A.M. José left Boston and followed the same route, driving at 60 mi/h. At what time did he overtake Lizzie? 1:50 P.M.

Study Skills Tip Encourage students to begin studying at least one week before the Chapter Test. Groups of two or more students could review their notes together and discuss what they have learned. They may find it helpful to review the properties of exponents and to summarize the major concepts of each lesson.

For Your Portfolio Have students gather samples from their project, homework, quizzes, and class work that portray efforts to meet each of their goals for this chapter. On a cover page for each representative work have students write the related goal, why the work is included in the portfolio, and what the teacher should look for when reviewing the work. On a general cover page have students write a self-evaluation of how well they have met each of their goals for this chapter. The general cover page should conclude with goals for the next chapter and the student's reasons for choosing these goals.

The Chapter Test is comprised of a variety of test-item types as follows:

writing	5
multiple choice	1, 6, 8, 11
traditional	2–4, 9–10
verbal	12–15
standardized test	1, 8

TEACHING TIP

The writing item provides an opportunity for students to demonstrate a knowledge of process as well as end result. Suggest that before they begin answering questions, students should look over the entire test and determine the order in which they will work. Some students may be more successful if they save the open-ended writing question until after they have completed the other test questions.

The table below correlates the Chapter Test items with the appropriate lesson(s).

Item	*Lesson*	Item	*Lesson*
1	*11.2, 11.6*	6–7	*11.2*
2	*11.2*	8–10	*11.4*
3	*11.8*	11	*11.3*
4	*11.6*	12–13	*11.8*
5	*11.8*	14	*11.3*
		15	*11.9*

CHAPTER ASSESSMENT

CHAPTER TEST

1. **STANDARDIZED TESTS** Which polynomials have a degree of 4? D

   I. $6x^2 + y^3z$ II. x^6y III. $2x + y^4 + z$

   A. I and II B. II and III

   C. I only D. I and III

Simplify.

2. $g^2h(g^3h^4)$ g^5h^5
3. $(2r + s)^2$ $4r^2 + 4rs + s^2$
4. How much greater is the expression $3x^2 - 2y$ than the expression $2x^2 - 3y$? $x^2 + y$
5. **WRITING MATHEMATICS** Write a paragraph explaining at least two different ways you can find the product $(x + 4)(2x - 1)$. See Additional Answers.
6. Which of the following expressions is *not* equivalent to $(-2x^3y)^2(-xy^3)$? C

   A. $-4x^7y^5$ B. $(4x^6y^2)(-xy^3)$

   C. $(-2)^2(x^3)^2(y^2)(-x)^3(y^3)$

   D. $(-2)^2(x^3)^2(y^2)(-xy^3)$
7. Express the surface area of the rectangular prism as an algebraic expression in simplest form. $10x^2 + 2x - 24$

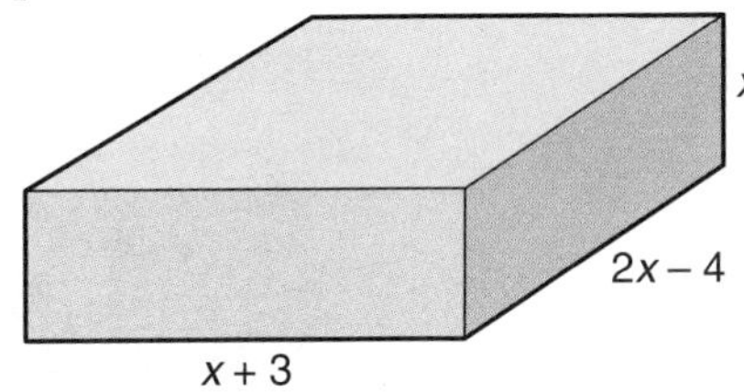

8. **STANDARIZED TESTS** Which of the following is the scientific notation for 0.000000215? B

   A. 21.5×10^{-8} B. 2.15×10^{-7}

   C. 21.5×10^{8} D. 2.15×10^{7}
9. Write 43 billion in scientific notation. 4.3×10^{10}
10. Evaluate. Write the answers in scientific notation.

    a. $(1.4 \times 10^6)(2.7 \times 10^8)$ 3.78×10^{14}

    b. $(7.3 \times 10^5)(4.6 \times 10^4)$ 3.358×10^{10}

    c. $(3 \times 10^7)^2$ 9×10^{14} d. $\dfrac{8 \times 10^9}{4 \times 10^3}$ 2×10^6
11. Which expressions are equivalent to $\left(\dfrac{2x^3y}{-xy^4}\right)^2$? B

    I. $4\left(\dfrac{x^3y}{-xy^4}\right)^2$ II. $-4\left(\dfrac{x^3y}{-xy^4}\right)^2$

    III. $\dfrac{4x^6y^2}{-x^2y^8}$ IV. $\dfrac{4x^4}{y^6}$ V. $4x^4y^{-6}$

    A. I and IV only B. I, IV, and V

    C. IV and V only D. I and III

Solve each problem.

12. A rectangle is four times as long as it is wide. Its width is $x + 1$. Express its area as an algebraic expression in simplest form. $4x^2 + 8x + 4$
13. Express the area of a rectangle whose length is three times its width as an algebraic expression in simplest form. If the area is 48 cm², what are the dimensions of the rectangle? See Additional Answers.
14. The volume of a rectangular prism is $8x^2y^2$. Find the width. $2y$

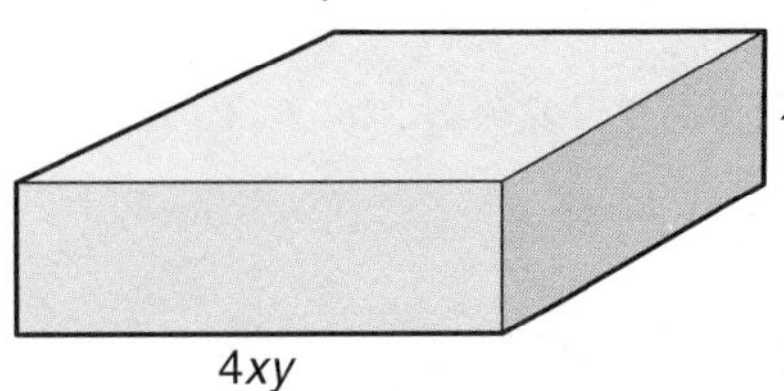

15. Joelle begins the 465 mi drive from Atlanta to Tampa at 6:30 A.M., driving at an average speed of 58 mi/h. Jason leaves Tampa at 8:00 A.M. the same day and travels to Atlanta on the opposite side of the same route. He drives at an average speed of 50 mi/h. At what time will the two drivers meet? 11:30 A.M.

For Performance Assessment see Additional Answers.

PERFORMANCE ASSESSMENT

USE ALGEBLOCKS Pick a variety of algebraic expressions that show addition and subtraction of polynomials as presented in this chapter. Show how to model each operation with Algeblocks. Then ask a partner to show the steps for completing each model. Check that each step is correct.

USE GRID PAPER Let each unit square on grid paper represent one unit, a strip of 5 unit squares represent x, and a 5×5 square represent x^2. The diagram shows that $x^2 + 2x$ is the area of the rectangle with width x and length $x + 2$. What happens if you substitute 5 for x? Draw pictures of rectangles to represent products of polynomials. Use different values for x. Have a partner express the width, length, and area as algebraic expressions and confirm that the area of each rectangle is the product of the length and width.

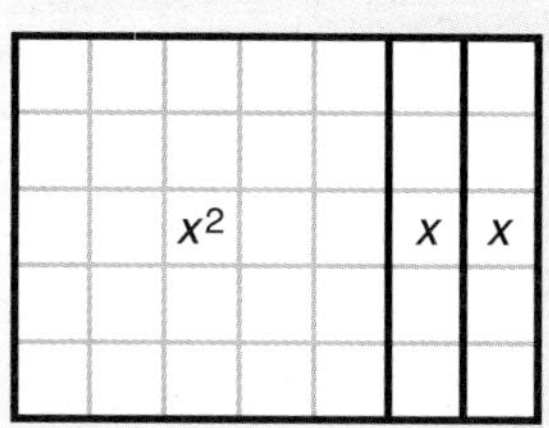

USE ALGEBLOCKS Use Algeblocks to model multiplying and dividing various polynomials. Have a partner write the algebraic expression to represent the multiplication or division and then show the steps for finding the product or quotient. Check that each step is correct.

CALCULATE COMPOUND INTEREST Investigate the different savings plans that various banks in your community offer. Use the formula $A = p(1 + r)^t$ to decide which plan would be best for you. Remember that A represents the amount of money in the account, p is the principal or the amount of money invested, r is the rate of interest per time period, and t is the number of time periods.

PROJECT ASSESSMENT

PROJECT Connection Have a two-part competition to determine which group has designed the paper airplane that will either fly the greatest distance or stay airborne the longest. Hold the competition in a large indoor area such as a gymnasium. Have each group introduce their entry with a short talk that explains the aerodynamic principles they applied to their design.

1. Decide how many trials each entry will be allowed. Will the results be averaged or will only the best distance or time be used?
2. As a class, record all data on the distances and times of each plane. Then have each group choose a different way to organize and present the data visually. For example, one group might make a bar graph of distances, another group might make a circle graph showing the percent of entries with flight times in certain intervals, and another group could make a scatterplot to see if there is a relationship between some aspect of the plane, such as wingspan, and the flight distance or time.
3. Interested students can extend the project by building more durable and sophisticated models.

Performance Assessment

The activities on page 565 give students with different learning styles opportunities to demonstrate their understanding of concepts in this chapter. The activities may be used in addition to or instead of the Chapter Test on the previous page.

Use Algeblocks (Kinesthetic/Visual) A student's ability to model an operation with Algeblocks is a good indicator of understanding. Be sure that the student finds the correct opposite of the expression when subtracting.

Use Grid Paper (Visual) Students can relate a pictorial representation of the area of a rectangle to multiplying polynomials. Check that students' rectangles match the algebraic expressions they have assigned to them.

Use Algeblocks (Kinesthetic/Visual) Check that the models match the algebraic expressions to be multiplied or divided. Students must write expressions that can be modeled using the blocks. Therefore, they cannot include items like $3x^4(-2x^5)$.

Calculate Compound Interest (Individual) This activity is especially appropriate for extension or extra credit work. Have students gather information about interest rates and compounding periods. Have them use the formula to evaluate the information. Encourage students to compare the results for each bank over time periods of 1 year, 5 years, and 10 years. Students will need a calculator.

Project Assessment

Project Connection Conduct the competition in class. Have the class discuss the differences and similarities in the teams' designs. Have them conjecture as to how the design features of the winning entries contributed to their success. They may want to suggest a better design using a combination of features from the best entries.

NAME ______ CLASS ______ DATE ______

FORM B

CHAPTER 11 TEST

Write the letter of the best answer for Questions 1–7.

1. What is the degree of $5x^3y^4$? — 1. a

a. 7 b. 5 c. 4 d. 3

NAME ______ CLASS ______ DATE ______

FORM A

CHAPTER 11 TEST

Write the letter of the best answer for Questions 1–7.

1. What is the degree of $6x^2y^3$? — 1. d
   a. 6 b. 2 c. 3 d. 5
2. Which expression is not equal to 1? — 2. c
   a. 8^0 b. $\frac{x^2}{x^2}$ c. $y^3 - y^3$ d. $(4x + 2) - (4x + 1)$
3. Which is the standard form for 8.3×10^{-4}? — 3. b
   a. 83,000 b. 0.00083 c. 0.000083 d. 830,000
4. Which polynomial has a degree of 5? — 4. c
   I. x^5y^5 II. $4xy^4 - 8x$ III. $x^2y^3 + 2z^2$
   a. only I b. only II c. II and III d. I and III
5. Which is scientific notation for 960,000,000? — 5. b
   a. 9.6×10^7 b. 9.6×10^8
   c. 9.6×10^{-7} d. 9.6×10^{-6}
6. Which is equivalent to $(x + 4)(x - 4)$? — 6. c
   a. $x^2 + 16$ b. $x^2 + 4x + 16$
   c. $x^2 - 16$ d. $x^2 + 4x$
7. Which expressions are equivalent to $(x^2)^4$? — 7. c
   I. x^6 II. x^8 III. $(x^4)^2$ IV. $x^3 \cdot x^5$
   a. II and III b. only I c. II, III, and IV d. only II

Simplify. Write with positive exponents.

8. $5x(-3x)$ — 8. $-15x^2$
9. $(m^2n)(m^4n^5)$ — 9. m^6n^6
10. $(a^2)^5$ — 10. a^{10}
11. $8x^3 \cdot 2x^2$ — 11. $16x^5$
12. $\frac{-6y^8}{-2y^2}$ — 12. $3y^6$
13. $\frac{5m^4n^5}{25mn^3}$ — 13. $\frac{m^3n^2}{5}$
14. $\left(\frac{2m^2}{3n^3}\right)^3$ — 14. $\frac{8m^6}{27n^9}$
15. $\frac{6x^4y^0}{-x^3}$ — 15. $-6x$

50 South-Western Algebra 1: AN INTEGRATED APPROACH

CHAPTER 11 TEST Form A, page 2 NAME ______

Evaluate. Write the answers in scientific notation.

16. $\frac{6.8 \times 10^9}{2 \times 10^4}$ — 16. 3.4×10^5
17. $(3.5 \times 10^5)(2.3 \times 10^4)$ — 17. 8.05×10^9
18. $480{,}000{,}000 \times 3$ — 18. 1.44×10^9
19. 0.0000091×2 — 19. 1.82×10^{-5}

Perform the indicated operation.

20. $7m + 3n + 6s$ $+ 8m - 5n + 2s$ — 20. $15m - 2n + 8s$
21. $8x^2 + 7xy - 6$ $-(2x^2 - 6xy + 5)$ — 21. $6x^2 + 13xy - 11$
22. $6x(3x + 5)$ — 22. $18x^2 + 30x$
23. $(5x + 1)(2x + 3)$ — 23. $10x^2 + 17x + 3$

Solve.

24. GEOMETRY A rectangle is five times as long as it is wide. Its width is $x + 2$. Express its area as an algebraic expression in simplest form. — 24. $5x^2 + 20x + 20$
25. CAR TRAVEL Al and Denise leave the same gas station on an interstate highway at the same time, but they travel in opposite directions without stopping. Al travels at an average speed that is 10 miles per hour faster than Denise's average speed. After 2 hours they are 220 miles apart. How fast is Denise traveling? — 25. 50 mi/h
26. GEOMETRY Find the surface area of the rectangular prism shown. — 26. $94x^2$

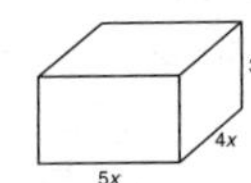

For Question 27, use a separate sheet of paper if necessary.

27. WRITING MATHEMATICS Explain why $(x + 3)^2 \neq x^2 + 9$ for all values of x.
    Possible answer: $(x + 3)^2$ is the square of a binomial, the result should be a trinomial. The polynomials will only be equal when $x = 0$.

52 South-Western Algebra 1: AN INTEGRATED APPROACH

CUMULATIVE REVIEW

Simplify each expression.

1. $y^3 \cdot y^5 \cdot y^2$ y^{10}; Lesson 11.2
2. $\frac{k^{16}}{k^8}$ k^8; Lesson 11.3
3. $(t^5)^8$ t^{40}; Lesson 11.2
4. $(3m^4n)^3$ $27m^{12}n^3$; Lesson 11.2
5. $\frac{x^7}{x^{10}}$ $\frac{1}{x^3}$; Lesson 11.3
6. $\left(\frac{-2a^5}{b^2}\right)^3$ $\frac{-8a^{15}}{b^6}$; Lesson 11.3

Use the quadratic formula to solve each equation. Round answers to the nearest hundredth.

7. $2x^2 - 5x = 11$ −1.41, 3.91; Lesson 10.5
8. $\frac{1}{2}x^2 + 6 = 13x$ 0.47, 25.53; Lesson 10.5

Solve each compound inequality. Then graph the solution. See Additional Answers for graphs.

9. $4n - 3 < 2n + 9$ and $1 - 2n < 5$ $-2 < n < 6$; Lesson 5.5
10. $6(2w - 1) \leq 3(3w - 5)$ or $w - 25 \geq -23$ $w \leq -3$ or $w \geq 2$; Lesson 5.5
11. $\frac{1}{4}z - 3 \leq 1 - \frac{3}{4}z$ and $2z - 2.7 > 5.3$ no solution; Lesson 5.5

Add or subtract. Lesson 11.6

12. $(4x^2 + 2x - 9) + (x^3 + x - 9) + (x^2 - 18)$ $x^3 + 5x^2 + 3x - 36$
13. $(5v^3 - 7v^2 + v - 4) - (8v^3 - 7v^2 - 3v + 10)$ $-3v^3 + 4v - 14$

Write each decimal as the quotient of two integers. Lesson 9.5

14. $0.\overline{36}$ $\frac{4}{11}$
15. 8.75 $\frac{35}{4}$
16. $2.1\overline{6}$ $\frac{13}{6}$

17. Determine an equation of the form $y = ax^2 + bx + c$ that passes through the points (1, 4), (−2, 25), and (7, 16). $y = x^2 - 6x + 9$; Lesson 10.2
18. Find the three greatest consecutive integers whose sum does not exceed 70. 22, 23, and 24; Lesson 5.7

Find each product. Lesson 11.8

19. $(x + 3)(x - 7)$ $x^2 - 4x - 21$
20. $(3t - 4)(3t + 4)$ $9t^2 - 16$
21. $(2z + 5)(2z + 5)$ $4z^2 + 20z + 25$
22. $-4mn^2(3m^4n + 2n^3)$ $-12m^5n^3 - 8mn^5$
23. $(x - 3)(2x^2 + 7x - 4)$ $2x^3 + x^2 - 25x + 12$

24. WRITING MATHEMATICS Explain why FOIL is only applicable when multiplying two binomials. See Additional Answers. Lesson 11.8
25. A farmer wants to enclose a rectangular area for some animals, using the side of a barn as one side. He has 80 feet of fencing available for the other three sides. What dimensions should the farmer make the enclosed area if he wants to maximize the space available? 20 ft by 40 ft; Lesson 10.6

Identify the property illustrated.

26. $8 + (-8) = 0$ additive inverse property; Lesson 2.5
27. If $7 \cdot 5 = 35$, then $35 = 7 \cdot 5$ symmetric property of equality; Lesson 9.6
28. $(82 + 75) + 54 = 54 + (82 + 75)$ commutative property of addition; Lesson 2.5
29. STANDARDIZED TESTS Which of the following expressions is equal to $2x^2 - x - 3$? B; Lessons 11.6 and 11.8
    I. $(2x + 3)(x - 1)$
    II. $(x^3 + 4x - 5) - (x^3 - 2x^2 + 5x - 2)$
    III. $(x^2 + 3x + 1) + (x^2 - 2x - 4)$

    A. I only B. II only
    C. I and II D. I, II, and III
30. WRITING MATHEMATICS Jorge and Consuela both make the same amount of money per month. One month, Jorge received a 10% raise while Consuela's salary was reduced by 10%. The next month Consuela received a 10% raise while Jorge's salary was reduced by 10%. Does Jorge still earn the same amount as Consuela? How does their current salary compare to their salary two months ago? Explain. See Additional Answers. Lesson 3.5

Write each number in scientific notation. Lesson 11.4

31. 40,500,000 $4.05 \cdot 10^7$
32. 0.0000000032 $3.2 \cdot 10^{-9}$
33. $(4.5 \cdot 10^6)(5.2 \cdot 10^6)$ $2.34 \cdot 10^{13}$

STANDARDIZED TEST

STANDARD FIVE-CHOICE Select the best choice for each question.

1. A boy starts out from home at 10:00 A.M. walking east at a rate of 4 miles per hour. His sister leaves from home at 10:30 A.M. running at 7 miles per hour, following the same route. At what time will the sister catch up to the brother? D; Lesson 11.9

A. 40 minutes
B. 10:40 A.M.
C. 11:00 A.M.
D. 11:10 A.M.
E. 11:40 A.M.

2. The slope of the line through points (a, b) and (c, d) is C; Lesson 6.2

A. $\frac{a-c}{b-d}$ **B.** $\frac{d-b}{a-c}$ **C.** $\frac{d-b}{c-a}$
D. $\frac{b-d}{c-a}$ **E.** $\frac{|b-d|}{|a-c|}$

3. The quadratic equation $x^2 - bx - c = 0$ will have how many real solutions if $b > 0$ and $c > 0$? D; Lesson 10.5

A. cannot be determined
B. 0
C. 1
D. 2
E. infinite

4. The vertex of the graph of $y = -2|x - 3| - 4$ is located at C; Lesson 9.2

A. $(-2, -4)$ **B.** $(-3, -4)$ **C.** $(3, -4)$
D. $(-2, 3)$ **E.** $(-4, 3)$

5. A football team scored these point totals during the season:

42, 27, 10, 13, 21, 16, 35, 7, 14, 24, 38

$Q_3 - Q_1 =$ A; Lesson 5.6

A. 22 **B.** 35 **C.** 21
D. 17.5 **E.** Q_2

6. Which of the following products simplifies to be $n^2 + 5n - 6$? E; Lesson 11.8

A. $(n + 3)(n - 2)$
B. $(n - 5)(n - 1)$
C. $(n - 6)(n + 1)$
D. $(n - 3)(n + 2)$
E. $(n - 1)(n + 6)$

7. An item is priced at \$42.50. A sale offers 20% off for this particular item. What is the item's sale price? B; Lesson 3.5

A. \$8.50
B. \$34.00
C. \$51.00
D. \$53.13
E. \$212.50

8. Consider statements I–III as each applies to the points in Quadrant III.

I. The product of the coordinates is positive.
II. Some of the points may lie on the line $y = -x$.
III. Some of the points may lie on the line $x + y = 4$.

Which statement is true? A; Lessons 4.3 and 6.4

A. I only **B.** II only **C.** III only
D. II and III **E.** none are true

9. Six oranges and five apples cost \$1.35. Five oranges and six apples cost \$1.40. What is the difference in price of one apple and one orange? B; Lesson 7.7

A. \$0.25 **B.** \$0.05 **C.** \$0.10
D. \$0.15 **E.** no difference

10. Multiply $(2.5 \cdot 10^8)(8.4 \cdot 10^{-3})$. In scientific notation, the product is C; Lesson 11.4

A. $21 \cdot 10^5$ **B.** $2.1 \cdot 10^4$ **C.** $2.1 \cdot 10^6$
D. $21 \cdot 10^{11}$ **E.** $2.1 \cdot 10^{12}$

Answers

1. E
2. E
3. A
4. B
5. B
6. B
7. D
8. A
9. B
10. B
11. C
12. A
13. C
14. D
15. C
16. B
17. A
18. A
19. C
20. C
21. A
22. D
23. 5
24. 156
25. 400
26. 0.4
27. 0.2
28. 15
29. 16

CHAPTER 11 Standardized Test, page 2 NAME ____________

Quantitative Comparison For Questions 11–22, fill in A if the quantity in Column 1 is greater, B if the quantity in Column 2 is greater, C if the two quantities are equal, and D if the relationship cannot be determined.

Grid Response For Questions 23–29, mark your answer on the answer grid provided.

23. The shaded area of the figure below is 65 square feet. Solve for x in feet.

NAME ____________ CLASS ________ DATE ________

CHAPTER 11 STANDARDIZED TEST

Standard Five-Choice For Questions 1–10, fill in the best choice on the answer grid provided.

1. What is the degree of the polynomial $5x^3y^4 + 2x^2y + 1$?

A. 3 **B.** 4 **C.** 5 **D.** 6 **E.** 7

2. Which expression is *not* equivalent to $(-6x^2y)^2(-xy^2)$?

A. $(36x^4y^2)(-xy^2)$ **B.** $-36x^5y^4$
C. $(-6)^2(x^2)^2(y^2)(-xy^2)$
D. $(-6)^2(x^2)^2(y^2)(-x)(y^2)$
E. $36x^5y^4$

3. Which expression shows the surface area of the prism?

A. $32x^2 - 2$
B. $16x^2 - 1$
C. $12x^3 - 3x$
D. $24x^3 - 6x$
E. $7x - 2$

3x
2x − 1
2x + 1

4. Which is scientific notation for 0.0000094?

A. 9.4×10^{-5} **B.** 9.4×10^{-6}
C. 9.4×10^5 **D.** 9.4×10^6
E. 9.4×10^{-5}

5. Evaluate $\frac{8.7 \times 10^6}{3 \times 10^3}$. Which shows the answer in scientific notation?

A. 2.9×10^2 **B.** 2.9×10^3
C. 2.9×10^{-2} **D.** 2.9×10^{-3}
E. 2.9×10^9

6. Find the product: $(3x + 1)(2x - 3)$

A. $6x^2 - 3$ **B.** $6x^2 - 7x - 3$
C. $6x^2 + 7x - 3$ **D.** $6x^2 + 7x + 3$
E. $6x^2 + 3$

7. Which expression is equivalent to $(x^2y^0z^{-2})^3$?

A. x^5y^3z **B.** $x^6 + y^3 + z$
C. $\frac{x^5}{z^6}$ **D.** $\frac{x^6}{z^6}$ **E.** x^5z

8. Which expressions are equivalent to $\left(\frac{3x^2y}{-xy^3}\right)^2$?

I. $\left(\frac{-3x}{y^2}\right)^2$ **II.** $\frac{9x^2}{y^4}$ **III.** $9x^2y^{-4}$
IV. $\frac{9x^2}{4}$ **V.** $9\left(\frac{x^2y}{-xy^3}\right)$

A. I, II, and III
B. I and II
C. I, III, and IV
D. I, II, III, and V
E. I, II, III, and V

9. Use the following information.

At 5:30 P.M., Alonzo left Chicago driving at 55 mi/h. At 5:45 P.M. Sarah left Chicago and followed the same route, driving at 60 mi/h.

Which equation could you use to find how long it would take Sarah to overtake Alonzo?

A. $55t = 60(t + 0.25)$
B. $55t = 60(t - 0.25)$
C. $55t = 60(t - 15)$
D. $55t = 60(t + 15)$
E. $55(t - 15) = 60t$

10. Which is equivalent to $(12x^2 + 6x) - (9x^2 - x)$?

A. $3x^2 - 5x$ **B.** $3x^2 + 7x$
C. $3x^2 + 6x$ **D.** $21x^2 + 5x$
E. None of these

South-Western Algebra 1: AN INTEGRATED APPROACH

57

Chapter Opener

DATA ACTIVITY, PAGES 514–515

1. 6.4 m **2.** 2.4 **3.** 78.6 cm
4. 74.0 ft **5.** 16,800 lb **6.** Answers will vary.

Algebra Workshop 11.1

EXPLORE, PAGE 517

12. 3^2; 9 units are needed for 3^2, but only 8 for 2^3

17. Place three *x*-blocks on the negative part of the horizontal axis and two *x*-blocks on the negative part of the vertical axis. Form a rectangular area using six x^2-blocks in the quadrant bounded by the blocks. Read the answer, $6x^2$, from the mat.

24. Correctly place the blocks that represent the length of the rectangle $-2y$.

25. Place two *x*-blocks on the positive side of the horizontal axis. Place two x^2-blocks on the positive quadrant bordering the divisor. Complete the vertical axis for the rectangle. Read the answer, *x*, from the vertical axis.

MAKE CONNECTIONS, PAGE 520

35. No; there is no way to model a fourth dimension.

36. Write each factor of $2x \bullet 3x^3$. You get $2 \bullet x \bullet 3 \bullet x \bullet x \bullet x$. When you use the commutative and associative properties, you see that the product is $6x^4$. That is, multiply the numerals, multiply the variables, then multiply these together.

37. Write each factor of the numerator and denominator of the fraction $\frac{5x^6}{10x}$. You get $\frac{5 \bullet x \bullet x \bullet x \bullet x \bullet x \bullet x}{10 \bullet x}$. Divide the numerator and denominator by the common factor 5x; $\frac{x^5}{2}$. That is, divide the numerals and the variables to get the final quotient.

SUMMARIZE, PAGE 520

40. Answers will vary. **41.** Answers will vary.

COMMUNICATING ABOUT ALGEBRA, PAGE 518

Answers will vary.

CHECK UNDERSTANDING, PAGE 519

yes;

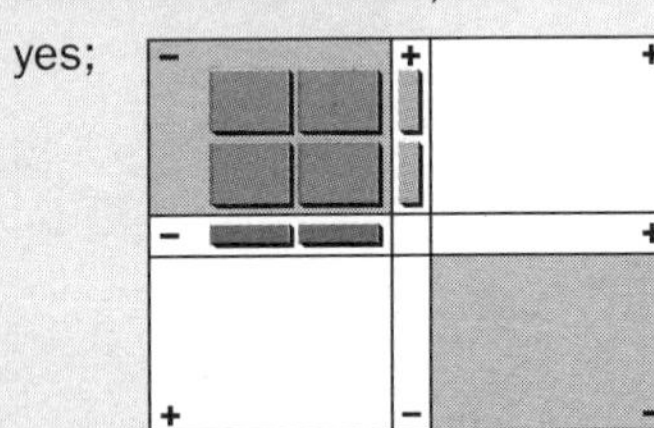

COMMUNICATING ABOUT ALGEBRA, PAGES 519

Answers will vary.

Lesson 11.2

EXPLORE/WORKING TOGETHER, PAGE 521

3. The regions double each time; the number of regions equals 2^f where *f* is the fold number.

COMMUNICATING ABOUT ALGEBRA, PAGES 523

In multiplying x^2 and x^3, the exponents are added to get the product x^5. In multiplying x^2 and y^3, the exponents cannot be added because the two terms have different bases.

TRY THESE, PAGE 524

17. (1) The product of powers: add exponents when multiplying variables with the same base; example: $y^4 \bullet y^5 = y^9$. (2) The power of a power: multiply exponents when raising a variable with an exponent to a power; example: $(a^2)^4 = a^8$. (3) The power of a product: each factor of a monomial raised to a power must be raised to that power; example: $(3x^3y^2)^3 = 27x^9y^6$.

PROJECT CONNECTION, PAGE 525

1. It is harder to run. The cardboard gives you a greater surface area affected by the force of the air.

Lesson 11.3

EXPLORE/WORKING TOGETHER, PAGE 527

5. $2^{-1}, \frac{1}{2}; 2^{-2}, \frac{1}{4}; 2^{-3}, \frac{1}{8}$

6. $2^{-1} = \frac{1}{2^1}; 2^{-2} = \frac{1}{2^2}; 2^{-3} = \frac{1}{2^3}$; possible response is that $2^{-k} = \frac{1}{2^k}$

TRY THESE, PAGE 530

18. *Quotient Rule*: When dividing variables with the same base, subtract the exponents. Example: $\frac{a^4}{a^2} = a^2$. *Zero Property*: Any variable or number raised to the zero power is 1. Example: $3^0 = 1$. *Property of Negative Exponents*: A variable or number with a negative exponent may be written as a reciprocal of the base raised to the positive power. Example: $r^{-4} = \frac{1}{r^4}$. *Power of a Quotient Rule*: To raise a quotient to a power, raise both the numerator and the denominator to that power. Example: $\left(\frac{a}{4}\right)^3 = \frac{a^3}{4^3} = \frac{a^3}{64}$.

EXTEND, PAGES 530–531

29. Possible response: Substitute $\frac{2}{3}$ for *K*, use the reciprocal of $\frac{2}{3}$ to get a positive exponent, $6\left(\frac{3}{2}\right)^2$. Now evaluate $6\left(\frac{3^2}{2^2}\right) = 6 \bullet \frac{9}{4} = \frac{54}{4} = 13\frac{1}{2}$.

32. The force is multiplied by 1.5. Replacing *m* by 2*m*, *M* by 3*M*, and *r* by 2*r*, you get $F = \frac{G(2m)(3M)}{(2r)^2}$. When you simplify it, you get $F = \frac{3GmM}{2r^2}$, So, F is $\frac{3}{2}$ or 1.5 times more than the original.

THINK CRITICALLY, PAGE 531

37. $p < q$; if *p* and *q* are positive and $n(p - q)$ is negative, then *p* must be less than *q*

MIXED REVIEW, PAGE 531

41.

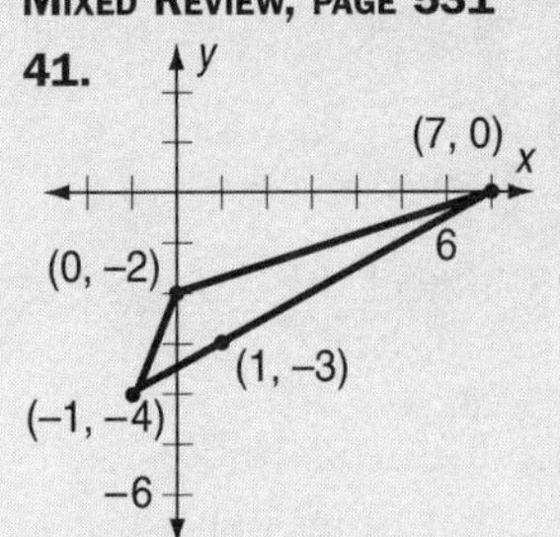

42. The points (–1, –4), (1, –3), and (7, 0) appear to result in one side of a triangle. To justify that the points are in a line, use the point slope formula to find the equation of the lines connecting them. Then substitute the values (1, –3) in that equation to see if they are a solution of the equation.

Lesson 11.4

TRY THESE, PAGES 534–535

16. Move the decimal point 4 places to the right. Write the number as 6.2×10^{-4}.

EXTEND, PAGES 535–536

33. $(3.7 \times 10^{-1})\frac{\text{m/s}}{°\text{C}}$ **34.** Answers will vary.

PROJECT CONNECTION, PAGE 536

5. The plane hangs level. If its weight is not balanced the plane may not fly properly.

Lesson 11.5

THINK BACK, PAGE 538

1. **3.**

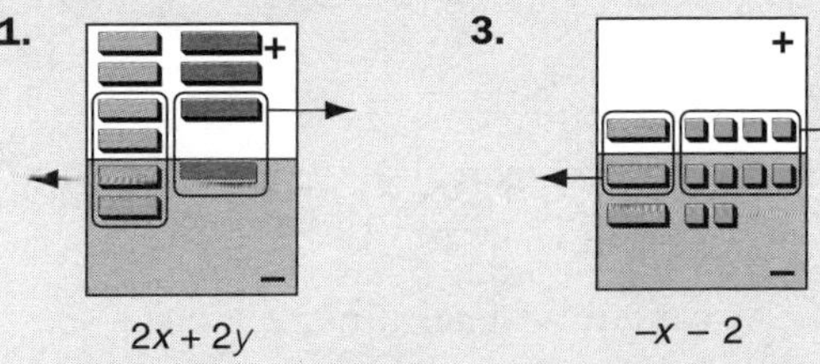

5. The number of different kinds of terms results in the same number of unlike terms after combining like terms.

6.

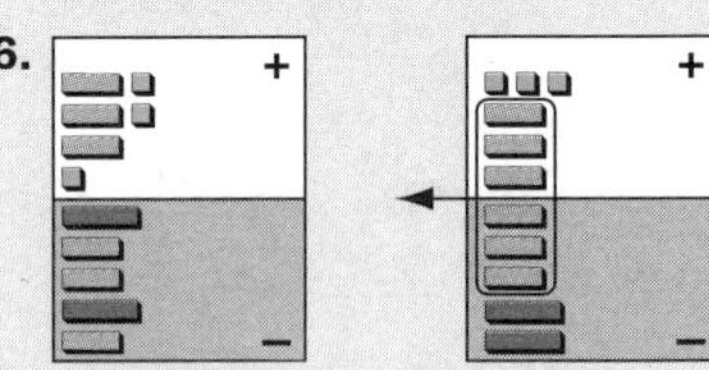

EXPLORE, PAGES 538–539

8.

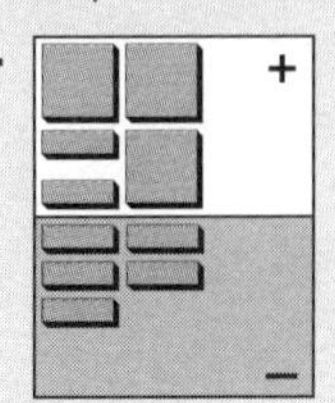

15. There are five zero pairs; the sum of the mat is 0

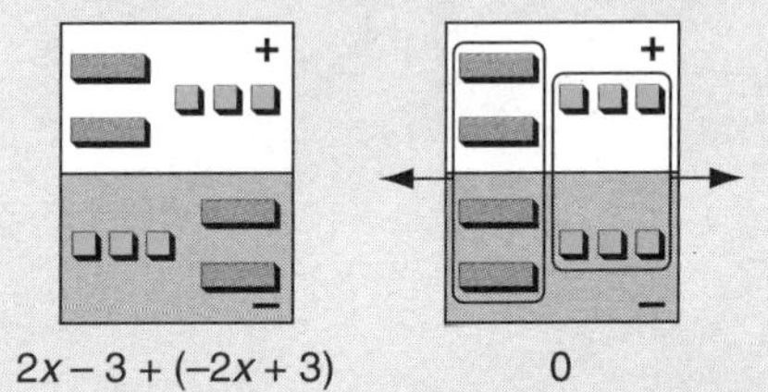

MAKE CONNECTIONS, PAGES 539–540

32. Like terms have the same variables and exponents.

34. North America 2.9×10^8, Latin America 4.7×10^8, Europe 7.28×10^8, Asia 3.392×10^9, Africa 7×10^8, Oceania 2.8×10^7

35. Rewrite the numbers for Asia and Oceania as 33.92×10^8 and 0.28×10^8. Add all the numbers by adding the first part of each notation.

SUMMARIZE, PAGE 540

37. **a.** Yes.

38. Answers will vary.

39. The opposite of an algebraic expression is the opposite of each term. If you add an algebraic expression and its opposite, you will get 0.

40. Answers will vary.

Lesson 11.6

EXPLORE, PAGE 541

4. $x = 17, x - 8 = 9, x - 7 = 10,$
$x - 6 = 11, x - 1 = 16, x + 1 = 18,$
$x + 6 = 23, x + 7 = 24, x + 8 = 25$

5. The sum of column 1 is $3x - 3$, the sum of column 2 is $3x$, and the sum of column 3 is $3x + 3$. So, $3x - 3 + 3x + 3x + 3 = 9x$.

CHECK UNDERSTANDING, PAGE 543

No; the sum of two binomials can have more or fewer terms than each of its addends. Example: $(2x + 3y) + (4x + 5z) = 6x + 3y + 5z$

TRY THESE, PAGE 545

8. On a basic mat, start with 2 x^2 blocks, 2 x blocks, and 1 unit block in the positive section, and 3 x^2 blocks and 4 unit blocks in the negative section. Remove 2 zero pairs of x's and 1 zero pair of 1's. The sum is $2x^2 - x - 3$.

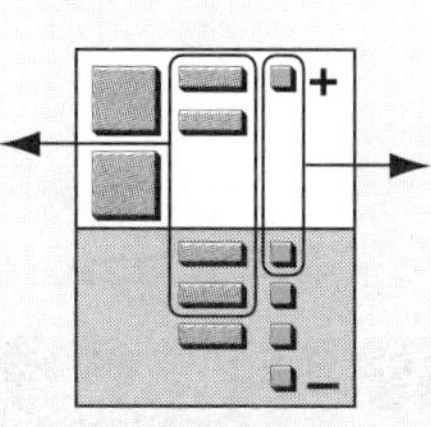

9. Answers will vary.

PRACTICE, PAGE 545

7. $12a - 2c$

8. $6r + 12s + 8t$

9. $-3p + 6q + 9$

10. $13x^2 - 10x$

11. $-4a + b - 6c$

12. $-2y + 2z$

13. $6y^4 + 8y^2 - 10$

14. $-2z^3 + 6z^2 - 6z$

EXTEND, PAGE 546

24. No. A car traveling at 40 mi/h needs 120 ft to stop. The rule of thumb says 80.

THINK CRITICALLY, PAGE 546

27. true; $(a - b) + (b - a) = 0$; therefore $b - a$ is the opposite of $a - b$.

PROJECT CONNECTION, PAGE 547

3. The area of a circle is $A = \pi r^2$, so $r = \sqrt{\frac{A}{\pi}}$.

The radius of the circle whose area equals that of an 8 × 8 in. square is $r = \sqrt{\frac{64}{\pi}}$ or 4.5 in.

7. Circular. The square chute allows air to escape out the sides, making it less stable. The circular chute holds air more uniformly, making it more stable.

Lesson 11.7

EXPLORE, PAGES 548–549

13. $2x^2 - 4x$. The Algeblocks model shows $2x(x)$ in Quadrant I and $(2x)(-2)$ in Quadrant IV.

MAKE CONNECTIONS, PAGE 550

24. Each term of the second factor is multiplied by each term of the first factor, and the result is the sum of these products.

30. Answers will vary.

SUMMARIZE, PAGE 550

32. Answers will vary.

35. Answers will vary.

Lesson 11.8

COMMUNICATING ABOUT ALGEBRA, PAGE 552

Multiply $(40 + 3)(20 + 5)$. Add the products $40 \bullet 20$, $40 \bullet 5$, $3 \bullet 20$, and $3 \bullet 5$.

TRY THESE, PAGE 555

16. Possible answer: since $(x + 5)^2$ is the square of a binomial, the result should be a trinomial.

EXTEND, PAGES 556–557

42. Shaded area
$= (a + b)(a - b)$
$= a(a - b) + b(a - b)$
$= a^2 - ab + ab - b^2$
$= a^2 - b^2$

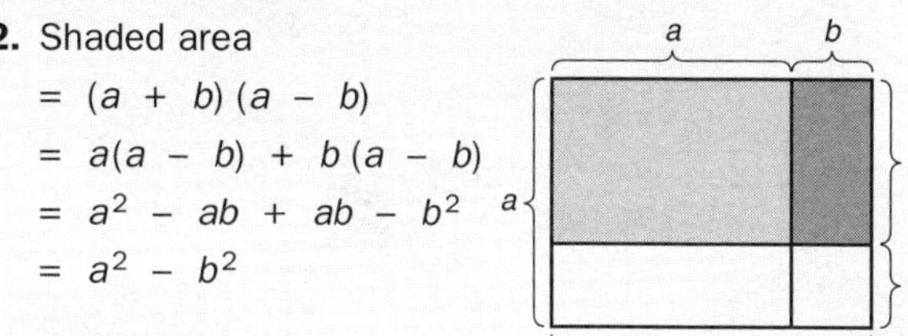

Lesson 11.9

EXPLORE THE PROBLEM, PAGE 558

3. Dan's distance plus Fran's distance will equal 200 mi; $55(t + 1) + 45t = 200$

4. $t = 1.45$ h or $1\frac{9}{20}$ h or 1 h 27 min, so the trucks pass at 9:27 A.M.

5. Dan's distance $= 55\left(1 + 1\frac{9}{20}\right) = 134\frac{3}{4}$ mi

Fran's distance $= 45\left(1\frac{9}{20}\right) = 65\frac{1}{4}$ mi

$134\frac{3}{4}$ mi $+ 65\frac{1}{4}$ mi $= 200$ mi

INVESTIGATE FURTHER, PAGE 559

12. Answers will vary.

APPLY THE STRATEGY, PAGE 560

15. Their distances are equal; $4(t + 0.5) = 6t$; $t = 1$ h; Ivan hikes for 1 h and covers 6 km; Darrell hikes for 1.5 h and also covers 6 km.

REVIEW PROBLEM SOLVING STRATEGIES, PAGE 561

THE EMPTY ENVELOPE PLEASE!

The envelopes all weigh the same, except the empty one is lighter. Divide them into 3 groups of 9. Weigh one group of 9 against another group of 9. If they balance, the empty envelope is in the leftover group of 9. If they do not, the empty one is in the group in the higher pan. Take the group with the empty envelope. Divide it into 3 groups of 3. Weigh one group of 3 against another group of 3. If they balance, the empty envelope is in the leftover group of 3. If they do not, the empty one is in the group in the higher pan. Take the group with the empty envelope. Weigh one envelope against another. If they balance, the empty one is the leftover envelope; if they don't, the empty one is in the higher pan. Exactly three weighings are necessary.

SWIMMER'S PUZZLE

Joel is in Lane 3, the third lane from the left. Methods will vary, but the problem can be solved by making a table as follows. 12 is 3 less than 15 and Lane 6 is 3 places to the right of Lane 3.

Lane	To right	To left	Product
1	8	0	0
2	7	1	7
3	6	2	12
4	5	3	15
5	4	4	16
6	3	5	15
7	2	6	12
8	1	7	7
9	0	8	0

SHOPPER'S SPECIAL

Under \$5, you save money at Bill's and not at Good Buys. You also save at Bill's for purchases of \$7–9 and \$14. For all other amounts over \$5, you save more at Good Buys.

Chapter Assessment, pages 564–565

CHAPTER TEST, PAGE 564

5. Answers will vary, but should include at least two of the following methods: distributive, FOIL, area model, Algeblocks, or vertical.

13. $3w^2$, where w represents the width; width: 4 cm, length: 12 cm

PERFORMANCE ASSESSMENT, PAGE 565

USE GRID PAPER

the sides measure $x = 5$ and $x + 2 = 7$; area is $x^2 + 2x = 35$ or 5×7

CUMULATIVE REVIEW, PAGE 566

9. $-2 < n < 6$

-3 -2 -1 0 1 2 3 4 5 6 7

10. $w \leq -3$ or $w \geq 2$

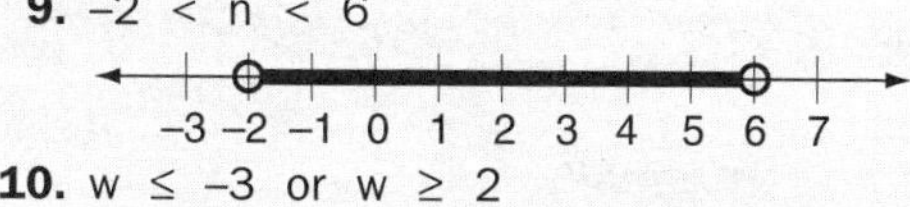

24. FOIL represents each of the four products to be found when multiplying binomials. Excluding monomials, any other combination of polynomials will yield more than four products, thus rendering FOIL useless as an aid.

30. If their original salary was \$1000, then after the first month Jorge made \$1100 and Consuela \$900. After the second month, Jorge's salary was \$990, as was Consuela's. So, yes, they still earn the same amount, but their salary is slightly less than it was originally.

CHAPTER 12 POLYNOMIALS AND FACTORING

High school graduates during the remainder of this century can expect to have four or more career changes. To develop the requisite adaptability, high school mathematics instruction must adopt broader goals for all students. It must provide experiences that encourage and enable students to value mathematics, gain confidence in their own mathematical ability, become mathematical problem solvers, communicate mathematically, and reason mathematically.

"Curriculum and Evaluation Standards for School Mathematics" NCTM, 1989, Reston, VA, page 123; Washington, D.C., page 1

The Big Question: Why study polynomials and factoring?

Factoring is an inverse process in which students take a polynomial product and rewrite it as the product of two or more factors. Even quadratic equations can be solved by factoring. Factoring is also a prerequisite to simplifying and dividing rational expressions, skills presented in Chapter 14. Polynomials can model real life situations. Although the theme of this chapter is rivers, students will also see applications from architecture, finance, gardening, geometry, history, machinery/metal work, magazine layout, packaging, physics, and recreation.

Using the Graphic Organizer

Project a copy of the Graphic Organizer Transparency for Chapter 12. Explain that the focus of this chapter is on factoring polynomials. Review the information on the graphic organizer, pointing out that polynomials can be factored in a number of different ways, including by a greatest common factor (GCF) and by recognizing patterns.

Ask some preview questions; for example, what does it mean to factor a number like 24?

One way to organize ideas about factoring polynomials is shown below.

Vocabulary

discriminant
factored
factored completely
factored form
leading coefficient
zero product property

One way to organize ideas about polynomials and factoring is shown.

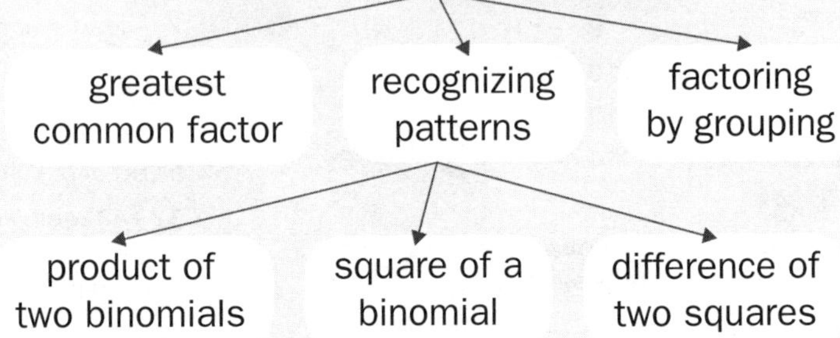

Try It **Use a different plan. Try organizing ideas around the number of terms in the polynomials.**

Explore the Chapter Theme:

U.S. Rivers

Rivers normally overflow their banks every year or two. The earliest civilizations were built along river banks because the flood plains were fertilized by silt from the rivers, and therefore, were productive for farming. However, dwellings built close to rivers are subject to damage from floods. Construction projects near river banks require planning to minimize flood damage. Scientists, engineers, and technicians contribute significantly to the planning, designing, and construction of buildings, roads, bridges, tunnels, dams, and water supply projects.

Skills Needed for Success in Jobs Related to U.S. Rivers

1. Gather data from many sources in order to understand the geological and climactic factors involved in a particular project.
2. Use analytical skills to understand data that includes many variables.
3. Use analytical skills to identify problems, causes, and solutions.
4. Have physical stamina for working outside.
5. Work cooperatively with a team.
6. Write and speak clearly.
7. Use computer simulations of geological problems, engineering projects, and/or water resource management.
8. Present technical information to the general public.
9. Use critical thinking skills in troubleshooting design problems.
10. Plan and work within a budget.
11. Manage people and resources for a complex project.
12. Read and understand government regulations about worker safety.
13. Make decisions based on government regulations.

Investigate Further

Have students identify a a career related to the study of rivers, geology, or civil engineering that interests them. Tell students to go to the library to find more information about this career. For example, students might find out about educational requirements including specific courses, degrees, examinations, or licenses required. Students should research the average salary range for the career. Have students share their findings in a class discussion about career opportunities.

Here is a list of jobs and educational requirements for careers related to U.S. Rivers.

Jobs Requiring 1 to 2 Years of Technical Training

Computer Operator

Surveyor

Inspector

Civil Engineering Technician

Water Resource Technician

Earth Science Field Assistant

Research Laboratory Technician

Jobs Requiring 4 + Years of College

Geologist

Hydrologist

Ecologist

Meteorologist

Civil Engineer

Engineering Manager

Environmental Consultant

Earth Science Teacher

Research Scientist

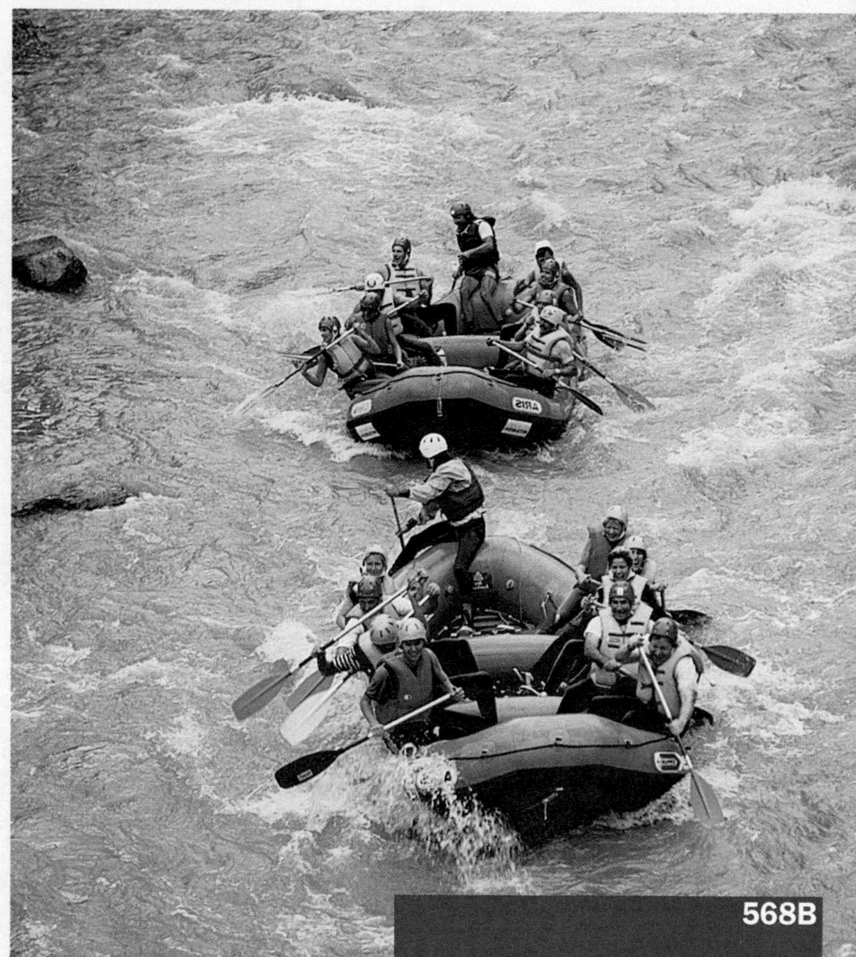

CHAPTER 12 PLANNING GUIDE

Lessons	Text Pages	NCTM Standards	ASSIGNMENTS Basic	Average	Enriched	Ancillaries	Manipulatives	Technology
Chapter Introduction	568–570	1, 2, 3, 4, 10				Video Discussion Guide		Video, Transparency 6
12.1 Algebra Workshop: Explore Patterns in Factoring	571–574	1, 2, 3, 4, 5, 8	1–47	1–47	1–48	S 29; M 12	Algeblocks, Quadrant Mats, 571–574	Transparencies 12, 21, 67
12.2 Factor Polynomials	575–581	1, 2, 3, 4, 5, 8	1–12, 15–33, 36, 38, 40, 43, PC1–3, AW1–4	3–13, 15–34, 36, 38–41, 43, PC1–3, AW1–4	4–44, PC1–3, AW1–4	W 12.2; R 12.2; P 12.2; E 12.2; Q 12.2; S 30; T 28	Algeblocks, Quadrant Mats, 576–578; Graph Paper	Graphing Utility Transparencies 12, 21, 67
12.3 Factoring Special Products	582–585	1, 2, 3, 4, 5, 8	1–20, 26, 28–29, MR33–39	3–24, 26, 28–31, MR33–39	4–32, MR33–39	W 12.3; R 12.3; P 12.3; E 12.3; Q 12.3	Algeblocks, Quadrant Mats, 583–584	Transparencies 12, 21
12.4 Factor by Grouping	586–590	1, 2, 3, 4, 5, 8	1–21, 25–26, 28, PC, AW1–4	2–26, 28, PC, AW1–4	3–30, PC, AW1–4	W 12.4; R 12.4; P 12.4; E 12.4; Q 12.4	Algeblocks, Quadrant Mats, 588	
12.5 Factoring Completely	591–594	1, 2, 3, 4, 5, 8	1–20, 34, MR36–39, PC1–3	4–30, 32–34, MR36–39, PC1–3	7–35, MR36–39, PC1–3	W 12.5; R 12.5; P 12.5; E 12.5; Q 12.5	Stopwatches; Algeblocks, Quadrant Mats, 593	Calculator, Transparency 6
12.6 Solve Quadratic Equations by Factoring	595–601	1, 2, 3, 4, 5, 8, 14	1–32, 36–37, MR42–50, AW1–6	3–34, 36–38, MR42–50, AW1–6	5–41, MR42–50, AW1–6	W 12.6; R 12.6; P 12.6; E 12.6; Q 12.6; T 29		Graphing Utility Transparency 6
12.7 Problem Solving File: Problems Involving Quadratic Equations.	602–605	1, 2, 3, 4, 5, 8, 11	1–19, RPSS1–3	1–23, RPSS1–3	1–24, RPSS1–3	R 12.7; P 12.7		Transparency 1

NCTM STANDARDS

1. Mathematics as Problem Solving
2. Mathematics as Communication
3. Mathematics as Reasoning
4. Mathematical Connections
5. Algebra
6. Functions
7. Geometry from a Synthetic Perspective
8. Geometry from an Algebraic Perspective
9. Trigonometry
10. Statistics
11. Probability
12. Discrete Mathematics
13. Conceptual Underpinnings of Calculus
14. Mathematical Structure

ANCILLARIES

W = Warm Up
R = Reteaching
P = Extra Practice
E = Enrichment
Q = Lesson Quiz
T = Technology Activity
M = Multicultural Connection
S = Study Skills Activity

ADDITIONAL RESOURCES

pplications	Career Connections	Cooperative Learning	Learning Styles	Strand Integration/ Math Connection
	Chapter Poster			
		Paired partners, 571 (Explore)	Linguistic/Interpersonal, Visual, 571–574; Tactile/Kinesthetic, 571–574	Problem Solving, Modeling, Writing, Patterns
eometry, 578, 579; achinery/Metal Work, 80; Physics, 579; ivers, 580	AlgebraWorks: Hydrologist, 581	Small groups, 580 (Project Connection)	Visual, 576–581; Tactile/Kinesthetic, 576–578; Linguistic/Interpersonal, 580	Problem Solving, Modeling, Writing, Geometry, Critical Thinking, Statistics
omputers, 585; eometry, 584, 585		Paired partners, 582 (Explore/Working Together)	Visual, 583–585; Tactile, 583–584; Linguistic/Interpersonal, 582	Problem Solving, Modeling, Geometry, Writing, Critical Thinking
eramic Tiling, 588; inance, 589; Geometry, 88, 589; History, 589; ivers, 589	AlgebraWorks: Civil Engineer, 590	Small groups, 589 (Project Connection)	Visual, 586–590; Linguistic/Interpersonal, 589; Tactile, 587–588	Problem Solving, Geometry, Modeling, Writing, Critical Thinking, Statistics
eometry, 592, 593; achinery/Metal Work, 93; Rivers, 594		Small groups, 591 (Explore/Working Together), 594 (Project Connection)	Linguistic/Interpersonal, 591, 592, 594; Visual, 592–594; Tactile, 593	Problem Solving, Modeling, Writing, Geometry, Critical Thinking
rchitecture, 598, 600; eometry, 599, 600; umber Theory, 599, 600	AlgebraWorks: Water Resources Technician, 601		Visual, 598, 601; Linguistic/Interpersonal, 597; Individual Learners, 596 (TE)	Problem Solving, Technology, Geometry, Number Theory, Writing, Critical Thinking
rt, 604; Gardening, 604; ome Furnishings, 603; achinery/Metal Work, 04; Magazine Layout, 03; Number Theory, 04; Packaging, 604; ecreation, 603			Visual, 602; Visual, 603 (TE)	Problem Solving, Logical Reasoning, Writing, Probability, Geometry, Number Theory

PACING GUIDE

Lessons	Regular Classes	2-year Algebra 1 Classes	Blocked Classes
12.1	1	2	½
12.2	1	2	½
12.3	1	2	½
12.4	1	2	½
12.5	1	2	½
12.6	1	2	½
12.7	1	2	1
Review	1	1	1
Test	1	1	1
Cumulative Test	1	1	1
Total Classes	10	17	7

SESSMENT OPTIONS

udent Edition
apter Assessment
Chapter Test
Performance Assessment
Project Assessment
ndardized Tests

Chapter Resource Book
Chapter Test, Form A
Chapter Test, Form B
Standardized Chapter Test
Portfolio Item: Self-Assessment
Portfolio Assessment Form

MicroExam II

PREVIEW THE CHAPTER

Take a Look Ahead Have students read the previewing suggestions and then scan the chapter looking for new and familiar things. Give students time to make notes in their journals. Discuss student answers to the preview questions.

Connecting to Career Opportunities Have students read the descriptions of the AlgebraWorks features for this chapter. Ask students to identify the careers mentioned. **hydrologists, civil engineers, and water resources technicians** Ask students if they know anyone who works at these jobs. Discuss the types of educational background required for each of the careers. For example, hydrologists and civil engineers have a college degree while water resources technicians usually have received additional technical training after high school.

Investigate Further Explain that as they study this chapter students should look for examples of other careers related to U.S. rivers. Ask students to determine one way in which algebra can be used in that career. Encourage students to write questions in their journals about other jobs related to rivers that they may want to learn more about.

USING THE DATA ACTIVITY

Introduce the Data Activity Have students read the introductory paragraph. Refer to a U.S. map to show the area identified as the Mississippi's drainage basin. Ask students to locate the Rocky and Appalachian Mountains.

Skill Focus Read the skills listed and discuss with students what they think each means. Ask students to suggest problems that might involve the skill being discussed.

Polynomials and Factoring

Take a Look AHEAD

Make notes about things that look new.

- Find an example to illustrate the difference between a common factor of two monomials and the greatest common factor of the same monomials.
- How do you apply the Distributive Property to multiply? How do you apply the Distributive Property to factor?

Make notes about things that look familiar.

- In Chapter 11, you learned to recognize special cases of polynomial multiplication. Identify examples of these special products in this chapter.
- How do you think factoring a polynomial will be similar to factoring an integer? How do you think the factoring process might be different?

DATA Activity

Where Do the Waters Go?

A river and its *tributaries*, smaller channels such as brooks or streams that merge into the river, form a *river system*. All the water in a river system eventually flows to one location—the main river. The area drained by a river system is called the system's *drainage basin*. As you can see from the table on the next page, the Mississippi River has the largest drainage area in the United States. Most of the rain that falls between the Rocky Mountains in the West to the Appalachian Mountains in the East drains into the Mississippi.

SKILL FOCUS

- Add, subtract, multiply, and divide and compare real numbers.
- Determine the range of a data set.
- Solve percent problems.
- Use scientific notation.
- Construct a boxplot.

568

In this chapter, you will see how

- **Hydrologists** create mathematical models of river activity using velocity and flow rate data. (Lesson 12.2, page 581)
- **Civil Engineers** design dams to provide both flood control and low-cost electrical power. (Lesson 12.4, page 590)
- **Water Resources Technicians** determine if the volume of water in a river is increasing toward flood levels. (Lesson 12.6, page 601)

Drainage Areas of U.S. Rivers

River	Drainage Area, 1000s of mi^2
Mississippi	1150
Ohio	203
Columbia	258
Yukon	328
Missouri	529
Mobile	44.6
Snake	108
Tennessee	40.9
Atchafalaya	95.1
Susquehanna	27.2

1–5 See Additional Answers.

Use the table at the right to answer the following questions.

1. What is the range of the drainage areas for the rivers shown?
2. Which river has a drainage area about four times the size of the drainage area of the Susquehanna River?
3. The drainage area of the Mississippi is about 40% of the total land area of the United States excluding Hawaii and Alaska. Determine the approximate total land area of the continental United States. Write your answer using scientific notation.
4. Consider the value for the Mississippi as an outlier. Make a boxplot of the data for the other rivers.
5. **Working Together** Research the size of the drainage areas of several major rivers of the world, such as the Amazon or the Nile. Write word problems that relate the size of the drainage area of a world river to the size of the basin of a United States river. Exchange problems with other groups and solve.

Study the Data The chart lists 10 different U.S. river systems and gives the drainage area in thousands of square miles. Point out that each number in the chart must be multiplied by 1000 to find the actual number of square miles.

Complete the Data Activity

For Item 1, remind students that the range is the difference between the largest and smallest areas. **1,150,000 – 27,200 = 1,122,800 mi²**

For Item 2, the drainage area of the Susquehanna River is 27.2 thousand square miles. Four times that is about 108 thousand square miles. Have students look in the chart for the number closest to 108 and find the corresponding river.

For Item 3, students can write an equation for the problem. Let x represent the total land area, in thousands of square miles, of the continental U.S. The problem can be translated into the equation $0.4x = 1150$. Then, $x = 2875$. So the total land area of the continental U.S. is approximately 2875 thousand square miles or 2,875,000 mi^2.

For Item 4, remind students that an outlier is a data value that is much greater or less than all of the other values. To construct the box-and-whisker plot for the rest of the data, students must find the median of the data (108), the median of each half (42.75, 293) and the least and greatest values (27.2, 529).

For Item 5, students will need access to almanacs and/or atlases. Encourage students to write a variety of problems.

South-Western Algebra 1 Chapter Theme Video or Videodisc

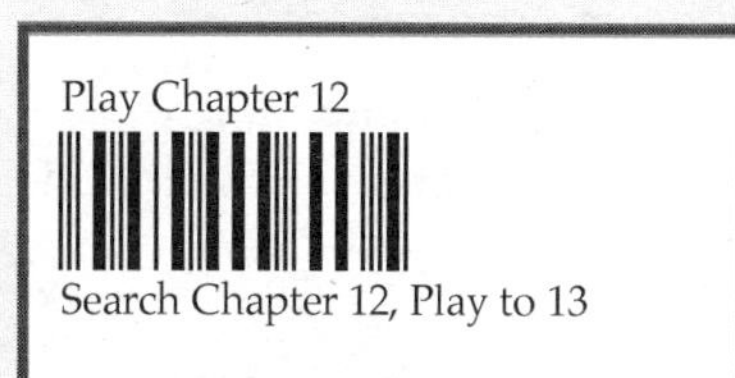

Play Chapter 12
Search Chapter 12, Play to 13

INTRODUCING THE PROJECT

Project Goal Discuss the project's big idea: What conditions contribute to white water rapids?

Getting Ready Collect pictures that show rivers with people white water rafting as well as quiet rivers with people fishing or boating. Use these as a springboard for discussion about differences in river currents. Encourage students to talk about rivers with which they are familiar and any boating experiences they have had.

FACILITATING THE PROJECT

Getting Started Help students identify what equipment they will need for the experiment, how much will be available from the science department, and how much students can contribute from home. Have students research earth science books about rivers.

Setting Project Benchmarks Make sure that students are aware of the project schedule in the Project Planning Calendar and the due dates for each of the benchmarks. You may find the TGT cooperative learning approach appropriate for the Project Assessment stage of this activity.

a. Build a river model and determine which river characteristics affect river flow. (Project/Chapter Opener)
b. Construct backwaters and eddies as features of the river model. (Project Connection 12.2)
c. Construct a souse hole as a feature of the river model. (Project Connection 12.4)
d. Explore the effect of a gradient on the speed of the river model flow. (Project Connection 12.5)
e. Complete the river model. Prepare a demonstration and presentation. (Project Assessment)

Suggest that students make subgoals for each goal and include subgoals in their calendar.

How Rapid Is Your River?

PROJECT GOAL

To construct a model of a white-water river.

You've probably seen pictures of white-water boating and perhaps even participated in this increasingly popular sport. The area of the United States between the Rocky Mountains and the Pacific Ocean is known for some of the best white-water rivers in the world, although good white-water boating is found throughout the country. In this project, you will explore some of the river conditions that lead to crashing rapids and thrilling rides.

Getting Started

Work with a group to build the river model.

1. If possible, borrow a *stream table* from the science department. You will also need large pails, rubber tubing, bricks or wooden blocks, sand to fill the stream table, a toy boat, a stopwatch, other materials such as rocks and clay to create special features in your model, lots of paper towels, and an approved working area. Consult a teacher or an earth science textbook for instructions on how to set up this equipment.
2. Research to find out which river characteristics affect the water flow. How do deep rivers compare with shallow ones? Does water flow faster in narrow channels or wide ones? How does a change in elevation affect water flow? How do different types of obstacles influence the water course?
3. Begin a glossary or special vocabulary list associated with rivers and white-water boating.

PROJECT Connections

Lesson 12.2, page 580: Find out how to model backwaters and eddies.
Lesson 12.4, page 589: Find out how to model souse holes.
Lesson 12.5, page 594: Determine the gradient of the river model and explore how gradient affects velocity.
Chapter Assessment, page 609: Demonstrate, evaluate, and compare each group's white-water river model.

12.1 Algebra Workshop
Explore Patterns in Factoring

Think Back

Algeblocks can be used to model multiplication of polynomials. The mat at the right shows the multiplication of two binomials.

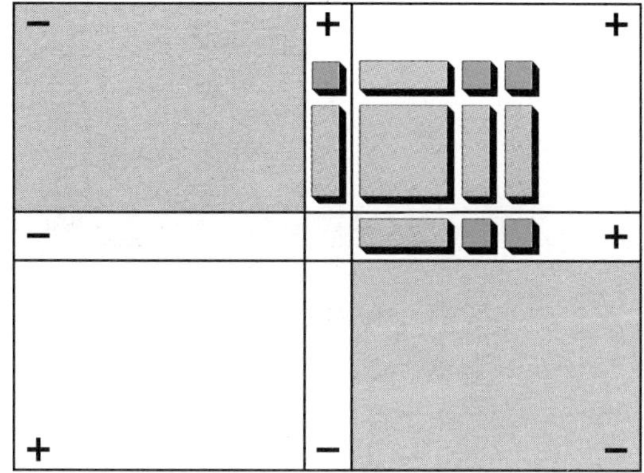

1. What two binomials are multiplied? $(x + 2)(x + 1)$
2. Describe how Algeblocks are used to form the product. See Additional Answers.
3. Read the product from the mat. $x^2 + 3x + 2$

Explore

Work with a partner and a set of Algeblocks.

4. Make a group of 8 unit blocks and another group of 12 unit blocks. For each group, form rectangles that have the length of one side in common. What is the greatest common length the two rectangles can have? 4
5. Model each of the monomials $2x^2$ and $4x$. See Additional Answers.
6. For each monomial in Question 5, form rectangles that have the length of one side in common. What is the greatest common length of the two rectangles? $2x$
7. Model the polynomial $2x^2 + 4x$ in one large rectangle in Quadrant I on a Quadrant Mat. Use the greatest common length that you found in Question 6 as the length of one side. Model that length on one axis. See Additional Answers.
8. Show the other length of the polynomial on the other axis. Read the dimensions from the mat. $2x$ and $(x + 2)$; see Additional Answers for model
9. Write $2x^2 + 4x$ as the product of a monomial and a binomial. $2x(x + 2)$
10. Explain why you think the product you wrote for Question 9 is called the factored form of $2x^2 + 4x$. See Additional Answers.

SPOTLIGHT ON LEARNING

WHAT? In this lesson you will learn
- to find the two binomial factors of a trinomial.
- to recognize special factoring patterns.

WHY? Algeblocks can help you to model patterns in factoring polynomials so you can solve problems in geometry, physics, and industry.

LESSON PLANNING

Objectives
- ▶ Find the two binomial factors of a trinomial.
- ▶ Recognize special factoring patterns.

Resources
Transparencies, 12, 21, 67
Student Handbook
Study Skills Activity 29
Multicultural Connection 12, African American: Focus on Construction

Materials/Manipulatives
Algeblocks
Quadrant Mats

ASSIGNMENTS

Basic: 1–47

Average: 1–47

Enriched: 1–48

1 MOTIVATE

Think Back After students have completed Questions 1–3, have them use Algeblocks to determine each product.

a. $(x + 2)(x - 1)$ $\mathbf{x^2 + x - 2}$

b. $(x - 2)(x + 1)$ $\mathbf{x^2 - x - 2}$

c. $(x - 2)(x - 1)$ $\mathbf{x^2 - 3x + 2}$

Ask students how the binomials are similar and how they are different. **The *x*-terms for each have a coefficient of 1 and the constant terms for each are 1 and 2; some constant terms are added and some are subtracted.** Ask how the products are similar and how they are different. **The first term of each product is x^2, the middle term is an *x*-term, and the third term is 2 or –2.**

2 FACILITATE

Explore Have students share their models for Question 7. Some students may have placed the x-blocks to the right of the x^2-blocks instead of above. Ask students if it makes any difference which way they modeled $2x^2 + 4x$. Why or why not? **no, because multiplication is commutative** For Question 13, tell students to use trial and error to form a rectangle. Have students share their answers. Some students may place the three x-blocks to the right of the x^2-block and the two x-blocks above it. Have students share their models for Questions 15–17. Some will have the factors reversed. For Question 26, some students may place the four x-blocks above the x^2-block in the first quadrant and one x-block and four unit blocks in the second quadrant. Ask students why there are always two ways to model the multiplication of two binomials. **because multiplication is commutative and so the factors can be reversed**

Make Connections After students have answered Question 45, ask how they determined whether both constants of the binomial factors should be positive or negative when the constant of the trinomial is positive. **When c is positive, both terms will be positive if b of $ax^2 + bx + c$ is positive and both will be negative if b is negative.** Ask them how they determined which constant of the binomial factors should be positive and which should be negative when the constant of the trinomial was negative. **Students will probably have used the FOIL method or the distributive method to check the product of the binomials.** Help students to see that for $(x + d)(x - e)$, if $d > e$ then b will be positive and if $d < e$ then b will be negative.

CHECK UNDERSTANDING

In Question 20, explain where to look on the mat when naming the terms of each binomial.

Use the blocks on the horizontal axis to name one factor and the blocks on the vertical axis to name the other factor.

Algebra Workshop

For each Algeblocks model, write the polynomial and its factored form.

11.

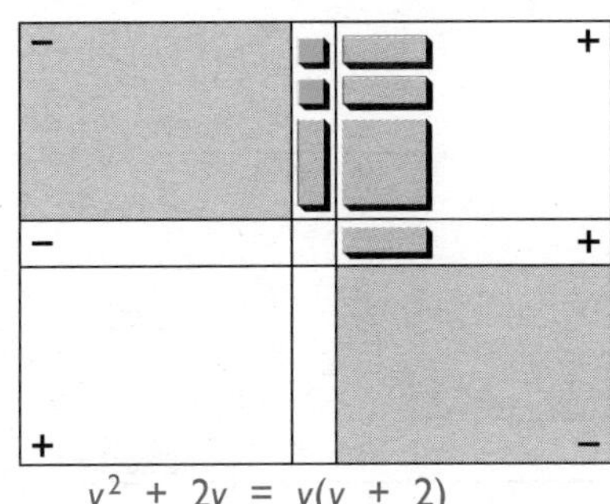

$y^2 + 2y = y(y + 2)$

12.

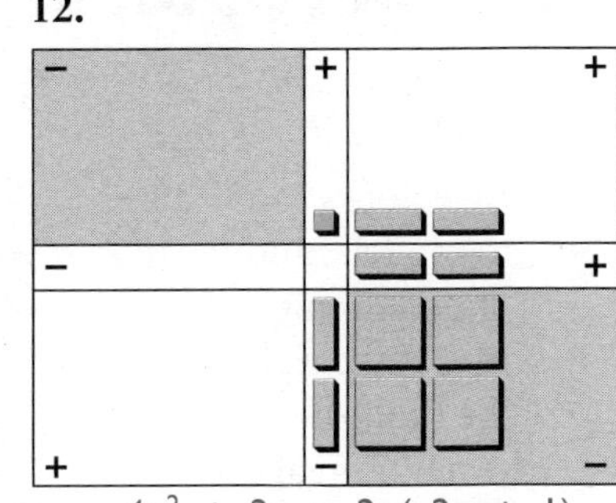

$-4x^2 + 2x = 2x(-2x + 1)$

The trinomial $x^2 + 5x + 6$ can be written as the product of two binomials. Use Algeblocks to find the two binomial factors.

13. Place Algeblocks for $x^2 + 5x + 6$ in Quadrant I on a Quadrant Mat. Arrange the blocks to form a rectangle. Draw a diagram of your work. See Additional Answers.

14. Place blocks along the horizontal and vertical axes of the rectangle you formed in Question 13. Read the two binomial factors of $x^2 + 5x + 6$. $(x + 2)$ and $(x + 3)$

Use Algeblocks to write the two binomial factors for each trinomial.

15. $x^2 + 4x + 3$ $(x + 3)$ and $(x + 1)$
16. $y^2 + 6y + 8$ $(y + 4)$ and $(y + 2)$
17. $y^2 + 9y + 8$ $(y + 1)$ and $(y + 8)$

18. What pattern do you notice for the terms of each trinomial in Questions 15–17? See Additional Answers.

19. Place Algeblocks for the trinomial $x^2 - 4x + 3$ on a Quadrant Mat. Arrange the blocks to form rectangles. (*Hint:* Use all four quadrants.) Place blocks for the dimensions of the rectangles on the horizontal and vertical axes. Draw a diagram to show your work. See Additional Answers.

20. Read the two binomial factors from the mat. $(x - 3)$ and $(x - 1)$

21. Compare your diagram for Question 19 with those of your classmates. Describe any differences you see. Did the differences affect the answer to Question 20? See Additional Answers.

Use Algeblocks to write the two binomial factors for each trinomial.

22. $x^2 - 2x + 1$ $(x - 1)$ and $(x - 1)$
23. $x^2 - 7x + 6$ $(x - 6)$ and $(x - 1)$
24. $y^2 - 3y + 2$ $(y - 2)$ and $(y - 1)$

25. What pattern do you notice for the terms of each trinomial in Questions 22–24? See Additional Answers.

26. Place Algeblocks for the trinomial $x^2 + 3x - 4$ on a Quadrant Mat. Arrange the blocks to form rectangles. (*Hint:* You may use zero pairs to complete the rectangles.) Place blocks for the dimensions of the rectangles on the horizontal and vertical axes. Draw a diagram to show your work. See Additional Answers.

27. Read the two binomial factors from the mat. $(x - 1)$ and $(x + 4)$

Use Algeblocks to write the two binomial factors for each trinomial.

28. $y^2 + y - 2$ $(y + 2)$ and $(y - 1)$
29. $x^2 + 2x - 3$ $(x + 3)$ and $(x - 1)$
30. $y^2 + 2y - 8$ $(y + 4)$ and $(y - 2)$
31. What pattern do you notice for the terms of each trinomial in Questions 28–30? See Additional Answers.

32. Place Algeblocks for the trinomial $x^2 - 3x - 4$ on a Quadrant Mat. Arrange the blocks to form rectangles. Place blocks for the dimensions of the rectangles on the horizontal and vertical axes. Draw a diagram to show your work. See Additional Answers.

33. Read the two binomial factors from the mat. $(x + 1)$ and $(x - 4)$

Use Algeblocks to write the two binomial factors for each trinomial.

34. $x^2 - x - 6$ $(x - 3)$ and $(x + 2)$
35. $y^2 - 4y - 5$ $(y - 5)$ and $(y + 1)$
36. $x^2 - 3x - 10$ $(x - 5)$ and $(x + 2)$
37. What pattern do you notice for the terms of each trinomial in Questions 34–36? Possible answers: the coefficient of the squared variable is 1; the first term is positive, and the middle and last (constant) terms are negative.

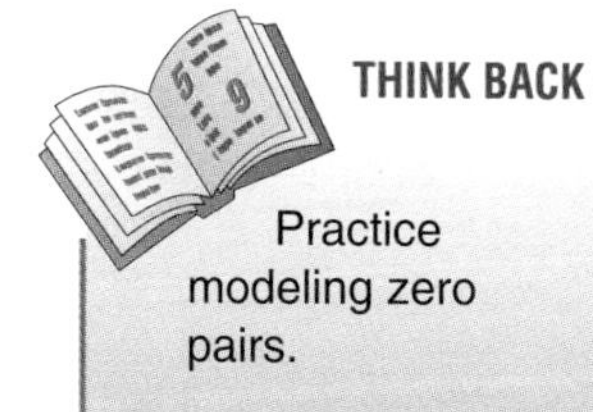

THINK BACK

Practice modeling zero pairs.

Manipulatives Have students use Algeblocks to model each of the four examples in Make Connections. Ask what Algeblocks patterns students notice for each of the four cases. **When all Algeblocks are in the first quadrant, *c* is positive and both factors are completely positive; when the Algeblocks are in all four quadrants, *c* is positive and both factors are differences; when the Algeblocks are in either the first and second or the first and fourth quadrants, *c* is negative and *b* is either negative or positive.**

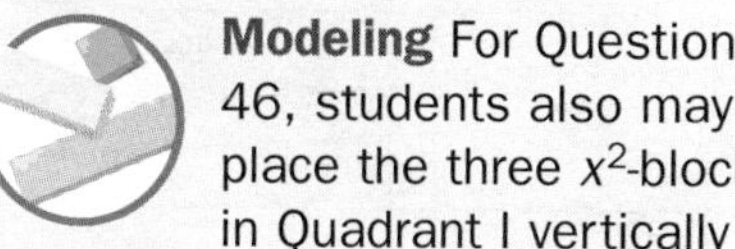

3 SUMMARIZE

Modeling For Question 46, students also may place the three x^2-blocks in Quadrant I vertically or horizontally and six x-blocks in Quadrant II or IV respectively to model the product $3x^2 - 6x$ as shown.

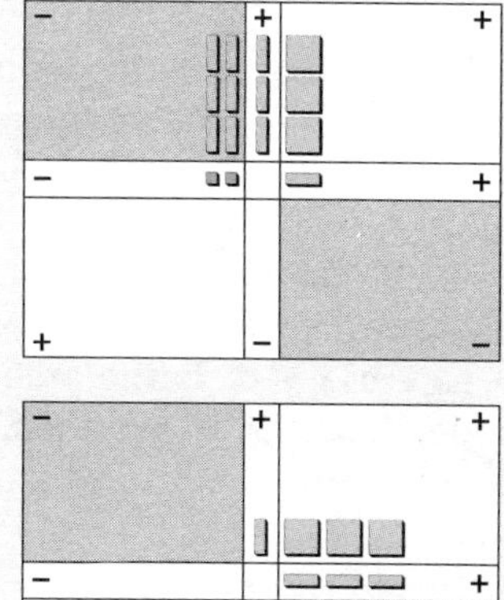

Writing Mathematics For Question 47, ask students how to determine the sign of each constant in the factors. **If the constant in the trinomial is positive, then the signs in each factor will both be positive or both be negative; if the constant in the trinomial is negative, then the**

sign in one factor will be positive and the sign in the other will be negative.

Going Further For Question 48, ask students to describe how Algeblocks can be used to model the product and factors of $2x^2 + 7x + 3$.

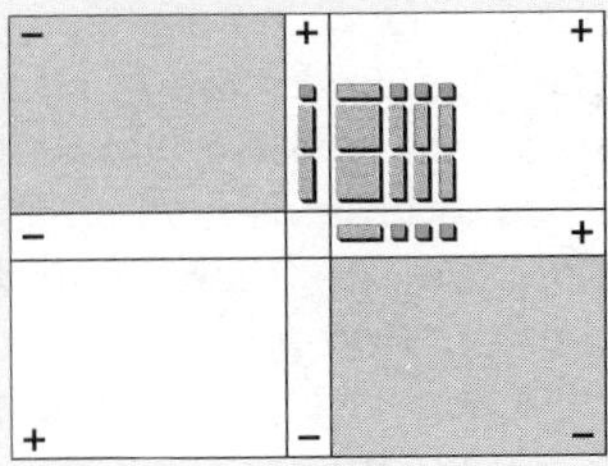

or

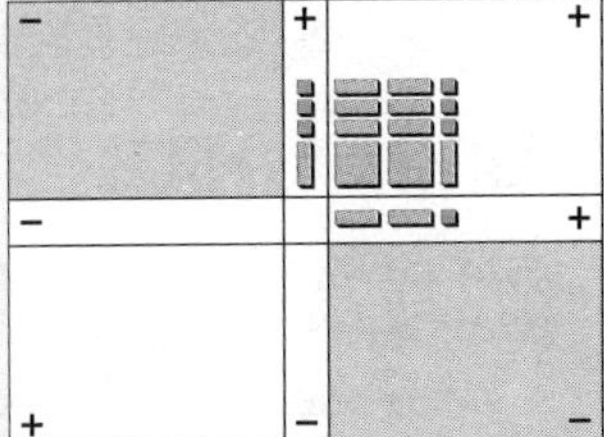

4 FOLLOW-UP

Other Explorations Have students devise a method for finding the factors of a trinomial $x^2 + bx + c$. Have them give the values for b if the factors of c are d and e. **The area model shows that $x^2 + ex + dx + de = x^2 + (e + d)x + de$ is the area of a rectangle. Thus, for $x^2 + bx + c$, $b = (e + d)$ and $c = de$.** Have students use an area model to find the two binomial factors of $x^2 + 7x + 12$. **$b = (e + d)$, $7 = (e + d)$ and $c = de$, $c = 12$; consider factors of 12: $1 \cdot 12$, $2 \cdot 6$, and $3 \cdot 4$; and the sums of the factors: $1 + 12 = 13$, $2 + 6 = 8$, and $3 + 4 = 7$.**

Algebra Workshop

Make Connections

There are four different patterns that you should be aware of when factoring a trinomial into two binomials. The table below shows the patterns and an example of each.

	Trinomial Pattern	Example	Binomial Factors
1.	$x^2 + bx + c$	$x^2 + 5x + 6$	$(x + 3)(x + 2)$
2.	$x^2 - bx + c$	$x^2 - 5x + 6$	$(x - 3)(x - 2)$
3.	$x^2 + bx - c$	$x^2 + x - 6$	$(x + 3)(x - 2)$
4.	$x^2 - bx - c$	$x^2 - x - 6$	$(x - 3)(x + 2)$

38. How are all four trinomials the same? See Additional Answers.

39. How are the trinomials for Patterns 1 and 2 similar? How are they different? See Additional Answers.

40. How are the trinomials for Patterns 3 and 4 similar? How are they different? See Additional Answers.

Match each trinomial with its binomial factors.

41. $x^2 - 3x - 28$ c	**a.** $(x + 7)(x + 4)$
42. $x^2 + 11x + 28$ a	**b.** $(x - 7)(x - 4)$
43. $x^2 + 3x - 28$ d	**c.** $(x - 7)(x + 4)$
44. $x^2 - 11x + 28$ b	**d.** $(x + 7)(x - 4)$

45. Describe how the patterns helped you to determine the binomial factors in Questions 41–44. See Additional Answers.

Summarize

46. **Modeling** Use Algeblocks to find the factored form of $3x^2 - 6x$. Sketch each step. See Additional Answers.

47. **Writing Mathematics** Write a paragraph describing how to find two binomial factors for a trinomial in which the coefficient of the x^2 term is 1. See Additional Answers.

48. **Going Further** Find the binomial factors of the trinomial $2x^2 + 7x + 3$. Use Algeblocks if you wish. $(2x + 1)(x + 3)$

12.2 Factor Polynomials

Explore

Jimmy wants to make two rectangular side-by-side enclosures for his pets. His rabbits need an area of 80 ft^2. The two puppies should have a 24-ft^2 area. Jimmy wants the enclosures to have one dimension in common so that one complete side of each pen shares the same fence.

1. List all the different ways that Jimmy can design rectangular enclosures that have a common dimension. Sketch the possible enclosures on graph paper to be sure your list is complete. See Additional Answers.
2. Find the total fencing needed for each design you listed. See Additional Answers.
3. Which design uses the least fencing? 8×3 and 8×10
4. What is the relationship between the possible common dimensions you found and the two given areas? They are common factors of the two areas.

SPOTLIGHT ON LEARNING

WHAT? In this lesson you will learn
- to factor polynomials whose terms have a common monomial factor.
- to factor a trinomial with a quadratic coefficient of 1.
- to factor a trinomial with an integral quadratic coefficient greater than 1.

WHY? Factoring polynomials can help you solve problems involving geometry, physics, and hydraulics.

Build Understanding

In Explore you saw several common dimensions or factors for two numbers. The terms of polynomials can also have common factors.

A polynomial is **factored**, or in **factored form**, when it is expressed as a product of other polynomials. Factoring is an important technique for many applications in advanced mathematics, science, and engineering. Factoring allows you to rewrite a complicated expression as the product of simpler expressions. To factor out a common monomial from the terms of a polynomial, you can use the distributive property in reverse.

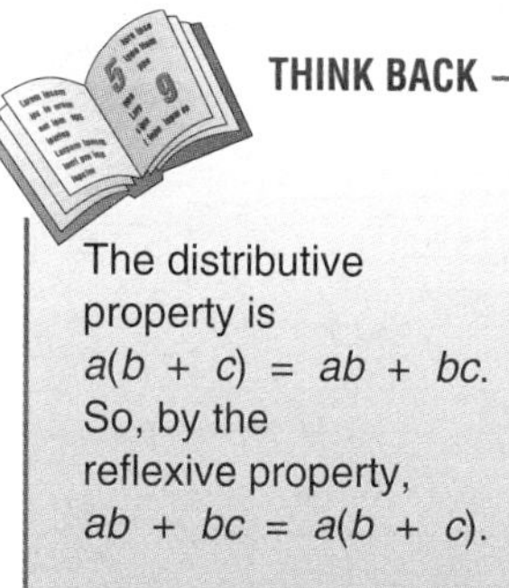

THINK BACK

The distributive property is $a(b + c) = ab + bc$. So, by the reflexive property, $ab + bc = a(b + c)$.

LESSON PLANNING

Objectives
- ▶ Factor polynomials whose terms have a common monomial factor.
- ▶ Factor trinomials with integral quadratic coefficients.

Vocabulary
factored
factored form
leading coefficient

Technology/Multimedia
graphing utility

Resources
Warm Up 12.2
Reteaching 12.2
Extra Practice 12.2
Enrichment 12.2
Transparencies 12, 21, 67
Student Handbook
Lesson Quiz 12.2
Study Skills Activity 30
Technology Activity 28

Materials/Manipulatives
Algeblocks
Graph paper
Quadrant Mats

ASSIGNMENTS

Basic: 1–12, 15–33, 36, 38, 40, 43, Project Connection 1–3, AlgebraWorks 1–4

Average: 3–13, 15–34, 36, 38–41, 43, Project Connection 1–3, AlgebraWorks 1–4

Enriched: 4–44, Project Connection 1–3, AlgebraWorks 1–4

1 MOTIVATE

Explore For Question 1, tell students that Jimmy is interested only in integer measurements for the dimensions.

2 TEACH

Use the Pages/Build Understanding Ask students to give examples of expressions using the distributive property. **possible example: $2x(x - 3) = 2x(x) - 2x(3)$** Ask students how they can find the GCF of 15 and 30. **List the factors of 15: 1 • 15, 3 • 5; list the factors of 30: 1 • 30, 2 • 15, 3 • 10, 5 • 6; 1, 3, 5, and 15 are common factors of each number, so 15 is the GCF.**

Example 1: Ask students why each term of $2x^3y + 6x^2 + 8xy$ is divided by $2x$. **to find the factor that gives each term when multiplied by $2x$** Explain that this is the distributive property in reverse. Have students check the factored form by multiplying them, which should yield the original trinomial.

Example 2: Make Connections Mathematics Ask students to find the product of 37 • 51 using a multiplication diagram.

	30	+7
50	1500	350
+1	30	7

1500 + 350 + 30 + 7 = 1887

Then ask students why 10 is written in the multiplication diagram in the example. **10 is the constant term in the trinomial and the product of the two constant terms of the two binomial factors.** Have students use Algeblocks to verify the answer. Ask how the Algeblocks Model compares with the multiplication diagram. **One dimension of each large rectangle is $x + 2$ and the other dimension is $x + 5$.**

ALGEBLOCKS MODEL

Factor the trinomial $x^2 + 7x + 10$. Place Algeblocks to model $x^2 + 7x + 10$ in Quadrant I. Arrange the blocks to form a rectangle.

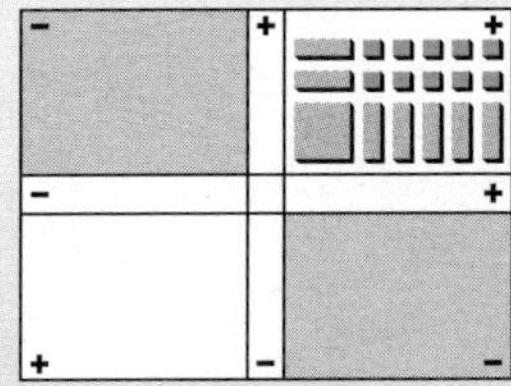

Place blocks along the horizontal and vertical axes to match the sides of the rectangle you formed.

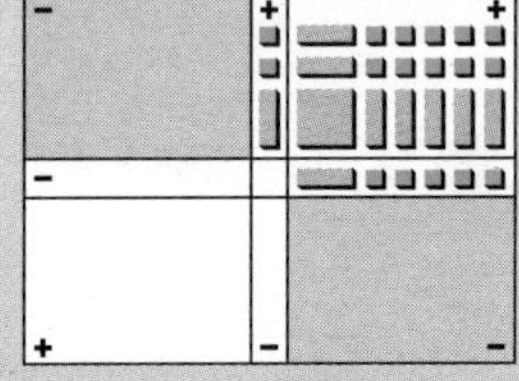

Read the two binomial factors of $x^2 + 7x + 10$ from the horizontal and vertical axes of the rectangle.

$(x + 5)(x + 2)$

When factoring out a monomial from a polynomial, list all the factors of each term of the polynomial to find the greatest common factor (GCF) of each term. The GCF allows you to factor a polynomial so that no common factors remain.

EXAMPLE 1

Factor $2x^3y + 6x^2 + 8xy$.

Solution

List all factors of each term.

$$2x^3y \quad + \quad 6x^2 \quad + \quad 8xy$$
$$2 \cdot x \cdot x \cdot x \cdot y \qquad 2 \cdot 3 \cdot x \cdot x \qquad 2 \cdot 2 \cdot 2 \cdot x \cdot y$$

Common factors of all three terms are 2 and x. So, the GCF is $2x$.

	x^2y +	$3x$ +	$4y$
$2x$	$2x^3y$	$6x^2$	$8xy$

Divide each term by the GCF, $2x$.

So, the factored form of $2x^3y + 6x^2 + 8xy$ is $2x(x^2y + 3x + 4y)$. ◄

Factoring a trinomial into two binomials is the reverse of multiplying two binomials whose product is a trinomial. Patterns you notice in multiplying two binomials will help you in factoring trinomials.

To factor a trinomial, you can use multiplication or you can use patterns of products of binomials, as in the next example.

EXAMPLE 2

Factor each trinomial.

a. $x^2 + 7x + 10$ **b.** $x^2 - 6x + 8$

Solution

a. *Multiplication diagram method* Use the multiplication diagram you used to multiply two polynomials. Fill in the products and terms you know for the product $x^2 + 7x + 10$.

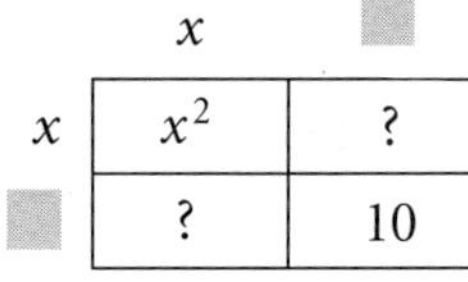

	x	■
x	x^2	?
■	?	10

The monomials that replace both ? must total $7x$, the x-term.

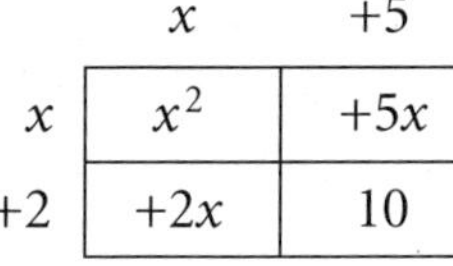

	x	$+5$
x	x^2	$+5x$
$+2$	$+2x$	10

Look for two factors having a sum of 7 and a product of 10. The factors 2 and 5 work.

The factored form of $x^2 + 7x + 10$ is $(x + 5)(x + 2)$.

Patterns of products method $x^2 + 7x + 10 = (x + \square)(x + \square)$

Factors of 10	Sum of the Factors
1, 10	11
−1, −10	−11
2, 5	7
−2, −5	−7

List all pairs of factors of 10. Then find the sum of each pair of factors. Look for the pair of factors whose sum is +7.

Since $2 + 5 = 7$, use 2 and 5 to complete the binomial factors.

So, $x^2 + 7x + 10$ factored is $(x + 2)(x + 5)$.

Multiply the factors to see that the product results in the original trinomial.

b. *Patterns of products method* $x^2 - 6x + 8 = (x + \square)(x + \square)$

Factors of 8	Sum of the Factors
1, 8	9
−1, −8	−9
2, 4	6
−2, −4	−6

Factors −2 and −4 have a sum of −6.

So, $x^2 - 6x + 8$ factored is $(x - 2)(x - 4)$.

Check by multiplying the factors. ◄

Example 3 shows that you can use the patterns of products method to factor a trinomial with a negative constant term. Also try using the multiplication diagram to see which method you prefer.

EXAMPLE 3

Factor each trinomial.

a. $x^2 - 4x - 5$ **b.** $x^2 + 2x - 15$

Solution

a. $x^2 - 4x - 5 = (x + \square)(x + \square)$

Factors of −5	Sum of the Factors
1, −5	−4
−1, 5	4

Factors 1 and −5 have a sum of −4.

So, $x^2 - 4x - 5$ factored is $(x + 1)(x - 5)$.

b. $x^2 + 2x - 15 = (x + \square)(x + \square)$

Factors of −15	Sum of the Factors
1, −15	−14
−1, 15	14
3, −5	−2
−3, 5	2

Factors −3 and 5 have a sum of 2.

So, $x^2 + 2x - 15$ factored is $(x - 3)(x + 5)$. ◄

CHECK UNDERSTANDING

In Example 2b, why weren't the factors −1, 8 or −2, 4 considered as possibilities?

Their products are −8, not 8.

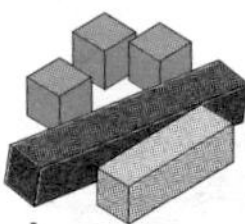

ALGEBLOCKS MODEL

Factor the trinomial $x^2 - 3x - 10$. Place Algeblocks to model $x^2 - 3x - 10$. Arrange the blocks to form rectangles. Use zero pairs to complete your rectangles if necessary.

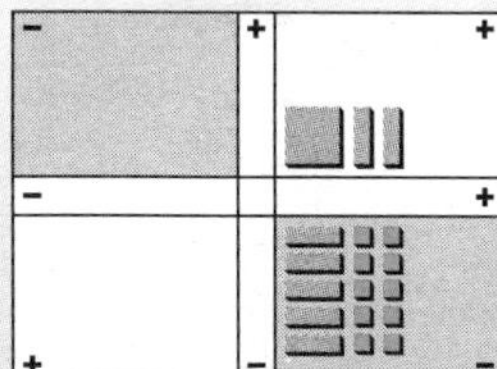

Place blocks along the horizontal and vertical axes to match the sides of the rectangle you formed.

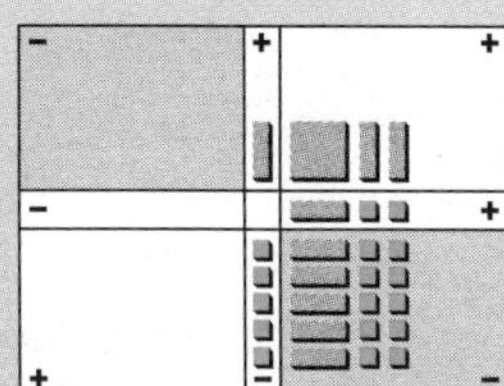

Read the two binomial factors of $x^2 - 3x - 10$ from the horizontal and vertical axes of the rectangle.

$(x - 5)(x + 2)$

Example 3: Have students use a multiplication diagram to find the binomial factors for both Example 3a and 3b.

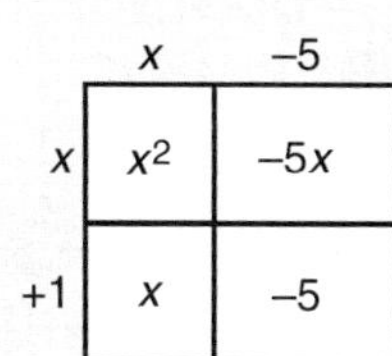

	x	-5
x	x^2	$-5x$
$+1$	x	-5

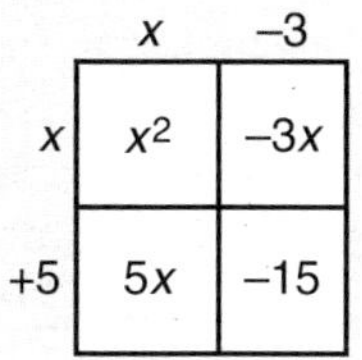

	x	-3
x	x^2	$-3x$
$+5$	$5x$	-15

Example 4: Ask what the possible combinations are for the pairs of factors 1 and 5 and −1 and −5. **The constant term of the first binomial can be 1, −1, 5, or −5 and that of the second binomial can be 5, −5, 1, or −1 respectively.**

Ongoing Assessment The important concepts and skills are factoring polynomials whose terms have a common monomial factor, factoring trinomials with a leading coefficient of 1, and factoring trinomials with a leading coefficient greater than 1. To assess these ideas, have students demonstrate how they have applied these concepts and skills in Exercises 2, 8, and 13 of the Try These section.

Guided Practice/Try These Have students share their answers for Exercise 4. For Exercises 5–12, remind students to write a list of the pairs of factors of the constant term and the sums of each pair of factors. Ask students how the trinomial in Exercise 13 differs from the trinomials in the previous exercises. **The leading coefficient is greater than 1.** Ask how they should find the factors of a trinomial with a leading coefficient greater than 1. **Determine the possible factors of the constant term, and then list all the possible factors and their products.**

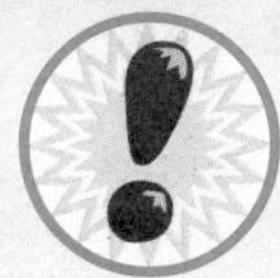

Error Alert Watch for students who forget to write 1 for the second term in the second factor for Exercise 1. When factoring $9x^2 + 3x$, these students will write $3x(3x)$ instead of the correct answer, $3x(3x + 1)$. Stress that the GCF is divided into each term and that $\frac{3x}{3x} = 1$.

3 SUMMARIZE

In the Math Journal Have students describe how to find the binomial factors of $3x^2 + 13x - 10$. **The first terms in each binomial factor must give the product of $3x^2$ when multiplied: $(3x + ?)(x + ?)$. Determine all the possible pairs of factors for the constant term of the trinomial: 1, −10; −1, 10; 2, −5; −2, 5. Then check the products of the possible combinations of binomial factors.**

4 PRACTICE

Practice For Exercises 1–14, stress that for each term in the second factor the GCF should be 1. For example, for Exercise 1, ask students if $2(a^4 + 4a)$ is completely factored and have them explain why or why not. **no, because the GCF of a^4 and $4a$ is a, not 1** For Exercises 15–35, remind students to list the possible pairs of factors of the constant term and then find the sum of the pairs to match the middle term of the trinomial.

So far you have seen how to factor trinomials whose **leading coefficient**, the coefficient of x^2, is 1. The following example shows how you can factor polynomials whose leading coefficient is greater than 1. Whether you use the multiplication diagram or the patterns of products method, you will need to guess and check to determine the factors.

PROBLEM SOLVING TIP

Guess and check is the process of listing all possible answers and then trying each answer one by one until the correct one is found.

EXAMPLE 4

GEOMETRY Find the dimensions of a rectangle in terms of x if the area of the rectangle is $2x^2 + 7x + 5$.

Solution

$$2x^2 + 7x + 5 = (2x + \square)(x + \square)$$

The factors of +5 are 1, 5 and −1, −5.

Check the product of every possible combination of binomial factors.

Trial Factors	Product	
$(2x + 1)(x + 5)$	$2x^2 + 11x + 5$	
$(2x - 1)(x - 5)$	$2x^2 - 11x + 5$	
$(2x + 5)(x + 1)$	$2x^2 + 7x + 5$	This is the product you want.
$(2x - 5)(x - 1)$	$2x^2 - 7x + 5$	

The required dimensions of the rectangle are $(2x + 5)$ and $(x + 1)$. ◄

TRY THESE

Factor.

1. $9x^2 + 3x$ $3x(3x + 1)$
2. $15y^4z + 10y^2z^2 - 20yz$ $5yz(3y^3 + 2yz - 4)$
3. $2y^3 - 16y^2$ $2y^2(y - 8)$
4. **WRITING MATHEMATICS** Write a paragraph explaining how you would determine the binomial factors of $x^2 - 4x + 3$. See Additional Answers.

Factor each trinomial.

5. $x^2 + 5x + 6$ $(x + 3)(x + 2)$
6. $x^2 + 6x + 8$ $(x + 4)(x + 2)$
7. $x^2 - 4x + 3$ $(x - 3)(x - 1)$
8. $x^2 - 11x + 30$ $(x - 6)(x - 5)$
9. $x^2 - 2x - 8$ $(x - 4)(x + 2)$
10. $x^2 - x - 12$ $(x - 4)(x + 3)$
11. $x^2 + 3x - 28$ $(x + 7)(x - 4)$
12. $x^2 + 5x - 14$ $(x + 7)(x - 2)$
13. $2x^2 + 5x + 3$ $(2x + 3)(x + 1)$
14. **GEOMETRY** Determine the dimensions of the rectangle at the right. $x + 1$ and $x + 6$
15. **MODELING** Use Algeblocks to show that $x^2 - 3x + 2 = (x - 2)(x - 1)$. See Additional Answers.

$A = x^2 + 7x + 6$

PRACTICE

Factor.

1. $2a^4 + 8a$ $2a(a^3 + 4)$
2. $7b^3 + 21b$ $7b(b^2 + 3)$
3. $8ab^2 - 12a^2b^3$ $4ab^2(2 - 3ab)$
4. $10c^3d^2 - 15cd^3$ $5cd^2(2c^2 - 3d)$
5. $6c^2 - 9d^2$ $3(2c^2 - 3d^2)$
6. $15f - 20g^2$ $5(3f - 4g^2)$
7. $4x^3 - 2x^2 + 14x$ $2x(2x^2 - x + 7)$
8. $3y^4 + 9y^2 - 15$ $3(y^4 + 3y^2 - 5)$
9. $2z^3 + 3z^2 + 4z$ $z(2z^2 + 3z + 4)$
10. $9mn - 3m^2 + 4mn^2$ $m(9n - 3m + 4n^2)$
11. $8abc^2 - 4b^2c + 12a^2bc$ $4bc(2ac - b + 3a^2)$
12. $6x^2yz + 2xy^2z - 4xyz$ $2xyz(3x + y - 2)$
13. $12a^4b^3c^2 - 4a^3bc^2 + 8a^2c - 16ab$ $4a(3a^3b^3c^2 - a^2bc^2 + 2ac - 4b)$
14. $9x^3yz^2 - 6x^2yz^2 + 12xyz^2 - 21yz^2$ $3yz^2(3x^3 - 2x^2 + 4x - 7)$

Factor each trinomial.

15. $x^2 + 5x + 4$ $(x + 1)(x + 4)$
16. $y^2 + 5y + 6$ $(y + 3)(y + 2)$
17. $z^2 + 8z + 15$ $(z + 5)(z + 3)$
18. $y^2 - 4y + 4$ $(y - 2)(y - 2)$
19. $x^2 - 6x + 9$ $(x - 3)(x - 3)$
20. $x^2 - 10x + 9$ $(x - 9)(x - 1)$
21. $z^2 - 10z + 9$ $(z - 9)(z - 1)$
22. $z^2 - 11z + 28$ $(z - 4)(z - 7)$
23. $y^2 + 7y - 8$ $(y + 8)(y - 1)$
24. $x^2 + x - 6$ $(x + 3)(x - 2)$
25. $y^2 + 11y - 12$ $(y + 12)(y - 1)$
26. $a^2 + 6a - 7$ $(a + 7)(a - 1)$
27. $b^2 + 3b - 4$ $(b + 4)(b - 1)$
28. $x^2 - x - 12$ $(x - 4)(x + 3)$
29. $x^2 - 2x - 35$ $(x - 7)(x + 5)$
30. $n^2 - 4n - 12$ $(n - 6)(n + 2)$
31. $c^2 - 3c - 18$ $(c - 6)(c + 3)$
32. $z^2 - 6z - 7$ $(z - 7)(z + 1)$
33. $5x^2 + 12x + 7$ $(5x + 7)(x + 1)$
34. $2a^2 + 13a - 7$ $(2a - 1)(a + 7)$
35. $2b^2 + 5b - 3$ $(2b - 1)(b + 3)$
36. GEOMETRY Determine the area of the shaded region at the right. Express your answer in factored form. $r^2(9 - \pi)$
37. GEOMETRY Determine the dimensions, in terms of x, of a rectangle if its area is $3x^2 + 13x - 10$. $3x - 2$ and $x + 5$

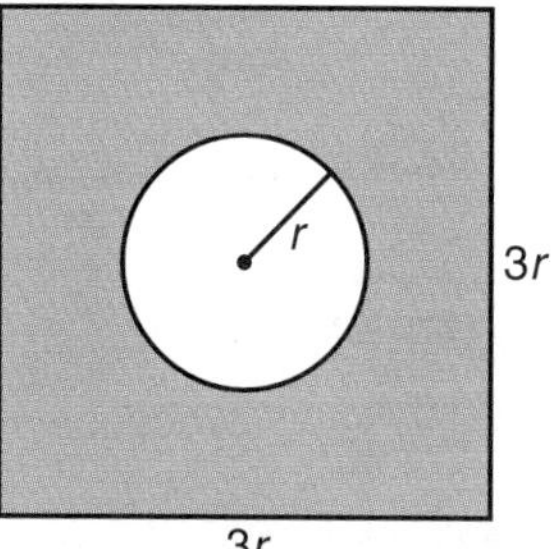

EXTEND

Find the missing factor.

38. $a^{n+4} + a^n = a^n(\quad)$ $a^4 + 1$
39. $6b^{2n} + 15b^{2n+2} = (\quad)(2 + 5b^2)$ $3b^{2n}$
40. GEOMETRY The area of a rectangle in square feet is $x^2 + 13x + 36$. How much longer is the length than the width of the rectangle? 5 ft
41. PHYSICS An expression that is used in connection with certain atomic particles is $Z\left(\frac{1}{2}\right) + N\left(-\frac{1}{2}\right)$, where Z is the number of protons and N is the number of neutrons in the nucleus. Factor this expression.
See Additional Answers.

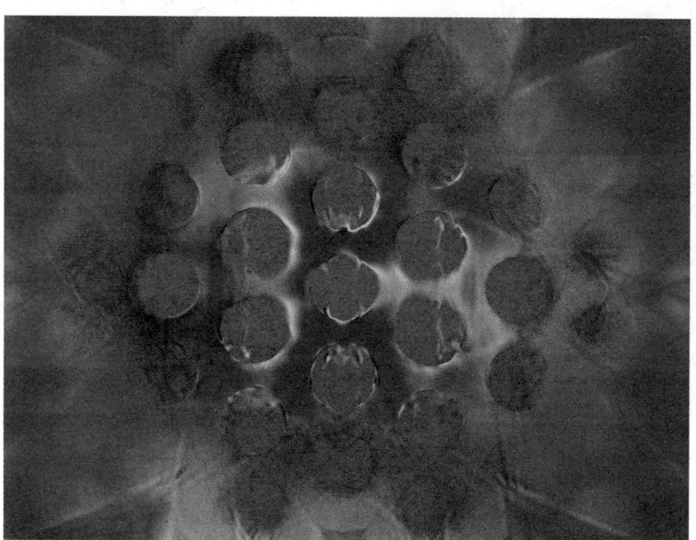

Extend For Exercise 38, ask students how they can rewrite a^{n+4} as a product of two factors. $\boldsymbol{a^{n+4} = a^n \cdot a^4}$ Ask a student to describe how he or she found the answer to Exercise 40. **Factor $x^2 + 13x + 36$ as $(x + 4)(x + 9)$. The width of the rectangle is $x + 4$ ft and the length is $x + 9$ ft, and $(x + 9) - (x + 4)$ is 5.**

Think Critically For Exercise 43, ask students how they can find the possible values of b that will make the trinomial factorable. **Consider the constant term 12 since *b* is the sum of the pair of factors of the constant term.** Have students list the possible pairs of factors of 12. **1, 12; –1, –12; 2, 6; –2, –6; 3, 4; –3, –4**

NAME ______ CLASS ______ DATE ______

RETEACHING

12.2 FACTOR POLYNOMIALS

Example Factor the trinomial $x^2 + 9x + 18$.

MULTIPLICATION DIAGRAM METHOD

Step 1: Fill in what you know.

	x	
x	x^2	?
	?	18

Step 2: Look for a factor pair of 18 that has a sum of 9.

	x	$+3$
x	x^2	$+3x$
$+6$	$+6x$	$+18$

The factored form is $(x + 3)(x + 6)$.

PATTERNS OF PRODUCTS METHOD

Step 1: List all the pairs of factors of 18. Find the sum of each pair.

Factors of 18	Sum
1, 18	19
–1, –18	–19
2, 9	11
–2, –9	–11
3, 6	9
–3, –6	–9

Step 2: Look for a sum of 9. Since $3 + 6 = 9$, use 3 and 6.
The factored form is $= (x + 3)(x + 6)$.

EXERCISES

Factor each trinomial. Use Algeblocks or one of the methods shown above.

1. $x^2 + 3x + 2$
2. $x^2 + 9x + 14$
3. $x^2 - 6x + 5$
4. $x^2 - 3x + 2$
5. $x^2 - x - 20$
6. $x^2 + 5x - 6$
7. $x^2 - 7x + 10$
8. $x^2 + 3x - 10$
9. $x^2 - 10x + 24$
10. $x^2 + x - 56$
11. $2x^2 - 7x - 15$
12. $3x^2 + 26x + 35$

Factor.

13. $5t - 20t^2$
14. $14cf^3 - 21cf^2 + 28c$
15. $x^3y^2z + x^4y^2 - x^2z^3 - x^3yz^3$
16. GEOMETRY Determine the dimensions, in terms of x, of a rectangle if its area is $3x^2 + 22x - 16$.

Answers:
1. $(x + 1)(x + 2)$
2. $(x + 7)(x + 2)$
3. $(x - 1)(x - 5)$
4. $(x - 2)(x - 1)$
5. $(x - 5)(x + 4)$
6. $(x + 6)(x - 1)$
7. $(x - 5)(x - 2)$
8. $(x - 2)(x + 5)$
9. $(x - 4)(x - 6)$
10. $(x + 8)(x - 7)$
11. $(2x + 3)(x - 5)$
12. $(3x + 5)(x + 7)$
13. $5t(1 - 4t)$
14. $7c(2f^3 - 3cf^2 + 4)$
15. $x^2(xy^2z + x^2y^2 - z^3 - xyz^3)$
16. $(x + 8)(3x - 2)$

5 FOLLOW-UP

Extension Have students explore using another method for finding binomial factors of a trinomial of the form $ax^2 + bx + c$. Ask them to follow the steps to factor $6x^2 + x - 2$.

- Find ac. $\mathbf{6(-2) = -12}$
- Write ac as a product of two factors whose sum is b. $\mathbf{2(-6) = -12}$ **and** $\mathbf{-3 + 4 = 1}$
- Use those factors to rewrite the trinomial.

$$\begin{aligned} &6x^2 + x - 2 \\ &= 6x^2 + 4x + (-3)x - 2 \end{aligned}$$

- Group the first two terms and the second two terms. Then use the reverse of the distributive property twice to factor each group.

$$\begin{aligned} &6x^2 + 4x + (-3)x - 2 \\ &= [6x^2 + 4x] + [(-3)x - 2] \\ &= 2x(3x + 2) - 1(3x + 2) \\ &= (2x - 1)(3x + 2) \end{aligned}$$

Have students try this method to factor $4x^2 + 5x - 6$. $\mathbf{(4x - 3)(x + 2)}$

NAME ____________ CLASS ________ DATE ________

EXTRA PRACTICE **12.2 FACTOR POLYNOMIALS**

Factor.

1. $8y + 2y^2$ **2.** $6c^4 + 18c$

3. $15a^2b^3 - 12ab^2 + 21a^2b^2$ **4.** $4n^3 - 18n + 14n^2$

5. $14r^2 + 7r - 28$ **6.** $24d^3 + 15g$

7. $24g^2h^3 + 32g^2 - 16gh^3 + 8g^3$

8. $12r^2st^3 - 9rs^3t^2 + 15rst^3 - 21s^2t^2$

Factor each trinomial.

9. $x^2 + 7x + 12$ **10.** $x^2 + 9x + 8$

11. $x^2 - 9x + 20$ **12.** $x^2 - 11x + 28$

13. $x^2 - 3x - 28$ **14.** $x^2 + 3x - 40$

15. $x^2 + 2x - 3$ **16.** $x^2 + 6x - 27$

17. $x^2 + 12x + 27$ **18.** $x^2 - 12x + 32$

19. $3x^2 + 22x + 7$ **20.** $2x^2 + 5x - 12$

21. $7x^2 + x - 8$ **22.** $5x^2 - 13x + 6$

23. GEOMETRY Determine the dimensions, in terms of x, of a rectangle if its area is $x^2 + 6x + 8$.

24. GEOMETRY Determine the area of the shaded region below. Express your answer in factored form.

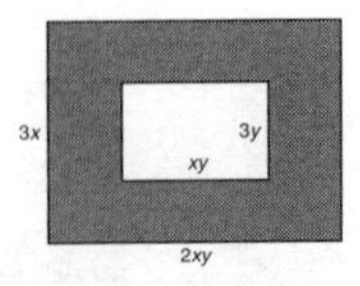

1. $2y(4 + y)$
2. $6c(c^3 + 3)$
3. $3ab^2(5ab - 4 + 7a)$
4. $2n(2n^2 - 9 + 7n)$
5. $7(2r^2 + r - 4)$
6. $3(8d^3 + 5g)$
7. $8g(3gh^3 + 4g - 2h^3 - g^2)$
8. $3st^2(4r^2t - 3rs^2 + 5rt - 7s)$
9. $(x + 3)(x + 4)$
10. $(x + 1)(x + 8)$
11. $(x - 5)(x - 4)$
12. $(x - 7)(x - 4)$
13. $(x - 7)(x + 4)$
14. $(x - 5)(x + 8)$
15. $(x + 3)(x - 1)$
16. $(x + 9)(x - 3)$
17. $(x + 3)(x + 9)$
18. $(x - 8)(x - 4)$
19. $(3x + 1)(x + 7)$
20. $(2x - 3)(x + 4)$
21. $(7x + 8)(x - 1)$
22. $(5x - 3)(x - 2)$
23. $x + 4, x + 2$
24. $3xy(2x - y)$

8 *South-Western Algebra 1: AN INTEGRATED APPROACH*

42. MACHINERY A hydraulic cylinder uses water power to turn a piston. The formula that applies to one type of hydraulic cylinder is

$$q = \frac{v\pi D^2 - v\pi d^2}{4}$$

where q is the flow rate in cubic inches per second, D is the diameter of the cylinder in inches, d is the diameter of the piston rod in inches, and v is the velocity of the piston in inches per second.

a. Rewrite the formula in factored form. See Additional Answers.

b. The velocity of the piston is 35 in./s, the diameter of the cylinder is 3 in., and the diameter of the rod is 0.75 in. Find the flow rate to the nearest whole number. 232 in.^{3}/s

THINK CRITICALLY

43. What are all the possible values of b that make $x^2 + bx + 12$ factorable? 7, –7, 13, –13, 8, –8

44. In the equation $x^2 + bx + 24 = (x + 3)(x + s)$, find all possible values of s and b. $s = 8, b = 11$

PROJECT Connection

Two features to include in your river model are *backwaters* and *eddies*. Both are the result of obstacles such as large rocks.

1. Look at the drawing of a backwater in Figure 1. In which direction is the main current A flowing? In which direction is the small current B behind the rock flowing? to the right; to the left

2. In Figure 1, the water at B is higher than the water at A. Because the water has a lot of speed as it goes from A to B, it continues to flow even as it moves upstream. The water behind the rock has only a little speed, so it flows as expected from high to low water. To construct a backwater, you need to give a portion of your model river a slight rise.

3. Eddies are similar to backwaters, but water flows along the boundary layer of the rock. Figure 2 shows the water flow. To construct an eddy, you need a rapid river flow.

Figure 1

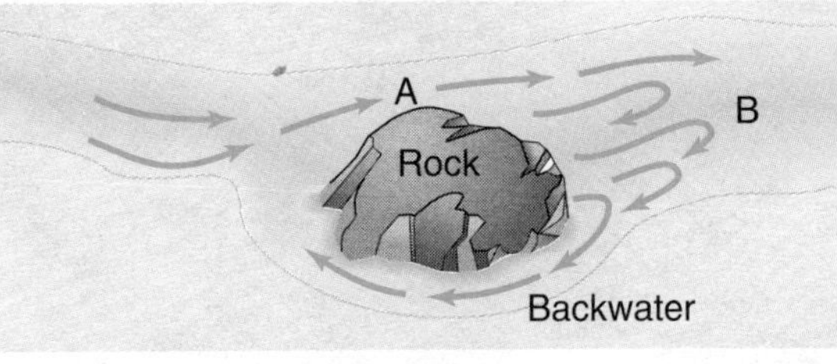

Figure 2

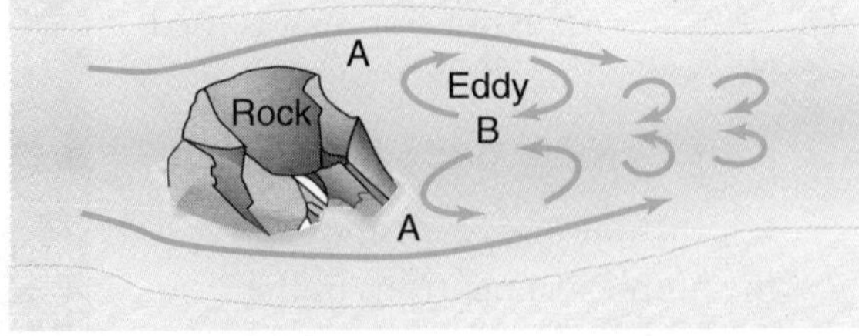

Career
Hydrologist

A hydrologist is a scientist who studies the distribution, circulation, and physical properties of underground and surface waters. Hydrologists are hired to observe and predict changes in many aspects of rivers, including the velocity of the river and its flow rate.

The Ohio River is the major eastern tributary of the Mississippi River. The word *Ohio* in Iroquois means "bright," "shining," or "great."

The table shows readings for the velocity and flow rate for four days on the Ohio River in Cincinnati.

Ohio River, Velocity and Flow Rate in Cincinnati				
Day	**1**	**2**	**3**	**4**
Velocity, mi/h	1.13	1.08	1.03	0.97
Flow rate, ft^3/s	52.8	50.0	46.7	43.7

A mathematical model of data is an equation that will provide a good estimate for one variable based on another variable. For the table, look at various models that relate x, the velocity of the river in miles per hour, to y, the flow rate in cubic feet per second.

A graphing utility can take the data points and give the following regression equations (coefficients rounded to the nearest tenth).

Linear regression equation: $y = 57.6x - 12.3$
Quadratic regression equation: $y = 35.8x^2 - 17.4x + 26.9$

Decision Making

Complete the tables. Round to the nearest hundredth.

1.

Linear Model				
x	**1.13**	**1.08**	**1.03**	**0.97**
$y = 57.6x - 12.3$				

52.79 49.91 47.03 43.57

2.

Quadratic Model				
x	**1.13**	**1.08**	**1.03**	**0.97**
$y = 35.8x^2 - 17.4x + 26.9$				

52.95 49.87 46.96 43.71

3. Which model do you think is best for the given data? Explain. See Additional Answers.
4. What information would the hydrologist look for if he or she wanted to improve the mathematical model for the river at this point? See Additional Answers.

Project Connection This activity presents further aspects of the project introduced on page 570. Have students study and discuss Figures 1 and 2. Be sure they understand the difference between the water flow in a backwater and in an eddy before they try to incorporate these features into their river model.

AlgebraWorks Ask students what a linear regression equation or a quadratic regression equation is. **An equation which gives the line or curve of best fit to the given data, that is, the x- and y-values.** Have students record the data into graphing utilities and verify the linear and quadratic regression equations. Have them discuss how they found the equations. **Answers will vary depending on the graphing utility used.**

NAME ______________ CLASS ________ DATE ________

12.2 FACTOR POLYNOMIALS

The trinomials you have factored so far have had a leading coefficient of either 1 or a prime number. When the leading coefficient is a composite number, more trials may be necessary before finding an answer.

Example
Factor: $6x^2 + 7x - 3$

Solution
The x-coefficients can be 6 and 1, –6 and –1, 2 and 3, or –2 and –3. The final term, –3, can be made with either –1 and 3 or 3 and –1. There are 16 possibilities. Start with one of the choices for the x-coefficients and one of the choices for the constant and solve.
$(6x - 1)(x + 3) = 6x^2 + 17x - 3$
The middle term needs to be smaller. Try another option.
$(6x + 3)(x - 1) = 6x^2 - 3x - 3$
Try another choice of factors for the x-coefficient.
$(2x - 3)(3x + 1) = 6x^2 - 7x - 3$
Try changing signs.
$(2x + 3)(3x - 1) = 6x^2 + 7x - 3$
These are the factors.

Use trial and error to factor each trinomial.

1. $4x^2 + 4x - 3$
2. $4x^2 + 7x + 3$
3. $14x^2 - x - 4$
4. $9x^2 - 18x + 8$
5. $6x^2 + 37x + 35$
6. $15x^2 - 34x + 15$
7. $6x^2 - 17x - 14$
8. $12x^2 + x - 63$
9. **Geometry** Determine the dimensions, in terms of x, of a rectangle if its area is $8x^2 + 18x + 9$.
10. **Geometry** Determine the perimeter, in terms of x, of a rectangle if its area is $12x^2 + 44x + 7$.
11. **Geometry** The area of a rectangle in square meters is $4x^2 + 12x + 5$. How much longer is the length than the width of the rectangle?

1. $(2x + 3)(2x - 1)$
2. $(4x + 3)(x + 1)$
3. $(2x + 1)(7x - 4)$
4. $(3x - 2)(3x - 4)$
5. $(6x + 7)(x + 5)$
6. $(3x - 5)(5x - 3)$
7. $(3x + 2)(2x - 7)$
8. $(4x - 9)(3x + 7)$
9. $4x + 3, 2x + 3$
10. $16x + 16$
11. 4 m

10 *South-Western Algebra 1: AN INTEGRATED APPROACH*

LESSON PLANNING

Objective

▶ Use patterns to factor the difference of two squares and perfect square trinomials.

Resources

Warm Up 12.3
Reteaching 12.3
Extra Practice 12.3
Enrichment 12.3
Transparencies 12, 21
Student Handbook
Lesson Quiz 12.3

Materials/Manipulatives

Algeblocks
Quadrant Mats

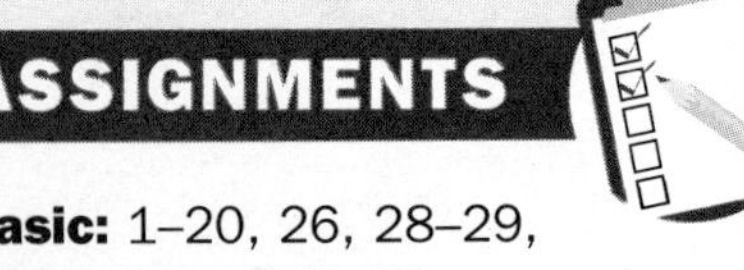

ASSIGNMENTS

Basic: 1–20, 26, 28–29, Mixed Review 33–39

Average: 3–24, 26, 28–31, Mixed Review 33–39

Enriched: 4–32, Mixed Review 33–39

1 MOTIVATE

Explore/Working Together After students have completed Questions 1–4, have them work with their partners to find other products of two even or two odd factors. Have students share their examples.

2 TEACH

Use the Pages/Build Understanding

Example 1: Ask students why an expression might not be factorable. **The terms of the expression may**

12.3 Factoring Special Products

SPOTLIGHT ON LEARNING

WHAT? In this lesson you will learn
- to use patterns to factor the difference of two squares.
- to use patterns to factor perfect square trinomials.

WHY? Factoring special products can help you solve problems involving geometry and computers.

Explore/Working Together

Work with a partner.

In ancient Iraq (about 2000 B.C.) the temple library had extensive tables of squares of whole numbers inscribed on clay tablets. It is thought that one way these tables were used was for multiplying two numbers. To find the product of two even numbers or two odd numbers, the Babylonians would compute the difference between the squares of two related numbers in the table. Then, they could multiply by subtracting! To find the product of 37 and 25, they would compute the difference between the square of 31 and the square of 6.

1. Show that $(37)(25) = 31^2 - 6^2$. $925 = 961 - 36$
2. Show that $(36)(28) = 32^2 - 4^2$. $1008 = 1024 - 16$
3. Explain how this method worked. (*Hint:* Find a relationship between each number that is squared and the original factors.) See Additional Answers.
4. Use this method to find the product $(51)(35)$. See Additional Answers.

Build Understanding

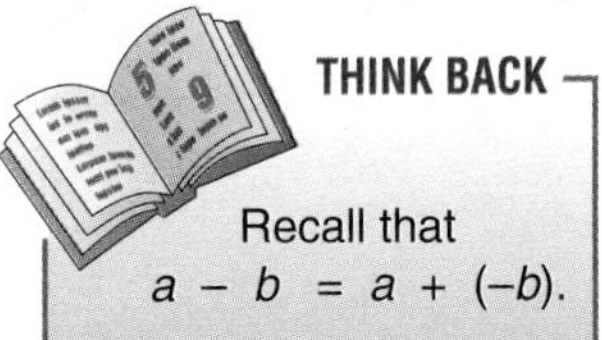

THINK BACK

Recall that $a - b = a + (-b)$.

Recall from Lesson 11.8 that the product of the sum and difference of the same two terms equals the difference between the squares of those terms.

$$(a + b)(a - b) = a^2 - b^2$$

By reversing the pattern, you can factor the difference of two squares.

EXAMPLE 1

Factor each expression if factorable.

a. $x^2 - 36$ **b.** $16a^2 - 49b^2$ **c.** $9y - 100$ **d.** $h^2 + 25$

Solution

Determine whether the polynomial is the difference of two squares. If it is, write it as the product of a sum and a difference.

a. $x^2 - 36$ is the difference of two squares, x^2 and 6^2.

So, $x^2 - 36 = (x + 6)(x - 6)$.

b. $16a^2 - 49b^2$ is the difference of two squares, $(4a)^2$ and $(7b)^2$.

So, $16a^2 - 49b^2 = (4a + 7b)(4a - 7b)$.

c. $9y - 100$ is *not* the difference of two squares. The two terms have no common factors, so the polynomial cannot be factored.

d. $h^2 + 25$ is the sum, rather than the difference, of two squares. The two terms have no common factors, so the polynomial cannot be factored.

Recall from Lesson 11.8 that the square of a binomial has special patterns.

$$(a + b)^2 = a^2 + 2ab + b^2 \text{ and } (a - b)^2 = a^2 - 2ab + b^2$$

Notice that the middle term in each trinomial is twice the product of the square roots of the first and last terms of the trinomial.

When you recognize either pattern in a trinomial, you can factor the trinomial into the square of a binomial.

EXAMPLE 2

Factor each polynomial.

a. $x^2 + 16x + 64$ **b.** $9y^2 - 30yz + 25z^2$

Solution

Test to see that the expression is a perfect square trinomial. First determine if the first and last terms are perfect squares. Then determine if the middle term is twice the product of the *square roots* of the first and last terms. Observe the sign of the middle term.

a. $x^2 + 16x + 64$

The first and last terms, x^2 and 64, are perfect squares.

The square root of the first term is x. The square root of the last term is 8. Twice the product of 8 and x is $16x$.

Therefore, $x^2 + 16x + 64$ is a perfect square trinomial.

Since the middle term of the trinomial is positive, the trinomial has the pattern $a^2 + 2ab + b^2 = (a + b)^2$.

So, $x^2 + 16x + 64 = (x + 8)^2$.

b. $9y^2 - 30yz + 25z^2$

The first and last terms, $9y^2$ and $25z^2$, are perfect squares.

The square root of the first term is $3y$. The square root of the last term is $5z$. Twice the product of $3y$ and $5z$ is $30yz$.

Therefore, $9y^2 - 30yz + 25z^2$ is a perfect square trinomial.

The trinomial fits the pattern $a^2 - 2ab + b^2 = (a - b)^2$.

So, $9y^2 - 30yz + 25z^2 = (3y - 5z)^2$.

ALGEBLOCKS MODEL

Factor the difference of two squares, $x^2 - 4$.

Step 1: Form rectangles to represent the terms in the expression. Use zero pairs where necessary.

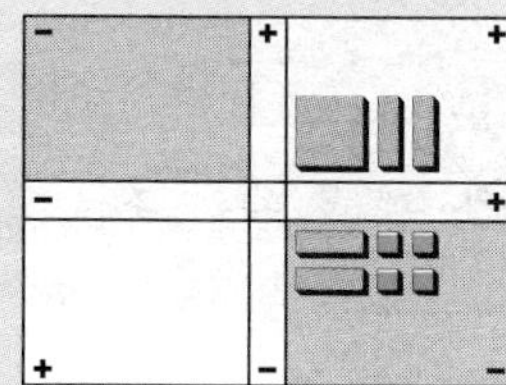

Step 2: Place Algeblocks in the axes to match the edges of the rectangles.

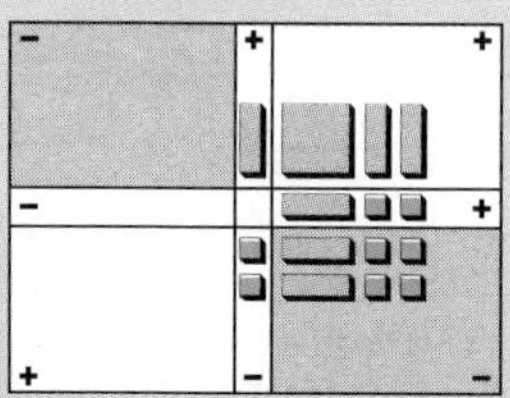

Read the factors from the mat.

$x^2 - 4 = (x + 2)(x - 2)$

CHECK UNDERSTANDING

Write a perfect square trinomial. Use Algeblocks to show that the model for your trinomial forms a square.

Answers will vary.

have no common factor other than 1 and it may not fit the patterns for factoring a trinomial or difference of squares.

Example 2: For part b, ask students how they know that $9y^2$ and $25z^2$ are perfect squares. Ask them what property of exponents they used. **$9y^2 = 3^2y^2 = (3y)^2$ and $25z^2 = 5^2z^2 = (5z)^2$; product of powers**

Example 3: Ask what the area of the large square is and what the area of the small square is. **x^2; $3^2 = 9$** Ask students what step they could include after $x^2 - 9$ to make it clear where the 3 comes from. **write $x^2 - 9$ as $x^2 - 3^2$**

Ongoing Assessment The important concepts and skills are using patterns to factor perfect square trinomials and the difference of two squares. To assess these ideas, have students demonstrate how they have applied these concepts and skills in Exercises 1 and 7 of the Try These section.

NAME ________ CLASS ________ DATE ________

RETEACHING

12.3 FACTORING SPECIAL PRODUCTS

DIFFERENCE OF TWO SQUARES

Factoring the difference of two squares follows the pattern

$$a^2 - b^2 = (a + b)(a - b)$$

To determine if a binomial is the difference of two squares, check the following:

1. Is the binomial a difference?
   This pattern doesn't work for a sum.
   $a^2 + b^2 \neq (a + b)(a - b)$
2. Are the two terms perfect squares?
   $36a^2 = 6a(6a)$ $46a^3 = 23a^2(2a)$
   $36a^2$ is a perfect square.
   $46a^3$ is not a perfect square.

SQUARE OF A BINOMIAL

Factoring the square of a binomial follows the pattern

$$a^2 + 2ab + b^2 = (a + b)^2$$
$$a^2 - 2ab + b^2 = (a - b)^2$$

To determine if a trinomial is the square of a binomial, check the following:

1. Are the two outside terms perfect squares? Find the square root of both terms.
2. Is the middle term exactly twice the product of the square roots of the outside terms?

If these two conditions hold, the trinomial is a square of a binomial. The binomial is $a - b$ if the middle term is negative. The binomial is $a + b$ if the middle term is positive.

EXERCISES

Are these binomials the difference of two squares? Write *yes* or *no*.

1. $x^2 - 49$ **2.** $c^2 + 25$

3. $5y^2 - 25$ **4.** $16g^2 - 36$

Are these trinomials the squares of binomials? Write *yes* or *no*.

5. $x^2 - 2x + 1$ **6.** $9z^2 + 42z + 49$

7. $m^2 + 4m + 4$ **8.** $4r^2 - 20r + 25$

Factor if possible.

9. $x^2 - 56$ **10.** $9g^2 - 25$

11. $2s^2 - 8s + 16$ **12.** $36h^2 - 120h + 100$

13. $25e^4 - 121$ **14.** $9x^2 - 12x + 4$

15. GEOMETRY Determine the dimensions, in terms of x, of a square if its area is $49x^2 + 42x + 9$.

1. yes
2. no
3. no
4. yes
5. yes
6. yes
7. yes
8. no
9. not factorable
10. $(3g - 5)(3g + 5)$
11. not factorable
12. $(6h - 10)^2$
13. $(5e^2 - 11)(5e^2 - 11)$
14. $(3x - 2)^2$
15. $(7x + 3)^2$

14 *South-Western Algebra 1: AN INTEGRATED APPROACH*

Guided Practice/Try These For Exercises 7–10, ask students to explain how they can determine whether a trinomial is a perfect square. **Check that the first and last terms are perfect squares, the middle term is twice the product of the square roots of the first and last terms, and signs follow the pattern.**

3 SUMMARIZE

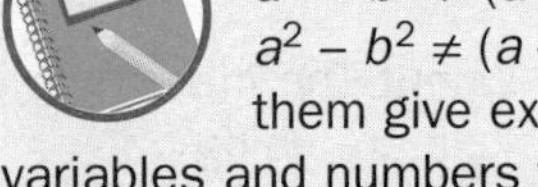

In the Math Journal Have students discuss why $a^2 + b^2 \neq (a + b)^2$ and why $a^2 - b^2 \neq (a - b)^2$. Have them give examples using variables and numbers to verify their statements. **Answers will vary but should include discussion of multiplying to show that in each case the two expressions are not equal. Possible numeric example: $3^2 + 4^2 = 9 + 16 = 25$, $(3 + 4)^2 = 7^2 = 49$, $25 \neq 49$**

NAME ______ CLASS ______ DATE ______

EXTRA PRACTICE **12.3 FACTORING SPECIAL PRODUCTS**

Factor if possible.

1. $x^2 + 8x + 16$ **2.** $n^2 - 6n + 9$

3. $c^2 - 10c - 25$ **4.** $d^2 - 14d + 49$

5. $4f^2 + 24f + 36$ **6.** $9f^2 + 21f + 49$

7. $64y^2 + 64y + 16$ **8.** $81b^2 - 90b + 25$

9. $x^2 - 36$ **10.** $g^2 - 144$

11. $x^2 + 25$ **12.** $4k^2 - 16$

13. $9j^2 - 1$ **14.** $49g - 24$

15. $121p^3 - 36$ **16.** $81e^4 - 64$

17. GEOMETRY Determine the perimeter, in terms of x, of a square if its area is $6x^4 + 24x^2 + 9$.

18. GEOMETRY Determine the area of the shaded region below. Express your answer in factored form.

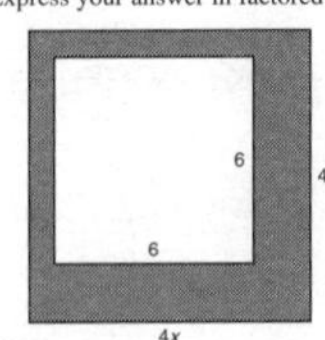

19. GEOMETRY In the figure shown for Exercise 18, suppose that the smaller square had sides of length y. What would be the area of the shaded region in factored form?

1. $(x + 4)^2$
2. $(n - 3)^2$
3. not factorable
4. $(d - 7)^2$
5. $(2f + 6)^2$
6. not factorable
7. $(8y + 4)^2$
8. $(9b - 5)^2$
9. $(x - 6)(x + 6)$
10. $(g - 12)(g + 12)$
11. not factorable
12. $(2k - 4)(2k + 4)$
13. $(3j - 1)(3j + 1)$
14. not factorable
15. not factorable
16. $(9e^2 - 8)(9e^2 + 8)$
17. $16x^2 + 12$
18. $(4x - 6)(4x + 6)$
19. $(4x - y)(4x + y)$

16 *South-Western Algebra 1: AN INTEGRATED APPROACH*

Some geometry problems can be solved by factoring.

EXAMPLE 3

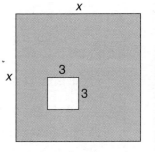

MODELING Find the dimensions in terms of x of a rectangle that has the same area as the shaded region at the right.

Solution

Write a polynomial for the area of the shaded region.

$$\text{area} = x^2 - 9$$

Factor $x^2 - 9$ as the difference of two squares.

$$x^2 - 9 = (x + 3)(x - 3)$$

Therefore, a rectangle with the same area as $x^2 - 9$ has dimensions $x + 3$ and $x - 3$.

TRY THESE

Factor if possible.

1. $a^2 - 16$ $(a + 4)(a - 4)$ **2.** $b^2 - 81$ $(b + 9)(b - 9)$ **3.** $c^4 + 49$ not factorable

4. $d^4 - 36$ $(d^2 + 6)(d^2 - 6)$ **5.** $9e^4 - 16f^2$ $(3e^2 + 4f)(3e^2 - 4f)$ **6.** $25g^2 - 21h^2$ not factorable

Determine if the trinomial is a perfect square. Factor if possible.

7. $a^2 - 10a + 25$ yes; $(a - 5)^2$ **8.** $b^2 + 14b + 49$ yes; $(b + 7)^2$ **9.** $c^4 - 4c^2 + 4$ yes; $(c^2 - 2)^2$ **10.** $9y^2 + 6y + 4$ no

11. MODELING For the Algeblocks diagram below, write the trinomial and its factors.

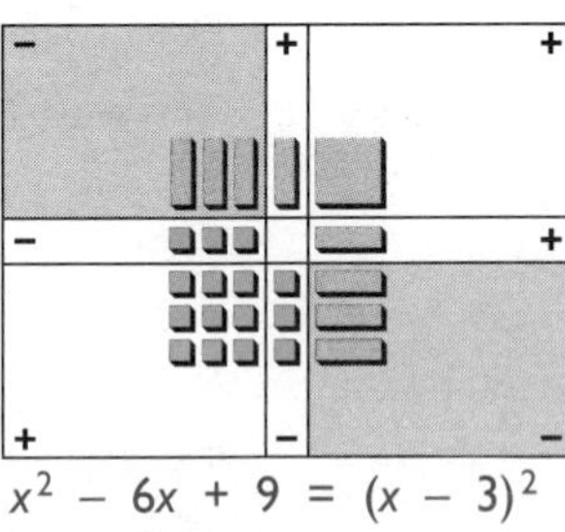

$x^2 - 6x + 9 = (x - 3)^2$

12. GEOMETRY Write the area of the shaded region as a polynomial. Factor if possible.

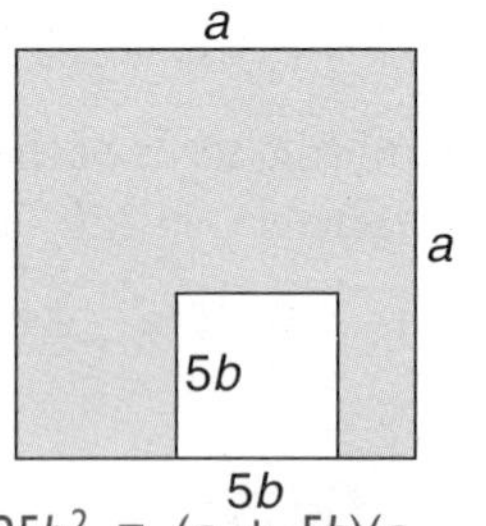

$a^2 - 25b^2 = (a + 5b)(a - 5b)$

13. WRITING MATHEMATICS Write a paragraph describing a perfect square trinomial. See Additional Answers.

PRACTICE

Factor if possible.

1. $a^2 - 16a + 64$ $(a - 8)^2$ **2.** $b^2 + 2b + 1$ $(b + 1)^2$ **3.** $c^2 + 6c + 9$ $(c + 3)^2$

4. $d^2 - 7d + 49$ not factorable **5.** $e^2 - 20e + 100$ $(e - 10)^2$ **6.** $f^4 + 10f^2 + 25$ $(f^2 + 5)^2$

7. $81h^2 + 36h + 4$ $(9h + 2)^2$ **8.** $25j^2 - 15j + 9$ not factorable **9.** $100p^2 + 60pq + 9q^2$ $(10p + 3q)^2$

10. $t^2 - 16$ $(t + 4)(t - 4)$

11. $v^2 - 121$ $(v + 11)(v - 11)$

12. $x^2 + 81$ not factorable

13. $y^2 - 1$ $(y + 1)(y - 1)$

14. $4z^2 - 49$ $(2z + 7)(2z - 7)$

15. $9a^2 - 12$ $3(3a^2 - 4)$

16. $25b^2 - 64$ $(5b + 8)(5b - 8)$

17. $36c^4 - d^2$ $(6c^2 + d)(6c^2 - d)$

18. $16p^2 - 21$ not factorable

19. **GEOMETRY** Find the dimensions of a rectangle that has the same area as the shaded region in the figure at the right. $2x + 5$ and $2x - 5$

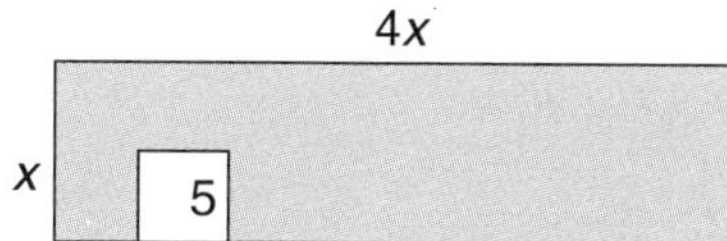

EXTEND

Factor if possible.

20. $g^6 + 12g^3 + 36$ $(g^3 + 6)^2$

21. $16r^4 - 8r^2s + s^2$ $(4r^2 - s)^2$

22. $9g^{10} - 100h^8$ $(3g^5 + 10h^4)(3g^5 - 10h^4)$

23. $400b^2 + 60b + 9$ not factorable

24. $900y^2 + 361$ not factorable

25. $121x^2 - 289$ $(11x + 17)(11x - 17)$

26. **GRAPHING** Recall from Lesson 10.2 that the graph of a function of the form $y = (x - a)^2$ is the same as the graph of $y = x^2$ moved a units to the right, as shown in the graph at the right. Describe the graph of $y = x^2 - 6x + 9$. See Additional Answers.

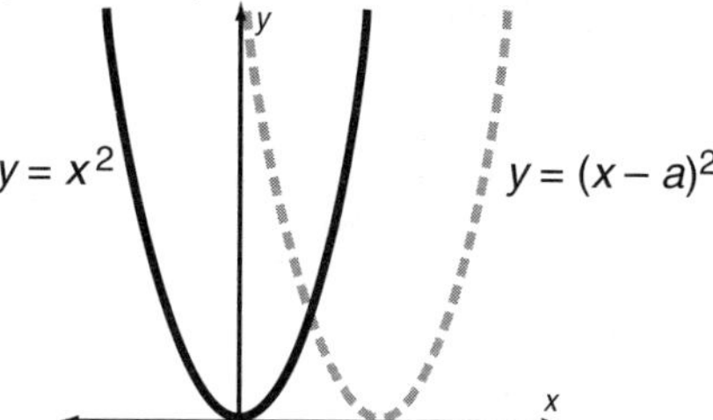

27. **COMPUTER SECURITY** Hard-to-crack codes are essential for computer security. Codes have been developed based on 200-digit numbers that are products of two prime numbers, which are difficult and time-consuming to determine. One time-saving approach is to find two numbers x and y such that $x^2 - y^2 = N$, the number to be factored.
   a. Determine two possible pairs of values of x and y for 24. 7 and 5 $(49 - 25 = 24)$; 5 and 1 $(25 - 1) = 24$
   b. Use these values of x and y to name two pairs of factors for 24. 12 and 2 $(7 + 5, 7 - 2)$; 6 and 4 $(5 + 1, 5 - 1)$

THINK CRITICALLY

Factor if possible.

28. $(x + y)^2 - z^2$ $(x + y + z)(x + y - z)$

29. $(a + b)^2 - (c + d)^2$ $(a + b + c + d)(a + b - c - d)$

30. $(p^2 - 2pq + q^2) - s^2$ $(p - q + s)(p - q - s)$

Find the value of N that makes the statement true.

31. $4x^2 - 3Ny^4 = (2x + 9y^2)(2x - 9y^2)$ 27

32. $16a^2 + 5Nb = (4a + 5b^3)(4a - 5b^3)$ $-5b^5$

MIXED REVIEW

Graph the solution. See Additional Answers. Lesson 5.5

33. $-3 < x \le 2$

34. $x < -1$ or $x > 2$

35. $0 \le x \le 3$

36. **STANDARDIZED TESTS** Which is the equation of the line through the points $(-2, 4)$ and $(3, -6)$? B; Lesson 6.4

A. $y = 2x$ B. $y = -2x$ C. $5y = 2x$ D. $5y = -2x$

Solve. Lesson 7.3

37. $\begin{cases} y = 2x \\ x + y = 24 \end{cases}$ $(8, 16)$

38. $\begin{cases} y = -x \\ 2x - 3y = 25 \end{cases}$ $(5, -5)$

39. $\begin{cases} y = 2x + 1 \\ 2x + 3y = 11 \end{cases}$ $(1, 3)$

4 PRACTICE

Practice Remind students to check answers by multiplying the factors to make sure the product is the original polynomial.

Extend For Exercise 20, ask students how g^6 could be rewritten as the square of a number or expression. $\mathbf{g^6 = (g^3)^2}$

Think Critically For Exercises 28–30, suggest that students use substitution to help factor.

5 FOLLOW-UP

Extra Practice Factor each.

1. $4x^4 + 4x$ $\mathbf{4x(x^3 + 1)}$
2. $25x^2 - 1$ $\mathbf{(5x - 1)(5x + 1)}$
3. $x^2 - 22x + 121$ $\mathbf{(x - 11)^2}$

NAME ______ CLASS ______ DATE ______

ENRICHMENT **12.3 FACTORING SPECIAL PRODUCTS**

Some polynomials may not at first appear to follow a factoring pattern. Suppose that you want to factor the trinomial $81x^4y^2 + 126x^2yz^3 + 49z^6$. This trinomial looks as if it could be the square of a binomial. It then would have the pattern $a^2 + 2ab + b^2 = (a + b)^2$. Compare the trinomial with the pattern.

$$81x^4y^2 + 126x^2yz^3 + 49z^6 = (? + ?)^2$$
$$a^2 + 2ab + b^2 = (a + b)^2$$

In order to fit the pattern, the following must be true: $a = 9x^2y$ and $b = 7z^3$.

The first term is $81x^4y^2$. Notice that each of the factors 81, x^4, and y^2 in this monomial is a square. So their product $81x^4y^2$ is a square: $81x^4y^2 = (9x^2y)^2$. This term fits the pattern.

The second term is $49x^6$. Each of the factors 49 and x is a square. So $49x^6 = (7z^3)^2$. This term also fits the pattern.

Finally, the middle term must fit the pattern $2ab$. Substitute for a and b:

$$2ab = 2(9x^2y)(7z^3) = 126x^2yz^3$$

Since this checks, replace a and b in the pattern for the square of a binomial with the terms above.

$$(a + b)^2 = (9x^2y + 7z^3)^2 = 81x^4y^2 + 126x^2yz^3 + 49z^6$$

Factor if possible.

1. $36x^{22} - 12x^{11}y^2z^4 + y^4z^8$ — 1. $(6x^{11} - y^2z^4)^2$
2. $k^6j^8 + 14k^3j^4m^5 + 49m^{10}$ — 2. $(k^3j^4 + 7m^5)^2$
3. $100n^6m^{14} - 20n^3p^{10}c^8 + p^{20}c^{16}$ — 3. $(10n^3 - p^{10}c^8)^2$
4. $v^8g^{24} + 8v^4g^{12}f^3r^{15} + 16f^6r^{30}$ — 4. $(v^4g^{12} + 4f^3r^{15})^2$
5. $16x^8y^4 + 32x^4y^4z^2 + 16y^4z^4$ — 5. $(4x^4y^2 + 4y^2z^2)^2$
6. $c^8d^{14} - 18c^9d^8 + 81c^{10}d^2$ — 6. $(c^4d^7 - 9c^5d)^2$
7. $f^{16}g^8h^6 - 6g^4h^3 + 9f^{32}$ — 7. not factorable
8. **GEOMETRY** Determine the perimeter, in terms of x, of a rectangle if its area is $121t^6x^8 - 64t^{12}x^{10}$. — 8. $44t^3x^4$
9. **GEOMETRY** The area of a rectangle in square meters is $216x^{30}y^{16} - 9x^{20}y^8$. How much greater is the length than the width? — 9. $6x^{10}y^4$

18 South-Western Algebra 1: AN INTEGRATED APPROACH

LESSON PLANNING

Objective

▶ Use the distributive property to factor polynomials by grouping.

Resources

Warm Up 12.4
Reteaching 12.4
Extra Practice 12.4
Enrichment 12.4
Student Handbook
Lesson Quiz 12.4

Materials/Manipulatives

Algeblocks
Quadrant Mats

ASSIGNMENTS

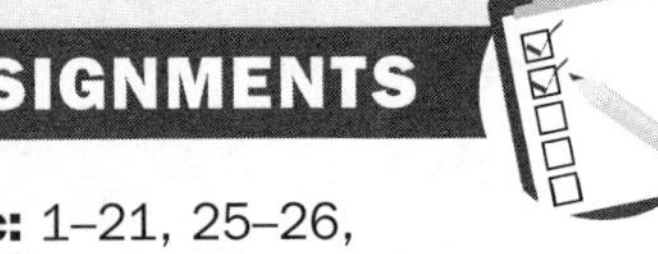

Basic: 1–21, 25–26, 28, Project Connection, AlgebraWorks 1–4

Average: 2–26, 28, Project Connection, AlgebraWorks 1–4

Enriched: 3–30, Project Connection, AlgebraWorks 1–4

1 MOTIVATE

Explore After students have completed Questions 1–4, ask them to find the dimensions of a rectangle with area $x^2 + 5x + 6$. **$(x + 2)(x + 3)$** Ask them to explain how they found the dimensions. **by factoring the expression representing the area** Ask them to explain how the expression for the area of this rectangle differs from that of the two expanded ones in the example. **It is a trinomial with one variable while the others are polynomials with four terms and two variables.**

12.4 Factor by Grouping

SPOTLIGHT ON LEARNING

WHAT? In this lesson you will learn

- to use the distributive property to factor polynomials by grouping.

WHY? Knowing how to factor polynomials by grouping can help you solve problems involving travel, geometry, installment loans, and history.

Explore

A rectangle with length x and width y will be expanded by 2 units in one dimension and 3 units in the other dimension.

1. Draw a diagram of the original rectangle and of the two possible expanded rectangles. See Additional Answers.
2. Compute the area of all three rectangles. xy, $xy + 2x + 3y + 6$, and $xy + 3x + 2y + 6$
3. Are the areas of the two expanded rectangles the same? Explain. no; $xy + 2x + 3y + 6 = xy + 3x + 2y + 6$ only if $x = y$
4. If $y > x$, which of the expanded areas is greater? Justify your answer. See Additional Answers.

Build Understanding

Recall from Lesson 12.2 that a polynomial can have a monomial as a factor of each of its terms. A polynomial can also have a binomial as a common factor. You can use the distributive property to factor out a common binomial just as you would use it to factor out a common monomial.

EXAMPLE 1

Factor each polynomial.

a. $y(a + b) + 3(a + b)$ **b.** $7(x^2 + 1) - y(x^2 + 1)$

Solution

a. The binomial $a + b$ is a common factor of both terms.

$$y(a + b) + 3(a + b) = (y + 3)(a + b)$$

b. The binomial $x^2 + 1$ is a common factor of both terms.

$$7(x^2 + 1) - y(x^2 + 1) = (7 - y)(x^2 + 1)$$

Look for common factors. Sometimes you will regroup terms.

EXAMPLE 2

Factor each polynomial.

a. $3ac + 6ab + 4c + 8b$ **b.** $4x^2 - 8y + 8xy - 4x$

Solution

a. The only common factor of the four terms in $3ac + 6ab + 4c + 8b$ is 1. Try to factor by grouping.

$$\begin{aligned} &3ac + 6ab + 4c + 8b \\ &= (3ac + 6ab) + (4c + 8b) && \text{Group the terms.} \\ &= 3a(c + 2b) + 4(c + 2b) && \text{Factor each group.} \\ &= (3a + 4)(c + 2b) && \text{Factor out the binomial.} \end{aligned}$$

So, $3ac + 6ab + 4c + 8b$ in factored form is $(3a + 4)(c + 2b)$.

Check by multiplying the binomials to see that the product is $3a + 6ab + 4c + b$.

b. Regroup the terms of the polynomial $4x^2 - 8y + 8xy - 4x$.

$$\begin{aligned} &4x^2 - 8y + 8xy - 4x \\ &= 4x^2 - 4x + 8xy - 8y && \text{Rearrange the polynomial.} \\ &= (4x^2 - 4x) + (8xy - 8y) && \text{Group the polynomial.} \\ &= 4x(x - 1) + 8y(x - 1) && \text{Factor each group.} \\ &= (4x + 8y)(x - 1) && \text{Factor out the binomial.} \\ &= 4(x + 2y)(x - 1) && \text{Factor out 4 from the first binomial.} \end{aligned}$$

In factored form $4x^2 - 8y + 8xy - 4x$ is $4(x + 2y)(x - 1)$. ◄

CHECK UNDERSTANDING

Describe how you can factor the two expressions in Examples 2a and 2b by starting with a different grouping of terms. Compare the results.

See Additional Answers.

It is helpful to recognize polynomials that are *additive inverses*, or *opposites*. Recall that multiplying x by -1 produces its opposite, $-x$. The opposite of a polynomial is one in which each term is the opposite of the corresponding term in the original polynomial. For example, the opposite of $x - y$ is $-1(x - y) = -x + y$. By the commutative property, $-x + y = y - x$. Therefore, $y - x$ is the opposite of $x - y$.

EXAMPLE 3

Factor: $y^2 - 7y + 21x - 3xy$

Solution

Group terms that have a common factor. Then factor each group.

$$y^2 - 7y + 21x - 3xy = y(y - 7) + 3x(7 - y)$$

Since $y - 7$ and $7 - y$ are opposites, you can replace $7 - y$ with $-1(y - 7)$.

$$\begin{aligned} y^2 - 7y + 21x - 3xy &= y(y - 7) + 3x(-1)(y - 7) \\ &= y(y - 7) - 3x(y - 7) \\ &= (y - 3x)(y - 7) \end{aligned}$$ ◄

PROBLEM SOLVING TIP

You can model factor-by-grouping problems using Algeblocks.

2 TEACH

Use the Pages/Build Understanding

Example 1: Tell students to let $x = a + b$ and rewrite the expression as $yx + 3x$. Have them factor the expression. $\mathbf{(y + 3)x}$ Then have them substitute $a + b$ for x. $\mathbf{(y + 3)(a + b)}$ Ask what substitution they could use in part b. **let $x^2 + 1 = a$**

Example 2: Tell students that they can also use a multiplication diagram to factor $4x^2 - 8y + 8xy - 4x$. Have them set up the model as shown, find the GCF for each column, and then write the terms of the missing factor.

	$4x$	$+8y$
x	$4x^2$	$8xy$
-1	$-4x$	$-8y$

$\mathbf{(4x + 8y)(x - 1)}$ Ask if the factors can be factored. **Yes, 4 is a common factor of $4x + 8y$.** Have them complete the factoring and compare their answer to the one in the example. **They are the same.**

Example 3: Ask students to explain why $y - 7$ and $7 - y$ are opposites. **The opposite of $y - 7$ is $(-1)(y - 7) = -y + 7 = 7 - y$.** Ask students to factor $y^2 - 7y + 21x - 3xy$ with a different grouping of terms. $\mathbf{(y^2 - 3xy) + (21x - 7y) = y(y - 3x) + 7(3x - y) = y(y - 3x) - 7(y - 3x) = (y - 7)(y - 3x)}$

Example 4: Explain that students can let $a = 2x + 3$. Have them write the expression in terms of a, factor, and then substitute $2x + 3$ for a. $\mathbf{a^2 - (5y)^2 = (a + 5y)(a - 5y) = (2x + 3 + 5y)(2x + 3 - 5y)}$

Ongoing Assessment The important concepts and skills involve factoring polynomials by grouping. To assess these ideas, have students demonstrate how they have applied these concepts and skills in Exercises 1, 4, and 8 of the Try These section.

Guided Practice/Try These Remind students to check their answers by multiplying the factors.

3 SUMMARIZE

In the Math Journal Have students discuss the possible groupings of $3x^2 - 3y + x - 9xy$ and whether or not it is factorable. **Students should realize that they may need to try several different groupings before finding a solution. Also they should realize that different groupings lead to the same factors. $3(x^2 - y) + x(1 - 9y)$ is not factorable; $3x(x - 3y) + x - 3y$ factors to $(x - 3y)(3x + 1)$.**

4 PRACTICE

Practice Remind students that they can substitute a single variable for a binomial.

NAME ______ CLASS ______ DATE ______

RETEACHING

12.4 FACTOR BY GROUPING

Example

Factor: $2xy + 3y - 2x - 3$

Solution

All four terms have no common factor other than 1, so you must factor by grouping together terms that have common factors. The first and third terms have $2x$ as a common factor. The second and fourth terms have a common factor of 3. Regroup these terms and then factor.

$$(2xy - 2x) + (3y - 3) = 2x(y - 1) + 3(y - 1)$$

Since each complex term has a factor of $y - 1$, $y - 1$ can be factored out.

The factored form is $(y - 1)(2x + 3)$.

EXERCISES

Factor.

1. $15(v - 7) - 8(v - 7)$ **$7(v - 7)$**
2. $3(d + r) + 7(d + r)$ **$10(d + r)$**
3. $p(f + 5) - x(f + 5)$ **$(p - x)(f + 5)$**
4. $5z + xt + zt + 5x$ **$(x + z)(t + 5)$**
5. $ns - 30 + 6n - 5s$ **$(n - 5)(s + 6)$**
6. $8 + cd - 4d - 2c$ **$(c - 4)(d - 2)$**
7. $2y^3 - 3y - 24 + 16y^2$ **$(y + 8)(2y^2 - 3)$**
8. $8b^2 - 10b - 5 + 4b$ **$(4b - 5)(2b + 1)$**
9. $p^2 + 8r + pr + 8p$ **$(8 + p)(p + r)$**
10. $w - v^2 - v + wv$ **$(w - v)(1 + v)$**
11. $pr + 2qs - qr - 2ps$ **$(p - q)(r - 2s)$**
12. $28x^2 - 8y^2 - 32xy + 7xy$ **$(4x + y)(7x - 8y)$**
13. GEOMETRY Find the dimensions of a rectangle with an area of $xy + 4 + 4x + y$. **$x + 1, y + 4$**
14. GEOMETRY Find the perimeter of a rectangle with an area of $3x + 2x^2 - 3 - 2x$. **$6x + 4$**

22 South-Western Algebra 1: AN INTEGRATED APPROACH

PROBLEM SOLVING TIP

In Example 4, you might have begun with the grouping $(4x^2 - 25y^2) + (12x + 9)$ and factored to get $(2x + 5y)(2x - 5y) + 3(4x + 3)$, which cannot be factored. You may need to try several approaches to factoring before you find one that works.

You may also group terms in special patterns to factor. You may have to factor twice, as in the following example, where you see the pattern of a perfect square trinomial as well as of a difference of two squares.

EXAMPLE 4

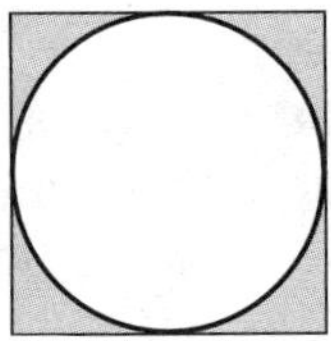

CERAMIC TILING The area of a square ceramic tile is $4x^2 + 12x + 9$ and the area of the circle is $25y^2$. Find the area of the shaded region in factored form.

Solution

The area of the shaded region = (area of square) − (area of circle). Notice that the area of the square, $4x^2 + 12x + 9$, is a perfect square trinomial and that the area of the circle, $25y^2$, is a perfect square.

$$A = 4x^2 + 12x + 9 - 25y^2$$

$$A = (2x + 3)^2 - (5y)^2 \quad \text{Factor the trinomial.}$$

$$A = (2x + 3 + 5y)(2x + 3 - 5y) \quad \text{Factor the difference of two squares.}$$

So, in factored form the area of the shaded region is $(2x + 3 + 5y)(2x + 3 - 5y)$.

TRY THESE

Factor.

1. $5(c + d) + 7(c + d)$ $12(c + d)$
2. $13(f^2 + 8) - 9(f^2 + 8)$ $4(f^2 + 8)$
3. $g(b + 3) - 4(b + 3)$ $(g - 4)(b + 3)$
4. $xz + 10x + yz + 10y$ $(x + y)(z + 10)$
5. $2h - 2k + gh - gk$ $(2 + g)(h - k)$
6. $x^2 - x + xy - y$ $(x + y)(x - 1)$
7. $y^4 - 2y^3 + 3y - 6$ $(y^3 + 3)(y - 2)$
8. $3a - 3b + ab - a^2$ $(3 - a)(a - b)$
9. $2wz - w + 3 - 6z$ $(w - 3)(2z - 1)$
10. GEOMETRY Find the dimensions of a rectangle with area $ab - 3a + 5b - 15$. $a + 5$ and $b - 3$
11. MODELING Use Algeblocks to find the factors of $xy - 2x + y - 2$. $(x + 1)(y - 2)$; see Additional Answers for Algeblocks model
12. WRITING MATHEMATICS Can $ax - bx - ay + by$ be factored? Write a paragraph explaining how you know. See Additional Answers.

PRACTICE

Factor.

1. $5(x + 1) + w(x + 1)$ $(5 + w)(x + 1)$
2. $z(y - 3) + 2(y - 3)$ $(z + 2)(y - 3)$
3. $xy + 5x + 2y + 10$ $(x + 2)(y + 5)$
4. $ab + 7a + 4b + 28$ $(a + 4)(b + 7)$
5. $xy + 2x - 7y - 14$ $(x - 7)(y + 2)$
6. $ab - 3a + 9b - 27$ $(a + 9)(b - 3)$
7. $ps - 2pt + qs - 2qt$ $(p + q)(s - 2t)$
8. $mw - mx - nw + nx$ $(m - n)(w - x)$
9. $12ab + 15a + 4b + 5$ $(3a + 1)(4b + 5)$
10. $2xy - 8x + 3y - 12$ $(2x + 3)(y - 4)$
11. $3wz + 12w - z - 4$ $(3w - 1)(z + 4)$
12. $cd - 8c - 3d + 24$ $(c - 3)(d - 8)$
13. GEOMETRY Find the dimensions of a rectangle if its area is $mn - 4m + 2n - 8$. $m + 2$ and $n - 4$

Factor.

14. $2fg + 4f - 7g - 14$ $(2f - 7)(g + 2)$
15. $yx - 2y + 8 - 4x$ $(y - 4)(x - 2)$
16. $gh - g + 3 - 3h$ $(g - 3)(h - 1)$
17. $pq - 7p + 35 - 5q$ $(p - 5)(q - 7)$
18. $st - 3s + 18 - 6t$ $(s - 6)(t - 3)$
19. $xy + 3x - 4y - 12$ $(x - 4)(y + 3)$
20. GEOMETRY Find the area of the shaded region shown at the right. The area of the square is $4x^2 + 4x + 1$ and the area of the circle is $36y^2$. Write the area in factored form. $(2x + 1 + 6y)(2x + 1 - 6y)$

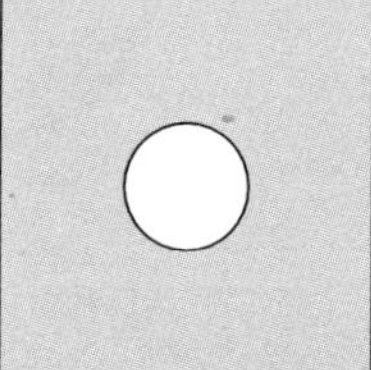

EXTEND

Factor by grouping.

21. $ax + bx + cx + 2a + 2b + 2c$ $(a + b + c)(x + 2)$
22. $xw + 2yw + 3zw - 4x - 8y - 12z$ $(x + 2y + 3z)(w - 4)$
23. $ap + aq - ar - bp - bq + br$ $(p + q - r)(a - b)$
24. $x^2 - cx - ax + ac - bx + bc$ $(x - a - b)(x - c)$
25. GEOMETRY Find the perimeter of a rectangle with an area of $xy - 5x + 4y - 20$. $2x + 2y - 2$

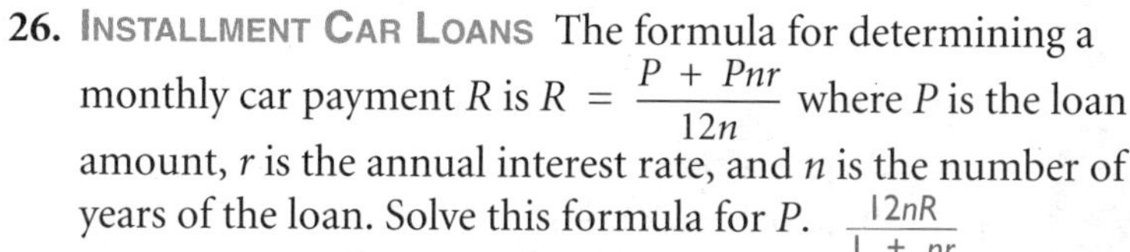

26. INSTALLMENT CAR LOANS The formula for determining a monthly car payment R is $R = \frac{P + Pnr}{12n}$ where P is the loan amount, r is the annual interest rate, and n is the number of years of the loan. Solve this formula for P. $\frac{12nR}{1 + nr}$

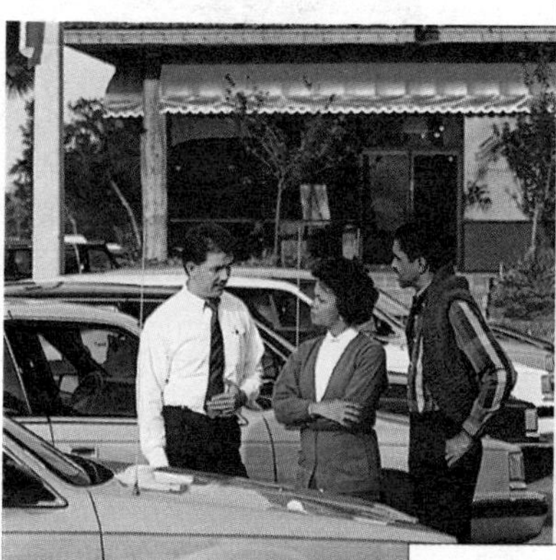

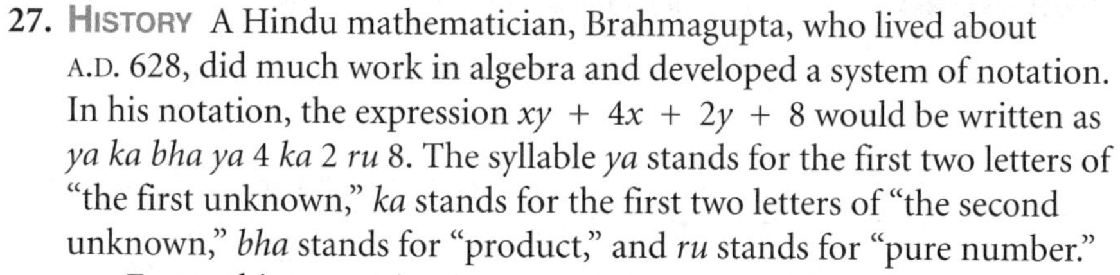

27. HISTORY A Hindu mathematician, Brahmagupta, who lived about A.D. 628, did much work in algebra and developed a system of notation. In his notation, the expression $xy + 4x + 2y + 8$ would be written as *ya ka bha ya* 4 *ka* 2 *ru* 8. The syllable *ya* stands for the first two letters of "the first unknown," *ka* stands for the first two letters of "the second unknown," *bha* stands for "product," and *ru* stands for "pure number."
   a. Factor this expression in our notation. $(x + 2)(y + 4)$
   b. How do you think Brahmagupta would write $3xy + 9y$? *ya ka 3 bha ka 9*

THINK CRITICALLY

Replace N with a number or monomial that will make the polynomial completely factorable. Then, factor the polynomial. See Additional Answers.

28. $2jk - 7j + N - 14$
29. $ab^2 + N + 3b^2 - 48$
30. $25q^2 + N + 16 - p^2$

PROJECT Connection

Another feature to include in your river model is a *hole* or *souse hole*. A hole occurs when there is a large drop behind a submerged obstruction.

As shown in the figure at the right, the fast water flowing over the obstacle collides with the slower, deeper water behind it and a wave, called a *roller*, forms. This wave can overflow into your boat or cause it to turn over. Create a hole in your model river using a submerged obstruction.

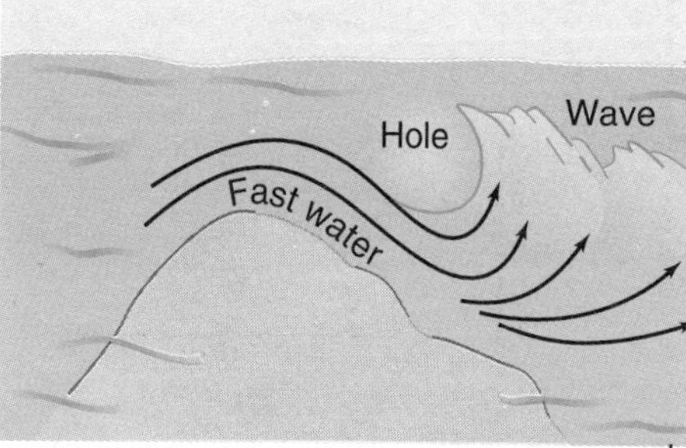

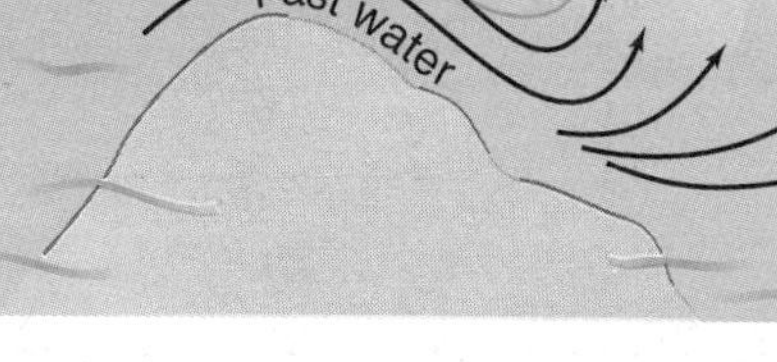

Error Alert For Exercise 11, watch for students who drop the last binomial term. These students will write $3w(z + 4)$. The correct answer is $(3w - 1)(z + 4)$.

Extend For Exercises 21–24, suggest that students try groupings of 3 terms.

Think Critically Ask students how they can determine a number or monomial for N. **Factor groups of two terms; then compare the binomials $(2k - 7)$ and $(N - 14)$ to find a value for N. $(N - 14) = (2)(2k - 7) = 4k - 14$, so $N = 4k$.**

NAME ______ CLASS ______ DATE ______

EXTRA PRACTICE **12.4 FACTOR BY GROUPING**

EXERCISES

Factor.

1. $6(y + 4) + 4(y + 4)$ **$10(y + 4)$**
2. $x(c + 15) - 7(c + 15)$ **$(x - 7)(c + 15)$**
3. $9(b + 7) - 12(b + 7)$ **$-3(b + 7)$**
4. $d(j + 3) + f(j + 3)$ **$(d + f)(j + 3)$**
5. $21 + ab + 7b + 3a$ **$(a + 7)(b + 3)$**
6. $kj - 60 + 10k - 6j$ **$(k - 6)(j + 10)$**
7. $15 - 3m + pm - 5p$ **$(5 - m)(3 - p)$**
8. $x^2 - 10y - 5x + 2xy$ **$(x + 2y)(x - 5)$**
9. $ac + bd - ad - bc$ **$(a - b)(c - d)$**
10. $w - v - v^2 + wv$ **$(w - v)(1 + v)$**
11. $3n^2 + 21np - 49p - 7n$ **$(3n - 7)(7p + n)$**
12. $2z^2 + 12x + 3z + 8xz$ **$(4x + z)(2z + 3)$**
13. $gh + 12h + 3h^2 - 4g$ **$(g + 3h)(h + 4)$**
14. $54 - 9r - 6s + rs$ **$(r - 6)(s - 9)$**
15. $3ts - 21 - 63s + t$ **$(t - 21)(3s + 1)$**
16. $56 - 32f - 21g + 12fg$ **$(4f - 7)(3g - 8)$**

17. GEOMETRY Determine the perimeter of a rectangle if its area is $cd + 5d - 5 - c$. **$2c + 2d + 8$**

18. GEOMETRY The area of a rectangle is $12x - 28y + 3xy$. A circle of area $7y^2$ is within the rectangle. Write an expression in factored form for the area of the rectangle outside the circle. **$(4 + y)(3x - 7y)$**

24 South-Western Algebra 1: AN INTEGRATED APPROACH

5 FOLLOW-UP

Extension Have students show the steps to factor $2a^2b + a^2 - 2b - 1$ into three factors. Suggest that they look for a difference of squares. $\mathbf{2a^2b + a^2 - 2b - 1 = (2a^2b + a^2) - (2b + 1) = a^2(2b + 1) - 1(2b + 1) = (a^2 - 1)(2b + 1) = (a + 1)(a - 1)(2b + 1)}$

Project Connection This activity presents further aspects of the project introduced on page 570. Be sure to have plenty of paper towels on hand for cleaning up.

AlgebraWorks For Question 1, ask students to describe how they can determine the percent increase of kilowatt capacity from 1952 until 1972. **Subtract to find the amount of increase; find what percent 157,500 is of 1,249,800: $157{,}500 = x/100 \cdot 1{,}249{,}800$, $x = 12.60201632$; the percent increase is about 12.6%.**

NAME ______________ CLASS ________ DATE ________

12.4 FACTOR BY GROUPING

Example
Factor $x^2 - 5x - 24$ by grouping.

Solution
When there seems to be no apparent way to break up a polynomial to factor by grouping, one of the terms may be rewritten. In this case, $-5x$ can be rewritten as a sum or difference to make this trinomial factorable by grouping.

Let's look at what you know:

- One of the terms must share a factor with x^2.
- One of the terms must share a factor with 24.
- The coefficients must have a product of 24.

$-5x = -8x + 3x$ This is the only option that works.

$x^2 - 8x + 3x - 24 = x(x - 8) + 3(x - 8) = (x + 3)(x - 8)$
Always check your answer by multiplying out the factors.

EXERCISES

Factor by grouping.

1. $t^2 + 3t - 18$ **$(t + 6)(t - 3)$**
2. $f^2 + 10f + 16$ **$(f + 8)(f + 2)$**
3. $g^2 - 7g + 12$ **$(g - 4)(g - 3)$**
4. $h^2 + 10h + 25$ **$(h + 5)^2$**
5. $m^2 - 9m + 8$ **$(m - 8)(m - 1)$**
6. $y^2 + yz + 2z^2$ **$(y - z)(y + 2z)$**
7. $2x^2 + x - 28$ **$(2x - 7)(x + 4)$**
8. $10n^2 + 8n - 24$ **$(5n - 6)(2n + 4)$**
9. $6a^2 + 17ab + 12b^2$ **$(2a + 3b)(3a + 4b)$**
10. $18k^2 + 15k - 3$ **$(6k - 1)(3k + 3)$**
11. GEOMETRY Determine the perimeter, in terms of x, of a rectangle if its area is $8x^2 + 30x + 13$. Factor by grouping and write the factors. **$(4x + 13)(2x + 1)$; $P = 12x + 28$**
12. GEOMETRY The area of a rectangle in square meters is $16x^2 + 54x - 7$. Find the dimensions and their difference. **$(8x - 1)(2x + 7)$; $6x - 8$**

26 *South-Western Algebra 1:* AN INTEGRATED APPROACH

Career
Civil Engineer

Civil engineers design and supervise the construction of roads, airports, tunnels, bridges, and dams. They often must solve problems, such as the one involving the Colorado River Basin in the early 1900s.

The Colorado River begins in Colorado and extends to California. The river used to flood low-lying areas in late spring and early summer. During other periods of the year, the river flow was so low that there was not enough water for irrigation or livestock. To alleviate this pattern of flood and drought, the Hoover Dam was built.

The dam, which is the highest concrete arch dam in the United States, is 726 feet high and contains 3.25 million cubic yards of concrete. It provides flood control; irrigation water; water for domestic, industrial, and municipal use; and low-cost electrical power for Arizona, Nevada, and southern California.

The energy generated by the dam is measured in kilowatt capacity. This table shows how the capacity has changed over the years.

Kilowatt Capacity—Hoover Dam

Year	1952	1961	1972	1989	1992
Kilowatts	1,249,800	1,344,800	1,407,300	1,920,000	2,217,000

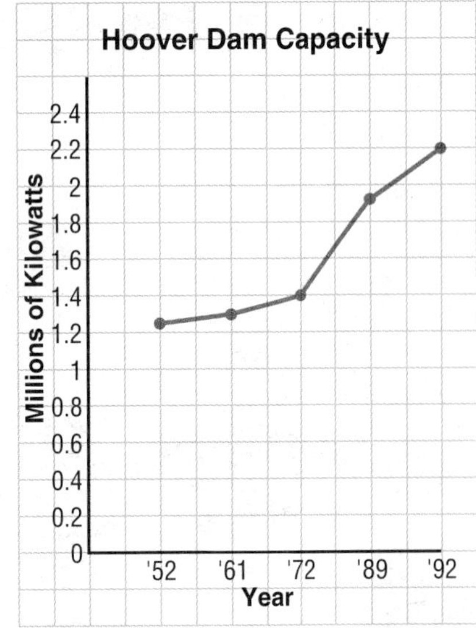

Decision Making

1. When the turbines were updated in 1972, what was the percent increase of kilowatt capacity from 1952? 12.6%
2. What is the total percent increase in kilowatt capacity from 1952 to 1992? 77.4%

Suppose the data in the table are graphed as shown at the left.

3. What does this graph seem to indicate about the future capacity of the dam? See Additional Answers.
4. Do you think this graph is a good representation for this data? Give reasons for your answer. See Additional Answers.

12.5 Factoring Completely

Explore/Working Together

Work in a small group. Each group should have a calculator.

1. Recall that the prime factorization of a number shows the number as a product of only prime numbers. For example, the prime factorization of 12 is $2 \cdot 2 \cdot 3$, or $2^2 \cdot 3$. Each group member should work independently with paper and pencil to find the prime factorization of 756.
   $756 = 2^2 \cdot 3^3 \cdot 7$
2. Compare your work with the work of other group members. Check with a calculator that each factorization is correct. Describe each person's method of factoring. See Additional Answers.
3. Which method appears to be the most efficient?
   See Additional Answers.

SPOTLIGHT ON LEARNING

WHAT? In this lesson you will learn
- to perform two or more types of factoring on the same polynomial.

WHY? Understanding how to factor polynomials completely can help you solve problems in geometry and metalwork.

Build Understanding

In this chapter, you have seen several ways of factoring polynomials.

Factor out a common monomial from a polynomial.

$$3x^3 - 12x^2 + 6x = 3x(x^2 - 4x + 2)$$

Factor a trinomial, including a perfect square binomial, as the product of two binomials.

$$x^2 + 4x + 3 = (x + 3)(x + 1)$$
$$4x^2 - 28x + 49 = (2x - 7)^2$$

Factor the difference of two squares as the product of two binomials.

$$16x^2 - 25 = (4x + 5)(4x - 5)$$

A polynomial is not considered "factored" until it is factored completely. A polynomial is **factored completely** only when it is expressed as the product of a monomial and one or more polynomial expressions that cannot be factored further. Some polynomials must be factored more than once before they are factored completely. You should check after each factoring step to see whether there are any expressions that can be factored further.

LESSON PLANNING

Objective
▶ Factor polynomials completely.

Vocabulary
factored completely

Technology/Multimedia
calculators

Resources
Warm Up 12.5
Reteaching 12.5
Extra Practice 12.5
Enrichment 12.5
Transparency 67
Student Handbook
Lesson Quiz 12.5

Materials/Manipulatives
calculators
stopwatches

ASSIGNMENTS

Basic: 1–20, 34, Mixed Review 36–39, Project Connection 1–3

Average: 4–30, 32–34, Mixed Review 36–39, Project Connection 1–3

Enriched: 7–35, Mixed Review 36–39, Project Connection 1–3

1 MOTIVATE

Explore/Working Together After students have completed Questions 1–3, ask them to find the prime factorization of 315. $3^2 \cdot 5 \cdot 7$

2 TEACH

Use the Pages/Build Understanding

Example 1: Ask students how they can tell that 2 is the GCF. **The terms left after factoring out 2 have no terms in common.**

Example 2: Have students check the answer by multiplying the factors to get the original polynomial.

Example 3: Tell students to check trinomials carefully to determine whether or not they can be factored.

Ongoing Assessment The important concepts and skills involve factoring polynomials completely. To assess these ideas, have students demonstrate how they have applied these concepts and skills in Exercises 1 and 3 of the Try These section.

Guided Practice/Try These Have students discuss their models for Exercise 9.

NAME ______________ CLASS ________ DATE ________

12.5 FACTORING COMPLETELY

Example

Factor: $6xy^2 - 6x + 12y^2 - 12$

Solution

Step 1: Look for a common factor. Each of the terms is divisible by 6. Factor out a 6. $6(xy^2 - x + 2y^2 - 2)$

Step 2: Factor by grouping.
$6[(xy^2 - x) + (2y^2 - 2)]$
$6[x(y^2 - 1) + 2(y^2 - 1)]$
$6(x + 2)(y^2 - 1)$

Step 3: Check to see if any factors can be factored further. Check for trinomials and the difference of two squares.

The factored form is $6(x + 2)(y + 1)(y - 1)$.

EXERCISES

Factor.

1. $3x^2 - 9x - 30$ **$3(x + 2)(x - 5)$**
2. $4y^2 + 28y + 24$ **$4(y + 6)(y + 1)$**
3. $6z^2 - 36z + 30$ **$6(z - 1)(z - 5)$**
4. $6cp^2 + 12cp - 288c$ **$6c(p - 6)(p + 8)$**
5. $5hj^2 - 45h$ **$5h(j - 3)(j + 3)$**
6. $7gm^2 + 28gm + 28g$ **$7g(m + 2)^2$**
7. $4nbc^2 - 4nb + 8nc^2 - 8n$ **$4n(b + 2)(c - 1)(c + 1)$**
8. $6k^2j^2 + 6kj - 12$ **$6(kj + 2)(kj - 1)$**
9. $14s^2t^4 - 224$ **$14(st - 4)(st + 4)$**
10. $6b^2c^2d + 12b^2c^2 - 54b^2d - 108b^2$ **$6b^2(c - 3)(c + 3)(d + 2)$**
11. $8mn^2 - 16n^2 + 48mn - 96n + 72m - 144$ **$8(m - 2)(n + 3)^2$**
12. $7pq^2 - 378 - 63p + 42q^2$ **$7(p + 6)(q - 3)(q + 3)$**
13. GEOMETRY Find the dimensions of a box if its volume is $a^2bc^2 + 8a^2bc + 12a^2b$. **$a^2b, c + 6, c + 2$**

30 *South-Western Algebra 1: AN INTEGRATED APPROACH*

COMMUNICATING ABOUT ALGEBRA

Review by making a list of all the types of factoring. Order them based on what to look for first when factoring completely.

Answers will vary.

EXAMPLE 1

Factor: $2x^2 - 14x + 24$

Solution

First, look for common monomial factors. Then try to factor the resulting polynomial.

$$\begin{aligned} &2x^2 - 14x + 24 \\ &= 2(x^2 - 7x + 12) && \text{Factor out 2, the GCF.} \\ &= 2(x - 3)(x - 4) && \text{Factor the trinomial.} \end{aligned}$$

Therefore, $2x^2 - 14x + 24 = 2(x - 4)(x - 3)$. ◄

Check by multiplying all the factors. Sometimes you need to factor more than twice.

EXAMPLE 2

Factor: $5x^2y + 20x^2 - 45y - 180$

Solution

$$\begin{aligned} &5x^2y + 20x^2 - 45y - 180 && \text{The GCF is 5.} \\ &= 5(x^2y + 4x^2 - 9y - 36) && \text{Factor out 5.} \\ &= 5[(x^2y + 4x^2) - (9y + 36)] && \text{Group.} \\ &= 5[(x^2(y + 4) - 9(y + 4)] && \text{Factor each group.} \\ &= 5(y + 4)(x^2 - 9) && \text{Factor out } y + 4. \\ &= 5(y + 4)(x + 3)(x - 3) && \text{Factor } x^2 - 9. \end{aligned}$$

Since no other terms can be factored,

$$5x^2y + 20x^2 - 45y - 180 = 5(y + 4)(x + 3)(x - 3)$$ ◄

Recall that the volume of a rectangular prism is the product of its length, width, and height.

EXAMPLE 3

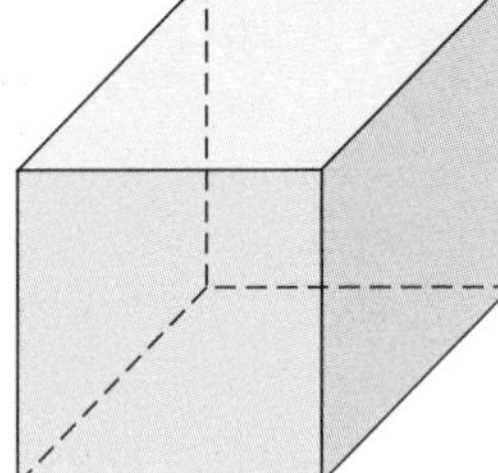

GEOMETRY The volume of a rectangular prism is $3ab^2 - 6ab - 45a$. Find the dimensions of the prism in terms of a and b.

Solution

$$\begin{aligned} &3ab^2 - 6ab - 45a \\ &= 3a(b^2 - 2b - 15) && \text{Factor out the GCF, } 3a. \\ &= 3a(b - 5)(b + 3) && \text{Factor the trinomial.} \end{aligned}$$

The three dimensions of the rectangular prism are $3a$, $b - 5$, and $b + 3$. ◄

TRY THESE

Factor.

1. $4x^2 + 8x - 32$ $4(x-2)(x+4)$
2. $3y^2 - 12y + 9$ $3(y-1)(y-3)$
3. $5x^2 - 20$ $5(x+2)(x-2)$
4. $7a^2 - 63$ $7(a+3)(a-3)$
5. $xy^2 - 16x + 2y^2 - 32$ $(x+2)(y+4)(y-4)$
6. $ab^2 - a + 9b^2 - 9$ $(a+9)(b+1)(b-1)$
7. GEOMETRY Find the dimensions of a box if its volume is $ab^2 + 13ab + 40a$. $a, b+5, b+8$
8. WRITING MATHEMATICS Write a paragraph describing how you know when a polynomial has been factored completely. See Additional Answers.
9. MODELING Use Algeblocks to build a three-dimensional model of a rectangular prism with a base equal to $x^2 + 2x + 1$ and a height of 3. How do the dimensions of the prism relate to the polynomial $3x^2 + 6x + 3$? See Additional Answers.

PRACTICE

Factor.

1. $2x^2 + 24x + 70$ $2(x+5)(x+7)$
2. $3y^2 + 21y + 36$ $3(y+4)(y+3)$
3. $5z^2 - 15z - 90$ $5(z-6)(z+3)$
4. $2a^2 - 4a - 160$ $2(a+8)(a-10)$
5. $4bc^2 + 12bc - 40b$ $4b(c-2)(c+5)$
6. $6gh^4 + 18gh^2 - 168g$ $6g(h^2+7)(h+2)(h-2)$
7. $3x^2 - 75$ $3(x+5)(x-5)$
8. $4m^2 - 144$ $4(m-6)(m+6)$
9. $4x^2 + 24x + 36$ $4(x+3)(x+3)$
10. $8y^2 - 160y + 800$ $8(y-10)(y-10)$
11. $5p^2q^2 - 500$ $5(pq+10)(pq-10)$
12. $3r^2s^4 - 147$ $3(rs^2+7)(rs^2-7)$
13. $2xy^2 - 32x$ $2x(y+4)(y-4)$
14. $3a^3b^4 - 192a^3$ $3a^3(b^2+8)(b^2-8)$
15. $2xy^2 - 2x + 4y^2 - 4$ $2(x+2)(y+1)(y-1)$
16. $5ab^2 - 20a + 30b^2 - 120$ $5(a+6)(b+2)(b-2)$
17. $4cd^2 - 4c - 12d^2 + 12$ $4(c-3)(d+1)(d-1)$
18. GEOMETRY Find the dimensions of a rectangular prism with the volume $3x^2 - 243$. $3, x+9, x-9$

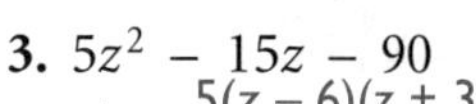

EXTEND

Factor.

19. $ab^2 + 8ab + 12a + 3b^2 + 24b + 36$ $(a+3)(b+6)(b+2)$
20. $xy^2 - 12xy + 36x + 4y^2 - 48y + 144$ $(x+4)(y-6)(y-6)$
21. $6pq^2 - 54p - 12q^2 + 108$ $6(p-2)(q+3)(q-3)$
22. $xy^2 + 7xy + 12x + 2y^2 + 14y + 24$ $(x+2)(y+3)(y+4)$
23. $ab^2 + 7ab + 10a + b^2 + 7b + 10$ $(a+1)(b+2)(b+5)$
24. $ac^2 + 5ac + 6a - bc^2 - 5bc - 6b$ $(a-b)(c+2)(c+3)$
25. $m^2n^2 + 9m^2n + 20m^2 - 4n^2 - 36n - 80$ $(m+2)(m-2)(n+5)(n+4)$
26. $a^4b^2 + 2a^4b + a^4 - 9b^2 - 18b - 9$ $(a^2+3)(a^2-3)(b+1)(b+1)$
27. METALWORK The formula for the volume of a hollow cylinder is $V = \pi R^2h - \pi r^2h$ where R is the radius of the cylinder, r is the radius of the hollow, and h is the height.
    a. Write the formula in factored form. $V = \pi h(R+r)(R-r)$
    b. The weight of aluminum is 168.5 lb/ft³. Find the weight, to the nearest tenth of a pound, of a hollow aluminum cylinder if $R = 3$ ft, $r = 2.5$ ft, and $h = 4$ ft. Use 3.14 for π. 5820.0 lb

3 SUMMARIZE

In the Math Journal Have students write a paragraph to describe what it means to factor a polynomial. **to express the polynomial as a product so that the GCF of each term in each factor is 1**

4 PRACTICE

Practice For Exercise 17, remind students to consider additive inverses when looking for common monomials or common binomials.

Extend For Exercises 28–31, have students multiply the factored part of the formulas to check that they give the original binomial.

Think Critically For Exercise 33, ask students how they can rewrite $16x^3 + 54y^3$ to use the formula. $\mathbf{2(8x^3 + 27y^3) = 2[(2x)^3 + (3y)^3]}$

NAME ________ CLASS ______ DATE ______

EXTRA PRACTICE **12.5 FACTORING COMPLETELY**

Factor.

1. $2x^2 + 20x + 48$ **$2(x+4)(x+6)$**
2. $4y^2 + 8y - 12$ **$4(y-1)(y+3)$**
3. $6g^2 - 12g - 378$ **$6(g+7)(g-9)$**
4. $2m^2k - 8k$ **$2k(m+2)(m-2)$**
5. $8s^2t + 48st + 72t$ **$8t(s+3)^2$**
6. $5c^4d - 15c^2d - 20d$ **$5d(c^2+1)(c-2)(c+2)$**
7. $10j^2 - 30j + 20$ **$10(j-2)(j-1)$**
8. $6b^2c^2 + 42bc - 264$ **$6(bc-4)(bc+11)$**
9. $7p^4q^2 + 56p^2q + 49$ **$7(p^2q+1)(p^2q+7)$**
10. $4xy^2 - 56xy + 196x$ **$4x(y-7)^2$**
11. $4m^3t^4 - 36m^3$ **$4m^3(t^2+3)(t^2-3)$**
12. $2ab^2 + 4ab + 2a + 8b^2 + 16b + 8$ **$2(a+4)(b+1)^2$**
13. $cd^2 - 2cd - 8c + 5d^2 - 10d - 40$ **$(d+2)(d-4)(c+5)$**
14. $4w^2y + 44wy + 112y - 32w^2 - 352w - 896$ **$4(w+4)(w+7)(y-8)$**
15. $8x^2y^5 - 128x^2y + 16x^2y^4 - 256x^2$ **$8x^2(y+2)(y^2+4)(y+2)(y-2)$**
16. GEOMETRY Find the dimensions of a box if its volume is $3xy^2 + 24xy + 45x$. **$3x, y+5, y+3$**
17. GEOMETRY Find the surface area of a box if its volume is $xy^2 - 9x + 2y^2 - 18$. (HINT: The surface area is the sum of the area of all six sides.) **$2y^2 + 4xy + 8y - 18$**

5 FOLLOW-UP

Extension Have students explore the factors for $x^2 + x + c$ where c is an integer. Have them write examples for different values of c. Ask students if the trinomial is factorable for all values of c and how many factors there are. Have them devise a formula to describe the factors. **Possible examples: $x^2 + x + 2$ is not factorable; $x^2 + x - 2 = (x + 2)(x - 1)$; it is not factorable for all values of c; there are infinitely many factors since there are infinitely many values of c. Some students may discover that the factors of c can be n and $1 - n$, where n is any real number, and that a formula for the factors is $x^2 + x + n - n^2 = (x + n)(x - n + 1)$.**

Project Connection This activity presents further aspects of the project introduced on page 570. Students may find it interesting to note that the steepness of a gradient of 50 feet per mile is about the same as a gradient of 0.11 inch per foot.

NAME ______________ CLASS ________ DATE ________

ENRICHMENT **12.5 FACTORING COMPLETELY**

Use what you have learned from previous enrichment pages to factor the following polynomials, most of which involve variables with coefficients greater than 1.

Factor.

1. $48bd^2 - 68bd - 20b$
   $4b(4d + 1)(3d - 5)$
2. $2a^2c^2 + 7abc^2 + 3b^2c^2 + 2a^2 + 7ab + 3b^2$
   $(2a + b)(a + 3b)(c^2 + 1)$
3. $12x^2y^2 - 2x^2y - 2x^2 + 36xy^2 - 6xy - 6x$
   $2x(x + 3)(2y - 1)(3y + 1)$
4. $36r^2s^2 - 81r^2 + 24rs^2 - 54r + 4s^2 - 9$
   $(3r + 1)^2(2s - 3)(2s + 3)$
5. $16a^3bc - ab^3c + 16a^3bd - ab^3d$
   $ab(c + d)(4a + b)(4a - b)$
6. $45mnp^4q - 45mnp^2 + 60mnp^3q - 60mnp + 20mnp^2q - 20mn$
   $5mn(3p + 2)^2(p^2q - 1)$
7. $8x^3z^3 - 24x^2yz^3 + 24xy^2z^3 - 8y^3z^3$
   (HINT: $(a - b)^3 = a^3 - 3a^2b + 3ab^2 - b^3$)
   $8z^3(x - y)^3$
8. $1024r^5s + 256r^4s - 64r^3s - 16r^2s$
   $16r^2s(4r + 1)^2(4r - 1)$
9. $81x^3z^2 + 81x^2yz^2 + 27xy^2z^2 + 3y^3z^2$
   (HINT: $(a + b)^3 = a^3 + 3a^2b + 3ab^2 + b^3$)
   $3z^2(3x + y)^3$
10. GEOMETRY The volume of a pyramid is found using the formula $V = \frac{1}{3}Bh$, where B = area of the base and h = height. If $h = 3$, write the dimensions of the base for a pyramid having a volume of $\frac{16}{3}xy + 36x + \frac{20}{3}xy - 2y - 6$.
   $2(6x - 1)(y + 3)$

34 *South-Western Algebra 1: AN INTEGRATED APPROACH*

The following formulas can be used to factor some third-degree polynomials.

$$x^3 - a^3 = (x - a)(x^2 + ax + a^2) \quad \text{and} \quad x^3 + a^3 = (x + a)(x^2 - ax + a^2)$$

Factor the given polynomial.

28. $x^3 + 2^3$ $(x + 2)(x^2 - 2x + 4)$
29. $x^3 - 1$ $(x - 1)(x^2 + x + 1)$
30. $x^3 + 64$ $(x + 4)(x^2 - 4x + 16)$
31. $y^6 - 2^6$ (*Hint:* Let $y^3 = u$ and $2^3 = v$.) $(y - 2)(y^2 + 2y + 4)(y + 2)(y^2 - 2y + 4)$

THINK CRITICALLY

32. Show that $a^3 + b^3 = (a + b)(a^2 - ab + b^2)$. See Additional Answers.
33. Use the pattern from Exercise 32 to factor $16x^3 + 54y^3$ completely.
    $2(2x + 3y)(4x^2 - 6xy + 9y^2)$

Find a value of n that makes the statement true.

34. $pq^2 - 14pq - 3np + 2q^2 - 28q - 30 = (p + 2)(q + 1)(q - 3n)$ 5
35. $8r^{5n-1} - 50s^2 = 2(2r^{2n+3} + 5s)(2r^{2n+3} - 5s)$ 7

MIXED REVIEW

36. STANDARDIZED TESTS 28% of what number is 42? B; Lesson 3.5

    A. 1.5 B. 150 C. 87.5 D. 11.76

Factor. Lesson 12.4

37. $xy - 5x + 2y - 10$
    $(x + 2)(y - 5)$
38. $2ab - 2a + 3b - 3$
    $(2a + 3)(b - 1)$
39. $4y^2z + 4y^2 - 9z - 9$
    $(2y + 3)(2y - 3)(z + 1)$

A river's *gradient*—how much it drops in vertical feet per mile—is a significant indicator of how rough the waterflow is likely to be. Rivers with a gradient of less than 20 feet per mile usually only have mild rapids, while those with a gradient over 50 feet per mile provide a dangerous ride.

1. Raise one end of your model using pieces of wood or other materials. Determine the average gradient or vertical drop in inches per foot along the entire course using the formula

$$g = \frac{\text{start elevation} - \text{end elevation (in inches)}}{\text{total length (in feet)}}$$

2. Sail a toy boat or piece of cork down the course. Use a stopwatch to time the trip. Then use the formula $d = rt$ to determine the speed.
3. Raise your model higher using another piece of wood. Determine the average gradient. Predict the time and speed for the course now. Then sail the boat again and check your predictions.

12.6 Solve Quadratic Equations by Factoring

Explore

1. Use a graphing utility to graph the function $y = x^2 + 5x - 6$. Set your calculator so that integers are displayed, and use the TRACE feature to locate the values of x for which $y = 0$. Substitute the values in the polynomial to check. $x = -6, x = 1$
2. Write the polynomial $x^2 + 5x - 6$ in factored form. $(x + 6), (x - 1)$
3. Describe how the factored form relates to the values of x for which $y = 0$. See Additional Answers.
4. Based on the example above, find the values of x for which $y = 0$ in the function $y = x^2 + 3x + 2$. Check these values by using the graphing utility or by substituting in the polynomial. $x = -1, x = -2$

SPOTLIGHT ON LEARNING

In this lesson you will learn
- to solve quadratic equations by factoring.

WHY? Solving quadratic equations by factoring can help you solve problems in geometry, number theory, architecture, and energy.

Build Understanding

You know that any time you multiply a number by zero, the product is zero. Therefore, if you know that a product is zero, then you can be sure that at least one of its factors is zero. This is stated in the **zero product property**.

THE ZERO PRODUCT PROPERTY

For any real numbers a and b, if $ab = 0$, then $a = 0$ or $b = 0$, or both $a = 0$ and $b = 0$.

The zero product property can be used in solving quadratic equations.

EXAMPLE 1

Find all the real solutions to each equation.

a. $y(2y - 3) = 0$ **b.** $(z + 2)(z - 5) = 0$

Solution

Use the zero product property.

a. $y(2y - 3) = 0$

$$y = 0 \quad \text{or} \quad 2y - 3 = 0$$
$$y = 0 \quad \text{or} \quad 2y - 3 + 3 = 0 + 3$$
$$y = 0 \quad \text{or} \quad \frac{2y}{2} = \frac{3}{2}$$
$$y = 0 \quad \text{or} \quad y = \frac{3}{2}$$

So, the solutions are 0 and $\frac{3}{2}$.

LESSON PLANNING

Objective
- ▶ Solve quadratic equations by factoring.

Vocabulary
discriminant
zero product property

Technology/Multimedia
graphing utility

Resources
Warm Up 12.6
Reteaching 12.6
Extra Practice 12.6
Enrichment 12.6
Transparency 68
Student Handbook
Lesson Quiz 12.6
Technology Activity 29

ASSIGNMENTS

Basic: 1–32, 36–37, Mixed Review 42–50, AlgebraWorks 1–6

Average: 3–34, 36–38, Mixed Review 42–50, AlgebraWorks 1–6

Enriched: 5–41, Mixed Review 42–50, AlgebraWorks 1–6

1 MOTIVATE

Explore For Question 4, ask students to factor $x^2 + 3x + 2$. **$(x + 1)(x + 2)$** Ask them to describe how they found the values of x for which $y = 0$. **solve $(x + 1) = 0$ and $(x + 2) = 0$; $(x + 1) = 0$ when $x = -1$ and $(x + 2) = 0$ when $x = -2$**

DIVERSITY IN THE CLASSROOM

Individual Learners Have students who are having difficulty factoring record the factoring steps in their math journals.

2 TEACH

Use the Pages/Build Understanding Have students read the section about the zero product property. Have them list as many pairs of factors of 6 as they can including rational and irrational factors. Then have them list as many pairs of factors of 0 as they can. Ask them what they notice about the factors of 0. **At least one factor must be 0.** Ask them what they notice about the factors of 6 in regard to 0. **None of the factors of 6 can be 0.**

Example 1: After students have read through the check, ask them how else they could check their solutions. **Use a graphing utility and determine the *x*-intercepts of the graph of $y = x(2x - 3)$.** Then have students check the solutions to both part a and part b using graphing utilities.

Technology Help students recall that they can solve quadratic equations using a graphing utility. Ask them to solve $x^2 + x - 7 = 5$ by letting $Y1 = x^2 + x - 7$ and $Y2 = 5$. Then, after finding their intersection points, they can use the *x*-values as the solutions to the equation. $x = -4$; $x = 3$

Example 2: Have students check the solutions to both part a and part b.

Ask students how all the equations in Examples 1 and 2 are alike. **They are all equal to 0.** Have students read the paragraph following Example 2.

ALGEBRA: WHO, WHERE, WHEN

People used to refer to 0's as "ciphers." The terms *cipher* and *zero* are, in fact, both terms for 0. They come from the same word, the Arabic term for 0, *zephirum*. The earliest use of the symbol 0 as a placeholder in numerals was in a Hindu inscription dated to 876 A.D.

Check

$$y = 0 \qquad 0(2 \cdot 0 - 3) \stackrel{?}{=} 0 \qquad 0 = 0 \checkmark$$

$$y = \frac{3}{2} \qquad \frac{3}{2}\left(2 \cdot \frac{3}{2} - 3\right) \stackrel{?}{=} 0 \qquad \frac{3}{2}(3 - 3) \stackrel{?}{=} 0 \qquad \frac{3}{2} \cdot 0 \stackrel{?}{=} 0 \qquad 0 = 0 \checkmark$$

b. $(z + 2)(z - 5) = 0$

$(z + 2) = 0$ or $(z - 5) = 0$

$z + 2 - 2 = 0 - 2$ or $z - 5 + 5 = 0 + 5$

$z = -2$ or $z = 5$

So, the solutions are –2 and 5.

Check

$$z = -2 \qquad (z + 2)(z - 5) \stackrel{?}{=} 0 \qquad (-2 + 2)(-2 - 5) = 0 \qquad 0(-7) = 0 \qquad 0 = 0 \checkmark$$

$$z = 5 \qquad (z + 2)(z - 5) \stackrel{?}{=} 0 \qquad (5 + 2)(5 - 5) = 0 \qquad 7 \cdot 0 = 0 \qquad 0 = 0 \checkmark$$

Some quadratic equations can be solved by factoring and using the zero product rule.

EXAMPLE 2

Solve each equation.

a. $x^2 - 7x = 0$ **b.** $x^2 - 9x + 20 = 0$

Solution

a. $x^2 - 7x = 0$

$x(x - 7) = 0$ Factor out the GCF.

$x = 0$ or $x - 7 = 0$

$x = 0$ or $x = 7$

So, the solutions are 0 and 7. Check each solution.

b. $x^2 - 9x + 20 = 0$

$(x - 4)(x - 5) = 0$ Factor into two binomials.

$x - 4 = 0$ or $x - 5 = 0$

$x = 4$ or $x = 5$

So, the solutions are 4 and 5. Check each solution.

It is important to remember that when you use the factoring method to solve quadratic equations, you are also using the zero product property. The factored polynomial *must* equal zero.

EXAMPLE 3

Solve each equation.

a. $a^2 = 8a$ **b.** $b^2 - 2b - 1 = 7$

Solution

a.

$$a^2 = 8a$$

$a^2 - 8a = 0$ Make one side of the equation equal to zero.

$a(a - 8) = 0$ Factor and solve.

$a = 0$ or $a - 8 = 0$

$a = 0$ or $a = 8$

The solutions are 0 and 8. Check the solutions.

b.

$$b^2 - 2b - 1 = 7$$

$b^2 - 2b - 1 - 7 = 0$ Make one side of the equation equal to zero.

$b^2 - 2b - 8 = 0$

$(b - 4)(b + 2) = 0$ Factor and solve.

$b - 4 = 0$ or $b + 2 = 0$

$b = 4$ or $b = -2$

The solutions are 4 and –2. Check the solutions. ◄

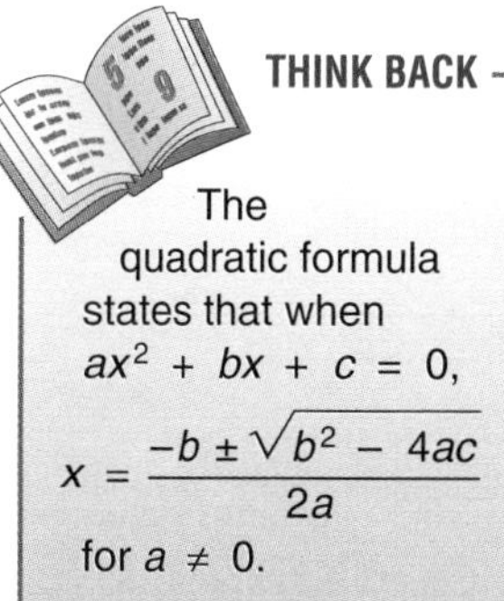

THINK BACK

The quadratic formula states that when $ax^2 + bx + c = 0$,

$$x = \frac{-b \pm \sqrt{b^2 - 4ac}}{2a}$$

for $a \neq 0$.

Remember that not all polynomials are factorable. You can use the *discriminant* of the quadratic formula to determine whether the polynomial is factorable. The **discriminant** is the expression under the radical symbol of the quadratic formula, $b^2 - 4ac$.

If $b^2 - 4ac < 0$, the equation has no real solution.

If $b^2 - 4ac = 0$, there is one, rational solution.

If $b^2 - 4ac > 0$, there are two real solutions.

Also, if $b^2 - 4ac > 0$ and is not a perfect square, then the solutions of the equation are irrational. If the discriminant is greater than zero and is a perfect square, then the solutions of the equation are rational numbers.

Therefore, for any polynomial $ax^2 + bx + c$, if $b^2 - 4ac \geq 0$ and is a perfect square, then the polynomial is factorable.

COMMUNICATING ABOUT ALGEBRA

Discuss why a polynomial is factorable only when the discriminant is a perfect square. You may want to start with two equations of the form $x = p$ and $x = q$ where p and q are rational numbers, and work backward to a polynomial.

See Additional Answers.

Example 3: Ask students what the standard form of a quadratic equation is. $\boldsymbol{ax^2 + bx + c = 0}$ Stress the importance of rewriting equations in standard form before solving.

Have students read Think Back. Ask how they could use the quadratic formula to check the Example 3 solutions. **Rewrite the equation in standard form, and then determine the values of *x* for the given equation.** Have students use the quadratic formula to check the solutions for part b.

$$x = \frac{-b \pm \sqrt{b^2 - 4ac}}{2a}$$

$$= \frac{-(-2) \pm \sqrt{(-2)^2 - 4(1)(-8)}}{2(1)}$$

$$= \frac{2 \pm \sqrt{4 + 32}}{2} = \frac{2 \pm \sqrt{36}}{2} = \frac{2 \pm 6}{2};$$

$$x = \frac{2 + 6}{2} \text{ or } \frac{2 - 6}{2};$$

$x = 4$ or $x = -2$

Have students discuss the paragraph following Example 3. Have them consider the polynomial $2x^2 - x - 6$ and tell what the values for *a*, *b*, and *c* are. **$a = 2$, $b = -1$, and $c = -6$** Have them determine the value of the discriminant for $2x^2 - x - 6$. **$(-1)^2 - 4(2)(-6) = 1 + 48 = 49$** Ask how many real solutions $y = 2x^2 - x - 6$ has. **2**

Example 4: After students have discussed part a, ask them to factor $2x^2 + x - 6$. **$(2x - 3)(x + 2)$**

Example 5: Ask students to list the possible factors for 84. **1, 84; 2, 42; 3, 28; 4, 21; 6, 14; 7, 12** Ask them which ones give the sum of 5 with the appropriate sign designations. **7, 12 when 12 is positive and 7 is negative**

Ongoing Assessment The important concepts and skills are solving quadratic equations by factoring and determining whether a polynomial is factorable. To assess these ideas, have students demonstrate how they have applied these concepts and skills in Exercises 1, 9, and 13 of the Try These section.

Guided Practice/Try These Ask students which exercises show equations that can be solved immediately without factoring. **Exercises 1–4** Ask which exercises show equations that can be factored immediately without moving any terms from one side of the equation to another. **Exercises 5–8** Have students explain what they must do to the equations in Exercises 9–12 and why. **Solve the equation for zero so that the zero product property can be applied.** Have students explain how to determine whether a polynomial is factorable. **Write the equation in standard form and determine the values for *a*, *b*, and *c*. Then substitute them in the determinant of the quadratic formula, $b^2 - 4ac$. If the result is greater than or equal to zero and a perfect square, then the polynomial is factorable.**

3 SUMMARIZE

In the Math Journal Have students list methods for solving a quadratic equation. Have them explain how to use each method to solve $2x^2 + 3x - 9 = -4$. Use a graphing utility to graph $Y1 = 2x^2 + 3x - 9$ and $Y2 = -4$; the *x*-intercepts of the intersection points are the solutions. **For all three other methods rewrite the equation in standard form: $2x^2 + 3x - 5 = 0$; (1) graphing utility: let $y = 2x^2 + 3x - 5$ and determine the *x*-intercepts; (2) factoring: $2x^2 + 3x - 5 = 0$, $(2x + 5)(x - 1) = 0$, solve both $2x + 5 = 0$ and $x - 1 = 0$ for *x*; (3) quadratic formula: $a = 2$, $b = 3$, and $c = -5$**

$$x = \frac{-3 \pm \sqrt{3^2 - [4 \cdot 2(-5)]}}{2 \cdot 2}$$

$$= \frac{-3 \pm \sqrt{9 + 40}}{4} = \frac{-3 \pm \sqrt{49}}{4}$$

$$= \frac{-3 \pm 7}{4},$$

$x = 1$ or $x = -2.5$

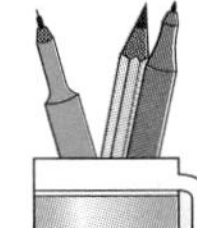

PROBLEM SOLVING TIP

Draw a diagram that helps you understand the problem.

EXAMPLE 4

Use the discriminant to determine whether each polynomial is factorable. Then, factor if possible.

a. $2x^2 + x - 6$ **b.** $x^2 + 10x + 2$

Solution

For each polynomial, identify *a*, *b*, and *c*. Then determine the value of $b^2 - 4ac$.

a. $2x^2 + x - 6$ $a = 2, b = 1, c = -6$

$$\begin{aligned} b^2 - 4ac &= (1)^2 - 4(2)(-6) \\ &= 1 + 48 \\ &= 49 \end{aligned}$$

Since 49 is a perfect square, the polynomial is factorable. By trial and error, you can find the factors.

$$2x^2 + x - 6 = (2x - 3)(x + 2)$$

b. $x^2 + 10x + 2$ $a = 1, b = 10, c = 2$

$$\begin{aligned} b^2 - 4ac &= 10^2 - 4(1)(2) \\ &= 100 - 8 \\ &= 92 \end{aligned}$$

Since 92 is not a perfect square, the polynomial cannot be factored.

Solving quadratic equations by factoring is often useful in solving problems about area.

EXAMPLE 5

ARCHITECTURE The length of a rectangle is 5 m more than its width. Find the dimensions of the rectangle if its area is 84 m^2.

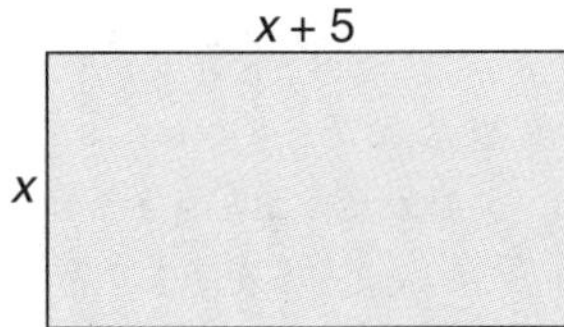

Solution

Let *x* represent the width of the rectangle. Let $(x + 5)$ represent the length.

$$\begin{aligned} (\text{length})(\text{width}) &= \text{area} \\ (x + 5)x &= 84 \\ x^2 + 5x &= 84 && \text{Multiply.} \\ x^2 + 5x - 84 &= 0 && \text{Make one side of the equation equal to zero.} \\ (x + 12)(x - 7) &= 0 && \text{Factor.} \end{aligned}$$

$x + 12 = 0$ or $x - 7 = 0$

$x = -12$ or $x = 7$

Since the width cannot be −12, use the positive solution, 7. The width is 7. The length is 7 + 5, or 12.

TRY THESE

Solve each equation.

1. $x(x + 3) = 0$ $x = 0, x = -3$
2. $y(y - 9) = 0$ $y = 0, y = 9$
3. $(x + 5)(x - 1) = 0$ $x = -5, x = 1$
4. $(x + 1)(x - 2) = 0$ $x = -1, x = 2$
5. $x^2 - 6x = 0$ $x = 0, x = 6$
6. $y^2 + 2y = 0$ $y = 0, y = -2$
7. $x^2 + 5x - 14 = 0$ $x = -7, x = 2$
8. $y^2 - 4y + 3 = 0$ $y = 3, y = 1$
9. $z^2 - z = 12$ $z = 4, z = -3$
10. $x^2 + 4x = 12$ $x = 2, x = -6$
11. $y^2 + 6y = -8$ $y = -4, y = -2$
12. $z^2 + 2z = 80$ $z = -10, z = 8$
13. **GEOMETRY** The length of a rectangle is 1 yd more than twice its width. The area is 55 yd^2. Find the dimensions of the rectangle. 5 yd, 11 yd

Determine whether the polynomial is factorable. Then factor, if possible.

14. $x^2 + 13x + 22$ yes; $(x + 2)(x + 11)$
15. $x^2 - 3x - 24$ not factorable
16. $x^2 - 20x + 36$ yes; $(x - 18)(x - 2)$
17. **WRITING MATHEMATICS** Write a paragraph explaining how some quadratic equations can be solved by factoring. Include directions for determining whether or not factoring can be used to solve a particular quadratic equation. See Additional Answers.

PRACTICE

Solve each equation.

1. $a(a + 1) = 0$ 0, −1
2. $b(b - 10) = 0$ 0, 10
3. $(c + 3)(c - 8) = 0$ −3, 8
4. $(d - 4)(d - 9) = 0$ 4, 9
5. $x^2 - 5x = 0$ 0, 5
6. $y^2 + 7y = 0$ 0, −7
7. $x^2 - 3x - 70 = 0$ 10, −7
8. $x^2 + 4x - 45 = 0$ −9, 5
9. $x^2 + 11x + 28 = 0$ −4, −7
10. $x^2 - 15x + 44 = 0$ 4, 11
11. $x^2 + 3x = 18$ −6, 3
12. $x^2 - 2x = 63$ −7, 9
13. $y^2 - 14 = 5y$ −2, 7
14. $z^2 + 10 = 11z$ 1, 10
15. $2x^2 + 7x = -3$ $-\frac{1}{2}, -3$
16. $3x^2 + 14x = 5$ $\frac{1}{3}, -5$
17. $x^2 - x = 3x + 12$ −2, 6
18. $y^2 + 3y - 2 = y + 1$ −3, 1
19. **GEOMETRY** The length of a rectangle is 7 m longer than its width. The area is 18 m^2. Find the dimensions of the rectangle. 2 m, 9 m

Determine whether the polynomial is factorable. Then factor, if possible.

20. $x^2 - 2x + 5$ not factorable
21. $x^2 - 12x + 32$ yes; $(x - 8)(x - 4)$
22. $x^2 - 13x - 48$ yes; $(x - 16)(x + 3)$
23. $x^2 - x - 90$ yes; $(x - 10)(x + 9)$
24. $2x^2 + 13x + 15$ yes; $(2x + 3)(x + 5)$
25. $2x^2 + x + 3$ not factorable
26. $x^2 - 5x - 84$ yes; $(x + 7)(x - 12)$
27. $x^2 - x + 4$ not factorable
28. $x^2 - 17x + 66$ yes; $(x - 11)(x - 6)$
29. **NUMBER THEORY** The product of two consecutive integers is 132. What are the integers? 11, 12; −12, −11
30. **NUMBER THEORY** The product of two consecutive odd integers is 143. What are the integers? 11, 13; −11, −13

4 PRACTICE

Practice Remind students to first rewrite each equation in standard form by making one side of the equation equal to zero. Have a student describe the steps to solve Exercise 16. **Rewrite in standard form: $3x^2 + 14x - 5 = 0$; factor: $(3x - 1)(x + 5) = 0$; $3x - 1 = 0$, $x = 1/3$ or $x + 5 = 0$, $x = -5$.** Ask a student to describe how to solve Exercise 29. **$x(x + 1) = 132$, $x^2 + x - 132 = 0$, $(x - 11)(x + 12) = 0$, $x = 11$ or $x = -12$; thus the consecutive numbers are $x = 11$ and $x + 1 = 12$ or $x = -12$ and $x + 1 = -11$**

For Exercise 30, ask students how to represent two consecutive even integers. **x and $x + 2$ or $2x$ and $2x + 2$**

NAME ______ CLASS ______ DATE ______

12.6 SOLVE QUADRATIC EQUATIONS BY FACTORING

Example
Solve: $x^2 - 11x = 12$

Solution
Step 1: Set the equation equal to zero.
$x^2 - 11x - 12 = 0$
Step 2: Identify a, b, and c.
$a = 1, b = -11, c = -12$
Step 3: Determine whether the polynomial is factorable by seeing if $b^2 - 4ac \geq 0$ and is a perfect square.
$b^2 - 4ac = (-11)^2 - 4(1)(-12)$
$= 121 + 48 = 169$
Since $169 = 13^2$, the polynomial is factorable.
Step 4: Factor the polynomial.
$x^2 - 11x - 12 = 0$
$(x + 1)(x - 12) = 0$
Step 5: Set each factor equal to zero and solve for x.
$x + 1 = 0$ or $x - 12 = 0$
$x = -1$ or $x = 12$

EXERCISES

Determine whether the polynomial is factorable. Write *yes* or *no*.

1. $x^2 - 4x - 32$
2. $x^2 - 9$
3. $x^2 - 6x + 10$
4. $x^2 - 12x - 13$
5. $x^2 - 12x + 48$
6. $x^2 - 3x - 70$

Solve each equation.

7. $y(y - 7) = 0$
8. $z(z + 6) = 0$
9. $(x - 7)(x + 4) = 0$
10. $(s - 11)(s - 10) = 0$
11. $c^2 - 2c = 0$
12. $d^2 + 6d = 0$
13. $x^2 - 4x - 12 = 0$
14. $x^2 + 6x + 5 = 0$

1. yes
2. yes
3. no
4. yes
5. no
6. yes
7. 0, 7
8. 0, −6
9. 7, −4
10. 11, 10
11. 0, 2
12. 0, −6
13. 6, −2
14. −5, −1

38 South-Western Algebra 1: AN INTEGRATED APPROACH

Extend Ask students how they can solve the equations in Exercises 31 and 32. **Find the products, combine like terms, and then solve each equation for zero.**

Think Critically For Exercises 36–39, ask students how they can write quadratic equations that have the given pair of solutions. **Write binomials equal to zero so that their solutions match the given solutions and then multiply the binomials to get a quadratic equation.** Ask a student how to solve Exercise 40. **Possible answer: Use a multiplication model**

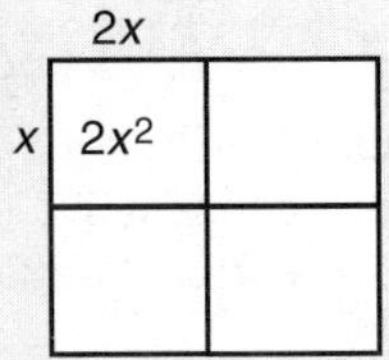

Solve by determining all combinations of pairs of factors for –10.

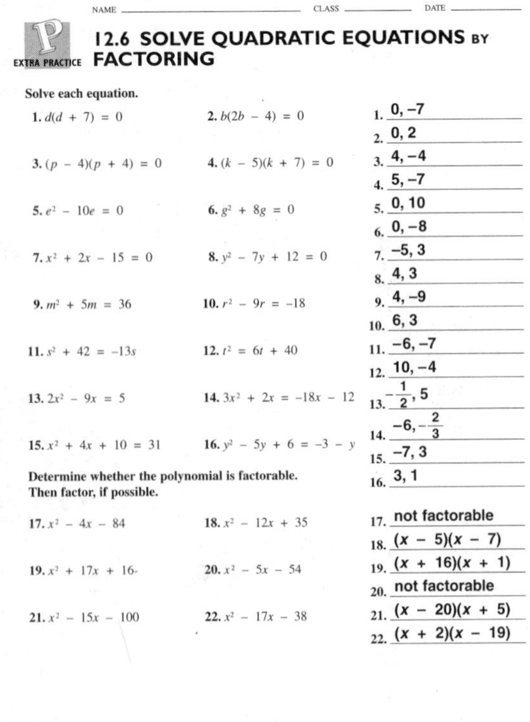

NAME ______ CLASS ______ DATE ______

EXTRA PRACTICE **12.6 SOLVE QUADRATIC EQUATIONS BY FACTORING**

Solve each equation.

1. $d(d + 7) = 0$
2. $b(2b - 4) = 0$
3. $(p - 4)(p + 4) = 0$
4. $(k - 5)(k + 7) = 0$
5. $e^2 - 10e = 0$
6. $g^2 + 8g = 0$
7. $x^2 + 2x - 15 = 0$
8. $y^2 - 7y + 12 = 0$
9. $m^2 + 5m = 36$
10. $r^2 - 9r = -18$
11. $s^2 + 42 = -13s$
12. $t^2 = 6t + 40$
13. $2x^2 - 9x = 5$
14. $3x^2 + 2x = -18x - 12$
15. $x^2 + 4x + 10 = 31$
16. $y^2 - 5y + 6 = -3 - y$

Determine whether the polynomial is factorable. Then factor, if possible.

17. $x^2 - 4x - 84$
18. $x^2 - 12x + 35$
19. $x^2 + 17x + 16$
20. $x^2 - 5x - 54$
21. $x^2 - 15x - 100$
22. $x^2 - 17x - 38$

Answers:
1. 0, –7
2. 0, 2
3. 4, –4
4. 5, –7
5. 0, 10
6. 0, –8
7. –5, 3
8. 4, 3
9. 4, –9
10. 6, 3
11. –6, –7
12. 10, –4
13. $-\frac{1}{2}$, 5
14. –6, $-\frac{2}{3}$
15. –7, 3
16. 3, 1
17. not factorable
18. $(x - 5)(x - 7)$
19. $(x + 16)(x + 1)$
20. not factorable
21. $(x - 20)(x + 5)$
22. $(x + 2)(x - 19)$

40 *South-Western Algebra 1: AN INTEGRATED APPROACH*

EXTEND

Solve each equation.

31. $(x + 1)^2 + (x - 5)^2 = 20$ 1, 3

32. $(x + 3)^2 - 2(x + 1) = 3$ –2

33. GEOMETRY The perimeter of a garden must be 40 m. The area of the garden must be 96 m^2. Find the length and width. 12 m, 8 m

34. NUMBER THEORY Find two consecutive even integers such that the square of the larger less five times the smaller is 60. 8 and 10

35. CHINESE ARCHITECTURE The floor plan of Toshodaiji, an eighth-century Japanese monastery, built under Chinese influence and supervision, is a rectangle. Its length is 1 unit less than twice its width, and the floor area is 28 square units. Find the dimensions in units. 4 units by 7 units

THINK CRITICALLY

Write a quadratic equation that has the given pair of solutions. Make all coefficients integers.

36. –2 and 8 $x^2 - 6x - 16 = 0$

37. 0 and –12 $x^2 + 12x = 0$

38. $\frac{1}{2}$ and –3 $2x^2 + 5x - 3 = 0$

39. $\frac{2}{3}$ and –1 $3x^2 + x - 2 = 0$

Find all integers, *n*, for which the polynomial has a binomial factor.

40. $2x^2 + nx - 10$ 0, 1, –1, 8, –8, 19, –19

41. $nx^2 + 2x - 4$ 0, 2, 6

MIXED REVIEW

Solve. Lesson 3.7

42. $7x + 8 = 3x - 20$ –7

43. $4(x - 3) = 3x + 11$ 23

44. $5x + 7 + 2x = 11 + 4x$ $\frac{4}{3}$

Find the range of the function given the domain {–2, 0, 3}. Lesson 4.2

45. $y = -3x$ {6, 0, –9}

46. $y = x + 5$ {3, 5, 8}

47. $y = x^2$ {4, 0, 9}

48. STANDARDIZED TESTS Which is the solution of the inequality $2 - x > 7$? D; Lesson 5.4

A. $x > 9$ **B.** $x > -5$ **C.** $x < -9$ **D.** $x < -5$

Simplify. Lesson 11.6

49. $(3x^2 + 4x - 2) + (4x^2 - 3)$ $7x^2 + 4x - 5$

50. $(4ab - 3a + b) - (2ab + a - 6b)$ $2ab - 4a + 7b$

Career
Water Resources Technician

The Mississippi River is an important waterway to the Gulf of Mexico and the Atlantic Ocean. *Mississippi* means "great river" in the language of the Ojibway, Native Americans of the Great Lakes region. Like all rivers, the Mississippi can be dangerous. In the summer of 1993, the Mississippi River overflowed, causing loss of life, property, and crops.

A water resources technician gathers data and makes computations for water projects, including flood control. These professionals pay close attention to river height as an indicator of flood potential. Even a small rise in a river can mean an increase in water volume of millions of gallons. The volume is determined by multiplying the length, width, and depth of the river ($V = lwd$). The table below models the change in volume when width, depth, or both are increased.

Length	Width	Depth	Volume	Change from Original
l	w	d	lwd	0
l	$w+x$	d	$lwd+xld$	$+xld$
l	w	$d+x$	$lwd+lwx$	$+lwx$
l	$w+x$	$d+x$	$lwd+lwx+lxd+lx^2$	$+lwx+lxd+lx^2$

Decision Making

Use the table to answer these questions.

1. The last line of the table shows the change in volume when both the width and the depth of the river are increased by the same amount. Rewrite this polynomial in factored form. $lx(w+d+x)$
2. Consider a stretch of the Mississippi that is $\frac{1}{2}$ mi wide. The depth of the river increases an average of $\frac{1}{2}$ ft along a 1-mi stretch. By how much does the volume of water (cubic feet) in the river increase along that stretch? [1 mi = 5280 ft]
   See Additional Answers.
3. Change your answer to Question 2, which is in cubic feet, to gallons. Round to the nearest whole gallon. [1 gal ≈ 0.13 ft³]
   about 53,612,308 gal
4. Compute the approximate increase in gallons of water for the same stretch as in Question 2, if the depth increases an average of $1\frac{1}{2}$ ft along that stretch. (Round to the nearest whole gallon.)
   The volume of water increases by about 160,836,923 gal.
5. How many more gallons of water are in that 1-mi stretch when the river's depth is increased by $1\frac{1}{2}$ ft than when it increases by $\frac{1}{2}$ ft?
   about 107,224,615 gal
6. Write a paragraph explaining the importance of a water resources technician, based on what you've learned from these exercises.
   See Additional Answers.

5 FOLLOW-UP

Extension Tell students that for any real numbers a, b, and c, if $abc = 0$, then $a = 0$, $b = 0$, or $c = 0$. Then have them solve the cubic equation $x^3 - 4x + 3x^2 - 12 = 0$ by grouping. Suggest that they use a graphing utility to check their solutions.

$(x^3 - 4x) + (3x^2 - 12) = 0;$
$x(x^2 - 4) + 3(x^2 - 4) = 0;$
$(x + 3)(x^2 - 4) = 0;$
$(x + 3)(x + 2)(x - 2) = 0;$
$x = -3$, $x = -2$, or $x = 2$.

AlgebraWorks Have students multiply the dimensions in each of the last three cases to verify the given volume. Ask how the change from the original volume was calculated. **Subtract the new volume from the original volume, *lwd*.** Ask a student to describe how to answer Question 2. **Change all units to feet. The increase in volume is shown by the third *Change from Original* expression since it is for a change of depth: $lwx = 5{,}280 \cdot 2{,}640 \cdot 1/2 = 6{,}969{,}600$.**

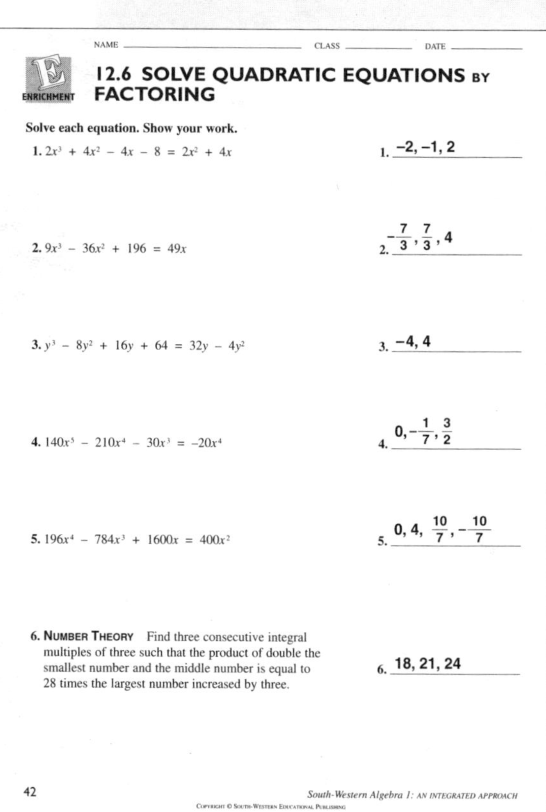
NAME ________ CLASS ________ DATE ________

ENRICHMENT

12.6 SOLVE QUADRATIC EQUATIONS BY FACTORING

Solve each equation. Show your work.

1. $2x^3 + 4x^2 - 4x - 8 = 2x^2 + 4x$ — 1. $-2, -1, 2$
2. $9x^3 - 36x^2 + 196 = 49x$ — 2. $-\frac{7}{3}, \frac{7}{3}, 4$
3. $y^3 - 8y^2 + 16y + 64 = 32y - 4y^2$ — 3. $-4, 4$
4. $140x^5 - 210x^4 - 30x^3 = -20x^4$ — 4. $0, -\frac{1}{7}, \frac{3}{2}$
5. $196x^4 - 784x^3 + 1600x = 400x^2$ — 5. $0, 4, \frac{10}{7}, -\frac{10}{7}$
6. **Number Theory** Find three consecutive integral multiples of three such that the product of double the smallest number and the middle number is equal to 28 times the largest number increased by three. — 6. 18, 21, 24

42 *South-Western Algebra 1:* AN INTEGRATED APPROACH

LESSON PLANNING

Objective

- Use quadratic equations and factoring to solve problems.

Resources

Reteaching 12.7
Extra Practice 12.7
Transparency 10
Student Handbook

ASSIGNMENTS

Basic: 1–19, Review Problem Solving Strategies 1–3

Average: 1–23, Review Problem Solving Strategies 1–3

Enriched: 1–24, Review Problem Solving Strategies 1–3

1 MOTIVATE

Introduction After students read the introductory paragraph, ask them to consider a rectangle with width x and length $x + 2$ and to describe how to find the dimensions if the area is 8 cm^2. **(width)(length) = area, $x(x + 2) = 8$, $x^2 + 2x - 8 = 0$, $(x - 2)(x + 4) = 0$, $x = 2$ or $x = -4$; width is 2 cm and the length is 4 cm** Ask students why they did not use -4 as one of the possible dimensions. **a width or length cannot be a negative quantity**

2 TEACH

Use the Pages/Problem Ask what information the problem gives. **The dimensions of the entire rectangular buckle, 80 mm by 60 mm, and the areas of the buckle and the silver rectangle.**

12.7 Problem Solving File

Use Variables

Problems Involving Quadratic Equations

SPOTLIGHT ON LEARNING

WHAT? In this lesson you will learn

- to use quadratic equations to solve problems.
- to determine which of two real solutions is an appropriate solution of a problem.

WHY? Solving quadratic equations can help you to solve problems involving home furnishings, recreation, magazine design, number theory, gardening, and metalwork.

In applied situations, the mathematical model often results in a quadratic equation. If the quadratic equation has two real solutions, it may be that only one of them makes sense in the problem. For example, a negative number cannot represent a length or elapsed time. Reject solutions that do not fit the physical situation.

Problem

A jewelry designer sketched a rectangular belt buckle 80 mm long and 60 mm wide. The belt buckle has a uniform strip of bronze around a smaller rectangle of silver. How wide should the bronze strip be if the area of the silver rectangle is to be half the area of the belt buckle?

Explore the Problem

Begin by drawing a diagram to help you analyze the problem.

x x x x 60 mm 80 mm

1. What will x represent?
   the width of the bronze strip
2. In terms of x, what are the dimensions of the silver rectangle?
   length = $80 - 2x$; width = $60 - 2x$
3. Express the area of the silver rectangle in terms of x.
   $A = (80 - 2x)(60 - 2x) = 4800 - 280x + 4x^2$
4. Write a quadratic equation that relates the areas of the two metals.
   See Additional Answers.
5. Solve the quadratic equation by factoring.
   $4(x - 60)(x - 10) = 0$; $x = 10$ or 60
6. Do both solutions make sense in the problem? Explain. What is the width of the bronze strip? See Additional Answers.
7. How can you check your solution? See Additional Answers.

Investigate Further

Cristina was curious to know how long her cousins Gustavo and Gloria have lived in Minneapolis. She asked her Uncle Hector, a skilled riddler. He replied, "Gustavo has lived in Minneapolis three years more than twice as long as Gloria has lived there. If you square the number of years each of them has lived in Minneapolis, the sum of the squares is 194." How long has each person lived in Minneapolis?

8. If y represents the number of years Gloria has lived in Minneapolis, what expression represents the number of years Gustavo has lived there? $2y + 3$

9. What information from the problem can you use to write an equation? Show your equation. See Additional Answers.

10. Can you solve the equation by factoring? How do you know? Yes, the discriminant is 3844, which is a perfect square (62^2).

11. Explain how the solutions you find by factoring relate to the problem. See Additional Answers.

12. How long has each person lived in Minneapolis? Check your answer. Gloria 5 years, Gustavo 13 years; $5^2 + 13^2 = 25 + 169 = 194$

13. Suppose Uncle Hector had responded, "Find two real numbers such that one number is 3 more than twice the second, and the sum of their squares is 194." Would your answer be different? Explain. See Additional Answers.

14. **WRITING MATHEMATICS** Think about different problems that could lead to the equation $x(x + 1) = 72$. Solve the equation by factoring and consider the values you obtain. Then write one problem for which both values would make sense and another problem for which only one value makes sense. See Additional Answers.

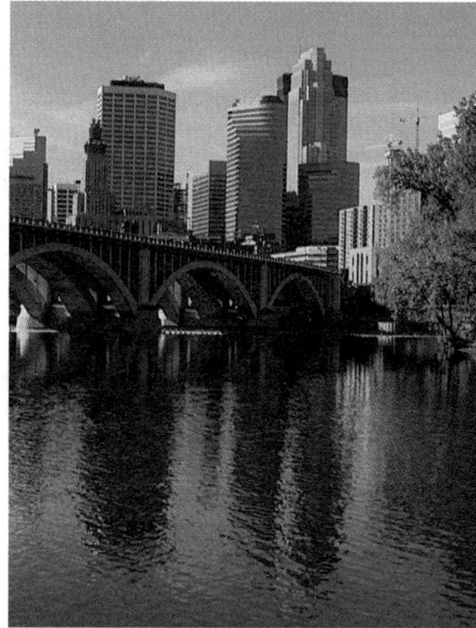

PROBLEM SOLVING PLAN

- Understand
- Plan
- Solve
- Examine

Apply the Strategy

15. **HOME FURNISHINGS** If the units are omitted, the sum of the area and perimeter of a square rug is 60.

    a. What equation can you use to find the length of one side of the rug? $s^2 + 4s - 60 = 0$

    b. What is the length, assuming the units are feet? $s = 6$ ft

16. **RECREATION** The area of a rectangular park is 1750 m^2. The park is 15 m longer than it is wide. What are the dimensions of the park? 35 m × 50 m

17. **MAGAZINE LAYOUTS** The perimeter of a rectangular photograph is 32 in. and the area is 63 in.^2 The photograph is positioned on a magazine page so that the only remaining space on the page is a $1\frac{1}{2}$-in. strip all around the photograph. (Assume length is the greater dimension.)

    a. What are the dimensions of the photograph? 7 in. × 9 in.

    b. What are the dimensions of the magazine page? 10 in. × 12 in.

Use the Pages/Explore the Problem Stress the usefulness of drawing a diagram to clarify a problem. For Question 2, ask a student to explain how the dimensions of $80 - 2x$ and $60 - 2x$ were determined. **Let w represent the width of the silver rectangle. The diagram shows that the width of the entire rectangle is $x + w + x$, which is 60 mm, $2x + w = 60$ and $w = 60 - 2x$. The length is found similarly.**

DIVERSITY IN THE CLASSROOM

Visual Learners Some students may find it helpful to make a chart to represent the data.

Use the Pages/Investigate Further Ask how the problem is similar to the one in the previous section. How is it different? **Both problems involve writing and solving quadratic equations. Also both problems require positive solutions. Although a diagram helped in the first problem, it does not help with this problem.** Ask what methods they can use to solve the problem. **Write a quadratic equation in terms of y, simplify it, factor it, and then solve for y.**

3 SUMMARIZE

In the Math Journal Remind students that in previous lessons they learned to check solutions of quadratic equations using several different methods. Have students discuss which method is best to check solutions of word problems and why. **Substitution in the original problem wording is an appropriate method since unreasonable answers can show up.**

4 PRACTICE

Apply the Strategy Remind students to define each variable and to draw a diagram or to make a chart to represent a problem whenever possible. For Problem 15, ask students how to write an equation to determine the length of one side of the rug. **Use the given information about the area and perimeter; area = s^2 and perimeter is $4s$; $s^2 + 4s = 60$ and $s^2 + 4s - 60 = 0$.** For Problem 20, remind students to factor out the GCF before trying to factor a trinomial into two binomial factors. For Problem 22, ask students how they can represent one side of each square. **Let s represent the perimeter of one square, and then the perimeter of the other square is $56 - s$; one side of each square is 1/4 its perimeter or $s/4$ and $(56 - s)/4$.**

Draw a Diagram | Write an Expression

18. **AGES** Yoshi is 1 year younger than Keiko. The product of their ages is 756. How old is each person? Yoshi is 27; Keiko is 28.

19. **NUMBER THEORY** Find two consecutive integers whose product is 1560. 39, 40 and −40, −39

20. **NUMBER THEORY** A positive integer is increased by 10. If the square of the resulting larger integer is nine times the square of the smaller integer, find the smaller integer. 5

21. **ART** A rectangular painting, with its wooden frame, measures 24 in. by 31 in. The width of the frame is equal all around. Without the frame, the painting has an area of 450 in.^{2}

    a. How wide is the frame? 3 in.

    b. What are the dimensions of the painting? 18 in. × 25 in.

22. **METALWORK** A piece of wire 56 in. long is cut into two pieces, each of which is formed into a square. If the sum of the areas of the squares is 106 in.^{2}, how long were the pieces of wire? 36 in. and 20 in.

23. **GARDENING** A circular garden covers an area of 400π ft^2. A paved path of constant width is to surround the garden. If the total area of the garden and path is 676π ft^2, how wide is the path? 6 ft

24. **PACKAGING** A square piece of cardboard has edges of 10 in. in length. A square piece is cut from each of the corners, and the remaining sides are folded up to form an open box. If the area of the bottom of the box is equal to the sum of the areas of the sides of the box, what is the length of the sides of the squares that were cut? $1\frac{2}{3}$ in.

NAME ______________ CLASS ________ DATE ________

RETEACHING

12.7 PROBLEM SOLVING FILE: PROBLEMS INVOLVING QUADRATIC EQUATIONS

Example
Find two integers such that their sum is 4 and their product is –96.

Solution

Step 1: Determine what the variable will represent.
x = one integer

Step 2: Write expressions to represent all other values in terms of x.
Since their sum is 4, the difference of the 4 and one integer should equal the other integer.
$4 - x$ = second integer

Step 3: Write an equation using the expressions and the information given. The information given about the product still has not been used. Use it to write an equation.
$x(4 - x) = -96$

Step 4: Solve the equation by setting the equation equal to zero and factoring.
$$x(4 - x) = -96$$
$$4x - x^2 = -96$$
$$x^2 - 4x - 96 = 0$$
$$(x - 12)(x + 8) = 0$$
$$x = 12 \text{ or } -8$$

Step 5: Put the values for x back into the expressions written to find the other values.
$$x = 12 \text{ or } -8$$
$$4 - x = -8 \text{ or } 12$$
The two integers are –8 and 12.

EXERCISES

NUMBER THEORY The sum of two integers is –1. Their product is –240.

1. Write expressions to represent the two integers. 1. $x, -1 - x$
2. Write an equation involving the two integers. 2. $x(-1 - x)$
3. What are the two integers? 3. −16, 15

ARCHITECTURE The blueprints for a rectangular office building show that the perimeter of the building will be 130 m. The amount of land the building will cover is 1,000 m^2.

4. Write expressions to describe the length and width of the building. 4. $y, 65 - y$
5. Write an equation concerning the area of the land. 5. $y(65 - y) = 1,000$
6. Find the length and width of the building. 6. 25 m, 40 m

44 South-Western Algebra 1: AN INTEGRATED APPROACH

Use a Model | Use a Formula | Use Logical Thinking

REVIEW PROBLEM SOLVING STRATEGIES

1–3 See Additional Answers.

CRAZY CARDS

1. A box contains three cards. One card is green on both sides, one card is yellow on both sides, and one card is green on one side and yellow on the other. You pick a card without looking and place it on the table. The card has a green side showing. What is the probability that the side not showing is also green? Before you (incorrectly) answer $\frac{1}{2}$, use the steps below to analyze the problem.

   a. Represent the cards as shown and consider the set of possible outcomes when a card is drawn and placed on the table. Use ordered pairs such as (G_1, G_2) where the first letter denotes the side placed face up and the second letter denotes the side not showing. How many ordered pairs are in the sample space?

   b. Since you know a green side is showing, what is the possible sample space now?

   c. So, if the side showing is green, what is the probability that the other side is also green?

   d. Now try this problem. Mrs. Long is the mother of two children. One of these children is a boy. What is the probability that they are both boys?

CUT CAREFULLY

2. Suppose you have two cords. One cord is 14 in. long and the other cord is 19 in. long.

   a. How can you cut one of the cords into two pieces so that the length of one of the three pieces of cord you now have will be the average of the lengths of the other two? What relationship to the original lengths do you notice?

   b. Generalize your results from 2a for any two cords. How can you cut one cord into two pieces so that the length of one of the three pieces is the average of the lengths of the other two? Explain.

FREQUENT FLIER

3. A northbound train starts traveling at the same time as a southbound train. The two trains, initially 150 kilometers apart, head toward each other on parallel tracks. The northbound train averages 33 km/h, and the southbound train averages 42 km/h. A bird is flying back and forth between the two trains at 8 km/h, leaving the northbound train just as it starts out. How far has the bird flown when the two trains pass? Explain your reasoning. (*Hint:* What formula can you use to determine the bird's distance? What do you know? What must you find?)

5 FOLLOW-UP

Extra Practice A rectangular rug is placed in a 16 ft by 13 ft room so that a uniform strip of flooring surrounds the rug. The area of the rug is 100 ft^2 less than the area of the room. How wide is the strip of flooring? **2 ft**

Review Problem Solving Strategies

Crazy Cards The strategy of using logical thinking will help the students solve the problem.

Cut Carefully The strategies of using logical thinking and writing an expression will help solve the problem.

Frequent Flier The strategy of using a formula will help the students solve the problem.

NAME ______ CLASS ______ DATE ______

12.7 PROBLEM SOLVING FILE: PROBLEMS INVOLVING QUADRATIC EQUATIONS

AUTOMOTIVES The following formula calculates an estimated number of feet d it takes to stop a car on a dry concrete road if the car is traveling s miles per hour. The distance covered in that time includes the amount of time it takes the driver to react.

$$1{,}000d = 42s^2 + 1{,}100s$$

1. If $d = 0$, what are the two possible values for s that would make the formula true? (Round to the nearest hundredth.) 1. **0, –26.19**

2. Do either of the values for s make sense? Which one(s) make sense? Explain your reasoning.
   Zero is the only answer that makes sense. If the car didn't require any time to stop, it must not have been moving.

PHYSICS A ball is thrown up into the air at the rate of 50 feet per second. The force of gravity pulls the ball down to the earth $16t^2$ feet in t seconds. The formula that gives the distance d above the earth after t seconds is $d = 50t - 16t^2$.

3. For what values of t will d equal 6? 3. **$\frac{1}{8}$, 3**

4. Do either of the values for t make sense? Which one(s) make sense? Explain your reasoning.
   Both values make sense. The ball will be 6 feet above the ground at both times, once on the way up and again on the way down.

5. At what time will the ball hit the ground? (Round to the nearest tenth.) 5. **3.1 seconds**

6. **PACKAGING** From a square piece of cardboard, 4 inch squares are cut from each corner. The sides are then folded up to make an open box. If the volume of the box needed is 100 in.³, what are the dimensions of the original piece of cardboard? 6. **13 in., 13 in.**

46 *South-Western Algebra 1: An Integrated Approach*

Introduction The Chapter Review emphasizes the major concepts, skills, and vocabulary presented in this chapter and can be used for diagnosing students' strengths and weaknesses. Page references direct students to appropriate sections for additional review and reteaching.

Using Pages 606–607 Ask students to scan the Chapter Review and ask questions about any section they find confusing. Exercises 1–4 review key vocabulary. Exercises 5–8 ask students to model factoring using Algeblocks.

Informal Evaluation Have students explain how they arrived at any incorrect answers. They may find their own mistakes and give you some clues as to the nature of their errors. Make sure students understand this material before moving on to the assessment stage.

Follow-Up Have students solve this problem: One positive number is 6 more than another positive number. The product of the two numbers is 27. Find the two numbers.

a. Let x represent the smaller positive number; then $x + 6$ represents the other positive number. The equation for the problem is $x(x + 6) = 27$.

b. Solve the equation $x = -9$, $x = 3$. Use $x = 3$ since it must be positive. **The two numbers are 3 and 9.**

Have students write problems that involve factoring polynomials. Students should exchange problems and solve them.

CHAPTER REVIEW

VOCABULARY

Choose the word from the list that completes each statement.

1. The __?__ states that if a product is zero, then at least one of its factors is zero. c
2. The __?__ is the number multiplying the first term in a polynomial written in standard form. a
3. A __?__ is a polynomial that is the square of a binomial. d
4. For a quadratic equation $ax^2 + bx + c$, the __?__ is the expression $b^2 - 4ac$. b

a. leading coefficient
b. discriminant
c. zero product property
d. perfect square trinomial

Lesson 12.1 EXPLORE PATTERNS IN FACTORING

pages 571–574

- Algeblocks may be used to model polynomials and find their factors.

Use Algeblocks to write the two binomial factors for each trinomial.

5. $x^2 + 4x + 3$ $(x + 1)(x + 3)$
6. $x^2 - 5x + 6$ $(x - 2)(x - 3)$
7. $x^2 + 2x - 8$ $(x + 4)(x - 2)$
8. $x^2 - 4x - 5$ $(x + 1)(x - 5)$

Lesson 12.2 FACTOR POLYNOMIALS

pages 575–581

- To factor out a monomial from a polynomial, find the greatest common factor and use the distributive property in reverse. To factor a trinomial, use a multiplication diagram or patterns of products.

Factor each polynomial.

9. $15d + 25d^2$ $5d(3 + 5d)$
10. $9xyz^2 - 3y^2z + 6x^2yz$ $3yz(3xz - y + 2x^2)$
11. $z^2 + 11z + 24$ $(z + 8)(z + 3)$
12. $y^2 + 8y - 9$ $(y + 9)(y - 1)$
13. Find the dimensions in terms of x of a rectangle if its area is $2x^2 + x - 15$. $2x - 5, x + 3$

Lesson 12.3 FACTORING SPECIAL PRODUCTS

pages 582–585

- Use patterns to factor the difference of two squares and perfect square trinomials.

Factor if possible.

14. $c^2 + 8c + 16$ $(c + 4)^2$
15. $x^2 - x + 1$ not factorable
16. $r^2 - 6r + 9$ $(r - 3)^2$
17. $w^2 - 100$ $(w + 10)(w - 10)$

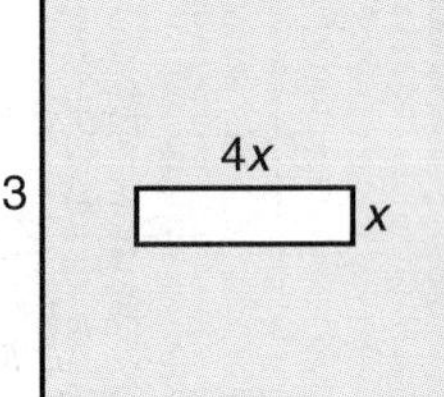

18. Find the dimensions of a rectangle that has the same area as the shaded region. $3 + 2x, 3 - 2x$

Lesson 12.4 FACTOR BY GROUPING pages 586–590

- To factor polynomials by grouping, use the distributive property.

Factor.

19. $4(x - 3) + y(x - 3)$ $(4 + y)(x - 3)$

20. $ab + 2a + 4b + 8$ $(a + 4)(b + 2)$

21. $pr - ps - qr + qs$ $(p - q)(r - s)$

22. $cd + 5c - 5 - d$ $(c - 1)(d + 5)$

23. Find the dimensions of a rectangle in terms of a and b if its area is $ab - 5a + 3b - 15$. $a + 3, b - 5$

Lesson 12.5 FACTORING COMPLETELY pages 591–594

- To factor completely, you may need to perform two or more types of factoring on the same polynomial.

Factor completely.

24. $3x^2 + 27x + 42$ $3(x + 2)(x + 7)$

25. $2ab^4 - 8ab^2 - 90a$ $2a(b^2 + 5)(b + 3)(b - 3)$

26. $6y^2 - 36y + 54$ $6(y - 3)(y - 3)$

27. $3xy^2 - 12x$ $3x(y + 2)(y - 2)$

28. Find the dimensions of a rectangular prism with the volume $4x^2 - 144$. $4, x + 6, x - 6$

Lesson 12.6 SOLVE QUADRATIC EQUATIONS BY FACTORING pages 595–601

- Use the zero property to solve quadratic equations by factoring.

Solve each equation.

29. $k(k + 5) = 0$ $0, -5$

30. $n(n - 9) = 0$ $0, 9$

31. $(y + 7)(y - 10) = 0$ $-7, 10$

32. $x^2 + 9x + 18 = 0$ $-6, -3$

33. The product of two consecutive even integers is 224. What are the integers? 14 and 16 or −14 and −16

Lesson 12.7 PROBLEMS INVOLVING QUADRATIC EQUATIONS pages 602–605

- You can use quadratic equations to solve problems, but you may have to reject a solution that is not reasonable.

Solve each problem.

34. A rectangular flag 30 in. by 20 in. has a partial border of equal width covering two of its sides as shown. Find the width of the border if the total area covered by the border is 264 in.^{2} 6 in.

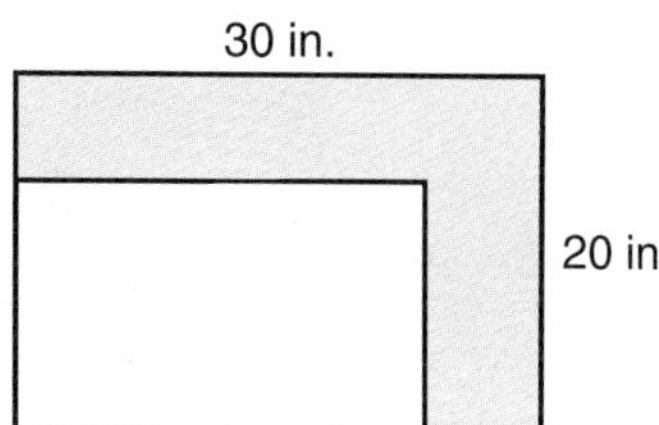

35. The difference of two positive numbers is 4. The sum of their squares is 170. What are the numbers? 7 and 11

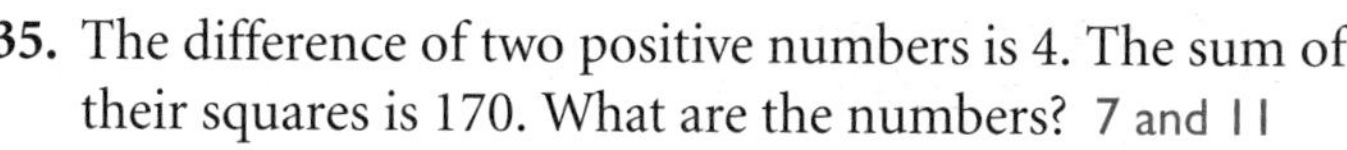

Study Skills Tip Suggest that students work in pairs. Each should make up some products like $(x + 1)(x - 3)$, $3x(4x - 5)$, $(x + 2)^2$ and $(x + 1)(x - 1)$. Then, the student gives his or her partner only the product and asks for the factors. Students can check each other's work. Similarly, they can make up problems like those in 12.7 and exchange them for solution.

For Your Portfolio Have students gather samples from their project, homework, quizzes, and class work that portray efforts to meet each of their goals for this chapter. On a cover page for each representative work have students write the related goal, why the work is included in the portfolio, and what the teacher should look for when reviewing the work. On a general cover page have students write a self-evaluation of how well they have met each of their goals for this chapter. The general cover page should conclude with the goals for the next chapter and the student's reason for choosing these goals.

The Chapter Test is comprised of a variety of test-item types as follows:

writing	5
traditional	1–4, 8–15, 18–24
verbal	6, 7, 25–30
standardized test	16, 17

TEACHING TIP

The writing item provides an opportunity for students to demonstrate a knowledge of process as well as end result. Suggest that before they begin answering questions, students should look over the entire test and determine the order in which they will work. Some students may be more successful if they save the open-ended writing question until after they have completed the other test questions.

The table below correlates the Chapter Test items with the appropriate lesson(s).

Item	*Lesson*	Item	*Lesson*
1–5	*12.2*	**25**	*12.4*
6	*12.6*	**26**	*12.5*
7–8	*12.3*	**27**	*12.6*
9–16	*12.2, 12.3*	**28–29**	*12.7*
17–24	*12.6*	***30***	*12.3*

CHAPTER ASSESSMENT

CHAPTER TEST

Factor completely.

1. $2g^3h^2 - 8gh$ $\quad 2gh(g^2h - 4)$

2. $6a^3b^2 - 3a^2b + 18ab^2$ $\quad 3ab(2a^2b - a + 6b)$

3. $4ab - 12b + 4a$ $\quad 4(ab - 3b + a)$

4. $3x^3y - 12xy^3 + 6x^2y^2$ $\quad 3xy(x^2 - 4y^2 + 2xy)$

5. WRITING MATHEMATICS Write a paragraph explaining how you can factor the polynomial $3x^3 + 9x^2 + 6x$. See Additional Answers.

6. The product of two consecutive odd whole numbers is 195. What are the numbers? 13 and 15

7. What is the difference between the expressions $4r^2$ and $16s^2$? Write your answer in factored form. $4(r + 2s)(r - 2s)$

Factor completely.

8. $x^2 - 81$ $\quad (x + 9)(x - 9)$

9. $x^3 - 16x$ $\quad x(x + 4)(x - 4)$

10. $50x^2 - 32$ $\quad 2(5x + 4)(5x - 4)$

11. $x^2 - 16x + 64$ $\quad (x - 8)(x - 8)$

12. $3z^2 - 2z - 1$ $\quad (3z + 1)(z - 1)$

13. $2x^2 - 28x + 98$ $\quad 4(x - 7)(x - 7)$

14. $a^4 - 6a^2 + 5$ $\quad (a^2 - 5)(a + 1)(a - 1)$

15. $2b^6c^6 - 7a^3b^3 - 4$ $\quad (2a^3b^3 + 1)(a^3b^3 - 4)$

16. STANDARDIZED TESTS Which expression does not have a difference of squares as at least one of its factors? C

A. $x^3 - 16x$ **B.** $4x^2 - 16$

C. $2x^2 - 4$ **D.** $2x^3 - 32x$

17. STANDARDIZED TESTS Which expressions are factorable? C

I. $3x^2 + 13x - 10$

II. $2x^2 + 11x + 14$

III. $4x^2 - 4x - 15$

IV. $2x^2 + 19x + 24$

A. I, II, and III only **B.** I and IV only

C. I, II, III, and IV **D.** I and III only

Solve each equation.

18. $r(r + 6) = 0$ $\quad 0, -6$

19. $16x^2 - 9 = 0$ $\quad \frac{3}{4}, -\frac{3}{4}$

20. $y^2 - 10y - 56 = 0$ $\quad 14, -4$

21. $x^2 + x - 0.75 = 0$ $\quad 0.5, -1.5$

22. $k(k + 4) - 3(k + 4) = 0$ $\quad 3, -4$

23. $n^2 - 7n + 10 = 0$ $\quad 2, 5$

24. $y^2 - 6y + 4 = 20$ $\quad -2, 8$

Solve each problem.

25. Find the area of the aqua region at the right and write it in factored form. $r^2(8 - \pi)$

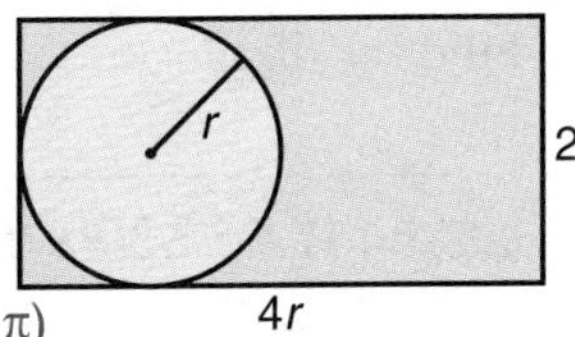

26. Find the dimensions of a rectangular prism with the volume $x^3 - 36x + 3x^2 - 108$. $x + 3, x + 6, x - 6$

27. The length of a rectangle is 7 cm longer than its width. The area is 120 cm². Find the dimensions of the rectangle. 15 cm, 8 cm

28. The perimeter of a rectangle is 38 m and its area is 84 m². What are the dimensions of the rectangle? 7 m, 12 m

29. A photograph is framed so that a uniform border surrounds the photograph. The entire framed photograph is 8 in. by 10 in. The area of the photograph is 32 in.² less than the area of the entire framed picture. How wide is the border? 1 in.

30. Find the dimensions of a rectangle that has the same area as the shaded region at the right. $5 + 2x, 5 - 2x$

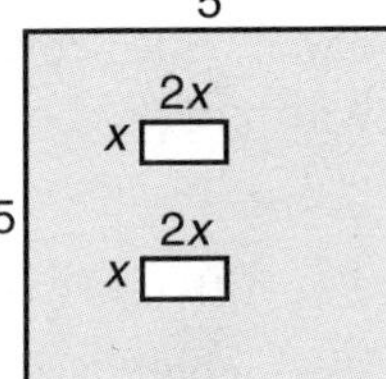

PERFORMANCE ASSESSMENT

Make a Flag Design a rectangular flag 12 in. by 16 in. with a uniform border surrounding a smaller rectangle inside. Make the area of the smaller rectangle a ratio of the area of the entire flag. For example, try $\frac{1}{4}$ the area, $\frac{1}{3}$ the area, or $\frac{1}{2}$ the area of the entire flag for the area of the smaller rectangle. Use a quadratic equation and factoring to help you find measurements that will work. You may wish to design flags of different sizes with similar conditions.

Use Multiplication Diagrams Select a variety of polynomials from this chapter. Draw multiplication diagrams and charts to find the factors as shown in the example for $x^2 + 2x - 8$. Draw a multiplication diagram and a chart.

	x	?
x	x^2	$?x$
?	$?x$	-8

Product, -8	Sum
$1, -8$	-7
$-1, 8$	7
$2, -4$	-2
$-2, 4$	2

	x	-2
x	x^2	$-2x$
$+4$	$4x$	-8

Use Algeblocks Use Algeblocks to build area models to determine factors of some polynomials. Select polynomials from this chapter that have all positive signs. Have a partner determine the factors. Follow the example below, a model of $x^2 + 4x + 3$. Remember the factors from the sides of the large rectangle are $(x + 3)$ and $(x + 1)$.

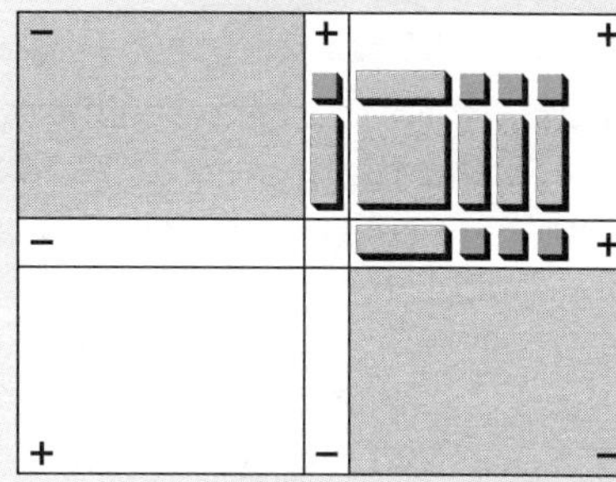

Use Algeblocks Pick a variety of polynomials from this chapter. Show how to model each polynomial with Algeblocks. Then ask a partner to show the steps for determining the factors of each polynomial. Check that each step is correct.

PROJECT ASSESSMENT

When each group has completed work on their river model, arrange a day for demonstrations.

1. Each group should name their water course and announce it when they begin the demonstration. Observers should take notes to be used later for comparison and evaluation of how well each group achieved its goal.
2. Each group should demonstrate three boat runs. These runs should be timed and averaged. The class can display the results in a bar graph and compare fastest and slowest times.
3. Geologists can estimate the age of a river based on its characteristics. Research and report on how they do so.

Performance Assessment

The activities on page 609 give students with different learning styles opportunities to demonstrate their understanding of concepts in this chapter. The activities may be used in addition to or instead of the Chapter Test on the previous page.

Make a Flag (Visual) Check that students have set up their quadratic equations correctly. Ask them to tell you how they know that the areas on their flags are in the stated ratio.

Using Multiplication Diagrams (Visual) Check that students have set up the diagram correctly. Check that they have considered all the possible different factors of the constant term.

Use Algeblocks (Tactile/Kinesthetic/Visual) A student's ability to model factoring with Algeblocks is a good indicator of understanding. Be sure that the students choose a polynomial with all positive signs.

Use Algeblocks (Tactile/Kinesthetic/Visual) Check that the models match the polynomials the students say are represented.

Project Assessment

Project Connection Have the students present their models to the class. Have the class discuss the differences and similarities in the models. Have them discuss what they learned about the river conditions that contribute to rapids.

NAME ____________ CLASS ________ DATE ________

FORM B

CHAPTER 12 TEST

Write the letter of the best answer for Questions 1–6.

1. Which is the factored form for $x^2 - 8x + 12$? 1. d

a. $(x + 6)(x - 2)$ b. $(x - 6)(x + 2)$

NAME ____________ CLASS ________ DATE ________

FORM A

CHAPTER 12 TEST

Write the letter of the best answer for Questions 1–6.

1. Which is the factored form for $x^2 - 7x + 10$? 1. c
   a. $(x + 5)(x - 2)$ b. $(x - 5)(x + 2)$
   c. $(x - 5)(x - 2)$ d. $(x + 5)(x + 2)$
2. Which is the greatest common monomial factor of $3x^3y + 9xy^2 + 12x^2y$? 2. b
   a. $3x^3$ b. $3xy$ c. 3 d. $3x^3y^2$
3. Which are the dimensions of a rectangle with area $2x^2 - x - 15$? 3. c
   a. $(2x + 3)(x + 5)$ b. $(x + 3)(2x - 5)$
   c. $(2x + 5)(x - 3)$ d. $(2x - 3)(x + 5)$
4. Which expression does *not* have a difference of squares as at least one of its factors? 4. c
   a. $x^3 - 36x$ b. $5x^2 - 45$ c. $3x^2 - 6$ d. $3x^3 - 48x$
5. Which is *not* a perfect square trinomial? 5. d
   a. $x^2 + 10x + 25$ b. $4x^2 + 12x + 9$
   c. $x^2 + 20x + 100$ d. $x^2 + 4x + 16$
6. Which is *not* factorable? 6. d
   a. $x^2 + 20x + 100$ b. $4x^2 + 3x - 1$
   c. $49x^2 - 64$ d. $x^2 + 100$

Factor completely.

7. $10x^2y + 20xy^2$ 7. $10xy(x + 2y)$
8. $14a^2b^2 - 7ab^2 + 21ab$ 8. $7ab(2a^2b - b + 3)$
9. $8ab + 12b - 16a$ 9. $4(2ab + 3b - 4a)$
10. $20x^2 - 36x$ 10. $4x(5x - 9)$
11. What is the difference between the expressions $8x^2$ and $32y^2$? Write your answer in factored form. 11. $8(x + 2y)(x - 2y)$
12. The product of two consecutive even numbers is 168. What are the numbers? 12. 12, 14 or −12, −14
13. GEOMETRY Find the dimensions in terms of x of a rectangle that has the same area as the shaded region at the right. 13. $(x + 5)(x - 5)$

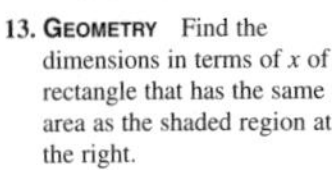

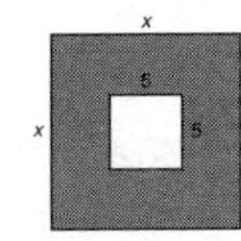

CHAPTER 12 TEST Form A, page 2 NAME ____________

Factor completely.

14. $y^2 - 144$ 14. $(y + 12)(y - 12)$
15. $x^3 - 81x$ 15. $x(x + 9)(x - 9)$
16. $2x^2 - 18$ 16. $2(x + 3)(x - 3)$
17. $x^2 - 14x + 49$ 17. $(x - 7)^2$
18. $3z^2 + 4z + 1$ 18. $(3z + 1)(z + 1)$
19. $5x^2 - 20x + 20$ 19. $5(x - 2)(x - 2)$
20. $x^4 - 7x^2 + 6$ 20. $(x^2 - 6)(x + 1)(x - 1)$
21. $ab + 5b + 3a + 15$ 21. $(a + 5)(b + 3)$

Solve each equation.

22. $s(s - 5) = 0$ 22. 0, 5
23. $4x^2 - 9 = 0$ 23. 1.5, −1.5
24. $x^2 - 3x - 54 = 0$ 24. 9, −6
25. $x(x + 2) - 3(x + 2) = 0$ 25. −2, 3
26. $x^2 + 10x = 0$ 26. 0, −10
27. $x^2 - 2x + 4 = 28$ 27. 6, −4

Solve.

28. GEOMETRY Find the dimensions of a rectangular prism with volume $x^3 - 4x + 5x^2 - 20$. 28. $(x + 5)(x + 2)$ $(x - 2)$
29. GEOMETRY The length of a rectangle is 3 ft longer than its width. The area is 130 square feet. Find the dimensions of the rectangle. 29. 10 ft by 13 ft
30. CRAFTS A cross-stitch design is framed so that a uniform border surrounds the design. The entire framed design is 5 inches by 7 inches. The area of the cross-stitch design is 20 in.² less than the area of the entire framed design. How wide is the border? 30. 1 inch

For Question 31, use a separate sheet of paper if necessary.

31. WRITING MATHEMATICS Think about different problems that could lead to the equation $x(x + 2) = 80$. Solve the equation by factoring and consider the values you obtain. Then write one problem for which both values would make sense.
    Answers will vary. The solutions are 8 and −10, so only the positive solution would make sense in an area problem, but both solutions would make sense in a problem about integers whose difference is 18.

CUMULATIVE REVIEW

Factor each polynomial. Lesson 12.2

1. $12x^2y + 8xy^3$ $4xy(3x + 2y^2)$
2. $h^2 + 13h + 30$ $(h + 3)(h + 10)$
3. $n^2 - 9n + 20$ $(n - 4)(n - 5)$
4. $g^2 + 10g - 56$ $(g - 4)(g + 14)$

Simplify each expression.

5. $\dfrac{x^8 \cdot x^7}{x^5}$ x^{10}; Lessons 11.2 and 11.3
6. $(x^3y)^3(xy^4)^2$ $x^{11}y^{11}$; Lesson 11.2
7. A chemist has 3 liters of a 24% alcohol solution. She wants to add some pure alcohol to the solution to bring it up to 28%. How much pure alcohol should the chemist add? $\frac{1}{6}$ of a liter; Lesson 3.9

Use the functions $f(x) = 5x - 2$ and $g(x) = 2x^2 + x - 1$ for Questions 8–11. 10, 11 Lesson 11.6

8. $f(-2) + g(-2)$ −7; Lessons 4.4 and 4.6
9. $\dfrac{f(4)}{g(2)}$ 2; Lessons 4.4 and 4.6
10. $f(x) + g(x)$ $2x^2 + 6x - 3$
11. $g(x) - f(x)$ $2x^2 - 4x + 1$

Factor each polynomial. 13–15 Lesson 12.3

12. $2x^2 + 7x + 3$ $(2x + 1)(x + 3)$; Lesson 12.2
13. $r^2 - 14r + 49$ $(r - 7)^2$
14. $9t^2 - 4$ $(3t + 2)(3t - 2)$
15. $16z^2 + 72z + 81$ $(4z + 9)^2$

Use the matrices for Questions 16–18. Lesson 1.6

$$A = \begin{bmatrix} 4 & -2 \\ -3 & 7 \end{bmatrix} \quad B = \begin{bmatrix} -5 & 4 \\ 3 & -9 \end{bmatrix}$$

16. $A + B$ $\begin{bmatrix} -1 & 2 \\ 0 & -2 \end{bmatrix}$
17. $B - A$ $\begin{bmatrix} -9 & 6 \\ 6 & -16 \end{bmatrix}$
18. (determinant of A) − (determinant of B) −11; Lesson 7.6
19. Ed's Car Rental charges $24.50 per day plus $0.18 a mile. Ralph's Rental charges $27.00 per day plus $0.16 per mile. Alice prefers to rent from Ralph's. For a one-day rental, how many miles would Alice have to travel so that Ralph's Rental would have the lesser charge? more than 125 miles; Lesson 5.7

Solve and graph each compound inequality. See Additional Answers for graphs. Lesson 5.5

20. $2x < -6$ or $x - 5 \geq -2$ $x < -3$ or $x \geq 3$
21. $-7 < 2x + 1 < 9$ $-4 < x < 4$

Factor each polynomial completely. 22, 23 Lesson 12.4; 24, 25 Lesson 12.5

22. $2x^2 + 6xy + 3x + 9y$ $(2x + 3)(x + 3y)$;
23. $x^3 - x^2 - 25x + 25$ $(x + 5)(x - 5)(x - 1)$;
24. $2p^4 - 8p^3 - 24p^2$ $2p^2(p - 6)(p + 2)$
25. $2z^4 - 32$ $2(z - 2)(z + 2)(z^2 + 4)$

Use the circle graph for Questions 26–28.

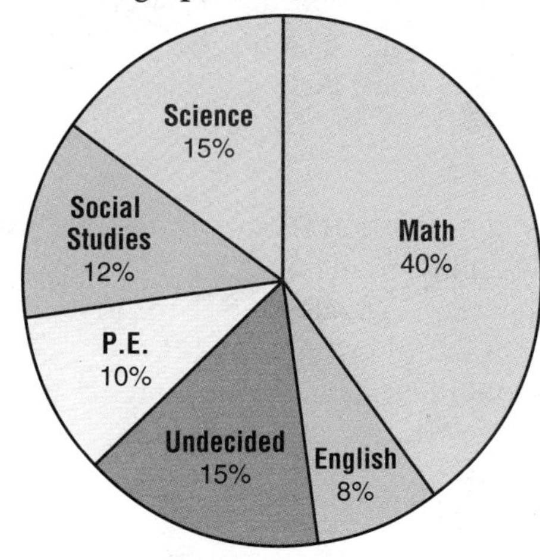

26. If 280 students gave their opinion, how many named Science as their favorite subject? 42; Lessons 1.4 and 3.5
27. If 45 students said that Social Studies was their favorite, how many students were part of the survey? 375; Lessons 1.4 and 3.5
28. WRITING MATHEMATICS Joe concluded that 40% of all the students at the school liked Mathematics best. Do you agree with Joe's conclusion? What questions might you like to ask Joe? See Additional Answers; Lesson 1.5

Solve each equation by factoring. Lesson 12.6

29. $x^2 + 8x = 20$ −10, 2
30. $3x^2 + 2 = 7x$ $\frac{1}{3}$, 2
31. $y^3 - y^2 - 2y = 0$ −1, 0, 2
32. $2n^2 + 12n = -18$ −3
33. TECHNOLOGY Fred was having trouble factoring the trinomial $x^2 - 4x - 45$. Wilma came by and suggested to Fred that he graph the trinomial on his graphing calculator. Fred was able to figure it out right away. How did Wilma's idea help? See Additional Answers. Lesson 12.6

STANDARDIZED TEST

QUANTITATIVE COMPARISON In each question compare the quantity in Column 1 with the quantity in Column 2. Select the letter of the correct answer from these choices:

A. The quantity in Column 1 is greater.
B. The quantity in Column 2 is greater.
C. The two quantities are equal.
D. The relationship cannot be determined by the information given.

Notes: In some questions, information which refers to one or both columns is centered over both columns. A symbol used in both columns has the same meaning in each column. All variables represent real numbers. Most figures are not drawn to scale.

	Column 1	Column 2
1.	 Area = $2x^2 + 7x + 6$	
	length of the longer side	twice the length of the shorter side
	D; Lesson 12.7	
2.	the line $y = mx + b$, with $m < 0$	
	slope of a line parallel to the one given	slope of a line perpendicular to the one given
	B; Lesson 6.3	
3.	product of the coordinates of the vertex of the graph of $y = 2\|x - 2\| - 2$	product of the coordinates of the vertex of the graph of $y = 2\|x + 2\| + 2$
	C; Lesson 9.2	
4.	$a < 0$	
	$a^5 \cdot a^3$	$(a^5)^3$
	A; Lessons 11.2 and 2.2	
5.	P(even number) rolling one number cube	P(tails) with one toss of a coin
	C; Lesson 8.6	
6.	$(8 \div 4) \div 2$	$8 \div (4 \div 2)$
	B; Lesson 2.8	
7.	$-3x < 12$	
	x	4
	D; Lesson 5.3	
8.	A total of 20 nickels and dimes amounts to $1.45.	
	number of nickels	number of dimes
	A; Lesson 7.7	
9.	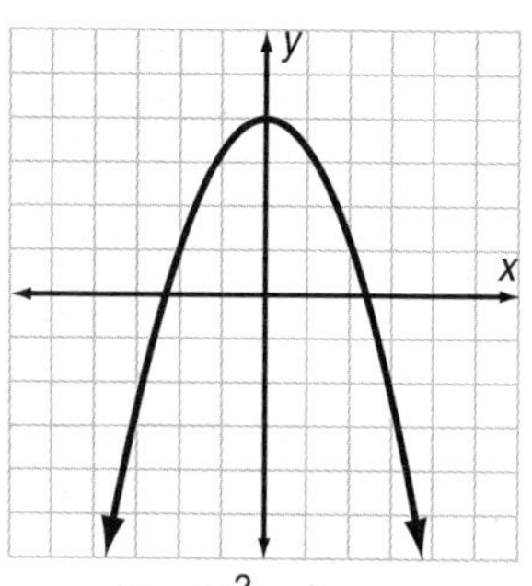 $y = ax^2 + bx + c$	
	a	c
	B; Lesson 10.2	
10.	83%	$\frac{5}{6}$
	B; Lessons 3.5 and 9.5	
11.	$\|x\| < 7, \|y\| > 7$	
	x	y
	D; Lesson 9.4	
12.	m and n are integers, $a > 0$	
	$a^{m - n}$	$\frac{1}{a^{n - m}}$
	C; Lesson 11.3	
13.	$x \neq 0, y \neq 0$	
	number of terms when $(x + y)(x - y)$ is multiplied	number of terms when $(x + y)(x + y)$ is multiplied
	B; Lesson 11.8	
14.	$4(x + 5) < 12, 3(2 - n) < 12$	
	x	n
	B; Lesson 5.4	

Answers

1. C	**13.** A
2. C	**14.** A
3. A	**15.** B
4. C	**16.** D
5. E	**17.** 12
6. B	**18.** 50
7. D	**19.** 16
8. B	**20.** 6
9. D	**21.** 12
10. A	**22.** 2
11. B	**23.** 11
12. C	**24.** 10

CHAPTER 12 Standardized Test, page 2 NAME ________

Quantitative Comparison For Questions 10–16, fill in A if the quantity in Column 1 is greater, B if the quantity in Column 2 is greater, C if the two quantities are equal, and D if the relationship cannot be determined.

Grid Response For Questions 17–24, mark your answer on the answer grid provided.

Solve each equation. Give the larger solution.

NAME ________ CLASS ________ DATE ________

CHAPTER 12 STANDARDIZED TEST

Standard Five Choice For Questions 1–9, fill in the best choice on the answer grid provided.

1. Which expressions are *not* factored completely?

I. $x^3 - 6x$ **II.** $x^2 - 100$
III. $x^2 + 4$ **IV.** $x^2 + 10x + 25$

A. I, II, and III **B.** II and III
C. I, II, and IV **D.** II, III, and IV
E. I, II, III, and IV

2. Which expression does *not* have a difference of two squares as at least one of its factors?

A. $3x^4 - 12x^2$ **B.** $x^3 - 9x$
C. $x^2 - 18x + 81$ **D.** $5x^2 - 20$
E. $2x^2 - 200$

3. Which shows the factored form of $6(x^2 + 1) - y(x^2 + 1)$?

A. $(6 - y)(x^2 + 1)$ **B.** $6x^2 + 6$
C. $(6 - x^2)(y + 1)$ **D.** $6y(x^2 + 1)$
E. $6x^2y$

4. Which is *not* a perfect square trinomial?

A. $4x^2 + 20x + 25$
B. $9x^2 - 24x + 16$
C. $9x^2 + 3x + 1$
D. $25x^2 + 10x + 1$
E. $x^4 - 6x^2y + 9y^2$

5. Which trinomials are *not* factorable?

I. $x^2 + 5x + 6$ **II.** $x^2 - 7x - 8$
III. $x^2 - 8x + 16$ **IV.** $x^2 - 2x - 1$

A. I and II **B.** II and III
C. III and IV **D.** only III
E. only IV

6. Which polynominals are factorable?

I. $4x^2 - 4x + 1$ **II.** $3x^2 - 8x - 3$
III. $4x^2 + 5x + 1$ **IV.** $x^2 + 2x + 2$

A. I and II only **B.** I, II, and III only
C. I only **D.** I and III only
E. II and III only

7. A rectangular painting, with its wooden frame, measures 24 inches by 30 inches. The width of the frame is equal all the way around. The area of the painting without the frame is 520 square inches. Which equation could you solve to find the width of the frame if x is the width of the frame?

A. $(24 - x)(30 - x) = 520$
B. $(24 + x)(30 + x) = 520$
C. $(24 + 2x)(30 + 2x) = 520$
D. $(24 - 2x)(30 - 2x) = 520$
E. None of these

8. To solve the equation $x^2 + 9x = -18$ by factoring, which polynomial would you factor?

A. $x^2 + 9x$ **B.** $x^2 + 9x + 18$
C. $x^2 + 9x - 18$ **D.** $x^2 + 18$
E. $x^2 - 18$

9. Which are the dimensions of a rectangle having the same area as the shaded region?

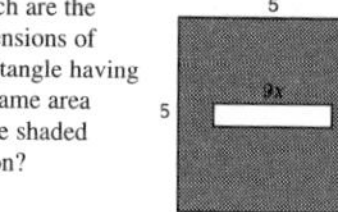

A. $5 - 3x, 5 - 3x$
B. $5 + 3x, 5 + 3x$
C. $5 + 4x, 5 - x$
D. $5 + 3x, 5 - 3x$
E. $25, 4x^2$

South-Western Algebra 1: AN INTEGRATED APPROACH 57

Chapter Opener

Data Activity, pages 568–569

1. 1122.8 mi^2
2. Snake River
3. 2.875 • 10^6 mi^2
4. **Drainage Area of U.S. Rivers**

5. Answers will vary.

Lesson 12.1

Think Back, page 571

2. Blocks showing $x + 2$ are placed along the horizontal axis. Blocks showing $x + 1$ are placed along the vertical axis. Within the quadrant, blocks are used to form a rectangle that has those dimensions.

Explore, pages 571–573

5. 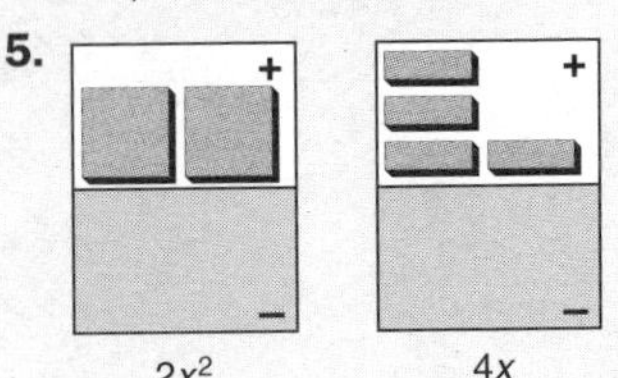

7. 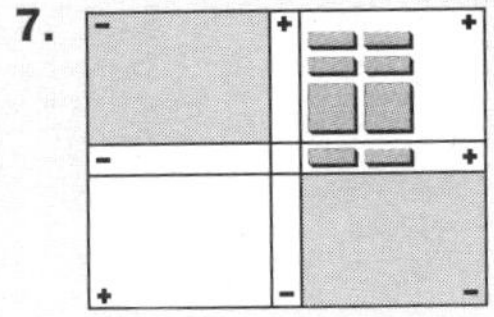

8. 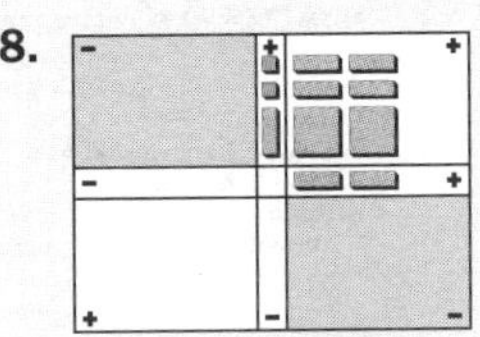

10. Answers will vary. Possible answer: $2x(x + 2)$ shows $2x^2 + 4x$ as the product of two factors.

13. 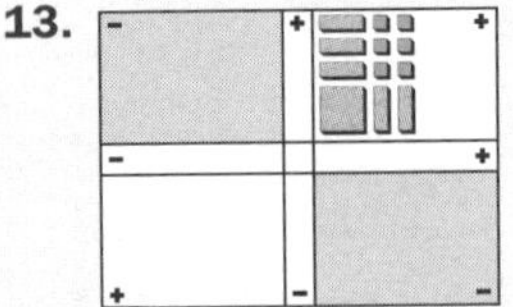

18. Possible answer: the coefficient of the squared variable is 1. All three terms are positive.

19. Arrangements will vary.

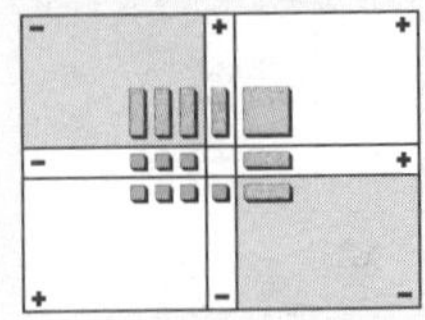

21. Students might place 3 negative x-blocks in Quadrant II and 1 negative x-block in Quadrant IV, or the reverse. The answer is not affected, but the order or factors may be different.

25. Possible answer: the coefficient of the squared variable is 1; the first and last (constant) terms are positive, and the middle term is negative.

26. 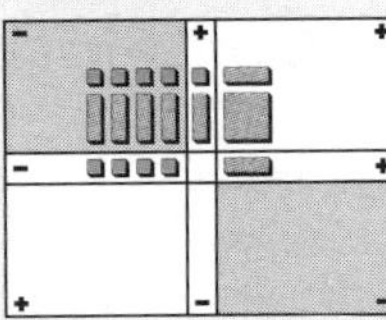

31. The coefficient of the squared variable is 1; the first and middle terms are positive, and the last (constant) term is negative.

32. Arrangements will vary. The 4 x-blocks and 4 unit blocks may be in Quadrant IV instead of in Quadrant II.

Make Connections, page 574

38. The coefficient of the x^2 term is 1; the constant term is ±6. The factors all include ±3 and ±2.
39. The first and last terms are positive, and the three terms in each are the same. The sign of the middle term is opposite.
40. The first terms are positive, the last terms are negative, and the three terms in each are the same. The sign of the middle term is opposite.
45. Answers will vary. Possible answer: If the constant term of the trinomial is positive, the constants in the binomial factors are both the same sign. If the constant term of the trinomial is negative, the constants in the binomial factors have different signs.

Summarize, page 574

46. Answers will vary. Possible answer: Model $3x^2$ and $-6x$. Make rectangles of each so that they have the greatest possible common dimension. The factored form of $3x^2 - 6x$ is $3x(x - 2)$.
47. Find two factors that give the constant term when multiplied and the coefficient of the middle term when added algebraically. Pay attention to the signs of the factors.

Lesson 12.2

Explore, page 575

1. 1×24 and 1×80; 2×12 and 2×40; 4×6 and 4×20; 8×3 and 8×10
2.

Dimensions	Total fencing
1×24 and 1×80	211 ft
2×12 and 2×40	110 ft
4×6 and 4×20	64 ft
8×3 and 8×10	50 ft

Try These, page 578

4. Determine what factors of 3 have a sum of −4. Since $(-3) + (-1) = -4$, $(x - 3)(x - 1) = x^2 - 4x + 3$.
15. Positions of some of the blocks will vary.

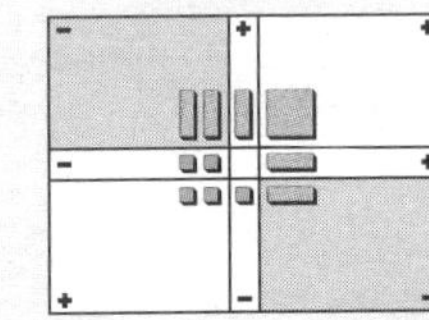

Extend, pages 579–580

41. $\left(\frac{1}{2}\right)(Z - N)$
42. a. $q = \frac{v\pi(D^2 - d^2)}{4}$

AlgebraWorks, page 581

3. Answers will vary, but students may prefer the linear model because it is easier to compute.
4. The hydrologist may gather more information and use that data to refine the model.

Lesson 12.3

Explore, page 582

3. The product equals the difference of two squares. Find the mean of the two factors. The other number to be squared is the difference between the mean and either of the two original factors.
4. $\frac{(51 + 35)}{2} = 43$; $51 - 43 = 8$
$(43 + 8)(43 - 8) = 1785$

Try These, page 584

13. The first and last terms are perfect squares and the middle term is twice the product of the square roots of the first and last terms.

Extend, page 585

26. The graph is the same as $y = x^2$ moved 3 units to the right.

Mixed Review, page 585

33. 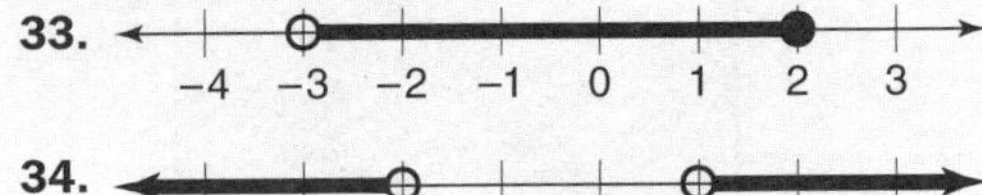

34. 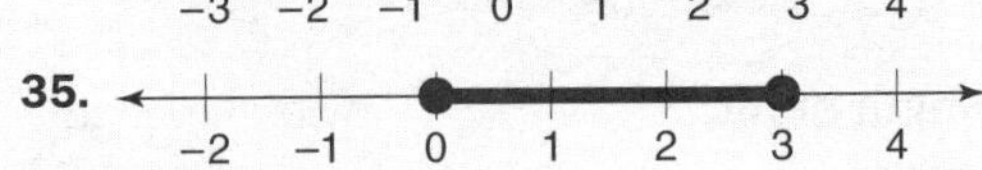

35. −2 −1 0 1 2 3 4

Lesson 12.4

Explore, page 586

1. 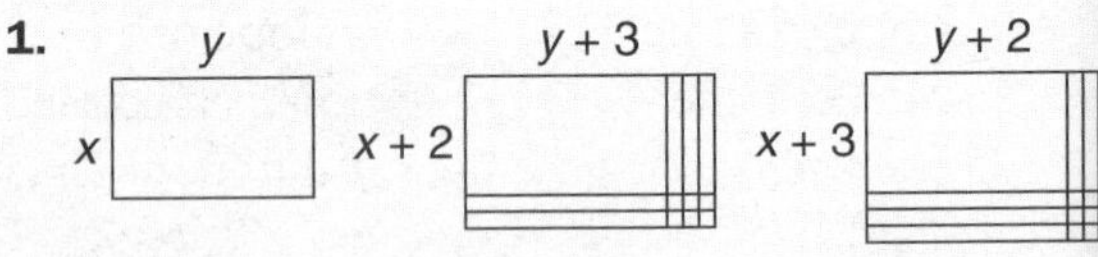

4. Answers will vary. Compare the areas. Subtract equal parts from each area.
$xy + 2x + 3y + 6$? $xy + 3x + 2y + 6$
$-xy - 2x - 2y - 6$? $-xy - 3x - 2y - 6$
y ? x
Since $y > x$, the rectangle with dimensions $x + 3$ and $y + 2$ is greater.

Check Understanding, page 587

2. a. Regroup the terms and factor:
$3ac + 4c + 6ab + 8b$
$= c(3a + 4) + 2b(3a + 4)$
$= (c + 2b)(3a + 4)$

b. Regroup the terms and factor:
$4x^2 - 8y + 8xy - 4x$
$= 4x^2 + 8xy - 4x - 8y$
$= 4x(x + 2y) - 4(x + 2y)$
$= 4(x - 1)(x + 2y)$
The results are the same with either grouping.

TRY THESE, PAGE 588

11. 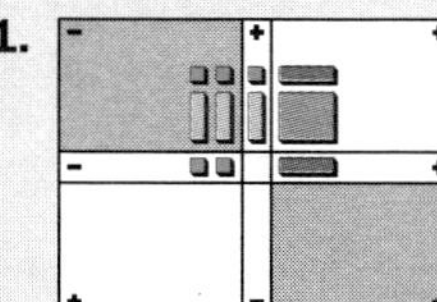

12. Yes; a polynomial can be factored by grouping if there are pairs of terms that have common factors, and factoring x from $(ax - bx)$ and $-y$ from $(-ay + by)$ leaves the common factor of $(a - b)$.

THINK CRITICALLY, PAGE 589

28. Answers will vary. $-2jk$, $-7(j - 2)$; $7j$, $2(jk - 7)$; 14, $j(2k - 7)$

29. Answers will vary. $-16a$, $(a + 3)(b + 4)(b - 4)$; $-ab^2$, $(3)(b + 4)(b - 4)$

30. Answers will vary. $40q$; $(5q + 4 + p)(5q + 4 - p)$; and $-40q$; $(5q - 4 + p)(5q - 4 - p)$; and $-25q^2$; $(4 + p)(4 - p)$ and -16; $(5q - p)(5q + p)$

ALGEBRAWORKS, PAGE 590

3. The capacity will increase at a faster rate.

4. No; the horizontal scale is not uniform; the change in capacity was caused by periodic upgradings of technology, which are not a function of time.

Lesson 12.5

EXPLORE, PAGE 591

2. Methods will vary.

3. Answers will vary.

TRY THESE, PAGE 593

8. Look for patterns, such as monomial factors, common factors, binomial factors, trinomials, perfect square trinomials, or a difference of squares. If you have been able to factor the polynomial as the product of two or more binomials, check to see whether you can factor still further.

9. Build a base of 1 x^2-block, 2 x-blocks, and 1 unit cube. Make three layers of this same base. The prism has the dimensions $x + 1$, $x + 1$, and 3. $3x^2 + 6x + 3$ is its volume.

THINK CRITICALLY, PAGE 594

32. $(a + b)(a^2 - ab + b^2)$
$= a^3 - a^2b + ab^2 + a^2b - ab^2 + b^3$. After like terms are combined, the result is $a^3 + b^3$.

Lesson 12.6

EXPLORE, PAGE 595

3. When $x^2 + 5x - 6 = 0$, then one or both factors are equal to zero.

COMMUNICATING ABOUT ALGEBRA, PAGE 597

If the discriminant is a perfect square, the roots are rational numbers, p and q. So, $x = p$ or $x = q$. Then, $x - p = 0$ or $x - q = 0$. So, $(x - p)(x - q) = 0$. Which, when multiplied, is a factorable trinomial.

TRY THESE, PAGE 599

17. The equation $ax^2 + bx + c = 0$ can be solved by factoring when $b^2 - 4ac$ is a perfect square. You can set each factor equal to zero and then solve for the unknown variable.

ALGEBRAWORKS, PAGE 601

2. The volume of water increases by 6,969,600 ft^3.

6. Since a small rise in river depth can produce a great increase in volume of water, water resources technicians need to keep careful watch over changes in the water depth.

Lesson 12.7

EXPLORE THE PROBLEM, PAGE 602

4. $4800 - 280x + 4x^2 = \frac{1}{2}(4800)$ or
$4x^2 - 280x + 2400 = 0$

6. $x = 60$ doesn't make sense because the strip would be larger than the actual buckle; the width is 10 mm.

7. Substitute 10 for x in the dimension of the silver rectangle; check that the area equals half the area of the buckle or 2400 $in.^2$; $(80 - 20)(60 - 20) = (60)(40) = 2400$, which checks.

INVESTIGATE FURTHER, PAGES 602–603

9. The sum of the squares is 194;
$y^2 + (2y + 3)^2 = 194$,
so $5y^2 + 12y - 185 = 0$.

11. The factored form is $(5y + 37)(y - 5) = 0$, so $y = 5$ and $y = -\frac{37}{5}$. Since the number of years cannot be negative, only the solution $y = 5$ makes sense for the problem.

13. The answer would include the numbers 5 and 13 and the numbers $-\frac{37}{5}$ and $-\frac{59}{5}$, since negative numbers also satisfy the conditions of this problem.

14. Answers will vary. The solutions are 8 and –9, so only the positive solution would make sense in an area problem; but both solutions would be acceptable for a problem that asked about consecutive integers.

REVIEW PROBLEM SOLVING STRATEGIES, PAGE 605

CRAZY CARDS

a. There are six pairs; (G1, G2) (G2, G1)(Y1, Y2)(Y2, Y1)(G1, Y2)(Y1, G2)

b. (G1, G2)(G2, G1)(G3, Y3)

c. $\frac{2}{3}$ **d.** $\frac{1}{3}$

CUT CAREFULLY

a. Cut the 19-in. cord into two pieces of 11 in. and 8 in. Then the 11-in. piece is the average of the 8-in. and the 14-in. pieces. The 11-in. piece is one-third the sum of the original lengths. $(19 + 14 = 33)$

b. If the two cords are unequal in length, cut from the longer piece. If equal in length, cut from either cord. Cut a piece that is one-third the sum of the lengths of the original pieces. Let the lengths be x and y $(y > x)$ and cut a length of b from y so you now have lengths, x, $y - b$, and b.
You want $\frac{x + (y - b)}{2} = b$,
so $x + y - b = 2b$, $x + y = 3b$, $b = \frac{x + y}{3}$

FREQUENT FLIER

16 km; Use $d = rt$. Find the length of time the bird flies. The bird's time equals the time it takes for the two trains to cover the 150 km.
So, $33t + 42t = 150$, $75t = 150$, $t = 2$. The bird's rate is 8 km/h, and $d = 8 \bullet 2 = 16$ km.

Chapter Assessment, pages 608-609

CHAPTER TEST, PAGE 608

5. Factor out the common monomial $3x$: $3x(x^2 + 3x + 2)$. Then factor the trinomial into two binomial factors such that the product of the first two binomial terms equals the first term of the trinomial, the product of the two last binomial terms equals the last term of the trinomial, and the sum of the products of the inner and outer terms equals the middle term: $3x(x + 2)(x + 1)$.

CUMULATIVE REVIEW, PAGE 610

20. $2x < -6$ or $x - 5 \geq -2$

–5 –4 –3 –2 –1 0 1 2 3 4 5

21. $-7 < 2x + 1 < 9$

–6 –5 –4 –3 –2 –1 0 1 2 3 4 5 6

28. Not necessarily; How many students did you ask? Was this a random sample, or possibly a cluster or convenience sample?

33. Fred knew that the product of the two factors would be zero only if one of the factors was zero. Where the graph crosses the x-axis (where $y = o$) are the values that would make the product zero. Since the graph crosses the x-axis at –5 and 9, the factors must be $9x + 50$ and $(x - 9)$.

CHAPTER 13 GEOMETRY AND RADICAL EXPRESSIONS

If their mathematics is to be both understandable and usable, students must learn to apply ideas from algebra and geometry together with statistics and discrete mathematics to the analysis of data. They can then use this analysis to pose problems, test hypotheses, construct mathematical models, and communicate their findings.

Mathematical Sciences Education Board. National Research Council Measuring What Counts. A Conceptual Guide for Mathematics Assessment. 1993, Washington, DC, page 22

The Big Question: Why study geometry and radical expressions?

Similar triangles and trigonometric ratios are used to make indirect measures, a technique used by surveyors and navigators. Although the theme of this chapter is travel and transportation, students will also see applications from auto mechanics, chemistry, construction, engineering, geography, plumbing, and surveying.

Vocabulary

acute triangle
amplitude
complementary angles
conjugates
converse of the Pythagorean theorem
corresponding angles
corresponding sides
cosine
crest
distance formula
equilateral triangle
geometric mean
isosceles triangle
like radicals
midpoint
midpoint formula
obtuse triangle
period
product and quotient properties of square roots
Pythagorean relationships
Pythagorean theorem
Pythagorean triple
radical equation
radical expression
radicand
rationalizing the denominator
right triangle
scale factor
scalene triangle
similar figures
similar triangles
simplest form
sine
sine curve
supplementary angles
tangent
trigonometric ratios
trigonometry
trough

Using the Graphic Organizer

Project a copy of the Graphic Organizer Transparency for Chapter 13. Explain that the focus of this chapter is on geometry and radical expressions. Review the information on the graphic organizer, pointing out that triangles can be classified in a variety of ways. Emphasize that the Pythagorean theorem and trigonometric ratios relate to right triangles.

Ask some preview questions; for example, how are triangles classified? What does it mean to say that lengths are proportional? Give an example.

One way to organize ideas about geometry and radical expressions is shown below.

One way to organize ideas about triangles is shown.

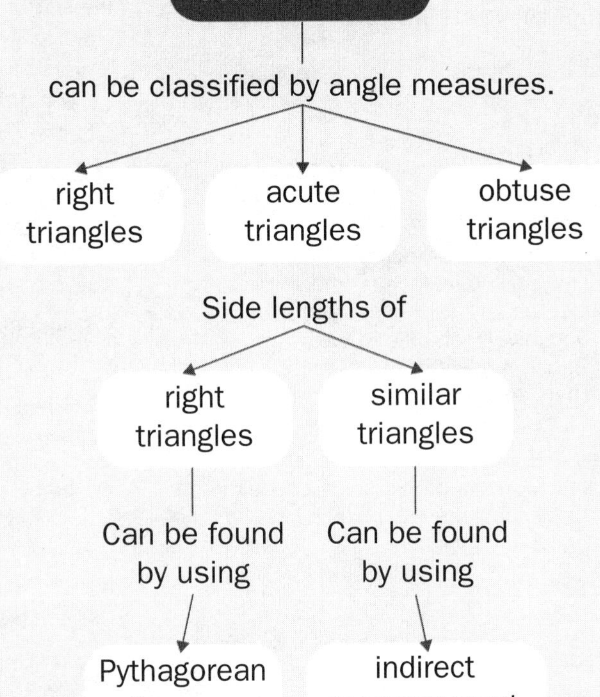

Try It Use a different plan. Try organizing ideas about radical expressions.

Explore the Chapter Theme:

Travel and Transportation

Travel and transportation have been important since ancient times. The ability to move people and goods from one place to another opens doors to learning and expanded opportunities. The transportation industry is a major part of our life today. More than 8 million workers are employed by the transportation industry in the United States alone.

The transportation industry includes travel and transport by automobiles, trucks, buses, railroads, mass transit systems, airplanes, ships, and pipelines.

Skills Needed for Success in Jobs in Travel and Transportation

Skills needed by people involved in designing transportation systems:

1. Work well with a group to design and implement a project.
2. Apply scientific and technical knowledge to a real situation.
3. Gather data about the movement of goods, mail, and freight.
4. Use computer simulations and modeling to test design ideas.
5. Use critical thinking skills to troubleshoot design and implementation problems.

Skills needed by people who operate transportation vehicles.

6. Have good vision and physical stamina.
7. Read and understand maps and/or navigational charts.
8. Know and use safety rules.
9. Communicate clearly to passengers and crew.

Investigate Further

Have students identify a career related to travel and transportation that interests them. Have students go to the library to find more information about this career. For example, students might find out about educational requirements including specific courses, degrees, examinations, or licenses required. Students should research the average salary range for the career. Have students share their findings in a class discussion about career opportunities.

Here is a list of jobs and educational requirements for careers in travel and transportation.

Jobs Requiring 1 to 2 Years of Technical Training

Road Developer

Mechanic

Computer Operator

Flight Attendant

Merchant Seaman

Electrician

Pipeline Equipment Operator

Inspector

Welder

Air Traffic Controller

Pilot

Jobs Requiring 4 + Years of College

Civil Engineer

Mechanical Engineer

Ship's Officer

Public Relations Specialist

Systems Analyst

Transportation Manager

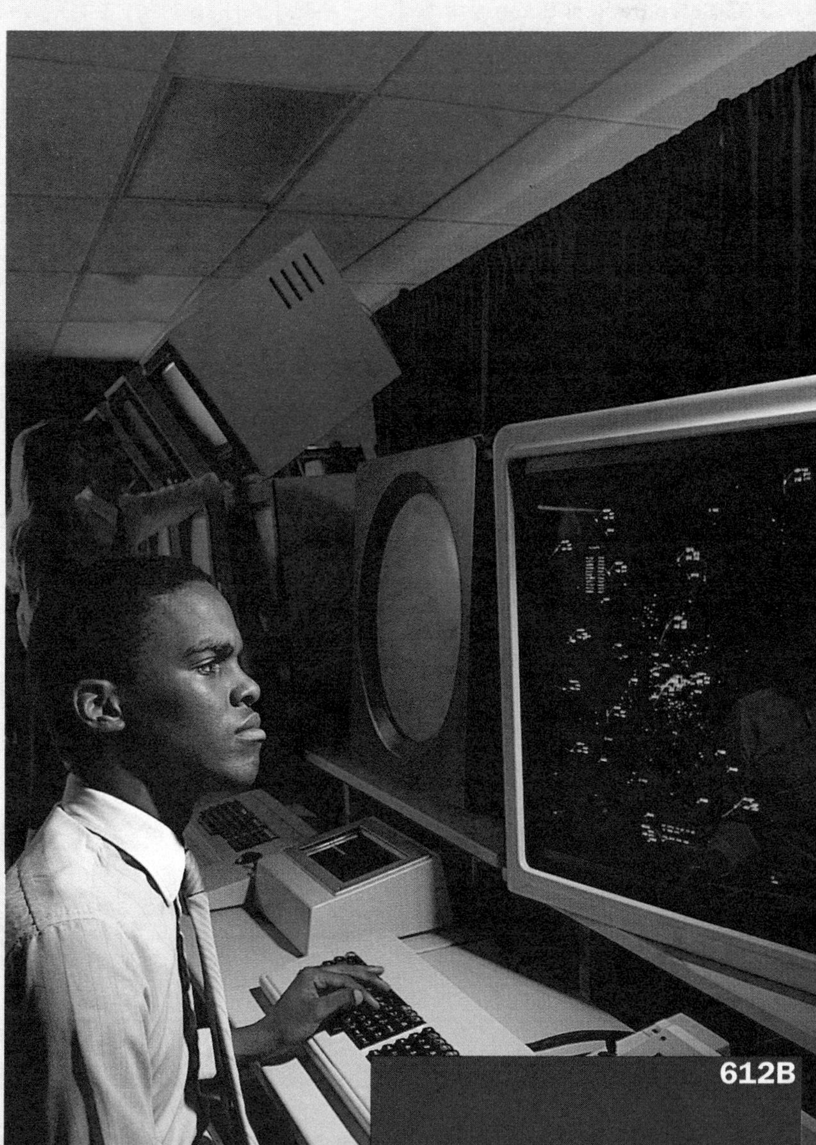

CHAPTER 13 PLANNING GUIDE

Lessons	Text Pages	NCTM Standards	ASSIGNMENTS			Ancillaries	Manipulatives	Technology
			Basic	Average	Enriched			
Chapter Introduction	612–614	1, 2, 3, 4, 5, 6, 10				Video Discussion Guide		Video, Transparency 69
13.1 Algebra Workshop: The Pythagorean Theorem	615–617	1, 2, 3, 4, 5, 8, 14	1–27	1–28	1–29	S 31; M 13	Geoboard, Graph Paper	Transparencies 27, 70
13.2 Triangles and the Pythagorean Theorem	618–624	1, 2, 3, 4, 5, 8	1–9, 12–15, MR16–25, PC1–3, AW1–4	1–10, 12–15, MR16–25, PC1–3, AW1–4	1–15, MR16–25, PC1–3, AW1–4	W 13.2; R 13.2; P 13.2; E 13.2; Q 13.2; S 32; T 30	Protractor, Scissors, Straightedge	Transparencies 70–72
13.3 Multiply and Divide Radicals	625–630	1, 2, 3, 4, 5, 8, 14	1–23, 25–35, MR38–44, AW1–6	3–36, MR38–44, AW1–6	4–37, MR38–44, AW1–6	W 13.3; R 13.3; P 13.3; E 13.3; Q 13.3	Protractor, Dot Paper or Graph Paper	Transparencies 27, 34
13.4 Add and Subtract Radicals	631–635	1, 2, 3, 4, 5, 8	1–17, 19–20, 22–25, 29, MR30–44, PC1–2	3–20, 22–26, 29, MR30–44, PC1–2	4–29, MR30–44, PC1–2	W 13.4; R 13.4; P 13.4; E 13.4; Q 13.4	Geoboard	Calculator, Transparency 27
13.5 Solve Radical Equations	636–641	1, 2, 3, 4, 5, 8	1–23, 27–32, 36, 38–40, 43–46, 48–50, MR52–61	3–41, 43–51, MR52–61	4–51, MR52–61	W 13.5; R 13.5; P 13.5; E 13.5; Q 13.5; T 31		Graphing Utility, Transparencies 78–80
13.6 The Distance and Midpoint Formulas	642–647	1, 2, 3, 4, 5, 8	1–19, 21–25, MR28–40, PC1–2, AW1–4	2–26, MR28–40, PC1–2, AW1–4	3–27, MR28–40, PC1–2, AW1–4	W 13.6: R 13.6: P 13.6: E 13.6: Q 13.6	Graph Paper, Straightedge	Calculator, Transparencies 32, 73, 78–80
13.7 Algebra Workshop: Similar Triangles	648–651	1, 2, 3, 4, 5, 8	1–17	1–17	1–18		Protractor, Ruler	Transparency 8
13.8 Sine, Cosine, and Tangent	652–658	1, 2, 3, 4, 5, 9	1–17, 19, 21–23, MR24–35	3–23, MR24–35	4–23, MR24–35	W 13.8; R 13.8; P 13.8; E 13.8; Q 13.8	Protractor, Straightedge	Graphing Utility, Transparencies 74, 75
13.9 Algebra Workshop: Explore Sine and Cosine Graphs	659–661	1, 2, 3, 4, 5, 6, 9	1–32	1–32	1–33		Graphing Utility	Graphing Utility, Transparencies 34, 74
13.10 Problem Solving File: Use Measures Indirectly	662–665	1, 2, 3, 4, 5, 8, 9	1–17	1–18	1–19	R 13.10; P 13.10		Calculator, Transparencies 10, 70, 74, 75

NCTM STANDARDS

1. Mathematics as Problem Solving
2. Mathematics as Communication
3. Mathematics as Reasoning
4. Mathematical Connections
5. Algebra
6. Functions
7. Geometry from a Synthetic Perspective
8. Geometry from an Algebraic Perspective
9. Trigonometry
10. Statistics
11. Probability
12. Discrete Mathematics
13. Conceptual Underpinnings of Calculus
14. Mathematical Structure

ANCILLARIES

W = Warm Up
R = Reteaching
P = Extra Practice
E = Enrichment
Q = Lesson Quiz
T = Technology Activity
M = Multicultural Connection
S = Study Skills Activity

ADDITIONAL RESOURCES

pplications	Career Connections	Cooperative Learning	Learning Styles	Strand Integration/ Math Connection
	Chapter Poster			
		Paired partners, 615 (Think Back/Working Together)	Tactile, 615, 617; Visual, 615–617; Interpersonal, 615; Kinesthetic, Visual, 616 (TE)	Modeling, Problem Solving, Geometry, Writing, Critical Thinking
lectronics, 621; lealth/Safety, 622	AlgebraWorks: Road Developer, 624	Small groups/TAI, 623 (Project Connection)	Visual, 618–624; Interpersonal, 623	Problem Solving, Geometry, Writing, Critical Thinking
hemistry, 628; eography, 628; eometry, 629; Sports, 28	AlgebraWorks: Highway Engineer, 630		Tactile, 625; Linguistic/Interpersonal, 625; Visual, 625, 628, 630	Modeling, Problem Solving, Geometry, Writing, Critical Thinking, Number Theory
eography, 634; eometry, 633; lealth/Safety, 634; lavigation, 634; Physics, 32, 634; Travel, 634	Police Investigator, 634	Small groups/TAI, 635 (Project Connection)	Tactile, 631; Visual, 631, 634, 635; Linguistic/Interpersonal, 635	Modeling, Problem Solving, Geometry, Writing, Critical Thinking
uto Mechanics, 640; eometry, 639, 641; lumbing, 640; Sports, 38		Paired partners, 636 (Explore/Working Together)	Linguistic/ Interpersonal, 636–637; Visual, 639–641	Problem Solving, Geometry, Writing, Critical Thinking, Technology, Statistics
eometry, 644, 645; lavigation, 645	AlgebraWorks: Air Traffic Controller, 647	Small groups/TAI, 646 (Project Connection)	Visual, 642–647; Linguistic/ Interpersonal, 642, 646	Problem Solving, Geometry, Writing, Critical Thinking, Technology
		Paired partners, 651 (Make Connections)	Visual, 648, 651	Problem Solving, Geometry, Writing
ngineering, 656; urveying, 651; Travel, 58			Visual, 652–658; Linguistic/ Interpersonal, 653; Individual, 652; Linguistic, 653 (TE)	Problem Solving, Geometry, Trigonometry, Writing, Critical Thinking, Technology
			Visual, 659–661	Problem Solving, Trigonometry, Functions, Modeling, Critical Thinking, Writing, Technology
onstruction, 664; eometry, 664; urveying, 663, 664; ravel, 663			Visual, 662–665	Problem Solving, Geometry, Trigonometry, Technology, Logical Reasoning, Patterns

PACING GUIDE

Lessons	Regular Classes	2-year Algebra 1 Classes	Blocked Classes
13.1	1	2	½
13.2	1	2	½
13.3	1	2	½
13.4	1	2	½
13.5	1	2	½
13.6	1	2	½
13.7	1	2	½
13.8	1	2	1
13.9	1	2	½
13.10	1	2	1
Review	1	1	1
Test	1	1	1
Cumulative Test	1	1	1
Total Classes	13	23	9

SESSMENT OPTIONS

udent Edition
apter Assessment
Chapter Test
Performance Assessment
Project Assessment
andardized Tests

Chapter Resource Book
Chapter Test, Form A
Chapter Test, Form B
Standardized Chapter Test
Portfolio Item: Self-Assessment
Portfolio Assessment Form

MicroExam II

PREVIEW THE CHAPTER

Take a Look Ahead Have students read the previewing suggestions and then scan the chapter looking for new and familiar things. Give students time to make notes in their journals. Discuss student answers to the previewing questions.

Connecting to Career Opportunities Have the students read the descriptions of the AlgebraWorks features for this chapter. Ask students to identify the careers mentioned. **road developers, highway engineers, and air traffic controllers** Ask students if they know anyone who works at these jobs. Discuss the types of educational background usually required for each of the careers. For example, highway engineers usually have an undergraduate or graduate degree; air traffic controllers may have a high school diploma and additional training.

Investigate Further Explain to students that as they study this chapter they should look for examples of other careers in travel and transportation as well as careers in other fields. Ask students to determine one way in which algebra can be used in that career. Encourage students to write questions in their journals about other travel and transportation jobs they would like to learn more about.

USING THE DATA ACTIVITY

Introduce the Data Activity Have students read the introductory copy and discuss why the original cost of an automobile dropped significantly during the first few years it was produced, but then the average cost of a new car started to increase again.

Skill Focus Read the skills listed and discuss with students what they think each means. Ask students to suggest problems that might involve the skill being discussed.

13 Geometry and Radical Expressions

Take a Look AHEAD

Make notes about things that look new.

- List the terms that are used to classify triangles according to the lengths of their sides. Make another list of terms that are used to classify triangles according to the measures of their angles.
- Identify the special ratios that are defined for corresponding sides of right triangles.

Make notes about things that look familiar.

- What does the radical symbol mean? What is the expression under the radical symbol called?
- Find a formula from this chapter that uses a radical symbol.
- In everyday language, when you describe two objects or ideas as being "similar," do you mean they are exactly alike? Use the word "similar" in a sentence. Find a sentence in this chapter that uses the word similar. How do you think their meanings compare?

DATA Activity

The Family Car

When Henry Ford began production of the Model T in 1908, the automobile's price was $850. By 1916 the price had dropped to $400 due to Ford's use of mass production methods. Since then, the cost of the average new car sold in the United States has risen significantly, and according to the Commerce Department, family income has not kept pace. The table on the next page shows average new car cost, in terms of the number of weeks' earnings of a median-income family. In addition to sticker price, costs include safety and pollution control equipment, dealer fees, registration fee, and taxes.

SKILL FOCUS

- Add, subtract, multiply, and divide real numbers.
- Interpret graphs.
- Write and solve an equation.
- Interpret the median of a data set.

ALGEBRAWORKS

TRAVEL and TRANSPORTATION

In this chapter, you will see how:

- **ROAD DEVELOPERS** apply the Pythagorean theorem to check that road intersections are perpendicular. (Lesson 13.2, page 624)
- **HIGHWAY ENGINEERS** use a formula involving a radical to design safe curves for freeway on-ramps. (Lesson 13.3, page 630)
- **AIR TRAFFIC CONTROLLERS** use a three-dimensional coordinate system when determining the distance between two airplanes. (Lesson 13.6, page 647)

1–5 See Additional Answers.

Use the table to answer the following questions.

1. In 1983, how many weeks' earnings would a median-income family have had to spend to purchase a new car?
2. How many more weeks' earnings were needed to purchase a new car in 1991 than in 1971?
3. Suppose the average new car price in 1994 was \$21,800. Write and solve an equation to determine the figure that was used as the median family income for that year.
4. If a family's income is below the median level, will the number of weeks' earnings required to purchase a new car be more or less than the weeks shown on the graph?
5. **WORKING TOGETHER** As a group, discuss possible reasons for the decreasing trend shown in the 1970s. Try to confirm your ideas by doing some research.

Study the Data Review the data in the table. You may wish to ask the following questions: What is meant by median income? How many people earn above the median income? **half** How many earn below? **half** Does the graph tell what the median income is for any given year? **no**

Complete the Data Activity Have students work individually or with partners to complete the questions.

For Item 1, be sure the students understand that the table does not tell the median income nor the price of a car for any given year. Instead it tells how many weeks' earnings would be required for a family earning the median income to buy a car with the average new car price for that year.

For Item 2, point out that the answer is obtained by first estimating the number of weeks for 1991 and 1971 and then subtracting.

For Item 3, point out that the graph applies to the *average* new car price for each given year. In 1991, if a median-income family decided to purchase a car with a price lower than the average price of \$21,800, then fewer weeks' earnings would be required.

For Item 4, students must realize that the graph applies to families earning exactly the median income. For families earning above the median income, fewer weeks' earnings would be required.

For Item 5, point out that many factors might contribute to the decreasing trend. Probably no one factor alone would account for the decrease.

South-Western Algebra 1
Chapter Theme Video or Videodisc

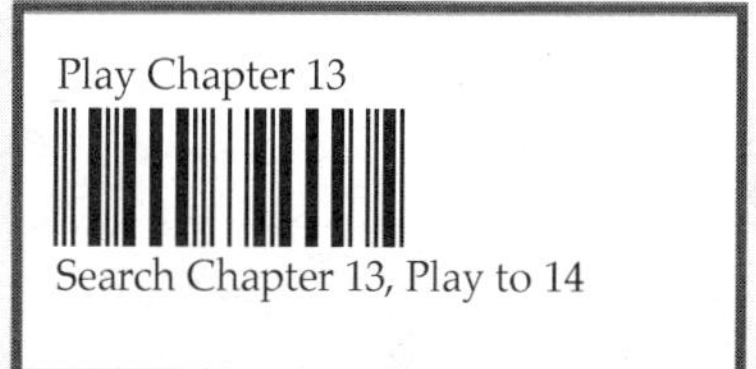

Play Chapter 13
Search Chapter 13, Play to 14

INTRODUCING THE PROJECT

Project Goal Discuss the project's big idea: How can information relating to automobiles be analyzed?

Getting Ready Collect several automotive magazines, as well as the automotive classified sections from several newspapers and consumer magazines. Also collect articles that pertain to cars, including topics such as car insurance, safety records, or car maintenance.

FACILITATING THE PROJECT

Getting Started Use automotive magazines as a springboard for discussion as to what kinds of cars students like. Suggest that students pick a car for which information is more readily available.

Setting Project Benchmarks Make sure that the students are aware of the project schedule in the Project Planning Calendar and the due dates for each of the benchmarks. You may find the TAI cooperative learning approach appropriate for this activity.

a. Collect newspaper ads and car dealer information for used cars of specific makes and model years. (Project/Chapter Opener)

b. Determine mean price, mode price, and percent of decrease from original price for cars being studied. (Project Connection 13.2)

c. Determine the maximum length of a package that will fit in the trunk of a car. (Project Connection 13.4)

d. Determine the distances and gasoline expenses along a triangular travel route. (Project Connection 13.6)

e. Design an ad for each used car being studied. (Project Assessment)

Suggest that students make subgoals for each goal and include subgoals in their calendar.

PROJECT

You "Auto" Find Out

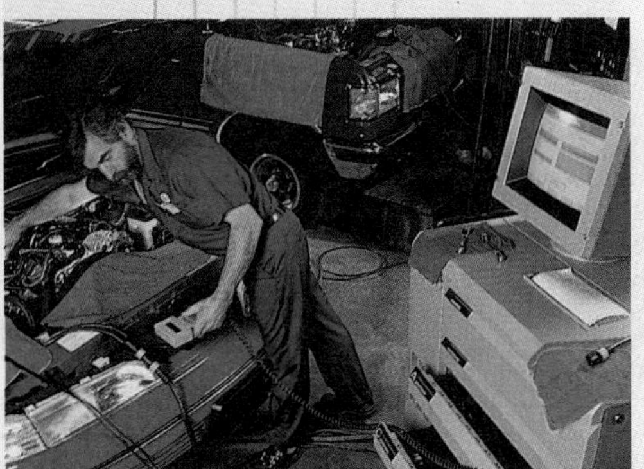

They cost many thousands of dollars to purchase, insure, and maintain, yet Americans own about 200,000,000 of them. People spend several hours each day inside them, possibly eating, listening to music, or talking on the telephone. No, it's not your home, it's your automobile, and it's the object under investigation in this project.

PROJECT GOAL

To analyze information relating to automobiles.

Getting Started

Work in groups.

1. Each group member should offer the name, make, and model year of a car for which he or she will collect information. This car might belong to a family member or a friend. Explain to the owners that you will need their help as you work on your project for the next few weeks.
2. Make a chart showing the cars to be analyzed by the group. List the options for each car, such as air conditioning, power windows, and stereo.
3. For the next two weeks, each group member should read the automotive classified section of one or more newspapers to find advertisements for cars of the same make and model year for sale. Collect the advertisements and bring them to the next group meeting. Some students should go to a car dealer and obtain prices.
4. Make a list of the abbreviations used in the advertisements. Explain the meaning of each abbreviation.

PROJECT Connections

Lesson 13.2, page 623:
Analyze data about features and prices of used cars.
Lesson 13.4, page 635:
Determine the maximum length of a package that will fit in a car's trunk.
Lesson 13.6, page 646:
Plan a triangular travel route, then determine distances and gasoline expense.
Chapter Assessment, page 669:
Use the information from the project to design classified advertisements for the used cars studied.

13.1 Algebra Workshop
The Pythagorean Theorem

Think Back/Working Together

Work with a partner.

1. Explain how this figure shows that $3^2 = 9$. See Additional Answers.

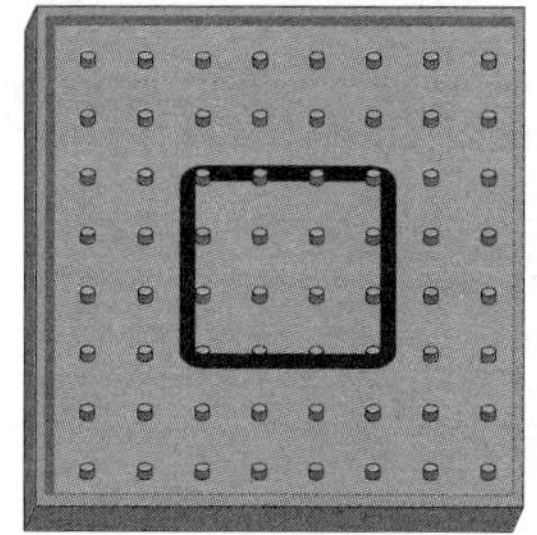

2. Explain how this figure shows that $\sqrt{4} = 2$. See Additional Answers.

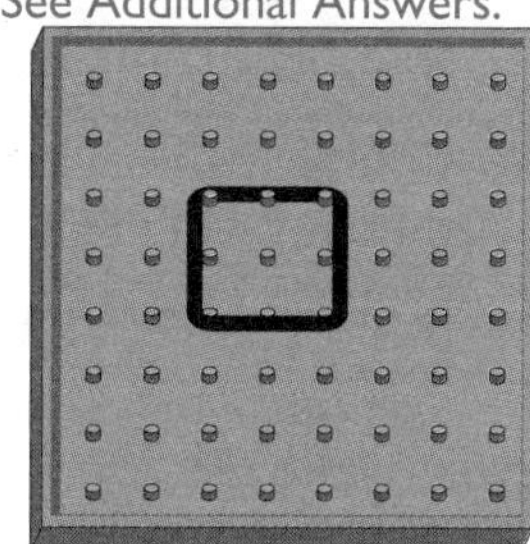

Find the area of each square. You may have to divide a square into smaller figures, calculate the area of each smaller figure, and then add to find the total area.

3.

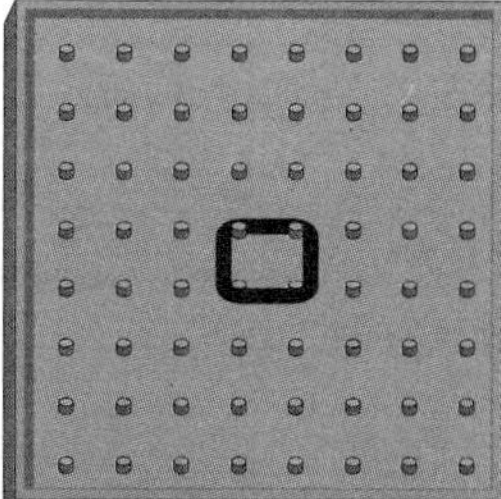

1 square unit

4.

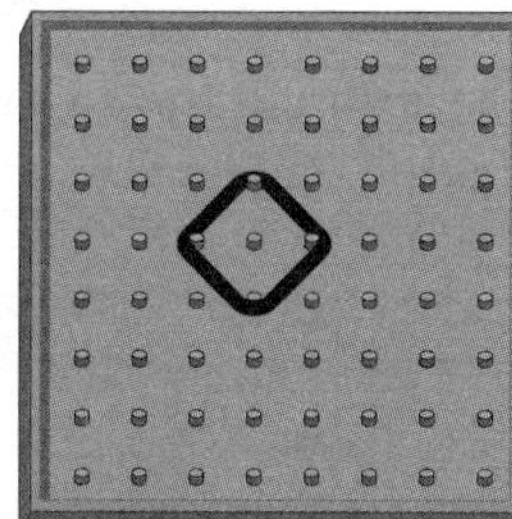

2 square units

5.

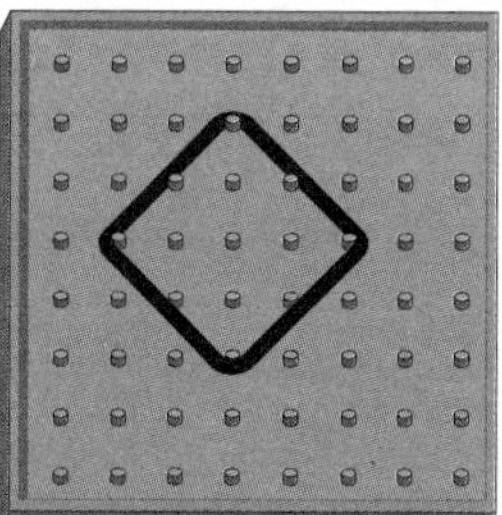

8 square units

Explore

6. Using graph paper, cut out three squares: 3×3, 4×4, and 5×5. Arrange the squares as shown at the right. Notice the triangle formed by this placement of the squares is a right triangle.

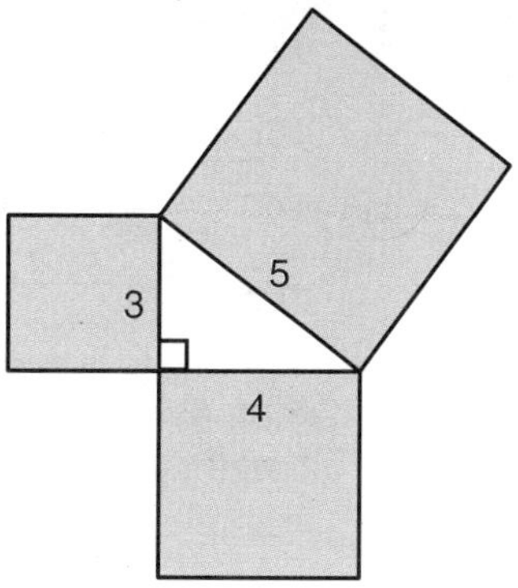

3
4
5

7. Find the area of each square in the figure. 9, 16, 25

Repeat Questions 6 and 7 for triangles with the following dimensions. Make a table of your results.

8. 5–12–13 25, 144, 169
9. 6–8–10 36, 64, 100
10. 8–15–17 64, 225, 289
11. Repeat Questions 6 and 7 for a triangle with dimensions of your choosing. Answers will vary.

SPOTLIGHT ON LEARNING

WHAT? In this lesson you will learn
- to use squares and square roots to find the lengths of the sides of a right triangle.

WHY? Finding the lengths of the sides of a right triangle helps you solve problems in geometry.

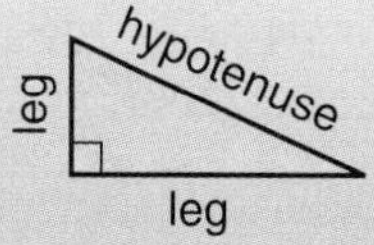

THINK BACK

A right triangle has a 90° angle. The side opposite the 90° angle is called the *hypotenuse*. The other two sides are called *legs*.

hypotenuse
leg
leg

LESSON PLANNING

Objective

▶ Use squares and square roots to find the lengths of the sides of a right triangle.

Vocabulary

Converse of the Pythagorean Theorem
Pythagorean Theorem
Pythagorean triples

Resources

Transparencies 27, 70
Student Handbook
Study Skills 31
Multicultural Connection 13, African: Focus on Pyramids

Materials/Manipulatives

graph paper
Geoboard

ASSIGNMENTS

Basic: 1–27

Average: 1–28

Enriched: 1–29

1 MOTIVATE

Think Back/Working Together Ask a student to explain how to show that $\sqrt{4} = 2$. **The area of a square equals the square of one side, $A = s^2$, so $\sqrt{A} = \sqrt{s^2}$ and $\sqrt{A} = s$. Since the square has an area of 4 square units and a side of 2 units, $\sqrt{4} = 2$.** Ask students how they found the area for each square. **Count the number of square units in each.**

2 FACILITATE

Explore For Question 7, ask how students found the area of each square. **counted the total number of square units or counted the number of units on a side and squared it**

DIVERSITY IN THE CLASSROOM

Kinesthetic/Visual Learners Students who do not understand that the sum of the squares of the legs of a right triangle equals the square of the hypotenuse may benefit from cutting out the squares of the legs. Then have them cut up the squares to fit them over the square of the hypotenuse.

Make Connections If students are having difficulty finding the relationship between the area of the largest square and the areas of the two smaller squares, suggest that they try adding, subtracting, multiplying, and dividing to look for a relationship.

For Question 13, students may answer that they squared each number to get the areas or they squared the numbers for each leg and then found their sum to get the area of the square of the hypotenuse. Have students read Question 14 and the section following. Students should note that the Pythagorean Theorem is true for right triangles only.

3 SUMMARIZE

Modeling For Question 26, ask students what they are being asked to show. **that the sum of the squares of the legs is equal to the square of the hypotenuse** Ask them to compare the two triangles of each square on the legs to the shaded triangle. **They are the same size and shape**

Algebra Workshop

ALGEBRA: WHO, WHERE, WHEN

Pythagoras (6th century B.C.) founded a secret society for the study of mathematics, philosophy, and natural science. So closely did the Pythagoreans guard their secrets that, according to legend, one member of the society, Hippasus, was drowned at sea for revealing the existence of irrational numbers.

The Pythagorean theorem, named after Pythagoras, was discovered at least 3000 years ago. Pythagoras made the first systematic study of the relationship stated in the theorem.

Make Connections

12. Examine the results of your exploration. For each triangle, what is the relationship between the area of the largest square and the areas of the two smaller squares? The area of the largest square equals the sum of the areas of the two smaller squares.

13. Suppose that you built squares on each leg of a 7–24–25 right triangle. Predict the areas of the squares. Explain how you made your prediction. See Additional Answers.

14. Complete the following statement: In a right triangle, the square of the length of the hypotenuse is equal to __?__ the squares of the lengths of the two legs. the sum of

The relationship between the sides of a right triangle is known as the *Pythagorean theorem.*

PYTHAGOREAN THEOREM

If a right triangle has lengths *a* and *b*, and a hypotenuse of length *c*, then

$$a^2 + b^2 = c^2$$

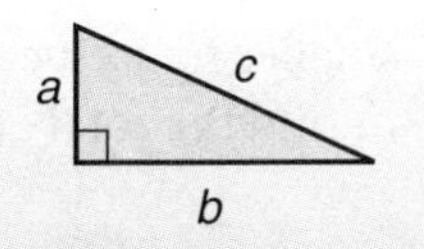

In Exercises 15–20, substitute known values in the equation $a^2 + b^2 = c^2$. Find the length of the missing side of each right triangle.

	Leg 1	Leg 2	Hypotenuse	
15.	3	4	■	5
16.	5	12	■	13
17.	■	12	15	9
18.	8	■	17	15
19.	■	40	41	9
20.	m	n	■	$\sqrt{m^2 + n^2}$

Suppose you know the length of the sides of a triangle. Substitute the lengths in the equation $a^2 + b^2 = c^2$. If this equation is true, then the triangle is a right triangle. This rule is called the *converse* of the Pythagorean theorem. So, you can use the converse of the Pythagorean theorem to determine if any triangle is a right triangle when you know the lengths of the sides.

Converse of the Pythagorean Theorem

Let *a*, *b*, and *c* represent the lengths of the sides of a triangle. If $a^2 + b^2 = c^2$, then the triangle is a right triangle.

The lengths of the sides of a triangle are given. State whether the triangle is a right triangle.

	Side 1	Side 2	Side 3	
21.	6	8	10	yes
22.	4	6	7	no
23.	2.5	6	6.5	yes
24.	12	35	37	yes
25.	14	22	26	no

Summarize

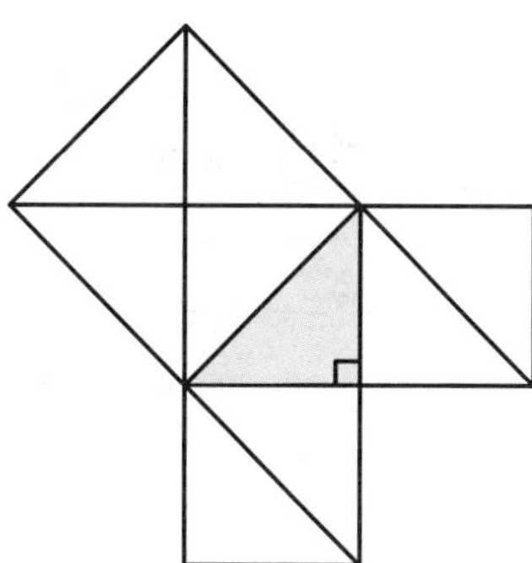

26. MODELING Explain how the figure at the right demonstrates the Pythagorean theorem as it relates to the shaded triangle. See Additional Answers.

27. WRITING MATHEMATICS Write a word problem that can be solved using the Pythagorean theorem. Then solve the problem. Answers will vary.

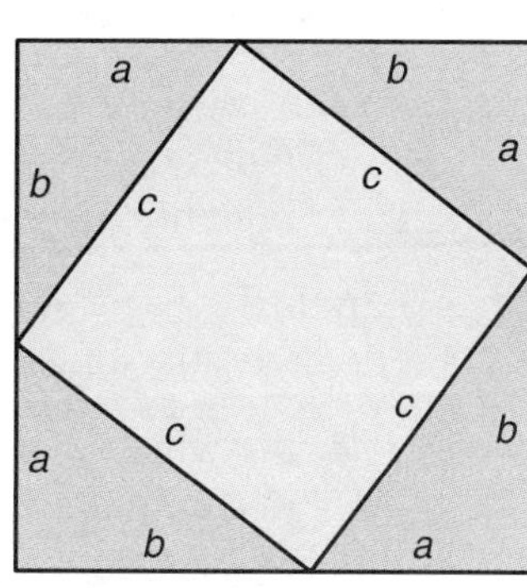

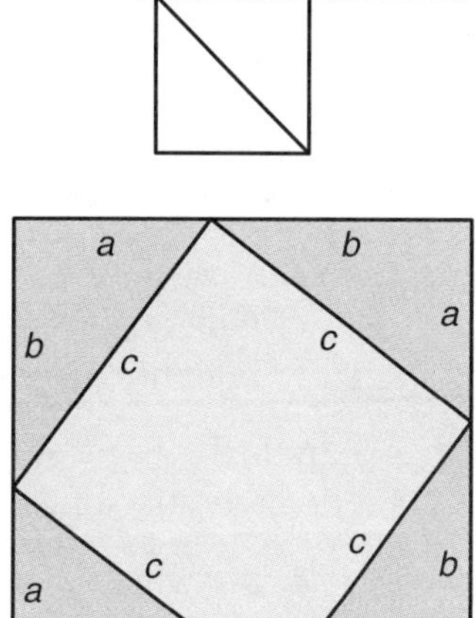

28. THINKING CRITICALLY Four right triangles with sides measuring *a*, *b*, and *c* are arranged to form a square as shown. Write the area of the large square as the sum of the areas of the four right triangles and smaller square. Set this sum equal to the area of the large square, $(a + b)^2$, and show that your results confirm the Pythagorean theorem. See Additional Answers.

29. GOING FURTHER A set of integers like {3, 4, 5} or {5, 12, 13} which satisfy the Pythagorean theorem is called a **Pythagorean triple**. Explore whether multiples (including fractional multiples) of Pythagorean triples are also Pythagorean triples. Describe your work and summarize your results. Methods will vary.

Writing Mathematics For Question 27, have students share their word problems with partners and solve their partners' problems.

Thinking Critically For Question 28, ask students to explain why the area of the large square is $(a + b)^2$. **because the length of each side of the large square is $(a + b)$**

Going Further For Question 29, ask students to discuss what they have discovered about Pythagorean triples. **Any multiple of a Pythagorean triple is itself a Pythagorean triple.** Have interested students evaluate the expressions $p^2 - q^2$, $2pq$, and $p^2 + q^2$ for different values of p and q and record their findings in a table. Ask what relationship they notice. **For all positive whole-number values greater than 1 of $p > q$, the expressions yield a Pythagorean triple.**

4 FOLLOW-UP

Other Explorations Have students consider the following figure.

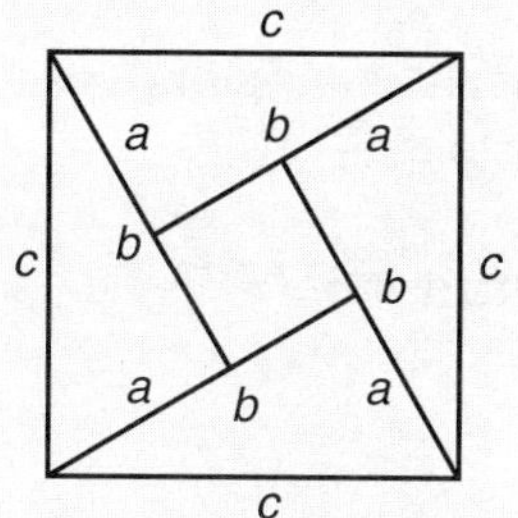

Ask them what the length of each side of the small square is. **$b - a$ units** Have students explain how the figure demonstrates the Pythagorean theorem. **The area of the large square is equal to the sum of the areas of the four triangles and of the small square.**

LESSON PLANNING

Objectives

- Classify triangles according to side lengths and angle measures.
- Solve problems involving sides and angles of triangles.

Vocabulary

acute triangle
complementary angles
equilateral triangle
isosceles triangle
obtuse triangle
Pythagorean relationships
right triangle
scalene triangle
supplementary angles

Resources

Warm Up 13.2
Reteaching 13.2
Extra Practice 13.2
Enrichment 13.2
Transparencies 70, 71, 72
Student Handbook
Lesson Quiz 13.2
Study Skills 32
Technology Activity 30

Materials/Manipulatives

protractor
scissors
straightedge

ASSIGNMENTS

Basic: 1–9, 12–15, Mixed Review 16–25, Project Connection 1–3, AlgebraWorks 1–4

Average: 1–10, 12–15, Mixed Review 16–25, Project Connection 1–3, AlgebraWorks 1–4

Enriched: 1–15, Mixed Review 16–25, Project Connection 1–3, AlgebraWorks 1–4

13.2 Triangles and the Pythagorean Theorem

SPOTLIGHT ON LEARNING

WHAT? In this lesson you will learn

- to classify triangles according to side lengths and angle measures.
- to solve problems involving sides and angles of triangles.

WHY? Understanding the relationship between angle and side measures of triangles can help you solve problems in electronics and home safety.

Explore

Square the measures of each side of each triangle below. Copy and complete the table.

1.
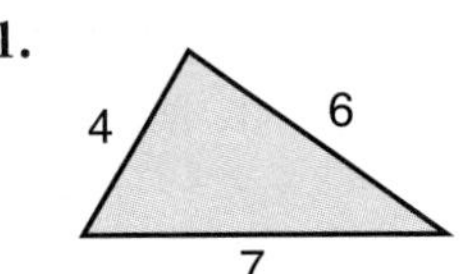

2.
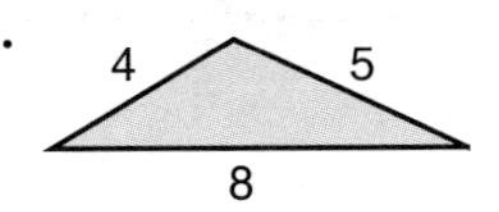

3.
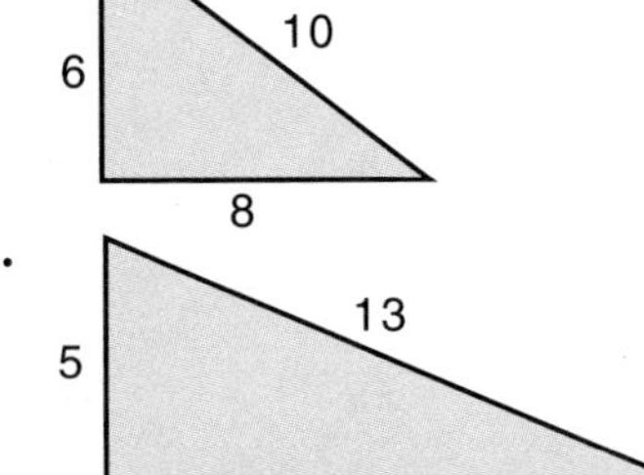

4.
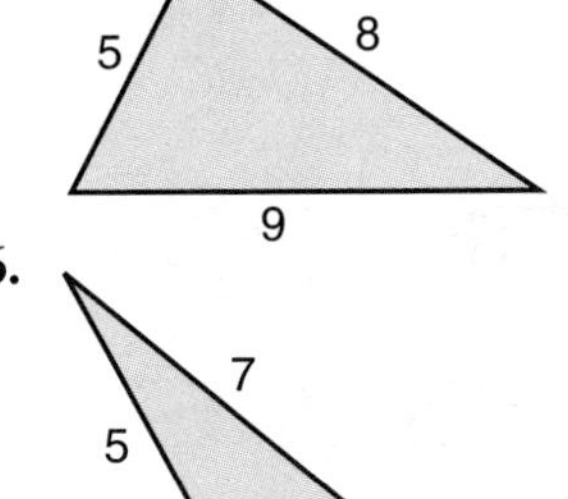

5.
5
13
12

6.
7
5
3

	Square of a short side (a^2)	Square of a short side (b^2)	Square of the longest side (c^2)	
1.				16, 36, 49
2.				16, 25, 64
3.				36, 64, 10
4.				25, 64, 81
5.				25, 144, 1
6.				9, 25, 49

7. Measure the angles of the triangles. Which of the triangles has a right angle? Which have an obtuse angle? Which have neither a right nor an obtuse angle? 3 and 5; 2 and 6; 1 and 4

THINK BACK

The measure of an acute angle is between 0° and 90°. The measure of a right angle is exactly 90°. The measure of an obtuse angle is between 90° and 180°.

In the Pythagorean theorem $a^2 + b^2 = c^2$, c is the hypotenuse, which is always the longest side of a right triangle.

8. For which triangles is $a^2 + b^2 = c^2$? What do these triangles have in common? 3 and 5; each has a right angle

9. For which triangles is $a^2 + b^2 < c^2$? What do these triangles have in common? 2 and 6; they have an obtuse angle

10. For which triangles is $a^2 + b^2 > c^2$? What do these triangles have in common? 1 and 4; they have neither an obtuse nor a right angle

Build Understanding

Triangles can be classified according to the measures of their angles.

An **acute triangle** has three acute angles.

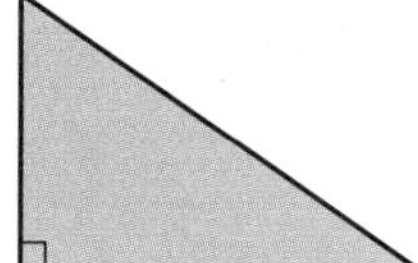
A **right triangle** has one right angle.

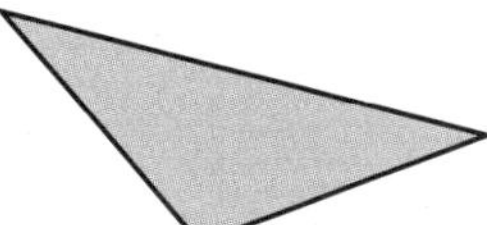
An **obtuse triangle** has one obtuse angle.

Triangles can be classified according to the length of their sides.

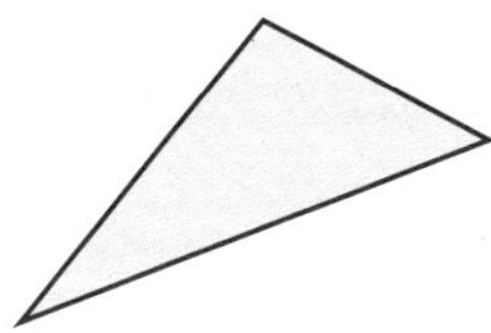
A **scalene triangle** has no sides equal in length.

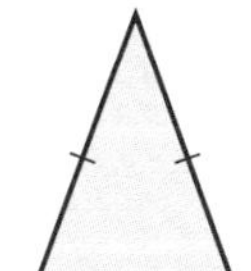
An **isosceles triangle** has at least two sides equal in length.

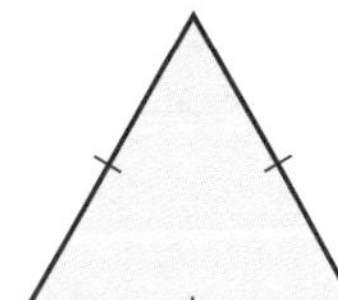
An **equilateral triangle** has three sides equal in length.

In an isosceles triangle, the measures of the angles opposite the equal sides are equal. In an equilateral triangle, the measures of all three angles are equal.

Triangle *PQR* can be written ΔPQR.

Classify each triangle according to its side lengths and angle measures.

a.
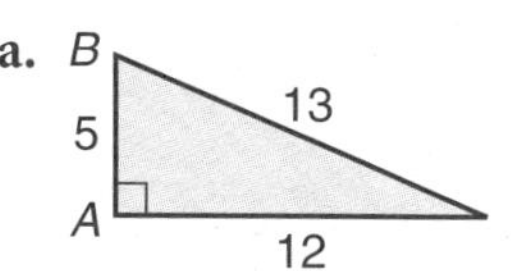

b.
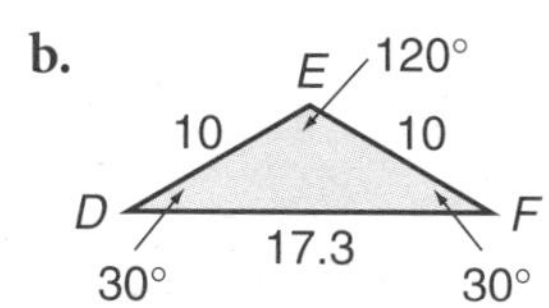

c.
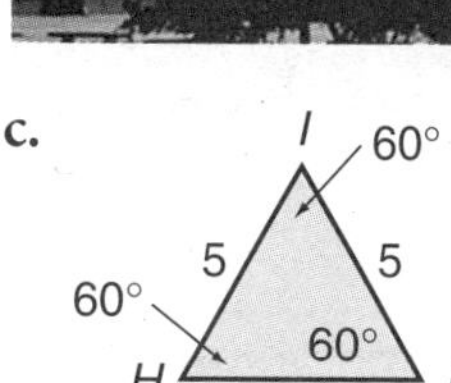

Solution

a. ΔABC has no sides equal and contains a right angle. It is scalene and right.

b. ΔDEF has two equal sides and one obtuse angle. It is isosceles and obtuse.

c. ΔHIJ has three equal sides and three equal angles. It is equilateral and acute. ◄

1 MOTIVATE

Explore Students should read Think Back before answering Question 7.

For Questions 8–10, have students draw other triangles of their own choosing. Then have them summarize the findings. **Students should conclude that the Pythagorean relationships on page 620 are true.**

2 TEACH

Use the Pages/Build Understanding Use the diagrams on page 619 to lead students to notice a relation between angle measure and length of the side opposite it. They should notice that if a triangle's sides are equal in measure, then so are its angles. They should notice that a scalene triangle has no angles equal. Help students to see that the longest side is opposite the biggest angle and that the shortest side is opposite the smallest angle.

Example 1: After students have discussed the examples, ask them if they can classify a triangle with one side measuring 12 cm, one angle measuring 70°, and the other two angles each measuring 55°. **Yes, the triangle is acute isosceles. It is acute because all the angle measures are less than 90°. It is isosceles because the measures of angles opposite the equal sides are equal.**

Example 2: Ask students if they can let $a = 24$, $b = 9$, and $c = 17$. Have them explain why or why not. **No, c must be the longest side to use the Pythagorean relationship.**

Ask students if they can assume that whenever $a^2 + b^2 < c^2$ the triangle is obtuse. Have students experiment with several acute, right, and obtuse triangles until they realize the Pythagorean relationships and their converses are true.

Manipulatives Have students draw and cut out a triangle with sides and angles of their own choosing. Have them fold the vertices together so that they meet at a point on one side of the triangle. Ask what they can conclude about the sum of the measures of the angles of a triangle. **The sum of the measures of the angles of a triangle must equal 180° since three angles form a 180° angle.**

Example 3: Before students read the solution, ask how they can find the measure of $\angle N$. **Since the sum of the measures of a triangle is 180°, you can set up an equation and solve for m $\angle N$.**

Ask students to explain why an angle measuring 90 – *x* is a complement of an angle measuring *x*. **Angles are complementary if the sum of their measures is 90. Since (90 – *x*) + *x* = 90, the two angles are complementary.**

Example 4: Stress the importance of defining the variable and writing an expression for the supplement.

Ongoing Assessment The important concepts and skills are classifying triangles according to side lengths and angle measures and solving problems involving sides and angles of triangles. To assess these ideas, have students demonstrate how they have applied these concepts and skills in Exercises 1, 8, and 10 of the Try These section.

Guided Practice/Try These For Exercise 2, ask students if they would have been able to classify the triangle if the side lengths had not been given. **Yes, two of the angle measures are equal and one angle is 90°, so the triangle is right isosceles.** After students have classified the triangle in Exercise 3, ask if they can classify the triangle using just angle measures and if so why. **Yes; none of the angle measures are equal, so the triangle must be scalene.**

For triangles having side *c* as the longest side, the following are true.

PYTHAGOREAN RELATIONSHIPS

If $a^2 + b^2 > c^2$, then the triangle is acute.
If $a^2 + b^2 = c^2$, then the triangle is right.
If $a^2 + b^2 < c^2$, then the triangle is obtuse.

EXAMPLE 2

Use the Pythagorean relationships to classify a triangle having side lengths 9, 17, and 24.

Solution

Let $a = 9$, $b = 17$, and $c = 24$. Then $a^2 = 81$, $b^2 = 289$, and $c^2 = 576$. Since $81 + 289 < 576$, the triangle is obtuse. ◄

For any triangle, regardless of how the triangle is classified by side lengths and angle measures, the following is true.

SUM OF THE ANGLES OF A TRIANGLE

The sum of the measures of the angles of a triangle is 180°.

Angle *Q* can be written $\angle Q$. The measure of $\angle Q$ can be written as $m\angle Q$.

EXAMPLE 3

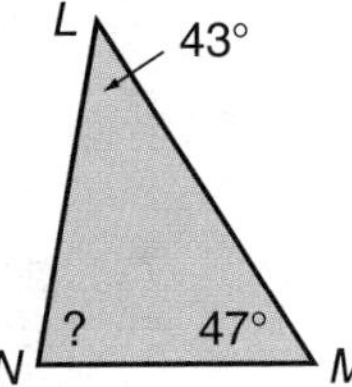

CITY PLANNING Roy is surveying a triangular plot of land for a city park. He determined that $m\angle L = 43°$ and $m\angle M = 47°$. Find $m\angle N$ and classify the triangle.

Solution

$$m\angle L + m\angle M + m\angle N = 180 \quad \text{Sum of the measures of the angles is } 180°.$$
$$43 + 47 + m\angle N = 180$$
$$90 + m\angle N = 180$$
$$m\angle N = 90$$

The measure of $\angle N$ is 90°. So, ΔLMN is a right triangle. ◄

As you could see in Example 3, ΔLMN is a right triangle and the sum of its two acute angles is 90°. Another way to say this is that the two acute angles are *complements* of each other.

COMPLEMENTARY ANGLES

A pair of angles is *complementary* if their sum is 90°. Each angle is said to be the *complement* of the other.

Another special pair of angles are *supplements* of each other.

SUPPLEMENTARY ANGLES

A pair of angles is *supplementary* if their sum is 180°. Each angle is said to be a *supplement* of the other.

EXAMPLE 4

The measure of an angle is 60° less than its supplement. Determine the measure of the two angles.

Solution

Let x equal the measure of the angle. Then $180 - x$ equals the measure of its supplement.

$$\begin{aligned} x &= (180 - x) - 60 \\ x &= 120 - x \\ 2x &= 120 \\ x &= 60 \end{aligned}$$

The measure of the angle is 60°. The measure of its complement is 120°. ◄

TRY THESE

Classify each triangle according to the lengths of its sides and the measures of its angles.

1. 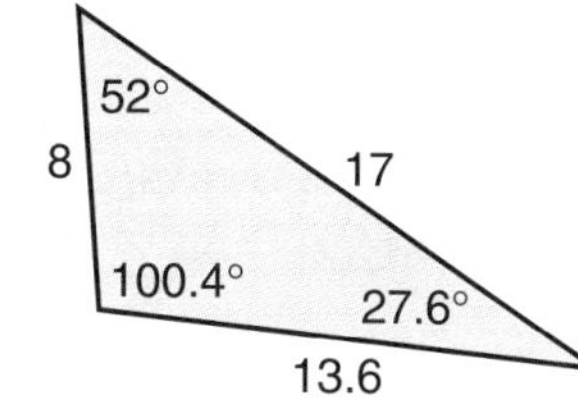

obtuse, scalene

2. 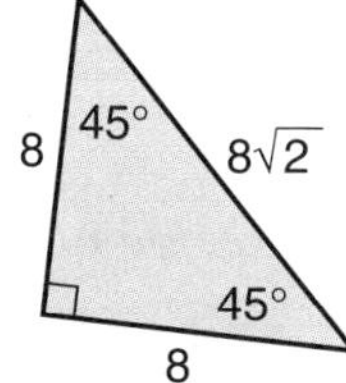 

right, isosceles

3. 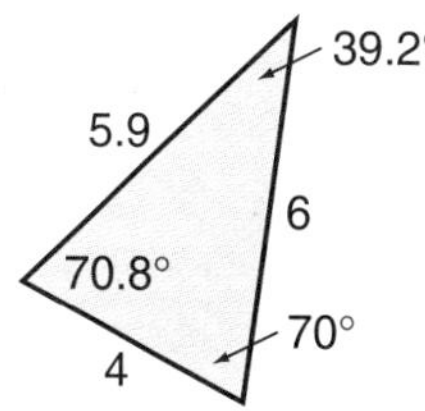

acute, scalene

Determine the measure of the third angle for each triangle.

4. m∠C = 42, m∠D = 81 57°
5. m∠C = 79, m∠D = 34 67°
6. m∠C = 108, m∠D = 29 43°
7. m∠C = 44, m∠D = 46 90°
8. In isosceles triangle RST, m∠R = 34, and m∠S = m∠T. Determine the measures of angles S and T. 73°
9. In right triangle NQR, one acute angle is 6° greater than three times the measure of its complement. Determine the measure of each angle. 90°, 69°, 21°

Use the Pythagorean relationship to classify each triangle .

10. 45, 108, 117 right
11. 39, 80, 90 obtuse
12. 15, 23, 24 acute
13. 80, 192, 208 right

3 SUMMARIZE

In the Math Journal Have students write a paragraph to answer the following questions.

1. Can a triangle be both obtuse and right? Explain. **No; if a triangle is obtuse and right, one angle has a measure greater than 90° and another angle is equal to 90°. The sum of just those two angles is greater than 180°. Since the sum of all three angles must equal 180°, an obtuse right triangle cannot exist.**
2. Can you classify triangles if you are given no angle measures and only the lengths of the three sides? Explain. **Yes, you can use the Pythagorean relationships.**

4 PRACTICE

Practice Have students share their work for Exercises 4–6.

Extend For Exercise 9 make sure that students use correct ratios for the sides of the triangle. AB:BC:AC is $1:\sqrt{3}:2$. Ask students what ratio they used to solve Exercise 9. $\frac{1}{\sqrt{3}} = \frac{x}{50.2}$, $x = 28.9829\ldots$ One way to solve Exercise 11 is to find the length of BC determine the length of the diagonal of the longer face. $\sqrt{10^2 + 65^2} \approx 65.76$ Then use the Pythagorean theorem again to determine the diagonal. $\sqrt{10^2 + 65.76^2} \approx 66.52$

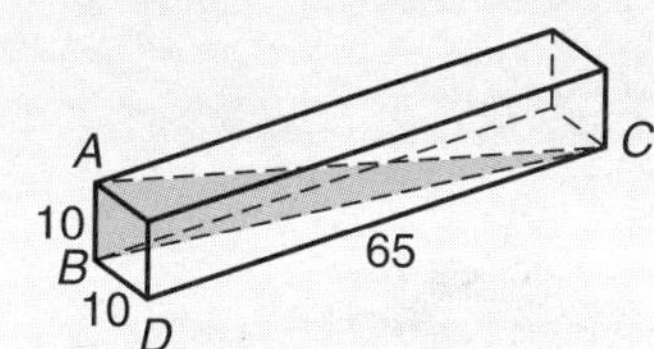

Think Critically Have students discuss their examples for Exercises 13 and 14. **Possible examples: (13)4, 7, and 9; (14)8, 9, 10**

5 FOLLOW-UP

Extension Have students work with partners to explore finding approximations for irrational square roots by following these steps.

- Draw right ΔABC with legs AB and BC each 1 cm in length. Use the Pythagorean theorem to determine the length of the hypotenuse $\overline{AC}$ **$\sqrt{2}$ cm**

NAME ______________ CLASS ________ DATE ________

RETEACHING

13.2 TRIANGLES AND THE PYTHAGOREAN THEOREM

The sum of the measures of a triangle is 180°. You can use this fact to determine unknown angle measures of a triangle.

Example
An obtuse isosceles triangle has one angle measure equal to 20°. What are the measures of the other angles of the triangle?

Solution
The triangle is isosceles, so two of the angle measures must be equal. There are two possibilities.

1. The other two angles have equal measures.

$180 = 20 + x + x$
$180 = 20 + 2x$
$160 = 2x$
$80 = x$
Angle measures: 20°, 80°, 80°

2. One of the two angles is equal to 20°.

$180 = 20 + 20 + x$
$180 = 40 + x$
$140 = x$
Angle measures: 20°, 20°, 140°

The triangle is obtuse, so one angle measure must be greater than 90°. The missing measures are 20° and 140°.

EXERCISES

Solve Exercises 1–3 for right triangle *ABC*.

1. If the measure of $\angle A$ is 37°, determine the measures of $\angle B$ and $\angle C$. 1. **53°, 90°**
2. If ΔABC is isosceles and the measure of $\angle C$ is 90°, determine the measures of $\angle A$ and $\angle B$. 2. **45°, 45°**
3. If the measure of $\angle A$ is half the measure of $\angle C$, and $\angle B$ is a right angle, determine the measure of each angle.
m – A = 30°, m – B = 90°, m – C = 60°

Solve Exercises 4–6 for each triangle.

4. ΔXYZ is an acute isosceles triangle. If the measure of $\angle Z$ is 32°, determine the measures of $\angle X$ and $\angle Y$. 4. **74°, 74°**
5. If ΔPQR is an obtuse scalene triangle and the measure of $\angle P$ is 95°, classify $\angle Q$ and $\angle R$. 5. **acute angles**
6. If ΔDEF is an acute isosceles triangle and the measure of $\angle D$ is 12°, determine the measures of $\angle E$ and $\angle F$. 6. **84°, 84°**

6 *South-Western Algebra 1: AN INTEGRATED APPROACH*

14. **ELECTRONICS** A guy wire attached to the top of a 200-ft radio antenna is bolted to the ground 75 ft from the base of the tower. Find the length of the guy wire to the nearest tenth. 213.6 ft
15. **HOME SAFETY** Safety experts recommend that the bottom of a 12-ft ladder should be at least 4 ft from the base of the wall. How high can the ladder safely reach? 11.3 ft
16. **WRITING MATHEMATICS** Assume you want to build a rectangular picture frame and hold it steady with a diagonal brace. Describe at least two ways by which you could test to see whether you have a true rectangle. See Additional Answers.

PRACTICE

Classify each triangle as either *acute, right,* or *obtuse* and as either *scalene, isosceles,* or *equilateral.*

1. 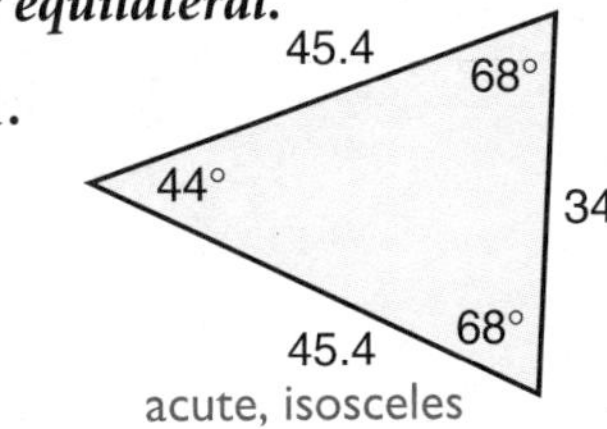

acute, isosceles

2. 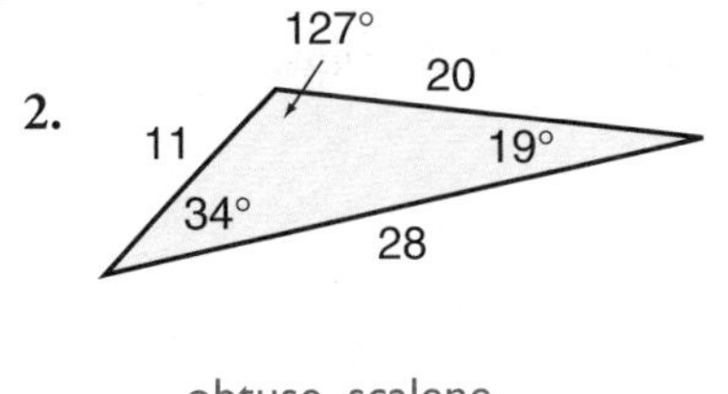

obtuse, scalene

3. 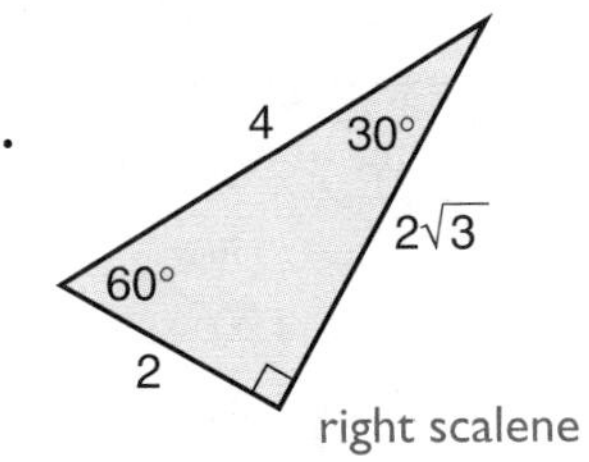

right scalene

4. In isosceles triangle ABC, if the measure of $\angle A$ is 92°, determine the measures of $\angle B$ and $\angle C$. 44°
5. In isosceles triangle DEF, the measure of each angle is a whole number of degrees. If one angle measures 35°, what are the measures of the other two angles? 35° and 110°
6. The measures of angles G and H are equal. If the measure of $\angle I$ is twice the measure of each of the other angles, determine each angle and describe the triangle. 45°, 45°, 90°; it is a right isosceles triangle
7. **WRITING MATHEMATICS** The measures of the angles of a triangle can be three consecutive integers. They can also be three consecutive even integers. Can the measures of the angles of a triangle be three consecutive odd integers? Explain your reasoning. they cannot: the sum of three odd numbers is odd, and 180 is even

EXTEND

A SPECIAL RIGHT TRIANGLE In right triangle ABC with 30° and 60° angles, the ratio of the side lengths is $1 : \sqrt{3} : 2$.

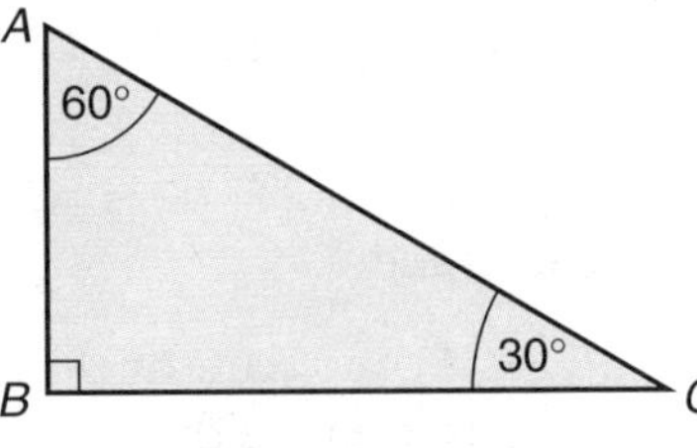

8. Name the sides of ΔABC in order from shortest to longest. $\overline{AB}, \overline{BC}, \overline{AC}$
9. **SHADOWS** Side $\overline{AB}$ represents a tree and $\overline{BC}$ the shadow it casts at a particular time of day. If the length of the shadow is 50.2 ft, how tall is the tree to the nearest tenth of a foot? 29 ft
10. In ΔPRS, the measure of $\angle P$ is 10° less than two-thirds the measure of $\angle R$. The measure of $\angle S$ is 3° greater than twice the measure of $\angle R$. Find the measures of the angles. $m\angle P = 24°, m\angle R = 51°, m\angle S = 105°$
11. **PACKING** Can a 66.5-in. fishing rod be packed in the carton shown at the right without bending the rod? Explain your reasoning. See Additional Answers.

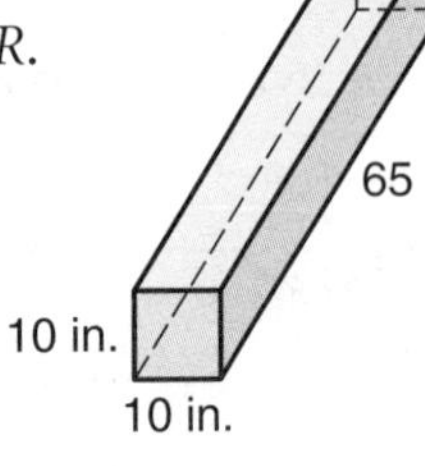

THINK CRITICALLY

12. PYTHAGOREAN TRIPLES Pythagorean triples are integers a, b, and c such that $a^2 + b^2 = c^2$. They can be generated using a formula known to the ancient Greeks. Where x is any odd whole number, the following numbers will always be a Pythagorean triple.

$$x, \frac{x^2 - 1}{2}, \frac{x^2 + 1}{2}$$

Verify the rule by applying the Pythagorean theorem to the three expressions. Assume that $\frac{(x^2 + 1)}{2}$ is the greatest number. See Additional Answers.

CREATING TRIANGLES In Exercises 13–15, make up side lengths for triangles that meet the given descriptions. (If necessary, round to the nearest hundredth.) In each case, explain how you know that you are correct. See Additional Answers.

13. obtuse and scalene **14.** acute and scalene **15.** acute and isosceles

MIXED REVIEW

Evaluate each expression. Lesson 2.3

16. $|12|$ 12 **17.** $-|17|$ −17 **18.** $|-41|$ 41

19. STANDARDIZED TESTS 30 is C; Lesson 3.5

A. 25% of 150 **B.** 20% of 140 **C.** 150% of 20 **D.** 150% of 25

Solve each system using the elimination method. Lesson 7.4

20. $\begin{cases} 3x - y = 2 \\ 2x + 3y = 16 \end{cases}$ 2, 4 **21.** $\begin{cases} x - y = 1 \\ 2x - y = 8 \end{cases}$ 7, 6 **22.** $\begin{cases} 4x + 3y = 3 \\ x - y = \frac{1}{6} \end{cases}$ $\frac{1}{2}, \frac{1}{3}$

Factor. Lesson 12.5

23. $3x^3 - 48x$ $3x(x + 4)(x - 4)$ **24.** $4x^2y - 4xy - 48y$ $4y(x - 6)(x + 2)$ **25.** $x^4 - 81$ $(x^2 + 9)(x + 3)(x - 3)$

PROJECT Connection In this activity, you will make some generalizations about the used cars you are studying. Answers will vary.

1. Assemble all the classified advertisements. Determine the mode option listed in them.
2. Sort the advertisements by make and model year. For each specific type of car, determine the mean price and mode price of the used cars offered for sale. If these prices differ, give reasons why.
3. If the owner will cooperate, find out the original purchase price of the car. (If not, you may be able to find out the original suggested retail price of the car as equipped.) Use the average selling price of similar used cars to determine the percent decrease from the original price. Compare and discuss the percents you obtain for different models.

- Draw right ΔACD with the hypotenuse of ΔABC as the leg AC and leg DC 1 cm in length. Use the Pythagorean theorem to determine the length of the hypotenuse of ΔACD. **$\sqrt{3}$ cm**
- Continue drawing triangles in this manner each with one leg the hypotenuse of the previous triangle and the other leg 1 cm in length. Determine the lengths of the hypotenuses for the next four triangles. **$\sqrt{4}$ cm = 2 cm, $\sqrt{5}$ cm, $\sqrt{6}$ cm, $\sqrt{7}$ cm**
- Use a ruler to measure each hypotenuse. What are the values of $\sqrt{2}$, $\sqrt{3}$, $\sqrt{5}$, $\sqrt{6}$, $\sqrt{7}$, to the nearest tenth? **1.4, 1.7, 2.2, 2.4, 2.6**

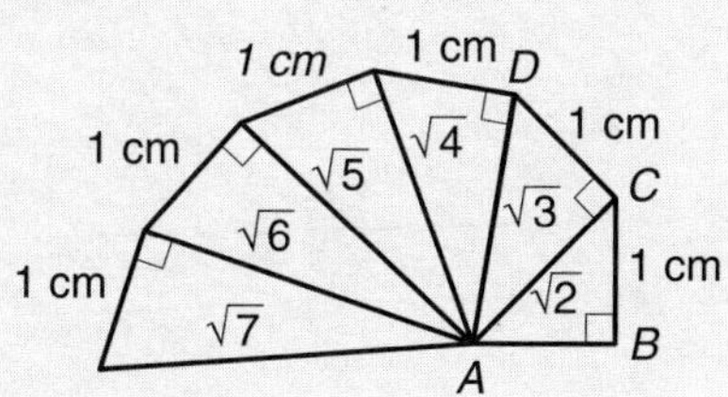

NAME ____ CLASS ____ DATE ____

EXTRA PRACTICE **13.2 TRIANGLES AND THE PYTHAGOREAN THEOREM**

Classify each triangle as *acute*, *right*, or *obtuse* and as *scalene*, *isosceles*, or *equilateral*.

1. 

obtuse, isosceles

2. 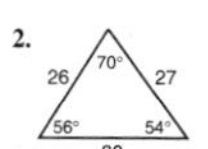

acute, scalene

3. 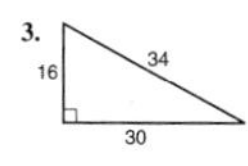

right, scalene

Determine the measure of the third angle for each triangle.

4. measure of $\angle A$ = 38°, measure of $\angle B$ = 76° **4.** 66°
5. measure of $\angle A$ = 17°, measure of $\angle B$ = 125° **5.** 38°
6. measure of $\angle A$ = 24°, measure of $\angle B$ = 51° **6.** 105°

Use the Pythagorean relationship to classify each triangle according to the lengths of the sides.

7. 18, 21, 27 **8.** 24, 32, 40 **9.** 38, 45, 60

10. 12, 36, 38 **11.** 16, 24, 28 **12.** 25, 60, 65

7. acute **8.** right **9.** obtuse **10.** obtuse **11.** acute **12.** right

13. In right ΔPQR, one angle is 12° less than twice the measure of its complement. Determine the measure of each angle. **13.** 56°, 34°, 90°

14. In isosceles ΔGHI, the measure of $\angle G = \angle I$, and the measure of $\angle H$ = 42°. Determine the measures of $\angle G$ and $\angle I$. **14.** 69°

15. In ΔDEF, the measure of $\angle D$ is one third the measure of $\angle E$, and the measure of $\angle F$ is 24°. Determine the measures of $\angle D$ and $\angle E$. **15.** 39°, 117°

16. In obtuse isosceles ΔABC, the measure of $\angle A$ is 16°. Determine the measures of $\angle B$ and $\angle C$. **16.** 16°, 148°

17. In acute isosceles ΔABC, the measure of $\angle A$ is 16°. Determine the measures of $\angle B$ and $\angle C$. **17.** 82°, 82°

8 *South-Western Algebra 1: An Integrated Approach*

Project Connection This activity presents further aspects of the project introduced on page 614. Review methods of determining the mean and mode and finding the percent of increase or decrease.

AlgebraWorks After students have completed Exercise 2, ask them to explain why this method works in assuring that intersecting roads are perpendicular. **6, 8, 10 is a Pythagorean triple since 36 + 64 = 100, so a right triangle is formed.**

NAME ____________ CLASS ________ DATE ________

13.2 TRIANGLES AND THE PYTHAGOREAN THEOREM

ENRICHMENT

The sum of the angle measures of a triangle is 180°. You can use this to determine the sum of the angle measures of polygons with more than three sides.

Example

Determine the sum of the angle measures of a pentagon.

Solution

Draw diagonal line segments from vertex *A* to vertices *C* and *D*. Number the angles in the interior of the figure, from 1 to 9.

Since the sum of the angle measures of a triangle is 180°,

$m\angle 3 + m\angle 4 + m\angle 5 = 180°$
$m\angle 1 + m\angle 8 + m\angle 9 = 180°$
$m\angle 2 + m\angle 6 + m\angle 7 = 180°$

By the associative and commutative properties,

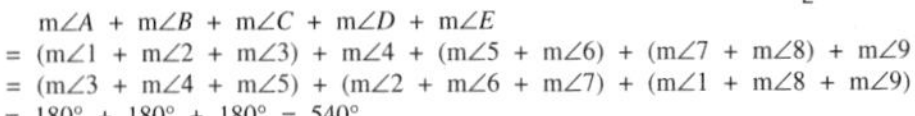

$m\angle A + m\angle B + m\angle C + m\angle D + m\angle E$
$= (m\angle 1 + m\angle 2 + m\angle 3) + m\angle 4 + (m\angle 5 + m\angle 6) + (m\angle 7 + m\angle 8) + m\angle 9$
$= (m\angle 3 + m\angle 4 + m\angle 5) + (m\angle 2 + m\angle 6 + m\angle 7) + (m\angle 1 + m\angle 8 + m\angle 9)$
$= 180° + 180° + 180° = 540°$

EXERCISES

Determine the sum of the angle measures of each figure. Then for each figure determine the measure of an angle if all the angle measures for that figure are equal.

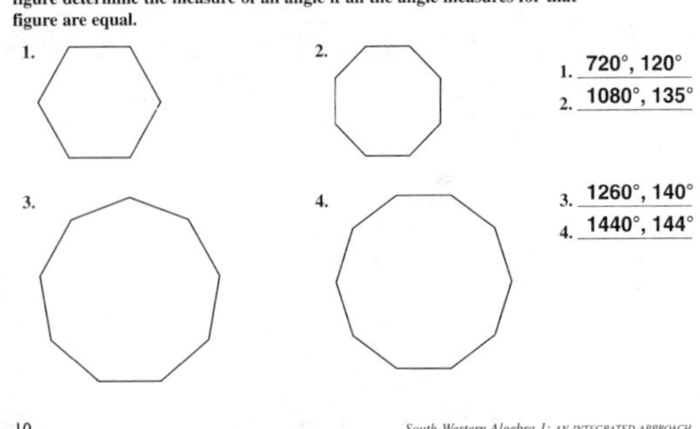

1. 720°, 120°
2. 1080°, 135°
3. 1260°, 140°
4. 1440°, 144°

10 South-Western Algebra 1: AN INTEGRATED APPROACH

Career
Road Developer

To be certain that road intersections are perpendicular, road developers use a procedure based on the Pythagorean theorem to create small scale layout documents to model a road system. You can model the procedure using string, tape, and a centimeter ruler.

1. Begin by taping both ends of a piece of string to your work surface. This string represents the first road. Make two marks on the string to represent two points *A* and *B* on the first road. You can do this with small additional pieces of tape.

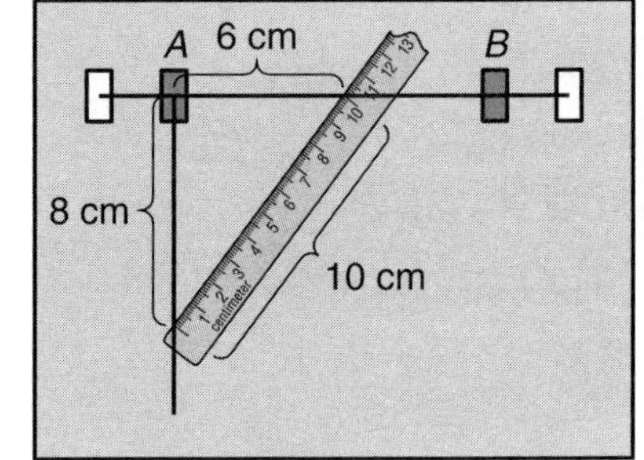

2. Tape one end of a second string at Point *A* on the first road and mark off 8 cm in the general direction of a right angle. Measure exactly 6 cm from Point *A* along the first road and mark the point. From that point, lay the end of a centimeter ruler toward the far end of the second road. Stretch the second string to form a triangle with the first road and the ruler. Tape the second string at the point where the 10 cm mark on the ruler meets the 8 cm mark of the second road. The second road must pass through this point.

3. Continue by repeating the process for each of the four corners where the roads are to intersect and form a right angle, by using a Pythagorean triple.

Decision Making

4. You can check the accuracy of your construction by measuring the diagonals of the rectangle you created. What should you look for? How will these measurements show whether you have constructed roads that meet at right angles?

The diagonals should be equal in length if the figure is a rectangle.

13.3 Multiply and Divide Radicals

Explore

In the figure, dots are 1 unit apart horizontally and vertically.

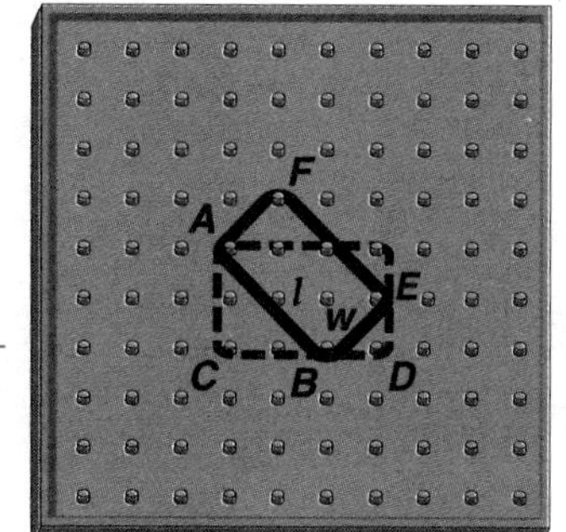

1. ΔABC is a right triangle with a hypotenuse of length l. Use the Pythagorean theorem to determine l. $\sqrt{8} = 2\sqrt{2}$
2. Find w, the hypotenuse of ΔBDE. $\sqrt{2}$
3. Find the area of rectangle $AFEB$ by counting the number of unit squares covered by the rectangle. 4
4. How does this exploration show that $\sqrt{8} \cdot \sqrt{2} = \sqrt{16}$?

   area of $AFEB$ = $lw = \sqrt{8} \cdot \sqrt{2} = 4 = \sqrt{16}$

Build Understanding

You have learned that the square root of a perfect square can be written in a simpler form, such as $\sqrt{36} = 6$. A **radical expression** (an expression containing a radical) is in **simplest form** if

1. the **radicand** (the expression under the radical symbol) contains no perfect-square factors other than 1
2. the radicand contains no fractions
3. no denominator contains a radical

Recall from Lesson 9.5 that you can use the following properties to simplify radical expressions.

PROPERTIES OF SQUARE ROOTS

For all real numbers a and b, where $a \geq 0$ and $b \geq 0$,

$\sqrt{ab} = \sqrt{a} \cdot \sqrt{b}$ PRODUCT PROPERTY

For all real numbers a and b, where $a \geq 0$ and $b > 0$,

$\sqrt{\frac{a}{b}} = \frac{\sqrt{a}}{\sqrt{b}}$ QUOTIENT PROPERTY

Recall that $\sqrt{}$ stands for the *principal*, or positive, square root of a positive number. Thus, $\sqrt{x^2} = x$ only if $x \geq 0$. In other words, $\sqrt{x^2} = |x|$. You can use this fact to simplify radical expressions.

SPOTLIGHT ON LEARNING

WHAT? In this lesson you will learn
- to multiply, divide, and simplify radicals.

WHY? Knowing how to multiply and divide radicals can help you solve problems in geography, sports, oceanography, and chemistry.

THINK BACK

A *perfect square* can be written as the square of an integer or a variable expression. Both 49 and y^2 are perfect squares because $49 = 7^2 = 7 \cdot 7$ and $y^2 = y \cdot y$.

COMMUNICATING ABOUT ALGEBRA

In your own words, explain the square root properties to another student.

See Additional Answers.

LESSON PLANNING

Objective
- Multiply, divide, and simplify radicals.

Vocabulary
conjugates
product and quotient properties of square roots
radical expression
radicand
rationalizing the denominator

Resources
Warm Up 13.3
Reteaching 13.3
Extra Practice 13.3
Enrichment 13.3
Transparencies 27, 34
Student Handbook
Lesson Quiz 13.3

Materials/Manipulatives
protractor
dot paper or graph paper

ASSIGNMENTS

Basic: 1–23, 25–35, Mixed Review 38–44, AlgebraWorks 1–6

Average: 3–36, Mixed Review 38–44, AlgebraWorks 1–6

Enriched: 4–37, Mixed Review 38–44, AlgebraWorks 1–6

1 MOTIVATE

Explore For Question 1, ask students to classify ΔABC. **right isosceles triangle** Then ask them to explain how they determined l. **Since dots are 1 unit apart, the lengths of the legs AB and BC are each 2 units. Thus $2^2 + 2^2 = l^2$, $8 = l^2$, $\sqrt{8} = l$**

Ask students to describe how they determined w. **The lengths of the legs BD and DE are each 1 unit. Thus, $1^2 + 1^2 = w^2$, $2 = l$, $\sqrt{2} = w$.** After students have discussed their answers to Question 4, ask them to draw on dot paper or graph paper a similar figure with AC and BC each equal to 3 units and BD and DE each equal to 2 units. Have them repeat Questions 1–4 for this new figure. **$l = \sqrt{18}$, $w = \sqrt{8}$; $A = 10 \cdot 1/2 + 7 = 12$ square units; $lw = \sqrt{18} \cdot \sqrt{8} = 12 = \sqrt{144}$**

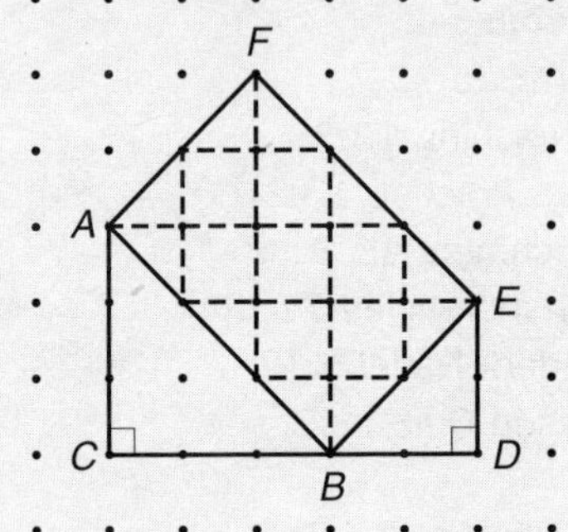

2 TEACH

Use the Pages/Build Understanding
Ask students which of these are in $\sqrt{x^2+1}$, $\sqrt{121}$, $3\sqrt{2}$, $\sqrt{5}/\sqrt{7}$. **$\sqrt{x^2+1}$, $3\sqrt{2}$.** Have them explain why the others are not. **121 is a perfect square; $\sqrt{7}$ is in the denominator**

Example 1: After students have discussed the example, have them read and discuss Problem Solving Tip and Check Understanding. Explain that for Problem Solving Tip, they should determine the greatest factor of the radicand that is a perfect square.

Example 2: Ask if $-\sqrt{6} \cdot \sqrt{15}$ could have been rewritten as $-\sqrt{-6} \cdot \sqrt{15}$ and to explain why or why not. **no; $\sqrt{-6}$ is not a real number.**

PROBLEM SOLVING TIP

To solve Example 1a mentally, look for a factor of the radicand that is a perfect square.

$54 = \boxed{9} \cdot 6$, so

$\sqrt{54} = \sqrt{9} \cdot \sqrt{6}$

$= 3\sqrt{6}$

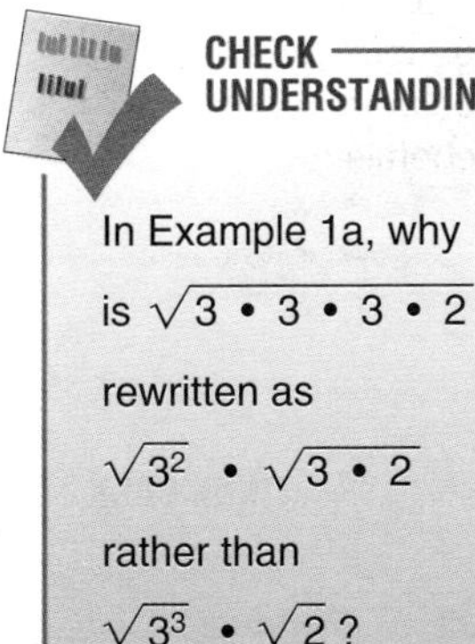

CHECK UNDERSTANDING

In Example 1a, why is $\sqrt{3 \cdot 3 \cdot 3 \cdot 2}$ rewritten as $\sqrt{3^2} \cdot \sqrt{3 \cdot 2}$ rather than $\sqrt{3^3} \cdot \sqrt{2}$?

The radicand should be grouped into factors that can be simplified. This means grouping even numbers of factors within radicals. Here, $\sqrt{3^2}$ can be simplified to 3, but $\sqrt{3^3}$ can be simplified only by further breaking $\sqrt{3^3}$ down into $\sqrt{3^2 \cdot 3}$.

EXAMPLE 1

Simplify.

a. $\sqrt{54}$ **b.** $\sqrt{98x^2y}$

Solution

a. $\sqrt{54} = \sqrt{3 \cdot 3 \cdot 3 \cdot 2}$ — Write the prime factorization of 54.

$= \sqrt{3^2} \cdot \sqrt{3 \cdot 2}$ — Use the product property of square roots.

$= 3\sqrt{6}$

b. $\sqrt{98x^2y} = \sqrt{7 \cdot 7 \cdot 2 \cdot x^2 \cdot y}$ — Write the prime factorization of 98.

$= \sqrt{7^2} \cdot \sqrt{x^2} \cdot \sqrt{2y}$ — Product property of square roots.

$= 7|x|\sqrt{2y}$ ◀

In Example 1, the product property of square roots was used to simplify radical expressions. The product property can also be used to multiply radical expressions.

EXAMPLE 2

Multiply and simplify.

a. $-\sqrt{6} \cdot \sqrt{15}$ **b.** $\sqrt{5y}(8 - \sqrt{35y})$

Solution

a. $-\sqrt{6} \cdot \sqrt{15}$

$= -\sqrt{6 \cdot 15}$ — Product property of square roots.

$= -\sqrt{2 \cdot 3 \cdot 3 \cdot 5}$ — Write the prime factorizations.

$= -\sqrt{3^2} \cdot \sqrt{2 \cdot 5}$ — Commutative property and product property of square roots.

$= -3\sqrt{10}$

b. $\sqrt{5y}(8 - \sqrt{35y})$

$= 8\sqrt{5y} - \sqrt{5y} \cdot \sqrt{35y}$ — Distributive property.

$= 8\sqrt{5y} - \sqrt{5y \cdot 35y}$

$= 8\sqrt{5y} - \sqrt{5 \cdot 5 \cdot 7 \cdot y^2}$ — Factor.

$= 8\sqrt{5y} - \sqrt{5^2 \cdot y^2 \cdot 7}$

$= 8\sqrt{5y} - 5y\sqrt{7}$ ◀

Notice that in Example 2b it is not necessary to write $|y|$ for $\sqrt{y^2}$. Since both $5y$ and $35y$ appear as radicands in the original problem, y must be greater than or equal to zero. Therefore, $\sqrt{y^2} = y$.

The quotient property of square roots can also be used to simplify radical expressions. Remember that in a radical expression in simplest form, no denominator should contain a radical.

EXAMPLE 3

Simplify.

a. $\frac{\sqrt{90}}{\sqrt{5}}$ **b.** $\sqrt{\frac{1}{2}}$

Solution

a. $\frac{\sqrt{90}}{\sqrt{5}} = \sqrt{\frac{90}{5}}$ Quotient property of square roots.

$= \sqrt{\frac{2 \cdot 3 \cdot 3 \cdot 5}{5}}$ Factor.

$= \sqrt{2 \cdot 3 \cdot 3}$ Divide by the common factor, 5.

$= 3\sqrt{2}$

b. $\sqrt{\frac{1}{2}} = \frac{\sqrt{1}}{\sqrt{2}}$ Quotient property of square roots.

$= \frac{1}{\sqrt{2}} \cdot \frac{\sqrt{2}}{\sqrt{2}}$ Multiply by $\frac{\sqrt{2}}{\sqrt{2}}$.

$= \frac{\sqrt{2}}{\sqrt{2 \cdot 2}}$ Product property.

$= \frac{\sqrt{2}}{2}$ ◄

CHECK UNDERSTANDING

What property assures that you can multiply the fraction $\frac{1}{\sqrt{2}}$ by $\frac{\sqrt{2}}{\sqrt{2}}$ without changing the value of the fraction?

See Additional Answers.

Notice that in Example 3b, the radical $\sqrt{2}$ was eliminated from $\frac{1}{\sqrt{2}}$ by multiplying the expression by $\frac{\sqrt{2}}{\sqrt{2}}$, which is equal to 1, and applying the product property. The process of eliminating the radical from the denominator is called **rationalizing the denominator**.

EXAMPLE 4

PHYSICS The formula $T = 2\pi\sqrt{\frac{L}{32}}$ gives the length of time T in seconds that it takes a pendulum of length L in feet to complete one swing. Approximate T for a pendulum 3 in. long.

Solution

$L = 3 \text{ in.} = 0.25 \text{ ft}$

$T = 2\pi\sqrt{\frac{L}{32}} = 2\pi\sqrt{\frac{0.25}{32}}$ Substitute 0.25 for L.

≈ 0.5553603673 Use a calculator.

≈ 0.56 Round.

The time is about 0.56 seconds. ◄

ALGEBRA: WHO, WHERE, WHEN

The Italian physicist Galileo discovered that the time for the swing of a pendulum depended on the pendulum length, not on the size of the arc. Simple pendulum clocks work on the principle that when a longer pendulum is used, the clock runs more slowly than it does with a shorter one.

Example 3: Ask students to explain why $\sqrt{(1/2)}$ is not in simplest form. **because the radicand contains a fraction** Have students discuss Check Understanding.

Example 4: Ask students to explain how 3 inches can be converted to feet. **Since 12 in. = 1 ft, 1 ft/12 in. = x/3 in. or x = 0.25 ft**

Ongoing Assessment The important concepts and skills are multiplying, dividing, and simplifying radicals. To assess these ideas, have students demonstrate how they have applied these concepts and skills in Exercises 2, 3, and 5 of the Try These section.

Guided Practice/Try These For Exercise 7, ask what students need to do to simplify the radical. **Use the quotient property to rewrite the expression as the quotient of two radical expressions: $\sqrt{5}/\sqrt{6}$; then rationalize the denominator**

3 SUMMARIZE

In the Math Journal Have students write a brief paragraph to summarize the three conditions that must be true for a radical expression to be in simplest form. **(1) The radicand contains no perfect square factors other than 1; (2) The radicand contains no fractions; (3) No radicals appear in the denominator.**

4 PRACTICE

Practice Remind students to write $\sqrt{x^2}$ as $|x|$ since square roots must be positive and to determine the greatest perfect square factors when simplifying. Ask how to simplify the expression. $-5\sqrt{(24x^3y)} = -5\sqrt{(4 \cdot 6 \cdot x^2 \cdot x \cdot y)} = -5\sqrt{4} \cdot \sqrt{6} \cdot \sqrt{x^2} \cdot \sqrt{x} \cdot \sqrt{y} = (-5 \cdot 2 \cdot x)\sqrt{(6xy)} = -10x\sqrt{(6xy)}$

Error Alert For Exercise 19, watch for students who mistakenly square the numerator and the denominator. These students make the following error:

$$\frac{2}{\sqrt{5}} = \left(\frac{2}{\sqrt{5}}\right)\left(\frac{2}{\sqrt{5}}\right) = \frac{4}{5}$$

The correct solution is

$$\frac{2}{\sqrt{5}} = \frac{2}{\sqrt{5}} \bullet \frac{\sqrt{5}}{\sqrt{5}} = \frac{2\sqrt{5}}{\sqrt{5} \bullet \sqrt{5}}$$
$$= \frac{2\sqrt{5}}{5}$$

Extend Ask students to give examples of radical expressions and their conjugates. **Possible examples: $\sqrt{3} + 4$ and $\sqrt{3} - 4$, $2\sqrt{5} - \sqrt{8}$ and $2\sqrt{5} + \sqrt{8}$** Ask students what the product of a pair of conjugates reminds them of. **the difference of squares**

Think Critically For Exercise 35, ask a student to describe how to set up equations to find the two numbers. **Let x and y represent the two numbers. Then $\sqrt{x + y} = 10$ and $\sqrt{x \bullet y} = 48$**

NAME ______ CLASS ______ DATE ______

RETEACHING **13.3 MULTIPLY AND DIVIDE RADICALS**

Use the properties of square roots to simplify radical expressions. Then look for factors that are perfect squares to simplify radicands.

Product property: $\sqrt{ab} = \sqrt{a} \cdot \sqrt{b}$ $(a \geq 0 \text{ and } b \geq 0)$

Quotient property: $\sqrt{\frac{a}{b}} = \frac{\sqrt{a}}{\sqrt{b}}$ $(a \geq 0 \text{ and } b > 0)$

Example 1
Simplify: $\sqrt{135}$
Solution
$\sqrt{135} = \sqrt{5 \cdot 27}$
$= \sqrt{5 \cdot 9 \cdot 3}$
$= \sqrt{9} \cdot \sqrt{5 \cdot 3}$
$= 3\sqrt{15}$

Example 2
Simplify: $\sqrt{3}(\sqrt{18} + \sqrt{12})$
Solution
$\sqrt{3}(\sqrt{18} + \sqrt{12})$
$= \sqrt{3} \cdot \sqrt{18} + \sqrt{3} \cdot \sqrt{12}$
$= \sqrt{3 \cdot 18} + \sqrt{3 \cdot 12}$
$= \sqrt{54} + \sqrt{36}$
$= \sqrt{9 \cdot 6} + 6$
$= \sqrt{9} \cdot \sqrt{6} + 6$
$= 3\sqrt{6} + 6$

Example 3
Simplify: $\sqrt{\frac{125}{2}}$
Solution
$\sqrt{\frac{125}{2}} = \frac{\sqrt{125}}{\sqrt{2}}$
$= \frac{\sqrt{25 \cdot 5}}{\sqrt{2}}$
$= \frac{5\sqrt{5}}{\sqrt{2}}$
$= \frac{5\sqrt{5}}{\sqrt{2}} \cdot \frac{\sqrt{2}}{\sqrt{2}}$
$= \frac{5\sqrt{5} \cdot \sqrt{2}}{2}$
$= \frac{5\sqrt{10}}{2}$

A radical expression in simplified form must have no radical in the denominator and no fraction within a radical.

EXERCISES

Simplify.

1. $\sqrt{48}$
2. $\sqrt{405}$
3. $\sqrt{192}$
4. $\sqrt{216}$
5. $\sqrt{2}(\sqrt{6} + \sqrt{8})$
6. $\sqrt{5}(4 + \sqrt{40})$
7. $\sqrt{3}(\sqrt{18} - \sqrt{6})$
8. $\sqrt{15}(2\sqrt{3} - \sqrt{5})$

1. $4\sqrt{3}$
2. $9\sqrt{5}$
3. $8\sqrt{3}$
4. $6\sqrt{6}$
5. $2\sqrt{3} + 4$
6. $4\sqrt{5} + 10\sqrt{2}$
7. $3\sqrt{6} - 3\sqrt{2}$
8. $6\sqrt{5} - 5\sqrt{3}$

14 South-Western Algebra 1: AN INTEGRATED APPROACH

TRY THESE

Simplify.

1. $\sqrt{50}$ $5\sqrt{2}$
2. $\sqrt{27k^2}$ $3|k|\sqrt{3}$
3. $2\sqrt{6} \cdot \sqrt{8}$ $8\sqrt{3}$
4. $\sqrt{2}(\sqrt{3} - \sqrt{8})$ $\sqrt{6} - 4$
5. $\frac{\sqrt{60}}{\sqrt{5}}$ $2\sqrt{3}$
6. $\frac{3}{\sqrt{3}}$ $\sqrt{3}$
7. $\sqrt{\frac{5}{6}}$ $\frac{\sqrt{30}}{6}$
8. $\frac{4\sqrt{3}}{\sqrt{8}}$ $\sqrt{6}$
9. **GEOGRAPHY** The formula $d = \sqrt{12h}$ can be used to approximate the distance d to Earth's horizon in kilometers from a point h meters above Earth's surface. Find and simplify a radical expression for the distance to the horizon from an elevation of 375 m. $30\sqrt{5}$ km
10. **SPORTS** A baseball "diamond" is really a square measuring 90 ft on a side. Determine a radical expression for the distance from home plate directly to second base. $90\sqrt{2}$ ft
11. **WRITING MATHEMATICS** Determine the prime factors of 30 and explain why $\sqrt{30}$ is in simplest form. The prime factors of 30 are $2 \cdot 3 \cdot 5$. Since none of the prime factors of 30 have exponents greater than 1, $\sqrt{30}$ is in simplest form.

PRACTICE

Simplify.

1. $\sqrt{18}$ $3\sqrt{2}$
2. $\sqrt{40}$ $2\sqrt{10}$
3. $\sqrt{300}$ $10\sqrt{3}$
4. $\sqrt{147}$ $7\sqrt{3}$
5. $\sqrt{9n^2}$ $3|n|$
6. $\sqrt{50p^2}$ $5|p|\sqrt{2}$
7. $3\sqrt{32c^3}$ $12c\sqrt{2c}$
8. $-5\sqrt{24x^3y}$ $-10x\sqrt{6xy}$
9. $\sqrt{3} \cdot \sqrt{3}$ 3
10. $\sqrt{7} \cdot \sqrt{7}$ 7
11. $5\sqrt{20} \cdot \sqrt{5}$ 50
12. $-3\sqrt{18} \cdot \sqrt{2}$ -18
13. $6(2 - \sqrt{3})$ $12 - 6\sqrt{3}$
14. $\sqrt{5}(5 + \sqrt{3})$ $5\sqrt{5} + \sqrt{15}$
15. $\sqrt{12}(2\sqrt{3} - \sqrt{5})$ $12 - 2\sqrt{15}$
16. $\frac{\sqrt{30}}{\sqrt{6}}$ $\sqrt{5}$
17. $\frac{\sqrt{72}}{\sqrt{8}}$ 3
18. $\frac{\sqrt{28a^2}}{\sqrt{8}}$ $\frac{|a|\sqrt{14}}{2}$
19. $\frac{2}{\sqrt{5}}$ $\frac{2\sqrt{5}}{5}$
20. $\frac{6}{\sqrt{2}}$ $3\sqrt{2}$

Determine the area of each figure.

21.

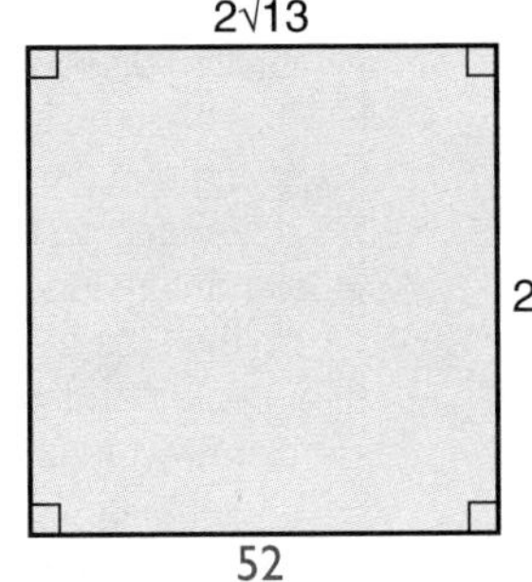

52

22.

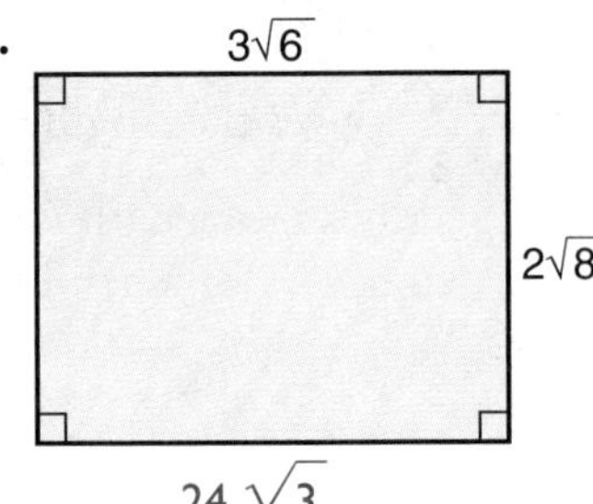

$24\sqrt{3}$

23.

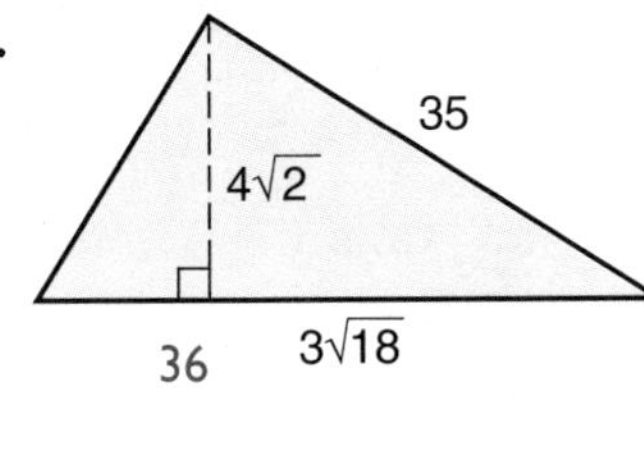

36

24. **CHEMISTRY** If two gases have masses of m_1 and m_2 respectively, the formula $\frac{r_1}{r_2} = \frac{\sqrt{m_1}}{\sqrt{m_2}}$ gives the ratio of the rates, r_1 and r_2, at which the gases diffuse (spread out to fill a space). Find and simplify the radical expression $\frac{r_1}{r_2}$ for two gases with $m_1 = 3$ mg and $m_2 = 2$ mg. $\frac{\sqrt{6}}{2}$
25. **WRITING MATHEMATICS** For each of the rules for simplification of radicals, give a radical and show how to simplify it. See Additional Answers.

EXTEND

26. **GEOMETRY** An equilateral triangle has sides measuring 12 cm. Find and simplify a radical expression for the height of the triangle. $6\sqrt{3}$

27. **GEOMETRY** Find and simplify a radical expression for the height of an equilateral triangle with sides measuring s units. $\frac{s\sqrt{3}}{2}$

If two radical expressions consist of the *sum* and *difference* of the same two terms, they are called **conjugates** of one another. The following expressions are conjugates.

$$\sqrt{2} + \sqrt{3} \text{ and } \sqrt{2} - \sqrt{3} \qquad 5 + 7\sqrt{13} \text{ and } 5 - 7\sqrt{13}$$

Give the conjugate of each radical expression. Then find the product of each pair of conjugates. See Additional Answers.

28. $4 + \sqrt{2}$
29. $\sqrt{5} - \sqrt{3}$
30. $2\sqrt{6} - 3\sqrt{2}$
31. $\sqrt{10} + 4$

To rationalize a denominator that is a binomial, multiply the numerator and denominator by the conjugate of the binomial.

Simplify.

32. $\frac{\sqrt{3} + \sqrt{2}}{\sqrt{3} - \sqrt{2}}$ $5 + 2\sqrt{6}$
33. $\frac{1 + \sqrt{2}}{3 - \sqrt{3}}$ $\frac{3 + \sqrt{3} + 3\sqrt{2} + \sqrt{6}}{6}$
34. $\frac{1 + \sqrt{3}}{2 + \sqrt{5}}$ $-2 + \sqrt{5} - 2\sqrt{3} + \sqrt{15}$

THINK CRITICALLY

35. Find two numbers such that the square root of their sum is 10 and the square root of their product is 48. 64, 36

36. Find the number such that the square root of the product of 7 and a number divided by the square root of the product of 28 and the number squared is $\frac{1}{2}$. 1

37. Suppose that m and n are rational numbers. Is the product $(m + \sqrt{n})(m - \sqrt{n})$ also a rational number? Explain. See Additional Answers.

MIXED REVIEW

Solve each equation for x. Lesson 3.7

38. $3x - 2 = 2x + 7$ 9
39. $6 - 3x = -5x + 2$ −2
40. $5(2x - 5) = -(x - 8)$ 3

Find the slope and y-intercept of the graph of each equation. Lesson 6.3

41. $y = -4x + 3$ −4; 3
42. $6x + 2y = 11$ −3; $\frac{11}{2}$
43. $3(y - 4) = 3x$ 1; 4

44. **STANDARDIZED TESTS** In simplest form $\sqrt{20n^2}$ is D; Lesson 13.3

A. $\pm 2n\sqrt{5}$
B. $|2n|\sqrt{5}$
C. $2n\sqrt{5}$
D. $2|n|\sqrt{5}$

5 FOLLOW-UP

Extension Have students work with partners to explore finding the area of an equilateral triangle with side s. Have them follow the steps below.

- Use the Pythagorean Theorem to determine the altitude h of an equilateral triangle with side s. (*Hint:* The altitude equally divides the base of the triangle.) $h^2 + [(1/2)s]^2 = s^2$, $h^2 + s^2/4 = s^2$, $4h^2 + s^2 = 4s^2$, $4h^2 = 3s^2$, $h^2 = (3s^2)/4$, $h = (s\sqrt{3})/2$
- Use this value for h to write the formula for the area of an equilateral triangle with side s. $A = 1/2(\text{base} \cdot \text{height})$; $A = 1/2[s \cdot (s \cdot \sqrt{3})/2]$, $A = (s^2\sqrt{3})/4$

Have students use this formula to find the area of an equilateral triangle with side $\sqrt{32}$. $8\sqrt{3}$

NAME ______ CLASS ______ DATE ______

EXTRA PRACTICE 13.3 MULTIPLY AND DIVIDE RADICALS

Simplify.

1. $\sqrt{52}$
2. $\sqrt{250}$
3. $\sqrt{320}$
4. $\sqrt{36z^2}$
5. $\sqrt{18m^3}$
6. $-4\sqrt{32x^2}$
7. $\sqrt{8} \cdot \sqrt{8}$
8. $3\sqrt{10} \cdot \sqrt{6}$
9. $-5\sqrt{12} \cdot \sqrt{3}$
10. $7(3 + \sqrt{5})$
11. $\sqrt{3}(6 + \sqrt{5})$
12. $\sqrt{18}(3\sqrt{2} + \sqrt{3})$
13. $\frac{\sqrt{63}}{\sqrt{7}}$
14. $\frac{\sqrt{40}}{\sqrt{5}}$
15. $\frac{\sqrt{18b^2}}{\sqrt{8}}$
16. $\frac{3}{\sqrt{6}}$
17. $\frac{\sqrt{8}}{\sqrt{2}}$
18. $\sqrt{\frac{2}{3}}$

Determine the area of each figure.

19. 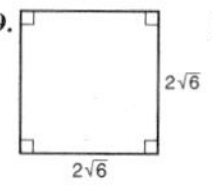

20. 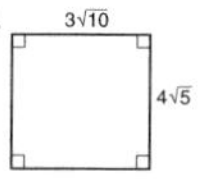

21. 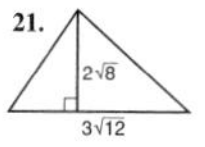

22. **GEOMETRY** The radius of a circle can be expressed in terms of its area by the formula $r = \sqrt{\frac{A}{\pi}}$. Determine the radius of a circle with an area of 3200π cm^2.

PHYSICS The velocity v of a tsunami or tidal wave in miles per hour can be approximated by the formula $v = \sqrt{15d}$, where d is the depth, in feet, of the water.

23. Find and simplify a radical expression for the velocity of a tsunami in 2500 feet of water.

24. A tsunami is unleashed by an earthquake at a depth of 18,000 feet. Use your calculator to determine the approximate speed of the wave.

Answers:

1. $2\sqrt{13}$
2. $5\sqrt{10}$
3. $8\sqrt{5}$
4. $6|z|$
5. $3m\sqrt{2m}$
6. $-16|x|\sqrt{2}$
7. 8
8. $6\sqrt{15}$
9. -30
10. $21 + 7\sqrt{5}$
11. $6\sqrt{3} + \sqrt{15}$
12. $18 + 3\sqrt{6}$
13. 3
14. $2\sqrt{2}$
15. $\frac{3|b|}{2}$
16. $\frac{\sqrt{6}}{2}$
17. $4\sqrt{2}$
18. $\frac{\sqrt{6}}{3}$
19. 24
20. $60\sqrt{2}$
21. $12\sqrt{6}$
22. $40\sqrt{2}$ cm
23. $50\sqrt{15}$ mi/h
24. 519.6 mi/h

16 *South-Western Algebra 1: AN INTEGRATED APPROACH*

Career
Highway Engineer

The United States, with 3.9 million miles of graded roads, has the most extensive highway system in the world. Within the U.S. highway system, Texas has the greatest number of miles of roads of any state, totalling about 306,000 mi. Highway engineers have the job of designing and building this massive network of highways and seeing to it that the roads are maintained in safe condition for the millions of commuters, truckers, tourists, and leisure drivers who use them.

Decision Making

1. What percent of U.S. highways are in Texas? about 7.8%
2. The earth's circumference is about 24,900 mi. If all the roads in the United States were laid end to end, how many times would they reach around the earth? about 157 times

In designing a curve for a freeway on-ramp, highway engineers must balance efficiency against safety. A short, sharp curve puts drivers on the freeway quickly but can be dangerous. If the curve is too sharp, a careless driver might drive off the edge of the road. A wide curve is safer but takes longer to drive. The formula for the relationship between the radius r in feet of an unbanked curve and the maximum velocity v in miles per hour at which a car can go around the curve without skidding is $v = \sqrt{2.5r}$.

3. As curve radius increases, does maximum safe velocity increase or decrease? Explain. Safe velocity increases; as r increases in the equation $v = \sqrt{2.5r}$, v increases.
4. Determine the maximum safe velocities achievable on curves of radii that are multiples of 10 ft, up to 100 ft. See Additional Answers.
5. Graph the equation $v = \sqrt{2.5r}$ for radii ranging from 0 ft to 2000 ft. See Additional Answers.

6. An unbanked curve with a radius of 4.1 mi would be needed to permit a no-skid turn by a car traveling at the fastest speed ever achieved at the Indianapolis 500 auto race. How fast was the race car moving? 232.6 mi/h

AlgebraWorks Ask students to explain how they can use scientific notation to find the percent for Exercise 1. **Think *306,000 is what percent of 3,900,000?* Write the equation 306,000 = x/100 • 3,900,000. Rewrite 306,000 as 3.06 x 10^5, 3,900,000 as 3.9 x 10^6, and 100 as 10^2 and substitute: 3.06 x $10^5 = \frac{x}{10^2}$ • 3.9 x 10^6 and solve for x. (3.06 x 10^5 x 10^2/3.9 x 10^6 = x. Simplify: (3.06 x 10^5) • (10^2)/(3.9 x 10^6) = (3.06 x 10^7)/(3.9 x 10^6) = 3.06/3.9 x 10 ≈ 7.8.** For Question 6, ask students what they need to do before substituting the distance of the radius in the formula to determine maximum velocity. **Convert 4.1 miles to feet since the formula represents the relationship between the radius in feet and the maximum velocity in miles per hour; 4.1 mi • 5280 ft/1 mi= 21,648.** Ask a student to describe the steps he or she used to find the velocity. **$v = \sqrt{(2.5 \cdot 21,648)}$ = 232.6370564... or about 232.6 mi/h**

NAME ______ CLASS ______ DATE ______

13.3 MULTIPLY AND DIVIDE RADICALS

A great circle of a sphere is a circle whose diameter goes through the center of the sphere and whose points lie on the sphere. The radius of a great circle is the same as the radius of the sphere. The surface area of a sphere is four times the area of one of its great circles. Thus, $A = 4\pi r^2$, where A represents the area of a sphere with radius r, and $r = \frac{A}{4\pi}$.

Example 1
Determine the surface area of a sphere with a radius of $2\sqrt{3}$ ft.

Solution

$$A = 4\pi r^2$$
$$= 4\pi \cdot (2\sqrt{3})^2$$
$$= 4\pi \cdot (2\sqrt{3}) \cdot (2\sqrt{3})$$
$$= 4\pi \cdot (2 \cdot 2) \cdot (\sqrt{3} \cdot \sqrt{3})$$
$$= 4\pi \cdot 4 \cdot 3$$
$$= 48\pi \text{ ft}^2$$

Example 2
Determine the radius of a sphere with surface area equal to 25π m.

Solution

$$r = \sqrt{\frac{A}{4\pi}}$$
$$= \sqrt{\frac{25\pi}{4\pi}}$$
$$= \sqrt{\frac{25}{4}}$$
$$= \frac{\sqrt{25}}{\sqrt{4}}$$
$$= \frac{5}{2} \text{ m}^2$$

EXERCISES

1. A sphere has a surface area of 1156π m². Determine the radius. 1. 17 m
2. A sphere has a surface area of 20π yd². Determine the radius. 2. $\sqrt{5}$ yd
3. A sphere has a surface area of 48π cm². Determine the radius. 3. $2\sqrt{3}$ cm
4. A sphere has a surface area of 96π in². Determine the diameter. 4. $4\sqrt{6}$ in.
5. A sphere has a surface area of 588π ft². Determine the diameter. 5. $14\sqrt{3}$ ft
6. The radius of a sphere is $3\sqrt{5}$ mm. Determine the surface area. 6. 180π mm²
7. The radius of a sphere is $2\sqrt{6}$ m. Determine the surface area. 7. 96π m²
8. The diameter of a sphere is $\sqrt{24}$ mi. Determine the surface area. 8. 24π mi²
9. The radius of a sphere is $2\sqrt{14}$ in. Determine the surface area. 9. 224π in.²
10. The radius of a sphere is $6\sqrt{7}$ cm. Determine the surface area. 10. 1008π cm²
11. The surface area of S_1 is 72π ft. The radius of sphere S_2 is half the radius of sphere S_1. Determine the radius and surface area of S_2. 11. $\frac{3\sqrt{2}}{2}$ ft; 36π ft²

18 South-Western Algebra 1: AN INTEGRATED APPROACH

13.4 Add and Subtract Radicals

Explore

In the figure below, dots are 1 unit apart horizontally and vertically.

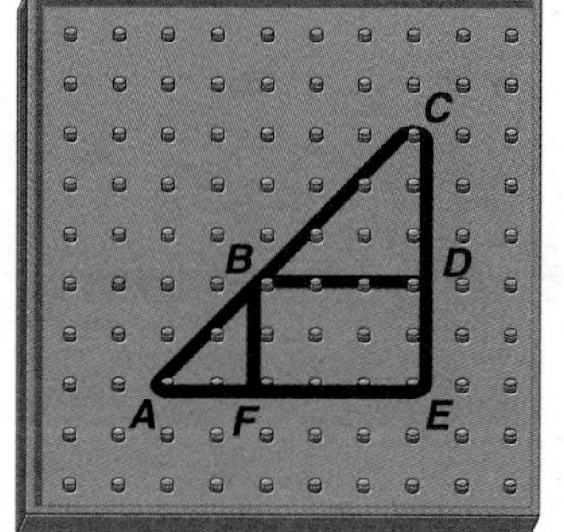

1. For ΔAFB, use the Pythagorean theorem to find and simplify a radical expression for AB. $2\sqrt{2}$
2. For ΔBDC, use the Pythagorean theorem to find and simplify a radical expression for BC. $3\sqrt{2}$
3. For ΔAEC, use the Pythagorean theorem to find and simplify a radical expression for AC. $5\sqrt{2}$
4. How does this exploration show that $2\sqrt{2} + 3\sqrt{2} = 5\sqrt{2}$?
   $AB + BC = AC$; by substitution, $2\sqrt{2} + 3\sqrt{2} = 5\sqrt{2}$

SPOTLIGHT ON LEARNING

WHAT? In this lesson you will learn
- to add and subtract radical expressions.

WHY? Knowing how to add and subtract radical expressions can help you solve problems in physics, traffic safety, geography, and navigation.

Build Understanding

Radical expressions with the same radicand are **like radicals.**

Like Radicals	**Unlike Radicals**
$2\sqrt{5}$ and $-3\sqrt{5}$	$\sqrt{6}$ and $4\sqrt{7}$
$3\sqrt{ab}$ and $12\sqrt{ab}$	$-5\sqrt{x}$ and $3\sqrt{y}$

You can combine radical expressions that are like radicals just as you can combine like terms in algebraic expressions.

Like Terms	**Like Radicals**
$8x - 3x = 5x$	$8\sqrt{2} - 3\sqrt{2} = 5\sqrt{2}$

Use the distributive property to add or subtract like radicals.

EXAMPLE 1

Simplify: $5\sqrt{3} + 7\sqrt{3} + 4\sqrt{6} - 2\sqrt{3}$

Solution

The terms containing $\sqrt{3}$ are like radicals.

$5\sqrt{3} + 7\sqrt{3} + 4\sqrt{6} - 2\sqrt{3}$

$= 5\sqrt{3} + 7\sqrt{3} - 2\sqrt{3} + 4\sqrt{6}$ Commutative property.

$= (5 + 7 - 2)\sqrt{3} + 4\sqrt{6}$ Distributive property.

$= 10\sqrt{3} + 4\sqrt{6}$ ◄

LESSON PLANNING

Objective

▶ Add and subtract radical expressions.

Vocabulary

like radicals

Resources

Warm Up 13.4
Reteaching 13.4
Extra Practice 13.4
Enrichment 13.4
Transparency 27
Student Handbook
Lesson Quiz 13.4

Materials/Manipulatives

Geoboard

ASSIGNMENTS

Basic: 1–17, 19–20, 22–25, 29, Mixed Review 30–44, Project Connection 1–2

Average: 3–20, 22–26, 29, Mixed Review 30–44, Project Connection 1–2

Enriched: 4–29, Mixed Review 30–44, Project Connection 1–2

1 MOTIVATE

Explore This Explore uses addition of segments to show that like radicals can be added. For Questions 1–3, ask students to describe how they found and simplified a radical expression for each hypotenuse. Be sure students understand the reasoning behind the answer to Question 4.

2 TEACH

Use the Pages/Build Understanding

Ask if $\sqrt{7}$ and $\sqrt{35}$ can be combined. **no, because they are not like radicals**

Example 1: Ask students to let $x = \sqrt{3}$ and $y = \sqrt{6}$ and substitute these variables into the original expression and simplify. **$5x + 7x + 4y - 2x$; $10x + 4y$** Have students compare simplifying radical expressions to simplifying variable expressions. **You can use the distributive property to add and subtract like variables or like radicals. Unlike variables cannot be combined. Similarly, unlike radicals cannot be combined.**

Example 2: Stress the importance of making sure that radicals are in simplified form before deciding whether they can be added or subtracted. Point out that although it appears that $2\sqrt{50} + 3\sqrt{18}$ cannot be added because they are unlike radicals, they can be once they are simplified. Ask students to show why. **$2\sqrt{50} + 3\sqrt{18} = 2\sqrt{(5^2 \cdot 2)} + 3\sqrt{(3^2 \cdot 2)} = 2 \cdot 5\sqrt{2} + 3 \cdot 3\sqrt{2} = 10\sqrt{2} + 9\sqrt{2} = 19\sqrt{2}$.**

Example 3: Have students discuss Check Understanding and then ask them how to subtract $2\sqrt{(45x^2)} - \sqrt{(20x^2)}$.

$$\begin{aligned}
&2\sqrt{(45x^2)} - \sqrt{(20x^2)} \\
&= 2\sqrt{(3^2 \cdot 5 \cdot x^2)} - \sqrt{(2^2 \cdot 5 \cdot x^2)} \\
&= 2 \cdot 3 \cdot \sqrt{5} \cdot |x| - 2 \cdot \sqrt{5}\,|x| \\
&= 6|x|\sqrt{5} - 2|x|\sqrt{5} \\
&= 4|x|\sqrt{5}
\end{aligned}$$

Example 4: Ask students what effect air has on a falling object. **Air causes the object to fall slower.**

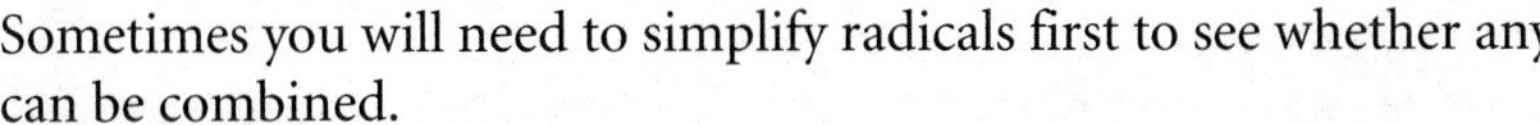

Sometimes you will need to simplify radicals first to see whether any can be combined.

EXAMPLE 2

Add: $2\sqrt{50} + 3\sqrt{18}$

Solution

$$\begin{aligned}
&2\sqrt{50} + 3\sqrt{18} \\
&= 2\sqrt{5^2 \cdot 2} + 3\sqrt{3^2 \cdot 2} && \text{Factor.} \\
&= 2 \cdot 5\sqrt{2} + 3 \cdot 3\sqrt{2} && \text{Simplify.} \\
&= 10\sqrt{2} + 9\sqrt{2} && \text{Multiply.} \\
&= 19\sqrt{2} && \text{Add.}
\end{aligned}$$

Radical expressions with variables in the radicand are added and subtracted in the same way as radicals having only real numbers in the radicand.

CHECK UNDERSTANDING

In Example 3, why is it not necessary to write the solution as $4|x|\sqrt{5x}$?

Absolute value bars are needed only when the variable might be negative. Because x^3 appears in each radicand in the problem, x cannot be negative.

EXAMPLE 3

Subtract: $2\sqrt{45x^3} - \sqrt{20x^3}$

Solution

$$\begin{aligned}
&2\sqrt{45x^3} - \sqrt{20x^3} \\
&= 2\sqrt{3^2 \cdot 5 \cdot x^2 \cdot x} - \sqrt{2^2 \cdot 5 \cdot x^2 \cdot x} \\
&= 2 \cdot 3x\sqrt{5x} - 2x\sqrt{5x} \\
&= 6x\sqrt{5x} - 2x\sqrt{5x} \\
&= 4x\sqrt{5x}
\end{aligned}$$

Real world problems involving square roots may require addition or subtraction of radicals.

EXAMPLE 4

PHYSICS The time t in seconds that it takes an object to fall d feet is given by $t = \frac{\sqrt{d}}{4}$. Two packages of equipment for Antarctic researchers are dropped simultaneously from two planes, one from an altitude of 4000 ft, the other from an altitude of 2560 ft. How long will one package be on the ground before the other one lands? Assume that air resistance is not a factor.

Solution

$$t_1 = \frac{\sqrt{4000}}{4} \qquad t_2 = \frac{\sqrt{2560}}{4}$$

difference in times: $t_1 - t_2$

$$\begin{aligned} & t_1 - t_2 \\ &= \frac{\sqrt{4000}}{4} - \frac{\sqrt{2560}}{4} \\ &= \frac{\sqrt{2^4 \cdot 5^2 \cdot 2 \cdot 5}}{4} - \frac{\sqrt{2^8 \cdot 2 \cdot 5}}{4} \\ &= \frac{20\sqrt{10}}{4} - \frac{16\sqrt{10}}{4} \\ &= 5\sqrt{10} - 4\sqrt{10} \\ &= \sqrt{10} \end{aligned}$$

The first package will land $\sqrt{10}$ seconds, or about 3.2 seconds, before the second package lands. ◄

TRY THESE

Simplify. See Additional Answers.

1. $5\sqrt{7} + 2\sqrt{7}$
2. $12\sqrt{5} - \sqrt{5}$
3. $10\sqrt{2} + 9\sqrt{2}$
4. $\sqrt{24} - \sqrt{6}$
5. $2\sqrt{10} - 3\sqrt{40} + 4\sqrt{5}$
6. $3\sqrt{b} - 5\sqrt{b}$
7. $7\sqrt{45} + 3\sqrt{20}$
8. $\sqrt{8x^2} + \sqrt{2x^2}$
9. $\sqrt{\frac{1}{2}} - \sqrt{\frac{1}{8}}$
10. GEOMETRY A rectangle is $\sqrt{54}$ in. long and $\sqrt{24}$ in. wide. Find the perimeter of the rectangle. $10\sqrt{6}$ in.
11. WRITING MATHEMATICS Write a paragraph that compares simplifying $7x^2 - 6x + 4x^2$ to simplifying $7\sqrt{6} - 6\sqrt{2} + 4\sqrt{6}$. See Additional Answers.

PRACTICE

Simplify. See Additional Answers.

1. $4\sqrt{3} + 5\sqrt{3}$
2. $8\sqrt{7} + 7\sqrt{7}$
3. $13\sqrt{5} - 5\sqrt{5}$
4. $\sqrt{10} + 3\sqrt{10} - \sqrt{5}$
5. $14\sqrt{3} + 6\sqrt{2} - 11\sqrt{3}$
6. $\sqrt{20} + \sqrt{80} - \sqrt{45}$
7. $11\sqrt{h} + 5\sqrt{h}$
8. $\sqrt{128y} - \sqrt{2y}$
9. $5\sqrt{18x} + 2\sqrt{8x}$
10. $2\sqrt{3} + 3\sqrt{12}$
11. $5\sqrt{50} - 4\sqrt{32}$
12. $\sqrt{200c^2} - \sqrt{98c^2}$
13. $\sqrt{8n + 8} + \sqrt{2n + 2}$
14. $\sqrt{2} + \sqrt{\frac{1}{2}}$
15. $\sqrt{\frac{2}{3}} - \sqrt{\frac{1}{6}}$

Ongoing Assessment The important concepts and skills are adding and subtracting radical expressions. To assess these ideas, have students demonstrate how they have applied these concepts and skills in Exercises 1, 3, and 4 of the Try These section.

Guided Practice/Try These

Error Alert For Exercise 4, watch for students who incorrectly subtract unlike radicals. These students make the following error:

$$\begin{aligned} \sqrt{24} - \sqrt{6} &= \sqrt{24 - 6} = \sqrt{18} \\ &= \sqrt{9 \cdot 2} = \sqrt{9} \cdot \sqrt{2} \\ &= 3\sqrt{2} \end{aligned}$$

The correct solution is

$$\begin{aligned} \sqrt{24} - \sqrt{6} &= \sqrt{4 \cdot 6} - \sqrt{6} \\ &= \sqrt{4} \cdot \sqrt{6} - \sqrt{6} \\ &= 2\sqrt{6} - \sqrt{6} = \sqrt{6} \end{aligned}$$

For Exercise 8, ask why an absolute value symbol is necessary in the solution. **because the square root must always be positive**

NAME ______ CLASS ______ DATE ______

RETEACHING **13.4 ADD AND SUBTRACT RADICALS**

Like radicals have the same radicand. When you add or subtract radical expressions you can only combine like radicals. To add or subtract radical expressions, follow these steps.

1. Make sure that each radical expression is in simplified form.
2. Use the distributive property to add or subtract the coefficients of any like radicals.

Example 1
Simplify: $5\sqrt{2} + \sqrt{8} - 3\sqrt{2}$

Solution
1. Simplify each radical.

$$\begin{aligned} & 5\sqrt{2} + \sqrt{8} - 3\sqrt{2} \\ &= 5\sqrt{2} + \sqrt{4 \cdot 2} - 3\sqrt{2} \\ &= 5\sqrt{2} + \sqrt{4} \cdot \sqrt{2} - 3\sqrt{2} \\ &= 5\sqrt{2} + 2\sqrt{2} - 3\sqrt{2} \end{aligned}$$

2. Use the distributive property to combine the coefficients of like radicals.

$$\begin{aligned} &= (5 + 2 - 3)\sqrt{2} \\ &= 4\sqrt{2} \end{aligned}$$

Example 2
Simplify: $3\sqrt{24x} - \sqrt{54x}$

Solution
1. Simplify each radical.

$$\begin{aligned} & 3\sqrt{24x} - \sqrt{54x} \\ &= 3\sqrt{4 \cdot 6 \cdot x} - \sqrt{9 \cdot 6 \cdot x} \\ &= 3(\sqrt{4} \cdot \sqrt{6} \cdot \sqrt{x}) - (\sqrt{9} \cdot \sqrt{6} \cdot \sqrt{x}) \\ &= 3(2 \cdot \sqrt{6x}) - (3 \cdot \sqrt{6x}) \\ &= 6\sqrt{6x} - 3\sqrt{6x} \end{aligned}$$

2. Use the distributive property to combine coefficients of like radicals.

$$\begin{aligned} &= (6 - 3)\sqrt{6x} \\ &= 3\sqrt{6x} \end{aligned}$$

EXERCISES

Simplify.

1. $2\sqrt{5} + 6\sqrt{5}$
2. $6\sqrt{5} + 4\sqrt{3} - 2\sqrt{5}$
3. $\sqrt{18} - \sqrt{2}$
4. $\sqrt{27} + \sqrt{54} - \sqrt{48}$
5. $11\sqrt{7} + 2\sqrt{28} - \sqrt{63}$
6. $3\sqrt{b} + 10\sqrt{b}$
7. $\sqrt{192z} - \sqrt{48z}$
8. $4\sqrt{32k} + 3\sqrt{18k}$
9. $\sqrt{125x^2} - \sqrt{20x^2}$
10. $\sqrt{6} - \sqrt{\frac{2}{3}}$

1. $8\sqrt{5}$
2. $4\sqrt{5} + 4\sqrt{3}$
3. $2\sqrt{2}$
4. $3\sqrt{6} - \sqrt{3}$
5. $12\sqrt{7}$
6. $13\sqrt{b}$
7. $4\sqrt{3z}$
8. $25\sqrt{2k}$
9. $3|x|\sqrt{5}$
10. $\frac{2\sqrt{6}}{3}$

22 *South-Western Algebra 1: AN INTEGRATED APPROACH*

3 SUMMARIZE

In the Math Journal Have students discuss how simplifying $\sqrt{a} \bullet \sqrt{b}$ is different from simplifying $\sqrt{a} + \sqrt{b}$. $\sqrt{a} \bullet \sqrt{b} = \sqrt{(a \bullet b)}$ **but** $\sqrt{a} + \sqrt{b} \neq \sqrt{(a + b)}$ Have them give examples to support their statements. **Examples will vary.**

4 PRACTICE

Practice For Exercise 6, ask whether there is a like radical or not and if so what it is. **yes, $\sqrt{5}$** For Exercises 14 and 15, ask students what they must do to each expression to simplify it. **Rewrite so that there are no fractions in a radicand and rationalize denominators.**

Extend For Exercise 23, ask what pattern they notice for right isosceles triangles. **The length of the hypotenuse of a right isosceles triangle is the length of one of its legs times $\sqrt{2}$.**

NAME ______ CLASS ______ DATE ______

EXTRA PRACTICE **13.4 ADD AND SUBTRACT RADICALS**

Simplify.

1. $7\sqrt{5} + 3\sqrt{5}$
2. $8\sqrt{7} - 3\sqrt{7}$
3. $11\sqrt{2} - 4\sqrt{6} + \sqrt{2}$
4. $\sqrt{3} - 8\sqrt{2} + 5\sqrt{3}$
5. $\sqrt{27} + \sqrt{12} - \sqrt{48}$
6. $\sqrt{18} + \sqrt{32} + \sqrt{8}$
7. $5\sqrt{y} - 2\sqrt{y}$
8. $\sqrt{6s} + \sqrt{54s}$
9. $4\sqrt{20a} - \sqrt{80a}$
10. $5\sqrt{3} + 2\sqrt{27}$
11. $3\sqrt{45} - 2\sqrt{20}$
12. $\sqrt{48x} - \sqrt{27x}$
13. $\sqrt{96x^2} + \sqrt{600x^2}$
14. $3\sqrt{40} + 2\sqrt{5} - \sqrt{10}$
15. $2\sqrt{18} - 3\sqrt{8} + \sqrt{12}$
16. $\sqrt{3z + 5} + \sqrt{12z + 20}$
17. $\sqrt{3} - \sqrt{\frac{1}{3}}$
18. $\sqrt{\frac{7}{8}} + \sqrt{14}$

Determine the area and perimeter of each figure.

19. 20. 21.

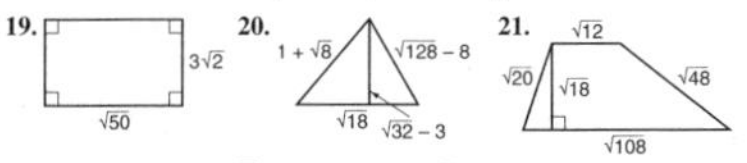

22. Rectangle A is $5\sqrt{3}$ cm long and $2\sqrt{8}$ cm wide. Rectangle B is $3\sqrt{18}$ cm long and $2\sqrt{3}$ cm wide. How much greater is the area of rectangle A than the area of rectangle B?

23. Determine the length of the hypotenuse of ΔABC with legs 4 cm and 8 cm and of ΔDEF with legs 8 cm and 16 cm. How much longer is the hypotenuse of ΔDEF than that of ΔABC?

24. The radius of a circle can be expressed in terms of its area by the formula $r = \sqrt{\frac{A}{\pi}}$. Two respective circles each have an area of 147π cm² and 48π cm². How much longer is the radius of one circle than the radius of the other circle?

1. $10\sqrt{5}$
2. $5\sqrt{7}$
3. $12\sqrt{2} - 4\sqrt{6}$
4. $6\sqrt{3} - 8\sqrt{2}$
5. $\sqrt{3}$
6. $9\sqrt{2}$
7. $3\sqrt{y}$
8. $4\sqrt{6s}$
9. $4\sqrt{5a}$
10. $11\sqrt{3}$
11. $5\sqrt{5}$
12. $\sqrt{3x}$
13. $14|x|\sqrt{6}$
14. $5\sqrt{10} + 2\sqrt{5}$
15. $2\sqrt{3}$
16. $3\sqrt{3z + 5}$
17. $\frac{2\sqrt{3}}{3}$
18. $\frac{5\sqrt{14}}{4}$
19. $30; 16\sqrt{2}$
20. $12 - \frac{9\sqrt{2}}{2}$; $13\sqrt{2} - 7$
21. $12\sqrt{6}$; $12\sqrt{3} + 2\sqrt{5}$
22. $2\sqrt{6}$ cm²
23. $4\sqrt{5}$ cm
24. $3\sqrt{3}$ cm

24 *South-Western Algebra 1: An Integrated Approach*

Determine the area and perimeter of each figure. See Additional Answers.

16. 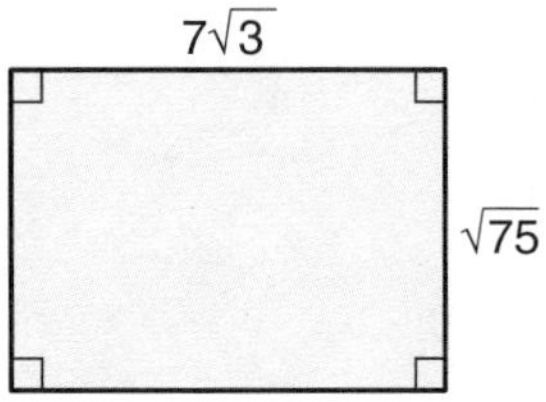

17. 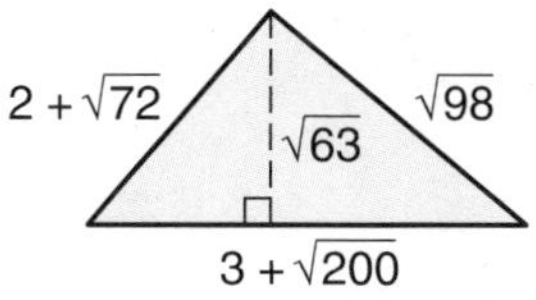

18. 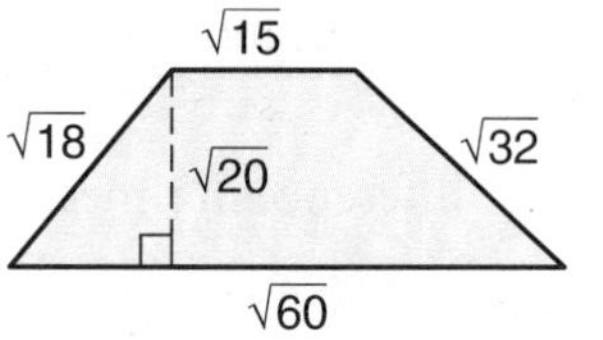

19. TRAFFIC SAFETY Police investigators can use the formula $s = 2\sqrt{5L}$ to approximate the rate of speed s in miles per hour of a car that leaves skids marks of length L in feet after the driver slams on the brakes to stop. Skid marks at a two-car accident measured 230.4 ft and 160 ft. Find the difference in speed of the two cars involved in the accident. $8\sqrt{2}$ mi/h

20. GEOGRAPHY The formula $d = \sqrt{12h}$ can be used to approximate the distance d in kilometers to Earth's horizon from a point h meters above Earth's surface. How much farther could you see from the top of New York City's Chrysler Bulding (height, 320 m) than you could see from the top of Cityspire (height, 245 m)? Assume that the views to the horizon are unobstructed. See Additional Answers.

21. PHYSICS The formula $T = 2\pi\sqrt{\frac{L}{32}}$ gives the length of time T in seconds that it takes a pendulum of length L in feet to complete one swing. Two pendulums, 4 ft and 1 ft in length respectively, begin a swing simultaneously.
    a. Which pendulum completes one swing first?
    b. How much less time does the faster pendulum take to complete one swing than the slower one takes?

    a. the 1-ft pendulum; b. See Additional Answers.

22. WRITING MATHEMATICS Explain how you can use a calculator to confirm that two radical expressions are equal. Provide an example to illustrate your explanation. See Additional Answers.

EXTEND

23. NAVIGATION To take advantage of the wind, a sailor boating from Portsmouth to Lakeview sailed south 3 mi and east 3 mi, then south 4 mi and east 4 mi, and finally south 7 mi and east 7 mi.
    a. Find the shortest distance from Portsmouth to Lakeview. $14\sqrt{2}$ mi.
    b. How much farther was it from Portsmouth to Lakeview by the route the sailor took? $28 - 14\sqrt{2}$ mi.

Decide whether the given value of x is a solution of the equation.

24. $x^2 + 4x + 2 = 0; x = -2 + \sqrt{2}$ yes
25. $x^2 - 4x - 7 = 0; x = 2 - \sqrt{11}$ yes
26. $x^2 - 3x - 5 = 0; x = 1 + \sqrt{6}$ no
27. $x^2 - 10x + 5 = 0; x = 5 + 2\sqrt{5}$ yes
28. a. Simplify: $\sqrt{x} + \sqrt{\frac{1}{x}}$ $\frac{x+1}{x}\sqrt{x}$
    b. Use your results to find $\sqrt{5} + \sqrt{\frac{1}{5}}$. $\frac{6}{5}\sqrt{5}$

THINK CRITICALLY

29. **a.** Use a calculator to evaluate the radical expressions $\sqrt{5} - 1$ and $\sqrt{6 - 2\sqrt{5}}$. What do you notice about your results? The expressions are equal.

b. Show that $\sqrt{5} - 1 = \sqrt{6 - 2\sqrt{5}}$ by squaring $\sqrt{5} - 1$. $(\sqrt{5} - 1)^2 = 6 - 2\sqrt{5}$

c. Simplify: $\sqrt{10 + 4\sqrt{6}}$ $\sqrt{6} + 2$

d. Simplify: $\sqrt{7 + 4\sqrt{3}}$ $\sqrt{3} + 2$

MIXED REVIEW

Evaluate each expression for the given value(s) of the variables. Lesson 2.2

30. $3x - 4y$, for $x = -2$ and $y = 5$ -26

31. $5a^2 + 7a$, for $a = -3$ 24

32. $6(x - 2y) + 5(x + y)$, for $x = 2$ and $y = -2$ 36

33. $m^3 - m^2 + 5m - 2$, for $m = -1$ -9

Evaluate the function $f(x) = 4x - 5$ for the given values of x. Lesson 4.2

34. $f(3)$ 7 **35.** $f(-5.5)$ -27 **36.** $f\left(\frac{1}{2}\right)$ -3 **37.** $f(x + 1)$ $4x - 1$

Solve each inequality. Lesson 9.4

38. $|x| < 3$ $-3 < x < 3$ **39.** $|x| \geq 6$ $x \leq -6$ or $x \geq 6$

40. STANDARDIZED TESTS The product of $(3 - \sqrt{5})(5 + 2\sqrt{5})$ is C; Lesson 13.3

A. $5 + 11\sqrt{5}$ **B.** $15 - \sqrt{5}$

C. $5 + \sqrt{5}$ **D.** $5 - 11\sqrt{5}$

Simplify. Lesson 13.4

41. $9\sqrt{7} - 3\sqrt{7}$ $6\sqrt{7}$ **42.** $\sqrt{18} - \sqrt{8}$ $\sqrt{2}$ **43.** $\sqrt{27} + 5\sqrt{3}$ $8\sqrt{3}$ **44.** $5\sqrt{x} + 2\sqrt{9x}$ $11\sqrt{x}$

In this activity, you will investigate what items can fit in your car's trunk compartment.

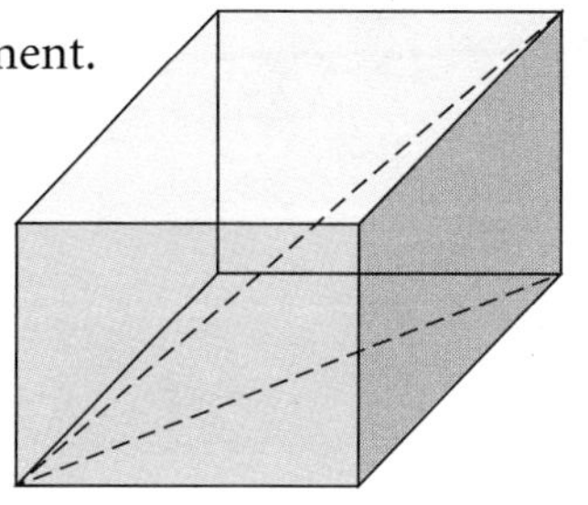

1. Obtain several large, empty cartons (such as those used for appliances). Experiment to determine the largest carton that will fit in the trunk with the hood securely closed. Then measure the dimensions of the carton (to the nearest tenth of a foot) and calculate the volume.
2. Next, use the dimensions of the carton to determine the length of the longest object that could be packed in it. What is the maximum length if the object lies flat in the carton? What is the maximum length if the object reaches from a bottom front corner to the diagonally opposite top back corner? Explain the steps you use. See Additional Answers.

Think Critically For Exercise 29c, have students describe a solution method.

Let $10 + 4\sqrt{6} = (\sqrt{6} + a)^2$. Then

$$10 + 4\sqrt{6} = 6 + 2a\sqrt{6} + a^2$$

$$4 + 4\sqrt{6} = 2a\sqrt{6} + a^2$$

$a^2 = 4$ and $2a = 4$; $a = 2$.

5 FOLLOW UP

Extension Have students show how to solve the following equation.

$2\sqrt{108} + 3x = 3\sqrt{75}$ **$2\sqrt{108} + 3x = 3\sqrt{75}$, $2\sqrt{(36 \cdot 3)} + 3x = 3\sqrt{(25 \cdot 3)}$, $12\sqrt{3} + 3x = 15\sqrt{3}$, $3x = 3\sqrt{3}$, $x = \sqrt{3}$**

Project Connection This activity presents further aspects of the project introduced on page 614. For Question 2, students will need to visualize the right triangle that has as one of its legs the maximum length they found for the object lying flat in the carton.

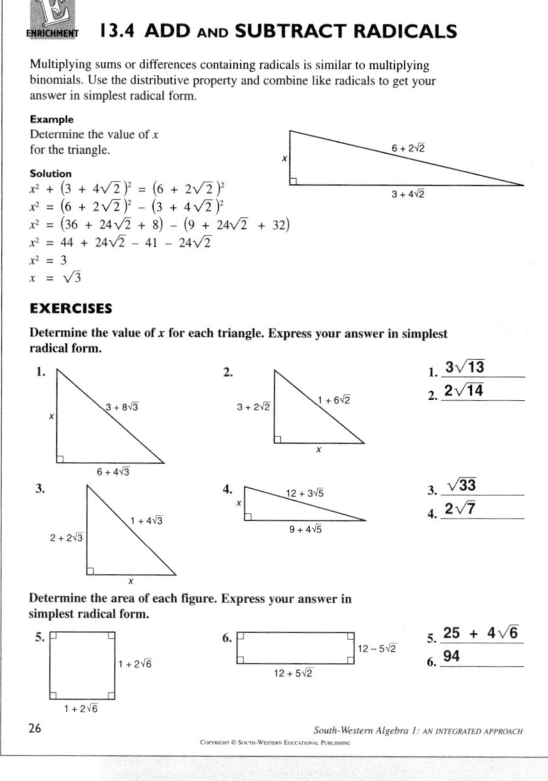

NAME ______ CLASS ______ DATE ______

ENRICHMENT **13.4 ADD AND SUBTRACT RADICALS**

Multiplying sums or differences containing radicals is similar to multiplying binomials. Use the distributive property and combine like radicals to get your answer in simplest radical form.

Example
Determine the value of x for the triangle.

Solution
$x^2 + (3 + 4\sqrt{2})^2 = (6 + 2\sqrt{2})^2$
$x^2 = (6 + 2\sqrt{2})^2 - (3 + 4\sqrt{2})^2$
$x^2 = (36 + 24\sqrt{2} + 8) - (9 + 24\sqrt{2} + 32)$
$x^2 = 44 + 24\sqrt{2} - 41 - 24\sqrt{2}$
$x^2 = 3$
$x = \sqrt{3}$

EXERCISES

Determine the value of x for each triangle. Express your answer in simplest radical form.

1. 2.

1. $3\sqrt{13}$
2. $2\sqrt{14}$

3. 4.

3. $\sqrt{33}$
4. $2\sqrt{7}$

Determine the area of each figure. Express your answer in simplest radical form.

5. 6.

5. $25 + 4\sqrt{6}$
6. 94

26 South-Western Algebra 1: AN INTEGRATED APPROACH

LESSON PLANNING

Objective

▶ Solve equations containing radical expressions.

Vocabulary

geometric mean
radical equation

Technology/Multimedia

graphing utility

Resources

Warm Up 13.5
Reteaching 13.5
Extra Practice 13.5
Enrichment 13.5
Transparencies 78–80
Student Handbook
Lesson Quiz 13.5
Technology Activity 31

ASSIGNMENTS

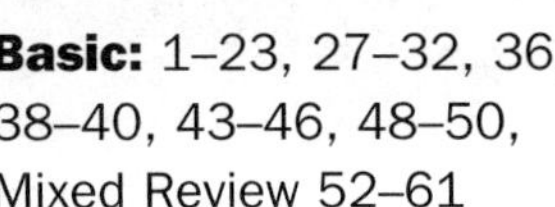

Basic: 1–23, 27–32, 36, 38–40, 43–46, 48–50, Mixed Review 52–61

Average: 3–41, 43–51, Mixed Review 52–61

Enriched: 4–51, Mixed Review 52–61

1 MOTIVATE

Explore/Working Together For Question 2, ask students why the solution –1 does not check. **because $-1 \neq \sqrt{[(5 \cdot -1) + 6]}$ since $\sqrt{[(5 \cdot -1) + 6]} = \sqrt{(-5 + 6)} = 1$ and $-1 \neq 1$** Students should note that in Question 5, –3 does not check because a square root cannot be negative; the solution is $x = 1/3$.

13.5 Solve Radical Equations

SPOTLIGHT ON LEARNING

WHAT? In this lesson you will learn
- to solve equations containing radical expressions.

WHY? Knowing how to solve radical equations can help you solve problems in plumbing, auto mechanics, and geometry.

Explore/Working Together

You and a partner will solve the equation $x = \sqrt{5x + 6}$ using two different methods. 1–6 See Additional Answers.

1. **a.** Use a graphing utility. How can you solve

$$x = \sqrt{5x + 6}$$

by graphing a system of equations?

b. Try your method and state the solution you determine. Remember to check each solution in the original equation.

2. **a.** Now solve $x = \sqrt{5x + 6}$ algebraically. How can you eliminate the radical on the right side?

b. What type of equation do you obtain? How can you solve this equation?

c. Check each solution in the original equation. What do you notice?

Solve and check each equation using both methods. Describe any patterns you notice.

3. $x = \sqrt{x + 2}$
4. $\sqrt{10 - 3x} = x$
5. $3x = \sqrt{3 - 6x}$
6. $2x = \sqrt{4x + 15}$

Build Understanding

An equation having a radical with a variable in the radicand, such as those you worked with in Explore, is a **radical equation**. The following are other examples of radical equations.

$$\sqrt{x} = 6 \qquad x + 2 = \sqrt{7x + 4}$$

As you discovered in Explore, you can use the following principle to solve radical equations.

PRINCIPLE OF SQUARING

If the equation $a = b$ is true, then the equation $a^2 = b^2$ is also true.

To solve a radical equation in the form $\sqrt{a} = b$, first square both sides. Then solve the resulting equation .

EXAMPLE 1

Solve and check: $\sqrt{2x - 1} = x$

Solution

$$\sqrt{2x-1} = x$$
$$(\sqrt{2x-1})^2 = x^2 \quad \text{Square both sides.}$$
$$2x - 1 = x^2$$
$$x^2 - 2x + 1 = 0$$
$$(x-1)(x-1) = 0$$
$$x = 1 \quad \text{Solve for } x.$$

Check

$$\sqrt{2x-1} = x$$
$$\sqrt{2(1)-1} \stackrel{?}{=} 1$$
$$\sqrt{1} \stackrel{?}{=} 1$$
$$1 = 1 \checkmark$$

The solution is $x = 1$.

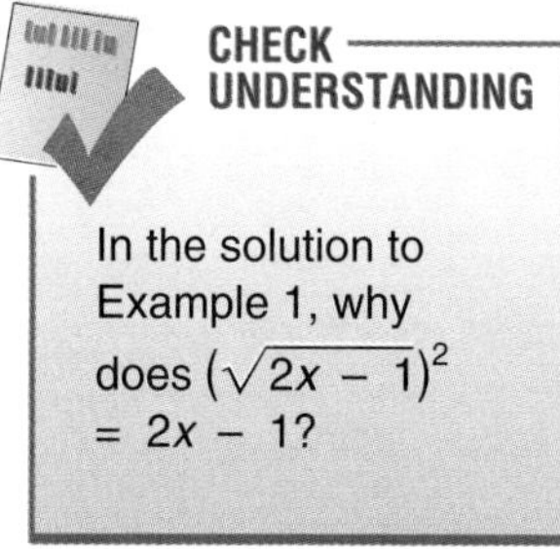

CHECK UNDERSTANDING

In the solution to Example 1, why does $(\sqrt{2x-1})^2 = 2x - 1$?

See Additional Answers.

To solve a radical equation of the form $\sqrt{a} + d = b$, first isolate the radical on one side of the equation. Then square both sides and solve the resulting equation. This step may introduce a number that appears to be a solution, but is not. Be sure to check all apparent solutions to see if they are actual solutions.

EXAMPLE 2

Solve and check: $\sqrt{2x - 1} - x = -2$

Solution

$$\sqrt{2x-1} - x = -2$$
$$\sqrt{2x-1} = x - 2 \quad \text{Isolate the radical.}$$
$$(\sqrt{2x-1})^2 = (x-2)^2 \quad \text{Square both sides of the equation.}$$
$$2x - 1 = x^2 - 4x + 4 \quad \text{Square the binomial.}$$
$$0 = x^2 - 6x + 5 \quad \text{Write the quadratic in standard form.}$$
$$0 = (x-1)(x-5) \quad \text{Factor.}$$
$$x - 1 = 0 \text{ or } x - 5 = 0 \quad \text{Use the zero product property.}$$
$$x = 1 \text{ or } x = 5$$

Check

$x = 1$

$$\sqrt{2x-1} - x = -2$$
$$\sqrt{2(1)-1} - 1 \stackrel{?}{=} -2$$
$$\sqrt{1} - 1 \stackrel{?}{=} -2$$
$$0 \neq -2$$

$x = 5$

$$\sqrt{2x-1} - x = -2$$
$$\sqrt{2(5)-1} - 5 \stackrel{?}{=} -2$$
$$\sqrt{9} - 5 \stackrel{?}{=} -2$$
$$-2 = -2 \checkmark$$

The solution is $x = 5$; $x = 1$ is not a solution.

COMMUNICATING ABOUT ALGEBRA

Explain to another student why it is easier to solve the equation in Example 2 by first isolating the radical than it would be to square both sides of the given equation.

See Additional Answers.

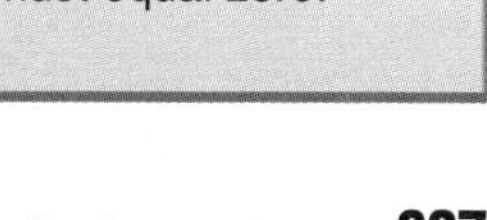

THINK BACK

The zero product property states that if the product of two quantities is zero, one or the other quantity, or both, must equal zero.

2 TEACH

Use the Pages/Build Understanding

Ask students to consider the radical equation $\sqrt{x} = x$. Ask them to identify what is wrong with this solution: $(\sqrt{x})^2 = x^2$, $x = x^2$, $1 = x$. **If a value for that variable is zero, you cannot solve the equation by dividing because you can't divide by zero.** Ask students to suggest another way to solve for x. **by factoring: $0 = x^2 - x$, $0 = x(x - 1)$, $x = 0$ or $x = 1$**

Example 1: Have students discuss Check Understanding. Ask them to give numerical examples of $(\sqrt{a^2}) = a$. **Possible examples: $(\sqrt{7})^2 = \sqrt{7} \cdot \sqrt{7} = 7$, $(\sqrt{2})^2 = \sqrt{2} \cdot \sqrt{2} = 2$**

Example 2: Have students discuss Communicating About Algebra. Ask them to square both sides of the equation before isolating the variable. **$2x - 1 - 2x\sqrt{(2x-1)} + x^2 = 4$** They should be able to see that they still would need to isolate the radical and square again. Stress the importance of isolating the radical first whenever possible. Also stress the importance of checking both solutions in the original equation to see whether either solution is extraneous.

Example 3: Ask students to rework the example and start by multiplying both sides of the equation by 2. **$1/2x = \sqrt{2x-3}$; $x = 2\sqrt{2x-3}$; $x^2 = 4(2x-3)$; $x^2 = 8x - 12$; $x = 6$ or $x = 2$.** Ask them which method they prefer and why. **Answers will vary.**

Example 4: Ask students to describe what the resulting equation would be like if they squared both sides before rewriting the equation with a radical on either side. **A trinomial with a radical as the middle term: $4(x - 9) - 4\sqrt{[(2x)(x-9)]} + 2x = 0$**

Example 5: Ask students to explain how the Pythagorean theorem gives $\sqrt{[h^2 + (0.3)^2]} = c$. **The legs and hypotenuse of the right triangle are h, 0.3, and c. Thus, by the Pythagorean theorem, $h^2 + (0.3)^2 = c^2$ can be solved to give $\sqrt{(h^2 + (0.3)^2)} = c$**

Make Connections

Science Explain that the lengths of the left and right arms of balance scales are not always *exactly* the same length. A technique that scientists use to make sure of an accurate weight is shown below. Have students follow the steps below to obtain the true weight W of an object.

- Place an object on the right side of the scale. Counterbalance the left side with weight W_1. Since the scale is in balance, the ratio of the object's true weight to W is equivalent to the ratio of the weight on the right side of the scale to the weight on the left side. Write this as $W/W_1 = R/L$.
- Place the object on the left side of the scale. Counterbalance the right side with Weight W_2. Then $W_2/W = R/L$.
- Substitute W/W_1 for R/L and write the equation $W/W_1 = W_2/W$. Solve for W: $\mathbf{W = \sqrt{W_1W_2}}$

Ongoing Assessment The important concepts and skills involve solving equations containing radical expressions. To assess this idea, have students demonstrate how they have applied it in Exercises 1, 3, and 7 of the Try These section.

Guided Practice/Try These Ask a student to describe how to solve the equation in Exercise 8. **Isolate the radical, square both sides of the equation, and solve for x; then check.** For Exercise 13, ask students how the equation $r = \sqrt{(A/\pi)}$ was obtained. **The formula for the area of a circle is $A = \pi r^2$. Thus, $\sqrt{A} = \sqrt{(\pi r^2)}$, $\sqrt{A} = \sqrt{\pi} \cdot \sqrt{r^2}$, $\sqrt{A}/\sqrt{\pi} = \sqrt{r^2}$, $\sqrt{A}/\sqrt{\pi} = r$, $\sqrt{(A/\pi)} = r$.** Have students share their answers to Exercise 14.

When solving a radical equation with a fraction, remember to multiply both sides by the denominator to clear the fractions.

EXAMPLE 3

Solve and check: $\frac{1}{2}x = \sqrt{2x - 3}$

Solution

$$\frac{1}{2}x = \sqrt{2x - 3}$$

$$\frac{x^2}{4} = 2x - 3 \quad \text{Square both sides.}$$

$$x^2 = 8x - 12 \quad \text{Multiply both sides by 4.}$$

$$x^2 - 8x + 12 = 0$$

$$(x - 6)(x - 2) = 0$$

$$x - 6 = 0 \quad \text{or} \quad x - 2 = 0$$

$$x = 6 \quad \text{or} \quad x = 2$$

The solutions are 6 and 2 since both check in the original equation.

PROBLEM SOLVING TIP

Remember that when you square both sides of the equation in Example 3, you must square not only the radical $\sqrt{x - 9}$, but also square the coefficient, $\frac{1}{2}$, as well.

When there are two different radicals, write the equation with one radical on each side before squaring both sides of the equation.

EXAMPLE 4

Solve and check: $2\sqrt{x - 9} - \sqrt{2x} = 0$

Solution

$$2\sqrt{x - 9} - \sqrt{2x} = 0$$

$$2\sqrt{x - 9} = \sqrt{2x} \quad \text{Add } \sqrt{2x} \text{ to both sides.}$$

$$(2\sqrt{x - 9})^2 = (\sqrt{2x})^2 \quad \text{Square both sides.}$$

$$4(x - 9) = 2x$$

$$4x - 36 = 2x \quad \text{Use the distributive property.}$$

$$2x = 36$$

$$x = 18 \quad \text{Solve for } x.$$

Check

$$2\sqrt{x - 9} - \sqrt{2x} = 0$$

$$2\sqrt{18 - 9} - \sqrt{2 \cdot 18} \stackrel{?}{=} 0 \quad \text{Substitute 18 for } x.$$

$$2\sqrt{9} - \sqrt{36} \stackrel{?}{=} 0$$

$$0 = 0$$

The solution is $x = 18$.

Real world problems may involve radical equations.

EXAMPLE 5

SKIING Both a chair lift and a gondola are used to transport skiers to the top of Triangle Mountain. The length of the gondola is 1.7 times the length of the chair lift cable, c. Use this information to determine h, the difference in elevation between the base of the mountain and the top.

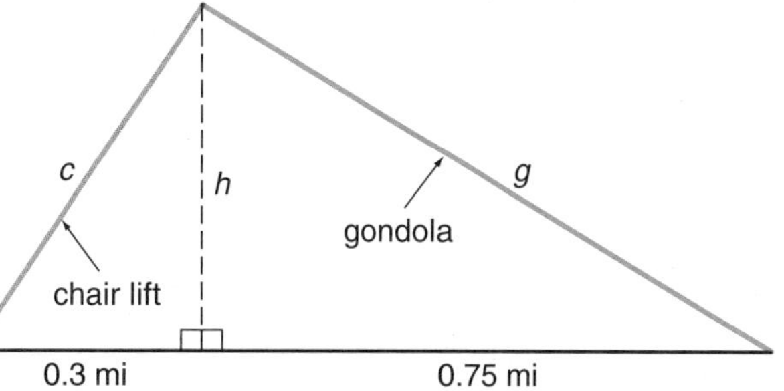

Solution

By the Pythagorean theorem,

$\sqrt{h^2 + (0.3)^2} = c$ **chair-lift triangle**

$\sqrt{h^2 + (0.75)^2} = g$ **gondola triangle**

$g = 1.7c$	Write an equation.
$\sqrt{h^2 + (0.75)^2} = 1.7\sqrt{h^2 + (0.3)^2}$	Substitute.
$\sqrt{h^2 + 0.5625} = 1.7\sqrt{h^2 + 0.09}$	Simplify the radicands.
$\left(\sqrt{h^2 + 0.5625}\right)^2 = \left(1.7\sqrt{h^2 + 0.09}\right)^2$	Square both sides.
$h^2 + 0.5625 = 2.89(h^2 + 0.09)$	
$h^2 + 0.5625 = 2.89h^2 + 0.2601$	Use the distributive property.
$0.3024 = 1.89h^2$	
$0.16 = h^2$	
$0.4 = h$	Solve for h.

From the base of the mountain to the top, the elevation is 0.4 mi. Check the solution. ◄

TRY THESE

Solve and check.

1. $\sqrt{x} = 3$ 9

2. $7 = \sqrt{x}$ 49

3. $\sqrt{x - 3} = 5$ 28

4. $\sqrt{2x - 5} = 11$ 63

5. $\sqrt{3x} = 6$ 12

6. $\sqrt{-5x} = 10$ −20

7. $7\sqrt{x + 3} - 6 = 22$ 13

8. $-3\sqrt{x - 5} + 15 = -6$ 54

9. $\sqrt{x + 7} = x - 5$ 9

10. $x - 5 = \sqrt{18 - 2x}$ 7

11. $\sqrt{5x - 9} - \sqrt{3x + 1} = 0$ 5

12. $\sqrt{5x - 4} - 3\sqrt{x - 4} = 0$ 8

13. **GEOMETRY** The formula $r = \sqrt{\frac{A}{\pi}}$ determines the radius of a circle with area A. Use the formula to write an equation to find the area of a circle with radius 11 cm. Then solve the equation. $11 = \sqrt{\frac{A}{\pi}}$; 121π cm^2

14. **WRITING MATHEMATICS** Explain how solving $2\sqrt{x - 1} + 5 = 15$ is similar to solving $2w + 5 = 15$. See Additional Answers.

3 SUMMARIZE

In the Math Journal Have students discuss if $a^2 = b^2$ is true, then is $a = b$ always true? Have them explain why or why not. Ask them to give examples. **It is not always true since if $a^2 = b^2$, then a could have the same value as b or have a value opposite to that of b; that is, $a = b$ or $a = -b$. Possible example: $(-3)^2 = 3^2$, but $-3 \neq 3$.**

4 PRACTICE

Practice For Exercises 9–35 remind students to check all solutions in the original equation. Ask students how Exercises 32–35 differ from the previous exercises. **In each equation at least one of the radicals is multiplied by a real number.** Remind students to square both the number and the radical when squaring both sides of the equation. Have students discuss their answers to Exercise 38.

NAME ____________ CLASS ________ DATE ________

RETEACHING **13.5 SOLVE RADICAL EQUATIONS**

The principle of squaring states that if $a = b$, then $a^2 = b^2$ for all real numbers a and b.

To solve a radical equation, follow these steps.

1. Be sure that the radical is isolated on one side of the equation.
2. Square both sides of the equation to eliminate the radical.
3. Solve the resulting equation.

Be sure to check all solutions by substituting in the *original* equation. Squaring both sides of the equation may introduce extraneous solutions—solutions that are true for the squared equation but not for the original equation.

Example

Solve: $\sqrt{x - 1} - x = -3$

Solution

$\sqrt{x - 1} - x = -3$

$\sqrt{x - 1} = x - 3$ Isolate the radical.

$(\sqrt{x - 1})^2 = (x - 3)^2$ Square both sides.

$x - 1 = x^2 - 6x + 9$ Square the binomial.

$0 = x^2 - 6x + 9 - x + 1$

$0 = x^2 - 7x + 10$

$0 = (x - 2)(x - 5)$ Factor.

$x = 2$ or $x = 5$

Check

$x = 2$	$x = 5$
$\sqrt{2 - 1} - 2 \stackrel{?}{=} -3$	$\sqrt{5 - 1} - 5 \stackrel{?}{=} -3$
$\sqrt{1} - 2 \stackrel{?}{=} -3$	$\sqrt{4} - 5 \stackrel{?}{=} -3$
$-1 \neq -3$	$2 - 5 \stackrel{?}{=} -3$
	$-3 = -3$ ✓

The only correct solution is $x = 5$.

EXERCISES

Solve and check.

1. $\sqrt{x} = 13$

2. $\sqrt{y} - 7 = 0$

3. $\sqrt{k} + 4 = 10$

4. $\sqrt{2z - 9} - 5 = 0$

5. $\sqrt{3y - 2} - 1 = 6$

6. $\sqrt{x + 6} = x$

7. $\sqrt{5x - 4} = x$

8. $\sqrt{3x - 2} - x = 0$

9. $\sqrt{2q + 8} - q = 0$

10. $\sqrt{r + 5} = r - 1$

11. $\sqrt{2x - 3} + 3 = x$

12. $\sqrt{8 - x} + x = 2$

1. 169
2. 49
3. 36
4. 17
5. 17
6. 3
7. 1, 4
8. 1, 2
9. 4
10. 4
11. 6
12. −1

30 *South-Western Algebra 1: AN INTEGRATED APPROACH*

Extend Have a volunteer describe how he or she solved the equation in Exercise 39. **$[\sqrt{(x+7)}]^2 = [\sqrt{(x-1)}+2]^2$, $x + 7 = x - 1 + 4\sqrt{(x-1)} + 4$, $4 = 4\sqrt{(x-1)}$, $1 = \sqrt{(x-1)}$, $1^2 = [\sqrt{(x-1)}]^2$, $1 = x - 1$, $2 = x$** For Exercises 44–47, after students have shared how to find values of n, ask them to write a general equation for n. **$n = \frac{b^2}{m}$**

Think Critically Have students discuss their answers to Exercises 48–50. Ask them to describe the general pattern of these equations. **If $y = \sqrt{x} + a$, the graph is the same as the graph of $y = \sqrt{x}$ except it is translated a units up for $a > 0$ and a units down for $a < 0$. If $y = \sqrt{(x+b)}$, the graph is the same as the graph of $y = \sqrt{x}$, except it is translated b units to the left for $b > 0$ and b units to the right for $b < 0$.**

NAME ______________ CLASS ________ DATE ________

EXTRA PRACTICE **13.5 SOLVE RADICAL EQUATIONS**

Solve and check.

1. $\sqrt{b} = 6$
2. $-\sqrt{y} = -9$
3. $\sqrt{k} - 12 = 0$
4. $\sqrt{y} - 7 = 0$
5. $8 - \sqrt{n} = 0$
6. $3\sqrt{z} = 18$
7. $-4\sqrt{c} = -44$
8. $\sqrt{x} + 5 = 12$
9. $\sqrt{y} - 10 = -5$
10. $\sqrt{x+9} = 5$
11. $\sqrt{3a} = 6$
12. $-\sqrt{4y} = -8$
13. $\sqrt{2s-6} = 8$
14. $\sqrt{2x-1} - 7 = 0$
15. $\sqrt{3k+1} - 4 = 6$
16. $\sqrt{2z+3} = z$
17. $\sqrt{4k-3} - k = 0$
18. $\sqrt{3z+4} - z = 0$
19. $\sqrt{x-5} = 5 - x$
20. $\sqrt{3x+1} + 3 = x$
21. $\sqrt{2x+3} + x = 6$
22. $\sqrt{x+3} = \sqrt{2x-5}$
23. $\sqrt{4x+1} = \sqrt{x+10}$
24. $2\sqrt{x-6} = \sqrt{3x-2}$

25. **GEOMETRY** The formula $r = \sqrt{\frac{V}{\pi h}}$ determines the radius r of a cylinder with volume V and height h. Use the formula to write an equation to find the height of a cylinder with radius 4 cm and volume 48π cm³. Then determine the height.
$4 = \sqrt{\frac{48\pi}{\pi h}}$; 3 cm

26. **PHYSICS** The formula $t = \sqrt{\frac{2d}{g}}$ determines the time it takes for a free-falling object to fall, where t is in seconds, $g = 9.8$ m/s², and d is the distance in meters. Use the formula to write an equation to determine the distance an object falls in 5 seconds. Then find the distance.
$5 = \sqrt{\frac{2d}{9.8}}$; 122.5 m

1. 36
2. 81
3. 144
4. 49
5. 64
6. 36
7. 121
8. 49
9. 25
10. 16
11. 12
12. 16
13. 35
14. 25
15. 33
16. 3
17. 1, 3
18. 4
19. 5
20. 8
21. 3
22. 8
23. 3
24. 22

32 *South-Western Algebra 1: AN INTEGRATED APPROACH*

PRACTICE

Write the square of each expression.

1. 9 81
2. –5 25
3. 1.2 1.44
4. –8.5 72.25
5. $\sqrt{6}$ 6
6. $\sqrt{27.13}$ 27.13
7. $\sqrt{x-5}$ $x - 5$
8. $\sqrt{3x^2+6}$ $3x^2 + 6$

Solve and check.

9. $\sqrt{a} = 2$ 4
10. $-\sqrt{x} = -11$ 121
11. $\sqrt{j} - 9 = 0$ 81
12. $\sqrt{m} - 4 = 0$ 16
13. $5\sqrt{p} = 30$ 36
14. $-28 = -4\sqrt{x}$ 49
15. $\sqrt{x} + 8 = 11$ 9
16. $\sqrt{n} - 3 = 7$ 100
17. $\sqrt{c+6} = 8$ 58
18. $\sqrt{s-9} = 5$ 34
19. $\sqrt{2d} = 12$ 72
20. $-\sqrt{5x} = -10$ 20
21. $\sqrt{2k-5} = 7$ 27
22. $\sqrt{4x+4} = 8$ 15
23. $\sqrt{3t-5} = 5$ 10
24. $\sqrt{6y-11} = 11$ 22
25. $\sqrt{3h} = \frac{1}{3}$ $\frac{1}{27}$
26. $\sqrt{5x-1} = \frac{1}{2}$ $\frac{1}{4}$
27. $\sqrt{z+18} = z - 2$ 7
28. $\sqrt{x+5} = 1 - x$ –1
29. $g + 1 = \sqrt{1-2g}$ 0
30. $\sqrt{x+7} = \sqrt{3x-19}$ 13
31. $\sqrt{5x+2} = \sqrt{-2x+23}$ 3
32. $2\sqrt{x+5} = \sqrt{6x-2}$ 11
33. $2\sqrt{6x+1} = 5\sqrt{x}$ 4
34. $3\sqrt{5x-4} - \sqrt{9x+9} = 0$ $\frac{5}{4}$
35. $4\sqrt{x-1} - \sqrt{13x+14} = 0$ 10

36. **PLUMBING** A circular pipe has an inner radius of r and a cross-sectional area of A. The outer radius R of the pipe is given by $R = \sqrt{\frac{A}{\pi} + r^2}$.

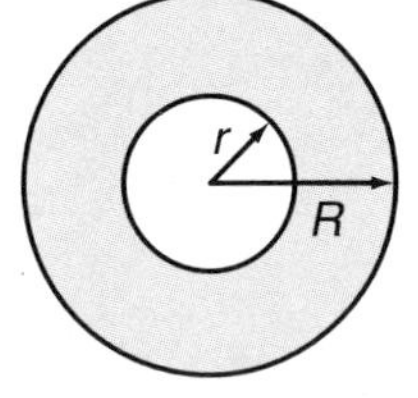

Use the formula to write an equation to find the inner radius of apipe with an outer radius of 2 cm and across-sectional area of 1.75π cm². Then solve the equation. $2 = \sqrt{\frac{1.75\pi}{\pi} + r^2}$; 1.5 cm

37. **AUTO MECHANICS** An engine piston is acted on by a force F producing pressure P. The diameter d of the piston is given by $d = \sqrt{\frac{5F}{4P}}$. Use the formula to write an equation you can use to find the force in pounds that produces a pressure of 80 lb/in.² on a piston with a diameter of 3 in. Then solve the equation. See Additional Answers.

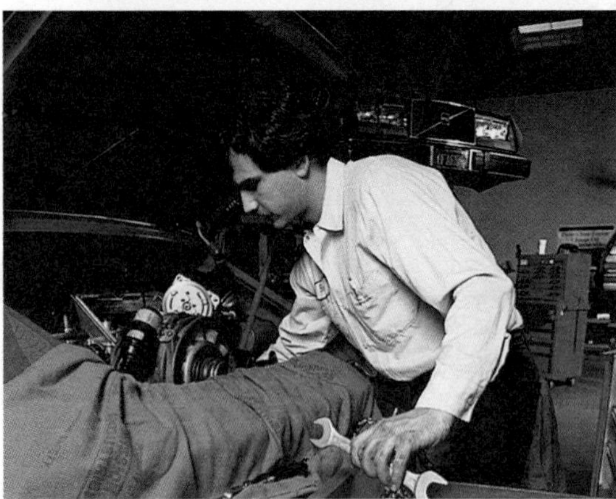

38. **WRITING MATHEMATICS** Explain why it is important to check solutions to a radical equation. Provide examples to illustrate your explanation. See Additional Answers.

EXTEND

After squaring both sides of a radical equation, the equation may still contain a radical. To solve, isolate the remaining radical and repeat the process.

Solve and check.

39. $\sqrt{x + 7} = \sqrt{x - 1} + 2$ 2

40. $5 - \sqrt{x} = \sqrt{x - 5}$ 9

41. $\sqrt{x} + \sqrt{x + 1} = 2$ $\frac{9}{16}$

42. $\sqrt{x + 4} = 1 + \sqrt{x}$ $\frac{9}{4}$

43. The perimeter of the rectangle is 42. Find the value of x. 218

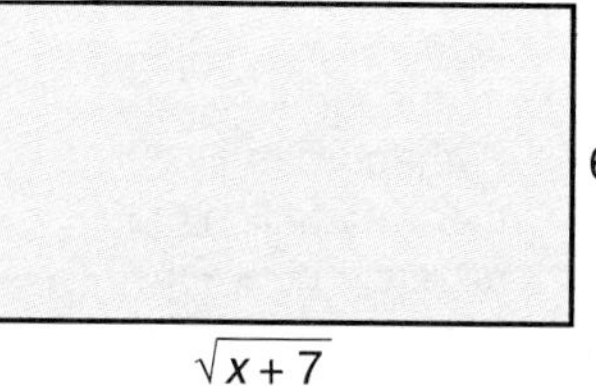

GEOMETRY A number b is the **geometric mean** between two numbers m and n if $\frac{m}{b} = \frac{b}{n}$. The geometric mean of two numbers m and n is $\sqrt{mn}$. Determine n, given m and the geometric mean of m and n.

44. $m = 5$, geometric mean $= 10$ 20

45. $m = 3$, geometric mean $= 6$ 12

46. $m = 16$, geometric mean $= 12$ 9

47. $m = 20$, geometric mean $= 30$ 45

THINK CRITICALLY

48. Graph $y_1 = \sqrt{x}$, $y_2 = \sqrt{x} + 2$, $y_3 = \sqrt{x} - 3$ on the same set of axes. How is the graph of y_2 related to the graph of y_1? How is the graph of y_3 related to the graph of y_1? See Additional Answers.

49. Graph $y_1 = \sqrt{x}$, $y_2 = \sqrt{x + 2}$, $y_3 = \sqrt{x - 3}$ on the same set of axes. How is the graph of y_2 related to the graph of y_1? How is the graph of y_3 related to the graph of y_1? See Additional Answers.

50. The graph of a certain function is translated 4 units up and 1 unit to the right from the graph of $y = \sqrt{x}$. Write the equation of the function. Check your answer by comparing the graph to the graph of $y = \sqrt{x}$. $y = \sqrt{x - 1} + 4$; See Additional Answers for graph.

51. When 8 times a number is decreased by 3, the square root of the result is 9. Find the number. 10.5

MIXED REVIEW

Find the mean, median, and mode of each set of data. Lesson 1.7

52. $\{9, 5, 4, 9, 8\}$ 7, 8, 9

53. $\{42, 48, 29, 37, 66, 28, 37, 45\}$ 41.5, 39.5, 37

Solve each inequality. Lesson 5.4

54. $4x - 5 \le 23$ $x \le 7$

55. $2x + 6 > 3x - 5$ $x < 11$

56. $7(3 - x) < -5(x - 5)$ $x > -2$

Solve each system by graphing. Lesson 7.2

57. $\begin{cases} y = 2x - 1 \\ y = -x + 5 \end{cases}$ 2, 3

58. $\begin{cases} y = -2x + 2 \\ y = x + 5 \end{cases}$ −1, 4

Solve each equation. Lesson 13.4

59. $\sqrt{3x - 2} = 5$ 9

60. $\sqrt{x^2 + 2} = \sqrt{x^2 + x}$ 2

61. $\sqrt{x + 2} - x = -4$ 7

5 FOLLOW-UP

Extension Have students graph the rational equation $y = \sqrt{x}$ and each of the equations below. Have them describe how each graph is related to the graph of $y = \sqrt{x}$.

a. $y = \sqrt{-x}$ **b.** $y = -\sqrt{x}$

c. $y = \sqrt{2x}$ **d.** $y = 2\sqrt{x}$

a. The graph of $y = \sqrt{-x}$ is the reflection of the graph of $y = \sqrt{x}$ over the y-axis.

b. The graph of $y = -\sqrt{x}$ is the reflection of the graph of $y = \sqrt{x}$ over the x-axis.

c. The graph of $y = \sqrt{2x}$ is $\sqrt{2}$ times as high for each value of x.

d. The graph of $y = 2\sqrt{x}$ is 2 times as high for each value of x.

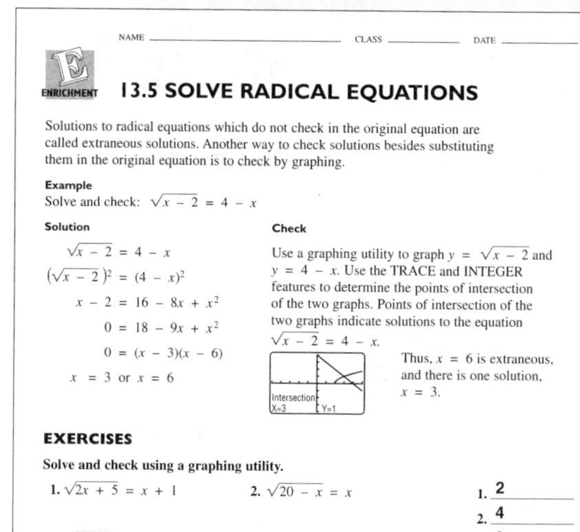

NAME ____________ CLASS ________ DATE ________

ENRICHMENT **13.5 SOLVE RADICAL EQUATIONS**

Solutions to radical equations which do not check in the original equation are called extraneous solutions. Another way to check solutions besides substituting them in the original equation is to check by graphing.

Example

Solve and check: $\sqrt{x - 2} = 4 - x$

Solution

$$\sqrt{x - 2} = 4 - x$$
$$(\sqrt{x - 2})^2 = (4 - x)^2$$
$$x - 2 = 16 - 8x + x^2$$
$$0 = 18 - 9x + x^2$$
$$0 = (x - 3)(x - 6)$$
$$x = 3 \text{ or } x = 6$$

Check

Use a graphing utility to graph $y = \sqrt{x - 2}$ and $y = 4 - x$. Use the TRACE and INTEGER features to determine the points of intersection of the two graphs. Points of intersection of the two graphs indicate solutions to the equation $\sqrt{x - 2} = 4 - x$.

Intersection X=3 Y=1

Thus, $x = 6$ is extraneous, and there is one solution, $x = 3$.

EXERCISES

Solve and check using a graphing utility.

1. $\sqrt{2x + 5} = x + 1$
2. $\sqrt{20 - x} = x$
3. $\sqrt{x + 7} = x - 5$
4. $\sqrt{6 - x} = x$
5. $\sqrt{3x + 4} - x = 0$
6. $\sqrt{2x - 1} = x - 8$
7. $\sqrt{8 - x} = x - 2$
8. $\sqrt{2x + 3} = x$
9. $\sqrt{2 - x} = x + 4$
10. $\sqrt{2x + 6} = x + 3$
11. $\sqrt{1 - x} = x + 5$
12. $\sqrt{x + 8} = x + 8$
13. $\sqrt{4x - 7} = x - 7$
14. $\sqrt{3x - 2} = x - 4$

1. 2
2. 4
3. 9
4. 2
5. 4
6. 13
7. 4
8. 3
9. −2
10. −1, −3
11. −3
12. −7, −8
13. 14
14. 9

34 *South-Western Algebra 1:* AN INTEGRATED APPROACH

LESSON PLANNING

Objective

- Use the Pythagorean theorem to find the distance between two points in the coordinate plane.

Vocabulary

distance formula
midpoint
midpoint formula

Technology/Multimedia

calculator

Resources

Warm Up 13.6
Reteaching 13.6
Extra Practice 13.6
Enrichment 13.6
Transparencies 32, 73, 78–80
Student Handbook
Lesson Quiz 13.6

Materials/Manipulatives

graph paper
straightedge

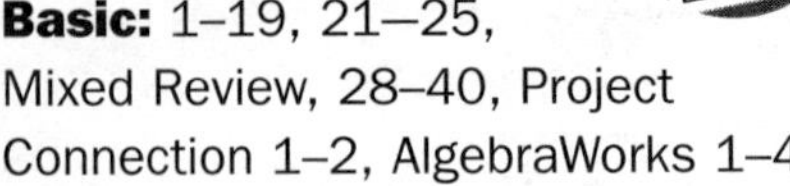

ASSIGNMENTS

Basic: 1–19, 21–25, Mixed Review, 28–40, Project Connection 1–2, AlgebraWorks 1–4

Average: 2–26, Mixed Review 28–40, Project Connection 1–2, AlgebraWorks 1–4

Enriched: 3–27, Mixed Review 28–40, Project Connection 1–2, AlgebraWorks 1–4

13.6 The Distance and Midpoint Formulas

SPOTLIGHT ON LEARNING

WHAT? In this lesson you will learn

- to use the Pythagorean theorem to find the distance between two points in the coordinate plane.
- to use the midpoint formula to find the midpoint of a segment.

WHY? Knowing the distance and midpoint formulas can help you solve problems in geometry and navigation.

Explore

Graph to determine the distance between each point.

1. (2, 3) and (8, 3) 6 units
2. (−7, −3) and (0, −3) 7 units
3. (−4, 5) and (5, 5) 9 units
4. (17, −1) and (−5, −1) 22 units
5. What is the distance between the points (a, c) and (b, c)? $|a - b|$

Graph to determine the distance between each point.

6. (4, 1) and (4, 11) 10 units
7. (0, −8) and (0, −12) 4 units
8. (−2, 9) and (−2, −5) 14 units
9. (1, −7) and (1, 2) 9 units
10. What is the distance between the points (a, b) and (a, c)? $|b - c|$
11. Graph the points (4, −1), (10, 7), and (4, 7). Describe the kind of triangle formed. Determine the length of each side of the triangle.
a right triangle; 6 units, 8 units, and 10 units

Build Understanding

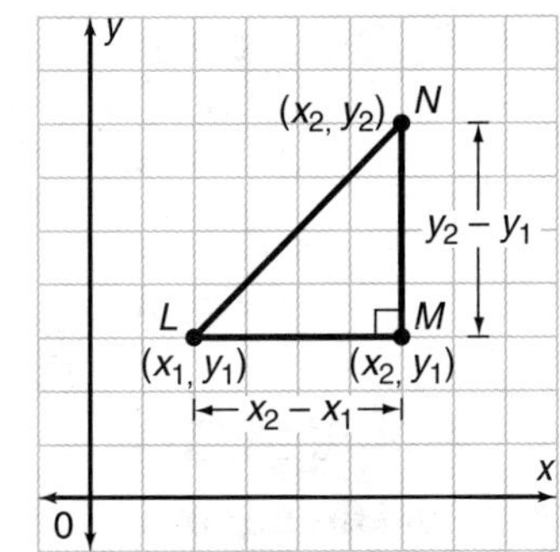

As you saw in Explore, you can determine the distance between two points in the coordinate plane. If the two points are on a vertical line, you can subtract the y-values. If the two points are on a horizontal line, you can subtract the x-values. If the two points are not on a vertical or horizontal line, you can think of the two points as endpoints of the hypotenuse of a right triangle. Then you can use the Pythagorean theorem to determine the distance.

The *distance formula* combines all the steps you used in Explore to determine the distance between two points in the coordinate plane.

DISTANCE FORMULA

If d is the distance between the two points (x_1, y_1) and (x_2, y_2) in the coordinate plane, then

$$d = \sqrt{(x_2 - x_1)^2 + (y_2 - y_1)^2}$$

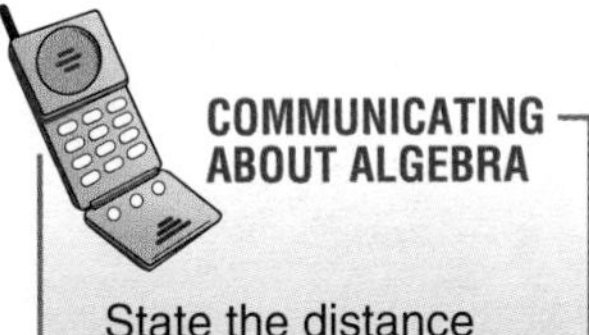

COMMUNICATING ABOUT ALGEBRA

State the distance formula in your own words.

See Additional Answers.

EXAMPLE 1

Use the distance formula to determine the distance between the points (2, –4) and (14, 1).

Solution

Let $(x_1, y_1) = (2, -4)$ and let $(x_2, y_2) = (14, 1)$. Then $x_1 = 2$, $x_2 = 14$, $y_1 = -4$, and $y_2 = 1$.

$$
\begin{aligned}
d &= \sqrt{(x_2 - x_1)^2 + (y_2 - y_1)^2} && \text{Distance formula.}\\
&= \sqrt{(14 - 2)^2 + (1 - (-4))^2} && \text{Substitute.}\\
&= \sqrt{12^2 + 5^2} && \text{Subtract.}\\
&= \sqrt{144 + 25} && \text{Square the terms.}\\
&= \sqrt{169} && \text{Add.}\\
&= 13 && \text{Simplify.}
\end{aligned}
$$

PROBLEM SOLVING TIP

You can choose either point for (x_1, y_1) and the other point for (x_2, y_2). In Example 1, (14, 1) was chosen for (x_2, y_2) to make the calculations easier.

With a calculator, enter the expression after you have substituted. Be sure to include parentheses.

$$\sqrt{((14 - 2)^2 + (1 - (-4))^2)} = 13$$

The distance between the points is 13 units. ◀

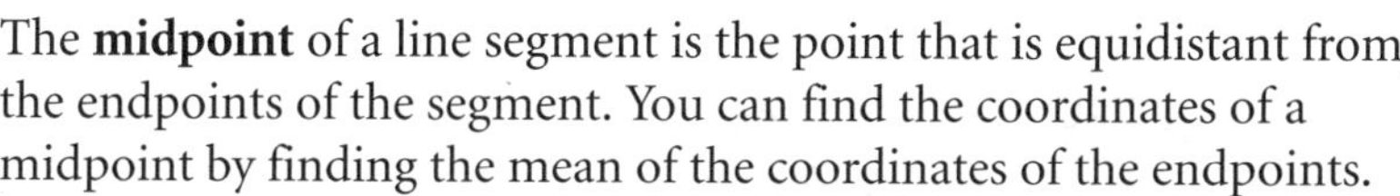

The **midpoint** of a line segment is the point that is equidistant from the endpoints of the segment. You can find the coordinates of a midpoint by finding the mean of the coordinates of the endpoints.

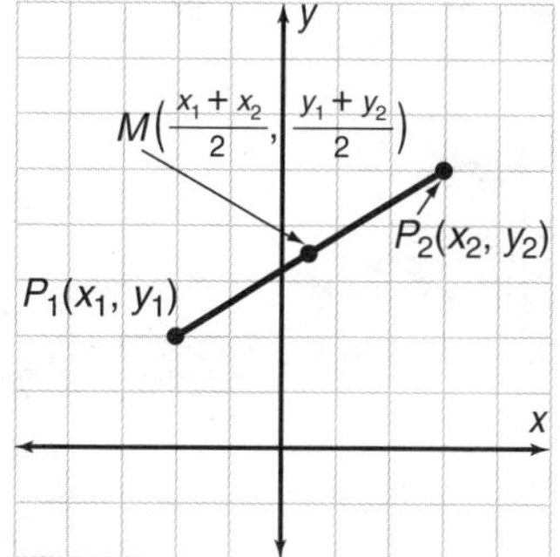

MIDPOINT FORMULA

The *midpoint* M of the line segment whose endpoints are $P_1(x_1, y_1)$ and $P_2(x_2, y_2)$ is

$$M\left(\frac{x_1 + x_2}{2}, \frac{y_1 + y_2}{2}\right)$$

EXAMPLE 2

Determine the midpoint of the segment with endpoints (–3, 5) and (11, –1).

Solution

Let $(x_1, y_1) = (-3, 5)$ and let $(x_2, y_2) = (11, -1)$. Then $x_1 = -3$, $x_2 = 11$, $y_1 = 5$, and $y_2 = -1$.

$$
\begin{aligned}
&\left(\frac{x_1 + x_2}{2}, \frac{y_1 + y_2}{2}\right) && \text{Midpoint formula.}\\
&= \left(\frac{-3 + 11}{2}, \frac{5 + (-1)}{2}\right)\\
&= (4, 2)
\end{aligned}
$$

The midpoint of the segment is (4, 2). ◀

CHECK UNDERSTANDING

In Example 2, how could you use the distance formula to verify that (4, 2) is the correct answer?

See Additional Answers.

1 MOTIVATE

Explore For Question 11, ask students how to determine the length of the sides of the triangle. **The length of one leg of the right triangle is the distance between (4, 7) and (4, –1), or 8; the length of the other leg is the distance between (4, 7) and (10, 7), or 6; by the Pythagorean theorem the hypotenuse is $\sqrt{(6^2 + 8^2)} = 10$.**

2 TEACH

Use the Pages/Build Understanding

Example 1: After students have discussed the example, ask them to graph (2, –4) and (14, 1). Use the Pythagorean theorem to verify that 13 is the distance between the two points. Ask students to name the three points forming the vertices and the lengths of each leg. **(2, –4), (14, 1), and either (2, 1), or (14, –4)** Point out that there are two possible right triangles that can be drawn. Each gives the same result.

Example 2: After students have discussed the example, have them consider the question in Check Understanding. Have them verify that (4, 2) is the midpoint of the line segment with endpoints (–3, 5) and (11, –1). **$d_1 = \sqrt{(4 + 3)^2 + (2 - 5)^2} = \sqrt{(49 + 9)} = \sqrt{58}$; $d_2 = \sqrt{(11 - 4)^2 + (-1 - 2)^2} = \sqrt{(49 + 9)} = \sqrt{58}$; $d_{1+2} = \sqrt{(11 + 3)^2 + (-1 - 5)^2} = \sqrt{(196 + 36)} = 2\sqrt{58}$; since $d_1 + d_2 = d_{1+2}$, (4, 2) is the midpoint**

Example 3: Point out that it is important in real world problems to check the reasonableness of all solutions.

Make Connections
Geometry Ask what figure would contain all the points on the coordinate plane equidistant from the point (4, 6). **a circle** Have students use the distance formula to determine an equation for all the points 6 units from the point (4, 6).
$6 = \sqrt{[(x - 4)^2 + (y - 6)^2]}$ or $36 = (x - 4)^2 + (y - 6)^2$ Explain that the equation of any circle on the coordinate plane with center at a point (h, k) and radius r is $r^2 = (x - h)^2 + (y - k)^2$.

Ongoing Assessment The important concepts and skills are finding the distance between two points and finding a midpoint of a segment joining two points in the coordinate plane. To assess these ideas, have students demonstrate how they have applied these concepts and skills in Exercises 1, 4, and 7 of the Try These section.

Guided Practice/Try These For Exercise 10, ask students how they know that the triangle is isosceles. **because two of the sides have equal measures**

3 SUMMARIZE

In the Math Journal Have students discuss how they can use the distance formula to determine an equation of the perpendicular bisector of the segment joined by the points (–1, 4) and (5, –2). (Hint: Any point on the perpendicular bisector of a line segment is equidistant from the endpoints of the segment.) **The distance between (–1, 4) and (x, y) is equal to the distance between (5, –2) and (x, y).**

$$\sqrt{[(x + 1)^2 + (y - 4)^2]} = \sqrt{[(x - 5)^2 + (y + 2)^2]}$$
$$x^2 + 2x + 1 + y^2 - 8y + 16 = x^2 - 10x + 25 + y^2 + 4y + 4$$
$$12x - 12y - 12 = 0$$
$$y = x - 1$$

To solve real world problems involving the distance formula, you may need to solve a radical equation.

EXAMPLE 3

A coordinate grid of Valley Park is drawn using Valley Creek as the positive x-axis and Park Road as the positive y-axis. (Units are in miles.) Park officials are laying out a straight-line race course from the Visitor Center (1, 1.4) to a point on Valley Creek $(x, 0)$. If the course must be exactly 5 mi long, where will it intersect Valley Creek?

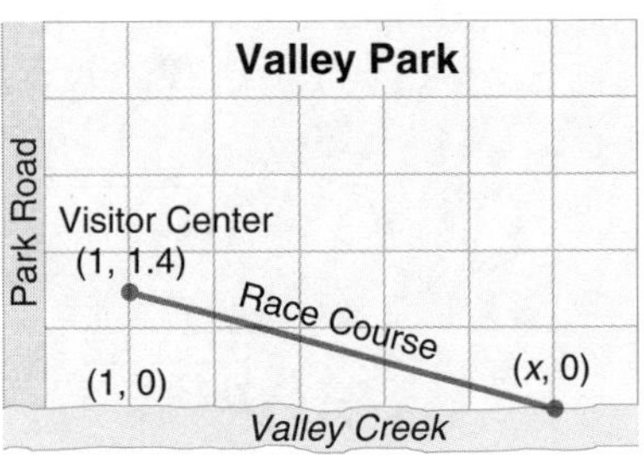

Solution

Let $d = 5, x_2 = 1, x_1 = x, y_2 = 1.4$, and $y_1 = 0$.

$d = \sqrt{(x_2 - x_1)^2 + (y_2 - y_1)^2}$ — Distance formula.

$5 = \sqrt{(1 - x)^2 + (1.4 - 0)^2}$ — Substitute.

$25 = (1 - x)^2 + (1.4 - 0)^2$ — Square both sides of the equation.

$25 = (1 - 2x + x^2) + 1.96$

$0 = x^2 - 2x - 22.04$ — Write the equation in standard form.

$x = \dfrac{2 \pm \sqrt{(-2)^2 - 4(1)(-22.04)}}{2(1)}$ — Use the quadratic formula.

$x = \dfrac{2 \pm \sqrt{92.16}}{2}$ — Simplify.

$x = 5.8$ or $x = -3.8$ — To the nearest tenth of a mile.

The race course intersects Valley Creek at (5.8, 0) or (–3.8, 0). Since (–3.8, 0) lies outside the park boundaries, the intersection point is (5.8, 0). ◄

TRY THESE

Determine the distance between the points. Write radicals in simplest form.

1. (5, –2) and (–5, –2) 10
2. (–7, 4) and (–7, –2) 6
3. (3, 7) and (8, –5) 13
4. (5, 9) and (–1, 6) $3\sqrt{5}$
5. (–6, –10) and (9, –2) 17
6. $(\sqrt{2}, \sqrt{6})$ and (0, 0) $2\sqrt{2}$

Determine the midpoint of the segment joining the two points.

7. (2, 5) and (6, 1) (4, 3)
8. (–7, 11) and (–1, 3) (–4, 7)
9. (3, 7) and (14, 20) $\left(\frac{17}{2}, \frac{27}{2}\right)$

10. GEOMETRY Determine the lengths of the sides of the triangle formed by connecting the points (5, 1), (1, –2), and (2, –3). Then state whether the triangle is *scalene*, *isosceles*, or *equilateral*. 5, 5, $\sqrt{2}$; isosceles

11. WRITING MATHEMATICS State whether you agree or disagree with this statement: the distance formula is an application of the Pythagorean theorem. Explain your reasoning. See Additional Answers.

PRACTICE

Determine the distance between the points. Write radicals in simplest form.

1. (12, 10) and (6, 2) 10
2. (9, 7) and (–6, 15) 17
3. (–2, –3) and (0, –7) $2\sqrt{5}$
4. (0, 0) and (5, 6) $\sqrt{61}$
5. (–8, 6) and (–1, 7) $5\sqrt{2}$
6. (5, 4) and (13, 8) $4\sqrt{5}$
7. (–9, –15) and (–2, 9) 25
8. (4, 4.5) and (0, 12) 8.5
9. $\left(2\frac{1}{2}, 4\frac{1}{2}\right)$ and $\left(-6\frac{1}{2}, 44\frac{1}{2}\right)$ 41

Determine the midpoint of the segment joining the two points.

10. (5, 6) and (3, 8) (4, 7)
11. (–1, –3) and (7, –11) (3, –7)
12. (8, 12) and (3, –2) (5.5, 5)
13. (–7, –9) and (2, –13) (–2.5, –11)
14. (–3, 0) and (2, 0) (–0.5, 0)
15. (m, n) and $(m, -n)$ $(m, 0)$

GEOMETRY For Exercises 16 and 17, state whether the triangle connecting the points is *scalene, isosceles*, or *equilateral*.

16. (3, 4), (8, –1), (10, 3) isosceles
17. $(-4, 0), (0, 4\sqrt{3}), (4, 0)$ equilateral

18. GEOMETRY The endpoints of a diameter of a circle are (–3, 6) and (9, 3). Find the coordinates of the center of the circle and the length of its radius. $\left(3, 4\frac{1}{2}\right)$; $\frac{3}{2}\sqrt{17}$

19. WRITING MATHEMATICS To find the distance between (4, 2) and (6, –1), must you use 4 for x_1? Explain. See Additional Answers.

EXTEND

20. NAVIGATION A tanker at (630, 21) on a coordinate grid of the Atlantic Ocean sets a straight-line course for Libreville, Gabon, on the equator 29 mi away. Find the coordinates of Libreville. (Units are in miles.) (650, 0)

21. Use the distance formula to verify that the midpoint of the segment joining the points $A(2, 5)$ and $B(12, -1)$ is $M(7, 2)$. $AM = MB = \sqrt{34}$

22. Determine the point on the x-axis that is equidistant from the points (–4, 5) and (3, 2). (–2, 0)

23. The point $(3, a)$ is 5 units from the point (7, 9). Find all values of a. 6 or 12

24. The point $(b, 12)$ is 17 units from the point (2, 4). Find all values of b. 17 or –13

4 PRACTICE

Practice Ask a student to determine the midpoint of the segment joining the two points in Exercise 15. **$[(m + m)/2, (n + (-n))/2]$, $[(2m)/2, 0/2]$, $(m, 0)$** For Exercises 16–17, ask students to explain how to determine whether the triangles are scalene, isosceles, or equilateral. **Use the distance formula to find the length of each side and classify each triangle according to the lengths of its sides.** Ask students how they can determine the center and the radius of the circle in Exercise 18. **center: determine the midpoint of the segment joining the two points; radius: determine the length of the segment joined by the center point and one endpoint.**

NAME ______ CLASS ______ DATE ______

13.6 THE DISTANCE AND MIDPOINT FORMULAS

The distance between any two points (x_1, y_1) and (x_2, y_2), is determined by the distance formula, $d = \sqrt{(x_2 - x_1)^2 + (y_2 - y_1)^2}$.

Example
Given two points A and B, find the distance between them.

Solution

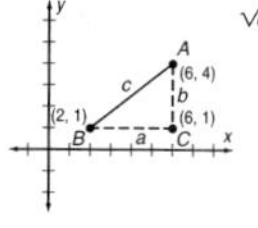

$$\sqrt{a^2 + b^2 = c^2} = \sqrt{(x_2 - x_1)^2 + (y_2 - y_1)^2}$$ Use distance formula.
$$= \sqrt{(6 - 2)^2 + (4 - 1)^2}$$ Substitute given values.
$$= \sqrt{4^2 + 3^2}$$ Simplify.
$$= \sqrt{16 + 9}$$
$$= \sqrt{25}$$
$$= \sqrt{5}$$

The distance between the points A and B is 5.

The midpoint of a line segment is the average of the x- and y-coordinates of the endpoints. The formula is

$$M\left(\frac{x_1 + x_2}{2}, \frac{y_1 + y_2}{2}\right)$$

Example
Find the coordinates of the midpoint of AB in the figure above.

Solution

$$\left(\frac{6 + 2}{2}, \frac{4 + 1}{2}\right) = \left(\frac{8}{2}, \frac{5}{2}\right) = (4, 2.5)$$

The coordinates of the midpoint of AB are (4, 2.5).

EXERCISES

Determine the distance between the points. Write radicals in simplest form.

1. (1, 6) and (8, 5)
2. (–3, –1) and (3, 4)
3. (–3, 0) and (7, 2)
4. (0, –6) and (–2, –3)
5. (–3, –12) and (1, –9)
6. (0, 0) and (–6, 8)

Determine the coordinates of the midpoint of the segment with the given coordinates.

7. (–6, –3) and (10, 5)
8. (8, –2) and (6, 2)
9. (–12, –6) and (12, –12)
10. (1, 0) and (9, 4)

1. $5\sqrt{2}$
2. $\sqrt{61}$
3. $2\sqrt{26}$
4. $\sqrt{13}$
5. 5
6. 10
7. (8, 1)
8. (7, 0)
9. (0, –9)
10. (5, 2)

38 *South-Western Algebra 1: AN INTEGRATED APPROACH*

Extend For Exercise 22, ask students to describe how they can determine the point that is equidistant from the two points. **Determine the length of the segment joining the points (−4, 5) and (*x*, 0) and the points (3, 2) and (*x*, 0); use the distance formula to write an expression for each length and set them equal to each other. Then solve for *x*. The equation will be $\sqrt{(x-3)^2+(0-2)^2} = \sqrt{(x+4)^2+(0-5)^2}$**

Think Critically For Exercise 25, students will need to draw a diagram on a grid to represent the problem. Ask how they solved part b. **substituted $x = 1$ and $y = 4$ in $y = 2x + b$ and solved for b** Ask how they solved part c. **solved the system $y = 2x + 2$ and $y = -x/2 - 3$ for the point of intersection** After students complete the problem, point out that the distance they determined along the perpendicular is the shortest distance from (1, 4) to $y = -x/2 - 3$.

THINK CRITICALLY

25. Use these steps to find the distance from the point (1, 4) to the line $y = -\frac{1}{2}x - 3$.
    a. Find the slope of the line through (1, 4) that is perpendicular to the given line. 2
    b. Find the equation of the line through (1, 4) that is perpendicular to the given line. $y = 2x + 2$
    c. Find the point of intersection of the line you have found and the given line. (−2, −2)
    d. Find the distance from the point (1, 4) to the point of intersection. $3\sqrt{5}$

26. A circle with its center at the origin has a radius of 3. Write the equation of the circle by using the distance formula to express the distance between the origin and any point (x, y) that is on the circle. $\sqrt{x^2 + y^2} = 3$, or $x^2 + y^2 = 9$

27. An ellipse is an oval or elongated circle. Each point (x, y) on a certain ellipse has the property that the sum of its distances from the points (−4, 0) and (4, 0) equals 12. Use the distance formula to write the equation of the ellipse. $\sqrt{(x+4)^2 + y^2} + \sqrt{(x-4)^2 + y^2} = 12$

MIXED REVIEW

Evaluate each expression. Lesson 2.8

28. $6 + 3 \cdot 2$ 12
29. $36 \div 18 \div 2$ 1
30. $20 - 10 \div 5$ 18
31. $24 - 19 - 3$ 2
32. $24 - (19 - 3)$ 8
33. $5 + 2^2$ 9

34. STANDARDIZED TESTS The equation of a vertical line passing through the point (5, 7) is D; Lesson 6.5
    A. $y = 7$ B. $y = -7$ C. $x = -5$ D. $x = 5$

Solve by using the quadratic formula. Write answers in simplest radical form. Lesson 10.5

35. $x^2 - 10x + 22 = 0$ $5 \pm \sqrt{3}$
36. $3x^2 - 4x - 2 = 0$ $\frac{2 \pm \sqrt{10}}{3}$
37. $4x^2 + 20x + 23 = 0$ $\frac{-5 \pm \sqrt{2}}{2}$

Determine the distance between the points. Lesson 13.5

38. (−5, 0) and (0, −5) $5\sqrt{2}$
39. (9, 3) and (−7, −9) 20
40. (6, −3) and (4, 2) $\sqrt{29}$

PROJECT Connection For this activity, you will need to know the average number of miles each car travels per gallon of gasoline (mpg). The owner may have a reliable value from past experience; otherwise, plan a test drive to collect the data you to need calculate the value.

1. Obtain a road map of the United States. Select three major cities that seem to form a right triangle when segments are drawn to connect them. Use the map scale to determine the distances represented by the legs of the triangle. Then use the Pythagorean theorem to calculate the longest distance. Compare your result with the distance you obtain by measuring and using the map scale. Also, look up the distances between your cities in a reference book. How can you account for any differences? See Additional Answers.
2. Use each car's mpg, determined earlier. How many gallons of gas would be necessary to drive from your hometown to the closest city on the triangle, travel on the perimeter of the triangle to visit the other two cities, and return home? Use an average per-gallon price to determine the gasoline expense for the trip. Answers will vary.

NAME ______ CLASS ______ DATE ______

P EXTRA PRACTICE

13.6 THE DISTANCE AND MIDPOINT FORMULAS

Determine the distance between the points. Write radicals in simplest form.

1. (2, −2) and (8, 6)
2. (3, 1) and (10, 2)
3. (−5, 0) and (−1, −3)
4. (−12, −4) and (−10, 0)
5. (6, 9) and (−9, 1)
6. (−7, −1) and (−4, −7)
7. (16, 4) and (−8, 11)
8. (12, 3) and (15, 8)
9. (−1, 7) and (2, −2)
10. (2, −5) and (8, −1)
11. (−4, −8) and (5, 4)
12. (3, −2) and (−2, 3)

Determine the midpoint of the segment joining the two points.

13. (3, 6) and (5, −2)
14. (−2, −1) and (0, −3)
15. (1, −7) and (11, 3)
16. (0, 12) and (5, 6)
17. (−2, 3) and (0, 8)
18. (8, 1) and (2, 5)
19. (−5, −2) and (−1, −8)
20. (4, −2) and (3, −7)
21. (−12, −1) and (−3, −5)

22. Determine the lengths of the sides of the triangle formed by connecting the points (−2, −3), (5, −4), and (−3, 4). Then state whether the triangle is *scalene*, *isosceles*, or *equilateral*.
    $8\sqrt{2}$, $5\sqrt{2}$, $5\sqrt{2}$; isosceles

23. Determine the perimeter of the triangle formed by connecting points (0, 1), (1, 3), and (3, −1).
    $3\sqrt{5} + \sqrt{13}$

24. The endpoints of a diameter of a circle are (−5, −4) and (8, 5). Determine the coordinates of the center of the circle and the length of its radius.
    $\left(1\frac{1}{2}, \frac{1}{2}\right)$; $\frac{5\sqrt{10}}{2}$

1. 10
2. $5\sqrt{2}$
3. 5
4. $2\sqrt{5}$
5. 17
6. $3\sqrt{5}$
7. 25
8. $\sqrt{34}$
9. $3\sqrt{10}$
10. $2\sqrt{13}$
11. 15
12. $5\sqrt{2}$
13. (4, 2)
14. (−1, −2)
15. (6, −2)
16. (2.5, 9)
17. (−1, 5.5)
18. (5, 3)
19. (−3, −5)
20. (3.5, −4.5)
21. (−7.5, −3)

40 South-Western Algebra 1: AN INTEGRATED APPROACH

Career
Air Traffic Controller

In 1992, a record 473,305,000 passengers flew on commercial airlines in the United States, accumulating a grand total of 478 *billion* miles in the air. Chicago's O'Hare Airport was the world's busiest, with more than 64 million passengers. Every day about 2300 planes take off or land at O'Hare.

Given so much daily traffic, the job of air traffic controller is certainly challenging. At any given moment a controller may be keeping track of a dozen or more planes traveling at different altitudes, speeds, and directions. Because of this, a keen ability to visualize three-dimensional relationships is a prerequisite for controllers.

Decision Making

1. Determine the mean number of miles flown by each airline passenger in 1992. $\approx$1,010 mi

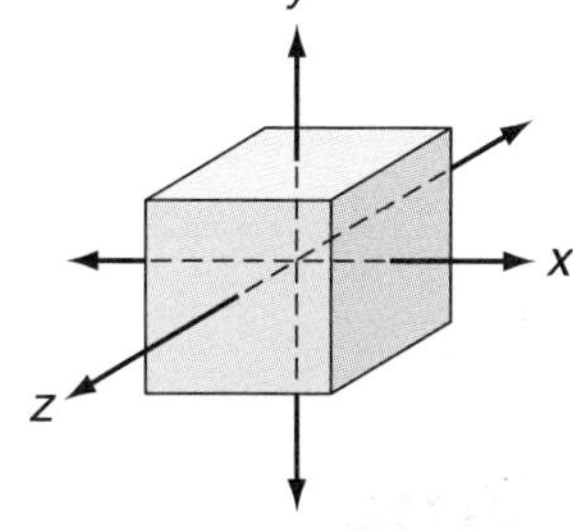

2. To determine the distance between two planes in the air, a three-coordinate system must be employed using ordered triplets (x, y, z). Each plane's position is measured in relation not only to a horizontal x-axis and a vertical y-axis, but also to a depth-measuring z-axis perpendicular to the other two axes. Place the origin $(0, 0, 0)$ of the three axes at the O'Hare Airport control tower and measure units in miles. Where is a plane with position coordinates $(8, 2, 5)$? See Additional Answers.
3. The space distance d between two points (x_1, y_1, z_1) and (x_2, y_2, z_2) is given by $d = \sqrt{(x_2 - x_1)^2 + (y_2 - y_1)^2 + (z_2 - z_1)^2}$. Two planes have position coordinates $(-3, 5, -4)$ and $(9, 2, 0)$. How far apart are they? 13 mi
4. A passenger jet is midway between two private aircraft with position coordinates $(6, 2, -13)$ and $(1, -8, -5)$. Find the coordinates of the jet. Explain how you found your answer. See Additional Answers.

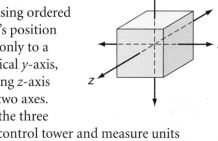

5 FOLLOW-UP

Extra Practice Determine the length and midpoint of the segment whose endpoints are the given points.

1. (0, 0) and (6, 8) **10; (3, 4)**
2. (–11, 2) and (–1, 26) **26; (–6, 14)**
3. (–5, –5) and (5, 5) **$10\sqrt{2}$; (0, 0)**

Project Connection This section presents further aspects of the project introduced on page 614. For Question 1, show students how to use a map scale.

AlgebraWorks Have students show other real world applications of ordered triplets. **Possible example: placement of items in a grocery store (aisle 7, row 2, shelf 3)**

NAME ______________ CLASS ________ DATE ________

13.6 THE DISTANCE AND MIDPOINT FORMULAS

An ellipse is the set of all points (x, y) such that the sum of the distances from any point $P(x, y)$ to two fixed points is a constant. Each fixed point is called a *focus* (plural: *foci*). If you know the coordinates of both foci and the constant, use the distance formula to write the equation of an ellipse.

Example

Determine an equation of the ellipse having foci at $F_1(-4, 0)$ and $F_2(4, 0)$. From any point $P(x, y)$ on the ellipse to the foci, the sum of the distances $\overline{PF_1}$ and $\overline{PF_2}$ is 12.

Solution

$12 = \overline{PF_1} + \overline{PF_2}$ Use the distance formula for $\overline{PF_1}$ and $\overline{PF_2}$.

$12 = \sqrt{(x - (-4))^2 + (y - 0)^2} + \sqrt{(x - 4)^2 + (y - 0)^2}$

$12 = \sqrt{(x + 4)^2 + y^2} + \sqrt{(x - 4)^2 + y^2}$

$12 - \sqrt{(x + 4)^2 + y^2} = \sqrt{(x - 4)^2 + y^2}$

$144 - 24\sqrt{(x + 4)^2 + y^2} + (x + 4)^2 + y^2 = (x - 4)^2 + y^2$ Square both sides.

$144 - 24\sqrt{(x + 4)^2 + y^2} + x^2 + 8x + 16 + y^2 = x^2 - 8x + 16 + y^2$

$16x + 144 = 24\sqrt{(x + 4)^2 + y^2}$

$2x + 18 = 3\sqrt{(x + 4)^2 + y^2}$ Divide both sides by 8.

$4x^2 + 72x + 324 = 9(x^2 + 8x + 16 + y^2)$ Square both sides.

$180 = 5x^2 + 9y^2$ Simplify.

$1 = \frac{x^2}{36} + \frac{y^2}{20}$ Divide both sides by 180.

EXERCISES

Determine an equation of the ellipse having the given points as foci and the given sum of the distances from any point (x, y) on the ellipse to the two foci. Write the equation so that one side is 1.

1. (–2, 0) and (2, 0), 8 — $1 = \frac{x^2}{16} + \frac{y^2}{12}$
2. (0, –2) and (0, 2), 8 — $1 = \frac{x^2}{12} + \frac{y^2}{16}$
3. (–1, 0) and (1, 0), 4 — $1 = \frac{x^2}{4} + \frac{y^2}{3}$
4. (0, –1) and (0, 1), 4 — $1 = \frac{x^2}{3} + \frac{y^2}{4}$
5. (–3, 0) and (3, 0), 8 — $1 = \frac{x^2}{16} + \frac{y^2}{7}$
6. (0, –3) and (0, 3), 8 — $1 = \frac{x^2}{7} + \frac{y^2}{16}$

42 *South-Western Algebra 1: AN INTEGRATED APPROACH*

LESSON PLANNING

Objectives

- Identify corresponding sides and corresponding angles of similar triangles.
- Use proportions and properties of similar triangles to solve problems.

Vocabulary

scale factor
similar
similar triangles

Resources

Transparency 8
Student Handbook

Materials/Manipulatives

protractor
ruler

ASSIGNMENTS

Basic: 1–17

Average: 1–17

Enriched: 1–18

1 MOTIVATE

Think Back For Question 3, ask students how they determined that the triangles in part *a* and part *b* are mathematically similar. **Answers will vary but should include that the triangles appear to be the same shape.**

13.7 Algebra Workshop
Similar Triangles

SPOTLIGHT ON LEARNING

WHAT? In this lesson you will learn

- to identify corresponding sides and corresponding angles of similar triangles.
- to use proportions and properties of similar triangles to solve problems.

WHY? Knowing the properties of similar triangles can help you find unknown measures of sides of triangles.

Think Back

The word *similar* is used in everyday language to describe objects or ideas that are alike in some way. In mathematics, figures are said to be **similar** if they have the same shape, but not necessarily the same size.

1. Name two objects which meet the everyday definition of the word *similar*, but not necessarily the mathematical definition. See Additional Answers.
2. Name two objects that meet the mathematical definition of similarity. See Additional Answers.
3. Examine each pair of triangles below. Decide whether the triangles in each pair are mathematically similar.

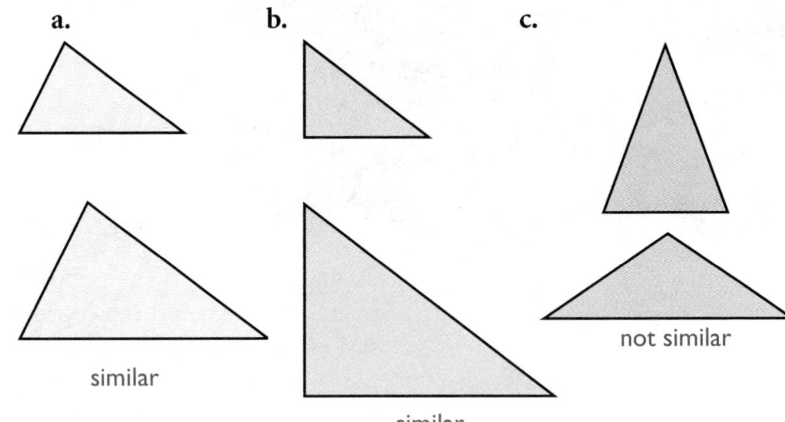

Explore

You can draw **similar triangles** using a projection point.

4. On a sheet of paper, draw any triangle ABC approximately in the center of the paper. Select a point P somewhere outside the triangle, as shown in the figure.
5. Measure the length of $\overline{PA}$ and draw $\overline{PA'}$ so that $\overline{PA'}$ passes through point A and is exactly twice as long as $\overline{PA}$.
6. Do the same with $\overline{PB}$ and $\overline{PC}$, making sure that $\overline{PB'}$ is twice the length of $\overline{PB}$ and $\overline{PC'}$ is twice the length of $\overline{PC}$.
7. Connect point A' to B', B' to C', and C' to A' to form $\Delta A'B'C'$.

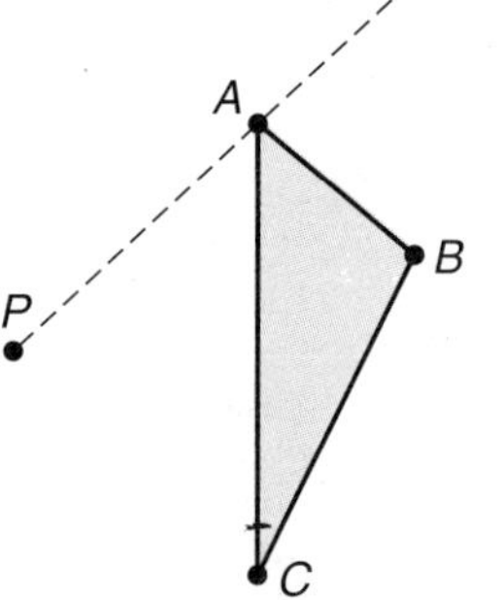

8. Use a ruler and protractor to measure the side lengths and angle measures of each triangle. Copy the table and enter your data. Answers will vary.

Side Lengths						Angle Measures					
$\overline{AB}$	$\overline{A'B'}$	$\overline{BC}$	$\overline{B'C'}$	$\overline{AC}$	$\overline{A'C'}$	$\angle A$	$\angle A'$	$\angle B$	$\angle B'$	$\angle C$	$\angle C'$

9. Compare your data with those of another student. What patterns do you notice? See Additional Answers.

10. Would the side and angle relationships be the same if you had begun with a different triangle? Draw a new triangle, choose a projection point, and test your prediction. See Additional Answers.

11. You can draw similar triangles by reducing, rather than enlarging, the original triangle. Draw another triangle, *ABC,* and choose a projection point *P* some distance from the triangle. Draw $\overline{PA}$ and measure its length. Locate the midpoint *A'* so that $\overline{PA'}$ is exactly half of $\overline{PA}$. Repeat to determine points *B'* and *C'*. Draw $\Delta A'B'C'$. How does this pair of triangles compare to previous pairs of similar triangles you have drawn? See Additional Answers.

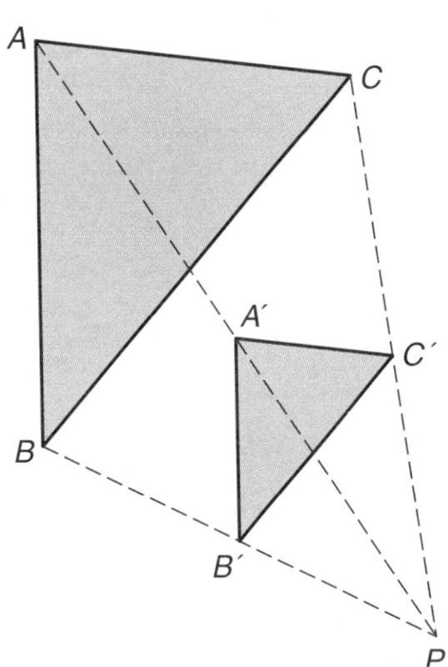

Make Connections

Triangle *JKM* and triangle *RST* are similar. Similar triangles have corresponding angles and sides. Triangles are similar if the measures of *corresponding angles* are equal and the ratios of *corresponding sides* form proportions. You can use this definition to find unknown measures in pairs of similar triangles or to determine whether a pair of triangles is similar.

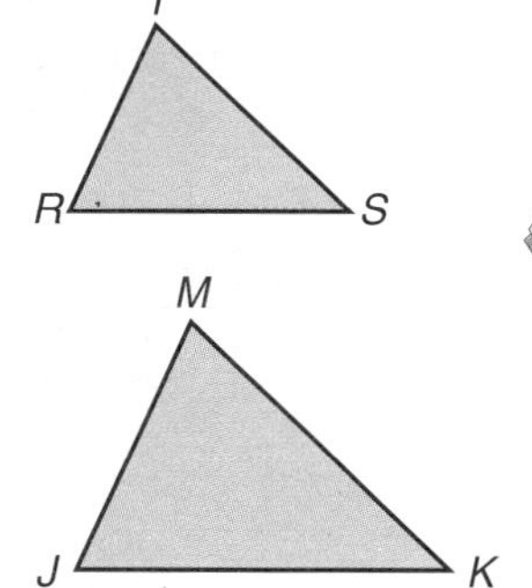

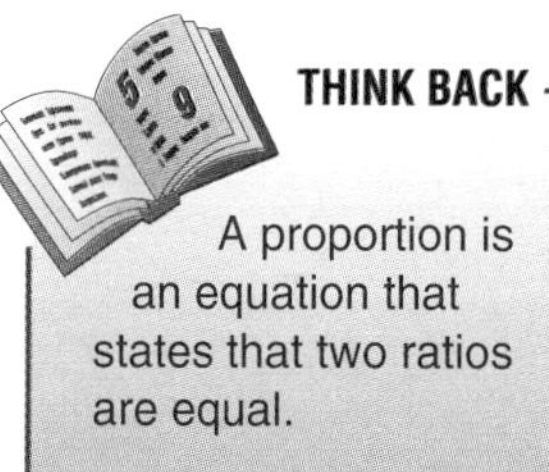

THINK BACK

A proportion is an equation that states that two ratios are equal.

Corresponding Angles	Corresponding Sides
$\angle J$ and $\angle R$	$\overline{JK}$ and $\overline{RS}$
$\angle K$ and $\angle S$	$\overline{KM}$ and $\overline{ST}$
$\angle M$ and $\angle T$	$\overline{MJ}$ and $\overline{TR}$

2 FACILITATE

Explore Tell students that *A'* (read *A* prime) is a point that corresponds to or relates to point *A*. Ask what segment *A'B'* corresponds to. $\overline{AB}$ Before students answer Question 8, ask them to name pairs of corresponding sides and angles of ΔABC and $\Delta A'B'C'$. **$\overline{AB}$ and $\overline{A'B'}$, $\overline{BC}$ and $\overline{B'C'}$, $\overline{AC}$ and $\overline{A'C'}$, $\angle A$ and $\angle A'$, $\angle B$ and $\angle B'$, $\angle C$ and $\angle C'$** For Question 9, students should find that the new triangle has corresponding side measures twice as long as those of the original triangle and measures of corresponding angles should be equal. Ask what the ratios of the side measures of ΔABC are to the corresponding side measures of $\Delta A'B'C'$. **$AB/A'B' = 1/2$, $BC/B'C' = 1/2$, $AC/A'C' = 1/2$** For Question 11, ask what the ratios of the side measures of ΔABC are to the corresponding side measures of $\Delta A'B'C'$. **$AB/A'B' = 2/1$, $BC/B'C' = 2/1$, $AC/A'C' = 2/1$**

Make Connections For Question 12 part a, ask students how they can determine the measures of the angles in $\Delta Q'R'S'$. **$180° - (50° + 65°) = 65°$; therefore, the corresponding angle measures are 50°, 65°, and 65°.** For part b, ask a student to describe the proportions he or she used to determine the missing side lengths. **$UT/U'T' = UV/U'V'$, $24/16 = 33/U'V'$, $U'V' = 16 \bullet 33/24 = 22$; $UT/U'T' = VT/V'T'$, $V'T' = 16 \bullet 48/24 = 32$** For Question 13, ask students to explain how they can determine whether the triangles in each case are similar. **(a.) $24/36 \neq 12/36$; (b.) Corresponding angle measures are equivalent; (c.) ratios of corresponding sides are in proportion: $26/39 = 30/45 = 40/60 = 2/3$.** After students have answered Question 14, ask them to explain why the scale factor is not 22/33 or 2/3. **Since the original triangle was enlarged, the scale factor must be greater than one: 33/22 or 3/2.**

DIVERSITY IN THE CLASSROOM

Visual/Tactile Learners Some students may have difficulty determining proportions and scale factors correctly because they do not identify corresponding sides and angles correctly. Have them trace each triangle and their measures on separate sheets of paper. Have them overlap the papers and hold them up to the light. Tell them to flip and rotate and slide one of the papers until all 3 sides of one triangle are parallel to all 3 sides of the other triangle. Then have them write the proportions to determine the scale factors.

3 SUMMARIZE

Writing Mathematics For Question 16, have students draw their own triangles by taking 1/2 of 20 and 34 respectively. Have them compare the results with those of their classmates. Have them discuss their explanations to this question. Ask them what additional information would be needed to draw a triangle similar to the original triangle. **Answers will vary. Students should indicate that more information about the angle measures or the measure of the third side is needed.**

Going Further For Question 18, ask students to describe the proportions they can set up for ΔABC and ΔADE. ***AB/AD = BC/DE, AB/AD = AC/AE, BC/DE = AC/AE*** Ask a student how he or she determined the unknown lengths.

Algebra Workshop

In the figure below, ΔABC is similar to ΔDEF. To determine the lengths of $\overline{BC}$ and $\overline{DE}$, use corresponding sides to write and solve proportions.

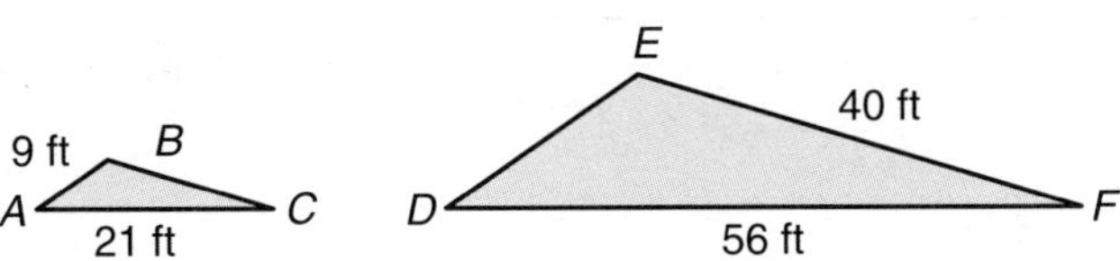

length of $\overline{DE}$:

$$\frac{AC}{DF} = \frac{AB}{DE}$$
$$\frac{21}{56} = \frac{9}{DE}$$
$$21DE = 504$$
$$DE = 24$$

The length of $\overline{DE}$ is 24 ft.

length of $\overline{BC}$:

$$\frac{BC}{EF} = \frac{AC}{DF}$$
$$\frac{BC}{40} = \frac{21}{56}$$
$$56BC = 840$$
$$BC = 15$$

The length of $\overline{BC}$ is 15 ft.

THINK BACK

The sum of the angles of a triangle is 180°.

12. Each pair of triangles is similar. Find all unknown side lengths and angle measures. See Additional Answers.

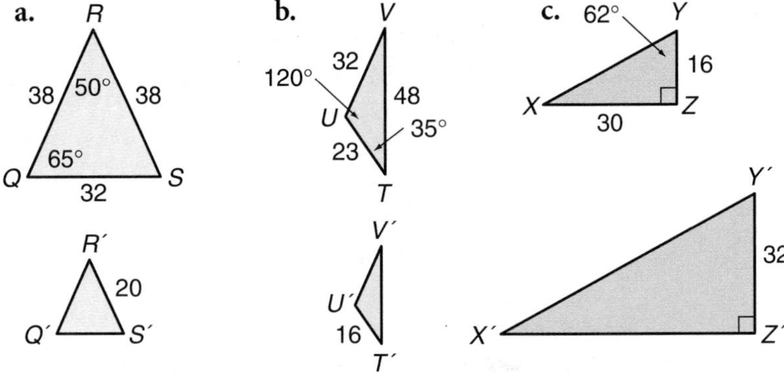

13. Use the given measures to determine whether each pair of triangles is similar.

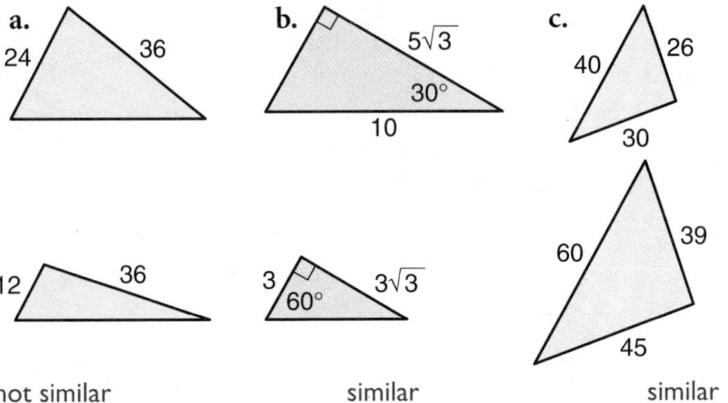

a. not similar b. similar c. similar

In Explore, you made enlargements and one reduction. In each case you created similar triangles. By measuring the lengths of one pair of corresponding sides of similar triangles and writing their ratio in simplest form, you can determine the **scale factor**, or multiplier, by which the original triangle is either enlarged or reduced.

14. Find the scale factor for each pair of similar triangles. For both pairs, assume that the smaller triangle is the original. All measures are given in millimeters.

a.

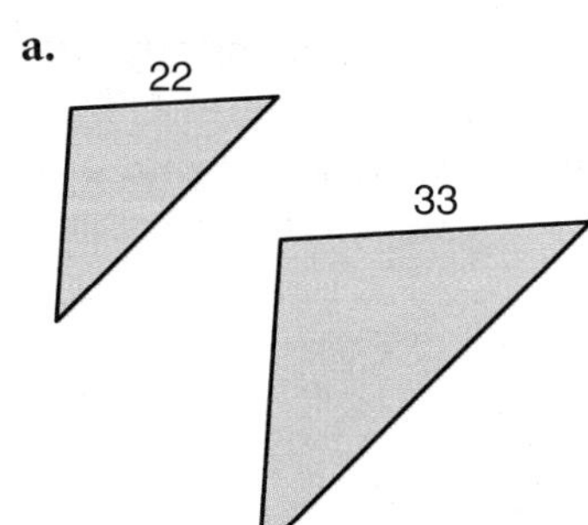

b.

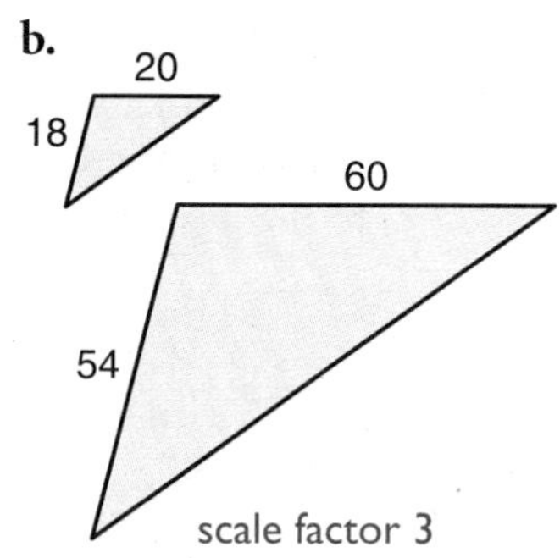

15. Draw a pair of similar triangles with a scale factor of your choosing. Exchange papers with a partner and have your partner determine the scale factor you used. Answers will vary.

Summarize

16. WRITING MATHEMATICS Two sides of a triangle are 20 units and 34 units. André and Ana each tried to draw a similar triangle by taking $\frac{1}{2}$ of 20 and 34, respectively. Their triangles are shown below. Who drew the correct similar triangle? Explain.
See Additional Answers.

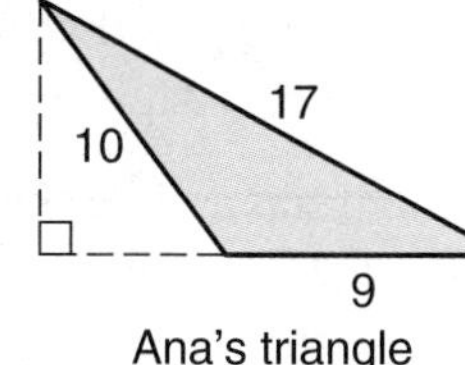

Ana's triangle

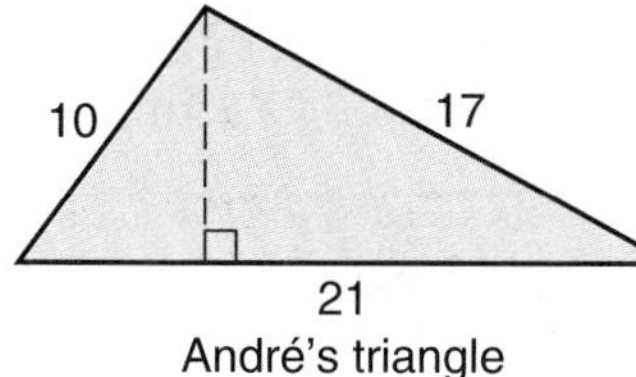

André's triangle

17. How many similar triangles can you find in the figure shown at the right? Explain your reasoning.
See Additional Answers.

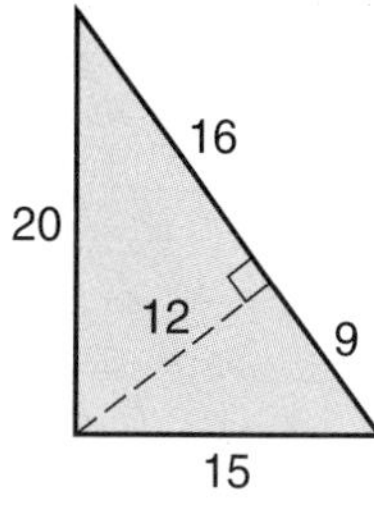

18. GOING FURTHER Triangles *ABC* and *ADE* are similar. The measures are as shown at the right. Determine the length of segments $\overline{BC}$ and $\overline{DB}$.
$BC = 40$ and $DB = 16.\overline{6}$

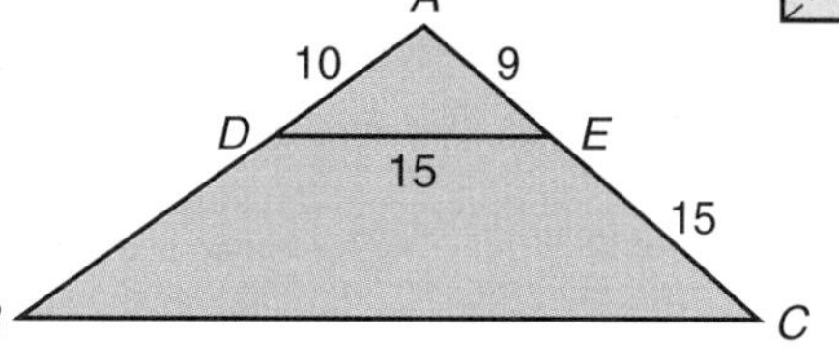

4 FOLLOW-UP

Extension Have students use similar triangles to determine the length of a pond. Explain that to find the length of the pond, a surveyor roped off two similar triangles as shown in the figure. Have students show two different methods to determine the length of the pond.

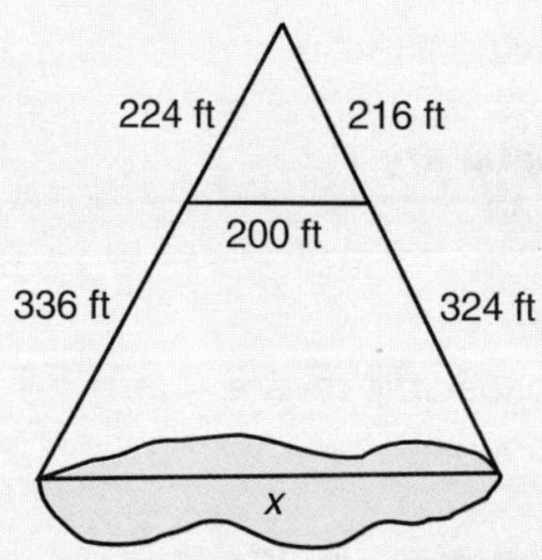

For Method 1, use proportions: (216 + 324 = 540) $x/200 = 540/216$, $x = 500$ ft; or (224 + 336 = 560) $x/200 = 560/224$, $x = 500$ ft;

For Method 2, determine the scale factor and multiply: 216 + 324 = 540; 540/216 = 5/2; 200 • 5/2 = 500 ft.

LESSON PLANNING

Objectives

- ▶ Determine trigonometric ratios for acute angles in a right triangle, given side lengths.
- ▶ Determine measures for acute angles, given the side lengths or the values of the trigonometric ratios.
- ▶ Use trigonometric ratios to measure indirectly.

Vocabulary

cosine
sine
tangent
trigonometric ratios
trigonometry

Technology/Multimedia

graphing utility

Resources

Warm Up 13.8
Reteaching 13.8
Extra Practice 13.8
Enrichment 13.8
Transparencies 74, 75
Student Handbook
Lesson Quiz 13.8

Materials/Manipulatives

protractor
straightedge

ASSIGNMENTS

Basic: 1–17, 19, 21–23, Mixed Review 24–35

Average: 3–23, Mixed Review 24–35

Enriched: 4–23, Mixed Review 24–35

13.8 Sine, Cosine, and Tangent

SPOTLIGHT ON LEARNING

WHAT? In this lesson you will learn

- to determine the sine, cosine, and tangent ratios for acute angles in a right triangle, given the side lengths.
- to determine the measure of acute angles in a right triangle, given the side lengths or value of the trigonometric ratios.

WHY? Knowing how to use trigonometric ratios can help you solve problems in engineering, home repair, and surveying.

Explore

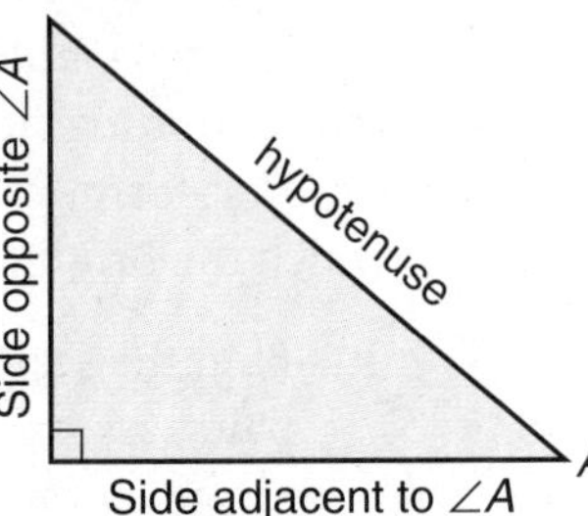

Examine the right triangle at the right. For either of the two acute angles, you can identify the side opposite the angle, the side adjacent to the angle, and the hypotenuse. In the figure, the sides are described in relation to $\angle A$.

1. Work independently. Using a protractor and straightedge, draw right triangle XYZ so that $\angle X$ has a measure of 30°, side XY is adjacent to $\angle X$, and $\angle Y$ is a right angle. Measure each side length to the nearest millimeter. Copy the table below. Enter the results.

Lengths of Sides		
XY (adjacent to $\angle X$)	YZ (opposite $\angle X$)	XZ (hypotenuse)
____ mm	____ mm	____ mm

2. Use the side lengths of your triangle to determine each of the following ratios. Copy the table below and enter the results. Round each ratio to the nearest thousandth.

Ratios of the Lengths of Sides		
$\frac{XY\text{ (adjacent)}}{XZ\text{ (hypotenuse)}}$	$\frac{YZ\text{ (opposite)}}{XZ\text{ (hypotenuse)}}$	$\frac{YZ\text{ (opposite)}}{XY\text{ (adjacent)}}$
____	____	____

3. Compare results with those of others in your group. What do you notice about the ratios of corresponding sides?
Values of the ratios should be close to one another.
4. What is the relationship between the triangles that members of the group have drawn? Explain. See Additional Answers.
5. Draw another right triangle, one that has a 45° angle. Measure side lengths. Copy and complete tables like those above for this triangle. What do you predict will be the relationship between your results and others' in your group?
Corresponding ratios will be equal.
6. In the right triangle with a 45° angle, what do you notice about the ratios of $\frac{\text{length of side opposite the angle}}{\text{length of hypotenuse}}$ and $\frac{\text{length of side adjacent to the angle}}{\text{length of hypotenuse}}$? Explain.
The two ratios are very close because the side opposite and the side adjacent to the 45° angle are equal.

Build Understanding

The word **trigonometry** comes from a Greek term meaning "measure of triangles." For any right triangle, there are three common **trigonometric ratios** of the lengths of the sides of the triangle. These ratios, called the **sine**, **cosine**, and **tangent**, are the same for all angles of equal measure in right triangles, even though the lengths of the sides of the triangles may be different.

For any right triangle, such as triangle ABC shown at the right, the following relationships apply to acute angle B.

TRIGONOMETRIC RATIOS	
Ratio	**Description**
sin B (read "sine of $\angle B$")	$\dfrac{\text{length of side opposite } \angle B}{\text{length of hypotenuse}}$
cos B (read "cosine of $\angle B$")	$\dfrac{\text{length of side adjacent to } \angle B}{\text{length of hypotenuse}}$
tan B (read "tangent of $\angle B$")	$\dfrac{\text{length of side opposite } \angle B}{\text{length of side adjacent to } \angle B}$

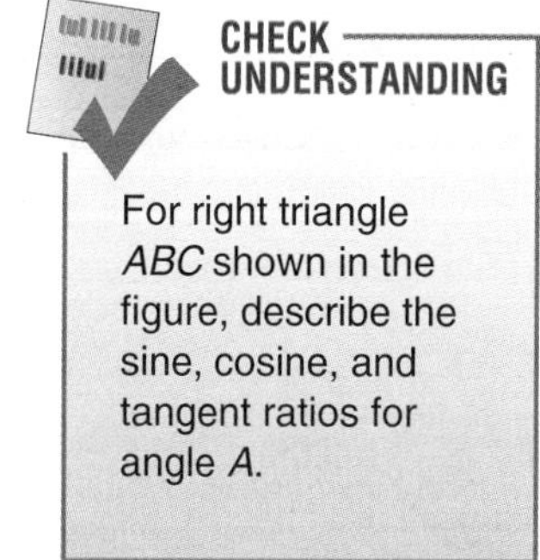

See Additional Answers.

EXAMPLE 1

Determine the sine, cosine, and tangent ratios for each acute angle in ΔQRS, shown at the right. Round to the nearest thousandth.

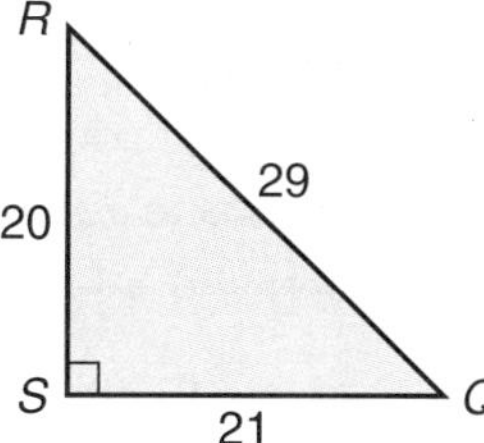

Solution

$$\sin Q = \frac{\text{opposite}}{\text{hypotenuse}} = \frac{20}{29} \approx 0.690$$

$$\cos Q = \frac{\text{adjacent}}{\text{hypotenuse}} = \frac{21}{29} \approx 0.724$$

$$\tan Q = \frac{\text{opposite}}{\text{adjacent}} = \frac{20}{21} \approx 0.952$$

$$\sin R = \frac{\text{opposite}}{\text{hypotenuse}} = \frac{21}{29} \approx 0.724$$

$$\cos R = \frac{\text{adjacent}}{\text{hypotenuse}} = \frac{20}{29} \approx 0.690$$

$$\tan R = \frac{\text{opposite}}{\text{adjacent}} = \frac{21}{20} = 1.05$$

COMMUNICATING ABOUT ALGEBRA

For the triangle in Example 1, the values of cos Q and sin R are equal and the values of cos R and sin Q are equal. Do you think this equality will be true for all right triangles? Explain.

See Additional Answers.

1 MOTIVATE

Explore For Question 1, have students draw ΔXYZ on graph paper to help them draw the right angle. For Question 3, accept any ratios that are close to $XY/XZ = 0.866$, $YZ/XZ = 0.5$, and $YZ/XY = 0.577$. Ask students what they can conclude regarding any differences in the ratios of the corresponding sides of their triangles. **The ratios vary slightly due to lack of exactness in measurement and rounding of numbers; actually the ratios should be equal.**

2 TEACH

Use the Pages/Build Understanding Ask students to discuss Check Understanding.

DIVERSITY IN THE CLASSROOM

Linguistic Learners Tell them that a helpful mnemonic device for remembering sine, cosine, and tangent ratios goes as follows:

Some **O**ld **H**ound	**S**ine = **O**pposite/**H**ypotenuse
Came **A**-**H**owling	**C**osine = **A**djacent/**H**ypotenuse
Through **O**ur **A**lley	**T**angent = **O**pposite/**A**djacent

Example 1: Have students identify the hypotenuse of ΔQRS, the side opposite $\angle Q$, and the side adjacent to $\angle Q$. **The hypotenuse is $\overline{QR}$; the side opposite $\angle Q$ is $\overline{RS}$; the side adjacent to $\angle Q$ is $\overline{QS}$.** Have students discuss Communicating About Algebra.

Example 2: Have students read Problem Solving Tip. Have them find the cos 74° and the tan 74° to the nearest ten thousandth. **cos 74° = 0.2756; tan 74° = 3.4874**

Example 3: Remind students that they will probably need to use parentheses when keying in 14/10 in their graphing calculators.

2nd $\tan^{-1}$ (14 ÷ 10)
ENTER 54.46232221

Otherwise the display will read 8.591438322. Ask students to explain why this happens. **because the calculator reads the expression to be evaluated as ($\tan^{-1}$ 14) ÷ 10; $\tan^{-1}$ 14 = 85.91438322; so ($\tan^{-1}$ 14) ÷ 10 = 8.591438322** Have students discuss Check Understanding.

Example 4: Ask students what distance they are being asked to find. **the length of the hypotenuse** Ask students to describe how they could use cosine to find the length of the hypotenuse. **Determine the measure of the third angle: 180° – (90° + 6°) = 84°; cos 84° = 350/hypotenuse, 0.1045284633 ≈ 350/hypotenuse, hypotenuse ≈ 350/0.1045284633 = 3348.370282.**

Example 5: Ask students to explain how they can determine the length of the wire. **By the Pythagorean theorem, $16^2 + 50^2 = c^2$, $c \approx 52.498$; or sin 72° = opposite/hypotenuse, sin 72° = 50/hypotenuse, hypotenuse = 50/sin 72°, hypotenuse ≈ 52.573 or 53 ft**

PROBLEM SOLVING TIP

Before entering data for trigonometric ratios be sure that the angle mode on your calculator is set for degrees (DEG).

CHECK UNDERSTANDING

What is the relationship between the tangent of $\angle X$ and the slope of the hypotenuse XY?

They are the same. The $\frac{\text{rise}}{\text{run}}$ is equivalent to $\frac{\text{side opposite}}{\text{side adjacent}}$, or tangent of $\angle X$.

You can use a calculator to find sine, cosine, and tangent values given an angle value. You can also use a calculator to find the angle value when given a sine, cosine, or tangent value.

EXAMPLE 2

Use a graphing calculator to compute.

a. Find the value of sin 74° to the nearest ten thousandth.

b. Given cos B = 0.5987. Find the measure of $\angle B$ to the nearest degree.

Solution

a. Enter: SIN 74 The result is 0.9612616959.
To the nearest ten thousandth, the value of sin 74° is 0.9613.

b. Enter: 2nd COS^{-1} 0.5987 The result is 53.22315137.
To the nearest ten thousandth, the measure of $\angle B$ is 53. ◄

If you know the lengths of two sides of a right triangle, you can use a trigonometric ratio to find the measure of an acute angle of the triangle.

EXAMPLE 3

Determine the measure of $\angle X$. Round to the nearest degree.

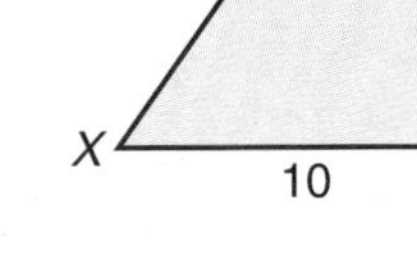

Solution

Because you have information about the side opposite and the side adjacent to $\angle X$, use the tangent ratio.

$$\tan X = \frac{\text{opposite}}{\text{adjacent}}$$

$$\tan X = \frac{14}{10} \qquad \text{Use a calculator.}$$

$$X \approx 54.46232221 \qquad 2^{nd}\ \text{TAN}^{-1}\ (14 \div 10)$$

To the nearest degree, the measure of $\angle X$ is 54°. ◄

Trigonometric ratios enable you to calculate distances or lengths that would otherwise be difficult to measure directly.

EXAMPLE 4

DRIVING The figure shows a truck at the top of an inclined road. Suppose that the brakes on the truck suddenly begin to fail. Over what distance must the driver keep control of the truck until the road levels out?

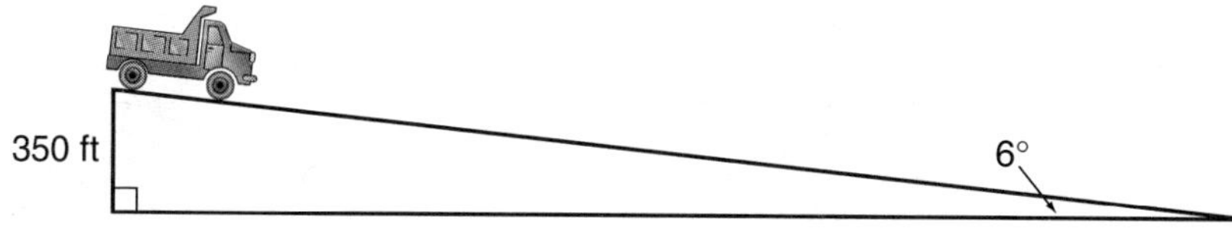

Solution

Suppose the measure of the angle is 6° and you know the measure of the side opposite. Use the sine ratio to find the measure of the hypotenuse.

$$\sin 6° = \frac{\text{opposite}}{\text{hypotenuse}}$$

$$\sin 6° = \frac{350}{\text{hypotenuse}}$$

$$\text{hypotenuse} \approx \frac{350}{\sin 6°}$$

$$\text{hypotenuse} \approx 3348.370282$$

To the nearest foot, the driver must keep control of the truck for a distance of 3348 ft before the road levels out. ◀

EXAMPLE 5

CONSTRUCTION A 32-ft antenna on a school building is attached to the roof and held in place by a wire from the top of the antenna to a roof 18 ft below the top of the building. To the nearest degree, what angle does the wire make with the roof to which it is attached?

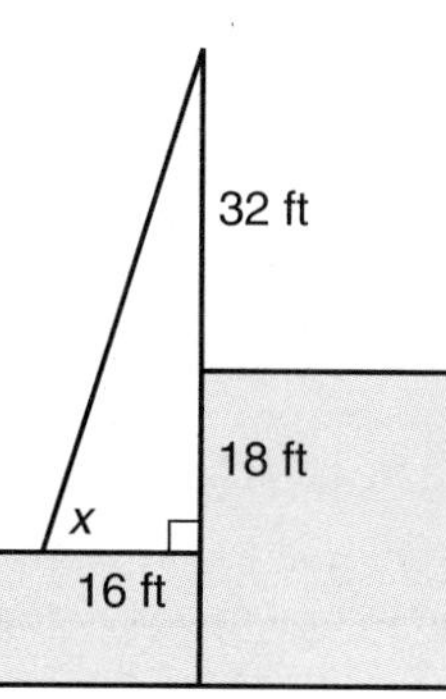

Solution

The information includes the side opposite and the side adjacent to $\angle x$. Use the tangent ratio.

$$\tan x = \frac{(18 + 32)}{16}$$

$$\tan x = \frac{50}{16} \qquad \text{Use a calculator.}$$

$$x \approx 72.2553287$$

To the nearest degree, the antenna wire makes a 72° angle with the roof to which it is attached. ◀

Ongoing Assessment The important concepts and skills involve trigonometric ratios and using trigonometric ratios to measure indirectly. To assess these ideas, have students demonstrate how they have applied these concepts and skills in Exercises 1, 8, and 11 of the Try These section.

Guided Practice/Try These For Exercises 1–4, ask students to name the hypotenuse of the triangle, the side adjacent to $\angle B$ and the side opposite $\angle B$. ***BC, AB, AC*** After students have discussed Exercises 1–4, ask them to explain how they can determine the measure of $\angle B$. **Since sin *B* = 24/25, find $\sin^{-1}$ (24/25): $\sin^{-1}$ (24/25) ≈ 73.7° or 74°.** For Exercise 12, ask students to explain how they can determine the measure of $\angle Z$. **First determine the measure of $\angle Y$: $\tan^{-1}$ 0.625 ≈ 32°; then subtract: 180° − (90° + 32°) = 58°.**

3 SUMMARIZE

In the Math Journal Have students draw right triangle *ABC* with $\angle B = 90°$ and with $AB = 4$, $BC = 3$, and $AC = 5$. Have them write the descriptions of the three trigonometric ratios in this lesson and the values for each for the acute angles of ΔABC. Then have them show each step in determining the angles of the triangle using either sine, cosine, or tangent. **sin *A* = 3/5, cos *A* = 4/5, tan *A* = 3/4, sin *C* = 4/5, cos *C* = 3/5, tan *C* = 4/3; m $\angle A$ is $\sin^{-1}$ (3/5) ≈ 36.8° or 37°; m $\angle C$ is 180° − (90° + 37°) = 53°**

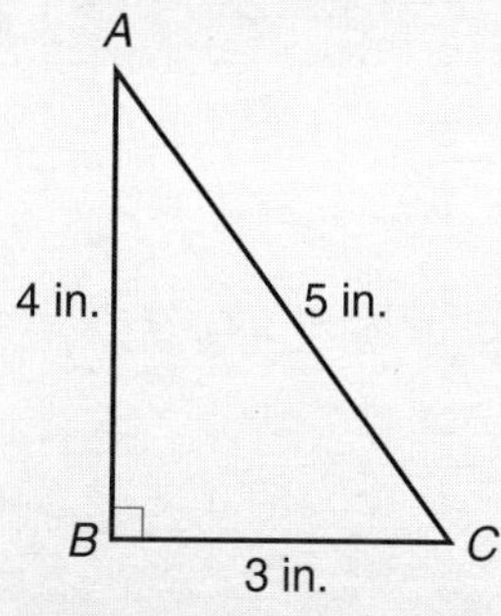

4 PRACTICE

Practice For Exercise 16, ask students what they need to find to determine whether the ladder is safe. **The measure of the angle formed by the ground and the ladder.** Ask a student to describe how to find this measure. **The length of the adjacent side and the hypotenuse are given. Use cos: cos $X = 1.5/8$; then $\cos^{-1}(1.5/8) \approx 79.2°$ or 79°; since 79 > 75, the ladder is safe.** For Exercise 17, ask a student to describe how to determine the maximum distance the ladder should be from the house. **Let d represent the distance; then $\cos 75° = d/9$, $d = \cos 75° \cdot 9 \approx 2.3$.**

Extend For Exercise 20, ask students what the slope of a linear equation represents. **rise/run** Suggest that they draw a diagram to represent the situation. Then ask a student to explain how to determine the measure of the angle. **Let x represent the angle of elevation.**

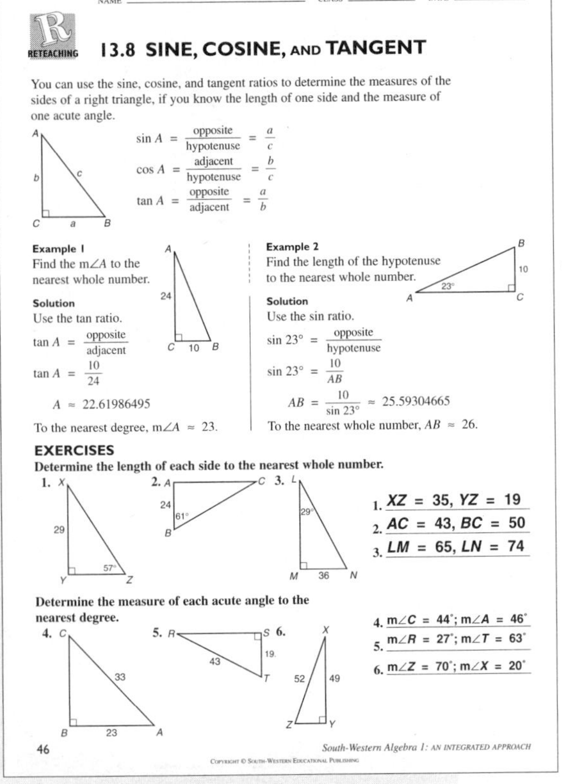

NAME ______ CLASS ______ DATE ______

RETEACHING

13.8 SINE, COSINE, AND TANGENT

You can use the sine, cosine, and tangent ratios to determine the measures of the sides of a right triangle, if you know the length of one side and the measure of one acute angle.

$\sin A = \frac{\text{opposite}}{\text{hypotenuse}} = \frac{a}{c}$

$\cos A = \frac{\text{adjacent}}{\text{hypotenuse}} = \frac{b}{c}$

$\tan A = \frac{\text{opposite}}{\text{adjacent}} = \frac{a}{b}$

Example 1
Find the m∠A to the nearest whole number.

Solution
Use the tan ratio.

$\tan A = \frac{\text{opposite}}{\text{adjacent}}$

$\tan A = \frac{10}{24}$

$A \approx 22.61986495$

To the nearest degree, m∠$A \approx 23$.

Example 2
Find the length of the hypotenuse to the nearest whole number.

Solution
Use the sin ratio.

$\sin 23° = \frac{\text{opposite}}{\text{hypotenuse}}$

$\sin 23° = \frac{10}{AB}$

$AB = \frac{10}{\sin 23°} \approx 25.59304665$

To the nearest whole number, $AB \approx 26$.

EXERCISES

Determine the length of each side to the nearest whole number.

1. $XZ = 35$, $YZ = 19$
2. $AC = 43$, $BC = 50$
3. $LM = 65$, $LN = 74$

Determine the measure of each acute angle to the nearest degree.

4. m∠C = 44°; m∠A = 46°
5. m∠R = 27°; m∠T = 63°
6. m∠Z = 70°; m∠X = 20°

46 South-Western Algebra 1: AN INTEGRATED APPROACH

TRY THESE

For triangle *ABC*, name the trigonometric ratio or ratios represented by the given fraction. Choose from *sine*, *cosine*, or *tangent*.

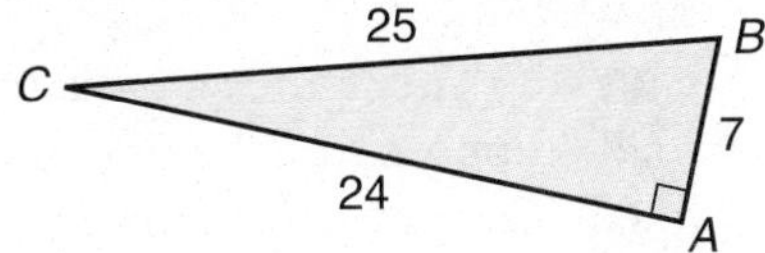

1. $\frac{7}{25}$ cos B or sin C
2. $\frac{24}{25}$ sin B or cos C
3. $\frac{24}{7}$ tan B
4. $\frac{7}{24}$ tan C

For triangle *FGH*, determine the value of each trigonometric ratio named. Write the ratio as a fraction.

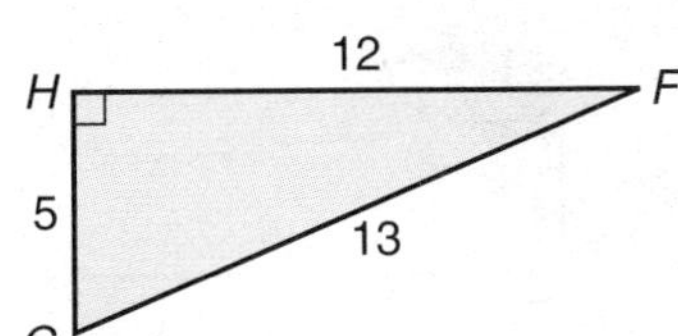

5. tan F $\frac{5}{12}$
6. cos G $\frac{5}{13}$

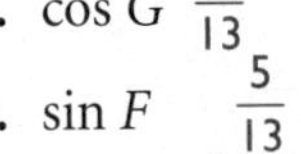

7. sin G $\frac{12}{13}$
8. sin F $\frac{5}{13}$
9. tan G $\frac{12}{5}$
10. cos F $\frac{12}{13}$

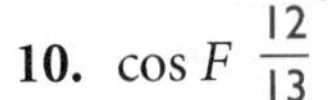

Determine the specified trigonometric ratio to the nearest ten thousandth.

11. sin X 0.8333

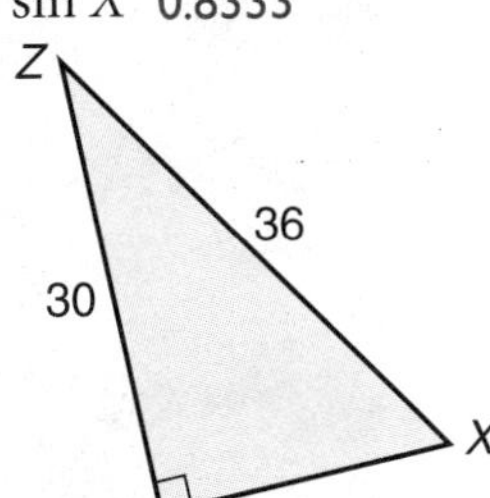

12. tan Y 0.6250

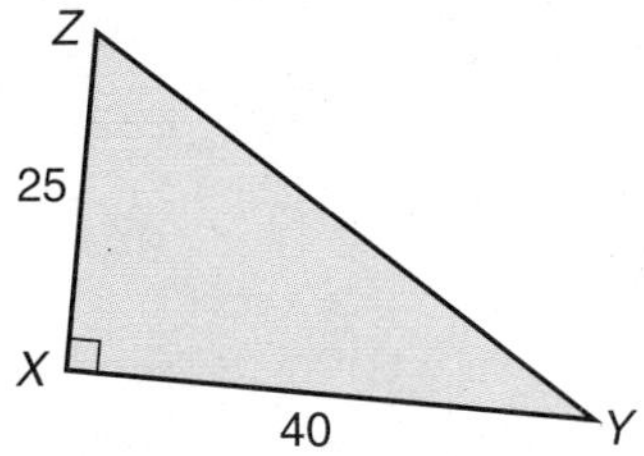

13. cos B 0.7879

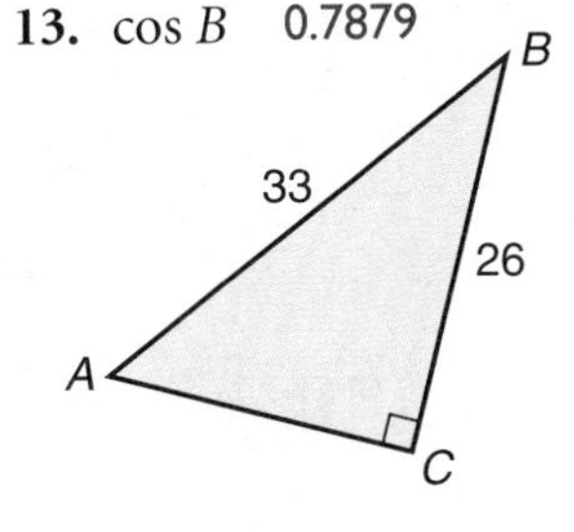

14. **ENGINEERING** What is the angle of elevation of the mountain in the figure below? 20°, to the nearest degree

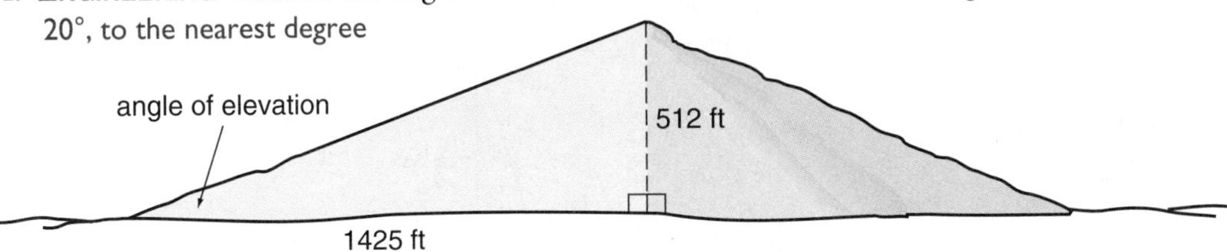

15. **WRITING MATHEMATICS** Is it true that in any right triangle, the tangents of the acute angles are reciprocals? Give several examples to support your answer. The statement is true, since for two acute angles, the numerator for one tangent ratio will be the denominator for the other.

PRACTICE

Determine the specified trigonometric ratio to the nearest ten thousandth.

1. tan W 0.5526

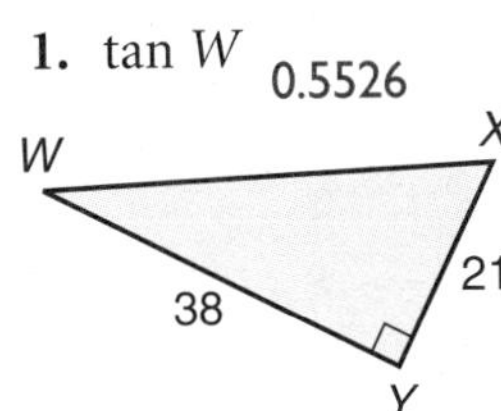

2. cos R 0.8772

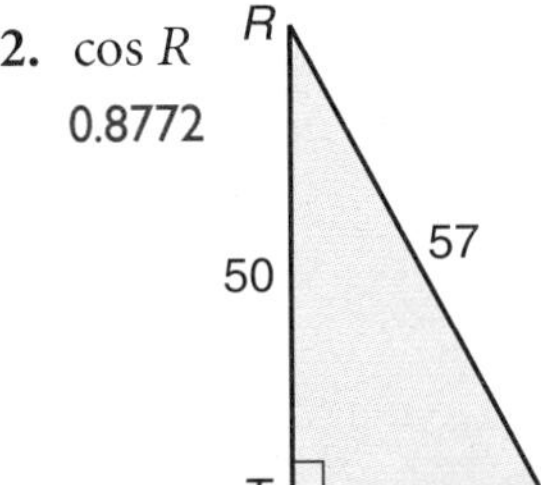

3. sin V 0.7778

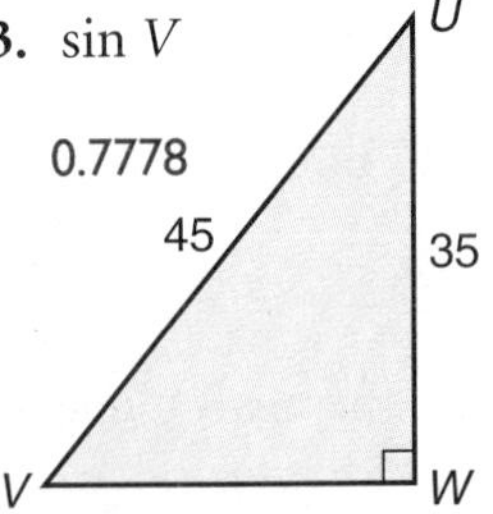

Determine the measure of each acute angle to the nearest degree.

4. 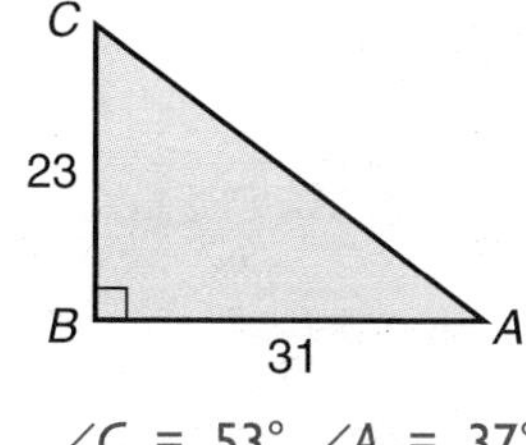

$\angle C = 53°, \angle A = 37°$

5. 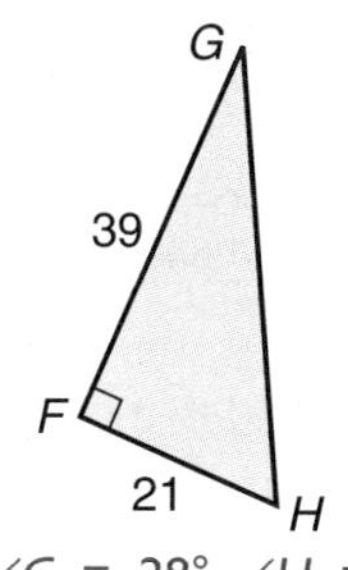

$\angle G = 28°, \angle H = 62°$

6. 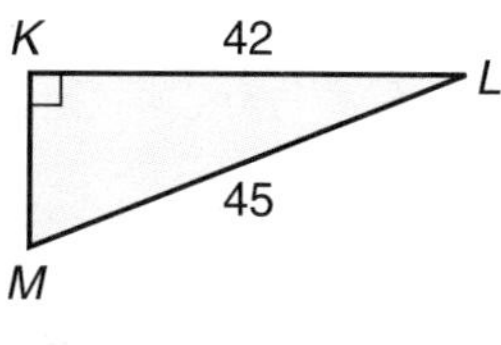

$\angle L = 21°, \angle M = 69°$

7. 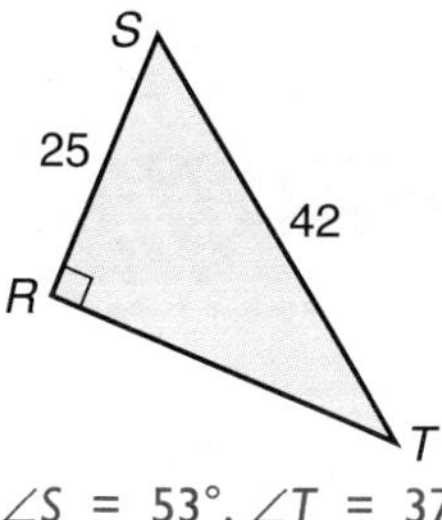

$\angle S = 53°, \angle T = 37°$

8. 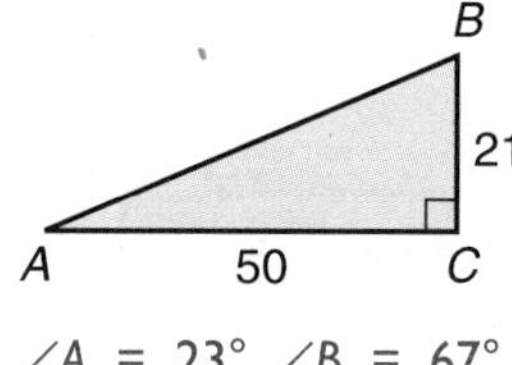

$\angle A = 23°, \angle B = 67°$

9. 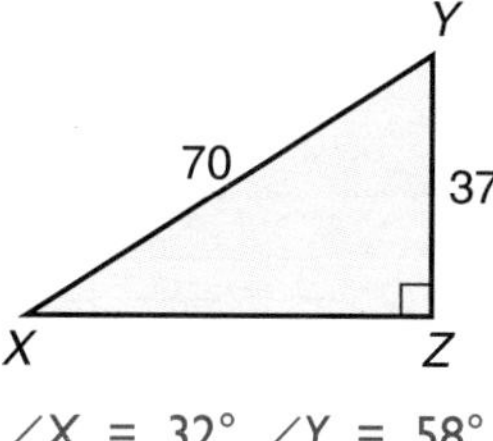

$\angle X = 32°, \angle Y = 58°$

For each trigonometric ratio, determine the measure of the angle named.

10. $\sin C = 0.8746$ 61°
11. $\tan D = 0.7002$ 35°
12. $\cos T = 0.7193$ 44°
13. $\tan G = 19.0811$ 87°
14. $\cos Y = 0.8988$ 26°
15. $\sin H = 0.2079$ 12°

HOME REPAIRS When you lean a ladder against a wall, it may be unstable at certain angles. Some home repair manuals recommend that the measure of the angle that an unsecured ladder makes with the ground should not be more than 75°.

16. The base of an 8-m ladder is placed 1.5 m from a wall. Is the ladder safe? no

17. An electrician places a ladder that is 9 m long against the outside wall of a house. At what distance should the base of the ladder be placed from the wall so that the ladder is safe to climb? Round to one decimal place. 2.3 m or more

18. **SURVEYING** As shown in the figure at the right, a surveyor finds that the distance from point M to point N is 350 m. The measure of the angle at point M is 43° To the nearest meter, what is the distance across the lake? 326 m

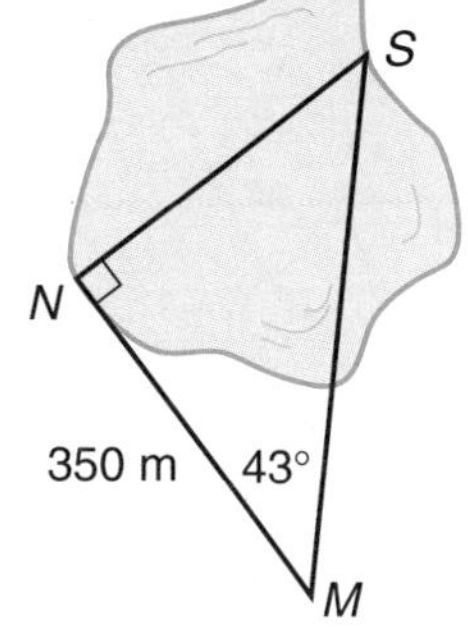

19. **WRITING MATHEMATICS** Using your calculator, a protractor, and a straightedge, draw right triangle RST in which the tangent value of $\angle R$ is 1.1503 (rounded to four decimal places) and $\angle T$ is a right angle. Describe the steps you used. See Additional Answers.

Then the slope = rise/run = opposite/adjacent = tan *x*. Thus, $\tan^{-1} 0.3154 = 17.50527445$ or 18°. For Exercise 21, ask a student to describe the steps he or she used to find the altitude. Remind students to convert miles to feet. **rise/run = tan *C* = 10/100 = 0.1, $\tan^{-1} 0.1 = 5.710593137$, or about 6°; sin 6° = *DE*/0.5. Since 0.5 mi = 2640 ft, 0.1045284633 = *DE*/2640, 0.1045284633 • 2640 = 275.955143 or about 276 ft**

Think Critically For Exercise 23, remind students to multiply both numerator and denominator by hypotenuse/adjacent side.

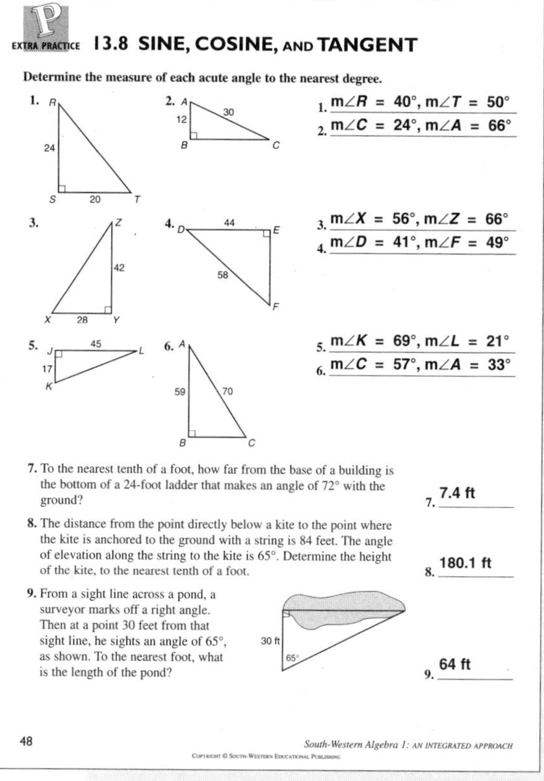

NAME ______ CLASS ______ DATE ______

EXTRA PRACTICE **13.8 SINE, COSINE, AND TANGENT**

Determine the measure of each acute angle to the nearest degree.

1. (triangle R, S, T: 24, 20)
2. (triangle A, B, C: 12, 30)
3. (triangle X, Y, Z: 42, 28)
4. (triangle D, E, F: 44, 58)
5. (triangle J, K, L: 45, 17)
6. (triangle A, B, C: 59, 70)

1. $m\angle R = 40°, m\angle T = 50°$
2. $m\angle C = 24°, m\angle A = 66°$
3. $m\angle X = 56°, m\angle Z = 66°$
4. $m\angle D = 41°, m\angle F = 49°$
5. $m\angle K = 69°, m\angle L = 21°$
6. $m\angle C = 57°, m\angle A = 33°$

7. To the nearest tenth of a foot, how far from the base of a building is the bottom of a 24-foot ladder that makes an angle of 72° with the ground? 7. 7.4 ft

8. The distance from the point directly below a kite to the point where the kite is anchored to the ground with a string is 84 feet. The angle of elevation along the string to the kite is 65°. Determine the height of the kite, to the nearest tenth of a foot. 8. 180.1 ft

9. From a sight line across a pond, a surveyor marks off a right angle. Then at a point 30 feet from that sight line, he sights an angle of 65°, as shown. To the nearest foot, what is the length of the pond? (30 ft, 65°) 9. 64 ft

48 *South-Western Algebra 1: AN INTEGRATED APPROACH*

5 FOLLOW-UP

Extension Explain that the equation $\sin^2 X + \cos^2 X = 1$ is a trigonometric identity because it is true for any angle. Have students use the Pythagorean theorem to show that the identity is true. **By the Pythagorean theorem, given any right triangle with an acute $\angle X$,**

$$\textbf{(side opposite } X)^2 + \textbf{(side adjacent } X)^2 = \textbf{hypotenuse}^2,$$

$$\frac{(\text{side opposite } X)^2}{\text{hypotenuse}^2} + \frac{(\text{side adjacent } X)^2}{\text{hypotenuse}^2} = \frac{\text{hypotenuse}^2}{\text{hypotenuse}^2}$$

$$\frac{(\text{side opposite } X)^2}{\text{hypotenuse}^2} + \frac{(\text{side adjacent } X)^2}{\text{hypotenuse}^2} = 1$$

$$\sin^2 X + \cos^2 X = 1$$

NAME ______ CLASS ______ DATE ______

ENRICHMENT

13.8 SINE, COSINE, AND TANGENT

Just as you can use trigonometric ratios to find side and angle measures for right triangles, you can use the law of cosines to find side and angle measures for any triangle.

The Law of Cosines

For any ΔABC, where a, b, and c are lengths of sides opposite angles A, B, and C, respectively,

$$a^2 = b^2 + c^2 - 2bc\cos A$$
$$b^2 = a^2 + c^2 - 2ac\cos B$$
$$c^2 = a^2 + b^2 - 2ab\cos C$$

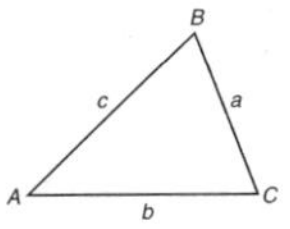

Example 1
In ΔABC, $a = 12$, $b = 15$, and the measure of $\angle C$ is 60°. Determine c to the nearest tenth.

Solution
$c^2 = a^2 + b^2 - 2ab\cos C$
$c^2 = 12^2 + 15^2 - 2(12)(15)\cos 60°$
$c^2 = 144 + 225 - 360(0.5)$
$c^2 = 369 - 180$
$c^2 = 189$
$c = \sqrt{189} \approx 13.7$

Example 2
In ΔABC, $b = 4$, $c = 6$, and the measure of $\angle A$ is 25°. Determine a to the nearest tenth.

Solution
$a^2 = b^2 + c^2 - 2bc\cos A$
$a^2 = 4^2 + 6^2 - 2(4)(6)\cos 25°$
$a^2 \doteq 16 + 36 - 48(0.906307787)$
$a^2 = 52 - 43.5027737378$
$a^2 = 8.49722622$
$a = \sqrt{8.49722622} \approx 2.9$

EXERCISES

1. In ΔABC, $a = 9$, $b = 12$, and the measure of $\angle C$ is 62°. Determine c to the nearest tenth.
2. In ΔABC, $b = 24$, $c = 8$, and the measure of $\angle A$ is 38°. Determine a to the nearest tenth.
3. In ΔABC, $a = 10$, $c = 15$, and the measure of $\angle B$ is 70°. Determine b to the nearest tenth.
4. In ΔABC, $a = 2$, $b = 6$, and the measure of $\angle C$ is 45°. Determine c to the nearest tenth.
5. In ΔABC, $b = 8$, $c = 12$, and the measure of $\angle A$ is 56°. Determine a to the nearest tenth.
6. In ΔABC, $a = 20$, $c = 30$, and the measure of $\angle B$ is 22°. Determine b to the nearest tenth.
7. In ΔABC, $a = 7$, $c = 5$, and the measure of $\angle B$ is 84°. Determine b to the nearest tenth.
8. In ΔABC, $a = 18$, $b = 22$, and the measure of $\angle C$ is 15°. Determine c to the nearest tenth.
9. In ΔABC, $a = 24$, $b = 32$, and the measure of $\angle C$ is 63°. Determine c to the nearest tenth.
10. In ΔABC, $a = 16$, $c = 4$, and the measure of $\angle B$ is 28°. Determine b to the nearest tenth.

1. 11.1
2. 18.4
3. 14.9
4. 4.8
5. 10
6. 13.7
7. 8.2
8. 6.6
9. 30
10. 12.6

50 *South-Western Algebra 1: AN INTEGRATED APPROACH*

EXTEND

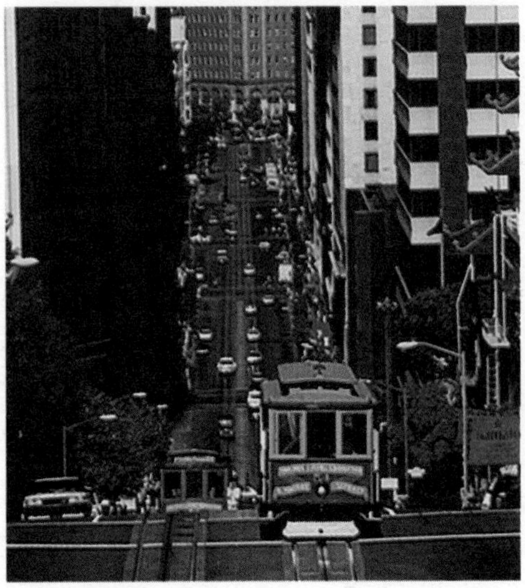

20. **STEEP STREETS** Filbert Street and 22nd Street in San Francisco are two of the world's steepest streets. Each has a slope of 0.3154. To the nearest degree, at what angle do these streets rise? 18°, to the nearest degree

21. **HIGHWAY DRIVING** For a road with a 10% grade, the road rises 10 ft for every 100 ft of horizontal distance. In driving from point C to point D, a distance of 0.5 mi, what will your altitude be at point D if point C is at sea level? (*Hint:* First use slope to find the measure of $\angle C$ to the nearest tenth of a degree.) See Additional Answers.

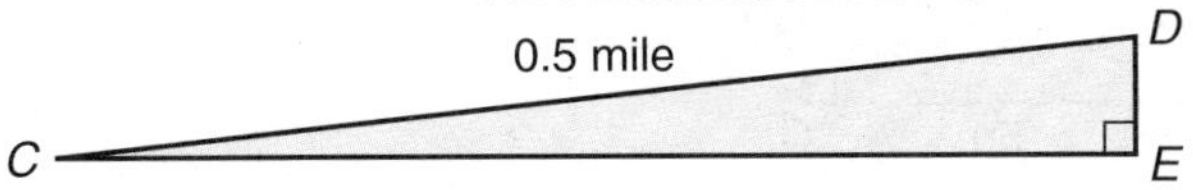

THINK CRITICALLY

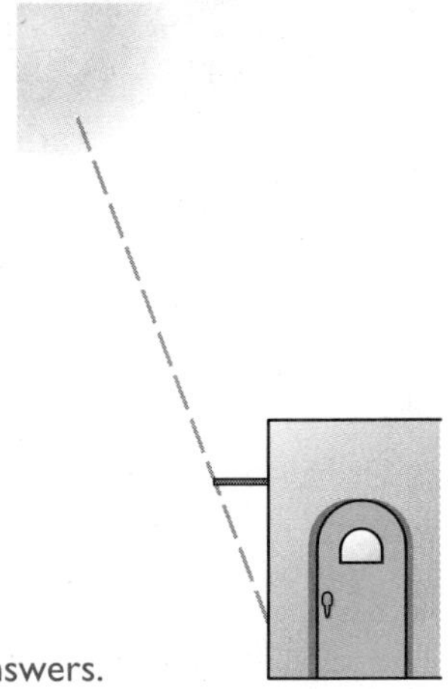

22. **SUNDIALS** Ancient Egyptians used the vertical shadow of a stick placed horizontally on the east side of a building to estimate the time of day. They kept a table of shadow lengths and hours of the morning. Describe what happened as the sun rose higher from early morning until noon. How is this an early use of the tangent concept? See Additional Answers.

23. Which of the following is a true equality?
$$\tan X = \frac{\sin X}{\cos X} \quad \text{or} \quad \tan X = \frac{\cos X}{\sin X}$$
Verify your answer by substituting the ratio for sine and cosine in each fraction and then simplifying the fraction. See Additional Answers.

MIXED REVIEW

Name the degree of each polynomial. Lesson 11.6

24. $5y$ 1
25. abc 3
26. $a^2b - 3$ 3
27. $-a^2 - 3b^4c^2 + a^4$ 6
28. $\frac{5w^2}{3} + \frac{w}{2}$ 2
29. $-2y^4 - 3x^2y^2$ 4

Solve each equation. Lesson 10.4

30. $2x^2 - 11x - 21 = 0$ $x = 7; x = \frac{-3}{2}$
31. $17x^2 - 7 = 418$ $x = 5; x = -5$
32. $x^2 - 7 = 4$ $x = \sqrt{11}; x = -\sqrt{11}$
33. $x^2 + 7x = -6$ $x = -1; x = -6$

34. The ratio of two numbers is 5 : 4. Their product is 980. Find the numbers. Lesson 10.4; 35, 28 and −35, −28

35. **STANDARDIZED TEST** The solution to the equation $2\sqrt{x + 3} = x$ is Lesson 13.5; B

A. 3 and −4 B. 6 C. −6 D. 6 and −2

13.9 Algebra Workshop
Explore Sine and Cosine Graphs

Think Back

Find each value. Round to hundredths.

1. sin 47° 0.73 **2.** cos 81° 0.16 **3.** sin 9° 0.16 **4.** cos 20° 0.94

Find the measure of the acute angle. Round to tenths.

5. $\sin x = 0.62$ 38.3°
6. $\cos y = 0.22$ 77.3°
7. $\sin z = 0.09$ 5.2°
8. $\cos w = 0.91$ 24.5°

9. Is $y = \sin x$ a function? Is $y = \cos x$ a function? Explain.
yes, yes; for each value of x, there is exactly one value of y.

Explore

You can graph the sine and cosine functions for an angle of any measure. The angle need not be acute or even less than 180°. The graphs of these functions show interesting patterns.

10. Copy the table and, using a graphing calculator, determine the sine for each angle. Round to hundredths where necessary.
See Additional Answers.

Angle Measure	Sine	Angle Measure	Sine	Angle Measure	Sine
0°	____	135°	____	270°	____
30°	____	150°	____	300°	____
45°	____	180°	____	315°	____
60°	____	210°	____	330°	____
90°	____	225°	____	360°	____
120°	____	240°	____		

11. Within what range of degrees is the value of the sine positive? For what range is it negative?
between 0° and 180°; between 180° and 360°

12. For any angle between 0° and 360°, what is the greatest sine value? Which is the least sine value? 1; −1

13. In graphing the function $y = \sin x$, which variable will be independent and which will be dependent? x; y

14. On graph paper, draw and label a set of axes for which the x-values range from 0° to 360° and the y-values range from −1 to 1. Using the table in Question 10, graph the data.
Graphs will vary.

SPOTLIGHT ON LEARNING

WHAT? In this lesson you will learn
- to graph the functions $y = \sin x$ and $y = \cos x$.
- to recognize how different parameters affect the appearance of these graphs.

WHY? Graphs of sine and cosine functions can help you solve problems in scientific experiments.

CHECK UNDERSTANDING

Does the graph of $y = \sin x$ pass the vertical line test? What does this mean?

A vertical line will touch the graph of $y = \sin x$ in exactly one place, so $y = \sin x$ is a function.

PROBLEM SOLVING TIP

Make sure your graphing utility is in DEG mode.

LESSON PLANNING

Objectives
- ▶ Graph the functions $y = \sin x$ and $y = \cos x$.
- ▶ Recognize how different parameters affect the appearance of these graphs.

Vocabulary
amplitude
crest
period
sine curve
trough

Technology/Multimedia
graphing utility

Resources
Transparencies 34, 74
Student Handbook

ASSIGNMENTS

Basic: 1–32

Average: 1–32

Enriched: 1–33

1 MOTIVATE

Think Back Ask students to determine the measure of the angle in Question 5. **$\sin^{-1}$ 0.62 = 38.31613447° or about 38.3°**

2 FACILITATE

Explore After students complete Question 10, ask them to describe any patterns in the table. **Possible patterns: Since values increase from 0° to 90°, decrease from 90° to 270°, and increase from 270° to 360°**

Explain that a function whose graph repeats for each given period is called a periodic function. For Question 17, ask students to explain how they can determine the period of a function. **Find where the graph first begins to repeat. For $y = \cos x$, the period is $0° < x < 360°$.** Emphasize that period and amplitude are always considered positive, i.e., they are absolute values.

Make Connections Ask a student to describe the steps used to determine the function in the form $y = a \cos bx$ in Question 23. **90° is 1/4 of 360°, so x should be multiplied by 4. The amplitude is 4 times that of $y = \cos x$, so multiply $\cos x$ by 4.**

3 SUMMARIZE

Writing Mathematics For Question 30, have students give an example of the function $y = a \sin bx$ and of $y = a \cos bx$ and state the period and amplitude for each. **Possible examples: $y = 5 \sin 2x$ with period 180° and amplitude 5; $y = 4 \cos 1/3\, x$ with period 1080° and amplitude 4.**

Modeling For Question 31, ask students what the amplitude of the curve is. **20°**

Thinking Critically For Question 32, suggest that students consider the values of x for which the two equations are equal. Then ask them to determine the values of x that are solutions to the equation $\sin 2x = \cos 2x$. **22.5°, 112.5°**

Going Further For Question 33, ask students what the line of symmetry is for the function $y = \sin x$. **the x-axis, $y = 0$**

Algebra Workshop

15. On your graphing utility, set the range values as in Question 14. Use an x scale of 90 and a y scale of 0.5. Graph $y = \sin x$. How do the two graphs compare? See Additional Answers.

16. Change the x_{max} range value to 720. Predict how the graph will look. Then graph the function and check your prediction. See Additional Answers.

The graph of the sine function is called a **sine curve**. The horizontal distance from any point on the graph to that point where the graph begins to repeat is called the **period** of the function. The period of the sine function is 360°.

The **amplitude** of the function is the distance from the middle line of the graph to either the **crest** (the maximum value) or **trough** (minimum value). The middle line for the graph of $y = \sin x$ is the x-axis. The amplitude of $y = \sin x$ is 1.

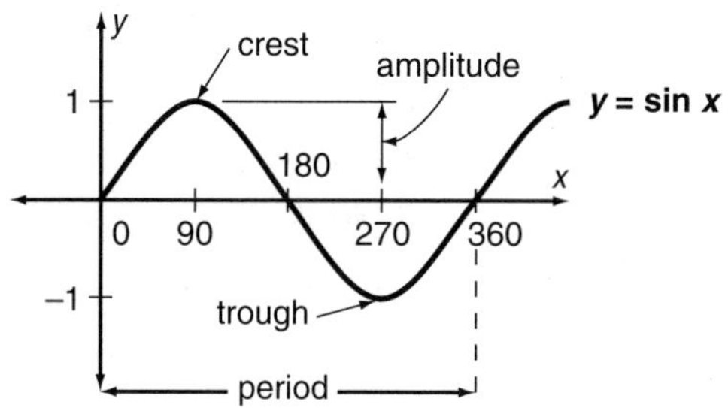

The function $y = \cos x$ is also a periodic function.

17. Graph the function of $y = \cos x$ for angles from 0° through 720°. Compare the period and amplitude to the graph of $y = \sin x$. You may wish to graph the two functions on the same screen. See Additional Answers.

18. For what values of x is $\sin x$ equal to 0? For what values of x is $\cos x$ equal to 0? See Additional Answers.

Make Connections

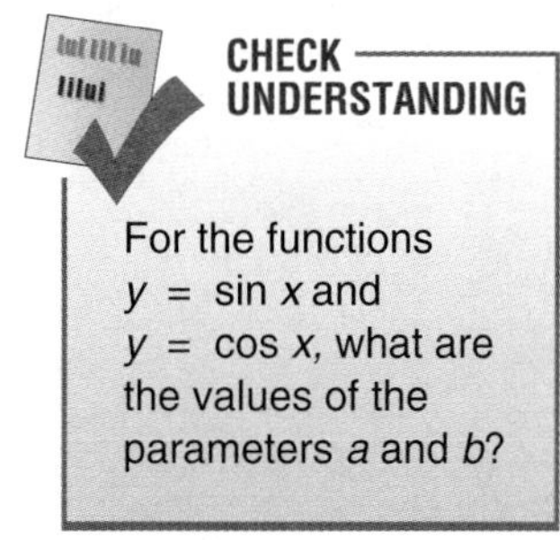

For the functions $y = \sin x$ and $y = \cos x$, what are the values of the parameters a and b?

$a = 1, b = 1$

In earlier lessons you used the graphs of $y = |x|$ and $y = x^2$ as references and explored the effect of different parameters. Now, you will use the graphs of $y = \sin x$ and $y = \cos x$ as references to compare graphs of general functions $y = a \sin bx$ and $y = a \cos bx$.

19–23 See Additional Answers for graphs.

19. Clear the graph screen. Graph the function of $y = 2 \sin x$ for x values from 0° through 720°. Compare the period and amplitude of $y = 2 \sin x$ with those of $y = \sin x$. period is 360°, amplitude is 2

20. Graph the function of $y = \sin 2x$ for values of x from 0° through 360°. Compare the period and amplitude of $y = \sin 2x$ with those of $y = \sin x$. period is 180°, amplitude is 1

21. Predict the period and amplitude of the function $y = 3 \sin 3x$. Check your answer by graphing the function. period is 120°, amplitude is 3
22. Graph the function $y = 2 \cos x$ for values of x from 0° through 720°. Compare the period and amplitude of this graph with those of $y = \cos x$. period is 360°, amplitude is 2
23. What function of the form $y = a \cos bx$ will have a period of 90° and an amplitude of 4? Check your answer by graphing the function. $y = 4 \cos 4x$

Identify the period and amplitude for each function. Check your answer by graphing the function.

24. $y = \frac{1}{2} \sin 2x$ 180°, $\frac{1}{2}$
25. $y = 4 \cos \frac{1}{2}x$ 720°, 4
26. $y = -3 \sin x$ 360°, 3
27. $y = 2 \cos 6x$ 60°, 2
28. $y = 3 \sin \frac{1}{3}x$ 1080°, 3
29. $y = 5 \cos 5x$ 72°, 5

Summarize

30. **Writing Mathematics** Explain how you determine the period and amplitude of the functions $y = a \sin bx$ and $y = a \cos bx$. Try to write general formulas that can be used to find the period and amplitude. Remember that the period and amplitude should always be positive numbers. period is $\frac{360}{|b|}$; amplitude is $|a|$
31. **Modeling** The graph below shows temperature fluctuations during a controlled experiment in a chemistry laboratory. What is the period of the curve? 90 minutes

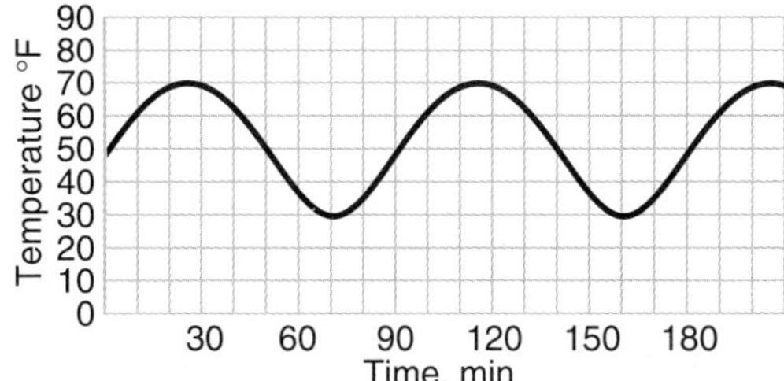

32. **Thinking Critically** Explain how you can use a graphing utility to find the values of x for the range $0 \le x \le 360°$ that are solutions to the equation $\sin x = \cos x$. Use your method to solve the equation. See Additional Answers.
33. **Going Further** Graph the function $y = \sin x + 2$ and compare it with $y = \sin x$. Then graph the function $y = \cos x - 4$ and compare it with $y = \cos x$. (*Hint*: Use a line of symmetry to determine the amplitude of the altered function.) See Additional Answers.

4 FOLLOW-UP

Other Explorations Have students make a table for the tangent function similar to the one they made for the sine function in Explore. Ask what happens when they try to find a value for tan 90° and for tan 270°. **The graphing utility indicates an error.**

Angle Measure	Tangent	Angle Measure	Tangent
0°	0.00		
30°	0.58	210°	0.58
45°	1.00	225°	1.00
60°	1.73	240°	1.73
90°		270°	
120°	–1.73	300°	–1.73
135°	–1.00	315°	–1.00
150°	–0.58	330°	–0.58
180°	0.00	360°	0.00

Have students set the range on their graphing utilities to Xmin = 0, Xmax = 360, Xscl = 90, Ymin = –5, Ymax = 5, and Yscl = 1 and then graph $y = \tan x$ for values of x between 0 and 360°. Ask what the period of the graph is. **180°** Ask students at what values of x the period begins to repeat. **180° and 360°** Ask if they can determine from the graph why their calculators give no value for the tangent function at 90° and 270°. **The values become infinitely small at the beginning of each period and infinitely large at the end of each period.**

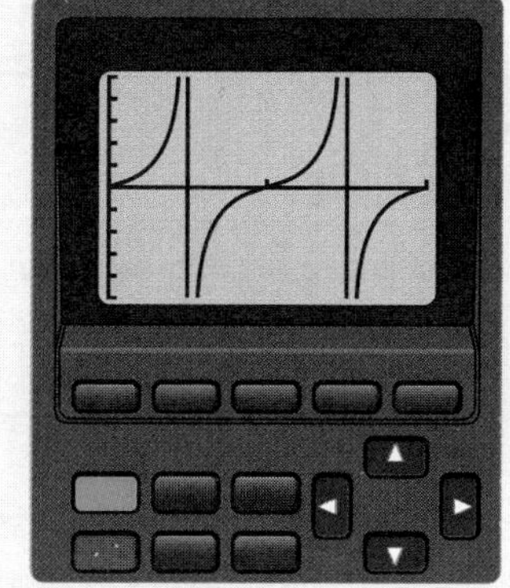

LESSON PLANNING

Objective

- Solve real world problems by choosing an appropriate method of indirect measurement.

Technology/Multimedia
calculator

Resources
Reteaching 13.10
Extra Practice 13.10
Transparencies 10, 70, 74, 74
Student Handbook

ASSIGNMENTS

Basic: 1–17

Average: 1–18

Enriched: 1–19

1 MOTIVATE

Introduction Ask students to explain what is meant by the term *indirect measurement.* **finding the measurements of items when measuring the actual object is difficult or impossible**

2 TEACH

Use the Pages/Problem Ask students what information is given in the problem. **the height of each mountain and the angle of elevation** Ask them how many triangles are drawn in the diagram and to classify and name them. **two right scalene triangles, $\triangle OAC$ and $\triangle OBD$.**

Use the Pages/Explore the Problem For Question 5, ask students to describe the steps they used to

Draw a Diagram

13.10 Problem Solving File

Use Measures Indirectly

SPOTLIGHT ON LEARNING

WHAT? In this lesson you will learn

- to solve real world problems by choosing an appropriate method of indirect measurement.

WHY?
Using indirect measurement can help you solve problems in surveying, construction, and geometry.

In some situations a measurement is needed that you cannot directly measure by hand. However, you can determine the measure indirectly by using the Pythagorean theorem, trigonometric ratios, or proportions in similar figures. For some problems, you may need to use more than one method of indirect measurement.

Problem

An electric power utility wants to run a cable between the summits of two mountains, from point C to point D. What is the distance from point C to point D?

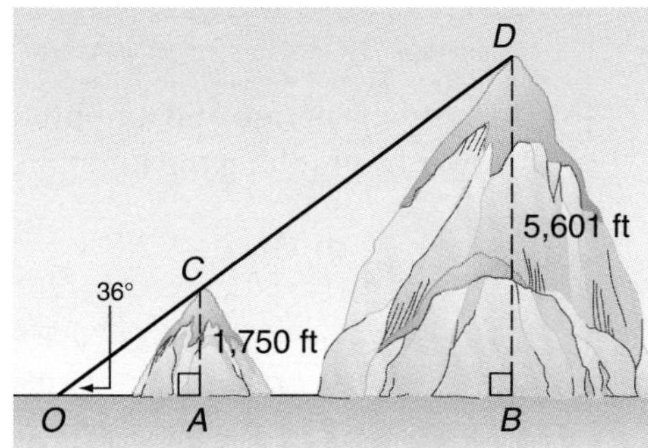

Explore the Problem

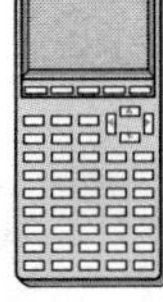

1. Which method of indirect measurement can you use to determine length OA? trigonometric ratios
2. What equation can you write? $\tan 36° = \frac{1750}{OA}$
3. Determine the length OA to the nearest foot. 2409 ft
4. What choice of methods do you have for finding the length of side OC of triangle OAC? either trigonometry, using the sine or cosine ratio, or the Pythagorean theorem
5. Find the length OC to the nearest foot using one of these methods. See Additional Answers.

6. With the information you have so far, how can you determine the length of $\overline{OD}$? How will this help you?

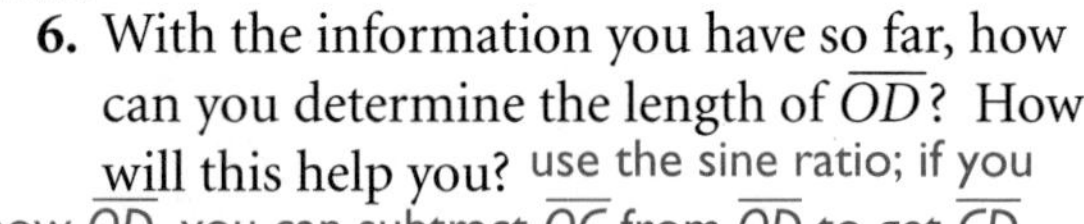

use the sine ratio; if you know $\overline{OD}$, you can subtract $\overline{OC}$ from $\overline{OD}$ to get $\overline{CD}$.

7. Use the plan you explained in Question 6. Determine the lengths of $\overline{OD}$ and $\overline{CD}$ to the nearest foot. $\overline{OD} = 9529$ ft, $\overline{CD} = 6551$ ft (or 6550 ft)
8. What if you also wanted to determine the distance from point A to point B. Describe a method you could use and carry out the steps. See Additional Answers.
9. WRITING MATHEMATICS Given a choice of methods for finding a particular length, which method did you choose? Why? See Additional Answers.

Investigate Further

CONSTRUCTION The wire supporting a radio transmitting tower touches the top of a 10-ft pole as shown in the diagram. Right triangles *ABC* and *ADE* are similar. Use this information to determine the height *h* of the tower.

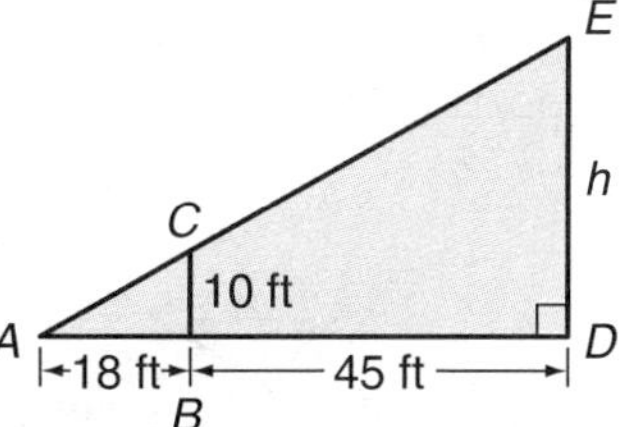

PROBLEM SOLVING PLAN

- Understand
- Plan
- Solve
- Examine

10. Describe how you could use principles of similar triangles to solve the problem. See Additional Answers.

11. Describe how you could use trigonometry to solve the problem. See Additional Answers.

12. Choose the method you prefer and carry out the steps to determine the height of the tower. 35 ft

13. Find a classmate who solved the problem differently than you did. Compare results and discuss the advantages and disadvantages of each method. Answers will vary.

Apply the Strategy

14. **SURVEYING** In the figure, triangles *JKL* and *MNL* are similar.
    a. To the nearest yard, find the distance *x* across the lake. 157.5 yd
    b. Could you use trigonometry to solve this problem? Why or why not? No, the triangles are not right triangles.

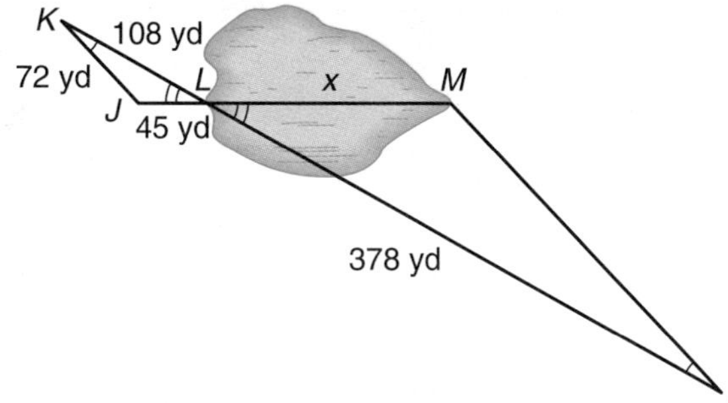

PROBLEM SOLVING TIP

Draw a diagram when one is not provided.

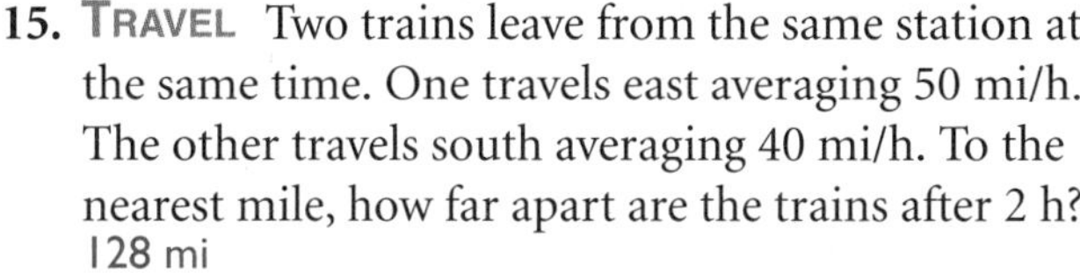

15. **TRAVEL** Two trains leave from the same station at the same time. One travels east averaging 50 mi/h. The other travels south averaging 40 mi/h. To the nearest mile, how far apart are the trains after 2 h? 128 mi

determine the length *OC*. **Use sin 36° = opp/hyp; sin 36° = 1750/*OC*; *OC* ≈ 2977 ft; or cos 36° = adj/hyp; cos 36° = 2409/*OC*; *OC* ≈ 2978 ft; or use the Pythagorean theorem $2409^2 + 1750^2 = OC^2$, $OC = \sqrt{8{,}865{,}781} = 2978$.**

Use the Pages/Investigate Further Ask students how the problem is similar to the one in the previous section. How is it different? **Both problems involve right triangles and determining the length of a side of at least one of the triangles; in this problem, it is given that the two triangles are also similar.** For Question 13, after students have discussed their methods with each other, ask students to describe the steps they used to determine *h*. **set up a proportion with corresponding sides or use the tangent function, $\tan A = 10/18 = \frac{h}{3}$ and solve for *h*.**

3 SUMMARIZE

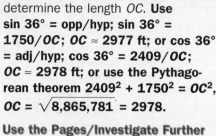

In the Math Journal Have students name the three methods of indirect measurement used in Explore the Problem and Investigate Further. **trigonometric ratios, similar triangles, proportions, and the Pythagorean theorem**

4 PRACTICE

Apply the Strategy Remind students to be sure to identify corresponding parts of similar triangles correctly.

For Problem 15, suggest that students draw a diagram. Ask a student to describe the steps he or she used to solve Problem 16. **Since the triangles are the same size, each base must be 1/2 of (2 + 28 + 2) or 16. Then, let *x* represent the length of the beam: tan 32° = opp/adj, tan 32° = *x*/16, tan 32° • 16 = *x*, 10 ≈ *x*.**

For Problem 17b, encourage students not to round until after they have determined the area.

Make Connections
Real Life Explain that astronomers, architects, and artists are just a few people who use indirect measurement. Have students investigate how right triangles and indirect measurement are used in each field.

5 FOLLOW UP

Extra Practice Use the following information to solve each problem.

A building casts an 18-foot shadow at the same time a 3-foot pole casts a 2-foot shadow forming similar triangles *ABC* and *DEF*

1. Find the approximate angle of the sun's rays by determining to the nearest degree the angle each hypotenuse makes with the ground. **56°**
2. Determine the height of the building. **27 ft**

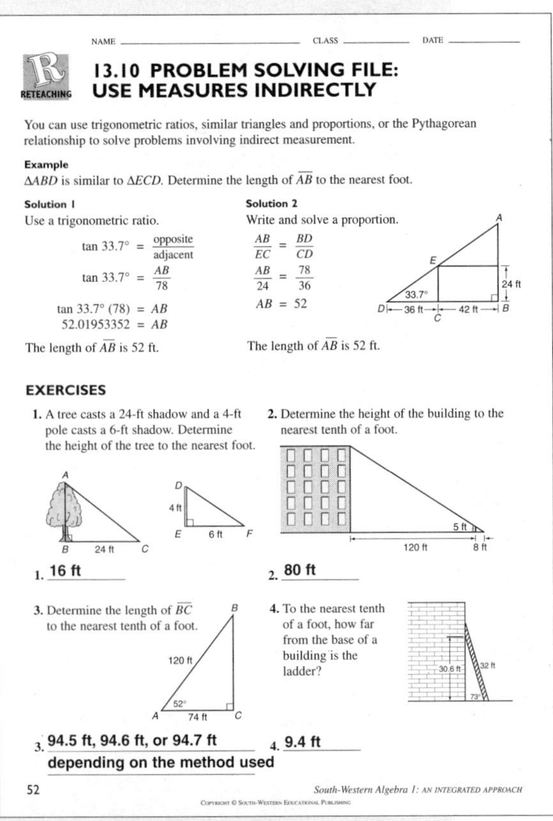

NAME ______ CLASS ______ DATE ______

RETEACHING

13.10 PROBLEM SOLVING FILE: USE MEASURES INDIRECTLY

You can use trigonometric ratios, similar triangles and proportions, or the Pythagorean relationship to solve problems involving indirect measurement.

Example

ΔABD is similar to ΔECD. Determine the length of $\overline{AB}$ to the nearest foot.

Solution 1

Use a trigonometric ratio.

$$\tan 33.7° = \frac{\text{opposite}}{\text{adjacent}}$$
$$\tan 33.7° = \frac{AB}{78}$$
$$\tan 33.7° (78) = AB$$
$$52.01953352 = AB$$

The length of $\overline{AB}$ is 52 ft.

Solution 2

Write and solve a proportion.

$$\frac{AB}{EC} = \frac{BD}{CD}$$
$$\frac{AB}{24} = \frac{78}{36}$$
$$AB = 52$$

The length of $\overline{AB}$ is 52 ft.

EXERCISES

1. A tree casts a 24-ft shadow and a 4-ft pole casts a 6-ft shadow. Determine the height of the tree to the nearest foot.

2. Determine the height of the building to the nearest tenth of a foot.

1. **16 ft**

2. **80 ft**

3. Determine the length of $\overline{BC}$ to the nearest tenth of a foot.

4. To the nearest tenth of a foot, how far from the base of a building is the ladder?

3. **94.5 ft, 94.6 ft, or 94.7 ft depending on the method used**

4. **9.4 ft**

52 South-Western Algebra 1: AN INTEGRATED APPROACH

16. **CONSTRUCTION** A vertical supporting beam divides the cross section of a roof into two right triangles of the same shape and size. If the slope of the roof is 32°, what is the length of the supporting beam b, to the nearest foot? 10 ft

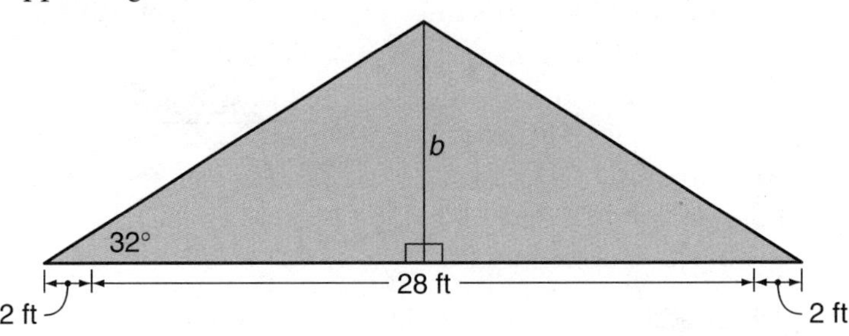

17. **GEOMETRY** Refer to rectangle *ABCD*.

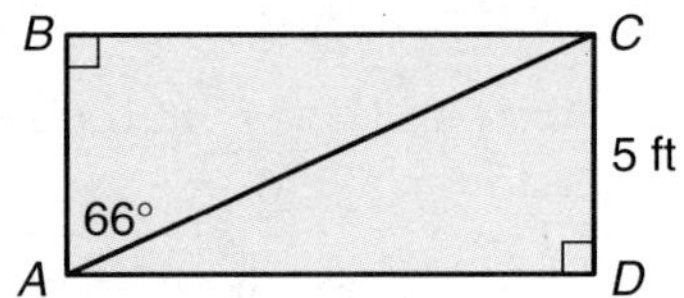

a. Find the length of the diagonal to the nearest foot. 12.3 ft

b. Find the area of the rectangle to the nearest tenth of a square foot. 56.2 ft^2

18. **SURVEYING** Find, to the nearest tenth of a foot, the height h of the antenna on top of the building shown in the figure below. $h \approx 14.1$ ft

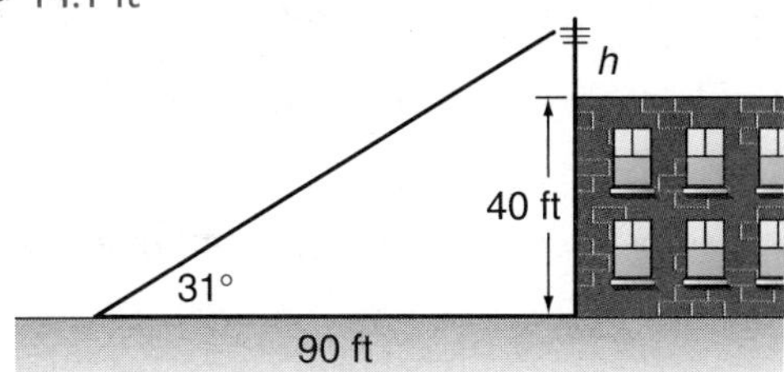

19. **MOVING** Some movers positioned a carton such that rectangle *RSTV* represents one side of the carton leaning against wall *TU* at point *T*. Triangle *RQV* is similar to triangle *VUT*. What is the distance from the corner *R* to the floor at *Q* to the nearest tenth of an inch? See Additional Answers.

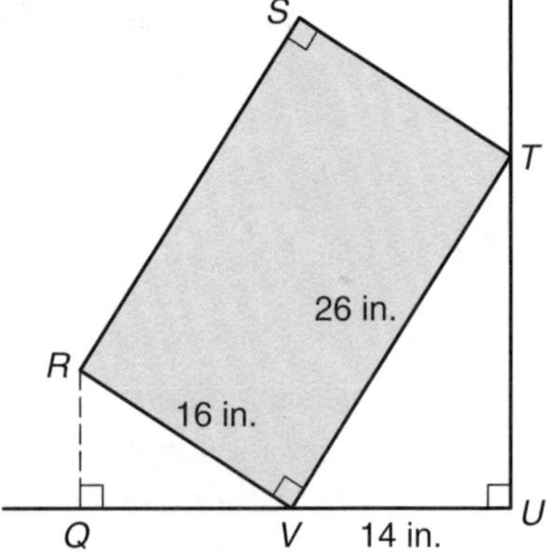

Guess and Check | Make a Table | Look for a Pattern

REVIEW PROBLEM SOLVING STRATEGIES

1–3 See Additional Answers.

ALGEBRA IS GREAT

1. The words that make up the triangle range from 2 through 15 letters. Let a, b, c and d be four different numbers. Choose four different words that are a, b, c, or d letters long so that $a^2 = bd$ and $ad = b^2c$. You can use guess and check or use the hint to help you solve the problem algebraically. (*Hint*: if $a^2 = bd$, then $a^2(ad) = bd(b^2c)$ or $a^3d = b^3dc$. Dividing by d, $a^3 = b^3c$. What does this imply about c? See what equations result from substituting the value you get for c and use logic.)

A M
L E T
G O O D
E X T R A
B E H I N D
R O O S T E R
A M I C A B L E
I N T E L L E C T
S T A T I O N A R Y
G R A S S H O P P E R
R E O R G A N I Z I N G
E X P O N E N T I A L L Y
A S T R O B I O L O G I S T
T O N S I L L E C T O M I E S

A TAXING PROBLEM

2. The country of Santa Taxita has an unusual tax plan. The tax rate is equal to the number of thousands of dollars of your income—that is, the rate is 3% on an income of \$3,000, 14% on \$14,000, and a maximum of 100% on income of \$100,000 or more.

   a. How much money will you have left if your income is \$18,000? Is there any other income for which you would be left with the same amount?

   b. Express the amount A you have left as a function of x, the number of thousands of dollars of income.

   c. At what income do you have the most money after taxes in Santa Taxita? Explain how you determined this amount.

The Power of Two

3. Without adding all the terms, how can you find the sum?

$$\frac{1}{2} + \frac{1}{4} + \frac{1}{8} + \frac{1}{16} + \ldots + \frac{1}{1024} = \square$$

Here are some questions to guide your thinking.

   a. What is the sum of the first two terms?

   b. How is the denominator of the sum of the first two terms related to the second addend?

   c. How is the numerator of the sum of the first two terms related to the denominator?

   d. What is the sum of the first three terms?

   e. What patterns do you see in how the addends are related to the sum?

   f. Without adding, find the sum of the original expression.

   g. Express the pattern you discovered as a general statement.

   h. How many terms are there in the series of addends that has the sum $\frac{32{,}767}{32{,}768}$? Write the last addend.

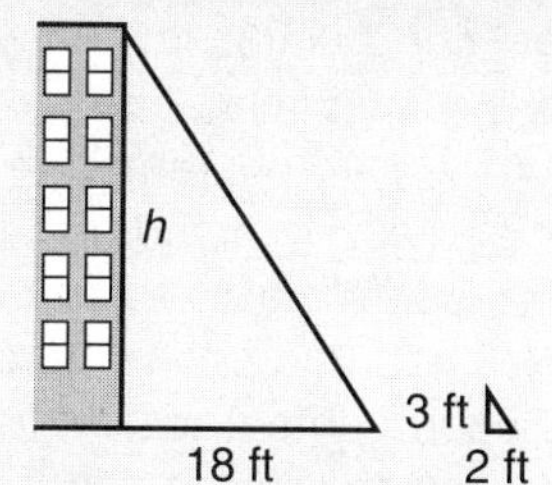

Review Problem Solving Strategies Have students work individually or in groups to solve these problems.

Algebra is Great Possible strategies for solving the problem are Guess and Check, or Use Logical Reasoning and Write an Expression.

A Taxing Problem Possible strategies for solving the problem are Write an Expression and Look for a Pattern.

The Power of 2 The strategy of Look for a Pattern will help the students solve the problem.

NAME ______ CLASS ______ DATE ______

13.10 PROBLEM SOLVING FILE: USE MEASURES INDIRECTLY

Use trigonometric ratios, similar triangles and proportions, or the Pythagorean relationship to solve each problem.

1. In isosceles ΔABC, $m\angle A$ and $m\angle B = 57$. The height is 48 cm. Find to the nearest tenth of a centimeter the length of each side of the triangle.
   $AB = 62.3$ cm, $AC = BC = 57.2$ cm

2. A surveyor marks off a right angle to the distance across a pond and finds a 58° angle as shown 75 ft from the line. To the nearest foot, what is the width of the pond?

3. A skier rides the ski lift 1500 ft to the summit of the mountain. Use the figure below to find to the nearest tenth of a foot the height h.

2. **120 ft**
3. **860.4 ft**

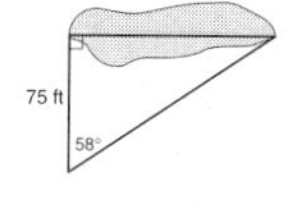

1500 ft
h
35°
1228.7 ft

4. In the figure triangles ABC and EDC are similar. Determine the distance AB across the lake.

5. Determine the height of the tree to the nearest tenth of a foot.

4. **350 m**
5. **48 ft**

A B
400 m
C 60 m
D E
52.5 m

6 ft
56.3°
28 ft 4 ft

6. To the nearest tenth of a foot, how far from the base of a building is the bottom of a 34-foot ladder that makes an angle of 75° with the ground?

6. **8.8 ft**

7. A carpenter needs to build a ramp that will have a 12° angle to the ground and reach a height of 2 ft. To the nearest tenth of a foot, how long must the ramp be?

7. **9.6 ft**

54 *South-Western Algebra 1:* AN INTEGRATED APPROACH

Introduction The Chapter Review emphasizes the major concepts, skills, and vocabulary presented in this chapter and can be used for diagnosing students' strengths and weaknesses. Page references direct students to appropriate sections for additional review and reteaching.

Using Pages 666–667 Ask students to scan the Chapter Review and ask questions about any section they find confusing. Exercises 1–3 review key vocabulary.

Informal Evaluation Have students explain how they arrived at any incorrect answers. They may find their own mistakes and give you some clues as to the nature of their errors. Make sure students understand this material before moving on to the assessment stage.

Follow-Up Have students solve this problem: A surveyor finds that the distance from point *A* to point *B* is 250 ft. The measure of the angle at point *B* is 19°.

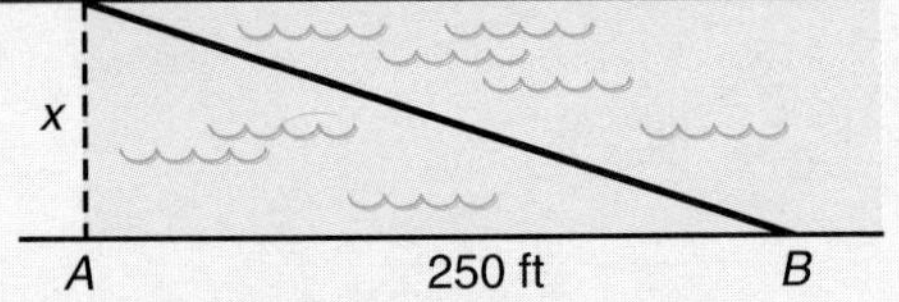

a. Let *x* represent the distance across the river. Use a trigonometric ratio to write an equation that could be used to find *x*. $\tan 19° = \frac{x}{250}$

b. Find the distance across the river to the nearest foot. **86 feet**

Have students write word problems that can be solved by using a trigonometric ratio. Students should exchange problems and solve each others' word problems.

CHAPTER REVIEW

VOCABULARY

Choose the word from the list that completes each statement.

1. In a right triangle, the ratio of the side opposite an acute angle to the hypotenuse is called the __?__ of the angle. b
2. The __?__ is the expression under the radical sign. c
3. A __?__ has no sides equal in length. a

a. scalene triangle
b. sine
c. radicand

Lessons 13.1, 13.2, and 13.7 TRIANGLES; THE PYTHAGOREAN THEOREM pages 615–624, 648–651

- Use the properties of triangles and Pythagorean relationships to classify triangles and to find measures of sides. Triangles are *similar* if the measures of corresponding angles are equal and the ratios of corresponding sides form proportions.

Classify each triangle according to its side lengths.

4. 11, 16, 32 since $11 + 16 < 32$, not a triangle
5. 21, 28, 35 right
6. 12, 15, 19 acute

For each pair of similar triangles find all unknown side lengths and angle measures. See Additional Answers.

7.

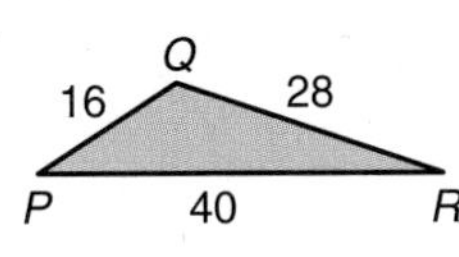

Y, 129°, 33°, X, 50, Z

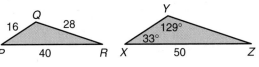

8.

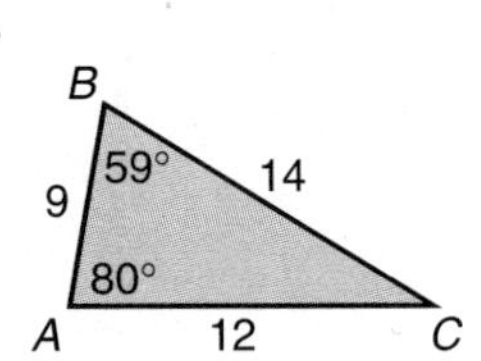

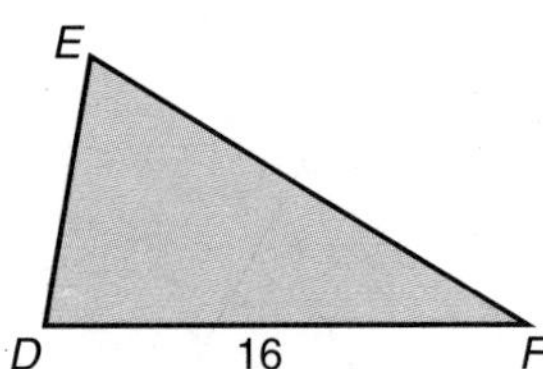

Lessons 13.3 and 13.4 MULTIPLY, DIVIDE, ADD, AND SUBTRACT RADICALS pages 625–635

- To multiply and divide radicals, use the product and quotient properties of square roots. Use the distributive property to add or subtract like radicals.

Simplify.

9. $\sqrt{28}$ $2\sqrt{7}$
10. $\sqrt{25y^2}$ $5|y|$
11. $2\sqrt{2} \cdot \sqrt{32}$ 16
12. $\sqrt{3}(4 + \sqrt{15})$ $4\sqrt{3} + 3\sqrt{5}$
13. $\frac{\sqrt{48}}{\sqrt{6}}$ $2\sqrt{2}$
14. $\sqrt{13} + 4\sqrt{13}$ $5\sqrt{13}$
15. $4\sqrt{5} - 3\sqrt{2} + 2\sqrt{5}$ $6\sqrt{5} - 3\sqrt{2}$
16. $\sqrt{128a} + 3\sqrt{8a}$ $14\sqrt{2a}$
17. $\sqrt{300r^2} - \sqrt{48r^2}$ $6|r|\sqrt{3}$

Lesson 13.5 SOLVE RADICAL EQUATIONS pages 636–641

- To solve a radical equation, isolate radicals and square both sides of the equation.

Solve and check.

18. $3\sqrt{m} = 15$ 25
19. $\sqrt{18k} - 4 = 2$ 2
20. $\sqrt{3s + 18} = s$ 6
21. $8\sqrt{x - 1} = 6\sqrt{3x - 14}$ 10

Lesson 13.6 THE DISTANCE AND MIDPOINT FORMULAS pages 642–647

- To determine the distance between two points (x_1, y_1) and (x_2, y_2), use the distance formula.
- To determine the midpoint between two points (x_1, y_1) and (x_2, y_2), use the midpoint formula.

Determine the distance between the two points. Then determine the midpoint of the segment joining them. Write radicals in simplest form.

22. (–12, 3) and (2, 5) $10\sqrt{2}$; (–5, 4)

23. (8, 1) and (7, –1) $\sqrt{5}$; (7.5, 0)

Lesson 13.8 SINE, COSINE, AND TANGENT pages 652–658

- Use the trigonometric ratios of sine, cosine, and tangent to determine the measure of an acute angle in a right triangle or to calculate distances or lengths indirectly.

Find the specified trigonometric ratio to the nearest ten thousandth.

24. sin J 0.4103

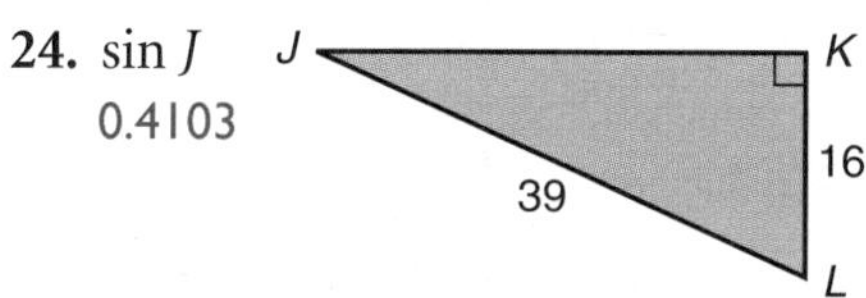

Determine the measure of each acute angle to the nearest degree.

25.

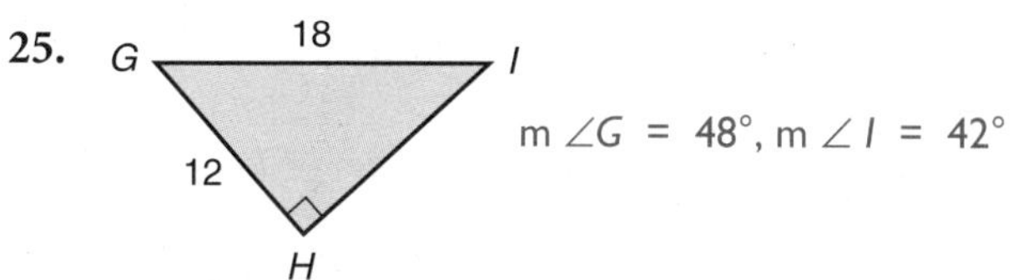

m $\angle G$ = 48°, m $\angle I$ = 42°

Lesson 13.9 EXPLORE SINE AND COSINE GRAPHS pages 659–661

- Use the graphs of $y = \sin x$ and $y = \cos x$ as basic references to graph functions of the form $y = a \sin bx$ and $y = a \cos bx$.

Match each equation to its graph. Each graph shows values for x between 0° and 360° and values for y between –4 and 4.

$y = \sin x$

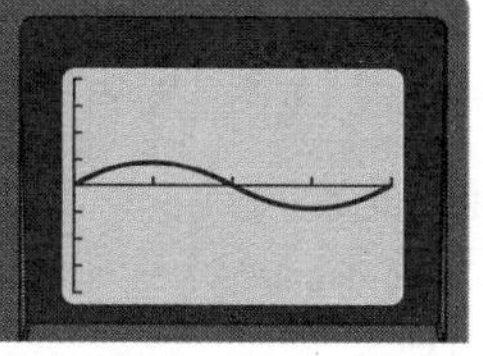

a.

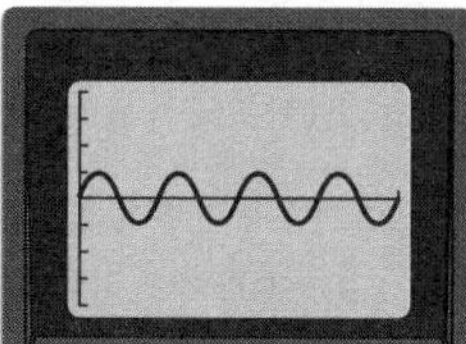

b.

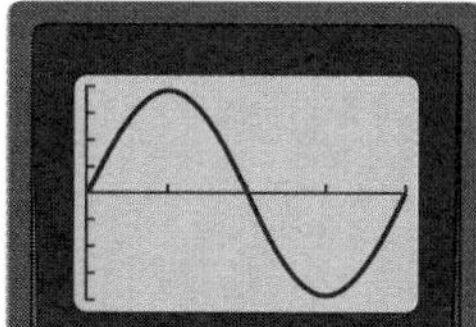

c.

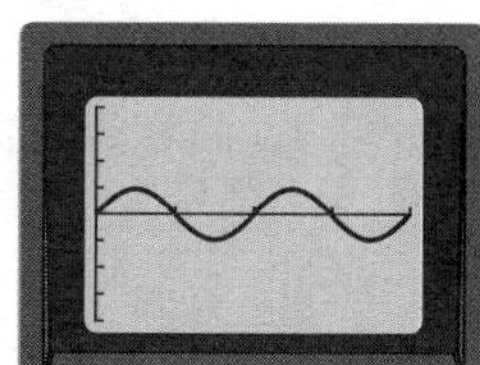

26. $y = \sin 2x$ c

27. $y = 4 \sin x$ b

28. $y = \sin 4x$ a

Lesson 13.10 USE MEASURES INDIRECTLY pages 662–665

- Indirect measurement can be used to solve problems.

29. To find the distance from the ground to the place on a pole where a support wire is connected, Rob has placed a 3-ft stick at right angles to the ground so that it just touches the wire. The distance BE is 3.75 ft and the distance EC is 1.25 ft. What is the distance AB? What is the length of the wire? 12 ft; 13 ft

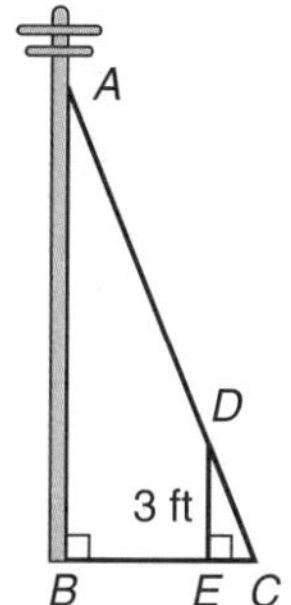

Study Skills Tip Remind students to read with a pencil in hand. Often it is helpful for students to study examples in the book, copy the examples (but not the solutions), and then close the book to see if they can work the problem without looking at the solutions.

For Your Portfolio Have students gather samples from their project, homework, quizzes, and class work that portray efforts to meet each of their goals for this chapter. On a cover page for each representative work have students write the related goal, why the work is included in the portfolio, and what the teacher should look for when reviewing the work. On a general cover page have students write a self-evaluation of how well they have met each of their goals for this chapter. The general cover page should conclude with goals for the next chapter and the student's reason for choosing these goals.

The Chapter Test is comprised of a variety of test-item types as follows:

writing	18
traditional	1–17, 20–25, 28–31
verbal	26–27, 32–35
standardized test	19

TEACHING TIP

The writing item provides an opportunity for students to demonstrate a knowledge of process as well as end result. Suggest that before they begin answering questions, students should look over the entire test and determine the order in which they will work. Some students may be more successful if they save the open-ended writing question until after they have completed the other test questions.

The table below correlates the Chapter Test items with the appropriate lesson(s).

Item	Lesson	Item	Lesson
1–6	13.2	28–31	13.8
7–12	13.3	32	13.2
13–19	13.4	33	13.4
20–25	13.5	34	13.2, 13.6
26	13.6		
27	13.7	35	13.10

CHAPTER ASSESSMENT

CHAPTER TEST

For the side lengths given, classify each triangle as *acute, right,* or *obtuse*.

1. 18, 24, 25 acute
2. 15, 20, 25 right
3. 9, 40, 42 obtuse

Determine the measure of the third angle of each triangle.

4. 32°, 50° 98°
5. 48°, 110° 22°
6. 63°, 99° 18°

Simplify each radical expression.

7. $\sqrt{12}$ $2\sqrt{3}$
8. $\frac{3\sqrt{6}}{\sqrt{3}}$ $3\sqrt{2}$
9. $\sqrt{\frac{4}{3}}$ $\frac{2\sqrt{3}}{3}$
10. $\sqrt{9x^3}$ $3x\sqrt{x}$
11. $\sqrt{8n^2}$ $2|n|\sqrt{2}$
12. $\sqrt{\frac{x}{3}}$ $\frac{\sqrt{3x}}{3}$
13. $5\sqrt{50} - 8\sqrt{32}$ $-7\sqrt{2}$
14. $4\sqrt{72a} - 3\sqrt{98a}$ $3\sqrt{2a}$
15. $\sqrt{48x} - \sqrt{27x}$ $\sqrt{3x}$
16. $\sqrt{5p} + 3\sqrt{45p^3}$ $(1 + 9|p|)\sqrt{5p}$
17. $\sqrt{12x + 12} + \sqrt{27x + 27}$ $5\sqrt{3x + 3}$

18. WRITING MATHEMATICS Write a paragraph explaining how the distributive property is used to add like radicals. Use an example to illustrate. See Additional Answers.

19. STANDARDIZED TESTS Which of the following radical expressions does *not* simplify to $4\sqrt{3}$? B

A. $3\sqrt{12} - 2\sqrt{3}$ B. $2\sqrt{75} + 2\sqrt{27}$
C. $4\sqrt{27} - 2\sqrt{48}$ D. $\sqrt{3} + \sqrt{27}$

Solve each radical equation.

20. $\sqrt{3x} = -6$ no solution
21. $3\sqrt{x - 5} - 7 = 5$ 21
22. $\sqrt{4r + 5} + r = 0$ -1
23. $\sqrt{3n - 2} - n = 0$ 2, 1
24. $\sqrt{3x + 1} = x - 3$ 8
25. $1 + 6\sqrt{y - 9} = y$ 13, 25

26. Determine the distance between the points (–3, –2) and (5, 4) and the midpoint of the line segment connecting them. 10; (1, 1)

27. Determine whether the two triangles shown are similar. yes

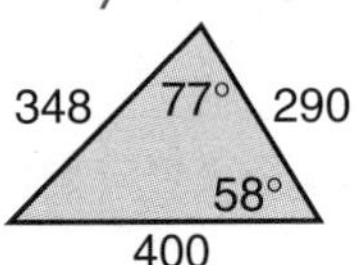

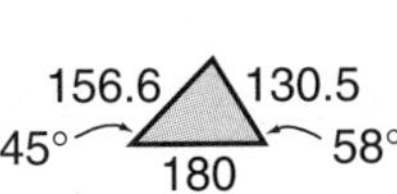

For ΔABC, find each trigonometric ratio.

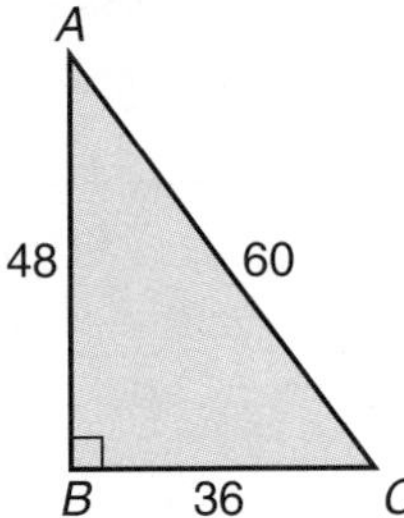

28. sin A 0.6
29. cos C 0.6
30. tan C 1.333 . . .
31. sin C 0.8

Solve each problem.

32. The measure of an angle is 48° less than its complement. Determine the measure of the angle and its complement. 21°, 69°

33. The formula $d = \sqrt{12h}$ can be used to approximate the distance d to Earth's horizon in kilometers from a point h meters above the Earth's surface. How much farther could you see from a height of 525 m than you could from a height of 336 m? $6\sqrt{7}$ km

34. Determine the lengths of the sides of the triangle formed by connecting the points (–2, 4), (4, 6), and (2, –2). Then state whether the triangle is *scalene, isosceles,* or *equilateral*. See Additional Answers.

35. Determine the width of the river given that ΔABC is similar to ΔEDC. 30 ft

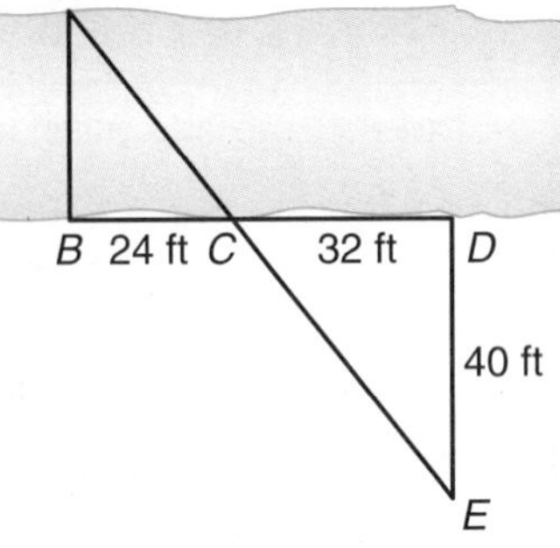

For Project Assessment see Additional Answers.

PERFORMANCE ASSESSMENT

DETERMINE HEIGHTS Work with a partner. Select a tall object such as a tree or building. Follow these steps to determine the height of the object using similar triangles.

- Select a point some distance from the object from which to sight a triangle and name it point C.
- Name the top of the object A and the bottom of the object B.

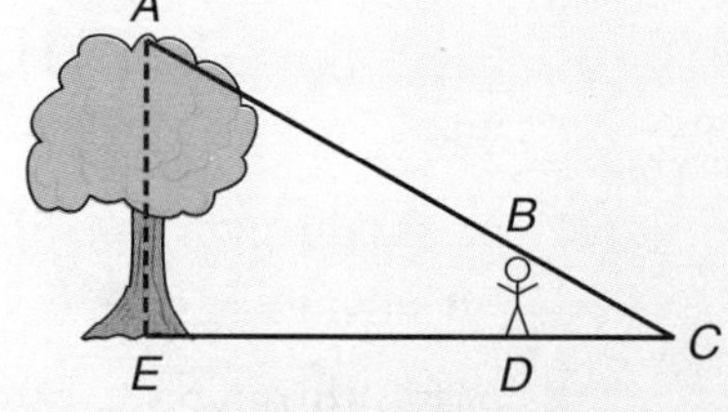

- Measure the distance from the sight point C to base E.
- While you look from the ground at sight point C, stand so that the sight line from the ground point to the top of the object grazes the top of your partner's head B. Make sure your partner stands so that he or she forms the same angle to the ground as that of the object. Then two similar triangles will be formed.
- Measure the distance CD to your partner.
- Determine the approximate height of the object.

USE A FLOWCHART Write a radical equation in the form $0 = a \pm b\sqrt{cx \pm d}$, where a, b, c, and d are real numbers greater than 0. Have a partner use the flowchart below to solve the radical equation. Check that each step is correct.

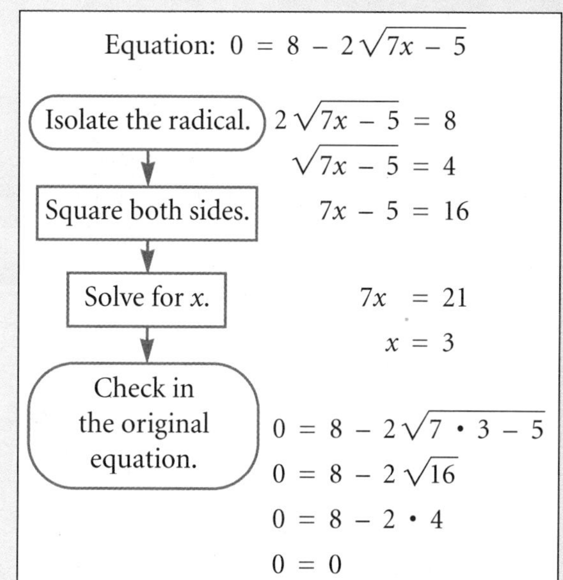

USE GRAPH PAPER Draw a right isosceles triangle ACE with side lengths of your own choosing on graph paper. Have a partner show at least two different ways to draw two right isosceles triangles ABF and BCD to show that $AB + BC = AC$. Check that each step is correct.

USE GRAPH PAPER Draw a right triangle on graph paper. Have a partner draw a similar right triangle either inside your triangle or containing it. Determine the scale factor your partner used. Show that it is true for each side of the pair of triangles.

PROJECT ASSESSMENT

PROJECT Connection It's time to sell your used cars. Assemble all the data and visuals you have collected during the project.

1. As a group, discuss each car you have studied. Decide on a fair price for the car and what features of the car you wish to highlight in an advertisement.
2. Have each group member work on a specific advertisement. He or she should use the correct abbreviations when developing the copy.
3. Contact one or more local newspapers to find out their automotive classified rates. Use these rates to determine the cost of running each advertisement for three days.
4. Compare your advertisements with those of other groups. Were some more attention-getting than others? Why?

Performance Assessment

The activities on page 669 give students with different learning styles opportunities to demonstrate their understanding of concepts in this chapter. The activities may be used in addition to or instead of the Chapter Test on the previous page.

Determine Heights (Kinesthetic/Visual) It will help students if they draw a diagram to illustrate their method for determining the height.

Use Graph Paper (Visual) Students should realize that point B must be located on the side of the triangle labeled AC. $\overline{BF}$ will be parallel to one side of the triangle, ACE and $\overline{BD}$ will be parallel to another side of triangle ACE.

Use a Flowchart (Visual) This flowchart can also be applied to other radical equations.

Use Graph Paper (Visual) Point out that one way to draw a triangle similar to another is to make each side of the new triangle parallel to a side of the original triangle.

Project Assessment

Project Connection As a class, have students consider and discuss the strengths and weaknesses of the various advertisements and how they might be made more effective.

NAME ______ CLASS ______ DATE ______

FORM B

CHAPTER 13 TEST

Write the letter of the best answer for Questions 1–6.

1. Which is not equal to $5\sqrt{2}$? 1. c

a. $\sqrt{10} \cdot \sqrt{5}$ b. $\sqrt{50}$

NAME ______ CLASS ______ DATE ______

FORM A

CHAPTER 13 TEST

Write the letter of the best answer for Questions 1–6.

1. Which is not equal to $5\sqrt{3}$? 1. d
   a. $\sqrt{15} \cdot \sqrt{5}$ b. $\sqrt{75}$
   c. $2\sqrt{3} + 3\sqrt{3}$ d. $\sqrt{3} + 5\sqrt{3}$
2. For the side lengths given, which represent the side lengths for an obtuse triangle? 2. c
   a. 12, 14, 16 b. 15, 20, 25
   c. 7, 9, 15 d. 10, 24, 26
3. Which is the distance between the points (6, –1) and (–2, 5)? 3. c
   a. 50 b. $4\sqrt{2}$
   c. 10 d. 4
4. Which is the midpoint for the segment joining (8, –10) and (12, –20)? 4. b
   a. (20, –30) b. (10, –15)
   c. (–4, 10) d. (–2, 5)
5. Which equals cos A? 5. a
   a. 0.6 b. 0.8
   c. 0.75 d. 1.333. . .
6. Which triangles are similar? 6. b
   I. II. III.
   a. I and II b. I and III
   c. II and III d. I, II, and III

For the sides given, classify each triangle as *acute*, *right*, or *obtuse*.

7. 12, 16, 20 8. 12, 18, 20 9. 12, 14, 20

Simplify each radical expression.

10. $\sqrt{80}$ 11. $\frac{12\sqrt{10}}{\sqrt{2}}$ 12. $\sqrt{\frac{5}{3}}$

13. $\sqrt{25x^3}$ 14. $\sqrt{48x^2}$ 15. $9\sqrt{32} - 2\sqrt{50}$

16. $\sqrt{8x + 8} + \sqrt{18x + 18}$ 17. $\sqrt{32x} + \sqrt{72x}$

7. right
8. acute
9. obtuse
10. $4\sqrt{5}$
11. $12\sqrt{5}$
12. $\frac{\sqrt{15}}{3}$
13. $5|x|\sqrt{x}$
14. $4|x|\sqrt{3}$
15. $26\sqrt{2}$
16. $5\sqrt{2x + 2}$
17. $10\sqrt{2x}$

58 *South-Western Algebra 1:* AN INTEGRATED APPROACH

CHAPTER 13 TEST Form A, page 2 NAME ______

Solve each radical equation.

18. $\sqrt{5x} = -4$ 19. $4\sqrt{x - 2} - 1 = 11$

20. $\sqrt{3y + 4} + y = 12$ 21. $\sqrt{4x + 5} - x = 0$

22. $\sqrt{2x + 1} = x - 7$ 23. $4 + 2\sqrt{y - 1} = y$

For ΔDEF, find each trigonometric ratio to the nearest thousandth.

24. sin D 25. cos D

26. tan E 27. sin E

Solve.

28. The measure of an angle is 32° less than its complement. Determine the measure of the angle and its complement.
29. **Travel Speed** The formula $s = \sqrt{24d}$ can be used to estimate the speed s a car was traveling if it skidded d feet on dry concrete. If a car skidded 100 feet on dry concrete, find and simplify a radical expression for the speed the car was traveling.
30. **Geometry** Determine the lengths of the sides of the triangle formed by connecting the points (10, 2), (2, –4), and (4, –6). Then state whether the triangle is *scalene*, *isosceles*, or *equilateral*.
31. **Surveying** Determine the distance across the pond given that ΔRST is similar to ΔPQT.

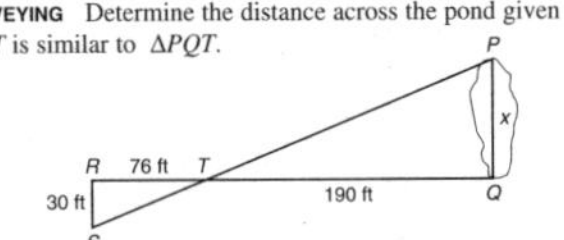

18. no solution
19. 11
20. 7
21. 5
22. 12
23. 10
24. 0.28
25. 0.96
26. 3.429
27. 0.96
28. 29°, 61°
29. $20\sqrt{6}$ mi/h
30. 10, 10, $2\sqrt{2}$; isosceles
31. 75 ft

For Question 32, use a separate sheet of paper if necessary.

32. **Writing Mathematics** Explain why a triangle cannot be both right and equilateral.
    Possible answer: If a triangle is equilateral, all the angles are equal and each must equal 60°. So the triangle cannot be a right triangle.

60 *South-Western Algebra 1:* AN INTEGRATED APPROACH

• • • CUMULATIVE REVIEW • • •

Simplify each radical expression. See Additional Answers.

1. $\sqrt{300}$ Lesson 13.3
2. $\sqrt{\frac{4}{5}}$
3. $\sqrt{15} \cdot \sqrt{5}$
4. $\frac{\sqrt{24}}{\sqrt{3}}$
5. Find two integers that differ by three and whose product is 54. –9, –6, or 6, 9 Lesson 12.7

Solve each equation. Round to the nearest hundredth.

6. $x^2 + 29x - 30 = 0$ –30, 1; Lesson 12.6
7. $4n - (5n - 8) = 8 - n$ all real numbers; Lesson 3.7
8. $x^2 - 11x + 25 = 0$ 3.21, 7.79; Lesson 10.5
9. $\frac{3}{4}d - 12 = 3 - \frac{1}{2}d$ 12; Lesson 3.7
10. **Writing Mathematics** You have learned three ways to solve quadratic equations: by factoring, by taking square roots, and using the quadratic formula. If you could choose only one of these methods for solving a particular quadratic equation, which would you choose? Why? See Additional Answers. Lessons 10.5 and 12.6

Simplify each radical expression. Lesson 13.4 See Additional Answers.

11. $\sqrt{48} + \sqrt{27} - \sqrt{75}$
12. $3\sqrt{24} + 2\sqrt{45} - \sqrt{150} + 6\sqrt{20}$
13. **Standardized Tests** The area of a rectangle is $2x^2 + 9x + 10$. What is the perimeter of the rectangle? A; Lessons 12.2 and 11.6
    - A. $6x + 14$
    - B. $3x + 7$
    - C. $2x^2 + 9x + 10$
    - D. 9
    - E. cannot be determined

Simplify each expression. Lessons 11.2 and 11.3

14. $\frac{(2x^2)^3}{(4x^5)^2}$ $\frac{1}{2x^4}$
15. $\frac{(a^2b^{-3})^6}{(a^3b^{-4})^4}$ $\frac{1}{b^2}$

Write the equation of each line described, in standard form.

16. passes through (4, –1) and parallel to the line $y = 2x - 3$ $2x - y = 9$; Lesson 6.4
17. passes through (–4, 5) and perpendicular to the line $3x - 2y = 8$ $2x + 3y = 7$; Lesson 6.4
18. passes through (3, –2) and perpendicular to the x axis $x = 3$; Lesson 6.5

Solve each equation. Lesson 13.5

19. $\sqrt{2x + 1} + 4 = 9$ 12
20. $\sqrt{x + 7} + 5 = x$ 9

Solve each system by graphing. See Additional Answers.

21. $\begin{cases} x - y = 1 \\ 2x + y = 5 \end{cases}$
22. $\begin{cases} 3x + 2y < 8 \\ 2x - y < 1 \end{cases}$
23. Find the length of the segment whose endpoints are (3, –5) and (–3, –1). See Additional Answers.
24. Find the midpoint of the segment whose endpoints are (10, 3) and (2, –5). (6, –1); Lesson 13.6
25. **Technology** Teri used the distance formula and came up with $\sqrt{36 + 16}$. She entered [√] 36 [+] 16 on her graphing calculator, but got an answer of 22, which she knew was not correct. Why did this happen, and how can Teri enter the calculation correctly? See Additional Answers. Lesson 13.6

Standardized Tests Determine whether the quantity in Column 1 is greater than, less than, or equal to the quantity in Column 2, or whether the relationship cannot be determined.

	Column 1	Column 2
26.	the discriminant of $2x^2 + 7x - 5 = 0$	the discriminant of $2x^2 - 7x - 5 = 0$
	They are equal; Lesson 10.5	
27.	the hypotenuse of a triangle with sides 10 and 24	the hypotenuse of a triangle with sides 15 and 20
	Column 1 is greater; Lesson 13.2	

• • • STANDARDIZED TEST • • •

STANDARD FIVE-CHOICE Select the best choice for each question.

1. Consider the expressions numbered I–IV.

   I. $2x^4 + 5$
   II. $x^4 + x^2y^2 + y^4$
   III. $4x^3 + 2x$
   IV. $7y^2 - 2y^4$

Which of the above is a fourth degree binomial?

A. IV only **B.** II and III **C.** I and IV
D. I and II **E.** I, II, and IV

C; Lesson 11.6

2. When factored correctly, the polynomial $x^2 - 13x - 30$ can be written as E; Lesson 12.2

A. $(x - 10)(x - 3)$
B. $(x - 10)(x + 3)$
C. $(x - 15)(x - 2)$
D. $(x + 15)(x - 2)$
E. $(x - 15)(x + 2)$

3. C; Lessons 13.2 and 13.8

B
8
A
15
C

$\cos A =$

A. cannot be determined

B. $\frac{8}{17}$ **C.** $\frac{15}{17}$ **D.** $\frac{15}{23}$ **E.** $\frac{8}{15}$

4. The value of $\frac{(-1)^{16}(-2)^5}{-4^2 - (-4)^2}$ is 2 and 2.7

A. 1 **B.** undefined **C.** 0
D. −32 **E.** 3

5. Darrell takes a $50 bill to the bank. He asks for change in bills. The teller returns 30 bills, all of which are $5's and $1's. How many $5's did Darrell get? C; Lesson 7.7

A. 1 **B.** 3 **C.** 5 **D.** 7 **E.** 9

6. What is the maximum area that can be enclosed by a rectangular region with 40 ft of fencing? D; Lesson 10.6

A. 10 ft^2 **B.** 20 ft^2 **C.** 40 ft^2
D. 100 ft^2 **E.** 160 ft^2

7. Which of the following numbers is between 5 and 6? C; Lesson 9.5

I. $\sqrt{31}$ **II.** 35%

III. 6.010010001. . . **IV.** $\frac{23}{4}$

A. I only **B.** II and IV **C.** I and IV
D. II and III **E.** I, II, and IV

8. A person is reading from a book. The sum of the two facing page numbers is 349. If each chapter in the book is 40 pages long, in what chapter is the person reading? B; Lesson 3.9

A. Chapter 4 **B.** Chapter 5 **C.** Chapter 6
D. Chapter 8 **E.** Chapter 9

9. If $f(x) = \frac{2}{3}x - 5$ and $g(x) = 2x^2 + 3x - 5$, find $f(6) + g(-2)$. B; Lessons 4.4 and 4.6

A. −20 **B.** −4 **C.** −2
D. 2 **E.** 10

10. The midpoint of a segment is (1,−3). If one endpoint of the segment is located at (4, −10), where is the other endpoint located? D; Lesson 13.6

A. (2.5, −6.5) **B.** (1.5, −3.5) **C.** (7, −17)
D. (−2, 4) **E.** the origin

11. An item had an original selling price of $24.00. First, it was marked $\frac{1}{3}$ off. Then it was further reduced, so that a customer only had to pay $12.00 for the item. What percent of the marked price was the second markdown? B; Lesson 3.5

A. 50% **B.** 25% **C.** $58\frac{1}{3}$%
D. $33\frac{1}{3}$% **E.** 40%

Answers

1. D	**14.** C
2. E	**15.** C
3. E	**16.** A
4. B	**17.** C
5. C	**18.** A
6. C	**19.** D
7. B	**20.** 2
8. D	**21.** 6
9. C	**22.** 0.28
10. A	**23.** 0.28
11. B	**24.** 0.29
12. B	**25.** 30
13. C	**26.** 41

CHAPTER 13 Standardized Test, page 2 NAME ______

Quantitative Comparison For Questions 11–19, fill in A if the quantity in Column 1 is greater, B if the quantity in Column 2 is greater, C if the two quantities are equal, or D if the relationship cannot be determined.

Grid Response For Questions 20–26, mark your answer on the answer grid provided.

Solve each equation.

20. $\sqrt{50x} - 4 = 6$

NAME ______ CLASS ______ DATE ______

CHAPTER 13 STANDARDIZED TEST

Standard Five Choice For Questions 1–10, fill in the best choice on the answer grid provided.

1. Which radical expression is *not* in simplest form?

A. $\sqrt{22}$ **B.** $\sqrt{15}$ **C.** $\sqrt{10}$
D. $\sqrt{45}$ **E.** $\sqrt{30}$

2. For the side lengths given, which could be lengths of the sides of a right triangle?

I. 15, 20, 25 **II.** 12, 15, 16
III. 18, 24, 30 **IV.** 10, 15, 20

A. only I **B.** only II
C. I and IV only **D.** I and II only
E. I and III only

3. Which does *not* simplify to $3\sqrt{3}$?

A. $\sqrt{27}$ **B.** $2\sqrt{3} + \sqrt{3}$
C. $\frac{9}{\sqrt{3}}$ **D.** $\sqrt{48} - \sqrt{3}$
E. $\sqrt{18}$

4. Which is the midpoint of the segment joining the points (10, −20) and (−20, 40)?

A. (15, −30) **B.** (−5, 10)
C. (−10, 20) **D.** (10, −5)
E. None of these

5. Which is simplest form for $\sqrt{40x^2}$?

A. $\pm 2|x|\sqrt{10}$ **B.** $2x\sqrt{10}$
C. $2|x|\sqrt{10}$ **D.** $-2x\sqrt{10}$
E. None of these

6. Which is simplest form $\sqrt{300} + \sqrt{48}$?

A. $\sqrt{348}$ **B.** 120 **C.** $14\sqrt{3}$
D. $14\sqrt{6}$ **E.** None of these

7. Which equals $\cos A$ (to the nearest hundredth)?

A. 0.28
B. 0.96
C. 0.29
D. 1.04
E. 3.57

25, 7, A, 24

8. Which radical equation has no solution?

A. $\sqrt{2x + 1} = 3$
B. $2\sqrt{x + 4} = 8$
C. $2\sqrt{x + 3} - x = 0$
D. $\sqrt{2x} = -4$
E. $\sqrt{x + 5} + x = 1$

9. Which triangles are similar?

I. 150, 95, 120 **II.** 100, 60, 80 **III.** 75, 45, 60

A. I and II **B.** I and III
C. II and III **D.** I, II, and III
E. None of these

10. For the given similar triangles, which proportion could you solve to find x?

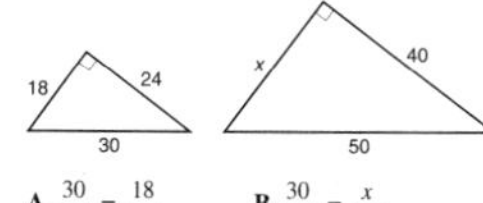

A. $\frac{30}{50} = \frac{18}{x}$ **B.** $\frac{30}{50} = \frac{x}{40}$
C. $\frac{18}{x} = \frac{50}{30}$ **D.** $\frac{x}{50} = \frac{30}{18}$
E. None of these

Chapter Opener

Data Activity, pages 612–613

1. about 22 weeks **2.** about 4 weeks

3. Answers will vary. $21{,}800 = \frac{24}{52}x$ where x is yearly income; income is about $47,233

4. more

5. Answers will vary. One explanation is that the average price of a new car dropped due to an increase in the number of low-priced imports during this period. Import prices have since risen.

Lesson 13.1

Think Back/Working Together, page 615

1. The area of a square equals the length of a side squared. This square has an area of 9 square units and a side of 3 units, so $3^2 = 9$.

2. The length of a side of a square equals the square root of the area. This square has a side of 2 units and an area of 4 square units, so $\sqrt{4} = 2$.

Make Connections, page 616–617

13. 49, 576, 625; The squares on the legs will have areas $7^2 = 49$ and $24^2 = 576$. The square on the hypotenuse will have area $49 + 576 = 625$.

Summarize, page 617

26. The square built on each leg of the shaded triangle consists of two triangles the same size and shape as the shaded triangle. The "sum" of these two squares consists of four triangles the same size and shape as the shaded triangle. The sum is equal to the square built on the hypotenuse, which also consists of four triangles the same size and shape as the shaded triangle.

28. The area of the large square is $(a + b)^2 = a^2 + 2ab + c^2$. The area of each of the four triangles is $\frac{1}{2}ab$. The small square in the middle with side c has an area of c^2. The combined area of the five polygons is

$$A = c^2 + 4\left(\frac{ab}{2}\right)$$
$$(a + b)^2 = c^2 + 2ab$$
$$a^2 + 2ab + b^2 = c^2 + 2ab$$
$$a^2 + b^2 = c^2$$

Lesson 13.2

Try These, page 621–622

16. Possible answers: (1) Measure the angles at opposite corners. They should be right angles. (2) Measure the lengths of the sides of one of the triangular regions formed by the frame and brace. If the triangle is a right triangle, the Pythagorean theorem should apply to those measures.

Extend, page 622

11. yes; the longest diagonal is 66.52 in.; find this length by squaring 65, adding 200 (the square of the diagonal of the square face) and finding the square root of the sum

Think Critically, page 623

12.
$$x^2 + \left(\frac{(x^2 - 1)}{2}\right)^2 = \left(\frac{(x^2 + 1)}{2}\right)^2$$
$$x^2 + \frac{(x^4 - 2x^2 + 1)}{4} = \frac{(x^4 - 2x^2 + 1)}{4}$$
$$4x^2 + x^4 - 2x^2 + 1 = x^4 + 2x^2 + 1$$
$$x^4 + 2x^2 + 1 = x^4 + 2x^2 + 1$$

13. Answers will vary, but there should be three different lengths and, if c is the longest side, $a^2 + b^2$ should be less than c^2.

14. three different lengths, with $a^2 + b^2 > c^2$

15. two lengths equal, with $a^2 + b^2 > c^2$; c can be either the longest side or one of two equal longer sides.

Lesson 13.3

Communicating About Algebra, page 625

Explanations will vary. Samples: (Product Property) The square root of a product equals the product of the square roots of the factors; (Quotient Property) The square root of a quotient equals the quotient of the square roots of the numerator and the denominator.

Check Understanding, page 627

multiplication property of 1; $\left(\frac{\sqrt{2}}{\sqrt{2}} = 1\right)$

Practice, page 628

25. Answers will vary. Samples:

1. the radicand contains no perfect-square factors other than 1: $\sqrt{75} = 5\sqrt{3}$
2. the radicand contains no fractions: $\sqrt{\frac{1}{3}} = \frac{\sqrt{3}}{3}$
3. no denominator contains a radical: $\frac{3}{\sqrt{2}} = \frac{3\sqrt{2}}{2}$

Extend, page 629

28. $4 - \sqrt{2}$; 14

29. $\sqrt{5} + \sqrt{3}$; 2

30. $2\sqrt{6} + 3\sqrt{2}$; 6

31. $\sqrt{10} - 4$; –6

Think Critically, page 629

37. $(m + \sqrt{n})(m - \sqrt{n}) = m^2 - n$. Since both m^2 and n are rational numbers, their difference is also a rational number. Therefore, the product is rational.

AlgebraWorks, page 630

4. (answers in mi/h)

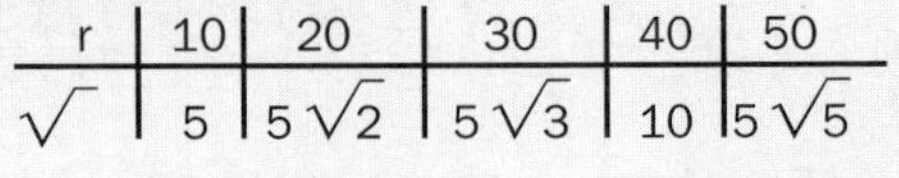

r	10	20	30	40	50
$\sqrt{\ }$	5	$5\sqrt{2}$	$5\sqrt{3}$	10	$5\sqrt{5}$

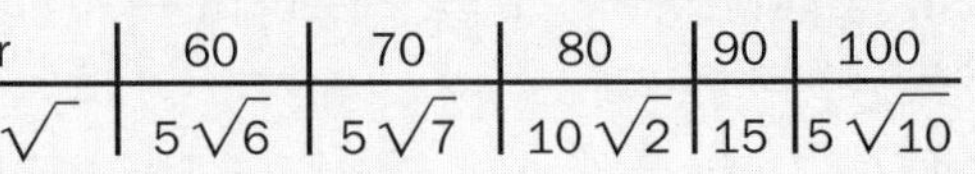

r	60	70	80	90	100
$\sqrt{\ }$	$5\sqrt{6}$	$5\sqrt{7}$	$10\sqrt{2}$	15	$5\sqrt{10}$

5.

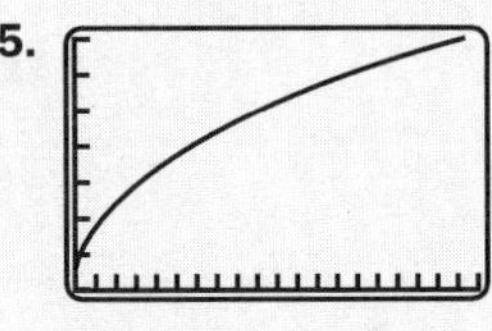

x scl = 100, y scl = 10

Lesson 13.4

Try These, page 633

1. $7\sqrt{7}$ **2.** $11\sqrt{5}$

3. $19\sqrt{2}$ **4.** $\sqrt{6}$

5. $-4\sqrt{10} + 4\sqrt{5}$ **6.** $-2\sqrt{b}$

7. $27\sqrt{5}$ **8.** $3|x|\sqrt{2}$

9. $\frac{\sqrt{2}}{4}$

11. In $7x^2 - 6x + 4x^2$, only $7x^2$ and $4x^2$ are like because they have the same exponent and base. So they can be combined to $11x^2$.
In $7\sqrt{6} - 6\sqrt{2} + 4\sqrt{6}$, $7\sqrt{6}$ and $4\sqrt{6}$ are like because the radicands are the same, so they can be combined to $11\sqrt{6}$.

Practice, pages 633–634

1. $9\sqrt{3}$ **2.** $15\sqrt{7}$

3. $8\sqrt{5}$ **4.** $4\sqrt{10} - \sqrt{5}$

5. $3\sqrt{3} + 6\sqrt{2}$ **6.** $3\sqrt{5}$

7. $16\sqrt{h}$ **8.** $7\sqrt{2y}$

9. $19\sqrt{2x}$ **10.** $8\sqrt{3}$

11. $9\sqrt{2}$ **12.** $3|c|\sqrt{2}$

13. $3\sqrt{2n + 2}$

14. $\frac{3\sqrt{2}}{2}$ **15.** $\frac{\sqrt{6}}{6}$

16. 105; $24\sqrt{3}$

17. $\frac{9\sqrt{7}}{2} + 15\sqrt{14}$; $23\sqrt{2} + 5$

18. $15\sqrt{3}$; $3\sqrt{15} + 7\sqrt{2}$

20. $2\sqrt{15}$ km **21.b.** $\frac{\pi\sqrt{2}}{4}$ seconds

22. Explanations will vary. Students should state that they can use a calculator to evaluate each expression and then compare the results.

ROJECT CONNECTION, PAGE 635

2. Students should explain that they use the Pythagorean theorem twice, first to determine the length of the diagonal along a flat surface of the carton, and then again to find the corner-to-corner diagonal.

esson 13.5

XPLORE/WORKING TOGETHER, PAGE 636

1. Let $y_1 = x$, $y_2 = \sqrt{5x + 6}$, ; determine the point of intersection of the graphs. The solution is $x = 6$.
2. Square both sides of the equation. The resulting quadratic, $x^2 - 5x - 6 = 0$ can be factored as $(x + 1)(x - 6) = 0$, giving solutions $x = 6$ and $x = -1$. The solution $x = 6$ checks in the original equation but $x = -1$ does not. Thus, the solution is $x = 6$ as above.
3. $x = 2$
4. $x = 2$
5. $x = \frac{1}{3}$; answers will vary; in each case the algebraic method introduces an extraneous solution of –1 that does not check
6. $x = \frac{5}{2}$; answers will vary; the algebraic method introduces an extraneous solution of $-\frac{3}{2}$

HECK UNDERSTANDING, PAGE 637

nswers will vary. Sample answer: Squaring and taking ne square root are inverse operations. Each operation ndoes the other, and when both are applied to $x - 1$, the result is $2x - 1$.

OMMUNICATING ABOUT ALGEBRA, PAGE 637

he given equation has a binomial on the left side. quaring the equation will produce a trinomial on the eft side. Furthermore, there will still be a radical on the eft side, in the middle term of the trinomial. The urpose of squaring both sides is to simplify the quation by ridding it of radicals by squaring once, but hat can occur only if the radical is isolated before quaring both sides.

RY THESE, PAGE 639

4. In each, you must begin by isolating one expression. In the radical equation you first isolate the radical expression $2\sqrt{x - 1}$. In the linear equation you first isolate the variable expression and then solve for the variable. Once you isolate the radical expression, you must then square both sides of the equation before solving for the variable.

RACTICE, PAGE 640

7. $3 = \sqrt{\frac{5F}{320}}$; 576 lb

8. Answers will vary. Students should point out that solving a radical equation by squaring both sides may produce extraneous solutions. The only way to know whether a possible solution is extraneous is to check it in the original equation.

THINK CRITICALLY, PAGE 641

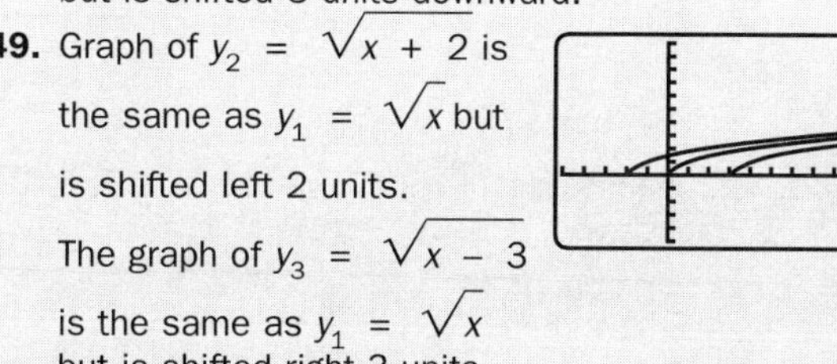

48. Graph of $y_2 = \sqrt{x} + 2$ same as $y_1 = \sqrt{x}$ but is shifted upward 2 units. Graph of $y_3 = \sqrt{x} - 3$ is the same as $y_1 = \sqrt{x}$ but is shifted 3 units downward.

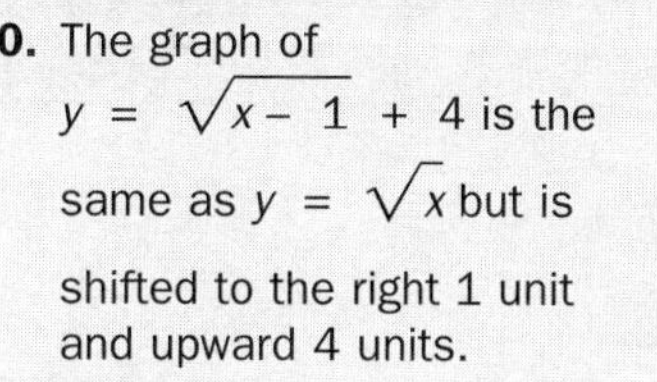

49. Graph of $y_2 = \sqrt{x + 2}$ is the same as $y_1 = \sqrt{x}$ but is shifted left 2 units. The graph of $y_3 = \sqrt{x - 3}$ is the same as $y_1 = \sqrt{x}$ but is shifted right 3 units.

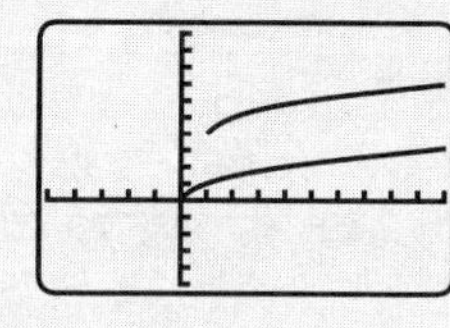

50. The graph of $y = \sqrt{x - 1} + 4$ is the same as $y = \sqrt{x}$ but is shifted to the right 1 unit and upward 4 units.

Lesson 13.6

COMMUNICATING ABOUT ALGEBRA, PAGE 642

Answers will vary. Possible answer: the distance between two points equals the square root of the sum of the square of the difference in the *x*-coordinates of the points and the square of the difference in the *y*-coordinates of the points.

CHECK UNDERSTANDING, PAGE 643

Find the distances from (4, 2) to (–3, 5) and from (4, 2) to (11, –1). If the distances are equal, then (4, 2) is the midpoint.

TRY THESE, PAGES 644–645

11. Students should agree with the statement. The distance formula is derived by drawing a right triangle with a hypotenuse having endpoints (x_1, y_1) and (x_2, y_2) and then using the Pythagorean theorem to determine the length of the hypotenuse.

PRACTICE, PAGE 645

19. Answers will vary. It is not necessary to use 4 for x_1. Since $(x_1 - x_2)^2 = (x_2 - x_1)^2$, *x*-coordinates may be subtracted in either order. For similar reasons, *y*-coordinates may be subtracted in either order. However, the same order must be followed for both *x*- and *y*-coordinates.

PROJECT CONNECTION, PAGE 646

1. Answers will vary. The triangle may not actually be a right triangle and this would affect the computation. Published distances may be based on driveable routes that are not necessarily straight-line distances and that may include driving over mountains.

ALGEBRAWORKS, PAGE 647

2. Measuring from the origin, 8 mi on the horizontal, 2 mi up, and from there, 5 mi out on the *z*-axis.
4. Answers will vary. Students might reason that since the space version of the distance formula is a simple extension of the plane version, the midpoint formula for space can likewise be extended from the plane version. This gives coordinates (3.5, –3, –9), which is, in fact, the correct answer.

Lesson 13.7

THINK BACK, PAGE 648

1. Answers will vary: family members, pieces of jewelry, articles of clothing, hairstyles; any objects which have some common element, such as color or pattern.
2. Answers will vary: for plane figures: circular plates or square rugs of different sizes, a photo and its enlargement, any two triangular objects that are equilateral; for space figures: any two spheres such as baseballs or basketballs, or any two cubes of different dimensions.

EXPLORE, PAGES 648–649

7.

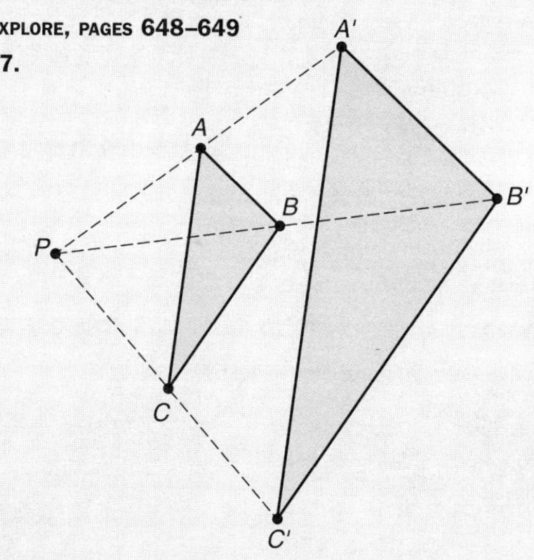

9. Sides of $\Delta A'B'C'$ are twice as long as corresponding sides of ΔABC; corresponding angles have the same measure.
10. Answers will vary. For all similar triangles, the ratios of the measures of corresponding sides will be equal, and the measures of corresponding angles will be equal.
11. Answers will vary. Corresponding sides form equal ratios and corresponding angles have the same measure.

MAKE CONNECTIONS, PAGES 649–651

12. a. $Q'R' = 20$, $Q'S' = 16.8$; $m\angle S = 65°$, $m\angle Q' = 65°$, $m\angle R' = 50°$, $m\angle S' = 65°$
    b. $U'V' = 22.3$, $T'V' = 33.4$; $m\angle V = 25°$, $m\angle T' = 35°$, $m\angle U' = 120°$, $m\angle V' = 25°$
    c. $XY = 34$, $X'Y' = 68$; $X'Z' = 60$, $m\angle X = 28°$, $m\angle X' = 28°$, $m\angle Y' = 62°$

SUMMARIZE, PAGE 651

16. Either one is correct. Since only two sides of the original triangle are given, more than one triangle is possible.

17. 3; ordering the measures of corresponding sides from least to greatest for each triangle produces 9–12–15, 12–16–20, and 15–20–25. The scale factor of the first to the second is 3 to 4. The scale factor of the second to the third is 4 to 5. The scale factor of the first to the third is 3 to 5.

Lesson 13.8

EXPLORE, PAGE 652

4. The triangles are similar, since corresponding angles have equal measures and ratios of corresponding sides are very close.

CHECK UNDERSTANDING, PAGE 653

$$\sin A = \frac{\text{length of side opposite } \angle A}{\text{length of hypotenuse}}$$

$$\cos A = \frac{\text{length of side adjacent to } \angle A}{\text{length of hypotenuse}}$$

$$\tan A = \frac{\text{length of side opposite } \angle A}{\text{length of side adjacent to } \angle A}$$

COMMUNICATING ABOUT ALGEBRA, PAGE 653

Yes. Answers will vary, but should include the fact that the ratios are using the same sides.

PRACTICE, PAGES 656–657

19. Find the angle whose tangent value is given (49°). Then construct $\angle R$ equal to 49°. Construct $\angle S$ equal to 90° − 49° or 41°. Complete the triangle and check to see that $\angle T$ is a right angle.

EXTEND, PAGE 658

21. $\tan C = \frac{10}{100} = 0.10$; $m\angle C = 5.7°$ to the nearest degree; Find side DE of ΔCDE:

$\sin 5.7° = \frac{DE}{CD}$; $\sin 5.7° = \frac{DE}{2640 \text{ ft}}$;

$DE = \sin 5.7°(2640) = 262.2$ ft, rounded to the nearest tenth of a foot.

THINK CRITICALLY, PAGE 658

22. Answers will vary. As the sun rose higher, the length of the shadow grew. For the Egyptians, a greater value of the tangent of the angle of the sun meant a later hour of the morning.

23. $\tan x = \frac{\sin x}{\cos x}$; $\tan x = \frac{\frac{opp.}{hyp.}}{\frac{adj.}{hyp.}}$

$= \frac{opp.}{hyp.} \times \frac{hyp.}{adj.} = \frac{opp.}{adj.}$, the tangent ratio

Lesson 13.9

EXPLORE, PAGES 659–660

10.

0°, 0	210°, − 0.5
30°, 0.5	225°, − 0.71
45°, 0.71	240°, − 0.87
60°, 0.87	270°, − 1
90°, 1	300°, − 0.87
120°, 0.87	315°, − 0.71
135°, 0.71	330°, − 0.5
150°, 0.5	360°, 0
180°, 0	

For 15–21 graphs, x-scale is 90, y-scale is 0.5; for 22–33 graphs, x-scale is 90, y-scale is 1.

15. Student graphs from Question 14 should approximate the graph of $y = \sin x$ on the utility.

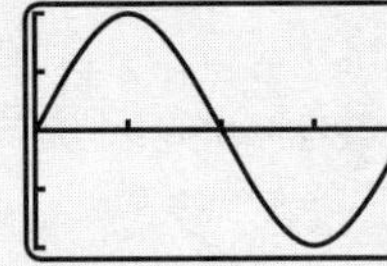

16. Predictions will vary

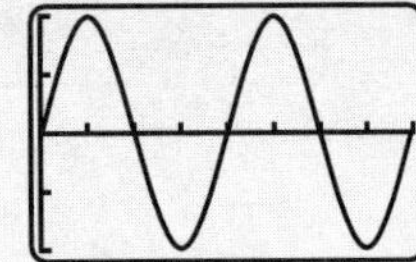

17. For $y = \cos x$, period is 360° and amplitude is 1. Both period and amplitude are the same for $y = \sin x$ and $y = \cos x$.

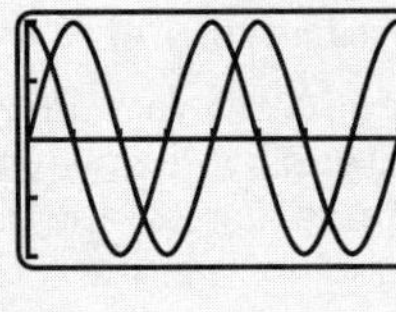

MAKE CONNECTIONS, PAGES 660-661

18. $\sin x$ is 0 at 0°, 180°, 360°, 540°, and 720°; $\cos x$ is 0 at 90°, 270°, 450°, and 630°

19. **21.**

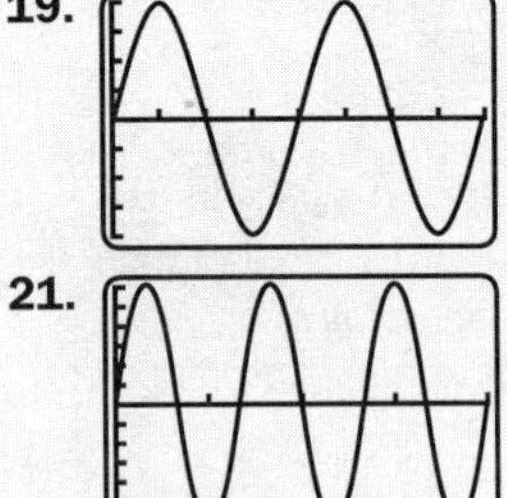

20.

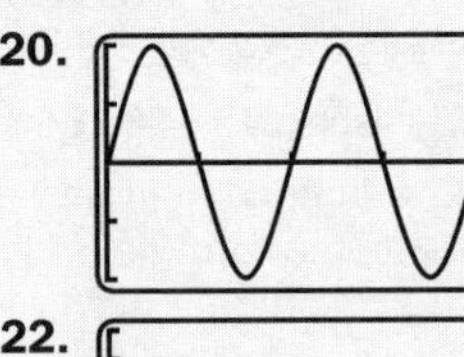

22.

23.

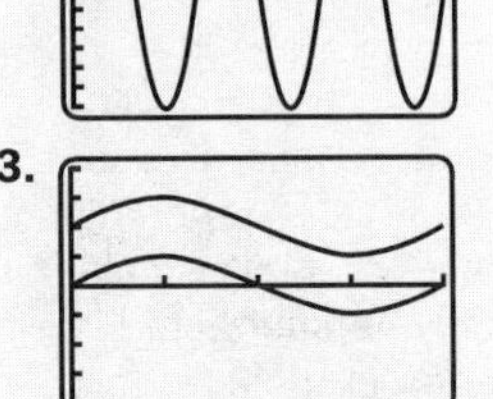

SUMMARIZE, PAGE 661

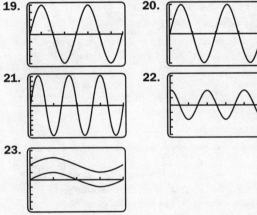

32. Graph $y_1 = \sin x$ and $y_2 = \cos x$ and find intersection points. Solutions are 45° and 225°.

33. $y = \sin x + 2$ represents a translation of $y = \sin x$ upward two units. The period is still 360° and the amplitude is 1 with regard to the li of symmetry $y = 2$. $y = \cos x - 4$ represent a translation of $y = \cos x$ downward 4 units. Th period is still 360° and the amplitude is 1 with regard to the line of symmetry $y = -4$.

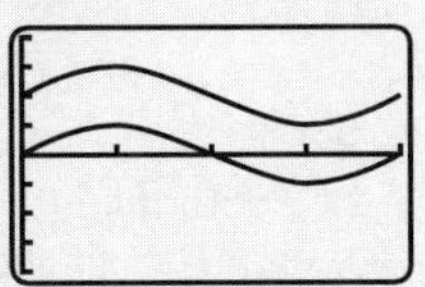

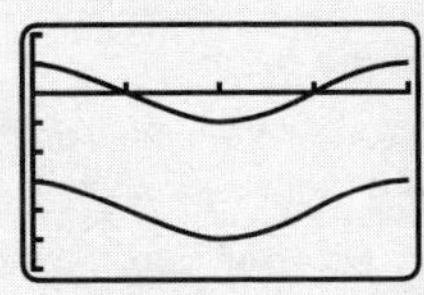

Lesson 13.10

EXPLORE THE PROBLEM, PAGE 662

5. 2977 ft using either the sine ratio or the cosine ratio, or 2978 using the Pythagorean theorem

8. Answers will vary. Determine $\overline{OB}$ using tan 36°, c 36°, or the Pythagorean theorem, then subtract t known length $\overline{OA}$ from $\overline{OB}$ to obtain 5300 ft.

9. Answers will vary. Students may feel that using similar triangles is most visual, but setting up ar solving a proportion involves too many terms anc leaves room for error; trigonometric functions are faster, but students may not be comfortable in choosing the correct function; the Pythagorean theorem allows students to use the same relationship, regardless of which side of a triang they are solving for.

10. Write and solve the proportion

$\frac{AB}{AD} = \frac{BC}{h}$; $\frac{18}{63} = \frac{10}{h}$

11. Determine the tan $\angle A$ using the small triangle, then determine the measure of angle A. Then us tan $\angle A$ and length AD to determine h.

APPLY THE STRATEGY, PAGES 663–664

19. 8.6 to 8.7 in., depending on whether the methoc of similar triangles or trigonometric ratios is usec

REVIEW PROBLEM SOLVING STRATEGIES, PAGE 665

ALGEBRA IS GREAT

Since $a^3 = b^3c$, c must be a perfect cube. The only cube from 2 to 15 is 8, so $c = 8$. Then $a^3 = 8b^3$; since $(2b)^3 = 8b^3$, $a = 2b$. Substitute into the firs given equation to get $4b^2 = bd$, so $4b = d$. In the given range of numbers, b must equal 2 or 3 and d must equal 8 or 12. Since c is already 8, d is 12 anc b is 3. Finally $a = 2b = 6$. The corresponding wo are LET, BEHIND, AMICABLE, and REORGANIZING.

A TAXING PROBLEM

a. $14,760; $82,000

b. $A = 1000x - 10x^2$

c. At $50,000 you are left with $25,000, and this the maximum possible. Students who graph the function A will find it is a parabola with maximum at (50, 25,000). An alternative approach is to make a table of amounts left for successive incomes and identify that the numbers are symmetric on either side of $50,000.

The Power of Two

a. $\frac{3}{4}$

b. The denominator of the sum is the same as the second addend.

c. The numerator is one less than the denominator.

d. $\frac{7}{8}$

e. The denominator is the same as the last addend; the numerator is 1 less than the denominator.

f. $\frac{1023}{1024}$

g. $\frac{1}{2^1} + \frac{1}{2^2} + \frac{1}{2^3} + \ldots + \frac{1}{2^n} = \frac{2^n - 1}{2^n}$

h. 15; $\frac{1}{2^{15}}$

Chapter Review, pages 666–667

7. $m\angle Z = 18°$, $m\angle P = 33°$, $m\angle Q = 129°$, $m\angle R = 18°$, XY is 20, YZ is 35

8. $m\angle C = 41°$, $m\angle D = 80°$, $m\angle E = 59°$, $m\angle F = 41°$, DE is 12, EF is 18.6

Chapter Assessment

Chapter Test, page 668

18. Answers will vary. The distributive property states that for all real numbers a, b, and c that $ac + bc = (a + b)c$. Since radicals are real numbers, you can let c represent any radical. Then the sum of the product of real numbers times like radicals is the product of the sum of real numbers and the radical. Therefore, if c is a radical such as $\sqrt{3}$, and $a = 2$ and $b = 5$, then $2\sqrt{3} + 5\sqrt{3} = (2 + 5)\sqrt{3} = 7\sqrt{3}$.

34. $2\sqrt{10}$, $2\sqrt{17}$, $2\sqrt{13}$; scalene

Project Connection, page 669

4. Answers will vary.

Cumulative Review, page 670

1. $10\sqrt{3}$

2. $\frac{2\sqrt{5}}{5}$

3. $5\sqrt{3}$

4. $2\sqrt{2}$

10. Answers will vary but the quadratic formula is the only method that can be applied to solving all quadratic equations.

11. $2\sqrt{3}$

12. $\sqrt{6} + 18\sqrt{5}$

21. $\begin{cases} x - y = 1 \\ 2x + y = 5 \end{cases}$

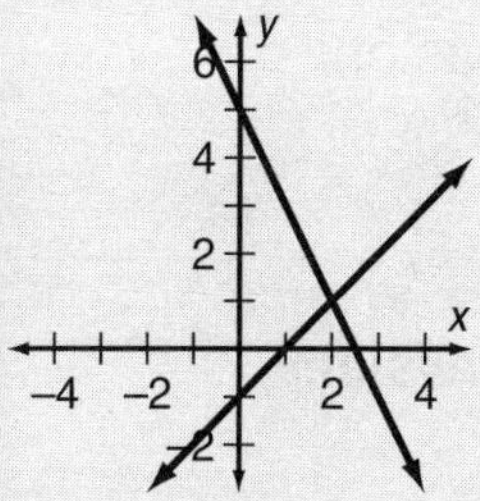

22. $\begin{cases} 3x + 2y < 8 \\ 2x - y < 1 \end{cases}$

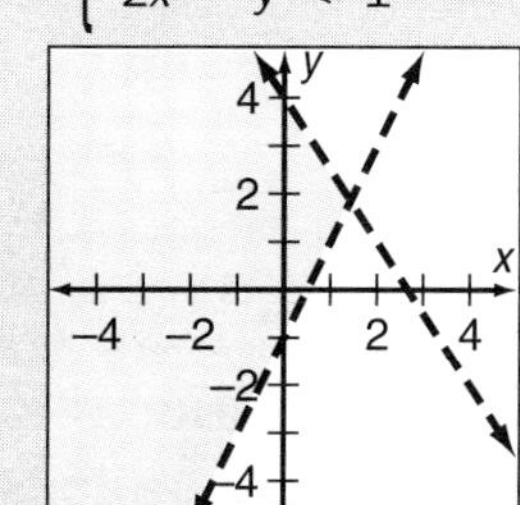

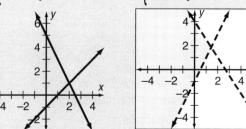

23. $2\sqrt{13}$ or about 7.21

25. The calculator figured $\sqrt{36} + 16 = 22$. Teri needs to use parentheses around the 36 + 16, so that the calculator will find the sum first, and then take the square root of that sum.

Additional Answers continued from Chapter 10, page 513B

Lesson 10.7

Try These, page 505

1.

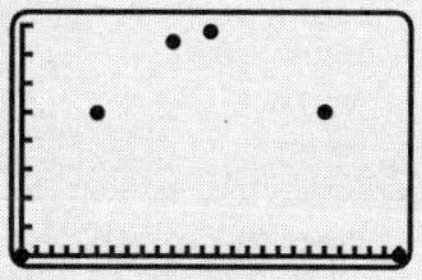

2.

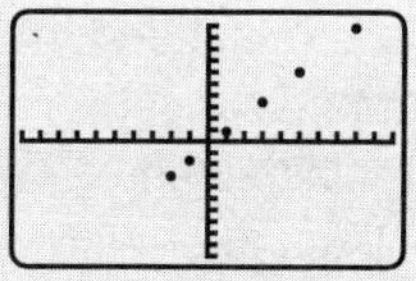

3.

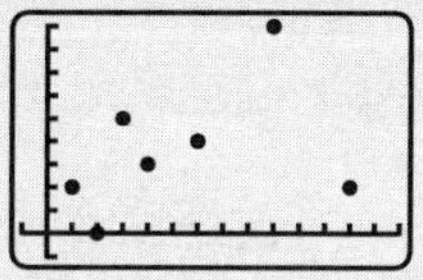

4.

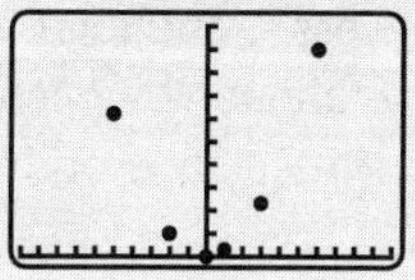

5.

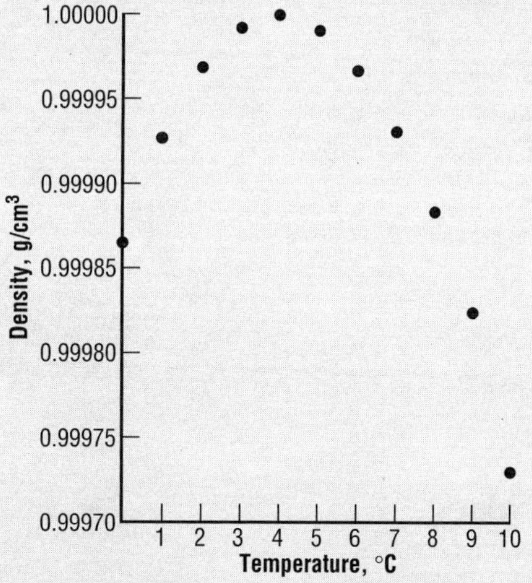

Practice, page 506

1. Answers will vary.

7. Answers will vary.

Mixed Review, page 507

16.

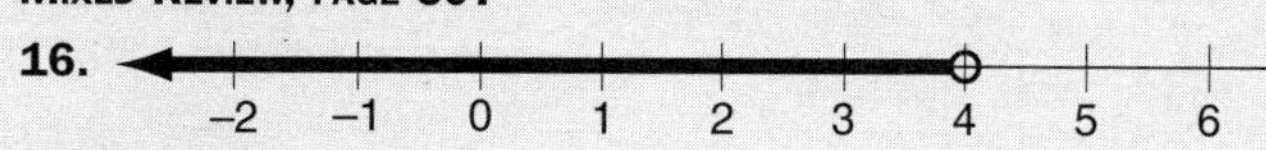

Chapter Assessment

Chapter Test, page 510

23. Answers will vary.

Performance Assessment, page 511

"Weightless" Equations

a. Neglecting air resistance, the two objects hit the ground at the same time.

b. Both objects hit the ground at the same time.

c. The time it takes for an object to fall from a height is independent of its mass.

Cumulative Review, page 512

1.

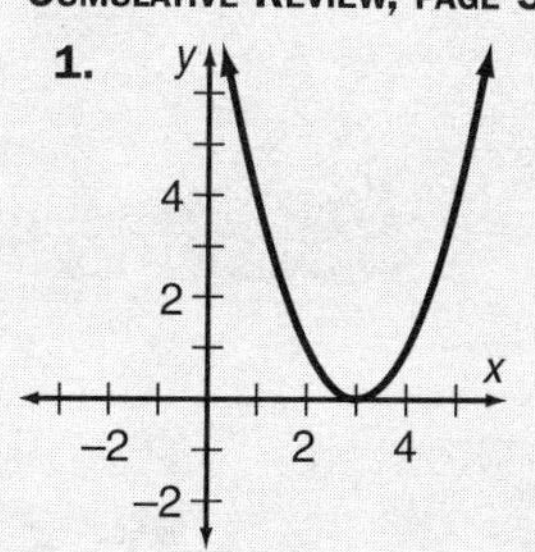

2.

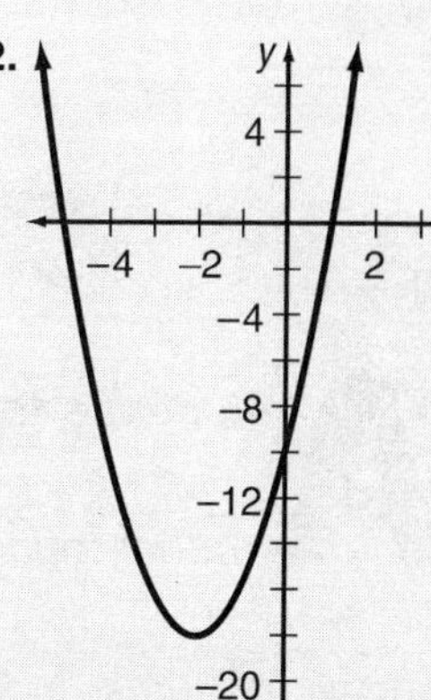

3.

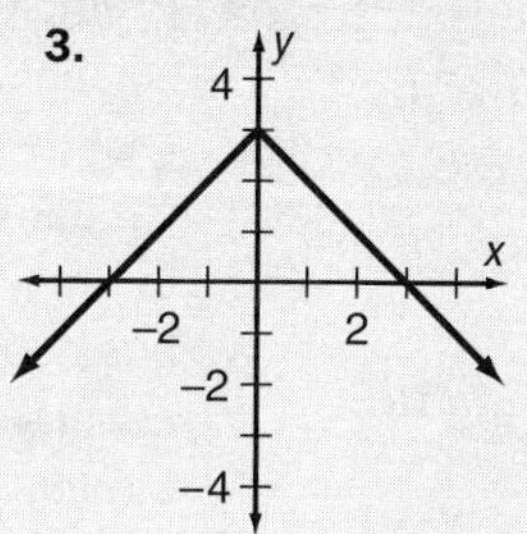

4.

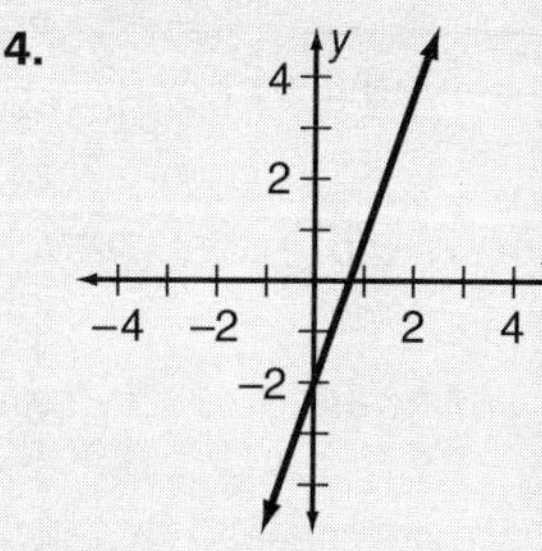

10. $-\sqrt{17}$, -3.943, -3.94, $\frac{-11}{3}$

18. Circle graph; the data show 100% of the day. The number of hours can be converted to a percent of 24 h.

19. $-1 \pm 2\sqrt{2}$

20. $\frac{\pm 2\sqrt{10}}{3}$

23.

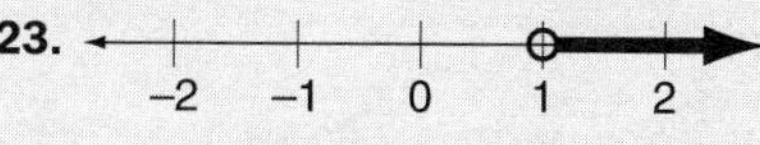

24.

CHAPTER 14 RATIONAL EXPRESSIONS

A student's feelings toward mathematics can be a strong influence in his or her decision to continue with or begin to avoid mathematics. Enjoyment, confidence, and anxiety about mathematics continue to reflect the student's attitude toward mathematics. In addition, the perceived usefulness of mathematics is an important factor in shaping the student's view of the subject.

***Jane M. Armstrong, "A National Assessment of Participation and Achievement of Women in Mathematics" in* Women and Mathematics: Balancing the Equation, *ed.* Susan F. Chipman, Lorelei R. Brush, Donna M. Wilson, 1985 Laurence Erlbaum Associates, Publishers, Hillsdale, N.J., pages 62–63**

The Big Question: Why study rational expressions?

The ability to simplify complex rational expressions is needed in more advanced mathematics; for example, in evaluating sums of certain series. This chapter also includes direct, inverse, and joint variation. These relationships occur in many situations in science and business. Although the theme of this chapter is agribusiness, the students will also see applications from biology, civics, cooking, finance, interior design, manufacturing, navigation, physics, travel, and water storage.

Vocabulary

- complex rational expression
- constant of variation
- conversion factor
- dimensional analysis
- dimensions
- direct variation
- extraneous solutions
- inverse variation
- joint variation
- mixed expression
- least common denominator (LCD)
- rational equation
- rational expression
- reciprocal
- restrictions on the variable
- simplest form

Using the Graphic Organizer

Project a copy of the Graphic Organizer Transparency for Chapter 14. Explain that the focus of this chapter is on operations with rational expressions. Review the information on the graphic organizer, pointing out that rational expressions are algebraic fractions and are simplified and operated on in a similar way as arithmetic fractions.

Ask some preview questions; for example, what does it mean that a fraction is in simplest form? How do you write a fraction in simplest form?

One way to organize ideas about rational expressions is shown below.

One way to organize ideas about rational expressions is shown.

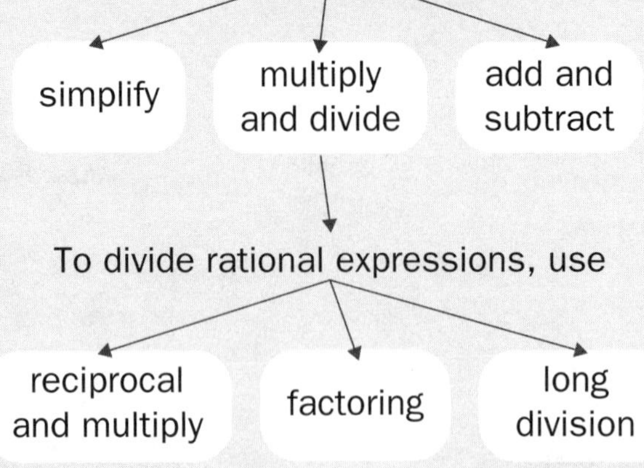

Try It Use a different plan. Try organizing ideas pertaining to rational expressions or rational equations.

Explore the Chapter Theme:

Agribusiness

Today's careers in agriculture extend from biologists to marketing managers. Biotechnology and information technology are among the fastest growing employment sectors in the field of agribusiness. Striving towards efficiency in food production has brought us giant farms, increased mechanization, and the application of many new technologies.

The person running a farm these days is an agribusiness manager who understands farming and business.

Skills Needed for Success in Jobs in Agribusiness

1. Organize, process, and maintain written or computerized records and other information about production and finances.
2. Use analytical skills to make decisions based on a variety of variables.
3. Understand and use principles of probability in dealing with weather and market forecasts.
4. Do long-range planning and scheduling.
5. Take pride in being involved in an industry vital to all people.
6. Be able to adapt to changes in growing conditions and in markets.
7. Have physical stamina for work outdoors.
8. Make decisions based on scientific and technological knowledge.
9. Understand and observe complex safety regulations.
10. Know and observe water and soil pollution regulations.

Investigate Further

Have students identify a career related to agribusiness that interests them. Have students go to the library to find more information about this career. For example, students might find out about educational requirements including specific courses, degrees, examinations, or licenses required. Students should research the average salary range for the career. Have students share their findings in a class discussion about career opportunities.

Here is a list of jobs and educational requirements for careers in agribusiness.

Jobs Requiring 1 to 2 Years of Technical Training

Agricultural Supply Sales Worker

Agricultural Technician

Food Processing Technician

Forest Products Technician

Forestry Technician

Jobs Requiring 4 + Years of College

Farm Manager

Agricultural Engineer

Agronomist

Forester

Horticulturist

Range Manager

Veterinarian

Water Resource Engineer

CHAPTER 14 PLANNING GUIDE

Lessons		Text Pages	NCTM Standards	ASSIGNMENTS Basic	Average	Enriched	Ancillaries	Manipulatives	Technology
	Chapter Introduction	672–674	1, 2, 3, 4, 10, 11				Video Discussion Guide		Video, Transparency 76
14.1	**Algebra Workshop: Inverse Variation**	675–678	1, 2, 3, 4, 5, 8	1–19, AW1–3	1–19, AW1–3	1–21, AW1–3	S 33, M 14	Grid Paper	Graphing Utility, Transparencies 32, 33, 35, 77
14.2	**Direct, Inverse, and Joint Variation**	679–685	1, 2, 3, 4, 5, 8	1–21, 23–24, MR27–33, PC1–4, AW1–4	3–25, MR27–33, PC1–4, AW1–4	4–26, MR27–33, PC1–4, AW1–4	W 14.2; R 14.2; P 14.2; E 14.2; Q 14.2, S 34		Transparencies 33, 35, 77
14.3	**Simplify Rational Expressions**	686–691	1, 2, 3, 4, 5, 8, 10	1–22, 24, 26, MR28–32, PC1–4, AW1–6	3–26, MR28–32, PC1–4, AW1–6	3–27, MR28–32, PC1–4, AW1–6	W 14.3; R 14.3; P 14.3; E 14.3; Q 14.3; S 35; T 32, T 33	Algeblocks, Basic Mats, 686	Transparencies 33, 35
14.4	**Multiply and Divide Rational Expressions**	692–696	1, 2, 3, 4, 5, 8	1–24, 26–30, MR33–39	1–32, MR33–39	5–32, MR33–39	W 14.4; R 14.4; P 14.4; E 14.4; Q 14.4		
14.5	**Divide Polynomials**	697–701	1, 2, 3, 4, 5, 8	1–15, 17–20, 22, MR25–28	1–23, MR25–28	1–24, MR25–28	W 14.5; R 14.5; P 14.5; E 14.5; Q 14.5; T 34	Algeblocks, Quadrant Mats, 697	Graphing Utility, Transparencies 12, 21, 78–80
14.6	**And and Subtract Rational Expressions**	702–706	1, 2, 3, 4, 5, 8	1–22, 25, 28–29, 33–34, MR35–43	2–30, 32–34, MR35–43	3, 6–34, MR35–43	W 14.6; R 14.6; P 14.6; E 14.6; Q 14.6		
14.7	**Complex Rational Expressions**	707–711	1, 2, 3, 4, 5, 8	1–20, 22–24, 27, 29–30	1–6, 8–25, 27–31	4–6, 9–32	W 14.7; R 14.7; P 14.7; E 14.7; Q 14.7		Graphing Utility, Transparencies 78–80
14.8	**Solve Rational Equations**	712–717	1, 2, 3, 4, 5, 8, 10	1–14, 16, 18, 22, PC1–3	3–18, 21–24, PC1–3	4–25, PC1–3	W 14.8; R 14.8; P 14.8; E 14.8; Q 14.8		Graphing Utility, Transparencies 78–80
14.9	**Problem Solving File: Use Dimensional Analysis**	718–721	1, 2, 3, 4, 5, 8	1–10, 12, RPSS1–3	1–14, RPSS1–3	1–15, RPSS1–3	R 14.9; P 14.9		Transparency 1[illegible]

NCTM STANDARDS

1. Mathematics as Problem Solving
2. Mathematics as Communication
3. Mathematics as Reasoning
4. Mathematical Connections
5. Algebra
6. Functions
7. Geometry from a Synthetic Perspective
8. Geometry from an Algebraic Perspective
9. Trigonometry
10. Statistics
11. Probability
12. Discrete Mathematics
13. Conceptual Underpinnings of Calculus
14. Mathematical Structure

ANCILLARIES

W = Warm Up
R = Reteaching
P = Extra Practice
E = Enrichment
Q = Lesson Quiz
T = Technology Activity
M = Multicultural Connection
S = Study Skills Activity

ADDITIONAL RESOURCES

pplications	Career Connections	Cooperative Learning	Learning Styles	Strand Integration/ Math Connection
	Chapter Poster			
	AlgebraWorks: Agribusiness Manager, 678	Paired partners, 675 (Think Back/Working Together); Paired partners, 675 (Explore/Working Together)	Linguistic/Interpersonal, 675; Visual, 675–678; Visual, 677 (TE)	Problem Solving, Technology, Geometry, Writing, Critical Thinking, Statistics
griculture, 684; Biology, 83; Electricity, 682; eometry, 683, 684; hysics, 682; Travel, 680	AlgebraWorks: Refrigeration System Engineer, 685	Small groups, 684 (Project Connection)	Linguistic/Interpersonal, 680, 684; Visual, 679, 684, 685; Tactile/ Kinesthetic, 681 (TE)	Problem Solving, Geometry, Writing, Critical Thinking
griculture, 690; Cooking, 89; Interior Design, 688; anufacturing, 689; ravel, 689	AlgebraWorks: Cattle Farmer, 691; Lawyers, 688	Small groups, 690 (Project Connection)	Visual, 686, 690–691; Linguistic/ Interpersonal, 688, 690; Tactile/Kinesthetic, 686	Problem Solving, Geometry, Writing, Critical Thinking
inance, 696; Geometry, 95; Physics, 694, 695			Visual, 695	Problem Solving, Geometry, Writing, Critical Thinking
utomobile Depreciation, 00; Biology, 701; eometry, 699, 700			Visual, 697, 699, 701; Tactile/ Kinesthetic, 697	Problem Solving, Modeling, Geometry, Writing, Critical Thinking, Technology
ooking, 704; Geometry, 06; Navigation, 704; hysics, 705	Window Washer, 706		Visual, 703, 705, 706; Individual, 704	Problem Solving, Number Theory, Writing, Geometry, Technology, Critical Thinking
griculture, 709, 710; ivics, 711; Education, 10; Electricity, 711; eometry, 711; Travel, 11	Gardener, 709		Linguistic/ Interpersonal, 708	Problem Solving, Geometry, Writing, Critical Thinking
griculture, 717; Boating, 16, 717; Finance, 716; terior Design, 717; ravel, 714, 715, 716; ater Storage, 717	Wallpaper Hanger, 717	Small Groups, 717 (Project Connection)	Visual, 713, 717; Linguistic/Interpersonal, 713, 715, 717	Problem Solving, Technology, Writing, Critical Thinking
usiness, 720; Physics, 20; Travel, 720			Visual, 721	Problem Solving, Measurement, Writing, Geometry, Logical Reasoning

PACING GUIDE

Lessons	Regular Classes	2-year Algebra 1 Classes	Blocked Classes
14.1	1	2	½
14.2	1	2	½
14.3	1	2	½
14.4	1	2	½
14.5	1	2	½
14.6	1	2	½
14.7	1	2	½
14.8	1	2	½
14.9	1	2	1
Review	1	1	1
Test	1	1	1
Cumulative Test	1	1	1
Total Classes	12	21	8

SESSMENT OPTIONS

udent Edition
apter Assessment
Chapter Test
Performance Assessment
Project Assessment
ndardized Tests

Chapter Resource Book
Chapter Test, Form A
Chapter Test, Form B
Standardized Chapter Test
Portfolio Item: Self-Assessment
Portfolio Assessment Form

MicroExam II

PREVIEW THE CHAPTER

Take a Look Ahead Have students read the previewing suggestions and then scan the chapter looking for new and familiar things. Allow students to make notes in their journals. Discuss student answers to the previewing questions.

Connecting to Career Opportunities Have students read the descriptions of the AlgebraWorks features for this chapter. Ask students to identify the careers mentioned. **agribusiness managers, refrigeration system engineers, and cattle farmers** Ask students if they know anyone who works at these jobs. Discuss the types of educational background usually required for each of the careers. For example, agribusiness managers and refrigeration system engineers usually have an undergraduate or graduate degree; farmers today frequently have college degrees.

Investigate Further Explain to students that as they study this chapter they should look for examples of other careers in agribusiness as well as careers in other fields. Ask students to determine one way in which algebra can be used in that career. Encourage students to write questions in their journals about other agribusiness jobs they would like to learn more about.

USING THE DATA ACTIVITY

Introduce the Data Activity Have students read the introductory paragraph and discuss why traditional family-owned farms are gradually disappearing.

Skill Focus Read the skills listed and discuss with students what they think each means. Ask students to suggest problems that might involve the skill being discussed.

14 Rational Expressions

Take a Look AHEAD

Make notes about things that look new.

- Find graphs that are different from other graphs that you have seen in this book. Describe the differences.
- What is "dimensional analysis" and why is it a useful problem solving strategy?

Make notes about things that look familiar.

- Find a lesson on multiplication and division. What will be multiplied and divided?
- Describe the equations you find in this chapter.

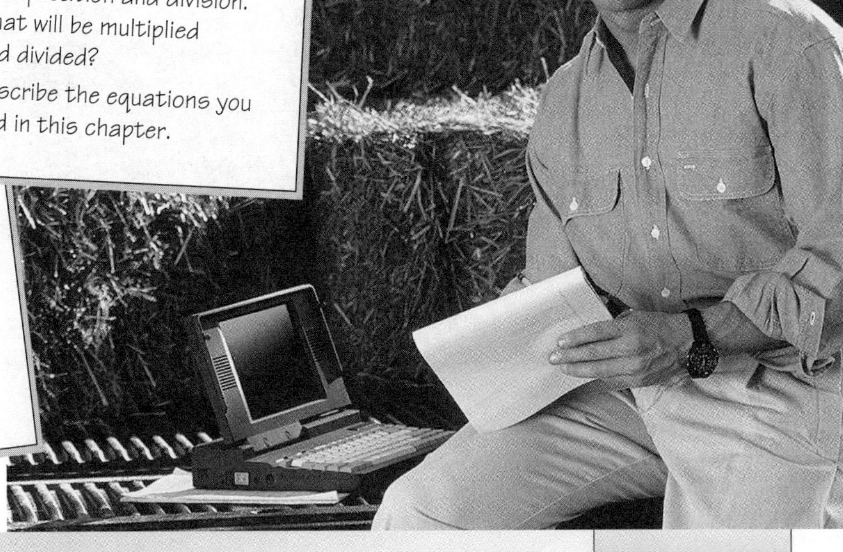

DATA Activity

Technology and Agribusiness

Technology has greatly reduced the farmer's workload. Huge plows and combines make planting and harvesting easier tasks. Automated systems may feed animals or distribute water, pesticides, and fertilizer to fields. However, the expense of such equipment is feasible only for a large-scale operation. Traditional family-owned farms are gradually disappearing, replaced by giant corporate-owned farms called *agribusinesses*.

Today's farmer is more likely to use a computer than go to the market to find out the latest product prices. The table on the next page shows farm product prices for a week in July 1995.

SKILL FOCUS

- Add, subtract, multiply, and divide real numbers.
- Determine percent decrease.
- Use probability.
- Read a table.

AGRIBUSINESS

In this chapter, you will see how:

- **Agribusiness Managers** work with several variables to determine break-even points, amount of profit, and sales goals. (Lesson 14.1, page 678)
- **Refrigeration System Engineers** use direct and inverse relationships when designing cooling systems. (Lesson 14.2, page 685)
- **Cattle Farmers** use rational expressions to select the most cost-effective feed mixture for their animals. (Lesson 14.3, page 691)

1–5 Data Activity, 1–4 Getting Started See Additional Answers.

Farm Product Prices, grain prices per bushel

Product	Mon	Tue	Wed	Thur	Fri
Eggs (large white doz.)	0.83	0.85	0.85	0.86	0.86
Corn (No. 2 yellow)	2.94	2.98	$2.96\frac{1}{2}$	$2.92\frac{1}{2}$	2.91
Soybeans (No. 1 yellow)	$6.25\frac{1}{2}$	$6.30\frac{1}{4}$	$6.31\frac{1}{4}$	$6.22\frac{1}{2}$	$6.21\frac{1}{2}$
Wheat (No. 2 soft)	4.73	$4.56\frac{1}{4}$	$4.55\frac{1}{2}$	$4.52\frac{1}{2}$	4.54
Wheat (No. 2 dark)	$5.85\frac{1}{2}$	5.76	$5.74\frac{1}{2}$	5.69	$5.60\frac{3}{4}$
Wheat (No. 2 hard)	$5.13\frac{1}{2}$	$4.97\frac{1}{2}$	4.94	4.84	$4.85\frac{1}{2}$
Oats (No. 2 heavy)	2.09	2.08	2.09	$2.07\frac{1}{2}$	2.06

Use the table to answer the following questions.

1. What was the change in the price of No. 2 dark wheat from Monday to Friday?
2. A farmer sold 10,000 bushels of No. 2 yellow corn on Tuesday. How much money did the farmer receive? How much more is this than if the sale had taken place on Thursday?
3. What was the percent decrease in the price of No. 2 soft wheat from Monday to Friday? Round to the nearest percent.
4. If a farmer sold one of the listed products on Wednesday, what is the probability the farmer received the best price of the week?
5. **Working Together** Research and report on how farm product prices have varied over the last 40 years. For which products have prices risen? Which product prices have declined? Use several graphs to present your findings.

Study the Data Review the data in the table. Ask the following questions: Which items represented in the table are sold by the bushel? **all except eggs** Which item has the widest range in price for the week? **wheat – no. 2 hard**

Complete the Data Activity Have students work individually or with partners to complete the questions.

For Item 1, remind students that the prices can be expressed without fractions for ease of calculation, but the method shown in the table (using fractions of a cent) is the customary way of listing agricultural prices.

For Item 2, point out that mental math skills are useful for multiplication by powers of ten.

For Item 3, review the algorithm for finding percent decrease.

For Item 4, to compute the probability, assume that each item in the table has an equal chance of being sold on Wednesday.

For Item 5, point out that many almanacs have information about farm prices.

South-Western Algebra 1 Chapter Theme Video or Videodisc

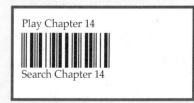

Play Chapter 14

Search Chapter 14

INTRODUCING THE PROJECT

Project Goal Discuss the project's big idea: How is the storage capacity of a cylindrical silo related to its base and height?

Getting Ready Collect as many photos of silos as you can find. Also have students bring to class or provide them with dried materials such as macaroni, popcorn, or beans.

FACILITATING THE PROJECT

Getting Started Use photos of silos as a springboard for discussion as to why they are usually cylindrical in shape. Before students actually construct their cylinders have them guess which cylinder will hold more, the one that is 11 inches high or the one that is $8\frac{1}{2}$ inches high.

Setting Project Benchmarks Make sure that the students are aware of the project schedule in the Project Planning Calendar and the due dates for each of the benchmarks.

a. Explore silo capacity by constructing models in which the surface area remains constant but the height and circumference of the base vary. (Project/Chapter Opener)
b. Determine the equation of a variation that relates to the construction of the silos. (Project Connection 14.2)
c. Explore volume as a function of the circumference and the base of the silo. (Project Connection 14.3)
d. Use dry matter tonnage to predict silo capacities for different moisture levels of silage. (Project Connection 14.8)
e. Assemble and analyze the results of exploring the storage capacity of silos. Prepare your final presentation. (Project Assessment)

Suggest that students make subgoals for each goal and include subgoals in their calendar.

PROJECT

Specialize in Silos

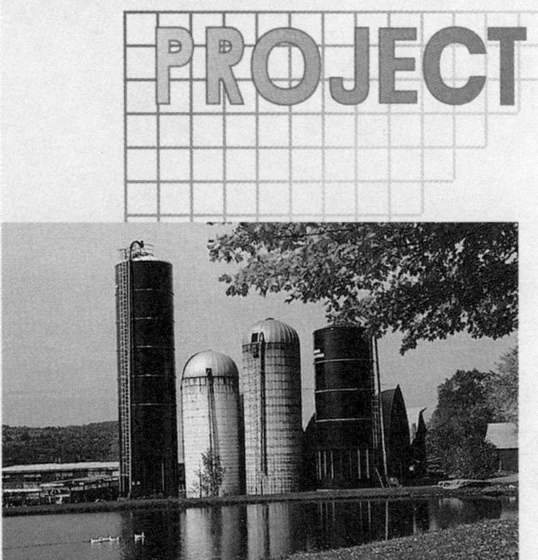

Farmers use silos to store livestock feed, grain, and other products. Early silos were just pits covered with boards. In 1873, Fred Hatch, an Illinois farmer, built the first above-ground silo. Because of its square shape, feed could not be packed tightly enough to prevent air pockets that lead to spoilage. In 1882, Franklin King, a Wisconsin agricultural scientist, constructed a round silo that proved to be airtight. Today, tall, cylindrical, glass-lined, steel silos provide year-round storage.

PROJECT GOAL

To investigate the storage capacity of a silo.

Getting Started

Suppose a farmer has only 93.5 yd^2 of material to use for the lateral sides of a silo. How can the farmer maximize the storage capacity?

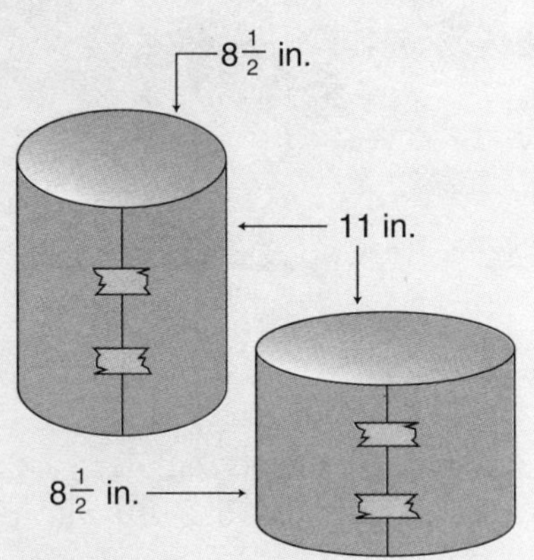

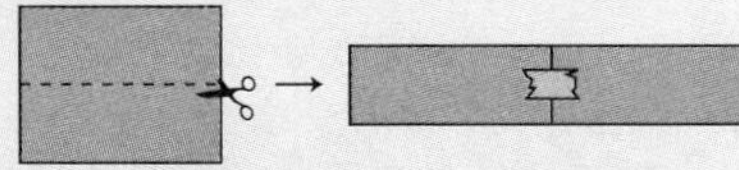

1. Why is an $8\frac{1}{2}$ in. by 11 in. sheet of paper convenient for solving this problem?
2. First roll and tape the paper lengthwise, then tape the paper widthwise. Be careful not to overlap the edges. Which "silo" holds more? (In each case, one dimension of the paper will be the height h and the other will be the circumference C of the base.) Stand each cylinder on a tabletop, then fill with macaroni, popcorn, beans, or other similar material to determine volume. Record your results.
3. Continue investigating by cutting your paper into strips and taping the strips to build wider and taller silos. How do the height and the circumference of the base change?
4. Make a table showing the circumference of the base, the height, and the volume for each silo.

PROJECT Connections

Lesson 14.2, page 684: Determine the equation of a variation that relates to the construction of the silos.
Lesson 14.3, page 690: Explore volume as a function of the circumference of the base of the silo.
Lesson 14.8, page 717: Use dry matter tonnage to predict silo capacities for different moisture levels of stored product.
Chapter Assessment, page 725: Use roleplaying to present results and recommendations of project investigation.

14.1 Algebra Workshop
Inverse Variation

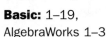

Think Back/Working Together

Work with a partner. Recall that a direct variation is a relation where y varies directly as x and can be written in the form $y = kx, k \neq 0$.

1. Copy and complete the table below for a car that travels at an average speed of 50 mi/h.

Number of Hours	1	2	3	4	5	x
Miles Traveled	50	100	150	200	250	$50x$

2. Write an equation that represents the information from the table above, letting x represent number of hours and y represent miles traveled. Is it an example of direct variation? $y = 50x$; yes

3. Use a graphing utility to graph the equation you wrote in Question 2. Set an appropriate range for the viewing window. See Additional Answers.

Explore/Working Together

Work with a partner.

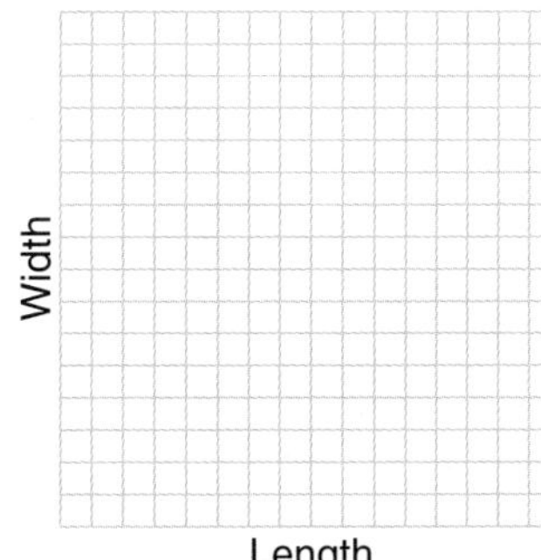
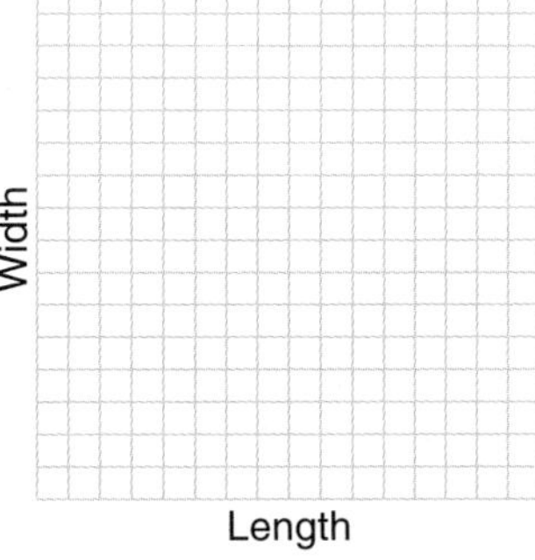

4. Use a grid similar to the one at the right to draw the different rectangles with lengths and widths that are whole numbers and having an area of 12 square units. See Additional Answers.

5. Use these rectangles to complete a table of the pairs of factors of 12.

Length	1	2	3	4	6	12
Width	12	6	4	3	2	1

6. Write an equation that represents the width of the rectangle, letting x represent the length and y represent the width. As x increases, what happens to y? As x decreases, what happens to y? Is this a direct variation? $y = \frac{12}{x}$; decreases; increases; no

7. Use a graphing utility to graph the equation you wrote in Question 6. Use a standard viewing window. See Additional Answers.

8. Trace along the portion of the graph in Quadrant I to investigate ordered pairs, other than those in your table, that satisfy the equation. Do these values make sense in this situation? Explain. See Additional Answers.

SPOTLIGHT ON LEARNING

WHAT? In this lesson you will learn
- to use area models to explore inverse variation.
- to recognize the equation of an inverse variation.
- to explore the graph of an inverse variation.

WHY? Writing and solving equations of inverse variation can help you solve problems in geometry, agriculture, and business.

LESSON PLANNING

Objective
- Explore inverse variation using area models and graphs.

Vocabulary
direct variation
hyperbola
inverse variation

Technology/Multimedia
graphing utility

Resources
Transparencies 32, 33, 35, 77
Student Handbook
Study Skills Activity 33
Multicultural Connection 14, African: Focus on Music

Materials/Manipulatives
grid paper

ASSIGNMENTS

Basic: 1–19, AlgebraWorks 1–3

Average: 1–19, AlgebraWorks 1–3

Enriched: 1–21, AlgebraWorks 1–3

1 MOTIVATE

Think Back/Working Together Ask students what is meant by the statement "y varies directly as x." **that y is directly proportional to x or that the ratio $\frac{y}{x}$ of the two quantities is constant** For Question 2, ask students to explain how they know $y = 50x$ is an equation of direct variation. **It is of the form $y = kx$ where $k = 50$.**

2 FACILITATE

Explore/Working Together In Questions 4–5, rectangles having dimensions $a \times b$ are different from those of $b \times a$. In Question 9, emphasize that a point satisfying the conditions of the function may not fit the situation. Ask students to describe what happens to the graph as the value of x approaches 0 and as x becomes infinitely large. **The graph approaches the x-axis for $y = 0$, and the y-axis for $x = 0$ but never touches either axis.** Have students repeat the questions for rectangles with an area of 36 square units. Ask students how the graphs of $y = 12/x$ and $y = 36/x$ are similar and how they are different. **They are both curves in the first and third quadrants approaching the x- and y-axes; the graph of $y = 12/x$ is closer to the x-axis for the same values of x.** Then ask students to graph the equation $y = -12/x$ and compare it with the graph of $y = 12/x$. **It is the same except that it is in Quadrants II and IV instead of Quadrants I and III.**

Make Connections Make sure that all students are using the equation $y = \frac{12}{x}$ to answer Question 11. Have students share their answers to Question 11 before having them answer Questions 12 and 13. For Question 16, ask students what it means for the values of x to increase infinitely. **There is no upper limit, or bound, to the value of x.** Have students discuss their answers to Questions 14 and 17. Have them graph the following equations of indirect variation: $y = 0.8/x$, $y = 5/x$, $y = 10/x$, and $y = 25/x$. Have them compare the graphs. **The smaller the constant value is, the closer the graph is to the axes; the greater the constant value is, the farther the graph is from the axes.**

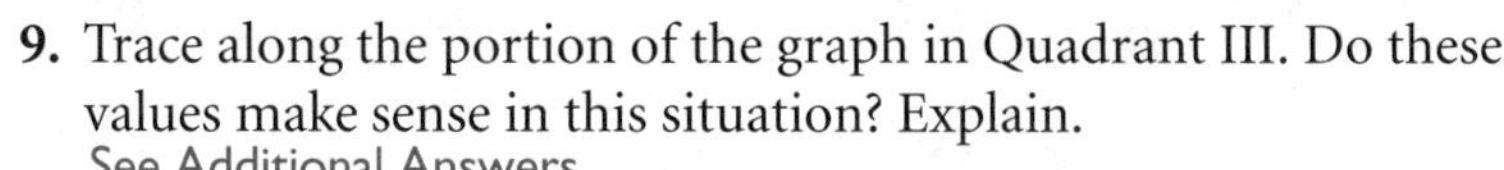

Algebra Workshop

9. Trace along the portion of the graph in Quadrant III. Do these values make sense in this situation? Explain.
   See Additional Answers.
10. Can you find a point on the curve for which x equals zero? Why or why not? Would $x = 0$ make sense in this situation? Explain.
   See Additional Answers.

The equation you wrote in Question 6 is of the form

$$y = \frac{k}{x}, k \neq 0, x \neq 0$$

It shows an *inverse variation*. The variable y varies inversely as x, or y is inversely proportional to x.

Make Connections

11. Use the equation you wrote in Question 6. Copy and complete Tables 1 and 2 by finding the width that corresponds to each length.

Table 1

Length, x	0.01	0.02	0.05	0.08	0.1	0.2	0.5	0.8	1
Width, y									

1200 600 240 150 120 60 24 15 12

Table 2

Length, x	12	24	36	48	60	72	84	96	100	120
Width, y										

1 0.5 0.333 0.25 0.2 0.167 0.143 0.125 0.12 0.1

12. Compare the change in the x-values to the change in the y-values in Table 1. What do you notice?
   See Additional Answers.
13. Compare the change in the x-values to the change in the y-values in Table 2. What do you notice?
   See Additional Answers.
14. What do you notice about the rate of change in y as x changes from 0.01 to 120? How does this compare to a direct variation?
   See Additional Answers.
15. What do you think happens to the values of y as the values of x get closer and closer to zero?
   They increase infinitely.
16. What do you think happens to the values of y as the values of x increase infinitely?
   They approach, but do not reach, zero.

ALGEBRA: WHO, WHERE, WHEN

American biologist Rachel Louise Carson (1907–1964) noticed that the thickness of egg shells of predatory birds varied indirectly as the exposure of the parent birds to DDT. This threatened the survival of the species. Her discovery launched ecology awareness as we know it today.

17. Compare the two groups of graphs below. Describe the differences between the graphs of equations having direct and inverse variations. See Additional Answers.

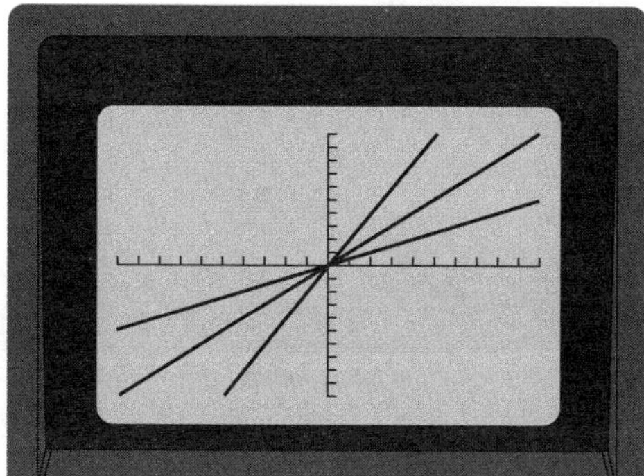

Direct: $y = x$, $y = 2x$, $y = 0.5x$

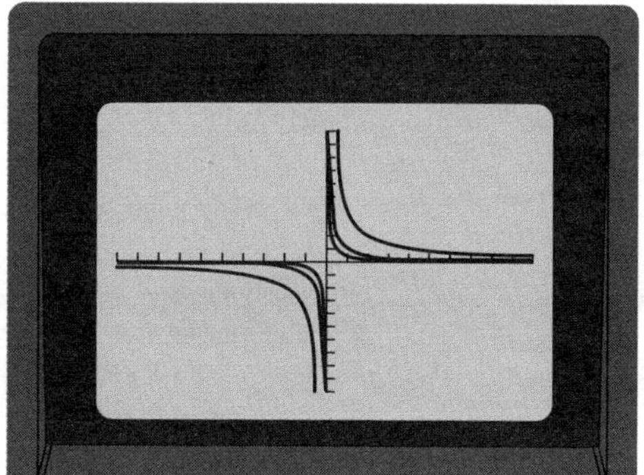

Inverse: $y = \frac{1}{x}$, $y = \frac{4}{x}$, $y = \frac{0.5}{x}$

Summarize

18. **Writing Mathematics** Summarize the characteristics of an inverse variation. Include the following information.
    - **a.** the general form of the equation
    - **b.** the shape of the graph
    - **c.** the value of y when x equals zero
    - **d.** the values of y when x gets infinitely small
    - **e.** the values of y when x gets infinitely large
    - **f.** how to find k given ordered pairs of x and y

    See Additional Answers.
19. **Thinking Critically** Will the graphs of $y = \frac{1}{x}$ and $y = \frac{10}{x}$ ever intersect? Explain your answer. See Additional Answers.
20. **Going Further** The graph of an inverse variation $xy = k$ is called a *hyperbola*. Use a graphing utility to explore the hyperbolas that correspond to different values of k. When k is positive, in which quadrants are the parts or *branches* of the hyperbola? What happens when k is negative? See Additional Answers.
21. **Going Further** Use a graphing utility to graph equations of the form $y = \frac{k}{x^2}$. Comment on the graphs of variations in which y varies inversely as the square of x. Answers will vary. The graphs are in Quadrants I and II for $k > 0$ and in Quadrants III and IV for $k < 0$.

Diversity in the Classroom

Visual Learners Have students draw on grid paper all the triangles with an area of 12 square units and heights and bases that are whole numbers. This will provide a visual model in which students can see that for the constant area 12, as the height increases, the base decreases.

3 SUMMARIZE

Writing Mathematics For Question 18, suggest that students include an example in their answer for some constant value of k. Students may give the general form of the equation as $xy = k$ or $y = k/x$. They should include in their answers that neither x nor y will ever equal 0, but that as x decreases, y increases infinitely, and as x increases, y decreases infinitely.

Thinking Critically For Question 19, ask students to describe how to determine at what point the two graphs intersect. **Solve the system of equations to find a point both graphs have in common.** Have a student describe how to solve the system. **By substitution $1/x = 10/x$, $x = 10x$, so $x = 0$, which cannot be true. By elimination:**

$$y = 1/x \qquad xy = 1$$
$$y = 10/x \qquad -\ (xy = 10)$$
$$0 = -9$$

The elimination method leads to an incorrect statement since $0 = -9$; therefore, there is no solution, and the graphs do not intersect.

Going Further For Question 21, ask students to compare graphs of $y = k/x^2$ as k increases. **As k increases, the graphs in both quadrants are farther away from the axes.**

4 FOLLOW-UP

Other Explorations Have students explore inverse variation with the number of coins needed to make one dollar. Have them complete the table.

Coin	Value in Cents	Number of Coins = \$1
Penny	1	100
Nickel	5	20
Dime	10	20
Quarter	25	4
Half-dollar	50	2
Dollar	100	1

Ask them to write an equation that represents the number of coins needed to make one dollar. Let x represent the value in cents of a coin and y the number of coins needed to make one dollar. **$y = 100/x$**

AlgebraWorks Ask students what symbols in the formula for the break-even point represent the equivalents of y, x, and k in the inverse variation $y = k/x$. **t, the break-even tonnage, represents the variable y, Fixed Costs represents the constant k, and the difference of the selling price per ton and the variable costs per ton represents the variable x.** For Exercise 1, ask students what happens to y when the value for x goes up if y is inversely proportional to x. **The value for y goes down.**

Career
Agribusiness Manager

An agribusiness manager supervises the welfare of farm animals or crops in the interest of profit. The manager of Agri-Feed wants to project profits for the upcoming selling period. She must consider fixed costs such as buildings, equipment, and taxes, and variable costs such as labor and utilities. She must also determine the break-even point when all costs are covered and profit can begin. The break-even point occurs when the profit is zero.

TONS OF FEED PRODUCED	TOTAL REVENUE (P = \$174/ton)	VARIABLE COST (C = \$167/ton)	FIXED COSTS	TOTAL COSTS	TOTAL PROFITS
(Tons)	Tons x \$174 (Dollars)	Tons x \$167 (Dollars)	(Dollars)	Variable Costs Fixed Costs (Dollars)	Total Revenue Total Costs (Dollars)
0	0	0	12,500	12,500	−12,500
1000	174,000	167,000	12,500	179,500	−5500
2000	348,000	334,000	12,500	346,000	1500

Decision Making

Determining that the fixed costs are \$12,500 and that the variable costs are \$167 per ton, the manager produced the table shown above.

Let t represent the number of tons produced. Recall from Lesson 7.3 that the break-even point occurs when

$$\begin{aligned} \text{Revenue} &= \text{Fixed Costs} + \text{Variable Costs} \\ 174t &= 12{,}500 + 167t \\ t &= \frac{12{,}500}{174 - 167} \approx 1785.7 \end{aligned}$$

Agri-Feed must sell approximately 1785.7 tons of feed to break even. The solution shows that the break-even point occurs when

$$t = \frac{\text{Fixed Costs}}{\text{Selling Price per ton} - \text{Variable Cost per ton}}$$

So, the break-even tonnage varies inversely as the difference of the selling price per ton and the variable costs per ton.

1. What happens to the break-even point t when the selling price per ton goes up and the variable costs per ton stay the same? The value for t decreases.
2. If Agri-Feed raises the price of feed to \$175 per ton, determine the new break-even point. 1562.5 tons
3. If the selling price is \$174 per ton, the variable costs are \$167 per ton, and Agri-Feed sells 2250 tons of feed, what is their profit? How many tons of feed must they sell to make a profit of \$6500? \$3250; 2714.3 tons

14.2 Direct, Inverse, and Joint Variation

Explore

In Lesson 14.1 you examined the difference between direct and inverse variation.

DIRECT VARIATION

When y varies directly as x and k is the constant of variation, an equation can be written in the form

$$y = kx, k \neq 0$$

INVERSE VARIATION

When y varies inversely as x and k is the constant of variation, an equation can be written in the form

$$y = \frac{k}{x}, k \neq 0, x \neq 0$$

Consider the equation $C = \pi d$ for the circumference of a circle with diameter d.

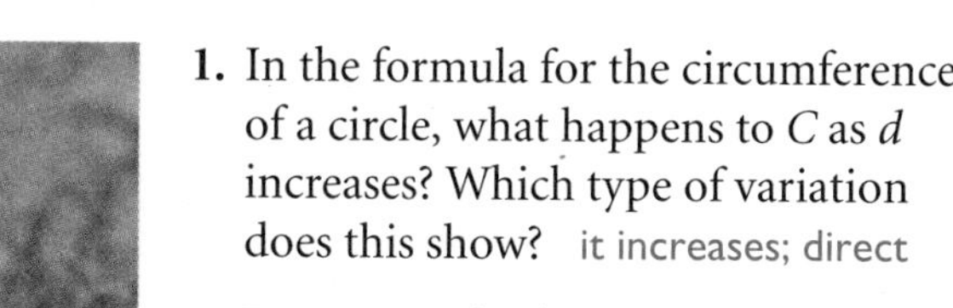

1. In the formula for the circumference of a circle, what happens to C as d increases? Which type of variation does this show? it increases; direct

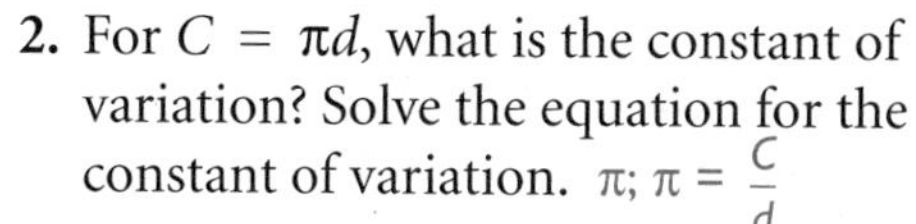

2. For $C = \pi d$, what is the constant of variation? Solve the equation for the constant of variation. π; $\pi = \frac{C}{d}$
3. Write the equation for the diameter d in terms of the radius r. As r increases, what happens to d? Does d vary directly as r? $d = 2r$; it increases; yes
4. If the circumference of a circle varies directly as the diameter, does it also vary directly as the radius? Explain. See Additional Answers.
5. Which would get you 4 mi from school in the least amount of time, walking or riding in a car? Which mode of transportation has the greater rate of speed? How does speed relate to time? Write an equation that relates speed and time to the distance of 4 mi.

riding in a car; car; speed varies inversely as time; $4 = st$

SPOTLIGHT ON LEARNING

WHAT? In this lesson you will learn
- to use direct variation, inverse variation, and joint variation.
- to apply the different forms of variation in real world settings.

WHY? Direct, inverse, and joint variation can help you solve problems about travel, electricity, and coordinate geometry.

THINK BACK

A radius is a segment from the center of a circle to any point on the circle.

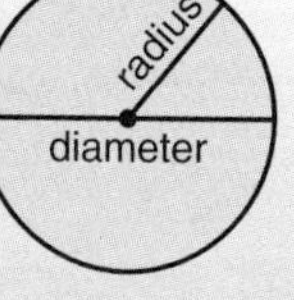

A diameter is a segment through the center of the circle which touches the circle at two points.

LESSON PLANNING

Objective

▶ Recognize and use direct, inverse, and joint variation.

Vocabulary

constant of variation
direct variation
inverse variation
joint variation

Resources

Warm Up 14.2
Reteaching 14.2
Extra Practice 14.2
Enrichment 14.2
Transparencies 33, 35, 77
Student Handbook
Lesson Quiz 14.2
Study Skills Activity 34

ASSIGNMENTS

Basic: 1–21, 23–24, Mixed Review 27–33, Project Connection 1–4, AlgebraWorks 1–4

Average: 3–25, Mixed Review 27–33, Project Connection 1–4, AlgebraWorks 1–4

Enriched: 4–26, Mixed Review 27–33, Project Connection 1–4, AlgebraWorks 1–4

1 MOTIVATE

Explore For Question 3, ask students how they know that d varies directly as r. **The equation $d = 2r$ is of the form $y = kx$ where $y = d$, $k = 2$, and $x = r$.** After students have answered Question 5, ask what it means to say that speed varies inversely as time. **As the rate of speed increases, the**

rate of time decreases. Ask how the equation 4 = *st* relates to the equation for inverse variation $y = k/x$. **The constant of variation *k* is the distance 4 and the variables *x* and *y* are represented by *s* and *t*.**

2 TEACH

Use the Pages/Build Understanding Ask how the equation $k = y/x$ was derived for direct variation and how the equation $k = xy$ was derived for inverse variation. **For direct variation divide both sides of the equation $y = kx$ by x to get $y/x = k$ or $k = y/x$; for inverse variation multiply both sides of the equation $y = k/x$ by x to get $xy = k$ or $k = xy$.**

Example 1: Before students read the solution, ask which formula in terms of *x*, *y*, and *k* they can use to determine whether the time varies inversely as the speed. **$xy = k$ where $x = s$, $y = t$, and *k* is unknown** After students have read the solution, ask what general formula they could use to show that time varies inversely as speed in this example. **$st = 120$**

Example 2: Explain that students can use either method to find the missing *x* or *y* value. Stress that if they use the proportion method they must place the values in the correct position. Have students read and answer Communicating About Algebra. Ask students to describe how the proportion $\frac{x_2}{x_1} = \frac{y_1}{y_2}$ can be derived.

Since $y_1 = k/x_1$, $y_1x_1 = k$ and since $y_2 = k/x_2$, $y_2x_2 = k$; therefore, $y_1x_1 = y_2x_2$ and $= \frac{x_2}{x_1} \cdot \frac{y_1}{y_2}$

Have students read Check Understanding. Ask them to give examples of triangles showing how the area increases as the base or height increases. **Possible example is shown.**

Base	4	6	6
Height	5	5	8
Area	10	15	24

Build Understanding

Explore describes two different kinds of variations, direct and inverse. Notice that when you solve for the constant of variation *k* in an equation of direct variation, $k = \frac{y}{x}$. When you solve for the constant of variation *k* in an equation of inverse variation, $k = xy$.

EXAMPLE 1

TRAVEL José recorded the time it took him to travel from home to the state capital driving at several different speeds. Do the results suggest that the time varies inversely as the speed?

Speed, *s* (mi/h)	60	50	40	30
Time, *t* (h)	2	2.4	3	4

Solution

If the time varies inversely as the speed, then the product *st* will be a constant. Calculate *st* for the given data.

$s \cdot t$

$60 \cdot 2 = 120$

$50 \cdot 2.4 = 120$

$40 \cdot 3 = 120$

$30 \cdot 4 = 120$

In each case, $st = 120$, which suggests that for any given distance, time varies inversely as the speed.

COMMUNICATING ABOUT ALGEBRA

Can you use the proportion $\frac{x_1}{x_2} = \frac{y_2}{y_1}$ to solve a direct variation? If so, explain why. If not, what proportion can you use?

No. Since $y_1 = kx_1$ and $y_2 = kx_2$, you would use the proportion $\frac{y_1}{x_1} = \frac{y_2}{x_2}$.

Proportions are useful when solving problems involving inverse variation. If the ordered pairs (x_1, y_1) and (x_2, y_2) satisfy the equation $xy = k$, then $x_1y_1 = k$ and $x_2y_2 = k$. Therefore,

$$x_1y_1 = x_2y_2$$

$$\frac{x_1}{x_2} = \frac{y_1}{y_2}$$

EXAMPLE 2

If *y* varies inversely as *x*, and $y = 2$ when $x = 50$, determine the value of *y* when $x = 200$. You can use the proportion method or the equation method.

Solution

Proportion Method

$$\frac{50}{200} = \frac{y}{2} \qquad \frac{x_1}{x_2} = \frac{y_2}{y_1}$$

$$\frac{50(2)}{200} = y$$

$$\frac{1}{2} = y$$

Equation Method

$xy = k$

$50(2) = k$ Substitute $x = 50, y = 2$.

$100 = k$

$xy = k$

$200y = 100$ Substitute 200 for x and 100 for k.

$y = \frac{100}{200}$

$y = \frac{1}{2}$ ◄

Sometimes one variable varies directly as the product of two or more variables. This is called *joint variation.*

JOINT VARIATION

When y varies directly as the product of w and x, and k is the constant of variation, an equation can be written in the form

$$y = kwx, k \neq 0$$

CHECK UNDERSTANDING

The formula for the area of a triangle, $A = \frac{1}{2}bh$, shows joint variation. The area increases as either the base or the height increases.

EXAMPLE 3

If y varies jointly as x and z, and $y = 144$ when $x = 3$ and $z = 12$, find y when $x = 5$ and $z = 11$.

Solution

$y = kxz$ Write the equation.

$144 = k(3)(12)$ Substitute $x = 3$ and $z = 12$.

$\frac{144}{(3)(12)} = k$ Solve for k.

$4 = k$ Simplify.

$y = kxz$ Write the equation.

$y = 4(5)(11)$ Substitute $k = 4$, $x = 5$, and $z = 11$.

$y = 220$ Simplify. ◄

Example 3: After students have discussed the example, ask them to consider what happens to y if the value of x is increased to 10 and the value of z stays the same. **It will increase.** Have them show how to find the value of y for $x = 10$. $\boldsymbol{y = kxz, y = 4(10)(11), y = 440}$

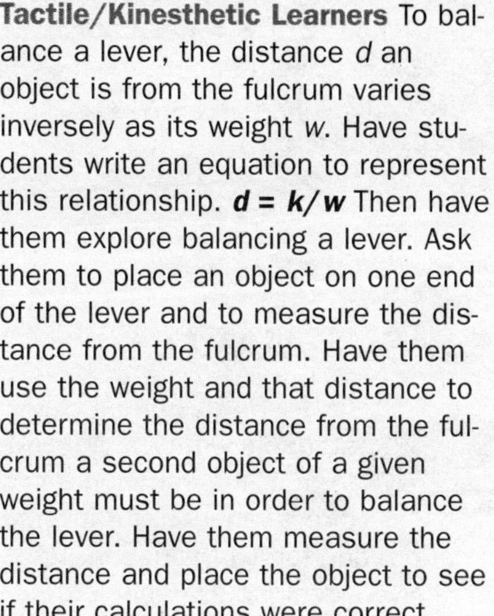

DIVERSITY IN THE CLASSROOM

Tactile/Kinesthetic Learners To balance a lever, the distance d an object is from the fulcrum varies inversely as its weight w. Have students write an equation to represent this relationship. $\boldsymbol{d = k/w}$ Then have them explore balancing a lever. Ask them to place an object on one end of the lever and to measure the distance from the fulcrum. Have them use the weight and that distance to determine the distance from the fulcrum a second object of a given weight must be in order to balance the lever. Have them measure the distance and place the object to see if their calculations were correct.

Ongoing Assessment The important concepts and skills involve recognizing and using direct, inverse, and joint variation. To assess these ideas, have students demonstrate how they have applied these concepts and skills in Exercises 1, 6, and 9 of the Try These section.

Guided Practice/Try These For Exercise 4, ask a student to describe how he or she determined whether the data in the table suggests that *y* varies inversely as *x*. **If *y* varies inversely as *x*, then *xy* = *k* where *k* is a constant not equal to zero. For every pair of *x*- and *y*-values, *xy* = 8. So 8 is the constant of variation.** After students have completed Exercise 13, ask them to describe how they solved the problem. **proportion method: 2/1.6 = *y*/12, 24/1.6 = *y*, 15*N* = *y*; equation method: *F* = *k*/*l*, 12 = *k*/2, 24 = *k*; *F* = 24/1.6, *F* = 15*N***

3 SUMMARIZE

In the Math Journal Have students write the general form of the equation for direct variation, for inverse variation, and for joint variation. Have them give a real life example for each. **Examples will vary. Direct variation: *y* = *kx*, the amount of money earned by a person who earns $10 an hour varies directly as the number of hours worked, *m* = 10*h*; Inverse variation: *xy* = *k*, the time it takes to drive 500 miles varies inversely as the speed at which the car travels, *st* = 500; joint variation: *y* = *kxz*, the volume of a box with height equal to 2 cm varies jointly as its length and width, *V* = 2*lw*.**

TRY THESE

State whether each equation represents *direct variation*, *inverse variation*, or *joint variation*. Also, state the constant of variation.

1. $s = 2qr$ joint; $k = 2$
2. $d = 2r$ direct; $k = 2$
3. $xy = 10$ inverse; $k = 10$

Determine whether the data in each table suggests that *y* varies inversely as *x*. If it does, state the constant of variation.

4.

x	1	2	4	8	16
y	8	4	2	1	$\frac{1}{2}$

yes; $k = 8$

5.

x	2	3	4	5	6
y	30	20	15	12	10

yes; $k = 60$

Write an equation for each variation using *k* as the constant of variation.

6. w varies inversely as x $w = \frac{k}{x}$
7. c varies inversely as the square of d $c = \frac{k}{d^2}$
8. f varies jointly as g and h $f = kgh$

In Exercises 9–10, *y* varies inversely as *x*.

9. If $y = 10$ when $x = 50$, find y when $x = 20$. 25
10. If $y = 8$ when $x = 12$, find x when $y = 6$. 16

In Exercises 11–12, *y* varies jointly as *x* and *z*.

11. If $y = 30$ when $x = 3$ and $z = 5$, find y when $x = 12$ and $z = \frac{1}{2}$. 12
12. If $y = 75$ when $x = 25$ and $z = 6$, find y when $x = 30$ and $z = 4$. 60

13. **SIMPLE MACHINES** The force F needed to pry open a crate varies inversely as the length l of the crowbar used. When the length is 2 m, the force needed is 12 N (newtons). What force would be needed if the crowbar was 1.6 m long? 15 N

14. **ELECTRICITY** The energy an appliance uses varies directly as the time it is in operation. A stereo that operates for 21 h a week uses 2.3 kWh (kilowatt-hours) of electrical energy. How much energy would the stereo use for 80 h of operation? Round to two decimal places. 8.76 kWh

15. **WRITING MATHEMATICS** The area of a triangle is 24 cm^2. Write a paragraph that describes how its base varies when the height increases or decreases. Determine the constant of variation and include that in your discussion. See Additional Answers.

PRACTICE

State whether each equation represents *direct variation*, *inverse variation*, or *joint variation*. State the constant of variation.

1. $a = 9.5b$ direct; $k = 9.5$

2. $c = \frac{1}{2}de$ joint; $k = \frac{1}{2}$

3. $lw = 72$ inverse; $k = 72$

4. $g = 4ef$ joint; $k = 4$

5. $u = 0.14v$ direct; $k = 0.14$

6. $q = \frac{16}{r}$ inverse; $k = 16$

In Exercises 7–10, y varies inversely as x.

7. If $y = 12$ when $x = 60$, find y when $x = 15$. 48

8. If $y = 15$ when $x = 20$, find y when $x = 30$. 10

9. If $y = 5$ when $x = 14$, find x when $y = 10$. 7

10. If $y = 9$ when $x = 50$, find x when $y = 15$. 30

In Exercises 11–14, y varies jointly as x and z.

11. If $y = 45$ when $x = 9$ and $z = 6$, find y when $x = 10$ and $z = 6$. 50

12. If $y = 75$ when $x = 25$ and $z = 6$, find y when $x = 30$ and $z = 4$. 60

13. If $y = 600$ when $x = 50$ and $z = 24$, find y when $x = 50$ and $z = 84$. 2100

14. If $y = 100$ when $x = 10$ and $z = 40$, find y when $x = 28$ and $z = 14$. 98

GEOMETRY Write an equation for each variation with k as the constant of variation.

15. The diameter of a circle varies directly as the radius of the circle. $d = kr$

16. The area of a triangle varies jointly as its base and height. $A = kbh$

17. In a rectangle with a constant area, the width varies inversely as the length. $w = \frac{k}{l}$

18. WRITING MATHEMATICS Write an equation such that y varies inversely as x. Describe a situation about agriculture for your equation. See Additional Answers.

EXTEND

In some cases, one quantity varies directly or inversely as the square of another. For example, the area of a circle varies directly as the square of the radius, as shown in the formula $A = \pi r^2$. This function is an example of **quadratic direct variation**.

19. Assume that y varies directly as x^2. When $x = 7$, $y = 245$. Find y when $x = 11$. 605

20. Assume that y varies inversely as x^2. When $x = 9$, $y = 16$. Find y when $x = 6$. 36

21. BIOLOGY The number of organisms in a culture varies directly as the square of the time the culture has been growing. A culture growing for 25 min has 5,000 organisms. About how long will it take for there to be 10,000 organisms? about 35 min

4 PRACTICE

Practice For Exercises 7–10, ask students what two methods they can use to find the missing variable. **proportion method, equation method** Suggest that students use one method to find the missing variable and then the other method to check. Ask a student to describe how he or she solved Exercise 11. **Substitute values for x, y, and z and solve for k: $y = kxz$, $45 = k(9)(6)$, $45 = k(54)$, $5/6 = k$; substitute values for x, z, and k and solve for y: $y = (5/6)(10)(6)$, $y = 50$.** Remind students using the proportion method to be sure that they are using the correct proportion.

Extend For Exercises 19 and 20, ask students what general formula they can use to find the value of y in each exercise. **$y = kx^2$, $y = k/x^2$** Have students show how to solve Exercise 21. **$y = kx^2$, $5000 = k(25)^2$, $5000/625 = k$, $8 = k$; $10{,}000 = 8x^2$, $1250 = x^2$, $x \approx 35$**

NAME ______________ CLASS ________ DATE ________

R RETEACHING

14.2 DIRECT, INVERSE, AND JOINT VARIATION

To identify direct, inverse, and joint variations, look for the following properties. The constant of variation is k and can be any number except 0.

- The equation for a **direct** variation is $y = kx$ where $k \neq 0$.
- The equation for an **inverse** variation is $y = \frac{k}{x}$, where $k \neq 0$.
- The equation for a **joint** variation is $y = kwx$ where $k \neq 0$.

You can use a proportion to solve a joint variation. Since a joint variation is in the form $y = kwx, k \neq 0$, it can be written as $k = \frac{y}{wx}$ and the proportion $\frac{y_1}{w_1x_1} = \frac{y_2}{w_2x_2}$ can be used.

Example
If y varies jointly as p and q, and $y = 45$ when $p = 3$ and $q = 5$, find y when $p = 4$ and $q = 7$.

Solution

$\frac{y_1}{w_1x_1} = \frac{y_2}{w_2x_2}$ Write a proportion.

$\frac{45}{3}(5) = \frac{y}{4}(7)$ Substitute.

$3 = \frac{y}{28}$ Simplify.

$3(28) = y$ Multiply both sides by 28.

$84 = y$

EXERCISES

In Exercises 1 and 2, y varies inversely as x.

1. If $y = 32$ when $x = 4$, find y when $x = 6$. 1. $\frac{64}{3}$

2. If $y = 60$ when $x = 15$, find y when $x = 9$. 2. 100

In Exercises 3–6, y varies jointly as x.

3. If $y = 90$ when $w = 2$ and $x = 5$, find y when $w = 3$ and $x = 8$. 3. 216

4. If $y = 1200$ when $w = 100$ and $x = 3$, find y when $w = 25$ and $x = 7$. 4. 700

5. If $y = 200$ when $w = 10$ and $x = 4$, find y when $w = 6$ and $x = 2$. 5. 60

6. If $y = 16$ when $w = 2$ and $x = 4$, find y when $w = 3$ and $x = 9$. 6. 54

6 *South-Western Algebra 1: AN INTEGRATED APPROACH*

Think Critically For Exercises 24–26, ask students on what line the point closest to the origin lies and to explain how they know this to be true. **$y = x$; since a line of symmetry for $xy = 1$ is $y = x$, the point that is on the graphs of both $xy = 1$ and $y = x$ must be the point on the graph of $xy = 1$ that is closest to the origin.** Ask students how they can find the point that is on both graphs. **Use substitution.**

5 FOLLOW-UP

Extension Have students explore combined variation. Explain that many real world applications require equations that combine inverse and joint variation. Tell students that one example involves heat loss through a window. Heat loss h through a window varies directly as the difference d between the inside and the outside temperatures and the area A of the window and inversely as the thickness of the window w. Have students

NAME ______ CLASS ______ DATE ______

P EXTRA PRACTICE 14.2 DIRECT, INVERSE, AND JOINT VARIATION

State whether each equation represents *direct variation*, *inverse variation*, or *joint variation*. State the constant of variation. Write D, I, or J.

1. $ab = 60$ **2.** $c = 2.5d$

3. $e = \frac{f}{3}$ **4.** $g = \frac{7}{h}$

5. $k = 8.1pq$ **6.** $r = \frac{3s}{t}$

1. I, 60
2. D, 2.5
3. D, $\frac{1}{3}$
4. I, 7
5. J, 8.1
6. J, 3

In Exercises 7–10, y varies inversely as x.

7. If $y = 16$ when $x = 3$, find y when $x = 4$. 7. 12

8. If $y = 7$ when $x = 4$, find y when $x = 2$. 8. 14

9. If $y = 20$ when $x = 3$, find y when $x = 10$. 9. 6

10. If $y = 15$ when $x = 4$, find x when $y = 5$. 10. 12

In Exercises 11–14, y varies jointly as x and z.

11. If $y = 100$ when $x = 2$ and $z = 10$, find y when $x = 30$ and $z = 6$. 11. 900

12. If $y = 36$ when $x = 3$ and $z = 6$, find y when $x = 7$ and $z = 4$. 12. 56

13. If $y = 480$ when $x = 5$ and $z = 4$, find y when $x = 8$ and $z = 6$. 13. 1152

14. If $y = 160$ when $x = 2$ and $z = 10$, find y when $x = 3$ and $z = 15$. 14. 360

GEOMETRY Write an equation for each variation with k as the constant of variation.

15. The circumference of a circle varies directly with the radius of the circle. 15. $c = kr$

16. The perimeter of a regular hexagon varies directly with the measure of a side of the hexagon. 16. $p = ks$

THINK CRITICALLY

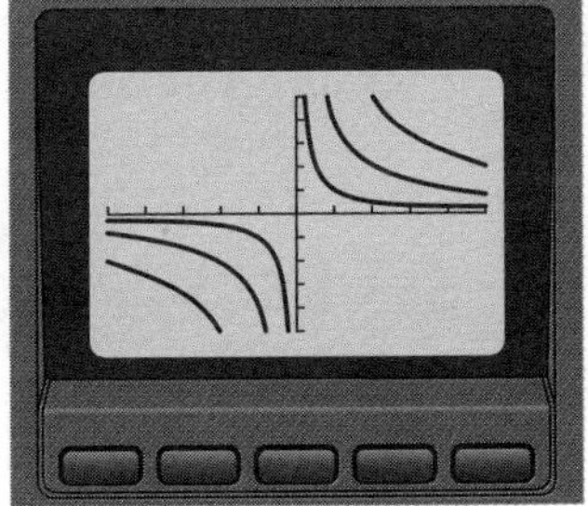

COORDINATE GEOMETRY The graph of an inverse variation of the form $y = \frac{k}{x}$ or $xy = k, x \neq 0, k \neq 0$ is a *hyperbola*. The graphs of $xy = 1$, $xy = 4$, and $xy = 10$ are displayed at the right.

22. In which quadrants is the graph of $xy = k$ located if k is greater than zero? if k is less than zero? I and III; II and IV

23. What are the lines of symmetry of the graph of $xy = k$? $y = x, y = -x$

24. Determine the Quadrant I point on the graph of $xy = 1$ that is closest to the origin. (*Hint:* On what line does the point closest to the origin lie? What is the relationship of the x- and y-coordinates of this point?) (1, 1)

25. Determine the Quadrant I point on the graph of $xy = 4$ that is closest to the origin. (2, 2)

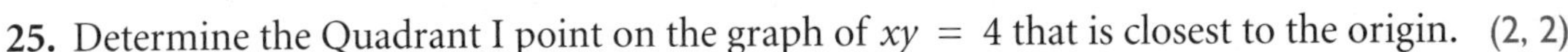

26. Determine the Quadrant I point on the graph of $xy = 10$ that is closest to the origin. $(\sqrt{10}, \sqrt{10})$

MIXED REVIEW

27. STANDARDIZED TESTS An 80-mL solution of water and acid contains 30% acid. How much water must you add to make it a 15% acid solution? B; Lesson 3.8

A. 40 mL **B.** 80 mL **C.** 24 mL **D.** 160 mL

Express the equation of each line in slope-intercept form. Lesson 6.4

28. $6x + 3y - 6 = 12$ $y = -2x + 6$

29. $2x + 15 = 3y + 9$ $y = \frac{2}{3}x + 2$

Use the algebraic method to solve each absolute value inequality. Lesson 9.4

30. $|2x - 6| > 12$ $x < -3$ or $x > 9$

31. $|4x + 8| < 16$ $-6 < x < 2$

In Exercises 32–33, y varies inversely as x. Lesson 14.2

32. If $y = 15$ when $x = 5$, find y when $x = 25$. 3

33. If $y = 45$ when $x = 5$, find x when $y = 9$. 25

PROJECT Connection Use the data collected during the Getting Started activity on page 674.

1. Determine the product of each pair of values for the height and circumference of the base. What do you notice? product always equals 93.5
2. Explain why this happens, in terms of the physical aspects of the situation. Surface area is constant; the amount of paper/lateral area does not change.
3. Express the height h as a function of the circumference C of the base. $h = \frac{93.5}{C}, C \neq 0$
4. Does the equation you wrote in Question 3 represent a variation and, if so, what type of variation? yes; an inverse variation

Career
Refrigeration System Engineer

Some branches of agribusiness require the use of refrigeration. Most refrigerators use a compression system that operates on two principles. First, as liquid evaporates, it absorbs heat from the surrounding air. Second, the temperature T of an enclosed gas varies jointly with the volume V and pressure P; that is, $T = kPV$. The diagram below shows the refrigeration process.

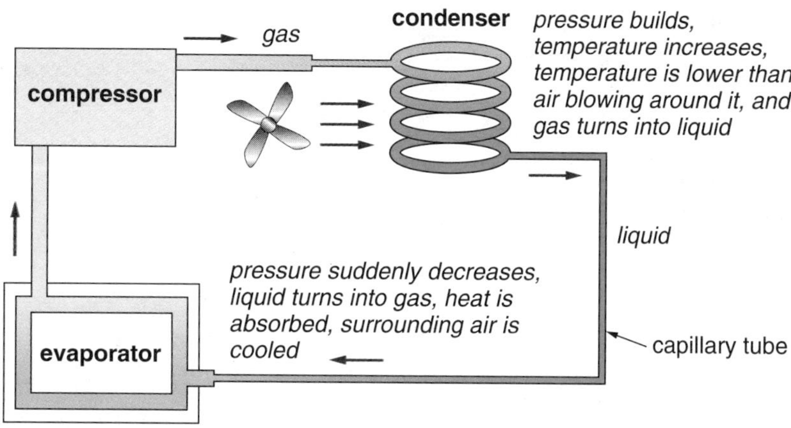

Decision Making

The engineer who designs the cooling system must choose the diameter of the capillary tube. For a given compressor and refrigerant, different diameters require different lengths of tubing. For example, the table shows the dimensions required to maintain high temperatures using a particular compressor and refrigerant.

Inside Diameter, in.	Length of Tubing, ft
0.031	1.1
0.036	2.2
0.040	3.5
0.042	4.5
0.049	9.0
0.055	15.0

1. Use the relationship $T = kPV$ to explain why a larger diameter requires more tubing to achieve the same temperature results. See Additional Answers.

One size capillary tube that is often used for refrigerant R-12 has an outside diameter of 0.114 in. and an inside diameter of 0.049 in.

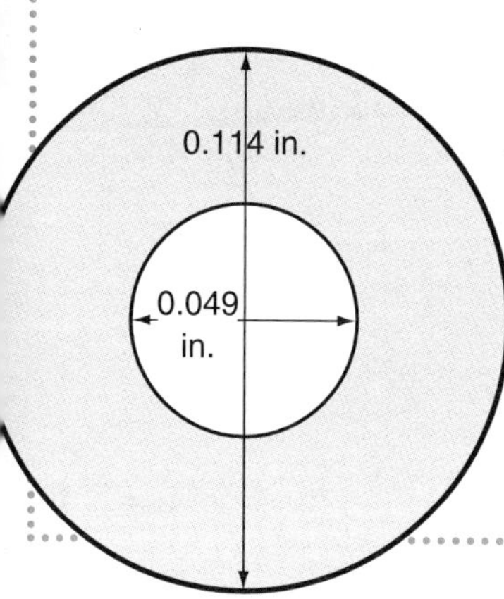

2. Determine the circumference of the inside and outside of the tube. inside: $0.049\pi \approx 0.154$ in.; outside: $0.114\pi \approx 0.358$ in.
3. If temperature is held constant, the volume of a gas varies inversely as the pressure. When the volume is 120 in.^{3}, the pressure is 30 lb/in.^{3} If the pressure changes to 20 lb/in.^{3}, what is the volume? 180 in.^{3}
4. If pressure is held constant, the volume of a gas varies directly with its temperature (in degrees Kelvin). If 10 m^3 of a gas is kept under constant pressure while its temperature drops from 405°K to 345°K, approximately what is its new volume? 8.52 m^3

write an equation representing this combined variation. $h = kdA/w$ Then have them solve the following problem: If the heat loss through a window with an area of 9 ft^2 and a width of 0.24 in. is 675 BTU per hour when the temperature difference is 60°F, what is the heat loss through the same window when the temperature difference is 40°F? **450 BTU**

Project Connection This activity presents further aspects of the project introduced on page 674. Have students explain why the equation represents an inverse variation. **As *C* increases *h* decreases, and as *C* decreases *h* increases.**

AlgebraWorks For Question 3, ask students what equation represents the relationship between the volume of a gas and the pressure, given constant temperature. ***VP* = *k* or *V* = *k*/*P*** For Question 4, ask students what equation represents the relationship between the volume of a gas and its temperature, given constant pressure. ***V*/*T* = *k* or *V* = *kT***

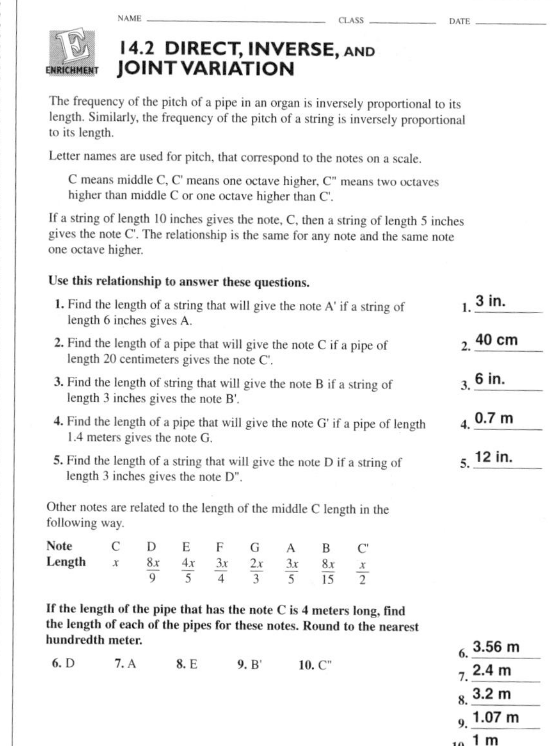

NAME ______ CLASS ______ DATE ______

ENRICHMENT

14.2 DIRECT, INVERSE, AND JOINT VARIATION

The frequency of the pitch of a pipe in an organ is inversely proportional to its length. Similarly, the frequency of the pitch of a string is inversely proportional to its length.

Letter names are used for pitch, that correspond to the notes on a scale.

C means middle C, C' means one octave higher, C'' means two octaves higher than middle C or one octave higher than C'.

If a string of length 10 inches gives the note, C, then a string of length 5 inches gives the note C'. The relationship is the same for any note and the same note one octave higher.

Use this relationship to answer these questions.

1. Find the length of a string that will give the note A' if a string of length 6 inches gives A. 1. 3 in.
2. Find the length of a pipe that will give the note C if a pipe of length 20 centimeters gives the note C'. 2. 40 cm
3. Find the length of string that will give the note B if a string of length 3 inches gives the note B'. 3. 6 in.
4. Find the length of a pipe that will give the note G' if a pipe of length 1.4 meters gives the note G. 4. 0.7 m
5. Find the length of a string that will give the note D if a string of length 3 inches gives the note D''. 5. 12 in.

Other notes are related to the length of the middle C length in the following way.

Note	C	D	E	F	G	A	B	C'
Length	x	$\frac{8x}{9}$	$\frac{4x}{5}$	$\frac{3x}{4}$	$\frac{2x}{3}$	$\frac{3x}{5}$	$\frac{8x}{15}$	$\frac{x}{2}$

If the length of the pipe that has the note C is 4 meters long, find the length of each of the pipes for these notes. Round to the nearest hundredth meter.

6. D 7. A 8. E 9. B' 10. C''

6. 3.56 m
7. 2.4 m
8. 3.2 m
9. 1.07 m
10. 1 m

10 South-Western Algebra 1: AN INTEGRATED APPROACH

LESSON PLANNING

Objective

▶ Simplify rational expressions and determine the values of the variable for which a rational expression is undefined.

Vocabulary

rational expression
restrictions
simplest form

Resources

Warm Up 14.3
Reteaching 14.3
Extra Practice 14.3
Enrichment 14.3
Transparencies 33, 35
Student Handbook
Lesson Quiz 14.3
Study Skills Activity 35
Technology Activities 32, 33

Materials/Manipulatives

Algeblocks

ASSIGNMENTS

Basic: 1–22, 24, 26, Mixed Review 28–32, Project Connection 1–4, AlgebraWorks 1–6

Average: 3–26, Mixed Review 28–32, Project Connection 1–4, AlgebraWorks 1–6

Enriched: 3–27, Mixed Review 28–32, Project Connection 1–4, AlgebraWorks 1–6

1 MOTIVATE

Explore Ask students how they can find the surface area of each rectangular prism. **Find the sum of the areas of all the faces.** Ask them to describe how they found the surface

14.3 Simplify Rational Expressions

SPOTLIGHT ON LEARNING

WHAT? In this lesson you will learn

- to determine the values of the variable for which a rational expression is undefined.
- to simplify rational expressions.

WHY? Simplifying rational expressions can help you solve problems about interior design, transportation, and farming.

Explore

Use Algeblocks to make the rectangular solids shown below. Determine the surface area and volume of each solid. Then write the ratio of the surface area to the volume. See Additional Answers.

1. 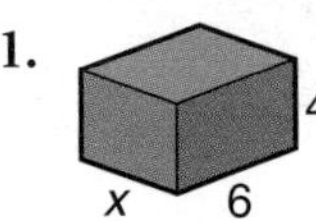

2. 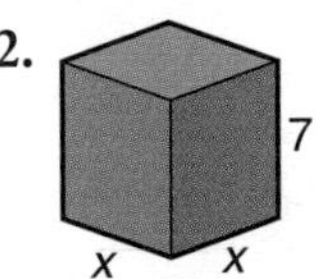

3. 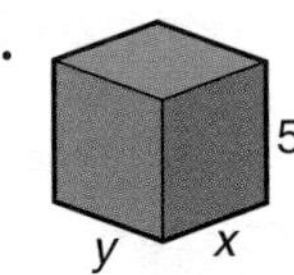

4. 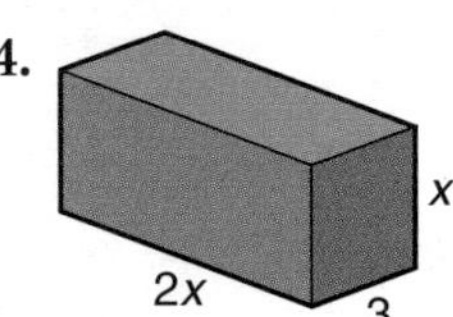

Build Understanding

Recall that a *rational number* is a number that can be expressed in the form $\frac{a}{b}$, where a and b are integers, $b \neq 0$. The denominator b cannot equal zero because division by zero is undefined. Examples of rational numbers include $\frac{0}{8}, -\frac{14}{42}, \frac{3}{1}$, 0.12121. . . , and 23.

RATIONAL EXPRESSION

A rational expression is an expression that can be written in the form $\frac{P}{Q}$ where P and Q are polynomials, $Q \neq 0$.

THINK BACK

A polynomial is a monomial or a sum or difference of monomials.

Examples of rational expressions include $\frac{1}{x}$, $4y + 2$, $\frac{x}{y^2 - 5}$, $\frac{3x^2 - 7}{x + 3}$, and $\frac{17}{77}$. When the denominator of a rational expression is zero, the expression is undefined. You sometimes need to factor the denominator to find the values of the variable that will make the denominator zero.

EXAMPLE 1

For which values of the variable is each expression undefined?

a. $\frac{2x^2y}{zw}$ b. $\frac{4xt}{t + 3}$ c. $\frac{3x}{4x^2 - 9}$

Solution

a. $zw = 0$

$z = 0 \quad w = 0$

b. $t + 3 = 0$

$t = -3$

c.

$$4x^2 - 9 = 0$$

$$(2x - 3)(2x + 3) = 0 \quad \text{Factor.}$$

$$2x - 3 = 0 \qquad 2x + 3 = 0$$

$$x = \frac{3}{2} \qquad x = -\frac{3}{2}$$

When you determine the values for a variable for which an expression is undefined, you determine the *restrictions* on that variable. The restrictions on x in Example 1c are $x \neq \frac{3}{2}$ and $x \neq -\frac{3}{2}$.

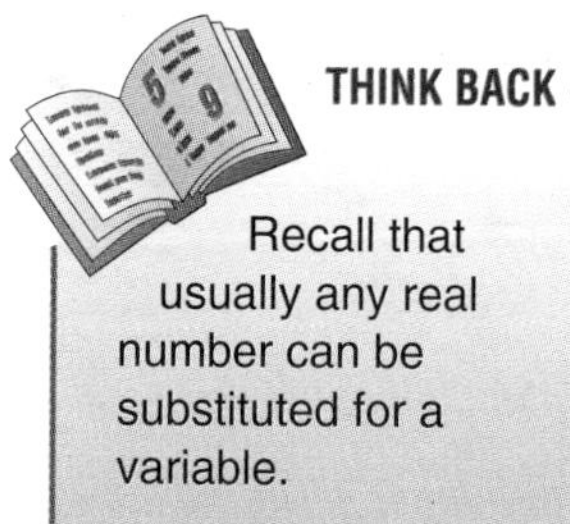

THINK BACK

Recall that usually any real number can be substituted for a variable.

When the numerator and denominator of a rational expression have no common factors other than 1, the rational expression is in **simplest form**. As with simplifying rational numbers, to simplify a rational expression, factor the numerator and denominator. Then divide each by the greatest common factor (GCF).

EXAMPLE 2

State any restrictions on the variable x. Then simplify: $\frac{4 + x}{2x^2 + 7x - 4}$

Solution

$$\frac{4 + x}{2x^2 + 7x - 4} = \frac{\overset{1}{\cancel{(4 + x)}}}{(2x - 1)\underset{1}{\cancel{(x + 4)}}} \quad \text{Factor the denominator and divide by } (x + 4) \text{, the GCF.}$$

$$= \frac{1}{2x - 1} \quad \text{Simplify.}$$

So, $\frac{4 + x}{2x^2 + 7x - 4} = \frac{1}{2x - 1}$.

Determine the restrictions on x. Set each factor in the denominator equal to zero.

$$2x - 1 = 0 \qquad x + 4 = 0$$

$$x = \frac{1}{2} \qquad x = -4$$

So, the restrictions on x are $x \neq \frac{1}{2}, x \neq -4$.

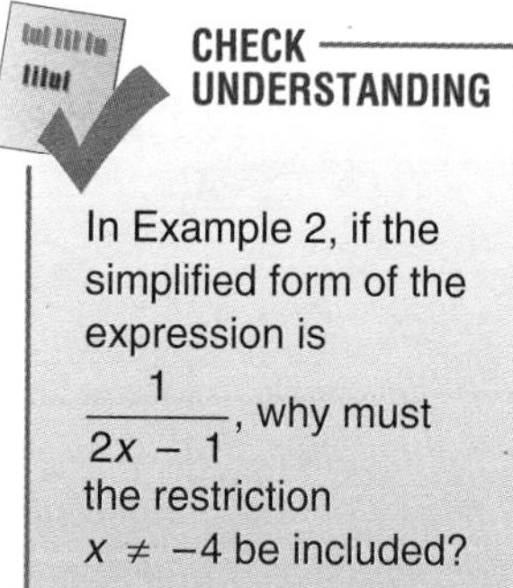

CHECK UNDERSTANDING

In Example 2, if the simplified form of the expression is $\frac{1}{2x - 1}$, why must the restriction $x \neq -4$ be included?

because $x \neq -4$ is a restriction on the original expression

Because of the property of -1, $y - x = -1(x - y)$. Therefore,

$$\frac{y - x}{x - y} = -1$$

So, you can replace $\frac{y - x}{x - y}$ with -1 in a rational expression.

area for the first rectangular prism. **$4x + 4x + 24 + 24 + 6x + 6x$ $= 20x + 48$ or $2(4x + 24 + 6x)$ $= 2(10x + 24) = 20x + 48$** Ask how they can find the volume of the rectangular prisms. **Count the total number of each type of block used in each prism or multiply the length times the width times the height.**

2 TEACH

Use the Pages/Build Understanding Ask why 0.12121... is included in the list of rational numbers. **because it is a repeating decimal and can be written in the form 4/33** Ask students to give other examples of rational expressions. **Examples will vary.**

Example 1: Ask students how they know when a rational expression is undefined. **when the value of the variable causes a denominator to be equal to zero** Ask how they can find the values of variables for which the denominator will be zero. **Set the denominator equal to zero and solve.** Ask what property is applied in part a. **zero product property, which states that if $ab = 0$, then $a = 0$ or $b = 0$** Explain that for part c, they need to factor the expression. Ask what special polynomial the denominator is. **the difference of two squares**

Example 2: Point out that students should look for such examples as $(4 + x)/(x + 4)$ when simplifying expressions. Ask them why $(4 + x) = (x + 4)$. **Addition is commutative and so $x + 4 = 4 + x$.** Have students read Check Understanding. Stress the importance of checking the restrictions on x in the original expression. Have students substitute -4 in the original ex-pression and explain what they find. **$(4 + (-4))/(2(-4)^2 + 7(-4) - 4) = = 0/0$; the expression is undefined for $x = -4$.**

Example 3: Ask students to verify that $(4 - x)/(x - 4)$ is equal to -1. **According to the property of -1, $y - x = (-1)(x - y)$, thus $4 - x = (-1)(x - 4)$.** Ask students to explain why $x \neq 4$ is included in the restrictions, since the simplified form of the expression is $3/(x + 3)$. **It makes the value of the denominator equal to zero in the original expression.**

Example 4: Ask students what restrictions they would apply to x in this case. **The restrictions would be $x \neq 0$ and $x \neq -3$; however, since length and width must be greater than zero, these restrictions are not meaningful.** Stress that it is important to always consider restrictions and determine whether they are necessary or not.

Ongoing Assessment The important concepts and skills are determining the values of the variable for which a rational expression is undefined and simplifying rational expressions. To assess these ideas, have students demonstrate how they have applied these concepts and skills in Exercises 4 and 8 of the Try These section.

Guided Practice/Try These For Exercise 3, ask students what property they use in determining values of x for which the expression is undefined. **zero product property which states that if $ab = 0$, then $a = 0$ or $b = 0$** For Exercise 14, ask what formula they can use. **distance = rate • time**

Error Alert For Try These Exercise 7, watch for students who incorrectly factor out 12 in the numerator and denominator:

$$\frac{4x - 12}{24} = \frac{4x - 1}{2}$$

The correct solution is

$$\frac{4x - 12}{24} = \frac{4(x - 3)}{24} = \frac{x - 3}{6}$$

COMMUNICATING ABOUT ALGEBRA

In Example 3, explain how the restrictions $x \neq -3$ and $x \neq 4$ were determined.

Set each factor in the denominator equal to zero and solve for x.

EXAMPLE 3

State any restrictions on the variable x. Then simplify: $\dfrac{12 - 3x}{x^2 - x - 12}$

Solution

$$\frac{12 - 3x}{x^2 - x - 12} = \frac{3(4 - x)}{(x + 3)(x - 4)} \qquad \text{Factor.}$$

$$= \frac{3(-1)\cancel{(x - 4)}}{(x + 3)\cancel{(x - 4)}} \qquad \text{Property of } -1. \text{ Divide out common factor.}$$

$$= -\frac{3}{x + 3} \qquad \text{Simplify.}$$

So, $\dfrac{12 - 3x}{x^2 - x - 12} = -\dfrac{3}{x + 3}, x \neq -3, x \neq 4.$

Rational expressions can be used in real world settings.

EXAMPLE 4

INTERIOR DESIGN When the law firm of C & V had only a few lawyers, partners and associates each received an office of dimensions x ft by x ft. Now that the firm has grown, they will be taking on more space in their building and enlarging the offices. Each office will be 3 ft wider, and partners' offices will also be 6 ft longer. Find a rational expression for the ratio of the new area of a partner's office to the new area of an associate's office. Evaluate the ratio if the current length of an office is 11 ft.

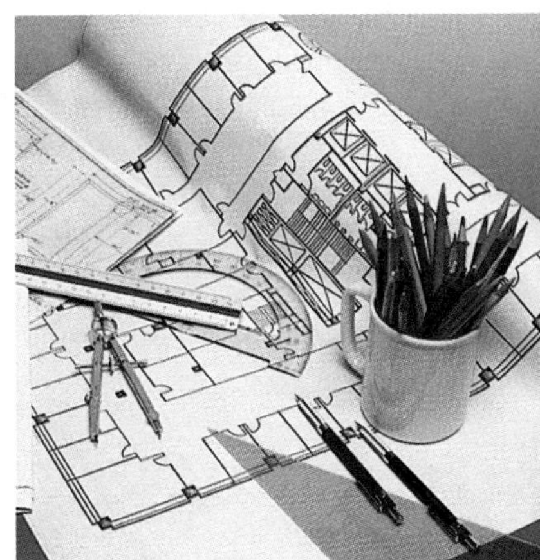

Solution

The area for a partner's office will be $(x + 6)(x + 3)$.
The area for an associate's office will be $x(x + 3)$.

$$\text{Ratio} = \frac{\text{Area of partner's office}}{\text{Area of associate's office}}$$

$$= \frac{(x + 6)\cancel{(x + 3)}}{x\cancel{(x + 3)}}$$

$$= \frac{(x + 6)}{x}$$

For $x = 11$, the ratio is $\frac{17}{11}$, the ratio of the partner's office area to the associate's office area.

TRY THESE

State the values of the variable for which each expression is undefined.

1. $\frac{6}{2x}$ $x = 0$
2. $\frac{x}{3x + 6}$ $x = -2$
3. $\frac{2x + 6}{(x + 3)(x - 7)}$ $x = -3, 7$
4. $\frac{x + 7}{x^2 - 2x - 35}$ $x = -5, 7$

Simplify each expression. State any restrictions on the variable.

5. $\frac{6x}{3x^2}$ $\frac{2}{x}; x \neq 0$
6. $\frac{5x^2}{25}$ $\frac{x^2}{5}$
7. $\frac{4x - 12}{24}$ $\frac{x - 3}{6}$
8. $\frac{6a - 12}{a - 2}$ $6; a \neq 2$
9. $\frac{a - 7}{7a - 49}$ $\frac{1}{7}; a \neq 7$
10. $\frac{3 - 2b}{6b - 9}$ $-\frac{1}{3}; b \neq \frac{3}{2}$
11. $\frac{5 + 2b}{-8b - 20}$ $-\frac{1}{4}; b \neq -\frac{5}{2}$
12. $\frac{3 + x}{x^2 - 2x - 15}$ $\frac{1}{x - 5}; x \neq -3, 5$
13. $\frac{4 + x}{x^2 + 10x + 24}$ $\frac{1}{x + 6}; x \neq -6, -4$
14. **TRANSPORTATION** Steve travels x miles each way in his car to visit his grandparents. It takes him y hours to get there and z hours to get home. Express his average speed for the round trip in terms of x, y, and z. $\frac{2x}{y + z}$
15. **WRITING MATHEMATICS** Explain why $\frac{y^2 - 25}{y - 5}$ is not the same as $y + 5$. See Additional Answers.

PRACTICE

State the values of the variable for which each expression is undefined.

1. $\frac{7}{9mn}$ $m = 0; n = 0$
2. $\frac{3}{pqr}$ $p = 0, q = 0, r = 0$
3. $\frac{y}{5y + 15}$ $y = -3$
4. $\frac{6x}{18x - 12}$ $x = \frac{2}{3}$
5. $\frac{z - 5}{(z - 1)(z + 8)}$ $z = 1, -8$
6. $\frac{3q + 8}{(q + 6)(q - 4)}$ $q = -6, 4$
7. $\frac{2x + 13}{x^2 + 2x - 48}$ $x = -8, 6$
8. $\frac{3y - 11}{y^2 - 10y - 56}$ $y = 14, -4$

Simplify each expression. State any restrictions on the variable.

9. $\frac{8x}{4x^2}$ $\frac{2}{x}; x \neq 0$
10. $\frac{10x}{5x^2}$ $\frac{2}{x}; x \neq 0$
11. $\frac{3y - 12}{15}$ $\frac{y - 4}{5}$
12. $\frac{6y + 15}{12}$ $\frac{2y + 5}{4}$
13. $\frac{4a - 16}{a - 4}$ $4; a \neq 4$
14. $\frac{a - 9}{9a - 81}$ $\frac{1}{9}; a \neq 9$
15. $\frac{4 - 8b}{40b - 20}$ $-\frac{1}{5}; b \neq \frac{1}{2}$
16. $\frac{4 - 3b}{9b - 12}$ $-\frac{1}{3}; b \neq \frac{4}{3}$
17. $\frac{2 + x}{x^2 - 5x - 14}$ $\frac{1}{x - 7}; x \neq -2, 7$
18. **BAKING** The baking time for a loaf of bread can be expressed as the ratio of the surface area to the volume. Calculate this ratio for a rectangular loaf of bread with dimensions $4x$ by x by x. $\frac{9}{2x}$
19. **MANUFACTURING** The efficiency of a machine is the ratio of the work output to the work input. Both are measured in joules. A machine has a work output of $4x^2 + 26x + 12$ joules and a work input of $2x + 1$ joules. Determine the efficiency. $2x + 12$
20. **WRITING MATHEMATICS** Compare simplifying $\frac{30x^3}{2x}$ to simplifying $\frac{6x^2 - 24x - 30}{4x - 20}$. See Additional Answers.

3 SUMMARIZE

In the Math Journal Have students describe how they can use what they have learned about simplifying rational expressions to solve the following equation for x in terms of n: $5nx + 2x = 25n^2 + 20n + 4$. **Factor each side of the equation: $x(5n + 2) = (5n + 2)(5n + 2)$; solve for x: $x = 5n + 2$, $n \neq -2/5$.**

4 PRACTICE

Practice For Exercises 9–17, students will need to look for opposites of polynomial factors. For Exercise 18, suggest that students draw a diagram to visualize the problem. Ask them to evaluate the ratio for $x = 3$. **3/2**

NAME ______ CLASS ______ DATE ______

RETEACHING **14.3 SIMPLIFY RATIONAL EXPRESSIONS**

If the denominator of a rational expression is zero, the expression is undefined. Values for a variable in the denominator must not be ones that will make the denominator zero. Any restrictions on the variable must be found for the original expression, before it is put in simplest form.

Example
State any restrictions on the variable. Then simplify: $\frac{3 + x}{x^2 + 5x + 6}$

Solution

$x^2 + 5x + 6 = 0$
$(x + 3)(x + 2) = 0$ Factor the denominator.
$x + 3 = 0$ $x + 2 = 0$ Set each factor equal to 0.
$x = -3$ $x = -2$

The restrictions on x are $x \neq -3$ and $x \neq -2$. These values would make the denominator zero.

Now, simplify:

$$\frac{3 + x}{x^2 + 5x + 6} = \frac{x + 3}{(x + 3)(x + 2)} = \frac{1}{x + 2}$$

EXERCISES
Simplify each expression. State any restrictions on the variable.

1. $\frac{5x}{20x^2}$ If $20x^2 = 0, x = 0$: $\frac{5x}{20x^2} = \frac{5 \cdot x}{4 \cdot 5 \cdot x \cdot x}$ — 1. $\frac{1}{4x}; x \neq 0$
2. $\frac{9x}{3x + 12}$ If $3x + 12 = 0, 3x = -12, x = -4$. — 2. $\frac{3x}{x + 4}; x \neq -4$
3. $\frac{4x^2}{2x^3}$ — 3. $\frac{2}{x}; x \neq 0$
4. $\frac{10y}{2y - 10}$ — 4. $\frac{5y}{y - 5}; y \neq 5$
5. $\frac{a - 6}{6 - a}$ — 5. $-1; a \neq 6$
6. $\frac{2b - 4}{2b}$ — 6. $\frac{b - 2}{b}; b \neq 0$
7. $\frac{e + 4}{e^2 - e - 20}$ — 7. $\frac{1}{e - 5}; e \neq -4, e \neq 5$
8. $\frac{f - 3}{f^2 + 2f - 15}$ — 8. $\frac{1}{f + 5}; f \neq -5, f \neq 3$

14 South-Western Algebra 1: AN INTEGRATED APPROACH

Extend Have a student describe how to simplify the expression in Exercise 21.

$((x^2 + 1)(x^2 - 1))/((x - 1)(x - 1))$
$= ((x^2 + 1)(x + 1)(x - 1))$
$/((x - 1)(x - 1))$
$= ((x^2 + 1)(x + 1))/(x - 1),$
$x \neq 1$

Think Critically For Exercise 26, ask students to show how they can write x^{2n} as a product of two factors. $x^{2n} = x^{n+n} = x^n x^n$

5 FOLLOW-UP

Extra Practice Simplify each expression. State any restrictions on the variable.

1. $(12x^2)/(2x^4)$ $6/x^2; x \neq 0$
2. $(4z + 8)/12$ $(z + 2)/3$
3. $(x + 1)/(x^2 - 7x - 8)$ $1/(x - 8);$ $x \neq -1, 8$

NAME ______________ CLASS ________ DATE ________

EXTRA PRACTICE **14.3 SIMPLIFY RATIONAL EXPRESSIONS**

State the values of the variable for which each expression is undefined.

1. $\frac{8}{ab}$
2. $\frac{x}{2yz}$
3. $\frac{6}{x + 2}$
4. $\frac{9a}{2a - 14}$
5. $\frac{-2}{(x - 2)(x + 1)}$
6. $\frac{x^2}{(x + 3)(x - 5)}$
7. $\frac{19}{x^2 - 4x + 3}$
8. $\frac{3x}{x^2 - 5x - 6}$

Simplify each expression. State any restrictions on the variable.

9. $\frac{3x}{9x^2}$
10. $\frac{15y^2}{10y^3}$
11. $\frac{4x - 20}{6}$
12. $\frac{5y + 15}{25}$
13. $\frac{2a + 6}{a + 3}$
14. $\frac{9b - 3}{6b - 2}$
15. $\frac{4 - c}{2c - 8}$
16. $\frac{15 - 3d}{4d - 20}$
17. $\frac{x + 5}{x^2 + 2x - 15}$
18. $\frac{y - 1}{y^2 - 2y + 1}$
19. $\frac{2x + 8}{x^2 + 7x + 12}$
20. $\frac{3x - 6}{x^2 - 6x + 8}$

1. $a \neq 0, b \neq 0$
2. $y \neq 0, z \neq 0$
3. $x \neq -2$
4. $a \neq 7$
5. $x \neq 2, x \neq -1$
6. $x \neq -3, x \neq 5$
7. $x \neq 3, x \neq 1$
8. $x \neq 6, x \neq -1$
9. $\frac{1}{3x}; x \neq 0$
10. $\frac{3}{2y}; y \neq 0$
11. $\frac{2(x - 5)}{3}$
12. $\frac{y + 3}{5}$
13. $2; a \neq -3$
14. $\frac{3}{2}; b \neq \frac{1}{3}$
15. $-\frac{1}{2}; c \neq 4$
16. $-\frac{3}{4}; d \neq 5$
17. $\frac{1}{x - 3}; x \neq -5, x \neq 3$
18. $\frac{1}{y - 1}; y \neq 1$
19. $\frac{2}{x + 3}; x \neq -3, x \neq -4$
20. $\frac{3}{x - 4}; x \neq 4, x \neq 2$

16 *South-Western Algebra 1:* AN INTEGRATED APPROACH

EXTEND

Recall that some polynomial expressions must be factored more than once before they are considered to be in simplest form. Be sure to factor completely when factoring rational expressions.

Simplify each expression. State any restrictions on the variable. See Additional Answers.

21. $\frac{x^4 - 1}{x^2 - 2x + 1}$

22. $\frac{x^3 - 6x^2 + 9x}{x^3 - 9x}$

23. $\frac{x^5 + 10x^4 + 25x^3}{x^3 + 4x^2 - 5x}$

THINK CRITICALLY

24. Write an algebraic expression for which the values $\frac{1}{2}$, $-\frac{1}{4}$, and 0 must be excluded. See Additional Answers.
25. Provide an example of a rational expression, the simplified form of which is $\frac{1}{x}$, and which has an x^3 term in the numerator. answers will vary; an example is $\frac{x^3}{x^4}$; $x \neq 0$
26. Simplify: $\frac{x^{2n} + 7x^n + 6}{x^{2n} + 9x^n + 8}$ $\frac{x^n + 6}{x^n + 8}$
27. Given the equation $\frac{(x + y)^q}{(x + y)^p} = x^2 + 2xy + y^2$, write an equation that expresses the relationship between p and q. $q = p + 2$

MIXED REVIEW

28. STANDARDIZED TESTS Choose the correct product. C; Lesson 11.7

$(4 \cdot 10^5)(1.5 \cdot 10^4)$

A. $5.5 \cdot 10^9$ **B.** $6 \cdot 10^{20}$ **C.** $6 \cdot 10^9$ **D.** $6 \cdot 10^{10}$

Write the equation of the line that contains each set of points. Lesson 6.4

29. (4, 7) and (–2, –3) $y = \frac{5}{3}x + \frac{1}{3}$
30. (3, 6) and (4, –8) $y = -14x + 48$

Tell whether the graph of each parabola opens upward or downward. Lesson 10.2

31. $y = -6x^2 + 3$ downward
32. $y = 4x^2 - 3$ upward

PROJECT Connection

In this activity, you will use the formula for the volume of a cylinder, $V = \pi r^2 h$. 1, 3–4 See Additional Answers.

1. In the formula $C = 2\pi r$, C represents the circumference and r represents the radius. Express r in terms of C. Then use your result to express V in terms of C and h.
2. In the Project Connection on page 684 you determined that $h = \frac{93.5}{C}$. Substitute this value for h into the new volume formula you wrote in Question 1. $V = \frac{93.5C}{4\pi}, C \neq 0$
3. Graph the rational function that represents the volume. What are the restrictions on C? Describe and interpret the graph.
4. What are the practical implications of your findings? What dimensions do you recommend for a silo? Justify your response.

Career
Cattle Farmer

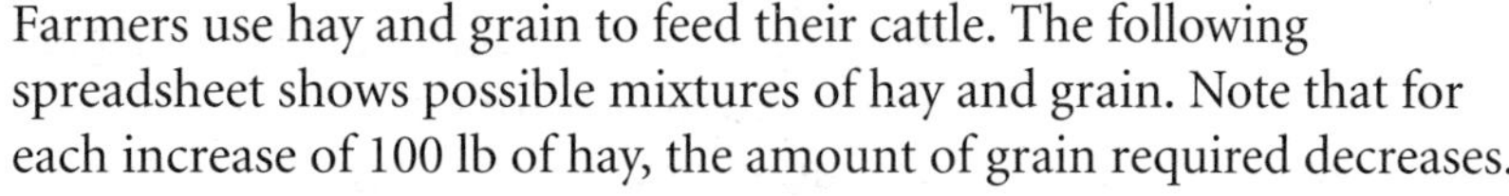

Farmers use hay and grain to feed their cattle. The following spreadsheet shows possible mixtures of hay and grain. Note that for each increase of 100 lb of hay, the amount of grain required decreases.

	A	B	C	D	E
1	Hay	Change in	Grain	Change in	Ratio of Change
2	(lb)	Hay (lb)	(lb)	Grain (lb)	in Grain to
3					Change in Hay
4	1000		1316		
5	1100	100	1259	57	0.57
6	1200	100	1208		
7	1300	100	1162		
8	1400	100	1120		
9	1500	100	1081		
10	1600	100	1046		
11	1700	100	1014		

Decision Making

1. Determine the change in the pounds of grain (Column D) for each 100-lb increase in hay. What formula could you use to calculate this in a spreadsheet? 51; 46; 42; 39; 35; 32; =C4–C5

2. Determine the change in pounds of grain per 100-lb change in hay (Column E). What formula could you use to calculate this in a spreadsheet? 0.51; 0.46; 0.42; 0.39; 0.35; 0.32; =D5/B5

The *price ratio* is the ratio of the price of hay to the price of grain. For example, if the price of grain is \$0.15/lb and the price of hay is \$0.06/lb, the price ratio of hay to grain is $0.06/0.15 = 0.4$. The lowest cost combination occurs when the ratio in Column E is equal to or slightly greater than the price ratio.

3. Determine the first number greater than or equal to 0.4 in Column E. How many pounds of hay and grain does that represent? 0.42; 1400 lb of hay and 1120 lb of grain
4. If the price of hay climbs to \$0.0725/lb, determine the lowest cost combination. 1200 lb of hay and 1208 lb of grain
5. If the price of grain climbs to \$0.165/lb and the price of hay is \$0.06/lb, determine the lowest cost combination. 1500 lb of hay and 1081 lb of grain
6. If the lowest cost combination is 1800 lb of hay and 984 lb of grain and the price of grain is \$0.175/lb, determine the price of hay. \$0.0525/lb

Project Connection This activity presents further aspects of the project introduced on page 674. Review transforming formulas.

AlgebraWorks After students have completed Questions 1 and 2 and have read the paragraph following those exercises, ask them to verify that the lowest cost combination occurs when the number in column 4 is equal to or slightly greater than the price ratio. **Find the cost of each combination by finding the sum of the product of the number of pounds of hay and \$0.06 and the number of pounds of grain and \$0.15.** Have them calculate the cost of each combination. **\$257.40, \$254.85, \$253.20, \$252.30, \$252, \$252.15, \$252.90, \$254.10; \$252, the cost for 1400 lb of hay and 1120 lb of grain, is the lowest**

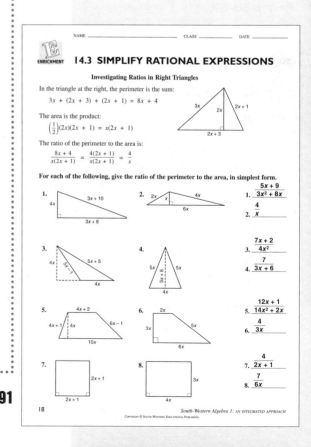

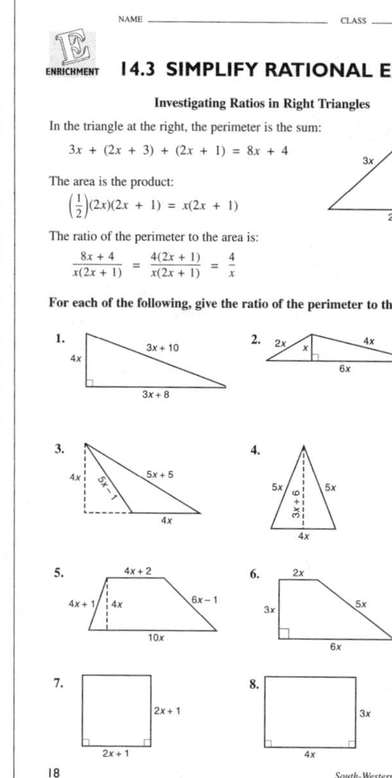

NAME ________ CLASS ________ DATE ________

ENRICHMENT **14.3 SIMPLIFY RATIONAL EXPRESSIONS**

Investigating Ratios in Right Triangles

In the triangle at the right, the perimeter is the sum:

$3x + (2x + 3) + (2x + 1) = 8x + 4$

The area is the product:

$\left(\frac{1}{2}\right)(2x)(2x + 1) = x(2x + 1)$

The ratio of the perimeter to the area is:

$\frac{8x + 4}{x(2x + 1)} = \frac{4(2x + 1)}{x(2x + 1)} = \frac{4}{x}$

For each of the following, give the ratio of the perimeter to the area, in simplest form.

1. $\frac{5x + 9}{3x^2 + 8x}$
2. $\frac{4}{x}$
3. $\frac{7x + 2}{4x^2}$
4. $\frac{7}{3x + 6}$
5. $\frac{12x + 1}{14x^2 + 2x}$
6. $\frac{4}{3x}$
7. $\frac{4}{2x + 1}$
8. $\frac{7}{6x}$

18 *South-Western Algebra 1:* AN INTEGRATED APPROACH

LESSON PLANNING

Objective
▶ Multiply and divide rational expressions.

Vocabulary
reciprocal

Resources
Warm Up 14.4
Reteaching 14.4
Extra Practice 14.4
Enrichment 14.4
Student Handbook
Lesson Quiz 14.4

ASSIGNMENTS

Basic: 1–24, 26–30, Mixed Review 33–39

Average: 1–32, Mixed Review 33–39

Enriched: 5–32, Mixed Review 33–39

1 MOTIVATE

Explore For Question 5, ask students what expression they got before simplifying. **($24x^2/48x$)** Ask them to describe how they simplified the expression. **Divide out the common monomial $24x$.** For Question 6, ask students what expression they got before simplifying. **$2(x + 6)/[x(x + 6)]$** Ask them to describe how they simplified the expression. **Factored out common expressions in the numerator and denominator: $(x + 6)/(x + 6)$** Tell students that in this lesson they will learn how to multiply and divide such expressions in the same way they multiply and divide rational numbers.

14.4 Multiply and Divide Rational Expressions

SPOTLIGHT ON LEARNING

WHAT? In this lesson you will learn
- to multiply and divide rational expressions.
- to find products and quotients of rational expressions in real world settings.

WHY? Multiplying and dividing rational expressions can help you solve problems about physics, geometry, and finance.

Explore

Let $x = 5$ for each of the following. Substitute the value for x. Then multiply the two rational numbers. Recall that to multiply two rational numbers, you multiply the numerators and then multiply the denominators. Simplify your answers. 1–3 See Additional Answers.

1. $\frac{x}{6} \cdot \frac{24}{x}$ **2.** $\frac{3x^2}{4} \cdot \frac{8}{12x}$ **3.** $\frac{x + 6}{x} \cdot \frac{2}{x + 6}$

4. Multiply $\frac{x}{6} \cdot \frac{24}{x}$ by multiplying the numerators and then multiplying the denominators as you would if you were multiplying two rational numbers. What is the result? Simplify the expression. How does the simplified expression compare to your answer for Question 1? $\frac{24x}{6x}$; 4; it is the same as when 5 is substituted for x

5. Multiply $\frac{3x^2}{4} \cdot \frac{8}{12x}$ by the process you used in Question 4. Simplify the expression. How does the simplified expression compare to your answer for Question 2? $\frac{x}{2}$; it is the same as when 5 is substituted for x

6. Use your answer for Question 2 to predict the expression resulting from multiplying the numerators and denominators of the factors in Question 3 and simplifying. Test your prediction.
The multiplied expressions should result in $\frac{2}{x}$.

Build Understanding

As you saw in Explore, the method for finding the product of rational expressions is similar to the method for finding the product of rational numbers.

EXAMPLE 1

Multiply: $\frac{6a^2}{5b} \cdot \frac{b}{3d}$

Solution

$$\frac{6a^2}{5b} \cdot \frac{b}{3d}$$

$$= \frac{6a^2 \cdot b}{5b \cdot 3d} \quad \text{Definition of multiplication.}$$

$$= \frac{\overset{2}{\cancel{6}}a^2 \cdot \cancel{b}}{5\cancel{b} \cdot \cancel{3}d} \quad \text{Divide out common factors.}$$

$$= \frac{2a^2}{5d} \quad \text{Simplify.}$$

When multiplying rational expressions, the polynomials need to be factored completely before you divide out any common factors.

EXAMPLE 2

Multiply: $\frac{x}{x + 2} \cdot \frac{3x + 6}{x^2 - 4x}$

Solution

$$\frac{x}{x + 2} \cdot \frac{3x + 6}{x^2 - 4x}$$

$$= \frac{x}{(x + 2)} \cdot \frac{3(x + 2)}{x(x - 4)} \quad \text{Factor.}$$

$$= \frac{\cancel{x}}{\cancel{(x + 2)}} \cdot \frac{3\cancel{(x + 2)}}{\cancel{x}(x - 4)} \quad \text{Divide out common factors.}$$

$$= \frac{3}{(x - 4)} \quad \text{Simplify.}$$

CHECK UNDERSTANDING

In Example 2, what is the GCF of the numerator and denominator?

$x(x + 2)$; the GCF consists of all those factors common to both polynomials, which may be divided out

The method for determining the quotient of rational expressions is similar to the method for determining the quotient of rational numbers. To divide one rational expression by another, multiply the first by the reciprocal of the second. After that, proceed as in multiplication, factoring polynomials completely and dividing out common factors.

EXAMPLE 3

Divide: $\frac{(x + 2)}{x} \div \frac{(x - 2)}{x^2}$

Solution

$$\frac{(x + 2)}{x} \div \frac{x - 2}{x^2}$$

$$= \frac{(x + 2)}{x} \cdot \frac{x^2}{(x - 2)} \quad \text{Multiply by the reciprocal of the divisor.}$$

$$= \frac{(x + 2)}{\cancel{x}} \cdot \frac{\cancel{x} \cdot x}{(x - 2)} \quad \text{Divide out } x \text{, the common factor.}$$

$$= \frac{x(x + 2)}{(x - 2)} \quad \text{Simplify.}$$

To multiply a rational expression by a polynomial such as $3x + 1$, for example, rewrite the polynomial as $\frac{3x + 1}{1}$. To divide a rational expression by $3x + 1$, multiply the rational expression by the reciprocal of $3x + 1$, or $\frac{1}{3x + 1}$.

ALGEBRA: WHO, WHERE, WHEN

In the early 17th century, German astronomer Johannes Kepler discovered that the orbits of the planets were not circular but elliptical. He also discovered the direct relation between the distance between the sun and a planet and the rate at which the planet moves in its orbit. Specifically, the cube of the mean distance d between a planet and the sun divided by the square of its orbital period t is constant $\left(\frac{d^3}{t^2}\right)$. This is critical in understanding the paths of moons, planets, and our satellites launched from Earth.

2 TEACH

Use the Pages/Build Understanding

Example 1: Ask students what common expression was factored out of the numerator and denominator. **3*b***

Example 2: Ask students what the GCF is. ***x*(*x* + 2).** Point out that those cancelled factors have a value of 1. Ask students to describe how to divide 45/64 by 18/24. **Multiply 45/64 by the reciprocal of 18/24 and factor out the GCF;**

$$\mathbf{\frac{15}{16}}$$

Example 3: Ask why the numerator and denominator were not factored further in the final step. **because the GCF of both the numerator and the denominator is 1** Ask why the 2's were not divided out to give $x^2/x = x$. **You can only divide out common factors, and 2 is not a factor (or multiple) of either numerator or denominator.**

Example 4: Ask what the reciprocal of $6x - 24$ is. **1/(6*x* – 24)** Ask why 2 is not factored out of the answer, $(x + 4)/(6x - 12)$. **Although 2 is a factor in the denominator 6*x* – 12, it is not a factor of the numerator *x* + 4.** Stress once again that you can only divide out common *factors* and 2 is not a factor of $x + 4$.

Ongoing Assessment The important concepts and skills are multiplying and dividing rational expressions. To assess these ideas, have students demonstrate how they have applied these concepts and skills in Exercises 6 and 7 of the Try These section.

Guided Practice/Try These Have a student describe how to find the quotient in Exercise 12. **Multiply by the reciprocal of the divisor and factor completely.**

For Exercise 14, ask students how they determined the expression for the work done. **multiplied force by distance:**

$$\frac{(x + 4)}{(x^2 - 16)} \cdot \frac{(x^2 + 13x + 42)}{(x + 6)}$$

TEACHING TIP

Suggest that students check their answers by substituting possible values for variables in the original expressions and in their answer. If they get the same result, the answer should be correct.

NAME ______ CLASS ______ DATE ______

RETEACHING

14.4 MULTIPLY AND DIVIDE RATIONAL EXPRESSIONS

Multiplying and dividing rational expressions is like multiplying and dividing fractions. You can divide out common factors from the numerator and denominator of a rational expression. To help you find all the common factors, write all polynomials in factored form.

Example
Multiply: $\frac{12x}{2x - 8} \cdot \frac{3x - 12}{14x^2}$

Solution
Rewrite $\frac{12x}{2x - 8} \cdot \frac{3x - 12}{14x^2}$ in factored form.

$$\frac{2 \cdot 2 \cdot 3 \cdot x}{2 \cdot (x - 4)} \cdot \frac{3 \cdot (x - 4)}{2 \cdot 7 \cdot x \cdot x}$$

$$= \frac{\cancel{2} \cdot \cancel{2} \cdot 3 \cdot \cancel{x}}{\cancel{2} \cdot \cancel{(x - 4)}} \cdot \frac{3 \cdot \cancel{(x - 4)}}{\cancel{2} \cdot 7 \cdot \cancel{x} \cdot x} \quad \text{Divide out common factors.}$$

$$= \frac{3}{1} \cdot \frac{3}{7x} = \frac{9}{7x} \quad \text{Simplify.}$$

EXERCISES

Perform the indicated operations.

1. $\frac{2x}{3} \cdot \frac{9x^2}{16x}$
2. $\frac{5x}{4x + 10} \cdot \frac{14x + 35}{25x}$
3. $\frac{4a^2}{3b} \cdot \frac{18b^3}{12a^4}$
4. $\frac{21y - 7}{8y + 16} \cdot \frac{4y + 8}{12y - 4}$
5. $\frac{15c^4}{5d} \div \frac{20c}{50d^2}$
6. $\frac{2x - 14}{8x - 16} \div \frac{x^2 - 8x + 7}{9x^2 - 18x}$

1. $\frac{3x^2}{8}$
2. $\frac{7}{10}$
3. $\frac{2b^2}{a^2}$
4. $\frac{7}{8}$
5. $\frac{15d}{2}$
6. $\frac{9x}{4(x - 1)}$

22 *South-Western Algebra 1: AN INTEGRATED APPROACH*

CHECK UNDERSTANDING

Express 1 N in the units of mass and acceleration.

$1 \text{ N} = 1 \text{ kg} \cdot \text{m/s}^2$

EXAMPLE 4

PHYSICS Newton's second law states that the force in newtons N is equal to the product of the mass in kg and the acceleration in m/s^2. So, $F = ma$.

If the force on an object is $\left(\frac{x^2 - 16}{x - 2}\right)$ newtons and the mass is $(6x - 24)$ kilograms, determine the acceleration of the object.

Solution

$$a = F \div m \qquad \text{Since } F = ma.$$

$$a = \frac{x^2 - 16}{x - 2} \div (6x - 24)$$

$$= \frac{x^2 - 16}{(x - 2)} \cdot \frac{1}{6x - 24} \qquad \text{Multiply by the reciprocal.}$$

$$= \frac{(x + 4)(x - 4)}{(x - 2)} \cdot \frac{1}{6(x - 4)} \qquad \text{Factor.}$$

$$= \frac{(x + 4)\cancel{(x - 4)}}{(x - 2)} \cdot \frac{1}{6\cancel{(x - 4)}} \qquad \text{Divide out common factors.}$$

$$= \frac{(x + 4)1}{(x - 2)6} \qquad \text{Multiply.}$$

$$= \frac{x + 4}{6x - 12}$$

The acceleration of the object is $\frac{x + 4}{6x - 12}$ m/s^2.

TRY THESE

Perform the indicated operation.

1. $\frac{3x}{5} \cdot \frac{10}{12x}$ $\frac{1}{2}$
2. $\frac{4x^2}{7} \cdot \frac{14}{5x}$ $\frac{8x}{5}$
3. $\frac{1}{4n} \div \frac{6n}{15}$ $\frac{5}{8n^2}$
4. $\frac{7r^2}{5} \div \frac{3r}{21}$ $\frac{49r}{5}$
5. $\frac{ab^2}{c} \cdot \frac{3c^2}{b}$ $3abc$
6. $\frac{2u^2}{v^2w} \cdot \frac{vw^2}{5}$ $\frac{2u^2w}{5v}$
7. $\frac{4d^2}{7e} \div \frac{8d}{e^2}$ $\frac{de}{14}$
8. $\frac{3q^2r^2}{4} \div \frac{9qr}{3}$ $\frac{qr}{4}$
9. $\frac{m - 3}{6(m + 4)} \cdot \frac{3(m + 4)}{m - 3}$ $\frac{1}{2}$
10. $\frac{x - 6}{8x + 12} \cdot \frac{10x + 15}{3x - 18}$ $\frac{5}{12}$
11. $\frac{(3x + 6)(x - 1)}{12x} \div \frac{(x + 2)}{8}$ $\frac{2x - 2}{x}$
12. $\frac{3x^2 - 10x - 8}{6x} \div \frac{2x^2 - 32}{-5x - 20}$ $-\frac{15x + 10}{12x}$
13. **WRITING MATHEMATICS** Write a paragraph that compares and contrasts multiplying $\frac{2}{3} \cdot \frac{1}{4}$ to multiplying $\frac{2}{3x} \cdot \frac{x}{4}$. See Additional Answers.

14. **Physics** In physics, the term *work* represents a force multiplied by the distance a body moves in the direction of the force applied. That is, $W = Fd$, where W represents work, or energy, in joules, F represents force in newtons, and d is the distance through which the force is applied (1 joule = 1 newton • 1 meter).

If a body moves $\frac{x^2 + 13x + 42}{(x + 6)}$ meters in the direction of a force of $\left(\frac{x + 4}{x^2 - 16}\right)$ newtons, determine the work. $\frac{x + 7}{x - 4}$ joules

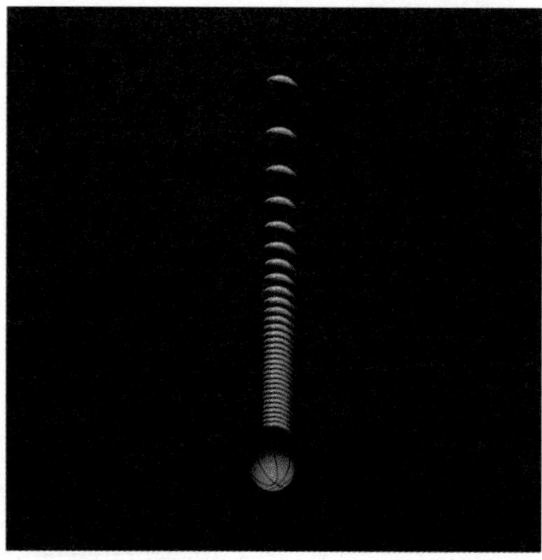

PRACTICE

Perform the indicated operation.

1. $\frac{5x}{7} \cdot \frac{14}{6x}$ $\quad \frac{5}{3}$
2. $\frac{1}{6x} \cdot \frac{18x^2}{11}$ $\quad \frac{3x}{11}$
3. $\frac{1}{5k} \div \frac{3}{20k^2}$ $\quad \frac{4k}{3}$
4. $\frac{8n}{5} \div \frac{5}{24n^2}$ $\quad \frac{192n^3}{25}$
5. $\frac{a^2b}{c} \cdot \frac{2ac^2}{a}$ $\quad 2a^2bc$
6. $\frac{wu^2}{v^2w} \cdot \frac{v^2w}{3u}$ $\quad \frac{wu}{3}$
7. $\frac{5c^2d}{9ce^2} \div \frac{15c^2d^2}{18e}$ $\quad \frac{2}{3cde}$
8. $\frac{8qr^2}{12qr} \div \frac{9qrs}{6s}$ $\quad \frac{4}{9q}$
9. $\frac{m - 5}{2(m + 6)} \cdot \frac{4(m + 6)}{8(m - 5)}$ $\quad \frac{1}{4}$
10. $\frac{x - 3}{6(2x + 1)} \cdot \frac{3(2x + 1)}{4(x - 3)}$ $\quad \frac{1}{8}$
11. $\frac{4(x + 3)(x - 2)}{6x} \div \frac{(x + 3)(x - 3)}{3(x - 3)}$ $\quad \frac{2x - 4}{x}$
12. $\frac{(2x + 3)(x - 5)}{4x} \div \frac{3(x + 5)(x - 5)}{6(x + 5)}$ $\quad \frac{2x + 3}{2x}$
13. $\frac{7x + 35}{3x^2 - 108} \cdot (6x + 36)$ $\quad \frac{14x + 70}{x - 6}$
14. $\frac{8x + 32}{4x^2 - 100} \cdot (3x - 15)$ $\quad \frac{6x + 24}{x + 5}$
15. $\frac{x^2 - 49}{x^2 - x - 42} \div (3x + 21)$ $\quad \frac{1}{3x + 18}$
16. $\frac{x^2 - 16}{x^2 - 7x + 12} \div (5x + 20)$ $\quad \frac{1}{5x - 15}$
17. $\frac{3x^2 - 17x - 6}{3x^2 - 108} \cdot \frac{5x}{-21x - 7}$ $\quad -\frac{5x}{21x + 126}$
18. $\frac{2x^2 + x - 10}{5x^2 - 20} \cdot \frac{5x}{-6x - 15}$ $\quad -\frac{x}{3x + 6}$
19. $\frac{x^2 + x - 6}{x^2 - 9} \div \frac{x^2 - 4}{7x - 21}$ $\quad \frac{7}{x + 2}$
20. $\frac{x^2 + 5x - 36}{x^2 - 81} \div \frac{x^2 - 16}{6x - 54}$ $\quad \frac{6}{x + 4}$

Geometry Find the area of each rectangle.

21. length: $\frac{6x - x^2}{2x + 4}$, width: $\frac{x^2 - 4}{36 - x^2}$ $\quad \frac{x^2 - 2x}{12 + 2x}$
22. length: $\frac{a^2 - 1}{ab^2 - b}$, width: $\frac{b}{3 - 3a}$ $\quad -\frac{a + 1}{3ab - 3}$

23. **Writing Mathematics** Explain or make a flowchart of the steps you would use to divide one rational expression by another rational expression. Answers will vary.

3 SUMMARIZE

In the Math Journal Have students explain why the answer to the following division is not correct.

$$\frac{x^2 + 3}{x + 3} = x + 1$$

The GCF is 1, so the two terms are already relatively prime. This expression cannot be divided.

4 PRACTICE

Practice For Exercise 9, ask a volunteer to explain how to simplify the expression.

$$= \frac{(m - 5) \cdot 4(m + 6)}{2(m + 6) \cdot 8(m - 5)}$$

$$= \frac{\cancel{(m - 5)} \cdot 4\cancel{(m + 6)}}{2\cancel{(m + 6)} \cdot 8\cancel{(m - 5)}}$$

$$= \frac{4}{16} = \frac{1}{4}$$

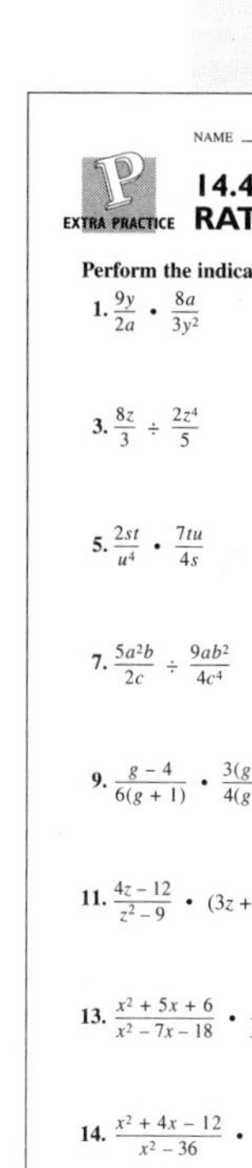
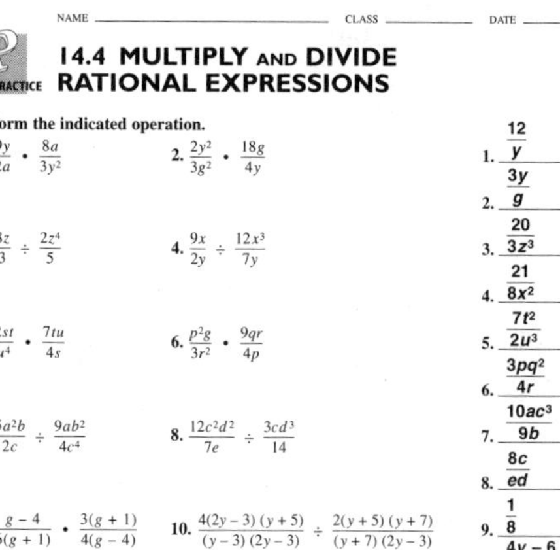
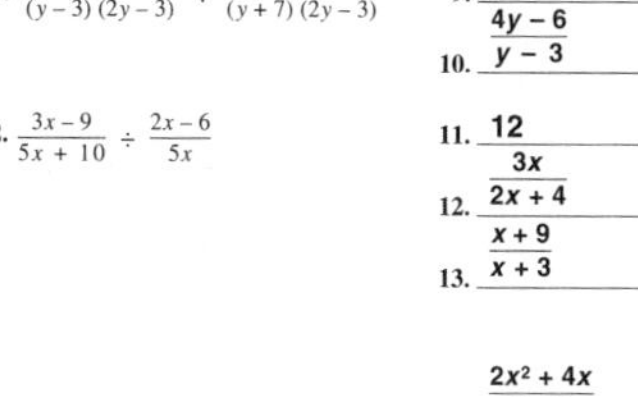

NAME ______________ CLASS ________ DATE ________

EXTRA PRACTICE
14.4 MULTIPLY AND DIVIDE RATIONAL EXPRESSIONS

Perform the indicated operation.

1. $\frac{9y}{2a} \cdot \frac{8a}{3y^2}$ — 1. $\frac{12}{y}$
2. $\frac{2y^2}{3g^2} \cdot \frac{18g}{4y}$ — 2. $\frac{3y}{g}$
3. $\frac{8z}{3} \div \frac{2z^4}{5}$ — 3. $\frac{20}{3z^3}$
4. $\frac{9x}{2y} \div \frac{12x^3}{7y}$ — 4. $\frac{21}{8x^2}$
5. $\frac{2st}{u^4} \cdot \frac{7tu}{4s}$ — 5. $\frac{7t^2}{2u^3}$
6. $\frac{p^2g}{3r^2} \cdot \frac{9qr}{4p}$ — 6. $\frac{3pq^2}{4r}$
7. $\frac{5a^2b}{2c} \div \frac{9ab^2}{4c^4}$ — 7. $\frac{10ac^3}{9b}$
8. $\frac{12c^2d^2}{7e} \div \frac{3cd^3}{14}$ — 8. $\frac{8c}{ed}$
9. $\frac{g - 4}{6(g + 1)} \cdot \frac{3(g + 1)}{4(g - 4)}$ — 9. $\frac{1}{8}$
10. $\frac{4(2y - 3)(y + 5)}{(y - 3)(2y - 3)} \div \frac{2(y + 5)(y + 7)}{(y + 7)(2y - 3)}$ — 10. $\frac{4y - 6}{y - 3}$
11. $\frac{4z - 12}{z^2 - 9} \cdot (3z + 9)$ — 11. 12
12. $\frac{3x - 9}{5x + 10} \div \frac{2x - 6}{5x}$ — 12. $\frac{3x}{2x + 4}$
13. $\frac{x^2 + 5x + 6}{x^2 - 7x - 18} \cdot \frac{x^2 - 81}{x^2 + 6x + 9}$ — 13. $\frac{x + 9}{x + 3}$
14. $\frac{x^2 + 4x - 12}{x^2 - 36} \cdot \frac{2x^2 - 12x}{x - 1}$ — 14. $\frac{2x^2 + 4x}{x - 1}$
15. **Geometry** The area of a rectangle can be represented by $\frac{x^2}{8}$. Write an expression for the width if the length is $\frac{2x}{3}$. — 15. $\frac{3x}{16}$

24 *South-Western Algebra 1: An Integrated Approach*

For Exercise 19, ask students to find the quotient. **Multiply by the reciprocal, factor, and simplify.**

Extend For Exercises 26–28, ask students how they can determine ratios. **Divide one rational expression by the other.**

Think Critically For Exercises 29 and 30, ask students how they found two different pairs of rational expressions with the given products. **Factor the numerator and the denominator. Then rearrange the factors.**

5 FOLLOW-UP

Extension Have students work with partners to simplify the expression.

$$\frac{\dfrac{3x^2 - 12}{x^2 - x - 2}}{\dfrac{x^2 + 3x + 2}{6x^2 - 6}}$$

NAME ______ CLASS ______ DATE ______

ENRICHMENT

14.4 MULTIPLY AND DIVIDE RATIONAL EXPRESSIONS

One way to check a product or quotient of rational numbers is to substitute a value for the variable or variables. Be sure that the value doesn't result in a denominator of 0.

Example

Use substitution to determine if the product is correct.

$$\frac{9x^2}{5x - 15} \cdot \frac{4x - 12}{18x} = \frac{2x}{5}$$

Solution

To check, let $x = 2$.

$$\frac{9(2)^2}{5(2) - 15} \cdot \frac{4(2) - 12}{18(2)} = \frac{2(2)}{5}$$

$$\frac{36}{10 - 15} \cdot \frac{8 - 12}{36} = \frac{4}{5}$$

$$\frac{1}{-5} \cdot \frac{-4}{1} = \frac{4}{5}$$

$$\frac{-4}{-5} = \frac{4}{5} \checkmark$$

So, the given product is correct.

Use substitution to determine whether each product or quotient is correct. If it is incorrect, give the correct answer.

1. $\frac{14x^4}{3x + 15} \cdot \frac{x^2 - 25}{7x^2 - 35x} = \frac{2x^4}{3}$ — 1. incorrect; $\frac{2x^3}{3}$
2. $\frac{10y - 5}{15} \cdot \frac{12y + 6}{8y^2 - 2} = 1$ — 2. correct
3. $\frac{6x + 3}{2x + 10} \cdot \frac{4x - 20}{12x + 6} = 2$ — 3. incorrect; $\frac{(x - 5)}{(x + 5)}$
4. $\frac{5x + 20}{x^2 + 7x + 12} \cdot \frac{x^2 - 9}{10x - 30} = \frac{1}{2}$ — 4. correct
5. $\frac{2x}{4x - 10} \div \frac{5x^2}{6x - 15} = \frac{3}{5x}$ — 5. correct
6. $\frac{3x^2}{2x + 8} \div \frac{9x}{3x + 12} = \frac{9x^3}{2x^2 + 16x + 12}$ — 6. incorrect; $\frac{x}{2}$
7. $\frac{3}{x^2 - 3x} \div \frac{3x + 6}{x^2 - x - 6} = x$ — 7. incorrect; $\frac{1}{x}$
8. $\frac{a^2 + 4a}{a^2 + 3a - 4} \div \frac{a^3}{2a - 2} = \frac{1}{a^2}$ — 8. incorrect; $\frac{2}{a^2}$

26 South-Western Algebra 1: AN INTEGRATED APPROACH

EXTEND

To simplify rational expressions that involve both multiplication and division, perform operations from left to right unless otherwise indicated by parentheses.

Perform the indicated operation.

24. $\frac{18 - 4x}{3x + 2} \div \frac{6x - 18}{-(6x + 4)} \cdot \frac{3x - 9}{81 - 4x^2}$ $-\frac{2}{9 + 2x}$

25. $\frac{t^2 - t}{t^2 - 2t - 3} \cdot \frac{t^2 + 2t + 1}{t^2 + 4t} \div \frac{t^2 - 3t - 4}{2t^2 - 32}$ $\frac{2t - 2}{t - 3}$

FINANCE Before making a loan to a company, a bank conducts a *ratio analysis* to determine how the company is doing in the marketplace.

26. The *current ratio*, the ratio of current assets to current liabilities, is one measure of the liquidity (convertibility of assets to cash) of the company. If the current assets can be represented by $\frac{2x^2 + 4x - 30}{2x^2 - 18}$ and the liabilities by $\frac{3x + 15}{4x + 12}$, determine the current ratio. $\frac{4}{3}$ or 4:3

27. *Leverage* is the firm's debt in relation to its equity. If the debt can be represented by $\frac{2x^2 - 2x - 4}{4x - 8}$ and the equity by $\frac{x^2 - 1}{4x - 4}$, determine the *debt to equity ratio*. 2 or 2:1

28. *Profitability ratios* measure how efficiently a company is managed. The *profit margin* is the ratio of the gross profit to the net sales. If the net sales can be represented by $10x^2 + 30x + 20$ and the gross profit by $\frac{x^3 + 3x^2 + 2x}{x}$, determine the profit margin. $\frac{1}{10}$ or 1:10

THINK CRITICALLY

See Additional Answers.

29. Find two different pairs of rational expressions whose product is $\frac{x^2 + 7x + 10}{3x^2 - 3}$.

30. Find two different pairs of rational expressions whose product is $\frac{m^2 - m - 6}{2m^2 + 5m - 3}$.

31. Find two different pairs of rational expressions whose quotient is $\frac{3x}{x - 5}$.

32. Find two different pairs of rational expressions whose quotient is $\frac{x + 4}{x + 6}$.

MIXED REVIEW

33. STANDARDIZED TESTS The absolute value equation $|3 - 4x| = 12$ can be expressed as C; Lesson 9.3

A. $3 - 4x = 12$ and $3 - 4x = -12$
B. $3 - 4x = 12$ or $-3 + 4x = -12$
C. $3 - 4x = 12$ or $3 - 4x = -12$
D. $3 - 4x > 12$ and $3 - 4x < -12$

Find the constant of variation *k* if *y* varies directly as *x*. Lesson 6.7

34. $y = 8.1, x = 9$ 0.9

35. $y = 9.9, x = 3.3$ 3

Solve each inequality. Lesson 5.3

36. $-3x > x - 16$ $x < 4$

37. $6x + 12 < 3x + 6$ $x < -2$

Perform the indicated operation. Lesson 14.4

38. $\frac{x^2 + 2x - 15}{25 - x^2} \cdot \frac{x^2 - 4x - 5}{x^2 - 2x - 3}$ -1

39. $\frac{x - 3}{x - 6} \div \frac{x^2 - 9}{x^2 - 2x - 24}$ $\frac{x + 4}{x + 3}$

14.5 Divide Polynomials

Explore

Use Algeblocks and the quadrant mat to divide a polynomial by a monomial .

Divide: $\frac{2x^2 - 4x}{2x}$

Place the divisor, $2x$, in the horizontal axis.

Use blocks for $2x^2 - 4x$ to form rectangular areas with $2x$ as their boundaries.

Determine the other dimension of the rectangular area. Read the answer from the mat: $x - 2$.

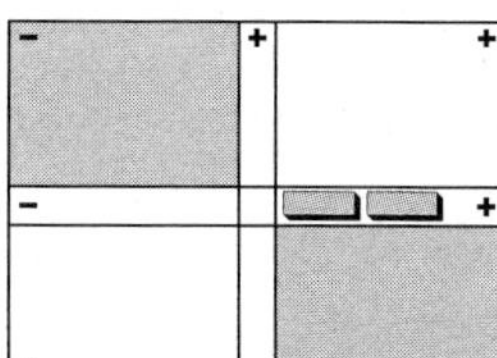

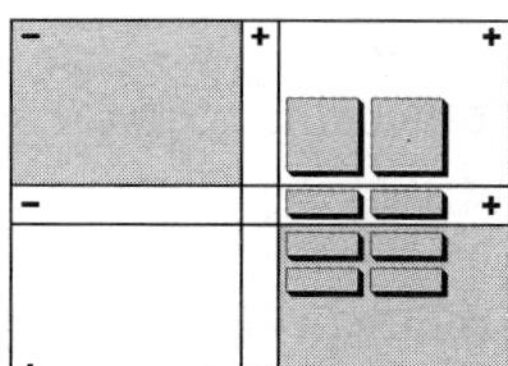

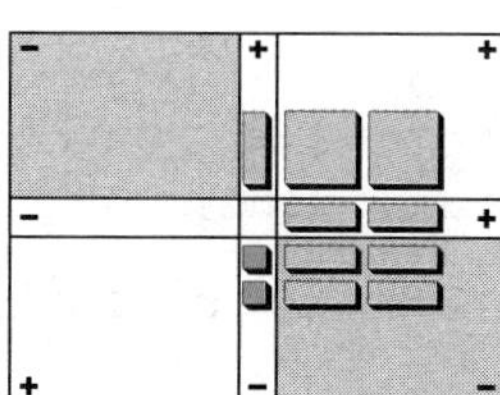

Using Algeblocks, you can divide a polynomial by a binomial.

Divide: $\frac{2x^2 - 8x}{x - 4}$

Place the divisor, $x - 4$, in the horizontal axis.

Use blocks for $2x^2 - 8x$ to form rectangular areas with $x - 4$ as their boundaries.

Determine the other dimension of the rectangular area. Read the answer from the mat, $2x$.

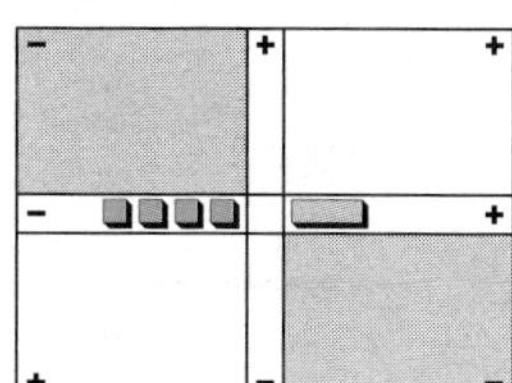

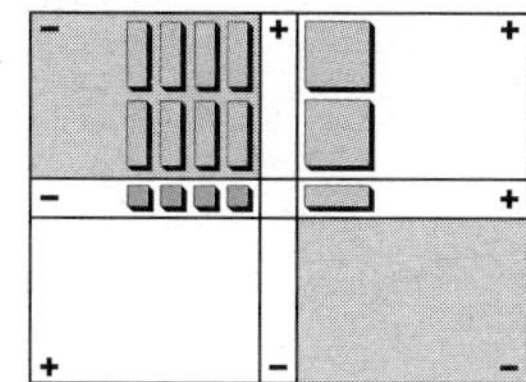

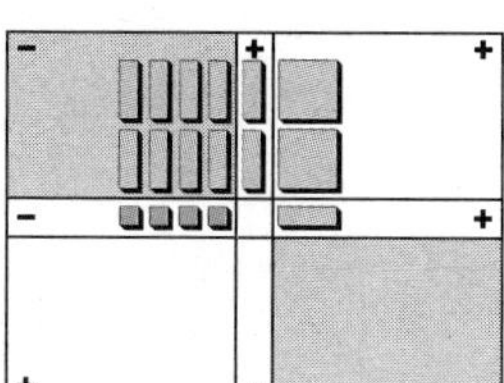

Use Algeblocks and a quadrant mat to divide.

1. $\frac{3x^2 - 6x}{3x}$ $x - 2$
2. $\frac{x^2 + 2x}{x}$ $x + 2$
3. $\frac{3x^2 + 6x}{x + 2}$ $3x$
4. $\frac{x^2 - x}{x - 1}$ x

SPOTLIGHT ON LEARNING

WHAT? In this lesson you will learn

- to divide one polynomial by another polynomial.

WHY? You can use division of polynomials to solve problems in geometry, automobile depreciation, and biology.

LESSON PLANNING

Objective

▶ Divide one polynomial by another polynomial.

Technology/Multimedia

graphing utility

Resources

Warm Up 14.5
Reteaching 14.5
Extra Practice 14.5
Enrichment 14.5
Transparencies 12, 21, 78–80
Student Handbook
Lesson Quiz 14.5
Technology Activity 34

Materials/Manipulatives

Algeblocks
Quadrant Mats

ASSIGNMENTS

Basic: 1–15, 17–20, 22, Mixed Review 25–28

Average: 1–23, Mixed Review 25–28

Enriched: 1–24, Mixed Review 25–28

1 MOTIVATE

Explore Remind students that they have used Algeblocks this way for a different procedure. Ask them what that procedure was. **factoring** Ask how factoring is like dividing. **In both you are looking for factors to place on the crosspiece of the Quadrant Mat.**

2 TEACH

Use the Pages/Build Understanding Ask students to show how to factor $4x^3 + 8x^2 - 6x$. $\mathbf{2x(2x^2 + 4x - 3)}$ Explain that to factor, each term of the polynomial is divided by $2x$.

Example 1: Ask students to explain how to simplify from step 2 to step 3. $\mathbf{(12x^4)/(4x^3) = (12/4)x^{4-3} = 3x;}$ $\mathbf{(4x^3)/(4x^3) = 1; -x^2/(4x^3) =}$ $\mathbf{-x^{2-3}/4 = -x^{-1}/4 = -1/4x}$

Example 2: Explain that dividing polynomials by long division is like using long division to divide whole numbers.

Ask students to arrange the terms of the polynomial $4x^2 - 3x + 2x^3 - 7$ in descending order of the exponents of the x variable. $\mathbf{2x^3 + 4x^2 - 3x - 7}$

Example 3: Ask students why the place holder of $0x^2$ is included in the polynomial. **As with whole numbers, each place must have a value.** Stress the importance of arranging both the dividend and the divisor in descending order of exponents and of inserting place holders for missing terms. Have students read Check Understanding to check the solution.

Example 4: Ask students to explain why they will get the surface area of the base of the prism by dividing the volume by the height of the cube. **because $V = lwh$, $lwh/h = lw$, which is the area of the base**

Ongoing Assessment The important concepts and skills involve dividing one polynomial by another polynomial. To assess this idea, have students demonstrate how they have applied it in Exercises 1 and 4 of the Try These section.

Guided Practice/Try These For Exercise 5, ask students how they can find the quotient. **by factoring** For Exercise 8, ask students to explain how they should write the dividend for long division. $\mathbf{d^3 + 0d^2 + 0d + 12}$

CHECK UNDERSTANDING

Explain the steps of dividing, multiplying, and subtracting used to complete this long division. Express the answer as a quotient plus a remainder.

$$
\begin{array}{r}
216 + \frac{41}{45} \\
45\,\overline{)\,9761} \\
\underline{90} \\
76 \\
\underline{45} \\
311 \\
\underline{270} \\
41
\end{array}
$$

See Additional Answers.

Build Understanding

Recall that to divide a polynomial by a monomial, each term of the polynomial must be divided by the monomial.

EXAMPLE 1

Divide: $(12x^4 + 4x^3 - x^2) \div 4x^3$

Solution

$$\frac{12x^4 + 4x^3 - x^2}{4x^3}$$

$$= \frac{12x^4}{4x^3} + \frac{4x^3}{4x^3} - \frac{x^2}{4x^3} \quad \text{Divide each term.}$$

$$= 3x + 1 - \frac{1}{4x}$$

To find the quotient of two polynomials with common factors, use the techniques you learned earlier in the chapter. To divide one polynomial by another when they have no common factors, use long division. Note that

$$\frac{\text{dividend}}{\text{divisor}} = \text{quotient} + \frac{\text{remainder}}{\text{divisor}}, \text{ or}$$

$$\text{dividend} = \text{quotient} \cdot \text{divisor} + \text{remainder}$$

EXAMPLE 2

Divide and check: $\dfrac{3a^2 + 2a + 4}{a - 2}$

Solution

$$
\begin{array}{r}
3a + 8 \\
a - 2\,\overline{)\,3a^2 + 2a + 4} \\
\underline{3a^2 - 6a} \\
8a + 4 \\
\underline{8a - 16} \\
20
\end{array}
$$

Divide: Think $3a^2 \div a = 3a$.
Multiply: $(a - 2)(3a) = 3a^2 - 6a$.
Subtract: $(3a^2 + 2a) - (3a^2 - 6a) = 8a$.
Bring down the 4.
Divide: Think $8a \div a = 8$.
Multiply: $(a - 2)(8) = 8a - 16$.
Subtract: $(8a + 4) - (8a - 16) = 20$.

So, $\dfrac{3a^2 + 2a - 4}{a - 2} = 3a + 8 + \dfrac{20}{a - 2}$. Write the remainder as a rational expression.

Check

$$\text{dividend} = \text{quotient} \cdot \text{divisor} + \text{remainder}$$

$$3a^2 + 2a + 4 \stackrel{?}{=} (3a + 8)(a - 2) + 20$$

$$\stackrel{?}{=} 3a^2 + 8a - 6a - 16 + 20$$

$$= 3a^2 + 2a + 4 \checkmark$$

Before dividing one polynomial by another, arrange the terms of the polynomials in descending order of the exponents of a variable. If the dividend or the divisor has missing terms, insert these terms with zero coefficients.

EXAMPLE 3

Divide: $(-5x - 3 + 4x^3) \div (3 + 2x)$

Solution

Arrange each expression in descending powers of exponents.

$$(4x^3 - 5x - 3) \div (2x + 3)$$

Use $0x^2$ as a place holder for the missing x^2 term.

$$(4x^3 + 0x^2 - 5x - 3) \div (2x + 3)$$

$$\begin{array}{rllll} & 2x^2 & -\ 3x & +\ 2 & \\ 2x + 3\,\big) & 4x^3 + 0x^2 & -\ 5x & -\ 3 & \\ & \underline{4x^3 + 6x^2} & & & \\ & -6x^2 & -\ 5x & & \\ & \underline{-6x^2} & \underline{-\ 9x} & & \\ & & 4x & -\ 3 & \\ & & \underline{4x} & \underline{+\ 6} & \\ & & & -9 & \end{array}$$

Use long division.

So, $\dfrac{-5x - 3 + 4x^3}{(3 + 2x)} = 2x^2 - 3x + 2 - \dfrac{9}{2x - 3}$. ◄

Division of polynomials can be applied to geometry.

EXAMPLE 4

GEOMETRY The volume of a rectangular prism is $(2x^3 + x^2 - 22x + 3)$ in.^{3} Find the surface area of the base of the rectangular prism if the height of the prism is $(x - 3)$ in.

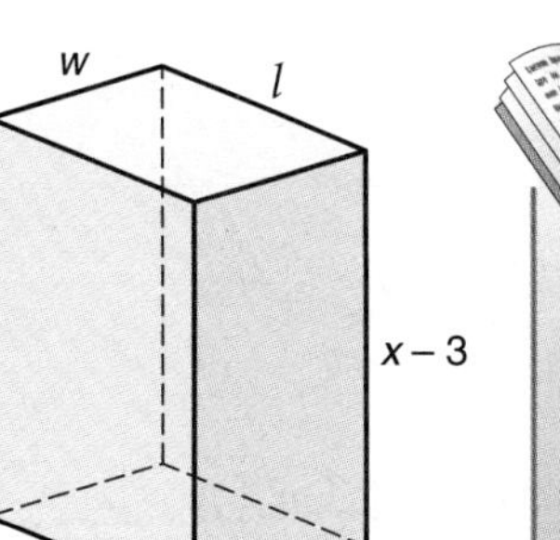

Solution

Find the surface area of the base lw by dividing the volume lwh by the height h.

$$\begin{array}{rllll} & 2x^2 & +\ 7x & -\ 1 & \\ x - 3\,\big) & 2x^3 + x^2 & -\ 22x & +\ 3 & \\ & \underline{2x^3 - 6x^2} & & & \\ & 7x^2 & -\ 22x & & \\ & \underline{7x^2} & \underline{-\ 21x} & & \\ & & -x & +\ 3 & \\ & & \underline{-x} & \underline{+\ 3} & \\ & & & 0 & \end{array}$$

The surface area of the base of the prism is $(2x^2 + 7x - 1)$ in.^{2} ◄

CHECK UNDERSTANDING

Check the solution for Example 3. Use the general equation that was given to check the solution for Example 2.

See Additional Answers.

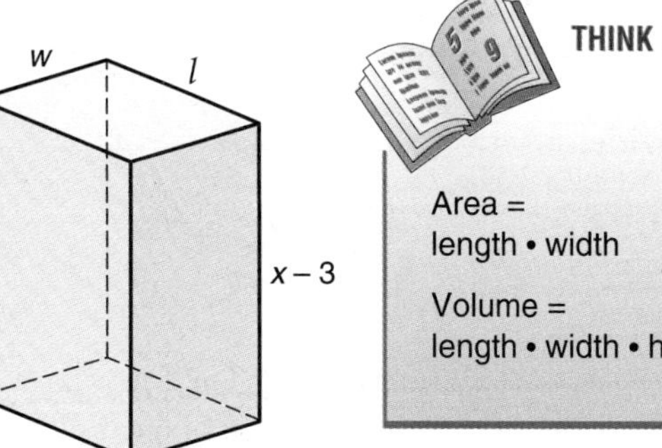

THINK BACK

Area = length • width

Volume = length • width • height

3 SUMMARIZE

In the Math Journal For *a* and *b* below, have students find each quotient and record each step in their journal. Ask them to write a paragraph explaining why they chose the method they did.

a. $(x^2 - x - 30) \div (x + 5)$ **$x - 6$**

b. $(x^2 + 2x - 3) \div (x + 5)$ **$x - 3 + 12/(x + 5)$**

4 PRACTICE

Practice Tell students that they may choose to factor rather than divide. Remind them to write the dividend and the divisor in descending order of the exponents and to use place-holders when necessary. For Exercises 14–16, ask students to define the term *depreciation*. **decrease in value**

NAME ____________ CLASS ________ DATE ________

RETEACHING

14.5 DIVIDE POLYNOMIALS

When dividing polynomials, remember that subtracting a polynomial means adding the opposite. Find the opposite of each term of the polynomial you want to subtract and add.

Example

Divide: $(3x^2 + x - 5) \div (x + 2)$

Solution

$$\begin{array}{rlll} & 3x & -\ 5 & \\ x + 2\,\big) & 3x^2 + x & -\ 5 & \text{Use long division.} \\ & \underline{3x^2 + 6x} & & \text{Multiply } (x + 2)(3x) \\ & -5x & -\ 5 & \text{Add the opposite: } -3x^2 - 6x \\ & \underline{-5x} & \underline{-\ 10} & \text{Add the opposite: } 5x + 10 \\ & & 5 & \end{array}$$

The quotient is $3x - 5 + \dfrac{5}{x + 2}$.

EXERCISES

Divide.

1. $x + 4\,\overline{\big)\,x^2 + 3x + 15}$; quotient $x - 1$; work: $x^2 + 4x$, **$-x + 15$**, **$-x - 4$**, **19**

   1. **$x - 1 + \dfrac{19}{x + 4}$**

2. $y - 3\,\overline{\big)\,y^2 - 5y + 1}$

   2. **$y - 2 - \dfrac{5}{y - 3}$**

3. $q + 1\,\overline{\big)\,2q^2 + 3q + 2}$

   3. **$2q + 1 + \dfrac{1}{q + 1}$**

4. $p - 5\,\overline{\big)\,3p^2 + 4p + 5}$

   4. **$3p + 19 + \dfrac{100}{p - 5}$**

30 *South-Western Algebra 1: AN INTEGRATED APPROACH*

Extend Ask students which variable they should choose for Exercises 17 and 18. ***m* and *n* respectively**

Think Critically Ask students to describe how they found the value of *k* that will make the divisor a factor of the dividend for Exercise 22. **In the final step of the long division $-x + k$ must be equal to the last term in the quotient times $x + 3$: $(-1)(x + 3) = -x - 3$. Therefore, $k = -3$. 23.**

5 FOLLOW-UP

Extension Ask students what happens to the values of the expression $(x^2 + 4)/(x + 2)$ as x gets very large. Ask them why this is so. **The value of $(x^2 + 4)/(x + 2)$ approaches the value of $x - 2$. The value of the remainder $8/(x + 2)$ approaches 0 as x gets very large.**

NAME ______ CLASS ______ DATE ______

EXTRA PRACTICE 14.5 DIVIDE POLYNOMIALS

In Exercise 1, list the dividend, the divisor, the quotient and the remainder in that order.

1. $\frac{x^2 + 8}{x - 2} = x + 2 + \frac{12}{x - 2}$ — 1. $x^2 + 8;\ x - 2;\ x + 2;\ \frac{12}{(x - 2)}$

Divide.

2. $(4x^2 + 2x + 12) \div 2x$ — 2. $2x - 1 + \frac{6}{x}$
3. $(16x^4 - 12x^3 + 8x^2) \div 4x^2$ — 3. $4x^2 - 3x + 2$
4. $(15y^3 - 10y^2 + 2y) \div 5y$ — 4. $3y^2 - 2y + \frac{2}{5}$
5. $(x^2 + 3x + 5) \div (x - 1)$ — 5. $x + 4 + \frac{9}{x + 1}$
6. $(x^2 - 10x + 1) \div (x + 2)$ — 6. $x - 12 + \frac{25}{x + 2}$
7. $(2a^2 + 3a + 6) \div (a + 4)$ — 7. $2a - 5 + \frac{26}{a + 4}$
8. $(c^2 - 4c + 12) \div (c - 6)$ — 8. $c + 2$
9. $(2x^2 - 3x + 1) \div (x - 1)$ — 9. $2x - 1$
10. $(6q^3 + 5q^2 + 10) \div (q - 1)$ — 10. $6q^2 + 11q + 11 + \frac{21}{q - 1}$
11. $(16 - x - x^2) \div (x + 2)$ — 11. $-x + 1 + \frac{14}{x + 2}$
12. $(y^2 - 7) \div (2 + y)$ — 12. $y - 2 - \frac{3}{y + 2}$
13. $(3 + 2z^2 - 4z) \div (z + 3)$ — 13. $2z - 10 + \frac{33}{z + 3}$
14. GEOMETRY A rectangle has an area represented by $x^2 - 8x + 15$. The length is $x - 3$. What is its width? — 14. $x - 5$

32 *South-Western Algebra 1:* AN INTEGRATED APPROACH

TRY THESE

In Exercises 1–2, list the dividend, the divisor, the quotient, and the remainder in that order.

1. $\frac{x^2 + 8}{x - 2} = x + 2 + \frac{12}{x - 2}$ $x^2 + 8,\ x - 2,\ x + 2,\ 12$
2. $\frac{x^2 + 16}{x + 4} = x - 4 + \frac{32}{x + 4}$ $x^2 + 16,\ x + 4,\ x - 4,\ 32$

Divide.

3. $(6x^3 + 2x^2 + x) \div 2x^2$ $3x + 1 + \frac{1}{2x}$
4. $(8x^3 + 4x^2 + 2x) \div 4x^2$ $2x + 1 + \frac{1}{2x}$
5. $(a^2 + 3a - 10) \div (a - 2)$ $a + 5$
6. $(4m^2 - 6m - 5) \div (m - 4)$ $4m + 10 + \frac{35}{m - 4}$
7. $(2p^3 + 3p^2 - 5p + 1) \div (2p + 1)$ $p^2 + p - 3 + \frac{4}{2p + 1}$
8. $(d^3 + 12) \div (d - 4)$ $d^2 + 4d + 16 + \frac{76}{d - 4}$
9. GEOMETRY The area of a rectangle is $8t^2 + 26t + 15$, and the width is $2t + 5$. Find the length. $4t + 3$
10. WRITING MATHEMATICS Discuss what it means if you get a remainder of zero when dividing one polynomial by another. Answers will vary. It means that zero quotient and divisor are factors of the dividend.

PRACTICE

In Exercises 1–2, list the dividend, the divisor, the quotient, and the remainder in that order.

1. $\frac{x^2 + 10}{x - 4} = x + 4 + \frac{26}{x - 4}$ $x^2 + 10,\ x - 4,\ x + 4,\ 26$
2. $\frac{x^2 + 12}{x - 3} = x + 3 + \frac{21}{x - 3}$ $x^2 + 12,\ x - 3,\ x + 3,\ 21$

Divide.

3. $(12x^3 + 6x^2 + x) \div 3x^2$ $4x + 2 + \frac{1}{3x}$
4. $(15x^3 + 10x^2 + x) \div 5x^2$ $3x + 2 + \frac{1}{5x}$
5. $(a^2 + 4a - 21) \div (a - 3)$ $a + 7$
6. $(b^2 + 6b - 16) \div (b + 8)$ $b - 2$
7. $(12m^2 - 2m - 2) \div (3m + 1)$ $4m - 2$
8. $(27y^3 + 27y^2 + 9y + 1) \div (3y + 1)$ $9y^2 + 6y + 1$
9. WRITING MATHEMATICS Explain how dividing a polynomial by a polynomial is similar to dividing an integer by an integer. See Additional Answers.

Divide. 10–13 See Additional Answers.

10. $(2p^3 + 9p^2 - 6p + 2) \div (2p + 1)$
11. $(3q^3 + 5q^2 + 4q - 3) \div (3q - 1)$
12. $(8x^2 + 16 + 4x^4) \div (-4 + x)$
13. $(5 + 10y^2 + 5y^4) \div (-5 + y)$

AUTOMOBILE DEPRECIATION The formula $A = A_0(r^3 + 3r^2 + 3r + 1)$ can be used to determine the value of a car after 3 years, where A_0 represents the original cost of the car and r represents the rate of depreciation (represented by a negative decimal in the formula).

14. If the original price of the car can be represented by $\frac{10{,}000}{r + 1}$, find an expression that represents the value of the car after 3 years. $10{,}000r^2 + 20{,}000r + 10{,}000$
15. Evaluate the expression you found in Exercise 14 if $r = -20\%$. $6400
16. If the original price of the car is $\frac{18{,}000}{r + 1}$ and $r = -15\%$, determine the value of the car after 3 years. $13,005

EXTEND

When a polynomial contains more than one variable, arrange the terms in descending order of one of the variables. To divide $(15mn^2 + 5m^2n + 10m^3 + 25n^3)$ by $(m - n)$, arrange the terms in descending order of m, the first variable in the divisor. Then,

$$(15mn^2 + 5m^2n + 10m^3 + 25n^3) \div (m - n) = 10m^2 + 15mn + 30n^2 + \frac{55n^3}{m - n}$$

Divide.

17. $(4m^2n + 12mn^2 + 8m^3 + 16n^3) \div (m - n)$ $8m^2 + 12mn + 24n^2 + \frac{40n^3}{m - n}$

18. $(4m^2n + 12mn^2 + 8m^3 + 16n^3) \div (2n - m)$ $8n^2 + 10mn + 7m^2 + \frac{15m^3}{2n - m}$

BIOLOGY The population of a bacteria colony after 4 days is represented by the formula $P = P_0(r^4 + 4r^3 + 6r^2 + 4r + 1)$, where P_0 represents the initial number of bacteria and r represents the rate of increase in the number of bacteria per day, expressed as a decimal.

19. If the original number of bacteria can be represented by $\frac{336}{1 + r}$, find an expression that represents the number of bacteria after 4 days. $336r^3 + 1008r^2 + 1008r + 336$

20. Evaluate to the nearest whole number the expression you found in Exercise 19 if $r = 12\%$. 472

21. If the original number of bacteria is $\frac{460}{1 + r}$ and $r = 15\%$, determine to the nearest whole number the number of bacteria after 4 days. 700

THINK CRITICALLY

Determine the value of k that will make the divisor a factor of the dividend.

22. $\frac{x^3 + 5x^2 + 5x + k}{x + 3}$ -3 **23.** $\frac{x^3 + 2x^2 + kx + 45}{x - 5}$ -44 **24.** $\frac{2x^3 + kx^2 + 18}{2x + 3}$ -5

MIXED REVIEW

25. STANDARDIZED TESTS Select the correct solution for the following set of equations. A; Lesson 7.4

$$3x - 5y + 6z = 54$$
$$2x - 5y + 8z = 61$$
$$2z = 10$$

A. $x = 3, y = -3, z = 5$ **B.** $x = -3, y = 3, z = 5$
C. $x = 9, y = -3, z = 5$ **D.** $x = 3, y = -1, z = 5$

In Exercises 26–28, match the equation with the graph. Lesson 10.2

26. $y = 2x^2 + 3x + 1$ c **27.** $y = -\frac{1}{2}x^2 - 4x - 2$ b **28.** $y = -\frac{1}{4}x^2 + 4x + 2$ a

a.
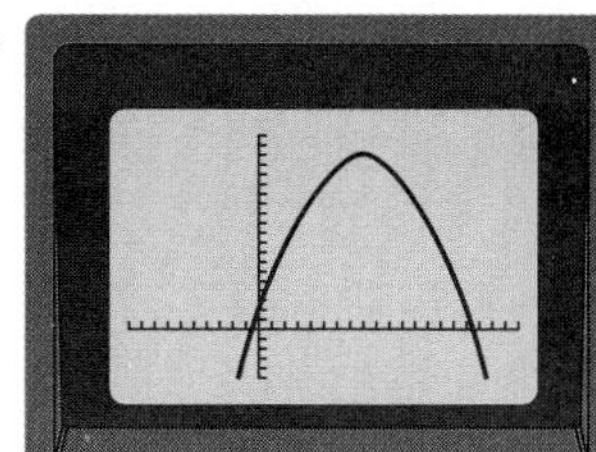

b.
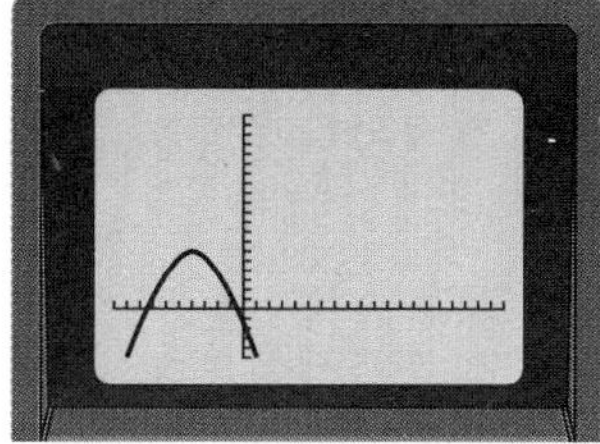

c.
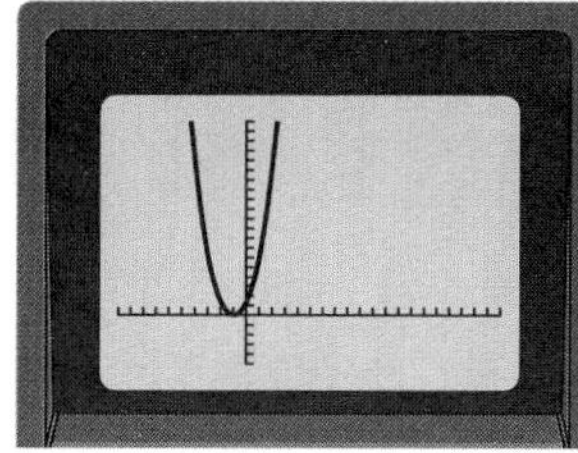

Technology Have students divide $3x + 15$ by $x + 2$. **3 + 9/(x + 2)** Ask them what they think will happen to the graph of $y = (3x + 15)/(x + 2)$ as x gets very large. **It will approach the graph of y = 3 as the value of the remainder approaches 0.** Then have students explore the graphs of $y = (3x + 15)/(x + 2)$ and $y = 3$ on their graphing utilities. Have them set the range: Xmin = –3, Xmax = 15, Xscl = 1, Ymin = 0, Ymax = 20, Yscl = 1. Ask them what happens as x approaches –2. **The value of (3x + 15)/(x + 2) gets very large.**

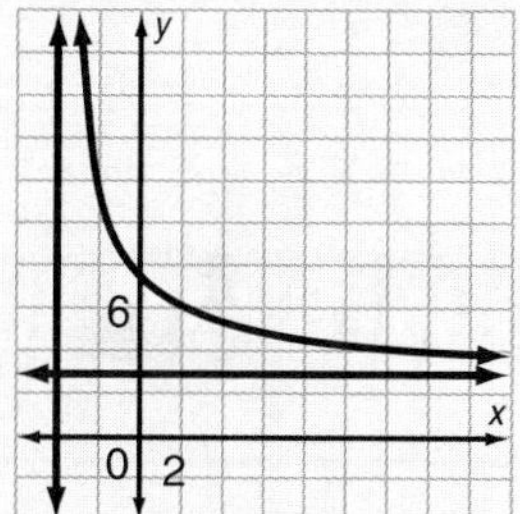

Point out that the graph is actually one half of the complete graph of $y = (3x + 15)/(x + 2)$. Ask students to graph the function using the standard range values.

NAME ________ CLASS ________ DATE ________

ENRICHMENT **14.5 DIVIDE POLYNOMIALS**

Find the values of the missing letters in each division below. Write those values on the answer blanks to the right.

1. $x + 5\,\overline{)\,x^2 + Ax - 11}$, quotient $x + 2$
$x^2 + 5x$
$Bx - 11$
$Bx + C$
D

1. A = 7, B = 2, C = 10, D = –21

2. $x + 7\,\overline{)\,x^2 + Fx - 13}$, quotient $x + E$
$x^2 + 7x$
$Ex - 13$
$Ex + G$
-34

2. E = 7, F = 10, G = 21

3. $x - 4\,\overline{)\,2x^2 + Jx + H}$, quotient $2x + K$
$2x^2 - 8x$
$Kx + H$
$Kx - 44$
41

3. H = –3, J = 3, K = 11

4. $x - 1\,\overline{)\,x^3 + Nx^2 + Lx + M}$, quotient $x^2 - x + 2$
$x^3 - x^2$
$-x^2 + Lx$
$-x^2 + x$
$2x + M$
$2x - 2$
-9

4. L = 3, M = –11, N = –2

5. $2x + 3\,\overline{)\,4x^2 + Qx + 2}$, quotient $2x + P$
$4x^2 - 6x$
$-2x + 2$
$P(2x) + P(3)$
5

5. P = –1, Q = 4

34 *South-Western Algebra 1:* AN INTEGRATED APPROACH

LESSON PLANNING

Objective

▶ Add and subtract rational expressions.

Vocabulary

least common denominator (LCD)

Resources

Warm Up 14.6
Reteaching 14.6
Extra Practice 14.6
Enrichment 14.6
Student Handbook
Lesson Quiz 14.6

ASSIGNMENTS

Basic: 1–22, 25, 28–29, 33–34, Mixed Review 35–43

Average: 2–30, 32–34, Mixed Review 35–43

Enriched: 3, 6–34, Mixed Review 35–43

1 MOTIVATE

Explore After students have answered Question 3, ask them to describe how they can find the least common multiple of two denominators. **Determine the prime factorization of each denominator, determine the maximum number of times each prime factor occurs, and multiply these factors.** Ask students to describe the steps they followed once they had determined the LCM of the denominators to find the sum in Question 3. **Multiply each fraction by a form of 1 to make each denominator equal to 18: 4/9 + 2/6 = (4/9)(2/2) + (2/6)(3/3) = 8/18 + 6/18 = 14/18 = 7/9.**

14.6 Add and Subtract Rational Expressions

SPOTLIGHT ON LEARNING

WHAT? In this lesson you will learn
- to find the least common denominator of rational expressions.
- to add and subtract rational expressions.

WHY? Adding and subtracting rational expressions can help you solve problems about cooking, the lens formula, and geometry.

Explore

Recall that to add two rational numbers, write equivalent rational numbers having the same denominator and then add the numerators.

Let $x = 10$ for each of the following. Substitute the value for x. Then add the two rational numbers. Simplify your answers and leave them in improper form.

1. $\frac{x}{5} + \frac{4}{x}$ $\frac{12}{5}$ **2.** $\frac{3x}{4} + \frac{1}{2x}$ $\frac{151}{20}$ **3.** $\frac{(x-6)}{(x-1)} + \frac{2}{(x-4)}$

4. When adding rational numbers, how do you determine what the denominator should be? See Additional Answers.

Determine the denominators you would use to add the following rational numbers.

5. $\frac{1}{2} + \frac{1}{3}$ 6 **6.** $\frac{1}{2} + \frac{1}{6}$ 6

7. $\frac{1}{x} + \frac{1}{x}$ x **8.** $\frac{1}{4} + \frac{1}{x}$ $4x$

9. $\frac{2}{3x} + \frac{4}{x}$ $3x$ **10.** $\frac{2}{x^2} + \frac{4}{3x}$ $3x^2$

11. $\frac{1}{(x-5)} + \frac{3}{8}$ $8(x-5)$ **12.** $\frac{6}{2x} + \frac{3}{2(x+1)}$ $2x(x+1)$

13. Determine the denominators you would use to add each of the rational expressions in Questions 1–3. $5x$; $4x$; $(x-1)(x-4)$

Build Understanding

Adding or subtracting rational expressions is similar to adding and subtracting rational numbers. When the denominators are the same, add or subtract the numerators.

EXAMPLE 1

Add: $\frac{6}{x+3} + \frac{4}{x+3}$

Solution

$$\frac{6}{x+3} + \frac{4}{x+3} = \frac{10}{x+3}$$

When the denominators of rational expressions are different, rewrite the expressions as equivalent expressions with a **least common denominator** (**LCD**) before adding or subtracting.

Use the following steps to determine the LCD.

- Determine the prime factorization for each denominator. Use exponents where needed.
- For each common prime factor, choose the factor with the greatest exponent.
- Multiply these factors.

THINK BACK

A common denominator of two fractions or rational numbers is a common multiple of their denominators. The least common denominator (LCD) is the least common multiple (LCM) of the denominators.

EXAMPLE 2

Determine the LCD of $\frac{5a}{12ab^2}$ and $\frac{7b}{15a^3b}$.

Solution

Factor each denominator: $12ab^2 = 2^2 \cdot 3 \cdot a \cdot b^2$
$15a^3b = 3 \cdot 5 \cdot a^3 \cdot b$

List the prime factors.	2	3	5	a	b
Determine the greatest exponent for each factor.	2	1	1	3	2

The LCD is $2^2 \cdot 3 \cdot 5 \cdot a^3 \cdot b^2$ or $60a^3b^2$. ◄

To add or subtract rational expressions, use the LCD to rewrite each expression as an equivalent rational expression having the LCD as its denominator. Then add or subtract the numerators.

EXAMPLE 3

Subtract: $\frac{5}{6m^2} - \frac{7 - 2m^2}{8m}$

Solution

$\frac{5}{6m^2} - \frac{7 - 2m^2}{8m}$ — The LCD is $2^3 \cdot 3 \cdot m^2 = 24m^2$.

$= \frac{5}{6m^2}\left(\frac{4}{4}\right) - \frac{(7 - 2m^2)}{8m}\left(\frac{3m}{3m}\right)$ — Write equivalent expressions that have the LCD.

$= \frac{20}{24m^2} - \frac{(21m - 6m^3)}{24m^2}$

$= \frac{20 - (21m - 6m^3)}{24m^2}$ — Subtract.

$= \frac{20 - 21m + 6m^3}{24m^2}$ — Simplify. ◄

2 TEACH

Use the Pages/Build Understanding

Example 1: After students have discussed Example 1, ask them to simplify $6/(x + 3) - 4/(x + 3)$. $\mathbf{6/(x + 3) - 4/(x + 3) = (6 - 4)/(x + 3) = 2/(x + 3)}$

Example 2: Have students simplify the given expressions and find the LCD of the new expressions. $\mathbf{60a^3b^2}$

Example 3: Ask students to describe the steps for finding the LCD. $\mathbf{6m^2 = 2 \cdot 3 \cdot m^2; 8m = 2^3 \cdot m;}$

LCD is $2^3 \cdot 3 \cdot m^2$ or $24m^2$

Ask students to explain why $5/6m^2$ is multiplied by $4/4$ and $(7 - 2m)/8m$ is multiplied by $3m/3m$. **to make the denominators the same**

Example 4: Have students evaluate the expression representing the total time when $t = 3$. **4 h** Ask how they can check if this is correct. **Find the time it takes the boat to travel upstream for $t = 3$ and downstream for $t = 3$, and then add the two times to get the round trip.**

Ongoing Assessment The important concepts and skills are adding and subtracting rational expressions. To assess these ideas, have students demonstrate how they have applied these concepts and skills in Exercises 6 and 9 of the Try These section.

Guided Practice/Try These For Exercise 8, ask students to show how they found the LCD. **$5a^2 = 5 \cdot a^2$, $15a = 3 \cdot 5 \cdot a$, $a = a$; make a table to determine the LCD:**

prime factors	3	5	a
greatest exponent	1	1	2

$3 \cdot 5 \cdot a^2 = 15a^2$

For Exercise 12, ask students how they can find how many hours before dinner time they must begin to prepare the meal. **Find the sum of $2/(x + 2)$ and $1/x$.**

NAME ______ CLASS ______ DATE ______

RETEACHING

14.6 ADD AND SUBTRACT RATIONAL EXPRESSIONS

To add or subtract rational expressions that do not have the same denominator, follow these steps:

1. Determine the least common denominator (LCD) of the expressions.
2. Compare each denominator with the LCD.
3. Multiply if necessary to write equivalent expressions with the LCD as its denominator.
4. Add or subtract as indicated.

Example
Add:

$\frac{4}{2x} + \frac{3}{2(x+4)}$ The LCD is $2x(x + 4)$

$\frac{4}{2x}\left(\frac{x+4}{x+4}\right) + \frac{3}{2(x+4)}\left(\frac{x}{x}\right)$ Write equivalent expressions that have the LCD.

$\frac{4x+16}{2x(x+4)} + \frac{3x}{2x(x+4)}$

$\frac{7x+16}{2x(x+4)}$ Add. Combine like terms in the numerator.

Add or subtract.

1. $\frac{3}{2x^2} + \frac{7}{6x^3}$ LCD: $6x^3$ — 1. $\frac{9x+7}{6x^2}$
2. $\frac{4a}{a+3} - \frac{2a}{a-2}$ LCD = $(a + 3)(a - 2)$ — 2. $\frac{2a^2 - 14}{(a+3)(a-2)}$
3. $\frac{7x}{3x^4} + \frac{5x+1}{2x}$ — 3. $\frac{15x^3 + 3x^2 + 14}{6x^3}$
4. $\frac{2}{5y} + \frac{1}{y+3}$ — 4. $\frac{7y+6}{5y(y+3)}$

38 South-Western Algebra 1: AN INTEGRATED APPROACH

You can add and subtract rational expressions to solve many real world applications.

EXAMPLE 4

NAVIGATION A boat takes $\frac{3}{t - 2}$ hours to travel upstream and $\frac{8 - t}{t + 2}$ hours to travel downstream. Write an expression for the time it takes for the round trip.

Solution

$$\frac{3}{t - 2} + \frac{8 - t}{t + 2}$$ The LCD is $(t + 2)(t - 2)$.

$$= \left(\frac{3}{t - 2}\right)\left(\frac{t + 2}{t + 2}\right) + \left(\frac{8 - t}{t + 2}\right)\left(\frac{t - 2}{t - 2}\right)$$ Write equivalent expressions.

$$= \frac{3(t + 2) + (8 - t)(t - 2)}{(t + 2)(t - 2)}$$

$$= \frac{3t + 6 + 8t - 16 - t^2 + 2t}{(t + 2)(t - 2)}$$

$$= \frac{-t^2 + 13t - 10}{(t + 2)(t - 2)}$$ Combine like terms in the numerator.

The total time is $\frac{-t^2 + 13t - 10}{(t + 2)(t - 2)}$ hours. ◄

TRY THESE

Determine the least common denominator for each set of expressions.

1. $\frac{5}{mn^2}, \frac{101}{mn}$ mn^2
2. $\frac{8}{a^2b}, \frac{3}{2ac}$ $2a^2bc$
3. $\frac{121}{x - 4}, \frac{199}{x - 5}$ $(x - 4)(x - 5)$

Add or subtract. Simplify if possible.

4. $\frac{a}{11} + \frac{7a}{11}$ $\frac{8a}{11}$
5. $\frac{5}{7y} - \frac{9}{7y}$ $-\frac{4}{7y}$
6. $\frac{3p}{p - 4} - \frac{12}{p - 4}$ 3
7. $\frac{6}{5x} + \frac{-2}{15x}$ $\frac{16}{15x}$
8. $\frac{6}{5a^2} + \frac{2}{15a} - \frac{5}{a}$ $\frac{-73a + 18}{15a^2}$
9. $\frac{4}{a + 4} + \frac{5}{a - 9}$ $\frac{9a - 16}{(a + 4)(a - 9)}$
10. $\frac{2x + 5}{(x + 2)(x - 2)} + \frac{-2}{x + 2}$ $\frac{9}{(x + 2)(x - 2)}$
11. $\frac{4z + 2}{16 - z^2} + \frac{4}{z - 4}$ $\frac{-14}{16 - z^2}$
12. **COOKING** It takes $\frac{2}{x + 2}$ hours to prepare a specific dinner and $\frac{1}{x}$ hours to cook it. If you want to serve the dinner at a certain time, how many hours before that time must you begin preparing it? $\frac{3x + 2}{x(x + 2)}$
13. **WRITING MATHEMATICS** Write a paragraph that explains in your own words how to add two rational expressions with unlike denominators.
See Additional Answers.

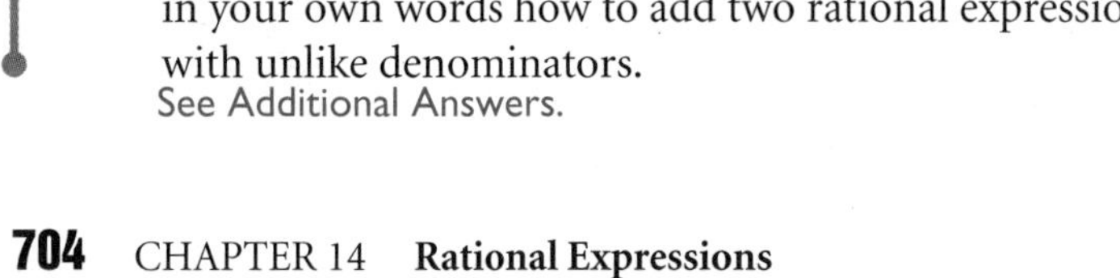

PRACTICE

Determine the least common denominator.

1. $\frac{3}{ab^2}, \frac{11}{b^3}$ ab^3
2. $\frac{101}{x-2}, \frac{19}{x-3}$ $(x-2)(x-3)$
3. $\frac{17}{3x}, \frac{13}{x(x+1)}$ $3x(x+1)$

Add or subtract. Simplify if possible.

4. $\frac{12}{5y} - \frac{7}{5y}$ $\frac{1}{y}$
5. $\frac{22}{7z} + \frac{6}{7z}$ $\frac{4}{z}$
6. $\frac{3}{p+2} + \frac{p-3}{p+2}$ $\frac{p}{p+2}$
7. $\frac{8d}{d-6} - \frac{d+42}{d-6}$ 7
8. $\frac{13e}{e-12} - \frac{e+144}{e-12}$ 12
9. $\frac{4}{b-4} - \frac{b}{b-4}$ -1
10. $\frac{9}{2x} + \frac{-5}{8x}$ $\frac{31}{8x}$
11. $\frac{8}{3x} + \frac{-1}{9x}$ $\frac{23}{9x}$
12. $\frac{5}{4t^2} - \frac{3}{8t} - \frac{2}{t}$ $\frac{-19t+10}{8t^2}$

13. **LIGHT** The *lens formula*, $\frac{1}{d_o} + \frac{1}{d_i} = \frac{1}{f}$, expresses the relationship between the location of an object serving as a light source d_o, the location of the image d_i, and the focal length of the lens f.

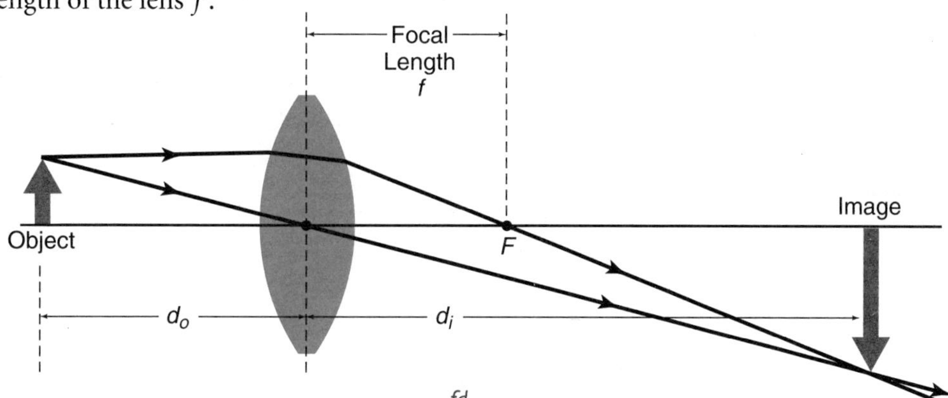

a. Solve the lens equation for d_i. $d_i = \frac{fd_o}{d_o - f}$

b. If the focal length of the cornea-lens part of your eye is approximately 1.65 cm and you look at an object 50 m (5000 cm) away, find d_i. Round to two decimal places. 1.65 cm

c. If the object is moved so that it is only 30 cm away (reading distance), find d_i. Round to two decimal places. 1.75 cm

Add or subtract. Simplify if possible. 20–24 See Additional Answers.

14. $\frac{3}{a+6} + \frac{2}{a-5}$ $\frac{5a-3}{(a+6)(a-5)}$
15. $\frac{5}{a+7} + \frac{4}{a-4}$ $\frac{9a+8}{(a+7)(a-4)}$
16. $\frac{t}{2(t+3)} - \frac{2}{3(t+3)}$ $\frac{3t-4}{6(t+3)}$
17. $\frac{r}{3(r+3)} - \frac{3}{4(r+3)}$ $\frac{4r-9}{12(r+3)}$
18. $\frac{4y+16}{(y+4)(y-4)} + \frac{-4}{y+4}$ $\frac{32}{y^2-16}$
19. $\frac{5x+3}{(5-x)(5+x)} + \frac{5}{x-5}$ $\frac{-22}{25-x^2}$
20. $\frac{6q-1}{81-q^2} - \frac{2q}{q+9}$
21. $\frac{10v-1}{100-v^2} - \frac{5v}{v+10}$
22. $\frac{11}{121-u^2} - \frac{u^2}{u+11}$
23. $\frac{3a}{6a^2+13a+2} + \frac{a+1}{a^2+5a+6}$
24. $\frac{5b}{3b^2-b-2} + \frac{b+2}{b^2+4b-5}$

25. **WRITING MATHEMATICS** When adding or subtracting two rational numbers, such as $\frac{5}{6} - \frac{1}{2}$, you can find a common denominator by multiplying the denominators instead of using the LCD. Why might you not want to do that for rational expressions?
Multiplying polynomials might get complicated, leaving great room for error in computation.

3 SUMMARIZE

In the Math Journal For

$$\frac{7x}{12x^3y} + \frac{5y}{18xy^2}$$

have students find the LCD and sum before simplifying either term. Then have them find the LCD and sum after simplifying both terms. Ask them to compare their answers. **The answers are both $(21 + 10x)/36x^2y$.** Ask which method they preferred and why. **Answers will vary.**

4 PRACTICE

Practice

Error Alert For Practice Exercise 7, watch for students who forget to multiply 42 by –1.

NAME ______ CLASS ______ DATE ______

EXTRA PRACTICE 14.6 ADD AND SUBTRACT RATIONAL EXPRESSIONS

Determine the least common denominator.

1. $\frac{3}{4x}, \frac{5}{18x^3}$
2. $\frac{24}{x+3}, \frac{2}{x-4}$
3. $\frac{14}{5a}, \frac{6}{a+10}$
4. $\frac{9}{x-2}, \frac{11}{4x}$

Add or subtract. Simplify if possible.

5. $\frac{2}{5x} + \frac{8}{5x}$
6. $\frac{13}{2g} - \frac{-5}{2g}$
7. $\frac{b}{b+1} - \frac{3}{b+1}$
8. $\frac{2a}{a-3} + \frac{5a-1}{a-3}$
9. $\frac{2x}{x+2} + \frac{3x+10}{x+2}$
10. $\frac{5}{y-5} - \frac{y}{y-5}$
11. $\frac{4}{3x} + \frac{-5}{6x}$
12. $\frac{a}{2(a+1)} + \frac{4}{3(a+1)}$
13. $\frac{2c+1}{c-3} + \frac{c-8}{c+3}$
14. $\frac{4g}{2-g} + \frac{3g+2}{g^2-4}$
15. $\frac{8h}{h^2-49} + \frac{h+1}{7-h}$
16. $\frac{7}{a^2+6a+8} + \frac{3}{a^2-a-6}$
17. **ELECTRONICS** The total resistance of a certain circuit can be found by the formula $R_1 + \frac{1}{R_2} + \frac{1}{R_3}$
If $R_1 = x$, $R_2 = 2x$ and $R_3 = 4x$, find the total resistance.

1. $18x^4$
2. $(x+3)(x-4)$
3. $5a(a+10)$
4. $4x(x-2)$
5. $\frac{2}{x}$
6. $\frac{9}{g}$
7. $\frac{b-3}{b+1}$
8. $\frac{7a-1}{a-3}$
9. 5
10. -1
11. $\frac{1}{2x}$
12. $\frac{3a+8}{6(a+1)}$
13. $\frac{3c^2-4c+27}{(c-3)(c+3)}$
14. $\frac{-4g^2-5g-2}{g^2-4}$
15. $\frac{-h^2-7}{h^2-49}$
16. $\frac{10a-9}{(a+2)(a+4)(a-3)}$
17. $\frac{(4x^2+3)}{4x}$

40 *South-Western Algebra 1: AN INTEGRATED APPROACH*

For Exercise 13, suggest that students substitute other variables for d_i and d_o before working the problem.

Extend Remind students to factor polynomials completely and to divide out common factors before multiplying or dividing rational expressions involving polynomials in the numerator and in the denominator.

Think Critically Have students share their answers for Exercises 32 and 33.

5 FOLLOW-UP

Extra Practice Add or subtract. Simplify if possible.

1. 5/(4*z*) + 11/(4*z*) **(4/*z*)**
2. 6/(*b* + 5) – 4/(*b* – 2) **[(2*b* – 32)/((*b* + 5)(*b* – 2))]**
3. *y*/[2(*y* + 1)] + 5/(3(*y* + 1)] **[(3*y* + 10)/ (6(*y* + 1))]**

NAME ________ CLASS ________ DATE ________

ENRICHMENT

14.6 ADD AND SUBTRACT RATIONAL EXPRESSIONS

To check a sum or difference, substitute a number for the variable in the rational expressions.

Example

Check the sum: $\frac{3a}{a+2} + \frac{a-1}{2a} = \frac{7a^2+a-2}{2a(a+2)}$

Solution

Substitute $a = 1$ in each expression. Do not to choose a value that will result in a denominator of 0.

$$\frac{3(1)}{1+2} + \frac{1-1}{2(1)} = \frac{7(1)^2+1-2}{2(1)(1+2)}$$

$$\frac{3}{3} + \frac{0}{2} = \frac{6}{6}$$

$1 + 0 = 1$ So, the sum is correct.

Check each addition and subtraction by substitution. If the given answer is incorrect, write the correct answer.

1. $\frac{4a}{7a^2} + \frac{3}{7a^2} = \frac{4a+3}{7a^2}$
2. $\frac{5}{2b} + \frac{4}{3b^2} = \frac{15b+3}{6b^2}$
3. $\frac{c+3}{3c} + \frac{c-8}{4c} = \frac{7c+36}{12c}$
4. $\frac{d+2}{5d} + \frac{d-1}{d^2} = \frac{d^2-3d+5}{5d^2}$
5. $\frac{7e}{e+1} + \frac{2e+1}{e-3} = \frac{9e^2+e-21}{(e+1)(e-3)}$
6. $\frac{f+2}{f^2-1} - \frac{f-4}{f+1} = \frac{-f^2+5f-5}{f^2-1}$
7. $\frac{g}{g^2-g-2} + \frac{3g}{g^2-4} = \frac{18g}{(g+1)(g^2-4)}$
8. $\frac{h-1}{h+3} - \frac{h-3}{h+1} = \frac{-10}{(h+3)(h+1)}$
9. $\frac{2k-1}{2k} + \frac{k-4}{3k} - \frac{3k+1}{4k} = \frac{7k-25}{12k}$
10. $\frac{m-2}{m+2} - \frac{1}{m} = \frac{m^2-m-4}{m(m+2)}$

1. correct
2. no; $\frac{15b+8}{6b^2}$
3. no; $\frac{7c-12}{12c}$
4. correct
5. no; $\frac{9e^2-18e+1}{(e+1)(e-3)}$
6. no; $\frac{-f^2+6f-2}{f^2-1}$
7. no; $\frac{4g^2+5g}{(g+1)(g^2-4)}$
8. no; $\frac{8}{(h+3)(h+1)}$
9. correct
10. no; $\frac{m^2-3m-2}{m(m^2-4)}$

42 *South-Western Algebra 1: AN INTEGRATED APPROACH*

EXTEND

Combine. Follow the order of operations.

26. $\left(\frac{2}{x+2} - \frac{1}{x+5}\right)\left(\frac{2x+10}{x^2+8x}\right)$ $\frac{2}{x(x+2)}$

27. $\left(\frac{3}{x-5} - \frac{1}{x^2-25}\right) \div \left(\frac{3x+14}{x-8}\right)$ $\frac{x-8}{x^2-25}$

GEOMETRY Write an expression for the perimeter of a triangle with sides of the given lengths.

28. $x, \frac{3}{x}, \frac{4x}{1-x}$ $\frac{-x^3+5x^2-3x+3}{x(1-x)}$

29. $\frac{1}{x}, \frac{2}{x+1}, \frac{x}{6x-1}$ $\frac{x^3+19x^2+3x-1}{x(x+1)(6x-1)}$

30. $\frac{2}{x}, \frac{3}{x+2}, \frac{x}{3x-1}$ $\frac{x^3+17x^2+7x-4}{x(x+2)(3x-1)}$

31. $x, \frac{4}{x}, \frac{10x}{1-2x}$ $\frac{-2x^3+11x^2-8x+4}{x(1-2x)}$

THINK CRITICALLY

32. Provide an original example of the addition or subtraction of two rational expressions in which using the LCD produces an answer that is not in simplest form.
See Additional Answers.

33. Provide an original example of the addition or subtraction of two rational expressions in which using the LCD produces an answer that is in simplest form.
See Additional Answers.

34. Write the complete group of rational expressions having k as the numerator and $2x - 6$ as the LCD. $\frac{k}{1}, \frac{k}{2}, \frac{k}{x-3}, \frac{k}{2(x-3)}$

MIXED REVIEW

35. STANDARDIZED TESTS A window washer dropped his ring from a window 72 m above the ground. If the acceleration due to gravity on Earth is approximately –9.8 m/s², how long will it take for the ring to reach the ground? Use the formula $d = \frac{1}{2}|a|t^2$. D; Lesson 10.4

A. 14.69 s **B.** 2.74 s **C.** 7.55 s **D.** 3.83 s

36. A mini-van dealer estimates that she sold 25 ± 4 green vans last year. Write an absolute value inequality that models the situation. $|x - 25| \le 4$; Lesson 9.4

Simplify each expression. Lesson 2.8

37. $3(12 - 3^2)^3 - 2(7 - 1)^2$ 9

38. $[1260 \div (4 - 2^8)]^2 - 6 + 5^3$ 144

In Exercises 39–41, match the equation with the graph. Lesson 10.2

39. $y = 2x^2$ c

40. $y = x^2 - 2$ a

41. $y = (x + 2)^2$ b

a.

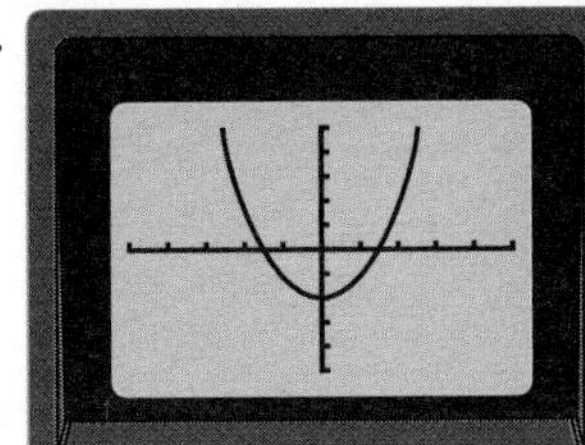

b.

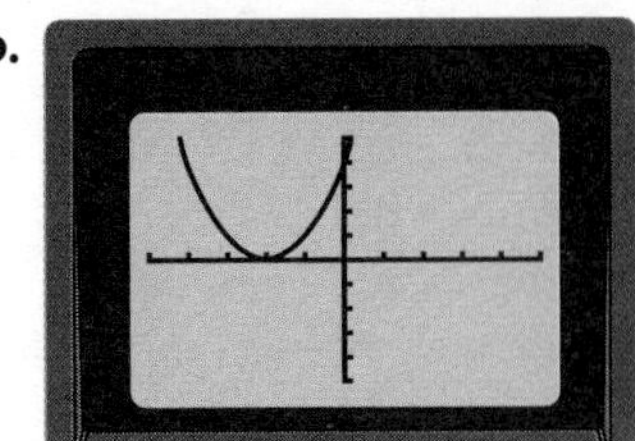

c.

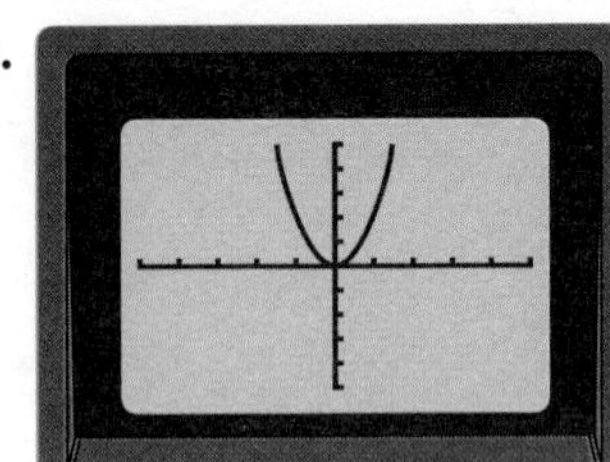

Add or subtract as indicated. Simplify if possible. Lesson 14.6

42. $\frac{7}{6t^2} + \frac{12}{12t} - \frac{3}{t}$ $\frac{-12t+7}{6t^2}$

43. $\frac{3}{8r^2} + \frac{8}{16r} - \frac{2}{r}$ $\frac{-12r+3}{8r^2}$

14.7 Complex Rational Expressions

Explore

Recall that a mixed number such as $4\frac{3}{5}$ is the sum of an integer and a fraction $\left(4 + \frac{3}{5}\right)$. You can express a mixed number as an improper fraction. For example,

$$\begin{aligned} 4\frac{3}{5} &= 4 + \frac{3}{5} \\ &= \frac{4}{1} \cdot \left(\frac{5}{5}\right) + \frac{3}{5} \\ &= \frac{20}{5} + \frac{3}{5} \\ &= \frac{23}{5} \end{aligned}$$

Evaluate each of the following for $x = 4$.

1. $3 - \frac{1}{x}$ $\frac{11}{4}$ **2.** $x + 3 + \frac{6}{x + 3}$ $\frac{55}{7}$ **3.** $2 + \frac{x^2 - 4}{x^2 - 9}$ $\frac{26}{7}$

4. Describe the procedure you would use to convert a mixed expression to a rational expression. Use an example to illustrate your point. See Additional Answers.

Recall that a fraction bar indicates division. For example, $\frac{3}{4} = 3 \div 4$. When you divide 4 into 3, the result is 0.75.

When both the numerator and denominator are rational numbers, you can divide the numerator by the denominator. For example,

$$\frac{\frac{2}{3}}{\frac{3}{4}} = \frac{2}{3} \div \frac{3}{4}$$

Write a division expression for each of the following. Then evaluate the expression.

5. $\frac{\frac{5}{3}}{\frac{15}{4}}$ $\frac{5}{3} \div \frac{15}{4}; \frac{4}{9}$ **6.** $\frac{\frac{1}{2}}{\frac{2}{3}}$ $\frac{1}{2} \div \frac{2}{3}; \frac{3}{4}$ **7.** $\frac{8}{\frac{1}{4}}$ $8 \div \frac{1}{4}; 32$

Build Understanding

A **mixed expression** is the sum or difference of a polynomial and a rational expression. Each of the following is a mixed expression.

$4 + \frac{3}{2x}$ $\qquad p - 3 - \frac{p}{p - 1}$

SPOTLIGHT ON LEARNING

WHAT? In this lesson you will learn
- to convert mixed expressions to rational expressions.
- to simplify complex rational expressions.

WHY? Knowing how to simplify complex rational expressions is useful for solving problems in agriculture, electricity, political science, and geometry.

LESSON PLANNING

Objectives
- ▶ Convert mixed expressions to rational expressions.
- ▶ Simplify complex rational expressions.

Vocabulary
complex rational expression
mixed expression

Technology/Multimedia
graphing utilities

Resources
Warm Up 14.7
Reteaching 14.7
Extra Practice 14.7
Enrichment 14.7
Transparencies 78–80
Student Handbook
Lesson Quiz 14.7

ASSIGNMENTS

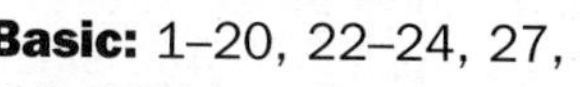

Basic: 1–20, 22–24, 27, 29–30

Average: 1–6, 8–25, 27–31

Enriched: 4–6, 9–32

1 MOTIVATE

Explore Ask students to give an example of another mixed number and to describe how to express it as an improper fraction. **Possible example: 2 5/8 = 2/1 + 5/8 = 2/1 • (8/8) + 5/8 = 16/8 + 5/8 = 21/8** After students have completed Questions 5–7, tell them that these fractions are called *complex fractions* and that they will be learning how to simplify similar rational expressions.

2 TEACH

Use the Pages/Build Understanding Ask students to explain what a rational expression is. **an expression that can be expressed in the form P/Q, where P and Q are polynomials and Q ≠ 0** Ask them how they could express *x* as a rational expression. ***x*/1**

Example 1: Ask students to explain what a rational number is. **a number that can be expressed in the form *a*/*b*, where *a* and *b* are integers and *b* ≠ 0** Ask them to explain why 3/1 is multiplied by *p*/*p*. **to convert the mixed expression 3 + 2/*p* to a rational expression whose terms can be added** After students have discussed the example, ask them to convert *p* + 2/*p* to a rational expression. $\mathbf{p(p/p) + 2/p = (p^2 + 2)/p}$

Example 2: After students have discussed the example, have them read Communicating About Algebra and try that method of simplifying the rational expression.

Example 3: Ask students to explain why (2/*m*)*mn* simplifies to 2*n* and why (4/*n*)*mn* simplifies to 4*m*. **Since *m*/*m* = 1, (2/*m*)*mn* = 2*n* • *m*/*m* = 2*n* • 1 = 2*n*; similarly, (4/*n*)*mn* = 4*m***

Example 4: Ask students why the expression in the second step of the solution is multiplied by *x*/*x*. **because *x* is the LCD of all the rational expressions in the complex rational expression**

Ongoing Assessment The important concepts and skills are converting mixed expressions to rational expressions and simplifying complex rational expressions. To assess these ideas, have students demonstrate how they have applied these concepts and skills in Exercises 2, 6, and 7 of the Try These section.

Guided Practice/Try These For Exercises 9 and 10, ask students to determine the LCD. **2*pq*, 3*rt***

COMMUNICATING ABOUT ALGEBRA

To simplify Example 2 another way, use the fact that

$$\frac{\frac{a}{b}}{\frac{c}{d}} = \frac{a}{b} \div \frac{c}{d} = \frac{a}{b} \cdot \frac{d}{c} = \frac{ad}{bc}$$

Begin by simplifying the numerator and the denominator into single rational expressions. Then divide the numerator by the denominator. Which method requires fewer steps?

See Additional Answers.

Converting mixed expressions to rational expressions is similar to converting mixed numbers to improper fractions.

EXAMPLE 1

Convert $3 + \frac{2}{p}$ to a rational expression.

Solution

$$3 + \frac{2}{p} = \frac{3}{1} \cdot \left(\frac{p}{p}\right) + \frac{2}{p} \quad \text{Express 3 as a rational number.}$$

$$= \frac{3p}{p} + \frac{2}{p} \quad \text{Write equivalent expressions with LCD} = p.$$

$$= \frac{3p + 2}{p} \quad \text{Add.}$$

A **complex rational expression** contains one or more rational expressions in its numerator or denominator. Examples include

$$\frac{\frac{2}{x}}{\frac{3}{y}} \qquad \frac{5 + \frac{4}{2x}}{x} \qquad \frac{\frac{4}{3b - 5}}{2b - \frac{3}{b - 5}} \qquad \frac{\frac{x - 3}{x}}{\frac{x - 2}{x - 3}}$$

To simplify a complex rational expression, determine the LCD of all the rational expressions in both the numerator and the denominator. Then multiply the numerator and the denominator by the LCD.

EXAMPLE 2

Simplify: $\dfrac{\frac{3}{x}}{\frac{6}{y}}$

Solution

$$\frac{\frac{3}{x}}{\frac{6}{y}} = \frac{\frac{3}{x}}{\frac{6}{y}} \cdot \frac{xy}{xy} \quad \text{The LCD is } xy\text{, so multiply by } \frac{xy}{xy}.$$

$$= \frac{\frac{3}{\cancel{x}} \cdot \frac{\cancel{x}y}{1}}{\frac{6}{\cancel{y}} \cdot \frac{x\cancel{y}}{1}} \quad \text{Divide out common factors.}$$

$$= \frac{3y}{6x}$$

$$= \frac{y}{2x} \quad \text{Simplify.}$$

Some complex rational expressions contain mixed expressions.

EXAMPLE 3

Simplify: $\dfrac{\frac{2}{m} + 3}{5 - \frac{4}{n}}$

Solution

$$\frac{\frac{2}{m} + 3}{5 - \frac{4}{n}} = \frac{\frac{2}{m} + 3}{5 - \frac{4}{n}} \cdot \frac{mn}{mn}$$ The LCD is mn, so multiply by $\frac{mn}{mn}$.

$$= \frac{\left(\frac{2}{m} \cdot mn\right) + (3 \cdot mn)}{(5 \cdot mn) - \left(\frac{4}{n} \cdot mn\right)}$$ Use the distributive property.

$$= \frac{2n + 3mn}{5mn - 4m}$$ ◄

Complex rational expressions can model real world situations.

EXAMPLE 4

AGRICULTURE In April, a gardener was able to purchase x sacks of fertilizer for \$600. In August, the fertilizer was on sale for \$10 less per sack. How many sacks at the sale price could the gardener purchase for \$600?

Solution

April price: p August price: $p - 10$

Sacks purchased in April: $x = \frac{600}{p}$, so $p = \frac{600}{x}$

Sacks that can be purchased in August $=$

$$\frac{600}{p - 10}$$

$$= \frac{600}{\frac{600}{x} - 10}$$ Substitute $\frac{600}{x}$ for p.

$$= \frac{600}{\frac{600}{x} - 10} \cdot \frac{x}{x}$$ The LCD is x, so multiply by $\frac{x}{x}$.

$$= \frac{600x}{600 - 10x}$$ Use the distributive property.

$$= \frac{10(60x)}{10(60 - x)}$$ Simplify.

$$= \frac{60x}{60 - x}$$

The farmer could purchase $\frac{60x}{60 - x}$ sacks. ◄

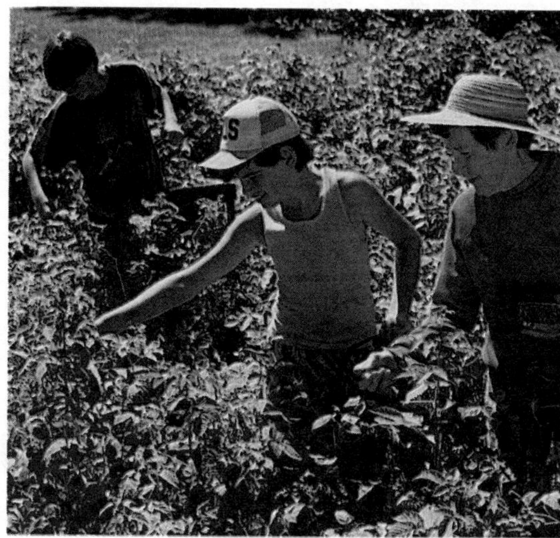

3 SUMMARIZE

In the Math Journal Have students write a paragraph explaining how to simplify the complex rational expression

$$\frac{\frac{1}{a} + \frac{1}{b}}{\frac{1}{2b}}$$

and to show the steps they describe. **Multiply the complex rational expression by $(2ab)/(2ab)$; then simplify.**

NAME ______ CLASS ______ DATE ______

RETEACHING

14.7 COMPLEX RATIONAL EXPRESSIONS

Example

Simplify: $\dfrac{\frac{1}{a} + a}{\frac{6}{5a} - 3}$

Solution

$$\frac{\frac{1}{a} + a}{\frac{6}{5a} - 3} = \frac{\frac{1 + a^2}{a}}{\frac{6 - 15a}{5a}}$$ Find the LCD of both numerator and denominator.

$$\frac{\frac{1 + a^2}{a}}{\frac{6 - 15a}{5a}} \cdot \frac{5a}{5a}$$ The LCD is $5a$. So, multiply by $\frac{5a}{5a}$.

$$= \frac{\frac{1 + a^2}{a} \cdot \frac{5a}{1}}{\frac{6 - 15a}{5a} \cdot \frac{5a}{1}}$$ Divide out common factors.

$$= \frac{(1 + a^2)5}{6 - 15a} = \frac{5 + 5a^2}{6 - 15a}$$ Distribute numerator.

Simplify. Write your answer in simplest form.

1. $\dfrac{\frac{7}{p} + \frac{3}{p^2}}{\frac{2}{7p^2}}$ — 1. $\dfrac{49p + 21}{2}$

2. $\dfrac{\frac{5}{x} + x}{\frac{1}{x} + \frac{3}{2x}}$ — 2. $\dfrac{10 + 2x^2}{5}$

3. $\dfrac{9 - \frac{1}{q}}{\frac{5}{q} + 2}$ — 3. $\dfrac{9q - 1}{5 + 2q}$

46 *South-Western Algebra 1: AN INTEGRATED APPROACH*

4 PRACTICE

Practice Remind students to be careful when multiplying by the LCD to apply the distributive property when necessary. Ask a student to describe how he or she converted the expression in Exercise 3. **Multiply $3z$ and -1 by $(3z)/(3z)$; then simplify.**

Extend For Exercises 27 and 28, ask students how they can determine the width of each rectangle. **Divide the area by the length.**

Think Critically For Exercise 30, ask students how they can verify that their example is its own reciprocal. **Multiply the expression by itself; the product should be 1.**

NAME ____________ CLASS ________ DATE ________

EXTRA PRACTICE **14.7 COMPLEX RATIONAL EXPRESSIONS**

Convert each mixed expression to a rational expression.

1. $2 + \frac{3}{a}$
2. $b + \frac{b+3}{b}$
3. $1 - \frac{8}{c}$
4. $5 - d - \frac{2}{d+1}$

Simplify. Write your answer in simplest form.

5. $\dfrac{\frac{7}{a}}{\frac{9}{b}}$
6. $\dfrac{\frac{2}{c}}{\frac{7}{d}}$
7. $\dfrac{\frac{1}{g} + \frac{1}{h}}{\frac{6}{g}}$
8. $\dfrac{\frac{2}{m} + \frac{3}{n}}{\frac{-5}{n}}$
9. $\dfrac{\frac{5}{3p}}{\frac{2}{21q}}$
10. $\dfrac{\frac{9}{r^2s}}{\frac{8}{rs^2}}$
11. $\dfrac{\frac{1}{t} + \frac{1}{u}}{\frac{3}{4t} + \frac{4}{5u}}$
12. $\dfrac{\frac{4}{x} + \frac{5}{y}}{\frac{1}{2x} - \frac{1}{3y}}$
13. $\dfrac{\frac{1}{a} + 7}{\frac{6}{a}}$
14. $\dfrac{\frac{2}{b} - 5}{\frac{3}{b}}$

15. ELECTRICITY In a parallel circuit with two light bulbs, the total resistance R, in ohms, can be found by the formula $R = \frac{R_1 \cdot R_2}{R_1 + R_2}$. Find R if $R_1 = \frac{2}{x}$ and and $R_2 = \frac{1}{2x}$.

Answers:
1. $\frac{2a+3}{a}$
2. $\frac{b^2+b+3}{b}$
3. $\frac{c-8}{c}$
4. $\frac{-d^2+4d+3}{d+1}$
5. $\frac{7b}{9a}$
6. $\frac{2d}{7c}$
7. $\frac{h+g}{6h}$
8. $\frac{2n+3m}{-5m}$
9. $\frac{35q}{2p}$
10. $\frac{9s}{8r}$
11. $\frac{20u+20t}{15u+16t}$
12. $\frac{24y+30x}{3y-2x}$
13. $\frac{1+7a}{6}$
14. $\frac{2-5b}{3}$
15. $\frac{2}{5x}$ ohms

48 South-Western Algebra 1: AN INTEGRATED APPROACH

TRY THESE

Convert each mixed expression to a rational expression.

1. $5 + \frac{9}{t}$ Answer: $\frac{5t + 9}{t}$
2. $2x - \frac{x+5}{x}$ Answer: $\frac{2x^2 - x - 5}{x}$
3. $3n + \frac{2n+3}{4n+5}$ Answer: $\frac{12n^2 + 17n + 3}{4n + 5}$
4. WRITING MATHEMATICS Explain how converting a mixed expression to a rational expression is similar to converting a mixed number to an improper fraction. Show an example of each and explain the steps. Answers will vary.
5. TESTING On a particular true-false examination, there were $\frac{100}{4x+1}$ true statements and $\frac{80}{3x+2}$ false statements. Determine the ratio of true statements to false statements. Answer: $\frac{15x + 10}{16x + 4}$

Simplify. Write your answer in simplest form.

6. $\dfrac{\frac{5}{x}}{\frac{7}{y}}$ Answer: $\frac{5y}{7x}$
7. $\dfrac{\frac{8}{c}}{\frac{3}{d}}$ Answer: $\frac{8d}{3c}$
8. $\dfrac{\frac{13}{2u}}{\frac{6}{5z}}$ Answer: $\frac{65z}{12u}$
9. $\dfrac{\frac{1}{p} - \frac{3}{q}}{\frac{11}{2q}}$ Answer: $\frac{2q - 6p}{11p}$
10. $\dfrac{\frac{1}{r} - \frac{1}{t}}{\frac{7}{3t}}$ Answer: $\frac{3t - 3r}{7r}$
11. $\dfrac{\frac{6}{a} - 5}{-2 - \frac{3}{a}}$ Answer: $\frac{-5a + 6}{-2a - 3}$
12. $\dfrac{7 - \frac{5}{g+3}}{14 - \frac{10}{g+3}}$ Answer: $\frac{1}{2}$
13. AGRICULTURE Refer to Example 4. Suppose the gardener had purchased 12 sacks of fertilizer in April. How many sacks could be purchased in August? 15

PRACTICE

Convert each mixed expression to a rational expression.

1. $11 - \frac{13}{b}$ Answer: $\frac{11b - 13}{b}$
2. $3x - \frac{x+2}{x}$ Answer: $\frac{3x^2 - x - 2}{x}$
3. $\frac{2z-5}{3z} + 3z - 1$ Answer: $\frac{9z^2 - z - 5}{3z}$
4. $n + \frac{n-4}{3n+4}$ Answer: $\frac{3n^2 + 5n - 4}{3n + 4}$
5. $t - 3 - \frac{5}{t+1}$ Answer: $\frac{t^2 - 2t - 8}{t + 1}$
6. $b + 5 + \frac{5}{b-5}$ Answer: $\frac{b^2 - 20}{b - 5}$

Simplify. Write your answer in simplest form.

7. $\dfrac{\frac{3}{x}}{\frac{4}{y}}$ Answer: $\frac{3y}{4x}$
8. $\dfrac{\frac{5}{m}}{\frac{6}{n}}$ Answer: $\frac{5n}{6m}$
9. $\dfrac{\frac{1}{p} - \frac{3}{q}}{\frac{4}{q}}$ Answer: $\frac{q - 3p}{4p}$
10. $\dfrac{\frac{2}{r} + \frac{3}{t}}{-\frac{5}{r}}$ Answer: $-\frac{2t + 3r}{5t}$
11. $\dfrac{\frac{7}{2u}}{\frac{8}{3v}}$ Answer: $\frac{21v}{16u}$
12. $\dfrac{\frac{5}{uv^2}}{\frac{2}{u^2v}}$ Answer: $\frac{5u}{2v}$
13. $\dfrac{\frac{1}{r} - \frac{1}{t}}{-\frac{6}{5t}}$ Answer: $\frac{-5t + 5r}{6r}$
14. $\dfrac{\frac{1}{m} - \frac{1}{n}}{\frac{3}{2m} - \frac{3}{2n}}$ Answer: $\frac{2}{3}$
15. $\dfrac{\frac{4}{p} + 5}{\frac{5}{q}}$ Answer: $\frac{4q + 5pq}{5p}$
16. $\dfrac{\frac{8}{a} - 9}{\frac{6}{b}}$ Answer: $\frac{8b - 9ab}{6a}$
17. $\dfrac{\frac{c}{d^2} + \frac{3}{d}}{\frac{c}{d} - 1}$ Answer: $\frac{c + 3d}{cd - d^2}$
18. $\dfrac{\frac{4}{e^2} + \frac{f}{e}}{\frac{2}{e} - 12}$ Answer: $\frac{4 + ef}{2e - 12e^2}$

19. **ELECTRICITY** In a parallel circuit with two light bulbs, the total resistance R can be determined by the formula $R = \frac{R_1 \cdot R_2}{R_1 + R_2}$. If $R_1 = \frac{5}{q}$ ohm and $R_2 = \frac{10}{q^2}$ ohm, determine R. $\frac{10}{q^2 + 2q}$

20. **TRAVEL** Stacey drives m km at 40 km/h and returns on the same route at 60 km/h. Determine Stacey's average speed for the round trip. 48 km/h

21. **VOTING** In Urbania, $\frac{250{,}000}{3x - 10}$ people voted yes on a bond issue and $\frac{4{,}000{,}000}{x^2}$ people voted no. Determine the ratio of yes votes to no votes. See Additional Answers.

22. **WRITING MATHEMATICS** Example 2 shows one procedure for simplifying a complex expression. Next to Example 2, Communicating About Algebra shows a different procedure. Choose the procedure you prefer and explain why you prefer it. Answers will vary.

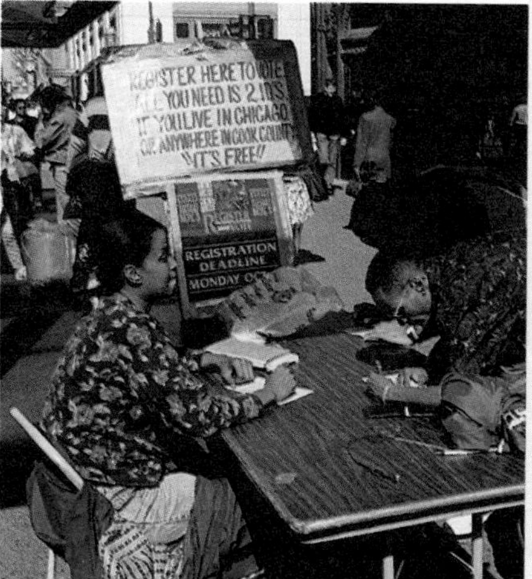

EXTEND

When the rational expressions in the numerator and denominator of the complex rational expression have denominators that are polynomials of more than one term, factor first, if possible. Then determine the LCD. For example,

$$\frac{\frac{4x}{x^2 - 25} + \frac{6}{x + 5}}{\frac{3}{2x + 10}} = \frac{\frac{4x}{(x + 5)(x - 5)} + \frac{6}{(x + 5)}}{\frac{3}{2(x + 5)}}$$

Factor: the LCD is $2(x + 5)(x - 5)$.

23. Simplify the expression above. $\frac{20x - 60}{3x - 15}$

Simplify.

24. $\dfrac{\frac{3x}{x^2 - 49} + \frac{7}{x + 7}}{\frac{1}{x - 7} - \frac{7}{2x + 14}}$ $\frac{20x - 98}{-5x + 63}$

25. $\dfrac{\frac{2b}{b - 4} - \frac{3}{b^2}}{\frac{5}{5b - 20} + \frac{3}{4b^2 - 16b}}$ $\frac{8b^3 - 12b + 48}{4b^2 + 3b}$

26. $\dfrac{\frac{6}{n^2 + n - 20} + \frac{3}{n - 4}}{\frac{2}{3n - 12} + \frac{3}{n + 5}}$ $\frac{9n + 63}{11n - 26}$

GEOMETRY Determine the width of each rectangle with the given length and area.

27. $\frac{x + 1}{x - 1}$ ft; $\frac{x^2 + 2x + 1}{4}$ ft^2 $\frac{x^2 - 1}{4}$ ft

28. $\frac{2x + 10}{3x + 18}$ ft; $\frac{x^2 + 14x + 45}{x^2 + 6x}$ ft^2 $\frac{3x + 27}{2x}$ ft

THINK CRITICALLY

29. Is $\frac{5}{6}$ a complex rational expression? Explain. yes; 5 and 6 are both rational expressions

30. Provide an example of a complex rational expression that is its own reciprocal. See Additional Answers.

Simplify.

31. $\dfrac{\frac{1}{a + 1}}{a - \frac{1}{a + \frac{1}{a}}}$ $\frac{a^2 + 1}{a^4 + a^3}$

32. $\dfrac{2}{c + \frac{1}{1 + \frac{c + 1}{5 - c}}}$ $\frac{12}{5c + 5}$

5 FOLLOW-UP

Extension Have students use graphing utilities to graph the following equation: $y = [x^{-1} - x(x^2 - 1)^{-1}] \div [(x + 1)^{-1} - (x - 1)^{-1}]$. Have them set the window for $-2 \le x \le 2$ and $-10 \le y \le 10$.

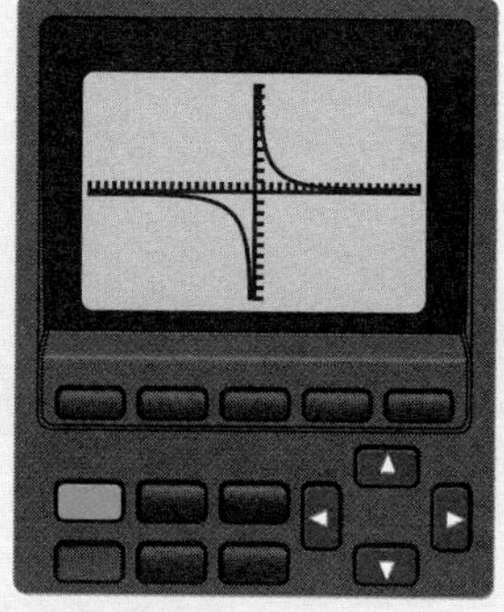

Then have them rewrite the expression with all positive exponents and simplify the result. Have them graph the resulting equation. **$y = [1/x - x/(x^2 - 1)]/[1/(x + 1) - 1/(x - 1)] = 1/2x$** Ask how the graph of the second equation compares with that of the first. **They are the same.**

ENRICHMENT

NAME ______ CLASS ______ DATE ______

14.7 COMPLEX RATIONAL EXPRESSIONS

Compute this sequence of continued fractions. Use the pattern to write Exercise 6.

1. $1 + \frac{1}{2}$ — 1. $\frac{3}{2}$
2. $1 + \frac{1}{1 + \frac{1}{2}}$ — 2. $\frac{5}{3}$
3. $1 + \frac{1}{1 + \frac{1}{1 + \frac{1}{2}}}$ — 3. $\frac{8}{5}$
4. $1 + \frac{1}{1 + \frac{1}{1 + \frac{1}{1 + \frac{1}{2}}}}$ — 4. $\frac{13}{8}$
5. $1 + \frac{1}{1 + \frac{1}{1 + \frac{1}{1 + \frac{1}{1 + \frac{1}{2}}}}}$ — 5. $\frac{21}{13}$
6. $1 + \frac{1}{1 + \frac{1}{1 + \frac{1}{1 + \frac{1}{1 + \frac{1}{1 + \frac{1}{2}}}}}}$ — 6. $\frac{34}{21}$
7. Predict the 10th sum in this pattern. — 7. $\frac{233}{144}$
8. What do you notice about this pattern? **Answers will vary. Possible answer: the numerator of the next sum is the sum of the numerator and denominator of the previous sum. The denominator is the numerator of the previous sum.**
9. Compute the decimal equivalent of each sum. What do you notice? **Each decimal is a closer approximation to 1.618, which is the golden ratio.**

50 South-Western Algebra 1: AN INTEGRATED APPROACH

LESSON PLANNING

Objectives

- ▶ Solve rational equations.
- ▶ Solve uniform motion and work problems.

Vocabulary

rational equation
extraneous solutions

Technology/Multimedia

graphing utility

Resources

Warm Up 14.8
Reteaching 14.8
Extra Practice 14.8
Enrichment 14.8
Transparencies 78–80
Student Handbook
Lesson Quiz 14.8

ASSIGNMENTS

Basic: 1–14, 16, 18, 22, Project Connection 1–3

Average: 3–18, 21–24, Project Connection 1–3

Enriched: 4–25, Project Connection 1–3

1 MOTIVATE

Explore For Question 1b, ask students to explain how they can find the LCD. **Factor each denominator: $4 = 2^2$ and $9 = 3^2$; since there are no common prime factors, multiply the factors of each to get 36.** For Questions 3 and 4, have students describe how they found the LCD for each. **Factor each denominator; for each common prime factor, choose the term with the greatest exponent and multiply.**

14.8 Solve Rational Equations

SPOTLIGHT ON LEARNING

WHAT? In this lesson you will learn

- to solve rational equations.
- to set up and solve uniform motion problems and work problems.

WHY? Knowing how to solve rational equations can help you to solve problems in travel, finance, water storage, and agriculture.

Explore

1. **a.** Determine the least integer that produces integral coefficients when you multiply both sides of the equation by the integer.

$$3 + \frac{x}{4} = \frac{x}{9}$$ 36

b. What way besides trial and error can you use to determine this number? Determine the LCD.

c. Write and solve the resulting equation. $108 + 9x = 4x$; $x = -\frac{108}{5}$

Solve for x.

2. $\frac{x}{2} + \frac{x}{5} = 50$ $\frac{500}{7}$
3. $\frac{2x}{7} = \frac{3x}{8} - \frac{5}{4}$ 14
4. $\frac{3x}{10} = \frac{2x}{15} + \frac{3}{2}$ 9

5. How would you solve an equation such as $\frac{4}{x} + \frac{8}{x} = 2$? See Additional Answers.
6. What method would you use to solve any equation that contains one or more rational expressions? Answers will vary. Multiply both sides of the equation by the LCD of the denominators of all the rational expressions.

Build Understanding

A **rational equation** is an equation that contains one or more rational expressions. To eliminate the denominators (other than 1), multiply both sides of the rational equation by the LCD of all the expressions. Then solve the resulting equation. Check each solution *in the original equation* to make sure that it is a solution.

EXAMPLE 1

Solve and check: $\frac{3}{x} + \frac{1}{2x} = 7$

Solution

Algebraic Method

$$\frac{3}{x} + \frac{1}{2x} = 7$$ The LCD is $2x$.

$$\frac{3}{x}(2x) + \frac{1}{2x}(2x) = 7(2x)$$ Multiply each term by the LCD.

$$6 + 1 = 14x$$

$$7 = 14x$$

$$\frac{1}{2} = x$$ Solve the resulting equation.

Check

$$\frac{3}{\frac{1}{2}} + \frac{1}{2\left(\frac{1}{2}\right)} \stackrel{?}{=} 7$$

$$6 + 1 \stackrel{?}{=} 7$$

$$7 = 7 \checkmark$$

The solution is $\frac{1}{2}$.

Graphing Method

Use a graphing utility to graph each side of the equation. Determine where the graphs of $y_1 = \frac{3}{x} + \frac{1}{2x}$ and $y_2 = 7$ intersect.

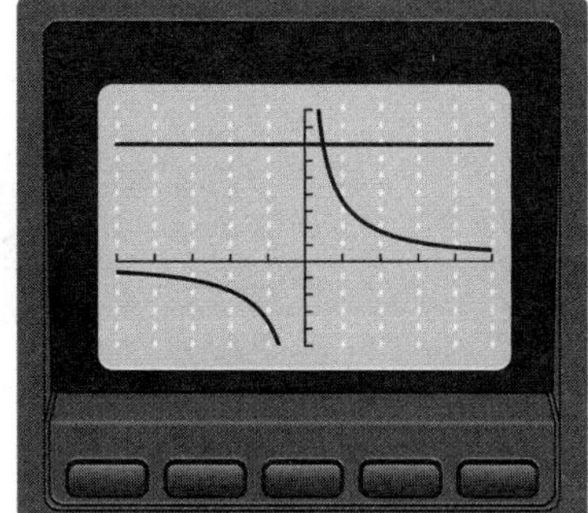

Since the value of y_1 and y_2 is 7 when $x = \frac{1}{2}$, the solution is $x = \frac{1}{2}$. ◄

When you multiply both sides of a rational equation by an LCD that contains a variable and then solve the resulting equation, you may find solutions that make the denominator of the original equation equal to zero. Such solutions are called *extraneous solutions.*

EXAMPLE 2

Solve and check: $\frac{3}{a-3} + 2 = \frac{a}{a-3}$

Solution

$$\frac{3}{a-3} + 2 = \frac{a}{a-3}$$ The LCD is $(a - 3)$.

$$\frac{3}{(a-3)}(a-3) + 2(a-3) = \frac{a}{(a-3)}(a-3)$$ Multiply each term by the LCD.

$$3 + 2a - 6 = a$$

$$3 = a$$ Solve the resulting equation.

Check

$$\frac{3}{3-3} + 2 \stackrel{?}{=} \frac{3}{3-3}$$

Since the denominator is zero when $a = 3$, 3 is an extraneous solution. The original equation has no solution. ◄

You may get two solutions to a rational equation. However, one or both of them may be extraneous.

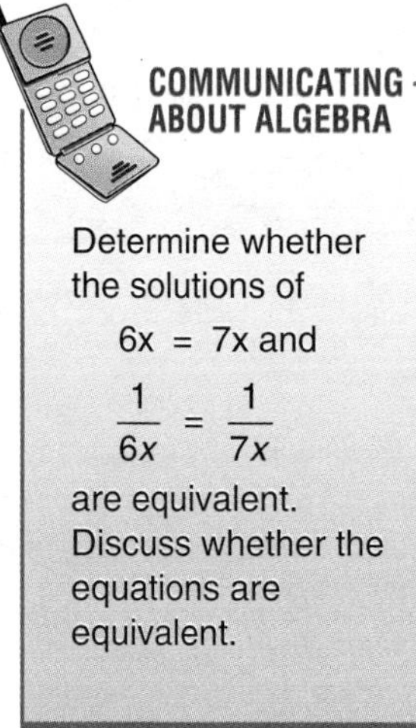

COMMUNICATING ABOUT ALGEBRA

Determine whether the solutions of

$6x = 7x$ and

$\frac{1}{6x} = \frac{1}{7x}$

are equivalent. Discuss whether the equations are equivalent.

See Additional Answers.

2 TEACH

Use the Pages/Build Understanding

Example 1: Ask what the restrictions on x are. $\mathbf{x \neq 0}$ For the algebraic method, point out the importance of multiplying each term on both sides of the equation by the LCD, in this case $2x$. Also emphasize that to check, students should substitute the solution in the original equation.

For the paragraph following Example 1, point out that an extraneous solution satisfied the transformed equation but not the original equation.

Example 2: Ask students what properties were applied in multiplying each term of both sides of the equation by the LCD. **the distributive property and the multiplicative identity property** Have students graph the system with a graphing utility, letting $x = a$. Have them try to determine the intersection points. Explain that although it looks as if the graphs might intersect as the value of x approaches 3, the value of Y_1 is always 2 greater than the value of Y_2. The graphs do not intersect, and so there is no solution.

Example 3: Point out that when students multiply by the LCD, the resulting equation may be quadratic with two solutions, one of which is extraneous.

Example 4: Some students might find it helpful to organize the information in a table.

	Distance	Rate	Time
Debbie	300	r	t
Mindy	300	$r-10$	$t+1$

Example 5: Be sure that students understand why the expressions for the rates are 140 + w and 140 – w. Ask students to explain why the time for the airplane flying 700 miles with a tail wind equals 700/(140 + w) and why the time for the airplane flying 420 miles against the wind equals 420/(140 – w). **Since distance = rate • time, time = distance ÷ rate.**

Ongoing Assessment The important concepts and skills are solving rational equations and solving uniform motion and work problems. To assess these ideas, have students demonstrate how they have applied these concepts and skills in Exercises 6, 7, and 11 of the Try These section.

Guided Practice/Try These For Exercise 5, have students explain why there is no solution. **An algebraic solution is b = 2, but b cannot equal 2, since it makes the denominator equal to zero.**

Make Connections

Sports Tell students that the batting average of a baseball player is the ratio of the number of hits to the number of official times at bat. If a batter has officially been at bat 120 times and had 30 hits, the current batting average is 30/120 or .250. Ask how many consecutive hits must be made to increase the average to .280. To solve, students will need to add the same number to the hits and to the times at bat to get the new average of .280. **Let x = the number of future hits and the number of future times at bat. Then, .280 = (30 + x)/(120 + x), x = 5. Thus you need 5 more hits in 5 more times at bat.**

3 SUMMARIZE

In the Math Journal Have students discuss whether the following equation is solved correctly.

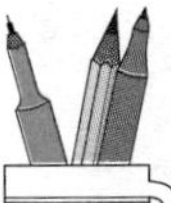

PROBLEM SOLVING TIP

When the denominators of a rational equation are polynomials of more than one term, factor if possible before finding the LCD.

EXAMPLE 3

Solve and check: $\dfrac{c}{c+3} - \dfrac{4}{c-3} = \dfrac{c-27}{c^2-9}$

Solution

$$\frac{c}{c+3} - \frac{4}{c-3} = \frac{c-27}{c^2-9} \qquad \text{The LCD is } (c+3)(c-3).$$

$$\frac{c}{\cancel{(c+3)}}\cancel{(c+3)}(c-3) - \frac{4}{\cancel{(c-3)}}(c+3)\cancel{(c-3)} = \frac{c-27}{\cancel{(c+3)(c-3)}}\cancel{(c+3)(c-3)}$$

$$\begin{aligned} c(c-3) - 4(c+3) &= c - 27 \\ c^2 - 3c - 4c - 12 &= c - 27 \\ c^2 - 8c + 15 &= 0 \\ (c-3)(c-5) &= 0 \qquad \text{Solve by factoring.} \\ c - 3 = 0 \text{ or } c - 5 &= 0 \\ c = 3 \qquad c &= 5 \end{aligned}$$

Check

Substitute 3 for c in the original equation.

$$\frac{3}{3+3} - \frac{4}{3-3} \stackrel{?}{=} \frac{3-27}{3^2-9}$$

Since two denominators in the original equation are 0 when $c = 3$, 3 is an extraneous solution.

Substitute 5 for c in the original equation.

$$\frac{5}{5+3} - \frac{4}{5-3} \stackrel{?}{=} \frac{5-27}{5^2-9}$$

$$\frac{5}{8} - \frac{4}{2} \stackrel{?}{=} \frac{-22}{16}$$

$$\frac{-11}{8} = \frac{-11}{8} \checkmark$$

Rational equations can be used to solve problems involving *uniform (constant) motion.*

EXAMPLE 4

TRAVEL Debbie and Mindy each traveled 300 mi to visit Lamb's Farm. Debbie drove at an average speed of 10 mi/h faster than Mindy drove and arrived 1 h earlier than Mindy. How fast did each woman drive?

Solution

Use the information given in the problem to set up a rational equation. You know that Debbie made the trip in 1 h less than Mindy.

Since distance = rate • time, time = distance ÷ rate. Let r represent the rate at which Debbie traveled. Therefore, $r - 10$ represents the rate at which Mindy traveled.

$$\text{Debbie's time} = \text{Mindy's time} - 1$$

$$\frac{300}{r} = \frac{300}{r - 10} - 1$$

Solve the equation using an LCD of $r(r - 10)$.

$$\frac{300}{\cancel{r}}(\cancel{r})(r - 10) = \frac{300}{\cancel{(r - 10)}}(r)\cancel{(r - 10)} - 1(r)(r - 10)$$

$$\begin{aligned} 300(r - 10) &= 300r - r(r - 10) \\ 300r - 3000 &= 300r - r^2 + 10r \\ r^2 - 10r - 3000 &= 0 \\ (r - 60)(r + 50) &= 0 \\ r - 60 = 0 \quad &\text{or } r + 50 = 0 \\ r = 60 \quad & \quad r = -50 \end{aligned}$$

Eliminate $r = -50$, since a negative rate of speed does not make sense in this situation. Debbie traveled at 60 mi/h and Mindy traveled at $60 - 10$ or 50 mi/h. ◄

CHECK UNDERSTANDING

In Example 4, check the solutions $r = 60$ and $r = -50$ in the original equation. Is either solution extraneous?

Both solutions work. Neither is extraneous for the equation, but –50 is eliminated because it does not make sense in the context of the problem.

$$\begin{aligned} 3(5) &= z(z - 2) \\ 15 &= z^2 - 2z \\ 0 &= z^2 - 2z - 15 \\ 0 &= (z + 3)(z - 5) \\ z &= -3, z = 5 \end{aligned}$$

Yes, because the LCD 5(z – 2) was multiplied correctly on both sides of the equation, the equation was correctly written in standard form, and it was factored correctly.

Rational equations can also be used to solve problems involving *wind speed*.

EXAMPLE 5

TRAVEL In calm air, a small airplane can fly at the rate of 140 mi/h. It can fly 700 mi with a tailwind in the same time it can fly 420 mi against the wind. Find the speed of the wind.

Solution

Let w represent the rate of the wind. Then $140 + w$ represents the rate with the wind and $140 - w$ the rate against the wind.

Since the time for the 700-mi trip equals the time for the 420-mi trip, you can write an equation.

$$\frac{700}{140 + w} = \frac{420}{140 - w} \qquad \text{The LCD is } (140 + w)(140 - w).$$

$$\frac{700}{\cancel{(140 + w)}}\cancel{(140 + w)}(140 - w) = \frac{420}{\cancel{(140 - w)}}(140 + w)\cancel{(140 - w)}$$

$$\begin{aligned} 700(140 - w) &= 420(140 + w) \\ 98{,}000 - 700w &= 58{,}800 + 420w \\ 39{,}200 &= 1{,}120w \\ 35 &= w \qquad \text{Solve the equation.} \end{aligned}$$

The speed of the wind was 35 mi/h. ◄

COMMUNICATING ABOUT ALGEBRA

Discuss how to organize the information for Example 5 using a table.

	d	r	t
With wind	700	140 + w	$\frac{700}{140 + w}$
Against wind	420	140 – w	$\frac{420}{140 - w}$

4 PRACTICE

Practice Remind students to check each solution in the original rational equation for possible extraneous solutions. Ask students to describe a table they could set up to solve the problem in Exercise 14.

	With a tail wind	Against the wind
Distance	2400	2000
Rate	550 + w	550 – w
Time	2400/(550 + w)	2000/(550 – w)

NAME ____________ CLASS ________ DATE ________

RETEACHING

14.8 SOLVE RATIONAL EQUATIONS

To solve a rational equation, change it to an equivalent equation that has no denominators. Do this by multiplying both sides of the equation by the least common denominator of all the denominators in the equation.

Example

Solve: $\frac{1}{2x} + \frac{2}{3x} = \frac{7}{12}$

Solution

The least common denominator of $2x$, $3x$, and 12 is $12x$. Multiply both sides by $12x$.

$$\begin{aligned} 12x\left(\frac{1}{2x}\right) + 12x\left(\frac{2}{3x}\right) &= 12x\left(\frac{7}{12}\right) \\ 6(1) + 4(2) &= x(7) \\ 6 + 8 &= 7x \\ 14 &= 7x \\ \frac{14}{7} &= \frac{7x}{7} \\ 2 &= x \end{aligned}$$

Check

$$\begin{aligned} \frac{1}{2(2)} + \frac{2}{3(2)} &= \frac{7}{12} \\ \frac{1}{4} + \frac{2}{6} &= \frac{7}{12} \\ \frac{3}{12} + \frac{4}{12} &= \frac{7}{12} \\ \frac{7}{12} &= \frac{7}{12} \checkmark \end{aligned}$$

EXERCISES

Solve and check.

1. $\frac{2}{x} + \frac{1}{2x} = \frac{5}{6}$ LCD $= 6x$

$6x\left(\frac{2}{x}\right) + 6x\left(\frac{1}{2x}\right) = 6x\left(\frac{5}{6}\right)$

$12 + 3 = 5x$

$\frac{15}{5} = x$

2. $\frac{3}{2} + \frac{3a}{5} = \frac{7a}{10}$

3. $\frac{4}{b} + \frac{3}{2b} = \frac{11}{14}$

4. $\frac{5}{c + 1} - \frac{2}{c} = \frac{7}{4c}$

5. $\frac{2}{d} - \frac{1}{d - 2} = \frac{11}{3d}$

1. **3**
2. **15**
3. **7**
4. **$\frac{11}{9}$**
5. **$\frac{5}{4}$**

54 *South-Western Algebra 1: AN INTEGRATED APPROACH*

Then ask what rational equation they can use to solve the problem. **Set the expressions for time equal to each other: 2400/(550 + *w*) = 2000/(550 – *w*).** For Exercise 15, ask students what rational equation they used to solve the problem. **(1500 + *x*)/(*x* + 450) = 23/17**

Extend For Exercises 16–17, remind students to factor each rational expression in the equation before trying to find the LCD. For Exercises 18–20, suggest that students organize the information in tables.

Think Critically For Exercise 21, ask students what it means for a solution to be extraneous. **When substituted in the original equation, it makes a denominator zero.** For Exercise 22, ask them when a rational equation has no solution. **When the only solution or solutions make a denominator of the original equation zero when substituted in that equation.**

NAME ______________ CLASS ________ DATE ________

EXTRA PRACTICE **14.8 SOLVE RATIONAL EQUATIONS**

Solve and check. If an equation has no solution, write *no solution*.

1. $2a + \frac{2}{3} = \frac{3}{4}$
2. $3b - \frac{4}{5} = -\frac{7}{8}$
3. $\frac{2c}{3} + \frac{4c}{5} = 44$
4. $\frac{3d}{2} - \frac{5d}{4} = 2$
5. $\frac{6}{g-3} + 2 = \frac{10}{g-3}$
6. $\frac{2h+3}{h+3} = \frac{-3}{h+3} - 1$
7. $2 + \frac{3}{j} = -10$
8. $\frac{4}{k} - 2 = 18$
9. $\frac{3}{5m} + \frac{7}{2m} = 2$
10. $\frac{1}{n} - \frac{3}{4n} = 1$
11. $\frac{p-1}{p-2} + \frac{3}{p-2} = 5$
12. $\frac{q+6}{q+1} + \frac{5q}{q+1} = 3$
13. $\frac{1}{r} + \frac{4}{5r} = \frac{9}{10}$
14. $\frac{1}{3s} - \frac{2}{s} = \frac{5}{6}$
15. $\frac{x}{x+1} - 3 = \frac{7}{x+1}$
16. $1 + \frac{3}{q-2} = \frac{2q}{q-2}$
17. $\frac{x}{5} + \frac{1}{x-1} = \frac{x+1}{x-1}$
18. $\frac{w+1}{w-1} - \frac{2}{w-1} = \frac{w}{8}$
19. **BOATING** A boat that sails at 30 kilometers per hour in still water can go 104 kilometers with the wind in the same time it takes to travel 91 kilometers against the wind. Find the wind speed.

1. $\frac{1}{24}$
2. $-\frac{1}{40}$
3. 30
4. 8
5. 5
6. no solution
7. $-\frac{1}{4}$
8. $\frac{1}{5}$
9. 2.05
10. $\frac{1}{4}$
11. 3
12. no solution
13. 2
14. –2
15. –5
16. 1
17. 0, 6
18. 8
19. 2 km/h

56 *South-Western Algebra 1: AN INTEGRATED APPROACH*

TRY THESE

1. **WRITING MATHEMATICS** Explain why it is necessary to check possible solutions of a rational equation in the original equation. See Additional Answers.

Solve and check. If an equation has no solution, write no solution.

2. $2x + \frac{4}{5} = \frac{17}{20}$ $\frac{1}{40}$
3. $\frac{3t}{4} - \frac{5t}{8} = 8$ 64
4. $\frac{7t}{3} - \frac{8t}{9} = 13$ 9
5. $\frac{b}{b-2} - 2 = \frac{2}{b-2}$ no solution
6. $4 + \frac{5}{c} = -11$ $-\frac{1}{3}$
7. $\frac{3}{4e} - \frac{5}{2e} = \frac{7}{2}$ $-\frac{1}{2}$
8. $\frac{h+8}{h} + \frac{3}{4h} = 11$ $\frac{7}{8}$
9. $\frac{2c+5}{c+10} = \frac{c-9}{c+10} + 1$ no solution
10. $\frac{4d-6}{d-11} = \frac{d+8}{d-11} + 2$ –8
11. **BOATING** A canoe can travel 16 mi/h in still water. Going with the current, it can travel 24 mi in the same amount of time that it can travel 12 mi going against the current. Determine the rate of the current. $5\frac{1}{3}$ mi/h

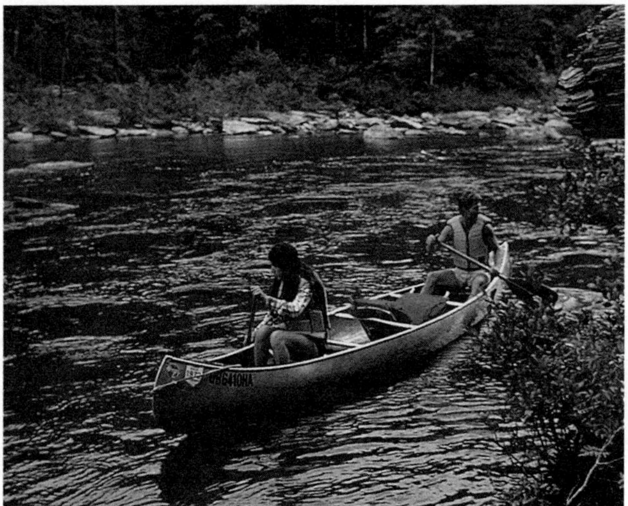

PRACTICE

Solve and check. If an equation has no solution, write no solution.

1. $2m + \frac{2}{3} = \frac{23}{10}$ $\frac{49}{60}$
2. $6a - \frac{7}{8} = -\frac{12}{5}$ $-\frac{61}{240}$
3. $\frac{3u}{4} + \frac{4u}{6} = 17$ 12
4. $\frac{4v}{15} + \frac{v}{5} = 14$ 30
5. $\frac{j}{j+6} = 3 - \frac{6}{j+6}$ no solution
6. $\frac{k}{k+2} - \frac{5}{k+2} = 8$ –3
7. $\frac{m}{m-5} - \frac{13}{m-5} = 7$ $\frac{11}{3}$
8. $4 - \frac{6}{n} = 5$ –6
9. $\frac{4}{5q} - \frac{2}{7q} = \frac{1}{35}$ 18
10. $\frac{w+3}{w} + \frac{2}{3w} = 12$ $\frac{1}{3}$
11. $\frac{x-3}{x} + \frac{3}{4x} = 16$ $-\frac{3}{20}$
12. $\frac{3d-8}{d-5} = \frac{d+6}{d-5} + 2$ no solution
13. **WRITING MATHEMATICS** In your own words, explain the procedure used to rewrite rational equations so they are easier to solve. Students should discuss determining and multiplying by the LCD.
14. **TRAVEL** A jet can fly 550 mi/h in calm air. With a tailwind, it can fly 2400 mi in the same time it can fly 2000 mi against the wind. Find the time it takes to make the 2400 mi trip with the tailwind. 4 h
15. **FINANCE** Rikuichi's checking account contains $1500 more than Keemo's. If Keemo makes a deposit of $450, the ratio of the amount in Rikuichi's account to the amount in Keemo's account will be 46 : 25. Determine the amount of money in each account. Rikuichi = $2300, Keemo = $1250

EXTEND

In Exercises 16–17, factor each denominator before determining the LCD. Then solve and check. Eliminate any extraneous solutions.

16. $\dfrac{2t - 5}{t^2 - t - 2} = \dfrac{t - 5}{t^2 - 4t - 5}$ 3

17. $\dfrac{x + 5}{x^2 + 4x - 5} = \dfrac{2x + 8}{x^2 + 3x - 4}$ no solution

18. **BOATING** A motorboat can travel 12 mi downstream in $\frac{3}{4}$ of the time it takes to travel the same distance upstream. Determine the rate of the motorboat in still water if the rate of the current is 4 mi/h. 28 mi/h

19. **WATER STORAGE** Two pipes can fill a storage tank in 12 h if they run at the same time. If the faster pipe runs 4 times as fast as the slower one, how long would it take for the faster one to fill the tank working alone? 15 h

20. **INTERIOR DECORATING** An experienced wallpaper hanger can hang paper twice as fast as his apprentice can. If they work together, they can paper a large room in 4 h. How long would it take each one working alone to do the job?
wallpaper hanger: 6 h; apprentice: 12 h

THINK CRITICALLY

21. Write a rational equation that has an extraneous solution of 4 and one other solution that is not extraneous. See Additional Answers.

22. Write an original rational equation that has no solution. See Additional Answers.

23. Write an original rational equation that has zero as its only solution. See Additional Answers.

Solve and check.

24. $\left(\dfrac{x - 3}{x + 6}\right)^2 \cdot \left(\dfrac{x + 6}{2x - 6}\right)^3 = 1$ $\dfrac{30}{7}$

25. $\left(\dfrac{x - 2}{x + 4}\right)^2 \div \left(\dfrac{3x - 6}{x + 4}\right)^3 = 1$ $\dfrac{29}{13}$

PROJECT *Connection*

The table shows the dry matter capacity for standard 12-ft-diameter silos.

Silage, the livestock feed stored in the silo, is usually moist material. Depending on the moisture level, the total tonnage for the silo will vary.

Size, ft (diameter × height)	Volume, ft^3	Dry Matter, approximate tons
12 × 30	3390	21
12 × 40	4520	31
12 × 50	5650	42

The total tonnage at different moisture levels is described by the following rational function where the moisture level is expressed as a percent.

$$\frac{\text{tons dry matter}}{1.00 - \text{percent moisture level}} = \text{tons in silo}$$

1. Determine how many tons of 50% moisture feed are in a 12-ft × 50-ft silo. How many tons will there be if the moisture level is 65%? 84 tons; 120 tons

2. At what moisture level will a 12-ft × 40-ft silo hold about 77.5 tons? 60%

3. Use a graphing utility to graph the function for a 12-ft × 30-ft silo. For what moisture levels is the function defined? Why? See Additional Answers.

5 FOLLOW-UP

Extension Have students explore the relationship between the length and width of rectangles when the perimeter is equal to the area. Have them consider rectangles with the dimensions 10 cm x 2.5 cm and 6 cm x 3 cm.

Ask them to write a rational equation expressing the length in terms of the width for a rectangle whose perimeter is equal to its area. ***A* = *lw* and *P* = 2(*l* + *w*); *l* = (2*w*)/(*w* – 2)**

Project Connection This activity presents further aspects of the project introduced on page 674. For Question 2, check that students have correctly substituted values in the equation: $\dfrac{31}{1 - x} = 77.5$ so $77.5(1 - x) = 31$ and $-77.5x = -46.5$, thus $x = 0.6 = 60\%$.

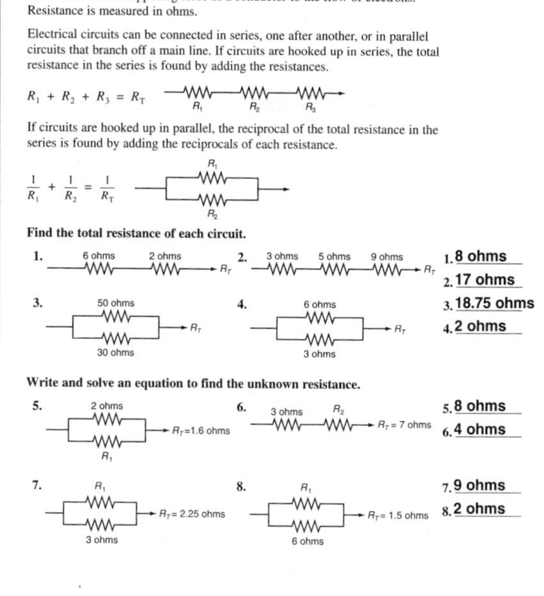

NAME ________ CLASS ________ DATE ________

ENRICHMENT **14.8 SOLVE RATIONAL EQUATIONS**

Electrical current is the flow of electrons through a conductor such as metal. The current flows more easily through some conductors than others. Resistance is a measure of the opposing force of a conductor to the flow of electrons. Resistance is measured in ohms.

Electrical circuits can be connected in series, one after another, or in parallel circuits that branch off a main line. If circuits are hooked up in series, the total resistance in the series is found by adding the resistances.

$R_1 + R_2 + R_3 = R_T$

If circuits are hooked up in parallel, the reciprocal of the total resistance in the series is found by adding the reciprocals of each resistance.

$\dfrac{1}{R_1} + \dfrac{1}{R_2} = \dfrac{1}{R_T}$

Find the total resistance of each circuit.

1. 6 ohms, 2 ohms → R_T
2. 3 ohms, 5 ohms, 9 ohms → R_T
3. 50 ohms, 30 ohms → R_T
4. 6 ohms, 3 ohms → R_T

1. 8 ohms
2. 17 ohms
3. 18.75 ohms
4. 2 ohms

Write and solve an equation to find the unknown resistance.

5. 2 ohms, R_1 → R_T=1.6 ohms
6. 3 ohms, R_2 → R_T = 7 ohms
7. R_1, 3 ohms → R_T= 2.25 ohms
8. R_1, 6 ohms → R_T= 1.5 ohms

5. 8 ohms
6. 4 ohms
7. 9 ohms
8. 2 ohms

58 *South-Western Algebra 1: AN INTEGRATED APPROACH*

LESSON PLANNING

Objective

▶ Use dimensional analysis to solve problems.

Vocabulary

conversion factor
dimensional analysis
dimensions

Resources

Reteaching 14.9
Extra Practice 14.9
Transparency 10
Student Handbook

ASSIGNMENTS

Basic: 1–10, 12, Review Problem Solving Strategies 1–3

Average: 1–14, Review Problem Solving Strategies 1–3

Enriched: 1–15, Review Problem Solving Strategies 1–3

1 MOTIVATE

Introduction After students have read the first two paragraphs, ask them to solve the following two problems. Have them explain how they found each solution.

1. If Aline drives for 3 h at 40 mi/h, how many miles will she travel? **d = 40 mi/h • 3 h = 40 • 3 • mi • h/h = 120 mi**
2. If a garden snail travels at about 31.7 in./min, how many inches can it travel in 5 minutes? **d = 31.7 in./min • 5 min = 31.7 • 5 • in. • min/min = 158.5 in.**

Tell students that dimensional analysis can help them set up equations for problems involving conversion.

14.9 Problem Solving File

Use Logical Thinking

Use Dimensional Analysis

SPOTLIGHT ON LEARNING

WHAT? In this lesson you will learn
- to solve problems involving the units or dimensions in which quantities are measured.
- to convert dimensions from one unit to another.

WHY? Analyzing dimensions of measurement can help you solve problems in chemistry, physics, astronomy, travel, and personnel management.

The **dimensions** of a quantity are the units in which it is measured. For example, consider the units of a distance formula.

$$\text{distance} = \text{rate} \cdot \text{time} \qquad \text{and} \qquad \text{rate} = \frac{\text{distance}}{\text{time}}$$

If the distance is in inches and the time is in minutes, the rate must be in inches per minute.

You can treat units as though they were variables. Substitute the units into the distance formula to check that both sides represent distance.

$$\text{inches} = \frac{\text{inches}}{\text{minute}} \cdot \text{minutes}$$

Because only identical units divide out, you may need to introduce a **conversion factor** if the units do not match. For example, suppose the rate in the equation above were feet/minute and your answer has to be in inches.

$$\text{inches} = \frac{\text{feet}}{\text{minute}} \cdot \text{minutes}$$

Since inches ≠ feet, you need to *convert* feet to inches to get an answer in inches. You can do this by multiplying the rate by 12 inches per foot. Since 12 in. = 1 ft, $\frac{12\text{ in.}}{\text{ft}} = 1$.

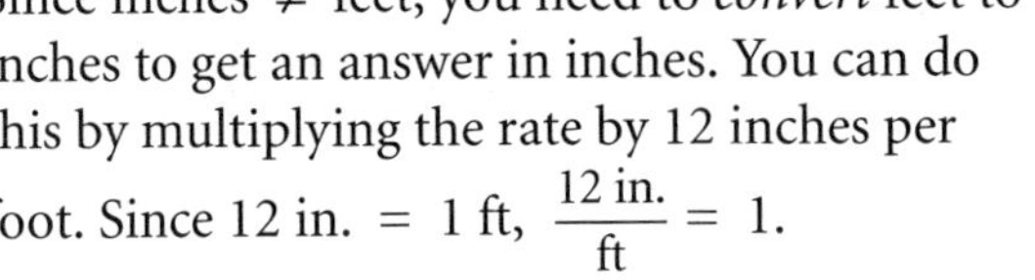

$$\text{inches} = \frac{\text{feet}}{\text{minute}} \cdot \frac{12\text{ in.}}{\text{foot}} \cdot \text{minutes}$$

This process of using units or dimensions in equations to solve problems is called **dimensional analysis**.

Problem

Each member of a class of 28 students needs 12.5 g of sodium chloride (salt) for a plant-growth experiment. The teacher provides a new 1.5-lb container of the salt. If each student uses the proper amount, what is the mass of the salt that will be left in the container?

CHECK UNDERSTANDING

Can you add or subtract quantities if they do not have the same units?
Can you multiply or divide quantities if they do not have the same units?

no; yes

Write an Equation

Use Variables

Explore the Problem

1. Reread the question in the problem. In what units should the final answer be? grams

2. First, find the total mass of salt used. The unit "students" is eliminated.

$$\text{mass used} = 28 \text{ students} \cdot 12.5 \frac{\text{g}}{\text{student}} = \blacksquare \text{ g} \quad 350\text{g}$$

3. Subtract the mass used from the mass in the container to find the mass of salt left. What additional information do you need? You need to know the number of grams in a pound.

4. Use 1 lb = 453.6 g as a conversion factor. Write it as a ratio that eliminates pound.

$$\text{mass in container} = 1.5 \text{ lb} \cdot \frac{453.6 \text{ g}}{\text{lb}} = \blacksquare \text{ g} \quad 680.4 \text{ g}$$

5. Subtract the mass used from the mass in the container. $680.4 - 350 = 330.4$

6. Suppose there were 24 students, each student used 8.5 g of salt, and the original container held 2.5 lb of salt. Write one equation to solve this problem. Include units and show cancellations. See Additional Answers.

7. **WRITING MATHEMATICS** Explain why multiplying one side of an equation by a conversion factor does not upset the equality. See Additional Answers.

PROBLEM SOLVING PLAN

- Understand
- Plan
- Solve
- Examine

Investigate Further

You can use dimensional analysis to help you set up an equation for a problem. The next problem requires several conversion factors.

The distance light travels through space in one year is called a *light-year*. If light travels 3.0×10^8 meters per second, determine the number of kilometers in a light-year. Assume a 365-day year.

8. Write the conversion factor you can use to change meters to kilometers. Use scientific notation. Then show how to find the number of kilometers light travels per second. See Additional Answers.

9. To solve this problem, you need to convert seconds to minutes, minutes to hours, and hours to days. Write the conversion factor for each. See Additional Answers.

10. Write the equation for the number of kilometers in a light-year that combines all the conversions and numerical operations. Show all units. Write the answer in scientific notation. See Additional Answers.

11. **WRITING MATHEMATICS** Explain what characteristics of a problem will help you decide whether the strategy of using dimensional analysis is appropriate. See Additional Answers.

2 TEACH

Use the Pages/Problem Ask what units are presented in the problem. **students, grams, and pounds** Ask what the problem asks them to find. **the mass of salt that will be left in the container**

Use the Pages/Explore the Problem For Question 1, ask why the answer should be in *grams* instead of pounds. **because the problem asks for mass and mass is represented by grams** For Question 2, ask why the unit *students* was eliminated. **because it appeared in both the numerator and the denominator** Have students discuss their answers to Question 7. Have them give examples. **possible examples: 1 foot = 12 inches, 1 foot/12 inches = 1; 60 minutes = 1 hour, 60 minutes/1 hour = 1; 1 pound = 16 ounces, 1 pound/16 ounces = 1**

Use the Pages/Investigate Further Ask students how the problem is similar to the one in the previous section. How is it different? **Both problems involve dimensional analysis requiring the use of conversion factors. This problem requires the use of several conversion factors while the first problem required only one conversion factor.** Ask them what methods they can use to solve the problem. **Use conversion factors to write an equation and to convert different units of measure to like units of measure.** For Problem 8, ask students how many meters are in a kilometer. **1000 m** Have students discuss their answers to Problem 11.

3 SUMMARIZE

In the Math Journal Have students discuss what dimensional analysis is and why it is useful. **Dimensional analysis is the process of using the units of measurement to ensure a correct computational set-up for a problem. It also helps to avoid multiplying large numbers since common factors can be eliminated first.**

4 PRACTICE

Apply the Strategy For Problem 14, ask what the problem is asking for. **the cost of gasoline for the planned route** Ask how they can find the cost of gasoline for the planned route. **find the distance in miles, since the cost of gasoline is in dollars per miles** Ask what conversion factor they will need to find the length of the route in miles. **1 mi/1.6 km**

NAME ______ CLASS ______ DATE ______

R RETEACHING

14.9 PROBLEM SOLVING FILE: USE DIMENSIONAL ANALYSIS

To change units, multiply by a ratio that is equivalent to 1. Divide out unit names as you would divide out common factors.

Example

Jim works as a word processor. It takes him 8 minutes to enter one page of a report on the computer. How many hours will it take him to produce a 500-page report?

Solution

Write the ratio you are given: $\frac{8 \text{ minutes}}{1 \text{ page}}$

Since minutes appears in the numerator and you want hours, write a ratio that has minutes in the denominator: $\frac{1 \text{ hour}}{60 \text{ min}}$

Multiply these ratios and 500 pages:

$$\frac{8 \text{ min}}{1 \text{ page}} \cdot \frac{1 \text{ hr}}{60 \text{ min}} \cdot 500 \text{ pages} = \frac{4000 \text{ hours}}{60} = 66\frac{2}{3} \text{ hours}$$

Here are some common conversion ratios you may need to use.

1 mile = 5280 feet
12 months = 1 year
16 ounces = 1 pound
1 hour = 60 minutes
1 ton = 2000 pounds

EXERCISES

1. A 5-mile stretch of highway will get a new guard rail. The rail will have steel posts every 4 feet. How many posts will be needed? $5 \text{ mi} \cdot \frac{5280 \text{ ft}}{1 \text{ mi}} \cdot \frac{1 \text{ post}}{4 \text{ ft}} = ? \text{ posts}$ — 1. **6600 posts**
2. The Wongs' water bill is $125 every 2 months. What is the average cost of the water they use per day? (Use 365 days in 1 year.) Round to the nearest cent. — 2. **$2.05/day**
3. Cable lines are supported every 10 feet. How many supports are needed for 3 miles of cable? — 3. **1584 supports**
4. A delivery truck can carry 2 tons of freight. The company wants to ship hammers that weigh 8 ounces each. The hammers are packed 20 to a box. How many boxes of hammers can the truck carry? — 4. **400 boxes**

60 *South-Western Algebra 1: An Integrated Approach*

Draw a Diagram | Write an Expression

Apply the Strategy

12. **Motion** Acceleration requires the dimensions of a length divided by the product of two times, $\frac{(\text{length})}{(\text{time})(\text{time})}$. State whether each of the following units can be used to measure acceleration.
    a. feet per second per second yes
    b. miles per hour per second yes
    c. meters per kilometer per hour no
    d. inches per day per minute yes

Travel Felipé is planning a car trip with his family through New Mexico, Arizona, and California. He marked their route on a map, measured the segments, and approximated the total length of the route to be 46 cm. He checked the map scale and found that 2 .5 cm = 100 km. The family car averages 22 miles per gallon of gasoline, and gasoline costs $1.16 per gallon.

13. What information do you need to calculate Felipé's family budget for gasoline? Use a reference book to find this information (correct to one decimal place). need number of km per mi; use 1 mi = 1.6 km
14. Show how to set up all the information to compute the answer and check the units by dimensional analysis. Find the answer. See Additional Answers.

Sales Force Organization Companies must balance the need for sales personnel to promote products with the goal of cost efficiency. One common method of determining the size of sales force is based on this **workload formula**:

$$S = \frac{C \cdot F \cdot L}{T}$$

where S is the number of salespeople, C is the number of product customers (such as supermarkets or department stores) served, F is the call frequency necessary to service a customer annually, L is the average length of a call, and T is the average amount of selling time a salesperson has per year.

15. Silver Spoon Foods sells its products to 258,000 supermarkets, grocery stores and so on. Assume salespersons call on these customers at least 50 times a year. The average sales call lasts 48 minutes and an average salesperson works 40 hours a week for 50 weeks, but 10 hours a week are taken up by travel and paperwork. Make any necessary conversions and use dimensional analysis to show that the units of the answer are salespeople and determine the number. See Additional Answers.

Guess and Check | Solve a Simpler Problem

REVIEW PROBLEM SOLVING STRATEGIES

1–3 See Additional Answers.

READING BETWEEN THE LINES

1. Rectangle $ABCD$ is shown. Point P is within the rectangle such that the distance from P to A is 3 units, from P to B is 4 units, and from P to C is 5 units. How far is P from D? Work in pairs to solve the problem.

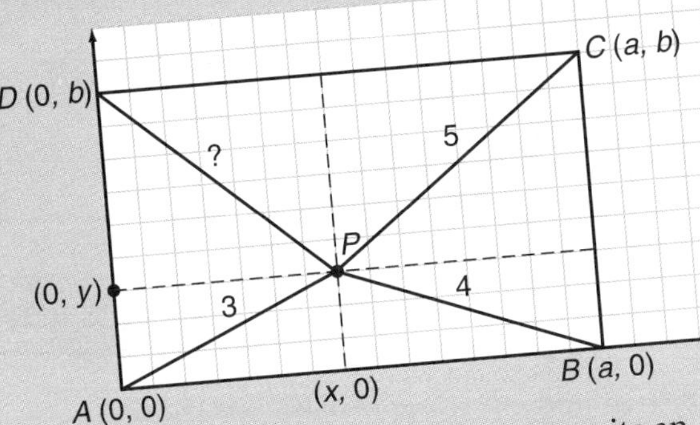

a. Use the known distance PA to write an equation for x and y. Call this Equation I.

b. $\overline{PB}$ is the hypotenuse of a right triangle. Express the length of one leg in terms of a and x and the other in terms of y. Use the Pythagorean theorem to write Equation II.

c. $\overline{PC}$ is the hypotenuse of a right triangle. Express the length of one leg in terms of a and x and the other in terms of b and y. Then write Equation III.

d. What do you want to find? What equation can you write? Call it IV.

e. Try to find a way of combining Equations I, II, and III so that the variable expression on one side of the resulting equation is exactly the same as one side of Equation IV.

f. Explain how to complete the problem.

A PERFECT 10

2. What is the smallest ten-digit number you can find that is made up of the digits 0, 0, 1, 1, 2, 2, 3, 3, 4, and 4? The 0s must be separated by zero digits, the 1s by one digit, the 2s by two digits, the 3s by three digits, and the 4s by four digits.

OLD TIMERS

3. Sonja needs to cook onions for exactly one minute. She has two old-fashioned timers. One of her timers takes 5 min to empty its top compartment. The other takes 8 min to empty its top compartment. How can she use her two timers to measure one minute?

5 FOLLOW–UP

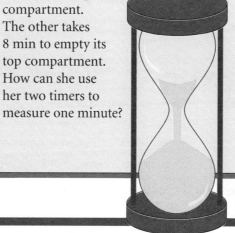

Extra Practice Solve the problem.

If a refrigerator uses 105 kWh (kilowatt-hours) of electricity per month and the cost of electricity is $0.126 per kWh, what is the operating cost of the refrigerator for one day in November? **$0.441/day or 44.1¢/day**

Review Problem Solving Strategies

Reading Between the Lines Strategies for solving this problem are use logical thinking and write an equation.

A Perfect 10 Strategies for solving this problem are use logical thinking and guess and check.

Old Timers The strategy for solving this problem is use logical thinking.

NAME ______ CLASS ______ DATE ______

EXTRA PRACTICE

14.9 PROBLEM SOLVING FILE: USE DIMENSIONAL ANALYSIS

EXERCISES

Use the following common conversion ratios to solve problems.

1 mile = 5280 feet	36 inches = 1 yard
1 hour = 60 minutes	1 minute = 60 seconds
1 mile = 1.6 kilometers	1 gallon = 128 ounces

Solve.

1. A 27-mile stretch of highway costs $12 million dollars. Find the cost per foot. Round your answer to the nearest cent. — 1. **$84.18**

2. Gwen is planning decorations for the school dance. She wants to make 9-inch long streamers to hang from the ceiling of the gym. She has 6 rolls of ribbon. Each roll contains 120 yards. How many streamers can she cut in all? — 2. **2,880 streamers**

3. A car is traveling at 60 miles per hour. What is its speed in feet per second? — 3. **88 ft/s**

4. A room measures 8 feet by 11 feet. Carpeting costs $19.50 per square yard. Find the cost to the nearest cent of carpeting the room. — 4. **$190.67**

5. A day care center serves 23 children breakfast each morning. Each child should get 4 ounces of orange juice. How many gallons of juice will be needed in one year? (Assume that the center is open 250 days per year.) Round your answer to the nearest gallon. — 5. **180 gal./y**

6. Jay is planning an automobile trip in Canada. The speedometer on his car gives miles per hour. The Canadian road map uses the scale 1 centimeter = 15 kilometers. How long will it take him to get from his hotel to Edmonton if the map distance is 9.2 cm and he can do most of the driving at 40 miles per hour? (Round to the nearest hour.) — 6. **2 hours**

7. A dripping faucet drips 1 ounce of water in 9 seconds. How many gallons of water will it waste in one year? (Use 365 days in 1 year.) — 7. **27,375 gal.**

62 *South-Western Algebra 1: AN INTEGRATED APPROACH*

Introduction The Chapter Review emphasizes the major concepts, skills, and vocabulary presented in this chapter and can be used for diagnosing students' strengths and weaknesses. Page references direct students to appropriate sections for additional review and reteaching.

Using Pages 722–723 Ask students to scan the Chapter Review and ask questions about any section they find confusing. Exercises 1–3 review key vocabulary.

Informal Evaluation Have students explain how they arrived at any incorrect answers. They may find their own mistakes and give you some clues as to the nature of their errors. Make sure students understand this material before moving on to the assessment stage.

Follow-Up Have students solve this problem: In calm air a small plane can fly 150 miles per hour. It can fly 350 miles with a tailwind in the same time it can fly 250 miles against the wind.

a. Write an equation that can be used to find the speed of the wind.
$\frac{350}{150 + w} = \frac{250}{150 - w}$

b. Find the speed of the wind.
25 mi/h

Have students write word problems that can be solved using a rational equation. Students should exchange and solve each others' word problems.

CHAPTER REVIEW

VOCABULARY

Choose the word from the list that completes each statement.

1. A relation written in the form $y = kxz, k \neq 0$, is a(n) __?__. b
2. A(n) __?__ is a fraction whose numerator and denominator are polynomials. a
3. A(n) __?__ is a relation written in the form $y = \frac{k}{x}$ where $k \neq 0, x \neq 0$. c

a. rational expression
b. joint variation
c. inverse variation

Lessons 14.1 and 14.2 DIRECT, INVERSE, AND JOINT VARIATION pages 675–685

- Use direct variation, inverse variation, or joint variation to find the value of a given variable or the constant of variation.

Find each variable.

4. If y varies inversely as x and $y = 16$ when $x = 20$, find y when $x = 64$. 5
5. If y varies jointly as x and z and $y = 60$ when $x = 30$ and $z = 4$, find y when $x = 12$ and $z = 3$. 18

Lesson 14.3 SIMPLIFY RATIONAL EXPRESSIONS pages 686–691

- A **rational expression** is an expression that can be written in the form $\frac{P}{Q}$ where P and Q are polynomials and $Q \neq 0$. To simplify a rational expression, factor both numerator and denominator and divide out the greatest common factor (GCF), so that the numerator and the denominator have no common factors other than 1.

Simplify each expression. State any restrictions on the variable.

6. $\frac{12x}{4x^2}$ $\frac{3}{x}; x \neq 0$
7. $\frac{6b + 18}{b + 3}$ $6; b \neq -3$
8. $\frac{2y - 1}{4 - 8y}$ $-\frac{1}{4}; y \neq \frac{1}{2}$

Lesson 14.4 MULTIPLY AND DIVIDE RATIONAL EXPRESSIONS pages 692–696

- To multiply rational expressions, factor and simplify each expression; then multiply the resulting factors. To multiply a rational expression by a polynomial P, rewrite the polynomial as $\frac{P}{1}$. To divide a rational expression by a polynomial P, multiply the expression by the reciprocal of P, $\frac{1}{P}$.

Perform the indicated operation.

9. $\frac{pq^2}{r} \cdot \frac{3p^2r}{p}$ $3p^2q^2$
10. $\frac{4}{3y} \div \frac{2}{9y^2}$ $6y$
11. $\frac{n + 7}{2n - 6} \div \frac{10(n + 7)}{5(n - 3)}$ $\frac{1}{4}$
12. $\frac{6x + 24}{2x^2 - 8} \cdot (3x + 6)$ $\frac{9x + 36}{x - 2}$
13. $\frac{x^2 - 36}{x^2 + 4x - 12} \div (3x - 18)$ $\frac{1}{3x - 6}$
14. $\frac{5x^2 + 5x}{x^2 - 3x - 4} \cdot (3x - 12)$ $15x$

Lesson 14.5 DIVIDE POLYNOMIALS — pages 697–701

- To divide a polynomial by a monomial, divide each term of the polynomial by the monomial. To divide one polynomial by another when there are no common factors, use long division.

Divide.

15. $(6x^3 - 8x^2 + x) \div 2x^2$ *$3x - 4 + \frac{1}{2x}$*

16. $(y^2 + y - 56) \div (y - 7)$ *$y + 8$*

17. $(5 - 7x^2 + 3x^4) \div (x - 1)$ *$3x^3 + 3x^2 - 4x - 4 + \frac{1}{x - 1}$*

18. The volume of a rectangular prism is $2x^3 + 5x^2 - x + 2$ and the length is $x + 3$. Find the area of the face bordered by the height and the width. *$2x^2 - x + 2 - \frac{4}{x + 3}$*

Lesson 14.6 ADD AND SUBTRACT RATIONAL EXPRESSIONS — pages 702–706

- To add rational expressions, rewrite the expressions as equivalent expressions with a least common denominator. Then add the numerators.

Add or subtract. Simplify if possible.

19. $\frac{7}{g + 2} - \frac{g + 6}{g + 2}$ *$\frac{1 - g}{g + 2}$*

20. $\frac{8}{3x} - \frac{2}{9x}$ *$\frac{22}{9x}$*

21. $\frac{5}{3z^2} - \frac{2}{z} + \frac{1}{6z}$ *$\frac{10 - 11z}{6z^2}$*

22. $\frac{t}{2t + 8} - \frac{5}{3t + 12}$ *$\frac{3t - 10}{6t + 24}$*

Lessons 14.7 and 14.8 COMPLEX RATIONAL EXPRESSIONS AND EQUATIONS — pages 707–717

- To simplify a complex rational expression, determine the LCD of all the rational expressions in both numerator and denominator and multiply each numerator and denominator by the LCD.
- To solve a rational equation, eliminate the denominators by multiplying both sides of the rational equation by the LCD of all the expressions. Then solve the resulting equation.

Simplify. Write your answer in simplest form.

23. $\frac{\frac{4}{a}}{\frac{7}{b}}$ *$\frac{4b}{7a}$*

24. $\frac{\frac{1}{m} - \frac{2}{n}}{\frac{4}{m}}$ *$\frac{n - 2m}{4n}$*

25. $\frac{\frac{2}{x} + \frac{3}{y}}{\frac{1}{2x} - \frac{1}{2y}}$ *$\frac{4y + 6x}{y - x}$*

26. $\frac{\frac{3}{r} + 2}{\frac{4}{s}}$ *$\frac{3s + 2rs}{4r}$*

Solve and check.

27. $2b + \frac{4}{5} = \frac{2}{3}$ *$-\frac{1}{15}$*

28. $\frac{y}{y - 2} - \frac{14}{y - 2} = 5$ *-1*

29. $\frac{k + 5}{k} - \frac{2}{5k} = 10$ *$\frac{23}{45}$*

Lesson 14.9 USE DIMENSIONAL ANALYSIS — pages 718–721

- You can use dimensional analysis to solve problems involving different units of measure.

Solve each problem.

30. On a map of the Mississippi, the distance between Biloxi and Jackson measures $6\frac{3}{8}$ in. The map scale is $\frac{3}{4}$ in. = 20 mi. Joyce's car averages 24 mi/gal of gasoline. If gasoline costs $1.29 a gallon, how much, to the nearest cent, will it cost in gasoline for Joyce to drive from Biloxi to Jackson? *$9.14*

Study Skills Tip Remind students that some vocabulary terms sound similar, but have different meanings. For example, rational expressions and rational equations are two different concepts. Have students record examples of terms that are similar in name and give an example to illustrate each.

For Your Portfolio Have students gather samples from their project, homework, quizzes, and class work that portray efforts to meet each of their goals for this chapter. On a cover page for each representative work have students write the related goal, why the work is included in the portfolio, and what the teacher should look for when reviewing the work. On a general cover page have students write a self-evaluation of how well they have met each of their goals for this chapter. The general cover page should conclude with goals for the next chapter and the student's reason for choosing these goals.

The Chapter Test is comprised of a variety of test-item types as follows:

writing	1, 19
traditional	3–18, 20–28
verbal	29–31
standardized test	2

TEACHING TIP

The writing items provide an opportunity for students to demonstrate a knowledge of process as well as end result. Suggest that before they begin answering the questions, students should look over the entire test and determine the order in which they will work. Some students may be more successful if they save the open-ended writing questions until after they have completed the other test questions.

The table below correlates the Chapter Test items with the appropriate lesson(s).

Item	Lesson	Item	Lesson
1–5	14.2	19	14.5
6–7	14.6	20–27	14.7
8–11	14.3	28	14.8
12–14	14.4	29	14.4
15–18	14.6	30–31	14.9

CHAPTER ASSESSMENT

CHAPTER TEST

1. WRITING MATHEMATICS Write a paragraph explaining what happens to the y-values in the inverse variation $y = \frac{24}{x}$ as the x-values increase and decrease. Give examples. See Additional Answers.

2. STANDARDIZED TESTS Which value of k indicates that y varies inversely as x when $y = 14$ and $x = 2$? B

   A. 7 B. 28 C. $\frac{1}{7}$ D. $\frac{1}{28}$

Tell whether each equation represents *direct*, *inverse*, or *joint variation*. State the constant of variation. See Additional Answers.

3. $y = \frac{4}{x}$ 4. $t = 5s$ 5. $A = 2\pi rh$

Determine the LCD for each set of expressions.

6. $\frac{15}{2x}, \frac{16}{x(x+2)}$ $2x(x+2)$ 7. $\frac{3}{8def^2}, \frac{8}{6d^2e}, \frac{12}{f^2}$ $24d^2ef^2$

Simplify each expression. State any restrictions on the variable. 9–11 See Additional Answers.

8. $\frac{5x+10}{15}$ $\frac{(x+2)}{3}$ 9. $\frac{x+3}{x^2-10x-39}$

10. $\frac{x^2+10x+25}{x^2+11x+30}$ 11. $\frac{c^2-c-56}{c^2-16c+64}$

Perform the indicated operation.

12. $\frac{3x^2-15x}{4x+2} \cdot \frac{8x+4}{125-5x^2}$ $-\frac{6x}{5x+25}$

13. $\frac{4x^2-8x}{3x+1} \cdot \frac{9x+3}{16-4x^2}$ $-\frac{3x}{x+2}$

14. $\frac{x^2+x-30}{x^2-36} \div \frac{x^2-25}{3x-18}$ $\frac{3}{x+5}$

Add or subtract. See Additional Answers.

15. $\frac{7}{5r^2} + \frac{9}{10r} - \frac{5}{r}$ 16. $\frac{6}{a+3} + \frac{14}{a-10}$

17. $\frac{21}{16a^2} - \frac{5}{24ab} - \frac{1}{6b^2}$ 18. $\frac{7q-5}{49-q^2} - \frac{7}{q-7}$

19. WRITING MATHEMATICS Write a paragraph explaining when and why you should use long division. See Additional Answers.

Convert each mixed expression into a rational expression. See Additional Answers.

20. $2p - \frac{4p-7}{4p-6}$ 21. $q - 5 - \frac{4}{q+3}$

22. $\frac{2k-1}{k+10} - k$ 23. $a + 4 + \frac{4}{a-4}$

Simplify. Write your answer in simplest form.

24. $\dfrac{\frac{1}{5c^2} - \frac{16}{5d^2}}{\frac{1}{c^2d} + \frac{4}{cd^2}}$ $\frac{d-4c}{5}$ 25. $\dfrac{\frac{1}{x} - \frac{1}{y}}{\frac{3}{2x} - \frac{3}{2y}}$ $\frac{2}{3}$

26. $\dfrac{\frac{6}{a^2} + \frac{6}{a}}{\frac{3}{a} - 18}$ $\frac{2+2a}{a-6a^2}$ 27. $\dfrac{5 - \frac{6}{x+9}}{10 - \frac{12}{x+9}}$ $\frac{1}{2}$

28. For what values of x is the equation $\frac{x+2}{3} = \frac{1}{2} + \frac{5}{2}x$ true? $\frac{5}{2}, -3$

Write and solve an equation for each problem.

29. Determine the area of a rectangle that has a length of $\frac{p^2-4}{p^2q-2p}$ cm and a width of $\frac{p^2-p}{p^2-3p+2}$ cm. $\frac{p+2}{pq-2}$ cm^2

30. In calm air an airplane can fly at the rate of 960 mi/h. It can fly 3000 mi with a tailwind in the same time it can fly 2760 mi against the wind. Find the speed of the wind. 40 mi/h

31. Earth is about 93,000,000 mi from the sun. If light travels at a speed of about 5.88×10^{12} mi/y, about how many minutes does it take light to travel from the sun to the Earth? Assume a 365-day year and use scientific notation. about 8.3 min

PERFORMANCE ASSESSMENT

USE ALGEBLOCKS Use Algeblocks and the Quadrant Mat to divide polynomials by monomials and binomials. Create division examples such that there is no remainder when the polynomial is divided by the monomial or binomial. Have a partner use Algeblocks to find the quotient. Check that each step is correct.

Examples:

$\frac{(x+3)(x+4)}{x+3}$ $\frac{x^2+7x+12}{x+3}$ Have a partner find $(x^2+7x+12) \div (x+3)$.

$\frac{4x(x-8)}{4x}$ $\frac{4x^2-32x}{4x}$ Have a partner find $(4x^2-32x) \div 4x$.

USE ALGEBLOCKS Use Algeblocks to make different rectangular solids. Have a partner determine the surface area and volume of each solid, write the ratio of the surface area to the volume, and then simplify the ratio if it can be simplified. Check that each step is correct.

USE A GRID Use a grid to draw different rectangles having a certain area and having lengths and widths that are whole numbers. Experiment with different areas and make a table to represent each area showing the lengths and widths which are factor pairs of each area.

PLAN A TRIP Plan a trip you would like to take. On a map, measure the distance of the route you could follow. Note the map scale. Find out the mileage that the car you would ride in gets to a gallon of gasoline. Decide whether you will use regular, mid-range, or high-test gasoline, and find out the cost per gallon. Then calculate how much in gasoline the trip would cost.

PROJECT ASSESSMENT

PROJECT Connection Prepare a report for the farmer summarizing your exploration of silos. Be sure to include an explanation of the methods you used, relevant tables, graphs, mathematical interpretations, and your results and recommendations.

1. Have one student in your group play the role of the farmer, asking questions about building the silo. The other students act as consultants using their reports to respond to questions and justify their recommendations. Both sides should agree on the silo that represents the best choice for the situation.

2. The consultants can propose other investigations that might be useful for the farmer. These investigations may involve geometric questions such as fencing an area or financial questions such as break-even/profit analysis of the farmer's business operations.

Performance Assessment

The activities on page 725 give students with different learning styles opportunities to demonstrate their understanding of concepts in this chapter. The activities may be used in addition to or instead of the Chapter Test on the previous page.

Use Algeblocks (Kinesthetic/Visual) Be sure that students understand that to create division examples so that there is no remainder, they can simply multiply any two binomials or a monomial and a binomial. Then they can divide the product by either of the original factors.

Use Algeblocks (Kinesthetic/Visual) Point out that not all ratios of surface area to volume can be simplified.

Use a Grid (Visual) Mention that prime numbers in the table will have exactly two factor pairs ($1 \times f$ and $f \times 1$ for any prime factor f). But all other numbers will have more than two pairs.

Plan a Trip (Visual) Students should realize that map distances are measured on a straight line, but in actuality, most roads are curved. Thus the estimated costs may vary from the actual costs.

Project Assessment

Project Connection Have the class discuss the various recommendations that were made to the farmer. Then have them try to agree on the best documented recommendation.

NAME ______ CLASS ______ DATE ______

FORM B

CHAPTER 14 TEST

Write the letter of the best answer for Questions 1–6.

1. Which represents a direct variation? 1. a

I. $y = 10x$ II. $xy = 10$ III. $x = \frac{y}{...}$ IV. $x = \frac{10}{...}$

NAME ______ CLASS ______ DATE ______

FORM A

CHAPTER 14 TEST

Write the letter of the best answer for Questions 1–6.

1. Which represents an inverse variation? 1. d

   I. $y = 10x$ II. $xy = 10$ III. $x = \frac{y}{10}$ IV. $x = \frac{10}{y}$

   a. only II b. only III c. II and III d. II and IV

2. Which is the LCD of $\frac{3}{x^3y^2}$ and $\frac{5}{xy^3}$? 2. d

   a. $15xy$ b. xy c. x^3y^2 d. x^3y^3

3. By which ratio would you multiply 180 lb to convert pounds to kg if the conversion factor is 1 kg = 2.2 lb.? 3. c

   a. $\frac{2.2 \text{ kg}}{1 \text{ lb}}$ b. $\frac{2.2 \text{ lb}}{1 \text{ kg}}$ c. $\frac{1 \text{ kg}}{2.2 \text{ lb}}$ d. $\frac{2.2 \text{ kg}}{2.2 \text{ lb}}$

4. By what would you multiply both sides of the equation to solve $\frac{x}{x+3} - \frac{5}{x-3} = \frac{x-10}{x^2-9}$? 4. c

   a. $x + 3$ b. $x - 3$ c. $(x - 3)(x + 3)$ d. $9x$

5. Which equals $(20x^6 - 10x^3 - x^2) \div 2x^3$? 5. c

   a. $10x^2 - 5 - \frac{1}{2x}$ b. $10x^2 - 5 - 2x$

   c. $10x^3 - 5 - \frac{1}{2x}$ d. $18x^3 - 8 - \frac{1}{2x}$

Find each variable.

6. If y varies inversely as x and $y = 30$ when $x = 4$, find y when $x = 12$. 6. 10
7. If y varies jointly as x and z and $y = 54$ when $x = 6$ and $z = 3$, find y when $x = 8$ and $z = 2$. 7. 48

Simplify each expression. State any restrictions on the variable.

8. $\frac{24y}{6y^3}$ 9. $\frac{6x-18}{x-3}$ 10. $\frac{2y-1}{2-4y}$

11. $\frac{m^4n}{8} \cdot \frac{4mn^2s^2}{n}$ 12. $(x^2 + 6x + 9) \cdot \frac{x-3}{x^2-9}$

13. $\frac{5}{9y^2} \div \frac{15}{27y}$ 14. $\frac{4x^2+4x}{x^2+3x+2} \div \frac{8x^2}{x^2-4}$

8. $\frac{4}{y^2}$; $y \neq 0$
9. 6; $x \neq 3$
10. $-\frac{1}{2}$; $x \neq \frac{1}{2}$
11. $\frac{m^5n^2s}{2}$
12. $x + 2$
13. $\frac{1}{y}$
14. $\frac{x-2}{2x}$

66 *South-Western Algebra 1: AN INTEGRATED APPROACH*

CHAPTER 14 TEST Form A, page 2 NAME ______

Perform the indicated operation.

Divide.

15. $(12x^4 + 8x^2 + x) \div 4x$ 16. $(5x^2 + 18x - 8) \div (x + 4)$

Add or subtract. Simplify if possible.

17. $\frac{5}{x+1} - \frac{x+4}{x+1}$ 18. $\frac{7}{2x} + \frac{1}{3x}$

19. $\frac{3}{8x^2} + \frac{1}{x} - \frac{1}{2x}$ 20. $\frac{4}{x-2} + \frac{2}{x+2}$

Simplify. Write your answer in simplest form.

21. $\frac{\frac{3}{x}}{\frac{8}{y}}$ 22. $\frac{\frac{2}{x} + \frac{5}{x}}{-\frac{3}{x}}$ 23. $\frac{\frac{3}{m} - \frac{2}{n}}{\frac{1}{2m} - \frac{1}{2n}}$

Solve and check.

24. $\frac{4x}{15} + \frac{x}{3} = 12$ 25. $\frac{5}{3x} + \frac{1}{x} = 8$ 26. $\frac{x}{x-3} - \frac{10}{x-3} = 2$

15. $3x^3 + 2x + \frac{1}{4}$
16. $5x - 2$
17. $\frac{1-x}{x+1}$
18. $\frac{23}{6x}$
19. $\frac{4x+3}{8x^2}$
20. $\frac{6x+4}{(x+2)(x-2)}$
21. $\frac{3y}{8x}$
22. $-\frac{7}{3}$
23. $\frac{6n-4m}{n-m}$
24. 20
25. $\frac{1}{3}$
26. -4
27. \$10.61

27. TRAVEL On a map, the distance between two cities measures $5\frac{1}{2}$ inches. The map scale is $\frac{1}{4}$ in. = 10 miles. Tyrone's car averages 28 miles/gal of gasoline. If gasoline costs \$1.35 a gallon, how much, to the nearest cent, will it cost in gasoline for Tyrone to drive between the two cities?

For Question 28, use a separate sheet of paper if necessary.

28. WRITING MATHEMATICS Explain how you can determine if a set of ordered pairs represents a direct variation.

    Possible answer: Find the ratio for each ordered pair. If the ratio is the same in each case, then $\frac{y}{x} = k$, where k is a constant. So the ordered pairs represent a direct variation.

68 *South-Western Algebra 1: AN INTEGRATED APPROACH*

CUMULATIVE REVIEW

1. If y varies jointly as x and z, and $y = 36$ when $x = 2$ and $z = 9$, find x when $y = 40$ and $z = 4$. 5; Lesson 14.2

Simplify each expression. State any restrictions on the variable. See Additional Answers. Lesson 14.3

2. $\dfrac{2x^3 - 18x}{4x - 12}$
3. $\dfrac{x^2 + x - 20}{x^2 + 3x - 10}$

Perform each operation. See Additional Answers.

4. $(3n^3 + 8n^2 - 23n + 5) + (9n^3 - 8n^2 - 15)$ Lesson 11.6
5. $(4y - 7)(2y^2 + 9y - 2)$ Lesson 11.8
6. $(6t^3 - 3t + 11) - (2t^3 - 5t^2 + 3t - 1)$ Lesson 11.6
7. $(x^4 + 5x^3 - 7x - 2) \div (x + 3)$ Lesson 14.5
8. WRITING MATHEMATICS Explain why $\dfrac{4x}{4y} = \dfrac{x}{y}$ but $\dfrac{x+4}{y+4} \neq \dfrac{x}{y}$. See Additional Answers. Lesson 14.3

Solve each equation or inequality.

9. $4x + 15 = 2x - 9\left(\frac{1}{3}x - 2\right)$ $\frac{3}{5}$; Lesson 3.7
10. $\frac{2}{3}x + 5 > 8 - \frac{5}{6}x$ $x > 2$; Lesson 5.4
11. $-3m \leq 12$ $m \geq -4$; Lesson 5.3
12. $5n^2 + 27n - 18 = 0$
13. $2y^2 + 5y = 4$ 12–13 See Additional Answers.
14. $\sqrt{x + 7} + 9 = x + 4$ 9; Lesson 13.5

Simplify each expression.

15. $\dfrac{x^3 - 16x}{x^2 + 3x - 10} \div \dfrac{x^2 + 2x - 8}{x^2 - 4x + 4}$ $\frac{x^2 - 4x}{x + 5}$; Lesson 14.4
16. $\dfrac{y + 4}{3y^2 - 27} + \dfrac{6}{y - 3} - \dfrac{4}{3y + 9}$ $\frac{15y + 70}{3y^2 - 27}$; Lesson 14.6
17. $4\sqrt{18} + 2\sqrt{72} - 4\sqrt{\frac{1}{2}}$ $22\sqrt{2}$; Lesson 13.4
18. $\dfrac{(x^2y^{-4})^6}{(x^{-4}y^8)^{-3}}$ 1; Lessons 11.2 and 11.3
19. $\dfrac{4ab^5c^{-2}}{12a^3b^{-4}c^{-3}}$ $\frac{b^9c}{3a^2}$; Lesson 11.3

Solve for *x*. Lesson 9.3

20. $|x + 2| = 2$ 0, −4
21. $|2x + 3| + 11 = 12$ −1, −2
22. $2|x - 5| - 6 = 0$ 2, 8
23. $-3|x + 4| = -12$ −8, 0

The data show how many pitches a baseball pitcher threw in consecutive starts. Use the data for Questions 24–26.

112, 75, 98, 140, 52, 101, 110, 94, 82

24. Find the mean number of pitches thrown. 96 pitches; Lesson 1.7
25. Make a boxplot representing the data. See Additional Answers. Lesson 5.6
26. WRITING MATHEMATICS Of bar graph, line graph, or circle graph, which type of graph would you choose to represent the data? Why? See Additional Answers. Lesson 1.4
27. Solve for x in the equation $xy - 5 = x + 4$. See Additional Answers. Lesson 13.8
28. A chemist has 450 mL of 25% saline solution. How much water should be added to dilute the solution to 20% saline? 112.5 mL; Lesson 3.9
29. Donald needs 3 hours more than Mickey to paint a room by himself. Working together, they can paint the room in 2 hours. How long would it take Donald to paint the room himself? 6 h; Lesson 14.8

Identify the domain and range of each function. See Additional Answers.

30. $y = 2x - 3$
31. $y = x^2 - 2$
32. $y = -|x - 3| + 1$
33. $y = \sqrt{x + 2} + 1$
34. STANDARDIZED TESTS If $n < 0$, the determinant $\begin{vmatrix} 5 & n \\ 2 & 4 \end{vmatrix}$ has the value A; Lesson 7.6

    A. $20 - 2n$ B. $20 + 2n$
    C. $2n - 20$ D. $5n - 8$
    E. $10 - 4n$

35. A concession stand manager adds pompoms and T-shirts to her inventory. There is room to store at most 1500 of the new items. The profit on pompoms is \$3.00 and the profit on T-shirts is \$5.00, so if x is pompoms and y is T-shirts then her profit is $P = 3x + 5y$. The manager can order no more than 800 pompoms and 1000 T-shirts. How many pompoms should she order? How many T-shirts? What is the maximum profit? 500 pompoms; 1000 T-shirts; \$6500; Lesson 8.5

• • • STANDARDIZED TEST • • •

STUDENT PRODUCED ANSWERS Solve each question and on the answer grid write your answer at the top and fill in the ovals.

Notes: Mixed numbers such as $1\frac{1}{2}$ must be gridded as 1.5 or 3/2. Grid only one answer per question. If your answer is a decimal, enter the most accurate value the grid will accommodate.

1. If $\sin A = \frac{3}{5}$, find the value of $\tan A$. $\frac{3}{4}$; Lesson 13.8
2. Solve the equation $x^2 - 4x - 2 = 0$. Find the product of the two solutions. −2; Lessons 10.5 and 13.3
3. Pedro has 12 more dimes than nickels. He has a total of \$2.70. Find the total number of coins that Pedro has. 32; Lesson 7.7
4. Find the slope of a line perpendicular to the line that passes through the points (−3, 4) and (5, 1). $\frac{8}{3}$; Lessons 6.2 and 6.3
5. Find the measure for the perimeter of the figure shown. 36; Lesson 13.6

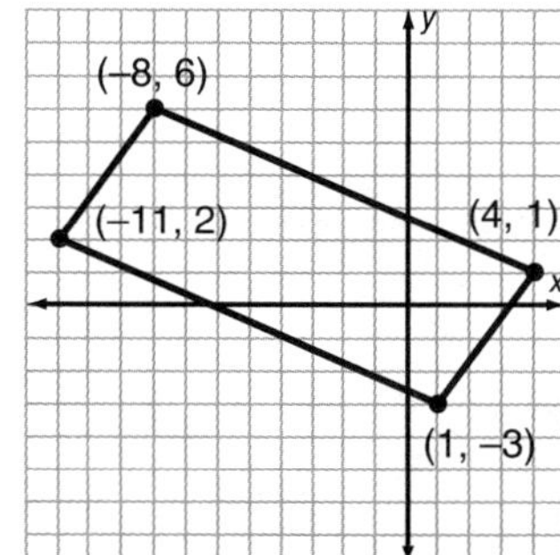

6. Suppose you toss a fair coin once and roll a die twice. Find the number of different outcomes there are in the sample space. 72; Lesson 8.6
7. If p varies jointly as m and n, and $p = 12$ when $m = 8$ and $n = 6$, find the value of m when $p = 20$ and $n = 5$. 16; Lesson 14.2
8. Find the remainder when $2x^3 - 54$ is divided by $x - 3$. 0; Lesson 14.5
9. Sum the solutions to the systems of equations. 5; Lesson 7.4

$$\begin{cases} x + 2y = 10 \\ 2x + y = 5 \end{cases}$$

10. Find the number of rows in matrix Q.

$$Q = \begin{bmatrix} 7 & 6 \\ 3 & 1 \\ 2 & 9 \\ 4 & 0 \end{bmatrix}$$ 4; Lesson 1.6

11. Simplify the expression. Enter the answer as a fraction.

$$\frac{\frac{2}{3} - \frac{3}{5}}{\frac{5}{6} + \frac{1}{4}}$$ $\frac{4}{65}$; Lesson 14.7

12. Find the degree of the monomial $(2x^3y^5)^4$. 32; Lesson 11.2
13. Every morning Sebastian runs 8 miles, then walks 2 miles. He runs 6 mi/h faster than he walks. If his total time yesterday was 1 hour, find Sebastian's rate running. 12; Lesson 14.8
14. So far, a survey taken asking people their favorite color has shown that 45 people prefer blue, 38 prefer red, 25 like green, 18 prefer yellow, and 24 people like various other colors. Find the probability, as a decimal, that the next person asked will choose yellow. 0.12; Lesson 1.8
15. Evaluate the expression. Enter the answer in decimal notation. 400; Lesson 11.4

$$\frac{(4.2 \cdot 10^7)(2 \cdot 10^{-9})}{(2.1 \cdot 10^{-4})}$$

16. Find the value of x in the determinant equation.

$$\begin{vmatrix} x & 4 \\ -3 & 5 \end{vmatrix} + \begin{vmatrix} -4 & 2 \\ x & 1 \end{vmatrix} = 11$$ 1; Lessons 3.6 and 7.6

17. If y varies inversely as x and x is 12 when y is 5 then what is x when y is 30? 2; Lesson 14.2
18. What is the mode of this set of data? 22; Lesson 1.7

24 22 22 20 25 21 23 23 21 20
22 25 24 20 22 23 22 25 21 25

19. Which of the following is the greatest?

$\frac{76}{16}$ $\sqrt{10}$ $\frac{159}{50}$ $3.\overline{15}$ $\frac{76}{16}$; Lesson 9.5

Answers

1. B	12. C
2. D	13. A
3. D	14. A
4. A	15. B
5. B	16. C
6. C	17. 36
7. B	18. 8
8. C	19. 0.5
9. B	20. 3.75
10. C	21. 9.80
11. B	22. 4

CHAPTER 14 Standardized Test, page 2 NAME ______

Quantitative Comparison For Questions 11–16, fill in A if the quantity in Column 1 is greater, B if the quantity in Column 2 is greater, C if the two quantities are equal, and D if the relationship cannot be determined.

Grid Response For Questions 17–22, mark your answer on the answer grid provided.

Solve each equation.

NAME ______ CLASS ______ DATE ______

CHAPTER 14 STANDARDIZED TEST

For Questions 1–10 fill in the best choice on the answer grid provided.

1. Which represents an inverse variation?
   A. $y = 100s$ **B.** $xy = 100$ **C.** $y = 100xz$ **D.** $\frac{y}{z} = 10$ **E.** None of these
2. If y varies jointly as x and z, and $y = 50$ when $x = 5$ and $z = 10$, find y when $x = 20$ and $z = 15$.
   A. 1 **B.** 50 **C.** 250 **D.** 300 **E.** None of these
3. Which rational expression is in simplest form?
   A. $\frac{x^2 - 4}{2x + 4}$ **B.** $\frac{6x}{18y}$ **C.** $\frac{3x - 1}{1 - 3x}$ **D.** $\frac{x^2 + 2}{3x + 2}$ **E.** All of these
4. Which shows $\frac{x + 3}{x} \div \frac{x + 3}{x^3}$ in simplest form?
   A. x^2 **B.** $\frac{1}{x^2}$ **C.** x^3 **D.** $\frac{x^2 + 6x + 9}{x^4}$ **E.** None of these
5. Which rational expression equals $3x - \frac{x + 3}{x}$?
   A. $\frac{3x^2 - x + 3}{x}$ **B.** $\frac{3x^2 - x - 3}{x}$ **C.** $\frac{9x^2 - x + 3}{3x}$ **D.** $3x^2 - 3$ **E.** None of these
6. If $\frac{x^2 + 16}{x - 2} = x + 18 + \frac{36}{x - 2}$, what is the quotient?
   A. $x^2 + 16$ **B.** $x - 2$ **C.** $x + 18$ **D.** 36 **E.** $\frac{36}{x - 2}$
7. Which is simplified form for $\frac{\frac{1}{x} + \frac{1}{y}}{\frac{1}{x}}$?
   A. $\frac{y}{x + y}$ **B.** $\frac{x + y}{y}$ **C.** $\frac{x + y}{x^2y}$ **D.** $\frac{2}{y}$ **E.** None of these
8. Which shows the solution for $\frac{2x}{15} + \frac{x}{5} = 2$?
   A. 15 **B.** $\frac{80}{3}$ **C.** 6 **D.** $\frac{1}{12}$ **E.** None of these
9. By which ratio would you multiply 2000 kilometers to convert kilometers to miles if the conversion factor is 1 mile = 1.6 km?
   A. $\frac{1.6 \text{ km}}{1 \text{ mi}}$ **B.** $\frac{1 \text{ mi}}{1.6 \text{ km}}$ **C.** $\frac{1.6 \text{ km}}{1.6 \text{ mi}}$ **D.** $\frac{1.6 \text{ mi}}{1.6 \text{ km}}$ **E.** None of these
10. Which products are equal?
    I. $\frac{3x + 12}{12x} \cdot \frac{4x}{x + 4}$ II. $\frac{20x^3}{y} \cdot \frac{y}{60x^3}$ III. $\frac{x^2 + 6x + 9}{3x + 9} \cdot \frac{x - 3}{x^2 - 9}$
    A. I and II **B.** I and III **C.** II and III **D.** I, II, and III **E.** None of these

South-Western Algebra 1: AN INTEGRATED APPROACH 73

Chapter Opener

DATA ACTIVITY, PAGES 672–673

1. $-0.24\frac{3}{4}$ **2.** \$29,800; \$550 **3.** 4% decrease

4. $\frac{2}{7}$ (oats or soybeans) **5.** Answers will vary.

GETTING STARTED, PAGE 674

1. $8.5 \cdot 11 = 93.5$ square units

2. Answers will vary.

3. One doubles while the other halves.

4. Answers will vary.

Lesson 14.1

THINK BACK, PAGE 675

3. Answers will vary.

Xmin: 0 Ymin: 0

Xmax: 10 Ymax: 500

Xscl: 1 Yscl: 50

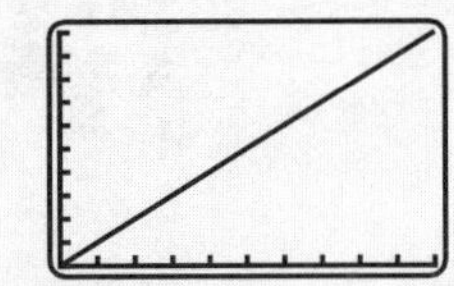

EXPLORE/WORKING TOGETHER, PAGES 675–676

4. Answers will vary.

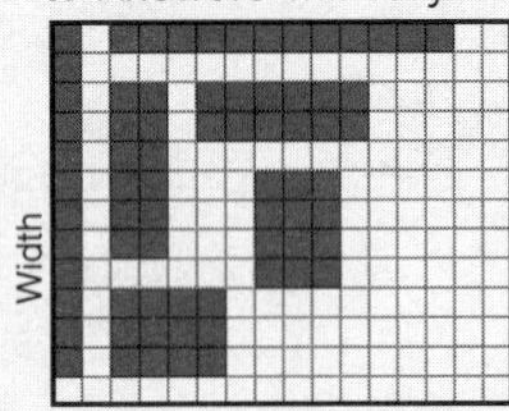

7.

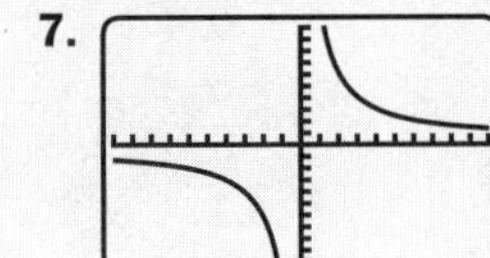

8. Yes, they make sense as possible dimensions of rectangles of area 12 square units.

9. No; they make sense as real number factors of 12 but not as rectangle dimensions.

10. No; division by zero is undefined; no; a rectangle cannot have a dimension that is equal to zero.

MAKE CONNECTIONS, PAGE 676–677

12. Small changes in x produce large changes in y.

13. Large changes in x produce small changes in y.

14. The rate of change in y is not constant in this inverse variation, but is in a direct variation.

17. Direct variations are linear, whereas inverse variations are curved. Direct variations always include (0, 0); inverse variations never do.

SUMMARIZE, PAGE 677

18. The equation is $y = \frac{k}{x}$. The graph shape is two curves in two quadrants (I and III or II and IV). y is undefined when $x = 0$. y becomes infinitely great as x becomes infinitely small. y becomes infinitely small as x becomes infinitely great. $k = xy$.

19. No. Setting $\frac{1}{x}$ equal to $\frac{10}{x}$ yields $x = 10x$. The only value of x that satisfies this equation is 0, and both equations are undefined for $x = 0$.

20. Branches are in Quadrants I and III when $k > 0$ and II and IV when $k < 0$.

Lesson 14.2

EXPLORE, PAGE 679

4. yes; substituting $2r$ for d in the equation $C = \pi d$ results in $C = 2\pi r$, and $k = 2\pi$.

TRY THESE, PAGE 682

15. The formula for the area of a triangle is $A = 0.5bh$. When the area is 24 cm^2, $0.5bh = 24$ and $bh = 48$. $k = 48$ and b varies inversely as h.

PRACTICE, PAGE 683

18. $y = \frac{k}{x}$; possible answer: if more weed killer is used in a field, fewer weeds grow there

ALGEBRAWORKS, PAGE 685

1. A wider tube causes the pressure to increase at a slower rate. Since P is smaller, V must be greater to maintain a particular temperature. Thus, a longer tube must be used to hold a greater volume.

Lesson 14.3

EXPLORE, PAGE 686

1. four layers of 6 x-blocks
$SA = 20x + 48$; $V = 24x$; $\frac{20x + 48}{24x}$

2. a stack of 7 x^2-blocks
$SA = 2x^2 + 28x$; $V = 7x^2$; $\frac{2x^2 + 28x}{7x^2}$

3. a stack of 5 xy-blocks
$SA = 10x + 2xy + 10y$; $V = 5xy$; $\frac{10x + 2xy + 10y}{5xy}$

4. 6 x^2-blocks in 2 stacks of 3 x^2-blocks.
$SA = 4x^2 + 18x$; $V = 6x^2$; $\frac{4x^2 + 18x}{6x^2}$

TRY THESE, PAGE 689

15. Answers will vary; $\frac{y^2 - 25}{y - 5}$ has the restriction $y \neq 5$ whereas $y + 5$ has no restrictions.

PRACTICE, PAGE 689

20. Both have restrictions on the variable. They are different because some factors of $\frac{6x^2 - 24x - 30}{4x - 20}$ are binomials but the factors of $\frac{30x^3}{2x}$ are monomials.

EXTEND, PAGE 690

21. $\frac{(x^2 + 1)(x + 1)}{(x - 1)}$; $x \neq 1$

22. $\frac{(x - 3)}{(x + 3)}$; $x \neq 0, 3, -3$

23. $\frac{x^2(x + 5)}{(x - 1)}$; $x \neq 0, 1, -5$

THINK CRITICALLY, PAGE 690

24. Answers will vary. An example is
$$\frac{1}{(2x - 1)(4x + 1)(x)} = \frac{1}{8x^3 - 2x^2 - x}$$

PROJECT CONNECTION, PAGE 690

1. $r = \frac{C}{2\pi}$; $V = \pi\left(\frac{C}{2\pi}\right)^2$; $h = \frac{C^2}{4\pi}h$

3. $C \neq 0$; the graph is a line with a hole at 0; the graph implies that the volume continues to increase as the cylinder gets wider and, therefore, shorter; C can't be negative

4. Answers will vary. Although the volume may be greater, an extremely wide silo may not be useful, because it would occupy a large piece of land and require a lot of material for a cover.

Lesson 14.4

EXPLORE, PAGE 692

1. 4 **2.** $\frac{5}{2}$ **3.** $\frac{2}{5}$

TRY THESE, PAGES 694–695

13. Answers will vary. In both products, you can divide out common factors; no denominator can be zero. The product of rational expressions can be a rational number or rational expression; the produc of rational numbers is always a rational number.

THINK CRITICALLY, PAGE 696

For 29–32, examples will vary.

29. $\frac{x + 2}{3x + 3} \cdot \frac{x + 5}{x - 1}$ or $\frac{x + 5}{3x + 3} \cdot \frac{2x + 4}{2x - 2}$

30. $\frac{m - 3}{2m - 1} \cdot \frac{m + 2}{m + 3}$ or $\frac{m - 3}{2m + 6} \cdot \frac{2m + 4}{2m - 1}$

31. $\frac{3x^2 + 18x}{x + 5} \div \frac{x^2 + x - 30}{x + 5}$
or $\frac{6x^2 + 42x}{2x + 16} \div \frac{x^2 + 2x - 35}{x + 8}$

32. $\frac{x^2 + 5x + 4}{x^2 - 2x - 3} \div \frac{x + 6}{x - 3}$
or $\frac{x^2 + 6x + 8}{x^2 + 3x - 18} \div \frac{x + 2}{x - 3}$

Lesson 14.5

PRACTICE, PAGE 700

9. Answers will vary.

10. $p^2 + 4p - 5 + \frac{7}{2p + 1}$

11. $q^2 + 2q + 2 - \frac{1}{3q - 1}$

12. $4x^3 + 16x^2 + 72x + 288 + \frac{1168}{-4 + x}$

13. $5y^3 + 25y^2 + 135y + 675 + \frac{3380}{-5 + y}$

Lesson 14.6

EXPLORE, PAGE 702

4. Answers will vary. Some may find the product of the denominators or the LCD.

TRY THESE, PAGE 704

13. Find a common denominator; write equivalent expressions with the same denominator; add the numerators; combine like terms.

RACTICE, PAGE 705

0. $\dfrac{2q^2 - 12q - 1}{81 - q^2}$ **21.** $\dfrac{5v^2 - 40v - 1}{100 - v^2}$

2. $\dfrac{u^3 - 11u^2 + 11}{121 - u^2}$

3. $\dfrac{9a^2 + 16a + 1}{(6a + 1)(a + 2)(a + 3)}$

4. $\dfrac{8b^2 + 33b + 4}{(3b + 2)(b - 1)(b + 5)}$

HINK CRITICALLY, PAGE 706

2. An example is $\dfrac{2}{x + 1} + \dfrac{6}{2x + 2} = \dfrac{10}{2x + 2}$, which can be simplified to $\dfrac{5}{x + 1}$.

3. An example is $\dfrac{2}{x + 1} + \dfrac{3}{2x + 2} = \dfrac{7}{2x + 2}$.

esson 14.7

XPLORE, PAGE 707

4. Express the polynomial using the same denominator as in the rational part of the expression and add the two expressions.

OMMUNICATING ABOUT ALGEBRA, PAGE 708

he method shown in Example 2 requires fewer steps.

RACTICE, PAGES 710–711

1. $\dfrac{x^2}{48x - 160}$

HINK CRITICALLY, PAGE 711

0. Answers will vary. Example: $\dfrac{\dfrac{x + 1}{x^2 - 3}}{\dfrac{x + 1}{x^2 - 3}}$

esson 14.8

XPLORE, PAGE 712

5. Answers will vary. Multiply each term by x and solve the resulting equation.

OMMUNICATING ABOUT ALGEBRA, PAGE 713

hey are not equivalent equations because their olutions are not equivalent. Zero satisfies the first quation but not the second.

RY THESE, PAGE 716

1. When you multiply by a variable, the resulting equation may have solutions that are not solutions of the original equations.

HINK CRITICALLY, PAGE 717

or 21–23, examples will vary.

1. $\dfrac{x}{x + 4} + \dfrac{8}{x - 4} = \dfrac{x + 60}{x^2 - 16}$

2. $\dfrac{2}{x + 1} = \dfrac{-2x}{x + 1} + 4$

3. $\dfrac{4}{x + 1} + \dfrac{6}{x - 2} = \dfrac{-2}{x^2 - x - 2}$

ROJECT CONNECTION, PAGE 717

3. $0 \le x < 1$;
Moisture cannot be greater than 1, or less than 0; $x \ne 1$ because the function is not defined at 1.

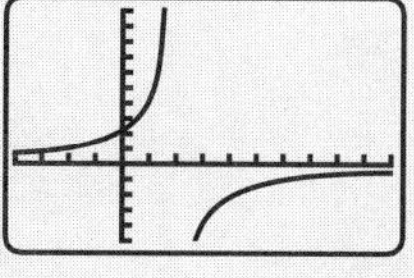

Lesson 14.9

EXPLORE THE PROBLEM, PAGE 719

6. mass left =

$$2.5\ \not{lb} \bullet \frac{453.6\text{ g}}{\not{lb}} - \left(\frac{8.5\text{ g}}{\not{\text{student}}} \times 24\ \not{\text{students}}\right)$$
$$= 1134\text{ g} - 204\text{ g} = 930\text{ g}$$

7. The value of any correct conversion factor is 1; multiplying by 1 does not change the value.

INVESTIGATE FURTHER, PAGE 719

8. $\dfrac{1\text{km}}{1 \times 10^3\text{ m}}$; $\dfrac{3 \times 10^8\ \not{m}}{1\text{s}} \bullet \dfrac{1\text{km}}{1 \times 10^3\ \not{m}} =$
$3 \bullet 10^5$ km/s

9. $\dfrac{60\text{ s}}{1\text{ min}}$; $\dfrac{60\text{ min}}{1\text{ h}}$; $\dfrac{24\text{ h}}{1\text{ day}}$

10. lt yr =

$$\frac{3.0 \times 10^8\ \not{m}}{1\ \not{s}} \bullet \frac{1\text{km}}{1 \times 10^3\ \not{m}} \bullet \frac{60\ \not{s}}{1\ \not{\text{min}}} \bullet \frac{60\ \not{\text{min}}}{1\ \not{h}} \bullet \frac{24\ \not{h}}{1\ \not{\text{day}}} \bullet 365\ \not{\text{days}} = 94608 \times 10^{12}\text{ km}$$

11. If units of measure or physical quantities are involved; many ratios and steps are involved; conversion of units is required.

APPLY THE STRATEGY, PAGE 720

14. $46\ \not{cm} \bullet \dfrac{100\ \not{km}}{2.5\ \not{cm}} \bullet \dfrac{1\ \not{mi}}{1.6\ \not{km}} \bullet \dfrac{1\ \not{gal}}{22\ \not{mi}} \bullet \dfrac{1.16\text{ dollars}}{1\ \not{gal}} = 60.64\text{ dollars or }\$60.64$

15. $\dfrac{258{,}000\text{ customers} \bullet \left(50\dfrac{\text{calls}}{\text{customers}}\right) \bullet \left(0.8\dfrac{\text{hours}}{\text{call}}\right)}{1500\dfrac{\text{hours}}{\text{salesperson}}}$

= 6880 salespersons

REVIEW PROBLEM SOLVING STRATEGIES, PAGE 721

READING BETWEEN THE LINES

a. $x^2 + y^2 = 9$ **b.** $(a - x)^2 + y^2 = 16$

c. $(a - x)^2 + (b - y)^2 = 25$

d. $x^2 + (b - y)^2 = (PD)^2$

e. Methods will vary. One method is to subtract Equation II from Equation III and add Equation I to the result.

f. Since $x^2 + (b - y)^2 = (DP)^2$ and $x^2 + (b - y)^2 = 18$, it follows that $(DP)^2 = 18$. So, $DP = \sqrt{18}$

A PERFECT 10

1,312,432,004

OLD TIMERS

Sonja can set both timers at the same time. As soon as the 5-min timer finishes, she turns it over. As soon as the 8-min timer finishes, she turns it over. As soon as the 5-min timer finishes the second time, she immediately turns it over again. The amount of time from when the 5-min timer finishes for the third time to when the 8-min timer finishes for the second time is 1 min.

Chapter Assessment

CHAPTER TEST, PAGE 724

1. Examples will vary. Students should state that as the x-values decrease, the y-values decrease, and as the x-values decrease, the y-values increase.

3. inverse, $k = 4$ **4.** direct, $k = 5$

5. joint, $k = 2\pi$ **9.** $\dfrac{1}{x - 13}$; $x \ne -3, 13$

10. $\dfrac{x + 5}{x + 6}$; $x \ne -6, -5$ **11.** $\dfrac{c + 7}{c - 8}$; $c \ne 8$

15. $\dfrac{-41r + 14}{10r^2}$ **16.** $\dfrac{20a - 18}{(a + 3)(a - 10)}$

17. $\dfrac{63b^2 - 10ab - 8a^2}{48a^2b^2}$ **18.** $\dfrac{14q + 44}{49 - q^2}$

19. When one polynomial is divided by another and the two expressions have no common factors other than 1, you must use long division.

20. $\dfrac{8p^2 - 16p + 7}{4p - 6}$ **21.** $\dfrac{q^2 - 2q - 19}{q + 3}$

22. $\dfrac{-k^2 - 8k - 1}{k + 10}$ **23.** $\dfrac{a^2 - 12}{a - 4}$

CUMULATIVE REVIEW, PAGE 726

2. $\dfrac{x^2 + 3x}{2}$; $x \ne 3$ **3.** $\dfrac{x - 4}{x - 2}$; $x \ne -5, 2$

4. $12n^3 - 23n - 10$

5. $8y^3 + 22y^2 - 71y + 14$

6. $4t^3 + 5t^2 - 6t + 12$

7. $x^3 + 2x^2 - 6x + 11 - \dfrac{35}{x + 3}$

8. In the first example, 4 is a factor of both the numerator and denominator. In the second example, 4 is a term but is not a factor.

12. $-6, \dfrac{3}{5}$ **13.** $\dfrac{-5 - \sqrt{57}}{4}$, $\dfrac{-5 + \sqrt{57}}{4}$

25.

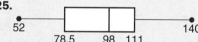

52 78.5 98 111 140

26. A line graph would best show the highs and lows and the differences from one game to the next.

27. $\dfrac{9}{y - 1}$

30. domain: all real numbers; range: all real numbers

31. domain: all real numbers; range: $y \ge -2$

32. domain: all real numbers; range: $y \le 1$

33. domain: $x \ge -2$; range: $y \ge 1$

Geometry

Quick Notes

Geometry Basics

All geometric figures are made up of at least one point.

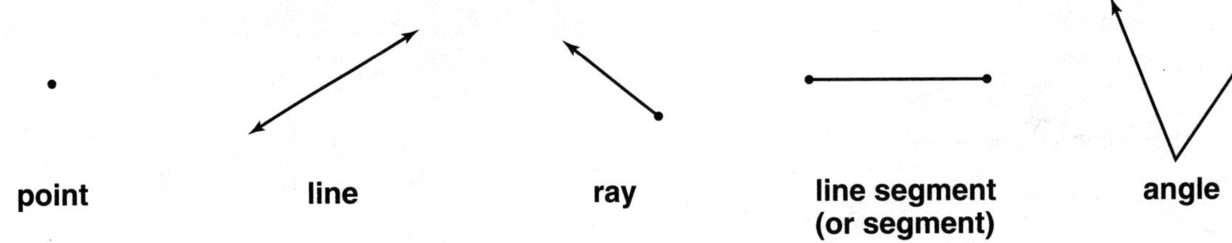

About Lines

Lines in a plane can be either parallel to each other or they can intersect each other.

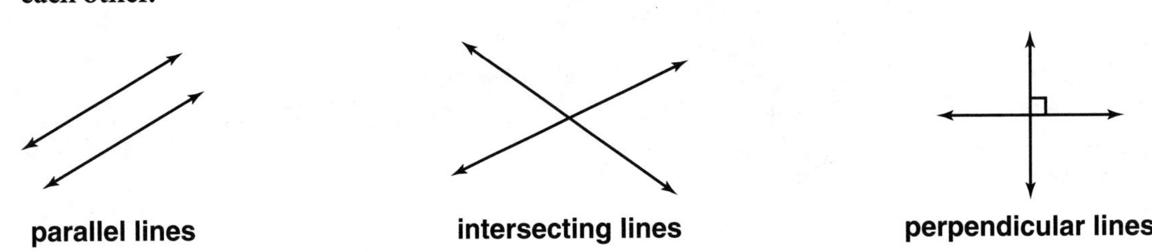

About Angles

Angles are measured in degrees.

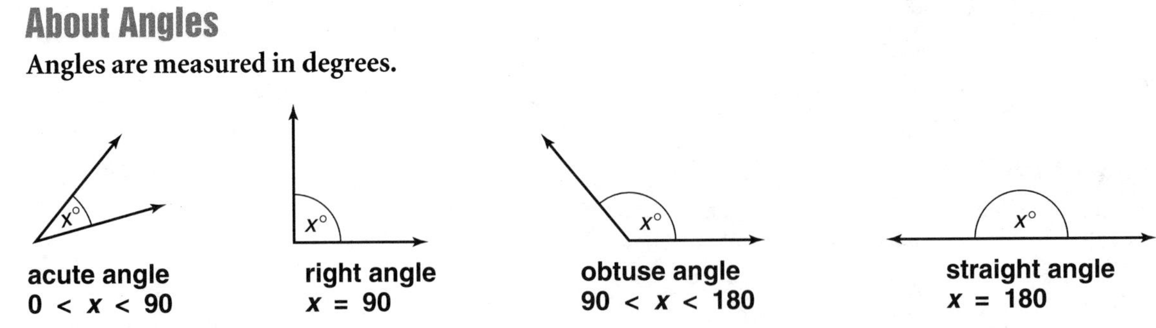

Complementary and Supplementary Angles

Two angles are complementary if the sum of their measures is exactly 90°.

Two angles are supplementary if the sum of their measures is exactly 180°.

728

About Triangles

Triangles are three-sided plane figures. They can be classified according to the measures of their sides or their angles.

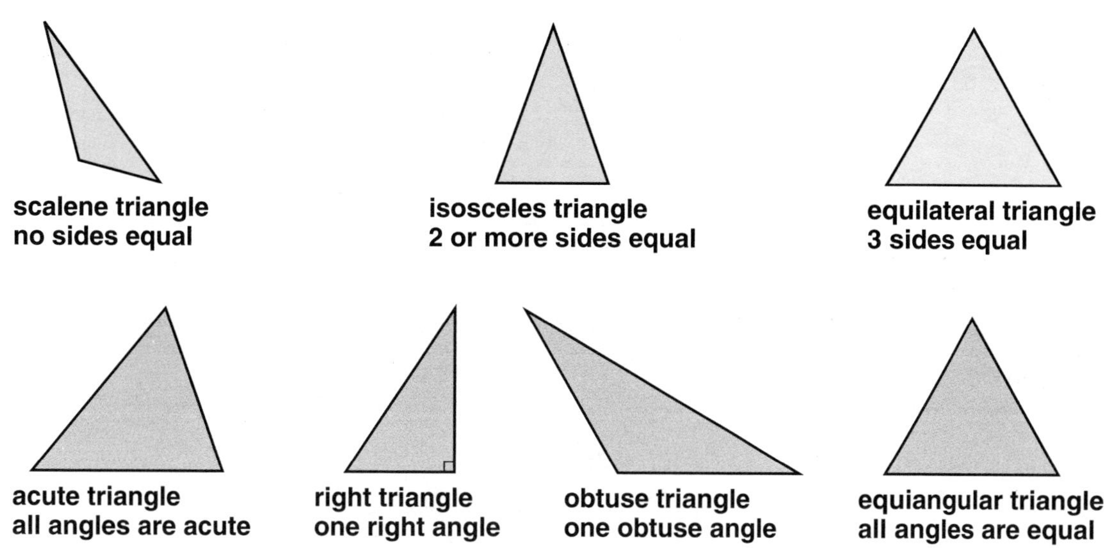

About Quadrilaterals

Quadrilaterals are four-sided plane figures. Each figure in the diagram has all the properties of the figures preceding it, including the properties listed with that figure.

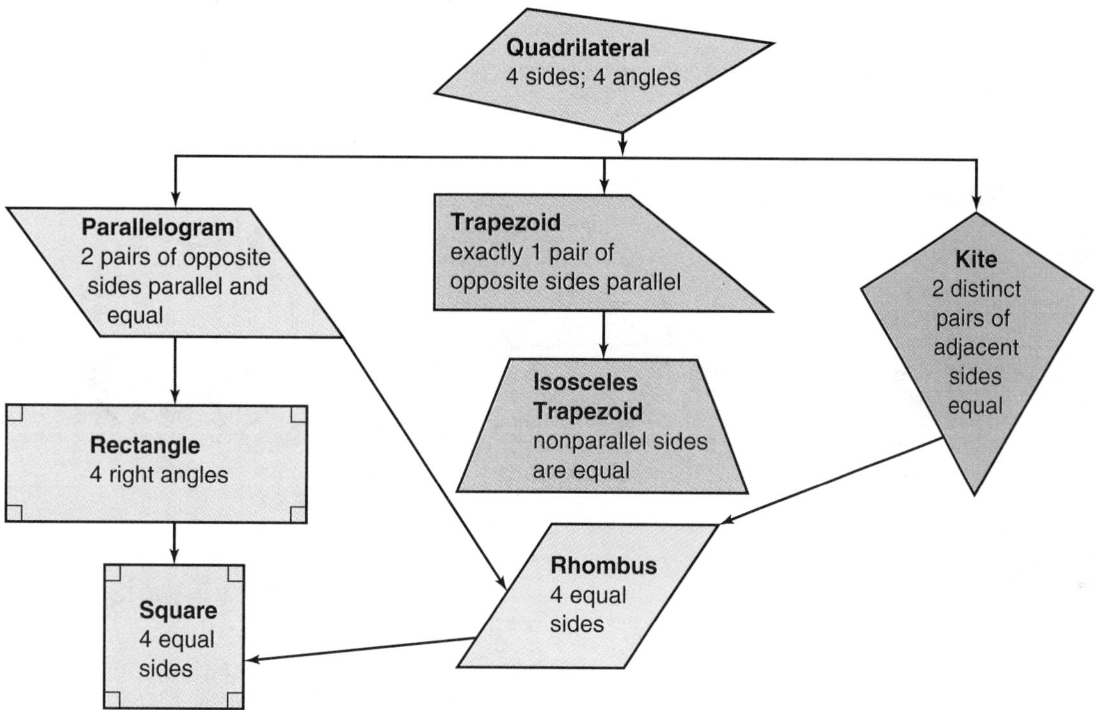

About Other Polygons

Polygons are plane figures made up of segments and angles. Triangles and four-sided figures are also polygons.

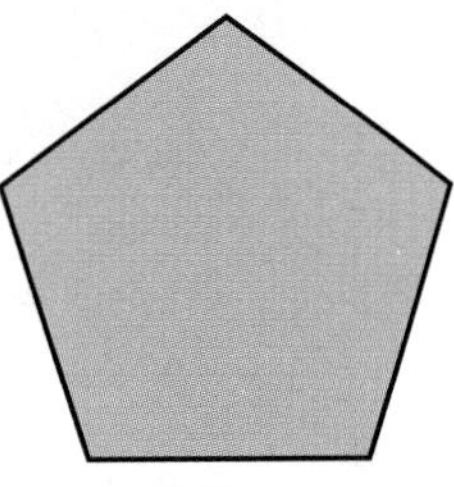
pentagon

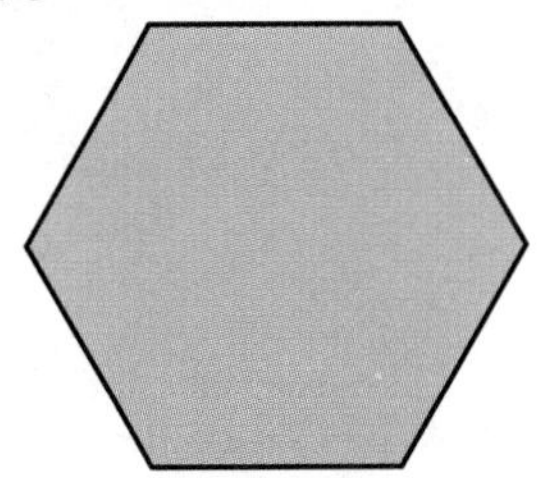
hexagon

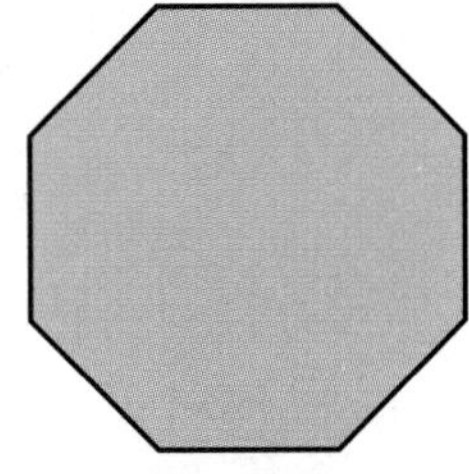
octagon

Perimeter Formulas

In the following formulas, l = length, w = width, s = side, and P = perimeter.

Perimeter of a rectangle	$P = 2l + 2w$
Perimeter of a square	$P = 4s$

Area Formulas

In the following formulas, b = base, B = long base, h = height, l = length, w = width, s = side, and A = area.

Area of a parallelogram	$A = bh$
Area of a rectangle	$A = lw$
Area of a square	$A = s^2$
Area of a trapezoid	$A = \frac{1}{2}(B + b)h$
Area of a triangle	$A = \frac{1}{2}bh$

About Circles and Spheres

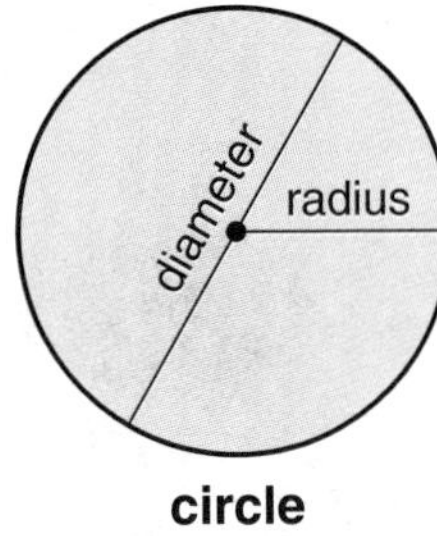

circle

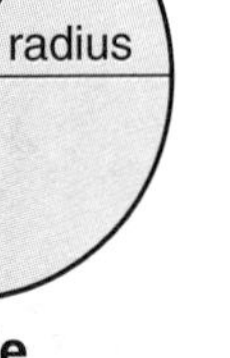
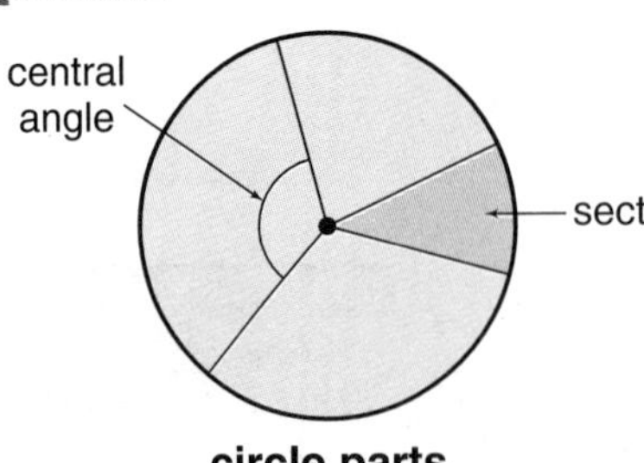

circle parts

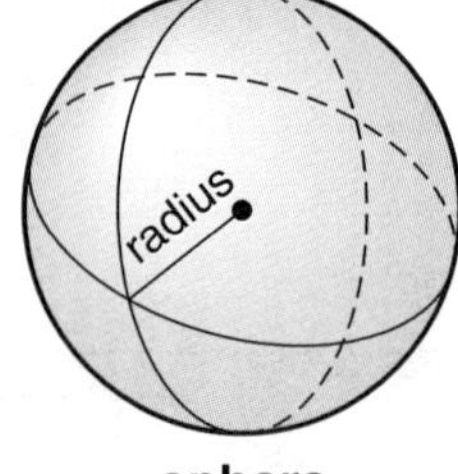

sphere

Circle Formulas

Circumference of a circle	$C = 2\pi r$ or $C = \pi d$
Area of a circle	$A = \pi r^2$

Sphere Formulas

Area of a sphere	$A = 4\pi r^2$
Volume of a sphere	$V = \frac{4}{3}\pi r^3$

About Geometric Solid Figures

Geometric solid figures are made up of plane polygons. Below are some geometric solid right figures.

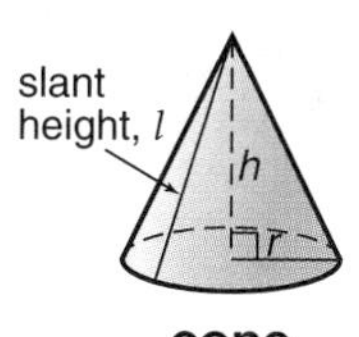

cone

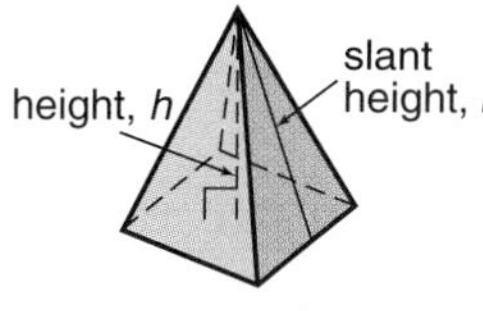

pyramid

cylinder

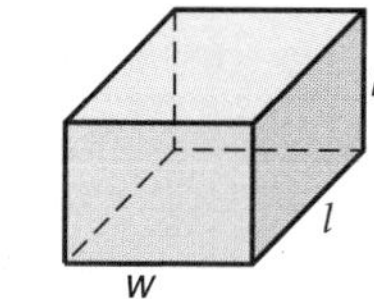

rectangular prism

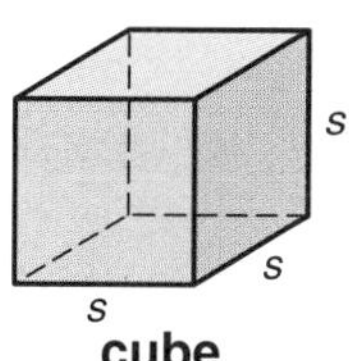

cube

Base

The cone and the pyramid have one base. The cylinder and the prism have two bases and they are parallel. The cone and cylinder have circular bases. The base of a pyramid or prism can be any polygonal shape.

Lateral Surface

The lateral surface is the side or sides of the solid figure other than a base. The cone and cylinder have one lateral surface. The lateral surface of a pyramid is made up of triangles. The lateral surface of a right prism is made up of rectangles.

Slant Height

The slant height of a cone is measured from the vertex of the cone to the edge of its base. The slant height of a pyramid is measured from the vertex to the center of one side of the base.

Formulas

Total surface area of a right circular cone	$T = \pi r(l + r)$
Volume of a cone	$V = \frac{1}{3}\pi r^2 h$
Total surface area of a right cylinder	$T = 2\pi r(r + h)$
Volume of a cylinder	$V = \pi r^2 h$
Total surface area of a rectangular prism	$T = 2(lw + lh + wh)$
Volume of a rectangular prism	$V = lwh$
Total surface area of a cube	$T = 6s^2$
Volume of a cube	$V = s^3$

Technology

Quick Notes

Using the Texas Instruments TI-82 Graphing Calculator

- **For additional features and instructions, consult your user's manual.**

  THE KEYBOARD The feature accessed when a key is pressed is shown in white on the key. To access the features in blue above each key, first press the 2ND key. To access what is in white above the keys, first press ALPHA.

  CALCULATIONS Calculations are performed in the Home Screen. This screen may be returned to at any time by pressing 2ND QUIT. The calculator evaluates according to the order of operations. Press ENTER to calculate. For $3 + 4 \times 5$ ENTER, the result is 23. You can replay the previous line by pressing 2ND ENTER. Use the arrow keys to edit.

Displaying Graphs

- **GRAPH FEATURE** To enter an equation, press Y=. Enter an equation such as $y = 2x + 3$ using the X, T, θ key for x. Then press GRAPH to display the graph in the viewing window.

  VIEWING WINDOW To set range values for the viewing window, press WINDOW. Press ▶ to access FORMAT where you can choose features such as Grid Off or Grid On.

  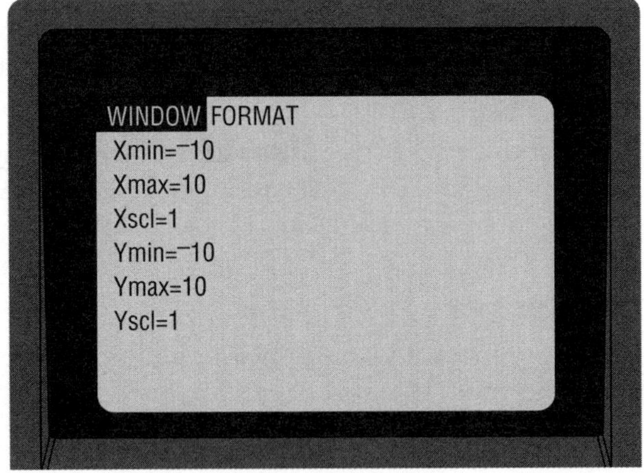

  ZOOM FEATURE Press ZOOM and then 6 (Standard) to set a standard viewing window. Press ZOOM 1 (Box) to highlight a particular area and zoom in on that part of the graph. Press ZOOM 8 (Integer) to set values for a friendly window.

  TRACE FEATURE Pressing TRACE places the cursor directly on the graph and shows the x- and y-coordinates of the point where the cursor is located. You can move the cursor along the graph using the right and left arrow keys.

  TABLE FEATURE Press 2ND TBLSET to set up the table. Then press 2ND TABLE to see a table of values for each equation.

Intersection Feature To determine the coordinates of the point of intersection of two graphs, press 2ND CALC, then 5 (Intersect). The calculator will then prompt you to identify the first graph. Use the right and left arrow keys to move the cursor to the first graph, close to the point of intersection. Repeat to identify the second graph and get the coordinates of the point of intersection.

Statistics

Entering Data Enter data into lists by pressing STAT 1 (Edit).

Calculating Statistics Return to the Home Screen by pressing 2ND QUIT. To calculate the mean of List 1, press 2ND LIST ▶ (MATH) 3 (Mean) 2ND L1 ENTER. To calculate the median, choose 4 instead of 3. To calculate statistics, press STAT ▶ (CALC) 1 (1 - Var Stats) ENTER. You can also choose 2 to calculate two variable statistics and 5 to calculate linear regression. To see the lower quartile of a boxplot, press VARS 5 (Statistics) ▶ ▶ ▶ (BOX) 1 (Q1). Use 2 for median and 3 for the upper quartile.

Graphing Data To graph your data, press 2ND STATPLOT and choose a scatter plot, a line graph, a boxplot, or a histogram. Then choose the data list. Then press GRAPH to draw the graph.

Using the Casio CFX-9800G Graphing Calculator

For additional features and instructions, consult your user's manual.

The Keyboard The feature accessed when a key is pressed is shown in white on the key. To access the features in gold above each key, first press the SHIFT key. To access what is in red above the keys, first press ALPHA.

The Main Menu This is the screen you see when you first turn the calculator on. Highlight and press EXE or press the number to choose the menu item. You can access the Main Menu at any time by pressing the MENU key.

Performing Calculations Calculations are performed by pressing 1 (for COMPutations) in the Main Menu. The calculator evaluates according to the order of operations. Press EXE (for EXEcute) to calculate. For $3 + 4 \times 5$ EXE, the result is 23. You can replay the previous line by pressing ◀. Use the arrow keys to edit.

Displaying Graphs

Comp Mode Press 1 in the Main Menu. To enter an equation, press GRAPH. Enter an equation such as $y = 2x + 3$ using the X, θ, T key for x. Then press EXE to display the graph in the viewing window.

Graph Mode Press 6 (GRAPH) in the Main Menu. Then press AC. Use the up or down arrows to choose a location to store the equation. Enter the equation as above. Then press F6 (DRW) to display the graph in the viewing window.

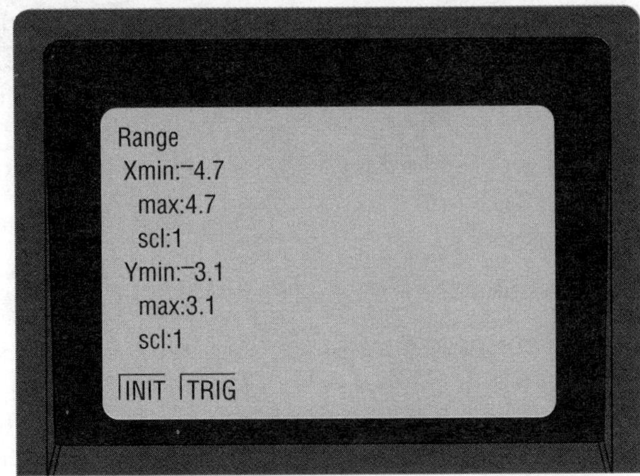

Viewing Window To set range values for the viewing window, press RANGE. You can use F1 (INIT) to set standard values for a viewing window.

Zoom Feature Press SHIFT F2 (ZOOM) to access this feature. Press F1 (BOX) to highlight a particular area and zoom in on that part of the graph. Press F5 (AUT) to set range values for a friendly window.

Trace Feature Pressing SHIFT F1 (TRACE) places the cursor directly on the graph and shows the x- and y-coordinates of the point where the cursor is located. You can move the cursor along the graph using the right arrow keys.

Table Feature Press 8 (TABLE) in the Main Menu. Press AC to clear the screen. Then press F1 (RANGE FUNC). Select the function. Then press F5 (RNG) to set up the table. Press F6 (TBL) to see the table of values. You can press SHIFT QUIT to return to a previous screen.

Intersection Feature To determine the coordinates of the point of intersection of two graphs, press SHIFT, then 9 (G-SOLV). Then press F5 (ISCT). The calculator will then prompt you to identify the graphs.

Statistics

Entering Data From the Main Menu, press 3 (SD). Press SHIFT SET UP and select STOre for S-data. Then press EXIT AC to clear the screen. Enter data, pressing F1 after each entry.

Calculating Statistics To calculate the mean ($\bar{x}$), press F4 (DEV) F1 ($\bar{x}$) EXE. To calculate the median, press F4 (DEV) F4 ▼ and F2 (Med) EXE.

Graphing Data To graph your data, press SHIFT SET UP and select DRAW for S-graph. Press EXIT and then GRAPH EXE.

Using the Hewlett-Packard 38G Graphing Calculator

For additional features and instructions, consult your user's manual.

The Keyboard The feature accessed when a key is pressed is shown in yellow on the key. To access the features in green above each key, first press the green key. To access what is in red below the keys, first press A...Z. The blank keys at the top of the keyboard are used for the menu items at the bottom of the screen. Pressing the Menu key at the far right will return menu items to the screen.

Calculations Calculations are performed in the Home Screen. This screen may be returned to at any time by pressing HOME. The calculator evaluates according to the order of operations. Press ENTER to calculate. For $3 + 4 \times 5$ ENTER, the result is 23. You can edit a previous line by using the arrow keys to choose a line you want to edit. Press the Copy key. Use the arrow keys to edit.

Displaying Graphs

Graph Feature To enter an equation, press LIBrary. Select Function. Press ENTER. Press the Edit key to enter an equation such as $y = 2x + 3$, using the X, T, θ key for x. Then press PLOT to display the graph in the viewing window.

Viewing Window Press the green key and VIEWS. Select Auto Scale to get a friendly window, or you can press the green key and PLOT to change the range in the viewing window. Next, press PLOT to show the graph.

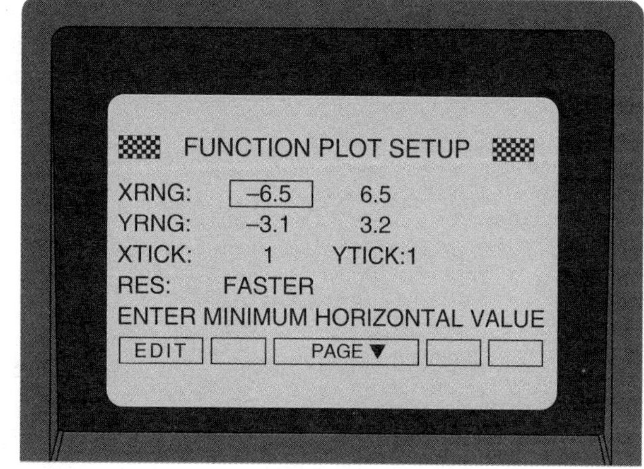

Zoom Feature Press the Menu key. Press the Zoom key. Then select Box... to highlight a particular area and zoom in on that part of the graph.

Trace Feature Pressing the Trace key puts the cursor directly on the graph and shows the x- and y-coordinates of the point of its location. You can move the cursor along the graph using the right and left arrow keys.

Table Feature To display a table of values for the graphed equation, press NUMber.

Intersection Feature To determine the coordinates of the point of intersection of two graphs, move the cursor close to the point of intersection. Press the Function key and select Intersection. This verifies one of your equations. Press ENTER. Then press the Function key and select Intersection to verify the other equation. Press ENTER.

Statistical Features

Entering Data Data may be entered into a list by pressing LIB and selecting Statistics.

Calculating Statistics To calculate mean, median, upper, and lower quartiles of the data entered in C1, press the Stats key and use the arrow keys to access all the information.

Graphing Data To graph your data, press the green key and then PLOT. Then press the Choos key. Select BoxWhisker or Histogram and ENTER. Then press the green key and VIEWS. Select Auto Scale.

735

GLOSSARY

A

absolute value (p. 68) The distance of a number from 0 on the number line. The absolute value of x is written as $|x|$. For any real number x, $|x| = x$ if $x > 0$ or $x = 0$ and $|x| = -x$ if $x < 0$.

absolute value function (p. 416) The function $f(x) = |x|$. The corresponding absolute value equation is $y = |x|$ where x is any real number and y is any number greater than or equal to zero.

absolute value inequality (p. 432) An inequality of the form $|ax \pm b| < c$ or $|ax \pm b| > c$.

acute triangle (p. 619) A triangle with three acute angles.

addition property of equality (p. 124) For all real numbers a, b, and c, if $a = b$, then $a + c = b + c$.

addition property of inequality (p. 230) For all real numbers a, b, and c, if $a > b$, then $a + c > b + c$ and if $a < b$, then $a + c < b + c$.

additive identity property (p. 80) For any real number a, $a + 0 = a$.

additive inverse property (p. 80) For any real number a, $a + (-a) = 0$. (See also **opposite**.)

Algeblocks (p. 56) Models that physically represent algebraic concepts and operations.

algebraic expression (p. 13, 60) An expression having at least one number, operation, and variable.

amplitude (of a function) (p. 660) The distance from the middle line of the graph of a function to the maximum or minimum value of the function.

associative property of addition (p. 80) For any real numbers a, b, and c, $(a + b) + c = a + (b + c)$.

associative property of multiplication (p. 89) For any real numbers a, b, and c, $(a \cdot b) \cdot c = a \cdot (b \cdot c)$.

average (p. 32) The mean of a set of data.

average rate of change (p. 271) The slope formula can be used to find average rate of change.

axis of symmetry (p. 469) A line, such as the vertical line passing through the vertex of a parabola, which divides a figure so that when folded, the two halves coincide.

B

bar graph (p. 19) A display of statistical information in which horizontal or vertical bars, or rectangles, represent data to be compared.

base (of a power) (p. 59) The repeating factor in a power. For example, in 4^3 the base is 4.

binomial (p. 541) A polynomial of two terms.

boundary (of two half-planes) (p. 374) The line, or graph of a linear equation, that divides the coordinate plane into two half-planes.

boxplot (p. 248) A graph that uses the three quartiles and the least and greatest values of a set of data to provide a visual display of the data.

C

cells (p. 14) The spaces formed by the horizontal rows and vertical columns on a computer spreadsheet, in which formulas or data can be entered.

circle graph (p. 19) A display of statistical information in which data is represented by sectors.

closed half-plane (p. 375) A half-plane that includes the boundary line.

cluster sampling (p. 22) A type of statistical sampling in which a specifically defined portion of a population is chosen at random and interviewed.

coefficient (p. 61) The numerical, nonvariable portion of a monomial.

coefficient of correlation (p. 299) The statistical measure r of how closely a set of data approximates a line. The range of the coefficient of correlation is from –1 to 1.

commutative property of addition (p. 80) For any real numbers a and b, $a + b = b + a$.

commutative property of multiplication (p. 89) For any real numbers a and b, $a \cdot b = b \cdot a$.

complementary angles (p. 620) Two angles the sum of whose measures is 90°. Each angle is the *complement* of the other.

complementary events (p. 400) The two possible outcomes in a random experiment in which the event occurs or the event does not occur. The probabilities of two complements total 1.

complex rational expression (p. 708) A rational expression that contains one or more rational expressions in its numerator or denominator.

compound inequality (p. 241, 430) Two inequalities connected by *and* or *or*.

computer spreadsheets (p. 14) Computer software programs that use formulas to calculate and analyze data and display it in columns and rows.

conjugates (p. 629) Two expressions that are the sum and difference of the same two terms, for example, $a + \sqrt{b}$ and $a - \sqrt{b}$.

conjunction (p. 241, 430) Two statements joined by the word *and*. A conjunction is true if and only if both of its statements are true.

consecutive integers (p. 107) Any integers in counting, or successive, order.

consistent (system) (p. 348) A system of equations with at least one solution.

constant (p. 61) In an algebraic expression, a number not multiplied or divided by a variable.

constant of variation (pp. 307, 679, 681) The constant k in the equation of a direct variation $y = kx$, an inverse variation $xy = k$, or a joint variation $y = kwx$.

constraints (p. 388) Conditions that limit business activity. In linear programming, constraints are represented by inequalities.

convenience sampling (p. 22) A type of statistical sampling in which a readily available portion of a population is chosen, and all members of that portion are surveyed.

conversion factor (p. 718) A ratio of two equal quantities used to convert one dimensional unit to another.

coordinate (p. 177) The real number that corresponds to a point on a number line; each of the two paired numbers corresponding to a given point in the coordinate plane.

coordinate plane (p. 177) A two-dimensional grid consisting of two perpendicular number lines called the x-axis and the y-axis.

corresponding elements (of a matrix) (p. 28) Elements in the same position in each of two matrices having the same dimensions.

cosine (p. 653) For either acute angle in a right triangle, the ratio of the length of the side adjacent to the angle to the length of the hypotenuse.

crest (of a graph) (p. 660) The maximum value of the graph of a periodic function.

D

data points (p. 169) Points on a coordinate plane that correspond to statistical information.

degree (of an expression) (p. 62) The greatest exponent of the variables in the expression in simplest form.

degree of a monomial (p. 521) The sum of the degrees of all the variable factors in a monomial.

degree of a polynomial (p. 542) The greatest degree of any of the terms of a polynomial.

degree of a variable (in a monomial) (p. 521) The number of times a variable occurs as a factor in a monomial.

dense (p. 446) A characteristic of real numbers because between any two real numbers there exists another real number.

dependent system (p. 349) A system of equations with the same graph.

dependent (variable) (p. 299) The output value of a relation.

determinant (p. 353) A numerical value associated with a square matrix. The determinant of a matrix is symbolized by using vertical bars in place of matrix brackets.

difference of two squares See **product of a sum and a difference.**

dimensional analysis (p. 718) The method of using units or dimensions in the solution of problems.

dimensions (of a matrix) (p. 27) The number of horizontal rows and the number of vertical columns in a matrix.

dimensions (of a quantity) (p. 718) The units in which a quantity is measured.

direct variation (p. 307, 679) When y varies directly as x and k is the constant of variation, an equation can be written in the form $y = kx$, $k \neq 0$.

GLOSSARY

discriminant (p. 491, 597) The expression $b^2 - 4ac$, under the radical symbol in the quadratic formula. The discriminant can be used to determine the number of real number solutions of any quadratic equation.

disjunction (p. 242, 425) Two statements joined by the word *or*. A disjunction is true if at least one of the statements is true.

distance formula (p. 642) The formula $d = \sqrt{(x_2 - x_1)^2 + (y_2 - y_1)^2}$ used to determine the distance d between any two points (x_1, y_1) and (x_2, y_2) in the coordinate plane.

distributive property of multiplication over addition (p. 96) For all real numbers a, b, and c, $a(b + c) = ab + ac$, and $(b + c)a = ba + ca$.

division (p. 90) For any real numbers a and b, $b \neq 0, a \div b = a \cdot \frac{1}{b}$.

division property of equality (p. 130) For all real numbers a, b, and c, if $a = b$, and $c \neq 0$, then $\frac{a}{c} = \frac{b}{c}$.

division property of inequality (p. 231) For all real numbers a, b, and c, if $a > b$, and $c > 0$, then $\frac{a}{c} > \frac{b}{c}$, and if $a > b$, and $c < 0$, then $\frac{a}{c} < \frac{b}{c}$.

domain (of a function) (p. 172) The input values of a function.

E

element (of a matrix) (p. 27) Each number or entry in a matrix.

element (of a set) (p. 437) An item or number that is part of a set. For example, 4 is an element of $\{2, 4, 6, 8\}$.

elimination method (p. 342) A method for solving a system of linear equations by using multiplication and addition to eliminate one of the variables.

equation (p. 115) A statement that two numbers or expressions are equal.

equilateral triangle (p. 619) A triangle having three sides equal in length.

equivalent equations (p. 124) Equations that have the same solution.

equivalent inequalities (p. 230) Inequalities that have the same solution.

evaluate (an expression) (p. 60) To find the value of an algebraic expression by substituting a given number for each variable and simplifying.

evaluate a function (p. 172) To find the output, $f(x)$, for a given input x.

event (p. 398) Any one of the possible outcomes of an experiment.

experimental probability (p. 38) The probability of an event determined by observation or measurement. The experimental probability, $P(E)$, of an event E is given by

$$P(E) = \frac{\text{number of times } E \text{ occurs}}{\text{total number of trials}}$$

exponent (p. 59) A superscript number showing how many times a base is used as a factor. For example, in 2^5, 5 is the exponent.

extraneous solution (p. 713) An apparent solution that does not satisy the original equation. Extraneous solutions often result from squaring both sides of an equation.

extremes (of a proportion) (p. 136) In the proportion $a{:}b = c{:}d$, a and d are the extremes.

F

factor (p. 88) Any of two or more numbers multiplied to produce a product. For example, in $3(4) = 12$, 3 and 4 are factors of 12.

factored completely (p. 591) A polynomial is factored completely when it cannot be factored further.

factored form (of a polynomial) (p. 575) A polynomial expressed as a product of other polynomials.

feasible region (p. 388) The intersection of the graphs of a system of constraints; the region of the coordinate plane that includes all possible solutions of the objective function.

finite (set) (p. 437) A set whose elements can be counted or listed.

FOIL (p. 553) A method for determining the product of two binomials by finding the product of the First terms, the Outside terms, the Inside terms, and the Last terms, and then simplifying the result.

formula (p. 152) A literal equation that expresses a relationship between two or more variables.

frequency (p. 8) The number of times an item occurs in a set of data.

frequency table (p. 8) A method of recording and organizing data using tally marks to show how often an item occurs in a set of data.

function (p. 171) A relation having exactly one output value for each input value in a set of paired values. In a function, more than one input value may have the same output value.

function notation (p. 172) The notation for representing a rule that associates an input value (independent variable) with an output value (dependent variable). The most commonly used function notation is the "f of x" notation, written "$f(x)$."

function rule (p. 172) The description of a function.

fundamental counting principle (p. 399) If one event can occur in m ways and, following that, a second event can occur in n ways, then the total number of possible outcomes equals $m \cdot n$.

G

geometric mean (p. 641) A number b is the geometric mean between two numbers m and n if $b = \sqrt{m \cdot n}$.

H

half-planes (p. 374) The two regions into which the graph of a linear equation divides the coordinate plane.

horizontal axis (p. 169) The x-axis of the coordinate plane.

horizontal shift (of a graph) (p. 417) The left or right translation of a graph in relation to another graph.

I

identity element for multiplication (p. 89) The number 1, because the product of any number and 1 is the number itself.

inconsistent (system) (p. 349) A system of equations with no solution.

independent (system) (p. 348) A system of equations that has exactly one solution.

independent (variable) (p. 299) The input value of a relation.

inequality (p. 67, 222) A statement that two numbers or expressions are not equal; a statement containing an inequality symbol.

inequality symbol (p. 67) A symbol used to compare, or order, real numbers. The inequality symbols are $<$, $>$, $\leq$, $\geq$, and $\neq$.

infinite (set) (p. 437) A set whose elements cannot be counted or listed, but go on forever. The set $\{0, 1, 2, 3, \ldots\}$ is an infinite set.

integer(s) (p. 56) All whole numbers and their opposites.

inverse operation (p. 90) An operation "undoing" what another operation does. For example, multiplication and division are inverse operations.

inverse variation (p. 679) When y varies inversely as x and k is the constant of variation, an equation can be written in the form $y = \frac{k}{x}, k \neq 0$.

irrational number (p. 65, 438) A number that cannot be expressed as the quotient of two integers, a terminating decimal, or a repeating decimal. For example, π and $\sqrt{2}$ are irrational numbers. (See also **perfect square.**)

isosceles triangle (p. 619) A triangle having at least two sides equal in length.

J

joint variation (p. 681) When y varies directly as the product of w and x and k is the constant of variation, an equation can be written in the form $y = kwx, k \neq 0$.

L

leading coefficient (p. 578) The coefficient of the first term in a polynomial in standard form.

least common denominator (LCD) (p. 703) The least positive common multiple of the denominators of two or more fractions or rational expressions.

like radicals (p. 631) Two or more radicals with the same radicand.

like terms (p. 97, 542) Two or more terms in an algebraic expression that have the same variable base and exponent.

linear equation in two variables (p. 183) An equation that can be written in the form $y = ax + b$, representing a linear function.

linear function (p. 183) A function that can be represented by a straight line or by a linear equation in two variables of the form $y = ax + b$, where x and y are variables and a and b are constants.

linear inequality in two variables (p. 373) An inequality that results when the equal symbol in a linear equation is replaced by $<$, $>$, $\leq$, $\geq$, or $\neq$.

linear programming (p. 388) A method used by business and government to maximize or minimize quantities such as profit and cost.

linear system (p. 328) Two or more linear equations that are considered together.

line graph (p. 19) A display of statistical information in which points representing data are plotted and then connected with line segments.

line of best fit (p. 299) The line that approximates a trend for the data on a scatter plot. Also called a *regression line*.

line of reflection (p. 416) The line over which a figure is reflected, or flipped.

line of symmetry (p. 413, 417, 469) A line that divides a figure so that when the figure is folded over that line, the two parts match exactly.

line plot (p. 19) A display of statistical information in which each item of data is represented by an X with X's stacked vertically in columns.

literal equation (p. 152) An equation that contains at least two different variables.

M

matrix *(plural: matrices)* (p. 27) A rectangular arrangement of numbers in rows and columns and enclosed with brackets.

maximize (an objective function) (p. 390) To determine the greatest possible value of an objective function. Maximums occur at or near a vertex of the feasible region of a linear programming graph.

maximum (point) (p. 468) See **vertex**.

mean (p. 32) The sum of the items in a set of data divided by the number of items. Also called the *average*.

means (of a proportion) (p. 136) In the proportion $a:b = c:d$, b and c are called the means.

measure of central tendency (p. 32) A statistical measurement, such as the mean, the median, or the mode, used to describe a set of data.

median (p. 33) The middle value of a set of data that are arranged in numerical order. When there are two middle values, the median is the average of these two values.

midpoint formula (p. 643) The point that is equidistant from the endpoints of a line segment. The midpoint M of the line segment whose endpoints are $P_1(x_1, y_1)$ and $P_2(x_2, y_2)$ is $M\left(\frac{x_1 + x_2}{2}, \frac{y_1 + y_2}{2}\right)$.

minimize (an objective function) (p. 390) To determine the least possible value of an objective function. Minimums occur at or near a vertex of the feasible region of a linear programming graph.

minimum (point) (p. 468) See **vertex**.

mixed expression (p. 707) The sum or difference of a polynomial and a rational expression.

mode (p. 33) The number or element in a set of data occurring most often.

model (p. 55) A physical or algebraic representation.

monomial (p. 521) A term that is a number, a variable, or the product of a number and one or more variables.

multiplication property of equality (p. 129) For all real numbers a, b, and c, if $a = b$, then $ca = cb$.

multiplication property of inequality (p. 231) For all real numbers a, b, and c, if $a > b$, and $c > 0$, then $ac > bc$, and if $a > b$ and $c < 0$, then $ac < bc$.

multiplicative identity property (p. 90) For any real number a, $a \cdot 1 = 1 \cdot a = a$.

multiplicative inverse (p. 90) The reciprocal of a number. For example, a and $\frac{1}{a}$ are multiplicative inverses.

multiplicative inverse property (p. 90) For any nonzero real number b, there exists a real number $\frac{1}{b}$ such that $b \cdot \frac{1}{b} = 1$.

multiplicative property of zero (p. 89) For any real number a, $a \cdot 0 = 0 \cdot a = 0$.

N

negative integers (p. 56) Integers less than zero.

negative reciprocal (p. 279) One of two fractions or ratios whose product is –1.

numerical expression (p. 59) Two or more numbers connected by operations such as addition, subtraction, multiplication, or division.

740

O

objective function (p. 390) An equation used to represent a quantity such as profit or cost.

obtuse triangle (p. 619) A triangle with one obtuse angle.

open half-plane (p. 375) A half-plane that does not include the boundary line.

open sentence (p. 115) An equation that contains one or more variables. An open sentence may be true or false, depending on what values of the variable are substituted.

opposite (p. 67, 74) The opposite of any real number x is $-x$. Two opposites have a sum of zero. For example, –27 and 27 are opposites. Also called the *additive inverse* of the number.

order (p. 67) To arrange numbers according to value, either from least to greatest or greatest to least.

ordered pair (p. 169) A pair of numbers named in a specific order; a pair of real numbers (x, y) corresponding to a point in the coordinate plane.

order of operations (p. 60, 95) Rules for evaluating algebraic expressions: Perform operations within grouping symbols first. Then perform all calculations involving exponents. Multiply or divide in order from left to right. Finally, add or subtract in order from left to right.

origin (p. 66, 169) The point that corresponds to 0 on a number line. The point in the coordinate plane where the horizontal and vertical axes intersect.

outcome (p. 398) The result of each trial of an experiment.

outlier (p. 248) A value far to the left of the first quartile or far to the right of the third quartile in a boxplot for a data set.

P

parabola (p. 463) The "U-shaped" graph of a quadratic equation of the form $y = ax^2 + bx + c$.

parallel lines (p. 279) Lines in the same coordinate plane that do not intersect. Two nonvertical lines are parallel if and only if they have the same slope.

percent discount (p. 136) The percent amount by which a price is reduced, as for a sale.

perfect square (p. 65) The product of a number or polynomial times itself. For example, 2^2, y^2, $(x + 2)^2$ are perfect squares. The square root of any number that is not a perfect square is an irrational number.

period (of a function) (p. 660) The horizontal distance from any point on the graph of a function to that point where the graph begins to repeat.

perpendicular lines (p. 279) Two lines that intersect to form right angles. The slopes of two perpendicular lines are negative reciprocals of each other.

pictograph (p. 18) A display of statistical information in which data is represented by symbols or pictures.

point of reflection (p. 469) The reflection of any point on a figure, such as a parabola, across its axis of symmetry. For example, for the graph of $y = x^2$, the point of reflection of (–3, 9) is (3, 9).

point-slope form (of a linear equation) (p. 287, 293) A linear equation in the form $(y - y_1) = m(x - x_1)$, where m is the slope and (x_1, y_1) are the coordinates of a given point on the line.

polynomial (p. 541) A monomial or the sum or difference of monomials.

population (p. 21) The total number of people making up a whole, considered for statistical purposes.

positive integers (p. 56) Integers that are greater than zero.

power (p. 59) A number that can be written as the product of equal factors. Powers can be expressed using exponents. The power $2 \cdot 2 \cdot 2$ can be written 2^3, read "two to the third power" or "two cubed."

principal square root (p. 439) The positive square root of a number k, written $\sqrt{k}$.

principle of squaring (p. 636) If the equation $a = b$ is true, then the equation $a^2 = b^2$ is also true.

probability (of an event) (p. 38, 398) The chance or likelihood that an event will occur. The value of a probability ranges from 0 to 1. An impossible event has a probability of 0. A certain event has a probability of 1. (See also **theoretical probability**.)

product (p. 88) The result when two or more factors are multiplied.

741

product of a sum and a difference (p. 554) The product of two binomials that are the sum and difference of the same two terms: $(a + b)(a - b) = a^2 - b^2$.

product property of square roots (p. 439, 625) For all real numbers a and b, where $a \geq 0$ and $b \geq 0$, $\sqrt{ab} = \sqrt{a} \cdot \sqrt{b}$.

proof (p. 446) A logical sequence of statements that show another statement to be true.

properties of equality (p. 446) For all real numbers a, b, and c,

Reflexive Property: $a = a$

Symmetric Property: If $a = b$, then $b = a$.

Transitive Property: If $a = b$ and $b = c$, then $a = c$.

Substitution Property: If $a = b$, then a may replace b or b may replace a in any statement.

property of exponents: power of a power (p. 523) For any real number a and for all positive integers m and n, $(a^m)^n = a^{mn}$.

property of exponents: power of a product (p. 523) For any real numbers a and b and for positive integer m, $(ab)^m = a^m b^m$.

property of exponents: power of a quotient rule (p. 529) For all real numbers a and b, $b \neq 0$, and for any positive integer m, $\left(\frac{a}{b}\right)^m = \frac{a^m}{b^m}$.

property of exponents: product of powers (p. 522) For any real number a and for all positive integers m and n, $a^m \cdot a^n = a^{m+n}$.

property of exponents: quotient rule (p. 528) For any real number a, $a \neq 0$, and for positive integers m and n, $\frac{a^m}{a^n} = a^{m-n}$.

property of negative exponents (p. 529) For any real number a, $a \neq 0$, and for any positive integer n, $a^{-n} = \frac{1}{a^n}$.

property of –1 for multiplication (p. 90) For any real number a, where $a \neq 0$, $a \cdot -1 = -1 \cdot a = -a$.

proportion (p. 136) An equation that states that two ratios are equal.

Pythagorean relationships (p. 620) For any triangle the following relationships between the lengths of the sides are true: If $a^2 + b^2 > c^2$, the triangle is acute. If $a^2 + b^2 = c^2$, the triangle is right. If $a^2 + b^2 < c^2$, the triangle is obtuse.

Pythagorean theorem (p. 616) If a right triangle has lengths a and b and a hypotenuse of length c, then $a^2 + b^2 = c^2$.

Pythagorean triple (p. 617) A set of three numbers, such as {3, 4, 5} or {5, 12, 13}, that satisfy the Pythagorean theorem.

Q

quadrants (p. 177) The four regions into which the x- and y-axes divide a coordinate plane.

quadratic direct variation (p. 683) A function in which one quantity varies directly as the square of another. For example, the area of a circle varies directly as the square of its radius: $A = \pi r^2$.

quadratic equation (p. 465) An equation in the form $y = ax^2 + bx + c$, where a, b, and c are real numbers, and $a \neq 0$.

quadratic formula (p. 490) For a quadratic equation of the form $ax^2 + bx + c = 0$ where a, b, and c are real numbers and $a \neq 0$,

$$x = \frac{-b \pm \sqrt{b^2 - 4ac}}{2a}.$$

quadratic function (p. 468) A function of the form $f(x) = ax^2 + bx + c$, where a, b, and c are real numbers, and $a \neq 0$.

qualitative graph (p. 202) A graph that shows general features of a function but does not use precise numerical scales.

quartiles (p. 247) Three numbers that divide a set of data into four equal parts, or quarters.

quotient property of square roots (p. 439, 625) For all real numbers a and b, where $a \geq 0$ and $b > 0$, $\sqrt{\frac{a}{b}} = \frac{\sqrt{a}}{\sqrt{b}}$.

R

radical (p. 439) A radical symbol $\sqrt{}$ and its radicand.

radical equation (p. 636) An equation that contains a radical with a variable in the radicand.

radical expression (p. 625) An expression containing a radical.

radicand (p. 439, 625) A number or expression under a radical symbol.

random sampling (p. 22) A type of statistical sampling in which each member of a population has an equal chance of being selected.

range (of values) (p. 20, 33) The difference between the greatest and the least values in a set of data.

range (of a function) (p. 172) The output values of a function.

rational equation (p. 712) An equation that contains one or more rational expressions.

rational expression (p. 686) An expression that can be written in the form $\frac{P}{Q}$, where P and Q are polynomials, $Q \neq 0$.

rational number (p. 65, 437) A number that can be expressed in the form $\frac{a}{b}$, where a and b are any integers and $b \neq 0$. A rational number may be expressed as a fraction, a terminating decimal, or a repeating decimal.

rationalizing the denominator (p. 627) The process of eliminating a radical from the denominator.

real number line (p. 66) A number line on which every point can be matched with a real number.

real numbers (p. 66, 439) All rational numbers and irrational numbers.

reciprocal (p. 90) The multiplicative inverse of a number. The product of a number and its reciprocal is 1.

reflection (p. 416) A transformation in which a figure is flipped over a line of reflection.

relation (p.171) A set of ordered pairs of data.

replacement set (p. 61) The set of numbers that can be substituted for a variable.

right triangle (p. 619) A triangle with one right angle.

root(s) (of an equation) (p. 477) The solution of an equation.

S

sample (p. 21) The representative portion of a population that is used for a statistical study, as in a survey.

sample space (p. 398) All the possible outcomes of an event.

scale factor (p. 650) The number by which the original dimensions of a figure are multiplied in order to enlarge or reduce the original figure proportionally. The scale factor is found by writing the ratio of a pair of corresponding sides.

scalene triangle (p. 619) A triangle having no sides equal in length.

scatter plot (p. 206) A graph in which the data are shown as points in a coordinate plane.

scientific notation (p. 532) A number written in the form $m \times 10^n$ where $1 \leq m < 10$ and n is any integer.

set (of numbers) (p. 437) Any group of numbers having one or more common attributes.

similar (figures) (p. 648) Two figures are similar if they have the same shape but not necessarily the same size.

simplest form (of a polynomial) (p. 544) A polynomial is in simplest form when it contains no like terms.

simplest form (of a radical) (p. 625) A radical expression in which the radicand has no perfect-square factors other than 1, has no fractions, and no denominator contains a radical.

simplest form (of a rational expression) (p. 687) A rational expression is in simplest form when the numerator and denominator of the expression have no common factors other than 1.

simplify (an expression) (p. 95) To change an expression to an equivalent expression with fewer terms.

sine (p. 653) For either acute angle in a right triangle, the ratio of the length of the side opposite the angle to the length of the hypotenuse.

sine curve (p. 660) The graph of the sine function.

slope (of a line) (p. 268, 269) The ratio of the number of units the line rises or falls vertically (the *rise*) to the number of units the line moves horizontally from left to right (the *run*). For a line connecting two points $P(x_1, y_1)$ and $Q(x_2, y_2)$, the

$$\text{slope of the line} = \frac{\text{rise}}{\text{run}} = \frac{y_2 - y_1}{x_2 - x_1}$$

The slope of a horizontal line is 0. The slope of a vertical line is undefined.

slope-intercept form (of a linear equation) (p. 277, 293) A linear equation in the form $y = mx + b$, where m is the slope and b is the y-intercept of the graph.

solution (p. 115) A value of a variable that makes an equation true.

solution (of a system of equations) (p. 329) An ordered pair that is a solution of all the equations in a system.

square matrix (p. 27) A matrix that has the same number of rows and columns.

743

square of a binomial (p. 554) A trinomial whose first and last terms are the squares of the terms of the binomial and whose middle term is twice the product of the two terms: $(a + b)^2 = a^2 + 2ab + b^2$ and $(a - b)^2 = a^2 - 2ab + b^2$.

square root method (p. 483) A method for solving an equation of the form $ax^2 + b = c$ that involves isolating the squared term on one side of the equation and then taking the square root of both sides.

square root property (p. 483) If $x^2 = k$, then $x = \sqrt{k}$ or $x = -\sqrt{k}$ for any real number k, $k > 0$. If $k = 0$, then $x^2 = 0$ has one solution, 0.

standard form (of a linear equation) (p. 294) An equation of the form $Ax + By = C$, where A, B, and C are integers and A and B are not both 0.

standard form (of a quadratic equation) (p. 477) An equation of the form $d = ax^2 + bx + c$ when $d = 0$.

standard notation (p. 532) The decimal form of any number, for example 12.45, 43, or 0.0087.

subset (p. 431) Set A is a subset of set B if every element of set A is also an element of set B.

substitution method (p. 335) An algebraic method for solving a system of linear equations.

subtraction of real numbers (p. 79) For all real numbers a and b, $a - b = a + (-b)$.

subtraction property of equality (p. 125) For all real numbers a, b, and c, if $a = b$, then $a - c = b - c$.

subtraction property of inequality (p. 230) For all real numbers a, b, and c, if $a > b$, then $a - c > b - c$, and if $a < b$, then $a - c < b - c$.

sum of the angles of a triangle (p. 620) The sum of the measures of the angles of a triangle is 180°.

supplementary angles (p. 621) Two angles whose sum is 180°. Each angle is the *supplement* of the other.

survey (p. 21) A study of the opinions or behavior of a population. Also, the collection of data through questioning or polling a population.

symmetry (p. 413) A figure is said to have symmetry if it has a line of symmetry.

systematic sampling (p. 22) A type of statistical sampling in which members of a population are chosen by a rule or pattern applied to the entire population.

system of linear equations (p. 328) Two or more linear equations that are considered together. Also called a *linear system.*

system of linear inequalities (p. 379) Two or more inequalities that are considered together.

• • T • •

tangent (p. 653) For either acute angle in a right triangle, the ratio of the length of the side opposite the angle to the length of the side adjacent to the angle (not the hypotenuse).

terms (p. 61) The parts of a variable expression that are separated by addition or subtraction signs. For example, the expression $x + y$ has two two terms, x and y.

theoretical probability (p. 398) The probability of an event, $P(E)$, assigned by determining the number of favorable outcomes and the number of possible outcomes in a sample space.

$$P(E) = \frac{\text{number of favorable outcomes}}{\text{number of possible outcomes}}$$

transformation (of a graph) (p. 418) A change in the position or shape of a graph as a result of an operation such as translation or reflection.

translation (of a graph) (p. 417) A slide or shift that moves the graph to a new position horizontally or vertically in the coordinate plane.

trend (p. 207) The general pattern formed by the points in a scatter plot.

trichotomy property (p. 221, 445) For all real numbers a and b, exactly one of the following is true: $a = b$, $a < b$, or $a > b$.

trigonometric ratios (p. 653) Ratios of the lengths of the sides of a right triangle. The three common ratios are the *sine, cosine,* and *tangent.*

trigonometry (p. 653) A word from a Greek term meaning "measure of triangles."

trinomial (p. 541) A polynomial of three terms.

trough (p. 660) The minimum value of the graph of a periodic function.

V

value (of a variable) (p. 115) The number assigned to or substituted for a variable.

variable (p. 13, 60) A letter or other symbol used to represent a number.

variable expression (p. 13, 60) An expression having at least one number, operation, and variable.

vertex (of a parabola) (p. 468) The point where a parabola has its maximum (highest) or minimum (lowest) point.

vertical axis (p. 169) The y-axis of the coordinate plane.

vertical line test (p. 178) A test used on the graph of a relation to determine whether the relation is also a function. If a vertical line drawn through the graph of a relation intersects the graph in more than one point, the graph does not represent a function.

vertical shift (of a graph) (p. 417) The up or down translation of a graph in relation to another graph.

W

whiskers (p. 248) Horizontal lines in a boxplot showing the range of the data.

X

x-axis (p. 178) The horizontal number line that divides the coordinate plane.

x-coordinate (p. 178) The first number in an ordered pair representing a point in the coordinate plane. The x-coordinate determines the horizontal location of the point.

x-intercept (p. 276, 477) The x-coordinate of the point where a graph crosses the x-axis.

Y

y-axis (p. 183) The vertical number line that divides the coordinate plane.

y-coordinate (p. 183) The second number in an ordered pair representing a point in the coordinate plane, also called the $f(x)$-coordinate for functions. The y-coordinate determines the vertical location of the point.

y-intercept (p. 269, 276) The y-coordinate of the point where a graph crosses the y-axis.

Z

zero pair (p. 74, 121) A pair of integers or algebraic terms whose sum is zero. Zero pairs are opposites.

zero product property (p. 595) For any real numbers a and b, if $ab = 0$, then $a = 0$ or $b = 0$, or both $a = 0$ and $b = 0$.

zero property of exponents (p. 528) For any real number a, $a \neq 0$, $a^0 = 1$.

745

GLOSSARY/GLOSARIO

A

absolute value/valor absoluto (p. 68) La distancia de un número desde 0 en la recta numérica. El valor absoluto de x se escribe como $|x|$. Para cualquier número real x, $|x| = x$ si $x > 0$ o $x = 0$ y $|x| = -x$ si $x < 0$.

absolute value function/función valor absoluto (p. 416) La función $f(x) = |x|$. La ecuación del valor correspondiente $y = |x|$ donde x es cualquier número real e y es cualquier número mayor de o igual a cero.

absolute value inequality/desigualdad de valor absoluto (p. 432) Una desigualdad de la forma $|ax \pm b| < c$ o $|ax \pm b| > c$.

acute triangle/triángulo acutángulo (p. 619) Un triángulo con tres ángulos agudos.

addition property of equality/propiedad aditiva de igualdad (p. 124) Para todos los números reales a, b y c, si $a = b$, entonces $a + c = b + c$.

addition property of inequality/propiedad aditiva de desigualdad (p. 230) Para todos los números reales a, b y c, si $a > b$, luego $a + c > b + c$ y si $a < b$, entonces $a + c < b + c$.

additive identity property/propiedad aditiva de identidad (p. 80) Para cualquier número real a, $a + 0 = a$.

additive inverse property/propiedad aditiva inversa (p. 80) Para cualquier número real a, $a + (-a) = 0$ (Véase también opuesto).

Algeblocks/bloques algebraicos (p. 56) Modelos que, físicamente, representan conceptos algebraicos.

algebraic expression/expresión algebraica (pp. 13, 60) Una expresión que tiene al menos, un número, una operación y una variable.

amplitude (of a function)/amplitud (de una función) (p. 660) La distancia desde la línea media de una gráfica de una función hasta el valor máximo o mínimo de la función.

associative property of addition/propiedad asociativa de la adición (p. 80) Para cualesquiera números reales a, b y c, $(a + b) + c = a + (b + c)$.

associative property of multiplication/propiedad asociativa de la multiplicación (p 89) Para cualesquiera números reales a, b y c, $(a \cdot b) \cdot c = a \cdot (b \cdot c)$.

average/promedio (p 32) La media de un conjunto de datos.

average rate of change/promedio del valor de cambio (p. 271) La fórmula de pendiente se puede usar para encontrar el promedio del valor de cambio.

axis of symmetry/eje de simetría (p. 469) Una línea como la vertical que pasa a través del vértice de una parábola la cual divide una figura de manera que cuando se dobla, las dos mitades coinciden.

B

bar graph/gráfica de barra (p. 19) Una muestra visual de estadística en la cual las barras horizontales y verticales o los rectángulos representan datos que se pueden comparar.

base (of a power)/base (de una potencia) (p. 59) El factor que se repite en una potencia. Por ejemplo, en 4^3, la base es 4.

binomial/binomio (p. 541) Un polinomio de dos términos.

boundary (of two half-plane)/frontera (de dos semiplanos) (p. 374) La línea o gráfica de una ecuación lineal que divide el plano coordenado en dos semiplanos.

boxplot/diagrama de bloque (p. 248) Una gráfica que usa los tres cuartiles y los valores menores y mayores de un conjunto de datos para representar visualmente los datos.

C

cells/células o celdas (p. 14) Los espacios formados por las filas horizontales y las columnas verticales en la hoja de cálculo de computadora en la cual se pueden poner fórmulas o datos.

circle graph/gráfica circular (p. 19) Una muestra visual de estadística en la cual los datos se representan por sectores.

closed half-plane/semiplano cerrado (p. 375) Un medio plano que incluye la frontera.

cluster sampling/muestra de grupo (p. 22) Un tipo de muestra de estadística en la cual se escoge, al azar, una porción determinada de una población para ser entrevistada.

coefficient/coeficiente (p. 61) La porción numérica no variable de un monomio.

coefficient of correlation/coeficiente de correlación (p. 299) La medida estadística r de lo cerca que pueden unos datos estar a una línea. El alcance del coeficiente de correlación es desde -1 a 1.

commutative property of addition/propiedad conmutativa de la adición (p. 80) Para cualesquiera números reales a, b y c, $a + b = b + a$.

commutative property of multiplication/propiedad conmutativa de la multiplicación (p. 89) Para cualesquiera númeroa reales a y b, $a \cdot b = b \cdot a$.

complementary angles/ángulos complementarios (p. 620) Dos ángulos, la suma de cuyas medidas es 90°. Cada ángulo es el *complemento* del otro.

complementary events/eventos complementarios (p. 400) Los dos resultados posibles en un experimento fortuito en el cual el evento ocurre o no ocurre. Las posibilidades de dos complementos suman 1.

complex rational expression/expresión racional compleja (p. 708) Una expresión racional que contiene una o más expresiones racionales en su numerador o denominador.

compound inequality/desigualdad compuesta (pp. 241, 430) Dos desigualdades unidas por *y* u *o*.

computer spreadsheets/hojas de cálculo de computadora (P. 14) Los programas para computadoras que usan fórmulas para calcular y analizar datos y lo muestran en columnas y filas.

conjugates/conjugadas (p. 629) Dos expresiones que son la suma y diferencia de los mismos dos términos, por ejemplo, $a + \sqrt{b}$ and $a - \sqrt{b}$.

conjunction/conjunción (pp. 241, 430) Dos declaraciones unidas por la palabra *y*. Una conjunción es verdadera si y solamente si ambas declaraciones son verdaderas.

consecutive integers/enteros consecutivos (p.107) Cualesquiera enteros en orden de conteo o sucesivo.

consistent (system)/consistente (sistema) (p. 348) Un sistema de ecuaciones con por lo menos una solución.

constant/constante (p. 61) En una expresión algebraica, un número no multiplicado o dividido por una variable.

constant of variation/constante de variación (pp. 307–308, 679, 681) La constante k en la ecuación de una variación directa $y = kx$, una variación inversa $xy = k$ o una variación conjunta $y = kwx$.

constraints/limitaciones (p. 388) Condiciones que limitan las actividades empresariales. En programación lineal las limitaciones se representan por desigualdades.

convenience sampling/muestra de conveniencia (p. 22) Un tipo de muestra estadística en la cual una porción disponible de la población es seleccionada y todos los miembros de esa porción son entrevistados.

conversion factor/factor de conversión (p. 718) Una razón de dos cantidades iguales que se usa para convertir una unidad dimensional a otra.

coordinate/coordenada (p.177) El número real que corresponde a un punto en una recta numérica; cada uno de los dos números apareados correspondientes a un punto dado en el plano coordenado.

coordinate plane/plano coordenado (p. 177) Una cuadrícula de dos dimensiones que consiste de dos rectas numéricas perpendiculares llamadas el eje de x y el eje de y.

corresponding elements (of a matrix)/elementos correspondientes (de una matriz) (p. 28) Elementos en la misma posición en cada una de dos matrices que tienen las mismas dimensiones.

cosine/coseno (p. 653) Para cualquier ángulo agudo en un triángulo rectángulo, la razón del largo del lado adyacente (cateto) al ángulo de la hipotenusa.

crest (of a graph)/cresta (de una gráfica) (p. 660) El valor máximo de la gráfica de una función periódica.

• • D • •

data points/puntos de datos (p. 62) Puntos en un plano coordenado que corresponden a medidas estadísticas.

degree (of an expression)/grado (de una expresión) (p. 62) El exponente mayor de las variables de la expresión en forma más simple.

degree of a monomial/grado de un monomio (p. 521) La suma de los grados de todos los factores variables en un monomio.

degree of a polynomial/grado de un polinomio (p. 542) El grado mayor de los términos del polinomio.

degree of a variable (in a monomial)/grado de una variable (en un monomio) (p. 521) El número de veces que una variable aparece como factor en un monomio.

dense/densidad (p. 446) Una característica de los números reales ya que existe un número real entre cualesquiera dos números reales existe otro número real.

dependent (variable)/dependiente (variable) (p. 299) El valor de salida de una relación.

dependent system/sistema dependiente (p. 349) Un sistema de ecuaciones con la misma gráfica.

determinant/determinante (p. 353) Un valor numérico asociado con una matriz cuadrada. La determinante de una matriz se representa usando barras verticales en lugar de corchetes de matriz.

difference of two squares/diferencia de dos cuadrados. Véase **producto de una suma y una diferencia.**

dimensional analysis/análisis dimensional (p. 718) El método de usar unidades o dimensiones en la solución de problemas.

dimensions (of a matrix)/dimensiones (de una matriz) (p. 27) El número de filas horizontales y el número de columnas verticales en una matriz.

dimensions (of a quantity)/dimensiones (de una cantidad) (p. 718) Las unidades en las cuales se mide una cantidad.

direct variation/variación directa (pp. 307, 679) Cuando y varía directamente como x y k es la constante de variación, se puede escribir una ecuación de la forma $y = kx$, $k \neq 0$.

discriminant/discriminante (pp. 491, 597) La expresión $b^2 - 4ac$, debajo del signo radical en la fórmula cuadrática. El discriminante se puede usar para determinar el número de soluciones reales de cualquier ecuación cuadrática.

disjunction/disyunción (pp. 242, 425) Dos declaraciones unidas por la palabra *o*. Una disyunción es verdadera si por lo menos una de sus declaraciones es verdadera.

distance formula/fórmula de distancia (p. 642) La fórmula $d = \sqrt{(x_2 - x_1)^2 + (y_2 - y_1)^2}$ que se usa para determinar la distancia d entre cualesquiera dos puntos (x_1, y_1) e (x_2, y_2) en el plano coordenado.

distributive property of multiplication over addition/propiedad distributiva de la multiplicación sobre la adición (p. 96) Para todos los números reales a, b y c, $a(b + c) = ab + ac$ y $(b + c)a = ba + ca$.

division/división (p. 90) Para cualquier número real a y b, $b \neq 0$, $a \div b = a \cdot 1/b$

division property of equality/propiedad de división de igualdad (p. 130) Para todos los números reales a, b y c, si $a = b$ y $c \neq 0$, entonces $a/c = b/c$

division property of inequality/propiedad de división de desigualdad (p. 231) Para todos los números reales a, b y c, si $a > b$ y $c > 0$, luego $a/c > b/c$ y si $a > b$ y $c < 0$, luego $a/c < b/c$

domain (of a function)/dominio (de una función) (p. 172) Los valores de entrada de una función.

• • E • •

element (of a matrix)/elemento (de una matriz) (p. 27) Cada número o entrada en una matriz.

element (of a set)/elemento (de un conjunto) (p. 437) Una cosa o un número que es parte de un conjunto. Por ejemplo, 4 es un elemento de {2, 4, 6, 8}.

elimination method/método de eliminación (p. 342) Un método para resolver un sistema de ecuaciones lineales usando la multiplicación y la adición para eliminar una de las variables.

equation/ecuación (p. 115) Una declaración que muestra que dos números o expresiones son iguales.

equilateral triangle/triángulo equilátero (p. 619) Un triángulo con tres lados iguales en longitud.

equivalent equations/ecuaciones equivalentes (p. 124) Ecuaciones que tienen la misma solución.

equivalent inequalities/desigualdades equivalentes (p. 230) Desigualdades que tienen la misma solución.

evaluate (an expression)/evaluar (una expresión) (p. 60) Encontrar el valor de una expresión algebraica sustituyendo un número dado para cada variable y simplificando.

evaluate a function/evaluar una función (p. 172) Encontrar el valor, $f(x)$ para un valor dado x.

event/evento o suceso (p. 398) Cualesquiera de los posibles resultados de un experimento.

experimental probability/probabilidad experimental (p. 38) La probabilidad de un evento determinada por observación o medida. La probabilidad experimental, $P(E)$ de un evento E se da por

$P(E) = \frac{\text{número de ocurrencias favorables a } E}{\text{número total ocurrencias}}$ posibles

exponent/exponente (p. 59) Un número sobrescrito que muestra las veces que una base se usa como factor. Por ejemplo, en 2^5, 5 es el exponente.

extraneous solution/solución extraña (p. 713) Una solución aparente que no satisface la ecuación original. Las soluciones extrañas generalmente resultan de elevar al cuadrado ambos lados de una ecuación.

extremes (of a proportion)/extremos (de una proporción) (p. 136) En la proporción $a:b = c:d$, a y d son los extremos.

• • F • •

factor/factor (p. 88) Cualesquiera de dos o más números multiplicados para hallar un producto. Por ejemplo, en $3(4) = 12$, 3 y 4 son factores de 12.

factored completely/factorización completa (p. 591) Un polinomio está totalmente factorizado cuando no se puede factorizar más.

factored form (of a polynomial)/forma factorizada (de un polinomio) (p. 575) Un polinomio expresado como un producto de otros polinomios.

feasible region/región viable (p. 388) La intersección de las gráficas de un sistema de limitaciones; la región del plano coordenado que incluye todas las soluciones posibles de la función objetiva.

finite (set)/finito (conjunto) (p. 437) Un conjunto cuyos elementos se pueden contar o enumerar en listas.

FOIL/PADU (p. 53) Un método para determinar el producto de dos binomios al encontrar el producto de los Primeros términos, los de Afuera, los de Dentro y los Últimos y luego simplificar el resultado.

formula/fórmula (p. 152) Una ecuación literal que expresa una relación entre dos o más variables.

frequency/frecuencia (p. 8) El número de veces que una cosa ocurre en un conjunto de datos.

frequency table/tabla de frecuencia (p. 8) Un método de anotar y organizar datos usando marcas de conteo para mostrar cuántas veces algo ocurre en un conjunto de datos.

function/función (p. 171) Una relación que tiene exactamente un valor de salida para cada valor de entrada en un conjunto de valores apareados. En una función, más de un valor de entrada puede tener el mismo valor de salida.

function notation/notación de función (p. 172) La notación que representa una regla que asocia el valor de entrada (variable independiente) con el valor de salida (variable dependiente). La notación de función más comúnmente usada es la notación "f de x" escrita "$f(x)$".

function rule/regla de función (p. 172) La descripción de una función.

fundamental counting principle/principio fundamental de conteo (p. 399) Si un evento puede ocurrir en m maneras y a continuación otro evento puede ocurrir en n maneras, luego el número total de resultados posibles es igual a $m \cdot n$.

• • G • •

geometric mean/media geométrica (p. 641) Un número b es la media geométrica entre dos números m y n si $b = \sqrt{m \cdot n}$

• • H • •

half-planes/semiplanos (p. 374) Las dos regiones en las cuales la gráfica de una ecuación lineal divide al plano coordenado.

horizontal axis/eje horizontal (p. 169) El eje de x del plano coordenado.

749

horizontal shift (of a graph)/cambio horizontal (de una gráfica) (p. 417) La traslación hacia la izquierda o la derecha de una gráfica en relación a otra gráfica.

I

identity element for multiplication/elemento de identidad para la multiplicación (p. 89) El número 1 porque el producto de cualquier número y 1 es el número mismo.

inconsistent (system)/inconsistente (sistema) (p. 349) Un sistema de ecuaciones sin solución.

independent (system)/independiente (sistema) (p. 348) Un sistema de ecuaciones que tiene exactamente una solución.

independent (variable)/independiente (variable) (p. 299) El valor de entrada de una relación.

inequality/desigualdad (pp. 67, 222) Una declaración de que dos números o expresiones no son iguales; una declaración que contiene un signo de desigualdad.

inequality symbol/signo de desigualdad (p. 67) Un signo que se usa para comparar u ordenar números reales. Los signos de desigualdad son $<, >, \leq, \geq$, y $\neq$.

infinite (set)/infinito (conjunto) (p. 437) Un conjunto cuyos elementos no se pueden contar ni enumerar en listas pero que continúan eternamente. El conjunto $\{0, 1, 2, 3, \ldots\}$ es un conjunto infinito.

integers/enteros (p. 56) Todos los números enteros no negativos y sus opuestos.

inverse operation/operación inversa (p. 90) Una operación que "deshace" lo que otra hace. Por ejemplo, la multiplicación y la división son operaciones inversas.

inverse variation/variación inversa (p. 679) Cuando y varía inversamente como x y k es la constante de variación, una ecuación se puede escribir en la forma $y = \frac{k}{x}, k \neq 0$.

irrational number/número irracional (pp. 65, 438) Un número que no puede expresarse como el cociente de dos enteros, un decimal finito o un decimal periódico. Por ejemplo π y $\sqrt{2}$ son números irracionales. (Véase también **raíz perfecta**).

isosceles triangle/triángulo isósceles (p. 619) Un triángulo con al menos dos lados iguales en longitud.

J

joint variation/variación conjunta (p. 681) Cuando y varía directamente como el producto de w y x y k es la constante de variación, una ecuación se puede escribir en la forma $y = kwx$, $k \neq 0$.

L

leading coefficient/coeficiente principal (p. 578) El coeficiente del primer término en un polinomio en forma estándar.

least common denominator (LCD)/mínimo común denominador (MCD) (p. 703) El menor múltiplo común positivo de los denominadores de dos o más fracciones o expresiones racionales.

like radicals/radicales semejantes (p. 631) Dos o más radicales con el mismo radicando.

like terms/términos semejantes (pp. 97, 542) Dos o más términos en una expresión algebraica que tienen la misma base variable y exponente.

line graph/gráfica de línea (p. 19) Una muestra visual de estadística en la cual los puntos que representan los datos se marcan y luego se conectan con segmentos de línea.

line of best fit/línea de mejor ajuste (p. 299) Una línea que se aproxima a una tendencia para datos en una gráfica de dispersión. También se le llama *línea de regresión*.

line of reflection/línea de reflexión (p. 416) La línea encima de la cual se refleja una figura.

line of symmetry/línea de simetría (pp. 413, 417, 469) Una línea que divide una figura de manera que cuando la figura se dobla encima de la línea, las dos partes concuerdan perfectamente.

line plot/diagrama de X (p. 19) Una muestra estadística en la cual los datos se representan por un X y éstas arregladas en columnas verticalmente.

linear equation in two variables/ecuación lineal en dos variables (p. 183) Una ecuación que se puede escribir en la forma $y = ax + b$ y que representa una función lineal.

linear function/función lineal (p. 183) Una función que puede representarse por una línea recta o por una ecuación lineal en dos variables de la forma $y = ax + b$ donde x e y son variables y a y b son constantes.

linear inequality in two variables/desiguladad lineal en dos variables (p. 373) Una desigualdad que resulta cuando el signo de igual en una ecuación lineal se reemplaza por $<$, $>$, $\leq$, $\geq$, o $\neq$.

linear programming/programación lineal (p. 388) Un método que usan los negocios y el gobierno para aumentar o disminuir cantidades como ganancia y costo.

linear system/sistema lineal (p. 328) Dos o más ecuaciones lineales consideradas juntas.

literal equation/ecuación literal (p. 152) Una ecuación que contiene por lo menos dos variables diferentes.

• • M • •

matrix *(plural: matrices)***/matriz** (p. 27) Números arreglados en forma rectangular en filas y columnas y encerrados en corchetes.

maximize (an objective function)/maximizar (una función objetiva) (p. 390) Determinar el mayor valor posible de una función objetiva. Los máximos ocurren en o cerca del vértice de la región viable de una gráfica de programación lineal.

maximum (point)/máximo (punto) (p. 468) Véase **vértice.**

mean/media (p. 32) La suma de los elementos en un conjunto de datos divididos entre el número de elementos. También se le llama el *promedio.*

means (of a proportion)/medias (de una proporción) (p. 136) En la proporción $a{:}b = c{:}d$, a b y c se les llama las medias.

measure of central tendency/medida de tendencia central (p. 32) Una medida estadística como la media, la mediana o la moda que se usa para describir un conjunto de datos.

median/mediana (p. 33) El valor medio de un conjunto de datos que están arreglados en orden numérico. Cuando hay dos valores medios, la mediana es el promedio de esos dos valores.

midpoint formula/fórmula de punto medio (p. 643) El punto que está equidistante de los puntos extremos de un segmento de línea. El punto medio M del segmento de línea cuyos puntos extremos son $P_1(x_1, y_1)$ y $P_2(x_2, y_2)$ es $M\left(\frac{x_1 + x_2}{2}, \frac{y_1 + y_2}{2}\right)$.

minimize (an objective function)/minimizar (una función objetiva) (p. 390) Para determinar el menor valor posible de una función objetiva. Los mínimos ocurren en o cerca de un vértice de la región viable de una gráfica de programación lineal.

minimum (point)/mínimo (punto) (p. 468) Véase **vértice.**

mixed expression/expresión mixta (p. 707) La suma o diferencia de un polinomio y una expresión racional.

mode/moda (p. 33) El número o elemento en un conjunto de datos que ocurre con mayor frecuencia.

model/modelo (p. 55) Una representación física o algebraica.

monomial/monomio (p. 521) Un término que es un número, una variable o el producto de un número y una o más variables.

multiplication property of equality/propiedad multiplicativa de la igualdad (p. 129) Para todos los números reales a, b y c, si $a = b$, entonces $ca = cb$.

multiplication property of inequality/propiedad multiplicativa de la desigualdad (p. 231) Para todos los números reales a, b y c, si $a > b$ y $c > 0$, entonces $ac > bc$ y si $a > b$ y $c < 0$, entonces $ac < bc$.

multiplicative identity property/propiedad multiplicativa de identidad (p. 90) Para cualquier número real a, $a \cdot 1 = 1 \cdot a = a$.

multiplicative inverse/inverso multiplicativo (p. 90) El recíproco de un número. Por ejemplo, a y $\frac{1}{a}$ son inversos multiplicativos.

multiplicative inverse property/propiedad multiplicativa inversa (p. 90) Para cualquier número real b que no sea cero, existe un número real $\frac{1}{b}$ de manera que $b \cdot \frac{1}{b} = 1$.

multiplicative property of zero/propiedad multiplicativa de cero (p. 89) Para cualquier número real a, $a \cdot 0 = 0 \cdot a = 0$.

N

negative integers/enteros negativos (p. 56) Enteros menores de cero.

negative reciprocal/recíproco negativo (p. 279) Una de dos fracciones o razones cuyo producto es -1.

numerical expression/expresión numérica (p. 59) Dos o más números conectados por operaciones como la adición, sustracción, multiplicación o división.

O

objective function/función objetiva (p. 390) Una ecuación que se usa para representar una cantidad como la ganancia o el costo.

obtuse triangle/triángulo obtusángulo (p. 619) Un triángulo con un ángulo obtuso.

open half-plane/medio plano abierto (p. 375) Un semiplano que no incluye la frontera.

open sentence/proposición abierta (p. 115) Una ecuación que contiene una o más variables. Una proposición abierta puede ser verdadera o falsa dependiendo de qué valores de la variable se sustituyen.

opposite/opuesto (pp. 67, 74) El opuesto de cualquier número real x es $-x$. Dos opuestos tienen una suma de cero. Por ejemplo, -27 y 27 son opuestos. También llamado el *inverso aditivo* del número.

order/orden (p. 67) Arreglar números de acuerdo a su valor, de menor a mayor o de mayor a menor.

order of operations/orden de las operaciones (pp. 60, 95) Reglas para evaluar expresiones algebraicas: Operaciones dentro de signos agrupados se hacen primero. Luego todos los cálculos relacionados con exponentes. Multiplicar o dividir en orden de izquierda a derecha. Finalmente, sumar o restar en orden de izquierda a derecha.

ordered pair/par ordenado (p. 169) Un par de números nombrados en orden específico; un par de números reales (x, y) que corresponde a un punto en el plano coordenado.

origen/origen (pp. 66, 169) El punto que corresponde a 0 en una recta numérica. El punto en el plano coordenado donde los ejes horizontal y vertical se intersecan.

outcome/salida (p. 398) El resultado de cada intento de un experimento.

outliers/datos extremos (p. 248) Un valor a la extrema izquierda del primer cuartil o a la extrema derecha del tercer cuartil en un diagrama de bloque para un conjunto de datos.

P

parabola/parábola (p. 463) La gráfica en la forma de "U" de una ecuación cuadrática en la forma $y = ax^2 + bx + c$.

parallel lines/líneas paralelas (p. 279) Líneas en el mismo plano coordenado que no se intersecan. Dos líneas no verticales son paralelas si y solamente si tienen la misma pendiente.

percent discount/por ciento de descuento (p. 136) La cantidad de por ciento por el cual se reduce un precio como para una venta.

perfect square/cuadrado perfecto (p. 65) El producto de un número o polinomio multiplicado por sí mismo. Por ejemplo, 2^2, y^2, $(x + 2)^2$ son cuadrados perfectos. La raíz cuadrada de cualquier número que no es un cuadrado perfecto es un número irracional.

period (of a function)/período (de una función) (p. 660) La distancia horizontal desde cualquier punto en la gráfica de una función a ese punto donde la gráfica comienza a repetirse.

perpendicular lines/líneas perpendiculares (p. 279) Dos líneas que se intersecan para formar ángulos rectos. Las pendientes de dos líneas perpendiculares son recíprocos negativos de cada una.

pictograph/pictografía (p. 18) Una muestra visual de estadística en la cual los datos se representan por símbolos o ilustraciones.

point of reflection/punto de reflexión (p. 469) La reflexión de cualquier punto en una figura como una parábola a través del eje de simetría. Por ejemplo, para la gráfica de $y = x^2$, el punto de reflexión de $(-3, 9)$ es $(3, 9)$.

point-slope form (of an linear equation)/forma de punto y pendiente (de una ecuación lineal) (pp. 287, 293) Una ecuación lineal en la forma $(y - y_1) = m(x - x_1)$ donde m es la pendiente y (x_1, y_1) son las coordenadas de un punto dado en la línea.

polynomial/polinomio (p. 541) Un monomio o la suma o diferencia de monomios.

population/población (p. 21) El número total de habitantes de un lugar considerado para estadísticas.

positive integers/enteros positivos (p. 56) Enteros que son mayores de cero.

power/potencia (p. 59) Un número que se puede escribir como el producto de factores iguales. Las potencias se pueden expresar usando exponentes. La potencia $2 \cdot 2 \cdot 2$ se puede escribir 2^3 y se lee dos elevado a la tercera potencia o dos al cubo.

principal square root/raíz cuadrada principal (p. 439) La raíz cuadrada positiva de un número k se escribe $\sqrt{k}$

principle of squaring/principio de cuadratura o de cuadrar (p. 636) Si la ecuación $a = b$ es verdadera, entonces la ecuación $a^2 = b^2$ es también verdadera.

probability (of an event)/probabilidad (de un evento) (pp. 38, 398) La posibilidad de que un evento ocurra. El valor de una probabilidad va desde 0 a 1. Un evento imposible tiene una probabilidad de 0. Un evento que ocurre tiene una probabilidad de 1. (Véase también **probabilidad teórica**).

product/producto (p. 88) El resultado cuando dos o más factores se multiplican.

product of a sum and a difference/producto de una suma y una diferencia (p. 554) El producto de dos binomios que son la suma y la diferencia de los dos mismos términos: $(a + b)(a - b) = a^2 - b^2$.

product property of square roots/propiedad del producto de raíces cuadradas (pp. 439, 625) Para todos los números reales a y b donde $a \geq 0$, y $b \geq 0$, $\sqrt{ab} = \sqrt{a} \cdot \sqrt{b}$.

proof/prueba (p. 446) Una secuencia lógica de declaraciones que muestran que otra declaración es verdadera.

properties of equality/propiedades de igualdad (p. 446) Para todos los números reales a, b y c,
Propiedad reflexiva: $a = a$
Propiedad simétrica: Si $a = b$, entonces $b = a$.
Propiedad transitiva: Si $a = b$ y $b = c$, entonces $a = c$.
Propiedad de sustitución: Si $a = b$, entonces a puede reemplazar a b o b puede reemplazar a a en cualquier declaración.

property of −1 for multiplication/propiedad multiplicativa para −1 (p. 90) Para cualquier número real a donde $a \neq 0$, $a \cdot -1 = 1- \cdot a = -a$.

property of exponents: power of a power/propiedad de los exponentes: potencia de una potencia (p. 523) Para cualquier número real a y para todos los enteros positivos m y n, $(am)^n = a^{mn}$.

property of exponents: power of a product/propiedad de los exponentes: potencia de un producto (p. 523) Para todos los números reales a y b y para el entero positivo m, $(ab)^m = a^m b^m$.

property of exponents: power of a quotient rule/propiedad de los exponentes: potencia de la regla del cociente (p. 529) Para todos los números reales a y b, $b \neq 0$ y para cualquier entero positivo m, $\left(\frac{a}{b}\right)^m = \frac{a^m}{b^m}$.

property of exponents: product of powers/propiedad de los exponentes: producto de potencias (p. 522) Para cualquier número a y para todos los enteros positivos m y n, $a^m \cdot a^n = a^{m+n}$.

property of exponents: quotient rule/propiedad de los exponentes: regla del cociente (p. 528) Para cualquier número real a, $a \neq 0$ y para todos los enteros positivos m y n, $\frac{a^m}{a^n} = a^{m-n}$.

property of negative exponents/propiedad de exponentes negativos (p. 529) Para cualquier número real a, $a \neq 0$ y para cualquier entero positivo n, $a^{-n} = \frac{1}{a^n}$.

proportion/proporción (p. 136) Una ecuación que declara que dos razones son iguales.

Pythagorean triple/triple pitagórico (p. 617) Un conjunto de tres números como {3, 4, 5} ó {5, 12, 13} que satisface el teorema de Pitágoras.

Pythagorean relations/relaciones pitagóricas (p. 620) Para cualquier triángulo, las siguientes relaciones entre las longitudes de los lados son verdaderas: si $a^2 + b^2 > c^2$, el triángulo es acutángulo. Si $a^2 + b^2 = c^2$, el triángulo es rectángulo. Si $a^2 + b^2 < c^2$, el triángulo es obtusángulo.

Pythagorean theorem/teorema de Pitágoras (p. 616) Si un triángulo rectángulo tiene longitudes a y b y una hipotenusa de longitud c, entonces $a^2 + b^2 = c^2$.

Q

quadrants/cuadrantes (p. 177) Las cuatro regiones en las cuales los ejes de x e y dividen un plano coordenado.

quadratic direct variation/variación cuadrática directa (p. 683) Una función en la cual una cantidad varía directamente como el cuadrado de otra. Por ejemplo, el área de un círculo varía directamente como el cuadrado de su radio: $A = \pi r^2$.

quadratic equation/ecuación cuadrática (p. 465) Una ecuación en la forma $y = ax^2 + bx + c$ donde a, b y c son números reales y $a \neq 0$.

quadratic formula/fórmula cuadrática (p. 490) Para una ecuación cuadrática de la forma $ax^2 + bx + c = 0$ donde a, b y c son números reales y $a \neq 0$, $x = \dfrac{-b \pm \sqrt{b^2 - 4ac}}{2a}$

quadratic function/función cuadrática (p. 468) Una función de la forma $f(x) = ax^2 + bx + c$ donde a, b y c son números reales y $a \neq 0$.

qualitative graph/gráfica cualitativa (p. 202) Una gráfica que muestra las características generales de una función pero no usa escalas numéricas precisas.

quartiles/cuartiles (p. 247) Tres números que dividen un conjunto de datos en cuatro partes iguales o en cuartos.

quotient property of square roots/propiedad del cociente de raíces cuadradas (pp. 439, 625) Para todos los números reales a y b donde $a \geq 0$ y $b > 0$, $\sqrt{\frac{a}{b}} = \frac{\sqrt{a}}{\sqrt{b}}$

R

radical/radical (p. 439) Un signo radical $\sqrt{\ }$ y su radicando.

radical equation/ecuación radical (p. 636) Una ecuación que contiene un radical con una variable en el radicando.

radical expression/expresión radical (p. 625) Una expresión que contiene un radical.

radicand/radicando (pp. 439, 625) Un número o expresión debajo del signo radical.

random sampling/muestra aleatoria (p. 22) Un tipo de muestra de estadística en la cual cada miembro de una población tiene una oportunidad igual de ser seleccionado.

range (of a function)/alcance (de una función) (p. 172) Los valores de salida de una función.

range (of values)/alcance (de valores) (pp. 20, 33) La diferencia entre los valores mayores y menores de un conjunto de datos.

rational equation/ecuación racional (p. 712) Una ecuación que contiene una o más expresiones racionales.

rational expression/expresión racional (p. 686) Una expresión que se puede escribir en la forma P/Q , donde P y Q son polinomios $Q \neq 0$.

rational number/número racional (pp. 65, 437) Un número que se puede expresar en la forma a/b donde a y b son cualesquier enteros y $b \neq 0$. Un número racional puede expresarse como una fracción, un decimal finito o un decimal periódico.

rationalizing the denominator/racionalizar el denominador (p. 627) El proceso de eliminar un radical del denominador.

real number line/recta numérica real (p. 66) Una recta numérica en la cual cada punto se puede aparear con un número real.

real numbers/números reales (pp. 66, 439) Todos los números racionales e irracionales.

reciprocal/recíproco (p. 90) El inverso multiplicativo de un número. El producto de un número y su recíproco es 1.

reflection/reflexión (p. 416) Una transformación en la cual una figura se invierte sobre una línea de reflexión.

relation/relación (p. 171) Un conjunto de pares ordenados (de datos).

replacement set/conjunto de sustitución (p. 61) El conjunto de números que se puede sustituir por una variable.

right triangle/triángulo rectángulo (p. 619) Un triángulo con un ángulo recto.

root (of an equation)/raíz (de una ecuación) (p. 477) La solución de una ecuación.

• • S • •

sample/muestra (p. 21) La porción representativa de una población que se usa para un estudio estadístico como una encuesta.

sample space/espacio de muestra (p. 398) Todos los resultados posibles de un evento.

scale factor/factor de escala (p. 650) El número por el cual las dimensiones originales de una figura se multiplican ya sea para agrandar o reducir la figura original proporcionalmente. El factor de escala se encuentra escribiendo la razón de un par de lados correspondientes.

scalene triangle/triángulo escaleno (p. 619) Un triángulo que no tiene lados iguales en longitud.

scatter plot/gráfica de dispersión (p. 206) Una gráfica en la cual los datos se muestran como puntos en un plano coordenado.

scientific notation/notación científica (p. 532) Un número escrito en la forma $m \times 10^n$ donde $1 \leq m < 10$ y n es cualquier entero.

set (of numbers)/conjunto (de números) (p. 437) Una colección de números con uno o más atributos comunes.

similar (figures)/semejantes (figuras) (p. 648) Dos figuras son semejantes si tienen la misma forma pero no necesariamente el mismo tamaño.

simplest form (of a polynomial)/forma reducida (de un polinomio) (p. 544) Un polinomio está en forma reducida cuando no contiene términos semejantes.

simplest form (of a radical)/forma reducida (de un radical) (p. 625) Una expresión radical en la cual el radicando no tiene factores cuadrados perfectos además 1, no tiene fracciones y ningún denominador contiene un radical.

simplest form (of a rational expression)/forma reducida (de una expresión racional) (p. 687) Una expresión racional está en la forma más simple cuando el numerador y el denominador de la expresión no tienen factores comunes además de 1.

simplify (an expression)/simplificar (una expresión) (p. 95) Cambiar una expresión a una expresión equivalente con menos términos.

sine/seno (p. 653) Para cualquier ángulo agudo en un triángulo rectángulo, la razón de la longitud del cateto opuesto a la hipotenusa.

sine curve/curva sinusoidal (p. 660) La gráfica de la función del seno.

slope (of a line)/pendiente (de una línea) (pp. 268, 269) La razón del número de unidades que la línea se eleva verticalmente (la elevación) al número de unidades que la línea se mueve horizontalmente de izquierda a derecha (el curso). Para una línea que conecta dos puntos $P(x_1,y_1)$ y $Q(x_2,y_2)$,
la pendiente de la línea $= \frac{\text{elevación}}{\text{curso}} = \frac{y_2 - y_1}{x_2 = x_1}$.
La pendiente de una linea horizontal es 0. La pendiente de una linea vertical no está definida (no tiene pendiente).

slope-intercept form (of a linear equation)/forma de pendiente e intersección (de una ecuación lineal) (pp. 277, 293) Una ecuación lineal en la forma $y = mx + b$ donde m es la pendiente y b es el intercepto y de la gráfica.

solution (of a system of equations)/solución (de un sistema de ecuaciones) (p. 329) Un par ordenado que es una solución a todas las ecuaciones en un sistema.

solution/solución (p. 115) Un valor de una variable que hace una ecuación verdadera.

square matrix/matriz cuadrada (p. 27) Una matriz que tiene el mismo número de filas y columnas.

square of a binomial/cuadrado de un binomio (p. 554) Un trinomio cuyos primero y último términos son los cuadrados de los términos del binomio y cuyo término medio es dos veces el producto de los dos términos: $(a + b)^2 = a^2 + 2ab + b^2$ y $(a - b)^2 = a^2 - 2ab + b^2$.

square root method/método de raíz cuadrada (p. 483) Un método para resolver una ecuación de la forma $ax^2 + b = c$ que requiere aislar el término al cuadrado en un lado de la ecuación y después sacar la raíz cuadrada de ambos lados.

square root property/propiedad de raíz cuadrada (p. 483) Si $x^2 = k$, entonces $x = \sqrt{k}$ o $x = -\sqrt{k}$ para cualquier número real k, $k > 0$. Si $k = 0$, entonces $x^2 = 0$ tiene una sola solución, 0.

standard form (of a linear equation)/forma estándar (de una ecuación lineal) (p. 294) Una ecuación de la forma $Ax + Bx = C$ donde A, B y C son enteros y A y B no son 0.

standard form (of a quadratic equation)/forma estándar (de una ecuación cuadrática) (p. 477) Una ecuación de la forma $d = ax^2 + bx + c$ cuando $d = 0$.

standard notation/notación estándar (p. 532) La forma decimal de cualquier número, por ejemplo 12.45, 43 o 0.0087.

subset/subconjunto (p. 431) Conjunto A es un subconjunto del conjunto B si cada elemento del conjunto A es también un elemento del conjunto B.

substitution method/método de sustitución (p. 335) Un método algebraico para resolver un sistema de ecuaciones lineales.

subtraction of real numbers/sustracción de números reales (p. 79) Para todos los números reales a y b, $a - b = a + (-b)$.

subtraction property of equality/propiedad de sustracción de la igualdad (p. 125) Para todos los números reales a, b y c si $a = b$, luego $a - c = b - c$.

subtraction property of inequality/propiedad de sustracción de la desigualdad (p. 230) Para todos los números reales a, b y c si $a > b$, luego $a - c > b$ y si $a < b$, luego $a - c < b - c$.

sum of the angles of a triangle/suma de los ángulos de un triángulo (p. 620) La suma de las medidas de los ángulos de un triángulo es 180°.

supplementary angles/ángulos suplementarios (p. 621) Dos ángulos cuya suma es 180°. Cada ángulo es el *suplemento* del otro.

survey/encuesta (p. 21) Un estudio de las opiniones o el comportamiento de una población. También la colección de datos a través de preguntas o escrutinio a una población.

symmetry/simetría (p. 413) Se dice que una figura tiene simetría si tiene una línea de simetría.

system of linear equations/sistema de ecuaciones lineales (p. 328) Dos o más ecuaciones lineales que se consideran juntas. También se les llama un *sistema lineal.*

system of linear inequalities/sistema de desigualdades lineales (p. 379) Dos o más desigualdades que se consideran juntas.

systematic sampling/muestra sistemática (p. 22) Un tipo de muestra de estadística en la cual los miembros de una población se escogen por una regla o patrón que se aplica a la población completa.

T

tangent/tangente (p. 653) Para cualquier ángulo agudo en un triángulo rectángulo, la razón de la longitud del cateto opuesto al ángulo a la longitud del cateto adyacente al ángulo (no la hipotenusa).

terms/términos (p. 61) Las partes de una expresión variable que están separadas por signos de suma o resta. Por ejemplo, la expresión $x + y$ tiene dos términos, x e y.

theoretical probability/probabilidad teórica (p. 398) La probabilidad de un evento, $P(E)$, asignada al determinar el número de resultados favorables y el número de resultados posibles en un espacio de muestra.

$$P(E) = \frac{\text{número de resultados favorables}}{\text{número de resultados posibles}}$$

transformation (of a graph)/transformación (de una gráfica) (p. 418) Un cambio en la posición o forma de una gráfica como un resultado de una operación como traslación o reflexión.

translation (of a graph)/traslación (de una gráfica) (p. 417) Un desliz o cambio que mueve una gráfica a una nueva posición horizontalmente o verticalmente en el plano coordenado.

trend/tendencia (p. 207) El patrón general formado por los puntos en una gráfica de dispersión.

trichotomy property/propiedad de tricotomía (pp. 221, 445) Para todos los números reales a y b, exactamente uno de lo siguiente es verdadero: $a = b$, $a < b$ o $a > b$.

trigonometric ratios/razones trigonométricas (p. 653) Razones de las longitudes de los lados de un triángulo rectángulo. Las tres razones comunes son el *seno*, el *coseno* y la *tangente.*

trigonometry/trigonometría (p. 653) Palabra derivada de un término griego que significa "medida de triángulos".

trinomial/trinomio (p. 541) Un polinomio de tres términos.

trough/depresión (p. 660) El valor mínimo de la gráfica de una función periódica.

V

value (of a variable)/valor (de una variable) (p. 115) El número asignado a o sustituido por una variable.

variable/variable (pp. 13, 60) Una letra u otro símbolo usado para representar un número.

variable expression/expresión variable (pp. 13, 60) Una expresión que tiene por lo menos un número, una operación y una variable.

vertex (of a parabola)/vértice (de una parábola) (p. 468) El punto donde una parábola tiene su punto máximo (el más alto) o mínimo (el más bajo).

vertical axis/eje vertical (p. 169) El eje de y en el plano coordenado.

vertical line test/prueba de verticalidad de línea (p. 178) Una prueba que se usa en la gráfica de una relación para determinar si la relación es también una función. Si una línea vertical, dibujada a través de la gráfica de la relación, interseca la gráfica en más de un punto, la gráfica no representa una función.

vertical shift (of a graph)/cambio vertical (de una gráfica) (p. 417) La traslación hacia arriba o hacia abajo de una gráfica en relación a otra gráfica.

W

whiskers/límite de la información (p. 248) Líneas horizontales en un diagrama de bloque que muestra el alcance de los datos.

X

x*-axis/eje de *x (p. 178) La recta numérica horizontal que divide el plano coordenado.

x*-coordinate/coordenada de *x (p. 178) El primer número en un par ordenado que representa un punto en el plano coordenado. La coordenada de *x* determina la localización horizontal del punto.

x*-intercept/intercepto de *x (pp. 276, 477) La coordenada de *x* del punto donde una gráfica cruza el eje de *x*.

Y

y*-axis/eje de *y (p. 183) La recta numérica vertical que divide el plano coordenado.

y*-coordinate/coordenada de *y (p. 183) El segundo número en un par ordenado que representa un punto en el plano coordenado, también llamado la coordenada $f(x)$ para funciones. La coordenada de *y* determina la localización vertical del punto.

y*-intercept/intercepto de *y (pp. 269, 276) La coordenada de *y* del punto donde una gráfica cruza el eje de *y*.

Z

zero pair/par cero (pp. 74, 121) Un par de enteros o términos algebraicos cuya suma es cero. Los pares cero son opuestos.

zero product property/propiedad de los productos iguales a cero (p. 595) Para cualesquiera números *a* y *b* si $ab = 0$, entonces $a = 0$ o $b = 0$ o ambos $a = 0$ y $b = 0$.

zero property of exponents/propiedad de los exponentes cero (p. 528) Para cualquier número a, $a \neq 0$, $a^0 = 1$.

• • • SELECTED ANSWERS • • •

Chapter 1 Data and Graphs

Lesson 1.2, pages 8–12

TRY THESE

1. **Number of Hours Health Club Members Exercise per Week**

Number of Hours	Tally	Frequency
0	||	2
1	|||	3
2	卌	5
3	|||	3
4	||	2
5	||	2
6	|	1
7	||	2

3. 2 h

5. **Number of Books Read During Summer Reading Program**

Number of Books	Tally	Frequency
0–4	||||	4
5–9	卌 ||	7
10–14	卌 |||	8
15–19	|||	3
20–24	|||	3

7. 88%

PRACTICE **1.** 10 **3.** 11% **5.** 8 more magazines

EXTEND **9.** 0.370 **13.** \$6.00–\$6.99; 11; 7

THINK CRITICALLY **15.** Yes; the exact number of free throws he had made would have been shown as well as the number of boys who had made that number.

Lesson 1.3, pages 13–17

TRY THESE **1.** 4 **3.** 3 **5.** 1 **9.** 46, 79

PRACTICE **1.** 25 **3.** 35 **5.** 12 **7.** 8 **9.** 6.4 **11.** Store 1 is 237; Store 2 is 150; Store 3 is 410. **13.** 717.5 **15.** Change line 20 to PRINT B * H. **17.** 212

EXTEND **23.** G is 208; PG is 173; PG-13 is 174; R is 242 **25.** 10 INPUT H, M, N

20 PRINT 0.5 * H * (M + N)

THINK CRITICALLY **27.** Possible answers: 2 * A; B − 2; A * B/C **29.** Possible answers: B * C; 45 + C **31.** Possible answers: 8 * (A * B) + 8 * C; 20 * B **33.** no; if X = 2, Y = 3, and Z = 4, X * Y + Z = 10, and X * (Y + Z) = 14

MIXED REVIEW **34.** 29% **35.** C

Lesson 1.5, pages 21–26

TRY THESE **1.** Convenience: people stopping in at campaign headquarters are likely to be strong supporters of the mayor. **3.** Systematic: only people with jobs and cars will be surveyed. **5.** 8 **7.** 56

PRACTICE **1.** Systematic: the only people surveyed will be those who enjoy popcorn. **3.** Convenience: most of the people surveyed are likely to enjoy popcorn; people taking a tour may feel obligated to answer more positively. **5.** 2 **7.** 3 **9.** 26 **11.** 1

EXTEND **15.** 12.5 million **17.** 121,200

THINK CRITICALLY **19.** 65%; 59%

Lesson 1.6, pages 27–31

TRY THESE **1.** 9, 15, 7, 2, 6; 1 × 5

3. $\begin{bmatrix} 2 & 7 & 7 & 0 \\ -24 & 4 & 15 & 21 \end{bmatrix}$

5. $A = \begin{bmatrix} 117 & 88 \\ 91 & 95 \end{bmatrix}$; $B = \begin{bmatrix} 38 & 35 \\ 25 & 40 \end{bmatrix}$; $C = \begin{bmatrix} 13 & 9 \\ 6 & 10 \end{bmatrix}$

PRACTICE **1.** 4, 5, 8, 3

3. $\begin{bmatrix} 3 & 11 \\ 10 & -4 \end{bmatrix}$ **5.** $\begin{bmatrix} 3 & 4 \\ 0 & 6 \\ 4 & 6 \end{bmatrix}$

7. $I = \begin{bmatrix} 317 & 490 & 166 \\ 555 & 207 & 181 \end{bmatrix}$; $N = \begin{bmatrix} 52 & 70 & 48 \\ 88 & 86 & 66 \end{bmatrix}$;

$S = \begin{bmatrix} 61 & 90 & 77 \\ 114 & 98 & 50 \end{bmatrix}$

9. $\begin{bmatrix} 992 & 1008 & 960 \\ 888 & 912 & 920 \\ 1184 & 1128 & 1152 \\ 816 & 872 & 824 \end{bmatrix}$

758

Extend 13. $\begin{bmatrix} 11 & 15 & 24 \\ 19 & 31 & 28 \end{bmatrix}$

Think Critically 15. Double each element.

17. Possible answer: 100 $\begin{bmatrix} 124 & 126 & 120 \\ 111 & 114 & 115 \\ 148 & 141 & 144 \\ 102 & 109 & 103 \end{bmatrix}$

Mixed Review 21. B 22. 2×3

23. $\begin{bmatrix} 265 & 205 & 370 \\ 244 & 144 & 160 \end{bmatrix}$ 24. $\begin{bmatrix} 37 & 23 & 26 \\ 68 & 14 & 0 \end{bmatrix}$

Lesson 1.7, pages 32–37

Try These 1. 84; 81; 77; 23 3. 207; 197; none; 86 5. 188.2 cm; 185 cm; 180 cm; 30 cm 7. 80.5 s; 80 s; 80 s and 85 s; 23 s

Practice 1. 27.25; 26.5; 23; 15 3. 240; 235; 235; 100 5. 4394; 4411.5; none; 279 7. \$13,685; \$13,715; none; \$3,020 11. 405.3 ft; 403 ft; 400 ft 13. 211.3; 210.8; 210.5; 3.7

Extend 17. mode 19. range 21. \$14 or \$15 23. \$12, because all values appear the same number of times

Think Critically 25. 15: 6; 16: 96; 17: 120; 18: 18 27. The data item must equal at least one item already in the set.

Mixed Review 30. 2 31. 4 32. 8 33. 42 34. A

Lesson 1.8, pages 38–41

Try These 1. about 1 3. about 0.375 5. 80,000 7. $\frac{21}{25} = 0.84$, or 84% 9. 0

Practice 1. $\frac{251}{365} = 0.688$, or 68.8% 3. $\frac{6}{25}$, or 24% 5. 0% 7. about 175,200 9. about 51.4% 11. about 21.6%

Lesson 1.9, pages 42–45

Apply the Strategy 15. 42 17. 42% 19. 32,374 copies/week 21. 2,343,750 ft^2

Chapter Review, pages 46–47

1. a 2. d 3. e 4. b 5. c 7. 40%

8.

	A	B	C	D
1		Regal	Ovenmaster	Total
2	Campus	38	52	90 (=B2+C2)
3	Eastwood	49	70	119 (=B3+C3)
4	Central	25	41	66 (=B4+C4)

9. 2956 10. convenience sampling 11. 18,000

12. $\begin{bmatrix} 10 & 7 & 17 & 10 \\ 4 & 9 & 1 & 10 \end{bmatrix}$ 13. $\begin{bmatrix} 13 & 6 & 10 & 3 \\ 23 & 30 & 2 & 10 \end{bmatrix}$

14. $\begin{bmatrix} 20 & 10 & 19 & 9 \\ 25 & 39 & 3 & 15 \end{bmatrix}$ 15. 81.7; 81.5; 80 and 84; 8

16. about 3.3; 3; 3; 5 17. 16% 18. about 26.1%

Chapter 2 Variables, Expressions, and Real Numbers

Lesson 2.2, pages 59–64

Try These 1. 12 3. 15 5. 13 7. 2 9. 9 11. 40 15. degree 2; 3 terms; –1 17. 4 19. 1 21. $-\frac{3}{4}$ 23. $8s - 4$

Practice 1. 35 3. 33 5. 17 7. 19 9. 40 11. 1 13. 33 15. 54 17. 73 19. 337 21. $3.50 + x$ 23. 48 25. 23 27. 7; 10; 13; 16 29. 1; 2; 3; 5 31. degree 4; 4 terms; –3 33. degree 6; 6 terms; 10 35. 9 37. –3 39. $\frac{y}{8}$

Extend 41. 18 43. 23 45. 37,543 47. 15.6 49. 622 51. $450 + 0.02x$ 53. 163.1 cm or about 5 ft 4 in.

Think Critically 55. no; possible example: $3^2 \neq 2^3$

Lesson 2.3, pages 65–72

Try These 1. yes; it is the ratio of two integers 3. no; 3 is not a perfect square so $\sqrt{3}$ is irrational 5. no; 11 is not a perfect square, so $\sqrt{11}$ is irrational 7. E 9. D 11. G 13. < 15. > 17. 9 19. 4.9 23. Fairbanks; $-4 > -20$

Practice 1. yes; $5\frac{1}{4} = \frac{21}{4}$ 3. no; it is a nonterminating, nonrepeating decimal 5. no; 5 is not a perfect square, so $\sqrt{5}$ is irrational 7. yes; $6.2 = \frac{62}{10}$ 9. yes; $\sqrt{49} = 7$ 11. yes; it is a nonterminating, repeating decimal 13. C 15. H 17. E 19. A 21. G 23. < 25. < 27. < 29. > 31. 2 33. $7\frac{2}{3}$ 35. –2.3

SELECTED ANSWERS

EXTEND
43. $\sqrt{3}, 0.51, 0.5, \frac{9}{20}, -\frac{3}{10}, -0.98, -1.1, -\sqrt{4}$
45. < **47.** < **49.** >

MIXED REVIEW **54.** $0.15x$ **55.** $\frac{x}{3}$ **56.** B **57.** <
58. > **59.** > **60.** <

Lesson 2.5, pages 77–83

TRY THESE **1.** –1 **3.** $-\frac{9}{11}$ **5.** 0.7 **7.** $\frac{7}{12}$
11. 7 **13.** $-\frac{1}{8}$ **15.** –9 **17.** 4.5 **19.** –\$8 **21.** –10
23. 5.6 **25.** $\frac{17}{20}$

PRACTICE **3.** 5 **5.** –17 **7.** –0.6 **9.** 1.5
11. –6.3 **13.** –12 **15.** $-\frac{3}{10}$ **17.** $2\frac{2}{3}$ **19.** $-1\frac{1}{6}$
21. $\frac{4}{9}$ **23.** –4 **25.** –11 **27.** –6 **29.** –9.3
31. 0.1 **33.** 0.93 **35.** $1\frac{5}{24}$ **37.** $-1\frac{1}{4}$ **39.** $-\frac{1}{10}$
41. 2747 y **43.** –7 **45.** 44 **47.** $\frac{2}{5}$ **49.** –0.67
51. at the 28-yd line

EXTEND **53.** –10 **55.** 2 **57.** –14 **59.** –7 **61.** –3
63. $13\frac{7}{8}$ **65.** 16°F

Lesson 2.7, pages 88–94

TRY THESE **3.** –3.2 **5.** $25\frac{1}{3}$
7. $-\frac{4}{3}$ **9.** $-\frac{5}{17}$ **11.** 1.55 **13.** $3\frac{1}{2}$
15. $-3(2) = -6$

PRACTICE **1.** –99 **3.** 105 **5.** –2.04 **7.** 0.0027
9. $-\frac{7}{16}$ **11.** $-\frac{33}{8}$ or $-4\frac{1}{8}$ **13.** $-\frac{1}{21}$ **15.** $-\frac{6}{19}$
19. –25 **21.** 17 **23.** –0.04 **25.** 80 **27.** $-2\frac{1}{7}$
29. $1\frac{1}{4}$ **31. a.** $1125m - 100m - 5m$ **b.** \$4080

EXTEND **33.** 19 **35.** 10 **37.** 13 **39.** –26

THINK CRITICALLY **45.** no; $-8 \div 3 = -\frac{8}{3}$, which is not an integer **47.** $|ab|$ **49.** $\left|\frac{a}{b}\right|$

Lesson 2.8, pages 95–101

TRY THESE **1.** –3 **3.** 71 **5.** 0.059 **7.** –26 **9.** –4
11. $4b - 12$ **13.** $-2m + 16$ **15.** no **17.** no
19. $41 - 4x$ **23.** –5°C

PRACTICE **1.** 27 **3.** –31 **5.** 10.28 **7.** –1.76
9. 0.292 **11.** $\frac{19}{50}$ **13.** 0 **15.** 33 **17.** –13
19. $2x - 7$ **21.** $9 - 24c$ **23.** $17a - 2b + 2c$
25. $2r - s + 6$ **27.** $P = 2(l + w)$

EXTEND **29.** –5 **31.** –1 **33.** 72 **35.** 30 **37.** 0

39. 8 **41.** $(7 + 1) \cdot 2 + 4$ **43.** 750.2 kilocalories

MIXED REVIEW **48.** both

49. $A + B$ $\begin{bmatrix} 5 & 6 & -6 \\ 13 & 0 & 5 \\ 0 & 6 & 5 \end{bmatrix}$ **50.** $A - B$ $\begin{bmatrix} 1 & 4 & -6 \\ 3 & -4 & 1 \\ -2 & 2 & 3 \end{bmatrix}$

51. D **52.** F **53.** C **54.** G **55.** B

Lesson 2.9, pages 102–105

APPLY THE STRATEGY **15. a.** $10a + b$; $10b + a$
b. $(10a + b) + (10b + a)$
c. $(10a + b) + (10b + a)$
$= 10a + b + 10b + a$ associative property
$= 10a + a + 10b + b$ commutative property
$= 11a + 11b$ Combine like terms.
$= 11(a + b)$ distributive property
$11(a + b)$ represents a whole number divisible by 11.

Chapter Review, pages 106–107

1. f **2.** b **3.** d **4.** c **5.** e **6.** a **7.** –2 **8.** $4x$
9. $-2y + 5$ **10.** 7 **11.** 112 **12.** 10
13–15.

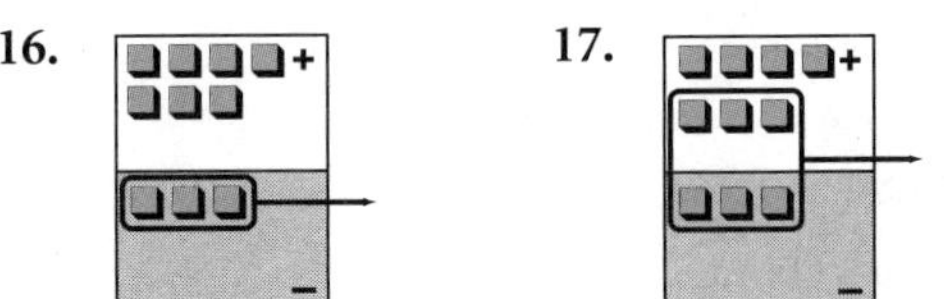

16. **17.**

18. **19.**

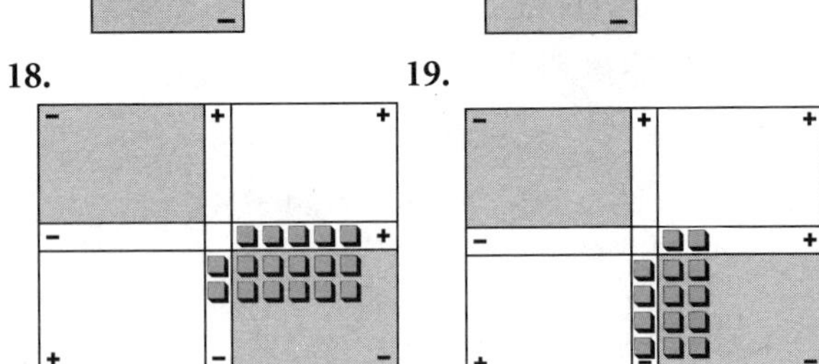

20. $-1\frac{3}{4}$ **21.** 9.8 **22.** –17 **23.** $12\frac{1}{2}$ **24.** –0.4
25. –44 **26.** –140 **27.** $-2\frac{2}{3}$ **28.** 16 **29.** –160
30. $-\frac{1}{6}$ **31.** –340 **32.** 0 **33.** $-8c + 4$
34. $x + 2y - 3z$ **35.** Let n and $n + 1$ represent consecutive whole numbers; $n + (n + 1) = 2n + 1$; $2n$ represents an even number, so $2n + 1$ represents an odd number.

Chapter 3 Linear Equations

Lesson 3.1, pages 115–119

Try These **1.** 16 **3.** 5 **5.** 28 **7.** 49 **9.** 4 **11.** –5 **13.** 8 **15.** 3 **17.** 9 **19.** 6 **21.** 2.1 **23.** 8 **25.** 3 **27.** height = 8 units; methods will vary

Practice **1.** 40 **3.** 480 **5.** 75 **7.** 14 **9.** 9.1 **11.** 52 **13.** 10 **15.** 5 **17.** 8 **19.** 38 **21.** Equations will vary. $13 - t = 12.5$; $t = 0.5$ g

Extend **25.** 38 **27.** 5 **29.** 6 **31.** –81 **35.** less **37.** less **39.** less **41.** 29 **43.** 4 **45.** no, since $3 \cdot 2.00 = 6.00$, almost the entire \$6.16 **47.** Possible answer: \$5.75 is approximately \$6.00; $15 \cdot 6.00 = 90.00$; \$89.95 is approximately \$90.00.

Think Critically **49.** The variable must be a negative number. **51.** 38 **53.** 77

Mixed Review **54.** mean = 7.2; median = 5; mode = 2; range = 21 **55.** C

Lesson 3.3, pages 124–128

Try These **1.** –3 **3.** 17 **5.** 6 **7.** –4 **9.** $x - 4 = 7$; $x = 11$;

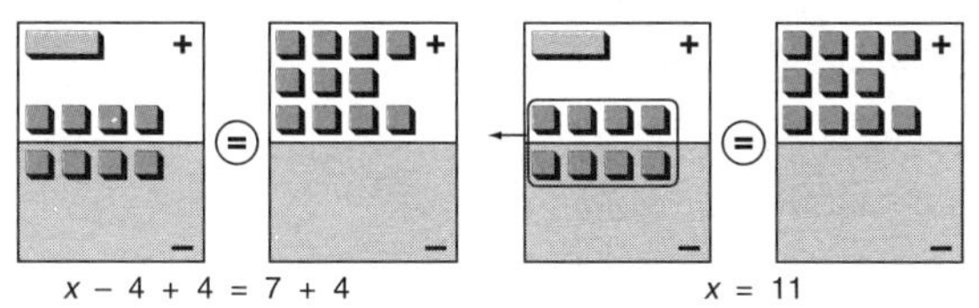

11. –5 **13.** –7 **15.** 16 **17.** 47 **19.** $4\frac{1}{4}$ **21.** 20

Practice **1.** 25 **3.** –20 **5.** 18 **7.** –3 **9.** –14 **11.** –48 **13.** equations will vary; possible response: $t + 14 = 71$; $t = 57$°F **15.** 7 **17.** 0 **19.** –3.6 **21.** $1\frac{5}{12}$ **23.** 2 **25.** 8

Extend **29.** –12.764 **31.** 5.0928 **33.** $3000 = C + 300$; 2700 Cal **35.** $220 = r - 130$; $r = 350$ Cal/h

Think Critically **37. a.** x decreases **b.** b increases **39.** $7\frac{1}{2}$

Lesson 3.4, pages 129–134

Try These **1.** divide by 7 **3.** multiply by 3 **5.** multiply by $\frac{3}{2}$ **7.** divide by 9 **9.** $3x = -9$ **11.** 15 **13.** 13 **15.** $b = \frac{32.2}{9.2}$ **17.** $d = 7.5(28.5)$

Practice **1.** divide by 6 **3.** divide by –4 **5.** divide by –7 **7.** multiply by 5 **9.** multiply by –12 **11.** multiply by $\frac{4}{3}$ **13.** 120 **15.** 12 **17.** –18 **19.** –17 **21.** 78 **23.** 3 **25.** –47.6 **27.** 2.5 **29.** $6x = 1008$; $x = 168$; 168 teams

Extend **33.** 2.5 **35.** –18 **37.** –0.4 or $-\frac{2}{5}$ **39.** 21.3 **41.** 108.24 **43.** –0.85 **45.** –1.33 **47.** 0.89 **49.** b; \$1242.20 **51.** $4x = 72$; $x = 18$; 18 in. **53.** $6.875g = 11$; 1.6 km **55.** $11{,}612m = 36{,}000{,}000$; about 3100 mi

Mixed Review **57.** D **58.** 6.5 **59.** 54 **60.** 13.5 **61.** 12.5 **62.** $8x = (-4)^2$; $x = 2$ **63.** $\frac{72}{2} = x + 15$; $x = 21$

Lesson 3.5, pages 135–139

Try These **1.** 48 **3.** 8.1 **5.** 130.2 **7.** 28.6% **9.** 166.7% **11.** 80 **13.** 104 **15.** $4\frac{1}{2}$ %

Practice **1.** 10.4 **3.** 166.7% **5.** 62.5% **7.** 529 **9.** 63.3% **11.** 2.6 **13.** 71% **15.** 3.8 g

Extend **17.** 23.8% **19.** 2.1 **21.** 51.2 **23.** 74.8 **25.** \$940; find the cost of the car in each state and subtract, or multiply the base price by the difference in states' tax rates

Think Critically **27.** true **29.** false; answers will vary **31.** The information is inconsistent. 3 g is 4% of 75 g, but 7 g is 15% of 46.7 g, giving the different RDA for protein.

Mixed Review **32.** $\frac{1}{2}$ **33.** $\frac{1}{6}$ **34.** $\frac{5}{12}$ **35.** $\frac{5}{12}$ **36.** $\frac{7}{12}$ **37.** $\frac{1}{3}$ **38.** B

Lesson 3.6, pages 140–145

Try These **1.** Add b to both sides. **3.** Add y to both sides. **5.** 9 **7.** 84 **9.** 30 **11.** –8 **13.** 7 **15.** –4 **19.** $14{,}000 - 1800x = 6800$; $x = 4$ yr

Practice **1.** 3 **3.** 3 **5.** 3 **7.** 9 **9.** 75 **11.** –10 **13.** 4 **15.** 11 **17.** –10 **19.** 2.5 **21.** 2 **23.** 56 **25.** 6 **27.** 9 **29.** 8

Extend **31.** –3 **33.** 3 **35.** $x + 3x = 1$; $P(\text{even}) = 0.75$; $P(\text{odd}) = 0.25$ **37.** 70°, 70°, 110°, 110°

Think Critically **39.** P = profit; x = the number of sweaters sold per month; $19x$ is the store's income; \$1300 is the store's expenses; 162 sweaters **41.** 27, 29, 31 **43.** 36 **45.** 28

Lesson 3.7, pages 146–151

Try These **1.** $a = 4$ **3.** $r = 7$ **5.** –3 **7.** 12 **9.** 5 **11.** 12 **13.** 1.5 **15.** –10

17. The accounts will be equal after 14 weeks.
19. $x = 4$; length $= 17$ mi; area $= 119$ mi^2

Practice **1.** -3 **3.** 1 **5.** 4 **7.** 7 **9.** -4 **11.** -9
15. $-\frac{1}{2}$ **17.** 2 **19.** -8 **21.** 8
23. $90 + 9x = 50 + 13x$; $x = 10$ yd^2 **25.** b

Extend **27.** 9 **29.** 6 **31.** $\frac{5}{7}$ **33.** Each board is 12 ft long; he needs 220 ft.

Think Critically **35.** The difference between the coefficients of the variable terms in each equation is 1.

Lesson 3.8, pages 152–155

Try These **1.** no **3.** yes **5.** subtract 7 from both sides **7.** add m to both sides **9.** divide both sides by 9 **11.** $w = \frac{P - 2l}{2}$ **13.** $N = \frac{60H}{15}$

Practice **1.** $m = \frac{gs^2}{G}$ **3.** $h = \frac{3V}{\pi r^2}$ **5.** $c = \frac{C}{1 + r}$
7. $m = \frac{E}{c^2}$ **9.** $\frac{y - 7}{3}$; $x = 4$ **11.** $\frac{V}{lw}$; $h = 3$
13. $\frac{E}{tI}$; $V = 6$ **15.** 13 h
17. 701.5 mi **19.** 3 cm **21.** 10.5%

Extend **23.** $Q = \frac{100A + 10B + C}{A + B + C}$ **25.** $Q = 56$

Think Critically **27.** Interest paid is zero.
29. divided by 4 rather than -4

Mixed Review **31.** $m = -3$ **32.** $x = -8$
33. $r = 9$ **34.** $b = 4$ **35.** D

Lesson 3.9, pages 156–159

Apply the Strategy **13.** 50 mL **15.** 60 lb **17.** 121 g **19. a.** 4 qt **b.** 1.6 **c.** 0.8 qt **d.** 4.8 qt

Chapter Review, pages 160–161

1. c **2.** d **3.** e **4.** a **5.** b **6.** 18 **7.** 15 **8.** -6
9. $x + 3 = 8$; $x = 5$ **10.** $x - 3 = 4$; $x = 7$
11. $x - 2 = -5$; $x = -3$ **12.** 9 **13.** -8 **14.** 19
15. -5 **16.** 4 **17.** 18 **18.** 11 **19.** $3\frac{2}{3}$ **20.** 6.5
21. 34.5 **22.** 450% **23.** 24% **24.** 6 **25.** -20
26. -15 **27.** 3 **28.** 9 **29.** -40 **30.** 6 **31.** 5
32. 2 **33.** -6 **34.** 1 **35.** $\frac{1}{3}$ **36.** $b = \frac{a + 3}{2}$
37. $r = \frac{12 - 7s}{8}$ **38.** $l = \frac{P - 2w}{2}$
39. \$1200 at 5%; \$900 at 7%

Chapter 4 Functions and Graphs

Lesson 4.2, pages 171–176

Try These **1.** function; domain: $-1, -2, -3, -4, -5$; range: 2 **3.** function; domain: 3, 4, 5, 6; range: 3, 4, 5, 6 **5.** -1; 0; 2 **7.** $f(x) = 2x - 2$; 4

Practice **1.** function; domain: \$0.50, \$0.60, \$0.70, \$0.80, \$0.90; range: \$0.02 **3.** function; domain: 2, 4, 6, 8, 10; range: 0 **5.** not a function **7.** function; domain: 1, 2, 3, 4, 5; range: 50, 100, 150, 200, 250
9. -2; 0.5; 10 **11.** 7; -1; 7 **13. a.** 4.5 Cal **b.** 18 Cal **c.** 153 Cal

Extend **15.** not a function **17.** function; domain: a, b, c, d; range: d, e, f, g
19. a. $f(\$3,500) = \$100 + 0.1(\$3,500) = \$450$
b. $f(\$2,000) = \$100 + 0.1(\$2,000) = \$300$
c. $f(\$1,900) = \$200 + 0.05(\$1,900) = \$295$

Think Critically **23.** $f(x) = 2x + 1$ **25.** Possible answer: cost of a pizza, where $x =$ number of toppings
27. -4 or 4

Mixed Review **28.** 46.2 cm **29.** 41 cm **30.** no mode **31.** 45 cm **32.** 294 **33.** -5 **34.** C

Lesson 4.3, pages 177–182

Try These **1.** $(-4, -2)$ **3.** $\left(-2\frac{1}{2}, 1\right)$ or $(-2.5, 1)$
9. function; domain: all real numbers; range: all real numbers ≥ 0 **11.** not a function

Practice **1.** x-axis **3.** Quadrant IV **5.** $(-2, -1)$
7. $\left(-3\frac{1}{2}, 0\right)$ **9.** $(0, -2.5)$ or $\left(0, -2\frac{1}{2}\right)$
15. function; domain: 0–120 in.; range 0–240 in.
19. not a function

Extend **21.** $f(x) = 20 - x$ where x is the number of minutes already played (Each period is $\frac{60}{3}$, or 20 min.)

Think Critically **27.** (a, b) **29.** $(a, -b)$
31. $(-a, b)$

Lesson 4.4, pages 183–188

Try These

1.

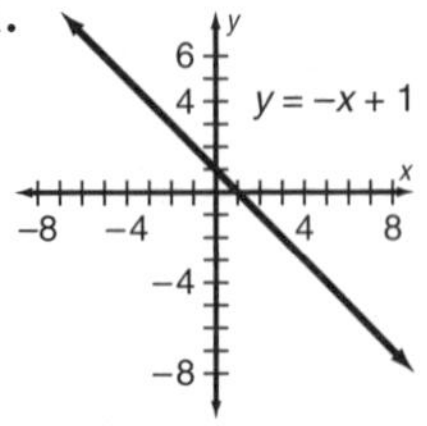

$y = -x + 1$

3.

$y = \frac{x}{2} - 4$

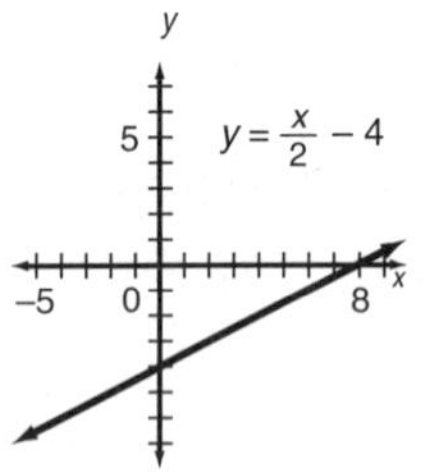

5. No; the point is not on the line. **7.** No; if the line were extended, the point would still not be on the line.
9. No; the point is not on the line.

PRACTICE

1. 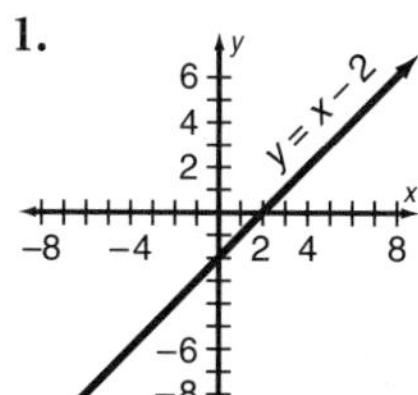

3. 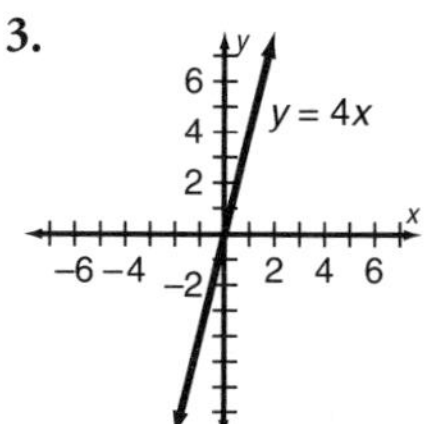

7. No; the point is not on the line. **9.** Yes; if the line were extended the point would be on the line. **11.** No; if the line were extended the point would still not be on the line. **13.** Nonlinear; as each income amount increases by $15,000, the tax rate increases by a different amount (13%, 0%, 3%, 0%)

EXTEND

15. 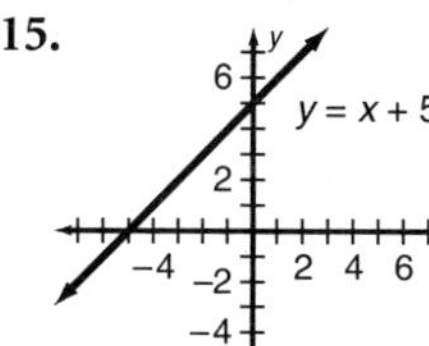

17. 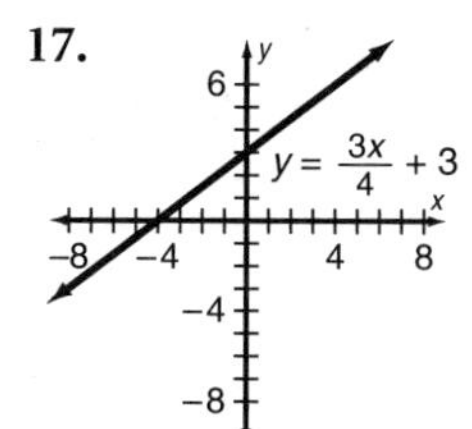

THINK CRITICALLY **21.** Not a linear function; this is not a function at all. If this were graphed, it would be a vertical line through the x-axis at 1. This indicates that, for the input 1, there are an infinite number of different outputs. **23.** Linear function

Lesson 4.6, pages 192–196

TRY THESE **1.** **3.** **5.**

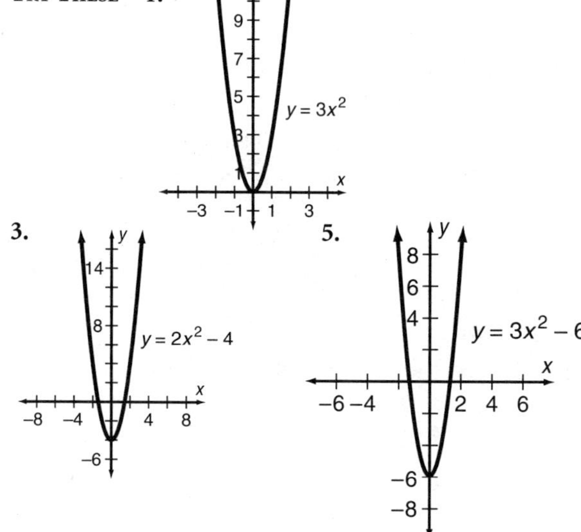

7. Yes; if the curve were extended, the point would be on the curve. **9.** Yes; the point is on the curve.

PRACTICE

1. 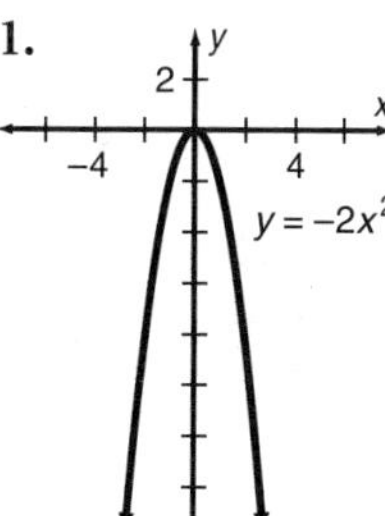

7. Accept 1992 or 1993.

9. nonlinear

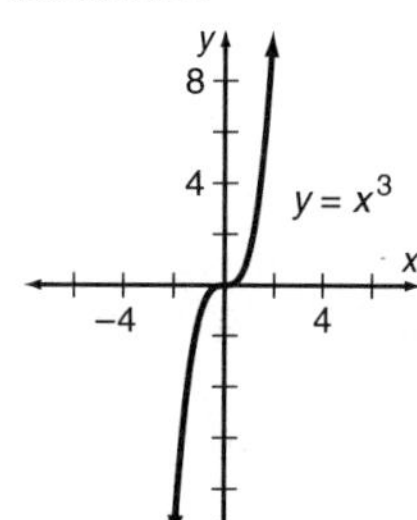

11. nonlinear

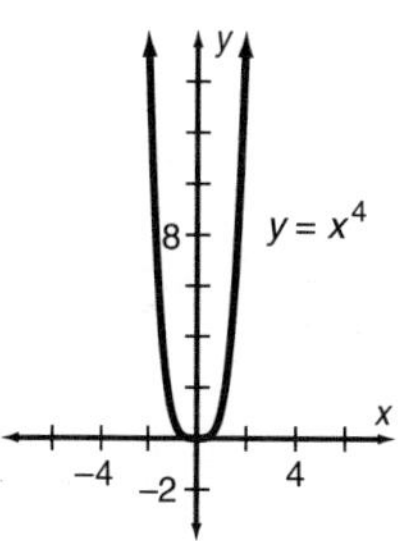

13. 700–800 ft^2 **15.** The charge per ft^2 decreases as the square footage increases.

EXTEND **17.**

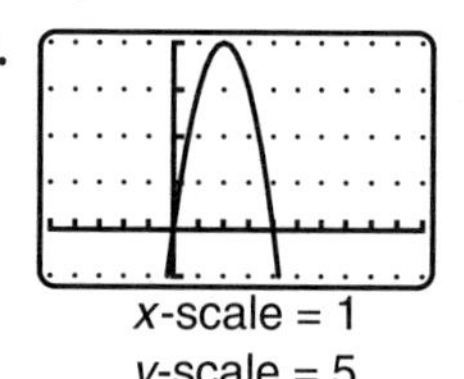

x-scale = 1
y-scale = 5

19. 4 s

THINK CRITICALLY **23.** One opens up and the other opens down.

MIXED REVIEW **25.** $76,000 **26.** $9a + 7b - 3ab$ **27.** $11r^2 + 3r - 3$ **28.** B **29.** Quadrant II **30.** Quadrant IV **31.** x-axis **32.** Quadrant III

Lesson 4.7, pages 197–201

TRY THESE **1.** $y = 9x - 5; y = 22$ **3.** $y = 3(x - 5); y = x + 7$ **5.** $x = -3$ **9.** $x = 2$

PRACTICE

1. $y = -3x + 5;$
$y = -10;$
$x = 5$

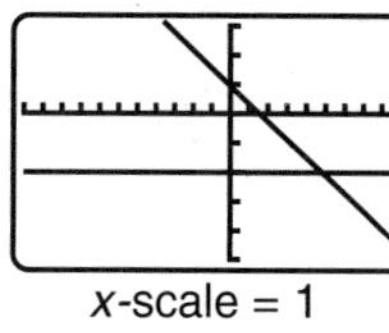

x-scale = 1
y-scale = 5

3. $y = 2x - 4;$
$y = 2(x - 2);$
$x =$ all real numbers

7. 3 h

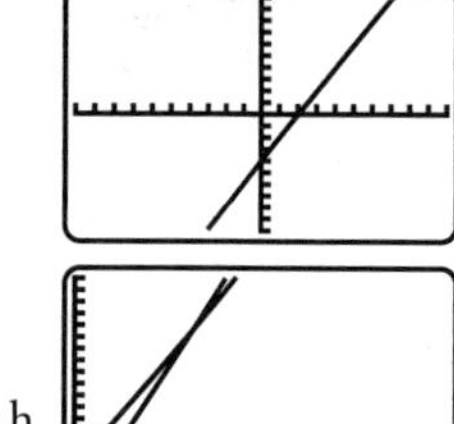

x-scale = 1
y-scale = 100

Extend **9.** $\$1.99x = 20 + 0.89x$ **11.** Plan A: \$37.81; Plan B: \$36.91

13. $x = 0$

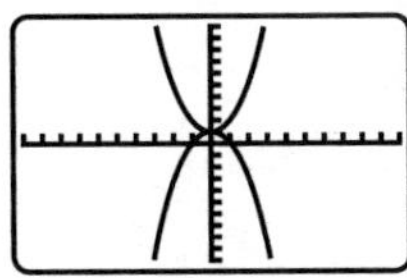

15. no solution

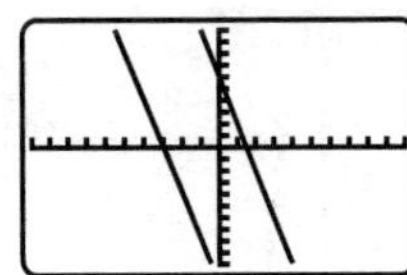

17. two solutions ($x = \pm\sqrt{2}$)

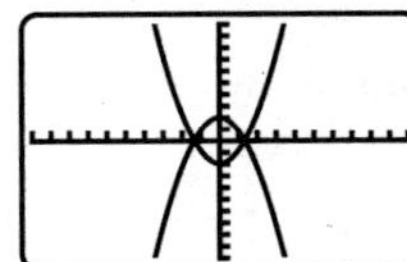

19. The graphs intersect at (6, 15), meaning that 6 min after the hot water was turned on, 15 gal of hot water and 15 gal of cold water, or 30 gal altogether, have run. This is 10 gal more than the sink will hold. Vinje guessed correctly.

Think Critically **21.** not possible **23.** one line (the two graphs coincide) **25.** a line and a curve that intersect in two points

Mixed Review **26.** D **27.** 144 **28.** 48 **29.** $-cde$ **30.** $\frac{mo}{np}$ **31.** −11 **32.** −5 **33.** 4

Lesson 4.8, pages 202–205

Apply the Strategy **15.** a; since the container is wider at the bottom and narrower at the top, the height rises gently at first, then more steeply later.

Lesson 4.9, pages 206–211

Try These

1. Number of Daily Newspapers in U.S.

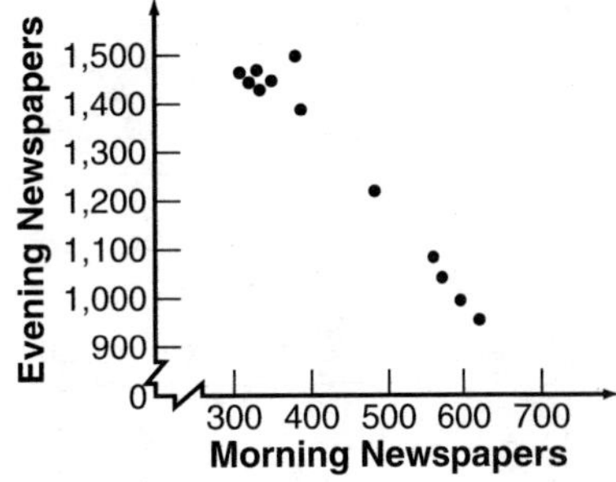

Practice

1. U.S. Energy Production and Imports

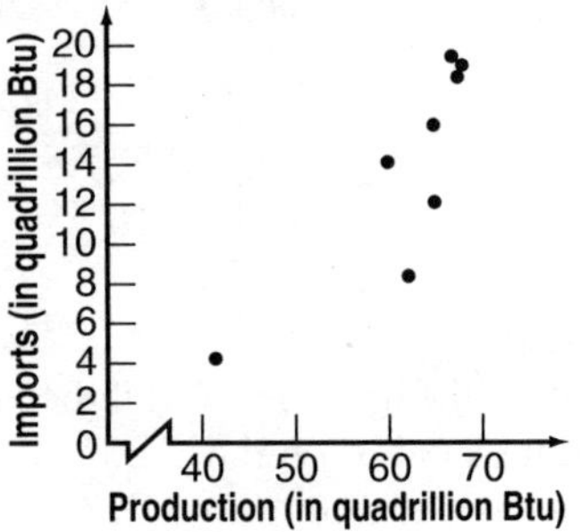

3. World Area and Population, 1992

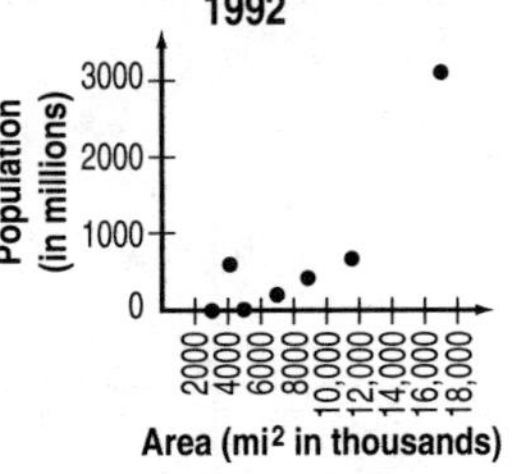

Extend **7.** As the number of miles increases, so does the number of stations.

Mixed Review

14. $\begin{bmatrix} 2 & 1 \\ 0 & 9 \\ 2 & 9 \end{bmatrix}$ **15.** $\begin{bmatrix} -4 & -9 \\ 8 & 5 \\ -2 & -7 \end{bmatrix}$

16. 20,000 **17.** 15 **18.** −15 **19.** −15 **20.** $y = 45$ **21.** $y = -3$ **22.** $y = -3$ **23.** $4x - 12$ **24.** $-3a + 21$ **25.** $4y + 16y^2$ **26.** $14x - 14$ **27.** C **28.** A **29.** $x = 3$ **30.** $x = 10$ **31.** $x = 72$ **32.** $x = 75$

Chapter Review, pages 212–213

1. b **2.** e **3.** d **4.** c **5.** a **6.** Function; domain: 3, 5, 7, 9, 11; range: 2, 4 **7.** Not a function **8.** Function; domain: 5, 10, 15, 20, 25; range: 5, 10, 15, 20, 25 **9.** (−4, −2) **10.** (−2, 3) **11.** (2, 1) **12.** (5, 0) **13.** (1, −2) **14.** Yes; possible explanations: a vertical line cannot be drawn through any two points; for every different x-value, there is only one $f(x)$-value

15. **16.**

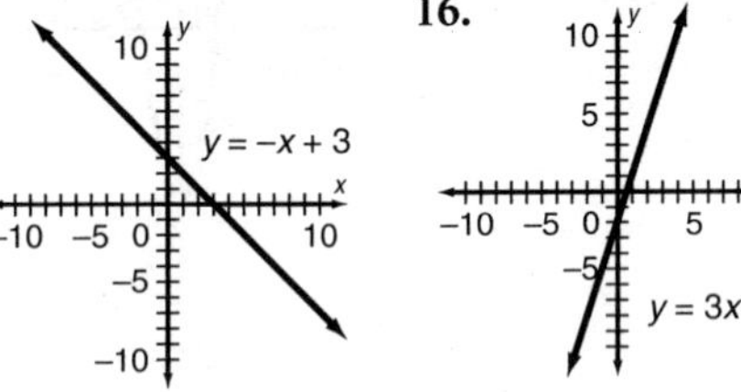

17.

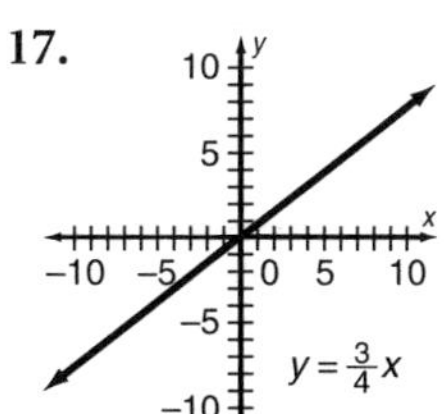

18.

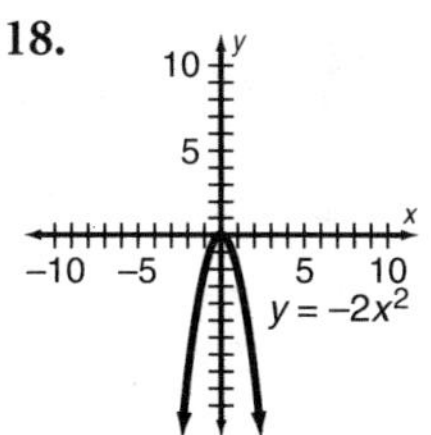

19.

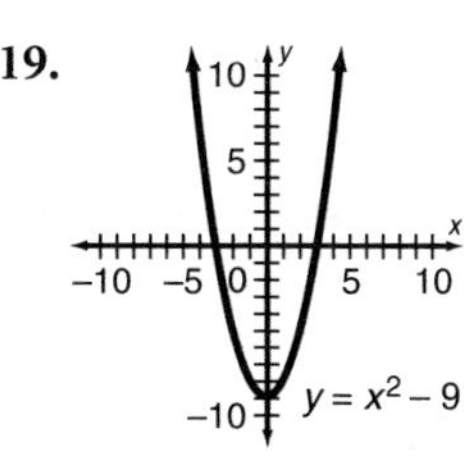

20.

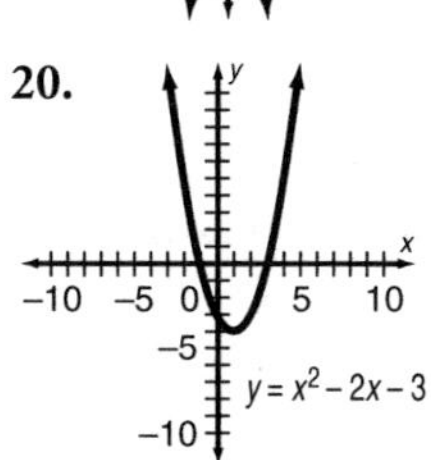

21. $y = 3x - 4$;
$y = 8; x = 4$

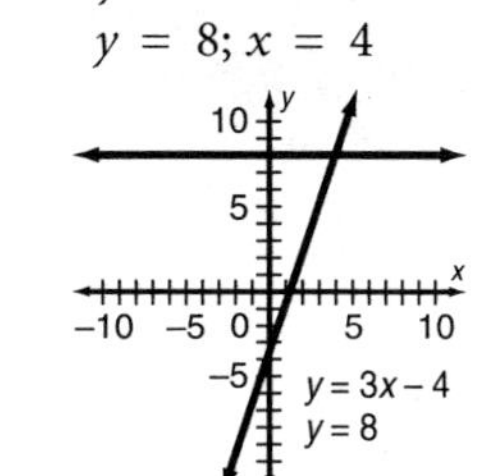

22. $y = -2x + 3$;
$y = 4x - 9; x = 2$

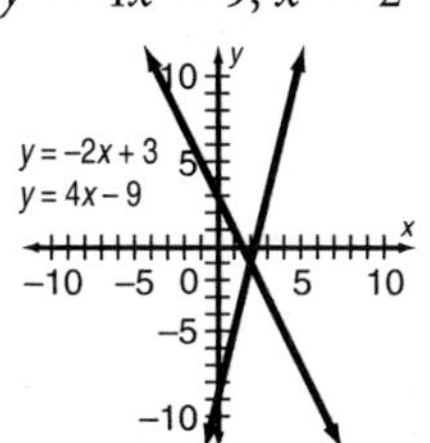

23. $y = 4(x - 1)$;
$y = 4x - 4$;
$x =$ all real numbers

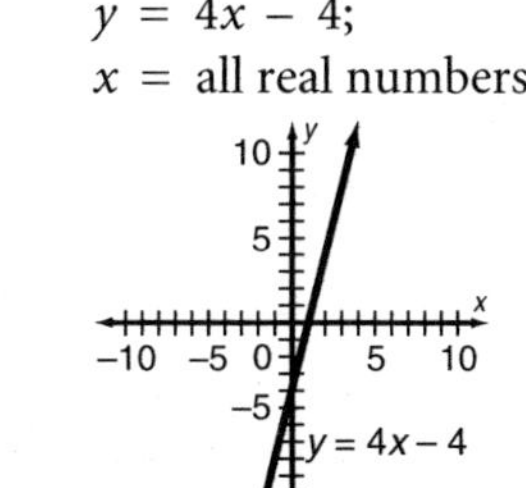

24. Possible graph:

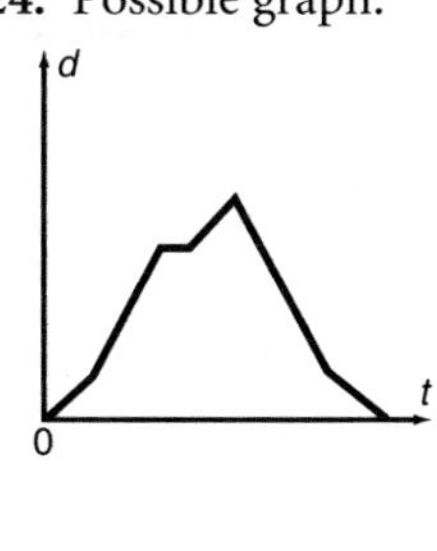

25.

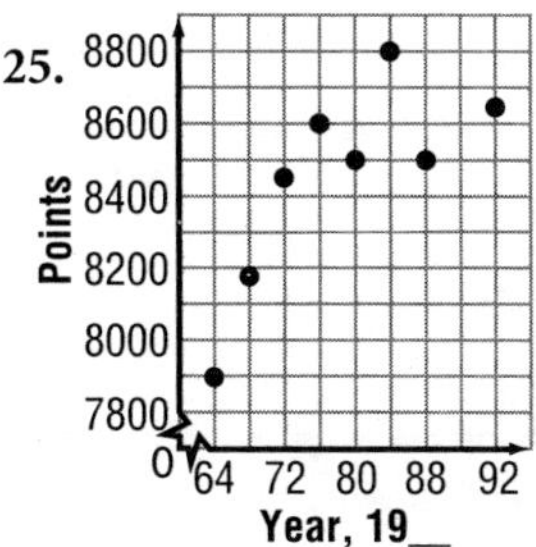

26. As the years increase, the number of points tend to increase.

Chapter 5 Linear Inequalities

Lesson 5.1, pages 221–226

TRY THESE **1.** $c > -3.5$ **3.** $c < -3.5$

5.

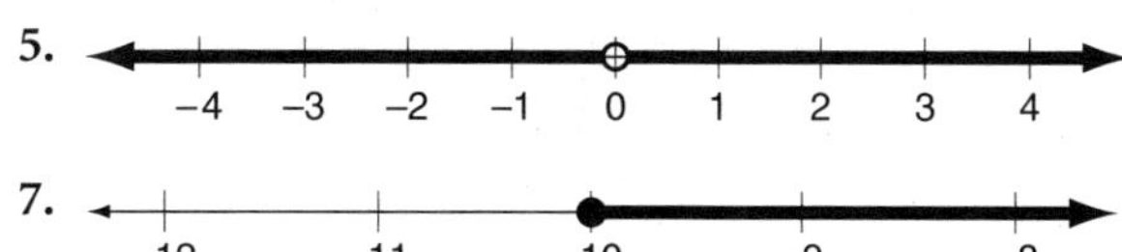

7.

PRACTICE **1.** yes **3.** no

7.

9.

EXTEND **17.** no; accept $g \le 7.3$ or $g \ge 7.3$ **19.** no; accept $v > 10$, $v \ge 10$, $v \ne 10$, $10 > v$, or $10 \ge v$

21. yes **23.** $x \ge 6$ **25.** $x \ne \frac{1}{2}$ **27.** $x \le 37.4$

29. a. $s \le 55$ **b.** No; it is impossible for a car to travel less than 0 mi/h.

THINK CRITICALLY **31.** always true **33.** never true; possible example: $2 < 3$ but 3 is not less than 2

35. sometimes; possible example: if $a = 2$, $b = 1$, then $2 < 3$ but 2 is not less than 1

Lesson 5.3, pages 230–234

TRY THESE

1. $a \le 7$

3. $c \ge 4.8$

5. $m \le 4$

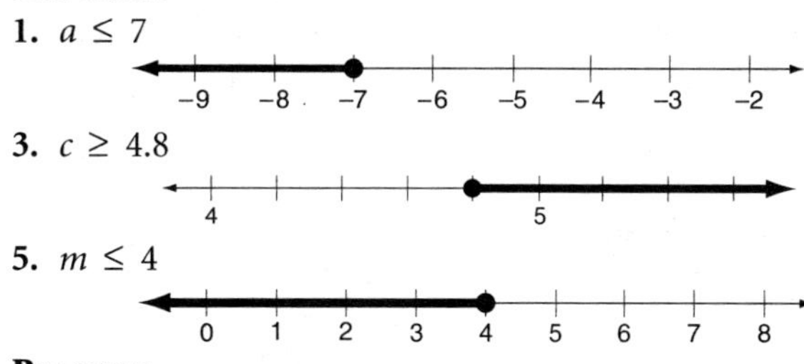

PRACTICE

1. $k \le 16$

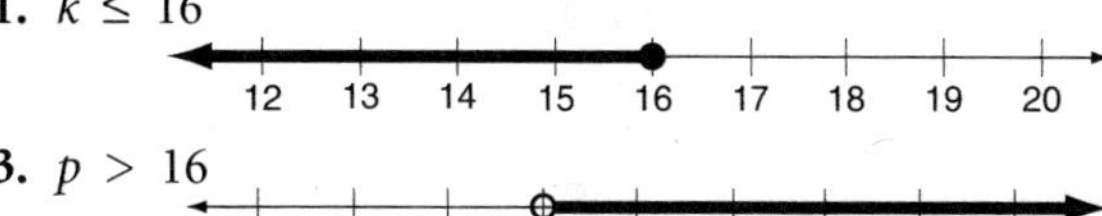

3. $p > 16$

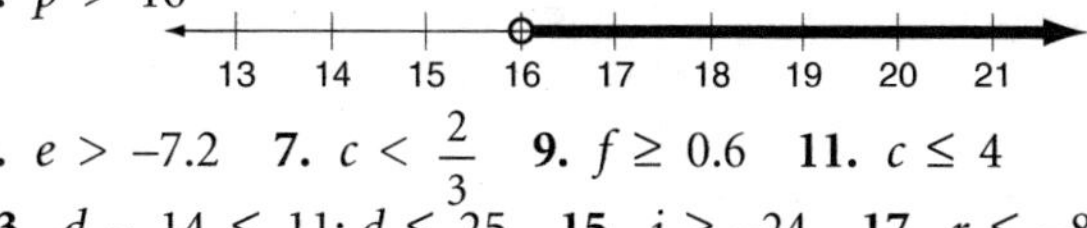

5. $e > -7.2$ **7.** $c < \frac{2}{3}$ **9.** $f \ge 0.6$ **11.** $c \le 4$

13. $d - 14 \le 11; d \le 25$ **15.** $j \ge -24$ **17.** $r \le -8$

19. $q \ge 8.6$ **21.** $z > 7.2$ **23.** $h > 13.5$

25. $t \le -\frac{1}{6}$ **27.** $s < 5$ **29.** $\frac{A}{12} \ge 10; A \ge 120$

EXTEND

31. $h \le 8$

33. $g \ge 3$

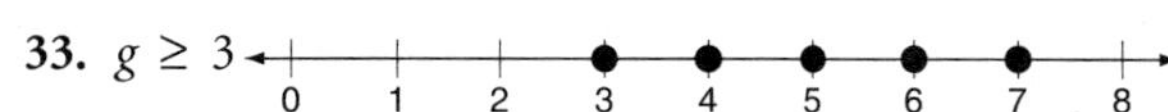

35. The graph of $y = x - 4$ is graphed for all values of x when $x < 3$. **37. a.** $\$0.75w \le 25$

b. $w \leq 33\frac{1}{3}$; 33, since only integers from 1 to 33 make sense as solutions to this problem

Think Critically **39.** always true

Mixed Review **43.** \$8.06 **44.** \$8.00 **45.** no mode **46.** \$2.30 **47.** $e = 1.6$ **48.** $k = -20$ **49.** $n = -36$ **50.** y-axis **51.** Quadrant II **52.** Quadrant IV **53.** C

Lesson 5.4, pages 235–240

Try These

1. $c \geq 4$

3. $s < -36$

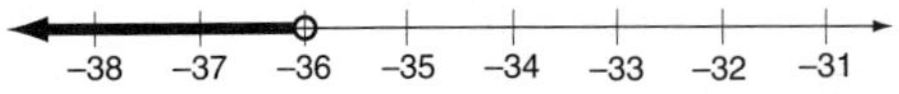

5. $1 \leq x$

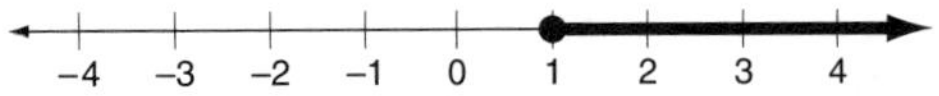

7. $x > -10$

9. $40 + 25h \geq 150$; 4.4 hours or more

Practice **1.** $-5 \leq d$ **3.** $c \geq 12$ **5.** $4 \geq p$ **7.** $e > -8$ **9.** $x < 7$ **11.** $k > 10$ **13.** no solution **15.** all real numbers **17.** $e \leq -1$ **19.** $b \leq 22$ **23.** The solution is $x \geq 5$. This will be graphed as a straight horizontal line beginning at (5, 1) and drawn to the right.

Extend **25.** distributed 2 over h but not over 4; $h \geq 2$ **27.** incorrectly thought that if all variables were eliminated, the solution is all real numbers; no solution **29.** $z + 27 < 4z - 6$; $z > 11$ **31.** $100 + 0.06s \geq \$360$; at least \$4333.34

Mixed Review **37.** \$1000 **38.** 8 **39.** −8 **40.** −8 **41.** B **42.** $x > 36$ **43.** $y > 1$

Lesson 5.5, pages 241–246

Try These

1.

3.

5.

7. $x < 2$ or $x > 2$ **9.** $0 < x < 4$ **11.** $x > -2$ and $x < 4$, or $-2 < x < 4$ **13.** $x < -9$ or $x > 4$

Practice **1.** no **3.** yes **5.** no **7.** $x < 0$ or $x > 0$ **9.** $0 \leq x \leq 5$

11.

13.

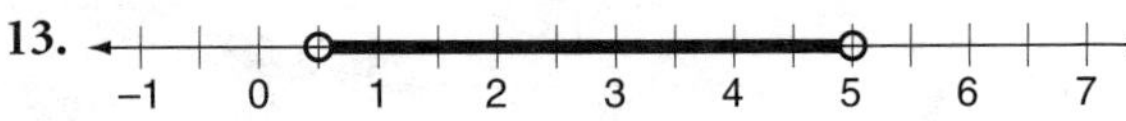

15.

17. $a < -5$ or $a \geq -1$

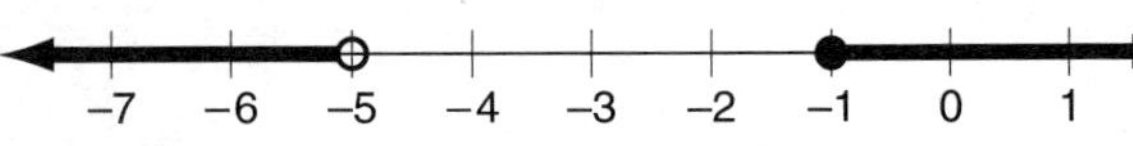

19. $j < 5$ or $j > 7$

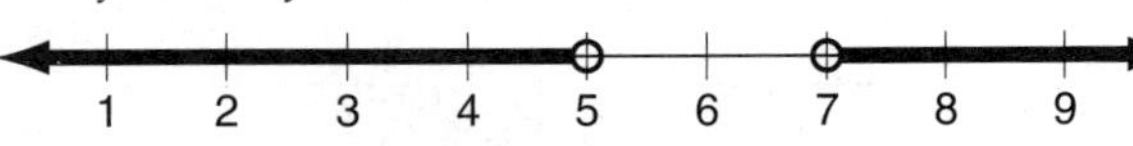

21. $24 < b < 32$

23. $50 \leq 7(n + 12) \leq 68$; $-4 \leq n \leq -3$ **25.** $x < 5$ or $x > 7$ **27.** $x < 8$ or $x > 13$ **29.** $x > 5$ and $x < 7$, or $5 < x < 7$ **31. a.** $t < 55$ or $t > 80$ **b.** temperatures less than 55°F or greater than 80°F;

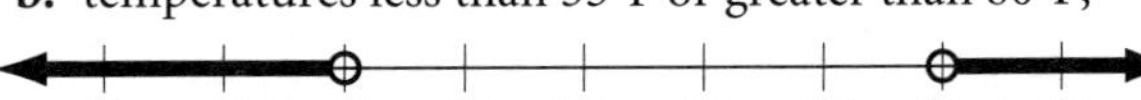

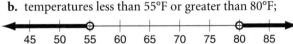

Extend

33. $2 \leq d < \frac{8}{3}$

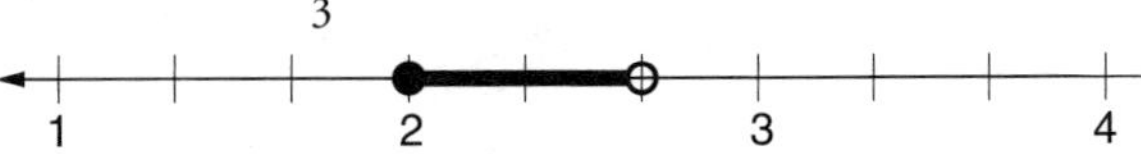

35. $x < 8$ or $x > 15$

37. $1 < b < 10$

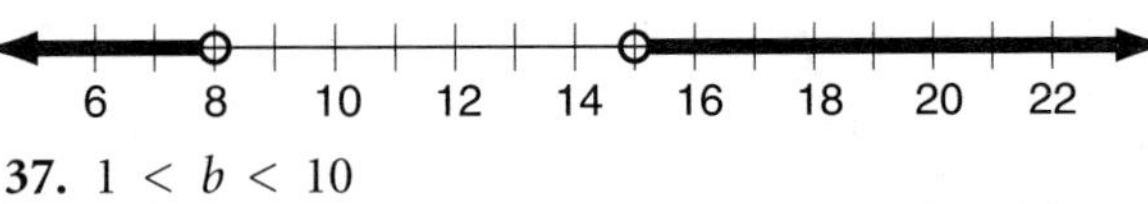

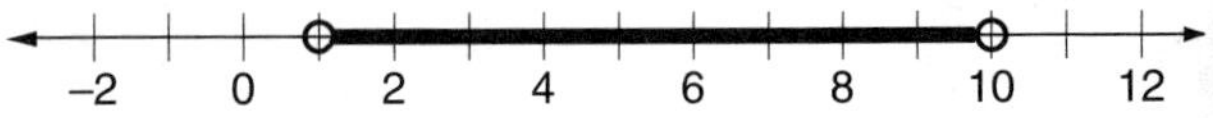

39. a. $155 \leq w - 30 \leq 199$

b. any weight between 185 and 229 lb;

Think Critically

41. a. $-1 < x < 6$

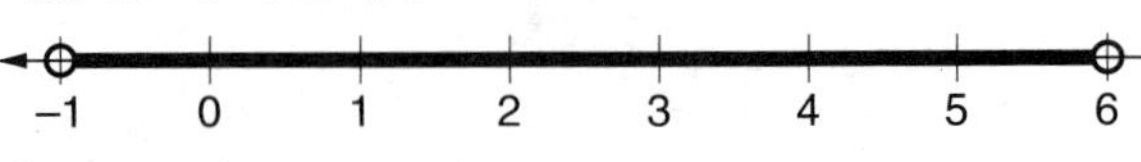

b. $x < -8$ or $x > -6$

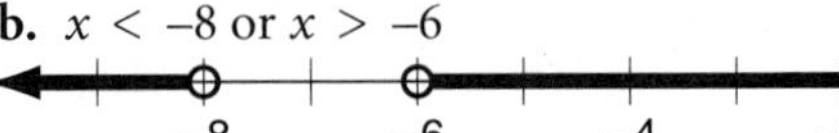

43. $2 < x < 10$

Mixed Review 44. 5:40 45. $b = -2$ 46. $m = 1$

47.

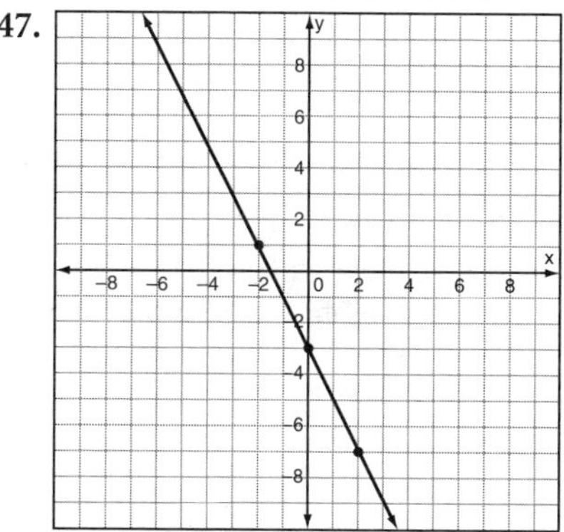

48.

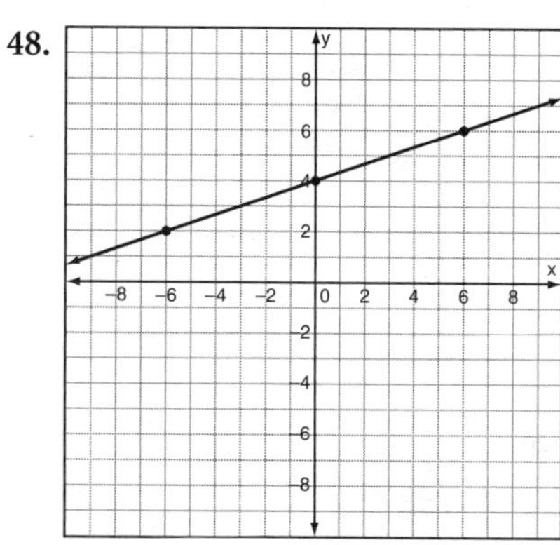

49. D

Lesson 5.6, pages 247–251

Try These 1. \$500, \$562.50, \$675
3. $400 \leq c < 500$

Practice 1. 24.5 (million), 28 (million), 45 (million)
3. $45 \leq p \leq 65$

5. No outliers. The range is 27.

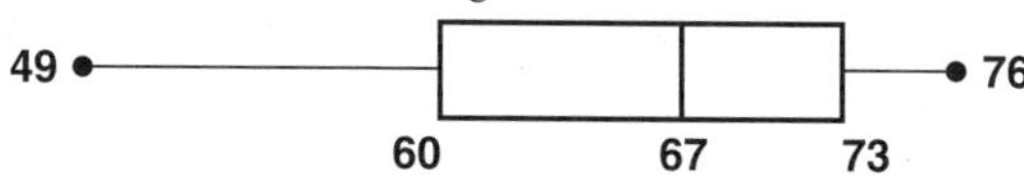

7. Team A; Team A; 130, 198

Extend 11. 4, 8, 12 13. a. $3 \leq v \leq 12$ or $4 \leq v \leq 54$ b. $3 \leq v \leq 8, 4 \leq v \leq 12$, or $8 \leq v \leq 54$ c. $3 \leq v \leq 54$

Think Critically 15. d; quite consistent temperatures year round 17. c; temperatures vary from cold to warm but not as much as do the temperatures for Minneapolis

Lesson 5.7, pages 252–255

Apply the Strategy 9. 5.2 h 11. maximum, 216 red; minimum, 144 blue 13. 6692°F ≤ t ≤ 7592°F
15. $m \geq 7$

Chapter Review, pages 256–257

1. e 2. d 3. a 4. c 5. b

6.

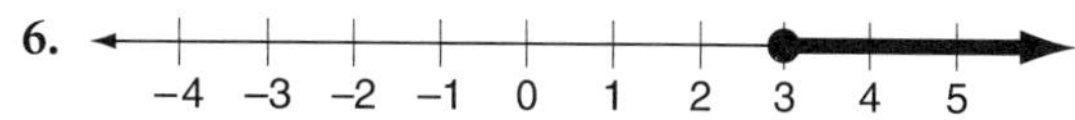

7.

8.

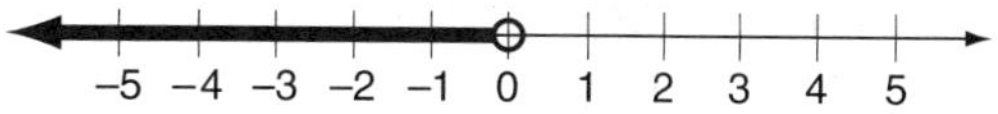

9.

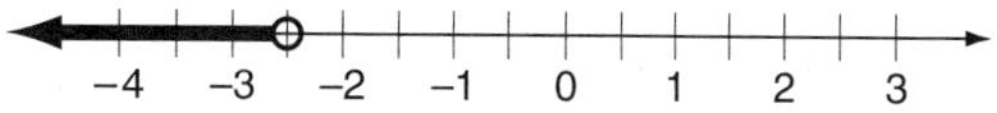

10. < 11. ≤ 12. < 13. >

14. $a > 5$

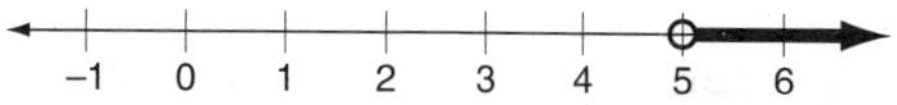

15. $x < 6$

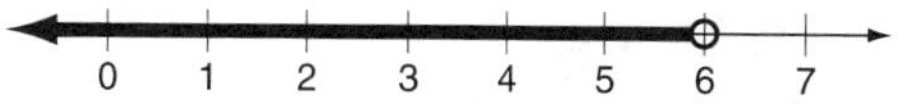

16. $-10 < y$

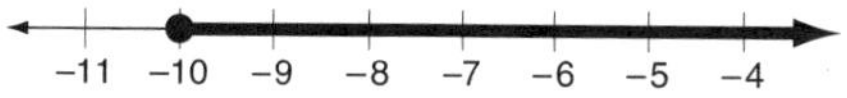

17. $3 < w$

18. $x > 20$ 19. $b > -6$ 20. $x \leq 15$ 21. $2 > r$
22. $x > 36$ 23. $x > 12$ 24. $x < \frac{1}{3}$ 25. $y \leq -4$

26. $-2 < x < 8$

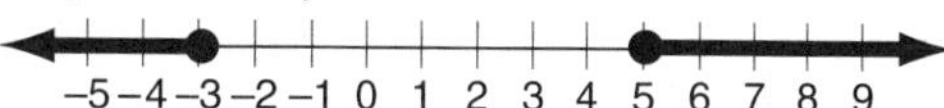

27. $x > 7$ or $x < 3$

28. $y \leq -3$ or $y \geq 5$

29. no solution

30. $x \leq -1$ or $x \geq 5$

31. $x \leq -3$ or $x \geq 2$

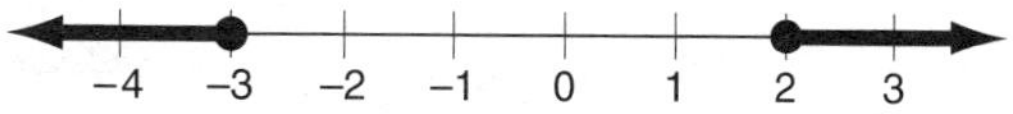

32.

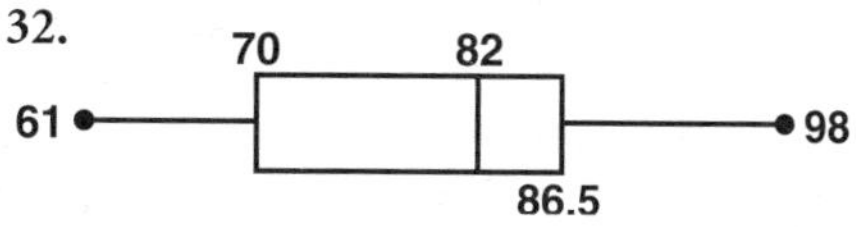

33. $70 \leq s \leq 86.5$ 34. $w \geq 7$ 35. length, 39 ft; width, 8ft

Chapter 6 Linear Functions and Graphs

Lesson 6.2, pages 268–274

Try These **1.** k **3.** j **5.** s **7.** 0.5 **9.** 0 **11.** undefined **13.** line a **15.** line e

Practice **1.** 0.5 **3.** $-\frac{8}{3}$ **5.** 3 **7.** –3 **9.** undefined **11.** line c **13.** line p **15.** 1

Extend **35.** The slope for each year of the graph is positive, except for 1987–88. The negative slope indicates that the number of flights decreased. **37.** 540,000 flights per year **39.** 2222.8 ft

Mixed Review **41.** –66 **42.** $-\frac{1}{7}$ **43.** 36 **44.** linear **45.** nonlinear **46.** nonlinear **47.** B

Lesson 6.3, pages 276–284

Try These **1.** 3, –2 **3.** 3, 3

5.

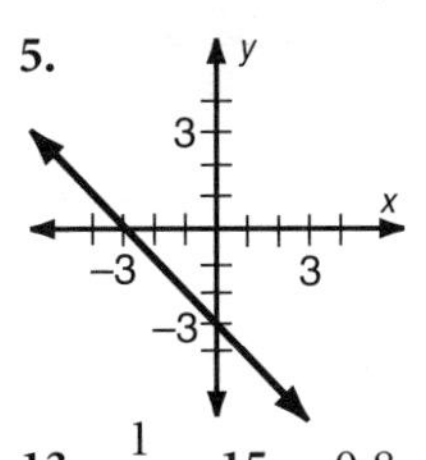

7.

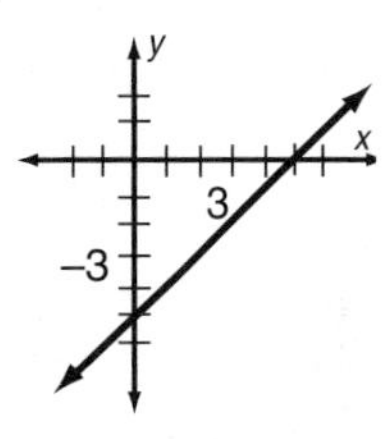

13. $\frac{1}{20}$ **15.** –0.8

Practice **1.**

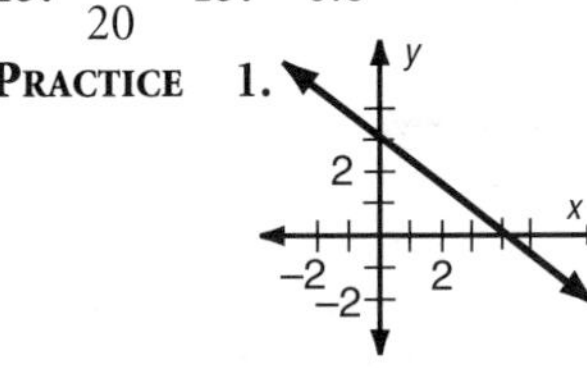

3.

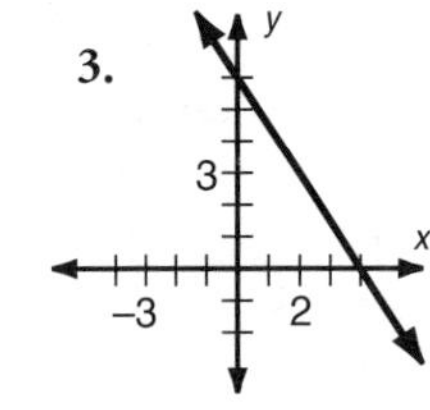

9. c **11.** b **13.** $y = -2.5x$ **15.** $y = -\frac{7}{8} + \frac{3}{5}$ **17.** 3 **19.** $\frac{1}{3}$ **21.** –1 **23.** –2

Extend **27.** $y = 3x$ **29.** $y = -2x - 3$ **31.** $y = -\frac{2}{3}x - 2$

Think Critically **39.** (–4, 2) **41.** the slopes are negative reciprocals; –1

Mixed Review **44.** Edgar **45.** approximately 57% (4 out of 7) **46.** $\frac{2}{5}$ **47.** $4\frac{1}{2}$ h **48.** distributive property of multiplication over addition **49.** associative property of addition **50.** commutative property of multiplication **51.** additive inverse property **52.** D

Lesson 6.4, pages 285–292

Try These **1.** $y = 0.5x + 3.5$ **3.** $y = -2x + 7$ **5.** $y = -6$ **7.** $y = 1.5x - 3.5$ **9.** $y = \frac{3}{2}x + 2$ **11.** $y - 4 = -3(x - 1); y = -3x + 7$ **13.** $y - 1 = \frac{1}{2}(x + 2); y = \frac{1}{2}x + 2$ **15.** $y = -0.5x + 20.17$

Practice **1.** $b = -2.5$ **3.** $b = 10.5$ **5.** $y = -4x + 2$ **7.** $y = -1.5x - 2.5$ **9.** $y = 6x - 18.5$ **11.** $y - 2 = -0.2(x + 3);$ $y = -0.2x + 1.4$ **13.** $y + 2 = -3(x + 4);$ $y = -3x - 14$ **15.** $y = 0.5x + 25$ **17.** $y = 1.4x - 38$

Extend **21.** $y = -0.25x - 0.5$ **23.** $y = 8x - 16$ **25.** $y = 1.25x - 6.25$ **27.** $y = 0.75x - 5.5$ **29.** $y - 2 = -\frac{7}{2}(x + 1)$ **31a.** $y = 10x + 75$ **31b.** 225 pairs

Think Critically **33.** write both in slope-intercept form: $y = x - 1$ **35.** $y = a + -3; y = -a - 9$

Mixed Review **36.** 1.75 **37.** 3.61 **38.** 6.29 **39.** 4.47 **40.** 4 **41.** $\frac{1}{3}$ **42.** 0 **43.** 9 **44.** –2.4 **45.** $2\frac{17}{40}$ **46.** $5\frac{3}{20}$ **47.** $8\frac{29}{30}$ **48.** D

Lesson 6.5, pages 293–298

Try These **1.** $-8x + y = 5$ or $8x - y = -5$ **3.** $3x - 2y = 0$ **5.** $y = 9$ **7.** $x = -7$ **9.** $-x + 6y = -4$ **11.** $x + y = 11$ **13.** $x = -3$ **15.** $x - y = 0$ **17.** $y = -3$ **19a.** $60x + 90y = 1260$ **19b.** The graph has y-intercept 14, x-intercept 21

Practice **1.** $-x - y = 0$ or $x + y = 0$ **3.** $-3x + 2y = -3$ **5.** $2x + y = 18$ **7.** $y = -3$ **9.** $-2x + y = 1$ **11.** $y = 0$ **13a.** $x + 2y = 18$

Extend **15.** $2x + 10y = 15$ **17.** $-18x + 5y = 40$ **19.** $27x + 20y = 3$ **21.** $-18x + 12y = -7$ **23.** $-15x + y = -75$ **25.** $10x + 16y = 75$

Think Critically **33.** horizontal: $y = -5$; vertical: $x = 2$ **35.** $x = 1, x = -1$ **37.** $y = -8$

Mixed Review **39.** B **40.** 43.8 **41.** 208.3% **42.** 920.8 **43.** 2.2 **44.** $x = 13$ **45.** $x = 40$ **46.** $x = -3$ **47.** 1250%

Lesson 6.6, pages 299–306

Try These **1.** pos **3.** pos **5.** neg **7.** 2005

Practice **1.** negative **3.** nonlinear **5.** positive **7.** $y = 4.75x + 4.025$ **9.** a; 0.99; data are positively correlated and each data point lies very close to what would be the line of best fit

Extend **11.** negatively correlated; as the number of

cans redeemed increases, the number found in the trash decreases **13.** –0.997 rounded to nearest thousandth; points for each pair of data lie close to the line of best fit **15.** 303, to the nearest integer **17.** The coefficient of correlation is –0.04, showing almost no relationship between the length of the drive and the number of cans collected weekly

Think Critically **19.** actual number = 149; estimated from the equation = 149.16; percent difference is 0.1%

Mixed Review

21. $\begin{bmatrix} 3 & -2 & 4 \\ 0 & 0 & 4 \\ 4 & 4 & -4 \end{bmatrix}$ **22.** $\begin{bmatrix} 2 & 1 & 4 \\ -1 & 1 & -2 \\ -7 & 10 & -9 \end{bmatrix}$

23. 25 **24.** 267 **25.** 99 **26.** $x > 8$ **27.** $x < 3$ **28.** $x \geq -5$ **29.** C **30.** $m = 0.25, b = -25$ **31.** $m = 4.2, b = 0.3$ **32.** $m = 1, b = 0$ **33.** $m = -1, b = -1$ **34.** parallel: $y = 1.2x + 19$; perpendicular: $y = -\frac{5}{6}x + 2\frac{14}{15}$

Lesson 6.7, pages 307–311

Try These **1.** $y = 50$ **3.** $y = 23.8$ **5.** $k = 0.8$; $y = 0.8x$ **7.** no **9.** yes **11.** yes **13.** no **15.** 170

Practice **1.** $k = 1.75, y = 1.75x$ **3.** $k = 2.4$, $y = 2.4x$ **5.** $k = 4; y = 4x$ **7.** $k = -0.2, y = -0.2x$ **9.** $k = -0.75, y = -0.75x$ **11.** 11.25 **13.** –35 **15. a.** 1.22 **b.** 3.66 **c.** 7.56 **17.** no

Extend **21.** 0.38

Think Critically **25.** Because an unidentified slope indicates a vertical line and means that k, the constant of variation, will be undefined.

Chapter Review, pages 316–317

1. b **2.** c **3.** a **4.** c **5.** $\frac{2}{5}$ **6.** 2 **7.** –3 **8.** $y = \frac{3}{4}x + 8$ **9.** $y = -2x + 3$ **10.** $y = -\frac{1}{3}x - 2$ **11.** perpedicular **12.** parallel **13.** neither **14.** $y - 2 = -9(x - 6); y = -9x + 56$ **15.** $m = 6; y - 3 = 6(x - 3); y = 6x - 15$ **16.** $y - 2 = -\frac{1}{2}(x - 9); y = \frac{1}{2}x + 6.5$ **17.** $-2x + y = 1$ **18.** $2x + y = 11$ **19.** $-3x + 8y = 17$ **20.** $3x + 2y = 8$ **21.** zero **22.** positive **23.** negative **24.** $k = \frac{2}{3}; y = \frac{2}{3}x$ **25.** $k = 3.2; y = 3.2x$ **26.** $k = -1.75; y = -1.75x$

27.

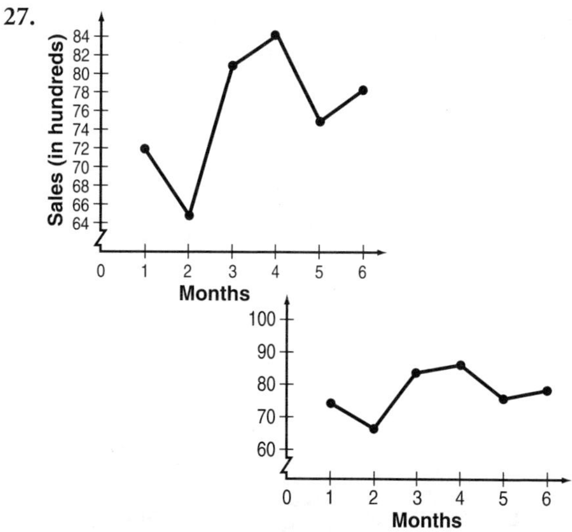

Chapter 7 Systems of Linear Equations

Lesson 7.2, pages 328–334

Try These **1.** yes **3.** yes

5.

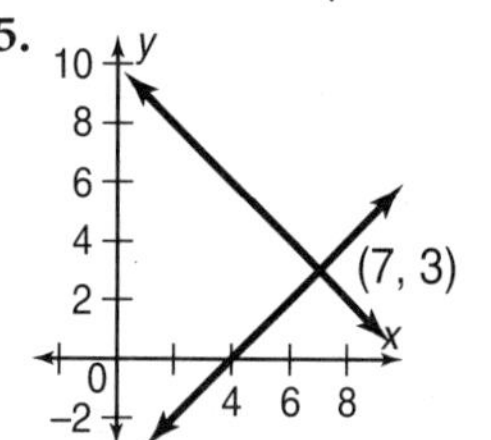

7.

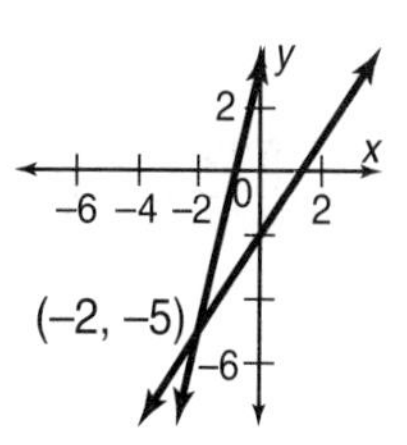

9. (3, $17)

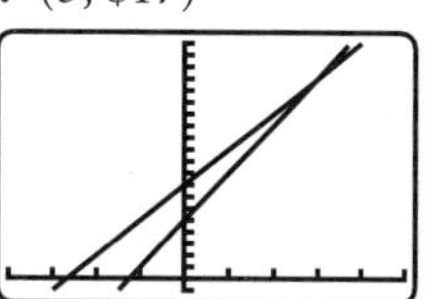

Practice **1.** yes **3.** no **5.** $3x + 2y = 28$, $2x + y = 17$ **7.** $6/yd for cotton; $5 yd for rayon

9. **11.**

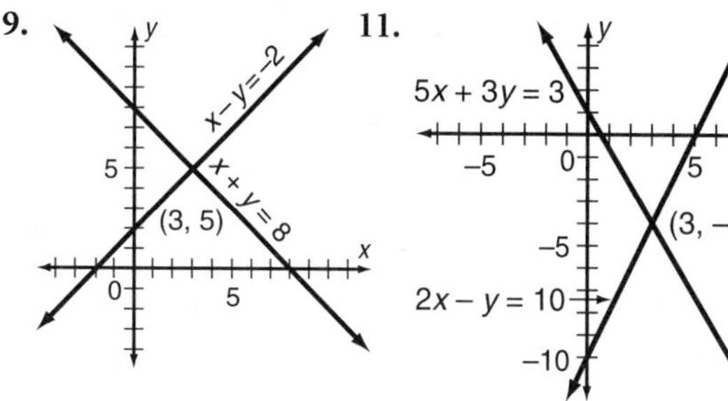

17. $y = 0.06x + 44, y = 0.09x + 35$ **21.** $y = 15x + 250, y = 20x + 200$ **23.** 10 weeks; $400

Extend **25.** (4, 3) **27.** 24 **29.** (–1, –5)

769

Think Critically **31.** no; because two distinct lines may intersect in, at most, one point; infinitely many **33.** $(0, b)$

Lesson 7.3, pages 335–341

Try These **1.** $(15, 3)$ **3.** $(3, 2)$ **5.** $\left(\frac{1}{3}, 2\right)$ **7.** $x + y = 8000, 0.06x + 0.08y = 530$

Practice **1.** $(2, -7)$ **3.** $(2, -3)$ **5.** $(0, 2)$ **7.** $(7, -1)$ **9.** $\left(-1, \frac{2}{7}\right)$ **11.** $(10, 1)$ **13.** $x + y = 90, x = 5y$ **15.** $y = 50 + 40x$, $y = 30 + 45x$ **17.** For a job lasting less than 4 h, Paula's is cheaper. For a job lasting more than 4 h, Reliable would be cheaper.

Extend **19.** $(0.5, 3)$ **23.** 35 **25.** rate of boat in still water is 3 mi/h; rate of current is 1 mi/h **27.** $(3, 2, 1)$

Think Critically **31.** $(4, 2)$ **33.** $A = 2, B = 5$

Lesson 7.4, pages 342–347

Try These **1.** Multiply equation 1 by 7 and equation 2 by 4, or multiply equation 1 by 3 and equation 2 by 5. **3.** $(8, 3)$ **5.** $(-2, 5)$ **7.** $(-6, -12)$ **9.** 3 at \$200, 13 at \$165

Practice **1.** Multiply equation 1 by 3 and equation 2 by 5, or multiply equation 1 by 7 and equation 2 by 6. **3.** $(1, -2)$ **5.** $(-1, 4)$ **7.** $(-3, -2)$ **9.** $(-1.5, 0.25)$ **11.** $(-0.5, 1)$ **13.** $(9, -7)$ **15.** 36 Mercurys, 53 Whirlwinds

Extend **19.** $(6, 10)$ **21.** $\left(\frac{58}{27}, -\frac{7}{9}\right)$ **23.** 1986 **25.** The first equation, $N = 1200 - 10t$ **27.** $N \approx 1010, t \approx 19.0$; the equilibrium point of about 1010 passengers per hour is reached when a bus completes the route in about 19 min.

Think Critically **29.** $(a + b, a - b)$ **31.** 42 **33.** $(2, 4), (-6, 0), (6, -2)$

Mixed Review **35.** $5a - 35$ **36.** $-2x + 12$ **37.** $2b + 6b^2$ **38.** $8m - 4$ **39.** 74,800 mi **40.** D **41.** $(6, 11)$

Lesson 7.5, pages 348–352

Try These **1.** $(9, 4)$ **3.** inconsistent **5.** independent **7.** Consolidated: $y = 5.6x - 35$; Co-op: $y = 5.6x - 25$

Practice **1.** inconsistent **3.** inconsistent **5.** dependent **7.** inconsistent **9.** independent

Extend **13.** 15; –25; because then it would be a dependent, consistent system **15.** –3

Think Critically **17.** The slopes are equal. The y-intercepts are unequal. **19.** A: 3,600; B: 4,100; C: 4,200

Lesson 7.6, pages 353–359

Try These **1.** –2 **3.** –22 **5.** 32 **7.** $(5, -4)$ **9.** $(2, -1)$

Practice **1.** –3 **3.** 0 **5.** –4 **7.** 2 **9.** –171 **11.** $-8k$ **15.** $(-1, 4)$ **17.** $(-1, 2)$ **19.** $\left(\frac{-28}{3}, \frac{-49}{9}\right)$ **21.** $(6, 9)$ **23.** $(4, 6)$ **25.** $(3, 7)$ **27.** 15 at \$30, 25 at \$22 **29.** 4 calories each

Extend **31.** –63 **33.** André, \$18; Franco, \$12 **35.** 0 **37.** $(6, 10)$

Think Critically

39. $\begin{vmatrix} a & b \\ c & d \end{vmatrix} = ad - bc = 4$
The value of $\begin{vmatrix} c & d \\ a & b \end{vmatrix}$ is $cb - ad$.
And $cb - ad = bc - ad$, which is the additive inverse of $ad - bc$. So $bc - ad = -(ad - bc) = -(4)$
41. $\begin{vmatrix} d & c \\ b & a \end{vmatrix} = da - bc$; since $da - bc = ad - bc$, and $ad - bc = 4, da - bc = 4$

Mixed Review **43.** 39% or 0.39 **44.** \$2800 **45–48.**

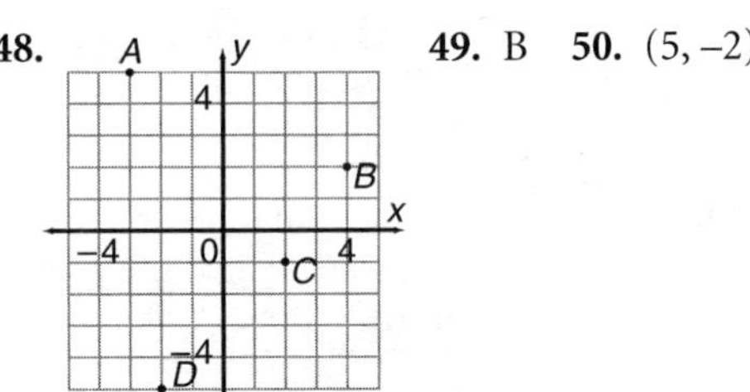

49. B **50.** $(5, -2)$

Lesson 7.7, pages 360–365

Apply the Strategy **19.** 56 dimes, 24 quarters **21.** 35, 69 **23.** $(29)(14) = 406$ **25.** \$26,500 **27.** $w = 5$ ft, $l = 14$ ft **29.** 24 \$10 bills, 34 \$5 bills, and 36 \$1 bills

Chapter Review, pages 364–365

1. c **2.** a **3.** d **4.** b **5.** yes **6.** no **7.** $(5, 7)$ **8.** $(4, 13)$

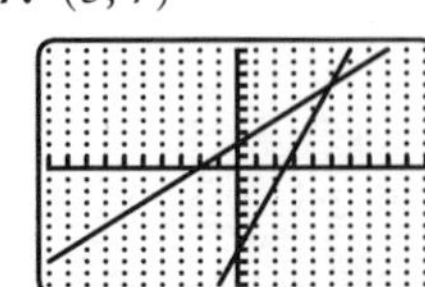

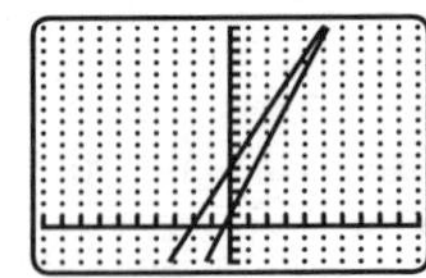

9. (1, 0) **10.** (–6, –5)

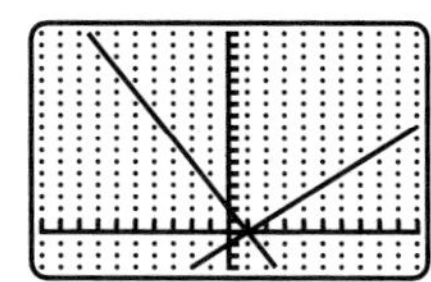

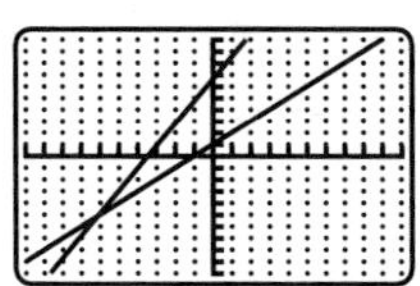

11. (1, –2) **12.** (–6, –8)

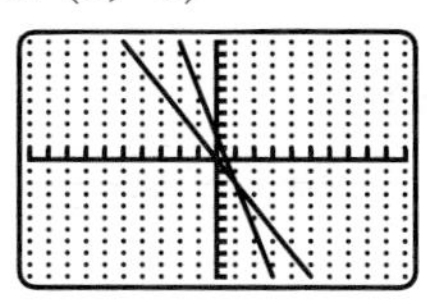

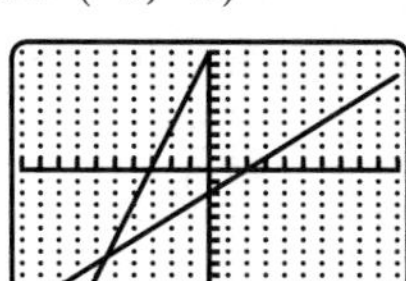

13. (2, –3) **14.** $\left(5, \frac{1}{2}\right)$ **15.** (3, –2) **16.** (2, 1)
17. 18 **18.** (3, 4.5) **19.** (8, –5) **20.** (–3, –1)
21. (–17, –14) **22.** Chen, \$53; Lisa, \$37 **23.** (5, –2)
24. inconsistent **25.** dependent **26.** (–1, –1)
27. (2, 1) **28.** (3, 4) **29.** w = 18 in., l = 72 in.
30. 16, 22

Chapter 8 Systems of Linear Inequalities

Lesson 8.1, pages 373–378

Try These **1.** no **3.** no

5.

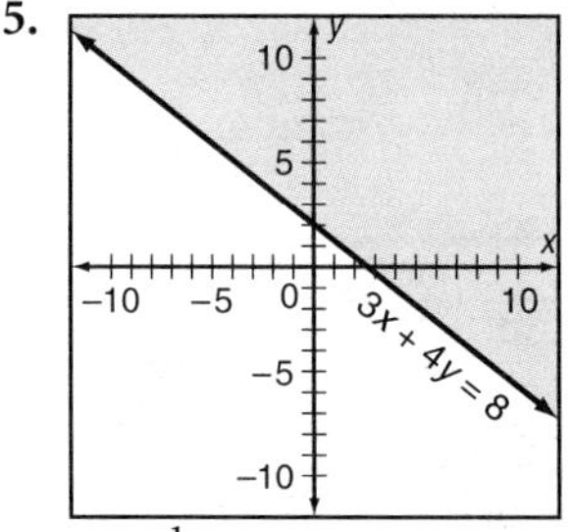

7. $y \geq \frac{1}{3}x + 3$ or $3y \geq x + 9$

Practice **1.** no **3.** yes

5.

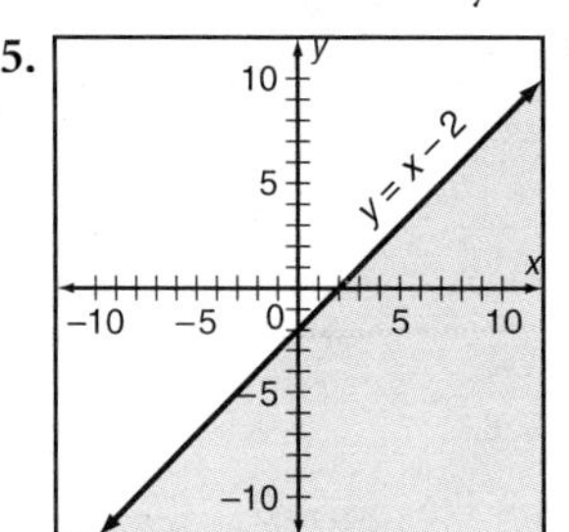

7. 3x + 5y = 20

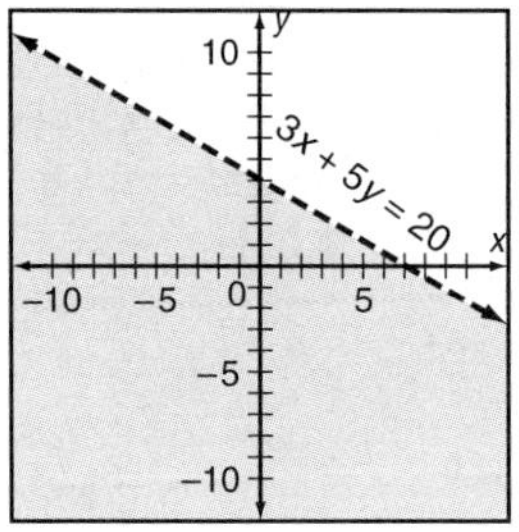

11. $y < x - 4$ **13.** $y \geq -2x + 1$

Extend **17.** not equivalent **19.** equivalent

Think Critically **25.** dashed line; half-plane above the line **27.** solid line; half-plane above the line
29. $x > 0$

Mixed Review **32.** B

33.

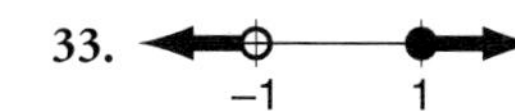

34. –2.3 6

35. (–3, 2) **36.** (1.5, 2.5)

37.

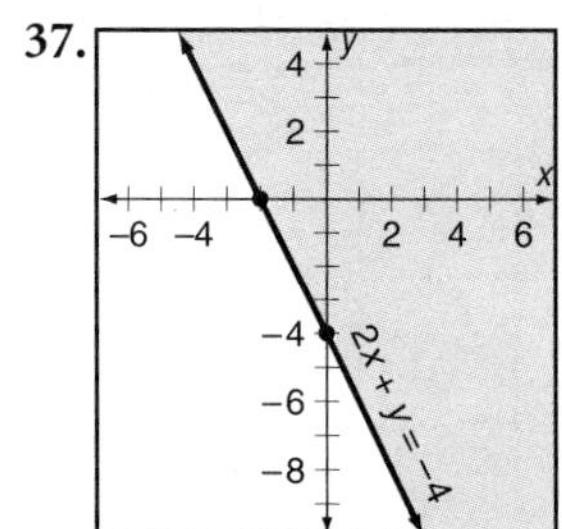

38. y = 3x – 2

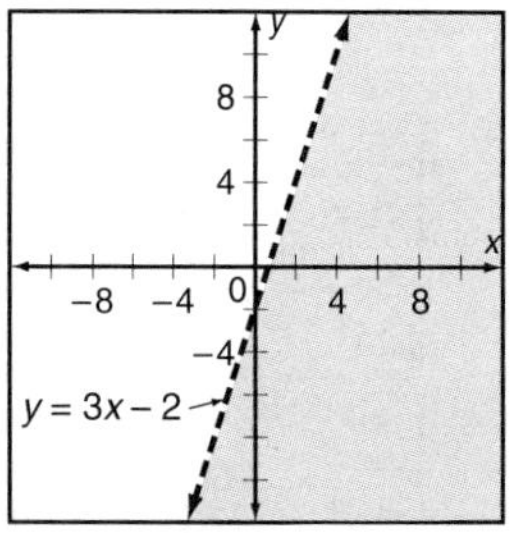

Lesson 8.2, pages 379–385

Try These

1.

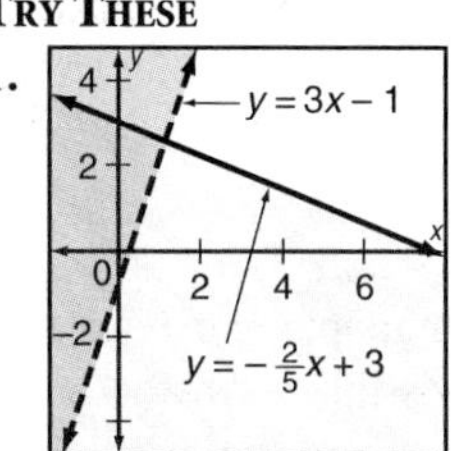

3. y = –x + 1; y = x

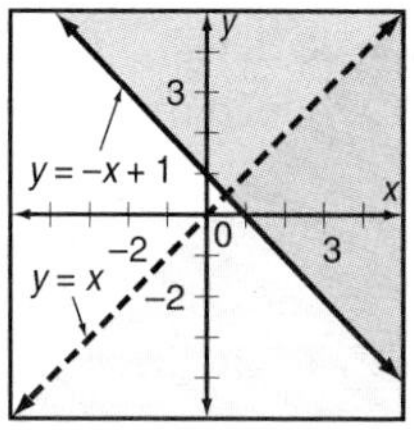

5.

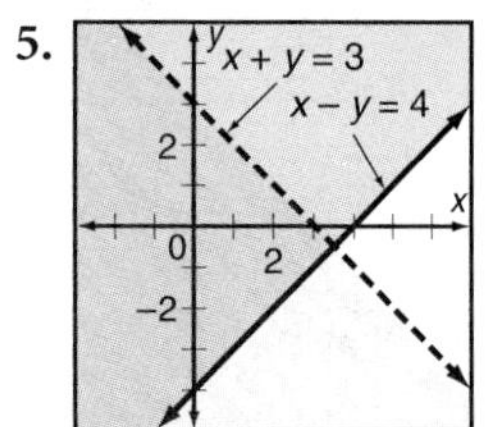

7. x + y = –1; 3x – y = 4

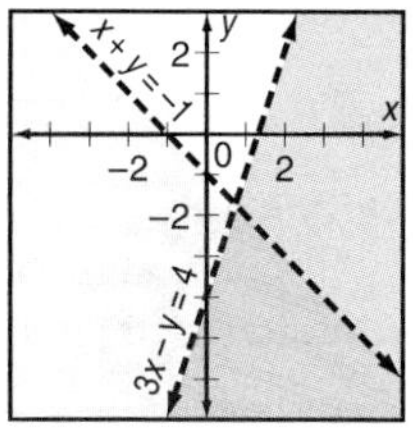

11a. no **11b.** no **11c.** yes **11d.** yes

Practice **1.** no **3.** no

5.

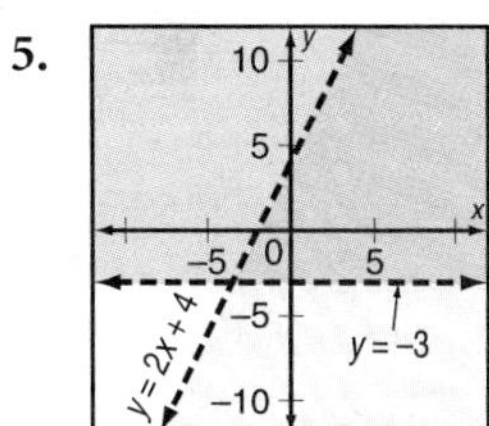

7. x – 2y = –6; x + 4y = –8

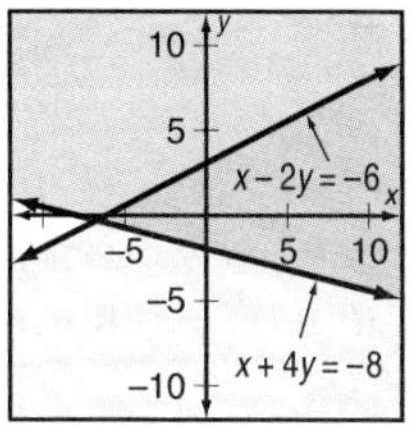

9.

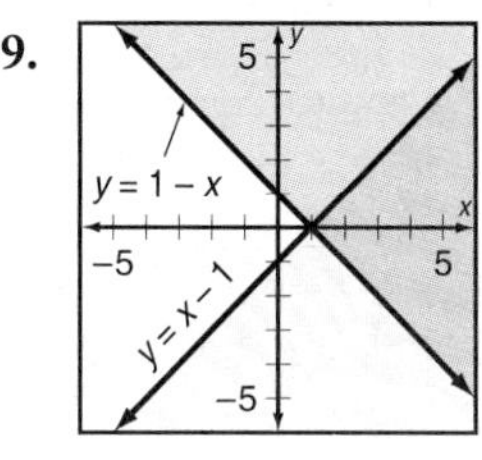

11. x + y = 9; x – y = 3

SELECTED ANSWERS

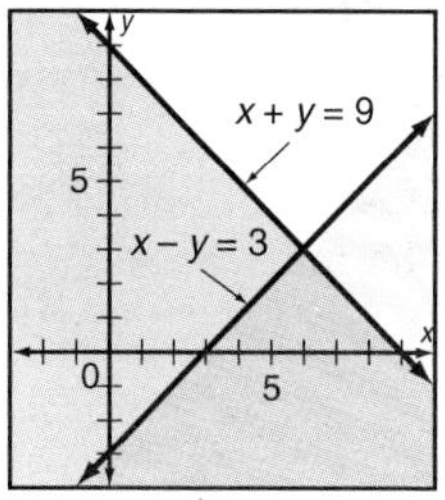

17. $\begin{cases} y < -2x + 4 \\ y > 2x - 1 \end{cases}$ **19.** $\begin{cases} y \geq x + 2 \\ y \leq \frac{3}{5}x + 3 \end{cases}$

21.b. possible combinations: 0 chairs and 50 tables, 10 chairs and 35 tables, 50 chairs and 10 tables

EXTEND **23.** $2x + y \leq 3$ **25.** both

27. $\begin{cases} x > 0 \\ y > 0 \end{cases}$ **29.** $\begin{cases} x \geq 0 \\ y < 0 \end{cases}$

31.

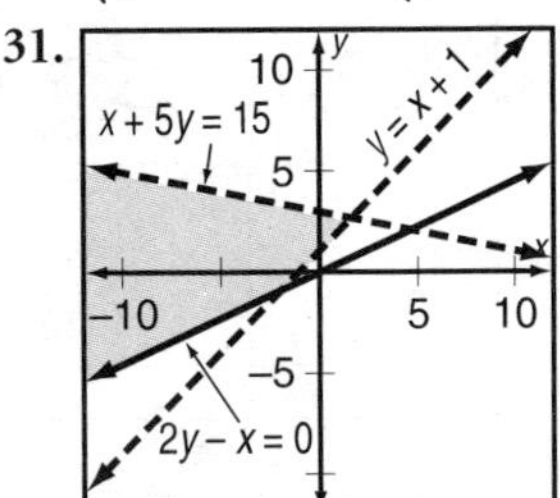

33.

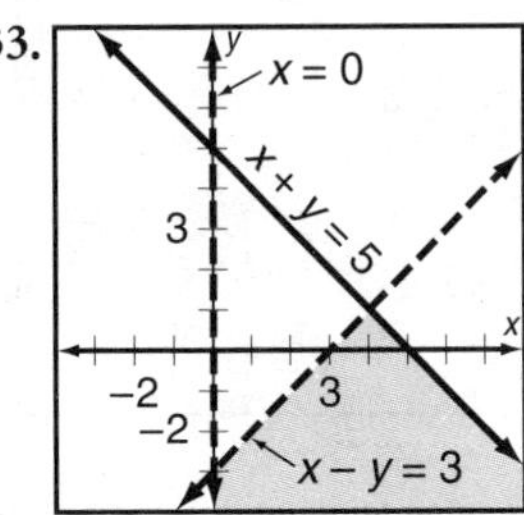

35. b. possible combinations: 5000 in mutual funds and 4000 in CD's, 6000 in mutual funds and 3000 in CD's, 7000 in mutual funds and 2500 in CD's.

THINK CRITICALLY

39. Not possible; because coordinate plane extends to infinity in all directions, it is impossible to write equations for boundary lines of a region that includes the entire plane.

Lesson 8.4, pages 388–393

TRY THESE **1.** The point is not within the region. **3.** minimum 0 at (0, 0); maximum 21 at (0, 7) **5.** minimum 2 at (0, 1); maximum 38 at (9, 1) **7.** minimum 0 at (0, 0); maximum 15 at (4, 3) and (5, 0) **9.** maximum is 16.5 at (3.5, 9.5)

PRACTICE **1.** The point lies within the region. **3.** The point lies within the region. **5.** minimum –15 at (0, 5); maximum 3 at (3, 1) **7.** minimum –15 at (–3, 3); maximum 0 at (0, 0) and (–2, –3) **9.** maximum is 12 at (0, 3) **11.** maximum is 69 at (16, 5) **14.** She should choose $C = 3x + 2y$. At the point (0, 2), this function has a minimum value of 4.

EXTEND

17. There is a minimum value but no maximum value because the graph of the constraints is unbounded above.

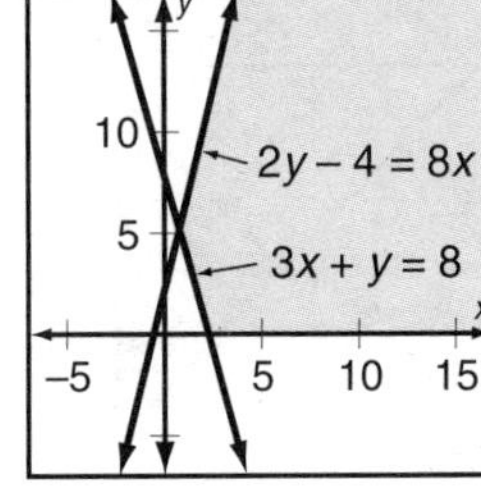

19. There is a minimum value but no maximum value, because the graph of the constraints is unbounded above.

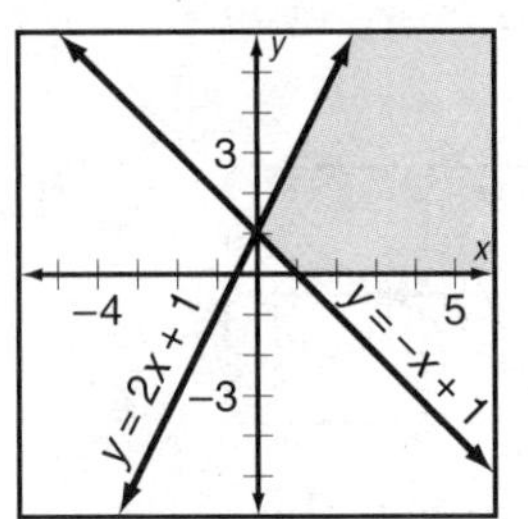

21. For any value less than *M*, the graph misses the feasible region.

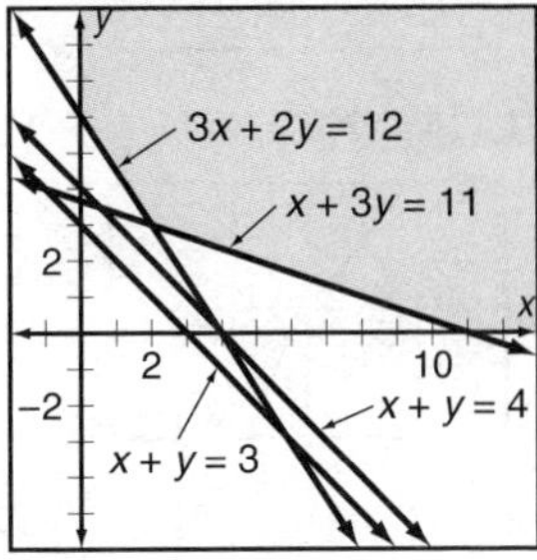

THINK CRITICALLY **23.** It represents that profit *P* is $1.00 on each bracelet and $2.00 on each necklace.

Lesson 8.5, pages 394–397

APPLY THE STRATEGY **15 a.** Let x = number of cross-country skis. Let y = number of slalom skis.

$6x + 4y \leq 96$

$x + y \leq 20$

$x \geq 0$

$y \geq 0$

15b.

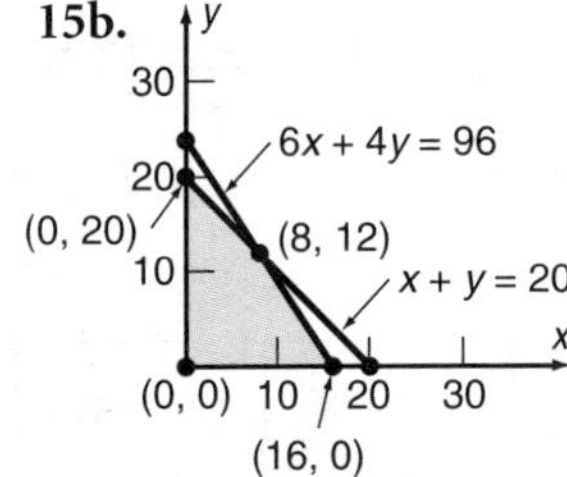

15c. $P = 45x + 30y$

vertex	$P = 45x + 30y$	Profit, *P*
(0, 0)	45(0) + 30(0)	$0
(0, 20)	45(0) + 30(20)	$600
(16, 0)	45(16) + 30(0)	$720
(8, 12)	45(8) + 30(12)	$720

15d. 16 pairs of cross-country skis and 0 pairs of slalom skis or 8 pairs of cross-country skis and 12 pairs of slalom skis; $720 **17.** 75 bicycles and 35 rowers; $P = 125(75) + 200(35) = \$16,375$

Lesson 8.6, pages 398–403

TRY THESE **1.** 104 **3.** $\frac{26}{104}$ or $\frac{1}{4}$ **5.** 360 shirts **7.** $\frac{1}{18}$

PRACTICE **1.** 26^3, which is 17,576 **3.** $90 \cdot 26^3$, which is 1,581,840 **5.** $26 \cdot 90$, which is 2340 **7.** $9 \cdot 2 \cdot 10$, which is 180 **9.** $6 \cdot 8 \cdot 5 = 240$ **11.** $\left(\frac{1}{2}\right)^5 = \frac{1}{32}$

EXTEND **13.** The game is unfair; $P(A\ wins) = \frac{27}{36}$ or $\frac{3}{4}$ of the time;

$P(B\ wins) = \frac{9}{36}$ or $\frac{1}{4}$ of the time

THINK CRITICALLY **15.** $\frac{1}{16}$ **17.** $\frac{1}{4}$; $\frac{1}{4}$

19. Exercises 16–18 include the sample space of all possible outcomes for a family with four children. The sum of all possible outcomes in a probability experiment is exactly 1.

Chapter Review, pages 404–405

1. d **2.** c **3.** b **4.** a **5.** no **6.** no **7.** yes

8. $y = x + 3$

9. $3x + 6y = 12$

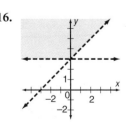

10. $3x - 2y = 6$

11. $y = x + 1$; $y = 2x - 2$

12. $y = -2x + 3$; $3y = x + 6$

13. $3x - 2y = 0$; $x - 4y = 4$

14.

15.

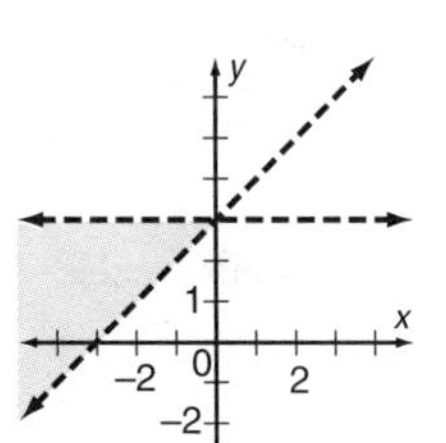

16.

17. maximum is 24 at (0, 8) **18. a.** $P = 3x + 2y$

18b. $x + y \geq 20, x + y \leq 40, y \geq x, y \leq 20$

18c. The maximum profit given the constraints is $100 earned by selling 20 apple pies and 20 blueberry pies.

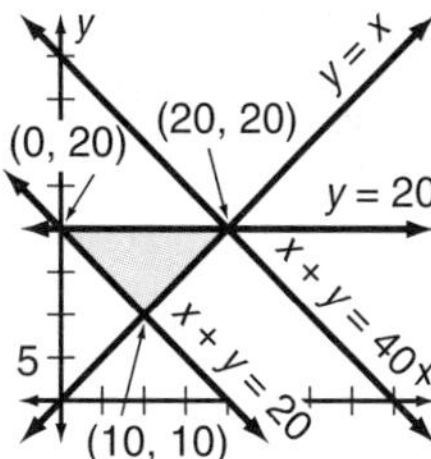

19. 216

Chapter 9 Absolute Value and the Real Number System

Lesson 9.2, pages 416–423

TRY THESE **1.** (2.5, 0); $x = 2.5$ **3.** (0, –1.5); $x = 0$ **5.** (–4, –9); $x = -4$ **7.** (–3, –1); $x = -3$ **9.** The rays that form the V in the graph of $y = 4|x|$ are farther from the x-axis than those of $y = |x|$. **11.** The rays that form the V in the graph of $y = -2|x|$ are farther from the x-axis than those of $y = |x|$. The graph opens downward, unlike the graph of $y = |x|$. **13.** d **15.** a

17.

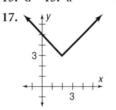

19.

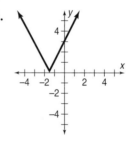

PRACTICE **1.** (0, –4); $x = 0$ **3.** (1.5, 0); $x = 1.5$ **5.** (4, –3); $x = 4$ **7.** (–1, –2); $x = -1$ **9.** The rays that form the V in the graph of $y = 3|x|$ are farther from the x-axis than those of $y = |x|$. **11.** The rays that form the V in the graph of $y = -\frac{1}{5}|x|$ are closer to the x-axis than those of $y = |x|$. The graph opens downward, unlike the graph of $y = |x|$. **13.** b **15.** c **17.** d **19.** a

21.

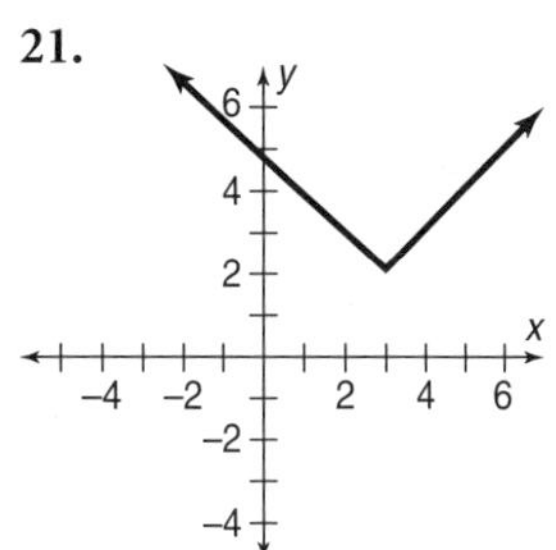

23.

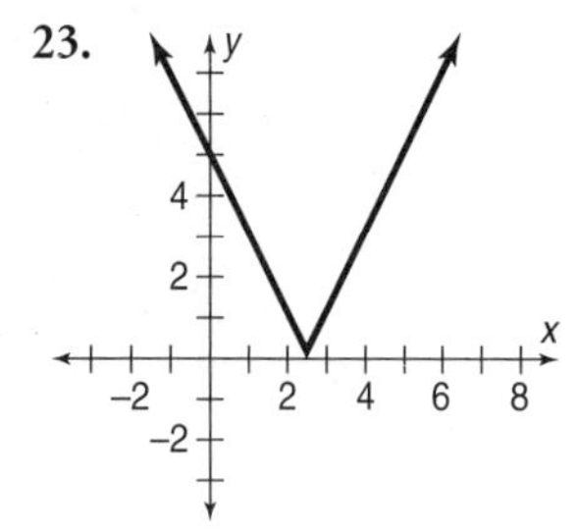

SELECTED ANSWERS

31. $y = -|x - 3| + 3$ **33.** A: $y = |x| - 3$, B: $y = 2|x| - 3$, C: $y = 3|x| - 3$

EXTEND **35.** (–1, 1); (1, 1) **37.** x-axis, y-axis **39.** x-axis, y-axis, $y = x$, $y = -x$ **41.** x-axis, y-axis **43.** any line passing through the center of the circle

45.

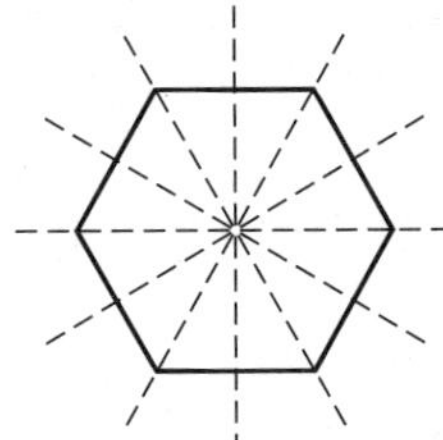

THINK CRITICALLY **47.** Quadrant IV is reflected into Quadrant I; x-axis **49.** no

Lesson 9.3, pages 424–429

TRY THESE **1.** $2x - 3 = 12$ or $2x - 3 = -12$ **3.** $2x + 5 = 17$ or $2x + 5 = -17$ **5.** –6, 12 **7.** 6, 10 **9.** –1, 10 **11.** –1, 7 **13.** $-1, \frac{3}{2}$ **15.** no solution **17.** –5, –1 **19.** $|x - 30| = 1.5$

PRACTICE **1.** $4x = 12$ or $4x = -12$ **3.** $3x + 4 = 11$ or $3x + 4 = -11$ **5.** $5x - 1.5 = 8.5$ or $5x - 1.5 = -8.5$ **7.** –8, 8 **9.** no solution **11.** 3, 13 **13.** –1, 6 **15.** $-\frac{4}{3}, \frac{2}{3}$ **17.** –13, 5 **19.** –6, 0 **21.** $-\frac{5}{2}, \frac{7}{2}$ **23.** –5, –1 **25.** –2, 12 **27.** $-\frac{8}{3}, \frac{16}{3}$ **29.** $|x - 9| = 3$; max 12 mo; min 6 mo

EXTEND **31.** $-\frac{5}{4}, \frac{5}{6}; -\frac{5}{4}; \frac{5}{6}$ **33.** $\frac{3}{5}$ **35.** –2, 6 **37.** 3, 14 **39.** $|x - 3.5| = 0.5$; max average 4.0, min average 3.0

THINK CRITICALLY **43.** y_1 would be V-shaped and y_2 would be a line that intersects y_1 in exactly one point. **45.** $\frac{d - e}{c}, \frac{d + e}{c}$ **47.** $\frac{4 - c}{3}, -c - 4$

Lesson 9.4, pages 430–436

TRY THESE **1.** $-6 < x + 3$ and $x + 3 < 6$ **3.** $2x - 4 \leq -6$ or $2x - 4 \geq 6$ **5.** $-8 < z < 2$ **7.** $t \leq 3$ or $t \geq 7$ **9.** c **11.** d **13.** $q \leq 3$ or $q \geq 4$ **15.** $-4 < t < \frac{2}{3}$ **17.** all reals **19.** $|x - 85| \leq 3$

PRACTICE **1.** $-5 < x + 1$ and $x + 1 < 5$ **3.** $x - 4 < -6$ or $x - 4 > 6$ **5.** $-6 \leq 2x - 2$ and $2x - 2 \leq 6$ **7.** $2x + 5 \leq -3$ or $2x + 5 > 3$ **9.** $-4 < z < 2$ **11.** $x < 3$ or $x > 7$ 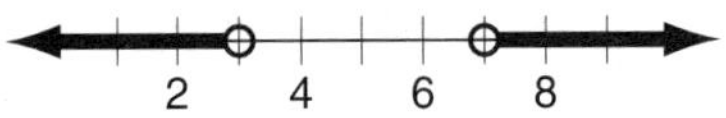 **13.** $-3 \leq x \leq 4$ 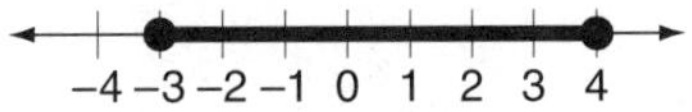 **15.** $w \leq -6$ or $w \geq 1$ 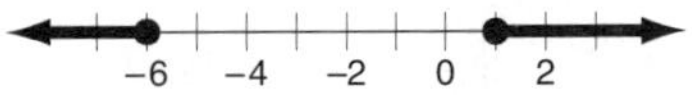 **17.** b **19.** c **21.** $q \leq -1$ or $q \geq 5$ **23.** $-5 < t < \frac{5}{3}$ **25.** $z < -2$ or $z > 6$  **27.** $-7 \leq q \leq 2$ 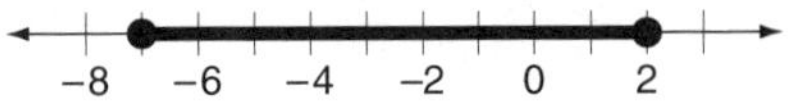 **29.** (all reals except $x = 0$) **31.** no solution **33.** (all x except $x = 2$) **35.** all reals **37.** $-3 < x < 9$ **39.** $x = -2$ **41.** $-\frac{3}{2} \leq z \leq \frac{1}{2}$ **43.** $2 \leq t \leq 8$ **45.** $\frac{1}{2} < x < \frac{7}{2}$ **47.** $|x - 21| \leq 10$

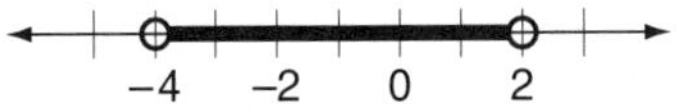

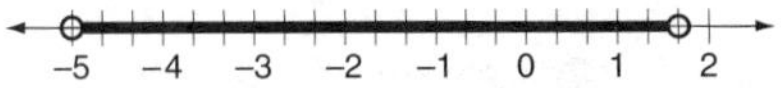

EXTEND **51.** $x > \frac{1}{3}$ **53.** $x \leq \frac{5}{4}$ **55.** $-7 < x \leq 11$ **57.** $x \leq 2$ or $x \geq 7$ **59.** $|x - 1.05| \leq 0.35$

THINK CRITICALLY **61.** $|x| > 0$ **63.** Since < includes all numbers that ≥ does not, any real number that does not satisfy $|x| < c$ must satisfy $|x| \geq c$.

MIXED REVIEW **65.** C **66.** $y = \frac{3}{4}x - \frac{5}{2}$ **67.** $y = \frac{2}{5}x + \frac{16}{5}$ **68.** (6, 3) **69.** (2, 4) **70.** $x < -10.5$ or $x > 4.5$ **71.** $-\frac{14}{3} < x < \frac{28}{3}$

Lesson 9.5, pages 437–444

TRY THESE **1.** [number line] **3.** irrationals, reals **5.** wholes, integers, rationals, reals **7.** $\frac{-3}{1}$ **9.** $\frac{38}{7}$ **11.** $\frac{1}{100}$ **13.** $\frac{35}{99}$ **15.** $\frac{41}{333}$ **17.** 0.45 **19.** –1.4 **21.** $0.\overline{81}$ **23.** not a real number **25.** 52 **27.** 9.06 **29.** –6.86 **31.** 0.94 **33.** $\frac{263}{100}$, 162

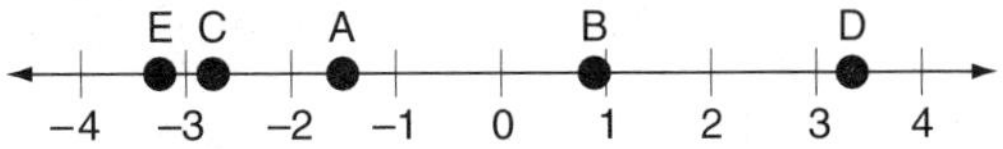

PRACTICE **1.** [number line] **3.** wholes, integers, rationals, reals **5.** rationals, reals **7.** rationals, reals **9.** irrationals, reals **11.** rationals, reals **13.** $\frac{522}{100}$ **15.** $\frac{78}{1000}$ **17.** $\frac{4}{33}$ **19.** $\frac{167}{999}$ **21.** $\frac{157}{999}$ **23.** 1.89 **25.** 52 **27.** $\frac{30}{23}$ **29.** –0.8 **31.** 1.7

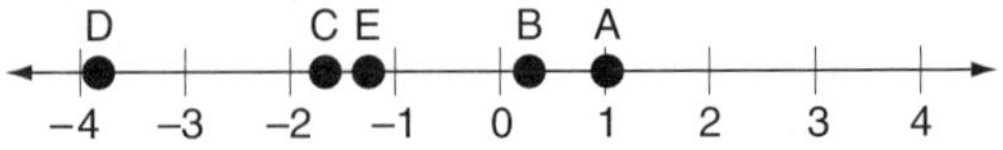

33. 12.29 **35.** –12.88 **37.** 0.75 **39.** 0.3 **41.** –47.25 **43.** about 0.45 s

Extend **45.** 3.00 **47.** –0.30 **49.** 4.22 **51.** 6.23 cm **53.** 81, 100, 121

Think Critically **55.** $\sqrt{\frac{1}{7}}$ **57.** $\sqrt[3]{0.064}$

59. false; answers will vary **61.** A rational number k is a perfect square if there is a rational number x such that $x^2 = k$. **63.** $x \geq -3$

Lesson 9.6, pages 445–451

Try These **1.** –3, –1, 0, 2, $\sqrt{5}$, 4

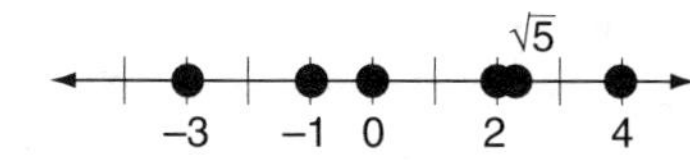

3. $\frac{3}{4}$, 1.2, $\frac{5}{4}$, $\frac{3}{2}$, 1.8

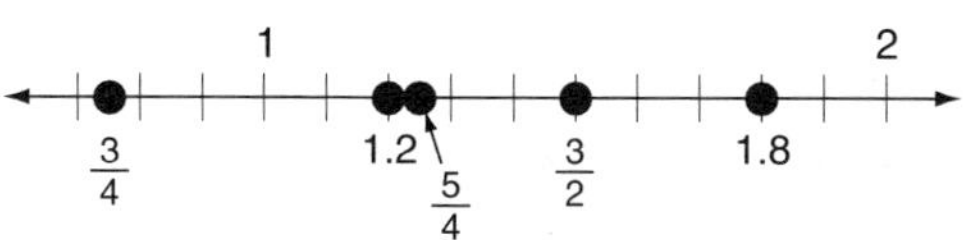

7. symmetric **9.** reflexive **11.** reflexive property; substitution property **13.** carpool

Practice **1.** –4, $-\sqrt{6}$, –2, 0, 3, 5

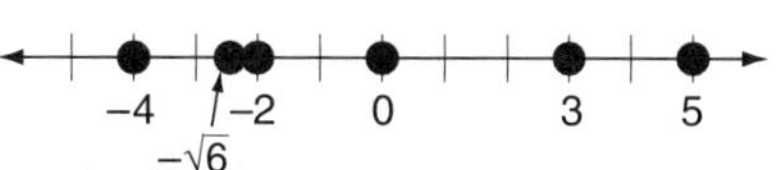

3. $\frac{6}{5}$, 1.3, $\frac{8}{5}$, 1.8, $\frac{19}{10}$ **5.** $\frac{4}{7}$, $\frac{5}{8}$, $\frac{6}{9}$ **7.** $1\frac{6}{7}$, 2.1, $\frac{15}{7}$

9. –0.1511, –0.151, –0.1501 **15.** reflexive **17.** symmetric **19.** reflexive property; substitution property **21.** Flora **23.** Flora, Vesta, Iris, Metis, Hebe, Astraea, Juno, Ceres, Pallas, Hygeia

Extend **27.** No; a number is not less than itself; 3 < 3 **29.** No; if 2 < 3 and 2 + 4 < 7, then 3 + 4 < 7 is a false statement. **31.** false **33.** true

Think Critically **35.** For all real numbers a and b, one and only one of the following properties is true: $a = b$; $a \neq b$. **37.** Yes; if $a \neq b$, then $b \neq a$. **39.** No; if $3 \neq 4$ and $3 + 5 \neq 9$, then $4 + 5 \neq 9$ is a false statement.

Mixed Review **41.** 85.5 **42.** 92 **43.** 88.5 **44.** 29 **45.** B **46.** $\frac{17}{21}$, $\frac{13}{16}$, $\frac{17}{19}$ **47.** –0.1611, –0.161, 0.1601

Lesson 9.7, pages 452–455

Apply the Strategy **13. a.** The slope of the transportation workers' graph would be less because the average yearly increase is less. The graph for Exercises 1 and 8 supports the prediction. **b.** \$15.45; $y = 15.45x + 133$ **c.** \$596.50

Chapter Review, pages 456–457

1. e **2.** c **3.** a **4.** d **5.** b

6.

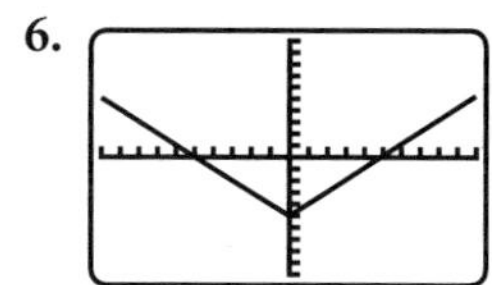

7.

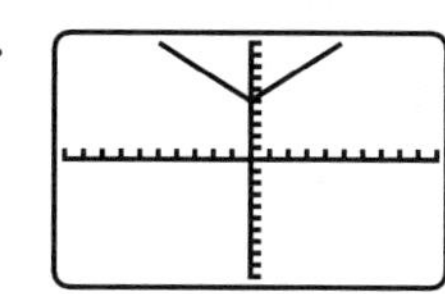

8.

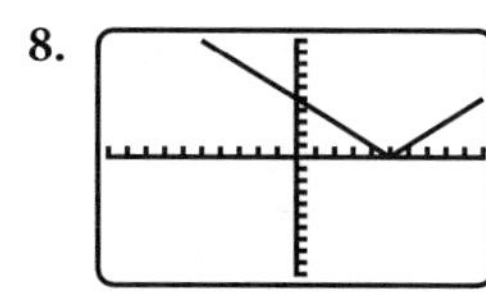

9.

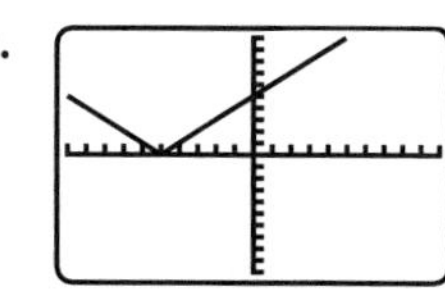

10.

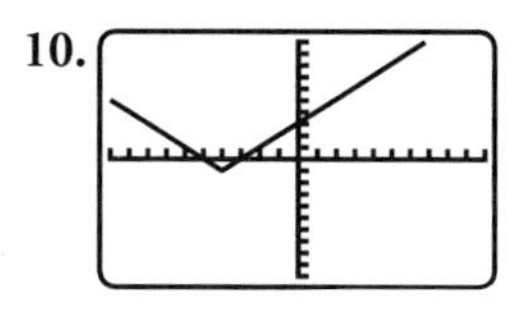

(–4, –1); $x = -4$

11.

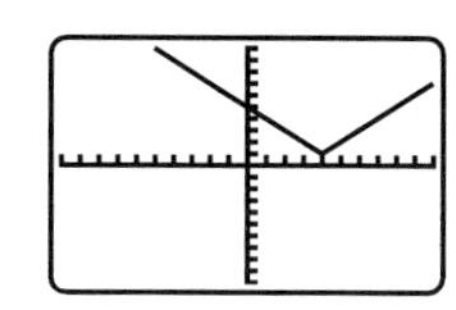

(4, 1); $x = 4$

12.

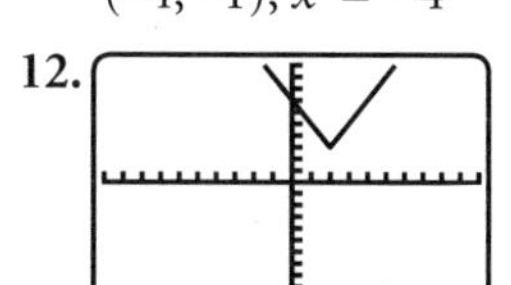

(2, 3); $x = 2$

13.

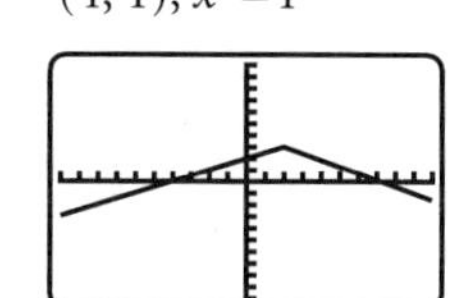

(2, 3); $x = 2$

14. –6, 6 **15.** –3, 13 **16.** –12, 6 **17.** no solution

18. $-5 < x < 9$

–7 –5 –3 –1 1 3 5 7 9 11

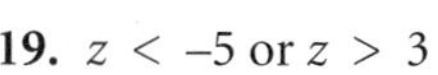

19. $z < -5$ or $z > 3$

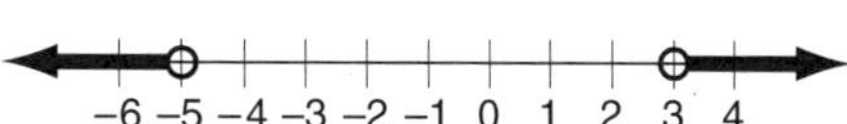

20. $-6 \leq w \leq 2$

–7 –6 –5 –4 –3 –2 –1 0 1 2 3

21. all reals; graph is the number line **22.** $|x - 97| \leq 3$ **23.** $0.1\overline{8}$ **24.** $0.\overline{5}$ **25.** 0.55 **26.** 17 **27.** $0.2\overline{7}$ **28.** –0.7 **29.** not a real number

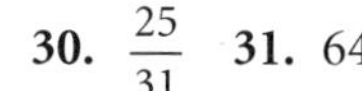

30. $\frac{25}{31}$ **31.** 64

32.

$-\sqrt{5}$ –2 $-\sqrt{2}$ $-\frac{2}{3}$ $-\sqrt{\frac{1}{9}}$ $\frac{3}{8}$

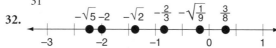

–3 –2 –1 0 1

33.

Statement	Reason
1. $a = b$	given
2. $a - c = a - c$	reflexive property
3. $a - c = b - c$	substitution property

34. 2800 million metric tons

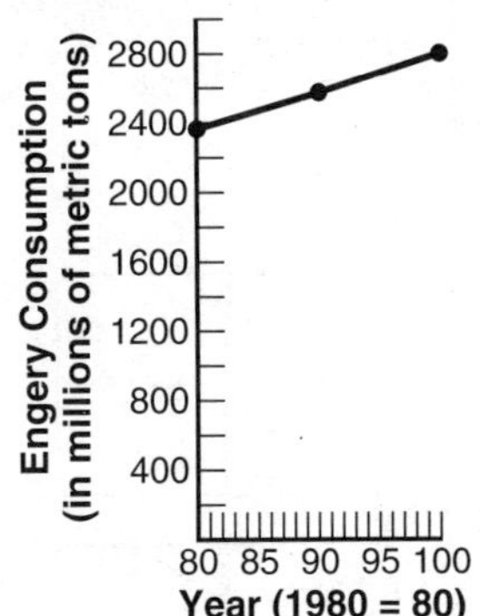

Chapter 10 Graphs of Quadratic Functions

Lesson 10.2, pages 468–476

Try These **1.** downward **3.** upward **5.** $(0, 0), x = 0$ **7.** $(0, 15), x = 0$ **9.** $\left(-\frac{5}{6}, -\frac{83}{12}\right), x = -\frac{5}{6}$ **11.** 6 units up **13.** wider **15.** 8 units left **17.** a

19.

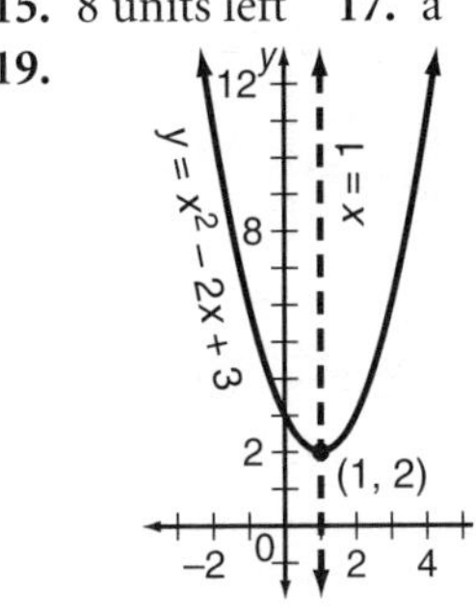

21.

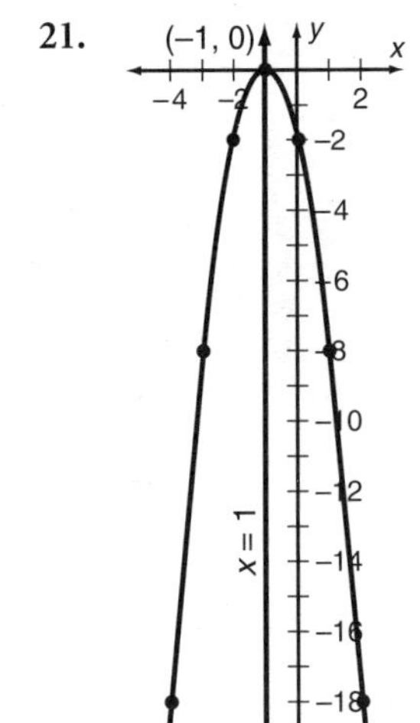

Practice **1.** upward **3.** upward **5.** $(0, 0), x = 0$ **7.** $(0, 14), x = 0$ **9.** $(-1, -10), x = -1$ **11.** $(-4, 22), x = -4$ **13.** 10 units down **15.** narrower **17.** 25 units left **19.** c **21.** *a* **23.** a

25.

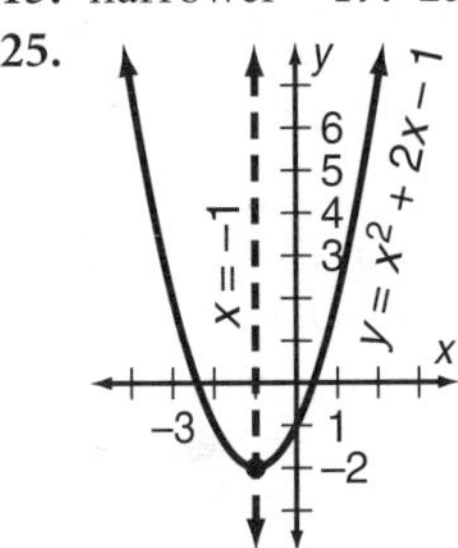

27.

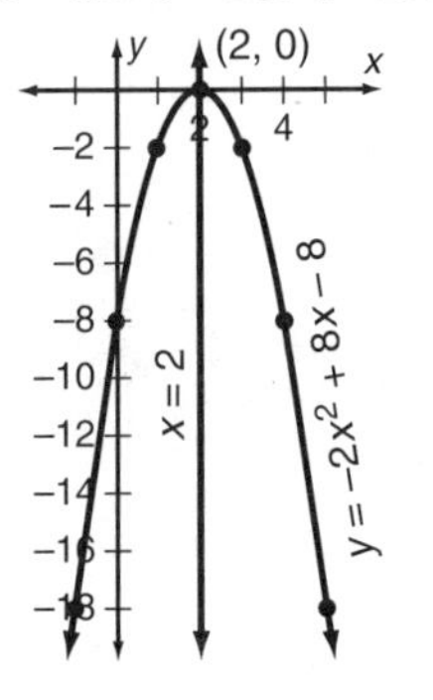

29. (312.50, 103.91); the elevation of the high point will be 3.9 ft greater than point *A* and 312.5 ft from a point directly above point *A*.

Extend **31.** $y = 3x^2 - 2x + 4$ **33.** $y = 2x^2 - x - 2$ **35.** $h = -16t^2 + 25t + 6$ **37.** about 1,093 million, or about 1.093 billion **39.** (–2.29, 0.25); (2.29, 0.25)

Think Critically **41.** $(0, c)$ **43.** c moves each graph up c units if c is positive and down c units if c is negative

Mixed Review **46.** $x = -13.5$ **47.** $x = -\frac{22}{5}$ **48.** C **49.** It is shifted up 3 units and to the right by 1 unit. The rays that form the V are closer to the *y*-axis. **50.** It is shifted down 1 unit and to the left by 3 units. The rays that form the V are farther away from the *y*-axis. **51.** $(2, -25); x = 2$ **52.** $(\frac{3}{2}, -13); x = \frac{3}{2}$

Lesson 10.3, pages 477–482

Try These **1.** $0 = 3x^2 - 4x + 8$ **3.** $0 = \frac{1}{2}x^2 - 3x$ **5.** equivalent **7.** –5, 3 **9.** 5 **11.** $0 = -x^2 + 6x - 7$; 1.59, 4.41 **13.** –3, 5 **15.** –1.68, 2.68 **17.** 0 **19.** 1.29 and 43.83

Practice **1.** $0 = 2x^2 - 5x + 3$ **3.** $0 = \frac{1}{4}x^2 - 5x$ **5.** equivalent **7.** –4, 6 **9.** –5, 2 **11.** 6 **13.** 0.31, 3.19 **15.** –0.78, 1.28 **17.** $0 = x^2 + 8x - 65$; 5, –13 **19.** $0 = -x^2 + 2x + 4$; –1.24, 3.24 **21.** $0 = 4x^2 - 2x - 4$; –0.78, 1.28 **23.** –2.27, 5.27 **25.** 1 **27.** 2 **29.** 2 **31.** April 1994

Extend **35.** 16 or 44 **37.** 60

Mixed Review **43.** C **44.** infinitely many **45.** one **46.** $\frac{-8}{1}$ **47.** $\frac{533}{100}$ **48.** $\frac{-19}{2}$ **49.** $\frac{19}{200}$ **50.** $0 = x^2 + 5x + 6$; –2, –3 **51.** $0 = -x^2 + 3x + 3$; –0.79, 3.79

Lesson 10.4, pages 483–489

Try These **1.** –9, 9 **3.** $\pm 4\sqrt{3}$ **5.** $\pm 2\sqrt{10}$ **7.** –4, 6 **9.** 8, –10 **11.** $-1, -\frac{1}{3}$ **13.** no real number solution **15.** ±2.29 **17.** ±2.58 **19.** 0.45, 3.55 **21.** –1.72, 0.72

Practice **1.** –7, 7 **3.** $\pm\frac{5}{9}$ **5.** $\pm\frac{19}{22}$ **7.** no real number solution **9.** $\pm 4\sqrt{5}$ **11.** $\pm 7\sqrt{2}$ **13.** –11, 19 **15.** $\pm 7\sqrt{10}$ **17.** –2, –10

19. $-4.5, \frac{11}{6}$ 21. $-1.2, 0.6$ 23. ± 2.65 25. ± 2.41
27. $\pm\sqrt{8.54}$ 29. 1.95,10.05 31. $-0.75, 2.35$

Extend 35. $x < -12$ or $x > 12$ 37. $x < -6$ or $x > 6$ 39. $0 < x < 4$ 41. 2.82 m 43. 7.64 m

Think Critically 45. 4 47. $A = P\left(1 + \frac{r}{100}\right)^4$
49. less; in the simple interest account, you would have \$929.60; in the compounded account, you would have \$933.12

Mixed Review 51. D 52. multiplicative inverse
53. multiplication property of zero 54. $(5, 1); x = 5$
55. $(-4, -2); x = -4$ 56. $-5.45, -0.55$
57. 2.31, 7.69

Lesson 10.5, pages 490–497

Try These 1. -56 3. 0 5. 0 7. 1 9. 0
11. $-1, 8$ 13. $-5, 2$ 15. $-3.12, 1.12$
17. $0.88, -0.68$ 19. 36 21. ± 8

Practice 1. -87 3. 0 5. 2 7. 1 9. 0
11. $-1, 7$ 13. 5, 6 15. $-3, 10$ 17. $-7, 3$
19. \$37.00 21. $-\frac{1}{2}, \frac{5}{7}$ 23. $-5.37, 0.37$
25. $-1.65, 3.65$ 27. $-2.87, -0.46$ 29. 49 31. ± 40

Extend 35. $x^2 - 4x - 21 = 0$
37. $2x^2 - 13x - 7 = 0$ 39. $x^2 - c^2 = 0$
41. $x^2 + 37x - 650 = 0$; 13, -50

Think Critically 43. $k < 9$ 45. $\frac{2a + 1 \pm \sqrt{21}}{2}$
47. The solutions are all rational numbers.

Mixed Review 49. C 50. function 51. not a function 52. $4 - 3x = 21$ or $4 - 3x = -21$
53. $2x - \frac{1}{2} = \frac{1}{4}$ or $2x - \frac{1}{2} = -\frac{1}{4}$ 54. $\frac{7}{2}$, 15
55. $-\frac{1}{2}, \frac{1}{3}$

Lesson 10.6, pages 498–501

Apply the Strategy 13a. $l = 120 - 2w$
13b. $A(w) = w(120 - 2w)$ or $120w - 2w^2$
13c. $l = 60$ ft, $w = 30$ ft, $A = 1800$ ft^2
13d. To make a square, divide the total amount of fencing by 3. Each side of fencing must be 40 ft; for a 40-ft square $A = 1600$ ft^2

Lesson 10.7, pages 502–507

Try These
1. quadratic 3. neither

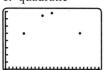

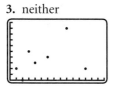

Practice 3. 74.121; 179.721
5. $y = 0.783x + 128.857$

Extend 9. $a = \frac{13}{640}$, $b = \frac{53}{80}$, $c = 179$;
11. 291.875, 448.375; the equation does not seem to be a good fit at higher temperatures

Think Critically 13. false

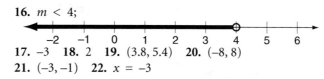

Mixed Review 15. D
16. $m < 4$;
17. -3 18. 2 19. (3.8, 5.4) 20. $(-8, 8)$
21. $(-3, -1)$ 22. $x = -3$

Chapter Review, pages 508–509

1. b 2. d 3. c 4. a 5. c 6. a 7. b
8. $(0, 5); x = 0$ 9. $(1, 9); x = 1$
10. $(-3, -10); x = -3$ 11. 1, 2 12. $-4, 5$
13. $1.32, -5.32$ 14. ± 7 15. $\pm 4\sqrt{2}$ 16. $\pm 4\sqrt{3}$
17. $-2, -5$ 18. 1.5 19. $2.79, -1.79$ 20. two
21. zero 22. two 23. 3 yards by 3 yards
24. 10%

Chapter 11 Polynomials and Exponents

Lesson 11.2, pages 521–526

Try These 1. 10 3. 1 5. $-6a^4$ 7. $18c^{11}d^3$
9. 729 11. z^{28} 13. $-27b^3$ 15. $-64m^6$

Practice 1. 2 3. 8 5. 1 7. 6 9. a^7
11. $-10x^5$ 13. $-20g^{10}$ 15. $18a^3b^6$

Extend 35. $-36x^9y^5$ 37. $-8p^9q^{19}$ 39. $W = I^2R$

Think Critically 41. 3 43. 5 45. $q = p + 1$

Lesson 11.3, pages 527–531

Try These 1. $3x^2$ 3. $3a^8b^2$ 5. 1 7. $\frac{1}{16}$ 9. $\frac{1}{3g^2h^2}$
11. $2q$ 13. $\frac{64}{125}$ 15. $\frac{32x^{20}}{y^{15}}$ 17. $4x^2 \div -2x = -2x$

Practice 1. $8a$ 3. $-3ab^3$ 5. $6y$ 7. $\frac{31}{7y^4}$ 9. 79
11. $\frac{3}{4}$ 13. $\frac{13x^4}{y^2}$ 15. $\frac{-3s}{t}$ 17. $\frac{16}{81}$ 19. $\frac{4c^8}{25d^2}$ 21. x

Extend 23. $\frac{64a^{13}b^5}{9}$ 25. $\frac{-gh}{2}$ 27. $\frac{25w^6x^4}{4}$
31. 7,467,802

Think Critically 33. 3 35. 2 37. If p and q are positive and $p - q$ is negative, then p must be less than q.

Mixed Review **38.** –6 **39.** 4 **40.** –4

41.

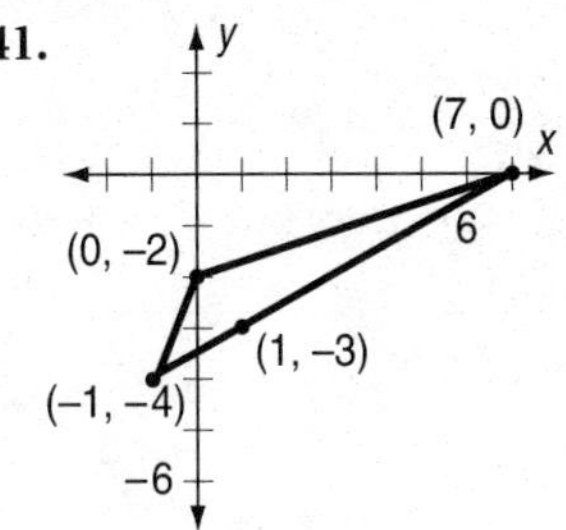

42. Connecting the points (–1, –4), (1, –3), and (7, 0) appears to result in a line that forms the side of a triangle. To justify the conclusion that all the points are in a line, you must use the point slope form and points (–1, –4) and (7, 0) to find the equation of the lines connecting them and then substitute the values (1, –3) in that equation to see whether they are a solution of the equation. **43.** $x > -3$ **44.** $x \le 7$ **45.** $x < -\frac{1}{2}$ **46.** $x < 1$ **47.** C **48.** $2b^2$ **49.** $\frac{-5}{x^2y}$ **50.** $\frac{64a^6}{27b^9}$ **51.** 81

Lesson 11.4, pages 532–537

Try These **1.** 3.25×10^9 **3.** 7.2×10^7 **5.** 3.15×10^{-3} **7.** 5.4×10^{-6} **9.** 7.35×10^9 **11.** 8×10^7 **13.** 5.776×10^9 **15.** 6.72×10^7

Practice **1.** 512,000,000 **3.** 0.000012 **5.** 3.14×10^5 **7.** 2.3×10^7 **9.** 4.15×10^{-4} **11.** 8×10^{-6} **13.** 3.12×10^{14} **15.** 3×10^3

Extend **27.** 1×10^{36} **29.** 3×10^5 **31.** 4×10^{17} **33.** $(3.7 \times 10^{-1})\ \frac{\text{m/s}}{°\text{C}}$

Think Critically **35.** 4 **37.** 53 **39.** $ab > 10$

Lesson 11.6, pages 541–547

Try These **1.** 6 **3.** 3 **5.** $-2x^4y + 3x^2y^2 + 6xy^3 + 9$ **7.** $2x^2 + 3x - 5$ **9.** $9x^2y + xy + 8y$ **11.** $-8a^2 - 2a + 7$ **13.** $-a - 2b - c$ **15.** $5b^2 + 9b - 5$ **17.** $9p^2 + 5p - 4q - 6q^2$

Practice **1.** 2 **3.** 4 **5.** 7 **7.** $12a - 2c$ **9.** $-3p + 6q + 9$ **11.** $-4a + b - 6c$ **13.** $6y^4 + 8y^2 - 10$ **15.** $5x + 10y - 24$ **17.** $4a + 3b + 4c$ **19.** $5d^3 - 9d^2 + 4d$ **21.** $2x^2 + 8xy - 2y^2$ **23.** $32x^2$

Extend **25.** $5x$ **27.** 1.72 **29.** $4g^2 - 4g - 3$ **31.** W_{st} and W_e **33.** 120 ft

Think Critically **35.** $-7x$ **37.** It is true; $(a - b) + (b - a) = 0$; therefore $b - a$ is the opposite of $a - b$.

Mixed Review **38.** 11 **39.** 17 **40.** 6.86 **41.** 10.15 **42.** $11,250 **43.** $19,500 **44.** 3,400,000 **45.** 102,000,000 **46.** 0.00000048 **47.** 0.0000303

Lesson 11.8, pages 551–557

Try These **1.** $3x^2 + 5x$ **3.** $-4y - 8$ **5.** $x^2 + 15x + 56$ **7.** $2x^2 - 7x - 4$ **9.** $a^3 - 5a^2 + 8a - 4$ **11.** $a^2 + 4a + 4$ **13.** $x^2 - 25$ **15.** $(x + 2)(2x + 1) = 2x^2 + 5x + 2$

Practice **1.** $x^2 - 5x$ **3.** $-10z^2 - 15z$ **5.** $-6m^2 + 12m$ **7.** $2x^3y - 2xy^3$ **9.** $x^2 + 7x + 10$ **11.** $a^2 - 10a + 24$ **13.** $c^2 - 2c - 15$ **15.** $g^4 + 5g^2 - 14$

Extend **35.** $q^3 - 6q^2 + 12q - 8$ **37.** $g^3 + g^2 - 5g + 3$ **39.** 4.5 m **41.** 6 ft **43.** 21,005,820

Think Critically **45.** $n = 7$ **47.** Since $(a + b)^2 = a^2 + 2ab + b^2$, it is $2ab$ greater than $a^2 + b^2$.

Lesson 11.9, pages 558–563

Apply the Strategy **13.** same direction **15.** Their distances are equal; $4(t + 0.5) = 6t$; $t = 1$ h; Ivan hikes for 1 h and covers 6 km; Darrell hikes for 1.5 h and also covers 6 km. **17.** 4:06 P.M. **19.** 9.75 or $9\frac{3}{4}$ mi

Chapter Review, pages 562–567

1. b **2.** c **3.** a **4.** $-3y^2$ **5.** $3x$ **6.** $6xy$ **7.** x **8.** z^6 **9.** $-6a^7$ **10.** $-12x^3y^7$ **11.** $6a^4b^4c^3$ **12.** $3x^2$ **13.** $-6a^3$ **14.** $\frac{p^5}{4q^2}$ **15.** $-5x$ **16.** $\frac{27g^6}{8h^{12}}$ **17.** $4.5 \cdot 10^{10}$ **18.** $3.15 \cdot 10^3$ **19.** $2.4 \cdot 10^9$ **20.** $6.9 \cdot 10^{-8}$ **21.** $2x + y$ **22.** $-2x^2 + 3y$ **23.** $3x - 5$ **24.** $4x - y$ **25.** $11r - s + t$ **26.** $3x^2 + 7x - 10$ **27.** $2a - 2b + 6c$ **28.** $3x^2 + 3xy + 3$ **29.** $2x^2 + 5x + 2$ **30.** $-x^2 + 3x - 2$ **31.** $x^2 + 2x - 3$ **32.** $k^2 + 4k$ **33.** $-15x^2 + 5xy$ **34.** $6a^2b - 8ab^3$ **35.** $a^2 + 4a + 3$ **36.** $x^2 + 2x - 8$ **37.** $2r^2 - rs - s^2$ **38.** $y^2 - 36$ **39.** $b^2 + 4b + 4$ **40.** $y^3 + y^2 - 10y + 8$ **41.** 1:50 P.M.

Chapter 12 Polynomials and Factoring

Lesson 12.2, pages 575–581

Try These **1.** $3x(3x + 1)$ **3.** $2y^2(y - 8)$ **5.** $(x + 3)(x + 2)$ **7.** $(x - 3)(x - 1)$

9. $(x - 4)(x + 2)$ **11.** $(x + 7)(x - 4)$
13. $(2x + 3)(x + 1)$

Practice **1.** $2a(a^3 + 4)$ **3.** $4ab^2(2 - 3ab)$
5. $3(2c^2 - 3d^2)$ **7.** $2x(2x^2 - x + 7)$
15. $(x + 1)(x + 4)$ **17.** $(z + 5)(z + 3)$
19. $(x - 3)(x - 3)$ **21.** $(z - 9)(z - 1)$
23. $(y + 8)(y - 1)$ **25.** $(y + 12)(y - 1)$

Extend **39.** $3b^{2n}$ **41.** $\left(\frac{1}{2}\right)(Z - N)$

Think Critically **43.** 7, –7, 13, –13, 8, –8

Lesson 12.3, pages 582–585

Try These **1.** $(a + 4)(a - 4)$ **3.** not factorable
5. $(3e^2 + 4f)(3e^2 - 4f)$ **7.** yes; $(a - 5)^2$ **9.** yes; $(c^2 - 2)^2$ **11.** $x^2 - 6x + 9 = (x - 3)^2$

Practice **1.** $(a - 8)^2$ **3.** $(c + 3)^2$ **5.** $(e - 10)^2$
7. $(9h + 2)^2$ **9.** $(10p + 3q)^2$
11. $(v + 11)(v - 11)$ **13.** $(y + 1)(y - 1)$
15. $3(3a^2 - 4)$ **17.** $(6c^2 + d)(6c^2 - d)$
19. $2x + 5$ and $2x - 5$

Extend **21.** $(4r^2 - s)^2$ **23.** not factorable
25. $(11x + 17)(11x - 17)$ **27a.** 7 and 5 $(49 - 25 = 24)$; 5 and 1 $(25 - 1) = 24$ **b.** 12 and 2 $(7 + 5, 7 - 5)$; 6 and 4 $(5 + 1, 5 - 1)$

Think Critically
29. $(a + b + c + d)(a + b - c - d)$ **31.** 27

Mixed Review

33. –4 –3 –2 –1 0 1 2 3

34. –3 –2 –1 0 1 2 3 4

35. –2 –1 0 1 2 3 4

36. B **37.** (8, 16) **38.** (5, –5) **39.** (1, 3)

Lesson 12.4, pages 586–590

Try These **1.** $12(c + d)$ **3.** $(g - 4)(b + 3)$
5. $(2 + g)(h - k)$ **7.** $(y^3 + 3)(y - 2)$
9. $(w - 3)(2z - 1)$ **11.** $(x + 1)(y - 2)$

Practice **1.** $(5 + w)(x + 1)$ **3.** $(x + 2)(y + 5)$
5. $(x - 7)(y + 2)$ **7.** $(p + q)(s - 2t)$
9. $(3a + 1)(4b + 5)$ **11.** $(3w - 1)(z + 4)$

Extend **21.** $(a + b + c)(x + 2)$
23. $(p + q - r)(a - b)$ **25.** $2x + 2y - 2$
27a. $(x + 2)(y + 4)$ **b.** *ya ka 3 bha ka 9*

Lesson 12.5, pages 591–594

Try These **1.** $4(x - 2)(x + 4)$ **3.** $5(z + 2)(z - 2)$
5. $(x + 2)(y + 4)(y - 4)$ **7.** $a, b + 5, b + 8$

Practice **1.** $2(x + 5)(x + 7)$ **3.** $5(z - 6)(z + 3)$
5. $4b(c - 2)(c + 5)$ **7.** $3(x + 5)(x - 5)$

Extend **19.** $(a + 3)(b + 6)(b + 2)$
21. $6(p - 2)(q + 3)(q - 3)$
23. $(a + 1)(b + 2)(b + 5)$
25. $(m + 2)(m - 2)(n + 5)(n + 4)$
27a. $V = \pi h(R + r)(R - r)$ **b.** 5820.0 lb
29. $(x - 1)(x^2 + x + 1)$
31. $(y - 2)(y^2 + 2y + 4)(y + 2)(y^2 - 2y + 4)$

Think Critically **33.** $2(2x + 3y)(4x^2 - 6xy + 9y^2)$
35. 7

Mixed Review **36.** B **37.** $(x + 2)(y - 5)$
38. $(2a + 3)(b - 1)$ **39.** $(2y + 3)(2y - 3)(z + 1)$

Lesson 12.6, pages 595–601

Try These **1.** $x = 0, x = -3$ **3.** $x = -5, x = 1$
5. $x = 0, x = 6$ **7.** $x = -7, x = 2$
9. $z = 4, z = -3$ **11.** $y = -4, y = -2$
13. 5 yd, 11 yd **15.** not factorable

Practice **1.** 0, –1 **3.** –3, 8 **5.** 0, 5 **7.** 10, –7
9. –4, –7 **11.** –6, 3 **13.** –2, 7 **15.** $-\frac{1}{2}, -3$
17. –2, 6 **19.** 2 m, 9 m **21.** yes; $(x - 8)(x - 4)$
23. yes; $(x - 10)(x + 9)$ **25.** not factorable
27. not factorable **29.** 11, 12; –12, –11

Extend **31.** 1, 3 **33.** 12 m, 8 m **35.** 4 units by 7 units

Think Critically **37.** $x^2 + 12x = 0$
39. $3x^2 + x - 2 = 0$ **41.** 0, 2, 6

Mixed Review **42.** –7 **43.** 23 **44.** $\frac{4}{3}$
45. {6, 0, –9} **46.** {3, 5, 8} **47.** {4, 0, 9} **48.** D
49. $7x^2 + 4x - 5$ **50.** $2ab - 4a + 7b$

Lesson 12.7, pages 602–605

Apply the Strategy **15a.** $s^2 + 4s - 60 = 0$
b. $s = 6$ ft **17a.** 7 in. × 9 in. **b.** 10 in. × 12 in.

19. 39, 40 and –40, –39 **21a.** 3 in.
b. 18 in. × 25 in. **23.** 6 ft

Chapter Review, pages 606–607

1. c **2.** a **3.** d **4.** b **5.** $(x + 1)(x + 3)$
6. $(x - 2)(x - 3)$ **7.** $(x + 4)(x - 2)$
8. $(x + 1)(x - 5)$ **9.** $5d(3 + 5d)$
10. $3yz(3xz - y + 2x^2)$ **11.** $(z + 8)(z + 3)$
12. $(y + 9)(y - 1)$ **13.** $2x - 5, x + 3$
14. $(c + 4)^2$ **15.** not factorable **16.** $(r - 3)^2$

17. $(w + 10)(w - 10)$ **18.** $3 + 2x, 3 - 2x$
19. $(4 + y)(x - 3)$ **20.** $(a + 4)(b + 2)$
21. $(p - q)(r - s)$ **22.** $(c - 1)(d + 5)$
23. $a + 3, b - 5$ **24.** $3(x + 2)(x + 7)$
25. $2a(b^2 + 5)(b + 3)(b - 3)$
26. $6(y - 3)(y - 3)$ **27.** $3x(y + 2)(y - 2)$
28. $4, x + 6, x - 6$ **29.** 0, –5 **30.** 0, 9 **31.** –7, 10
32. –6, –3 **33.** 14 and 16 or –14 and –16 **34.** 6 in.
35. 7 and 11

Chapter 13 Geometry and Radical Expressions

Lesson 13.2, pages 618–624

TRY THESE **1.** obtuse, scalene **3.** acute, scalene **5.** 67° **7.** 90° **9.** 90°, 69°, 21° **11.** obtuse **13.** right **15.** 11.3 ft

PRACTICE **1.** acute, isosceles **3.** right, scalene **5.** 35° and 110°

EXTEND **9.** 29.0 ft **11.** yes; the longest diagonal is 66.52.; find this length by squaring 65, adding 200 (the square of the diagonal of the square face) and finding the square root of the sum.

THINK CRITICALLY **15.** two lengths equal, with $a^2 + b^2 > c^2$; c can be either the longest side or one of two equal longer sides.

MIXED REVIEW **16.** 12 **17.** –17 **18.** 41 **19.** C

20. 2, 4 **21.** 7, 6 **22.** $\frac{1}{2}, \frac{1}{3}$ **23.** $3x(x + 4)(x - 4)$

24. $4y(x - 4)(x + 3)$ **25.** $(x^2 + 9)(x + 3)(x - 3)$

Lesson 13.3, pages 625–630

TRY THESE **1.** $5\sqrt{2}$ **3.** $8\sqrt{3}$ **5.** $2\sqrt{3}$ **7.** $\frac{\sqrt{30}}{6}$ **9.** $30\sqrt{5}$ km

PRACTICE **1.** $3\sqrt{2}$ **3.** $10\sqrt{3}$ **5.** $3|n|$ **7.** $12c\sqrt{2c}$ **9.** 3 **11.** 50 **13.** $12 - 6\sqrt{3}$ **15.** $12 - 2\sqrt{15}$ **17.** 3 **19.** $\frac{2\sqrt{5}}{5}$ **21.** 52 **23.** 36

EXTEND **27.** $\frac{s\sqrt{3}}{2}$ **29.** $\sqrt{5} + \sqrt{3}; 2$ **31.** $\sqrt{10} - 4; -6$ **33.** $\frac{3 + \sqrt{3} + 3\sqrt{2} + \sqrt{6}}{6}$

THINK CRITICALLY **35.** 64, 36 **37.** $(m + \sqrt{n})(m - \sqrt{n}) = m^2 - n$. Since both m^2 and n are rational numbers, their difference is also a rational number. Therefore, the product is rational.

MIXED REVIEW **38.** 9 **39.** –2 **40.** 3 **41.** –4; 3 **42.** $-3; \frac{11}{2}$ **43.** 1; 4 **44.** D

Lesson 13.4, pages 631–635

TRY THESE **1.** $7\sqrt{7}$ **3.** $19\sqrt{2}$ **5.** $-4\sqrt{10} + 4\sqrt{5}$ **7.** $27\sqrt{5}$ **9.** $\frac{\sqrt{2}}{4}$

PRACTICE **1.** $9\sqrt{3}$ **3.** $8\sqrt{5}$ **5.** $3\sqrt{3} + 6\sqrt{2}$ **7.** $16\sqrt{h}$ **9.** $19\sqrt{2x}$ **11.** $9\sqrt{2}$ **13.** $3\sqrt{2n + 2}$

EXTEND **23a.** $14\sqrt{2}$ mi **23b.** $28 - 14\sqrt{2}$ mi **25.** yes **27.** yes **29a.** The expressions are equal. **29b.** $(\sqrt{5} - 1)^2 = 6 - 2\sqrt{5}$ **29c.** $\sqrt{6} + 2$ **29d.** $\sqrt{3} + 2$

MIXED REVIEW **30.** –26 **31.** 24 **32.** 36 **33.** –9 **34.** 7 **35.** –27 **36.** –3 **37.** $4x - 1$ **38.** $-3 < x < 3$ **39.** $x \le -6$ or $x \ge 6$ **40.** C **41.** $6\sqrt{7}$ **42.** $\sqrt{2}$ **43.** $8\sqrt{3}$ **44.** $11\sqrt{x}$

Lesson 13.5, pages 636–641

TRY THESE **1.** 9 **3.** 28 **5.** 12 **7.** 13 **9.** 9 **11.** 5 **13.** $11 = \sqrt{\frac{A}{\pi}}$; 121π cm²

PRACTICE **1.** 81 **3.** 1.44 **5.** 6 **7.** $x - 5$ **9.** 4 **11.** 81 **13.** 36 **15.** 9 **17.** 58 **19.** 72

EXTEND **39.** 2 **41.** $\frac{9}{16}$ **43.** 218 **45.** 12 **47.** 45 **51.** 10.5

THINK CRITICALLY **49.** Graph of $y_2 = \sqrt{x + 2}$ same as $y_1 = \sqrt{x}$ but is shifted left 2 units.

Graph of $y_3 = \sqrt{x - 3}$ is the same as $y_1 = \sqrt{x}$ but is shifted right 3 units **51.** 10.5

MIXED REVIEW **52.** 7, 8, 9 **53.** 41.5, 39.5, 37 **54.** $x \le 7$ **55.** $x < 11$ **56.** $x > -2$ **57.** 2, 3 **58.** –1, 4 **59.** 9 **60.** 2 **61.** 7

Lesson 13.6, pages 642–647

TRY THESE **1.** 10 **3.** 13 **5.** 17 **7.** (4, 3) **9.** $\left(\frac{17}{2}, \frac{27}{2}\right)$

780

Practice **1.** 10 **3.** $2\sqrt{5}$ **5.** $5\sqrt{2}$ **7.** 25 **9.** 41 **11.** (3, –7) **13.** (–2.5, –11) **15.** $(m, 0)$ **17.** equilateral

Extend **21.** $AM = MB = \sqrt{34}$ **23.** 6 or 12

Think Critically **25a.** 2 **25b.** $y = 2x + 2$ **25c.** (–2, –2) **25d.** $3\sqrt{5}$

Mixed Review **28.** 12 **29.** 1 **30.** 18 **31.** 2 **32.** 8 **33.** 9 **34.** D **35.** $5 \pm \sqrt{3}$ **36.** $\frac{2 \pm \sqrt{10}}{3}$ **37.** $\frac{-5 \pm \sqrt{2}}{2}$ **38.** $5\sqrt{2}$ **39.** 20 **40.** $\sqrt{29}$

Lesson 13.8, pages 652–658

Try These **1.** $\cos B$ or $\sin C$ **3.** $\tan B$ **5.** $\frac{5}{12}$ **7.** $\frac{12}{13}$ **9.** $\frac{12}{5}$ **11.** 0.8333 **13.** 0.7879

Practice **1.** 0.5526 **3.** 0.7778 **5.** $\angle G = 28°, \angle H = 62°$ **7.** $\angle S = 53°, \angle T = 37°$ **9.** $\angle X = 32°, \angle Y = 58°$ **11.** 35° **13.** 87° **15.** 12° **17.** 2.3 m or less

Extend **21.** $\text{Tan } C = \frac{10}{100} = 0.10$; $m\angle C = 5.7°$ to the nearest tenth of a degree; Find side DE of ΔCDE: $\sin 5.7° = \frac{DE}{CD}$; $\sin 5.7° = \frac{DE}{2{,}640 \text{ ft}}$; $DE = \sin 5.7°(2{,}640) = 262.2$ ft to the nearest tenth.

Think Critically **23.** $\tan x = \frac{\sin x}{\cos x}$;

$$\tan x = \frac{\frac{opp.}{hyp.}}{\frac{adj.}{hyp.}} = \frac{opp.}{hyp.} \times \frac{hyp.}{adj.} = \frac{opp.}{adj.},$$

the tangent ratio

Mixed Review **24.** 1 **25.** 3 **26.** 3 **27.** 6 **28.** 2 **29.** 4 **30.** $x = 7; x = \frac{-3}{2}$ **31.** $x = 5; x = -5$ **32.** $x = \sqrt{11}; x = -\sqrt{11}$ **33.** $x = -1; x = -6$ **34.** 35, 28 and –35, –28 **35.** B

Lesson 13.10, pages 662–665

Apply The Strategy **15.** 128 mi **17a.** 12.3 ft **17b.** 56.2 ft^2 **19.** 8.6 in.

Chapter Review, pages 666–667

1. b **2.** c **3.** a **4.** obtuse **5.** right **6.** acute **7.** $m\angle Z = 18°, m\angle P = 33°, m\angle Q = 129°$, $m\angle R = 18°$, XY is 20, YZ is 35 **8.** $m\angle C = 41°, m\angle D = 80°, m\angle E = 59°$, $m\angle F = 41°$, DE is 12, EF is 18.7 **9.** $2\sqrt{7}$ **10.** $5|y|$ **11.** 16 **12.** $4\sqrt{3} + 3\sqrt{5}$ **13.** $2\sqrt{2}$ **14.** $5\sqrt{13}$ **15.** $6\sqrt{5} - 3\sqrt{2}$ **16.** $14\sqrt{2a}$ **17.** $6|r|\sqrt{3}$ **18.** 25 **19.** 2 **20.** 6 **21.** 10 **22.** $10\sqrt{2}$; (–5, 4) **23.** $\sqrt{5}$; (7.5, 0) **24.** 0.4103 **25.** $m\angle G = 48°, m\angle I = 42°$ **26.** c **27.** b **28.** a **29.** 12 ft; 13 ft

Chapter 14 Rational Expressions

Lesson 14.2, pages 679–685

Try These **1.** joint; $k = 2$ **3.** inverse; $k = 10$ **5.** yes; $k = 60$ **7.** $c = \frac{k}{d^2}$ **9.** 25 **11.** 12 **13.** 15 N

Practice **1.** direct; $k = 9.5$ **3.** inverse; $k = 72$ **5.** direct; $k = 0.14$ **7.** 48 **9.** 7 **11.** 50 **13.** 2100 **15.** $d = kr$ **17.** $w = \frac{k}{l}$

Extend **19.** 605 **21.** about 35 min

Think Critically **23.** $y = x, y = -x$ **25.** (2, 2)

Mixed Review **27.** B **28.** $y = -2x + 6$ **29.** $y = \frac{2}{3}x + 2$ **30.** $x < -3$ or $x > 9$ **31.** $-6 < x < 2$ **32.** 3 **33.** 25

Lesson 14.3, pages 686–691

Try These **1.** $x = 0$ **3.** $x = -3, 7$ **5.** $\frac{2}{x}, x \neq 0$ **7.** $\frac{x-3}{6}$ **9.** $\frac{1}{7}; a \neq 7$

Practice **1.** $m = 0; n = 0$ **3.** $y = -3$ **5.** $z = 1, -8$ **7.** $x = -8, 6$ **9.** $\frac{2}{x}; x \neq 0$

Extend **21.** $\frac{(x^2 + 1)(x + 1)}{(x - 1)}; x \neq 1$ **23.** $\frac{x^2(x + 5)}{(x - 1)}; x \neq 0, 1, -5$

Think Critically **27.** $q = p + 2$

Mixed Review **28.** C **29.** $y = \frac{5}{3}x + \frac{1}{3}$ **30.** $y = -14x + 48$ **31.** downward **32.** upward

Lesson 14.4, pages 692–696

Try These **1.** $\frac{1}{2}$ **3.** $\frac{5}{8n^2}$ **5.** $3abc$ **7.** $\frac{de}{14}$ **9.** $\frac{1}{2}$ **11.** $\frac{2x - 2}{x}$

Practice 1. $\frac{5}{3}$ 3. $\frac{4k}{3}$ 5. $2a^2bc$ 7. $\frac{2}{3cde}$ 9. $\frac{1}{4}$ 11. $\frac{2x-4}{x}$ 13. $\frac{14x+70}{x-6}$ 15. $\frac{1}{3x+18}$ 17. $-\frac{5x}{21x+126}$ 19. $\frac{7}{x+2}$ 21. $\frac{x^2-2x}{12+2x}$

Extend 25. $\frac{2t-2}{t-3}$ 27. 2 or 2:1

Mixed Review 33. C 34. 0.9 35. 3 36. $x < 4$ 37. $x < -2$ 38. -1 39. $\frac{x+4}{x+3}$

Lesson 14.5, pages 697–701

Try These 1. $x^2 + 8, x - 2, x + 2, 12$ 3. $3x + 1 + \frac{1}{2x}$ 5. $a + 5$ 7. $p^2 + p - 3 + \frac{4}{2p+1}$ 9. $4t + 3$

Practice 1. $x^2 + 10, x - 4, x + 4, 26$ 3. $4x + 2 + \frac{1}{3x}$ 5. $a + 7$ 7. $4m - 2$

Extend 17. $8m^2 + 12mn + 24n^2 + \frac{40n^2}{m-n}$ 19. $336r^2 + 1008r^2 + 1008r + 336$ 21. 700

Think Critically 23. -44

Mixed Review 25. A 26. c 27. b 28. a

Lesson 14.6, pages 702–706

Try These 1. mn^2 3. $(x-4), (x-5)$ 5. $-\frac{4}{7y}$ 7. $-\frac{16}{15x}$ 9. $\frac{9a-16}{(a+4)(a-9)}$ 11. $\frac{-14}{16-x^2}$

Practice 1. ab^3 3. $3x(x+1)$ 5. $\frac{4}{z}$ 7. 7 9. -1 11. $\frac{23}{9x}$

Extend 27. $\frac{x-8}{x^2-25}$ 29. $\frac{x^3+19x^2+3x-1}{x(x+1)(6x-1)}$ 31. $\frac{-2x^3+11x^2-8x+4}{x(1-2x)}$

Mixed Review 35. D 36. $|x - 25| \leq 4$ 37. 9 38. 144 39. c 40. a 41. b 42. $\frac{-12t+7}{6t^2}$ 43. $\frac{-12r+3}{8r^2}$

Lesson 14.7, pages 707–711

Try These 1. $\frac{5t+9}{t}$ 3. $\frac{12n^2+17n+3}{4n+5}$ 5. $\frac{15x+10}{16x+4}$ 7. $\frac{8d}{3c}$ 9. $\frac{2q-6p}{11p}$

Practice 1. $\frac{11b-13}{b}$ 3. $\frac{9z^2-z-5}{3z}$ 5. $\frac{t^2-2t-8}{t+1}$ 7. $\frac{3y}{4x}$ 9. $\frac{q-3p}{4p}$

Extend 23. $\frac{20x-60}{3x-15}$ 25. $\frac{8b^3-12b+48}{4b^2+3b}$ 27. $\frac{x^2-1}{4}$ ft

Think Critically 29. yes; 5 and 6 are both rational expressions 31. $\frac{a^2+1}{a^4+a^3}$

Lesson 14.8, pages 712–717

Try These 3. 64 5. no solution 7. $-\frac{1}{2}$ 9. no solution 11. $5\frac{1}{3}$ mi/h

Practice 1. $\frac{49}{60}$ 3. 12 5. no solution 7. $\frac{11}{3}$ 9. 18 11. $-\frac{3}{20}$ 15. Rikuichi = \$2300, Keemo = \$1250

Extend 17. no solution 19. 15 h

Think Critically 25. $\frac{29}{13}$

Lesson 14.9, pages 718–721

Apply the Strategy 13. need number of km per mi; use 1 mi = 1.6 km

Chapter Review, pages 722–723

1. b 2. a 3. c 4. 5 5. 18 6. $\frac{3}{x}; x \neq 0$ 7. 6; $b \neq -3$ 8. $-\frac{1}{4}; y \neq \frac{1}{2}$ 9. $3p^2q^2$ 10. $6y$ 11. $\frac{1}{4}$ 12. $\frac{9x+36}{x-2}$ 13. $\frac{1}{3x-6}$ 14. $15x$ 15. $3x - 4 + \frac{1}{2x}$ 16. $y + 8$ 17. $3x^3 + 3x^2 - 4x - 4 + \frac{1}{x-1}$ 18. $2x^2 - x + 2 - \frac{4}{x+3}$ 19. $\frac{1-g}{g+2}$ 20. $\frac{22}{9x}$ 21. $\frac{10-11z}{6z^2}$ 22. $\frac{3t-10}{6t+24}$ 23. $\frac{4b}{7a}$ 24. $\frac{n-2m}{4n}$ 25. $\frac{4y+6x}{y-x}$ 26. $\frac{3s+2rs}{4r}$ 27. $-\frac{1}{15}$ 28. -1 29. $\frac{23}{45}$ 30. \$9.14

INDEX

INDEX

• • B • •

C

D

E

• • J • •

• • L • •

• • M • •

• • N • •

• • O • •

INDEX

• • P • •

INDEX

T

U

V

W

X

Y

Z

790

Photo Credits

CONTENTS
p. vi: Lillian Gee/Picture It Corp.; p. vii: Terry Qing/FPG International Corp.; p. viii: Michael Hart/FPG International Corp.; p. ix: Jacob Taposchaner/FPG International Corp.; p. x: Lillian Gee/Picture It Corp.; p. xi: DL-FC/FPG International Corp.; p. xii: Lillian Gee/Picture It Corp.; p. xiii: Comstock; p. xiv: John Terence Turner/FPG International Corp.; p. xv: Lillian Gee/Picture It Corp.; p. xvi: Lillian Gee/Picture It Corp.; p. xvii: Lillian Gee/Picture It Corp.; p. xviii: Suzanne Murphy/FPG International Corp.; p. xix: Lillian Gee/Picture It Corp.

CHAPTER 1
p. 2: Ken Chernus/FPG International Corp. (top); David Hamilton/The Image Bank (bottom); p. 3: Bruce Forster/Tony Stone Images; p. 4: Grandadam/Photo Researchers, Inc.; p. 5: Jeff Greenberg/Photo Researchers; p. 6: Lawrence Fried/The Image Bank; p. 7: Steven W. Jones/FPG International Inc. (top); Richard Laird/FPG International Corp. (bottom); p. 8: Blair Seitz/Photo Researchers, Inc.; p. 10: Marc Romanelli/The Image Bank; p. 11: Michael Melford/The Image Bank (top); Telegraph Colour Library/FPG International Corp. (bottom); p. 12: Porterfield/Chickering/Photo Researchers, Inc.; p. 14: Ira Block/The Image Bank; p. 15: Lillian Gee/Picture It Corp.; p. 16: Gerard Champlong/The Image Bank; p. 18: The Image Bank; p. 19: John Lewis Stage/The Image Bank; p. 20: Jeff Isaac Greenberg/Photo Researchers, Inc.; p. 21: Skip Hine; p. 23: Roger Miller Photo, Ltd. (top); F. Roiter/The Image Bank (bottom); p. 24: Ken Huang/The Image Bank; p. 26: McDonald Studios/FPG International Corp. (left); P. Harris/Shooting Star (right); p. 27: Duomo Photo/The Image Bank; p. 28: David De Lossy/The Image Bank; p. 29: Anthony Meshkinyar/Tony Stone Images; p. 30: Sauzereau O/Explorer/Photo Researchers, Inc.; p. 32: Kevin Forest/The Image Bank; p. 34: Lou Jones/The Image Bank; p. 39: Grant Faint/The Image Bank; p. 42: Richard Mackson/FPG International Corp.; p. 44: Steve Dunwell/The Image Bank

CHAPTER 2
p. 52: Stim/Photri, Inc. (top); NSS/LAB/The Image Bank (bottom); p. 53: Mark Burnett/Photo Researchers, Inc.; p. 54: Mark C. Burnett/Photo Researchers, Inc.; p. 55: Ted Kawalerski/The Image Bank; p. 56: Erik von Fisher/Photonics (top); Les Riess/Photri, Inc. (bottom); p. 58 Keith Kent/Science Photo Library/Photo Researchers, Inc.; p. 59: J. P. Pieuchot/The Image Bank; p. 60: Terje Rakke/The Image Bank; p. 63: Romilly Lockyer/The Image Bank; p. 64: Alvis Upitis/The Image Bank (bottom); p. 66: Bachmann/Photo Researchers, Inc.; p. 69: Farrell Grehan/Photo Researchers, Inc.; p. 71: Syd Greenberg/Photo Researchers, Inc. (top); Photo Researchers, Inc. (top middle); Tom Burnside/Photo Researchers, Inc. (bottom middle); Courtesy of Oldsmobile (bottom); p. 72: Science Photo Library/Photo Researchers, Inc.; p. 73: Lillian Gee/Picture It Corp.; p. 81: Harald Sund/The Image Bank; p. 82: Bill Billingham/Photri, Inc.; p. 87: Roger Miller Photo, Ltd.; p. 91: Rosenthal/Superstock; p. 92: Photri, Inc.; p. 93: Photri, Inc.; p. 94: David R. Frazier Photolibrary/Photo Researchers, Inc.; p. 96: Stephen J. Krasemann/Photo Researchers, Inc.; p. 99: Tom Wilson/FPG International Corp.; p. 101: Scott Markewitz/FPG International Corp.; p. 102: Art Stein/Photo Researchers, Inc. (top and bottom); p. 104: Bruce Roberts/Photo Researchers, Inc.

CHAPTER 3
p. 112: Eunice Harris/Science Source/Photo Researchers, Inc. (top); Ken Lax/Photo Researchers, Inc. (bottom); p. 113: Will & Deni McIntyre/Photo Researchers, Inc.; p. 114: Ron Chapple/FPG International Corp.; p. 115: Lillian Gee/Picture It Corp.; p. 116: Lillian Gee/Picture It Corp.; p. 118: Schneps/The Image Bank; p. 119: Courtesy of International Business Machines Corp.; p. 120: Benn Mitchell/The Image Bank; p. 124: Photri, Inc.; p. 127: Renee Lynn/Photo Researchers, Inc.; p. 128: Charles D. Winters/Photo Researchers, Inc.; p. 130: Lillian Gee/Picture It Corp; p. 133: Photri, Inc.; p. 134: Marc Romanelli/The Image Bank; p. 135: Lillian Gee/Picture It; p. 136: Gilda Schiff/Photo Researchers, Inc.; p. 139: John Clark/Photri, Inc.; p. 142: Robert E Daemmich/Tony Stone Images; p. 143: Dean Siracusa/FPG International Corp.; p. 144:

Jeff Greenberg; p. 145: Charles D. Winters/Photo Researchers, Inc.; p. 147: Will & Deni McIntyre/The Image Bank; p. 149: Nancy Brown/The Image Bank; p. 151: Richard Anderson (bottom); p. 152: Lillian Gee/Picture It Corp.; p. 153: Lillian Gee/Picture It Corp.; p. 156: Diane Padys/FPG International Corp.; p. 157: Lillian Gee/Picture It Corp.; p. 158: Bill Varie/The Image Bank (top); Thomas Digory/The Image Bank (bottom); p. 159: Obremski/The Image Bank

CHAPTER 4

p. 166: Robert E. Daemmrich/Tony Stone Images (top); Jim McNee/FPG International Corp. (bottom); p. 167: Tetrel/Photo Researchers, Inc.; p. 168: Robert E. Daemmrich/Tony Stone Images; p. 169: Duomo Photography/The Image Bank; p. 170: Larry Dale Gordon Studio/The Image Bank; p. 171: Wachter/Photri, Inc.; p. 175: Al Hamdan/The Image Bank; p. 177: Joseph Devenney/The Image Bank; p. 179: Anne-Marie Weber/FPG International Corp.; p. 184: Lillian Gee/Picture It Corp.; p. 186: Maria Taglienti/The Image Bank; p.187: Nick Sebastian/Photri, Inc.; p. 191: Lillian Gee/Picture It Corp.; p. 195: David Madison/Tony Stone Images; p. 196: Jeff Greenberg; p. 198: Mel Digiacomo/The Image Bank; p. 200: Peter Gridley/FPG International Corp.; p. 201: Stephen Simpson/FPG International Corp.; p. 202: Aram Gesar/The Image Bank; p. 204: Ed Braverman/FPG International Corp.; p. 206: Lillian Gee/Picture It Corp.; p. 207: Telegraph Colour Library/FPG International Corp.; p. 208: Vince Streano/Tony Stone Images (top); Art Montes De Oca/FPG International Corp. (bottom); p. 209: Brett Froomer/The Image Bank; p. 210: Lonnie Duka/Tony Stone Images; p. 211: Lou Jones/The Image Bank

CHAPTER 5

p. 218: Joseph Nettis/Photo Researchers, Inc. (top); Michael Salas/The Image Bank (middle); Bruce Ayres/Tony Stone Images (bottom); p. 219: William McCoy/Rainbow; p. 220: Will & Deni McIntyre/Photo Researchers, Inc.; p. 221: Obremski/The Image Bank; p. 223: Takeshi Takahara/Photo Researchers Inc.; p. 224: Robert E. Daemmrich/Tony Stone Images (top); Alex Stewart/The Image Bank (bottom); p. 225: Lani Novak Howe/Photri Inc., p. 226: Will McIntrye/Photo Reasearchers Inc.; p. 228: Lillian Gee/Picture It Corp.; p. 233: Margot Granitsas/Photo Researchers, Inc.; p. 235: Blair Seitz/Photo Reasearchers, Inc.; p. 237: Gatzen/Photri, Inc., p. 238: Rafael Macia/Photo Researchers, Inc.; p. 240: Blair Seitz/Photo Researchers Inc.; p. 241: Alan Carruthers/Photo Researchers Inc.; p. 243: Ken Cavanagh/Photo Researchers Inc.; p. 246: Philippe Sion/The Image Bank; p. 247: Courtesy of International Business Machines Corp.; p. 251: Jay Freis/The Image Bank; p. 252: Lillian Gee/Picture It Corp., p. 253: Dick Luria/FPG International Corp.; p. 254: Michael Ventura/Tony Stone Images

CHAPTER 6

p. 262: Patti McConville/The Image Bank (top); Yellow Dog Prods./The Image Bank (bottom); p. 263: Ron Chapple/FPG International Corp.; p. 264: Renee Lynn/Photo Researchers, Inc.; p. 265: Jeff Greenberg; p. 268: David Brownell/The Image Bank; p. 270: Luis Castaneda/The Image Bank (top); Grant Faint/The Image Bank (bottom); p. 271: Jeffrey Sylvester/FPG International Corp., p. 275: Mosallem/ FPG International Corp.; p. 277: Andre Gallant/The Image Bank; p. 278: Jurgen Vogt/The Image Bank (top); Robert Kristofik/The Image Bank (bottom); p. 280: Roger Miller Photo, Ltd.; p. 281: Maria Taglienti/The Image Bank; p. 284: Walter Bibikow/The Image Bank; p. 287: Paul Simcock/The Image Bank; p. 288: Greater Houston Partnership; p. 289: U. S. Department of Agriculture; p. 290: Dr. C. W. Biedel/Photri, Inc.; p. 292: Aluminum Company of America (top); Veina Brainard/Photri, Inc. (bottom); p. 295: Robert E. Daemmrich/Tony Stone Images; p. 302: Larry Fried/The Image Bank; p. 304: Jeff Cadge/The Image Bank; p. 305: Kaz Mori/The Image Bank; p. 308: Alberto Incrocci/The Image Bank; p. 310: U.S. Department of Commerce/American Petroleum Institute; p. 313: Holiday Inn, Inc. (top); Courtesy of Hewlett-Packard Co. (bottom); p. 314: HMS Images/The Image Bank

CHAPTER 7

p. 322: Alcoa (top); Telegraph Colour Library/FPG International Corp. (bottom); p. 323: Charles Thatcher/Tony Stone Images (top); Lawrence Migdale/Photo Researchers, Inc. (bottom); p. 324: Tourism British Columbia; p. 326: Lillian Gee/Picture It Corp.; p. 327: Photri, Inc.; p. 328: Roger Miller Photo, Ltd.; p. 330: Comstock; p. 331: Theodore Anderson/The Image Bank; p. 332: Ron Chapple/FPG International Corp.; p. 333:

Sebastian/Photri, Inc.; p. 334: Photri, Inc.; p. 335: Lori Adamski Peek/Tony Stone Images; p. 337: Lou Jones/The Image Bank; p. 338: Michael Krasowitz/FPG International Corp.; p. 339: B. Kulik/Photri, Inc.; p. 340: Comstock; p. 341: InnerLight/The Image Bank; p. 343: Lani Novak Howe/Photri, Inc.; p. 345: Photri, Inc. (top); Dick Luria/FPG International Corp. (bottom); p. 347: Photri, Inc.; p. 348: Photri, Inc.; p. 351: Comstock; p. 355: Ken Kaminsky/Photri, Inc.; p. 356: Blair Seitz/Photo Researchers, Inc.; p. 358: Dick Luria/FPG International Corp.; p. 359: Photri, Inc.; p. 360: Bennett/Photri, Inc.; p. 361: Jack Novak/Photri, Inc.; p. 362: Michael Melford/The Image Bank

CHAPTER 8

p. 370: Don Smeltzer/Tony Stone Images (top); Michael Krasowitz/FPG International Corp. (bottom); p. 371: Jon Riley/Tony Stone Images (left); p. 372: David Young Wolff/Tony Stone Images; p. 373: David R. Frazier Photolibrary/Photo Researchers, Inc.; p. 377: Ken Lax/Photo Researchers, Inc.; p. 378: Jeff Isaac Greenberg/Photo Researchers, Inc.; p. 379: Alvis Upitis/The Image Bank; p. 380: Superstock; p. 381: Burton McNeely/The Image Bank; p. 382: Steve Niedorf/The Image Bank; p. 383: Photri, Inc.; p. 384: Alan Brown/Photonics; p. 385: Gregory Heisler/The Image Bank (top and top center); Jay Brousseau/The Image Bank (bottom center); Larry Gatz/The Image Bank (bottom); p. 386: Lillian Gee/Picture It Corp.; p. 389: Alvis Upitis/The Image Bank; p. 392: Dick Luria/FPG International Corp.; p. 393: Rafael Macia/Photo Researchers, Inc.; p. 396: Jean-Marc Barey/Agence Vandystadt/Photo Researchers, Inc. (top); Jeff Greenberg/Photo Researchers, Inc. (bottom); p. 398: Lillian Gee/Picture It Corp.; p. 401: Richard Nowitz/Photo Researchers, Inc.; p. 402: Image Makers/The Image Bank

CHAPTER 9

p. 410: Baron Wolman/Tony Stone Images (top); Superstock (bottom); p. 411: Steve Dunwell/The Image Bank; p. 412: R. W. Jones/Westlight (top); Peter Gridley/FPG International Corp. (bottom); p. 415: Andy Caulfield/The Image Bank; p. 416: Lani Novak Howe/Photri, Inc.; p. 420: Lani Novak Howe/Photri, Inc.; p. 423: Elaine Sulle/The Image Bank; p. 425: Art Stein/Photo Researchers, Inc. (top); Harald Sund/The Image Bank (center); Art Stein/The Image Bank (bottom); p. 427: Gary Bistram/The Image Bank; p. 428: Comstock (top); Rafael Macia/Photo Researchers, Inc. (bottom); p. 432: Geoff Gove/The Image Bank; p. 433: Blair Seitz/Photo Researchers, Inc.; p. 435: Donal Philby/FPG International Corp.; p. 436: Michael Hart/FPG International Corp.; p. 438: Alberto Incrocci/The Image Bank; p. 441: Patti McConville/The Image Bank; p. 442: Sergio Duarte/The Image Bank; p. 443: David Doody/FPG International Corp.; p. 444: Robert J. Bennett/Photri, Inc. (top); Mark Scott/FPG International Corp. (bottom); p. 447: Frank Cezus/Tony Stone Images; p. 448: Grant V. Faint/The Image Bank; p. 449: NASA/Science Photo Library/Photo Researchers, Inc.; p. 451: Tom Wilson/FPG International Corp.; p. 453: Comstock

CHAPTER 10

p. 462: Telegraph Colour Library/FPG International Corp. (top); Andy Sacks/Tony Stone Images (bottom); p. 463: John Banagan/The Image Bank; p. 464: Gerard Loucel/Tony Stone Images; p. 465: Kathleen Campbell/Tony Stone Images; p. 470: Donovan Reese/Tony Stone Images; p. 471: Tom Wilson/FPG International Corp.; p. 473: Bernard Roussel/The Image Bank; p. 474: Courtesy of Johnson Controls, Inc.; p; 475: Comstock; p. 476: Richard Hutchings/Photo Researchers, Inc.; p. 477: Lillian Gee/Picture It Corp.; p. 480: Photri, Inc.; p. 481: Philip & Karen Smith/Tony Stone Images; p. 485: B. Kulik/Photri, Inc.; p. 489: Chuck Kuhn/The Image Bank; p. 491: F. Roiter/The Image Bank; p. 493: Keith Wood/Tony Stone Images; p. 497: Bill Howe/Photri, Inc.; p. 498: James Kirby/Photri, Inc.; p. 499: Hans Reinhard/OKAPIA/Photo Researchers, Inc.; p. 500: Michael P. Gadomski/Photo Researchers, Inc.; p. 502: G. Randall/FPG International Corp. (top); Stan Osolinski/FPG International Corp. (bottom); p. 506: Blair Seitz/Photo Researchers, Inc.

CHAPTER 11

p. 514: NASA/Science Photo Library/Photo Researchers, Inc. (top); Kay Chernish/The Image Bank (bottom); p. 515: Stephen Derr/The Image Bank; p. 516: Stephen Dalton/Photo Researchers, Inc. (top); Frank Whitney/The Image Bank (bottom); p. 518: Lillian Gee/Picture It Corp.; p. 523: Lillian Gee/Picture It Corp.; p. 526: P. & G. Bowater/The Image Bank; p. 527: Marvin E. Newman/The Image Bank; p. 531:

Superstock; p. 533: Steven Hunt/The Image Bank; p. 535: NASA/Science Source/Photo Reseachers, Inc. (top); Rich LaSalle/Tony Stone Images (bottom); p. 536: Gerard Christopher/Viacom/Shooting Star; p. 537: Wendt Worldwide; p. 539: Photri, Inc.; p. 540: M. Keller/Superstock; p. 541: Erik Simonsen/The Image Bank; p. 542: Trevor Bonderud/Westlight; p. 543: Lillian Gee/Picture It Corp.; p. 546: Melissa Grimes-Guy/Photo Researchers, Inc.; p. 547: Guy Sauvage/Agence Vandystadt/Photo Researchers, Inc.; p. 548: Lillian Gee/Picture It Corp.; p. 551: M. Rutherford/Superstock; p. 552: Walter Hodges/Westlight; p. 557: Superstock; p. 558: Frank Whitney/The Image Bank; p. 559: Hugh Sitton/Tony Stone Images (top); Randy Faris/Westlight (bottom); p. 560: Jim Zuckerman/Westlight; p. 561: C. Aurness/Westlight

CHAPTER 12
p. 570: Keith Wood/Tony Stone Images; p. 571: Luis Casteneda/The Image Bank; p. 572: Michael O'Leary/Tony Stone Images; p. 573: Lillian Gee/Picture It Corp; p. 575: Renee Lynn/Photo Researchers, Inc.; p. 579: Dr. David Wexler, colored by Dr. Jeremy Burgess/Science Photo Library/Photo Researchers, Inc.; p. 581: Colin Molyneux/The Image Bank (left); Photri, Inc. (right); p. 584: Photri, Inc.; p. 586: Tim Bieber/The Image Bank; p. 587: D. & I. McDonald/Photri, Inc.; p. 589: Photri, Inc.; p. 590: Photri, Inc.; p. 592: Comstock; p. 594: Tim Davis/Photo Reseachers, Inc.; p. 595: Bachmann/Photo Researchers, Inc.; p. 597: Roger Miller Photo, Ltd.; p. 600: Obremski/The Image Bank; p. 601: Photri, Inc.; p. 603: Garry McMichael/Photo Researchers, Inc. (top); Blair Seitz/Photo Researchers, Inc. (bottom); p. 604: Harald Sund/The Image Bank (bottom)

CHAPTER 13
p. 612: Maria Taglienti/The Image Bank; p. 613: Tim Bieber/The Image Bank; p. 614: Blair Seitz/Photo Researchers, Inc. (top); Marc Romanelli/The Image Bank (bottom); p. 615: Lillian Gee/Picture It Corp.; p. 617: Peter Miller/The Image Bank; p. 619: John Grant/Photri, Inc. (top); Lani Novak Howe/Photri, Inc. (bottom); p. 624: Mark Burnett/Photo Researchers, Inc. (top); Laima Druskis/Photo Researchers, Inc. (bottom); p. 628: Photri, Inc.; p. 630: Derek Redfearn/The Image Bank (top); Marc Romanelli/The Image Bank (bottom); p. 632: Harald Sund/The Image Bank; p. 634: Photri, Inc.; p. 639: Marcel Isy-Schwart/The Image Bank; p. 640: Francesco Ruggeri/The Image Bank (top); Weinberg/Clark/The Image Bank (bottom); p. 644: Marc Romanelli/The Image Bank; p. 647: Photri, Inc.; p. 648: Lillian Gee/Picture It Corp; p. 654: Photri, Inc.; p. 655: Steve Krongard/The Image Bank; p. 658: Grant V. Faint/The Image Bank; p. 661: Lillian Gee/Picture It Corp.; p. 662: Anne Rippy/The Image Bank; p. 663: Photri, Inc.

CHAPTER 14
p. 672: Comstock; p. 673: U. S. Department of Agriculture; p. 674: David W. Hamilton/The Image Bank; p. 676: Lillian Gee/Picture It Corp., p. 677: Bob Thomason/Tony Stone Images; p. 678: Courtesy of New Idea, Coldwater, OH; p. 680: Marc Grimberg/The Image Bank; p. 681: U.S. Dept. of Housing & Urban Development; p. 682: Kristin Finnegan/Tony Stone Images; p. 688: David Jeffrey/The Image Bank; p. 689: Michael Neveux/Westlight; p. 691: Photri, Inc. (top); Alvis Upitis/The Image Bank (bottom); p. 695: Ben Rose/The Image Bank; p. 704: Ron Chapple/FPG International Corp.; p. 709: U. S. Dept. of Agriculture; p. 711: Lee Balterman/FPG International Corp.; p. 714: Grant Faint/The Image Bank; p. 713: Wendt Worldwide; p. 716: Burton McNeely/The Image Bank; p. 718: Lillian Gee/Picture It Corp.; p. 719: Lou Jones/The Image Bank; p. 720: E. Burciaga/Photri, Inc.

TEACHER'S ANNOTATED EDITION
p. T33: Loren Santow/Tony Stone Images; p. T35: Loren Santow/Tony Stone Images; p. T36: Bob Krist/Tony Stone Images; p. T39: David Young Wolff/Tony Stone Images; p. T41: Bill Losh/FPG International Corp.; p. T43: Jeffrey Myers/FPG International Corp.; p. T45: Lillian Gee/Picture It Corp.; p. T46: Lillian Gee/Picture It Corp.; p. 12B: Lawrence Migdale/Photo Researchers, Inc.; p. 52B: Mark Burnett/Photo Researchers, Inc.; p. 112B: Ken Lax/Photo Researchers, Inc.; p. 166B: Mel DiGiacomo/The Image Bank; p. 218B: Linda Phillips/Photo Researchers, Inc.; p. 262B: Chris Michaels/Photo Researchers, Inc.; p. 322B: Stephen Simpson/FPG International Corp.; p. 370B: Marc Grimberg/The Image Bank; p. 410B: Eric Schweikardt/The Image Bank; p. 462B: Arthur Tilley/FPG International Corp.; p. 514B: Guy Sauvage/Photo Researchers, Inc.; p. 568B: Guy Marche/FPG International Corp.; p. 612B: Charles Fiel/FPG International Corp.; p. 672B: Alain Choisnet/The Image Bank

794